56th Annual Meeting of the Association for Computational Linguistics (ACL 2018)

Short Papers

Melbourne, Australia
15 – 20 July 2018

ISBN: 978-1-5108-6706-2

ACL 2018

The 56th Annual Meeting of the
Association for Computational Linguistics

Proceedings of the Conference, Vol. 2 (Short Papers)

July 15 - 20, 2018
Melbourne, Australia

Message from the General Chair

It is an honor to write the initial words of this proceedings as General Chair of the 56th Annual Meeting of the Association for Computational Linguistics! This is only the second time that an ACL conference has been held in Australia — the first time was for the joint COLING/ACL conference in June of 2006 in Sydney, and I was one of its Program Chairs. For ACL 2018 we have tried to maintain the welcoming and intimate spirit and the relaxed and genial character of the much smaller ACL conferences of the past in spite of the ever-growing number of researchers in the field and participants in our conferences.

It is my pleasure here to express gratitude to all those without whom this conference would not exist. My biggest thanks go to the Program Chairs Iryna Gurevych and Yusuke Miyao, as well as to Local Chairs Tim Baldwin, Trevor Cohn and Karin Verspoor. They have done a tremendous job to manage the submission and review process, and the local arrangement details, respectively.

I also want to thank all of the other chairs for their very hard work: Workshops Chairs Brendan O'Connor and Eva Maria Vecchi; Tutorials Chairs Yoav Artzi and Jacob Eisenstein; Demo Chairs Fei Liu and Thamar Solorio; Student Research Workshop Organizers Vered Shwartz, Jeniya Tabassum and Rob Voigt; Faculty Advisors to the Student Research Workshop Marie-Catherine de Marneffe, Wanxiang Che and Malvina Nissim; Publications Chairs Shay Cohen, Kevin Gimpel and Wei Lu; Exhibits Coordinator Karin Vespoor; Student Volunteer Coordinator Karin Vespoor; Conference Handbook Chairs Jey Han Lau and Trevor Cohn; Publicity Chair Sarvnaz Karimi; Local Sponsorship Chair Cecile Paris; Webmaster Andrew MacKinlay; and Priscilla Rasmussen, giver of advice and wisdom to all of us as ACL Business Manager.

I also warmly thank the ACL Executive Committee for its guidance and advice on many important issues and concerns as they arose.

I am also extremely grateful to all the sponsors for their great support to the conference.

Many thanks to the area chairs, the reviewers, the invited speakers, the authors of the various papers, posters and presentations.

And, finally, many many thanks to all the participants who will put the final touches on making ACL 2018 an exciting, stimulating and inspiring event!

Claire Cardie
ACL 2018 General Chair
July 2018

Message from the Program Committee Co-Chairs

Welcome to the 56th Annual Meeting of the Association for Computational Linguistics 2018 – or ACL 2018 for short.

In September 2017, Program Committee Co-Chairs (PCs) posted the call for nominations of Area Chairs (AC), Reviewers and Invited Speakers. We received 752 responses in total. Overall, out of 388 valid nominations for area chairs, 299 unique persons were suggested; 110 persons were self-nominations. About 70% of the 56 selected area chairs (later expanded to 61 area chairs due to the high number of submissions) were nominated by the community. For the reviewers, we collected 936 valid nominations. At the PhD level, 139 persons were self-nominations and 129 were nominated by others. At the Postdoc/Ass.Prof. level, 160 were self-nominated, 112 nominated by others. At the Prof. level, 221 persons were self-nominated, 175 nominated by others.

We received 138 unique nominations for invited speakers, from which two invited speakers of the conference were selected:

- Carolyn Penstein Rosé, Language Technologies Institute at Carnegie Mellon University, USA

- Anton van den Hengel, Australian Centre for Visual Technologies at University of Adelaide, Australia

Our community is steadily growing: in total, 1621 submissions were received right after the submission deadline: 1045 long, 576 short papers. 13 erroneous submissions were deleted or withdrawn in the preliminary checks by PCs. 25 papers were rejected without review (16 long, 9 short); the reasons are the violation of the ACL 2018 style and dual submission guidelines. 32 papers were withdrawn before the review period started; the main reason was that the papers have been accepted as the short papers at NAACL HLT 2018. In total, 1551 papers went into the reviewing phase: 1021 long, 530 short papers. 1610 reviewers (1473 primary and 137 secondary reviewers) were involved in the reviewing process; each reviewer has reviewed about 3 papers on average. 3 long and 4 short papers were withdrawn during the reviewing period, and finally 1018 long and 526 short papers were considered during the acceptance decision phase.

The assignment of papers to areas and reviewers has been done in multiple rounds. First round: Initial assignments of papers to areas were determined automatically with the help of the authors' input, while PCs went through all submissions and moved papers to other areas, considering COI and the topical fit. PCs assigned one AC as a meta-reviewer to each paper using Toronto Paper Matching System (TPMS) scores. Second round: ACs looked into the papers in their area, and adjusted meta-reviewer assignments. ACs sent a report to PCs if they found any problems. Third round: PCs made the final decision, considering the workload balance, possible COIs and the topical fit. Fourth round: ACs decided which reviewers would review each paper, based on AC's knowledge about the reviewers, TPMS scores, reviewers' bids, and COI.

We have introduced several innovations to the reviewing process. One of them is an argument-based review form. The reviewers were asked to provide arguments for and against the paper. This has been tremendously helpful for ACs and PCs to analyze the reviews and come up with final recommendations. The authors were asked to respond to the con arguments during the rebuttal. In coordination with the NAACL HLT 2018 PCs, we plan to do some analytics on anonymized reviews and rebuttal statements, with the consent of the reviewers and authors. Our purpose is to improve the quality of the review process. The data will be compiled into a unique corpus for NLP, and will be made available to the research community after appropriate anonymization checks, at the earliest in 2 years after ACL 2018.

We hope to provide data on *how to review* to younger researchers, and to improve the transparency of the reviewing process in general.

The ACL 2018 conference is super-competitive: We accepted 256 out of 1018 submitted long papers and 125 out of 526 short papers, with an overall acceptance rate of 24.7%. The details of the review process are available at the conference homepage. Criteria of acceptance were mainly:

- strengths/weaknesses raised by reviewers and their significance;

- the result of discussions and author responses;

- contribution to CL as the science of language: whether the paper advances (or contributes to) our understanding of language in any way;

- diversity: we do not want to fill ACL with similar papers like achieving 1% improvement on a well-known task.

We also considered the balance of paper types, topics and contributions and re-considered the acceptance when reviewers reported any problem in preliminary checks (*Appropriateness* to *Handling of Human Participants*).

Continuing the tradition, ACL 2018 will feature 20 papers which were accepted for publication in the Transactions of the Association for Computational Linguistics (TACL). The TACL papers were split into 10 oral presentations and 10 poster presentations.

There are many people to thank for who have worked diligently to make ACL 2018 possible. All names are listed in the Program Committee section of the Front Matter.

Since the conference size continues to grow and the organizational complexity increases, we have introduced the role of Program Committee Co-Chair Assistants. In total, 5 senior researchers have supported the PCs during most intensive work phases to handle the communication in a timely manner, draft various documents and effectively prepare decisions.

Thanks to our area chairs for their hard work on recruiting reviewers, managing reviews, leading discussions, and making recommendations.

This program certainly would not be possible without the help of the 1610 reviewers. In particular, 192 reviewers from this list were recognized by the area chairs as outstanding reviewers who have turned in exceptionally well-written and constructive reviews and who have actively engaged themselves in the post-rebuttal discussions.

We are also deeply indebted to the best paper selection committee which consists of 22 members. They had to additionally review 6-8 papers according to the best paper criteria on short notice. Their time and effort in recommending the best paper awards is much appreciated.

We also would like to thank many colleagues for generously sharing their experience in organizing prior ACL conferences and for their advice. We are grateful for the guidance and the support of the ACL presidents Joakim Nivre and Marti Hearst, and the ACL board. We also would like to thank the publication co-chairs Shay Cohen, Kevin Gimpel and Wei Lu (Advisory) and the handbook chair Jey Han Lau for putting together the proceedings and the conference handbook; and Rich Gerber from Softconf for always being responsive to our requests. We would like to thank the ACL Business Manager Priscilla Rasmussen for helping us to sort important things out. Finally, this conference could not have happened without the efforts of the general chair, Claire Cardie. We thank her for the leadership and advice, especially when matters got complicated.

We hope you will enjoy ACL 2018 and contribute to the future success of our community!

ACL 2018 Program Committee Co-Chairs
Iryna Gurevych, TU Darmstadt, Germany
Yusuke Miyao, National Institute of Informatics, Japan

The process for selecting best papers and honourable mentions

The Program Committee Co-Chairs (PCs) have defined a multi-step process. Area Chairs (ACs) were asked to select a number of top papers in their areas satisfying as many as possible of the following criteria:

- high quality

- nominated for the award by at least one primary reviewer

- bringing disruptive ground-breaking innovation as compared to the current mainstream

ACs re-read their finalists and discussed among themselves the merits of the nominee's work with the help of the primary reviews. ACs then submitted the papers to the PCs along with their selection decisions. PCs balanced ACs' nominations for diversity and representativeness among areas and the review consistency. They prepared the papers in Softconf for best-paper reviewing and selection. There were 52 best paper candidates.

In parallel, PCs formed the best paper selection committee (BPC) from 22 experts in the field with a mix of expertise and backgrounds and at a good seniority level. In case of COIs, the BPC member was excluded from the further evaluation process. BPC members reviewed 6-8 papers each and provided a short review with respect to the best paper criteria.

Based on BPC recommendations, there were about 20 papers left in the pool. PCs then re-read those papers and discussed their particular merits. Finally, 6 long papers and 2 short papers were selected as honourable mentions. For the best papers, 3 long papers and 2 short papers were selected for presentation in the closing conference session.

The selected honourable mentions and best papers emphasize the diversity of the ACL in terms of research questions, methods, and interdisciplinarity.

Best Long Papers

- *Finding syntax in human encephalography with beam search.* John Hale, Chris Dyer, Adhiguna Kuncoro and Jonathan Brennan.

- *Learning to Ask Good Questions: Ranking Clarification Questions using Neural Expected Value of Perfect Information.* Sudha Rao and Hal Daumé III.

- *Let's do it "again": A First Computational Approach to Detecting Adverbial Presupposition Triggers.* Andre Cianflone, Yulan Feng, Jad Kabbara and Jackie Chi Kit Cheung.

Best Short Papers

- *Know What You Don't Know: Unanswerable Questions for SQuAD.* Pranav Rajpurkar, Robin Jia and Percy Liang.

- *'Lighter' Can Still Be Dark: Modeling Comparative Color Descriptions.* Olivia Winn and Smaranda Muresan.

Invited Talk: Deep Neural Networks, and what they're not very good at

Anton van den Hengel

Professor, School of Computer Science, University of Adelaide

Abstract: Deep Neural Networks have had an incredible impact in a variety of areas within machine learning, including computer vision and natural language processing. Deep Neural Networks use implicit representations that are very high-dimensional, however, and are thus particularly well suited to problems that can be solved by associative recall of previous solutions. They are ill-suited to problems that require human-interpretable representations, explicit manipulation of symbols, or reasoning. The dependency of Deep Neural Networks on large volumes of training data, also means that they are typically only applicable when the problem itself, and the nature of the test data, are predictable long in advance.

The application of Deep Neural Networks to Visual Question Answering has achieved results that would have been thought impossible only a few years ago. It has also thrown a spotlight on the shortcomings of current Deep Nets in solving problems that require explicit reasoning, the use of a knowledge base, or the ability to learn on the fly. In this talk I will illustrate some of the steps being taken to address these problems, and a new learning-to-learn approach that we hope will combine the power of Deep Learning with the significant benefits of explicit-reasoning-based methods.

Bio: Anton van den Hengel is a Professor in the School of Computer Science at the University of Adelaide, the Director of the Australian Institute for Machine Learning, and a Chief Investigator of the Australian Centre for Robotic Vision. Prof. van den Hengel has been a CI on over \$60m in external research funding from sources including Google, Canon, BHP Billiton and the ARC, and has won a number of awards, including the Pearcey Foundation Entrepreneur Award, the SA Science Excellence Award for Research Collaboration, and the CVPR Best Paper prize in 2010. He has authored over 300 publications, had 8 patents commercialised, formed 2 start-ups, and has recently had a medical technology achieve first-in-class FDA approval. Current research interests include Deep Learning, vison and language problems, interactive image-based modelling, large-scale video surveillance, and learning from large image databases.

Invited Talk: Who is the Bridge Between the What and the How

Carolyn Penstein Rosé
Professor, School of Computer Science, Carnegie Mellon University

Abstract: This talk reports on over a decade of research where theoretical foundations motivate computational models that produce real world impact in online spaces. Both the earliest philosophers of language and the most recent researchers in computational approaches to social media analysis have acknowledged the distinction between the what of language, namely its propositional content, and the how of language, or its form, style, or framing. What bridges between these realms are social processes that motivate the linguistic choices that result in specific realizations of propositional content situated within social interactions, designed to achieve social goals. These insights allow researchers to make sense of the connection between discussion processes and outcomes from those discussions. These findings motivate on the one hand design of computational approaches to real time monitoring of discussion processes and on the other hand the design of interventions that support interactions in online spaces with the goal of increasing desired outcomes, including learning, health, and wellbeing.

As an example, in this talk we probe into a specific quality of discussion referred to as Transactivity. Transactivity is the extent to which a contribution articulates the reasoning of the speaker, that of an interlocutor, and the relation between them. In different contexts, and within very distinct theoretical frameworks, this construct has been associated with solidarity, influence, expertise transfer, and learning. Within the construct of Transactivity, the cognitive and social underpinnings are inextricably linked such that modeling the who enables prediction of the connection between the what and the how.

Bio: Dr. Carolyn Rosé is a Professor of Language Technologies and Human-Computer Interaction in the School of Computer Science at Carnegie Mellon University. Her research program is focused on better understanding the social and pragmatic nature of conversation, and using this understanding to build computational systems that can improve the efficacy of conversation between people, and between people and computers. In order to pursue these goals, she invokes approaches from computational discourse analysis and text mining, conversational agents, and computer supported collaborative learning. Her research group's highly interdisciplinary work, published in 200 peer reviewed publications, is represented in the top venues in 5 fields: namely, Language Technologies, Learning Sciences, Cognitive Science, Educational Technology, and Human-Computer Interaction, with awards in 3 of these fields. She serves as Past President and Inaugural Fellow of the International Society of the Learning Sciences, Chair of the International Alliance to Advance Learning in the Digital Era, and Executive Editor of the International Journal of Computer-Supported Collaborative Learning.

Organising Committee

General Chair:

Claire Cardie, Cornell University

Program Chairs:

Iryna Gurevych, TU Darmstadt
Yusuke Miyao, National Institute of Informatics

Workshop Chairs:

Brendan O'Connor, University of Massachusetts Amherst
Eva Maria Vecchi, University of Cambridge

Tutorial Chairs:

Yoav Artzi, Cornell University
Jacob Eisenstein, Georgia Institute of Technology

Demo Chairs:

Fei Liu, University of Central Florida
Thamar Solorio, University of Houston

Publications Chairs:

Shay Cohen, University of Edinburgh
Kevin Gimpel, Toyota Technological Institute at Chicago
Wei Lu, Singapore University of Technology and Design (Advisory)

Exhibits Coordinator:

Karin Verspoor, University of Melbourne

Conference Handbook Chairs:

Jey Han Lau, IBM Research
Trevor Cohn, University of Melbourne

Publicity Chair:

Sarvnaz Karimi, CSIRO

Local Sponsorship Chair:

Cecile Paris, CSIRO

Local Chairs:

Tim Baldwin, University of Melbourne
Karin Verspoor, University of Melbourne
Trevor Cohn, University of Melbourne

Student Research Workshop Organisers:

Vered Shwartz, Bar-Ilan University
Jeniya Tabassum, Ohio State University
Rob Voigt, Stanford University

Faculty Advisors to the Student Research Workshop:

Marie-Catherine de Marneffe, Ohio State University
Wanxiang Che, Harbin Institute of Technology
Malvina Nissim, University of Groningen

Webmaster:

Andrew MacKinlay, Culture Amp / University of Melbourne

Program Committee

Program Committee Co-Chairs

Iryna Gurevych, TU Darmstadt, Germany
Yusuke Miyao, National Institute of Informatics, Japan

Program Committee Co-Chair Assistants

Yang Gao, TU Darmstadt, Germany
Ivan Habernal, TU Darmstadt, Germany
Sang Phan, National Institute of Informatics, Japan
Steffen Eger, TU Darmstadt, Germany
Christian Meyer, TU Darmstadt, Germany

Area Chairs

Senior Area Chairs are indicated in boldface.

Dialogue and Interactive Systems

Asli Celikyilmaz
Verena Rieser
Milica Gasic
Jason Williams

Discourse and Pragmatics

Manfred Stede
Ani Nenkova

Document Analysis

Hang Li
Yiqun Liu
Eugene Agichtein

Generation

Ioannis Konstas
Claire Gardent

Information Extraction and Text Mining

Feiyu Xu
Kevin Cohen
Zhiyuan Liu
Ralph Grishman
Yi Yang
Nazli Goharian

Linguistic Theories, Cognitive Modeling and Psycholinguistics

Shuly Wintner
Tim O'Donnell

Machine Learning

Andre Martins
Ariadna Quattoni
Jun Suzuki

Machine Translation

Yang Liu (Tsinghua University)
Matt Post
Lucia Specia
Dekai Wu

Multidisciplinary and Area Chair COI

Yoav Goldberg
Anders Søgaard
Mirella Lapata

Multilinguality

Bernardo Magnini
Tristan Miller

Phonology, Morphology and Word Segmentation

Graham Neubig
Hai Zhao

Question Answering

Lluís Màrquez
Teruko Mitamura
Zornitsa Kozareva
Richard Socher

Resources and Evaluation

Gerard de Melo
Sara Tonelli
Karën Fort

Sentence-level Semantics

Luke Zettlemoyer
Ellie Pavlick
Jacob Uszkoreit

Sentiment Analysis and Argument Mining

Smaranda Muresan
Benno Stein
Yulan He

Social Media

David Jurgens

Jing Jiang

Summarization

Kathleen McKeown
Xiaodan Zhu

Tagging, Chunking, Syntax and Parsing

Liang Huang
Weiwei Sun
Željko Agić
Yue Zhang

Textual Inference and Other Areas of Semantics

Michael Roth
Fabio Massimo Zanzotto

Vision, Robotics, Multimodal, Grounding and Speech

Yoav Artzi
Shinji Watanabe
Timothy Hospedales

Word-level Semantics

Ekaterina Shutova
Roberto Navigli

Best Paper Selection Committee

Timothy Baldwin
Pushpak Bhattacharyya
Phil Blunsom
Johan Bos
Jordan Boyd-Graber
Trevor Cohn
Vera Demberg
Kevin Duh
Katrin Erk
Mark Johnson
Yang Liu (Tsinghua University)
Yuji Matsumoto
Jong Park
Ellie Pavlick
Simone Paolo Ponzetto
Sebastian Riedel
Carolyn Penstein Rosé
Noah A. Smith
Anders Søgaard
Ivan Titov
Benjamin Van Durme
Ming Zhou

Primary Reviewers

Outstanding reviewers are indicated in boldface.

Mourad Abbas, Ahmed Abdelali, Asad Abdi, **Muhammad Abdul-Mageed**, **Omri Abend**, Gilles Adda, Heike Adel, Stergos Afantenos, Apoorv Agarwal, Arvind Agarwal, Rodrigo Agerri, Roee Aharoni, Murat Akbacak, Mohammad Akbari, Alan Akbik, Ahmet Aker, Elif Aktolga, Mohamed Al-Badrashiny, Firoj Alam, Chris Alberti, Hanan Aldarmaki, **Enrique Alfonseca**, David Alfter, Afra Alishahi, Laura Alonso Alemany, Ashjan Alsulaimani, David Alvarez-Melis, Carlos Alzate, **Maxime Amblard**, Daniel Andrade, **Jacob Andreas**, Nicholas Andrews, Ion Androutsopoulos, Anietie Andy, Galia Angelova, Jean-Yves Antoine, **Marianna Apidianaki**, **Emilia Apostolova**, Jun Araki, Kenji Araki, Yuki Arase, Philip Arthur, Masayuki Asahara, Ramón Astudillo, John Atkinson, Giuseppe Attardi, Isabelle Augenstein, Eleftherios Avramidis, Amittai Axelrod, Wilker Aziz, AmirAli Bagher Zadeh, JinYeong Bak, Collin Baker, Simon Baker, Omid Bakhshandeh, Alexandra Balahur, Mithun Balakrishna, Vevake Balaraman, Niranjan Balasubramanian, Timothy Baldwin, Kalika Bali, Miguel Ballesteros, David Bamman, Rafael E. Banchs, Srinivas Bangalore, Mohit Bansal, Roy Bar-Haim, Libby Barak, Ken Barker, Marco Baroni, Alberto Barrón-Cedeño, Sabine Bartsch, Pierpaolo Basile, Valerio Basile, Roberto Basili, Daniel Bauer, Timo Baumann, **Rachel Bawden**, Frederic Bechet, Daniel Beck, Srikanta Bedathur, **Beata Beigman Klebanov**, Núria Bel, Yonatan Belinkov, Meriem Beloucif, Iz Beltagy, Anja Belz, Yassine Benajiba, **Jonathan Berant**, Raffaella Bernardi, Yevgeni Berzak, Laurent Besacier, Steven Bethard, Rahul Bhagat, Archna Bhatia, Sumit Bhatia, Pushpak Bhattacharyya, Ergun Biçici, Ann Bies, Lidong Bing, **Joachim Bingel**, **Or Biran**, Alexandra Birch, Arianna Bisazza, Yonatan Bisk, Johannes Bjerva, Anders Björkelund, Philippe Blache, Frédéric Blain, Eduardo Blanco, Michael Bloodgood, Bernd Bohnet, Ondřej Bojar, Danushka Bollegala, Daniele Bonadiman, Claire Bonial, Francesca Bonin, Kalina Bontcheva, Georgeta Bordea, **Benjamin Börschinger**, Johan Bos, Elizabeth Boschee, **Antoine Bosselut**, Fethi Bougares, Pierrette Bouillon, **Gerlof Bouma**, **Samuel Bowman**, Cem Bozsahin, David Bracewell, James Bradbury, S.R.K. Branavan, António Branco, Chloé Braud, Ted Briscoe, **Chris Brockett**, Julian Brooke, Thomas Brovelli (Meyer), Christian Buck, Paweł Budzianowski, Michael Bugert, Paul Buitelaar, Harry Bunt, Franck Burlot, Hendrik Buschmeier, Miriam Butt, Jan Buys, José G. C. de Souza, Deng Cai, Iacer Calixto, Chris Callison-Burch, Jose Camacho-Collados, **Erik Cambria**, Leonardo Campillos Llanos, B Rosario Campomanes-Alvarez, **Burcu Can**, Yuan Cao, Yunbo Cao, Giuseppe Carenini, Marine Carpuat, Xavier Carreras, John Carroll, Paula Carvalho, Vitor Carvalho, Francisco Casacuberta, Iñigo Casanueva, Helena Caseli, **Tommaso Caselli**, Taylor Cassidy, Giuseppe Castellucci, Daniel Cer, Christophe Cerisara, Özlem Çetinoğlu, Mauro Cettolo, Joyce Chai, Yllias Chali, **Nathanael Chambers**, Muthu Kumar Chandrasekaran, Akshay Chandrashekaran, **Angel Chang**, Baobao Chang, Chia-Hui Chang, Kai-Wei Chang, Yin-Wen Chang, Snigdha Chaturvedi, Wanxiang Che, **Ciprian Chelba**, Bin Chen, Boxing Chen, Chen Chen, Danqi Chen, Hsin-Hsi Chen, Qian Chen, Qingcai Chen, Wenliang Chen, Xinchi Chen, Yubo Chen, **Yun-Nung Chen**, Zhiyuan Chen, Fei Cheng, **Hao Cheng**, Jianpeng Cheng, Pu-Jen Cheng, Colin Cherry, Jackie Chi Kit Cheung, David Chiang, Christian Chiarcos, Jen-Tzung Chien, Hai Leong Chieu, Dokook Choe, Eunsol Choi, Yejin Choi, Kostadin Cholakov, Grzegorz Chrupała, Chenhui Chu, Tagyoung Chung, Kenneth Church, Mark Cieliebak, Philipp Cimiano, Volkan Cirik, Alexander Clark, Stephen Clark, Guillaume Cleuziou, Ann Clifton, **Maximin Coavoux**, **Anne Cocos**, **Arman Cohan**, Kevin Cohen, Shay B. Cohen, Michael Collins, John Conroy, Matthieu Constant, Danish Contractor, Paul Cook, Marta R. Costa-jussà, Ryan Cotterell, **Alain Couillault**, Benoit Crabbé, Danilo Croce, **Paul Crook**, James Cross, Montse Cuadros, Heriberto Cuayahuitl, Silviu-Petru Cucerzan, Lei Cui, Xiaodong Cui, Aron Culotta, Shane Culpepper, Anna Currey, Luis Fernando D'Haro, Giovanni Da San Martino, Walter Daelemans, Xin-Yu Dai, Beatrice Daille, Fahim Dalvi, Cristian Danescu-Niculescu-Mizil, Falavigna Daniele, Kareem Darwish, Abhishek Das, Amitava Das, Dipanjan Das, Tirthankar Dasgupta, Johannes Daxenberger, Gaël de Chalendar, Munmun De Choudhury, Adrià de Gispert, Daniël de Kok, Eric De La Clergerie, **Marie-Catherine de Marneffe**, Renato de Mori, Thierry Declerck, Luciano Del Corro, Louise Deléger, Felice Dell'Orletta, **Claudio Delli Bovi**, Rodolfo Delmonte, Vera Demberg, Dina Demner-Fushman, Lingjia Deng, Pascal Denis, Michael Denkowski, Tejaswini Deoskar, Valeria dePaiva, Nina Dethlefs, **Chris Develder**, Barry Devereux, Bhuwan Dhingra, Luigi Di Caro, Giuseppe Di Fabbrizio, Emanuele Di Rosa, Mona Diab, Gaël Dias, Jana Diesner, Shuoyang Ding, Georgiana Dinu, Stefanie Dipper, Nemanja Djuric, Dmitriy Dligach, Simon Dobnik, Jesse Dodge, A. Seza Doğruöz, Tobias Domhan, Daxiang Dong, **Li Dong**, Shichao Dong, Doug Downey, Mark Dras, Markus Dreyer, Patrick Drouin, Lan Du, Xinya Du, Nan Duan, Xiangyu Duan, Pablo Duboue, Shiran Dudy, **Kevin Duh**, Stefan Daniel Dumitrescu, **Greg Durrett**, **Ondřej Dušek**, Chris Dyer, Hiroshi Echizen'ya, **Judith Eckle-Kohler**, Markus Egg, Patrick Ehlen, Maud Ehrmann, Vladimir Eidelman, Andreas Eisele, **Jacob Eisenstein**, Layla El Asri, Shady Elbassuoni, Mohamed Eldesouki, Michael Elhadad, Desmond Elliott, **Guy Emerson**, Erkut Erdem, **Mihail Eric**, Tomaž Erjavec, **Katrin Erk**, Arash Eshghi, Ramy Eskander, Cristina España-Bonet, Luis Espinosa Anke, Miquel Esplà-Gomis, Kilian Evang, **Ingrid Falk**, Hao Fang, Hui Fang, Licheng Fang, Meng Fang, Benamara Farah, Stefano Faralli, Richárd Farkas, Maryam Fazel-Zarandi, Afsaneh Fazly, Marcello Federico, Christian Federmann, Anna Feldman, Yansong Feng, Olivier Ferret, Alejandro Figueroa, Elena Filatova, Simone Filice, Denis Filimonov, Katja Filippova, Andrew Finch, Mark Finlayson, Orhan Firat, Mark Fishel, Nicholas FitzGerald, Jeffrey Flanigan, **Margaret Fleck**, Lucie Flekova, Radu Florian, Antske Fokkens, Eric Fosler-Lussier, **George Foster**, **James Foulds**, Marc Franco-Salvador, Thomas Francois, Stella Frank, Dayne Freitag, Markus Freitag, André Freitas, **Lea Frermann**, **Daniel Fried**, Annemarie Friedrich, Hagen Fuerstenau, Akinori Fujino, Fumiyo Fukumoto, Sadaoki Furui, Robert Gaizauskas, Olivier Galibert, Irina Galinskaya, Matthias Gallé, Michel Galley, Kuzman Ganchev, Octavian-Eugen Ganea, Bin Gao, Jianfeng Gao, **Wei Gao**, Claire Gardent, **Dan Garrette**, **Albert Gatt**, Eric Gaussier, Tao Ge, **Lieke Gelderloos**, Spandana Gella, Kallirroi Georgila, Pablo Gervás, Marjan Ghazvininejad, Debanjan Ghosh, Sucheta Ghosh, Daniela Gifu, Daniel Gildea, C Lee Giles, Kevin Gimpel, Roxana Girju, **Dimitra Gkatzia**, **Goran Glavaš**, Dan Goldwasser, **Carlos Gómez-Rodríguez**, Hugo Gonçalo Oliveira, Jibing Gong, Yeyun Gong, Graciela Gonzalez-Hernandez, Jesús González-Rubio, Kyle Gorman, Matthew R. Gormley, **Cyril Goutte**, Kartik Goyal, Natalia Grabar, Joao Graca, Jorge Gracia, Yvette Graham, Roger Granada, **Christophe Gravier**, **Gregory Grefenstette**, Cyril Grouin, Marco Guerini, Anupam Guha, Lin Gui, Bruno Guillaume, Curry Guinn, **Kristina Gulordava**, Weiwei Guo, Yuhong Guo, **Arpit Gupta**, Joakim Gustafson, **E. Dario Gutierrez**, Francisco Guzmán, Jeremy Gwinnup, Maryam Habibi, Ben Hachey, Christian Hadiwinoto, Gholamreza Haffari, Udo Hahn, Hannaneh Hajishirzi, Dilek Hakkani-Tur, Keith Hall, **William L. Hamilton**, Michael Hammond, Thierry Hamon, Ting Han, Xianpei Han, Sanda Harabagiu, Christian Hardmeier, Orin Hargraves, Sadid A. Hasan, Kazuma Hashimoto, Eva Hasler, Ahmed Hassan Awadallah, Hany Hassan, Helen Hastie, Katsuhiko Hayashi, He He, Hua He, **Luheng He**, Shizhu He, Xiangnan He, Kenneth Heafield, James Henderson, Matthew Henderson, **Lisa Anne Hendricks**, **Aurélie Herbelot**, Jonathan Herzig, **Jack Hessel**, **John Hewitt**, Felix Hieber, Ryuichiro Higashinaka, Tsutomu Hirao, **Julia Hirschberg**, **Graeme Hirst**, Julian Hitschler, Lydia-Mai Ho-Dac, Vu Cong Duy Hoang, Johannes Hoffart, Chris Hokamp, Chester Holtz, **Ari Holtzman**, Yu Hong, Chiori Hori, Takaaki Hori, Ehsan Hosseini-Asl, Yufang Hou, Julian Hough, Dirk Hovy, Eduard Hovy, **David M. Howcroft**, Renfen Hu, Yuheng Hu, Zhiting Hu, Fei Huang, Hen-Hsen Huang, Lifu Huang, Minlie Huang, Po-Sen Huang, Ruihong Huang, Shujian Huang, Xuanjing Huang, Matthias Huck, Mans Hulden, **Tim Hunter**, Jena D. Hwang, Seung-won Hwang, Ignacio Iacobacci, Nancy Ide, Marco Idiart, Adrian Iftene, Ryu Iida, Naoya Inoue, Kentaro Inui, **Srinivasan Iyer**, Mohit Iyyer, Tommi Jaakkola, **Cassandra L. Jacobs**, **Aaron Jaech**, Kokil Jaidka, **Laura Jehl**, **Yacine Jernite**, Rahul Jha, Donghong Ji, Yangfeng Ji, Robin Jia, Sittichai Jiampojamarn, Hui Jiang, Antonio Jimeno Yepes, Hongyan Jing, **Charles Jochim**, Richard Johansson, Kristiina Jokinen, Gareth Jones, **Aditya Joshi**, Shafiq Joty, Marcin Junczys-Dowmunt, Ákos Kádár, Sylvain Kahane, **Hetunandan Kamisetty**, **Herman Kamper**, Jaap Kamps, Min-Yen Kan, Hiroshi Kanayama, **Dongyeop Kang**, Katharina Kann, Diptesh Kanojia, Dimitri Kartsaklis, Makoto P. Kato, David Kauchak, Daisuke Kawahara, Tatsuya Kawahara, Anna Kazantseva, **Hideto Kazawa**, Chris Kedzie, **Andrew Kehler**, Simon Keizer, Ruth Kempson, Casey Kennington, Fabio Kepler, Nitish Shirish Keskar, Mitesh M. Khapra, Huda Khayrallah, **Douwe Kiela**, Yuta Kikuchi, **Halil Kilicoglu**, Jin-Dong Kim, Sun Kim, **Yoon Kim**, Young-Bum Kim, **Brian Kingsbury**, Eliyahu Kiperwasser, Svetlana Kiritchenko, Chunyu Kit, Dietrich Klakow, Alexandre Klementiev, Manfred Klenner, Sigrid Klerke, **Ro-**

man Klinger, Julien Kloetzer, Kevin Knight, Sosuke Kobayashi, Thomas Kober, **Ekaterina Kochmar**, Philipp Koehn, **Alexander Koller**, Kazunori Komatani, **Rik Koncel-Kedziorski**, **Grzegorz Kondrak**, Lingpeng Kong, **Maximilian Köper**, Stefan Kopp, Selcuk Kopru, Parisa Kordjamshidi, Valia Kordoni, Anna Korhonen, Yannis Korkontzelos, Leila Kosseim, Katsunori Kotani, Lili Kotlerman, Emiel Krahmer, Martin Krallinger, Julia Kreutzer, **Jayant Krishnamurthy**, Kriste Krstovski, Canasai Kruengkrai, **Ivana Kruijff-Korbayova**, **Germán Kruszewski**, Lun-Wei Ku, Marco Kuhlmann, Roland Kuhn, Ashish Kulkarni, Gaurav Kumar, **Shankar Kumar**, Anil Kumar Singh, **Jonathan K. Kummerfeld**, Adhiguna Kuncoro, Souvik Kundu, Gakuto Kurata, Sadao Kurohashi, Nate Kushman, Andrey Kutuzov, Polina Kuznetsova, Majid Laali, Gorka Labaka, Anirban Laha, Mathias Lambert, Vasileios Lampos, **Gerasimos Lampouras**, Ian Lane, Ni Lao, Mirella Lapata, Shalom Lappin, Romain Laroche, Kornel Laskowski, Alberto Lavelli, Alon Lavie, Phong Le, **Joseph Le Roux**, Robert Leaman, Gianluca Lebani, **Chia-ying Lee**, Hung-yi Lee, John Lee, Kenton Lee, Lin-shan Lee, Moontae Lee, Sungjin Lee, Yoong Keok Lee, **Young-Suk Lee**, **Els Lefever**, Fabrice Lefevre, Wenqiang Lei, Jochen L. Leidner, Gaël Lejeune, Alessandro Lenci, Piroska Lendvai, Yves Lepage, Johannes Leveling, Tomer Levinboim, Omer Levy, **Roger Levy**, Mike Lewis, Baoli Li, Cheng-Te Li, Chenliang Li, Chunyuan Li, Fangtao Li, Haizhou Li, Jing Li, Juanzi Li, Junhui Li, Junyi Jessy Li, Piji Li, Qing Li, **Shaohua Li**, Sheng Li, Shoushan Li, Sujian Li, Wenjie Li, Xiangsheng Li, Xiaoli Li, **Xiujun Li**, Yanran Li, Zhenghua Li, Zhixing Li, Zichao Li, **Maria Liakata**, Chen Liang, **Timm Lichte**, Anne-Laure Ligozat, Nut Limsopatham, **Chenghua Lin**, Chin-Yew Lin, Jimmy Lin, Shou-de Lin, Xi Victoria Lin, Xiao Ling, **Tal Linzen**, Zachary Lipton, Pierre Lison, Diane Litman, Marina Litvak, Bing Liu, Changsong Liu, Fei Liu, Jing Liu, Kang Liu, Lemao Liu, Qian Liu, Qiaoling Liu, Qun Liu, Shujie Liu, Ting Liu, Xiaobing Liu, Yang Liu (University of Texas at Dallas), Yang Liu (University of Edinburgh), Yang Liu (Tsinghua University), Yijia Liu, Zhiyuan Liu, Elena Lloret, **Sharid Loáiciga**, José Lopes, Lucelene Lopes, Marcos Lopes, Oier Lopez de Lacalle, Aurelio Lopez-Lopez, Annie Louis, Samuel Louvan, Bin Lu, Qin Lu, **Wei Lu**, Xiaofei Lu, Yanbin Lu, Zhiyong Lu, Yi Luan, **Andy Luecking**, **Stephanie M. Lukin**, Cheng Luo, Jiaming Luo, Xiaoqiang Luo, Zhunchen Luo, Franco M. Luque, Anh Tuan Luu, Teresa Lynn, Ji Ma, Jianqiang Ma, Mingbo Ma, Xuezhe Ma, Wolfgang Macherey, Pranava Swaroop Madhyastha, Nitin Madnani, Pierre Magistry, Simone Magnolini, **Wolfgang Maier**, **Jean Maillard**, Prodromos Malakasiotis, Alfredo Maldonado, Andreas Maletti, Igor Malioutov, Radhika Mamidi, Suresh Manandhar, Gideon Mann, Christopher D. Manning, Diego Marcheggiani, Daniel Marcu, David Mareček, **Matthew Marge**, Alex Marin, Erwin Marsi, Scott Martin, Héctor Martínez Alonso, Bruno Martins, David Martins de Matos, Yuval Marton, **Yann Mathet**, Prashant Mathur, Shigeki Matsubara, Yuji Matsumoto, Yoichi Matsuyama, Takuya Matsuzaki, Austin Matthews, Jonathan May, Karen Mazidi, David McAllester, Diana McCarthy, **R. Thomas Mccoy**, **John Philip McCrae**, Stephen McGregor, Tara McIntosh, Louise McNally, Yashar Mehdad, Sameep Mehta, **Hongyuan Mei**, Oren Melamud, Nurit Melnik, Arul Menezes, Fandong Meng, Slim Mesfar, **Florian Metze**, Haitao Mi, Yishu Miao, Antonio Valerio Miceli Barone, Claudiu Mihăilă, Todor Mihaylov, Elena Mikhalkova, Timothy Miller, Tristan Miller, Bonan Min, **Anne-Lyse Minard**, Michael Minock, Toben Mintz, Shachar Mirkin, Seyed Abolghasem Mirroshandel, Paramita Mirza, **Abhijit Mishra**, Dipendra Misra, Prasenjit Mitra, Vikramjit Mitra, Arpit Mittal, Makoto Miwa, Junta Mizuno, Daichi Mochihashi, Ashutosh Modi, Marie-Francine Moens, Samaneh Moghaddam, Abdelrahman Mohamed, **Saif Mohammad**, Behrang Mohit, Michael Mohler, Mitra Mohtarami, Karo Moilanen, Luis Gerardo Mojica de la Vega, Helena Moniz, Johanna Monti, **Nafise Sadat Moosavi**, Roser Morante, Erwan Moreau, Shinsuke Mori, Hajime Morita, Andrea Moro, David R. Mortensen, Alessandro Moschitti, Nasrin Mostafazadeh, Lili Mou, Diego Moussallem, Nikola Mrkšić, Arjun Mukherjee, Tanmoy Mukherjee, Philippe Muller, Yugo Murawaki, Gabriel Murray, Kenton Murray, Elena Musi, Sung-Hyon Myaeng, Maria Nadejde, Masaaki Nagata, Ajay Nagesh, Tetsuji Nakagawa, Yukiko Nakano, Ndapa Nakashole, Preslav Nakov, Courtney Napoles, Jason Naradowsky, Karthik Narasimhan, **Shashi Narayan**, Shrikanth Narayanan, Masha Naslidnyk, Alexis Nasr, Vivi Nastase, Borja Navarro-Colorado, Adeline Nazarenko, Arvind Neelakantan, Matteo Negri, Aida Nematzadeh, Guenter Neumann, Aurélie Névéol, Denis Newman-Griffis, **Dominick Ng**, Hwee Tou Ng, Jun-Ping Ng, Vincent Ng, Dong Nguyen, Thien Huu Nguyen, Truc-Vien T. Nguyen, Viet-An Nguyen, Garrett Nicolai, Massimo Nicosia, Vlad

Niculae, **Jian-Yun Nie**, Jan Niehues, Ivelina Nikolova, Kristina Nilsson Björkenstam, **Sergiu Nisioi**, **Joakim Nivre**, Cicero Nogueira dos Santos, Hiroshi Noji, Joel Nothman, Damien Nouvel, **Diarmuid Ó Séaghdha**, Stephan Oepen, Kemal Oflazer, Alice Oh, Jong-Hoon Oh, Kiyonori Ohtake, Hidekazu Oiwa, Naoaki Okazaki, Hiroshi G. Okuno, Shereen Oraby, Constantin Orasan, Vicente Ordonez, Petya Osenova, Simon Ostermann, Robert Östling, Myle Ott, Jessica Ouyang, Katja Ovchinnikova, Arzucan Özgür, Muntsa Padró, **Alexis Palmer**, Martha Palmer, Alessio Palmero Aprosio, Joao Palotti, Boyuan Pan, Sinno Jialin Pan, Xiaoman Pan, Alexander Panchenko, Alexandros Papangelis, Denis Paperno, Ankur Parikh, Cecile Paris, **Seong-Bae Park**, Yannick Parmentier, Patrick Paroubek, **Carla Parra Escartín**, Tommaso Pasini, Peyman Passban, **Panupong Pasupat**, Siddharth Patwardhan, Michael J. Paul, Adam Pauls, Romain Paulus, Adam Pease, Pavel Pecina, Bolette Pedersen, Anselmo Peñas, Baolin Peng, Hao Peng, Haoruo Peng, Nanyun Peng, Xiaochang Peng, Laura Perez-Beltrachini, **Isaac Persing**, Casper Petersen, Fabio Petroni, Slav Petrov, Miriam R L Petruck, Hieu Pham, Nghia The Pham, Karl Pichotta, Roberto Pieraccini, Olivier Pietquin, **Mohammad Taher Pilehvar**, Juan Pino, Yuval Pinter, Emily Pitler, Paul Piwek, Barbara Plank, Massimo Poesio, Thierry Poibeau, Heather Pon-Barry, Edoardo Maria Ponti, Simone Paolo Ponzetto, Andrei Popescu-Belis, Maja Popović, Fred Popowich, François Portet, **Christopher Potts**, Vinodkumar Prabhakaran, Daniel Preoţiuc-Pietro, Laurent Prévot, Emily Prud'hommeaux, Matthew Purver, James Pustejovsky, Valentina Pyatkin, **Ashequl Qadir**, Vahed Qazvinian, Peng Qi, Longhua Qian, Lianhui Qin, Long Qiu, Minghui Qiu, Xipeng Qiu, Lizhen Qu, Uwe Quasthoff, Chris Quirk, **Alessandro Raganato**, Altaf Rahman, Jonathan Raiman, Taraka Rama, Vikram Ramanarayanan, Maya Ramanath, Rohan Ramanath, Carlos Ramisch, Jinfeng Rao, Ari Rappoport, Mohammad Sadegh Rasooli, Pushpendre Rastogi, Soumya Ray, Manny Rayner, Simon Razniewski, Livy Real, Siva Reddy, Chris Reed, **Ines Rehbein**, Georg Rehm, Marek Rei, Roi Reichart, Julia Reinspach, Ehud Reiter, **Steffen Remus**, Xiang Ren, Zhaochun Ren, Christian Retore, Corentin Ribeyre, Kyle Richardson, Matthew Richardson, Mark Riedl, Martin Riedl, Jason Riesa, Stefan Riezler, German Rigau, Ellen Riloff, **Laura Rimell**, Fabio Rinaldi, Alan Ritter, Kirk Roberts, Molly Roberts, Ina Roesiger, Marcus Rohrbach, Oleg Rokhlenko, Laurent Romary, Salvatore Romeo, Carolyn Penstein Rosé, Andrew Rosenberg, **Sara Rosenthal**, Sophie Rosset, **Paolo Rosso**, Benjamin Roth, **Michael Roth**, Sascha Rothe, Johann Roturier, Jacobo Rouces, Subhro Roy, Alla Rozovskaya, Raphael Rubino, Sebastian Ruder, **Rachel Rudinger**, Maja Rudolph, Pablo Ruiz, Anna Rumshisky, Josef Ruppenhofer, Vasile Rus, Irene Russo, Delia Rusu, Attapol Rutherford, Mrinmaya Sachan, Kugatsu Sadamitsu, Markus Saers, Kenji Sagae, Benoît Sagot, Saurav Sahay, Cem Sahin, Magnus Sahlgren, Patrick Saint-Dizier, Hassan Sajjad, Keisuke Sakaguchi, Sakriani Sakti, Mohammad Salameh, Elizabeth Salesky, Avneesh Saluja, Rajhans Samdani, Mark Sammons, Germán Sanchis-Trilles, **Marina Santini**, Ruhi Sarikaya, Kamal Sarkar, **Agata Savary**, Asad Sayeed, Carolina Scarton, **Tatjana Scheffler**, **Christian Scheible**, Niko Schenk, Yves Scherrer, Frank Schilder, David Schlangen, Natalie Schluter, Allen Schmaltz, Helmut Schmid, Alexandra Schofield, William Schuler, Björn Schuller, Sabine Schulte im Walde, Claudia Schulz, Sebastian Schuster, Didier Schwab, H. Andrew Schwartz, Lane Schwartz, Roy Schwartz, Donia Scott, Djamé Seddah, Joao Sedoc, Abigail See, Frederique Segond, Satoshi Sekine, Ethan Selfridge, Mark Seligman, Jean Senellart, Rico Sennrich, Minjoon Seo, Christophe Servan, Burr Settles, Armin Seyeditabari, Lei Sha, Izhak Shafran, Kashif Shah, Pararth Shah, Samira Shaikh, Igor Shalyminov, Lifeng Shang, Yan Shao, Ehsan Shareghi, Rebecca Sharp, Lanbo She, Shiqi Shen, Shuming Shi, Hiroyuki Shindo, Koichi Shinoda, Eyal Shnarch, **Vered Shwartz**, Advaith Siddharthan, Avi Sil, Carina Silberer, Max Silberztein, Sameer Singh, Kairit Sirts, Gabriel Skantze, **Noam Slonim**, Kevin Small, **Noah A. Smith**, Jan Šnajder, Richard Socher, Artem Sokolov, **Luca Soldaini**, **Swapna Somasundaran**, Wei Song, Yangqiu Song, Radu Soricut, Aitor Soroa, **Daniil Sorokin**, René Speck, Jennifer Spenader, **Manuela Speranza**, Matthias Sperber, Caroline Sporleder, **Vivek Srikumar**, Somayajulu Sripada, Shashank Srivastava, **Christian Stab**, Sanja Štajner, **Gabriel Stanovsky**, Mark Steedman, Pontus Stenetorp, **Mitchell Stern**, Mark Stevenson, Brandon Stewart, Sebastian Stober, Matthew Stone, Svetlana Stoyanchev, Veselin Stoyanov, Karl Stratos, **Kristina Striegnitz**, **Jannik Strötgen**, **Emma Strubell**, Tomek Strzalkowski, Sara Stymne, Hui Su, Jinsong Su, Keh-Yih Su, Yu Su, David Suendermann-Oeft, Alane Suhr, Ang Sun, Huan Sun, Le Sun, Lin Sun, Weiwei Sun, Xu Sun, Hanna Suominen, Mihai Surdeanu, Simon Suster, Hisami Suzuki, **Swabha**

Swayamdipta, **John Sylak-Glassman**, Stan Szpakowicz, Idan Szpektor, Oscar Täckström, Prasad Tadepalli, Kaveh Taghipour, Nina Tahmasebi, Sho Takase, David Talbot, Aleš Tamchyna, **Akihiro Tamura**, Chenhao Tan, Liling Tan, Niket Tandon, Duyu Tang, Jiliang Tang, Jintao Tang, **Chris Tanner**, Fangbo Tao, Marta Tatu, Christoph Teichmann, Serra Sinem Tekiroglu, Irina Temnikova, Joel Tetreault, Simone Teufel, Kapil Thadani, Stefan Thater, Jesse Thomason, Sam Thomson, Fei Tian, Ran Tian, Jörg Tiedemann, Ivan Titov, Takenobu Tokunaga, Katrin Tomanek, Gaurav Singh Tomar, Marc Tomlinson, Antonio Toral, Kentaro Torisawa, Isabel Trancoso, David Traum, Rocco Tripodi, Alexander Trott, Chen-Tse Tsai, Ming-Feng Tsai, Reut Tsarfaty, Yuta Tsuboi, Oren Tsur, Yoshimasa Tsuruoka, Yulia Tsvetkov, Kewei Tu, Zhaopeng Tu, Dan Tufis, Don Tuggener, Gokhan Tur, Marco Turchi, Ferhan Ture, Francis Tyers, Kateryna Tymoshenko, Kiyotaka Uchimoto, Stefan Ultes, **Shyam Upadhyay**, Olga Uryupina, Dmitry Ustalov, Masao Utiyama, Alessandro Valitutti, Tim Van de Cruys, **Benjamin Van Durme**, Paul Van Eecke, **Menno van Zaanen**, Vincent Vandeghinste, Clara Vania, Tony Veale, Mihaela Vela, Paola Velardi, Sumithra Velupillai, Subhashini Venugopalan, Patrick Verga, Marc Verhagen, Rakesh Verma, Karin Verspoor, **Tim Vieira**, David Vilar, **David Vilares**, **Serena Villata**, Aline Villavicencio, Sami Virpioja, **Andreas Vlachos**, Svitlana Volkova, Elena Volodina, Ngoc Thang Vu, **Thuy Vu**, **Ivan Vulić**, V.G.Vinod Vydiswaran, Ekaterina Vylomova, **Henning Wachsmuth**, Joachim Wagner, **Byron Wallace**, Matthew Walter, Xiaojun Wan, Baoxun Wang, Chenguang Wang, Di Wang, Hai Wang, Hongning Wang, Houfeng Wang, Hua Wang, Jin Wang, Josiah Wang, Linlin Wang, Lu Wang, Mingxuan Wang, Quan Wang, Shaojun Wang, Shuohang Wang, Suge Wang, Tong Wang, Wei Wang, William Yang Wang, Xiaolong Wang, Yu-Chun Wang, Zhichun Wang, Zhongqing Wang, **Zhuoran Wang**, Leo Wanner, Nigel Ward, Zeerak Waseem, Patrick Watrin, Bonnie Webber, Ingmar Weber, Julie Weeds, Furu Wei, Zhongyu Wei, Gerhard Weikum, Marion Weller-Di Marco, **Tsung-Hsien Wen**, Michael White, Antoine Widlöcher, **Michael Wiegand**, **John Wieting**, Derry Tanti Wijaya, Adina Williams, Philip Williams, Sam Wiseman, Marcin Woliński, Derek F. Wong, Kam-Fai Wong, Tak-Lam Wong, Bowen Wu, Chun-Kai Wu, Wei Wu, Yu Wu, Zhaohui Wu, Joern Wuebker, Yunqing Xia, Min Xiao, Tong Xiao, Xinyan Xiao, Yanghua Xiao, **Boyi Xie**, Pengtao Xie, Shasha Xie, Caiming Xiong, Chenyan Xiong, Deyi Xiong, Hua Xu, Ruifeng Xu, Wei Xu, Wenduan Xu, Nianwen Xue, Semih Yagcioglu, Yadollah Yaghoobzadeh, Mohamed Yahya, Takehiro Yamamoto, Rui Yan, Zhao Yan, Bishan Yang, Grace Hui Yang, **Jie Yang**, Liu Yang, Qian Yang, Weiwei Yang, Yaqin Yang, Zhilin Yang, Roman Yangarber, Helen Yannakoudakis, Andrew Yates, Mark Yatskar, Lana Yeganova, Meliha Yetisgen, Pengcheng Yin, Wenpeng Yin, Dani Yogatama, Naoki Yoshinaga, Koichiro Yoshino, Steve Young, Bei Yu, Dian Yu, Jianfei Yu, Kai Yu, Liang-Chih Yu, Mo Yu, Zhengtao Yu, Zhou Yu, **François Yvon**, Wlodek Zadrozny, Virginie Zampa, **Amir Zeldes**, Daojian Zeng, Xiaodong Zeng, Kalliopi Zervanou, Torsten Zesch, Deniz Zeyrek, Biao Zhang, Chao Zhang, Congle Zhang, Dongdong Zhang, Hu Zhang, Jiajun Zhang, Justine Zhang, Li Zhang, Meishan Zhang, Min Zhang, Qi Zhang, Sicong Zhang, Wei-Nan Zhang, **Xingxing Zhang**, Yongfeng Zhang, Bing Zhao, Dongyan Zhao, Hai Zhao, Jun Zhao, Sendong Zhao, Tiancheng Zhao, **Tianyu Zhao**, Tiejun Zhao, Wayne Xin Zhao, Zhou Zhao, Guoqing Zheng, Vincent W. Zheng, Victor Zhong, Deyu Zhou, Guodong Zhou, Xiaobing Zhou, Yingbo Zhou, Muhua Zhu, Xiaodan Zhu, Fuzhen Zhuang, Heike Zinsmeister, Ayah Zirikly, Chengqing Zong, Guido Zuccon, Willem Zuidema, Pierre Zweigenbaum.

Secondary Reviewers

Peter A. Rankel, Ranit Aharonov, Domagoj Alagić, Anusha Balakrishnan, Somnath Banerjee, Joost Bastings, Giannis Bekoulis, Gayatri Bhat, Yonatan Bilu, Filip Boltužić, Svetla Boytcheva, Dominique Brunato, Gaëtan Caillaut, Iacer Calixto, Thiago Castro Ferreira, Dhivya Chinnappa, Arman Cohan, Joana Correia, Sujatha Das Gollapalli, Tobias Daudert, Hugues de Mazancourt, Maksym Del, Thomas Demeester, Ying Ding, Zhang Dong, Seth Ebner, Roxanne El Baff, Akiko Eriguchi, Nawshad Farruque, Quentin Feltgen, Elisa Ferracane, Qiaozi Gao, Pepa Gencheva, Bilal Ghanem, Frederic Godin, Nitish Gupta, Shachi H Kumar, Mareike Hartmann, Zhengqiu He, Irazú Hernández, Geert Heyman, Parag Jain, Sarthak Jain, Jyun-Yu Jiang, Xisen Jin, Vidur Joshi, Meizhi Ju, Joo-Kyung Kim, Jooyeon Kim, Elena Kochkina, Bhushan Kotnis, Florian Kreyssig, Sachin Kumar, Ronja Laarmann-Quante, Patrick Lange, Jihwan Lee, Shasha Li, Xinyi Li, Chen Liang, Yuping Lin, Haochen Liu, Qiuzhi Liu, Tong Liu,

Jing Lu, Yen-Fu Luo, Veronica Lynn, Jing Ma, Sean MacAvaney, Arjun Magge, Nona Naderi, Jingzhi Pang, Sunghyun Park, Peyman Passban, Hao Peng, Yifan Peng, Nina Poerner, Hanieh Poostchi, Paul Pu Liang, Robert Pugh, Niklas Rach, Shiya Ren, Ricardo Rodrigues, Sean Rosario, Adam Roussel, Keisuke Sakaguchi, Zahra Sarabi, Marijn Schraagen, Hannes Schulz, Royal Sequiera, Aliaksei Severyn, Piyush Sharma, Shikhar Sharma, Dinghan Shen, Miikka Silfverberg, Kiril Simov, Devendra Singh Sachan, Youngseo Son, Manuela Speranza, Pei-Hao Su, Remi Tachet des Combes, Andre Tattar, Yi Tay, Suzushi Tomori, Adam Tsakalidis, Bo-Hsiang Tseng, Yi-lin Tuan, Antonio Uva, Alakananda Vempala, Giulia Venturi, Natalia Viani, Chao Wang, Guoyin Wang, Huaming Wang, Longyue Wang, Shuang Wang, Wenya Wang, Xiang Wang, Xinyi Wang, Zongsheng Wang, Sarah Wiegreffe, Ji Xin, Jun Xu, Qiuling Yan, Xiao Yang, Yinfei Yang, Ziyu Yao, Hai Ye, Junjie Yu, Roberto Zanoli, Ziqian Zeng, Sheng Zha, Biao Zhang, Dong Zhang, Yijia Zhang, He Zhao, Huan Zhao, Suyan Zhu.

Table of Contents

Conference Program

Monday, July 16, 2018

9:00–10:00   *Welcome Session & Presidential Address*

10:00–10:30   *Coffee Break*

12:30–14:00   *Poster Session 1A: Machine Learning*

Continuous Learning in a Hierarchical Multiscale Neural Network
Thomas Wolf, Julien Chaumond and Clement Delangue

Restricted Recurrent Neural Tensor Networks: Exploiting Word Frequency and Compositionality
Alexandre Salle and Aline Villavicencio

Deep RNNs Encode Soft Hierarchical Syntax
Terra Blevins, Omer Levy and Luke Zettlemoyer

Word Error Rate Estimation for Speech Recognition: e-WER
Ahmed Ali and Steve Renals

Towards Robust and Privacy-preserving Text Representations
Yitong Li, Timothy Baldwin and Trevor Cohn

HotFlip: White-Box Adversarial Examples for Text Classification
Javid Ebrahimi, Anyi Rao, Daniel Lowd and Dejing Dou

Domain Adapted Word Embeddings for Improved Sentiment Classification
Prathusha K Sarma, Yingyu Liang and Bill Sethares

12:30–14:00   *Poster Session 1B: Semantics*

Active learning for deep semantic parsing
Long Duong, Hadi Afshar, Dominique Estival, Glen Pink, Philip Cohen and Mark Johnson

Learning Thematic Similarity Metric from Article Sections Using Triplet Networks
Liat Ein Dor, Yosi Mass, Alon Halfon, Elad Venezian, Ilya Shnayderman, Ranit
Aharonov and Noam Slonim

Unsupervised Semantic Frame Induction using Triclustering
Dmitry Ustalov, Alexander Panchenko, Andrey Kutuzov, Chris Biemann and Simone Paolo Ponzetto

12:30–14:00   ***Poster Session 1C: Information Extraction, Text Mining***

Identification of Alias Links among Participants in Narratives
Sangameshwar Patil, Sachin Pawar, Swapnil Hingmire, Girish Palshikar, Vasudeva
Varma and Pushpak Bhattacharyya

Named Entity Recognition With Parallel Recurrent Neural Networks
Andrej Zukov Gregoric, Yoram Bachrach and Sam Coope

Type-Sensitive Knowledge Base Inference Without Explicit Type Supervision
Prachi Jain, Pankaj Kumar, Mausam - and Soumen Chakrabarti

A Walk-based Model on Entity Graphs for Relation Extraction
Fenia Christopoulou, Makoto Miwa and Sophia Ananiadou

*Ranking-Based Automatic Seed Selection and Noise Reduction for Weakly Super-
vised Relation Extraction*
Van-Thuy Phi, Joan Santoso, Masashi Shimbo and Yuji Matsumoto

Automatic Extraction of Commonsense LocatedNear Knowledge
Frank F. Xu, Bill Yuchen Lin and Kenny Zhu

12:30–14:00   ***Poster Session 1D: Discourse, Linguistics, Cognitive Modeling***

*Neural Coreference Resolution with Deep Biaffine Attention by Joint Mention De-
tection and Mention Clustering*
Rui Zhang, Cicero Nogueira dos Santos, Michihiro Yasunaga, Bing Xiang and
Dragomir Radev

Fully Statistical Neural Belief Tracking
Nikola Mrkšić and Ivan Vulić

Some of Them Can be Guessed! Exploring the Effect of Linguistic Context in Predicting Quantifiers
Sandro Pezzelle, Shane Steinert-Threlkeld, Raffaella Bernardi and Jakub Szymanik

12:30–14:00   *Poster Session 1E: Resources and Evaluation*

A Named Entity Recognition Shootout for German
Martin Riedl and Sebastian Padó

A dataset for identifying actionable feedback in collaborative software development
Benjamin S Meyers, Nuthan Munaiah, Emily Prud'hommeaux, Andrew Meneely, Josephine Wolff, Cecilia Ovesdotter Alm and Pradeep Murukannaiah

SNAG: Spoken Narratives and Gaze Dataset
Preethi Vaidyanathan, Emily T. Prud'hommeaux, Jeff B. Pelz and Cecilia O. Alm

Analogical Reasoning on Chinese Morphological and Semantic Relations
Shen Li, Zhe Zhao, Renfen Hu, Wensi Li, Tao Liu and Xiaoyong Du

Construction of a Chinese Corpus for the Analysis of the Emotionality of Metaphorical Expressions
Dongyu Zhang, Hongfei Lin, Liang Yang, Shaowu Zhang and BO XU

Automatic Article Commenting: the Task and Dataset
Lianhui Qin, Lemao Liu, Wei Bi, Yan Wang, Xiaojiang Liu, Zhiting Hu, Hai Zhao and Shuming Shi

Improved Evaluation Framework for Complex Plagiarism Detection
Anton Belyy, Marina Dubova and Dmitry Nekrasov

12:30–14:00   *Poster Session 1F: Summarization, Social Media*

Global Encoding for Abstractive Summarization
Junyang Lin, Xu SUN, Shuming Ma and Qi Su

A Language Model based Evaluator for Sentence Compression
Yang Zhao, Zhiyuan Luo and Akiko Aizawa

Identifying and Understanding User Reactions to Deceptive and Trusted Social News Sources
Maria Glenski, Tim Weninger and Svitlana Volkova

Content-based Popularity Prediction of Online Petitions Using a Deep Regression Model
Shivashankar Subramanian, Timothy Baldwin and Trevor Cohn

Fighting Offensive Language on Social Media with Unsupervised Text Style Transfer
Cicero Nogueira dos Santos, Igor Melnyk and Inkit Padhi

Diachronic degradation of language models: Insights from social media
Kokil Jaidka, Niyati Chhaya and Lyle Ungar

Tuesday, July 17, 2018

9:00–10:00　　*Invited Talk 1: Carolyn Penstein Rosé*

10:00–10:30　　*Coffee Break*

12:30–14:00　　*Poster Session 2B: Dialog and Interactive Systems, Multilinguality*

Task-oriented Dialogue System for Automatic Diagnosis
Zhongyu Wei, Qianlong Liu, Baolin Peng, Huaixiao Tou, Ting Chen, Xuanjing Huang, Kam-Fai Wong and Xiangying Dai

Transfer Learning for Context-Aware Question Matching in Information-seeking Conversations in E-commerce
Minghui Qiu, Liu Yang, Feng Ji, Wei Zhou, Jun Huang, Haiqing Chen, Bruce Croft and Wei Lin

A Multi-task Approach to Learning Multilingual Representations
Karan Singla, Dogan Can and Shrikanth Narayanan

Characterizing Departures from Linearity in Word Translation
Ndapa Nakashole and Raphael Flauger

Filtering and Mining Parallel Data in a Joint Multilingual Space
Holger Schwenk

12:30–14:00　　*Poster Session 2C: Information Extraction, Text Mining*

Hybrid semi-Markov CRF for Neural Sequence Labeling
Zhixiu Ye and Zhen-Hua Ling

A Study of the Importance of External Knowledge in the Named Entity Recognition Task
Dominic Seyler, Tatiana Dembelova, Luciano Del Corro, Johannes Hoffart and Gerhard Weikum

Improving Topic Quality by Promoting Named Entities in Topic Modeling
Katsiaryna Krasnashchok and Salim Jouili

Obligation and Prohibition Extraction Using Hierarchical RNNs
Ilias Chalkidis, Ion Androutsopoulos and Achilleas Michos

12:30–14:00　　*Poster Session 2D: Generation*

Paper Abstract Writing through Editing Mechanism
Qingyun Wang, Zhihao Zhou, Lifu Huang, Spencer Whitehead, Boliang Zhang, Heng Ji and Kevin Knight

Conditional Generators of Words Definitions
Artyom Gadetsky, Ilya Yakubovskiy and Dmitry Vetrov

12:30–14:00　　*Poster Session 2E: Question Answering*

CNN for Text-Based Multiple Choice Question Answering
Akshay Chaturvedi, Onkar Pandit and Utpal Garain

Narrative Modeling with Memory Chains and Semantic Supervision
Fei Liu, Trevor Cohn and Timothy Baldwin

Injecting Relational Structural Representation in Neural Networks for Question Similarity
Antonio Uva, Daniele Bonadiman and Alessandro Moschitti

12:30–14:00   *Poster Session 2F: Machine Translation*

A Simple and Effective Approach to Coverage-Aware Neural Machine Translation
Yanyang Li, Tong Xiao, Yinqiao Li, Qiang Wang, Changming Xu and Jingbo Zhu

Dynamic Sentence Sampling for Efficient Training of Neural Machine Translation
Rui Wang, Masao Utiyama and Eiichiro Sumita

Compositional Representation of Morphologically-Rich Input for Neural Machine Translation
Duygu Ataman and Marcello Federico

Extreme Adaptation for Personalized Neural Machine Translation
Paul Michel and Graham Neubig

Multi-representation ensembles and delayed SGD updates improve syntax-based NMT
Danielle Saunders, Felix Stahlberg, Adrià de Gispert and Bill Byrne

Learning from Chunk-based Feedback in Neural Machine Translation
Pavel Petrushkov, Shahram Khadivi and Evgeny Matusov

Bag-of-Words as Target for Neural Machine Translation
Shuming Ma, Xu SUN, Yizhong Wang and Junyang Lin

Improving Beam Search by Removing Monotonic Constraint for Neural Machine Translation
Raphael Shu and Hideki Nakayama

Session 5A: Semantics 1 (Short)

14:00–14:15   *Leveraging distributed representations and lexico-syntactic fixedness for token-level prediction of the idiomaticity of English verb-noun combinations*
Milton King and Paul Cook

14:15–14:30   *Using pseudo-senses for improving the extraction of synonyms from word embeddings*
Olivier Ferret

14:30–14:45   *Hearst Patterns Revisited: Automatic Hypernym Detection from Large Text Corpora*
Stephen Roller, Douwe Kiela and Maximilian Nickel

14:45–15:00   *Jointly Predicting Predicates and Arguments in Neural Semantic Role Labeling*
Luheng He, Kenton Lee, Omer Levy and Luke Zettlemoyer

Session 5B: Machine Translation, Multilinguality 1 (Short)

14:00–14:15   *Sparse and Constrained Attention for Neural Machine Translation*
Chaitanya Malaviya, Pedro Ferreira and André F. T. Martins

14:15–14:30   *Neural Hidden Markov Model for Machine Translation*
Weiyue Wang, Derui Zhu, Tamer Alkhouli, Zixuan Gan and Hermann Ney

14:30–14:45   *Bleaching Text: Abstract Features for Cross-lingual Gender Prediction*
Rob van der Goot, Nikola Ljubešić, Ian Matroos, Malvina Nissim and Barbara Plank

14:45–15:00   *Orthographic Features for Bilingual Lexicon Induction*
Parker Riley and Daniel Gildea

Session 5C: Information Extraction 1 (Short)

14:00–14:15   *Neural Cross-Lingual Coreference Resolution And Its Application To Entity Linking*
Gourab Kundu, Avi Sil, Radu Florian and Wael Hamza

14:15–14:30   *Judicious Selection of Training Data in Assisting Language for Multilingual Neural NER*
Rudra Murthy, Anoop Kunchukuttan and Pushpak Bhattacharyya

14:30–14:45   *Neural Open Information Extraction*
Lei Cui, Furu Wei and Ming Zhou

14:45–15:00   *Document Embedding Enhanced Event Detection with Hierarchical and Supervised Attention*
Yue Zhao, Xiaolong Jin, Yuanzhuo Wang and Xueqi Cheng

Session 5D: Dialog System, Discourse (Short)

14:00–14:15   *Learning Matching Models with Weak Supervision for Response Selection in Retrieval-based Chatbots*
Yu Wu, wei wu, Zhoujun Li and Ming Zhou

14:15–14:30   *Improving Slot Filling in Spoken Language Understanding with Joint Pointer and Attention*
Lin Zhao and Zhe Feng

14:30–14:45   *Large-Scale Multi-Domain Belief Tracking with Knowledge Sharing*
Osman Ramadan, Paweł Budzianowski and Milica Gasic

14:45–15:00   *Modeling discourse cohesion for discourse parsing via memory network*
Yanyan Jia, Yuan Ye, Yansong Feng, Yuxuan Lai, Rui Yan and Dongyan Zhao

Session 5E: Vision, Linguistics, Resource and Evaluation (Short)

14:00–14:15   *SciDTB: Discourse Dependency TreeBank for Scientific Abstracts*
An Yang and Sujian Li

14:15–14:30   *Predicting accuracy on large datasets from smaller pilot data*
Mark Johnson, Peter Anderson, Mark Dras and Mark Steedman

14:30–14:45   *The Influence of Context on Sentence Acceptability Judgements*
Jean-Philippe Bernardy, Shalom Lappin and Jey Han Lau

14:45–15:00   *Do Neural Network Cross-Modal Mappings Really Bridge Modalities?*
Guillem Collell and Marie-Francine Moens

Session 5F: Parsing, Morphology (Short)

14:00–14:15   *Policy Gradient as a Proxy for Dynamic Oracles in Constituency Parsing*
Daniel Fried and Dan Klein

14:15–14:30   *Linear-time Constituency Parsing with RNNs and Dynamic Programming*
Juneki Hong and Liang Huang

14:30–14:45   *Simpler but More Accurate Semantic Dependency Parsing*
Timothy Dozat and Christopher D. Manning

14:45–15:00   *Simplified Abugidas*
Chenchen Ding, Masao Utiyama and Eiichiro Sumita

15:00–15:30   *Coffee Break*

17:20–18:50   *ACL Business Meeting*

Learning with Structured Representations for Negation Scope Extraction
Hao Li and Wei Lu

End-Task Oriented Textual Entailment via Deep Explorations of Inter-Sentence Interactions
Wenpeng Yin, Dan Roth and Hinrich Schütze

Sense-Aware Neural Models for Pun Location in Texts
Yitao Cai, Yin Li and Xiaojun Wan

A Rank-Based Similarity Metric for Word Embeddings
Enrico Santus, Hongmin Wang, Emmanuele Chersoni and Yue Zhang

Addressing Noise in Multidialectal Word Embeddings
Alexander Erdmann, Nasser Zalmout and Nizar Habash

GNEG: Graph-Based Negative Sampling for word2vec
Zheng Zhang and Pierre Zweigenbaum

Unsupervised Learning of Style-sensitive Word Vectors
Reina Akama, Kento Watanabe, Sho Yokoi, Sosuke Kobayashi and Kentaro Inui

12:30–14:00   ***Poster Session 3D: Sentiment Analysis and Argument Mining***

Exploiting Document Knowledge for Aspect-level Sentiment Classification
Ruidan He, Wee Sun Lee, Hwee Tou Ng and Daniel Dahlmeier

Modeling Sentiment Association in Discourse for Humor Recognition
Lizhen Liu, Donghai Zhang and Wei Song

Double Embeddings and CNN-based Sequence Labeling for Aspect Extraction
Hu Xu, Bing Liu, Lei Shu and Philip S. Yu

Will it Blend? Blending Weak and Strong Labeled Data in a Neural Network for Argumentation Mining
Eyal Shnarch, Carlos Alzate, Lena Dankin, Martin Gleize, Yufang Hou, Leshem Choshen, Ranit Aharonov and Noam Slonim

12:30–14:00 *Poster Session 3E: Vision, Multimodal, Grounding, Speech*

Investigating Audio, Video, and Text Fusion Methods for End-to-End Automatic Personality Prediction
Onno Kampman, Elham J. Barezi, Dario Bertero and Pascale Fung

12:30–14:00 *Poster Session 3F: Morphology, Tagging, Parsing*

An Empirical Study of Building a Strong Baseline for Constituency Parsing
Jun Suzuki, Sho Takase, Hidetaka Kamigaito, Makoto Morishita and Masaaki Nagata

Parser Training with Heterogeneous Treebanks
Sara Stymne, Miryam de Lhoneux, Aaron Smith and Joakim Nivre

Generalized chart constraints for efficient PCFG and TAG parsing
Stefan Grünewald, Sophie Henning and Alexander Koller

Session 8A: Semantics 2 (Short)

14:00–14:15 *Exploring Semantic Properties of Sentence Embeddings*
Xunjie Zhu, Tingfeng Li and Gerard de Melo

14:15–14:30 *Scoring Lexical Entailment with a Supervised Directional Similarity Network*
Marek Rei, Daniela Gerz and Ivan Vulić

14:30–14:45 *Extracting Commonsense Properties from Embeddings with Limited Human Guidance*
Yiben Yang, Larry Birnbaum, Ji-Ping Wang and Doug Downey

14:45–15:00 *Breaking NLI Systems with Sentences that Require Simple Lexical Inferences*
Max Glockner, Vered Shwartz and Yoav Goldberg

Session 8B: Machine Translation, Multilinguality 2 (Short)

14:00–14:15 *Adaptive Knowledge Sharing in Multi-Task Learning: Improving Low-Resource Neural Machine Translation*
Poorya Zaremoodi, Wray Buntine and Gholamreza Haffari

14:15–14:30 *Automatic Estimation of Simultaneous Interpreter Performance*
Craig Stewart, Nikolai Vogler, Junjie Hu, Jordan Boyd-Graber and Graham Neubig

14:30–14:45 *Polyglot Semantic Role Labeling*
Phoebe Mulcaire, Swabha Swayamdipta and Noah A. Smith

14:45–15:00 *Learning Cross-lingual Distributed Logical Representations for Semantic Parsing*
Yanyan Zou and Wei Lu

Session 8C: Information Extraction 2 (Short)

14:00–14:15 *Enhancing Drug-Drug Interaction Extraction from Texts by Molecular Structure Information*
Masaki Asada, Makoto Miwa and Yutaka Sasaki

14:15–14:30 *diaNED: Time-Aware Named Entity Disambiguation for Diachronic Corpora*
Prabal Agarwal, Jannik Strötgen, Luciano Del Corro, Johannes Hoffart and Gerhard Weikum

14:30–14:45 *Examining Temporality in Document Classification*
Xiaolei Huang and Michael J. Paul

14:45–15:00 *Personalized Language Model for Query Auto-Completion*
Aaron Jaech and Mari Ostendorf

Session 8D: Generation, Summarization (Short)

14:00–14:15   *Personalized Review Generation By Expanding Phrases and Attending on Aspect-Aware Representations*
Jianmo Ni and Julian McAuley

14:15–14:30   *Learning Simplifications for Specific Target Audiences*
Carolina Scarton and Lucia Specia

14:30–14:45   *Split and Rephrase: Better Evaluation and Stronger Baselines*
Roee Aharoni and Yoav Goldberg

14:45–15:00   *Autoencoder as Assistant Supervisor: Improving Text Representation for Chinese Social Media Text Summarization*
Shuming Ma, Xu SUN, Junyang Lin and Houfeng WANG

Session 8E: Machine Learning, Question Answering (Short)

14:00–14:15   *Long Short-Term Memory as a Dynamically Computed Element-wise Weighted Sum*
Omer Levy, Kenton Lee, Nicholas FitzGerald and Luke Zettlemoyer

14:15–14:30   *On the Practical Computational Power of Finite Precision RNNs for Language Recognition*
Gail Weiss, Yoav Goldberg and Eran Yahav

14:30–14:45   *A Co-Matching Model for Multi-choice Reading Comprehension*
Shuohang Wang, Mo Yu, Jing Jiang and Shiyu Chang

14:45–15:00   *Tackling the Story Ending Biases in The Story Cloze Test*
Rishi Sharma, James Allen, Omid Bakhshandeh and Nasrin Mostafazadeh

Continuous Learning in a Hierarchical Multiscale Neural Network

Thomas Wolf, Julien Chaumond & Clement Delangue
Hugging Face Inc.
81 Prospect St.
Brooklyn, New York 11201, USA
`{thomas, julien, clement}@huggingface.co`

Abstract

We reformulate the problem of encoding a multi-scale representation of a sequence in a language model by casting it in a continuous learning framework. We propose a hierarchical multi-scale language model in which short time-scale dependencies are encoded in the hidden state of a lower-level recurrent neural network while longer time-scale dependencies are encoded in the dynamic of the lower-level network by having a meta-learner update the weights of the lower-level neural network in an online meta-learning fashion. We use elastic weights consolidation as a higher-level to prevent catastrophic forgetting in our continuous learning framework.

1 Introduction

Language models are a major class of natural language processing (NLP) models whose development has lead to major progress in many areas like translation, speech recognition or summarization (Schwenk, 2012; Arisoy et al., 2012; Rush et al., 2015; Nallapati et al., 2016). Recently, the task of language modeling has been shown to be an adequate proxy for learning unsupervised representations of high-quality in tasks like text classification (Howard and Ruder, 2018), sentiment detection (Radford et al., 2017) or word vector learning (Peters et al., 2018).

More generally, language modeling is an example of online/sequential prediction task, in which a model tries to predict the next observation given a sequence of past observations. The development of better models for sequential prediction is believed to be beneficial for a wide range of applications like model-based planning or reinforcement learning as these models have to encode some form of memory or causal model of the world to accurately predict a future event given past events.

One of the main issues limiting the performance of language models (LMs) is the problem of capturing long-term dependencies within a sequence.

Neural network based language models (Hochreiter and Schmidhuber, 1997; Cho et al., 2014) learn to implicitly store dependencies in a vector of hidden activities (Mikolov et al., 2010). They can be extended by attention mechanisms, memories or caches (Bahdanau et al., 2014; Tran et al., 2016; Graves et al., 2014) to capture long-range connections more explicitly. Unfortunately, the very local context is often so highly informative that LMs typically end up using their memories mostly to store short term context (Daniluk et al., 2016).

In this work, we study the possibility of combining short-term representations, stored in neural activations (hidden state), with medium-term representations encoded in a set of dynamical weights of the language model. Our work extends a series of recent experiments on networks with dynamically evolving weights (Ba et al., 2016; Ha et al., 2016; Krause et al., 2017; Moniz and Krueger, 2018) which show improvements in sequential prediction tasks. We build upon these works by formulating the task as a hierarchical online meta-learning task as detailed below.

The motivation behind this work stems from two observations.

On the one hand, there is evidence from a physiological point of view that time-coherent processes like working memory can involve differing mechanisms at differing time-scales. Biological neural activations typically have a 10 ms coherence timescale, while short-term synaptic plasticity can temporarily modulate the dynamic of the neural network it-self on timescales of 100 ms to minutes. Longer time-scales (a few minutes

1

Proceedings of the 56th Annual Meeting of the Association for Computational Linguistics (Short Papers), pages 1–7
Melbourne, Australia, July 15 - 20, 2018. ©2018 Association for Computational Linguistics

to several hours) see long-term learning kicks in with permanent modifications to neural excitability (Tsodyks et al., 1998; Abbott and Regehr, 2004; Barak and Tsodyks, 2007; Ba et al., 2016). Interestingly, these psychological observations are paralleled, on the computational side, by a series of recent works on recurrent networks with dynamically evolving weights that show benefits from dynamically updating the weights of a network during a sequential task (Ba et al., 2016; Ha et al., 2016; Krause et al., 2017; Moniz and Krueger, 2018).

In parallel to that, it has also been shown that temporal data with multiple time-scales dependencies can naturally be encoded in a hierarchical representation where higher-level features are changing slowly to store long time-scale dependencies and lower-level features are changing faster to encode short time-scale dependencies and local timing (Schmidhuber, 1992; El Hihi and Bengio, 1995; Koutnìk et al., 2014; Chung et al., 2016).

As a consequence, we would like our model to encode information in a multi-scale hierarchical representation where

1. *short time-scale dependencies* can be encoded in fast-updated neural activations (hidden state),

2. *medium time-scale dependencies* can be encoded in the dynamic of the network by using dynamic weights updated more slowly, and

3. *a long time-scale memory* can be encoded in a static set of parameters of the model.

In the present work, we take as dynamic weights the full set of weights of a RNN language model (usually word embeddings plus recurrent, input and output weights of each recurrent layer).

2 Dynamical Language Modeling

Given a sequence of T discrete symbols $S = (w_1, w_2, \ldots, w_T)$, the language modeling task consists in assigning a probability to the sequence $P(S) = p(w_1, \ldots, w_T)$ which can be written, using the chain-rule, as

$$P(S \mid \theta) = \prod_{t=1}^{T} P(w_t \mid w_{t-1}, \ldots, w_0, \theta) P(w_0 \mid \theta).$$

$$(1)$$

where θ is a set of parameters of the language model.

In the case of a neural-network-based language model, the conditional probability $P(w_t \mid w_{t-1}, \ldots, w_0, \theta)$ is typically parametrized using an autoregressive neural network as

$$P(w_t \mid w_{t-1}, \ldots, w_0, \theta) = f_\theta(w_{t-1}, \ldots, w_0)$$

$$(2)$$

where θ are the parameters of the neural network.

In a dynamical language modeling framework, the parameters θ of the language model are not tied over the sequence S but are allowed to evolve. Thus, prior to computing the probability of a future token w_t, a set of parameters θ_t is estimated from the past parameters and tokens as $\theta_t = \operatorname*{argmax}_\theta P(\theta \mid w_{t-1}, \ldots, w_0, \theta_{t-1} \ldots \theta_0)$ and the updated parameters θ_t are used to compute the probability of the next token w_t.

In our hierarchical neural network language model, the updated parameters θ_t are estimated by a higher level neural network g parametrized by a set of (static) parameters ϕ:

$$\theta_t = g_\phi(w_{t-1}, \ldots, w_0, \theta_{t-1} \ldots \theta_0) \qquad (3)$$

2.1 Online meta-learning formulation

The function computed by the higher level network g, estimating θ_t from an history of parameters $\theta_{<t}$ and data points $w_{<t}$, can be seen as an online meta-learning task in which a high-level meta-learner network is trained to update the weights of a low-level network from the loss of the low-level network on a previous batch of data.

Such a meta-learner can be trained (Andrychowicz et al., 2016) to reduce the loss of the low-level network with the idea that it will generalize a gradient descent rule

$$\theta_t = \theta_{t-1} - \alpha_t \nabla_{\theta_{t-1}} \mathcal{L}_t \qquad (4)$$

where α_t is a learning rate at time t and $\nabla_{\theta_{t-1}} \mathcal{L}_t^{LM}$ is the gradient of the loss $\mathcal{L}_t^{LM}$ of the language model on the t-th dataset with respect to previous parameters θ_{t-1}.

Ravi and Larochelle (2016) made the observation that such a gradient descent rule bears similarities with the update rule for LSTM cell-states

$$c_t = f_t \odot c_{t-1} + i_t \odot \tilde{c}_t \qquad (5)$$

when $c_t \to \theta_t$, $i_t \to \alpha_t$ and $\tilde{c}_t \to -\nabla_{\theta_{t-1}} \mathcal{L}_t$

We extend this analogy to the case of a multi-scale hierarchical recurrent model illustrated on figure 1 and composed of:

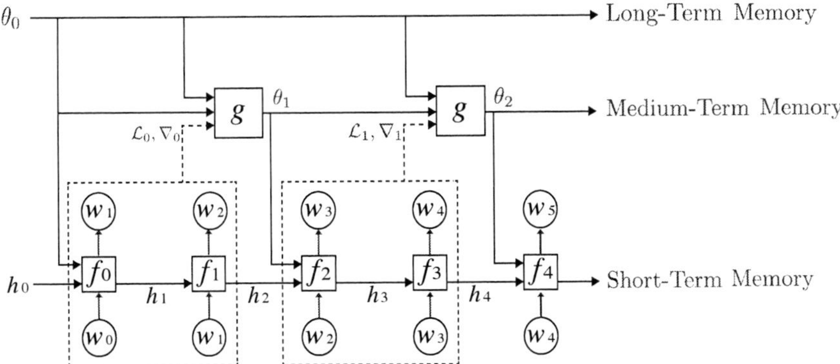

Figure 1: A diagram of the Dynamical Language Model. The lower-level neural network f (short-term memory) is a conventional word-level language model where $w_0, \ldots, w_5$ are words tokens. The medium-level language model g is a feed-forward or recurrent neural network while the higher-level memory is formed by a static set of consolidated pre-trained weights (see text).

1. *Lower-level / short time-scale*: a RNN-based language model f encoding representations in the activations of a hidden state,

2. *Middle-level / medium time-scale*: a meta-learner g updating the set of weights of the language model to store medium-term representations, and

3. *Higher-level / long time-scale*: a static long-term memory of the dynamic of the RNN-based language model (see below).

The meta-learner g is trained to update the lower-level network f by computing $f_t, i_t, z_t = g_\phi(\theta_{t-1}, \mathcal{L}_t^{LM}, \nabla_{\theta_{t-1}}\mathcal{L}_t^{LM}, \theta_0)$ and updating the set of weights as

$$\theta_t = f_t \odot \theta_{t-1} + i_t \odot \nabla_{\theta_{t-1}}\mathcal{L}_t^{LM} + z_t \odot \theta_0 \quad (6)$$

This hierarchical network could be seen as an analog of the hierarchical recurrent neural networks (Chung et al., 2016) where the gates f_t, i_t and z_t can be seen as controlling a set of COPY, FLUSH and UPDATE operations:

1. COPY (f_t): part of the state copied from the previous state θ_{t-1},

2. UPDATE (i_t): part of the state updated by the loss gradients on the previous batch, and

3. FLUSH (z_t): part of the state reset from a static long term memory θ_0.

One difference with the work of (Chung et al., 2016) is that the memory was confined to the hidden in the later while the memory of our hierarchical network is split between the weights of the lower-level network and its hidden-state.

The meta-learner can be a feed-forward or a RNN network. In our experiments, simple linear feed-forward networks lead to the lower perplexities, probably because it was easier to regularize and optimize. The meta-learner implements coordinate-sharing as described in (Andrychowicz et al., 2016; Ravi and Larochelle, 2016) and takes as input the loss $\mathcal{L}_t^{LM}$ and loss-gradients $\nabla_{\theta_{t-1}}\mathcal{L}_t^{LM}$ over a previous batch B_i (a sequence of M tokens $w_0, \ldots, w_M$ as illustrated on figure 1). The size M of the batch adjusts the trade-off between the noise of the loss/gradients and updating frequency of the medium-term memory, smaller batches leading to faster updates with higher noise.

2.2 Continual learning

The interaction between the meta-learner and the language model implements a form of continual-learning and the language model thus faces a phenomenon known as catastrophic forgetting (French, 1999). In our case, this correspond to the lower-level network over-specializing to the lexical field of a particular topic after several updates of the meta-learner (e.g. while processing a long article on a specific topic).

To mitigate this effect we use a higher-level static memory initialized using "elastic weight consolidation" (EWC) introduced by Kirkpatrick

3

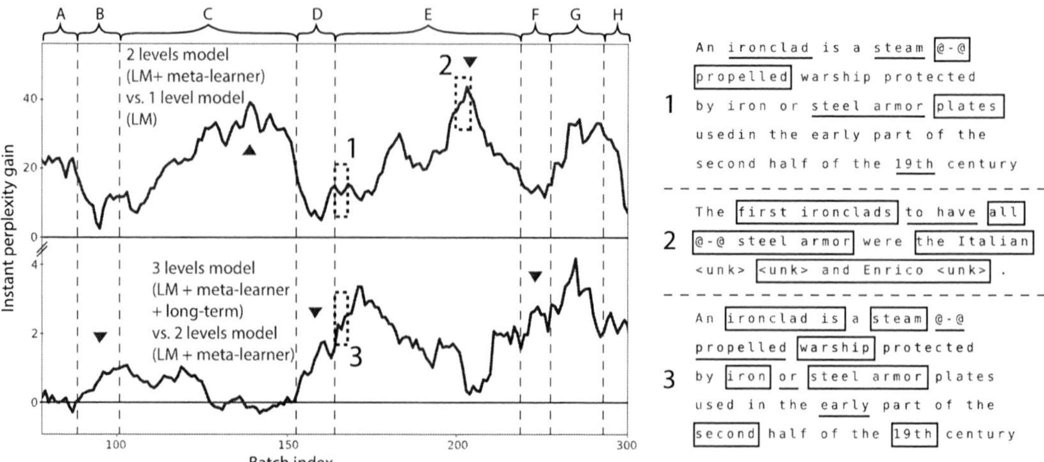

Figure 2: Medium and long-term memory effects on a sample of Wikitext-2 test set with a sequence of Wikipedia articles (letters $A - H$). (Left) Instantaneous perplexity gain: difference in batch perplexity between models. Higher values means the first model has locally a lower perplexity than the second model. (Top curve) Comparing a two-levels model (LM + meta-learner) with a one-level model (LM). (Bottom curve) Comparing a three-levels model (LM + meta-learner + long-term memory) with a two-levels model. (Right) Token loss difference on three batch samples indicated on the left curves. A squared (resp. underlined) word means the first model has a lower (resp. higher) loss on that word than the second model. We emphasize only words associated with a significant difference in loss by setting a threshold at 10 percent of the maximum absolute loss of each sample.

et al. (2017) to reduce forgetting in multi-task reinforcement learning.

Casting our task in the EWC framework, we define a task A which is the language modeling task (prediction of next token) when no context is stored in the weights of the lower-level network. The solution of task A is a set of weights toward which the model could advantageously come back when the context stored in the weights become irrelevant (for example when switching between paragraphs on different topics). To obtain a set of weights for task A, we train the lower-level network (RNN) alone on the training dataset and obtain a set of weights that would perform well on average, i.e. when no specific context has been provided by a context-dependent weight update performed by the meta-learner.

We then define a task B which is a language modeling task when a context has been stored in the weights of the lower-level network by an update of the meta-learner. The aim of EWC is to learn task B while retaining some performance on task A.

Empirical results suggest that many weights configurations result in similar performances (Sussmann, 1992) and there is thus likely a solution for task B close to a solution for task A. The idea behind EWC is to learn task B while protecting the performance in task A by constraining the parameters to stay around the solution found for task A.

This constraint is implemented as a quadratic penalty, similarly to spring anchoring the parameters, hence the name elastic. The stiffness of the springs should be greater for parameters that most affect performance in task A. We can formally write this constrain by using Bayes rule to express the conditional log probability of the parameters when the training dataset $\mathcal{D}$ is split between the training dataset for task A ($\mathcal{D}_A$) and the training dataset for task B ($\mathcal{D}_B$):

$$\log p(\theta \mid \mathcal{D}) = \log p(\mathcal{D}_B \mid \theta) + \log p(\theta \mid \mathcal{D}_A) - \log p(\mathcal{D}_B) \tag{7}$$

The true posterior probability on task A $p(\theta \mid \mathcal{D}_A)$ is intractable, so we approximate the posterior as a Gaussian distribution with mean given by the parameters and a diagonal precision given by the diagonal of the Fisher information matrix F which is equivalent to the second derivative of the loss near a minimum and can be computed from first-order derivatives alone.

3 Related work

Several works have been devoted to dynamically updating the weights of neural networks during inference. A few recent architectures are the Fast-Weights of Ba et al. (2016), the Hypernetworks of Ha et al. (2016) and the Nested LSTM of Moniz and Krueger (2018). The weights update rules of theses models use as inputs one or several of (i) a previous hidden state of a RNN network or higher level network and/or (ii) the current or previous inputs to the network. However, these models do not use the predictions of the network on the previous tokens (i.e. the loss and gradient of the loss of the model) as in the present work. The architecture that is most related to the present work is the study on dynamical evaluation of Krause et al. (2017) in which a loss function similar to the loss function of the present work is obtained empirically and optimized using a large hyper-parameter search on the parameters of the SGD-like rule.

4 Experiments

4.1 Architecture and hyper-parameters

As mentioned in 2.2, a set of pre-trained weights of the RNN language model is first obtained by training the lower-level network f and computing the diagonal of the Fisher matrix around the final weights.

Then, the meta-learner g is trained in an online meta-learning fashion on the validation dataset (alternatively, a sub-set of the training dataset could be used). A training sequence S is split in a sequence of mini-batches B_i, each batch B_i containing M inputs tokens $(w_{i \times M}, \ldots, w_{i \times M+M})$ and M associated targets $(w_{i \times M+1}, \ldots, w_{i \times M+M+1})$. In our experiments we varied M between 5 and 20.

The meta-learner is trained as described in (Andrychowicz et al., 2016; Li and Malik, 2016) by minimizing the sum over the sequence of LM losses: $\mathcal{L}_{meta} = \sum_{i>0} \mathcal{L}_i^{LM}$. The meta-learner is trained by truncated back-propagation through time and is unrolled over at least 40 steps as the reward from the medium-term memory is relatively sparse (Li and Malik, 2016).

To be able to unroll the model over a sufficient number of steps while using a state-of-the-art language model with over than 30 millions parameters, we use a memory-efficient version of back propagation through time based on gradient checkpointing as described by Grusly et al. (2016).

4.2 Experiments

We performed a series of experiments on the Wikitext-2 dataset (Merity et al., 2016) using an AWD-LSTM language model (Merity et al., 2017) and a feed-forward and RNN meta-learner.

The test perplexity are similar to perplexities obtained using dynamical evaluation (Krause et al., 2017), reaching 46.9 with a linear feed-forward meta-learner when starting from a one-level language model with test perplexity of 64.8.

In our experiments, the perplexity could not be improved by using a RNN meta-learner or a deeper meta-learner. We hypothesis that this may be caused by several reasons. First, storing a hidden state in the meta-learner might be less important in an online meta-learning setup than it is in a standard meta-learning setup (Andrychowicz et al., 2016) as the target distribution of the weights is non-stationary. Second, the size of the hidden state cannot be increased significantly without reducing the number of steps along which the meta-learner is unrolled during meta-training which may be detrimental.

Some quantitative experiments are shown on Figure 2 using a linear feed-forward network to illustrate the effect of the various layers in the hierarchical model. The curves shows differences in batch perplexity between model variants.

The top curve compares a one-level model (language model) with a two-levels model (language model + meta-learner). The meta-learner is able to learn medium-term representations to progressively reduce perplexity along articles (see e.g. articles C and E). Right sample 1 (resp. 2) details sentences at the begging (resp. middle) of article E related to a warship called "Ironclad". The addition of the meta-learner reduces the loss on a number of expression related to the warship like "ironclad" or "steel armor".

Bottom curve compares a three-levels model (language model + meta-learner + long-term memory) with the two-levels model. The local loss is reduced at topics changes and beginning of new topics (see e.g. articles B, D and F). The right sample 3 can be contrasted with sample 1 to illustrate how the hierarchical model is able to better recover a good parameter space following a change in topic.

References

L. F. Abbott and Wade G. Regehr. 2004. Synaptic computation. *Nature*, 431(7010):796–803.

Marcin Andrychowicz, Misha Denil, Sergio Gomez, Matthew W. Hoffman, David Pfau, Tom Schaul, Brendan Shillingford, and Nando de Freitas. 2016. Learning to learn by gradient descent by gradient descent. *arXiv:1606.04474 [cs]*. ArXiv: 1606.04474.

Ebru Arisoy, Tara N. Sainath, Brian Kingsbury, and Bhuvana Ramabhadran. 2012. Deep neural network language models. In *Proceedings of the NAACL-HLT 2012 Workshop: Will We Ever Really Replace the N-gram Model? On the Future of Language Modeling for HLT*, pages 20–28. Association for Computational Linguistics.

Jimmy Ba, Geoffrey Hinton, Volodymyr Mnih, Joel Z. Leibo, and Catalin Ionescu. 2016. Using Fast Weights to Attend to the Recent Past. *arXiv:1610.06258 [cs, stat]*. ArXiv: 1610.06258.

Dzmitry Bahdanau, Kyunghyun Cho, and Yoshua Bengio. 2014. Neural machine translation by jointly learning to align and translate. *arXiv preprint arXiv:1409.0473*.

Omri Barak and Misha Tsodyks. 2007. Persistent activity in neural networks with dynamic synapses. *PLoS computational biology*, 3(2):e35.

Kyunghyun Cho, Bart van Merrienboer, Caglar Gulcehre, Dzmitry Bahdanau, Fethi Bougares, Holger Schwenk, and Yoshua Bengio. 2014. Learning Phrase Representations using RNN Encoder-Decoder for Statistical Machine Translation. *arXiv:1406.1078 [cs, stat]*. ArXiv: 1406.1078.

Junyoung Chung, Sungjin Ahn, and Yoshua Bengio. 2016. Hierarchical Multiscale Recurrent Neural Networks. *arXiv:1609.01704 [cs]*. ArXiv: 1609.01704.

Micha Daniluk, Tim Rocktschel, Johannes Welbl, and Sebastian Riedel. 2016. Frustratingly Short Attention Spans in Neural Language Modeling.

Salah El Hihi and Yoshua Bengio. 1995. Hierarchical Recurrent Neural Networks for Long-term Dependencies. In *Proceedings of the 8th International Conference on Neural Information Processing Systems*, NIPS'95, pages 493–499, Cambridge, MA, USA. MIT Press.

Robert M. French. 1999. Catastrophic forgetting in connectionist networks. *Trends in Cognitive Sciences*, 3(4):128–135.

Alex Graves, Greg Wayne, and Ivo Danihelka. 2014. Neural turing machines. *arXiv preprint arXiv:1410.5401*.

Audrnas Gruslys, Remi Munos, Ivo Danihelka, Marc Lanctot, and Alex Graves. 2016. Memory-Efficient Backpropagation Through Time. *arXiv:1606.03401 [cs]*. ArXiv: 1606.03401.

David Ha, Andrew Dai, and Quoc V. Le. 2016. HyperNetworks. *arXiv:1609.09106 [cs]*. ArXiv: 1609.09106.

Sepp Hochreiter and Jrgen Schmidhuber. 1997. Long Short-Term Memory. *Neural Comput.*, 9(8):1735–1780.

Jeremy Howard and Sebastian Ruder. 2018. Fine-tuned Language Models for Text Classification. *arXiv:1801.06146 [cs, stat]*. ArXiv: 1801.06146.

James Kirkpatrick, Razvan Pascanu, Neil Rabinowitz, Joel Veness, Guillaume Desjardins, Andrei A. Rusu, Kieran Milan, John Quan, Tiago Ramalho, Agnieszka Grabska-Barwinska, Demis Hassabis, Claudia Clopath, Dharshan Kumaran, and Raia Hadsell. 2017. Overcoming catastrophic forgetting in neural networks. *Proceedings of the National Academy of Sciences*, 114(13):3521–3526.

Jan Koutnk, Klaus Greff, Faustino Gomez, and Jrgen Schmidhuber. 2014. A Clockwork RNN. In *Proceedings of the 31st International Conference on International Conference on Machine Learning - Volume 32*, ICML'14, pages II–1863–II–1871, Beijing, China. JMLR.org.

Ben Krause, Emmanuel Kahembwe, Iain Murray, and Steve Renals. 2017. Dynamic Evaluation of Neural Sequence Models. *arXiv:1709.07432 [cs]*. ArXiv: 1709.07432.

Ke Li and Jitendra Malik. 2016. Learning to Optimize. *arXiv:1606.01885 [cs, math, stat]*. ArXiv: 1606.01885.

Stephen Merity, Nitish Shirish Keskar, and Richard Socher. 2017. Regularizing and Optimizing LSTM Language Models. *arXiv:1708.02182 [cs]*. ArXiv: 1708.02182.

Stephen Merity, Caiming Xiong, James Bradbury, and Richard Socher. 2016. Pointer Sentinel Mixture Models. *arXiv:1609.07843 [cs]*. ArXiv: 1609.07843.

Tomas Mikolov, Martin Karafit, Lukas Burget, Jan Cernock, and Sanjeev Khudanpur. 2010. *Recurrent neural network based language model*, volume 2.

Joel Ruben Antony Moniz and David Krueger. 2018. Nested LSTMs. *arXiv:1801.10308 [cs]*. ArXiv: 1801.10308.

Ramesh Nallapati, Bowen Zhou, Caglar Gulcehre, and Bing Xiang. 2016. Abstractive text summarization using sequence-to-sequence rnns and beyond. *arXiv preprint arXiv:1602.06023*.

Matthew E. Peters, Mark Neumann, Mohit Iyyer, Matt Gardner, Christopher Clark, Kenton Lee, and Luke Zettlemoyer. 2018. Deep contextualized word representations. *arXiv:1802.05365 [cs]*. ArXiv: 1802.05365.

Alec Radford, Rafal Jozefowicz, and Ilya Sutskever. 2017. Learning to Generate Reviews and Discovering Sentiment. *arXiv:1704.01444 [cs]*. ArXiv: 1704.01444.

Sachin Ravi and Hugo Larochelle. 2016. Optimization as a Model for Few-Shot Learning.

Alexander M. Rush, Sumit Chopra, and Jason Weston. 2015. A neural attention model for abstractive sentence summarization. *arXiv preprint arXiv:1509.00685*.

J. Schmidhuber. 1992. Learning Complex, Extended Sequences Using the Principle of History Compression. *Neural Computation*, 4(2):234–242.

Holger Schwenk. 2012. Continuous space translation models for phrase-based statistical machine translation. *Proceedings of COLING 2012: Posters*, pages 1071–1080.

Hctor J. Sussmann. 1992. Uniqueness of the weights for minimal feedforward nets with a given input-output map. *Neural Networks*, 5(4):589–593.

Ke Tran, Arianna Bisazza, and Christof Monz. 2016. Recurrent Memory Networks for Language Modeling. *arXiv:1601.01272 [cs]*. ArXiv: 1601.01272.

Misha Tsodyks, Klaus Pawelzik, and Henry Markram. 1998. *Neural Networks with Dynamic Synapses*.

Restricted Recurrent Neural Tensor Networks: Exploiting Word Frequency and Compositionality

Alexandre Salle[1] Aline Villavicencio[1,2]
[1]Institute of Informatics, Federal University of Rio Grande do Sul (Brazil)
[2]School of Computer Science and Electronic Engineering, University of Essex (UK)
alex@alexsalle.com avillavicencio@inf.ufrgs.br

Abstract

Increasing the capacity of recurrent neural networks (RNN) usually involves augmenting the size of the hidden layer, with significant increase of computational cost. Recurrent neural tensor networks (RNTN) increase capacity using distinct hidden layer weights for each word, but with greater costs in memory usage. In this paper, we introduce restricted recurrent neural tensor networks (r-RNTN) which reserve distinct hidden layer weights for frequent vocabulary words while sharing a single set of weights for infrequent words. Perplexity evaluations show that for fixed hidden layer sizes, r-RNTNs improve language model performance over RNNs using only a small fraction of the parameters of unrestricted RNTNs. These results hold for r-RNTNs using Gated Recurrent Units and Long Short-Term Memory.

1 Introduction

Recurrent neural networks (RNN), which compute their next output conditioned on a previously stored hidden state, are a natural solution to sequence modeling. Mikolov et al. (2010) applied RNNs to word-level language modeling (we refer to this model as s-RNN), outperforming traditional n-gram methods. However, increasing capacity (number of tunable parameters) by augmenting the size H of the hidden (or recurrent) layer — to model more complex distributions — results in a significant increase in computational cost, which is $O(H^2)$.

Sutskever et al. (2011) increased the performance of a character-level language model with a multiplicative RNN (m-RNN), the factored approximation of a recurrent neural tensor network (RNTN), which maps each symbol to separate hidden layer weights (referred to as recurrence matrices from hereon). Besides increasing model capacity while keeping computation constant, this approach has another motivation: viewing the RNN's hidden state as being transformed by each new symbol in the sequence, it is intuitive that different symbols will transform the network's hidden state in different ways (Sutskever et al., 2011). Various studies on compositionality similarly argue that some words are better modeled by matrices than by vectors (Baroni and Zamparelli, 2010; Socher et al., 2012). Unfortunately, having separate recurrence matrices for each symbol requires memory that is linear in the symbol vocabulary size ($|V|$). This is not an issue for character-level models, which have small vocabularies, but is prohibitive for word-level models which can have vocabulary size in the millions if we consider surface forms.

In this paper, we propose the Restricted RNTN (r-RNTN) which uses only $K < |V|$ recurrence matrices. Given that $|V|$ words must be assigned K matrices, we map the most frequent $K - 1$ words to the first $K - 1$ matrices, and share the K-th matrix among the remaining words. This mapping is driven by the statistical intuition that frequent words are more likely to appear in diverse contexts and so require richer modeling, and by the greater presence of predicates and function words among the most frequent words in standard corpora like COCA (Davies, 2009). As a result, adding K matrices to the s-RNN both increases model capacity and satisfies the idea that some words are better represented by matrices. Results show that r-RNTNs improve language model performance over s-RNNs even for small K with no computational overhead, and even for small K approximate the performance of RNTNs using a fraction of the parameters. We also exper-

8

Proceedings of the 56th Annual Meeting of the Association for Computational Linguistics (Short Papers), pages 8–13
Melbourne, Australia, July 15 - 20, 2018. ©2018 Association for Computational Linguistics

iment with r-RNTNs using Gated Recurrent Units (GRU) (Cho et al., 2014) and Long Short-Term Memory (LSTM) (Hochreiter and Schmidhuber, 1997), obtaining lower perplexity for fixed hidden layer sizes. This paper discusses related work (§2), and presents r-RNTNs (§3) along with the evaluation method (§4). We conclude with results (§5), and suggestions for future work.

2 Related Work

We focus on related work that addresses language modeling via RNNs, word representation, and conditional computation.

Given a sequence of words $(x_1, ..., x_T)$, a language model gives the probability $P(x_t|x_{1...t-1})$ for $t \in [1, T]$. Using a RNN, Mikolov et al. (2010) created the s-RNN language model given by:

$$h_t = \sigma(W_h x_t + U_h h_{t-1} + b_h) \quad (1)$$

$$P(x_t|x_{1...t-1}) = x_t^T Softmax(W_o h_t + b_o) \quad (2)$$

where h_t is the hidden state represented by a vector of dimension H, $\sigma(z)$ is the pointwise logistic function, W_h is the $H \times V$ embedding matrix, U_h is the $H \times H$ recurrence matrix, W_o is the $V \times H$ output matrix, and b_h and b_o are bias terms. Computation is $O(H^2)$, so increasing model capacity by increasing H quickly becomes intractable.

The RNTN proposed by Sutskever et al. (2011) is nearly identical to the s-RNN, but the recurrence matrix in eq. (1) is replaced by a tensor as follows:

$$h_t = \sigma(W_h x_t + U_h^{i(x_t)} h_{t-1} + b_h) \quad (3)$$

where $i(z)$ maps a hot-one encoded vector to its integer representation. Thus the U_h tensor is composed of $|V|$ recurrence matrices, and at each step of sequence processing the matrix corresponding to the current input is used to transform the hidden state. The authors also proposed m-RNN, a factorization of the $U_h^{i(x_t)}$ matrix into $U_{lh} diag(v_{x_t}) U_{rh}$ to reduce the number of parameters, where v_{x_t} is a *factor* vector of the current input x_t, but like the RNTN, memory still grows linearly with $|V|$. The RNTN has the property that input symbols have both a vector representation given by the embedding and a matrix representation given by the recurrence matrix, unlike the s-RNN where symbols are limited to vector representations.

The integration of both vector and matrix representations has been discussed but with a focus on representation learning and not sequence modeling (Baroni and Zamparelli, 2010; Socher et al., 2012). For instance, Baroni and Zamparelli (2010) argue for nouns to be represented as vectors and adjectives as matrices.

Irsoy and Cardie (2014) used m-RNNs for the task of sentiment classification and obtained equal or better performance than s-RNNs. Methods that use conditional computation (Cho and Bengio, 2014; Bengio et al., 2015; Shazeer et al., 2017) are similar to RNTNs and r-RNTNs, but rather than use a static mapping, these methods train gating functions which do the mapping. Although these methods can potentially learn better policies than our method, they are significantly more complex, requiring the use of reinforcement learning (Cho and Bengio, 2014; Bengio et al., 2015) or additional loss functions (Shazeer et al., 2017), and more linguistically opaque (one must learn to interpret the mapping performed by the gating functions).

Whereas our work is concerned with updating the network's hidden state, Chen et al. (2015) introduce a technique that better approximates the output layer's Softmax function by allocating more parameters to frequent words.

3 Restricted Recurrent Neural Tensor Networks

To balance expressiveness and computational cost, we propose restricting the size of the recurrence tensor in the RNTN such that memory does not grow linearly with vocabulary size, while still keeping dedicated matrix representations for a subset of words in the vocabulary. We call these Restricted Recurrent Neural Tensor Networks (r-RNTN), which modify eq. (3) as follows:

$$h_t = \sigma(W_h x_t + U_h^{f(i(x_t))} h_{t-1} + b_h^{f(i(x_t))}) \quad (4)$$

where U_h is a tensor of $K < |V|$ matrices of size $H \times H$, b_h is a $H \times K$ bias matrix with columns indexed by f. The function $f(w)$ maps each vocabulary word to an integer between 1 and K.

We use the following definition for f:

$$f(w) = min(rank(w), K) \quad (5)$$

where $rank(w)$ is the rank of word w when the vocabulary is sorted by decreasing order of unigram frequency.

This is an intuitive choice because words which appear more often in the corpus tend to have more

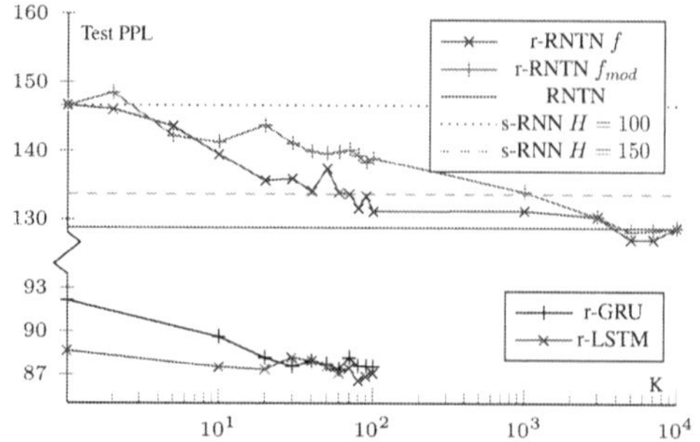

Figure 1: PTB test PPL as K varies from 1 to 10000 (100 for gated networks). At $K = 100$, the r-RNTN with f mapping already closely approximates the much bigger RNTN, with little gain for bigger K, showing that dedicated matrices should be reserved for frequent words as hypothesized.

variable contexts, so it makes sense to dedicate a large part of model capacity to them. A second argument is that frequent words tend to be predicates and function words. We can imagine that predicates and function words transform the meaning of the current hidden state of the RNN through matrix multiplication, whereas nouns, for example, add meaning through vector addition, following Baroni and Zamparelli (2010).

We also perform initial experiments with r-RNTNs using LSTM and GRUs. A GRU is described by

$$r_t = \sigma(W_h^r x_t + U_h^r h_{t-1} + b_h^r) \qquad (6)$$

$$z_t = \sigma(W_h^z x_t + U_h^z h_{t-1} + b_h^z) \qquad (7)$$

$$\tilde{h}_t = \tanh(W_h^h x_t + U_h^h (r_t \odot h_{t-1}) + b_h^h) \qquad (8)$$

$$h_t = z_t \odot h_{t-1} + (1 - z_t) \odot \tilde{h}_t \qquad (9)$$

and an LSTM by

$$f_t = \sigma(W_h^f x_t + U_h^f h_{t-1} + b_h^f) \qquad (10)$$

$$i_t = \sigma(W_h^i x_t + U_h^i h_{t-1} + b_h^i) \qquad (11)$$

$$o_t = \sigma(W_h^o x_t + U_h^o h_{t-1} + b_h^o) \qquad (12)$$

$$\tilde{c}_t = \tanh(W_h^c x_t + U_h^c h_{t-1} + b_h^c) \qquad (13)$$

$$c_t = i_t \odot \tilde{c}_t + f_t \odot c_{t-1} \qquad (14)$$

$$h_t = o_t \odot tanh(c_t) \qquad (15)$$

We create r-RNTN GRUs (r-GRU) by making U_h^h and b_h^h input-specific (as done in eq. (4)). For r-RNTN LSTMs (r-LSTM), we do the same for U_h^c and b_h^c.

4 Materials

We evaluate s-RNNs, RNTNs, and r-RNTNs by training and measuring model perplexity (PPL) on the Penn Treebank (PTB) corpus (Marcus et al., 1994) using the same preprocessing as Mikolov et al. (2011). Vocabulary size is 10000.

For an r-RNTN with $H = 100$, we vary the tensor size K from 1, which corresponds to the s-RNN, all the way up to 10000, which corresponds to the unrestricted RNTN. As a simple way to evaluate our choice of rank-based mapping function f, we compare it to a pseudo-random variant:

$$f_{mod}(w) = rank(w) \bmod K \qquad (16)$$

We also compare results to 1) an s-RNN with $H = 150$, which has the same number of parameters as an r-RNTN with $H = 100$ and $K = 100$. 2) An m-RNN with $H = 100$ with the size of factor vectors set to 100 to match this same number of parameters. 3) An additional r-RNTN with $H = 150$ is trained to show that performance scales with H as well.

We split each sentence into 20 word subsequences and run stochastic gradient descent via backpropagation through time for 20 steps without mini-batching, only reseting the RNN's hidden state between sentences. Initial learning rate (LR) is 0.1 and halved when the ratio of the validation perplexity between successive epochs is less than 1.003, stopping training when validation improvement drops below this ratio for 5 consecutive epochs. We use Dropout (Srivastava et al., 2014) with $p = .5$ on the softmax input to reduce overfitting. Weights are drawn from $\mathcal{N}(0, .001)$; gradients are not clipped. To validate our proposed method, we also evaluate r-RNTNs using the much larger text8[1] corpus with a 90MB-5MB-5MB train-validation-test split, mapping words which appear less than 10 times to $\langle unk \rangle$ for a total vocabulary size of 37751.

Finally, we train GRUs, LSTMs, and their r-RNTN variants using the PTB corpus and parameters similar to those used by Zaremba et al. (2014). All networks use embeddings of size 650 and a single hidden layer. Targeting $K = 100$, we set $H = 244$ for the r-GRU and compare with a GRU with $H = 650$ which has the same number of parameters. The r-LSTM has $H = 254$ to match the number of parameters of an LSTM

---

[1] http://mattmahoney.net/dc/textdata.html

Method	H	PTB		text8		Method	H	PTB	
		# Params	Test PPL	# Params	Test PPL			# Params	Test PPL
s-RNN	100	2M	146.7	7.6M	236.4	GRU	244	9.6M	92.2
r-RNTN f	100	3M	131.2	11.4M	190.1	GRU	650	15.5M	90.3
RNTN	100	103M	128.8	388M	-	r-GRU f	244	15.5M	**87.5**
m-RNN	100	3M	164.2	11.4M	895.0	LSTM	254	10M	88.8
s-RNN	150	3M	133.7	11.4M	207.9	LSTM	650	16.4M	**84.6**
r-RNTN f	150	5.3M	**126.4**	19.8M	**171.7**	r-LSTM f	254	16.4M	87.1

Table 1: Comparison of validation and test set perplexity for r-RNTNs with f mapping ($K = 100$ for PTB, $K = 376$ for text8) versus s-RNNs and m-RNN. r-RNTNs with the same H as corresponding s-RNNs significantly increase model capacity and performance with no computational cost. The RNTN was not run on text8 due to the number of parameters required.

with $H = 650$. The training procedure is the same as above but with mini-batches of size 20, 35 timestep sequences without state resets, initial LR of 1, Dropout on all non-recurrent connections, weights drawn from $\mathcal{U}(-.05, .05)$, and gradients norm-clipped to 5.

5   Results

Results are shown in fig. 1 and table 1.

Comparing the r-RNTN to the baseline s-RNN with $H = 100$ (fig. 1), as model capacity grows with K, test set perplexity drops, showing that r-RNTN is an effective way to increase model capacity with no additional computational cost. As expected, the f mapping outperforms the baseline f_{mod} mapping at smaller K. As K increases, we see a convergence of both mappings. This may be due to matrix sharing at large K between frequent and infrequent words because of the modulus operation in eq. (16). As infrequent words are rarely observed, frequent words dominate the matrix updates and approximate having distinct matrices, as they would have with the f mapping.

It is remarkable that even with K as small as 100, the r-RNTN approaches the performance of the RNTN with a small fraction of the parameters. This reinforces our hypothesis that complex transformation modeling afforded by distinct matrices is needed for frequent words, but not so much for infrequent words which can be well represented by a shared matrix and a distinct vector embedding. As shown in table 1, with an equal number of parameters, the r-RNTN with f mapping outperforms the s-RNN with a bigger hidden layer. It appears that heuristically allocating increased model capacity as done by the f based r-RNTN is a better way to increase performance than simply increasing hidden layer size, which also incurs a computational penalty.

Although m-RNNs have been successfully employed in character-level language models with small vocabularies, they are seldom used in word-level models. The poor results shown in table 1 could explain why.[2]

For fixed hidden layer sizes, r-RNTNs yield significant improvements to s-RNNs, GRUs, and LSTMs, confirming the advantages of distinct representations.

6   Conclusion and Future Work

In this paper, we proposed restricted recurrent neural tensor networks, a model that restricts the size of recurrent neural tensor networks by mapping frequent words to distinct matrices and infrequent words to shared matrices. r-RNTNs were motivated by the need to increase RNN model capacity without increasing computational costs, while also satisfying the ideas that some words are better modeled by matrices rather than vectors (Baroni and Zamparelli, 2010; Socher et al., 2012). We achieved both goals by pruning the size of the recurrent neural tensor network described by Sutskever et al. (2011) via sensible word-to-matrix mapping. Results validated our hypothesis that frequent words benefit from richer, dedicated modeling as reflected in large perplexity improvements for low values of K.

Interestingly, results for s-RNNs and r-GRUs suggest that given the *same number of parameters*, it is possible to obtain higher performance by increasing K and reducing H. This is not the

---

[2]It should be noted that Sutskever et al. (2011) suggest m-RNNs would be better optimized using second-order gradient descent methods, whereas we employed only first-order gradients in all models we trained to make a fair comparison.

case with r-LSTMs, perhaps to due to our choice of which of the recurrence matrices to make input-specific. We will further investigate both of these phenomena in future work, experimenting with different combinations of word-specific matrices for r-GRUs and r-LSTMs (rather than only U_h^h and U_h^c), and combining our method with recent improvements to gated networks in language modeling (Jozefowicz et al., 2016; Merity et al., 2018; Melis et al., 2018) which we believe are orthogonal and hopefully complementary to our own.

Finally, we plan to compare frequency-based and additional, linguistically motivated f mappings (for example different inflections of a verb sharing a single matrix) with mappings learned via conditional computing to measure how external linguistic knowledge contrasts with knowledge automatically inferred from training data.

Acknowledgments

This research was partly supported by CAPES and CNPq (projects 312114/2015-0, 423843/2016-8, and 140402/2018-7).

References

Marco Baroni and Roberto Zamparelli. 2010. Nouns are vectors, adjectives are matrices: Representing adjective-noun constructions in semantic space. In *Proceedings of the 2010 Conference on Empirical Methods in Natural Language Processing*. Association for Computational Linguistics, pages 1183–1193.

Emmanuel Bengio, Pierre-Luc Bacon, Joelle Pineau, and Doina Precup. 2015. Conditional computation in neural networks for faster models. *arXiv preprint arXiv:1511.06297* .

Welin Chen, David Grangier, and Michael Auli. 2015. Strategies for training large vocabulary neural language models. *arXiv preprint arXiv:1512.04906* .

Kyunghyun Cho and Yoshua Bengio. 2014. Exponentially increasing the capacity-to-computation ratio for conditional computation in deep learning. *arXiv preprint arXiv:1406.7362* .

Kyunghyun Cho, Bart van Merrienboer, aglar Gülehre, Dzmitry Bahdanau, Fethi Bougares, Holger Schwenk, and Yoshua Bengio. 2014. Learning phrase representations using rnn encoder-decoder for statistical machine translation. In *EMNLP*.

Mark Davies. 2009. The 385+ million word corpus of contemporary american english (1990–2008+): Design, architecture, and linguistic insights. *International journal of corpus linguistics* 14(2):159–190.

Sepp Hochreiter and Jürgen Schmidhuber. 1997. Long short-term memory. *Neural computation* 9 8:1735–80.

Ozan Irsoy and Claire Cardie. 2014. Modeling compositionality with multiplicative recurrent neural networks. *arXiv preprint arXiv:1412.6577* .

Rafal Jozefowicz, Oriol Vinyals, Mike Schuster, Noam Shazeer, and Yonghui Wu. 2016. Exploring the limits of language modeling. *arXiv preprint arXiv:1602.02410* .

Mitchell P. Marcus, Beatrice Santorini, and Mary A. Marcinkiewicz. 1994. Building a large annotated corpus of English: The Penn Treebank. *Computational Linguistics* 19(2):313–330.

Gbor Melis, Chris Dyer, and Phil Blunsom. 2018. On the state of the art of evaluation in neural language models. In *International Conference on Learning Representations*.

Stephen Merity, Nitish Shirish Keskar, and Richard Socher. 2018. Regularizing and optimizing LSTM language models. In *International Conference on Learning Representations*.

T. Mikolov, A. Deoras, S. Kombrink, L. Burget, and J. Cernocký. 2011. Empirical evaluation and combination of advanced language modeling techniques. In *INTERSPEECH*. pages 605–608.

Tomas Mikolov, Martin Karafiát, Lukas Burget, Jan Cernockỳ, and Sanjeev Khudanpur. 2010. Recurrent neural network based language model. In *INTERSPEECH 2010, 11th Annual Conference of the International Speech Communication Association, Makuhari, Chiba, Japan, September 26-30, 2010*. pages 1045–1048.

Noam Shazeer, Azalia Mirhoseini, Krzysztof Maziarz, Andy Davis, Quoc Le, Geoffrey Hinton, and Jeff Dean. 2017. Outrageously large neural networks: The sparsely-gated mixture-of-experts layer. *arXiv preprint arXiv:1701.06538* .

Richard Socher, Brody Huval, Christopher D Manning, and Andrew Y Ng. 2012. Semantic compositionality through recursive matrix-vector spaces. In *Proceedings of the 2012 Joint Conference on Empirical Methods in Natural Language Processing and Computational Natural Language Learning*. Association for Computational Linguistics, pages 1201–1211.

Nitish Srivastava, Geoffrey E Hinton, Alex Krizhevsky, Ilya Sutskever, and Ruslan Salakhutdinov. 2014. Dropout: a simple way to prevent neural networks from overfitting. *Journal of Machine Learning Research* 15(1):1929–1958.

Ilya Sutskever, James Martens, and Geoffrey E Hinton. 2011. Generating text with recurrent neural networks. In *Proceedings of the 28th International Conference on Machine Learning (ICML-11)*. pages 1017–1024.

Wojciech Zaremba, Ilya Sutskever, and Oriol Vinyals.
2014. Recurrent neural network regularization.
arXiv preprint arXiv:1409.2329 .

Deep RNNs Encode Soft Hierarchical Syntax

Terra Blevins, Omer Levy, and Luke Zettlemoyer
Paul G. Allen School of Computer Science & Engineering
University of Washington
Seattle, WA
`{blvns, omerlevy, lsz}@cs.washington.edu`

Abstract

We present a set of experiments to demonstrate that deep recurrent neural networks (RNNs) learn internal representations that capture soft hierarchical notions of syntax from highly varied supervision. We consider four syntax tasks at different depths of the parse tree; for each word, we predict its part of speech as well as the first (parent), second (grandparent) and third level (great-grandparent) constituent labels that appear above it. These predictions are made from representations produced at different depths in networks that are pre-trained with one of four objectives: dependency parsing, semantic role labeling, machine translation, or language modeling. In every case, we find a correspondence between network depth and syntactic depth, suggesting that a soft syntactic hierarchy emerges. This effect is robust across all conditions, indicating that the models encode significant amounts of syntax even in the absence of an explicit syntactic training supervision.

1 Introduction

Deep recurrent neural networks (RNNs) have effectively replaced explicit syntactic features (e.g. parts of speech, dependencies) in state-of-the-art NLP models (He et al., 2017; Lee et al., 2017; Klein et al., 2017). However, previous work has shown that syntactic information (in the form of either input features or supervision) is useful for a wide variety of NLP tasks (Punyakanok et al., 2005; Chiang et al., 2009), even in the neural setting (Aharoni and Goldberg, 2017; Chen et al., 2017). In this paper, we show that the internal representations of RNNs trained on a variety of NLP tasks encode these syntactic features without explicit supervision.

We consider a set of feature prediction tasks drawn from different depths of syntactic parse trees; given a word-level representation, we attempt to predict the POS tag and the parent, grandparent, and great-grandparent constituent labels of that word. We evaluate how well a simple feedforward classifier can detect these syntax features from the word representations produced by the RNN layers from deep NLP models trained on the tasks of dependency parsing, semantic role labeling, machine translation, and language modeling. We also evaluate whether a similar classifier can predict if a dependency arc exists between two words in a sentence, given their representations.

We find that, across all four types of supervision, the representations learned by these models encode syntax beyond the explicit information they encounter during training; this is seen in both the word-level tasks and the dependency arc prediction task. Furthermore, we also observe that features associated with different levels of syntax tree correlate with word representations produced by RNNs at different depths. Largely speaking, we see that deeper layers in each model capture notions of syntax that are higher-level and more abstract, in the sense that higher-level constituents cover a larger span of the underlying sentence.

These findings suggest that models trained on NLP tasks are able to induce syntax even when direct syntactic supervision is unavailable. Furthermore, the models are able to differentiate this induced syntax into a soft hierarchy across different layers of the model, perhaps shedding some light on why *deep* RNNs are so useful for NLP.

2 Methodology

Given a model that uses multi-layered RNNs, we collect the vector representation $\mathbf{x}_i^l$ of each word i at each hidden layer l. To determine what syntactic information is stored in each word vector, we try to predict a series of constituency-based prop-

14

Proceedings of the 56th Annual Meeting of the Association for Computational Linguistics (Short Papers), pages 14–19
Melbourne, Australia, July 15 - 20, 2018. ©2018 Association for Computational Linguistics

Training Signal	Dataset	RNN Layers	Input Dims	Hidden Dims
Dependency Parsing	English Universal Dependencies	4 parallel bidirectional LSTMs	200	400
Semantic Role Labeling	CoNLL-2012	8 alternating-direction LSTMs with highways	100	300
Machine Translation	WMT-2014 English-German	4 parallel bidirectional LSTMs	500	500
Language Modeling	CoNLL-2012	2 sets of 4 unidirectional LSTMs with highways	1000	1000

Table 1: The training data, recurrent architecture, and hyperparameters of each model.

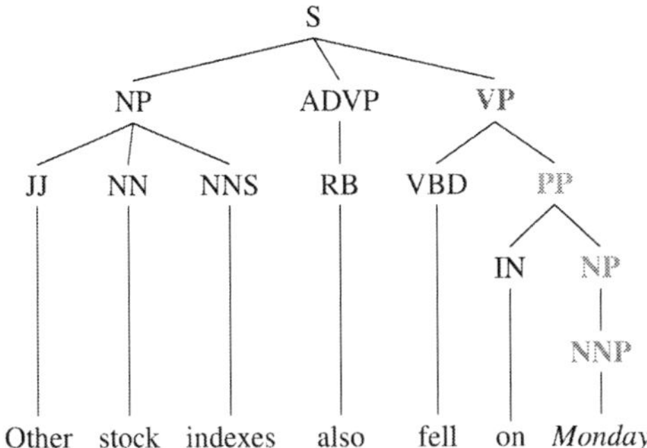

Figure 1: Constituency tree with labels for the word "Monday" for the POS (green), parent constituent (blue), grandparent constituent (orange), and great-grandparent constituent (red) tasks.

erties from the vector alone. Specifically, we predict the word's part of speech (POS), as well as the first (parent), second (grand-parent), and third level (great-grandparent) constituent labels of the given word. Figure 1 shows how these labels correspond to an example constituency tree.

Our methodology follows Shi et al. (2016), who run syntactic feature prediction experiments over a number of different shallow machine translation models, and Belinkov et al. 2017a; 2017b, who use a similar process to study the morphological, part-of-speech, and semantic features learned by deeper machine translation encoders. We extend upon prior work by considering training signals for models other than machine translation, and by applying more stratified word-level syntactic tasks.

2.1 Experiment Setup

We predict each syntactic property with a simple feed-forward network with a single 300-dimensional hidden layer activated by a ReLU:

$$\mathbf{y}_i^l = \text{SoftMax}(W_2\text{ReLU}(W_1\mathbf{x}_i^l)) \qquad (1)$$

where i is the word index and l is the layer index within a model. To ensure that the classifiers are not trained on the same data as the RNNs, we train the classifier for each layer l separately using the development set of CoNLL-2012 and evaluate on the test set (Pradhan et al., 2013).

In addition, we compare performance with word-level baselines. We report the per-word majority class baseline; at the POS level, for example, "cat" will be classified as a noun and "walks" as a verb. This baseline outperforms the pre-trained GloVe (Pennington et al., 2014) embeddings on every task. We also consider a contextual baseline, in which we concatenate each word's embedding with the average of its context's embeddings; however, this baseline also performed worse that the reported one.

2.2 Analyzed Models

We consider four different forms of supervision. Table 1 summarizes the differences in data, architecture, and hyperparameters.[1]

Dependency Parsing We train a four-layer version of the Stanford dependency parser (Dozat and Manning, 2017) on the Universal Dependencies English Web Treebank (Silveira et al., 2014). We ran the parser with 4 bidirectional LSTM layers (the default is 3), yielding a UAS of 91.5 and a weighted LAS of 82.18, consistent with the state of the art on CoNLL 2017. Since the parser receives syntactic features as input (POS) and is trained on an explicit syntactic signal, we expect

---

[1]While we control for some variables, we mainly rely on existing architectures and hyperparameters that were tuned for the original tasks, limiting the cross-model comparability of absolute performance levels on our syntactic evaluations.

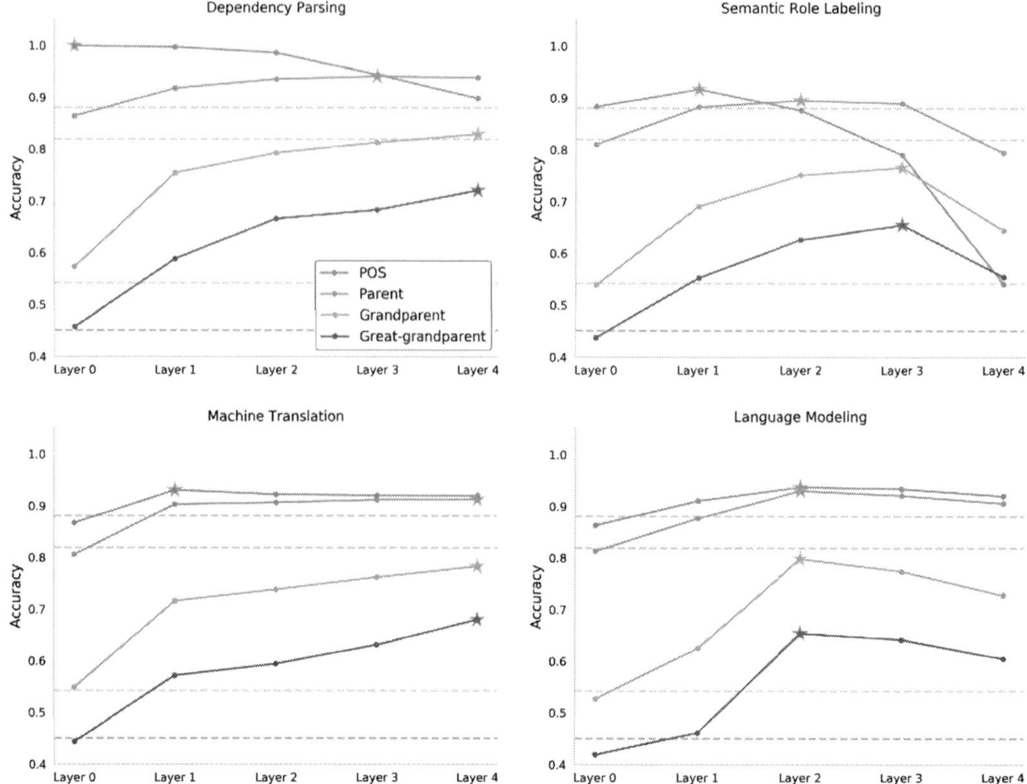

Figure 2: Results of syntax experiments. The best performing layer for each experiment is annotated with a star, and the per-word majority baseline for each task is shown with a dashed line.

its intermediate representations to contain a high amount of syntactic information.

Semantic Role Labeling We use the pre-trained DeepSRL model from (He et al., 2017), which was trained on the training data from the CoNLL-2012 dataset. This model is an alternating bidirectional LSTM, where the model consists of eight total layers that alternate between a forward layer and backward layer. We concatenate the representations from each pair of directional layers in the model for consistency with other models.

Machine Translation We train a machine translation model using OpenNMT (Klein et al., 2017) on the WMT-14 English-German dataset. The encoder (which we examine in our experiments) is a 4-layer bidirectional LSTM; we use the defaults for every other setting. The model achieves a BLEU score of 21.37, which is in the ballpark of other vanilla encoder-decoder attention models on this benchmark (Bahdanau et al., 2015).

Language Modeling We train two separate language models on CoNLL-2012's training set, one going forward and another backward. Each model is a 4-layer LSTM with highway connections, variational dropout, and tied input-output embeddings. After training, we concatenate the forward and backward representations for each layer.[2]

3 Constituency Label Prediction

Figure 2 shows our results (see supplementary material for numerical results). We make several observations:

RNNs can induce syntax. Overall, each model outperforms the baseline and its respective input embeddings on every syntax task, indicating that their internal representations encode some notions

---

[2]The model achieved perplexities of 50.56 (forward) and 51.24 (backward) on CoNLL-2012's test set. Since we are not familiar with other perplexity results on this data, we note that retraining the architecture on Penn TreeBank achieved 64.39 perplexity, which is comparable to other high-performing language models.

of syntax. The only exception to this observation is POS prediction with dependency parsing representations; in this case the parser is provided gold POS tags as input, and cannot improve upon them. This result confirms the findings of Shi et al. (2016) and Belinkov et al. (2017b), who demonstrate that neural machine translation encoders learn syntax, and shows that RNNs trained on other NLP tasks also induce syntax.

Deeper layers reflect higher-level syntax. In 11 out of 16 cases, performance improves up to a certain layer and then declines, suggesting that the deeper layers encode less syntactic information that earlier ones in these cases. Strikingly, the higher-level a syntactic task is, the deeper in the network the peak performance occurs; for example, in SRL we see that the parent constituent task peaks one layer after POS, and the grand-parent and great-grandparent tasks peak on the layer after that. One possible explanation is that each layer leverages the shallower syntactic information learned in the previous layer in order to construct a more abstract syntactic representation. In SRL and language modeling, it seems as though the syntactic information is then replaced by task-specific information (semantic roles, word probabilities), perhaps making it redundant.

This observation may also explain a modeling decision in ELMo (Peters et al., 2018), where injecting the contextualized word representations from a pre-trained language model was shown to boost performance on a wide variety of NLP tasks. ELMo represents each word using a task-specific weighted sum of the language model's hidden layers, i.e. rather than use only the top layer, it selects which of the language model's internal layers contain the most relevant information for the task at hand. Our results confirm that, in general, different types of information manifest at different layers, suggesting that post-hoc layer selection can be beneficial.

Language models learn some syntax. We compare the performance of language model representations to those learned with dependency parsing supervision, in order to gauge the amount of syntax induced. While this comparison is not ideal (the models were trained with slightly different architectures and hyperparameters), it does provide evidence that the language model's representations encode some amount of syntax implic-

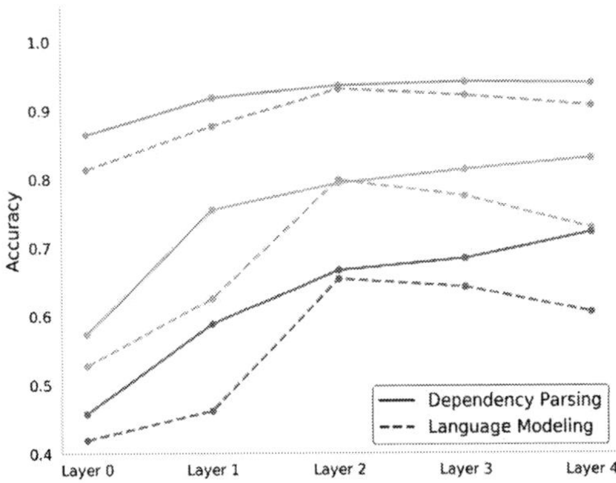

Figure 3: Comparison between the LM and dependency parser on the parent (blue), grandparent (yellow), and great-grandparent (red) constituent prediction tasks.

itly. Specifically, we observe in Figure 3 that the language model and dependency parser perform nearly identically on the three constituent prediction tasks in the second layer of their respective networks. In deeper layers the parser continues to improve, while the language model peaks at layer 2 and drops off afterwards.

These results may be surprising given the findings of Linzen et al. (2016), which found that RNNs trained on language modeling perform below baseline levels on the task of subject-verb agreement. However, the more recent investigation by Gulordava et al. (2018) are in line with our results. They find that language models trained on a number of different languages assign higher probabilities to valid long-distance dependencies than to incorrect ones. Therefore, LMs seem able to induce syntactic information despite being provided with no linguistic annotation.

4 Dependency Arc Prediction

We run an additional experiment that seeks to clarify if the representations learned by deep NLP models capture information about syntactic structure. Using the internal representations from a deep RNN, we train a classifier to predict whether two words share an dependency arc (have a parent-child relationship) in the in the dependency parse tree over a sentence. We find that, similarly to the previous set of tasks, deep RNNs trained on various linguistic signals encode notions of the syntactic relationships between words in a sentence.

Source Model	GloVe	L0	L1	L2	L3	L4
DP	0.50	0.68	0.77	0.81	0.88	**0.95**
SRL	0.50	0.58	0.69	0.76	**0.79**	0.74
MT	0.50	0.61	**0.73**	0.63	0.63	0.63
LM	0.50	0.62	0.74	0.78	**0.80**	0.73

Table 2: Results of the dependency arc prediction task. L0–L4 denote the different layers of the model. DP refers to the RNN trained with dependency parsing supervision.

Setup We use the same pretrained deep RNNs and feed-forward prediction network paradigm. However, we change the input from the previous experiments, as this task is not at the word-level, but rather concerns the relationship between two words; therefore, given a word pair w_c, w_p for which we have a dependency arc label, we input $[w_c; w_p; w_c \circ w_p]$ into the classifier.

We use the Universal Dependencies dataset for this task, such that we train each classifier on the development set of this dataset and evaluate on the test set. We set up the task by generating two pairs of examples for each word in the UD dataset: a positive pair that consists of the word and its parent in the dependency tree, and a negative pair that matches the word with another randomly chosen word from the sentence.

Results The results for this prediction task are given in Table 2. We see the best performance from the dependency parser, finding that the performance for the dependency parser's representations continue to improve in the deepest layers, with a maximum performance of approximately 95% on the last layer. This result is unsurprising, as this closely related to the task on which the model was explicitly trained. In the three other models, we find peaks that occur 12 to 20 accuracy points above the input layer's performance. These results support the findings from the constituency label prediction task and show that these findings hold up across syntactic formalisms.

Similarly to the word-level tasks, we see the best performance from deeper layers in the models, with both SRL and LM performance peaking on the third layer. For the LM, we find that the best performing layer outperforms the initial layer by 18%. This is consistent with our finding in the previous set of experiments, that RNNs encode significant amounts of syntax information even when trained on linguistic tasks without any explicit annotations.

5   Conclusions

In this paper, we run a series of prediction tasks on the internal representations of deep NLP models, and find these RNNs are able to induce syntax without explicit linguistic supervision. We also observe that the representations taken from deeper layers of the RNNs perform better on higher-level syntax tasks than those from shallower layers, suggesting that these recurrent models induce a soft hierarchy over the encoded syntax. These results provide some insight as to why deep RNNs are able to model NLP tasks without annotated linguistic features. Further characterizing the exact aspects of syntax which these models can capture (and perhaps more importantly, those they cannot) is an interesting area for future work.

Acknowledgments

The research was supported in part by the ARO (W911NF-16-1-0121) and the NSF (IIS-1252835, IIS-1562364). We also thank Yonatan Bisk, Yoav Goldberg, and the UW NLP group for helpful conversations and comments on the work.

References

Roee Aharoni and Yoav Goldberg. 2017. Towards string-to-tree neural machine translation. In *Proceedings of the 55th Annual Meeting of the Association for Computational Linguistics (Volume 2: Short Papers)*. Association for Computational Linguistics, pages 132–140. https://doi.org/10.18653/v1/P17-2021.

Dzmitry Bahdanau, Kyunghyun Cho, and Yoshua Bengio. 2015. Neural machine translation by jointly learning to align and translate. In *Proceedings of the Third International Conference on Learning Representations (ICLR)*. https://arxiv.org/abs/1409.0473.

Yonatan Belinkov, Nadir Durrani, Fahim Dalvi, Hassan Sajjad, and James Glass. 2017a. What do neural machine translation models learn about morphology? In *Proceedings of the 55th Annual Meeting of the Association for Computational*

Linguistics (Volume 1: Long Papers). Association for Computational Linguistics, pages 861–872. https://doi.org/10.18653/v1/P17-1080.

Yonatan Belinkov, Lluís Màrquez, Hassan Sajjad, Nadir Durrani, Fahim Dalvi, and James Glass. 2017b. Evaluating layers of representation in neural machine translation on part-of-speech and semantic tagging tasks. In *Proceedings of the Eighth International Joint Conference on Natural Language Processing (Volume 1: Long Papers)*. Asian Federation of Natural Language Processing, pages 1–10. http://aclweb.org/anthology/I17-1001.

Danqi Chen, Adam Fisch, Jason Weston, and Antoine Bordes. 2017. Reading wikipedia to answer open-domain questions. In *Proceedings of the 55th Annual Meeting of the Association for Computational Linguistics (Volume 1: Long Papers)*. Association for Computational Linguistics, Vancouver, Canada, pages 1870–1879. http://aclweb.org/anthology/P17-1171.

David Chiang, Kevin Knight, and Wei Wang. 2009. 11,001 new features for statistical machine translation. In *Proceedings of Human Language Technologies: The 2009 Annual Conference of the North American Chapter of the Association for Computational Linguistics*. Association for Computational Linguistics, pages 218–226. http://www.aclweb.org/anthology/N09-1025.

Timothy Dozat and Christopher D. Manning. 2017. Deep biaffine attention for neural dependency parsing. In *Proceedings of the Fifth International Conference on Learning Representations (ICLR)*. http://arxiv.org/abs/1611.01734.

Kristina Gulordava, Piotr Bojanowski, Edouard Grave, Tal Linzen, and Marco Baroni. 2018. Colorless green recurrent networks dream hierarchically. In *Proceedings of NAACL-HLT*. https://arxiv.org/pdf/1803.11138.pdf.

Luheng He, Kenton Lee, Mike Lewis, and Luke Zettlemoyer. 2017. Deep semantic role labeling: What works and what's next. In *Proceedings of the 55th Annual Meeting of the Association for Computational Linguistics (Volume 1: Long Papers)*. Association for Computational Linguistics, pages 473–483. https://doi.org/10.18653/v1/P17-1044.

Guillaume Klein, Yoon Kim, Yuntian Deng, Jean Senellart, and Alexander Rush. 2017. Opennmt: Open-source toolkit for neural machine translation. In *Proceedings of ACL 2017, System Demonstrations*. Association for Computational Linguistics, pages 67–72. http://www.aclweb.org/anthology/P17-4012.

Kenton Lee, Luheng He, Mike Lewis, and Luke Zettlemoyer. 2017. End-to-end neural coreference resolution. In *Proceedings of the 2017 Conference on Empirical Methods in Natural Language Processing*. Association for Computational Linguistics, pages 188–197. http://aclweb.org/anthology/D17-1018.

Tal Linzen, Emmanuel Dupoux, and Yoav Goldberg. 2016. Assessing the ability of LSTMs to learn syntax-sensitive dependencies. *Transactions of the Association of Computational Linguistics* 4:521–535. http://www.aclweb.org/anthology/Q16-1037.

Jeffrey Pennington, Richard Socher, and Christopher Manning. 2014. Glove: Global vectors for word representation. In *Proceedings of the 2014 Conference on Empirical Methods in Natural Language Processing (EMNLP)*. Association for Computational Linguistics, pages 1532–1543. https://doi.org/10.3115/v1/D14-1162.

Matthew E Peters, Mark Neumann, Mohit Iyyer, Matt Gardner, Christopher Clark, Kenton Lee, and Luke Zettlemoyer. 2018. Deep contextualized word representations. In *Proceedings of NAACL-HLT*. https://arxiv.org/pdf/1802.05365.pdf.

Sameer Pradhan, Alessandro Moschitti, Nianwen Xue, Hwee Tou Ng, Anders Björkelund, Olga Uryupina, Yuchen Zhang, and Zhi Zhong. 2013. Towards robust linguistic analysis using ontonotes. In *Proceedings of the Seventeenth Conference on Computational Natural Language Learning*. Association for Computational Linguistics, pages 143–152. http://www.aclweb.org/anthology/W13-3516.

Vasin Punyakanok, Dan Roth, and Wen-tau Yih. 2005. The necessity of syntactic parsing for semantic role labeling. In *International Joint Conference on Artificial Intelligence (IJCAI)*. volume 5, pages 1117–1123. http://cogcomp.org/papers/PunyakanokRoYi05.pdf.

Xing Shi, Inkit Padhi, and Kevin Knight. 2016. Does string-based neural MT learn source syntax? In *Proceedings of the 2016 Conference on Empirical Methods in Natural Language Processing*. Association for Computational Linguistics, pages 1526–1534. https://doi.org/10.18653/v1/D16-1159.

Natalia Silveira, Timothy Dozat, Marie-Catherine de Marneffe, Samuel Bowman, Miriam Connor, John Bauer, and Christopher D. Manning. 2014. A gold standard dependency corpus for English. In *Proceedings of the Ninth International Conference on Language Resources and Evaluation (LREC-2014)*. https://nlp.stanford.edu/pubs/Gold_LREC14.pdf.

Word Error Rate Estimation for Speech Recognition: e-WER

Ahmed Ali
Qatar Computing Research Institute
QCRI
Doha, Qatar
amali@qf.org.qa

Steve Renals
Centre for Speech Technology Research
University of Edinburgh
UK
s.renals@ed.ac.uk

Abstract

Measuring the performance of automatic speech recognition (ASR) systems requires manually transcribed data in order to compute the word error rate (WER), which is often time-consuming and expensive. In this paper, we propose a novel approach to estimate WER, or e-WER, which does not require a gold-standard transcription of the test set. Our e-WER framework uses a comprehensive set of features: ASR recognised text, character recognition results to complement recognition output, and internal decoder features. We report results for the two features; black-box and glass-box using unseen 24 Arabic broadcast programs. Our system achieves 16.9% WER root mean squared error (RMSE) across 1,400 sentences. The estimated overall WER e-WER was 25.3% for the three hours test set, while the actual WER was 28.5%.

1 Introduction

Automatic Speech Recognition (ASR) has made rapid progress in recent years, primarily due to advances in deep learning and powerful computing platforms. As a result, the quality of ASR has improved dramatically, leading to various applications, such as speech-to-speech translation, personal assistants, and broadcast media monitoring. Despite this progress, ASR performance is still closely tied to how well the acoustic model (AM) and language model (LM) training data matches the test conditions. Thus, it is important to be able to estimate the accuracy of an ASR system in a particular target environment.

Word Error Rate (WER) is the standard approach to evaluate the performance of a large vo-cabulary continuous speech recognition (LVCSR) system. The word sequence hypothesised by the ASR system is aligned with a reference transcription, and the number of errors is computed as the sum of substitutions (S), insertions (I), and deletions (D). If there are N total words in the reference transcription, then the word error rate WER is computed as follows:

$$\text{WER} = \frac{I + D + S}{N} \times 100. \qquad (1)$$

To obtain a reliable estimate of the WER, at least two hours of test data are required for a typical LVCSR system. In order to perform the alignment, the test data needs to be manually tran-scribed at the word level – a time-consuming and expensive process. It is, thus, of interest to de-velop techniques which can estimate the quality of an automatically generated transcription with-out requiring a gold-standard reference.

Such quality estimation techniques have been extensively investigated for machine translation (Specia et al., 2013), with extensions to spoken language translation (Ng et al., 2015, 2016). Although there is a long history of exploring word-level confidence measures for speech recognition (Evermann and Woodland, 2000; Cox and Das-mahapatra, 2002; Jiang, 2005; Seigel et al., 2011; Huang et al., 2013), there has been less work on the direct estimation of speech recognition errors.

Seigel and Woodland (2014) studied the detection of deletions in ASR output using a condi-tional random field (CRF) sequence model to de-tect one or more deleted word regions in ASR output. Ghannay et al. (2015) used word embed-dings to build a confidence classifier which labeled each word in the recognised word sequence with an error or a correct label. Tam et al. (2014) in-vestigated the use of a recurrent neural network (RNN) language model (LM) with complementary deep neural network (DNN) and Gaussian Mix-

Proceedings of the 56th Annual Meeting of the Association for Computational Linguistics (Short Papers), pages 20–24
Melbourne, Australia, July 15 - 20, 2018. ©2018 Association for Computational Linguistics

ture Model (GMM) acoustic models in order to identify ASR errors, based on the assumption that when two ASR systems disagree on an utterance region, then it is most likely an error.

Ogawa and Hori (2015) investigated using deep bidirectional recurrent neural networks (DBRNNs) to detect errors in ASR results. They explored four tasks for ASR error detection and recognition rate estimation: confidence estimation, out-of-vocabulary (OOV) word detection, error type classification, and recognition rate estimation. In an extension to this work, Ogawa et al. (2016); Ogawa and Hori (2017) investigated the estimation of speech recognition accuracy based on the classification of error types, in which sequence classification was performed by a CRF. Each word in a hypothesised word sequence was classified into one of three categories: correct, substitution error, or insertion error. Their study did not estimate the presence of deletions, and consequently cannot estimate the WER.

Jalalvand et al. (2016) developed a tool for ASR quality estimation, TranscRater, which is capable of predicting WER per utterance. This approach is based on a large set of extracted features (which do not require internal access to the ASR system) used to train a regression model (e.g., extremely randomised trees), and can also rank different transcriptions from multiple sources (Negri et al., 2014; de Souza et al., 2015; Jalalvand and Falavigna, 2015; Jalalvand et al., 2015a,b). TranscRater provides a WER per utterance, reporting the results as the MAE with respect to a reference transcription. This work did not report WER estimates for complete recordings or test sets, although it is possible that this could be done using utterance length estimates.

In this paper, we build on these contributions to develop a system to directly estimate the WER of an ASR output hypothesis. Our contributions are: (*i*) a novel approach to estimate WER per sentence and to aggregate them to provide WER estimation per recording or for a whole test set; (*ii*) an evaluation of our approach which compares the use of "black-box" features (without ASR decoder information) and "glass-box" features which use internal information from the decoder; and (*iii*) a release of the code and the data used for this paper for further research[1].

[1] https://github.com/qcri/e-wer

2   e-WER Framework

Estimating the probability of error of each word in a recognised word sequence has been successfully used to detect insertions, substitutions, and interword deletions (Ogawa et al., 2016; Ogawa and Hori, 2015; Ghannay et al., 2015; Jalalvand and Falavigna, 2015; Seigel and Woodland, 2014). However, these local estimates do not provide an estimate of the overall pattern of error, such as the total number of deletions in an utterance.

In our framework, we use two speech recognition systems; a word-based LVCSR system and a grapheme-sequence based system. Following Tam et al. (2014), we assume that when two corresponding ASR systems disagree on a sentence or part of a sentence, there is a pattern of error to be learned. Our architecture also benefits from utterance-based LVCSR decoder features including the total number of frames, the average log likelihood and the duration. Intuitively, we correlate short sentences with less context and assume that LM scoring will not be able to capture long context. Therefore, e-WER is defined as follows:

$$\text{e-WER} = \frac{\text{ERR}}{\hat{N}} \times 100\% \qquad (2)$$

Our model is required to predict two values for each utterance: ERR and $\hat{N}$. Given that each is integer-valued, we decided to frame their estimation as a classification task rather than a regression problem as shown in equations 3 and 4. Each class represents a specific word count. We limit the total number of classes to a maximum of C in ERR, with range from 0 to C. However, the total number of classes for $\hat{N}$ is $C - K$ to avoid estimating an utterance length of zero, with a range from K to C. If an utterance has more than C words or less than K words, it will thus be penalised by the loss function,

$$\text{ERR} = \underset{c_j \in C}{\arg\max}\, P(c_j | x_1, x_2, ..., x_n) \qquad (3)$$

$$\hat{N} = \underset{k_j \in C-K}{\arg\max}\, P(k_j | x_1, x_2, ..., x_n) \qquad (4)$$

Table 1 shows that fewer than 5% of the sentences have more than 20 words, and it is very unlikely to have an utterance with fewer than 2 words. We trained our system with $C = 20$ and $K = 2$. Since our approach predicts ERR and $\hat{N}$ for each sentence, it is possible to aggregate each of the two values across the entire test set in order to estimate the overall WER, as shown in section 3.

2.1 e-WER features

To estimate e-WER, we combine features from the word-based LVCSR system with features from the grapheme-based system. By running both word-based and character-based ASR systems, we are able to align their outputs against each other. We split the studied features into four groups

- L: lexical features – the word sequence extracted from the LVCSR.
- G: grapheme features – character sequence extracted from the grapheme recognition.
- N: numerical features – basic features about the speech signal, as well as grapheme alignment error details.
- D: decoder features – total frame count, average log-likelihood, total acoustic model likelihood and total language model likelihood.

Similar to previous research in ASR quality estimation, we refer to $\{L,G,N\}$ as the black-box features, and $\{L,G,N,D\}$ as the glass-box features, which are used to estimate the total number of words $\hat{N}$, and the total number of errors ERR in a given sentence.

2.2 Classification Back-end

We deployed a feed-forward neural network as a backend classifier for e-WER. The deployed network in this work has two fully-connected hidden layers (ReLU activation function), with 128 neurons in the first layer and 64 neurons in the second layer followed by a softmax layer. A minibatch size of 32 was used, and the number of epochs was up to 50 with an early stopping criterion.

2.3 Data

The e-WER training and development data sets are the same as the Arabic MGB-2 development and evaluation sets (Ali et al., 2016; Khurana and Ali, 2016), which is comprised of audio extracted from Al-Jazeera Arabic TV programs recorded in the last months of 2015. To test whether our approach generalises to test sets from a different source, and not tuned to the MGB-2 data set, we validated our results on three hours test set collected by BBC Monitoring during November 2016, as part of the SUMMA project[2].

---

[2]`http://summa-project.eu`

	Train	Dev	Test
Number of programs in corpus	17	17	24
Utterances	58K	56K	1.4K
Duration (in hours)	9.9	10.2	3.2
2-20 words sentences	96%	95%	96%
Word count (N)	**75K**	**69K**	**20K**
ASR word count (hyp)	58K	60K	18K
WER	42.6%	33.1%	28.5%
Total INS	1.9K	1.8K	130
Total DEL	19.1K	10.2K	2.6K
Total SUB	11.1K	10.8K	2.9K
ERR count (ERR)	**32.1K**	**22.8K**	**5.7K**

Table 1: Analysis of the train, dev and test data.

	MAE/Dev			MAE/Test		
	ERR	$\hat{N}$	e-WER	ERR	$\hat{N}$	e-WER
glass-box	1.6	1.8	13.8	1.7	1.7	12.3
black-box	1.8	2.2	28.4	1.9	2.3	24.7

Table 2: MAE per sentence reported for the glass-box and black-box features.

3 Experiments and discussions

We trained two DNN systems to estimate $\hat{N}$ and ERR separately. We explored training both a black-box based DNN system (without the decoder features) and a glass-box system using the decoder features. Overall, four systems were trained: two glass-box systems and two black-box systems. We used the same hyper-parameters across the four systems. Tables 2 and 3 present the e-WER performance in terms of the mean absolute error (MAE) and root mean squared error (RMSE) per sentence for ERR, $\hat{N}$ and the estimated WER for the dev and test sets with reference to the errors computed using a gold-standard reference. As expected, the glass-box features help to reduce MAE and RMSE for both ERR and $\hat{N}$. Although the difference between the black-box estimation and the glass-box results is not big for ERR and N, we can see that the impact becomes substantial on the estimated WER per sentence, which is almost double the error in both MAE and RMSE per sentence.

Table 4 reports the overall performance on the dev and on the test set. Across the 17 programs in the MGB-2 dev data, the actual WER is 33.1%, and the glass-box e-WER is 29.3%, while the black-box e-WER is 30.9%. Evaluating the same models on the 24 programs in the test data set results in an actual WER of 28.5%, while the glass-box e-WER is 25.3%, and the black-box e-WER is 30.3%.

Tables 2 and 3 show the glass-box features outperformed the black-box features in predicting both ERR and $\hat{N}$. Furthermore, the performance

	RMSE/Dev			RMSE/Test		
	ERR	$\hat{N}$	e-WER	ERR	$\hat{N}$	e-WER
glass-box	2.2	2.1	18.3	2.3	2.2	16.9
black-box	2.4	2.7	36.1	2.6	2.9	35.0

Table 3: RMSE per sentence reported for the glass-box and the black-box features.

Data	Reference	glass-box	black-box
	Actual/estimated WER		
Dev	33.1%	29.3%	30.9%
Test	28.5%	25.3%	30.3%

Table 4: Overall WER across the dev and the test data set.

of the estimated WER per sentence in the glass-box is substantially better than the black-box for both development and test sets. Table 4 indicates that the glass-box estimate is systematically lower than the black-box estimate. To further visualise these results, figure 1 plots the cumulative WER and e-WER across the three hours test set. This plot indicates that the glass-box estimate is continually lower than the black-box estimate. The large difference during the first 30 minutes arises owing the glass-box system is capable of better estimation with less data compared to the black-box system.

We estimate $\hat{N}$ and ERR separately. Therefore, our system is capable of estimating the WER at different levels of granularity. We visualise the prediction per program. In scenarios such as media-monitoring, where the main objective is to have a robust monitoring system for specific programs, we plot the WER across the 24 programs in the test set, and we can see in figure 2 that both the glass-box and black-box estimation are following the gold-standard WER per program. However, unlike predicting word count $\hat{N}$ or error count ERR, we can see that the black-box, in general, over-estimates the WER, while the glass-box system under-estimates WER similar to figure 1. One can argue from figure 2 that the decoder features are not helping in programs with high WER. We found both systems to be useful for reporting WER per program.

4   Conclusions

This paper presents our efforts in predicting speech recognition word error rate without requiring a gold-standard reference transcription. We presented a DNN based classifier to predict the total number of errors per utterance and the to-

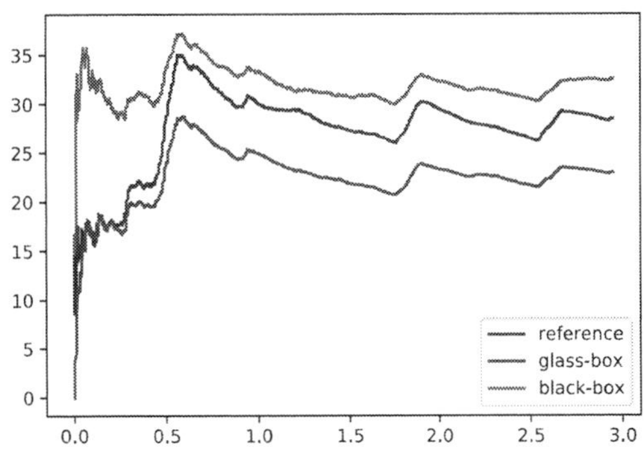

Figure 1: Test set cumulative WER over all sentences (X-axis is duration in hours and Y-axis is WER in %).

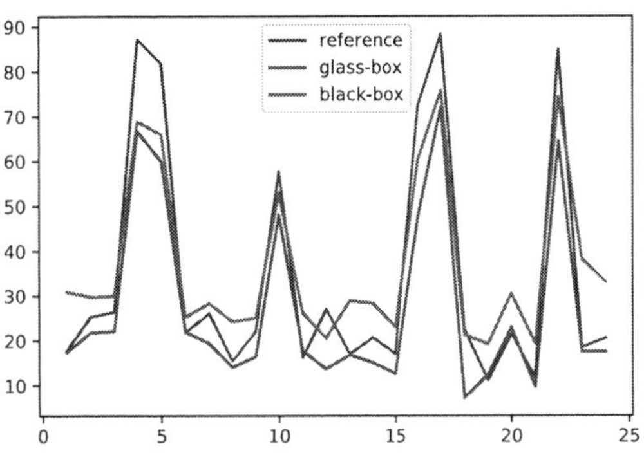

Figure 2: WER estimated over 24 programs on the test data.

tal word count separately. Our approach benefits from combining word-based and grapheme-based ASR results for the same sentence, along with extracted decoder features. We evaluated our approach per sentences and per program. Our experiments have shown that this approach is highly promising to estimate WER per sentence and we have aggregated the estimated results to predict WER for complete recordings, programs or test sets without the need for a reference transcription. For our future work, we shall continue our investigation into approaches that can estimate the word error rate using convolutional neural networks. In particular, we would like to explore combining the DNN numerical features with the CNN word embedding features.

References

Ahmed Ali, Peter Bell, James Glass, Yacine Messaoui, Hamdy Mubarak, Steve Renals, and Yifan Zhang. 2016. The MGB-2 challenge: Arabic multi-dialect broadcast media recognition. In *Proc IEEE SLT*.

Stephen Cox and Srinandan Dasmahapatra. 2002. High-level approaches to confidence estimation in speech recognition. *IEEE Transactions on Speech and Audio processing* 10(7):460–471.

José GC de Souza, Hamed Zamani, Matteo Negri, Marco Turchi, and Daniele Falavigna. 2015. Multitask learning for adaptive quality estimation of automatically transcribed utterances. In *HLT-NAACL*. pages 714–724.

Gunnar Evermann and PC Woodland. 2000. Posterior probability decoding, confidence estimation and system combination. In *Proc. Speech Transcription Workshop*. Baltimore, volume 27, page 78.

Sahar Ghannay, Yannick Esteve, and Nathalie Camelin. 2015. Word embeddings combination and neural networks for robustness in asr error detection. In *Signal Processing Conference (EUSIPCO), 2015 23rd European*. IEEE, pages 1671–1675.

Po-Sen Huang, Kshitiz Kumar, Chaojun Liu, Yifan Gong, and Li Deng. 2013. Predicting speech recognition confidence using deep learning with word identity and score features. In *Acoustics, Speech and Signal Processing (ICASSP), 2013 IEEE International Conference on*. IEEE, pages 7413–7417.

Shahab Jalalvand and Daniele Falavigna. 2015. Stacked auto-encoder for ASR error detection and word error rate prediction. In *Interspeech*.

Shahab Jalalvand, Daniele Falavigna, Marco Matassoni, Piergiorgio Svaizer, and Maurizio Omologo. 2015a. Boosted acoustic model learning and hypotheses rescoring on the chime-3 task. In *Automatic Speech Recognition and Understanding (ASRU), 2015 IEEE Workshop on*. IEEE, pages 409–415.

Shahab Jalalvand, Matteo Negri, Falavigna Daniele, and Marco Turchi. 2015b. Driving rover with segment-based asr quality estimation. In *Proceedings of the 53rd Annual Meeting of the Association for Computational Linguistics and the 7th International Joint Conference on Natural Language Processing (Volume 1: Long Papers)*. volume 1, pages 1095–1105.

Shahab Jalalvand, Matteo Negri, Marco Turchi, José GC de Souza, Daniele Falavigna, and Mohammed RH Qwaider. 2016. Transcrater: a tool for automatic speech recognition quality estimation. *ACL 2016* page 43.

Hui Jiang. 2005. Confidence measures for speech recognition: A survey. *Speech Communication* 45(4):455–470.

Sameer Khurana and Ahmed Ali. 2016. QCRI advanced transcription system (QATS) for the Arabic Multi-Dialect Broadcast Media Recognition: MGB-2 Challenge. In *SLT*.

Matteo Negri, Marco Turchi, José GC de Souza, and Daniele Falavigna. 2014. Quality estimation for automatic speech recognition. In *COLING*. pages 1813–1823.

Raymond WM Ng, Kashif Shah, Lucia Specia, and Thomas Hain. 2015. A study on the stability and effectiveness of features in quality estimation for spoken language translation. In *Sixteenth Annual Conference of the International Speech Communication Association*.

Raymond WM Ng, Kashif Shah, Lucia Specia, and Thomas Hain. 2016. Groupwise learning for asr k-best list reranking in spoken language translation. In *Acoustics, Speech and Signal Processing (ICASSP), 2016 IEEE International Conference on*. IEEE, pages 6120–6124.

Atsunori Ogawa and Takaaki Hori. 2015. Asr error detection and recognition rate estimation using deep bidirectional recurrent neural networks. In *ICASSP*.

Atsunori Ogawa and Takaaki Hori. 2017. Error detection and accuracy estimation in automatic speech recognition using deep bidirectional recurrent neural networks. *Speech Communication* 89:70–83.

Atsunori Ogawa, Takaaki Hori, and Atsushi Nakamura. 2016. Estimating speech recognition accuracy based on error type classification. *IEEE/ACM Transactions on Audio, Speech, and Language Processing* 24(12):2400–2413.

Matthew Stephen Seigel and Philip C Woodland. 2014. Detecting deletions in asr output. In *ICASSP*. IEEE, pages 2302–2306.

Matthew Stephen Seigel, Philip C Woodland, et al. 2011. Combining information sources for confidence estimation with crf models. In *Interspeech*. pages 905–908.

Lucia Specia, Kashif Shah, Jose G.C. de Souza, and Trevor Cohn. 2013. QuEst – a translation quality estimation framework. In *ACL: System Demonstrations*. pages 79–84.

Yik-Cheung Tam, Yun Lei, Jing Zheng, and Wen Wang. 2014. Asr error detection using recurrent neural network language model and complementary asr. In *ICASSP*. IEEE, pages 2312–2316.

Towards Robust and Privacy-preserving Text Representations

Yitong Li   **Timothy Baldwin**   **Trevor Cohn**
School of Computing and Information Systems
The University of Melbourne, Australia
`yitongl4@student.unimelb.edu.au`
`{tbaldwin,tcohn}@unimelb.edu.au`

Abstract

Written text often provides sufficient clues to identify the author, their gender, age, and other important attributes. Consequently, the authorship of training and evaluation corpora can have unforeseen impacts, including differing model performance for different user groups, as well as privacy implications. In this paper, we propose an approach to explicitly obscure important author characteristics at training time, such that representations learned are invariant to these attributes. Evaluating on two tasks, we show that this leads to increased privacy in the learned representations, as well as more robust models to varying evaluation conditions, including out-of-domain corpora.

1 Introduction

Language is highly diverse, and differs according to author, their background, and personal attributes such as gender, age, education and nationality. This variation can have a substantial effect on NLP models learned from text (Hovy et al., 2015), leading to significant variation in inferences across different types of corpora, such as the author's native language, gender and age. Training corpora are never truly representative, and therefore models fit to these datasets are biased in the sense that they are much more effective for texts from certain groups of user, e.g., middle-aged white men, and considerably poorer for other parts of the population (Hovy, 2015). Moreover, models fit to language corpora often fixate on author attributes which correlate with the target variable, e.g., gender correlating with class skews (Zhao et al., 2017), or translation choices (Rabinovich et al., 2017). This signal, however, is rarely fundamental to the task of modelling language, and is better considered as a confounding influence. These auxiliary learning signals can mean the models do not adequately capture the core linguistic problem. In such situations, removing these confounds should give better generalisation, especially for out-of-domain evaluation, a similar motivation to research in domain adaptation based on selection biases over text domains (Blitzer et al., 2007; Daumé III, 2007).

Another related problem is privacy: texts convey information about their author, often inadvertently, and many individuals may wish to keep this information private. Consider the case of the *AOL search data leak*, in which AOL released detailed search logs of many of their users in August 2006 (Pass et al., 2006). Although they de-identified users in the data, the log itself contained sufficient personally identifiable information that allowed many of these individuals to be identifed (Jones et al., 2007). Other sources of user text, such as emails, SMS messages and social media posts, would likely pose similar privacy issues. This raises the question of how the corpora, or models built thereupon, can be distributed without exposing this sensitive data. This is the problem of *differential privacy*, which is more typically applied to structured data, and often involves data masking, addition or noise, or other forms of corruption, such that formal bounds can be stated in terms of the likelihood of reconstructing the protected components of the dataset (Dwork, 2008). This often comes at the cost of an accuracy reduction for models trained on the corrupted data (Shokri and Shmatikov, 2015; Abadi et al., 2016).

Another related setting is where latent representations of the data are shared, rather than the text itself, which might occur when sending data from a phone to the cloud for processing, or trusting a third party with sensitive emails for NLP

Proceedings of the 56th Annual Meeting of the Association for Computational Linguistics (Short Papers), pages 25–30
Melbourne, Australia, July 15 - 20, 2018. ©2018 Association for Computational Linguistics

processing, such as grammar correction or translation. The transfered representations may still contain sensitive information, however, especially if an adversary has preliminary knowledge of the training model, in which case they can readily reverse engineer the input, for example, by a GAN attack algorithm (Hitaj et al., 2017). This is true even when differential privacy mechanisms have been applied.

Inspired by the above works, and recent successes of adversarial learning (Goodfellow et al., 2014; Ganin et al., 2016), we propose a novel approach for privacy-preserving learning of unbiased representations.[1] Specially, we employ Ganin et al.'s approach to training deep models with adversarial learning, to explicitly obscure individuals' private information. Thereby the learned (hidden) representations of the data can be transferred without compromising the authors' privacy, while still supporting high-quality NLP inference. We evaluate on the tasks of POS-tagging and sentiment analysis, protecting several demographic attributes — gender, age, and location — and show empirically that doing so does not hurt accuracy, but instead can lead to substantial gains, most notably in out-of-domain evaluation. Compared to differential privacy, we report gains rather than loss in performance, but note that we provide only empirical improvements in privacy, without any formal guarantees.

2 Methodology

We consider a standard supervised learning situation, in which inputs $\mathbf{x}$ are used to compute a representation $\mathbf{h}$, which then forms the parameterisation of a generalised linear model, used to predict the target $\mathbf{y}$. Training proceeds by minimising a differentiable loss, e.g., cross entropy, between predictions and the ground truth, in order to learn an estimate of the model parameters, denoted θ_M.

Overfitting is a common problem, particular in deep learning models with large numbers of parameters, whereby $\mathbf{h}$ learns to capture specifics of the training instances which do not generalise to unseen data. Some types of overfitting are insidious, and cannot be adequately addressed with standard techniques like dropout or regularisation. Consider, for example, the authorship of each sen-

---

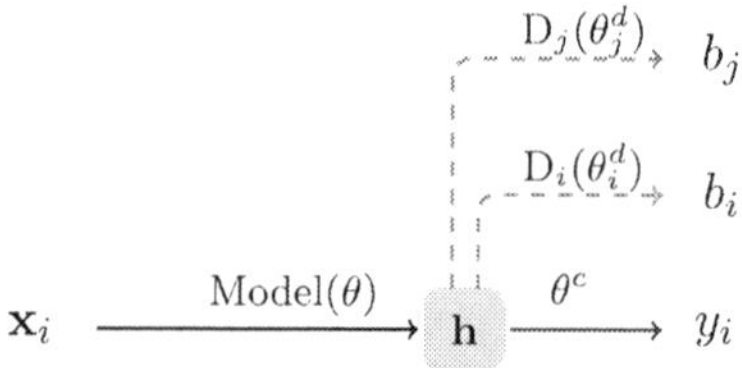

Figure 1: Proposed model architectures, showing a single training instance $(\mathbf{x}_i, y_i)$ with two protected attributes, b_i and b_j. D indicates a discriminator, and the red dashed and blue lines denote adversarial and standard loss, respectively.

tence in the training set in a sentiment prediction task. Knowing the author, and their general disposition, will likely provide strong clues about their sentiment wrt any sentence. Moreover, given the ease of authorship attribution, a powerful learning model might learn to detect the author from their text, and use this to predict the sentiment, rather than basing the decision on the semantics of each sentence. This might be the most efficient use of model capacity if there are many sentences by this individual in the training dataset, yet will lead to poor generalisation to test data authored by unseen individuals.

Moreover, this raises privacy issues when $\mathbf{h}$ is known by an attacker or malicious adversary. Traditional privacy-preserving methods, such as added noise or masking, applied to the representation will often incur a cost in terms of a reduction in task performance. Differential privacy methods are unable to protect the user privacy of $\mathbf{h}$ under adversarial attacks, as described in Section 1.

Therefore, we consider how to learn an unbiased representations of the data with respect to specific attributes which we expect to behave as confounds in a generalisation setting. To do so, we take inspiration from adversarial learning (Goodfellow et al., 2014; Ganin et al., 2016). The architecture is illustrated in Figure 1.

2.1 Adversarial Learning

A key idea of adversarial learning, following Ganin et al. (2016), is to learn a discriminator model D jointly with learning the standard supervised model. Using gender as an example, a discriminator will attempt to predict the gender, b, of each instance from $\mathbf{h}$, such that training involves joint learning of both the model parameters, θ_M, and the discriminator parameters θ_D. However, the aim of learning for these components are in opposition – we seek a $\mathbf{h}$ which leads to a good predictor of the target $\mathbf{y}$, while being a poor representation for prediction of gender. This leads to the objective (illustrated for a single training instance),

$$\hat{\theta} = \min_{\theta_M} \max_{\theta_D} \; \mathcal{X}(\hat{\mathbf{y}}(\mathbf{x}; \theta_M), \mathbf{y}) \tag{1}$$
$$- \lambda \cdot \mathcal{X}(\hat{b}(\mathbf{x}; \theta_D), b) \,,$$

where $\mathcal{X}$ denotes the cross entropy function. The negative sign of the second term, referred to as the adversarial loss, can be implemented by a gradient reversal layer during backpropagation (Ganin et al., 2016). To elaborate, training is based on standard gradient backpropagation for learning the main task, but for the auxiliary task, we start with standard loss backpropagation, however gradients are reversed in sign when they reach $\mathbf{h}$. Consequently the linear output components are trained to be good predictors, but $\mathbf{h}$ is trained to be maximally good for the main task and maximally poor for the auxiliary task.

Furthermore, Equation 1 can be expanded to scenarios with several (N) protected attributes,

$$\hat{\theta} = \min_{\theta_M} \max_{\{\theta_{D^i}\}_{i=1}^{N}} \; \mathcal{X}(\hat{\mathbf{y}}(\mathbf{x}; \theta_M), \mathbf{y}) \tag{2}$$
$$- \sum_{i=1}^{N} \left(\lambda_i \cdot \mathcal{X}(\hat{b}(\mathbf{x}; \theta_{D^i}), b_i) \right) \,.$$

3 Experiments

In this section, we report experimental results for our methods with two very different language tasks.

3.1 POS-tagging

This first task is part-of-speech (POS) tagging, framed as a sequence tagging problem. Recent demographic studies have found that the author's gender, age and race can influence tagger performance (Hovy and Søgaard, 2015; Jørgensen et al., 2016). Therefore, we use the POS tagging to demonstrate that our model is capable of eliminating this type of bias, thereby leading to more robust models of the problem.

Model Our model is a bi-directional LSTM for POS tag prediction (Hochreiter and Schmidhuber,

1997), formulated as:

$$\mathbf{h}_i = \text{LSTM}(\mathbf{x}_i, \mathbf{h}_{i-1}; \theta_h)$$
$$\mathbf{h}_i' = \text{LSTM}(\mathbf{x}_i, \mathbf{h}_{i+1}'; \theta_h')$$
$$\mathbf{y}_i \sim \text{Categorical}(\phi([\mathbf{h}_i; \mathbf{h}_i']); \theta_o) \,,$$

for input sequence $\mathbf{x}_i|_{i=1}^{n}$ with terminal hidden states $\mathbf{h}_0$ and $\mathbf{h}_{n+1}'$ set to zero, where ϕ is a linear transformation, and $[\cdot; \cdot]$ denotes vector concatenation.

For the adversarial learning, we use the training objective from Equation 2 to protect gender and age, both of which are treated as binary values. The adversarial component is parameterised by 1-hidden feedforward nets, applied to the final hidden representation $[\mathbf{h}_n; \mathbf{h}_0']$. For hyperparameters, we fix the size of the word embeddings and $\mathbf{h}$ to 300, and set all λ values to 10^{-3}. A dropout rate of 0.5 is applied to all hidden layers during training.

Data We use the TrustPilot English POS tagged dataset (Hovy and Søgaard, 2015), which consists of 600 sentences, each labelled with both the sex and age of the author, and manually POS tagged based on the Google Universal POS tagset (Petrov et al., 2012). For the purposes of this paper, we follow Hovy and Søgaard's setup, categorising SEX into female (F) and male (M), and AGE into over-45 (O45) and under-35 (U35). We train the taggers both with and without the adversarial loss, denoted ADV and BASELINE, respectively.

For evaluation, we perform a 10-fold cross validation, with a train:dev:test split using ratios of 8:1:1. We also follow the evaluation method in Hovy and Søgaard (2015), by reporting the tagging accuracy for sentences over different slices of the data based on SEX and AGE, and the absolute difference between the two settings.

Considering the tiny quantity of text in the TrustPilot corpus, we use the Web English Treebank (WebEng: Bies et al. (2012)), as a means of pre-training the tagging model. WebEng was chosen to be as similar as possible in domain to the TrustPilot data, in that the corpus includes unedited user generated internet content.

As a second evaluation set, we use a corpus of African-American Vernacular English (AAVE) from Jørgensen et al. (2016), which is used purely for held-out evaluation. AAVE consists of three very heterogeneous domains: LYRICS, SUBTITLES and TWEETS. Considering the substantial

	SEX			AGE		
	F	M	Δ	O45	U35	Δ
BASELINE	90.9	91.1	0.2	91.4	89.9	1.5
ADV	**92.2**	**92.1**	**0.1**	**92.3**	**92.0**	**0.3**

Table 1: POS prediction accuracy [%] using the Trustpilot test set, stratified by SEX and AGE (higher is better), and the absolute difference (Δ) within each bias group (smaller is better). The best result is indicated in **bold**.

difference between this corpus and WebEng or TrustPilot, and the lack of any domain adaptation, we expect a substantial drop in performance when transferring models, but also expect a larger impact from bias removal using ADV training.

Results and analysis Table 1 shows the results for the TrustPilot dataset. Observe that the disparity for the BASELINE tagger accuracy (the Δ column), for AGE is larger than for SEX, consistent with the results of Hovy and Søgaard (2015). Our ADV method leads to a sizeable reduction in the difference in accuracy across both SEX and AGE, showing our model is capturing the bias signal less and more robust to the tagging task. Moreover, our method leads to a substantial improvement in accuracy across all the test cases. We speculate that this is a consequence of the regularising effect of the adversarial loss, leading to a better characterisation of the tagging problem.

Table 2 shows the results for the AAVE heldout domain. Note that we do not have annotations for SEX or AGE, and thus we only report the overall accuracy on this dataset. Note that ADV also significantly outperforms the BASELINE across the three heldout domains.

Combined, these results demonstrate that our model can learn relatively gender and age *debiased* representations, while simultaneously improving the predictive performance, both for in-domain and out-of-domain evaluation scenarios.

3.2 Sentiment Analysis

The second task we use is sentiment analysis, which also has broad applications to the online community, as well as privacy implications for the authors whose text is used to train our models. Many user attributes have been shown to be easily detectable from online review data, as used extensively in sentiment analysis results (Hovy et al., 2015; Potthast et al., 2017). In this paper, we fo-

	LYRICS	SUBTITLES	TWEETS	Average
BASELINE	73.7	81.4	59.9	71.7
ADV	**80.5**	**85.8**	**65.4**	**77.0**

Table 2: POS predictive accuracy [%] over the AAVE dataset, stratified over the three domains, alongside the macro-average accuracy. The best result is indicated in **bold**.

cus on three demographic variables of gender, age, and location.

Model Sentiment is framed as a 5-class text classification problem, which we model using Kim (2014)'s convolutional neural net (CNN) architecture, in which the hidden representation is generated by a series of convolutional filters followed a maxpooling step, simply denote as $\mathbf{h} = \mathrm{CNN}(\mathbf{x}; \theta_M)$. We follow the hyper-parameter settings of Kim (2014), and initialise the model with word2vec embeddings (Mikolov et al., 2013). We set the λ values to 10^{-3} and apply a dropout rate of 0.5 to $\mathbf{h}$.

As the discriminator, we also use a feed-forward model with one hidden layer, to predict the private attribute(s). We compare models trained with zero, one, or all three private attributes, denoted BASELINE, ADV-*, and ADV-all, respectively.

Data We again use the TrustPilot dataset derived from Hovy et al. (2015), however now we consider the RATING score as the target variable, not POS-tag. Each review is associated with three further attributes: gender (SEX), age (AGE), and location (LOC). To ensure that LOC cannot be trivially predicted based on the script, we discard all non-English reviews based on LANGID.PY (Lui and Baldwin, 2012), by retaining only reviews classified as English with a confidence greater than 0.9. We then subsample 10k reviews for each location to balance the five location classes (US, UK, Germany, Denmark, and France), which were highly skewed in the original dataset. We use the same binary representation of SEX and AGE as the POS task, following the setup in Hovy et al. (2015).

To evaluate the different models, we perform 10-fold cross validation and report test performance in terms of the F_1 score for the RATING task, and the accuracy of each discriminator. Note that the discriminator can be applied to test data, where it plays the role of an adversarial attacker, by trying to determine the private attributes of

	F_1		Discrim. [%]		
	dev	test	AGE	SEX	LOC
Majority class			57.8	62.3	20.0
BASELINE	41.9	40.1	65.3	66.9	53.4
ADV-AGE	**42.7**	40.1	**61.1**	65.6	41.0
ADV-SEX	42.4	39.9	61.8	62.9	42.7
ADV-LOC	42.0	**40.2**	62.2	66.8	**22.1**
ADV-all	42.0	**40.2**	61.8	**62.5**	28.1

Table 3: Sentiment F_1-score [%] over the RAT-ING task, and accuracy [%] of all the discriminator across three private attributes. The best score is indicated in **bold**. The majority class with respect to each private attribute is also reported.

users based on their hidden representation. That is, lower discriminator performance indicates that the representation conveys better privacy for individuals, and vice versa.

Results Table 3 shows the results of the different models. Note that all the privacy attributes can be easily detected in BASELINE, with results that are substantially higher than the majority class, although AGE and SEX are less well captured than LOC. The ADV trained models all maintain the task performance of the BASELINE method, however they clearly have a substantial effect on the discrimination accuracy. The privacy of SEX and LOC is substantially improved, leading to discriminators with performance close to that of the majority class (conveys little information). AGE proves harder, although our technique leads to privacy improvements. Note that AGE appears to be related to the other private attributes, in that privacy is improved when optimising an adversarial loss for the other attributes (SEX and LOC).

Overall, these results show that our approach learns hidden representations that hide much of the personal information of users, without affecting the sentiment task performance. This is a surprising finding, which augurs well for the use of deep learning as a privacy preserving mechanism when handling text corpora.

4   Conclusion

We proposed a novel method for removing model biases by explicitly protecting private author attributes as part of model training, which we formulate as deep learning with adversarial learning. We evaluate our methods with POS tagging and senti-

ment classification, demonstrating our method results in increased privacy, while also maintaining, or even improving, task performance, through increased model robustness.

Acknowledgements

We thank Benjamin Rubinstein and the anonymous reviewers for their helpful feedback and suggestions, and the National Computational Infrastructure Australia for computation resources. We also thank Dirk Hovy for providing the Trustpilot dataset. This work was supported by the Australian Research Council (FT130101105).

References

Martin Abadi, Andy Chu, Ian Goodfellow, H Brendan McMahan, Ilya Mironov, Kunal Talwar, and Li Zhang. 2016. Deep learning with differential privacy. In *Proceedings of the 2016 ACM SIGSAC Conference on Computer and Communications Security*, pages 308–318.

Ann Bies, Justin Mott, Colin Warner, and Seth Kulick. 2012. English Web Treebank. *Linguistic Data Consortium, Philadelphia, USA*.

John Blitzer, Mark Dredze, and Fernando Pereira. 2007. Biographies, bollywood, boom-boxes and blenders: Domain adaptation for sentiment classification. In *Proceedings of the 45th Annual Meeting of the Association of Computational Linguistics*, pages 440–447.

Hal Daumé III. 2007. Frustratingly easy domain adaptation. In *Proceedings of the 45th Annual Meeting of the Association of Computational Linguistics*, pages 256–263.

Cynthia Dwork. 2008. Differential privacy: A survey of results. In *International Conference on Theory and Applications of Models of Computation*, pages 1–19. Springer.

Yaroslav Ganin, Evgeniya Ustinova, Hana Ajakan, Pascal Germain, Hugo Larochelle, François Laviolette, Mario Marchand, and Victor Lempitsky. 2016. Domain-adversarial training of neural networks. *Journal of Machine Learning Research*, 17:59:1–59:35.

Ian J. Goodfellow, Jean Pouget-Abadie, Mehdi Mirza, Bing Xu, David Warde-Farley, Sherjil Ozair, Aaron C. Courville, and Yoshua Bengio. 2014. Generative adversarial nets. In *Advances in Neural Information Processing Systems 27*, pages 2672–2680.

Briland Hitaj, Giuseppe Ateniese, and Fernando Pérez-Cruz. 2017. Deep models under the gan: information leakage from collaborative deep learning. In *Proceedings of the 2017 ACM SIGSAC Conference on Computer and Communications Security*, pages 603–618. ACM.

Sepp Hochreiter and Jürgen Schmidhuber. 1997. Long short-term memory. *Neural computation*, 9(8):1735–1780.

Dirk Hovy. 2015. Demographic factors improve classification performance. In *Proceedings of the 53rd Annual Meeting of the Association for Computational Linguistics and the 7th International Joint Conference on Natural Language Processing (Volume 1: Long Papers)*, volume 1, pages 752–762.

Dirk Hovy, Anders Johannsen, and Anders Søgaard. 2015. User review sites as a resource for large-scale sociolinguistic studies. In *Proceedings of the 24th International Conference on World Wide Web*, pages 452–461.

Dirk Hovy and Anders Søgaard. 2015. Tagging performance correlates with author age. In *Proceedings of the 53rd Annual Meeting of the Association for Computational Linguistics and the 7th International Joint Conference on Natural Language Processing (Volume 2: Short Papers)*, volume 2, pages 483–488.

Rosie Jones, Ravi Kumar, Bo Pang, and Andrew Tomkins. 2007. I know what you did last summer: query logs and user privacy. In *Proceedings of the Sixteenth ACM Conference on Conference on Information and Knowledge Management (CIKM 2007)*, pages 909–914.

Anna Jørgensen, Dirk Hovy, and Anders Søgaard. 2016. Learning a POS tagger for AAVE-like language. In *Proceedings of the 2016 Conference of the North American Chapter of the Association for Computational Linguistics: Human Language Technologies*, pages 1115–1120.

Yoon Kim. 2014. Convolutional neural networks for sentence classification. In *Proceedings of the 2014 Conference on Empirical Methods in Natural Language Processing*, pages 1746–1751.

Marco Lui and Timothy Baldwin. 2012. langid.py: An off-the-shelf language identification tool. In *Proceedings of ACL 2012 System Demonstrations*, pages 25–30.

Tomas Mikolov, Ilya Sutskever, Kai Chen, Greg S. Corrado, and Jeff Dean. 2013. Distributed representations of words and phrases and their compositionality. In *Advances in Neural Information Processing Systems 26*, pages 3111–3119.

Greg Pass, Abdur Chowdhury, and Cayley Torgeson. 2006. A picture of search. In *The First International Conference on Scalable Information Systems*, volume 152, page 1.

Slav Petrov, Dipanjan Das, and Ryan McDonald. 2012. A universal part-of-speech tagset. In *Proceedings of the Eighth International Conference on Language Resources and Evaluation*.

Martin Potthast, Francisco Rangel, Michael Tschuggnall, Efstathios Stamatatos, Paolo Rosso, and Benno Stein. 2017. Overview of PAN17: Author identification, author profiling, and author obfuscation. In *8th International Conference of the CLEF on Experimental IR Meets Multilinguality, Multimodality, and Visualization*.

Ella Rabinovich, Raj Nath Patel, Shachar Mirkin, Lucia Specia, and Shuly Wintner. 2017. Personalized machine translation: Preserving original author traits. In *Proceedings of the 15th Conference of the European Chapter of the Association for Computational Linguistics: Volume 1, Long Papers*, pages 1074–1084.

Reza Shokri and Vitaly Shmatikov. 2015. Privacy-preserving deep learning. In *Proceedings of the 22nd ACM SIGSAC Conference on Computer and Communications Security*, pages 1310–1321.

Jieyu Zhao, Tianlu Wang, Mark Yatskar, Vicente Ordonez, and Kai-Wei Chang. 2017. Men also like shopping: Reducing gender bias amplification using corpus-level constraints. In *Proceedings of the 2017 Conference on Empirical Methods in Natural Language Processing*, pages 2979–2989.

HotFlip: White-Box Adversarial Examples for Text Classification

Javid Ebrahimi*, **Anyi Rao**[†], **Daniel Lowd***, **Dejing Dou***
*Computer and Information Science Department, University of Oregon, USA
{javid, lowd, dou}@cs.uoregon.edu
[†]School of Electronic Science and Engineering, Nanjing University, China
{anyirao}@smail.nju.edu.cn

Abstract

We propose an efficient method to generate white-box adversarial examples to trick a character-level neural classifier. We find that only a few manipulations are needed to greatly decrease the accuracy. Our method relies on an atomic flip operation, which swaps one token for another, based on the gradients of the one-hot input vectors. Due to efficiency of our method, we can perform adversarial training which makes the model more robust to attacks at test time. With the use of a few semantics-preserving constraints, we demonstrate that HotFlip can be adapted to attack a word-level classifier as well.

1 Introduction

Adversarial examples are inputs to a predictive machine learning model that are maliciously designed to cause poor performance (Goodfellow et al., 2015). Adversarial examples expose regions of the input space where the model performs poorly, which can aid in understanding and improving the model. By using these examples as training data, adversarial training learns models that are more robust, and may even perform better on non-adversarial examples. Interest in understanding vulnerabilities of NLP systems is growing (Jia and Liang, 2017; Zhao et al., 2018; Belinkov and Bisk, 2018; Iyyer et al., 2018). Previous work has focused on heuristics for creating adversarial examples in the *black-box* setting, without any explicit knowledge of the model parameters. In the *white-box* setting, we use complete knowledge of the model to develop worst-case attacks, which can reveal much larger vulnerabilities.

We propose a white-box adversary against differentiable text classifiers. We find that only a few

South Africa's historic Soweto township marks its 100th birthday on Tuesday in a mood of optimism. 57% **World**
South Africa's historic Soweto township marks its 100th birthday on Tuesday in a moo**P** of optimism. 95% **Sci/Tech**
Chancellor Gordon Brown has sought to quell speculation over who should run the Labour Party and turned the attack on the opposition Conservatives. 75% **World**
Chancellor Gordon Brown has sought to quell speculation over who should run the Labour Party and turned the attack on the o**B**position Conservatives. 94% **Business**

Table 1: Adversarial examples with a single character change, which will be misclassified by a neural classifier.

manipulations are needed to greatly increase the misclassification error. Furthermore, fast generation of adversarial examples allows feasible adversarial training, which helps the model defend against adversarial examples and improve accuracy on clean examples. At the core of our method lies an atomic *flip* operation, which changes one token to another by using the directional derivatives of the model with respect to the one-hot vector input.

Our contributions are as follows:

1. We propose an efficient gradient-based optimization method to manipulate discrete text structure at its one-hot representation.

2. We investigate the robustness of a classifier trained with adversarial examples, by studying its resilience to attacks and its accuracy on clean test data.

2 Related Work

Adversarial examples are powerful tools to investigate the vulnerabilities of a deep learning model (Szegedy et al., 2014). While this line of research has recently received a lot of attention in the deep learning community, it has a long history

31

Proceedings of the 56th Annual Meeting of the Association for Computational Linguistics (Short Papers), pages 31–36
Melbourne, Australia, July 15 - 20, 2018. ©2018 Association for Computational Linguistics

in machine learning, going back to adversarial attacks on linear spam classifiers (Dalvi et al., 2004; Lowd and Meek, 2005). Hosseini et al. (2017) show that simple modifications, such as adding spaces or dots between characters, can drastically change the toxicity score from Google's `perspective` API [1]. Belinkov and Bisk (2018) show that character-level machine translation systems are overly sensitive to random character manipulations, such as keyboard typos. They manipulate every word in a sentence with synthetic or natural noise. However, throughout our experiments, we care about the degree of distortion in a sentence, and look for stronger adversaries which can increase the loss within a limited budget. Instead of randomly perturbing text, we propose an efficient method, which can generate adversarial text using the gradients of the model with respect to the input.

Adversarial training interleaves training with generation of adversarial examples (Goodfellow et al., 2015). Concretely, after every iteration of training, adversarial examples are created and added to the mini-batches. A projected gradient-based approach to create adversarial examples by Madry et al. (2018) has proved to be one of the most effective defense mechanisms against adversarial attacks for image classification. Miyato et al. (2017) create adversarial examples by adding noise to word embeddings, without creating real-world textual adversarial examples. Our work is the first to propose an efficient method to generate real-world adversarial examples which can also be used for effective adversarial training.

3 HotFlip

HotFlip is a method for generating adversarial examples with character substitutions ("flips"). HotFlip also supports insertion and deletion operations by representing them as sequences of character substitutions. It uses the gradient with respect to a one-hot input representation to efficiently estimate which individual change has the highest estimated loss, and it uses a beam search to find a set of manipulations that work well together to confuse a classifier.

3.1 Definitions

We use $J(\mathbf{x}, \mathbf{y})$ to refer to the loss of the model on input $\mathbf{x}$ with true output $\mathbf{y}$. For example,

[1] https://www.perspectiveapi.com

for classification, the loss would be the log-loss over the output of the softmax unit. Let V be the alphabet, $\mathbf{x}$ be a text of length L characters, and $x_{ij} \in \{0, 1\}^{|V|}$ denote a one-hot vector representing the j-th character of the i-th word. The character sequence can be represented by

$$\mathbf{x} = [(x_{11}, .. \ x_{1n}); ..(x_{m1}, .. \ x_{mn})]$$

wherein a semicolon denotes explicit segmentation between words. The number of words is denoted by m, and n is the number of maximum characters allowed for a word.

3.2 Derivatives of Operations

We represent text operations as vectors in the input space and estimate the change in loss by directional derivatives with respect to these operations. Based on these derivatives, the adversary can choose the best loss-increasing direction. Our algorithm requires just one function evaluation (forward pass) and one gradient computation (backward pass) to estimate the best possible flip.

A **flip** of the j-th character of the i-th word $(a \rightarrow b)$ can be represented by this vector:

$$\vec{v}_{ijb} = (\vec{0}, ..; (\vec{0}, ..(0, ..-1, 0, .., 1, 0)_j, ..\vec{0})_i; \vec{0}, ..)$$

where -1 and 1 are in the corresponding positions for the a-th and b-th characters of the alphabet, respectively, and $x_{ij}^{(a)} = 1$. A first-order approximation of change in loss can be obtained from a directional derivative along this vector:

$$\nabla_{\vec{v}_{ijb}} J(\mathbf{x}, \mathbf{y}) = \nabla_x J(\mathbf{x}, \mathbf{y})^T \cdot \vec{v}_{ijb}$$

We choose the vector with biggest increase in loss:

$$\max \nabla_x J(\mathbf{x}, \mathbf{y})^T \cdot \vec{v}_{ijb} = \max_{ijb} \frac{\partial J}{\partial x_{ij}}^{(b)} - \frac{\partial J}{\partial x_{ij}}^{(a)} \tag{1}$$

Using the derivatives as a surrogate loss, we simply need to find the best change by calling the function mentioned in eq. 1, to *estimate* the best character change $(a \rightarrow b)$. This is in contrast to a naive loss-based approach, which has to query the classifier for every possible change to compute the *exact* loss induced by those changes. In other words, apart from the overhead of calling the function in eq. 1, one backward pass saves the adversary a large number of forward passes.

Character **insertion**[2] at the j-th position of the i-th word can also be treated as a character flip, followed by more flips as characters are shifted to the right until the end of the word.

$$\max \nabla_x J(\mathbf{x}, \mathbf{y})^T \cdot \vec{v}_{ijb} = \max_{ijb} \frac{\partial J}{\partial x_{ij}}^{(b)} - \frac{\partial J}{\partial x_{ij}}^{(a)}$$
$$+ \sum_{j'=j+1}^{n} \left(\frac{\partial J}{\partial x_{ij'}}^{(b')} - \frac{\partial J}{\partial x_{ij'}}^{(a')} \right)$$

where $x_{ij'}^{(a')} = 1$ and $x_{ij'-1}^{(b')} = 1$. Similarly, character **deletion** can be written as a number of character flips as characters are shifted to the left. Since the magnitudes of direction vectors (operations) are different, we normalize by the L_2 norm of the vector i.e., $\frac{\vec{v}}{\sqrt{2N}}$, where N is the number of total flips.

3.3 Multiple Changes

We explained how to estimate the best single change in text to get the maximum increase in loss. A greedy or beam search of r steps will give us an adversarial example with a maximum of r flips, or more concretely an adversarial example within an L_0 distance of r from the original example. Our beam search requires only $\mathcal{O}(br)$ forward passes and an equal number of backward passes, with r being the budget and b, the beam width. We elaborate on this with an example: Consider the loss function $J(.)$, input x_0, and an individual change c_j. We estimate the score for the change as $\frac{\partial J(x_0)}{\partial c_j}$. For a sequence of 3 changes $[c_1, c_2, c_3]$, we evaluate the "score" as follows.

$$\text{score}([c_1, c_2, c_3]) = \frac{\partial J(x_0)}{\partial c_1} + \frac{\partial J(x_1)}{\partial c_2} + \frac{\partial J(x_2)}{\partial c_3}$$

where x_1 and x_2 are the modified input after applying $[c_1]$ and $[c_1, c_2]$ respectively. We need b forward and backward passes to compute derivatives at each step of the path, leading to $\mathcal{O}(br)$ queries. In contrast, a naive loss-based approach requires computing the exact loss for every possible change at every stage of the beam search, leading to $\mathcal{O}(brL|V|)$ queries.

4 Experiments

In principle, HotFlip could be applied to any differentiable character-based classifier. Here, we focus on the CharCNN-LSTM architecture (Kim

et al., 2016), which can be adapted for classification via a single dense layer after the last recurrent hidden unit. We use the AG's news dataset[3], which consists of 120,000 training and 7,600 test instances from four equal-sized classes: World, Sports, Business, and Science/Technology. The architecture consists of a 2-layer stacked LSTM with 500 hidden units, a character embedding size of 25, and 1000 kernels of width 6 for temporal convolutions. This classifier was able to outperform (Conneau et al., 2017), which has achieved the state-of-the-art result on some benchmarks, on AG's news. The model is trained with SGD and gradient clipping, and the batch size was set to 64. We used 10% of the training data as the development set, and trained for a maximum of 25 epochs. We only allow character changes if the new word does not exist in the vocabulary, to avoid changes that are more likely to change the meaning of text. The adversary uses a beam size of 10, and has a budget of maximum of 10% of characters in the document. In Figure 1, we plot the success rate of the adversary against an acceptable confidence score for the misclassification. That is, we consider the adversary successful only if the classifier misclassifies the instance with a given confidence score. For this experiment, we create adversarial examples for 10% of the test set.

We compare with a (greedy) black-box adversary, which does not have access to model parameters, and simply queries the classifier with random character changes. Belinkov and Bisk (2018) define an attack, Key, in which a character is replaced with an adjacent character in the keyboard. We allow a stronger black-box attacker to change a character to any character in the alphabet, and we call it Key*. As expected a white-box adversary is much more damaging, and has a higher success rate. As can be seen, the beam-search strategy is very effective in fooling the classifier even with an 0.9 confidence constraint, tricking the classifier for more than 90% of the instances. A greedy search is less effective especially in producing high-confidence scores. We use a maximum of 10% of characters in the document as the budget for the adversary, but our adversary changes an average of 4.18% of the characters to trick the classifier at confidence 0.5. The adversary picks the flip operation around 80% of the times, and favors delete over insert by two to one.

---

[2]For ease in exposition, we assume that the word size is at most n-1, leaving at least one position of padding at the end.

[3]https://www.di.unipi.it/~gulli/

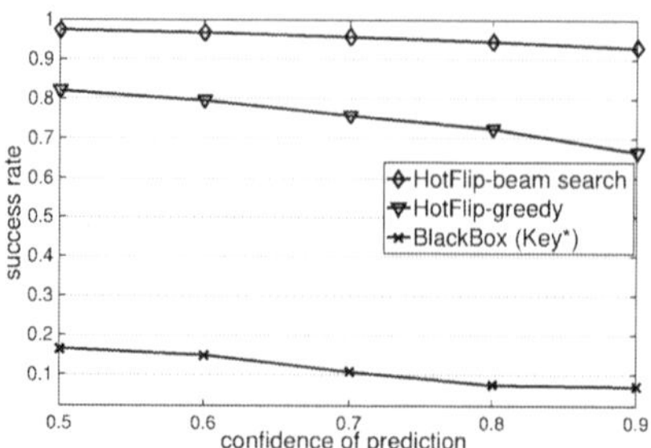

Figure 1: Adversary's success as a function of confidence.

Method	Misc. error	Success rate
Baseline	8.27%	98.16%
Adv-tr (Miyato et al., 2017)	8.03%	87.43%
Adv-tr (black-box)	8.60%	95.63%
Adv-tr (white-box)	**7.65%**	**69.32%**

Table 2: Comparison based on misclassification error on clean data and adversary's success rate.

4.1 Robustness

For our adversarial training, we use only use the flip operation, and evaluate models' robustness to this operation only. This is because insert and delete manipulations are n times slower to generate, where n is the number of maximum characters allowed for a word. For these experiments, we have no constraint on confidence score. We flip r characters for each training sample, which was set to 20% of the characters in text after tuning, based on the accuracy on the development set. In addition, for faster generation of adversarial examples, we directly apply the top r flips after the first backward pass, simultaneously[4].

We use the full test set for this experiment, and we compare HotFlip adversarial training with the white-box (supervised) adversarial training (Miyato et al., 2017) that perturbs word embeddings, which we adapt to work with character embeddings. Specifically, the adversarial noise per character is constrained by the Frobenius norm of the embedding matrix composed of the sequence of characters in the word. We also create another baseline where instead of white-box adversarial examples, we add black-box adversarial examples (Key*) to the mini-batches. As shown in Table 2, our approach decreases misclassification error and dramatically decreases the adversary's success rate. In particular, adversarial training on real adversarial examples generated by HotFlip, is more effective than training on *pseudo*-adversarial examples created by adding noise to the embeddings.

The current error of our adversarially trained model is still beyond an acceptable rate; this is mainly because the adversary that we use at test time, which uses beam search, is strictly stronger than our model's internal adversary. This has been observed in computer vision where strongest ad-

---

[4]The adversary at test time would still use beam search.

versaries are not efficient enough for adversarial training, but can break models trained with weaker adversaries (Carlini and Wagner, 2017).

4.2 Human Perception

Our human evaluation experiment shows that our character-based adversarial examples rarely alter the meaning of a sentence. We conduct an experiment of annotating 600 randomly-picked instances annotated by at least three crowd workers in Amazon Mechanical Turk. This set contains 150 examples of each class of AG's-news dataset, all of which are correctly classified by the classifier. We manipulate half of this set by our algorithm, which can successfully trick the classifier to misclassify these 300 adversarial examples. The median accuracy of our participants decreased by 1.78% from 87.49% on clean examples to 85.71% on adversarial examples. Similar small drops in human performance have been reported for image classification (Papernot et al., 2016) and text comprehension (Jia and Liang, 2017).

5 HotFlip at Word-Level

HotFlip can naturally be adapted to generate adversarial examples for word-level models, by computing derivatives with respect to one-hot word vectors. After a few character changes, the meaning of the text is very likely to be preserved or inferred by the reader (Rawlinson, 1976), which was also confirmed by our human subjects study. By contrast, word-level adversarial manipulations are much more likely to change the meaning of text, which makes the use of semantics-preserving constraints necessary. For example, changing the word *good* to *bad* changes the sentiment of the sentence *"this was a good movie"*. In fact, we expect the model to predict a different label after such a change.

To showcase the applicability of HotFlip to a word-level classifier, we use Kim's CNN (2014) trained for binary sentiment classification on the SST dataset (Socher et al., 2013). In order to create adversarial examples, we add constraints so that

one hour photo is an intriguing (**interesting**) snapshot of one man and his delusions it's just too bad it doesn't have more flashes of insight.
'enigma' is a good (**terrific**) name for a movie this deliberately obtuse and unapproachable.
an intermittently pleasing (**satisfying**) but mostly routine effort.
an atonal estrogen opera that demonizes feminism while gifting the most sympathetic male of the piece with a nice (**wonderful**) vomit bath at his wedding.
culkin exudes (**infuses**) none of the charm or charisma that might keep a more general audience even vaguely interested in his bratty character.

Table 3: Adversarial examples for sentiment classification. The bold words replace the words before them.

past → pas!t	Alps → llps	talk → taln	local → loral	you → yoTu	ships → hips	actor → actr	lowered → owered
pasturing	lips	tall	moral	Tutu	dips	act	powered
pasture	laps	tale	Moral	Hutu	hops	acting	empowered
pastor	legs	tales	coral	Turku	lips	actress	owed
Task	slips	talent	morals	Futurum	hits	acts	overpowered

Table 4: Nearest neighbor words (based on cosine similarity) of word representations from CharCNN-LSTM, picked at the output of the highway layers. A single adversarial change in the word often results in a big change in the embedding, which would make the word more similar to other words, rather than to the original word.

the resulting sentence is likely to preserve the original meaning; we only flip a word w_i to w_j only if these constraints are satisfied:

1. The cosine similarity between the embedding of words is bigger than a threshold (0.8).

2. The two words have the same part-of-speech.

3. We disallow replacing of stop-words, as for many of the stop-words, it is difficult to find cases where replacing them will still render the sentence grammatically correct. We also disallow changing a word to another word with the same lexeme for the same purpose.

Table 3 shows a few adversarial examples with only one word flip. In the second and the fourth examples, the adversary flips a positive word (i.e., *good, nice*) with highly positive words (i.e., *terrific, wonderful*) in an overall very negative review. These examples, albeit interesting and intuitive, are not abundant, and thus pose less threat to an NLP word-level model. Specifically, given the strict set of constraints, we were able to create only 41 examples (2% of the correctly-classified instances of the SST test set) with one or two flips.

For a qualitative analysis of relative brittleness of character-level models, we study the change in word embedding as an adversarial flip, insert, or delete operation occurs in Table 4. We use the output of the highway layer as the word representation, and report the embedding for a few adversarial words, for which the original word is not among their top 5 nearest neighbors.

In a character-level model, the lookup operation to pick a word from the vocabulary is replaced by a character-sequence feature extractor which gives an embedding for any input, including OOV words which would be mapped to an UNK token in a word-level model. This makes the embedding space induced in character-level representation more dense, which makes character-level models more likely to misbehave under small adversarial perturbations.

6 Conclusion and Future Work

White-box attacks are among the most serious forms of attacks an adversary can inflict on a machine learning model. We create white-box adversarial examples by computing derivatives with respect to a few character-edit operations (i.e., flip, insert, delete), which can be used in a beam-search optimization. While character-edit operations have little impact on human understanding, we found that character-level models are highly sensitive to adversarial perturbations. Employing these adversarial examples in adversarial training renders the models more robust to such attacks, as well as more robust to unseen clean data.

Contrasting and evaluating robustness of different character-level models for different tasks is an important future direction for adversarial NLP. In addition, the discrete nature of text makes it a more challenging task to understand the landscape of adversarial examples. Research in this direction can shed light on vulnerabilities of NLP models.

7 Acknowledgement

This work was funded by ARO grant W911NF-15-1-0265.

References

Yonatan Belinkov and Yonatan Bisk. 2018. Synthetic and natural noise both break neural machine translation. In *Proceedings of ICLR*.

Nicholas Carlini and David Wagner. 2017. Towards evaluating the robustness of neural networks. In *Security and Privacy (SP), 2017 IEEE Symposium on*, pages 39–57. IEEE.

Alexis Conneau, Holger Schwenk, Loïc Barrault, and Yann Lecun. 2017. Very deep convolutional networks for text classification. In *Proceedings of EACL*, volume 1, pages 1107–1116.

Nilesh Dalvi, Pedro Domingos, Sumit Sanghai, Deepak Verma, et al. 2004. Adversarial classification. In *Proceedings of KDD*, pages 99–108.

Ian J Goodfellow, Jonathon Shlens, and Christian Szegedy. 2015. Explaining and harnessing adversarial examples. In *Proceedings of ICLR*.

Hossein Hosseini, Sreeram Kannan, Baosen Zhang, and Radha Poovendran. 2017. Deceiving google's perspective api built for detecting toxic comments. *arXiv preprint arXiv:1702.08138*.

Mohit Iyyer, John Wieting, Kevin Gimpel, and Luke Zettlemoyer. 2018. Adversarial example generation with syntactically controlled paraphrase networks. *arXiv preprint arXiv:1804.06059*.

Robin Jia and Percy Liang. 2017. Adversarial examples for evaluating reading comprehension systems. In *Proceedings of EMNLP*.

Yoon Kim. 2014. Convolutional neural networks for sentence classification. In *Proceedings of EMNLP*.

Yoon Kim, Yacine Jernite, David Sontag, and Alexander M Rush. 2016. Character-aware neural language models. *Proceedings of AAAI*.

Daniel Lowd and Christopher Meek. 2005. Adversarial learning. In *Proceedings of KDD*, pages 641–647.

Aleksander Madry, Aleksandar Makelov, Ludwig Schmidt, Dimitris Tsipras, and Adrian Vladu. 2018. Towards deep learning models resistant to adversarial attacks. In *Proceedings of ICLR*.

Takeru Miyato, Andrew M Dai, and Ian Goodfellow. 2017. Adversarial training methods for semi-supervised text classification. In *Proceedings of ICLR*.

Nicolas Papernot, Patrick McDaniel, Somesh Jha, Matt Fredrikson, Z Berkay Celik, and Ananthram Swami. 2016. The limitations of deep learning in adversarial settings. In *Security and Privacy (EuroS&P), 2016 IEEE European Symposium on*, pages 372–387. IEEE.

Graham Ernest Rawlinson. 1976. *The Significance of Letter Position in Word Recognition*. Ph.D. thesis, University of Nottingham.

Richard Socher, Alex Perelygin, Jean Wu, Jason Chuang, Christopher D Manning, Andrew Ng, and Christopher Potts. 2013. Recursive deep models for semantic compositionality over a sentiment treebank. In *Proceedings of EMNLP*, pages 1631–1642.

Christian Szegedy, Wojciech Zaremba, Ilya Sutskever, Joan Bruna, Dumitru Erhan, Ian Goodfellow, and Rob Fergus. 2014. Intriguing properties of neural networks. In *Proceedings of ICLR*.

Zhengli Zhao, Dheeru Dua, and Sameer Singh. 2018. Generating natural adversarial examples. In *Proceedings of ICLR*.

Domain Adapted Word Embeddings for Improved Sentiment Classification

Prathusha K Sarma, Yingyu Liang and William A Sethares

University of Wisconsin-Madison
{kameswarasar,sethares}@wisc.edu,
yliang@cs.wisc.edu

Abstract

Generic word embeddings are trained on large-scale generic corpora; *Domain Specific* (DS) word embeddings are trained only on data from a domain of interest. This paper proposes a method to combine the breadth of generic embeddings with the specificity of domain specific embeddings. The resulting embeddings, called *Domain Adapted* (DA) word embeddings, are formed by aligning corresponding word vectors using Canonical Correlation Analysis (CCA) or the related nonlinear Kernel CCA. Evaluation results on sentiment classification tasks show that the DA embeddings substantially outperform both generic and DS embeddings when used as input features to standard or state-of-the-art sentence encoding algorithms for classification.

1 Introduction

Generic word embeddings such as Glove and word2vec (Pennington et al., 2014; Mikolov et al., 2013) which are pre-trained on large sets of raw text, have demonstrated remarkable success when used as features to a supervised learner in various applications such as the sentiment classification of text documents. There are, however, many applications with domain specific vocabularies and relatively small amounts of data. The performance of generic word embedding in such applications is limited, since word embeddings pre-trained on generic corpora do not capture domain specific semantics/knowledge, while embeddings learned on small data sets are of low quality.

A concrete example of a small-sized domain specific corpus is the Substances User Disorders (SUDs) data set (Quanbeck et al., 2014; Litvin et al., 2013), which contains messages on discussion forums for people with substance addictions.

These forums are part of a mobile health intervention treatment that encourages participants to engage in sobriety-related discussions. The goal of such treatments is to analyze content of participant's digital media content and provide human intervention via machine learning algorithms. This data is both domain specific and limited in size. Other examples include customer support tickets reporting issues with taxi-cab services, product reviews, reviews of restaurants and movies, discussions by special interest groups and political surveys. In general they are common in domains where words have different sentiment from what they would have elsewhere.

Such data sets present significant challenges for word embedding learning algorithms. First, words in data on specific topics have a different distribution than words from generic corpora. Hence using generic word embeddings obtained from algorithms trained on a corpus such as Wikipedia, may introduce considerable errors in performance metrics on specific downstream tasks such as sentiment classification. For example, in SUDs, discussions are focused on topics related to recovery and addiction; the sentiment behind the word 'party' may be very different in a dating context than in a substance abuse context. Thus domain specific vocabularies and word semantics may be a problem for pre-trained sentiment classification models (Blitzer et al., 2007). Second, there is insufficient data to completely retrain a new set of word embeddings. The SUD data set consists of a few hundred people and only a fraction of these are active (Firth et al., 2017), (Naslund et al., 2015). This results in a small data set of text messages available for analysis. Furthermore, content is generated spontaneously on a day to day basis, and language use is informal and unstructured. Fine-tuning the generic word embedding also leads to noisy outputs due to the highly non-convex training objective and the small amount of data. Since

37

Proceedings of the 56th Annual Meeting of the Association for Computational Linguistics (Short Papers), pages 37–42
Melbourne, Australia, July 15 - 20, 2018. ©2018 Association for Computational Linguistics

such data sets are common, a simple and effective method to adapt word embedding approaches is highly valuable. While existing work (Yin and Schütze, 2016), (?), (?), (?), (?) combines word embeddings from different algorithms to improve upon intrinsic tasks such as similarities, analogies etc, there does not exist a concrete method to combine multiple embeddings to perform domain adaptation or improve on extrinsic tasks.

This paper proposes a method for obtaining high quality word embeddings that capture domain specific semantics and are suitable for tasks on the specific domain. The new Domain Adapted (DA) embeddings are obtained by combining generic embeddings and Domain Specific (DS) embeddings via CCA/KCCA. Generic embeddings are trained on large corpora and do not capture domain specific semantics, while DS embeddings are obtained from the domain specific data set via algorithms such as Latent Semantic Analysis (LSA) or other embedding methods. The two sets of embeddings are combined using a linear CCA (Hotelling, 1936) or a nonlinear kernel CCA (KCCA) (Hardoon et al., 2004). They are projected along the directions of maximum correlation, and a new (DA) embedding is formed by averaging the projections of the generic embeddings and DS embeddings. The DA embeddings are then evaluated in a sentiment classification setting. Empirically, it is shown that the CCA/KCCA combined DA embeddings improve substantially over the generic embeddings, DS embeddings and a concatenation-SVD (concSVD) based baseline.

The remainder of this paper is organized as follows. Section 2 briefly introduces the CCA/KCCA and details the procedure used to obtain the DA embeddings. Section 3 describes the experimental set up. Section 4 discusses the results from sentiment classification tasks on benchmark data sets using standard classification as well as using a sophisticated neural network based sentence encoding algorithm. Section 5 concludes this work.

2 Domain Adapted Word Embeddings

Training word embeddings directly on small data sets leads to noisy outputs while embeddings from generic corpora fail to capture specific local meanings within the domain. Here we combine DS and generic embeddings using CCA KCCA, which projects corresponding word vectors along the directions of maximum correlation.

Let $\mathbf{W}_{DS} \in \mathbb{R}^{|V_{DS}| \times d_1}$ be the matrix whose columns are the domain specific word embeddings (obtained by, e.g., running the LSA algorithm on the domain specific data set), where V_{DS} is its vocabulary and d_1 is the dimension of the embeddings. Similarly, let $\mathbf{W}_G \in \mathbb{R}^{|V_G| \times d_2}$ be the matrix of generic word embeddings (obtained by, e.g., running the GloVe algorithm on the Common Crawl data), where V_G is the vocabulary and d_2 is the dimension of the embeddings. Let $V_\cap = V_{DS} \cap V_G$. Let $\mathbf{w}_{i,DS}$ be the domain specific embedding of the word $i \in V_\cap$, and $\mathbf{w}_{i,G}$ be its generic embedding. For one dimensional CCA, let ϕ_{DS} and ϕ_G be the projection directions of $\mathbf{w}_{i,DS}$ and $\mathbf{w}_{i,G}$ respectively. Then the projected values are,

$$\bar{w}_{i,DS} = \mathbf{w}_{i,DS}\,\phi_{DS}$$
$$\bar{w}_{i,G} = \mathbf{w}_{i,G}\,\phi_G. \tag{1}$$

CCA maximizes the correlation between $\bar{w}_{i,DS}$ and $\bar{w}_{i,G}$ to obtain ϕ_{DS} and ϕ_G such that

$$\rho(\phi_{DS}, \phi_G) = \max_{\phi_{DS}, \phi_G} \frac{\mathbb{E}[\langle \bar{w}_{i,DS}, \bar{w}_{i,G}\rangle]}{\sqrt{\mathbb{E}[\bar{w}_{i,DS}^2]\mathbb{E}[\bar{w}_{i,G}^2]}} \tag{2}$$

where ρ is the correlation between the projected word embeddings and $\mathbb{E}$ is the expectation over all words $i \in V_\cap$.

The d-dimensional CCA with $d > 1$ can be defined recursively. Suppose the first $d-1$ pairs of canonical variables are defined. Then the dth pair is defined by seeking vectors maximizing the same correlation function subject to the constraint that they be uncorrelated with the first $d-1$ pairs. Equivalently, matrices of projection vectors $\mathbf{\Phi}_{DS} \in \mathbb{R}^{d_1 \times d}$ and $\mathbf{\Phi}_G \in \mathbb{R}^{d_2 \times d}$ are obtained for all vectors in $\mathbf{W}_{DS}$ and $\mathbf{W}_G$ where $d \leq \min\{d_1, d_2\}$. Embeddings obtained by $\bar{\mathbf{w}}_{i,DS} = \mathbf{w}_{i,DS}\,\mathbf{\Phi}_{DS}$ and $\bar{\mathbf{w}}_{i,G} = \mathbf{w}_{i,G}\,\mathbf{\Phi}_G$ are projections along the directions of maximum correlation.

The final domain adapted embedding for word i is given by $\hat{\mathbf{w}}_{i,DA} = \alpha\bar{\mathbf{w}}_{i,DS} + \beta\bar{\mathbf{w}}_{i,G}$, where the parameters α and β can be obtained by solving the following optimization,

$$\min_{\alpha,\beta} \|\bar{\mathbf{w}}_{i,DS} - (\alpha\bar{\mathbf{w}}_{i,DS} + \beta\bar{\mathbf{w}}_{i,G})\|_2^2 +$$

$$\|\bar{\mathbf{w}}_{i,G} - (\alpha\bar{\mathbf{w}}_{i,DS} + \beta\bar{\mathbf{w}}_{i,G})\|_2^2. \tag{3}$$

Solving (3) gives a weighted combination with $\alpha = \beta = \frac{1}{2}$, i.e., the new vector is equal to the average of the two projections:

$$\hat{\mathbf{w}}_{i,DA} = \frac{1}{2}\bar{\mathbf{w}}_{i,DS} + \frac{1}{2}\bar{\mathbf{w}}_{i,G}. \tag{4}$$

Because of its linear structure, the CCA in (2) may not always capture the best relationships between the two matrices. To account for nonlinearities, a kernel function, which implicitly maps the data into a high dimensional feature space, can be applied. For example, given a vector $\mathbf{w} \in \mathbb{R}^d$, a kernel function K is written in the form of a feature map φ defined by $\varphi : \mathbf{w} = (\mathbf{w}_1, \ldots, \mathbf{w}_d) \mapsto \varphi(\mathbf{w}) = (\varphi_1(\mathbf{w}), \ldots, \varphi_m(\mathbf{w}))(d < m)$ such that given $\mathbf{w}_a$ and $\mathbf{w}_b$

$$K(\mathbf{w}_a, \mathbf{w}_b) = \langle \varphi(\mathbf{w}_a), \varphi(\mathbf{w}_b) \rangle.$$

In kernel CCA, data is first projected onto a high dimensional feature space before performing CCA. In this work the kernel function used is a Gaussian kernel, i.e.,

$$K(\mathbf{w}_a, \mathbf{w}_b) = \exp\left(- \frac{\|\mathbf{w}_a - \mathbf{w}_b\|^2}{2\sigma^2} \right).$$

The implementation of kernel CCA follows the standard algorithm described in several texts such as (Hardoon et al., 2004); see reference for details.

3 Experimental Evaluation

This section evaluates DA embeddings in binary sentiment classification tasks on four standard data sets. Document embeddings are obtained via (i) a standard framework, i.e document embeddings are a weighted combination of their constituent word embeddings and (ii) by initializing a state of the art sentence encoding algorithm InferSent (Conneau et al., 2017) with word embeddings to obtain sentence embeddings. Encoded sentences are then classified using a Logistic Regressor.

3.1 Datasets

The following balanced and imbalanced data sets are used for experimentation,

- **Yelp:** This is a balanced data set consisting of 1000 restaurant reviews obtained from Yelp. Each review is labeled as either 'Positive' or 'Negative'. There are a total of 2049 distinct word tokens in this data set.

Data Set		Embedding	Avg Precision	Avg F-score	Avg AUC
Yelp	$\mathbf{W}_{DA}$	KCCA(Glv, LSA)	85.36± 2.8	81.89±2.8	82.57±1.3
		CCA(Glv, LSA)	83.69± 4.7	79.48±2.4	80.33±2.9
		KCCA(w2v, LSA)	87.45± 1.2	83.36±1.2	84.10±0.9
		CCA(w2v, LSA)	84.52± 2.3	80.02±2.6	81.04±2.1
		KCCA(GlvCC, LSA)	**88.11± 3.0**	**85.35±2.7**	**85.80±2.4**
		CCA(GlvCC, LSA)	83.69± 3.5	78.99±4.2	80.03±3.7
		KCCA(w2v, DSw2v)	78.09± 1.7	76.04±1.7	76.66±1.5
		CCA(w2v, DSw2v)	86.22± 3.5	84.35±2.4	84.65±2.2
		concSVD(Glv, LSA)	80.14± 2.6	78.50±3.0	78.92±2.7
		concSVD(w2v, LSA)	85.11± 2.3	83.51±2.2	83.80±2.0
		concSVD(GlvCC, LSA)	84.20± 3.7	80.39±3.7	80.83±3.9
	$\mathbf{W}_G$	GloVe	77.13± 4.2	72.32±7.9	74.17±5.0
		GloVe-CC	82.10± 3.5	76.74±3.4	78.17±2.7
		word2vec	82.80± 3.5	78.28±3.5	79.35±3.1
	$\mathbf{W}_{DS}$	LSA	75.36± 5.4	71.17±4.3	72.57±4.3
		word2vec	73.08± 2.2	70.97±2.4	71.76±2.1
Amazon	$\mathbf{W}_{DA}$	KCCA(Glv, LSA)	86.30±1.9	83.00±2.9	83.39±3.2
		CCA(Glv, LSA)	84.68±2.4	82.27±2.2	82.78±1.7
		KCCA(w2v, LSA)	87.09±1.8	82.63±2.6	83.50±2.0
		CCA(w2v, LSA)	84.80±1.5	81.42±1.9	82.12±1.3
		KCCA(GlvCC, LSA)	**89.73±2.4**	85.47±2.4	85.56±2.6
		CCA(GlvCC, LSA)	85.67±2.3	83.83±2.3	84.21±2.1
		KCCA(w2v, DSw2v)	85.68±3.2	81.23±3.2	82.20±2.9
		CCA(w2v, DSw2v)	83.50±3.4	81.31±4.0	81.86±3.7
		concSVD(Glv, LSA)	82.36±2.0	81.30±3.5	81.51±2.5
		concSVD(w2v, LSA)	87.28±2.9	**86.17±2.5**	**86.42±2.0**
		concSVD(GlvCC, LSA)	84.93±1.6	77.81±2.3	79.52±1.7
	$\mathbf{W}_G$	GloVe	81.58±2.5	77.62±2.7	78.72±2.7
		GloVe-CC	79.91±2.7	81.63±2.8	81.46±2.6
		word2vec	84.55±1.9	80.52±2.5	81.45±2.0
	$\mathbf{W}_{DS}$	LSA	82.65±4.4	73.92±3.8	76.40±3.2
		word2vec	74.20±5.8	72.49±5.0	73.11±4.8
IMDB	DA	KCCA(Glv, LSA)	73.84±1.3	73.07±3.6	73.17±2.4
		CCA(Glv, LSA)	73.35±2.0	73.00±3.2	73.06±2.0
		KCCA(w2v, LSA)	**82.36±4.4**	**78.95±2.7**	**79.66±2.6**
		CCA(w2v, LSA)	80.66±4.5	75.95±4.5	77.23±3.8
		KCCA(GlvCC, LSA)	54.50±2.5	54.42±2.9	53.91±2.0
		CCA(GlvCC, LSA)	54.08±2.0	53.03±3.5	54.90±2.1
		KCCA(w2v, DSw2v)	60.65±3.5	58.95±3.2	58.95±3.7
		CCA(w2v, DSw2v)	58.47±2.7	57.62±3.0	58.03±3.9
		concSVD(Glv, LSA)	73.25±3.7	74.55±3.2	73.02±4.7
		concSVD(w2v, LSA)	53.87±2.2	51.77±5.8	53.54±1.9
		concSVD(GlvCC, LSA)	78.28±3.2	77.67±3.7	74.55±2.9
	$\mathbf{W}_G$	GloVe	64.44±2.6	65.18±3.5	64.62±2.6
		GloVe-CC	50.53±1.8	62.39±3.5	49.96±2.3
		word2vec	78.92±3.7	74.88±3.1	75.60±2.4
	$\mathbf{W}_{DS}$	LSA	67.92±1.7	69.79±5.3	69.71±3.8
		word2vec	56.87±3.6	56.04±3.1	59.53±8.9
A-CHESS	DA	**KCCA(Glv, LSA)**	32.07±1.3	39.32±2.5	**65.96±1.3**
		CCA(Glv, LSA)	32.70±1.5	35.48±4.2	62.15±2.9
		KCCA(w2v, LSA)	33.45±1.3	**39.81±1.0**	65.92±0.6
		CCA(w2v, LSA)	33.06±3.2	34.02±1.1	60.91±0.9
		KCCA(GlvCC, LSA)	36.38±1.2	34.71±4.8	61.36±2.6
		CCA(GlvCC, LSA)	32.11±2.9	36.85±4.4	62.99±3.1
		KCCA(w2v, DSw2v)	25.59±1.2	28.27±3.1	57.25±1.7
		CCA(w2v, DSw2v)	24.88±1.4	29.17±3.1	57.76±2.0
		concSVD(Glv, LSA)	27.27±2.9	34.45±3.0	61.59±2.3
		concSVD(w2v, LSA)	29.84±2.3	36.32±3.3	62.94±1.1
		concSVD(GlvCC, LSA)	28.09±1.9	35.06±1.4	62.13±2.6
	$\mathbf{W}_G$	GloVe	30.82±2.0	33.67±3.4	60.80±2.3
		GloVe-CC	**38.13±0.8**	27.45±3.1	57.49±1.2
		word2vec	32.67±2.9	31.72±1.6	59.64±0.5
	$\mathbf{W}_{DS}$	LSA	27.42±1.6	34.38±2.3	61.56±1.9
		word2vec	24.48±0.8	27.97±3.7	57.08±2.5

Table 1: This table shows results from the classification task using sentence embeddings obtained from weighted averaging of word embeddings. Metrics reported are average Precision, F-score and AUC and the corresponding standard deviations (STD). Best results are attained by KCCA (GlvCC, LSA) and are highlighted in boldface.

- **Amazon:** In this balanced data set there are 1000 product reviews obtained from Amazon. Each product review is labeled either 'Positive' or 'Negative'. There are a total of 1865 distinct word tokens in this data set.

- **IMDB:** This is a balanced data set consisting of 1000 reviews for movies on IMDB. Each movie review is labeled either 'Positive' or 'Negative'. There are a total of 3075 distinct

Data Set	Embedding	Avg Precision	Avg F-score	Avg AUC
Yelp	GlvCC	86.47±1.9	83.51±2.6	83.83±2.2
	KCCA(GlvCC, LSA)	**91.06±0.8**	**88.66±2.4**	**88.76±2.4**
	CCA(GlvCC, LSA)	86.26±1.4	82.61±1.1	83.99±0.8
	concSVD(GlvCC,LSA)	85.53±2.1	84.90±1.7	84.96±1.5
	RNTN	83.11±1.1	-	-
Amazon	GlvCC	87.93±2.7	82.41±3.3	83.24±2.8
	KCCA(GlvCC, LSA)	**90.56±2.1**	**86.52±2.0**	**86.74±1.9**
	CCA(GlvCC, LSA)	87.12±2.6	83.18±2.2	83.78±2.1
	concSVD(GlvCC, LSA)	85.73±1.9	85.19±2.4	85.17±2.6
	RNTN	82.84±0.6	-	-
IMDB	GlvCC	54.02±3.2	53.03±5.2	53.01±2.0
	KCCA(GlvCC, LSA)	59.76±7.3	**53.26±6.1**	56.46±3.4
	CCA(GlvCC, LSA)	53.62±1.6	50.62±5.1	**58.75±3.7**
	concSVD(GlvCC, LSA)	52.75±2.3	53.05±6.0	53.54±2.5
	RNTN	**80.88±0.7**	-	-
A-CHESS	GlvCC	52.21±5.1	**55.26±5.6**	**74.28±3.6**
	KCCA(GlvCC, LSA)	**55.37±5.5**	50.67±5.0	69.89±3.1
	CCA(GlvCC, LSA)	54.34±3.6	48.76±2.9	68.78±2.4
	concSVD(GlvCC, LSA)	40.41±4.2	44.75±5.2	68.13±3.8
	RNTN	-	-	-

Table 2: This table shows results obtained by using sentence embeddings from the InferSent encoder in the sentiment classification task. Metrics reported are average Precision, F-score and AUC along with the corresponding standard deviations (STD). Best results are obtained by KCCA (GlvCC, LSA) and are highlighted in boldface.

word tokens in this data set.

- **A-CHESS:** This is a proprietary data set[1] obtained from a study involving users with alcohol addiction. Text data is obtained from a discussion forum in the A-CHESS mobile app (Quanbeck et al., 2014). There are a total of 2500 text messages, with 8% of the messages indicative of relapse risk. Since this data set is part of a clinical trial, an exact text message cannot be provided as an example. However, the following messages illustrate typical messages in this data set, *"I've been clean for about 7 months but even now I still feel like maybe I won't make it."* Such a message is marked as 'threat' by a human moderator. On the other hand there are other benign messages that are marked 'not threat' such as *"30 days sober and counting, I feel like I am getting my life back."* The aim is to eventually automate this process since human moderation involves considerable effort and time. This is an unbalanced data set (8% of the messages are marked 'threat') with a total of 3400 distinct work tokens.

The first three data sets are obtained from (Kotzias et al., 2015).

3.2 Word embeddings and baselines:

This section briefly describes the various generic and DS embeddings used. We also compare against a basic DA embedding baseline in both the standard framework and while initializing the neural network baseline.

- **Generic word embeddings:** Generic word embeddings used are GloVe[2] from both Wikipedia and common crawl and the word2vec (Skip-gram) embeddings[3]. These generic embeddings will be denoted as Glv, GlvCC and w2v.

- **DS word embeddings:** DS embeddings are obtained via Latent Semantic Analysis (LSA) and via retraining word2vec on the test data sets using the implementation in gensim[4]. DS embeddings via LSA are denoted by LSA and DS embeddings via word2vec are denoted by DSw2v.

- **concatenation-SVD baseline:** Generic and DS embeddings are concatenated to form a single embeddings matrix. SVD is performed on this matrix and the resulting singular vectors are projected onto the d largest singular values to form resultant word embeddings. These meta-embeddings proposed by (Yin and Schütze, 2016) have demonstrated considerable success in intrinsic tasks such as similarities, analogies etc.

Details about dimensions of the word embeddings and kernel hyperparameter tuning are found in the supplemental material.

The following neural network baselines are used in this work,

- **InferSent:** This is a bidirectional LSTM based sentence encoder (Conneau et al., 2017) that learns sentence encodings in a supervised fashion on a natural language inference (NLI) data set. The aim is to use the sentence encoder trained on the NLI data set to learn generic sentence encodings for use in transfer learning applications.

- **RNTN:** The Recursive Neural Tensor Network (**?**) baseline is a neural network based dependency parser that performs sentiment analysis. Since the data sets considered in our experiments have binary sentiments we compare against this baseline as well.

Note that InferSent is fine-tuned with a combination of GloVe common crawl embeddings and DA embeddings, and concSVD. The choice of GloVe common crawl embeddings is in keeping with the experimental conditions of the authors of InferSent. Since the data sets at hand do not contain all the tokens required to retrain InferSent, we replace word tokens that are common across our test data sets and InferSent training data with the DA embeddings and concSVD.

Since we have a combination of balanced and unbalanced test data sets, test metrics reported are Precision, F-score and AUC. We perform 10-fold cross validation to determine hyperparameters and so we report averages of the performance metrics along with the standard deviation.

4   Results and Discussion

From Tables 1 and 2 we see that DA embeddings perform better than concSVD as well as the generic and DS word embeddings, when used in a standard classification task as well as when used to initialize a sentence encoding algorithm. As expected, LSA DS embeddings provide better results than word2vec DS embeddings. Note that on the imbalanced A-CHESS data set, on the standard classification task, KCCA embeddings perform better than the other baselines across all three performance metrics. However from Table 2, GlvCC embeddings achieve a higher average F-score and AUC over KCCA embeddings that obtain the highest precision.

While one can argue that when evaluating a classifier, the F-score and AUC are better indicators of performance, it is to be noted that A-CHESS is highly imbalanced and precision is calculated on the minor (positive) class that is of most interest. Also note that, InferSent is retrained on the balanced NLI data set that is much larger in size than the A-CHESS test set. Certainly such a training set has more instances of positive samples. Thus when using generic word embeddings to initialize the sentence encoder, which uses the outputs in the classification task, the overall F-score and AUC are better.

From our hypothesis, KCCA embeddings are expected to perform better than the others because CCA/KCCA provides an intuitively better technique to preserve information from both the generic and DS embeddings. On the other hand the concSVD based embeddings do not exploit information in both the generic and DS embeddings. Furthermore, in their work (Yin and Schütze, 2016) propose to learn an 'ensemble' of meta-embeddings by learning weights to combine different generic word embeddings via a simple neural network. We determine the proper weight for combination of DS and generic embeddings in the CCA/KCCA space using the simple optimization problem given in Equation (3).

Thus, task specific DA embeddings formed by a proper weighted combination of DS and generic word embeddings are expected to do better than the concSVD embeddings and individual generic and/or DS embeddings and this is verified empirically. Also note that the LSA DS embeddings do better than the word2vec DS embeddings. This is expected due to the size of the test sets and the nature of the word2vec algorithm. We expect similar observations when using GloVe DS embeddings owing to the similarities between word2vec and GloVe.

5   Conclusion

This paper presents a simple yet effective method to learn Domain Adapted word embeddings that generally outperform generic and Domain Specific word embeddings in sentiment classification experiments on a variety of standard data sets. CCA/KCCA based DA embeddings generally outperform even a concatenation based methods.

Acknowledgments

We would like to thank Ravi Raju for lending computing support for training our neural network baselines. We also thank the anonymous reviewers for their feedback and suggestions.

References

Natalia Y Bilenko and Jack L Gallant. 2016. Pyrcca: regularized kernel canonical correlation analysis in python and its applications to neuroimaging. *Frontiers in neuroinformatics* 10.

John Blitzer, Mark Dredze, Fernando Pereira, et al. 2007. Biographies, bollywood, boom-boxes and blenders: Domain adaptation for sentiment classification. In *ACL*. volume 7, pages 440–447.

Alexis Conneau, Douwe Kiela, Holger Schwenk, Loic Barrault, and Antoine Bordes. 2017. Supervised learning of universal sentence representations from natural language inference data. *arXiv preprint arXiv:1705.02364* .

Joseph Firth, John Torous, Jennifer Nicholas, Rebekah Carney, Simon Rosenbaum, and Jerome Sarris. 2017. Can smartphone mental health interventions reduce symptoms of anxiety? a meta-analysis of randomized controlled trials. *Journal of Affective Disorders* .

Seth Flaxman, Dino Sejdinovic, John P Cunningham, and Sarah Filippi. 2016. Bayesian learning of kernel embeddings. *arXiv preprint arXiv:1603.02160* .

David R Hardoon, Sandor Szedmak, and John Shawe-Taylor. 2004. Canonical correlation analysis: An overview with application to learning methods. *Neural computation* 16(12):2639–2664.

Harold Hotelling. 1936. Relations between two sets of variates. *Biometrika* 28(3/4):321–377.

Dimitrios Kotzias, Misha Denil, Nando De Freitas, and Padhraic Smyth. 2015. From group to individual labels using deep features. In *Proceedings of the 21th ACM SIGKDD International Conference on Knowledge Discovery and Data Mining*. ACM, pages 597–606.

Erika B Litvin, Ana M Abrantes, and Richard A Brown. 2013. Computer and mobile technology-based interventions for substance use disorders: An organizing framework. *Addictive behaviors* 38(3):1747–1756.

Tomas Mikolov, Ilya Sutskever, Kai Chen, Greg S Corrado, and Jeff Dean. 2013. Distributed representations of words and phrases and their compositionality. In *Advances in neural information processing systems*. pages 3111–3119.

John A Naslund, Lisa A Marsch, Gregory J McHugo, and Stephen J Bartels. 2015. Emerging mhealth and ehealth interventions for serious mental illness: a review of the literature. *Journal of mental health* 24(5):321–332.

Jeffrey Pennington, Richard Socher, and Christopher Manning. 2014. Glove: Global vectors for word representation. In *Proceedings of the 2014 conference on empirical methods in natural language processing (EMNLP)*. pages 1532–1543.

Andrew Quanbeck, Ming-Yuan Chih, Andrew Isham, Roberta Johnson, and David Gustafson. 2014. Mobile delivery of treatment for alcohol use disorders: A review of the literature. *Alcohol research: current reviews* 36(1):111.

Wenpeng Yin and Hinrich Schütze. 2016. Learning word meta-embeddings. In *Proceedings of the 54th Annual Meeting of the Association for Computational Linguistics (Volume 1: Long Papers)*. volume 1, pages 1351–1360.

Active learning for deep semantic parsing

Long Duong, Hadi Afshar, Dominique Estival, Glen Pink, Philip Cohen, Mark Johnson
Voicebox Technologies
`{longd,hadia,dominiquee,glenp,philipc,markj}@voicebox.com`

Abstract

Semantic parsing requires training data that is expensive and slow to collect. We apply active learning to both traditional and "overnight" data collection approaches. We show that it is possible to obtain good training hyperparameters from seed data which is only a small fraction of the full dataset. We show that uncertainty sampling based on least confidence score is competitive in traditional data collection but not applicable for overnight collection. We evaluate several active learning strategies for overnight data collection and show that different example selection strategies per domain perform best.

1 Introduction

Semantic parsing maps a natural language query to a logical form (LF) (Zettlemoyer and Collins, 2005, 2007; Haas and Riezler, 2016; Kwiatkowksi et al., 2010). Producing training data for semantic parsing is slow and costly. Active learning is effective in reducing costly data requirements for many NLP tasks. In this work, we apply active learning to deep semantic parsing and show that we can substantially reduce the data required to achieve state-of-the-art results.

There are two main methods for generating semantic parsing training data. The traditional approach first generates the input natural language utterances and then labels them with output LFs. We show that active learning based on uncertainty sampling works well for this approach.

The "overnight" annotation approach (Wang et al., 2015) generates output LFs from a grammar, and uses crowd workers to paraphrase these LFs into input natural language queries. This approach is faster and cheaper than traditional annotation. However, the difficulty and cost of data generation and validation are still substantial if we need a large amount of data for the system to achieve high accuracy; if the logical forms can express complex combinations of semantic primitives that must be covered; or if the target language is one with relatively few crowd workers.

Applying active learning to the overnight approach is even more compelling, since the unlabelled LFs can be generated essentially for free by a grammar. However, conventional active learning strategies are not compatible with the overnight approach, since the crowd annotators produce inputs (utterances) rather than labels (LFs).

In order to apply active learning to deep semantic parsing, we need a way of selecting hyperparameters without requiring the full training dataset. For optimal performance, we should re-run hyperparameter tuning for each active learning round, but this is prohibitively expensive computationally. We show that hyperparameters selected using a random subset of the data (about 20%) perform almost as well as those from the full set.

Our contributions are (1) a simple hyperparameter selection technique for active learning applied to semantic parsing, and (2) straightforward active learning strategies for both traditional and overnight data collection that significantly reduce data annotation requirements. To the best of our knowledge we are the first to investigate active learning for overnight data collection.

2 Related work

Sequence-to-sequence models are currently the state-of-the-art for semantic parsing (Jia and Liang, 2016; Dong and Lapata, 2016; Duong et al., 2017). In this paper, we also exploit a sequence-to-sequence model to minimise the amount of la-

Proceedings of the 56th Annual Meeting of the Association for Computational Linguistics (Short Papers), pages 43–48
Melbourne, Australia, July 15 - 20, 2018. ©2018 Association for Computational Linguistics

belled training data required to achieve state-of-the-art semantic parsing results.

Active learning has been applied to a variety of machine learning and NLP tasks (Thompson et al., 1999; Tang et al., 2002; Chenguang Wang, 2017) employing various algorithms such as least confidence score (Culotta and McCallum, 2005), large margin (Settles and Craven, 2008), entropy based sampling, density weighting method (Settles, 2012), and reinforcement learning (Fang et al., 2017). Nevertheless, there has been limited work applying active learning for deep semantic parsing with the exception of Iyer et al. (2017). Different from conventional active learning, they used crowd workers to select what data to annotate for traditional semantic parsing data collection.

In this paper, we apply active learning for both traditional and overnight data collection with the focus on overnight approach. In addition, a limitation of prior active learning work is that the hyperparameters are usually predefined in some way, mostly from different work on the same or similar dataset, or from the authors experience (Wang et al., 2017; Fang et al., 2017). In this paper, we investigate how to efficiently set the hyperparameters for the active learning process.

3 Base S2S Model

We base our approach on the attentional sequence-to-sequence model (S2S) of Bahdanau et al. (2014). This attentional model uses a bidirectional recurrent neural network (RNN) to encode a source as a sequence of vectors, which are used by another RNN to generates output. Given the source utterance $x = [x_1, x_2, ... x_n]$ and target LF $y = [y_1, y_2, ... y_m]$, we train the model to minimize the loss under model parameters θ.

$$\text{loss} = -\sum_{i=1}^{m} \log P(y_i | y_1, .. y_{i-1}, x; \theta) \quad (1)$$

Additionally, we apply the UNK replacement technique in Duong et al. (2017), keeping the original sentence in the data.[1]

4 Active learning models

There is a diversity of strategies for active learning. A simple and effective active learning strategy is based on **least confidence score** (Culotta

and McCallum, 2005). This strategy selects utterance x' to label from the unlabelled data U_x as follows:

$$x' = \underset{x \in U_x}{\operatorname{argmin}} \left[\max_{y^*} P(y^* | x; \theta) \right]$$

where y^* is the most likely output. We found that this least confidence score works well across datasets, even better than more complicated strategies in traditional data collection (described below).

4.1 Traditional data collection

In the traditional (forward) approach, we start with the list of unlabelled utterances and an initial seed of utterances paired with LFs. We gradually select utterances to annotate with the aim of maximizing the test score as early as possible. We use forward S2S sentence loss as defined in Equation (1) as the least confidence score measurement (i.e. select the instance with higher loss).

The drawback of a least confidence score strategy (and strategies based on other measurements such as large margin), is that they only leverage a single measurement to select utterances (Settles and Craven, 2008). To combine multiple measurements, we build a classifier to predict if the model will wrongly generate the LF given the utterance, and select those utterances for annotation. The classifier is trained on the data generated by running 5-fold cross validation on annotated data.[2] We exploit various features, including sentence log loss, the margin between the best and second best solutions, source sentence frequency, source encoder last hidden state and target decoder last hidden state (see supplementary material §A.1 for more detail) and various classifier architectures including logistic regression, feedforward networks and multilayer convolutional neural networks. On the development corpus, we observed that the least confidence score works as well as the classifier strategy.

4.2 Overnight data collection

In the overnight (backward) approach, we start with the set of all unlabelled LFs (U_y), and an initial randomly-selected seed of LFs paired with utterances (i.e. labelled LFs L_y). The aim is to select

---

[1] We call S2S model applied to traditional data collection and overnight data collection as forward S2S and backward S2S respectively. The forward S2S model estimates $P(y|x)$, the backward S2S model estimates $P(x|y)$.

[2] This classifier is complementary to the approach proposed in Iyer et al. (2017) where we use this classifier instead of user feedback.

LFs for which we should obtain utterances, maximizing the test score as early as possible. In the overnight approach, we can't use the least confidence score (i.e. the forward S2S sentence loss) directly since we can't estimate $P(y|x)$ because we don't know the utterance x. We have to somehow approximate this probability with regard to the performance on test.

A simple strategy is just to apply the backward S2S model and estimate $P(x|y)$, e.g. we select LF y' to label from the unlabelled data U_y as follows:

$$y' = \operatorname*{argmin}_{y \in U_y} \left[\max_{x^*} P(x^*|y;\theta) \right]$$

Essentially, we train the S2S model to predict the utterance given the LF. The motivation is that if we can reconstruct the utterance from the LF then we could possibly generate LFs from utterances. However, this strategy ignores one important aspect of semantic parsing, which is that LFs are an abstraction of utterances. One utterance is mapped to only one LF, but one LF corresponds to many utterances.

Since the forward S2S loss performs so well, another strategy is to approximate the selections made by this score. We train a linear binary classifier[3] to predict selections, using features which can be computed from LFs only. We extract two set of features from the LF model and the backward S2S model. The LF model is an RNN language model but trained on LFs (Zaremba et al., 2014).[4] We extract the LF sentence log probability i.e. $\log P(y)$, feature from this model. The backward S2S model, as mentioned above, is the model trained to predict an utterance given a LF. We extracted the same set of features as mentioned in §4.1 including LF sentence log loss, margin between best and second best solutions, and LF frequencies.

On the development corpus, we first run one active learning round using forward S2S model sentence loss (i.e. modelling $P(y|x)$) on the initial annotated data L_y. The set of selected LFs based on forward S2S loss will be the positive examples, and all other LFs that are not selected will be the negative examples for training the binary classifier. Our experiments show that the classifier which uses the combination of two features (source LF frequencies and the margin of best and

second best solution) are the best predictor of what is selected by forward S2S model log loss (i.e. modelling $P(y|x)$). It is interesting to see that absolute score of backward S2S model loss is not a good indicator as it is not selected. This may be due to the fact that utterance-LF mapping is one-to-many and the model probability is distributed to all valid output utterances. Hence, low probability is not necessary an indicator of bad prediction. We use the linear combination of the two features mentioned above with the weights from the binary classifier as a means of selecting the LF for overnight active learning on different corpora without retraining the classifier.

5 Experiment

5.1 Datasets

We experiment with the NLMaps corpus (Haas and Riezler, 2016) which was collected using the traditional approach. We tokenize following Kočiský et al. (2016). We also experiment with the Social Network corpus from the Overnight dataset (Wang et al., 2015) (which was collected using the overnight approach). Social Network was chosen as being the largest dataset available. Since neither corpora have a separate development set, we use 10% of the training set as development data for early stopping. We select ATIS (Zettlemoyer and Collins, 2007) as our development corpus for all feature selection and experiments with classifiers in §4.1 and §4.2.

For evaluation, we use full LF exact match accuracy for all experiments (Kočiský et al., 2016). Note that this is a much stricter evaluation compared with running through database evaluator as in Wang et al. (2015).

5.2 Hyperparameter tuning

Hyperparameter tuning is important for good performance. We tune the base S2S model (§3) on the development data by generating 100 configurations using Adam optimizer (Kingma and Ba, 2014) and a permutation of different source and target RNN sizes, RNN cell types, initializer, dropout rates and mini-batch sizes.

As mentioned, hyperparameter tuning is often overlooked in active learning. The common approach is just to use the configuration from a similar problem, from prior work on the same dataset,

---

[3] Instead of binary classifier, it would also be possible to train a logistic model. However, we leave this for future work.
[4] We use the configuration from Zaremba et al. (2014).

[5] The exact match accuracy for Social Network is extracted from logs from (Jia and Liang, 2016).

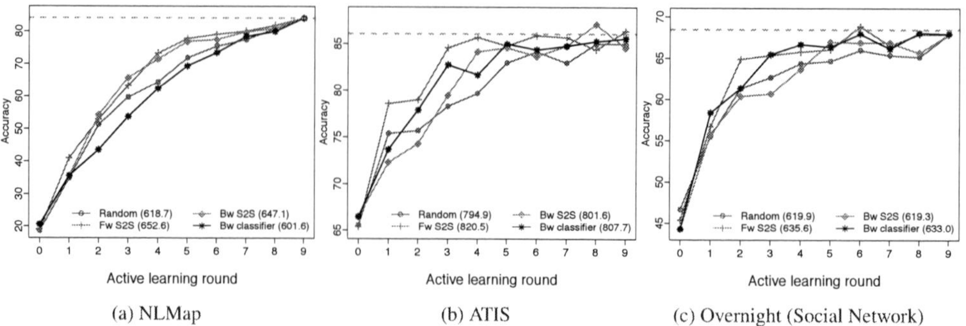

	NLMap	ATIS	Overnight (Social Network)
(a) NLMap	(b) ATIS	(c) Overnight (Social Network)

Figure 1: Active learning for various selection criteria. *Random* baseline randomly select the training data at each round. *Fw S2S* is used for traditional data collection using forward S2S loss score. *Bw S2S* is used for overnight data collection using backward S2S loss score. *Bw classifier* is used also for the overnight approach but linearly combines several scores together as mentioned in §4.2. The scores in parentheses measure the area under the curve. The dashed lines are the SOTA from Table 1.

	NLMap	Social	ATIS
From ATIS	76.0	65.8	86.0
Small subset	84.2	68.9	85.7
Full data	84.2	69.1	86.0
SOTA	84.1	68.8	86.1

Table 1: The LF exact match accuracy on NLMap, Social Network and ATIS with configurations from ATIS, from hyperparameter tuning on small subset of data (10% + dev) or on the full training data. The supervised SOTA for NLMap and ATIS (Duong et al., 2017) and Social Network (Jia and Liang, 2016) are provided for reference.[5]

or based on the authors own experience. However, in practice we don't have any prior work to copy the configuration from. Table 1 shows the experiments with the NLMap and Social Network corpora with configurations: 1) copied from another dataset (ATIS), 2) tuned on a small subset (10% of train data plus development data) and 3) tuned on the full dataset. We can see that copying from a different dataset results in a suboptimal solution, which is expected since the different datasets are significantly different. It is surprising that tuning on small subset of the data performs as well as tuning on all the data and, more importantly, it achieves similar results as the state of the art (SOTA).

5.3 Active Learning Results

Figure 1 shows the active learning curve for NLMap, ATIS and Overnight (Social Network) datasets. 10% of data is randomly selected as initial seed data for active learning and hyperparameter tuning. We run active learning for 10 rounds, selecting 10% of the data at each round. Round 0 reports the result trained on the initial seed data and round 9 is the result on the whole training data. For reference, we also report *Fw S2S* for Social Network, treating that corpus as if they were collected using the traditional approach, and *Bw S2S/classifier* for NLMap and ATIS treating those corpora as if they were collected using the overnight approach.

For traditional data collection (forward direction), S2S loss consistently outperforms the random baselines on both datasets. The differences are as high as 9% for NLMap (at round 4). Applying this strategy for ATIS, we reach SOTA results at round 4, using only 50% of data. We also experimented with the large margin baseline and classifier strategies as mentioned in §4.1. The least confidence strategy using S2S loss outperforms large margin and achieves similar performance with the more complicated classifier strategy, thus we omit those results for brevity.

On the overnight data collection active learning (backward direction), the results are split. The backward S2S loss performs particularly well on the NLMap corpus, approximating the forward S2S performance. However, it performs similar to the random baseline in the other corpora. On the other hand, the classifier strategy performs well on both ATIS and Social Network but poorly on NLMap. Using this strategy, we approximate the SOTA for both ATIS and Social Network at round 5 and 6 respectively (saving 40% and 30% of data). We suspect that backward S2S loss performs so well on NLMap since there is a one-to-one mapping between utterance and LF. The number of unique LFs in the training data for NLMap, ATIS and Overnight are 95.4%, 28.4% and 19.5% respectively. All in all, our proposed strategies for "overnight" active learning are nearly as good as traditional active learning, showing in similar area under the curve value in Figure 1.

6 Conclusion

We have discussed practical active learning for deep semantic parsing. We have empirically shown that it is possible to get good hyperparameters from only a small subset of annotated data. We applied active learning for both traditional and overnight semantic parsing data collection. For traditional data collection, we show that least confidence score based on S2S log loss performs well across datasets. Applying active learning for overnight data collection is challenging, and the best performing strategy depends on the domain. We recommend that applications explore both the backward S2S and classifier strategies.

References

Dzmitry Bahdanau, Kyunghyun Cho, and Yoshua Bengio. 2014. Neural machine translation by jointly learning to align and translate. *CoRR* abs/1409.0473.

Laura Chiticariu Yunyao Li Chenguang Wang. 2017. Active learning for black-box semantic role labeling with neural factors. In *Proceedings of the Twenty-Sixth International Joint Conference on Artificial Intelligence, IJCAI-17*. pages 2908–2914. https://doi.org/10.24963/ijcai.2017/405.

Aron Culotta and Andrew McCallum. 2005. Reducing labeling effort for structured prediction tasks. In *Proceedings of the 20th National Conference on Artificial Intelligence - Volume 2*. pages 746–751.

Li Dong and Mirella Lapata. 2016. Language to logical form with neural attention. In *Proceedings of the 54th Annual Meeting of the Association for Computational Linguistics (Volume 1: Long Papers)*. Association for Computational Linguistics, pages 33–43.

Long Duong, Hadi Afshar, Dominique Estival, Glen Pink, Philip Cohen, and Mark Johnson. 2017. Multilingual semantic parsing and code-switching. In *Proceedings of the 21st Conference on Computational Natural Language Learning (CoNLL 2017)*. Association for Computational Linguistics, pages 379–389. https://doi.org/10.18653/v1/K17-1038.

Meng Fang, Yuan Li, and Trevor Cohn. 2017. Learning how to active learn: A deep reinforcement learning approach. In *Proceedings of the 2017 Conference on Empirical Methods in Natural Language Processing*. Association for Computational Linguistics, pages 595–605. http://aclweb.org/anthology/D17-1063.

Carolin Haas and Stefan Riezler. 2016. A corpus and semantic parser for multilingual natural language querying of openstreetmap. In *Proceedings of the 2016 Conference of the North American Chapter of the Association for Computational Linguistics: Human Language Technologies*. Association for Computational Linguistics, pages 740–750.

Srinivasan Iyer, Ioannis Konstas, Alvin Cheung, Jayant Krishnamurthy, and Luke Zettlemoyer. 2017. Learning a neural semantic parser from user feedback. *CoRR* abs/1704.08760. http://arxiv.org/abs/1704.08760.

Robin Jia and Percy Liang. 2016. Data recombination for neural semantic parsing. In *Proceedings of the 54th Annual Meeting of the Association for Computational Linguistics (Volume 1: Long Papers)*. Association for Computational Linguistics, pages 12–22.

Diederik P. Kingma and Jimmy Ba. 2014. Adam: A method for stochastic optimization. *CoRR* abs/1412.6980. http://arxiv.org/abs/1412.6980.

Tomáš Kočiský, Gábor Melis, Edward Grefenstette, Chris Dyer, Wang Ling, Phil Blunsom, and Karl Moritz Hermann. 2016. Semantic parsing with semi-supervised sequential autoencoders. In *Proceedings of the 2016 Conference on Empirical Methods in Natural Language Processing*. Association for Computational Linguistics, pages 1078–1087.

Tom Kwiatkowksi, Luke Zettlemoyer, Sharon Goldwater, and Mark Steedman. 2010. Inducing probabilistic CCG grammars from logical form with higher-order unification. In *Proceedings of the 2010 Conference on Empirical Methods in Natural Language Processing*. Association for Computational Linguistics, pages 1223–1233.

Burr Settles. 2012. *Active Learning*. Morgan & Claypool Publishers.

Burr Settles and Mark Craven. 2008. An analysis of active learning strategies for sequence labeling tasks. In *Proceedings of the Conference on Empirical Methods in Natural Language Processing*. Association for Computational Linguistics, Stroudsburg, PA, USA, pages 1070–1079.

Min Tang, Xiaoqiang Luo, and Salim Roukos. 2002. Active learning for statistical natural language parsing. In *Proceedings of the 40th Annual Meeting on Association for Computational Linguistics*. Association for Computational Linguistics, Stroudsburg, PA, USA, ACL '02, pages 120–127. https://doi.org/10.3115/1073083.1073105.

Cynthia A. Thompson, Mary Elaine Califf, and Raymond J. Mooney. 1999. Active learning for natural language parsing and information extraction. In *Proceedings of the Sixteenth International Conference on Machine Learning*. Morgan Kaufmann Publishers Inc., San Francisco, CA, USA, ICML '99, pages 406–414. http://dl.acm.org/citation.cfm?id=645528.657614.

Keze Wang, Dongyu Zhang, Ya Li, Ruimao Zhang, and Liang Lin. 2017. Cost-effective active learning for deep image classification. *CoRR* abs/1701.03551. http://arxiv.org/abs/1701.03551.

Yushi Wang, Jonathan Berant, and Percy Liang. 2015. Building a semantic parser overnight. In *Proceedings of the 53rd Annual Meeting of the Association for Computational Linguistics and the 7th International Joint Conference on Natural Language Processing (Volume 1: Long Papers)*. Association for Computational Linguistics, pages 1332–1342.

Wojciech Zaremba, Ilya Sutskever, and Oriol Vinyals. 2014. Recurrent neural network regularization. *CoRR* abs/1409.2329. http://arxiv.org/abs/1409.2329.

Luke Zettlemoyer and Michael Collins. 2007. Online learning of relaxed CCG grammars for parsing to logical form. In *Proceedings of the 2007 Joint Conference on Empirical Methods in Natural Language Processing and Computational Natural Language Learning (EMNLP-CoNLL)*. pages 678–687.

Luke S. Zettlemoyer and Michael Collins. 2005. Learning to map sentences to logical form: Structured /classification with probabilistic categorial grammars. In *UAI '05, Proceedings of the 21st Conference in Uncertainty in Artificial Intelligence, Edinburgh, Scotland, July 26-29, 2005*. pages 658–666.

Learning Thematic Similarity Metric Using Triplet Networks

Liat Ein Dor,* Yosi Mass,* Alon Halfon, Elad Venezian, Ilya Shnayderman, Ranit Aharonov and Noam Slonim
IBM Research, Haifa, Israel
{liate,yosimass,alonhal,eladv,ilyashn,ranita,noams}@il.ibm.com

Abstract

In this paper we suggest to leverage the partition of articles into sections, in order to learn thematic similarity metric between sentences. We assume that a sentence is thematically closer to sentences within its section than to sentences from other sections. Based on this assumption, we use Wikipedia articles to automatically create a large dataset of weakly labeled sentence triplets, composed of a pivot sentence, one sentence from the same section and one from another section. We train a triplet network to embed sentences from the same section closer. To test the performance of the learned embeddings, we create and release a sentence clustering benchmark. We show that the triplet network learns useful thematic metrics, that significantly outperform state-of-the-art semantic similarity methods and multi-purpose embeddings on the task of thematic clustering of sentences. We also show that the learned embeddings perform well on the task of sentence *semantic* similarity prediction.

1 Introduction

Text clustering is a widely studied NLP problem, with numerous applications including collaborative filtering, document organization and indexing (Aggarwal and Zhai, 2012). Clustering can be applied to texts at different levels, from single words to full documents, and can vary with respect to the clustering goal. In this paper, we focus on the problem of clustering sentences based on thematic similarity, aiming to group together sentences that discuss the same theme, as opposed to the related task of clustering sentences that represent paraphrases of the same core statement.

Thematic clustering is important for various use cases. For example, in multi-document summarization, one often extracts sentences from multiple documents that have to be organized into meaningful sections and paragraphs. Similarly, within the emerging field of computational argumentation (Lippi and Torroni, 2016), arguments may be found in a widespread set of articles (Levy et al., 2017), which further require thematic organization to generate a compelling argumentative narrative.

We approach the problem of thematic clustering by developing a dedicated sentence similarity measure, targeted at a comparative task – Thematic Distance Comparison (TDC): given a pivot sentence, and two other sentences, the task is to determine which of the two sentences is thematically closer to the pivot. By training a deep neural network (DNN) to perform TDC, we are able to learn a thematic similarity measure.

Obtaining annotated data for training the DNN is quite demanding. Hence, we exploit the natural structure of text articles to obtain weakly-labeled data. Specifically, our underlying assumption is that sentences belonging to the same section are typically more thematically related than sentences appearing in different sections. Armed with this observation, we use the partition of Wikipedia articles into sections to automatically generate sentence triplets, where two of the sentences are from the same section, and one is from a different section. This results in a sizable training set of weakly labeled triplets, used to train a triplet neural network (Hoffer and Ailon, 2015), aiming to predict which sentence is from the same section as the pivot in each triplet. Table 1 shows an example of a triplet.

To test the performance of our network on the-

---

* These authors contributed equally to this work.

49

Proceedings of the 56th Annual Meeting of the Association for Computational Linguistics (Short Papers), pages 49–54
Melbourne, Australia, July 15 - 20, 2018. ©2018 Association for Computational Linguistics

matic clustering of sentences, we create a new clustering benchmark based on Wikipedia sections. We show that our methods, combined with existing clustering algorithms, outperform state-of-the-art general-purpose sentence embedding models in the task of reconstructing the original section structure. Moreover, the embeddings obtained from the triplet DNN perform well also on standard semantic relatedness tasks. The main contribution of this work is therefore in proposing a new approach for learning thematic relatedness between sentences, formulating the related TDC task and creating a thematic clustering benchmark. To further enhance research in these directions, we publish the clustering benchmark on the IBM Debater Datasets webpage [1].

2 Related Work

Deep learning via triplet networks was first introduced in (Hoffer and Ailon, 2015), and has since become a popular technique in metric learning(Zieba and Wang, 2017; Yao et al., 2016; Zhuang et al., 2016). However, previous usages of triplet networks were based on supervised data and were applied mainly to computer vision applications such as face verification. Here, for the first time, this architecture is used with *weakly-supervised* data for solving an *NLP* related task. In (Mueller and Thyagarajan, 2016), a supervised approach was used to learn *semantic* sentence similarity by a Siamese network, that operates on pairs of sentences. In contrast, here the triplet network is trained with weak supervision, aiming to learn *thematic* relations. By learning from triplets, rather than pairs, we provide the DNN with a context, that is crucial for the notion of similarity. (Hoffer and Ailon, 2015) show that triplet networks perform better in metric learning than Siamese networks, probably due to this valuable context. Finally, (Palangi et al., 2016) used click-through data to learn sentence similarity on top of web search engine results. Here we propose a different type of weak supervision, targeted at learning *thematic* relatedness between sentences.

3 Data Construction

We present two weakly-supervised triplet datasets. The first is based on sentences appearing in same vs. different sections, and the second is based on section titles. The datasets are extracted from the Wikipedia version of May 2017.

3.1 Sentence Triplets

For generating the sentence triplet dataset, we exploit the Wikipedia partitioning into sections and paragraphs, using OpenNLP[2] for sentence extraction. We then apply the following rules and filters, in order to reduce noise and to create a high-quality dataset, 'triplets-sen': i) The maximal distance between the intra-section sentences is limited to three paragraphs. ii) Sentences with less than 5, or more than 50 tokens are filtered out. iii) The first and the "Background" sections are removed due to their general nature. iv) The following sections are removed: "External links", "Further reading", "References", "See also", "Notes", "Citations" and "Authored books". These sections usually list a set of items rather than discuss a specific subtopic of the article's title. v) Only articles with at least five remaining sections are considered, to ensure focusing on articles with rich enough content. An example of a triplet is shown in Table 1.

<table>
<tr><td>1. McDonnell resigned from Martin in 1938
and founded McDonnell Aircraft Corporation in 1939</td></tr>
<tr><td>2. In 1967, McDonnell Aircraft merged with the
Douglas Aircraft Company to create McDonnell Douglas</td></tr>
<tr><td>3. Born in Denver, Colorado, McDonnell was raised in
Little Rock, Arkansas, and graduated from Little Rock
High School in 1917</td></tr>
</table>

Table 1: Example of a section-sen triplet from the article 'James Smith McDonnell'. The first two sentences are from the section 'Career' and the third is from 'Early life'

In use-cases such as multi-document summarization(Goldstein et al., 2000), one often needs to organize sentences originating from different documents. Such sentences tend to be standalone sentences, that do not contain the syntactic cues that often exist between adjacent sentences (e.g. co-references, discourse markers etc.). Correspondingly, to focus our weakly labeled data on sentences that are typically stand-alone in nature, we consider only paragraph opening sentences.

An essential part of learning using triplets, is the mining of difficult examples, that prevent quick stagnation of the network (Hermans et al., 2017). Since sentences in the same article essentially discuss the same topic, a deep understanding of se-

---

[1] http://www.research.ibm.com/haifa/dept/vst/debating_data.shtml

[2] https://opennlp.apache.org/

mantic nuances is necessary for the network to correctly classify the triplets. In an attempt to obtain even more challenging triplets, the third sentence is selected from an adjacent section. Thus, for a pair of intra-section sentences, we create a maximum of two triplets, where the third sentence is randomly selected from the previous/next section (if exists). The selection of the third sentence from both previous and next sections is intended to ensure the network will not pick up a signal related to the order of the sentences. In Section 5 we compare our third-sentence-selection method to two alternatives, and examine the effect of the selection method on the model performance.

Out of the $5.37M$ Wikipedia articles, $809K$ yield at least one triplet. We divide these articles into three sets, training (80%), validation and test (10% each). In terms of number of triplets, the training set is composed of $1.78M$ triplets, whereas the validation and test are composed of $220K$ and $223K$ triplets respectively.

3.2 Triplets with Section Titles

Incorporating the section titles into the training data can potentially enhance the network performance. Correspondingly, we created another triplets data, 'triplets-titles', where in each triplet the first sentence in the section (the 'pivot') is paired with the section title[3], as well as with the title of the previous/next sections (if exists), where the former pair is assumed to have greater thematic similarity. After applying the filters described above we end up with $1.38M$, $172K$ and $173K$ triplets for the training, validation and test set respectively. An example of a triplet is shown in Table 2.

Note, that for this variation of the triplets data, the network is expected to find a sentence embedding which is closer to the embedding of the true section title, than to the embedding of the title of the previous/next section. The learned representation is expected to encode information about the themes of the different sections to which the sentence can potentially belong. Thus, thematically related sentences are expected to have similar representations.

---

[3]We define the section title to be the article title concatenated to the section title. For example, the title of the section "Pricing" in the article "Black Market" is "Black Market Pricing".

| 1. Bishop was appointed Minister for Ageing in 2003. |
| 2. Julie Bishop Political career |
| 3. Julie Bishop Early life and career |

Table 2: Example of a triplet from the triplet-titles dataset, generated from the article 'Julie Bishop'.

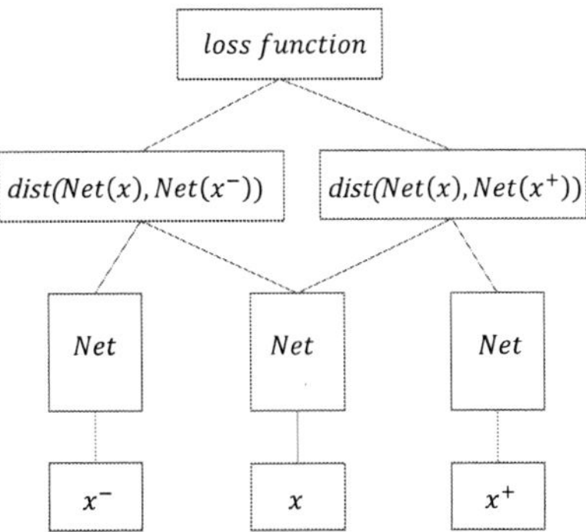

Figure 1: Triplet Network

3.3 Sentence Clustering Benchmark (SCB)

Our main goal is to successfully partition sentences into subtopics. Unfortunately, there is still no standard evaluation method for sentence clustering, which is considered a very difficult task for humans (Geiss, 2009). Correspondingly, we leverage again the partition of Wikipedia articles into sections. We assume that this partition, as performed by the Wikipedia editors, can serve as ground truth for the clustering of the article sentences. Based on this assumption we create a sentence clustering benchmark (SCB). SCB includes 692 articles that were not used in the training and validation sets of 'triplet-sen' and 'triplet-titles'. The number of sections (and correspondingly clusters) per article ranges from 5 to 12. The number of clustered sentences ranges from 17 to 1614, with an average of 67 sentences per article.

4 Model Architecture

We adopt the triplet network architecture (Hoffer and Ailon, 2015) (Figure 1) for obtaining sentence embeddings via metric learning as follows.

Assume a training data of sentences, arranged into triplets (x, x^+, x^-), where the pair (x, x^+) is presumably more similar than the pair (x, x^-). To train the model, each of the three sentences of each triplet, is fed into the same network (Net), as a sequence of word embeddings. The layer outputs their representations Net(x), Net(x⁺) and

$\text{Net}(x^-)$ respectively. Our objective is to make the representations of x and x^+ closer than the representations of x and x^-. Thus the next layer uses a distance function, denoted by 'dist', to compute two distances

$$d^+ = \text{dist}(\text{Net}(x), \text{Net}(x^+))$$
$$d^- = \text{dist}(\text{Net}(x), \text{Net}(x^-))$$

The final layer applies softmax on (d^+, d^-) that results in $p(d^+)$ and $p(d^-)$. Finally, the loss function is given by:

$$\text{loss} = |p(d^+)| + |1 - (p(d^-)|$$

Net is composed of a Bi-directional LSTM with hidden size 300 and 0.8 dropout followed by an attention (Yang et al., 2016) layer of size 200. The input to Net are the pre-trained glove word embeddings of 300d trained on 840B tokens (Pennington et al., 2014). For $dist$ and the loss function we use the $L1$ distance, which we found to yield better results than $L2$ and cosine-similarity. The selected loss function outperformed the popular triplet loss suggested in (Schroff et al., 2015). Finally, we use Adam optimizer with initial learning rate of 0.001. Given a sentence s, $\text{Net}(s)$ provides a sentence embedding of dimension 600.

5 Experiments

5.1 Reconstructing Article Sections

As mentioned, our main objective task is clustering sentences into subtopics. As a preliminary step, we first evaluate our method on the triplet-sen test set. We compare the model trained on triplet-sen to two well known methods. The first, mean-vectors, is simply the mean of the GloVe embeddings of the sentence words (Tai et al., 2015), which is considered a strong unsupervised baseline. The second, skip-thoughts (Ryan Kiros, 2015), is among the state-of-the-art unsupervised models for semantic similarity, and the most popular multi-purpose embedding method. We address two versions of skip-thoughts: one is based on the original 4800-dimensional vectors (skip-thoughts-cs), and the other, skip-thoughts-SICK, is based on the similarity function learned from the SICK semantic similarity dataset, as described in (Ryan Kiros, 2015). The aim of assessing skip-thoughts-SICK is to examine how well a state-of-the-art semantic similarity function performs on the thematic clustering task. In the case of mean-vectors and skip-thoughts-CS, the similarity between the sentences is computed using the cosine

similarity (CS) between the embedding vectors.

Table 3 indicates that our method, denoted by triplet-sen, clearly outperforms the other tested methods. Surprizingly, skip-thoughts-SICK is in-

Method	accuracy
mean-vectors	0.65
skip-thoughts-CS	0.615
skip-thoughts-SICK	0.547
triplets-sen	**0.74**

Table 3: Results on the triplets data

ferior to skip-thoughts-CS. Note that an additional interesting comparison is to a skip-thought version obtained by learning a linear transformation of the original vectors using the triplet datasets. However, no off-the-shelf algorithm is available for learning such transformation, and we leave this experiment for future work.

Next we report results on the clustering benchmark, SCB (Section 3.3). We evaluate three triplet-based models. Triplets-sen and triplets-titles are the models trained on triplets-sen and triplets-titles datasets respectively. Triplets-sen-titles is a concatenation of the representations of our two models. In addition we compare to mean-vectors and skip-thoughts-CS.

The evaluation procedure is performed as follows: for each method, we first compute for the sentences of each article, a similarity matrix, by calculating the CS between the embedding vectors of all pairs of sentences. We then use Iclust (Yom-Tov and Slonim, 2009; Slonim et al., 2005) and k-means to cluster the sentences, where the number of clusters is set to the number of sections in SCB[4]. Since the clustering algorithms themselves are not the focus of this study, we choose the classical, simple k-means, and one more advanced algorithm, Iclust. For the same reason, we also set the number of clusters to the correct number. Finally, we use standard agreement measures, MI, Adjusted MI (AMI) (Vinh et al., 2009), Rand Index (RI) and Adjusted Rand Index (ARI) (Rand, 1971), to quantify the agreement between the ground truth and the clustering results.

As exhibited in Table 4, our models significantly outperform the two other methods for both clustering algorithms, where the best performance is achieved by the concatenated representations (triplets-sen-titles), suggesting the two models,

---

[4]For k-means, using L1 as the distance metric gave similar results

triplets-sen and triplets-titles, learned complementary features. The performance of skip-thoughts-SICK on this task (not shown) was again inferior to skip-thoughts-CS.

As mentioned in Section 3.1, the third sentence in triplet-sen was selected from the sections adjacent to the pivot section, aiming to obtain more difficult triplets. We use the clustering task to examine the effect of the selection method on the model performance. We compare to two alternative methods: one that chooses the third sentence from a random section within the *same* article, and another (triplets-sen-rand-art), that chooses it randomly from a random *different* article. Results show that the first method leads to the same performance as our method, whereas triplets-sen-rand-art yields inferior results (see Table 4). A possible explanation is that the within-article triplets are difficult enough to prevent stagnation of the learning process without the need for further hardening of the task. However, the cross-article triplets are too easy to classify, and do not provide the network with the challenge and difficulty required for obtaining high quality representations.

| | iclust | | | |
Method	MI	AMI	RI	ARI
mean-vectors	0.811	0.222	0.774	0.154
skip-thoughts-CS	0.656	0.125	0.747	0.087
triplets-sen-rand-art	0.885	0.266	0.787	0.192
triplets-sen	0.935	0.296	0.801	0.224
triplets-titles	0.904	0.273	0.799	0.206
triplets-sen-titles	**0.945**	**0.303**	**0.803**	**0.230**
	kmeans			
mean-vectors	0.706	0.153	0.7760	0.103
skip-thoughts-CS	0.624	0.099	0.745	0.067
triplets-sen-rand-art	0.793	0.205	0.775	0.145
triplets-sen	0.873	0.257	0.791	0.195
triplets-titles	0.836	0.231	0.786	0.172
triplets-sen-titles	**0.873**	**0.258**	**0.791**	**0.194**

Table 4: Results on the clustering task

5.2 Semantic Relatedness

As evident from the clustering results, our models learned well to capture *thematic* similarity between sentences. Here we investigate the performance of our model in the more classical task of semantic relatedness of sentences. Specifically, we examine the SemEval 2014 Task 1: semantic relatedness SICK dataset (Marelli et al., 2014). We adopt the experimental setup of (Ryan Kiros, 2015) and learn logistic regression classifiers on top of the absolute difference and the component-wise product for all sentence pairs in the train-

ing data. The evaluation measures are Pearson r, Spearman ρ, and mean square error (MSE). Table 5 shows that like in the clustering task, best results are achieved by the concatenated embedding triplets-sen-titles, which performs in the range between mean-vector and skip-thoughts-SICK.

Method	r	ρ	MSE
mean-vectors	0.757	0.673	0.4557
skip-thoughts-SICK	**0.858**	**0.791**	**0.287**
triplets-sen	0.797	0.704	0.372
triplets-titles	0.786	0.685	0.393
triplets-sen-titles	0.818	0.724	0.339

Table 5: Results on the SICK semantic relatedness subtask.

Table 6 presents some examples of predictions of triplets-sen-titles compared to the ground truth and to skip-thoughts-SICK predictions. The first pair is semantically equivalent as both methods detect. In the second pair, the first sentence is a negation of the second, but from the thematic point of view they are rather similar, thus assigned a relatively high score by our model.

sentences	GT	Tr	Sk
1. A sea turtle is hunting for fish 2. A sea turtle is hunting for food	4.5	4.2	4.5
1. A sea turtle is not hunting for fish 2. A sea turtle is hunting for fish	3.4	4.1	3.8

Table 6: Example predictions on the SICK data. GT = groundtruth, Tr=triplets-sen, Sk=skip-thoughts-SICK

6 Summary

In this paper we suggest a new approach for learning thematic similarity between sentences. We exploit the Wikipedia section structure to generate a large dataset of weakly labeled triplets of sentences with no human involvement. Using a triplet network, we learn a high quality sentence embeddings, tailored to reveal thematic relations between sentences. Furthermore, we take a first step towards exploring the versatility of these embeddings, by showing their good performance on the semantic similarity task. An interesting direction for future work is further exploring this versatility, by examining the performance of the embeddings on a variety of other NLP tasks.

Acknowledgments

We would like to thank Yoav Goldberg for helpful advise.

References

Charu C Aggarwal and ChengXiang Zhai. 2012. A survey of text clustering algorithms. In *Mining text data*, pages 77–128. Springer.

Johanna Geiss. 2009. Creating a gold standard for sentence clustering in multi-document summarization. In *Proceedings of the ACL-IJCNLP Student Research Workshop*.

Jade Goldstein, Vibhu Mittal, Jaime Carbonell, and Mark Kantrowitz. 2000. Multi-document summarization by sentence extraction. In *Proceedings of the 2000 NAACL-ANLP Workshop on Automatic summarization*, pages 40–48. Association for Computational Linguistics.

Alexander Hermans, Lucas Beyer, and Bastian Leibe. 2017. In Defense of the Triplet Loss for Person Re-Identification. *ArXiv e-prints*.

Elad Hoffer and Nir Ailon. 2015. DEEP METRIC LEARNING USING TRIPLET NETWORK. *ArXiv e-prints*.

Ran Levy, Shai Gretz, Benjamin Sznajder, Shay Hummel, Ranit Aharonov, and Noam Slonim. 2017. Unsupervised corpus–wide claim detection. In *Proceedings of the 4th Workshop on Argument Mining*, pages 79–84, Copenhagen, Denmark. Association for Computational Linguistics.

Marco Lippi and Paolo Torroni. 2016. Argumentation mining: State of the art and emerging trends. *ACM Transactions on Internet Technology (TOIT)*, 16(2):10.

Marco Marelli, Luisa Bentivogli, Marco Baroni, Raffaella Bernardi, Stefano Menini, and Roberto Zamparelli. 2014. Semeval-2014 task 1: Evaluation of compositional distributional semantic models on full sentences through semantic relatedness and textual entailment.

Jonas Mueller and Aditya Thyagarajan. 2016. Siamese recurrent architectures for learning sentence similarity. In *AAAI*, pages 2786–2792.

Hamid Palangi, Li Deng, Yelong Shen, Jianfeng Gao, Xiaodong He, Jianshu Chen, Xinying Song, and Rabab Ward. 2016. Deep Sentence Embedding Using Long Short-Term Memory Networks: Analysis and Application to Information Retrieval. *ArXiv e-prints*.

Jeffrey Pennington, Richard Socher, and Christopher D. Manning. 2014. GloVe: Global Vectors for Word Representation.

William M Rand. 1971. Objective criteria for the evaluation of clustering methods. *Journal of the American Statistical association*, 66(336):846–850.

Ruslan Salakhutdinov Richard S. Zemel Antonio Torralba Raquel Urtasun Sanja Fidler Ryan Kiros, Yukun Zhu. 2015. Skip-Thought Vectors. *ArXiv e-prints arXiv:1506.06726*.

Florian Schroff, Dmitry Kalenichenko, and James Philbin. 2015. Facenet: A unified embedding for face recognition and clustering. In *Proceedings of the IEEE conference on computer vision and pattern recognition*, pages 815–823.

Noam Slonim, Gurinder Singh Atwal, Gaper Tkaik, and William Bialek. 2005. Information-based clustering. *PNAS*.

Kai Sheng Tai, Richard Socher, and Christopher D Manning. 2015. Improved semantic representations from tree-structured long short-term memory networks. *arXiv preprint arXiv:1503.00075*.

N. X. Vinh, J. Epps, and J. Bailey. 2009. Information theoretic measures for clusterings comparison. In *Proceedings of the 26th Annual International Conference on Machine Learning - ICML*.

Zichao Yang, Diyi Yang, Chris Dyer, Xiaodong He, Alex Smola, and Eduard Hovy. 2016. Hierarchical attention networks for document classification. In *Proceedings of NAACL-HLT*, pages 1480–1489.

Ting Yao, Fuchen Long, Tao Mei, and Yong Rui. 2016. Deep semantic-preserving and ranking-based hashing for image retrieval. In *IJCAI*, pages 3931–3937.

Elad Yom-Tov and Noam Slonim. 2009. Parallel pairwise clustering. In *SIAM International Conference on Data Mining*.

Bohan Zhuang, Guosheng Lin, Chunhua Shen, and Ian Reid. 2016. Fast training of triplet-based deep binary embedding networks. In *Proceedings of the IEEE Conference on Computer Vision and Pattern Recognition*, pages 5955–5964.

Maciej Zieba and Lei Wang. 2017. Training triplet networks with gan. *arXiv preprint arXiv:1704.02227*.

Unsupervised Semantic Frame Induction using Triclustering

**Dmitry Ustalov[†], Alexander Panchenko[‡], Andrei Kutuzov[⋆],
Chris Biemann[‡], and Simone Paolo Ponzetto[†]**

[†]University of Mannheim, Germany
`{dmitry,simone}@informatik.uni-mannheim.de`
[⋆]University of Oslo, Norway
`andreku@ifi.uio.no`
[‡]University of Hamburg, Germany
`{panchenko,biemann}@informatik.uni-hamburg.de`

Abstract

We use dependency triples automatically extracted from a Web-scale corpus to perform unsupervised semantic frame induction. We cast the frame induction problem as a *triclustering* problem that is a generalization of clustering for *triadic* data. Our replicable benchmarks demonstrate that the proposed graph-based approach, *Triframes*, shows state-of-the art results on this task on a FrameNet-derived dataset and performing on par with competitive methods on a verb class clustering task.

1 Introduction

Recent years have seen much work on Frame Semantics (Fillmore, 1982), enabled by the availability of a large set of frame definitions, as well as a manually annotated text corpus provided by the FrameNet project (Baker et al., 1998). FrameNet data enabled the development of wide-coverage frame parsers using supervised learning (Gildea and Jurafsky, 2002; Erk and Padó, 2006; Das et al., 2014, *inter alia*), as well as its application to a wide range of tasks, ranging from answer extraction in Question Answering (Shen and Lapata, 2007) and Textual Entailment (Burchardt et al., 2009; Ben Aharon et al., 2010).

However, frame-semantic resources are arguably expensive and time-consuming to build due to difficulties in defining the frames, their granularity and domain, as well as the complexity of the construction and annotation tasks requiring expertise in the underlying knowledge. Consequently, such resources exist only for a few languages (Boas, 2009) and even English is lacking domain-specific frame-based resources. Possible inroads are cross-lingual semantic annotation transfer (Padó and Lapata, 2009; Hartmann

FrameNet	Role	Lexical Units (LU)
Perpetrator	Subject	kidnapper, alien, militant
FEE	Verb	snatch, kidnap, abduct
Victim	Object	son, people, soldier, child

Table 1: Example of a LU tricluster corresponding to the "Kidnapping" frame from FrameNet.

et al., 2016) or linking FrameNet to other lexical-semantic or ontological resources (Narayanan et al., 2003; Tonelli and Pighin, 2009; Laparra and Rigau, 2010; Gurevych et al., 2012, *inter alia*). But while the arguably simpler task of PropBank-based Semantic Role Labeling has been successfully addressed by unsupervised approaches (Lang and Lapata, 2010; Titov and Klementiev, 2011), fully unsupervised frame-based semantic annotation exhibits far more challenges, starting with the preliminary step of automatically inducing a set of semantic frame definitions that would drive a subsequent text annotation. In this work, we aim at overcoming these issues by automatizing the process of FrameNet construction through unsupervised frame induction techniques.

Triclustering. In this work, we cast the frame induction problem as a *triclustering* task (Zhao and Zaki, 2005; Ignatov et al., 2015), namely a generalization of standard clustering and biclustering (Cheng and Church, 2000), aiming at simultaneously clustering objects along three dimensions (cf. Table 1). First, using triclustering allows to avoid sequential nature of frame induction approaches, e.g. (Kawahara et al., 2014), where two independent clusterings are needed. Second, benchmarking frame induction as triclustering against other methods on dependency triples allows to abstract away the evaluation of the frame induction algorithm from other factors, e.g., the input corpus or pre-processing steps, thus allowing a fair comparison of different induction models.

Proceedings of the 56th Annual Meeting of the Association for Computational Linguistics (Short Papers), pages 55–62
Melbourne, Australia, July 15 - 20, 2018. ©2018 Association for Computational Linguistics

The **contributions of this paper** are three-fold: (1) we are the *first to apply* triclustering algorithms for unsupervised frame induction, (2) we propose a *new approach to triclustering*, achieving state-of-the-art performance on the frame induction task, (3) we propose a *new method for the evaluation* of frame induction enabling straightforward comparison of approaches. In this paper, we focus on the simplest setup with *subject-verb-object* (SVO) triples and two roles, but our evaluation framework can be extended to more roles.

In contrast to the recent approaches like the one by Jauhar and Hovy (2017), our approach induces semantic frames without any supervision, yet capturing only two core roles: the subject and the object of a frame triggered by verbal predicates. Note that it is not generally correct to expect that the SVO triples obtained by a dependency parser are necessarily the core arguments of a predicate. Such roles can be implicit, i.e., unexpressed in a given context (Schenk and Chiarcos, 2016). Keeping this limitation in mind, we assume that the triples obtained from a Web-scale corpus cover most core arguments sufficiently.

Related Work. *LDA-Frames* (Materna, 2012, 2013) is an approach to inducing semantic frames using LDA (Blei et al., 2003) for generating semantic frames and their respective frame-specific semantic roles at the same time. The authors evaluated their approach against the CPA corpus (Hanks and Pustejovsky, 2005). *ProFinder* (Cheung et al., 2013) is another generative approach that also models both frames and roles as latent topics. The evaluation was performed on the in-domain information extraction task MUC-4 (Sundheim, 1992) and on the text summarization task TAC-2010.[1] Modi et al. (2012) build on top of an unsupervised semantic role labeling model (Titov and Klementiev, 2012). The raw text of sentences from the FrameNet data is used for training. The FrameNet gold annotations are then used to evaluate the labeling of the obtained frames and roles, effectively clustering instances known during induction. Kawahara et al. (2014) harvest a huge collection of verbal predicates along with their argument instances and then apply the Chinese Restaurant Process clustering algorithm to group predicates with similar arguments. The approach was evaluated on the verb

cluster dataset of Korhonen et al. (2003).

A major issue with unsupervised frame induction task is that these and some other related approaches, e.g., (O'Connor, 2013), were all evaluated in completely different incomparable settings, and used different input corpora. In this paper, we propose a methodology to resolve this issue.

2   The Triframes Algorithm

Our approach to frame induction relies on graph clustering. We focused on a simple setup using two roles and the SVO triples, arguing that it still can be useful, as frame roles are primarily expressed by subjects and objects, giving rise to semantic structures extracted in an unsupervised way with high coverage.

Input Data. As the input data, we use SVO triples extracted by a dependency parser. According to our statistics on the dependency-parsed FrameNet corpus of over 150 thousand sentences (Bauer et al., 2012), the SUBJ and OBJ relationships are the two most common shortest paths between frame evoking elements (*FEEs*) and their roles, accounting for 13.5 % of instances of a heavy-tail distribution of over 11 thousand different paths that occur three times or more in the FrameNet data. While this might seem a simplification that does not cover prepositional phrases and frames filling the roles of other frames in a nested fashion, we argue that the overall frame inventory can be induced on the basis of this restricted set of constructions, leaving other paths and more complex instances for further work.

The Method. Our method constructs embeddings for SVO triples to reduce the frame induction problem to a simpler graph clustering problem. Given the vocabulary V, a d-dimensional word embedding model $v \in V \rightarrow \vec{v} \in \mathbb{R}^d$, and a set of SVO triples $T \subseteq V^3$ extracted from a syntactically analyzed corpus, we construct the triple similarity graph $\mathcal{G}$. Clustering of $\mathcal{G}$ yields sets of triples corresponding to the instances of the semantic frames, thereby clustering frame-evoking predicates and roles simultaneously.

We obtain dense representations of the triples T by concatenating the word vectors corresponding to the elements of each triple by transforming a triple $t = (s, p, o) \in T$ into the $(3d)$-dimensional vector $\vec{t} = \vec{s} \oplus \vec{p} \oplus \vec{o}$. Subsequently, we use the triple embeddings to generate the undirected graph

---

[1] https://tac.nist.gov/2010/
Summarization

Algorithm 1 *Triframes* frame induction

Input: an embedding model $v \in V \to \vec{v} \in \mathbb{R}^d$,
    a set of SVO triples $T \subseteq V^3$,
    the number of nearest neighbors $k \in \mathbb{N}$,
    a graph clustering algorithm CLUSTER.
Output: a set of triframes F.

1: $S \leftarrow \{t \to \vec{t} \in \mathbb{R}^{3d} : t \in T\}$
2: $E \leftarrow \{(t, t') \in T^2 : t' \in \mathrm{NN}_k^S(\vec{t}), t \neq t'\}$
3: $F \leftarrow \emptyset$
4: **for all** $C \in \text{CLUSTER}(T, E)$ **do**
5:     $f_s \leftarrow \{s \in V : (s, v, o) \in C\}$
6:     $f_v \leftarrow \{v \in V : (s, v, o) \in C\}$
7:     $f_o \leftarrow \{o \in V : (s, v, o) \in C\}$
8:     $F \leftarrow F \cup \{(f_s, f_v, f_o)\}$
9: **return** F

$\mathcal{G} = (T, E)$ by constructing the edge set $E \subseteq T^2$. For that, we compute $k \in \mathbb{N}$ nearest neighbors of each triple vector $\vec{t} \in \mathbb{R}^{3d}$ and establish cosine similarity-weighted edges between the corresponding triples.

Then, we assume that the triples representing similar contexts appear in similar roles, which is explicitly encoded by the concatenation of the corresponding vectors of the words constituting the triple. We use graph clustering of $\mathcal{G}$ to retrieve communities of similar triples forming frame clusters; a clustering algorithm is a function $\text{CLUSTER} : (T, E) \to \mathbb{C}$ such that $T = \bigcup_{C \in \mathbb{C}} C$. Finally, for each cluster $C \in \mathbb{C}$, we aggregate the subjects, the verbs, and the objects of the contained triples into separate sets. As the result, each cluster is transformed into a *triframe*, which is a triple that is composed of the subjects $f_s \subseteq V$, the verbs $f_v \subseteq V$, and the objects $f_o \subseteq V$.

Our frame induction approach outputs a set of triframes F as presented in Algorithm 1. The hyper-parameters of the algorithm are the number of nearest neighbors for establishing edges (k) and the graph clustering algorithm CLUSTER. During the concatenation of the vectors for words forming triples, the ($|T| \times 3d$)-dimensional vector space S is created. Thus, given the triple $t \in T$, we denote the k nearest neighbors extraction procedure of its concatenated embedding from S as $\mathrm{NN}_k^S(\vec{t}) \subseteq T$. We used $k = 10$ nearest neighbors per triple.

To cluster the nearest neighbor graph of SVO triples $\mathcal{G}$, we use the WATSET *fuzzy graph clustering* algorithm (Ustalov et al., 2017). It treats the vertices T of the input graph $\mathcal{G}$ as the SVO triples, induces their senses, and constructs an intermedi-

ate sense-aware representation that is clustered using the Chinese Whispers (CW) hard clustering algorithm (Biemann, 2006). We chose WATSET due to its performance on the related synset induction task, its fuzzy nature, and the ability to find the number of frames automatically.

3 Evaluation

Input Corpus. In our evaluation, we use triple frequencies from the DepCC dataset (Panchenko et al., 2018) , which is a dependency-parsed version of the Common Crawl corpus, and the standard 300-dimensional word embeddings model trained on the Google News corpus (Mikolov et al., 2013). All evaluated algorithms are executed on the same set of triples, eliminating variations due to different corpora or pre-processing.

Datasets. We cast the complex multi-stage frame induction task as a straightforward triple clustering task. We constructed a gold standard set of triclusters, each corresponding to a FrameNet frame, similarly to the one illustrated in Table 1. To construct the evaluation dataset, we extracted frame annotations from the over 150 thousand sentences from the FrameNet 1.7 (Baker et al., 1998). Each sentence contains data about the frame, FEE, and its arguments, which were used to generate triples in the form $(\text{word}_i : role_1, \text{word}_j : FEE, \text{word}_k : role_2)$, where $\text{word}_{i/j/k}$ correspond to the roles and FEE in the sentence. We omitted roles expressed by multiple words as we use dependency parses, where one node represents a single word only.

For the sentences where more than two roles are present, all possible triples were generated. Sentences with less than two roles were omitted. Finally, for each frame, we selected only two roles, which are most frequently co-occurring in the FrameNet annotated texts. This has left us with about 100 thousand instances for the evaluation. For the evaluation purposes, we operate on the intersection of triples from DepCC and FrameNet. Experimenting on the full set of DepCC triples is only possible for several methods that scale well (WATSET, CW, k-means), but is prohibitively expensive for other methods (LDA-Frames, NOAC).

In addition to the frame induction evaluation, where subjects, objects, and verbs are evaluated together, we also used a dataset of polysemous verb classes introduced in (Korhonen et al., 2003) and employed by Kawahara et al. (2014). Statis-

Dataset	# instances	# unique	# clusters
FrameNet Triples	99,744	94,170	383
Poly. Verb Classes	246	110	62

Table 2: Statistics of the evaluation datasets.

tics of both datasets are summarized in Table 2. Note that the polysemous verb dataset is rather small, whereas the FrameNet triples set is fairly large, enabling reliable comparisons.

Evaluation Measures. Following the approach for verb class evaluation by Kawahara et al. (2014), we employ *normalized modified purity* (nmPU) and *normalized inverse purity* (niPU) as the clustering quality measures. Given the set of the obtained clusters K and the set of the gold clusters G, normalized modified purity quantifies the clustering precision as the average of the weighted overlap $\delta_{K_i}(K_i \cap G_j)$ between each cluster $K_i \in K$ and the gold cluster $G_j \in G$ that maximizes the overlap with K_i:
$$\text{nmPU} = \frac{1}{N} \sum_{i \text{ s.t. } |K_i|>1}^{|K|} \max_{1 \leq j \leq |G|} \delta_{K_i}(K_i \cap G_j),$$
where the weighted overlap is the sum of the weights c_{iv} for each word v in i-th cluster: $\delta_{K_i}(K_i \cap G_j) = \sum_{v \in K_i \cap G_j} c_{iv}$. Note that nmPU counts all the singleton clusters as wrong. Similarly, normalized inverse purity (collocation) quantifies the clustering recall:
$$\text{niPU} = \frac{1}{N} \sum_{j=1}^{|G|} \max_{1 \leq i \leq |K|} \delta_{G_j}(K_i \cap G_j).$$
nmPU and niPU are combined together as the harmonic mean to yield the overall clustering F-score (F_1), which we use to rank the approaches.

Our framework can be extended to evaluation of more than two roles by generating more roles per frame. Currently, given a set of gold triples generated from the FrameNet, each triple element has a role, e.g., *"Victim"*, *"Predator"*, and *"FEE"*. We use fuzzy clustering evaluation measure which operates not on triples, but instead on a set of tuples. Consider for instance a gold triple (Freddy: *Predator*, kidnap: *FEE*, kid: *Victim*). It will be converted to three pairs (Freddy, *Predator*), (kidnap, *FEE*), (kid, *Victim*). Each cluster in both K and G is transformed into a union of all constituent typed pairs. The quality measures are finally calculated between these two sets of tuples, K, and G. Note that one can easily pull in more than two core roles by adding to this gold standard set of tuples other roles of the frame, e.g., (forest, *Location*). In our experiments, we focused on two main roles as our contribution is related to the application of triclustering methods. However, if more advanced methods of clustering are used, yielding clusters of arbitrary modality (n-clustering), one could also use our evaluation schema.

Baselines. We compare our method to several available state-of-the-art baselines applicable to our dataset of triples.

LDA-Frames by Materna (2012, 2013) is a frame induction method based on topic modeling. We ran 500 iterations of the model with the default parameters. *Higher-Order Skip-Gram (HOSG)* by Cotterell et al. (2017) generalizes the Skip-Gram model (Mikolov et al., 2013) by extending it from word-context co-occurrence matrices to tensors factorized with a polyadic decomposition. In our case, this tensor consisted of SVO triple counts. We trained three vector arrays (for subjects, verbs and objects) on the 108,073 SVO triples from the *FrameNet* corpus, using the implementation by the authors. Training was performed with 5 negative samples, 300-dimensional vectors, and 10 epochs. We constructed an embedding of a triple by concatenating embeddings for subjects, verbs, and objects, and clustered them using k-means with the number of clusters set to 10,000 (this value provided the best performance). *NOAC* (Egurnov et al., 2017) is an extension of the Object Attribute Condition (OAC) triclustering algorithm (Ignatov et al., 2015) to numerically weighted triples. This incremental algorithm searches for dense regions in triadic data. A minimum density of 0.25 led to the best results. In the *Triadic* baselines, independent word embeddings of subject, object, and verb are concatenated and then clustered using a *hard clustering algorithm*: k-means, spectral clustering, or CW.

We tested various hyper-parameters of each of these algorithms and report the best results overall per clustering algorithm. Two trivial baselines are *Singletons* that creates a single cluster per instance and *Whole* that creates one cluster for all elements.

4 Results

We perform two experiments to evaluate our approach: (1) a frame induction experiment on the FrameNet annotated corpus by Bauer et al. (2012); (2) the polysemous verb clustering experiment on the dataset by Korhonen et al. (2003). The first is based on the newly introduced frame induction evaluation schema (cf. Section 3). The second one evaluates the quality of verb clusters only on a standard dataset from prior work.

Method	Verb			Subject			Object			Frame		
	nmPU	niPU	F_1	nmPU	niPU	F_1	nmPU	niPU	F_1	nmPU	niPU	F_1
Triframes WATSET	42.84	88.35	**57.70**	54.22	81.40	65.09	53.04	83.25	64.80	55.19	60.81	**57.87**
HOSG (Cotterell et al., 2017)	44.41	68.43	53.86	52.84	74.53	61.83	54.73	74.05	62.94	55.74	50.45	52.96
NOAC (Egurnov et al., 2017)	20.73	88.38	33.58	57.00	80.11	**66.61**	57.32	81.13	**67.18**	44.01	63.21	51.89
Triadic Spectral	49.62	24.90	33.15	50.07	41.07	45.13	50.50	41.82	45.75	52.05	28.60	36.91
Triadic k-Means	**63.87**	23.16	33.99	**63.15**	38.20	47.60	**63.98**	37.43	47.23	**63.64**	24.11	34.97
LDA-Frames (Materna, 2013)	26.11	66.92	37.56	17.28	83.26	28.62	20.80	90.33	33.81	18.80	71.17	29.75
Triframes CW	7.75	6.48	7.06	3.70	14.07	5.86	51.91	76.92	61.99	21.67	26.50	23.84
Singletons	0.00	25.23	0.00	0.00	25.68	0.00	0.00	20.80	0.00	32.34	22.15	26.29
Whole	3.62	**100.0**	6.98	2.41	**98.41**	4.70	2.38	**100.0**	4.64	2.63	**99.55**	5.12

Table 3: Frame evaluation results on the triples from the FrameNet 1.7 corpus (Baker et al., 1998). The results are sorted by the descending order of the Frame F_1-score. Best results are boldfaced.

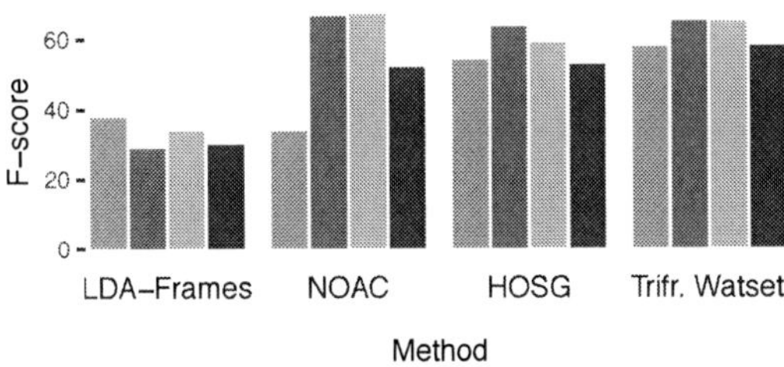

Figure 1: F_1-scores for ■ verbs, ■ subjects, ■ objects, ■ frames corresponding to Table 3.

Method	nmPU	niPU	F_1
LDA-Frames	**52.60**	45.84	**48.98**
Triframes WATSET	40.05	62.09	48.69
NOAC	37.19	64.09	47.07
HOSG	38.22	43.76	40.80
Triadic Spectral	35.76	38.96	36.86
Triadic k-Means	52.22	27.43	35.96
Triframes CW	18.05	12.72	14.92
Whole	24.14	**79.09**	36.99
Singletons	0.00	27.21	0.00

Table 4: Evaluation results on the dataset of polysemous verb classes by Korhonen et al. (2003).

Frame Induction Experiment. In Table 3 and Figure 1, the results of the experiment are presented. Triframes based on WATSET clustering outperformed the other methods on both Verb F_1 and overall Frame F_1. The *HOSG*-based clustering proved to be the most competitive baseline, yielding decent scores according to all four measures. The *NOAC* approach captured the frame grouping of slot fillers well but failed to establish good verb clusters. Note that *NOAC* and *HOSG* use only the graph of syntactic triples and do not rely on pre-trained word embeddings. This suggests a high complementarity of signals based on distributional similarity and global structure of the triple graph. Finally, the simpler *Triadic* baselines relying on hard clustering algorithms showed low performance, similar to that of *LDA-Frames*, justifying the more elaborate WATSET method.

While triples are intuitively less ambiguous than words, still some frequent and generic triples like (she, make, it) can act as hubs in the graph, making it difficult to split it into semantically plausible clusters. The poor results of the Chinese Whispers hard clustering algorithm illustrate this. Since the hubs are ambiguous, i.e., can belong to multiple clusters, the use of the WATSET fuzzy clustering algorithm that splits the hubs by disambiguating them leads to the best results (see Table 3).

Verb Clustering Experiment. Table 4 presents results on the second dataset for the best models identified on the first dataset. The *LDA-Frames* yielded the best results with our approach performing comparably in terms of the F_1-score. We attribute the low performance of the Triframes method based on CW clustering to its hard partitioning output, whereas the evaluation dataset contains fuzzy clusters. Different rankings also suggest that frame induction cannot simply be treated as a verb clustering and requires a separate task.

5 Conclusion

In this paper, we presented the first application of *triclustering* for unsupervised *frame induction*. We designed a dataset based on the FrameNet and SVO triples to enable fair corpus-independent evaluations of frame induction algorithms. We tested several triclustering methods as the baselines and proposed a new graph-based triclustering algorithm that yields state-of-the-art results. A promising direction for future work is using the induced frames in applications, such as Information Extraction and Question Answering.

Additional illustrations and examples of extracted frames are available in the supplementary materials. The source code and the data are available online under a permissive license.[2]

---

[2] https://github.com/uhh-lt/triframes

Acknowledgments

We acknowledge the support of DFG under the "JOIN-T" and "ACQuA" projects and thank three anonymous reviewers for their helpful comments. Furthermore, we thank Dmitry Egurnov, Dmitry Ignatov, and Dmitry Gnatyshak for help in operating the NOAC method using the multimodal clustering toolbox. Besides, we are grateful to Ryan Cotterell and Adam Poliak for a discussion and an implementation of the HOSG method. Finally, we thank Bonaventura Coppolla for discussions and preliminary work on graph-based frame induction.

References

Collin F. Baker, Charles J. Fillmore, and John B. Lowe. 1998. The Berkeley FrameNet Project. In *Proceedings of the 36th Annual Meeting of the Association for Computational Linguistics and 17th International Conference on Computational Linguistics - Volume 1*, ACL '98, pages 86–90, Montreal, QC, Canada. Association for Computational Linguistics.

Daniel Bauer, Hagen Fürstenau, and Owen Rambow. 2012. The Dependency-Parsed FrameNet Corpus. In *Proceedings of the Eight International Conference on Language Resources and Evaluation*, LREC 2012, pages 3861–3867, Istanbul, Turkey. European Language Resources Association (ELRA).

Roni Ben Aharon, Idan Szpektor, and Ido Dagan. 2010. Generating Entailment Rules from FrameNet. In *Proceedings of the ACL 2010 Conference Short Papers*, pages 241–246, Uppsala, Sweden. Association for Computational Linguistics.

Chris Biemann. 2006. Chinese Whispers: An Efficient Graph Clustering Algorithm and Its Application to Natural Language Processing Problems. In *Proceedings of the First Workshop on Graph Based Methods for Natural Language Processing*, TextGraphs-1, pages 73–80, New York, NY, USA. Association for Computational Linguistics.

David M. Blei, Andrew Y. Ng, and Michael I. Jordan. 2003. Latent Dirichlet Allocation. *Journal of Machine Learning Research*, 3:993–1022.

Hans C. Boas. 2009. *Multilingual FrameNets in Computational Lexicography: Methods and Applications*. Trends in Linguistics. Studies and Monographs. Mouton de Gruyter.

Aljoscha Burchardt, Marco Pennacchiotti, Stefan Thater, and Manfred Pinkal. 2009. Assessing the impact of frame semantics on textual entailment. *Natural Language Engineering*, 15(4):527–550.

Yizong Cheng and George M. Church. 2000. Biclustering of Expression Data. In *Proceedings of the Eighth International Conference on Intelligent Systems for Molecular Biology*, pages 93–103. AAAI Press.

Jackie C. K. Cheung, Hoifung Poon, and Lucy Vanderwende. 2013. Probabilistic Frame Induction. In *Proceedings of the 2013 Conference of the North American Chapter of the Association for Computational Linguistics: Human Language Technologies*, pages 837–846, Atlanta, GA, USA. Association for Computational Linguistics.

Ryan Cotterell, Adam Poliak, Benjamin Van Durme, and Jason Eisner. 2017. Explaining and Generalizing Skip-Gram through Exponential Family Principal Component Analysis. In *Proceedings of the 15th Conference of the European Chapter of the Association for Computational Linguistics: Volume 2, Short Papers*, pages 175–181, Valencia, Spain. Association for Computational Linguistics.

Dipanjan Das, Desai Chen, André F. T. Martins, Nathan Schneider, and Noah A. Smith. 2014. Frame-Semantic Parsing. *Computational Linguistics*, 40(1):9–56.

Dmitry Egurnov, Dmitry Ignatov, and Engelbert M. Nguifo. 2017. Mining Triclusters of Similar Values in Triadic Real-Valued Contexts. In *14th International Conference on Formal Concept Analysis - Supplementary Proceedings*, pages 31–47, Rennes, France.

Katrin Erk and Sebastian Padó. 2006. SHALMANESER — A Toolchain For Shallow Semantic Parsing. In *Proceedings of the Fifth International Conference on Language Resources and Evaluation*, LREC 2006, pages 527–532, Genoa, Italy. European Language Resources Association (ELRA).

Charles J. Fillmore. 1982. Frame Semantics. In *Linguistics in the Morning Calm*, pages 111–137. Hanshin Publishing Co., Seoul, South Korea.

Daniel Gildea and Martin Jurafsky. 2002. Automatic Labeling of Semantic Roles. *Computational Linguistics*, 28(3):245–288.

Iryna Gurevych, Judith Eckle-Kohler, Silvana Hartmann, Michael Matuschek, Christian M. Meyer, and Christian Wirth. 2012. UBY – A Large-Scale Unified Lexical-Semantic Resource Based on LMF. In *Proceedings of the 13th Conference of the European Chapter of the Association for Computational Linguistics*, EACL '12, pages 580–590, Avignon, France. Association for Computational Linguistics.

Patrick Hanks and James Pustejovsky. 2005. A Pattern Dictionary for Natural Language Processing. *Revue Française de linguistique appliquée*, 10(2):63–82.

Silvana Hartmann, Judith Eckle-Kohler, and Iryna Gurevych. 2016. Generating Training Data for Semantic Role Labeling based on Label Transfer from Linked Lexical Resources. *Transactions of the Association for Computational Linguistics*, 4:197–213.

Dmitry I. Ignatov, Dmitry V. Gnatyshak, Sergei O. Kuznetsov, and Boris G. Mirkin. 2015. Triadic Formal Concept Analysis and triclustering: searching for optimal patterns. *Machine Learning*, 101(1-3):271–302.

Sujay Kumar Jauhar and Eduard Hovy. 2017. Embedded Semantic Lexicon Induction with Joint Global and Local Optimization. In *Proceedings of the 6th Joint Conference on Lexical and Computational Semantics (*SEM 2017)*, pages 209–219, Vancouver, Canada. Association for Computational Linguistics.

Daisuke Kawahara, Daniel W. Peterson, and Martha Palmer. 2014. A Step-wise Usage-based Method for Inducing Polysemy-aware Verb Classes. In *Proceedings of the 52nd Annual Meeting of the Association for Computational Linguistics Volume 1: Long Papers*, ACL 2014, pages 1030–1040, Baltimore, MD, USA. Association for Computational Linguistics.

Anna Korhonen, Yuval Krymolowski, and Zvika Marx. 2003. Clustering Polysemic Subcategorization Frame Distributions Semantically. In *Proceedings of the 41st Annual Meeting on Association for Computational Linguistics - Volume 1*, ACL '03, pages 64–71, Sapporo, Japan. Association for Computational Linguistics.

Joel Lang and Mirella Lapata. 2010. Unsupervised Induction of Semantic Roles. In *Human Language Technologies: The 2010 Annual Conference of the North American Chapter of the Association for Computational Linguistics*, pages 939–947, Los Angeles, CA, USA. Association for Computational Linguistics.

Egoitz Laparra and German Rigau. 2010. eXtended WordFrameNet. In *Proceedings of the Seventh International Conference on Language Resources and Evaluation*, LREC 2010, pages 1214–1219, Valletta, Malta. European Language Resources Association (ELRA).

Jiří Materna. 2012. LDA-Frames: An Unsupervised Approach to Generating Semantic Frames. In *Computational Linguistics and Intelligent Text Processing, Proceedings, Part I*, CICLing 2012, pages 376–387, New Delhi, India. Springer Berlin Heidelberg.

Jiří Materna. 2013. Parameter Estimation for LDA-Frames. In *Proceedings of the 2013 Conference of the North American Chapter of the Association for Computational Linguistics: Human Language Technologies*, pages 482–486, Atlanta, GA, USA. Association for Computational Linguistics.

Tomas Mikolov, Ilya Sutskever, Kai Chen, Greg S. Corrado, and Jeffrey Dean. 2013. Distributed Representations of Words and Phrases and their Compositionality. In *Advances in Neural Information Processing Systems 26*, pages 3111–3119. Curran Associates, Inc., Harrahs and Harveys, NV, USA.

Ashutosh Modi, Ivan Titov, and Alexandre Klementiev. 2012. Unsupervised Induction of Frame-Semantic Representations. In *Proceedings of the NAACL-HLT Workshop on the Induction of Linguistic Structure*, pages 1–7, Montréal, Canada. Association for Computational Linguistics.

Srini Narayanan, Collin Baker, Charles Fillmore, and Miriam Petruck. 2003. FrameNet Meets the Semantic Web: Lexical Semantics for the Web. In *The Semantic Web - ISWC 2003: Second International Semantic Web Conference, Sanibel Island, FL, USA, October 20-23, 2003. Proceedings*, pages 771–787, Heidelberg, Germany. Springer Berlin Heidelberg.

Brendan O'Connor. 2013. Learning Frames from Text with an Unsupervised Latent Variable Model. arXiv preprint arXiv:1307.7382.

Sebastian Padó and Mirella Lapata. 2009. Cross-lingual Annotation Projection of Semantic Roles. *Journal of Artificial Intelligence Research*, 36(1):307–340.

Alexander Panchenko, Eugen Ruppert, Stefano Faralli, Simone Paolo Ponzetto, and Chris Biemann. 2018. Building a Web-Scale Dependency-Parsed Corpus from Common Crawl. In *Proceedings of the Eleventh International Conference on Language Resources and Evaluation*, LREC 2018, pages 1816–1823, Miyazaki, Japan. European Language Resources Association (ELRA).

Niko Schenk and Christian Chiarcos. 2016. Unsupervised Learning of Prototypical Fillers for Implicit Semantic Role Labeling. In *Proceedings of the 2016 Conference of the North American Chapter of the Association for Computational Linguistics: Human Language Technologies*, pages 1473–1479, San Diego, CA, USA. Association for Computational Linguistics.

Dan Shen and Mirella Lapata. 2007. Using Semantic Roles to Improve Question Answering. In *Proceedings of the 2007 Joint Conference on Empirical Methods in Natural Language Processing and Computational Natural Language Learning (EMNLP-CoNLL)*, pages 12–21, Prague, Czech Republic. Association for Computational Linguistics.

Beth M. Sundheim. 1992. Overview of the Fourth Message Understanding Evaluation and Conference. In *Proceedings of the 4th Conference on Message Understanding*, MUC4 '92, pages 3–21, Stroudsburg, PA, USA. Association for Computational Linguistics.

Ivan Titov and Alexandre Klementiev. 2011. A Bayesian Model for Unsupervised Semantic Parsing. In *Proceedings of the 49th Annual Meeting of the Association for Computational Linguistics: Human Language Technologies*, pages 1445–1455, Portland, OR, USA. Association for Computational Linguistics.

Ivan Titov and Alexandre Klementiev. 2012. A Bayesian Approach to Unsupervised Semantic Role Induction. In *Proceedings of the 13th Conference of the European Chapter of the Association for Computational Linguistics*, pages 12–22, Avignon, France. Association for Computational Linguistics.

Sara Tonelli and Daniele Pighin. 2009. New Features for FrameNet - WordNet Mapping. In *Proceedings of the Thirteenth Conference on Computational Natural Language Learning (CoNLL-2009)*, pages 219–227, Boulder, CO, USA. Association for Computational Linguistics.

Dmitry Ustalov, Alexander Panchenko, and Chris Biemann. 2017. Watset: Automatic Induction of Synsets from a Graph of Synonyms. In *Proceedings of the 55th Annual Meeting of the Association for Computational Linguistics (Volume 1: Long Papers)*, ACL 2017, pages 1579–1590, Vancouver, Canada. Association for Computational Linguistics.

Lizhuang Zhao and Mohammed J. Zaki. 2005. TRICLUSTER: An Effective Algorithm for Mining Coherent Clusters in 3D Microarray Data. In *Proceedings of the 2005 ACM SIGMOD International Conference on Management of Data*, SIGMOD '05, pages 694–705, New York, NY, USA. ACM.

Identification of Alias Links among Participants in Narratives

Sangameshwar Patil[*] **Sachin Pawar**[*] **Swapnil Hingmire**[*] **Girish K. Palshikar**
{sangameshwar.patil,sachin7.p}@tcs.com
{swapnil.hingmire,gk.palshikar}@tcs.com
TCS Research, Tata Consultancy Services, India

Vasudeva Varma
vv@iiit.ac.in
IIIT Hyderabad, India

Pushpak Bhattacharyya
pb@cse.iitb.ac.in
IIT Patna, India

Abstract

Identification of distinct and independent participants (entities of interest) in a narrative is an important task for many NLP applications. This task becomes challenging because these participants are often referred to using multiple aliases. In this paper, we propose an approach based on linguistic knowledge for identification of aliases mentioned using proper nouns, pronouns or noun phrases with common noun headword. We use Markov Logic Network (MLN) to encode the linguistic knowledge for identification of aliases. We evaluate on four diverse history narratives of varying complexity as well as newswire subset of ACE 2005 dataset. Our approach performs better than the state-of-the-art.

1 Introduction

Identifying aliases of participants in a narrative is crucial for many NLP applications like timeline creation, question-answering, summarization, and information extraction. For instance, to answer a question (in the context of Table 1) *When did Napoleon defeat the royalist rebels?*, we need to identify Napoleon and the young lieutenant as aliases of Napoleon Bonaparte. Similarly, timeline for Napoleon Bonaparte will be inconsistent with the text, if the young lieutenant is not identified as an alias Napoleon Bonaparte. This will further affect any analysis of the timeline (Bedi et al., 2017).

In the context of narrative analysis, we define –

• A *participant* as an entity of type PERSON (PER), LOCATION (LOC), or ORGANIZATION (ORG). A participant has a *canonical mention*,

```
[Napoleon Bonaparte]_{P1} was quite [a short man]_{A1}
just five feet three inches tall. When [he]_{A1}
was nine years old, [his parents]_{P2} sent [him]_{A1}
to [a military school in France]_{P3}. In 1785,
[he]_{A1} became [a lieutenant]_{A1}. When the
Revolution broke out, [Napoleon]_{A1} joined [the
army of the new government]_{P4}. When [royalist
rebels]_{P5} marched on [the National Convention]_{P6},
[a government official]_{P7} told [the young
lieutenant]_{A1} to defend [the delegates]_{P8}.
```

Table 1: Example narrative excerpt with only independent participant mentions marked. For the i-th participant, canonical mention is marked with Pi and all its aliases are marked with Ai.

which is a standardized reference to that participant (e.g., Napoleon Bonaparte). Further, it may have several *aliases*, which are different mentions referring to the same participant.

• A *basic participant mention* can be a sequence of proper nouns (e.g., Napoleon or N. Bonaparte), a pronoun (e.g., he) or a *generic NP*[1] (e.g., a short man or the young lieutenant).

• *Independent basic mentions* of a participant play primary role in the narrative. *Dependent basic mentions* play supporting role by qualifying or elaborating independent basic mentions. For each independent mention, we merge all its dependent mentions to create its *composite mention*.

Note that our notion of dependency is syntactic. A basic mention can be either dependent or independent. A basic mention is said to be *dependent* if its governor in the dependency parse tree is itself a participant mention; otherwise it is called as *independent* mention. An independent mention can be a basic (if it does not have any dependent mentions) or a composite mention. An in-

---

[*]These authors contributed equally.

[1]NP with a common noun headword

Proceedings of the 56th Annual Meeting of the Association for Computational Linguistics (Short Papers), pages 63–68
Melbourne, Australia, July 15 - 20, 2018. ©2018 Association for Computational Linguistics

dependent composite mention is created by recursively merging all its dependent mentions. For instance, for the phrases `his parents` and `parents of Napoleon`, following are the basic participant mentions - `his`, `Napoleon`, and `parents`. In the dependency parse trees, `parents` is the governor in both cases. Hence, `his` and `Napoleon` would be basic dependent mentions. Final independent composite mentions `his parents` or `parents of Napoleon` are created by merging the dependent mentions with the independent mention `parents`.

In this paper, we focus on identification of independent mentions (basic as well as composite) for any participant in a narrative. The problem of identifying aliases of participants is challenging because even though the standard NLP toolkits work well to resolve the coreferences among pronouns and named entities, we observed that they perform poorly for generic NPs. For instance, Stanford CoreNLP does not identify `the young lieutenant` and `Napoleon Bonaparte` as the same participant (Table 1); a task we aim to do. This task can be considered as a sub-problem of the standard coreference resolution (Ng, 2017). We build upon output from any standard coreference resolution algorithm, and improve it significantly to detect the missing aliases.

Our goal is to identify the canonical mentions of all independent participants and their aliases. In this paper, we propose a linguistically grounded algorithm for alias detection. Our algorithm utilizes WordNet hypernym structure for identifying participant mentions. It encodes linguistic knowledge in the form of first order logic rules and performs inference in Markov Logic Networks (MLN) (Richardson and Domingos, 2006) for establishing alias links among these mentions.

2   Related Work

Traditionally, alias detection restricts the focus on aliases of named entities which occur as proper nouns (Sapena et al., 2007; Hsiung et al., 2005) using lexical, semantic, and social network analysis. This ignores the aliases which occur as generic NPs. Even in the coreference resolution, recently (Peng et al., 2015a,b) the focus has come back to generic NP aliases by detecting mention heads. Peng et al. (2015b) propose a notion of *Predicate Schemas* to capture interaction between entities at predicate level and instantiate them using knowledge sources like Wikipedia. These in-

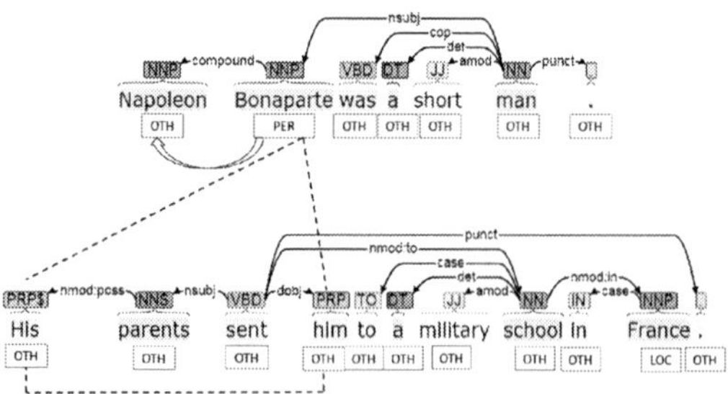

Figure 1: Input ULDG initialized with NER + Coreference. (Note: alias edges(E_a) are shown using dotted lines; participant edges (E_p) are shown using thick arrows; dependency edges (E_d) are shown using thin labelled arrows.)

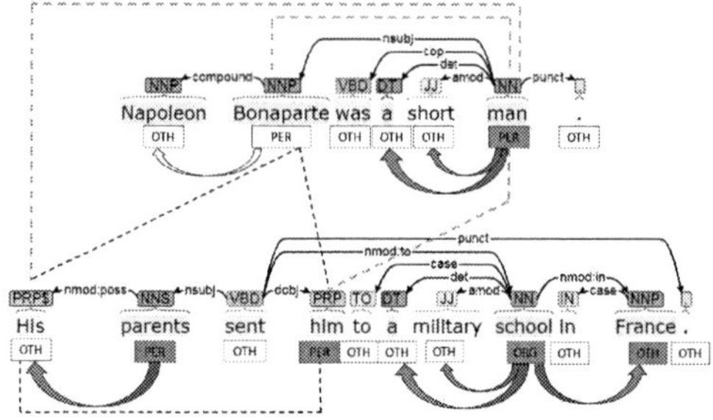

Figure 2: Output ULDG after applying Algorithm 1 on input ULDG in Figure 1. New E_a edges: ⟨man, Bonaparte⟩, ⟨man, him⟩, & ⟨man, His⟩ are added. Newly added E_p edges are highlighted with thick, filled arrows. Participant types of `man` & `school` are changed to PER & ORG respectively; type of `France` is changed to OTH.

stances of Predicate Schemas are then compiled into constraints in an Integer Linear Programming (ILP) based formulation to resolve coreferences. In addition to pronouns, our approach focuses on identification of common noun based aliases of a participant using MLN.

MLN has been used to solve the problem of coreference resolution (Poon and Domingos, 2008; Song et al., 2012). Our work differs from them as we build upon output of off-the-shelf coreference resolution system, rather than identifying aliases/coreferences from scratch. This helps in exploiting the strengths (such as linking pronoun mentions to their antecedents) of the existing systems and overcome the weaknesses (such as resolving generic NP mentions) by incorporating additional linguistic knowledge.

A more general and challenging problem involves resolution of bridging descriptions which study relationships between a definite description and its antecedent. As noted in (Vieira and Teufel, 1997; Poesio et al., 1997), bridging descriptions consider many different types of relationships between a definite description (definite generic NP) and its antecedent; e.g., synonymy, hyponymy, meronymy, events, compound nouns, etc. However, in this paper we focus on *identity* type of relationships only. Further, Vieira and Teufel (1997) use WordNet to identify these relationship types between definite descriptions. As described in Phase-I of algorithm 1 (Section 3), we use Word-Net for a completely different purpose of identifying participant type.[2] Gardent and Kow (2003) presented a corpus study of bridging definite descriptions and their typologies. They have identified several types of bridging relations like set-subset, event-argument etc.

3   Our Approach

Our approach has three broad phases: (I) Identification of participants, (II) MLN based formulation to identify aliases, and (III) Composite mention creation. We use a *Unified Linguistic Denotation Graph (ULDG)* representation of NLP-processed sentences in the input narrative. The ULDG unifies output from various stages of NLP pipeline such as dependency parsing, NER and coreference resolution, e.g., Figure 1 shows a sample ULDG.

Definition: A ULDG $G(V, E_d, E_p, E_a)$, corresponding to a set S of n sentences, is a vertex-labeled and edge-labeled graph. A node $u \in V$ corresponds to a token in S and its label is defined as: $L_u = (s, t, token, POS, p, a)$; where s : sentence index, t : token index, $token$, POS : part-of-speech tag of $token$, p denotes participant type ($p \in \{PER, ORG, LOC, OTHER (OTH)\}$) if u is a headword of a participant mention and a denotes canonical participant mention of corresponding group of aliases. There are three types of edges –

• $E_d = \{\langle u, v, dep \rangle$: directed dependency edge labelled with dep (dependency relation), which connects a governor (parent) token u to its dependent token $v\}$; e.g., $\langle$sent, parent, nsubj$\rangle$

• $E_p = \{\langle u, v \rangle$: directed edge, which connects headword u of a participant phrase to its each constituent word $v\}$; e.g., $\langle$Bonaparte, Napoleon$\rangle$

• $E_a = \{\langle u, v \rangle$: undirected edge, which connects nodes u and v which are headwords of aliases of the same participant $\}$; e.g., $\langle$him, Bonaparte$\rangle$

Our approach has been summarized in Algorithm 1. Its input is an ULDG $G(V, E_d, E_p, E_a)$ for a set S of given sentences. We initialize V, E_d, E_p and E_a using any standard dependency parser, NER and coreference resolution techniques[3].

---

input : G = ULDG for set of sentences S
output: G with updated participant and alias edges
```
// Phase-I: Basic participant mention
   identification
```
foreach $n \in G.nodes$ **do**
  if $n.POS$ *is noun* $\wedge\ n.p = OTH\ \wedge$
  $is\_generic\_NP\_head(G, n)$ **then**
    $n.p :=$
      $checkWordNetHypernyms(n.token)$
    if $n.p = OTH$ **then** continue
    foreach $\langle n, x, dep \rangle \in E_d$ **do**
      if $dep \in \{$**amod, compound, det**$\}$
      then $E_p := E_p \cup \{\langle n, x \rangle\}$

foreach $n \in G.nodes$ **do**
  if $n.POS$ *is pronoun* $\wedge\ (\exists x : \langle n, x \rangle \in E_a$ *such that* $x.p \neq OTH)$ **then** $n.p := x.p$

$G := resolveParticipantTypeConflict(G)$
```
// Phase-II: MLN-based alias detection
```
$E_a := E_a \cup \{\langle u, v \rangle$: where u and v are detected as aliases by $MLN\_encoded\_Linguistic\_Constraints()\}$
```
// Phase-III: Composite mention creation by
   merging dependent participant mentions
```
$G'(V', E') :=$ Subgraph of G, such that
$V' := \{n \in G : n.p \neq OTH\}$ and
$E' = \{\langle u, v, dep \rangle \in E_d : dep \in \{$**appos, nmod**$\}\}$
foreach $n \in G.nodes$ **do**
  if $n.p = OTH$ **then** continue
  $indParticipant := True$
  foreach $\langle x, n, dep \rangle \in E_d$ **do**
    if $dep \in \{$**appos, nmod**$\} \wedge x.p \neq OTH$
    then $indParticipant := False$

  if $\neg indParticipant$ **then** continue
  $depParticipants := DFS(G', n)$
  foreach $y \in depParticipants$ **do**
    $E_p := E_p \cup \{\langle n, y \rangle\}$
    foreach $\langle y, x \rangle \in E_p$ **do**
      $E_p := E_p \cup \{\langle n, x \rangle\}$
    $y.p := OTH$
    Drop from E_p all outgoing edges from y

foreach *clique* c *in subgraph* $(V, E_a) \subset G$ **do**
  foreach $n \in c.nodes$ **do**
    n.a := earliest participant mention in $c.nodes$

Algorithm 1: $identify\_participants\_\&\_aliases$

Our algorithm modifies the input ULDG in-place by updating node labels, E_p and E_a. Figure 1 shows an example of initialized input ULDG, which gets transformed by our algorithm to the output ULDG shown in Figure 2.

Phase-I: In this phase, we update participant type

---

[2]Further details are available in Figure A.1 and Table A.2 in the supplementary material.

[3]We use Stanford CoreNLP Toolkit (Manning et al., 2014)

Predicates	Description
$NEType(x, y)$	y is entity type of participant x
$CopulaConnect(x, y)$	Participants x and y are connected through a copula verb or a "copula-like" verb in E_d (e.g., become)
$Conj(x, y)$	Participants x and y are connected by a conjunction in E_d
$DiffVerbConnect(x, y)$	Participants x and y are connected through a "differentiating" verb or a copula-like verb in E_d (e.g. `tell`)
$LexSim(x, y)$	Participants x and y are lexically similar, i.e. having low edit distance
$Alias(x, y)$	Participants x and y are aliases of each other (used as a query predicate)

Hard rules	Description
$Alias(x, x)$; $Alias(x, y) \Rightarrow Alias(y, x)$	Reflexivity and symmetry of aliases
$Alias(x, y) \land Alias(y, z) \Rightarrow Alias(x, z)$ $Alias(x, y) \land \neg Alias(y, z) \Rightarrow \neg Alias(x, z)$	Transitivity of aliases
$Alias(x, y) \Rightarrow (NEType(x, z) \Leftrightarrow NEType(y, z))$	If x and y are aliases, their entity types should be same
$Conj(x, y) \Rightarrow \neg Alias(x, y)$	If x and y are conjuncts, then they are less likely to be aliases

Soft rules	Description
$CopulaConnect(x, y) \Rightarrow Alias(x, y)$	If x and y are connected though a copula or copula-like verb in E_d, then they are aliases of each other
$LexSim(x, y) \Rightarrow Alias(x, y)$	If x and y are lexically similar, then they are likely to be aliases
$DiffVerbConnect(x, y) \Rightarrow \neg Alias(x, y)$	If x and y are subjects / objects of a "differentiating" verb, then they are not likely to be aliases of each other

Table 2: MLN Predicates and Rules

of headword h of a generic NP if its Word-Net hypernyms contain PER/ORG/LOC indicating synsets. We also add new E_p edges from h to dependent nodes of h using dependency relations `compound`, `amod` or `det` (de Marneffe et al., 2014) to get corresponding mention boundaries. The function $resolveParticipantTypeConflict()$ ensures that participant types of all nodes in a single clique in E_a are same by giving higher priority to NER-induced type than WordNet-induced type.

Phase-II: In this phase, we encode linguistic rules in MLN to add new E_a edges. As elaborated by Mojica and Ng (2016), MLN gives the benefits of (i) ability to employ soft constraints, (ii) compact representation, and (iii) ease of specification of domain knowledge.

The predicates and key first-order logic rules are described in Table 2. Here, $Alias(x, y)$ is the only query predicate. Others are evidence predicates, whose observed groundings are specified using G. As we use a combination of hard rules (i.e., rules with infinite weight) and soft rules (i.e., rules with finite weights), probabilistic inference in MLN is necessary to get find most likely groundings of the predicate-$Alias(x, y)$. As the goal is to minimize supervision and to avoid dependence on annotated data, we rely on domain knowledge in the current version to set the MLN rule weights.

Phase-III: In this phase, we extract an auxiliary subgraph $G'(V', E') \subset G$; where V' contains only those nodes which correspond to headwords of basic participant mentions and E' contains only those edges incident on nodes in V' and labeled

with `appos` or `nmod`. We identify each independent participant mention in G' and merge its dependent mentions using depth first search (DFS) on G'.

Finally, each clique in E_a represents aliases of an unique participant. We use the earliest non-pronoun mention in text order as the canonical mention for that clique.

4 Experimental Analysis

Datasets: We evaluate our approach on history narratives as they are replete with challenging cases of alias detection. We choose public narratives of varying linguistic complexity to cover a spectrum of history: (i) famous personalities: Napoleon (**Nap**) (Littel, 2008), and Mao Zedong (**Mao**) (Wikipedia, 2018), (ii) a key event: Battle of Haldighati (**BoH**) (Chandra, 2007), and (iii) a major phenomenon: Fascism (**Fas**) (Littel, 2008). We manually annotated these datasets for the independent participant mentions and their aliases. For each alias group of participant mentions we use earliest non-pronoun mention as its canonical mention[4].

We also evaluate it on the newswire subset (**ACE**$_{nw}$) of standard ACE 2005 dataset (Walker et al., 2006). Entity mention annotations were transformed[5] such that only independent entity mentions and their aliases are used. We relied on **Nap** dataset to develop intuition for designing

---

[4]The annotated datasets are released with this draft.

[5]Transformation scripts are released as supplementary material.

the algorithm and tuning of MLN rules. All other datasets (**ACE**, **BoH**, **Fas**, and **Mao**) are unseen, independent test datasets.

Baselines: B1 is a standard approach to this problem where output of NER and coreference components of Stanford CoreNLP toolkit are combined to detect aliases. B2 is the state-of-the-art coreference resolution system based on (Peng et al., 2015a,b). M is our proposed alias detection approach (Algorithm 1).

Evaluation: The performance of all the approaches is evaluated at two levels: all independent participant mentions (i.e., *participant detection*) and their links with canonical mentions (i.e., *participant linking*). We use the standard F1 metric to measure performance of *participant detection*. For *participant linking*, we evaluate (Pradhan et al., 2014) the combined performance of participant mention identification and alias detection using the standard evaluation metrics, MUC (Vilain et al., 1995), BCUB (Bagga and Baldwin, 1998), Entity-based CEAF (CEAFe) (Luo, 2005) and their average.

Results: Results of the quantitative evaluation are summarized in Table 3. We observe that the proposed approach outperforms other baselines on all datasets.

Dataset & Approach		Participant mentions	Canonical mentions & aliases		
			BCUB	MUC	CEAFe
ACE$_{nw}$	B1	53.1	38.3	49.4	30.3
	B2	62.9	45.0	50.2	42.5
	M	**70.2**	**52.0**	**56.7**	**50.5**
Nap	B1	60.5	49.4	69.4	32.3
	B2	73.9	56.4	70.2	50.1
	M	**86.4**	**74.1**	**79.0**	**63.6**
BoH	B1	61.7	39.9	56.2	36.2
	B2	65.6	45.0	56.9	40.8
	M	**73.5**	**50.9**	**66.9**	**46.3**
Fas	B1	56.8	40.1	59.3	31.8
	B2	61.6	41.0	54.6	40.3
	M	**70.3**	**55.3**	**64.6**	**51.5**
Mao	B1	60.1	47.4	62.4	38.1
	B2	49.1	29.0	41.9	29.8
	M	**78.9**	**64.1**	**73.9**	**60.2**

Table 3: Experimental results (F_1 metric in %). B1 is combined output of NER and Coreference modules of (Manning et al., 2014). B2 is (Peng et al., 2015a). M is proposed method.

Correct identification of generic NPs as participant mentions, and accurate addition of alias edges due to MLN formulation lead to improved performance of Algorithm 1; e.g., in Table 1, the baselines fail to detect `a lieutenant` as an alias for `Napoleon Bonaparte`, but the pro-

posed approach succeeds as it exploits MLN rule $CopulaConnect(x, y) \Rightarrow Alias(x, y)$. As an illustration of the proposed approach, Table 4 shows the participant mentions and their corresponding canonical mentions for the example text in Table 1.

Sent. no.	Participant Mention	Canonical Mention
1	Napoleon Bonaparte	Napoleon Bonaparte
1	a short man	**Napoleon Bonaparte**
2	he	**Napoleon Bonaparte**
2	his parents	his parents
2	him	**Napoleon Bonaparte**
2	a military school in France	a military school in France
3	he	**Napoleon Bonaparte**
3	a lieutenant	**Napoleon Bonaparte**
4	Napoleon	**Napoleon Bonaparte**
4	the army of the new government	the army of the new government
5	royalist rebels	royalist rebels
5	the National Convention	the National Convention
5	a government official	a government official
5	the young lieutenant	**Napoleon Bonaparte**
5	the delegates	the delegates

Table 4: Output of Algorithm 1 for sentences in Table 1

5 Conclusions

Alias detection is an important and challenging NLP problem. We proposed a linguistically grounded approach to identify aliases of participants in a narrative. We observed that WordNet hypernym tree helps in identification of participant aliases mentioned using generic NPs. MLN proved to be an effective framework to encode linguistic knowledge and achieve better alias detection performance. Our approach was evaluated on history narratives which pose challenging alias detection cases and demonstrated better performance than the state-of-the-art approach. Our goal in current paper was to improve the output by exploiting the strengths (such as linking pronoun mentions to their antecedents) of off-the-shelf coreference algorithms and to overcome their weaknesses (such as resolving generic noun phrase mentions). As part of future work, we are planning to enhance existing MLN frameworks for coreference resolution by integrating the proposed MLN predicates and rules.

References

Amit Bagga and Breck Baldwin. 1998. Algorithms for scoring coreference chains. In *The first international conference on language resources and evaluation workshop on linguistics coreference*. Granada, volume 1, pages 563–566.

Harsimran Bedi, Sangameshwar Patil, Swapnil Hingmire, and Girish Palshikar. 2017. Event timeline generation from history textbooks. In *Proceedings of the 4th Workshop on Natural Language Processing Techniques for Educational Applications (NLPTEA 2017)*. pages 69–77.

Satish Chandra. 2007. *Medieval India: From Sultanat to the Mughals- Mughal Empire: Part Two*. Har Anand Publications.

Marie-Catherine de Marneffe, Timothy Dozat, Natalia Silveira, Katri Haverinen, Filip Ginter, Joakim Nivre, and Christopher D. Manning. 2014. Universal Stanford dependencies: A cross-linguistic typology. In *LREC 2014*. pages 4585–4592.

Claire Gardent, Hélène Manuélian, and Eric Kow. 2003. Which bridges for bridging definite descriptions? In *Proceedings of 4th International Workshop on Linguistically Interpreted Corpora (LINC-03) at EACL 2003*.

Paul Hsiung, Andrew Moore, Daniel Neill, and Jeff Schneider. 2005. Alias detection in link data sets. In *Proceedings of the International Conference on Intelligence Analysis*. volume 4.

McDougal Littel. 2008. *World History: Patterns of Interaction*. World History: Patterns of Int. Houghton Mifflin Harcourt Publishing Company.

Xiaoqiang Luo. 2005. On coreference resolution performance metrics. In *HLT/EMNLP 2005*. Association for Computational Linguistics, pages 25–32.

Christopher D. Manning, Mihai Surdeanu, John Bauer, Jenny Rose Finkel, Steven Bethard, and David McClosky. 2014. The Stanford CoreNLP Natural Language Processing Toolkit. In *ACL 2014*. pages 55–60.

Luis Gerardo Mojica and Vincent Ng. 2016. Markov logic networks for text mining: A qualitative and empirical comparison with integer linear programming. In *LREC 2016*.

Vincent Ng. 2017. Machine learning for entity coreference resolution: A retrospective look at two decades of research. In *AAAI, 2017*. pages 4877–4884.

Haoruo Peng, Kai-Wei Chang, and Dan Roth. 2015a. A Joint Framework for Coreference Resolution and Mention Head Detection. In *CoNLL 2015*. pages 12–21.

Haoruo Peng, Daniel Khashabi, and Dan Roth. 2015b. Solving Hard Coreference Problems. In *NAACL HLT 2015*. pages 809–819.

Massimo Poesio, Renata Vieira, and Simone Teufel. 1997. Resolving bridging references in unrestricted text. In *Proceedings of a Workshop on Operational Factors in Practical, Robust Anaphora Resolution for Unrestricted Texts*. ANARESOLUTION '97, pages 1–6.

Hoifung Poon and Pedro M. Domingos. 2008. Joint Unsupervised Coreference Resolution with Markov Logic. In *EMNLP 2008*.

Sameer Pradhan, Xiaoqiang Luo, Marta Recasens, Eduard Hovy, Vincent Ng, and Michael Strube. 2014. Scoring coreference partitions of predicted mentions: A reference implementation. In *Proceedings of the conference. Association for Computational Linguistics. Meeting*. volume 2014, pages 30–35.

Matthew Richardson and Pedro M. Domingos. 2006. Markov logic networks. *Machine Learning* 62(1-2):107–136.

Emili Sapena, Lluís Padró, and Jordi Turmo. 2007. Alias Assignment in Information Extraction. *Procesamiento del Lenguaje Natural* 39.

Yang Song, Jing Jiang, Wayne Xin Zhao, Sujian Li, and Houfeng Wang. 2012. Joint learning for coreference resolution with markov logic. In *EMNLP-CoNLL 2012*. pages 1245–1254.

Renata Vieira and Simone Teufel. 1997. Towards resolution of bridging descriptions. In *ACL-EACL 1997*. pages 522–524.

Marc Vilain, John Burger, John Aberdeen, Dennis Connolly, and Lynette Hirschman. 1995. A model-theoretic coreference scoring scheme. In *Proceedings of the 6th conference on Message understanding*. Association for Computational Linguistics, pages 45–52.

Christopher Walker, Stephanie Strassel, Julie Medero, and Kazuaki Maeda. 2006. Ace 2005 multilingual training corpus. *Linguistic Data Consortium, Philadelphia* 57.

Wikipedia. 2018. Mao zedong — Wikipedia, the free encyclopedia. [Online; accessed 22-Feb-2018]. https://en.wikipedia.org/wiki/Mao_Zedong.

Named Entity Recognition With Parallel Recurrent Neural Networks

Andrej Žukov-Gregorič[*‡], Yoram Bachrach[*†], and Sam Coope[*]

[*]DigitalGenius, 1 Canada Square, London E14 5AB
[‡]Department of Computer Science, Royal Holloway, University of London, Egham TW20 0EX
andrej.zukovgregoric.2010@live.rhul.ac.uk
yorambac@gmail.com
sam@digitalgenius.com

Abstract

We present a new architecture for named entity recognition. Our model employs multiple independent bidirectional LSTM units across the same input and promotes diversity among them by employing an inter-model regularization term. By distributing computation across multiple smaller LSTMs we find a reduction in the total number of parameters. We find our architecture achieves state-of-the-art performance on the CoNLL 2003 NER dataset.

1 Introduction

The ability to reason about entities in text is an important element of natural language understanding. Named entity recognition (NER) concerns itself with the identification of such entities. Given a sequence of words, the task of NER is to label each word with its appropriate corresponding entity type. Examples of entity types include *Person*, *Organization*, and *Location*. A special *Other* entity type is often added to the set of all types and is used to label words which do not belong to any of the other entity types.

Recently, neural network based approaches which use no language-specific resources, apart from unlabeled corpora for training word embeddings, have emerged. There has been a shift of focus from handcrafting better features to designing better neural architectures for solving NER.

In this paper, we propose a new parallel recurrent neural network model for entity recognition. We show that rather than using a single LSTM component, as many other recent architecture have, we instead resort to using multiple

[†] Now at Google DeepMind, 6 Pancras Square, London N1C 4AG.

smaller LSTM units. This has the benefit of reducing the total number of parameters in our model. We present results on the CoNNL 2003 English dataset and achieve the new state of the art results for models without help from an outside lexicons.

1.1 Related Work

Various approaches have been proposed to NER. Many of these approaches rely on hand-crafted feature engineering or language-specific or domain-specific resources (Zhou and Su, 2002; Chieu and Ng, 2002; Florian et al., 2003; Settles, 2004; Nadeau and Sekine, 2007). While such approaches can achieve high accuracy, they may fail to generalize to new languages, new corpora or new types of entities to be identified. Thus, applying such techniques in new domains requires making a heavy engineering investment.

Over time neural methods such as (Chiu and Nichols, 2015; Ma and Hovy, 2016; Luo et al., 2015; Lample et al., 2016) emerged. More recently (Peters et al., 2017; Reimers and Gurevych, 2017; Sato et al., 2017) have set the top benchmarks in the field.

Architecturally, our model is similar to those of (Zhu et al., 2017; Hidasi et al., 2016) with the most pronounced difference being that we (1) apply our parallel RNN units across the same input (2) explore a new regularization term for promoting diversity across what features our parallel RNNs extract and (3) explicitly motivate the architecture with a discussion about parameter complexity.

The need for a wider discussion on parameter complexity in the deep learning community is being pushed by the need to make complex neural models runnable in constrained environment such as field-programmable gate arrays (FPGAs) - for a great discussion relating to running LSTMs on FPGAs see (Guan et al., 2017). Additionally, complex models have proven difficult to use in certain

Proceedings of the 56th Annual Meeting of the Association for Computational Linguistics (Short Papers), pages 69–74
Melbourne, Australia, July 15 - 20, 2018. ©2018 Association for Computational Linguistics

domains such as embedded systems or finance due to their slowness. Our architecture lends itself to parallelization and attempts to tackle this problem.

2 Named Entity Recognition

Named Entity Recognition can be posited as a standard sequence classification problem where the dataset $D = \{(\mathbf{X}_i, \mathbf{y}_i)\}_{i=1}^k$ consists of example label pairs where both the examples and the labels are themselves sequences of word vectors and entity types, respectively.

Specifically, an input example $\mathbf{X}_i = (\mathbf{x}_{i,1}, \ldots, \mathbf{x}_{i,|X_i|})$ is a variable-length sequence of word vectors $\mathbf{x}_{i,j} \in \mathbb{R}^d$; the example's corresponding label $\mathbf{y}_i = (y_{i,1}, \ldots, y_{i,|X_i|})$ is a equal-length sequence of entity-type labels $y_{i,j} \in Y$ where Y is the set of all entity type labels and includes a special other 'O'-label with which all words that are not entities are labeled.

The goal is then to learn a parametrized mapping $f_\theta : \mathbf{X} \to \mathbf{y}$ from input words to output entity labels. One of the most commonly used class of models that handle this mapping are recurrent neural networks.

2.1 LSTM complexity

Long short term memory (LSTM) models belong to the family of recurrent neural network (RNN) models. They are often used as a component of much larger models, particularly in many NLP tasks including NER.

Classically, an LSTM cell is defined as follows (biases excluded for brevity):

$$
\begin{aligned}
\mathbf{i}_t &= \sigma(\boldsymbol{W}_i \mathbf{h}_{t-1} + \boldsymbol{U}_i \mathbf{x}_t) \\
\mathbf{f}_t &= \sigma(\mathbf{W}_f \mathbf{h}_{t-1} + \boldsymbol{U}_f \mathbf{x}_t) \\
\mathbf{o}_t &= \sigma(\boldsymbol{W}_o \mathbf{h}_{t-1} + \boldsymbol{U}_o \mathbf{x}_t) \\
\tilde{\mathbf{c}}_t &= \tanh(\boldsymbol{W}_c \mathbf{h}_{t-1} + \boldsymbol{U}_c \mathbf{x}_t) \\
\mathbf{c}_t &= \mathbf{f}_t \odot \mathbf{c}_{t-1} + \mathbf{i}_t \odot \tilde{\mathbf{c}}_t \\
\mathbf{h}_t &= \mathbf{o}_t \odot \tanh(\mathbf{c}_t)
\end{aligned}
$$

One way of measuring the complexity of a model is through its total number of parameters. Looking at the above, we note there are two parameter matrices, $\mathbf{W}$ and $\mathbf{U}$, for each of the three input gates and during cell update. If we let $\mathbf{W} \in \mathbb{R}^{n \times n}$ and $\mathbf{U} \in \mathbb{R}^{n \times m}$ then the total number of parameters in the model (excluding the bias terms) is $4(nm+n^2)$ which grows quadratically as n grows. Thus, increases in LSTM size can substantially increase the number of parameters.

3 Parallel RNNs

To reduce the total number of parameters we split a single LSTM into multiple equally-sized smaller ones:

$$
h_{k,t} = \text{LSTM}_k(h_{k,t-1}, \mathbf{x})
$$

where $k \in \{1, ..., K\}$. This has the effect of dividing the total number of parameters by a constant factor. The final hidden state h_t is then a concatenation of the hidden states of the smaller LSTMS:

$$
h_t = [h_{1,t}; h_{2,t}; ...; h_{K,t}]
$$

3.1 Promoting Diversity

To promote diversity amongst the constituent smaller LSTMs we add a orthogonality penalty *across* the smaller LSTMs. Recent research has used similar methods but applied to single LSTMs (Vorontsov et al., 2017).

We take the cell update recurrence parameters $\mathbf{W}_i$ across LSTMs (we omit the c in the subscript for brevity; the index i runs across the smaller LSTMs) and for any pair we wish the following to be true:

$$
\langle \text{vec}(W_c^{(i)}), \text{vec}(W_c^{(j)}) \rangle \approx 0
$$

.

To achieve this we pack the vectorized parameters into a matrix:

$$
\Phi = \begin{pmatrix} \text{vec}(W_c^{(1)}) \\ \text{vec}(W_c^{(2)}) \\ \vdots \\ \text{vec}(W_c^{(N)}) \end{pmatrix}
$$

and apply the following regularization term to our final loss:

$$
\lambda \sum_i \|\Phi\Phi^\top - I\|_F^2 \tag{1}
$$

3.2 Output and Loss

The concatenated output h_t is passed through a fully connected layer with bias before being passed through a final softmax layer:

$$
o_t = \text{softmax}(\mathbf{W}_{\text{out}} \hat{h}_t + b_{\text{out}})
$$

To extract a predicted entity type $\hat{y}_t$ at time t, we select the entity type corresponding to the most probable output:

$$\hat{y}_t = argmax(o_t)$$

The loss is defined as the sum of the softmax cross-entropy losses along the words in the input sequence. More precisely, we denote by $y_t^j \in 0, 1$ a binary indicator variable indicating whether word x_t truly is an entity of type j. The loss at time t is then defined to be $\mathcal{L}_t = -\sum_j y_t^j \log(o_t^j)$. Thus the overall loss is:

$$\mathcal{L} = -\sum_t \sum_j y_t^j \log(o_t^j)$$

3.3 Implementation Details

We use bidirectional LSTMs as our base recurrent unit and use pretrained word embeddings of size 100. These are the same embeddings used in (Lample et al., 2016). We concatenate to our word embeddings character-level embeddings similar to (Lample et al., 2016) but with a max pooling layer instead. Unlike with the parallel LSTMs, we only use a single character embedding LSTM.

Parameters are initialized using the method described by Glorot and Bengio (Glorot and Bengio, 2010). This approach scales the variance of a uniform distribution with regard to the root of the number of parameters in a layer. This approach has been found to speed up convergence compared to using a unit normal distribution for initialization.

Our model uses variational dropout (Gal and Ghahramani, 2016) between the hidden states of the parallel LSTMs. Recent work has shown this to be very effective at training LSTMs for language models (Merity et al., 2017). In our experiments, we use $p = 0.1$ as our dropping probability.

We experiment with different values of the regularization term parameter but settled on $\lambda = 0.01$.

Although vanilla stochastic gradient descent has been effective at training RNNs on language problems (Merity et al., 2017), we found that using the ADAM optimizer (Kingma and Ba, 2014) to be more effective at training our model. We experimented with different values for the learning rate α, increasing α from 10^{-3} to as high as 5×10^{-3} and still obtained good results.

Similarly, we kept a constant size for the character-level embeddings, using a unit bidirectional LSTM output size of $\dim(e^{\text{char}}) = 50$.

As previously discussed, we trained the network parameters using stochastic gradient descent (Werbos, 1990), augmented with the Adam optimizer (Kingma and Ba, 2014).

3.4 Relation to Ensemble Methods

Our model bears some resemblance to ensemble methods (Freund et al., 1996; Dietterich et al., 2000), which combine multiple "weak learners" into a single "strong learner"; One may view each of the parallel recurrent units of our model as a single "weak" neural network, and may consider our architecture as a way of combining these into a single "strong" network.

Despite the similarities, our model is very different from ensemble methods. First, as opposed to many boosting algorithms (Freund et al., 1996; Schapire and Singer, 1999; Dietterich et al., 2000) we do not "reweigh" training instances based on the loss incurred on them by a previous iteration. Second, unlike ensemble methods, our model is trained *end-to-end*, as a single large neural network. All the subcomponents are co-trained, so different subparts of the network may focus on different aspects of the input. This avoids redundant repeated computations across the units (and indeed, we encourage diversity between the units using our inter-module regularization). Finally, we note that our architecture does not simply combine the *prediction* of multiple classifiers; rather, we take the final *hidden layer* of each of the LSTM units (which contains more information than merely the entity class prediction), and combine this information using a feedforward network. This allows our architecture to examine inter-dependencies between pieces of information computed by the various components.

4 Experiments

We achieve state-of-the-art results on the CoNNL 2003 English NER dataset (see Table 1). Although we do not employ additional external resources (language specific dictionaries or gazetteers), our model is competitive even with some of the models that do.

To gain a better understanding of the performance of our model including how its various components affect performance we prepared four additional tables of runs.

Table 2 shows performance as a function of the number of RNN units with a fixed unit size. The

Model	F1
(Chieu and Ng, 2002)	88.31
(Florian et al., 2003)	88.76
(Ando and Zhang, 2005)	89.31
(Collobert et al., 2011)[‡]	89.59
(Huang et al., 2015)[‡]	90.10
(Chiu and Nichols, 2015)[‡]	90.77
(Ratinov and Roth, 2009)	90.80
(Lin and Wu, 2009)	90.90
(Passos et al., 2014)[‡*]	90.90
(Lample et al., 2016)[‡]	90.94
(Luo et al., 2015)[‡]	91.20
(Ma and Hovy, 2016)[‡]	91.21
(Sato et al., 2017)	91.28
(Chiu and Nichols, 2015)[‡*]	91.62
(Peters et al., 2017)[‡*]	91.93
This paper[‡]	**91.48** $\pm$0.22

Table 1: English NER F1 score of our model on the test set of CoNLL-2003 (English). During training we optimize for the development set and report test set results for our best performing development set model. The bounded F1 results we report ($\pm$0.22) are taken after 10 runs. For the purpose of comparison, we also list F1 scores of previous top-performance systems. ‡ marks the neural models. * marks model which use external resources.

number of units is clearly a hyperparameter which must be optimized for. We find good performance across the board (there is no catastrophic collapse in results) however when using 16 units we do outperform other models substantially. Even with very small unit sizes of 8 (Table 3) our models performs relatively well without a significant degradation in results. Table 4 shows and 5 show additional results for unit size and component impact on our best performing model.

5 Conclusion

We achieve state-of-the-art results on the CoNLL 2003 English dataset and introduce a new model motivated primarily by its ability to be easily distributable and reduce the total number of parameters. Further work should be done on evaluating it across different classification and sequence classification tasks to study its performance. Additionally, a run-time analysis show be conducted to compare speedups if the model is parallelized across CPU cores.

# RNN units	F_1
1	90.53 $\pm$0.31
2	90.79 $\pm$0.18
4	90.64 $\pm$0.24
8	91.09 $\pm$0.28
16	91.48 $\pm$0.22
32	90.68 $\pm$0.18

Table 2: Performance as a function of the number of RNN units with a fixed unit size of 64; averaged across 5 runs apart from the 16 unit (average across 10 runs).

# RNN units	Unit size	F_1
1	1024	87.54
2	512	91.25
4	256	91.29
8	128	91.31
16	64	91.48 $\pm$0.22
32	32	90.60
64	16	90.79
128	8	90.41

Table 3: Performance of our model with various unit sizes resulting in a fixed final output size h_t. Single runs apart from 16 unit.

Unit size	F_1
8	89.78
16	89.77
32	90.26
64	91.48 $\pm$0.22
128	89.28

Table 4: Performance as a function of the unit size for our best performing model (16 biLSTM units). Single runs apart from with size 64.

Component	F_1
No character embeddings	90.39
No orthogonal regularization	90.79
No Xavier initialization	91.09
No variational dropout	91.03
Mean pool instead of concat	90.49

Table 5: Impact of various architectural decisions on our best performing model (16 biLSTM units, 64 unit size). Single runs.

References

Rie Kubota Ando and Tong Zhang. 2005. A framework for learning predictive structures from multiple tasks and unlabeled data. *Journal of Machine Learning Research* 6(Nov):1817–1853.

Hai Leong Chieu and Hwee Tou Ng. 2002. Named entity recognition: a maximum entropy approach using global information. In *Proceedings of the 19th international conference on Computational linguistics-Volume 1*. Association for Computational Linguistics, pages 1–7.

Jason PC Chiu and Eric Nichols. 2015. Named entity recognition with bidirectional lstm-cnns. *arXiv preprint arXiv:1511.08308* .

Ronan Collobert, Jason Weston, Léon Bottou, Michael Karlen, Koray Kavukcuoglu, and Pavel Kuksa. 2011. Natural language processing (almost) from scratch. *Journal of Machine Learning Research* 12(Aug):2493–2537.

Thomas G Dietterich et al. 2000. Ensemble methods in machine learning. *Multiple classifier systems* 1857:1–15.

Radu Florian, Abe Ittycheriah, Hongyan Jing, and Tong Zhang. 2003. Named entity recognition through classifier combination. In *Proceedings of the seventh conference on Natural language learning at HLT-NAACL 2003-Volume 4*. Association for Computational Linguistics, pages 168–171.

Yoav Freund, Robert E Schapire, et al. 1996. Experiments with a new boosting algorithm. In *Icml*. volume 96, pages 148–156.

Yarin Gal and Zoubin Ghahramani. 2016. Dropout as a bayesian approximation: Representing model uncertainty in deep learning. In Maria Florina Balcan and Kilian Q. Weinberger, editors, *Proceedings of The 33rd International Conference on Machine Learning*. PMLR, New York, New York, USA, volume 48 of *Proceedings of Machine Learning Research*, pages 1050–1059. http://proceedings.mlr.press/v48/gal16.html.

Xavier Glorot and Yoshua Bengio. 2010. Understanding the difficulty of training deep feedforward neural networks. In *Proceedings of the Thirteenth International Conference on Artificial Intelligence and Statistics*. pages 249–256.

Yijin Guan, Zhihang Yuan, Guangyu Sun, and Jason Cong. 2017. Fpga-based accelerator for long short-term memory recurrent neural networks. In *Design Automation Conference (ASP-DAC), 2017 22nd Asia and South Pacific*. IEEE, pages 629–634.

Balázs Hidasi, Massimo Quadrana, Alexandros Karatzoglou, and Domonkos Tikk. 2016. Parallel recurrent neural network architectures for feature-rich session-based recommendations. In *Proceedings of the 10th ACM Conference on Recommender Systems*. ACM, pages 241–248.

Zhiheng Huang, Wei Xu, and Kai Yu. 2015. Bidirectional lstm-crf models for sequence tagging. *arXiv preprint arXiv:1508.01991* .

Diederik Kingma and Jimmy Ba. 2014. Adam: A method for stochastic optimization. *arXiv preprint arXiv:1412.6980* .

Guillaume Lample, Miguel Ballesteros, Sandeep Subramanian, Kazuya Kawakami, and Chris Dyer. 2016. Neural architectures for named entity recognition. *arXiv preprint arXiv:1603.01360* .

Dekang Lin and Xiaoyun Wu. 2009. Phrase clustering for discriminative learning. In *Proceedings of the Joint Conference of the 47th Annual Meeting of the ACL and the 4th International Joint Conference on Natural Language Processing of the AFNLP: Volume 2-Volume 2*. Association for Computational Linguistics, pages 1030–1038.

Gang Luo, Xiaojiang Huang, Chin-Yew Lin, and Zaiqing Nie. 2015. Joint named entity recognition and disambiguation. In *Proc. EMNLP*. pages 879–880.

Xuezhe Ma and Eduard Hovy. 2016. End-to-end sequence labeling via bi-directional lstm-cnns-crf. *arXiv preprint arXiv:1603.01354* .

Stephen Merity, Nitish Shirish Keskar, and Richard Socher. 2017. Regularizing and optimizing lstm language models. *arXiv preprint arXiv:1708.02182* .

David Nadeau and Satoshi Sekine. 2007. A survey of named entity recognition and classification. *Lingvisticae Investigationes* 30(1):3–26.

Alexandre Passos, Vineet Kumar, and Andrew McCallum. 2014. Lexicon infused phrase embeddings for named entity resolution. *arXiv preprint arXiv:1404.5367* .

Matthew E Peters, Waleed Ammar, Chandra Bhagavatula, and Russell Power. 2017. Semi-supervised sequence tagging with bidirectional language models. *arXiv preprint arXiv:1705.00108* .

Lev Ratinov and Dan Roth. 2009. Design challenges and misconceptions in named entity recognition. In *Proceedings of the Thirteenth Conference on Computational Natural Language Learning*. Association for Computational Linguistics, pages 147–155.

Nils Reimers and Iryna Gurevych. 2017. Reporting score distributions makes a difference: Performance study of lstm-networks for sequence tagging. *arXiv preprint arXiv:1707.09861* .

Motoki Sato, Hiroyuki Shindo, Ikuya Yamada, and Yuji Matsumoto. 2017. Segment-level neural conditional random fields for named entity recognition. In *Proceedings of the Eighth International Joint Conference on Natural Language Processing (Volume 2: Short Papers)*. volume 2, pages 97–102.

Robert E Schapire and Yoram Singer. 1999. Improved boosting algorithms using confidence-rated predictions. *Machine learning* 37(3):297–336.

Burr Settles. 2004. Biomedical named entity recognition using conditional random fields and rich feature sets. In *Proceedings of the International Joint Workshop on Natural Language Processing in Biomedicine and its Applications*. Association for Computational Linguistics, pages 104–107.

Eugene Vorontsov, Chiheb Trabelsi, Samuel Kadoury, and Chris Pal. 2017. On orthogonality and learning recurrent networks with long term dependencies. *arXiv preprint arXiv:1702.00071* .

Paul J Werbos. 1990. Backpropagation through time: what it does and how to do it. *Proceedings of the IEEE* 78(10):1550–1560.

GuoDong Zhou and Jian Su. 2002. Named entity recognition using an hmm-based chunk tagger. In *proceedings of the 40th Annual Meeting on Association for Computational Linguistics*. Association for Computational Linguistics, pages 473–480.

Danhao Zhu, Si Shen, Xin-Yu Dai, and Jiajun Chen. 2017. Going wider: Recurrent neural network with parallel cells. *arXiv preprint arXiv:1705.01346* .

Type-Sensitive Knowledge Base Inference
Without Explicit Type Supervision

Prachi Jain[*1] and **Pankaj Kumar**[*1] and **Mausam**[1] and **Soumen Chakrabarti**[2]

[1]Indian Institute of Technology, Delhi
{p6.jain, k97.pankaj}@gmail.com, mausam@cse.iitd.ac.in
[2]Indian Institute of Technology, Bombay
soumen@cse.iitb.ac.in

Abstract

State-of-the-art knowledge base completion (KBC) models predict a score for every known or unknown fact via a latent factorization over entity and relation embeddings. We observe that when they fail, they often make entity predictions that are incompatible with the type required by the relation. In response, we enhance each base factorization with two type-compatibility terms between entity-relation pairs, and combine the signals in a novel manner. *Without* explicit supervision from a type catalog, our proposed modification obtains up to 7% MRR gains over base models, and new state-of-the-art results on several datasets. Further analysis reveals that our models better represent the latent types of entities and their embeddings also predict supervised types better than the embeddings learned by baseline models.

1 Introduction

Knowledge bases (KBs) store facts in the form of relations (r) between subject entity (s) and object entity (o), e.g., $\langle$Obama, born-in, Hawaii$\rangle$. Since KBs are typically incomplete (Bollacker et al., 2008), the task of KB Completion (**KBC**) attempts to infer new tuples from a given KB. Neural approaches to KBC, e.g., Complex (Trouillon et al., 2016) and DistMult (Yang et al., 2015), calculate the score $f(s, r, o)$ of a tuple (s, r, o) via a latent factorization over entity and relation embeddings, and use these scores to predict the validity of an unseen tuple.

A model is evaluated over queries of the form $\langle s^*, r^*, ?\rangle$. It ranks all entities o in the descend-ing order of tuple scores $f(s^*, r^*, o)$, and credit is assigned based on the rank of gold entity o^*. Our preliminary analysis of DistMult (**DM**) and Complex (**CX**) reveals that they make frequent errors by ranking entities that are not compatible with types expected as arguments of r^* high. In **19.5%** of predictions made by DM on FB15K, the top prediction has a type different from what is expected (see Table 1 for illustrative examples).

In response, we propose a modification to base models (DM, Complex) by explicitly modeling type compatibility. Our modified function $f'(s, r, o)$ is the product of three terms: the original tuple score $f(s, r, o)$, subject type-compatibility between r and s, and object type-compatibility between r and o. Our type-sensitive models, **TypeDM** and **TypeComplex**, do not expect any additional type-specific supervision — they induce all embeddings using only the original KB.

Experiments over three datasets show that all typed models outperform base models by significant margins, obtaining new state-of-the-art results in several cases. We perform additional analyses to assess if the learned embeddings indeed capture the type information well. We find that embeddings from typed models can predict known symbolic types better than base models.

Finally, we note that an older model called E (Riedel et al., 2013) can be seen as modeling type compatibilities. Moreover, previous work has explored additive combinations of DM and E (Garcia-Duran et al., 2015b; Toutanova and Chen, 2015). We directly compare against these models and find that, our proposal outperforms both E, DM and their linear combinations.

We contribute open-source implementations[1] of all models and experiments discussed in this paper

---

*Equal contribution.

[1]https://github.com/dair-iitd/KBI

Proceedings of the 56th Annual Meeting of the Association for Computational Linguistics (Short Papers), pages 75–80
Melbourne, Australia, July 15 - 20, 2018. ©2018 Association for Computational Linguistics

for further research.

2   Background and Related Work

We are given an incomplete KB with entities $\mathcal{E}$ and relations $\mathcal{R}$. The KB also contains $\mathcal{T} = \{\langle s, r, o \rangle\}$, a set of known valid tuples, each with subject and object entities $s, o \in \mathcal{E}$, and relation $r \in \mathcal{R}$. Our goal is to predict the validity of any tuple not present in $\mathcal{T}$. Popular top performing models for this task are Complex and DM.

In Complex, each entity e (resp., relation r) is represented as a complex vector $\boldsymbol{a}_e \in \mathbb{C}^D$ (resp., $\boldsymbol{b}_r \in \mathbb{C}^D$). Tuple score $f_{\text{CX}}(s, r, o) = \Re\left(\sum_{d=1}^{D} a_{sd} b_{rd} a_{od}^{\star}\right)$, where $\Re(z)$ is real part of z, and $z^{\star}$ is complex conjugate of z. Holographic embeddings (Nickel et al., 2016) are algebraically equivalent to Complex. In DM, each entity e is represented as a vector $\boldsymbol{a}_e \in \mathbb{R}^D$, each relation r as a vector $\boldsymbol{b}_r \in \mathbb{R}^D$, and the tuple score $f_{\text{DM}}(s, r, o) = \langle \boldsymbol{a}_s, \boldsymbol{b}_r, \boldsymbol{a}_o \rangle = \sum_{d=1}^{D} a_{sd} b_{rd} a_{od}$. Earlier, Riedel et al. (2013) proposed a different model called E: relation r is represented by two vectors $\boldsymbol{v}_r, \boldsymbol{w}_r \in \mathbb{R}^D$, and the tuple score $f_{\text{E}}(s, r, o) = \boldsymbol{a}_s \cdot \boldsymbol{v}_r + \boldsymbol{a}_o \cdot \boldsymbol{w}_r$. E may be regarded as a relation prediction model that depends purely on type compatibility checking.

Observe that, in $\langle \boldsymbol{a}_s, \boldsymbol{b}_r, \boldsymbol{a}_o \rangle$, $\boldsymbol{b}_r$ mediates a direct compatibility between s and o for relation r, whereas, in $\boldsymbol{a}_s \cdot \boldsymbol{v}_r + \boldsymbol{a}_o \cdot \boldsymbol{w}_r$, we are scoring how well s can serve as subject and o as object of the relation r. Thus, in the second case, $\boldsymbol{a}_e$ is expected to encode the type(s) of entity e, where, by 'type', we loosely mean "information that helps decide if e can participate in a relation r, as subject or object." Heuristic filtering of the entities that do not match the desired type at test time has been known to improve accuracy (Toutanova et al., 2015; Krompaß et al., 2015). Our typed models formalize this within the embeddings and allow for discovery of latent types without additional data. Krompaß et al. (2015) also use heuristic typing of entities for generating negative samples while training the model. Our experiment finds that this approach is not very competitive against our typed models.

3   TypeDM and TypeComplex

Representation: We start with DM as the base model; the Complex case is identical. The first key modification (see Figure 1) is that each entity e is now represented by *two* vectors: $\boldsymbol{u}_e \in \mathbb{R}^K$ to encode *type* information, and $\boldsymbol{a}_e \in \mathbb{R}^{D'}$ to encode

information. Typically, $K \ll D'$. The second, concomitant modification is that each relation r is now associated with *three* vectors: $\boldsymbol{b}_r \in \mathbb{R}^{D'}$ as before, and also $\boldsymbol{v}_r, \boldsymbol{w}_r \in \mathbb{R}^K$. $\boldsymbol{v}_r$ and $\boldsymbol{w}_r$ encode the expected types for subject and object entities.

An ideal way to train type embeddings would be to provide canonical type signatures for each relation and entity. Unfortunately, these aspects of realistic KBs are themselves incomplete (Neelakantan and Chang, 2015; Murty et al., 2018). Our models train all embeddings using $\mathcal{T}$ only and don't rely on any explicit type supervision.

DM uses $(E + R)D$ model weights for a KB with R relations and E entities, whereas TypeDM uses $E(D' + K) + R(D' + 2K)$. To make comparisons fair, we set D' and K so that the total number of model weights (real or complex) are about the same for base and typed models.

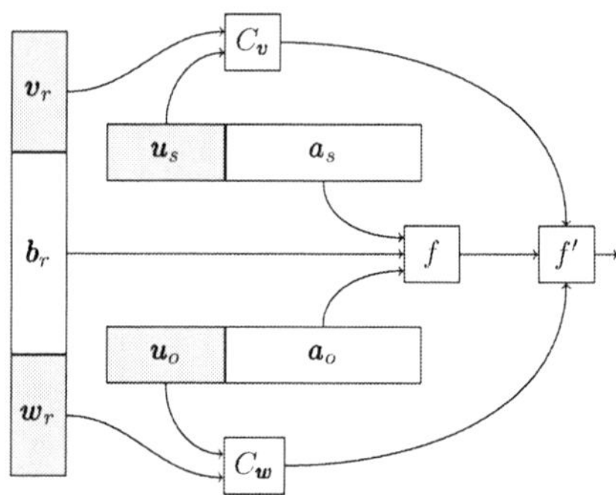

Figure 1: TypeDM and TypeComplex.

Prediction: DM's base prediction score for tuple (s, r, o) is $\langle \boldsymbol{a}_s, \boldsymbol{b}_r, \boldsymbol{a}_o \rangle$. We apply a (sigmoid) nonlinearity:

$$f(s, r, o) = \sigma(\langle \boldsymbol{a}_s, \boldsymbol{b}_r, \boldsymbol{a}_o \rangle), \qquad (1)$$

and then combine with two additional terms that measure type compatibility between the subject and the relation, and the object and the relation:

$$f'(s, r, o) = f(s, r, o)\, C_{\boldsymbol{v}}(s, r)\, C_{\boldsymbol{w}}(o, r), \qquad (2)$$

where $C_{\boldsymbol{x}}(e, r)$ is a function that measures the compatibility between the type embedding of e for a given argument slot of r:

$$C_{\boldsymbol{x}}(e, r) = \sigma(\boldsymbol{x}_r \cdot \boldsymbol{u}_e) \qquad (3)$$

If each of the three terms in Equation 2 is interpreted as a probability, $f'(s, r, o)$ corresponds to a simple logical AND of the three conditions.

We want $f'(s, r, o)$ to be almost 1 for positive instances (tuples known to be in the KG) and close to 0 for negative instances (tuples not in the KG). For a negative instance, one or more of the three terms may be near zero. There is no guidance to the learner on which term to drive down.

Subject s	Relation r	Gold Object o	Prediction 1	Prediction 2
Howard Leslie Shore	follows-religion	Jewism (religion)	Walk Hard (film)	21 Jump Street (film)
Spyglass Entertainment	headquarter-located-in	El lay (location)	The Real World (tv)	Contraband (film)
Les Fradkin	born-in-location	New York (location)	Federico Fellini (person)	Louie De palma (person)
Eugene Alden Hackman	studied	Rural Journalism (education)	Loudon Snowden Wainwright III (person)	The Bourne Legacy (film)
Chief Phillips (film)	released-in-region	Yankee land (location)	Akira Isida (person)	Presidential Medal of Freedom (award)

Table 1: Samples of top two DM predictions (having inconsistent types) on FB15K. TypeDM predicts entities of the correct type in top positions in the corresponding examples.

Contrastive Sampling: Training data consist of positive gold tuples (s, r, o) and negative tuples, which are obtained by perturbing each positive tuple by replacing either s or o with a randomly sampled s' or o'. This offers the learning algorithm positive and negative instances. The models are trained such that observed tuples have higher scores than unobserved ones.

Loss Functions: We implement two common loss objectives. The log-likelihood loss first computes the probability of predicting a response o for a query $(s, r, ?)$ as follows:

$$\Pr(o|s, r) = \frac{\exp(\beta f'(s, r, o))}{\sum_{o'} \exp(\beta f'(s, r, o'))} \quad (4)$$

Because $f' \in [0, 1]$ for typed models, we scale it with a hyper-parameter $\beta > 0$ (a form of inverse temperature) to allow $\Pr(o|s, r)$ to take values over the full range $[0, 1]$ in loss minimization.

The sum over o' in the denominator is sampled based on contrastive sampling, so the left hand side is not a formal probability (exactly as in DM). A similar term is added for $\Pr(s|r, o)$. The **log-likelihood loss** minimizes:

$$- \sum_{\langle s,r,o \rangle \in \mathcal{P}} \Big(\log Pr(o|s, r; \theta) + \log Pr(s|o, r; \theta) \Big) \quad (5)$$

The summation is over $\mathcal{P}$ which is the set of all positive facts. Following Trouillon et al. (2016), we also implement the **logistic loss**

$$\sum_{\langle s,r,o \rangle \in \mathcal{T}} \log \left[1 + e^{-Y_{sro} f'(s,r,o)} \right] \quad (6)$$

Here Y_{sro} is 1 if the fact (s, r, o) is true and -1 otherwise. Also, $\mathcal{T}$ is the set of all positive facts along with the negative samples. With logistic loss, model weights θ are L2-regularized and gradient norm is clipped at 1.

4 Experiments

Datasets: We evaluate on three standard data sets, FB15K, FB15K-237, and YAGO3-10 (Bor-

des et al., 2013; Toutanova et al., 2015; Dettmers et al., 2017). We retain the exact train, dev and test folds used in previous works. TypeDM and TypeComplex are competitive on the WN18 data set (Bordes et al., 2013), but we omit those results, as WN18 has 18 very generic relations (e.g., hyponym, hypernym, antonym, meronym), which do not give enough evidence for inducing types.

Model	Embedding dimensions	Number of parameters
E	200	3,528,200
DM+E	100+100	3,393,700
DM	200	3,259,200
TypeDM	180+19	3,268,459
Complex	200	6,518,400
TypeComplex	180+19	6,201,739

Table 2: Sizes were approximately balanced between base and typed models (FB15K).

Metrics: As is common, we regard test instances $(s, r, ?)$ as a task of ranking o, with gold o^* known. We report MRR (Mean Reciprocal Rank) and the fraction of queries where o^* is recalled within rank 1 and rank 10 (HITS). The *filtered* evaluation (Garcia-Duran et al., 2015a) removes valid train or test tuples ranking above (s, r, o^*) for scoring purposes.

Hyperparameters: We run AdaGrad for up to 1000 epochs for all losses, with early stopping on the dev fold to prevent overfitting. All the models generally converge after 300-400 epochs, except TypeDM that exhausts 1000 epochs. E, DM, DM+E and Complex use 200 dimensional vectors. All except E perform best with logistic loss and 20 negative samples (obtained by randomly corrupting s and r) per positive fact. This is determined by doing a hyperparameter search on a set $\{10, 20, 50, 100, 200, 400\}$.

For typed models we first perform hyperparameter search for size of type embeddings (K) such that total entity embedding size remains 200. We get the best results at $K = 20$, from among values in $\{10, 20, 30, 50, 80, 100, 120\}$. This hyperparameter search is done for the TypeDM model (which is faster to train than TypeComplex) on FB15k dataset, and the selected split is used for

Model	FB15K			FB15K237			YAGO3-10		
	MRR	HITS@1	HITS@10	MRR	HITS@1	HITS@10	MRR	HITS@1	HITS@10
E	23.40	17.39	35.29	21.30	14.51	36.38	7.87	6.22	10.00
DM+E	60.84	49.53	79.70	38.15	28.06	58.02	52.48	38.72	**77.40**
DM	67.47	56.52	84.86	37.21	27.43	56.12	55.31	46.80	70.76
TypeDM	75.01	66.07	87.92	38.70	29.30	57.36	58.16	51.36	70.08
Complex	70.50	61.00	86.09	37.58	26.97	55.98	54.86	46.90	69.08
TypeComplex	**75.44**	**66.32**	**88.51**	**38.93**	**29.57**	**57.50**	**58.65**	**51.62**	70.42

Table 3: KBC performance for base, typed, and related formulations. Typed models outperform their base models across all datasets.

all the typed models. To balance total model sizes (Table 2), we choose $K = 19$ dimensions for u_e, v_r, w_r and 180 dimensions for a_e, b_r.[2]

Typed models and E perform best with 400 negative samples per positive tuple while using log-likelihood loss (robust to a larger number of negative facts as opposed to logistic loss, which falls for class imbalance). FB15K and YAGO3-10 use L2 regularization coefficient of 2.0, and it is 5.0 for FB15K-237. Note that the L2 regularization penalty is applied to only those entities and relations that are a part of that batch update, as proposed by Trouillon et al. (2016). β is set to 20.0 for the typed models, and 1.0 for other models if they use the log-likelihood loss. Entity embeddings are unit normalized at the end of every epoch, for the type models. Also, we find that in TypeDM scaling the embeddings of the base model to unit norm performs better than using L2 regularization.

Results: Table 3 shows that TypeDM and TypeComplex dominate across all data sets. E by itself is understandably weak, and DM+E does not lift it much. Each typed model improves upon the corresponding base model on all measures, underscoring the value of type compatibility scores.[3] To the best of our knowledge, the results of our typed models are competitive with various reported results for models of similar sizes that do not use any additional information, e.g., soft rules (Guo et al., 2018), or textual corpora (Toutanova et al., 2015).

We also compare against the heuristic genera-

tion of type-sensitive negative samples (Krompaß et al., 2015). For this experiment, we train a Complex model using this heuristically generated negative set, and use standard evaluation, as in all other models. We find that all the models reported in Table 3 outperform this approach.

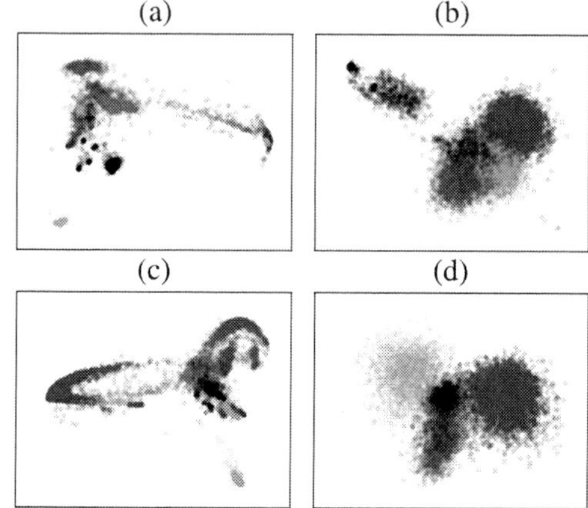

Figure 2: Projection of vectors representing entities belonging to frequent KB types- {**people**, location, **organisation**, film, **sports**}: a: TypeDM,u_e; b: TypeDM,a_e; c: TypeComplex,u_e; d: DM,a_e.

5   Analysis of Typed Embeddings

We perform two further analyses to assess whether the embeddings produced by typed models indeed capture type information better. For these experiments, we try to correlate (and predict) known symbolic types of an entity using the unsupervised embeddings produced by the models. We take a fine catalog of most frequent 90 freebase types over the 14,951 entities in the FB15k dataset (Xie et al., 2016). We exclude `/common/topic` as it occurs with most entities. On an average each entity has 12 associated types.

1. Clustering Entity/Type Embeddings: For this experiment we subselect entities in FB15k that

---

[2] Notice that a typed model has a slightly higher number of parameters for relation embeddings, because it needs to maintain *two* type embeddings of size K, over and above b_r. Using $K = 19$ reduced and brought the total number of parameters closer to that of the base model, for a fair direct comparison. The model performance did not differ by much when using either of the options (i.e., $K = 19$ or 20).

[3] For direct comparisons with published work, we choose 200 and 400 parameters per entity for DM and Complex respectively (Complex model has two 200 dimensional embeddings per entity). DM and TypeDM, on increasing the dimensionality to 400, yield MRR scores of 69.79 and 78.91, respectively, for FB15K.

Method	Embed-ding	Size	H	C	Type F1
TypeDM	u_e	19	66.72	66.29	81.77
TypeDM	a_e	180	57.89	59.67	75.96
TypeDM	Both	199	**66.75**	**66.29**	82.57
DM	a_e	200	51.40	48.12	81.34
TypeComplex	u_e	19	65.90	62.97	82.70
TypeComplex	a_e	180x2	50.76	48.57	74.75
TypeComplex	Both	379	66.03	63.09	84.14
Complex	a_e	200x2	51.56	47.20	81.58
DM+E	u_e	19	0.48	2.05	74.66
DM+E	a_e	180	49.62	47.24	82.72
DM+E	Both	199	49.66	47.26	82.68
E	a_e	200	39.83	37.62	74.23

Table 4: Interpretation of embeddings wrt supervised types: cluster homogeneity H, completeness C, and type prediction F1 score.

belong to one of the 5 types (people, location, organization, film, and sports) from the freebase dataset. These cover 84.88% of FB15K entities. We plot the FB15K entities e using the PCA projection of u_e and a_e in Figure 2, color-coding their types. We observe that u_e separates the type clusters better than a_e, suggesting that u_e vectors indeed collect type information. We also perform k-means clustering of u_e and a_e embeddings of these entities, as available from different models. We report cluster homogeneity and completeness scores (Rosenberg and Hirschberg, 2007) in Table 4. Typed models yield superior clusters.

2. Prediction of Symbolic Types: We train a single-layer network that inputs embeddings from various models and predicts a set of symbolic types from the KB. This tells us the extent to which the embeddings capture KB type information (that was not provided explicitly during training). Table 4 reports average macro F1 score (5-fold cross validation). Embeddings from TypeDM and TypeComplex are generally better predictors than embeddings learned by Complex, DM and E. $u_e \in \mathbb{R}^{19}$ is often better than $a_e \in \mathbb{R}^{180}$ or more, for typed models. DM+E with 199 model weights narrowly beats TypeDM with 19 weights, but recall that it has poorer KBC scores.

6 Conclusion and Future Work

We propose an unsupervised typing gadget, which enhances top-of-the-line base models for KBC (DistMult, Complex) with two type-compatibility functions, one between r and s and another between r and o. Without explicit supervision from any type catalog, our typed variants (with similar number of parameters as base models) substan-tially outperform base models, obtaining up to 7% MRR improvements and over 10% improvements in the correctness of the top result. To confirm that our models capture type information better, we correlate the embeddings learned without type supervision with existing type catalogs. We find that our embeddings indeed separate and predict types better. In future work, combining type-sensitive embeddings with a focus on less frequent relations (Xie et al., 2017), more frequent entities (Dettmers et al., 2017), or side information such as inference rules (Guo et al., 2018; Jain and Mausam, 2016) or textual corpora (Toutanova et al., 2015) may further increase KBC accuracy. It may also be of interest to integrate the typing approach here with the combinations of tensor and matrix factorization models for KBC (Jain et al., 2018).

Acknowledgements

This work is supported by Google language understanding and knowledge discovery focused research grants, a Bloomberg award, an IBM SUR award, and a Visvesvaraya faculty award by Govt. of India to the third author. It is also supported by a TCS Fellowship to the first author. We thank Microsoft Azure sponsorships, IIT Delhi HPC facility and the support of nVidia Corporation for computational resources.

References

Kurt Bollacker, Colin Evans, Praveen Paritosh, Tim Sturge, and Jamie Taylor. 2008. Freebase: a collaboratively created graph database for structuring human knowledge. In *SIGMOD Conference*. pages 1247–1250. http://ids.snu.ac.kr/w/images/9/98/sc17.pdf.

Antoine Bordes, Nicolas Usunier, Alberto Garcia-Duran, Jason Weston, and Oksana Yakhnenko. 2013. Translating embeddings for modeling multi-relational data. In *NIPS Conference*. pages 2787–2795. http://papers.nips.cc/paper/5071-translating-embeddings-for-modeling-multi-relational-data.pdf.

Tim Dettmers, Pasquale Minervini, Pontus Stenetorp, and Sebastian Riedel. 2017. Convolutional 2d knowledge graph embeddings. *arXiv preprint arXiv:1707.01476* .

Alberto Garcia-Duran, Antoine Bordes, and Nicolas Usunier. 2015a. Composing relationships with translations. In *EMNLP Conference*. pages 286–290. http://www.aclweb.org/anthology/D15-1034.

Alberto Garcia-Duran, Antoine Bordes, Nicolas Usunier, and Yves Grandvalet. 2015b. Combining two and three-way embeddings models for link prediction in knowledge bases. *arXiv preprint arXiv:1506.00999* https://arxiv.org/pdf/1506.00999.

Shu Guo, Quan Wang, Lihong Wang, Bin Wang, and Li Guo. 2018. Knowledge graph embedding with iterative guidance from soft rules. In *Proceedings of the Thirty-Second AAAI Conference on Artificial Intelligence*.

Prachi Jain and Mausam. 2016. Knowledge-guided linguistic rewrites for inference rule verification. In *Proceedings of the 2016 Conference of the North American Chapter of the Association for Computational Linguistics: Human Language Technologies*. pages 86–92.

Prachi Jain, Shikhar Murty, Mausam, and Soumen Chakrabarti. 2018. Mitigating the effect of out-of-vocabulary entity pairs in matrix factorization for kb inference. In *Proceedings of the Twenty-Sixth International Joint Conference on Artificial Intelligence, IJCAI-18*.

Denis Krompaß, Stephan Baier, and Volker Tresp. 2015. Type-constrained representation learning in knowledge graphs. In *International Semantic Web Conference*. Springer, pages 640–655.

Shikhar Murty, Patrik Verga, Luke Vilnis, Irena Radovanovic, and Andrew McCallum. 2018. Hierarchical losses and new resources for fine-grained entity typing and linking. In *Proceedings of the 56th Annual Meeting of the Association for Computational Linguistics*. Association for Computational Linguistics.

Arvind Neelakantan and Ming-Wei Chang. 2015. Inferring missing entity type instances for knowledge base completion: New dataset and methods. *In NAACL*.

Maximilian Nickel, Lorenzo Rosasco, Tomaso A Poggio, et al. 2016. Holographic embeddings of knowledge graphs. In *AAAI Conference*. pages 1955–1961. https://arxiv.org/abs/1510.04935.

Sebastian Riedel, Limin Yao, Andrew McCallum, and Benjamin M Marlin. 2013. Relation extraction with matrix factorization and universal schemas. In *NAACL Conference*. pages 74–84. http://www.anthology.aclweb.org/N/N13/N13-1008.pdf.

Andrew Rosenberg and Julia Hirschberg. 2007. V-measure: A conditional entropy-based external cluster evaluation measure. In *EMNLP Conference*. http://aclweb.org/anthology/D/D07/D07-1043.pdf.

Kristina Toutanova and Danqi Chen. 2015. Observed versus latent features for knowledge base and text inference. In *Proceedings of the 3rd Workshop on Continuous Vector Space Models and their Compositionality*. pages 57–66. http://www.aclweb.org/anthology/W15-4007.

Kristina Toutanova, Danqi Chen, Patrick Pantel, Hoifung Poon, Pallavi Choudhury, and Michael Gamon. 2015. Representing text for joint embedding of text and knowledge bases. In *EMNLP Conference*. pages 1499–1509. https://www.aclweb.org/anthology/D/D15/D15-1174.pdf.

Théo Trouillon, Johannes Welbl, Sebastian Riedel, Éric Gaussier, and Guillaume Bouchard. 2016. Complex embeddings for simple link prediction. In *ICML*. pages 2071–2080. http://arxiv.org/abs/1606.06357.

Qizhe Xie, Xuezhe Ma, Zihang Dai, and Eduard Hovy. 2017. An interpretable knowledge transfer model for knowledge base completion. *arXiv preprint arXiv:1704.05908* https://arxiv.org/pdf/1704.05908.pdf.

Ruobing Xie, Zhiyuan Liu, and Maosong Sun. 2016. Representation learning of knowledge graphs with hierarchical types. In *IJCAI*. pages 2965–2971.

Bishan Yang, Wen-tau Yih, Xiaodong He, Jianfeng Gao, and Li Deng. 2015. Embedding entities and relations for learning and inference in knowledge bases. In *ICLR*.

A Walk-based Model on Entity Graphs for Relation Extraction

Fenia Christopoulou[1,3], **Makoto Miwa**[2,3], **Sophia Ananiadou**[1,3]

[1]National Centre for Text Mining

[1]School of Computer Science, The University of Manchester, United Kingdom

[2]Toyota Technological Institute, Nagoya, 468-8511, Japan

[3]Artificial Intelligence Research Center (AIRC),

National Institute of Advanced Industrial Science and Technology (AIST), Japan

{efstathia.christopoulou, sophia.ananiadou}@manchester.ac.uk

makoto-miwa@toyota-ti.ac.jp

Abstract

We present a novel graph-based neural network model for relation extraction. Our model treats multiple pairs in a sentence simultaneously and considers interactions among them. All the entities in a sentence are placed as nodes in a fully-connected graph structure. The edges are represented with position-aware contexts around the entity pairs. In order to consider different relation paths between two entities, we construct up to l-length walks between each pair. The resulting walks are merged and iteratively used to update the edge representations into longer walks representations. We show that the model achieves performance comparable to the state-of-the-art systems on the ACE 2005 dataset without using any external tools.

1 Introduction

Relation extraction (RE) is a task of identifying typed relations between known entity mentions in a sentence. Most existing RE models treat each relation in a sentence individually (Miwa and Bansal, 2016; Nguyen and Grishman, 2015). However, a sentence typically contains multiple relations between entity mentions. RE models need to consider these pairs simultaneously to model the dependencies among them. The relation between a pair of interest (namely "target" pair) can be influenced by other pairs in the same sentence. The example illustrated in Figure 1 explains this phenomenon. The relation between the pair of interest *Toefting* and *capital*, can be extracted directly from the target entities or indirectly by incorporating information from other related pairs in the sentence. The person entity (PER) *Toefting* is directly related with *teammates* through the

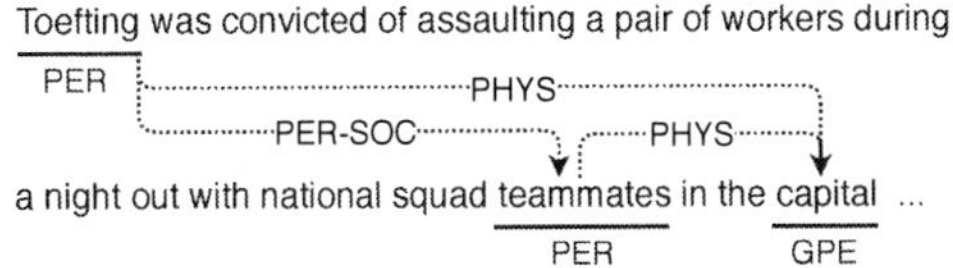

Figure 1: Relation examples from ACE (Automatic Content Extraction) 2005 dataset (Doddington et al., 2004).

preposition *with*. Similarly, *teammates* is directly related with the geopolitical entity (GPE) *capital* through the preposition *in*. *Toefting* and *capital* can be directly related through *in* or indirectly related through *teammates*. Substantially, the path from *Toefting* to *teammates* to *capital* can additionally support the relation between *Toefting* and *capital*.

Multiple relations in a sentence between entity mentions can be represented as a graph. Neural graph-based models have shown significant improvement in modelling graphs over traditional feature-based approaches in several tasks. They are most commonly applied on knowledge graphs (KG) for knowledge graph completion (Jiang et al., 2017) and the creation of knowledge graph embeddings (Wang et al., 2017; Shi and Weninger, 2017). These models rely on paths between existing relations in order to infer new associations between entities in KGs. However, for relation extraction from a sentence, related pairs are not predefined and consequently all entity pairs need to be considered to extract relations. In addition, state-of-the-art RE models sometimes depend on external syntactic tools to build the shortest dependency path (SDP) between two entities in a sentence (Xu et al., 2015; Miwa and Bansal, 2016). This dependence on external tools leads to domain dependent models.

Proceedings of the 56th Annual Meeting of the Association for Computational Linguistics (Short Papers), pages 81–88
Melbourne, Australia, July 15 - 20, 2018. ©2018 Association for Computational Linguistics

In this study, we propose a neural relation extraction model based on an entity graph, where entity mentions constitute the nodes and directed edges correspond to ordered pairs of entity mentions. The overview of the model is shown in Figure 2. We initialize the representation of an edge (an ordered pair of entity mentions) from the representations of the entity mentions and their context. The context representation is achieved by employing an attention mechanism on context words. We then use an iterative process to aggregate up-to l-length walk representations between two entities into a single representation, which corresponds to the final representation of the edge.

The contributions of our model can be summarized as follows:

- We propose a graph walk based neural model that considers multiple entity pairs in relation extraction from a sentence.
- We propose an iterative algorithm to form a single representation for up-to l-length walks between the entities of a pair.
- We show that our model performs comparably to the state-of-the-art without the use of external syntactic tools.

2 Proposed Walk-based Model

The goal of the RE task is given a sentence, entity mentions and their semantic types, to extract and classify all related entity pairs (target pairs) in the sentence. The proposed model consists of five stacked layers: embedding layer, BLSTM Layer, edge representation layer, walk aggregation layer and finally a classification layer.

As shown in Figure 2, the model receives word representations and produces simultaneously a representation for each pair in the sentence. These representations combine the target pair, its context words, their relative positions to the pair entities and walks between them. During classification they are used to predict the relation type of each pair.

2.1 Embedding Layer

The embedding layer involves the creation of n_w, n_t, n_p-dimensional vectors which are assigned to words, semantic entity types and relative positions to the target pairs. We map all words and semantic types into real-valued vectors $\mathbf{w}$ and $\mathbf{t}$ respectively. Relative positions to target entities are created based on the position of words in the sen-

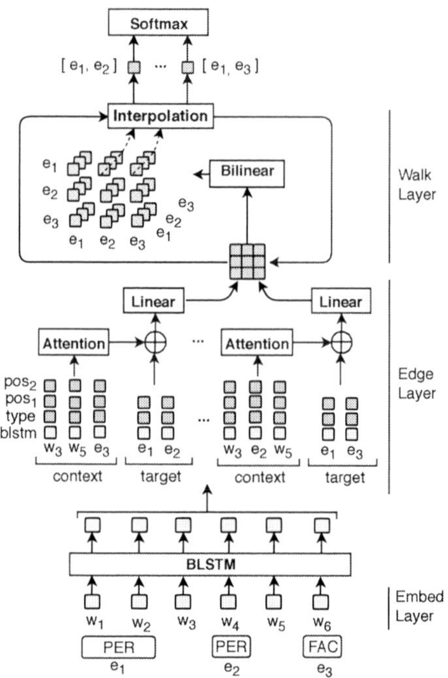

Figure 2: Overview of the walk-based model.

tence. In the example of Figure 1, the relative position of *teammates* to *capital* is -3 and the relative position of *teammates* to *Toefting* is $+16$. We embed real-valued vectors $\mathbf{p}$ to these positions.

2.2 Bidirectional LSTM Layer

The word representations of each sentence are fed into a Bidirectional Long-short Term Memory (BLSTM) layer, which encodes the context representation for every word. The BLSTM outputs new word-level representations $\mathbf{h}$ (Hochreiter and Schmidhuber, 1997) that consider the sequence of words.

We avoid encoding target pair-dependent information in this BLSTM layer. This has two advantages: (i) the computational cost is reduced as this computation is repeated based on the number of sentences instead of the number of pairs, (ii) we can share the sequence layer among the pairs of a sentence. The second advantage is particularly important as it enables the model to indirectly learn hidden dependencies between the related pairs in the same sentence.

For each word t in the sentence, we concatenate the two representations from left-to-right and right-to-left pass of the LSTM into a n_e-dimensional vector, $\mathbf{e}_t = [\overrightarrow{\mathbf{h}_t}; \overleftarrow{\mathbf{h}_t}]$.

2.3 Edge Representation Layer

The output word representations of the BLSTM are further divided into two parts: (i) target pair representations and (ii) target pair-specific context representations. The context of a target pair can be expressed as all words in the sentence that are not part of the entity mentions. We represent a related pair as described below.

A target pair contains two entities e_i and e_j. If an entity consists of N words, we create its BLSTM representation as the average of the BLSTM representations of the corresponding words, $\mathbf{e} = \frac{1}{|I|} \sum_{i \in I} \mathbf{e}_i$, where I is a set with the word indices inside entity e.

We first create a representation for each pair entity and then we construct the representation for the context of the pair. The representation of an entity e_i is the concatenation of its BLSTM representation $\mathbf{e}_i$, the representation of its entity type $\mathbf{t}_i$ and the representation of its relative position to entity e_j, $\mathbf{p}_{ij}$. Similarly, for entity e_j we use its relative position to entity e_i, $\mathbf{p}_{ji}$. Finally, the representations of the pair entities are as follows: $\mathbf{v}_i = [\mathbf{e}_i; \mathbf{t}_i; \mathbf{p}_{ij}]$ and $\mathbf{v}_j = [\mathbf{e}_j; \mathbf{t}_j; \mathbf{p}_{ji}]$.

The next step involves the construction of the representation of the context for this pair. For each context word w_z of the target pair e_i, e_j, we concatenate its BLSTM representation $\mathbf{e}_z$, its semantic type representation $\mathbf{t}_z$ and two relative position representations: to target entity e_i, $\mathbf{p}_{zi}$ and to target entity e_j, $\mathbf{p}_{zj}$. The final representation for a context word w_z of a target pair is, $\mathbf{v}_{ijz} = [\mathbf{e}_z; \mathbf{t}_z; \mathbf{p}_{zi}; \mathbf{p}_{zj}]$. For a sentence, the context representations for all entity pairs can be expressed as a three-dimensional matrix $\mathbf{C}$, where rows and columns correspond to entities and the depth corresponds to the context words.

The context words representations of each target pair are then compiled into a single representation with an attention mechanism. Following the method proposed in Zhou et al. (2016), we calculate weights for the context words of the target-pair and compute their weighted average,

$$
\begin{aligned}
\mathbf{u} &= \mathbf{q}^{\top} \tanh(\mathbf{C}_{ij}), \\
\alpha &= \text{softmax}(\mathbf{u}), \\
\mathbf{c}_{ij} &= \mathbf{C}_{ij}\, \alpha^{\top},
\end{aligned}
\tag{1}
$$

where $\mathbf{q} \in \mathbb{R}^{n_d}, n_d = n_e + n_t + 2n_p$ denotes a trainable attention vector, α is the attended weights vector and $\mathbf{c}_{ij} \in \mathbb{R}^{n_d}$ is the context representation of the pair as resulted by the weighted

average. This attention mechanism is independent of the relation type. We leave relation-dependent attention as future work.

Finally, we concatenate the representations of the target entities and their context ($\in \mathbb{R}^{n_m}$). We use a fully connected linear layer, $\mathbf{W}_s \in \mathbb{R}^{n_m \times n_s}$ with $n_s < n_m$ to reduce the dimensionality of the resulting vector. This corresponds to the representation of an edge or a one-length walk between nodes i and j: $\mathbf{v}_{ij}^{(1)} = \mathbf{W}_s\,[\mathbf{v}_i; \mathbf{v}_j; \mathbf{c}_{ij}] \in \mathbb{R}^{n_s}$.

2.4 Walk Aggregation Layer

Our main aim is to support the relation between an entity pair by using chains of intermediate relations between the pair entities. Thus, the goal of this layer is to generate a single representation for a finite number of different lengths walks between two target entities. To achieve this, we represent a sentence as a directed graph, where the entities constitute the graph nodes and edges correspond to the representation of the relation between the two nodes. The representation of one-length walk between a target pair $\mathbf{v}_{ij}^{(1)}$, serves as a building block in order to create and aggregate representations for one-to-l-length walks between the pair. The walk-based algorithm can be seen as a two-step process: walk construction and walk aggregation. During the first step, two consecutive edges in the graph are combined using a modified bilinear transformation,

$$
f(\mathbf{v}_{ik}^{(\lambda)}, \mathbf{v}_{kj}^{(\lambda)}) = \sigma\left(\mathbf{v}_{ik}^{(\lambda)} \odot (\mathbf{W}_b\,\mathbf{v}_{kj}^{(\lambda)})\right), \tag{2}
$$

where $\mathbf{v}_{ij}^{(\lambda)} \in \mathbb{R}^{n_b}$ corresponds to walks representation of lengths one-to-λ between entities e_i and e_j, $\odot$ represents element-wise multiplication, σ is the sigmoid non-linear function and $\mathbf{W}_b \in \mathbb{R}^{n_b \times n_b}$ is a trainable weight matrix. This equation results in walks of lengths two-to-2λ.

In the walk aggregation step, we linearly combine the initial walks (length one-to-λ) and the extended walks (length two-to-2λ),

$$
\mathbf{v}_{ij}^{(2\lambda)} = \beta\mathbf{v}_{ij}^{(\lambda)} + (1 - \beta) \sum_{k \neq i,j} f(\mathbf{v}_{ik}^{(\lambda)}, \mathbf{v}_{kj}^{(\lambda)}), \tag{3}
$$

where β is a weight that indicates the importance of the shorter walks. Overall, we create a representation for walks of length one-to-two using Equation (3) and $\lambda = 1$. We then create a representation for walks of length one-to-four by re-applying the equation with $\lambda = 2$. We repeat this process until the desired maximum walk length is reached, which is equivalent to $2\lambda = l$.

2.5 Classification Layer

For the final layer of the network, we pass the resulted pair representation into a fully connected layer with a softmax function,

$$\mathbf{y} = \mathrm{softmax}(\mathbf{W}_r \mathbf{v}_{ij}^{(l)} + \mathbf{b}_r), \qquad (4)$$

where $\mathbf{W}_r \in \mathbb{R}^{n_b \times n_r}$ is the weight matrix, n_r is the total number of relation types and b_r is the bias vector.

We use in total $2r+1$ classes in order to consider both directions for every pair, i.e., left-to-right and right-to-left. The first argument appears first in a sentence in a left-to-right relation while the second argument appears first in a right-to-left relation. The additional class corresponds to non-related pairs, namely "no relation" class. We choose the most confident prediction for each direction and choose the positive and most confident prediction when the predictions contradict each other.

3 Experiments

3.1 Dataset

We evaluate the performance of our model on ACE 2005[1] for the task of relation extraction. ACE 2005 includes 7 entity types and 6 relation types between named entities. We follow the pre-processing described in Miwa and Bansal (2016).

3.2 Experimental Settings

We implemented our model using the Chainer library (Tokui et al., 2015).[2] The model was trained with Adam optimizer (Kingma and Ba, 2015). We initialized the word representations with existing pre-trained embeddings with dimensionality of 200.[3] Our model did not use any external tools except these embeddings.

The forget bias of the LSTM layer was initialized with a value equal to one following the work of Jozefowicz et al. (2015). We use a batchsize of 10 sentences and fix the pair representation dimensionality to 100. We use gradient clipping, dropout on the embedding and output layers and L2 regularization without regularizing the biases, to avoid

<hr>

[1] https://catalog.ldc.upenn.edu/ldc2006t06
[2] https://chainer.org/
[3] https://github.com/tticoin/LSTM-ER

Model	P	R	F1 (%)
SPTree	70.1	61.2	65.3
Baseline	72.5	53.3	61.4*
No walks $l = 1$	71.9	55.6	62.7
+ Walks $l = 2$	69.9	58.4	63.6$^\diamond$
+ Walks $l = 4$	69.7	59.5	64.2$^\diamond$
+ Walks $l = 8$	71.5	55.3	62.4

Table 1: Relation extraction performance on ACE 2005 test dataset. * denotes significance at p < 0.05 compared to SPTree, $\diamond$ denotes significance at p < 0.05 compared to the Baseline.

overfitting. We also incorporate early stopping with patience equal to five, to chose the number of training epochs and parameter averaging. We tune the model hyper-parameters on the respective development set using the RoBO Toolkit (Klein et al., 2017). Please refer to the supplementary material for the values.

We extract all possible pairs in a sentence based on the number of entities it contains. If a pair is not found in the corpus, it is assigned the "no relation" class. We report the micro precision, recall and F1 score following Miwa and Bansal (2016) and Nguyen and Grishman (2015).

4 Results

Table 1 illustrates the performance of our proposed model in comparison with *SPTree* system Miwa and Bansal (2016) on ACE 2005. We use the same data split with *SPTree* to compare with their model. We retrained their model with gold entities in order to compare the performances on the relation extraction task. The *Baseline* corresponds to a model that classifies relations by using only the representations of entities in a target pair.

As it can be observed from the table, the *Baseline* model achieves the lowest F1 score between the proposed models. By incorporating attention we can further improve the performance by 1.3 percent point (pp). The addition of 2-length walks further improves performance (0.9 pp). The best results among the proposed models are achieved for maximum 4-length walks. By using up-to 8-length walks the performance drops almost by 2 pp. We also compared our performance with Nguyen and Grishman (2015) (*CNN*) using their data split.[4] For the comparison, we applied our

<hr>

[4] The authors kindly provided us with the data split.

# Entities	$l = 1$	$l = 2$	$l = 4$	$l = 8$
2	71.2	69.8	72.9	71.0
3	70.1	67.5	67.8	63.5*
$[4, 6)$	56.5	59.7	59.3	59.9
$[6, 12)$	59.2	64.2*	62.2	60.4
$[12, 23)$	54.7	59.3	62.3*	55.0

Table 2: Relation extraction performance (F1 %) on ACE 2005 development set for different number of entities. * denotes significance at $p < 0.05$ compared to $l = 1$.

best performing model ($l = 4$).[5] The obtained performance is 65.8 / 58.4 / 61.9 in terms of P / R / F1 (%) respectively. In comparison with the performance of the *CNN* model, 71.5 / 53.9 / 61.3, we observe a large improvement in recall which results in 0.6 pp F1 increase.

We performed the Approximate Randomization test (Noreen, 1989) on the results. The best walks model has no statistically significant difference with the state-of-the-art *SPTree* model as in Table 1. This indicates that the proposed model can achieve comparable performance without any external syntactic tools.

Finally, we show the performance of the proposed model as a function of the number of entities in a sentence. Results in Table 2 reveal that for multi-pair sentences the model performs significantly better compared to the no-walks models, proving the effectiveness of the method. Additionally, it is observed that for more entity pairs, longer walks seem to be required. However, very long walks result to reduced performance ($l = 8$).

5   Related Work

Traditionally, relation extraction approaches have incorporated a large variety of hand-crafted features to represent related entity pairs (Hermann and Blunsom, 2013; Miwa and Sasaki, 2014; Nguyen and Grishman, 2014; Gormley et al., 2015). Recent models instead employ neural network architectures and achieve state-of-the-art results without heavy feature engineering. Neural network techniques can be categorized into recurrent neural networks (RNNs) and convolutional neural networks (CNNs). The former is able to encode linguistic and syntactic properties of long word sequences, making them preferable for sequence-related tasks, e.g. natural language generation (Goyal et al., 2016), machine translation (Sutskever et al., 2014).

State-of-the-art systems have proved to achieve good performance on relation extraction using RNNs (Cai et al., 2016; Miwa and Bansal, 2016; Xu et al., 2016; Liu et al., 2015). Nevertheless, most approaches do not take into consideration the dependencies between relations in a single sentence (dos Santos et al., 2015; Nguyen and Grishman, 2015) and treat each pair separately. Current graph-based models are applied on knowledge graphs for distantly supervised relation extraction (Zeng et al., 2017). Graphs are defined on semantic types in their method, whereas we built entity-based graphs in sentences. Other approaches also treat multiple relations in a sentence (Gupta et al., 2016; Miwa and Sasaki, 2014; Li and Ji, 2014), but they fail to model long walks between entity mentions.

6   Conclusions

We proposed a novel neural network model for simultaneous sentence-level extraction of related pairs. Our model exploits target and context pair-specific representations and creates pair representations that encode up-to l-length walks between the entities of the pair. We compared our model with the state-of-the-art models and observed comparable performance on the ACE2005 dataset without any external syntactic tools. The characteristics of the proposed approach are summarized in three factors: the encoding of dependencies between relations, the ability to represent multiple walks in the form of vectors and the independence from external tools. Future work will aim at the construction of an end-to-end relation extraction system as well as application to different types of datasets.

Acknowledgments

This research has been carried out with funding from AIRC/AIST, the James Elson Studentship Award, BBSRC grant BB/P025684/1 and MRC MR/N00583X/1. Results were obtained from a project commissioned by the New Energy and Industrial Technology Development Organization (NEDO). We would finally like to thank the anonymous reviewers for their helpful comments.

---

[5] We kept the same parameters when we apply our model to the this data split. We did not remove any negative examples unlike the *CNN* model.

References

Rui Cai, Xiaodong Zhang, and Houfeng Wang. 2016. Bidirectional recurrent convolutional neural network for relation classification. In *Proceedings of the 54th Annual Meeting of the Association for Computational Linguistics (Volume 1: Long Papers)*, volume 1, pages 756–765.

George R Doddington, Alexis Mitchell, Mark A Przybocki, Lance A Ramshaw, Stephanie Strassel, and Ralph M Weischedel. 2004. The automatic content extraction (ace) program-tasks, data, and evaluation. In *Proceedings of the Fourth International Conference on Language Resources and Evaluation (LREC)*, volume 2, page 1.

Matthew R. Gormley, Mo Yu, and Mark Dredze. 2015. Improved relation extraction with feature-rich compositional embedding models. In *Proceedings of the Conference on Empirical Methods in Natural Language Processing (EMNLP)*, pages 1774–1784. Association for Computational Linguistics.

Raghav Goyal, Marc Dymetman, and Eric Gaussier. 2016. Natural language generation through character-based rnns with finite-state prior knowledge. In *Proceedings of COLING, the 26th International Conference on Computational Linguistics: Technical Papers*, pages 1083–1092.

Pankaj Gupta, Hinrich Schütze, and Bernt Andrassy. 2016. Table filling multi-task recurrent neural network for joint entity and relation extraction. In *Proceedings of COLING, the 26th International Conference on Computational Linguistics: Technical Papers*, pages 2537–2547.

Karl Moritz Hermann and Phil Blunsom. 2013. The role of syntax in vector space models of compositional semantics. In *Proceedings of the 51st Annual Meeting of the Association for Computational Linguistics (Volume 1: Long Papers)*, volume 1, pages 894–904.

Sepp Hochreiter and Jürgen Schmidhuber. 1997. Long short-term memory. *Neural computation*, 9(8):1735–1780.

Xiaotian Jiang, Quan Wang, Baoyuan Qi, Yongqin Qiu, Peng Li, and Bin Wang. 2017. Attentive path combination for knowledge graph completion. In *Asian Conference on Machine Learning*, pages 590–605.

Rafal Jozefowicz, Wojciech Zaremba, and Ilya Sutskever. 2015. An empirical exploration of recurrent network architectures. In *International Conference on Machine Learning*, pages 2342–2350.

Diederik P Kingma and Jimmy Ba. 2015. Adam: A method for stochastic optimization.

A. Klein, S. Falkner, N. Mansur, and F. Hutter. 2017. Robo: A flexible and robust bayesian optimization framework in python. In *Proceedings of Workshop on Bayesian Optimization in the Conference on Neural Information Processing Systems (NIPS)*.

Qi Li and Heng Ji. 2014. Incremental joint extraction of entity mentions and relations. In *Proceedings of the 52nd Annual Meeting of the Association for Computational Linguistics (Volume 1: Long Papers)*, pages 402–412. Association for Computational Linguistics.

Yang Liu, Furu Wei, Sujian Li, Heng Ji, Ming Zhou, and Houfeng WANG. 2015. A dependency-based neural network for relation classification. In *Proceedings of the 53rd Annual Meeting of the Association for Computational Linguistics and the 7th International Joint Conference on Natural Language Processing (Volume 2: Short Papers)*, pages 285–290. Association for Computational Linguistics.

Makoto Miwa and Mohit Bansal. 2016. End-to-end relation extraction using lstms on sequences and tree structures. In *Proceedings of the 54th Annual Meeting of the Association for Computational Linguistics (Volume 1: Long Papers)*, pages 1105–1116. Association for Computational Linguistics.

Makoto Miwa and Yutaka Sasaki. 2014. Modeling joint entity and relation extraction with table representation. In *Proceedings of the Conference on Empirical Methods in Natural Language Processing (EMNLP)*, pages 1858–1869. Association for Computational Linguistics.

Thien Huu Nguyen and Ralph Grishman. 2014. Employing word representations and regularization for domain adaptation of relation extraction. In *Proceedings of the 52nd Annual Meeting of the Association for Computational Linguistics (Volume 2: Short Papers)*, volume 2, pages 68–74.

Thien Huu Nguyen and Ralph Grishman. 2015. Relation extraction: Perspective from convolutional neural networks. In *Proceedings of the 1st Workshop on Vector Space Modeling for Natural Language Processing*, pages 39–48. Association for Computational Linguistics.

Eric W Noreen. 1989. *Computer-intensive methods for testing hypotheses*. Wiley New York.

Cicero dos Santos, Bing Xiang, and Bowen Zhou. 2015. Classifying relations by ranking with convolutional neural networks. In *Proceedings of the 53rd Annual Meeting of the Association for Computational Linguistics and the 7th International Joint Conference on Natural Language Processing (Volume 1: Long Papers)*, pages 626–634. Association for Computational Linguistics.

Baoxu Shi and Tim Weninger. 2017. Proje: Embedding projection for knowledge graph completion. In *Proceedings of AAAI Conference on Artificial Intelligence*, volume 17, pages 1236–1242.

Ilya Sutskever, Oriol Vinyals, and Quoc V Le. 2014. Sequence to sequence learning with neural networks. In *Advances in neural information processing systems*, pages 3104–3112.

Seiya Tokui, Kenta Oono, Shohei Hido, and Justin Clayton. 2015. Chainer: a next-generation open source framework for deep learning. In *Proceedings of Workshop on Machine Learning Systems (LearningSys) in the twenty-ninth Annual Conference on Neural Information Processing Systems (NIPS)*, volume 5.

Quan Wang, Zhendong Mao, Bin Wang, and Li Guo. 2017. Knowledge graph embedding: A survey of approaches and applications. *IEEE Transactions on Knowledge and Data Engineering*, 29(12):2724–2743.

Kun Xu, Yansong Feng, Songfang Huang, and Dongyan Zhao. 2015. Semantic relation classification via convolutional neural networks with simple negative sampling. In *Proceedings of the Conference on Empirical Methods in Natural Language Processing (EMNLP)*, pages 536–540. Association for Computational Linguistics.

Yan Xu, Ran Jia, Lili Mou, Ge Li, Yunchuan Chen, Yangyang Lu, and Zhi Jin. 2016. Improved relation classification by deep recurrent neural networks with data augmentation. In *Proceedings of COLING, the 26th International Conference on Computational Linguistics: Technical Papers*, pages 1461–1470.

Wenyuan Zeng, Yankai Lin, Zhiyuan Liu, and Maosong Sun. 2017. Incorporating relation paths in neural relation extraction. In *Proceedings of the Conference on Empirical Methods in Natural Language Processing (EMNLP)*, pages 1768–1777. Association for Computational Linguistics.

Peng Zhou, Wei Shi, Jun Tian, Zhenyu Qi, Bingchen Li, Hongwei Hao, and Bo Xu. 2016. Attention-based bidirectional long short-term memory networks for relation classification. In *Proceedings of the 54th Annual Meeting of the Association for Computational Linguistics (Volume 2: Short Papers)*, volume 2, pages 207–212.

A Hyper-parameter Settings

We tuned our proposed model using the RoBO toolkit (`https://github.com/automl/RoBO`). Table 3 provides the selected options we used for tuning the model.

Optimization Options	
Optimization method	Bohamiann
Maximizer	scipy
Acquisition function	log_ei
Number of iterations	50
Initial points	3

Table 3: Hyper-parameters optimization options.

The parameters that gave the best performance for the different models can be found in Tables 4a-4e.

Parameter	Baseline
Position dimension n_p	25
Type dimension n_t	15
LSTM dimension n_e	100
Input layer dropout	0.3
Output layer dropout	0.03
Learning rate	0.0018
Regularization	$3.2 \cdot 10^{-5}$
Gradient clipping	25.63

(a)

Parameter	$l = 1$
Position dimension n_p	25
Type dimension n_t	25
LSTM dimension n_e	100
Input layer dropout	0.13
Output layer dropout	0.38
Learning rate	0.0017
Regularization	$6.1 \cdot 10^{-5}$
Gradient clipping	30

(b)

Parameter	$l = 2$
Position dimension n_p	25
Type dimension n_t	20
LSTM dimension n_e	100
β	0.72
Input layer dropout	0.25
Output layer dropout	0.37
Learning rate	0.003
Regularization	0.0001
Gradient clipping	8.6

(c)

Parameter	$l = 4$
Position dimension n_p	25
Type dimension n_t	20
LSTM dimension n_e	100
β	0.77
Input layer dropout	0.11
Output layer dropout	0.32
Learning rate	0.002
Regularization	$5.7 \cdot 10^{-5}$
Gradient clipping	24.4

(d)

Parameter	$l = 8$
Position dimension n_p	25
Type dimension n_t	20
LSTM dimension n_e	100
β	0.88
Input layer dropout	0.49
Output layer dropout	0.36
Learning rate	0.001
Regularization	$1.88 \cdot 10^{-5}$
Gradient clipping	10.5

(e)

Table 4: Best hyper-parameters settings for proposed models.

Ranking-Based Automatic Seed Selection and Noise Reduction for Weakly Supervised Relation Extraction

Van-Thuy Phi[1], Joan Santoso[2], Masashi Shimbo[1] and Yuji Matsumoto[1,3]

[1] Nara Institute of Science and Technology
[2] Sekolah Tinggi Teknik Surabaya
[3] RIKEN Center for Advanced Intelligence Project (AIP)
[1]{*phi.thuy.ph8, shimbo, matsu*}*@is.naist.jp*
[2]*joan@stts.edu*

Abstract

This paper addresses the tasks of automatic seed selection for bootstrapping relation extraction, and noise reduction for distantly supervised relation extraction. We first point out that these tasks are related. Then, inspired by ranking relation instances and patterns computed by the HITS algorithm, and selecting cluster centroids using the K-means, LSA, or NMF method, we propose methods for selecting the initial seeds from an existing resource, or reducing the level of noise in the distantly labeled data. Experiments show that our proposed methods achieve a better performance than the baseline systems in both tasks.

1 Introduction

Bootstrapping for relation extraction (RE) (Brin, 1998; Riloff et al., 1999; Agichtein and Gravano, 2000) is a class of minimally supervised methods frequently used in machine learning: initialized by a small set of example instances called *seeds*, to represent a particular semantic relation, the bootstrapping system operates iteratively to acquire new instances of a target relation. Selecting *"good"* seeds is one of the most important steps to reduce *semantic drift*, which is a typical phenomenon of the bootstrapping process.

Another approach, called *"distant supervision"* (DS) (Mintz et al., 2009), does not require any labels on the text. The assumption of DS is that if two entities participate in a known Freebase relation, any sentence that contains those two entities might express that relation. However, this technique often introduces noise to the generated training data. As a result, DS is still limited by the quality of training data, and noise existing in positively labeled data may affect the performance of supervised learning.

In this study, we propose methods that can be applied for both automatic seed selection and noise reduction by formulating these tasks as ranking problems according to different ranking criteria. Our methods are inspired by ranking instances and patterns computed by the HITS algorithm, and selecting cluster centroids using K-means, latent semantic analysis, or the non-negative matrix factorization method. The main contributions of this paper are (a) an annotated dataset of 5,727 part-whole relations[1], which contains 8 subtypes for the bootstrapping RE system; (b) methods for automatic seed selection for bootstrapping RE and noise reduction for distant supervised RE; and (c) experimental results showing that the proposed models outperform baselines on two datasets.

2 Related Work

2.1 Automatic Seed Selection for Bootstrapping RE

As manually selecting the seeds requires tremendous effort, some research proposed methods to select the seed automatically. Eisner and Karakos (2005) used a "strapping" approach to evaluate many candidate seeds automatically for a word sense disambiguation task. Kozareva and Hovy (2010) proposed a method for measuring seed quality using a regression model and applied it to the extraction of unary semantic relations, such as*"people"* and *"city"*. Kiso et al. (2011) suggested a HITS-based approach to ranking the seeds, based on Komachi et al. (2008)'s analysis of the Espresso algorithm (Pantel and Pennacchiotti,

---

[1] We release our annotated dataset at https://github.com/pvthuy/part-whole-relations.

Proceedings of the 56th Annual Meeting of the Association for Computational Linguistics (Short Papers), pages 89–95
Melbourne, Australia, July 15 - 20, 2018. ©2018 Association for Computational Linguistics

2006). Movshovitz-Attias and Cohen (2012) generated a ranking based on pointwise mutual information (PMI) to pick up the seeds from existing resources in the biomedical domain. Given the seed set of a target relation, the goal of the bootstrapping method is to find *instances* similar to initial seeds by harvesting *instances* and *patterns* iteratively over large corpora, e.g., Wikipedia or ClueWeb.

2.2 Noise Reduction for Distantly Supervised RE

The DS assumption is too strong and leads to wrongly labeled data that affects performance. Many studies focused on methods of noise reduction in DS. Intxaurrondo et al. (2013) filtered out noisy mentions from the distantly supervised dataset using their frequencies, PMI, or the similarity between the centroids of all relation mentions and each individual mention. Xiang et al. (2016) introduced ranking-based methods according to different strategies to select effective training groups. Li et al. (2017) proposed three novel heuristics that use lexical and syntactic information to remove noise in the biomedical domain. The data generated by the noise reduction process can be used by supervised learning algorithms to train models.

3 Problem Formulation

Let R^* be the set of target relations. The goal is to find instances, or pairs of entities, upon which the relation holds. For each target relation $r \in R^*$, we assume there is a set D_r of triples representing the relation r. The triples in D_r have the form (e_1, p, e_2), where e_1 and e_2 denote entities, and p denotes the *pattern* that connects the two entities. A pair of entities (e_1, e_2) is called an *instance*. This terminology is similar to the one used in open information extraction systems, such as *Reverb* (Fader et al., 2011). For example, in triple $(Barack\ Obama, was\ born\ in, Honolulu)$, $(Barack\ Obama, Honolulu)$ is the instance, and *"was born in"* is the pattern.

The two tasks we address are defined as follows:

Seed Selection for Bootstrapping RE: In automatic seed selection, a set R^* of target relations and sets of instance-pattern triples $D_r = \{(e_1, p, e_2)\}$ representing each target relation $r \in R^*$ are given as input. These triples are extracted from existing corpus or database, e.g., WordNet.

With these inputs, the task is to choose *good* seeds from the instances appearing in D_r for each $r \in R^*$, such that they work effectively in bootstrapping RE.

Noise Reduction for Distantly Supervised RE: In noise reduction for distantly supervised RE, the input is the target relations R^* and the sets D_r of triples[2] generated automatically by DS for each relation $r \in R^*$. Because the data is generated automatically by DS, D_r may contain noise, i.e., triples (e_1, p, e_2) for which relation r does not actually hold between e_1 and e_2. The goal of noise reduction is to filter out these noisy triples, so that they do not deteriorate the quality of the triple classifier trained subsequently.

Formulation as Ranking Tasks: As we can see from the task definitions above, both seed selection and noise reduction are the task of selecting triples from a given collection. Indeed, the two tasks essentially have a similar goal in terms of the ranking-based perspective. We thus formulate them as the task of ranking instances (in seed selection) or triples (in noise reduction), given a set of (possibly noisy) triples. In the seed selection task, we use the k highest ranked instances as the seeds for bootstrapping RE. Likewise, in noise reduction for DS, we only use the k highest ranked triples from the DS-generated data to train a classifier. Note that the value of k in noise reduction may be much larger than in seed selection.

4 Approaches to Automatic Seed Selection and Noise Reduction

In this section, we propose several methods that can be applied for both automatic seed selection and noise reduction tasks, inspired by ranking relation instances and patterns computed by the HITS algorithm, and picking cluster centroids using the K-means, latent semantic analysis (LSA), or non-negative matrix factorization (NMF) method.

4.1 K-means-based Approach

The first method we describe is a K-means-based approach. It is described as follows: **(1)** De-

---

[2] To be precise, in each triple (e_1, s, e_2) generated by DS, s is not a pattern but a sentence that contains entities e_1 and e_2. However, we can easily convert each instance-sentence triple (e_1, s, e_2) to an instance-pattern triple (e_1, p, e_2) by looking for a pattern p that connects two entities in sentence s.

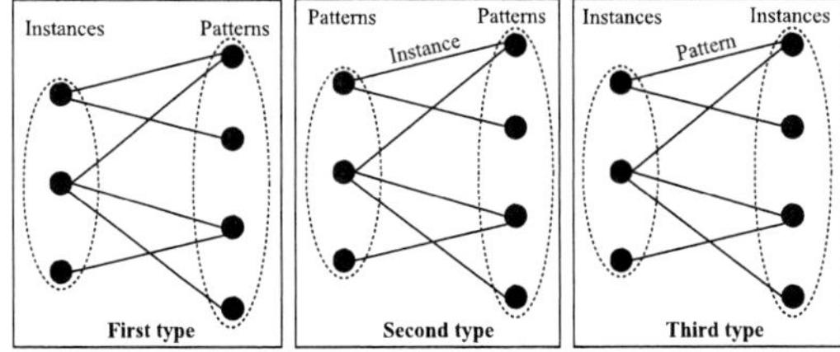

Figure 1: Graph representations of instances and patterns using the HITS algorithm.

termine the number k of instances/triples that should be selected[3]. (**2**) Run the K-means clustering algorithm to partition all instances in the input triples (see Section 3) into k clusters. Each data point is represented by the embedding vector difference between its entities; e.g., the instance $I = (Barack\ Obama, Honolulu)$ corresponds to: $\text{vec}(I) = \text{vec}(\text{"Barack Obama"}) - \text{vec}(\text{"Honolulu"})$. We use pre-trained vectors published by Mikolov et al. (2013). (**3**) The instance closest to the centroid is selected in each cluster. Given that the number of clusters is k, the same number of instances/triples will be chosen.

4.2 HITS-based Approach

Hypertext-induced topic search (HITS) (Kleinberg, 1999), also known as the *hubs-and-authorities* algorithm, is a link analysis method for ranking web pages. In HITS, a good hub is a page that points to many good authorities and vice versa; a good authority is a page that is pointed to by many good hubs. These hubs and authorities form a *bipartite* graph, where we can compute the hubness score of each node.

In our task, let $\mathbf{A}$ be the instance-pattern co-occurrence matrix. We can compute the hubness score for each instance on the bipartite graph of instances and patterns induced by the matrix $\mathbf{A}$. Inspired by the way HITS ranks hubs and authorities, our HITS-based seed selection strategy can be explained as follows: (**1**) Determine the number k of triples that should be selected.(**2**) Build the bipartite graph of instances and patterns based on the instance-pattern co-occurrence matrix $\mathbf{A}$. Figure 1 presents three possible ways of building a bipartite graph. For the first type of graph, we consider

each instance/pattern as a node in the graph. This representation is similar to that used by Kiso et al. (2011). In the second graph representation, patterns and instances are treated as nodes and edges, respectively. Similarly, instances and patterns are treated as nodes and edges, respectively in the last representation. (**3**) For the first and third types, we simply retain the top-k instances with the highest hubness scores as the outputs (we sort the instances in descending order based on their hubness scores). For the second type, k instances associated with the highest scoring patterns are chosen (we first sort the patterns in descending order based on their hubness scores).

4.3 HITS- and K-means-based Approach

In the combined method of HITS and K-means algorithms, we first rank the instances and patterns based on their bipartite graph and then run K-means to cluster instances in our annotated dataset. However, instead of choosing the instance nearest to the centroid, we retain the one that has the highest HITS hubness score in each cluster.

4.4 LSA-based Approach

Latent semantic analysis (LSA) (Deerwester et al., 1990) is also a widely used method for the automatic clustering of data along multiple dimensions. Singular value decomposition (SVD) is used to construct a low-rank approximation of the instance-pattern co-occurrence matrix $\mathbf{A}$. The SVD projection is performed by decomposing the matrix $\mathbf{A} \in \mathbb{R}^{M \times N}$ into the product of three matrices, namely an SVD instance matrix $\mathbf{I} \in \mathbb{R}^{M \times K}$, a diagonal matrix of singular values $\mathbf{S} \in \mathbb{R}^{K \times K}$, and an SVD pattern matrix $\mathbf{P} \in \mathbb{R}^{K \times N}$:

$$\mathbf{A} \approx \mathbf{I}\mathbf{S}\mathbf{P}^{T}$$

Our LSA-based seed selection strategy is as follows: (**1**) Specify the desired number k of triples. (**2**) Use the LSA algorithm to decompose the instance-pattern co-occurrence matrix $\mathbf{A}$ into three matrices $\mathbf{I}$, $\mathbf{S}$, and $\mathbf{P}$. We set the number of LSA dimensions to $K = k$. (**3**) We can consider LSA as a form of soft clustering, with each column of the SVD instance matrix $\mathbf{I}$ corresponding to a cluster. Then, we select the k instances that have the highest absolute values from each column of $\mathbf{I}$.

4.5 NMF-based Approach

Non-negative matrix factorization (NMF) (Paatero and Tapper, 1994; Lee and Seung, 1999) is an-

---

[3] Depending on the task, instances or triples will be selected: instances for the automatic seed selection task, and triples for the noise reduction task. As instances are pairs of entities which are included in triples, we can simply convert between the instance and the triple, and apply a proposed method to both tasks.

Subtype	Freq
Component-Of	643 (11.23%)
Member-Of	1,272 (22.21%)
Portion-Of	555 (9.69%)
Stuff-Of	1,082 (18.89%)
Located-In	534 (9.32%)
Contained-In	272 (4.75%)
Phase-Of	497 (8.68%)
Participates-In	872 (15.23%)
TOTAL	5,727 triples

Table 1: Statistics of our part-whole dataset.

Method	Average P@50
K-means	0.96
HITS_Graph1	0.90
HITS_Graph2	0.85
HITS_Graph3	0.90
HITS+K-means_Graph1	0.92
HITS+K-means_Graph2	0.85
HITS+K-means_Graph3	0.94
LSA	0.90
NMF	0.89
Random	0.75

Table 2: Performance of seed selection methods.

other method for approximate non-negative matrix factorization. The non-negative data matrix $\mathbf{A} \in \mathbb{R}^{M \times N}$ is represented by two non-negative factors $\mathbf{W} \in \mathbb{R}^{M \times K}$ and $\mathbf{H} \in \mathbb{R}^{K \times N}$, which, when multiplied, approximately reconstruct $\mathbf{A}$:

$$\mathbf{A} \approx \mathbf{WH}$$

The non-negativity constraint is the main difference between NMF and LSA. Similarly to the LSA-based method, we set the NMF parameter K to k, the desired number of instances to select. We then select the k instances that have the highest values from each column of $\mathbf{W}$.

5 Experiments

5.1 Datasets and Settings

We provide an annotated dataset of part-whole relations as a reliable resource for selecting seeds. Our dataset was collected from Wikipedia and ClueWeb, and annotated by two annotators. One of its special characteristics is that the part-whole relation is a collection of relations, not a single relation (Iris, 1989; Winston et al., 1987).

Table 1 gives the frequencies of each subtype of part-whole relations. There are 5,727 instances of 8 subtypes that were annotated with the same labels by both annotators. We use *Espresso+Word2vec* (Phi and Matsumoto, 2016), which is an improved version for the original Espresso algorithm (Pantel and Pennacchiotti, 2006). *Espresso+Word2vec* outperformed the Espresso system for harvesting part-whole relations by utilizing the *Similarity Ranker*, which uses the embedded vector difference between instance pairs of relations. The performance is measured with *Precision@N* (Manning et al., 2008), $N = 50$. In total, 5,000 instances are checked by annotators to ascertain whether they express part-whole relations. We vary the number k of seeds between 5 and 50 with a step of 5 to report the average P@50 of each seed selection method.

For the noise reduction task, we use the training and testing set developed by (Riedel et al., 2010), which contains 53 relation classes. This dataset was generated by aligning Freebase relations with the New York Times corpus. After removing noisy triples from the dataset using the proposed methods, we use the filtered data to train two kinds of convolutional neural networks (CNN) (the CNN model in (Zeng et al., 2014) and the PCNN model in (Zeng et al., 2015)) with at-least-one multi-instance learning (ONE) used in (Zeng et al., 2015), and the sentence-level attention (ATT) used in (Lin et al., 2016). Finally, we report the area under the precision-recall (AUCPR) of each noise reduction method.

5.2 Performance on Automatic Seed Selection Task

The performances of the seed selection methods are presented in Table 2. For the HITS-based and HITS+K-means-based methods, we display the P@50 with three types of graph representation as shown in Section 4.2. We use random seed selection as the baseline for comparison. As Table 2 shows, the random method achieved a precision of 0.75. The relation extraction system that uses the random method has the worst average P@50 among all seed selection strategies. The HITS-based method's P@50s when using Graph1 and Graph3 are confirmed to be better than when using Graph2. This indicates that relying on reliable instances is better than reasoning over patterns (recall that for the Graph2, we first choose

System	Original	+HITS	+LSA	+NMF	+Ensemble
CNN+ONE	0.180	**0.183**	0.173	0.178	0.181
CNN+ATT	0.234	0.235	0.235	0.233	**0.236**
PCNN+ONE	0.231	0.234	0.233	0.234	**0.235**
PCNN+ATT	0.248	0.253	0.250	0.252	**0.255**

Table 3: Performance (AUCPR) of each noise reduction method; in bold are the best scores.

the patterns, then select the instances associated with those patterns), as there is a possibility that a pattern can be ambiguous, and therefore, instances linked to that pattern can be incorrect. The K-means-based seed selection method provides the best average P@50 with a performance of 0.96. The HITS+K-means-based method performs better than using only the HITS strategy, while the LSA-based and NMF-based methods have a comparable performance.

5.3 Performance on Noise Reduction Task

Table 3 presents the performance of noise reduction methods. Recall that the K-means-based method achieves a high P@50 for the seed selection method. Our assumption is that each cluster may represent a set in which elements have similar semantic properties. However, we observed that as the number of relations is relatively high and there is no distinct definition between some relations in the distantly labeled data (e.g., the following three relations are quite similar: */location/country/capital*, */location/province/capital*, and */location/us_state/capital*, we decided not to perform the K-means-based method for our noise reduction task. The performances of the HITS-based, LSA-based, and NMF-based noise reduction methods are presented in Table 3. We experimentally set the portion of retained data from the distantly labeled data to 90%, given that the performance can be affected if too many sentences are removed from the original data. We also perform experiments with an ensemble method that combines the HITS-based and LSA-based strategies to merge rankings from their outputs, with half of the triples coming from the LSA-based method and the other half from the HITS-based method. Table 3 indicates that our proposed methods improved the performance of all CNN and PCNN models. Our ensemble method achieved the best improvements for three out of four systems, except that the HITS-based

method obtained the best score for *CNN+ONE*.

6 Conclusion

We formulated the seed selection and noise reduction tasks as ranking problems. In addition, we proposed several methods, inspired by ranking instances and patterns computed by the HITS algorithm, and selecting clusters centroids using the K-means, LSA, or NMF method. Experiments demonstrated that our proposed methods improved the baselines in both tasks.

Acknowledgments

This work was partly supported by JST CREST Grant Number JPMJCR1513 and MEXT/JSPS Kakenhi Grant Number JP15H02749. We are grateful to the members of the Computational Linguistics Laboratory, NAIST and the anonymous reviewers for their insightful comments.

References

Eugene Agichtein and Luis Gravano. 2000. Snowball: Extracting relations from large plain-text collections. In *Proceedings of the 5th ACM Conference on Digital Libraries*, pages 85–94. ACM.

Sergey Brin. 1998. Extracting patterns and relations from the world wide web. In *International Workshop on the World Wide Web and Databases*, pages 172–183. Springer.

Scott Deerwester, Susan T. Dumais, George W. Furnas, Thomas K. Landauer, and Richard Harshman. 1990. Indexing by latent semantic analysis. *Journal of the American Society for Information Science*, 41(6):391.

Jason Eisner and Damianos Karakos. 2005. Bootstrapping without the boot. In *Proceedings of the 2005 Human Language Technology Conference and Conference on Empirical Methods in Natural Language Processing*.

Anthony Fader, Stephen Soderland, and Oren Etzioni. 2011. Identifying relations for open information extraction. In *Proceedings of the 2011 Conference on*

Empirical Methods in Natural Language Processing, pages 1535–1545. Association for Computational Linguistics.

Ander Intxaurrondo, Mihai Surdeanu, Oier Lopez de Lacalle, and Eneko Agirre. 2013. Removing noisy mentions for distant supervision. *Procesamiento del lenguaje natural*, 51.

Madelyn Anne Iris. 1989. Problems of the part-whole relation. In *Relational Models of the Lexicon*, pages 261–288. Cambridge University Press.

Tetsuo Kiso, Masashi Shimbo, Mamoru Komachi, and Yuji Matsumoto. 2011. HITS-based seed selection and stop list construction for bootstrapping. In *Proceedings of the 49th Annual Meeting of the Association for Computational Linguistics: Human Language Technologies*, pages 30–36. Association for Computational Linguistics.

Jon M. Kleinberg. 1999. Authoritative sources in a hyperlinked environment. *Journal of the ACM*, 46(5):604–632.

Mamoru Komachi, Taku Kudo, Masashi Shimbo, and Yuji Matsumoto. 2008. Graph-based analysis of semantic drift in Espresso-like bootstrapping algorithms. In *Proceedings of the 2008 Conference on Empirical Methods in Natural Language Processing*, pages 1011–1020. Association for Computational Linguistics.

Zornitsa Kozareva and Eduard Hovy. 2010. Not all seeds are equal: Measuring the quality of text mining seeds. In *Human Language Technologies: The 2010 Annual Conference of the North American Chapter of the Association for Computational Linguistics*, pages 618–626. Association for Computational Linguistics.

Daniel D Lee and H. Sebastian Seung. 1999. Learning the parts of objects by non-negative matrix factorization. *Nature*, 401(6755):788–791.

Gang Li, Cathy Wu, and K. Vijay-Shanker. 2017. Noise reduction methods for distantly supervised biomedical relation extraction. In *SIGBioMed Workshop on Biomedical Natural Language Processing (BioNLP '17)*, pages 184–193. Association for Computational Linguistics.

Yankai Lin, Shiqi Shen, Zhiyuan Liu, Huanbo Luan, and Maosong Sun. 2016. Neural relation extraction with selective attention over instances. In *Proceedings of the 54th Annual Meeting of the Association for Computational Linguistics (Volume 1: Long Papers)*, pages 2124–2133. Association for Computational Linguistics.

Christopher D. Manning, Prabhakar Raghavan, and Hinrich Schütze. 2008. *Introduction to Information Retrieval*. Cambridge University Press.

Tomas Mikolov, Ilya Sutskever, Kai Chen, Greg S Corrado, and Jeff Dean. 2013. Distributed representations of words and phrases and their compositionality. In *Advances in Neural Information Processing Systems 26*, pages 3111–3119.

Mike Mintz, Steven Bills, Rion Snow, and Daniel Jurafsky. 2009. Distant supervision for relation extraction without labeled data. In *Proceedings of the Joint Conference of the 47th Annual Meeting of the ACL and the 4th International Joint Conference on Natural Language Processing of the AFNLP*, pages 1003–1011. Association for Computational Linguistics.

Dana Movshovitz-Attias and William W. Cohen. 2012. Bootstrapping biomedical ontologies for scientific text using nell. In *BioNLP: Proceedings of the 2012 Workshop on Biomedical Natural Language Processing*, pages 11–19. Association for Computational Linguistics.

Pentti Paatero and Unto Tapper. 1994. Positive matrix factorization: A non-negative factor model with optimal utilization of error estimates of data values. *Environmetrics*, 5(2):111–126.

Patrick Pantel and Marco Pennacchiotti. 2006. Espresso: Leveraging generic patterns for automatically harvesting semantic relations. In *Proceedings of the 21st International Conference on Computational Linguistics and 44th Annual Meeting of the Association for Computational Linguistics*, pages 113–120. Association for Computational Linguistics.

Van-Thuy Phi and Yuji Matsumoto. 2016. Integrating word embedding offsets into the Espresso system for part-whole relation extraction. In *Proceedings of the 30th Pacific Asia Conference on Language, Information and Computation: Oral Papers*, pages 173–181.

Sebastian Riedel, Limin Yao, and Andrew McCallum. 2010. Modeling relations and their mentions without labeled text. In *Proceedings of the 2010 Joint European Conference on Machine Learning and Principles of Knowledge Discovery in Databases (ECML PKDD)*, pages 148–163. Springer.

Ellen Riloff, Rosie Jones, et al. 1999. Learning dictionaries for information extraction by multi-level bootstrapping. In *Proceedings of the 16th National Conference on Artificial Intelligence and the 11th Innovative Applications of Artificial Intelligence Conference (AAAI/IAAI)*, pages 474–479.

Morton E. Winston, Roger Chaffin, and Douglas Herrmann. 1987. A taxonomy of part-whole relations. *Cognitive Science*, 11(4):417–444.

Yang Xiang, Qingcai Chen, Xiaolong Wang, and Yang Qin. 2016. Distant supervision for relation extraction with ranking-based methods. *Entropy*, 18(6):204.

Daojian Zeng, Kang Liu, Yubo Chen, and Jun Zhao. 2015. Distant supervision for relation extraction via piecewise convolutional neural networks. In *Proceedings of the 2015 Conference on Empirical Methods in Natural Language Processing*, pages 1753–1762. Association for Computational Linguistics.

Daojian Zeng, Kang Liu, Siwei Lai, Guangyou Zhou, and Jun Zhao. 2014. Relation classification via convolutional deep neural network. In *Proceedings of COLING 2014, the 25th International Conference on Computational Linguistics: Technical Papers*, pages 2335–2344. Dublin City University and Association for Computational Linguistics.

Automatic Extraction of Commonsense LocatedNear Knowledge

Frank F. Xu[*]   **Bill Yuchen Lin**[*]   **Kenny Q. Zhu**
Department of Computer Science and Engineering
Shanghai Jiao Tong University
Shanghai, China
{frankxu, yuchenlin}@sjtu.edu.cn, kzhu@cs.sjtu.edu.cn

Abstract

LOCATEDNEAR relation is a kind of commonsense knowledge describing two physical objects that are typically found near each other in real life. In this paper, we study how to automatically extract such relationship through a sentence-level relation classifier and aggregating the scores of entity pairs from a large corpus. Also, we release two benchmark datasets for evaluation and future research.

1 Introduction

Artificial intelligence systems can benefit from incorporating commonsense knowledge as background, such as *ice is cold* (HASPROPERTY), *chewing is a sub-event of eating* (HASSUBEVENT), *chair and table are typically found near each other* (LOCATEDNEAR), etc. These kinds of commonsense facts have been used in many downstream tasks, such as textual entailment (Dagan et al., 2009; Bowman et al., 2015) and visual recognition tasks (Zhu et al., 2014). The commonsense knowledge is often represented as relation triples in commonsense knowledge bases, such as *Concept-Net* (Speer and Havasi, 2012), one of the largest commonsense knowledge graphs available today. However, most commonsense knowledge bases are manually curated or crowd-sourced by community efforts and thus do not scale well.

This paper aims to automatically extract the commonsense LOCATEDNEAR relation between physical objects from textual corpora. LOCATEDNEAR is defined as the relationship between two objects typically found near each other in real life. We focus on LOCATEDNEAR relation for these reasons:

1. LOCATEDNEAR facts provide helpful prior knowledge to object detection tasks in com-

Figure 1: LOCATEDNEAR facts assist the detection of vague objects: if a set of knife, fork and plate is on the table, one may believe there is a glass beside based on the commonsense, even though these objects are hardly visible due to low light.

plex image scenes (Yatskar et al., 2016). See Figure 1 for an example.

2. This commonsense knowledge can benefit reasoning related to spatial facts and physical scenes in reading comprehension, question answering, etc. (Li et al., 2016)

3. Existing knowledge bases have very few facts for this relation (*ConceptNet 5.5* has only 49 triples of LOCATEDNEAR relation).

We propose two novel tasks in extracting LO-CATEDNEAR relation from textual corpora. One is a sentence-level relation classification problem which judges whether or not a sentence describes two objects (mentioned in the sentence) being physically close by. The other task is to produce a ranked list of LOCATEDNEAR facts with the given classified results of large number of sentences. We believe both two tasks can be used to automatically populate and complete existing commonsense knowledge bases.

Additionally, we create two benchmark datasets for evaluating LOCATEDNEAR relation extraction

---

[*]Both authors contributed equally.

Proceedings of the 56th Annual Meeting of the Association for Computational Linguistics (Short Papers), pages 96–101
Melbourne, Australia, July 15 - 20, 2018. ©2018 Association for Computational Linguistics

systems on the two tasks: one is 5,000 sentences each describing a scene of two physical objects and with a label indicating if the two objects are co-located in the scene; the other consists of 500 pairs of objects with human-annotated scores indicating confidences that a certain pair of objects are commonly located near in real life.[1]

We propose several methods to solve the tasks including feature-based models and LSTM-based neural architectures. The proposed neural architecture compares favorably with the current state-of-the-art method for general-purpose relation classification problem. From our relatively smaller proposed datasets, we extract in total 2,067 new LOCATEDNEAR triples that are not in *ConceptNet*.

2 Sentence-level LOCATEDNEAR Relation Classification

Problem Statement Given a sentence s mentioning a pair of physical objects $<e_i, e_j>$, we call $<s, e_i, e_j>$ an *instance*. For each instance, the problem is to determine whether e_i and e_j are located near each other in the physical scene described in the sentence s. For example, suppose e_i is "dog", e_j is "cat", and s = *"The King puts his dog and cat on the table."*. As it is true that the two objects are located near in this sentence, a successful classification model is expected to label this instance as *True*. However, if s_2 = *"My dog is older than her cat."*, then the label of the instance $<s_2, e_i, e_j>$ is *False*, because s_2 just talks about a comparison in age. In the following subsections, we present two different kinds of baseline methods for this binary classification task: feature-based methods and LSTM-based neural architectures.

2.1 Feature-based Methods

Our first baseline method is an SVM classifier based on following features commonly used in many relation extraction models (Xu et al., 2015):

1. *Bag of Words (BW)*: the set of words that ever appeared in the sentence.
2. *Bag of Path Words (BPW)*: the set of words that appeared on the shortest dependency path between objects e_i and e_j in the dependency tree of the sentence s, plus the words in the two subtrees rooted at e_i and e_j in the tree.
3. *Bag of Adverbs and Prepositions (BAP)*: the existence of adverbs and prepositions in the

sentence as binary features.
4. *Global Features (GF)*: the length of the sentence, the number of nouns, verbs, adverbs, adjectives, determiners, prepositions and punctuations in the whole sentence.
5. *Shortest Dependency Path features (SDP)*: the same features as with GF but in dependency parse trees of the sentence and the shortest path between e_i and e_j, respectively.
6. *Semantic Similarity features (SS)*: the cosine similarities between the pre-trained *GloVe* word embeddings (Pennington et al., 2014) of the two object words.

We evaluate *linear* and *RBF* kernels with different parameter settings, and find the *RBF* kernel with $\{C = 100, \gamma = 10^{-3}\}$ performs the best overall.

2.2 LSTM-based Neural Architectures

We observe that the existence of LOCATEDNEAR relation in an instance $<s, e_1, e_2>$ depends on two major information sources: one is from the semantic and syntactical features of sentence s and the other is from the object pair $<e_1, e_2>$. By this intuition, we design our LSTM-based model with two parts, shown in lower part of Figure 2. The left part is for encoding the syntactical and semantic information of the sentence s, while the right part is encoding the semantic similarity between the pre-trained word embeddings of e_1 and e_2.

Solely relying on the original word sequence of a sentence s has two problems: (i) the irrelevant words in the sentence can introduce noise into the model; (ii) the large vocabulary of original sentences induce too many parameters, which may cause over-fitting. For example, given two sentences *"The king led the dog into his nice garden."* and *"A criminal led the dog into a poor garden."*. The object pair is $<dog, garden>$ in both sentences. The two words *"lead"* and *"into"* are essential for determining whether the object pair is located near, but they are not attached with due importance. Also, the semantic differences between irrelevant words, such as "king" and "criminal", "beautiful" and "poor", are not useful to the co-location relation between the "dog" and "garden", and thus tend to act as noise.

To address the above issues, we propose a normalized sentence representation method merging the three most important and relevant kinds of information about each instance: lemmatized forms, POS (Part-of-Speech) tags and dependency roles.

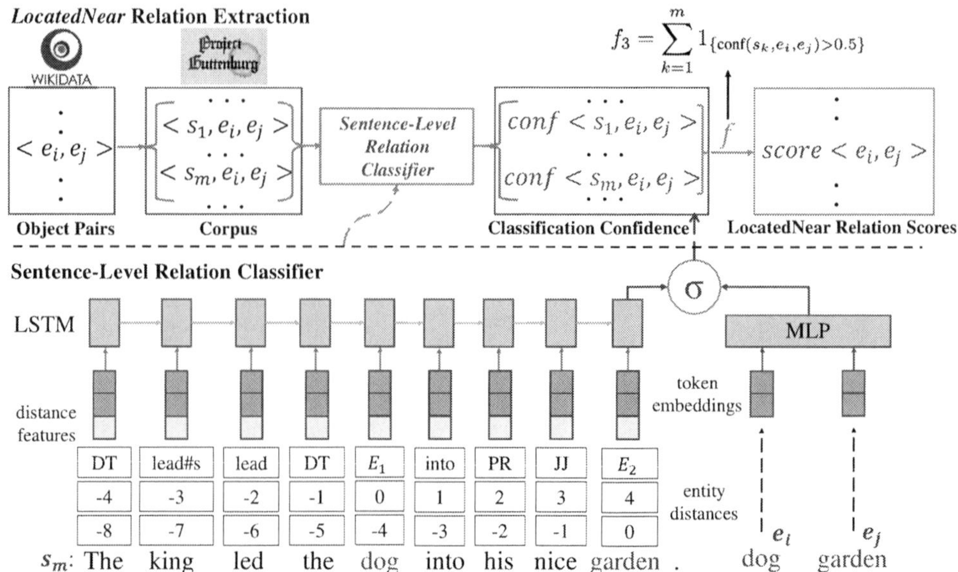

Figure 2: Framework with a LSTM-based classifier

Level	Examples
Objects	E_1, E_2
Lemma	open, lead, into, ...
Dependency Role	open#s, open#o, into#o, ...
POS Tag	DT, PR, CC, JJ, ...

Table 1: Examples of four types of tokens during sentence normalization. (#s stands for subjects and #o for objects)

We first replace the two nouns in the object pair as "E_1" and "E_2", and keep the lemmatized form of the original words for all the *verbs, adverbs and prepositions*, which are highly relevant to describing physical scenes. Then, we replace the *subjects and direct objects* of the *verbs and prepositions* (`nsubj, dobj` for verbs and `case` for prepositions in dependency parse trees) with special tokens indicating their dependency roles. For the remaining words, we simply use their POS tags to replace the originals. The four kinds of tokens are illustrated in Table 1. Figure 2 shows a real example of our normalized sentence representation, where the object pair of interest is *<dog, garden>*.

Apart from the normalized tokens of the original sequence, to capture more structural information, we also encode the distances from each token to E_1 and E_2 respectively. Such *position embeddings* (position/distance features) are proposed by (Zeng et al., 2014) with the intuition that information needed to determine the relation between two target nouns normally comes from the words which are close to the target nouns.

Then, we leverage LSTM to encode the whole sequence of the tokens of normalized representation plus position embedding. In the meantime, two pretrained *GloVe* word embeddings (Pennington et al., 2014) of the original two physical object words are fed into a hidden dense layer.

Finally, we concatenate both outputs and then use `sigmoid` activation function to obtain the final prediction. We choose to use the popular binary cross-entropy as our loss function, and RMSProp as the optimizer. We apply a dropout rate (Zaremba et al., 2014) of 0.5 in the LSTM and embedding layer to prevent overfitting.

3 LOCATEDNEAR Relation Extraction

The upper part of Figure 2 shows the overall workflow of our automatic framework to mine Located-Near relations from raw text. We first construct a vocabulary of physical objects and generate all candidate instances. For each sentence in the corpus, if a pair of physical objects e_i and e_j appear as nouns in a sentence s, then we apply our sentence-level relation classifier on this instance. The relation classifier yields a probabilistic score s indicating the confidence of the instance in the existence of LO-CATEDNEAR relation. Finally, all scores of the instances from the corpus are grouped by the object pairs and aggregated, where each object pair is associated with a final score. These mined physical pairs with scores can easily be integrated into existing commonsense knowledge base.

More specifically, for each object pair $<e_i, e_j>$, we find all the m sentences in our corpus mentioning both objects. We classify the m instances with the sentence-level relation classifier and obtain confidence scores for each instance, then feed them into a heuristic scoring function f to obtain the final aggregated score for the given object pair. We propose the following 5 choices of f considering accumulation and threshold:

$$f_0 = m \tag{1}$$

$$f_1 = \sum_{k=1}^{m} \text{conf}(s_k, e_i, e_j) \tag{2}$$

$$f_2 = \frac{1}{m} \sum_{k=1}^{m} \text{conf}(s_k, e_i, e_j) \tag{3}$$

$$f_3 = \sum_{k=1}^{m} \mathbb{1}_{\{\text{conf}(s_k,e_i,e_j)>0.5\}} \tag{4}$$

$$f_4 = \frac{1}{m} \sum_{k=1}^{m} \mathbb{1}_{\{\text{conf}(s_k,e_i,e_j)>0.5\}} \tag{5}$$

4 Datasets

Our proposed vocabulary of single-word physical objects is constructed by the intersection of all ConceptNet concepts and all entities that belong to "physical object" class in *Wikidata* (Vrandečić and Krötzsch, 2014). We manually filter out some words that have the meaning of an abstract concept, which results in 1,169 physical objects in total.

Afterwards, we utilize a cleaned subset of the Project Gutenberg corpus (Lahiri, 2014), which contains 3,036 English books written by 142 authors. An assumption here is that sentences in fictions are more likely to describe real life scenes. We sample and investigate the density of LOCATEDNEAR relations in Gutenberg with other widely used corpora, namely *Wikipedia*, used by Mintz et al. (2009) and *New York Times* corpus (Riedel et al., 2010). In the English *Wikipedia* dump, out of all sentences which mentions at least two physical objects, 32.4% turn out to be positive. In the *New York Times* corpus, the percentage of positive sentences is only 25.1%. In contrast, that percentage in the Gutenberg corpus is 55.1%, much higher than the other two corpora, making it a good choice for LOCATEDNEAR relation extraction.

From this corpus, we identify 15,193 pairs that co-occur in more than 10 sentences. Among these pairs, we randomly select 500 object pairs and 10 sentences with respect to each pair for annotators to label their commonsense LOCATEDNEAR. Each instance is labeled by at least three annotators who are college students and proficient with English. The final truth labels are decided by majority voting. The Cohen's Kappa among the three annotators is 0.711 which suggests substantial agreement (Landis and Koch, 1977). This dataset has almost double the size of those most popular relations in the SemEval task (Hendrickx et al., 2010), and the sentences in our data set tend to be longer. We randomly choose 4,000 instances as the training set and 1,000 as the test set for evaluating the sentence-level relation classification task. For the second task, we further ask the annotators to label whether each pair of objects are likely to locate near each other in the real world. Majority votes determine the final truth labels. The inter-annotator agreement here is 0.703 (substantial agreement).

5 Evaluation

In this section, we first present our evaluation of our proposed methods and the state-of-the-art general relation classification model on the first task. Then, we evaluate the quality of the new LOCATEDNEAR triples we extracted.

5.1 Sentence-level LOCATEDNEAR Relation Classification

We evaluate the proposed methods against the state-of-the-art general domain relation classification model (DRNN) (Xu et al., 2016). The results are shown in Table 2. For feature-based SVM, we do feature ablation on each of the 6 feature types. For LSTM-based model, we experiment on variants of input sequence of original sentence: "LSTM+Word" uses the original words as the input tokens; "LSTM+POS" uses only POS tags as the input tokens; "LSTM+Norm" uses the tokens of sequence after sentence normalization. Besides, we add two naive baselines: "Random" baseline method classifies the instances into two classes with equal probability. "Majority" baseline method considers all the instances to be positive.

From the results, we find that the SVM model without the Global Features performs best, which indicates that bag-of-word features benefit more in shortest dependency paths than on the whole sen-

	Random	Majority	SVM	SVM(-BW)	SVM(-BPW)	SVM(-BAP)	SVM(-GF)
Acc.	0.500	0.551	0.584	0.577	0.556	0.563	**0.605**
P	0.551	0.551	0.606	0.579	0.567	0.573	**0.616**
R	0.500	1.000	0.702	0.675	0.681	**0.811**	0.751
F1	0.524	0.710	0.650	0.623	0.619	0.672	**0.677**

	SVM(-SDP)	SVM(-SS)	DRNN	LSTM+Word	LSTM+POS	LSTM+Norm
Acc.	0.579	0.584	0.635	0.637	0.641	**0.653**
P	0.597	0.605	**0.658**	0.635	0.650	0.654
R	0.728	0.708	0.702	**0.800**	0.751	0.784
F1	0.656	0.652	0.679	0.708	0.697	**0.713**

Table 2: Performance of baselines on co-location classification task with ablation. (Acc.=Accuracy, P=Precision, R=Recall, "-" means without certain feature)

f	MAP	P@50	P@100	P@200	P@300
f_0	0.42	0.40	0.44	0.42	0.38
f_1	0.58	**0.70**	0.60	0.53	**0.44**
f_2	0.48	0.56	0.52	0.49	0.42
f_3	**0.59**	0.68	**0.63**	**0.55**	**0.44**
f_4	0.56	0.40	0.48	0.50	0.42

Table 3: Ranking results of scoring functions.

(door, room)	(boy, girl)	(cup, tea)
(ship, sea)	(house, garden)	(arm, leg)
(fire, wood)	(house, fire)	(horse, saddle)
(fire, smoke)	(door, hall)	(door, street)
(book, table)	(fruit, tree)	(table, chair)

Table 4: Top object pairs returned by best performing scoring function f_3

tence. Also, we notice that DRNN performs best (0.658) on precision but not significantly higher than LSTM+Norm (0.654). The experiment shows that LSTM+Word enjoys the highest recall score, while LSTM+Norm is the best one in terms of the overall performance. One reason is that the normalization representation reduces the vocabulary of input sequences, while also preserving important syntactical and semantic information. Another reason is that the LOCATEDNEAR relation are described in sentences decorated with prepositions/adverbs. These words are usually descendants of the object word in the dependency tree, outside of the shortest dependency paths. Thus, DRNN cannot capture the information from the words belonging to the descendants of the two object words in the tree, but this information is well captured by LSTM+Norm.

5.2 LOCATEDNEAR Relation Extraction

Once we have obtained the probability score for each instance using LSTM+Norm, we can extract LOCATEDNEAR relation using the scoring function f. We compare the performance of 5 different heuristic choices of f, by quantitative results. We rank 500 commonsense LOCATEDNEAR object pairs described in Section 3. Table 3 shows the ranking results using *Mean Average Precision* (MAP) and *Precision* at K as the metrics. Accumulative scores (f_1 and f_3) generally do better. Thus, we choose $f = f_3$ with a MAP score of 0.59 as the scoring function.

Qualitatively, we show 15 object pairs with some of the highest f_3 scores in Table 4. Setting a threshold of 40.0 for f_3, which is the minimum non-zero f_3 score for all true object pairs in the LOCATEDNEAR object pairs data set (500 pairs), we obtain a total of 2,067 LOCATEDNEAR relations, with a precision of 68% by human inspection.

6 Conclusion

In this paper, we present a novel study on enriching LOCATEDNEAR relationship from textual corpora. Based on our two newly-collected benchmark datasets, we propose several methods to solve the sentence-level relation classification problem. We show that existing methods do not work as well on this task and discovered that LSTM-based model does not have significant edge over simpler feature-based model. Whereas, our multi-level sentence normalization turns out to be useful.

Future directions include: 1) better leveraging distant supervision to reduce human efforts, 2) incorporating knowledge graph embedding techniques, 3) applying the LOCATEDNEAR knowledge into downstream applications in computer vision and natural language processing.

Acknowledgment

Kenny Q. Zhu is the contact author and was supported by NSFC grants 91646205 and 61373031. Thanks to the annotators for manual labeling, and the anonymous reviewers for valuable comments.

References

Samuel R. Bowman, Gabor Angeli, Christopher Potts, and Christopher D. Manning. 2015. A large annotated corpus for learning natural language inference. In *Proceedings of the 2015 Conference on Empirical Methods in Natural Language Processing*, pages 632–642. Association for Computational Linguistics.

Ido Dagan, Bill Dolan, Bernardo Magnini, and Dan Roth. 2009. Recognizing textual entailment: Rational, evaluation and approaches. *Natural Language Engineering*, 15(4):i–xvii.

Iris Hendrickx, Su Nam Kim, Zornitsa Kozareva, Preslav Nakov, Diarmuid Ó Séaghdha, Sebastian Padó, Marco Pennacchiotti, Lorenza Romano, and Stan Szpakowicz. 2010. Semeval-2010 task 8: Multi-way classification of semantic relations between pairs of nominals. In *Proceedings of the 5th International Workshop on Semantic Evaluation*, pages 33–38. Association for Computational Linguistics.

Shibamouli Lahiri. 2014. Complexity of word collocation networks: A preliminary structural analysis. In *Proceedings of the Student Research Workshop at the 14th Conference of the European Chapter of the Association for Computational Linguistics*, pages 96–105. Association for Computational Linguistics.

J. Richard Landis and Gary G. Koch. 1977. The measurement of observer agreement for categorical data. *Biometrics*, 33 1:159–74.

Xiang Li, Aynaz Taheri, Lifu Tu, and Kevin Gimpel. 2016. Commonsense knowledge base completion. In *Proceedings of the 54th Annual Meeting of the Association for Computational Linguistics (ACL), Berlin, Germany, August. Association for Computational Linguistics*, pages 1445–1455.

Mike Mintz, Steven Bills, Rion Snow, and Daniel Jurafsky. 2009. Distant supervision for relation extraction without labeled data. In *Proceedings of the Joint Conference of the 47th Annual Meeting of the ACL and the 4th International Joint Conference on Natural Language Processing of the AFNLP*, pages 1003–1011. Association for Computational Linguistics.

Jeffrey Pennington, Richard Socher, and Christopher Manning. 2014. Glove: Global vectors for word representation. In *Proceedings of the 2014 Conference on Empirical Methods in Natural Language Processing (EMNLP)*, pages 1532–1543. Association for Computational Linguistics.

Sebastian Riedel, Limin Yao, and Andrew McCallum. 2010. Modeling relations and their mentions without labeled text. *Machine learning and knowledge discovery in databases*, pages 148–163.

Robert Speer and Catherine Havasi. 2012. Representing general relational knowledge in conceptnet 5. In *Proceedings of the Eighth International Conference on Language Resources and Evaluation (LREC-2012)*. European Language Resources Association (ELRA).

Denny Vrandečić and Markus Krötzsch. 2014. Wikidata: A free collaborative knowledgebase. *Communications of ACM*, 57:78–85.

Yan Xu, Ran Jia, Lili Mou, Ge Li, Yunchuan Chen, Yangyang Lu, and Zhi Jin. 2016. Improved relation classification by deep recurrent neural networks with data augmentation. In *Proceedings of COLING 2016, the 26th International Conference on Computational Linguistics: Technical Papers*, pages 1461–1470. The COLING 2016 Organizing Committee.

Yan Xu, Lili Mou, Ge Li, Yunchuan Chen, Hao Peng, and Zhi Jin. 2015. Classifying relations via long short term memory networks along shortest dependency paths. In *Proceedings of the 2015 Conference on Empirical Methods in Natural Language Processing*, pages 1785–1794. Association for Computational Linguistics.

Mark Yatskar, Vicente Ordonez, and Ali Farhadi. 2016. Stating the obvious: Extracting visual common sense knowledge. In *Proceedings of the 2016 Conference of the North American Chapter of the Association for Computational Linguistics: Human Language Technologies*, pages 193–198. Association for Computational Linguistics.

Wojciech Zaremba, Ilya Sutskever, and Oriol Vinyals. 2014. Recurrent neural network regularization. *arXiv preprint arXiv:1409.2329*.

Daojian Zeng, Kang Liu, Siwei Lai, Guangyou Zhou, and Jun Zhao. 2014. Relation classification via convolutional deep neural network. In *Proceedings of COLING 2014, the 25th International Conference on Computational Linguistics: Technical Papers*, pages 2335–2344. Dublin City University and Association for Computational Linguistics.

Yuke Zhu, Alireza Fathi, and Li Fei-Fei. 2014. Reasoning about object affordances in a knowledge base representation. In *European conference on computer vision*, pages 408–424. Springer.

Neural Coreference Resolution with Deep Biaffine Attention by Joint Mention Detection and Mention Clustering

Rui Zhang *
Yale University
r.zhang@yale.edu

Cícero Nogueira dos Santos
IBM Research
cicerons@us.ibm.com

Michihiro Yasunaga
Yale University
michihiro.yasunaga@yale.edu

Bing Xiang
IBM Watson
bingxia@us.ibm.com

Dragomir R. Radev
Yale University
dragomir.radev@yale.edu

Abstract

Coreference resolution aims to identify in a text all mentions that refer to the same real-world entity. The state-of-the-art end-to-end neural coreference model considers all text spans in a document as potential mentions and learns to link an antecedent for each possible mention. In this paper, we propose to improve the end-to-end coreference resolution system by (1) using a biaffine attention model to get antecedent scores for each possible mention, and (2) jointly optimizing the mention detection accuracy and the mention clustering log-likelihood given the mention cluster labels. Our model achieves the state-of-the-art performance on the CoNLL-2012 Shared Task English test set.

1 Introduction

End-to-end coreference resolution is the task of identifying and grouping *mentions* in a text such that all mentions in a cluster refer to the same entity. An example is given below (Björkelund and Kuhn, 2014) where mentions for two entities are labeled in two clusters:

> [Drug Emporium Inc.]$_{a1}$ said [Gary Wilber]$_{b1}$ was named CEO of [this drugstore chain]$_{a2}$. [He]$_{b2}$ succeeds his father, Philip T. Wilber, who founded [the company]$_{a3}$ and remains chairman. Robert E. Lyons III, who headed the [company]$_{a4}$'s Philadelphia region, was appointed president and chief operating officer, succeeding [Gary Wilber]$_{b3}$.

Many traditional coreference systems, either rule-based (Haghighi and Klein, 2009; Lee et al., 2011)

---

*Work done during the internship at IBM Watson.

or learning-based (Bengtson and Roth, 2008; Fernandes et al., 2012; Durrett and Klein, 2013; Björkelund and Kuhn, 2014), usually solve the problem in two separate stages: (1) a mention detector to propose entity mentions from the text, and (2) a coreference resolver to cluster proposed mentions. At both stages, they rely heavily on complicated, fine-grained, conjoined features via heuristics. This pipeline approach can cause cascading errors, and in addition, since both stages rely on a syntactic parser and complicated handcraft features, it is difficult to generalize to new data sets and languages.

Very recently, Lee et al. (2017) proposed the first state-of-the-art end-to-end neural coreference resolution system. They consider all text spans as potential mentions and therefore eliminate the need of carefully hand-engineered mention detection systems. In addition, thanks to the representation power of pre-trained word embeddings and deep neural networks, the model only uses a minimal set of hand-engineered features (speaker ID, document genre, span distance, span width).

The core of the end-to-end neural coreference resolver is the scoring function to compute the mention scores for all possible spans and the antecedent scores for a pair of spans. Furthermore, one major challenge of coreference resolution is that most mentions in the document are singleton or non-anaphoric, i.e., not coreferent with any previous mention (Wiseman et al., 2015). Since the data set only have annotations for mention clusters, the end-to-end coreference resolution system needs to detect mentions, detect anaphoricity, and perform coreference linking. Therefore, research questions still remain on good designs of the scoring architecture and the learning strategy for both mention detection and antecedent scoring given only the gold cluster labels.

To this end, we propose to use a biaffine atten-

Proceedings of the 56th Annual Meeting of the Association for Computational Linguistics (Short Papers), pages 102–107
Melbourne, Australia, July 15 - 20, 2018. ©2018 Association for Computational Linguistics

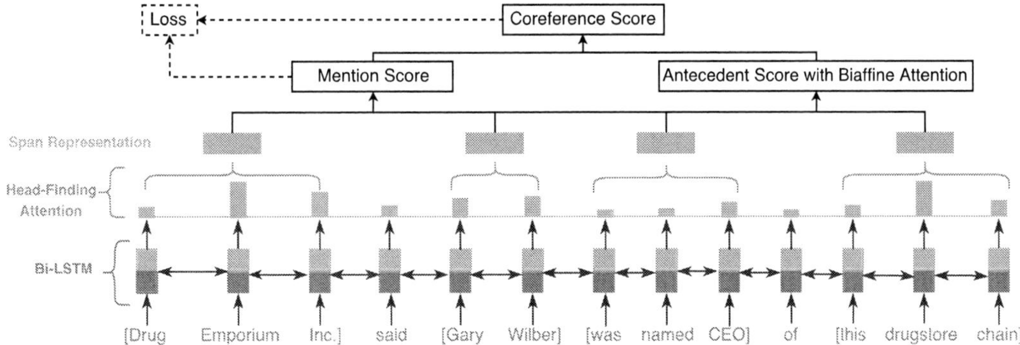

Figure 1: Model architecture. We consider all text spans up to 10-word length as possible mentions. For brevity, we only show three candidate antecedent spans ("Drug Emporium Inc.", "Gary Wilber", "was named CEO") for the current span "this drugstore chain".

tion model instead of pure feed forward networks to compute antecedent scores. Furthermore, instead of training only to maximize the marginal likelihood of gold antecedent spans, we jointly optimize the mention detection accuracy and the mention clustering log-likelihood given the mention cluster labels. We optimize mention detection loss explicitly to extract mentions and also perform anaphoricity detection.

We evaluate our model on the CoNLL-2012 English data set and achieve new state-of-the-art performances of 67.8% F1 score using a single model and 69.2% F1 score using a 5-model ensemble.

2   Task Formulation

In end-to-end coreference resolution, the input is a document D with T words, and the output is a set of mention clusters each of which refers to the same entity. A possible *span* is an N-gram within a single sentence. We consider all possible spans up to a predefined maximum width. To impose an ordering, spans are sorted by the start position $\text{START}(i)$ and then by the end position $\text{END}(i)$. For each span i the system needs to assign an antecedent a_i from all preceding spans or a dummy antecedent ϵ: $a_i \in \{\epsilon, 1, \ldots, i-1\}$. If a span j is a true antecedent of the span i, then we have $a_i = j$ and $1 \le j \le i-1$. The dummy antecedent ϵ represents two possibilities: (1) the span i is not an entity mention, or (2) the span i is an entity mention but not coreferent with any previous span. Finally, the system groups mentions according to coreference links to form the mention clusters.

3   Model

Figure 1 illustrates our model. We adopt the same span representation approach as in Lee et al. (2017) using bidirectional LSTMs and a head-finding attention. Thereafter, a feed forward network produces scores for spans being entity mentions. For antecedent scoring, we propose a biaffine attention model (Dozat and Manning, 2017) to produce distributions of possible antecedents. Our training data only provides gold mention cluster labels. To make best use of this information, we propose to jointly optimize the mention scoring and antecedent scoring in our loss function.

Span Representation Suppose the current sentence of length L is $[w_1, w_2, \ldots, w_L]$, we use $\mathbf{w}_t$ to denote the concatenation of fixed pretrained word embeddings and CNN character embeddings (dos Santos and Zadrozny, 2014) for word w_t. Bidirectional LSTMs (Hochreiter and Schmidhuber, 1997) recurrently encode each w_t:

$$\overrightarrow{\mathbf{h}}_t = \text{LSTM}^{\text{forward}}(\overrightarrow{\mathbf{h}}_{t-1}, \mathbf{w}_t)$$
$$\overleftarrow{\mathbf{h}}_t = \text{LSTM}^{\text{backward}}(\overleftarrow{\mathbf{h}}_{t+1}, \mathbf{w}_t) \qquad (1)$$
$$\mathbf{h}_t = [\overrightarrow{\mathbf{h}}_t, \overleftarrow{\mathbf{h}}_t]$$

Then, the head-finding attention computes a score distribution over different words in a span s_i:

$$\alpha_t = \mathbf{v}_\alpha^\mathsf{T} \text{FFNN}_\alpha(\mathbf{h}_t)$$
$$s_{i,t} = \frac{\exp(\alpha_t)}{\sum_{k=\text{START}(i)}^{\text{END}(i)} \exp(\alpha_k)} \qquad (2)$$
$$\mathbf{w}_i^{\text{head-att}} = \sum_{t=\text{START}(i)}^{\text{END}(i)} s_{i,t} \mathbf{w}_t$$

where FFNN is a feed forward network outputting a vector.

Effective span representations encode both contextual information and internal structure of spans. Therefore, we concatenate different vectors, including a feature vector $\phi(i)$ for the span size, to produce the span representation $\mathbf{s}_i$ for s_i:

$$\mathbf{s}_i = [\mathbf{h}_{\text{START}(i)}, \mathbf{h}_{\text{END}(i)}, \mathbf{w}_i^{\text{head-att}}, \phi(i)] \quad (3)$$

Mention Scoring The span representation is input to a feed forward network which measures if it is an entity mention using a score $m(i)$:

$$m(i) = \mathbf{v}_m^\mathsf{T} \text{FFNN}_m(\mathbf{s}_i) \quad (4)$$

Since we consider all possible spans, the number of spans is $O(T^2)$ and the number of span pairs is $O(T^4)$. Due to computation efficiency, we prune candidate spans during both inference and training. We keep λT spans with highest mention scores.

Biaffine Attention Antecedent Scoring Consider the current span s_i and its previous spans s_j ($1 \leq j \leq i - 1$), we propose to use a biaffine attention model to produce scores $c(i, j)$:

$$\begin{aligned} \hat{\mathbf{s}}_i &= \text{FFNN}_{\text{anaphora}}(\mathbf{s}_i) \\ \hat{\mathbf{s}}_j &= \text{FFNN}_{\text{antecedent}}(\mathbf{s}_j), 1 \leq j \leq i - 1 \quad (5) \\ c(i, j) &= \hat{\mathbf{s}}_j^\mathsf{T} \mathbf{U}_{\text{bi}} \hat{\mathbf{s}}_i + \mathbf{v}_{\text{bi}}^\mathsf{T} \hat{\mathbf{s}}_i \end{aligned}$$

$\text{FFNN}_{\text{anaphora}}$ and $\text{FFNN}_{\text{antecedent}}$ reduce span representation dimensions and only keep information relevant to coreference decisions. Compared with the traditional FFNN approach in Lee et al. (2017), biaffine attention directly models both the compatibility of s_i and s_j by $\hat{\mathbf{s}}_j^\mathsf{T} \mathbf{U}_{\text{bi}} \hat{\mathbf{s}}_i$ and the prior likelihood of s_i having an antecedent by $\mathbf{v}_{\text{bi}}^\mathsf{T} \hat{\mathbf{s}}_i$.

Inference The final coreference score $s(i, j)$ for span s_i and span s_j consists of three terms: (1) if s_i is a mention, (2) if s_j is a mention, (3) if s_j is an antecedent for s_i. Furthermore, for dummy antecedent ϵ, we fix the final score to be 0:

$$s(i, j) = \begin{cases} m(i) + m(j) + c(i, j), & j \neq \epsilon \\ 0, & j = \epsilon \end{cases} \quad (6)$$

During inference, the model only creates a link if the highest antecedent score is positive.

Joint Mention Detection and Mention Cluster During training, only mention cluster labels are available rather than antecedent links. Therefore, Lee et al. (2017) train the model end-to-end by

maximizing the following marginal log-likelihood where $\text{GOLD}(i)$ are gold antecedents for s_i:

$$\mathcal{L}_{\text{cluster}}(i) = \log \frac{\sum_{j' \in \text{GOLD}(i)} \exp(s(i, j'))}{\sum_{j = \epsilon, 0, \dots, i-1} \exp(s(i, j))} \quad (7)$$

However, the initial pruning is completely random and the mention scoring model only receives distant supervision if we only optimize the above mention cluster performance. This makes learning slow and ineffective especially for mention detection. Based on this observation, we propose to directly optimize mention detection:

$$\mathcal{L}_{\text{detect}}(i) = y_i \log \hat{y}_i + (1 - y_i) \log(1 - \hat{y}_i) \quad (8)$$

where $\hat{y}_i = \text{sigmoid}(m(i))$, $y_i = 1$ if and only if s_i is in one of the gold mention clusters. Our final loss combines mention detection and clustering:

$$\mathcal{L}_{\text{loss}} = -\lambda_{\text{detect}} \sum_{i=1}^{N} \mathcal{L}_{\text{detect}}(i) - \sum_{i'=1}^{N'} \mathcal{L}_{\text{cluster}}(i')$$

where N is the number of all possible spans, N' is the number of unpruned spans, and $\lambda_{\text{detection}}$ controls weights of two terms.

4 Experiments

Data Set and Evaluation We evaluate our model on the CoNLL-2012 Shared Task English data (Pradhan et al., 2012) which is based on the OntoNotes corpus (Hovy et al., 2006). It contains 2,802/343/348 train/development/test documents in different genres.

We use three standard metrics: MUC (Vilain et al., 1995), B^3 (Bagga and Baldwin, 1998), and CEAF_{ϕ_4} (Luo, 2005). We report Precision, Recall, F1 for each metric and the average F1 as the final CoNLL score.

Implementation Details For fair comparisons, we follow the same hyperparameters as in Lee et al. (2017). We consider all spans up to 10 words and up to 250 antecedents. $\lambda = 0.4$ is used for span pruning. We use fixed concatenations of 300-dimension GloVe (Pennington et al., 2014) embeddings and 50-dimension embeddings from Turian et al. (2010). Character CNNs use 8-dimension learned embeddings and 50 kernels for each window size in $\{3,4,5\}$. LSTMs have hidden size 200, and each FFNN has two hidden layers with 150 units and ReLU (Nair and Hinton, 2010) activations. We include (speaker ID, document

	MUC			B^3			CEAF$_{\phi_4}$			
	P	R	F1	P	R	F1	P	R	F1	Avg. F1
Our work (5-model ensemble)	82.1	73.6	77.6	73.1	62.0	67.1	67.5	59.0	62.9	**69.2**
Lee et al. (2017) (5-model ensemble)	81.2	73.6	77.2	72.3	61.7	66.6	65.2	60.2	62.6	68.8
Our work (single model)	79.4	73.8	76.5	69.0	62.3	65.5	64.9	58.3	61.4	**67.8**
Lee et al. (2017) (single model)	78.4	73.4	75.8	68.6	61.8	65.0	62.7	59.0	60.8	67.2
Clark and Manning (2016a)	79.2	70.4	74.6	69.9	58.0	63.4	63.5	55.5	59.2	65.7
Clark and Manning (2016b)	79.9	69.3	74.2	71.0	56.5	63.0	63.8	54.3	58.7	65.3
Wiseman et al. (2016)	77.5	69.8	73.4	66.8	57.0	61.5	62.1	53.9	57.7	64.2
Wiseman et al. (2015)	76.2	69.3	72.6	66.2	55.8	60.5	59.4	54.9	57.1	63.4
Fernandes et al. (2014)	75.9	65.8	70.5	77.7	65.8	71.2	43.2	55.0	48.4	63.4
Clark and Manning (2015)	76.1	69.4	72.6	65.6	56.0	60.4	59.4	53.0	56.0	63.0
Martschat and Strube (2015)	76.7	68.1	72.2	66.1	54.2	59.6	59.5	52.3	55.7	62.5
Durrett and Klein (2014)	72.6	69.9	71.2	61.2	56.4	58.7	56.2	54.2	55.2	61.7
Björkelund and Kuhn (2014)	74.3	67.5	70.7	62.7	55.0	58.6	59.4	52.3	55.6	61.6
Durrett and Klein (2013)	72.9	65.9	69.2	63.6	52.5	57.5	54.3	54.4	54.3	60.3

Table 1: Experimental results on the CoNLL-2012 Englisth test set. The F1 improvements are statistical significant with $p < 0.05$ under the paired bootstrap resample test (Koehn, 2004) compared with Lee et al. (2017).

	Avg. F1
Our model (single)	67.8
without mention detection loss	67.5
without biaffine attention	67.4
Lee et al. (2017)	67.3

Table 2: Ablation study on the development set.

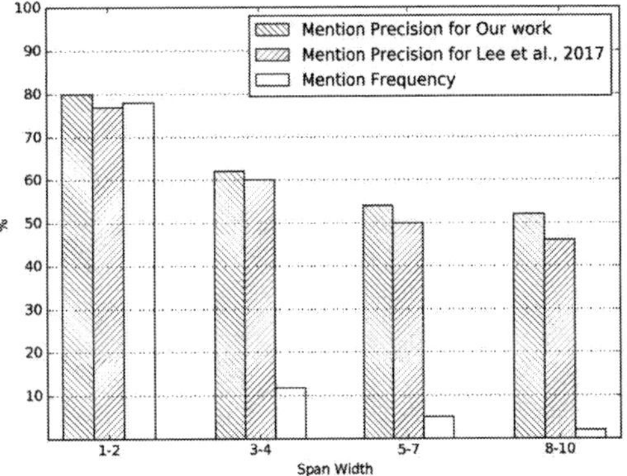

Figure 2: Mention detection subtask on development set. We plot accuracy and frequency breakdown by span widths.

genre, span distance, span width) features as 20-dimensional learned embeddings. Word and character embeddings use 0.5 dropout. All hidden layers and feature embeddings use 0.2 dropout. The batch size is 1 document. Based on the results on the development set, $\lambda_{\text{detection}} = 0.1$ works best from $\{0.05, 0.1, 0.5, 1.0\}$. Model is trained with ADAM optimizer (Kingma and Ba, 2015) and converges in around 200K updates, which is faster than that of Lee et al. (2017).

Overall Performance In Table 1, we compare our model with previous state-of-the-art systems. We obtain the best results in all F1 metrics. Our single model achieves 67.8% F1 and our 5-model ensemble achieves 69.2% F1. In particular, compared with Lee et al. (2017), our improvement mainly results from the precision scores. This indicates that the mention detection loss does produce better mention scores and the biaffine attention more effectively determines if two spans are coreferent.

Ablation Study To understand the effect of different proposed components, we perform ablation study on the development set. As shown in Table 2, removing the mention detection loss term or the biaffine attention decreases 0.3/0.4 final F1 score, but still higher than the baseline. This shows that both components have contributions and when they work together the total gain is even higher.

Mention Detection Subtask To further understand our model, we perform a mention detection subtask where spans with mention scores higher than 0 are considered as mentions. We show the mention detection accuracy breakdown by span widths in Figure 2. Our model indeed performs better thanks to the mention detection loss. The advantage is even clearer for longer spans which consist of 5 or more words.

In addition, it is important to note that our model can detect mentions that do not exist in the training data. While Moosavi and Strube (2017) observe that there is a large overlap between the gold mentions of the training and dev (test) sets, we find that our model can correctly detect 1048 mentions which are not detected by Lee et al. (2017), consisting of 386 mentions existing in training data and 662 mentions not existing in training data. From those 662 mentions, some examples are (1) a suicide murder (2) Hong Kong Island (3) a US Airforce jet carrying robotic undersea vehicles (4) the investigation into who was behind the apparent suicide attack. This shows that our mention loss helps detection by generalizing to new mentions in test data rather than memorizing the existing mentions in training data.

5   Related Work

As summarized by Ng (2010), learning-based coreference models can be categorized into three types: (1) Mention-pair models train binary classifiers to determine if a pair of mentions are coreferent (Soon et al., 2001; Ng and Cardie, 2002; Bengtson and Roth, 2008). (2) Mention-ranking models explicitly rank all previous candidate mentions for the current mention and select a single highest scoring antecedent for each anaphoric mention (Denis and Baldridge, 2007b; Wiseman et al., 2015; Clark and Manning, 2016a; Lee et al., 2017). (3) Entity-mention models learn classifiers to determine whether the current mention is coreferent with a preceding, partially-formed mention cluster (Clark and Manning, 2015; Wiseman et al., 2016; Clark and Manning, 2016b).

In addition, we also note latent-antecedent models (Fernandes et al., 2012; Björkelund and Kuhn, 2014; Martschat and Strube, 2015). Fernandes et al. (2012) introduce coreference trees to represent mention clusters and learn to extract the maximum scoring tree in the graph of mentions.

Recently, several neural coreference resolution systems have achieved impressive gains (Wiseman et al., 2015, 2016; Clark and Manning, 2016b,a). They utilize distributed representations of mention pairs or mention clusters to dramatically reduce the number of hand-crafted features. For example, Wiseman et al. (2015) propose the first neural coreference resolution system by training a deep feed-forward neural network for mention ranking. However, these models still employ the two-stage pipeline and require a syntactic parser or a separate designed hand-engineered mention detector.

Finally, we also note the relevant work on joint mention detection and coreference resolution. Daumé III and Marcu (2005) propose to model both mention detection and coreference of the Entity Detection and Tracking task simultaneously. Denis and Baldridge (2007a) propose to use integer linear programming framework to model anaphoricity and coreference as a joint task.

6   Conclusion

In this paper, we propose to use a biaffine attention model to jointly optimize mention detection and mention clustering in the end-to-end neural coreference resolver. Our model achieves the state-of-the-art performance on the CoNLL-2012 Shared Task in English.

Acknowledgments

We thank Kenton Lee and three anonymous reviewers for their helpful discussion and feedback.

References

Amit Bagga and Breck Baldwin. 1998. Algorithms for scoring coreference chains. In *The first international conference on language resources and evaluation workshop on linguistics coreference*.

Eric Bengtson and Dan Roth. 2008. Understanding the value of features for coreference resolution. In *EMNLP*.

Anders Björkelund and Jonas Kuhn. 2014. Learning structured perceptrons for coreference resolution with latent antecedents and non-local features. In *ACL*.

Kevin Clark and Christopher D. Manning. 2015. Entity-centric coreference resolution with model stacking. In *ACL*.

Kevin Clark and Christopher D. Manning. 2016a. Deep reinforcement learning for mention-ranking coreference models. In *EMNLP*.

Kevin Clark and Christopher D. Manning. 2016b. Improving coreference resolution by learning entity-level distributed representations. In *ACL*.

Hal Daumé III and Daniel Marcu. 2005. A large-scale exploration of effective global features for a joint entity detection and tracking model. In *Proceedings of Human Language Technology Conference and Conference on Empirical Methods in Natural Language Processing*.

Pascal Denis and Jason Baldridge. 2007a. Joint determination of anaphoricity and coreference resolution using integer programming. In *NAACL*.

Pascal Denis and Jason Baldridge. 2007b. A ranking approach to pronoun resolution. In *IJCAI*.

Timothy Dozat and Christopher D Manning. 2017. Deep biaffine attention for neural dependency parsing. In *ICLR*.

Greg Durrett and Dan Klein. 2013. Easy victories and uphill battles in coreference resolution. In *EMNLP*.

Greg Durrett and Dan Klein. 2014. A joint model for entity analysis: Coreference, typing, and linking. *Transactions of the Association for Computational Linguistics*, 2:477–490.

Eraldo Rezende Fernandes, Cícero Nogueira Dos Santos, and Ruy Luiz Milidiú. 2012. Latent structure perceptron with feature induction for unrestricted coreference resolution. In *Joint Conference on EMNLP and CoNLL-Shared Task*.

Eraldo Rezende Fernandes, Cícero Nogueira dos Santos, and Ruy Luiz Milidiú. 2014. Latent trees for coreference resolution. *Computational Linguistics*.

Aria Haghighi and Dan Klein. 2009. Simple coreference resolution with rich syntactic and semantic features. In *EMNLP*.

Sepp Hochreiter and Jürgen Schmidhuber. 1997. Long short-term memory. *Neural computation*, 9(8):1735–1780.

Eduard Hovy, Mitchell Marcus, Martha Palmer, Lance Ramshaw, and Ralph Weischedel. 2006. Ontonotes: the 90% solution. In *NAACL*.

Diederik Kingma and Jimmy Ba. 2015. Adam: A method for stochastic optimization. In *ICLR*.

Philipp Koehn. 2004. Statistical significance tests for machine translation evaluation. In *EMNLP*.

Heeyoung Lee, Yves Peirsman, Angel Chang, Nathanael Chambers, Mihai Surdeanu, and Dan Jurafsky. 2011. Stanford's multi-pass sieve coreference resolution system at the conll-2011 shared task. In *Proceedings of the fifteenth conference on computational natural language learning: Shared task*, pages 28–34.

Kenton Lee, Luheng He, Mike Lewis, and Luke Zettlemoyer. 2017. End-to-end neural coreference resolution. In *EMNLP*.

Xiaoqiang Luo. 2005. On coreference resolution performance metrics. In *EMNLP*.

Sebastian Martschat and Michael Strube. 2015. Latent structures for coreference resolution. *Transactions of the Association for Computational Linguistics*, 3:405–418.

Nafise Sadat Moosavi and Michael Strube. 2017. Lexical features in coreference resolution: To be used with caution. In *ACL*.

Vinod Nair and Geoffrey E Hinton. 2010. Rectified linear units improve restricted boltzmann machines. In *ICML*.

Vincent Ng. 2010. Supervised noun phrase coreference research: The first fifteen years. In *ACL*.

Vincent Ng and Claire Cardie. 2002. Improving machine learning approaches to coreference resolution. In *ACL*.

Jeffrey Pennington, Richard Socher, and Christopher D. Manning. 2014. Glove: Global vectors for word representation. In *EMNLP*.

Sameer Pradhan, Alessandro Moschitti, Nianwen Xue, Olga Uryupina, and Yuchen Zhang. 2012. Conll-2012 shared task: Modeling multilingual unrestricted coreference in ontonotes. In *Joint Conference on EMNLP and CoNLL-Shared Task*.

Cícero Nogueira dos Santos and Bianca Zadrozny. 2014. Learning character-level representations for part-of-speech tagging. In *Proceedings of the 31st International Conference on Machine Learning (ICML), JMLR: W&CP volume 32*.

Wee Meng Soon, Hwee Tou Ng, and Daniel Chung Yong Lim. 2001. A machine learning approach to coreference resolution of noun phrases. *Computational linguistics*, 27(4):521–544.

Joseph Turian, Lev Ratinov, and Yoshua Bengio. 2010. Word representations: a simple and general method for semi-supervised learning. In *ACL*.

Marc Vilain, John Burger, John Aberdeen, Dennis Connolly, and Lynette Hirschman. 1995. A model-theoretic coreference scoring scheme. In *Proceedings of the 6th conference on Message understanding*.

Sam Wiseman, Alexander M Rush, and Stuart M Shieber. 2016. Learning global features for coreference resolution. In *NAACL*.

Sam Joshua Wiseman, Alexander Matthew Rush, Stuart Merrill Shieber, and Jason Weston. 2015. Learning anaphoricity and antecedent ranking features for coreference resolution. In *ACL*.

Fully Statistical Neural Belief Tracking

Nikola Mrkšić[1] and **Ivan Vulić[1,2]**
[1] PolyAI
[2] Language Technology Lab, University of Cambridge
nikola@poly-ai.com   ivan@poly-ai.com

Abstract

This paper proposes an improvement to the existing data-driven Neural Belief Tracking (NBT) framework for Dialogue State Tracking (DST). The existing NBT model uses a hand-crafted belief state update mechanism which involves an expensive manual retuning step whenever the model is deployed to a new dialogue domain. We show that this update mechanism can be *learned* jointly with the semantic decoding and context modelling parts of the NBT model, eliminating the last rule-based module from this DST framework. We propose two different statistical update mechanisms and show that dialogue dynamics can be modelled with a very small number of additional model parameters. In our DST evaluation over three languages, we show that this model achieves competitive performance and provides a robust framework for building resource-light DST models.

1 Introduction

The problem of language understanding permeates the deployment of statistical dialogue systems. These systems rely on dialogue state tracking (DST) modules to model the user's intent at any point of an ongoing conversation (Young, 2010). In turn, DST models rely on domain-specific Spoken Language Understanding (SLU) modules to extract turn-level user goals, which are then incorporated into the *belief state*, the system's internal probability distribution over possible dialogue states.

The dialogue states are defined by the domain-specific *ontology*: it enumerates the constraints the users can express using a collection of slots (e.g. *price range*) and their slot values (e.g. *cheap, expensive* for the aforementioned slots). The be-

lief state is used by the downstream dialogue management component to choose the next system response (Su et al., 2016, 2017).

A large number of DST models (Wang and Lemon, 2013; Sun et al., 2016; Liu and Perez, 2017; Vodolán et al., 2017, *inter alia*) treat SLU as a separate problem: the detached SLU modules are a dependency for such systems as they require large amounts of annotated training data. Moreover, recent research has demonstrated that systems which treat SLU and DST as a single problem have proven superior to those which decouple them (Williams et al., 2016). Delexicalisation-based models, such as the one proposed by (Henderson et al., 2014a,b) offer unparalleled generalisation capability.

These models use *exact matching* to replace occurrences of slot names and values with generic tags, allowing them to share parameters across all slot values. This allows them to deal with slot values not seen during training. However, their downside is shifting the problem of dealing with linguistic variation back to the system designers, who have to craft *semantic lexicons* to specify rephrasings for ontology values. Examples of such rephrasings are [*cheaper, affordable, cheaply*] for slot-value pair FOOD=CHEAP, or [*with internet, has internet*] for HAS INTERNET=TRUE. The use of such lexicons has a profound effect on DST performance (Mrkšić et al., 2016). Moreover, such lexicons introduce a design barrier for deploying these models to large real-world dialogue domains and other languages.

The Neural Belief Tracker (NBT) framework (Mrkšić et al., 2017a) is a recent attempt to overcome these obstacles by using dense word embeddings in place of traditional n-gram features. By making use of semantic relations embedded in the vector spaces, the NBT achieves DST performance competitive to lexicon-supplemented delexicalisation-based models without relying on any hand-crafted resources. Moreover, the NBT

108

Proceedings of the 56th Annual Meeting of the Association for Computational Linguistics (Short Papers), pages 108–113
Melbourne, Australia, July 15 - 20, 2018. ©2018 Association for Computational Linguistics

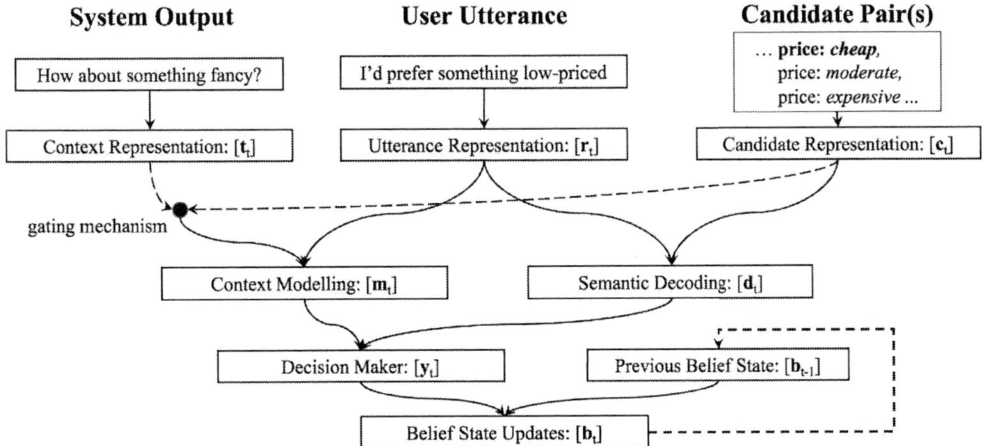

Figure 1: The architecture of the fully statistical neural belief tracker. Belief state updates are not rule-based but learned jointly with the semantic decoding and context modelling parts of the NBT model.

framework enables deployment and bootstrapping of DST models for languages other than English (Mrkšić et al., 2017b). As shown by Vulić et al. (2017), phenomena such as morphology make DST a substantially harder problem in linguistically richer languages such as Italian and German.

The NBT models decompose the (per-slot) multi-class value prediction problem into many binary ones: they iterate through all slot values defined by the ontology and decide which ones have just been expressed by the user. To differentiate between slots, they take as input the word vector of the slot value that it is making a decision about. In doing that, the previous belief state is discarded. However, the previous state may contain pertinent information for making the turn-level decision.

Contribution In this work, we show that cross-turn dependencies can be learned automatically: this eliminates the rule-based NBT component and effectively yields a fully statistical dialogue state tracker. Our competitive results on the benchmarking WOZ dataset for three languages indicate that the proposed fully statistical model: **1)** is robust with respect to the input vector space, and **2)** is easily portable and applicable to different languages.

Finally, we make the code of the novel NBT framework publicly available at: *https://github.com/nmrksic/neural-belief-tracker*, in hope of helping researchers to overcome the initial high-cost barrier to using DST as a real-world language understanding task.

2 Methodology

Neural Belief Tracker: Overview The NBT models are implemented as multi-layer neural networks. Their input consists of three components: **1)** the list of vectors for words in the last user utterance; **2)** the word vectors of the slot name and value (e.g. FOOD=INDIAN) that the model is currently making a decision about; and **3)** the word vectors which represent arguments of the preceding system acts.[1] To perform belief state tracking, the NBT model iterates over all candidate slot-value pairs as defined by the ontology, and decides which ones have just been expressed by the user.

The first layer of the NBT (see Figure 1) learns to map these inputs into intermediate distributed representations of: **1)** the current utterance representation $\mathbf{r}$; **2)** the current candidate slot-value pair $\mathbf{c}$; and **3)** the preceding system act $\mathbf{m}$. These representations then interact through the *context modelling* and *semantic decoding* downstream components, and are finally coalesced into the decision about the current slot value pair by the final *binary decision making* module. For full details of this setup, see the original NBT paper (Mrkšić et al., 2017a).

2.1 Statistical Belief State Updates

The NBT framework effectively recasts the per-slot multi-class value prediction problem as multiple

---

[1]Following Mrkšić et al. (2017a), we also consider only *system requests* and *system confirmations*, which ask the user to specify the value of a given slot (e.g. *'What kind of venue are you looking for?'*), or to confirm whether a certain intent is part of their belief state (*'Are you looking for Chinese food?'*).

binary ones: this enables the model to deal with slot values unseen in the training data. It iterates through all slot values and decides which ones have just been expressed by the user.

In the original NBT framework (Mrkšić et al., 2017a), the model for turn-level prediction is trained using SGD, maximising the accuracy of turn-level slot-value predictions. These predictions take preceding system acts into account, but *not* the previous belief state. Note that these predictions are done *separately for each slot value*.

Problem Definition   For any given slot $s \in V_s$, let $\mathbf{b}_s^{t-1}$ be the true belief state at time $t-1$ (this is a vector of length $|V_s| + 2$, accounting for all slot values and two special values, *dontcare* and *NONE*). At turn t, let the intermediate representations representing the preceding system acts and the current user utterance be $\mathbf{m}^t$ and $\mathbf{r}^t$. If the model is currently deciding about slot value $v \in V_s$, let the intermediate candidate slot-value representation be $\mathbf{c}_v^t$. The NBT binary-decision making module produces an estimate $\mathbf{y}_{s,v}^t = P(s, v|\mathbf{r^t}, \mathbf{m^t})$. We aim to combine this estimate with the previous belief state estimate for the entire slot s, $\mathbf{b}_s^{t-1}$, so that:

$$\mathbf{b}_s^t = \phi(\mathbf{y}_s^t, \mathbf{b}_s^{t-1}) \qquad (1)$$

where $\mathbf{y}_s^t$ is the vector of probabilities for each of the slot values $v \in V_s$.

Previously: Rule-Based   The original NBT framework employs a convoluted programmatic rule-based update which is hand-crafted and cannot be optimised or learned with gradient descent methods. For each slot value pair (s, v), its new probability $\mathbf{b}_{s,v}^t$ is computed as follows:

$$\mathbf{b}_{s,v}^t = \lambda \mathbf{y}_{s,v}^t + (1 - \lambda)\mathbf{b}_{s,v}^{t-1} \qquad (2)$$

λ is a tunable coefficient which determines the relative weight of the turn-level and previous turns' belief state estimates, and is maximised according to DST performance on a validation set. For slot s, the set of its *detected values* at turn t is then given as follows:

$$V_s^t = \{v \in V_s | \mathbf{b}_{s,v}^t \geq 0.5\} \qquad (3)$$

For informables (i.e., goal-tracking slots), which unlike requestable slots require belief tracking across turns, if $V_s^t \neq \emptyset$ the value in V_s^t with the highest probability is selected as the current goal.

This effectively means that the value with the highest probabilities $\mathbf{b}_{s,v}^t$ at turn t is then chosen as the new goal value, but *only* if its new probability $\mathbf{b}_{s,v}^t$ is greater than 0.5. If no value has probability greater than 0.5, the predicted goal value stays the same as the one predicted in the previous turn - even if its probability $\mathbf{b}_{s,v}^t$ is now less than 0.5.

In the rule-based method, tuning the hyper-parameter λ adjusts how likely any predicted value is to override previously predicted values. However, the "belief state" produced in this manner is not a valid probability distribution. It just predicts the top value using an ad-hoc rule that was empirically verified by Mrkšić et al. (2017a).[2]

This rule-based approach comes at a cost: the NBT framework with such updates is little more than an SLU decoder capable of modelling the preceding system acts. Its parameters do not learn to handle the previous belief state, which is essential for probabilistic modelling in POMDP-based dialogue systems (Young et al., 2010; Thomson and Young, 2010). We now show two update mechanisms that extend the NBT framework to (learn to) perform statistical belief state updates.

1. One-Step Markovian Update   To stay in line with the NBT paradigm, the criteria for the belief state update mechanism ϕ from Eq. (1) are: **1)** it is a differentiable function that can be backpropagated during NBT training; and **2)** it produces a valid probability distribution $\mathbf{b}_s^t$ as output. Figure 1 shows our fully statistical NBT architecture.

The first learned statistical update mechanism, termed One-Step Markovian Update, combines the previous belief state $\mathbf{b}_s^{t-1}$ and the current turn-level estimate $\mathbf{y}_s^t$ using a one-step belief state update:

$$\mathbf{b}_s^t = softmax\left(W_{curr}\mathbf{y}_s^t + W_{past}\mathbf{b}_s^{t-1}\right) \qquad (4)$$

W_{curr} and W_{past} are matrices which learn to combine the two signals into a new belief state. This variant violates the NBT design paradigm: each row of the two matrices learns to operate over *specific slot values*.[3]   Even though turn-level NBT

---

[2]We have also experimented with a simple model conducting statistical updates which tunes the parameter λ jointly during training and produces a valid probability distribution for the belief state at each turn t. The belief state update is performed as follows: $\mathbf{b}_s^t = \lambda \mathbf{y}_s^t + (1 - \lambda)\mathbf{b}_s^{t-1}$. We note that this simplistic statistical update mechanism performs poorly in practice, with joint goal accuracy on the English DST task in the 0.22-0.25 interval (compare it to the results from Table 1).

[3]This means the model will not learn to predict or maintain

output $\mathbf{y}_s^t$ may contain the right prediction, the parameters of the corresponding row in W_{curr} will not be trained to update the belief state, since its parameters (for the given value) will not have been updated during training. Similarly, the same row in W_{past} will not learn to maintain the given slot value as part of the belief state.

To overcome the data sparsity and preserve the NBT model's ability to deal with unseen values, one can use the fact that there are fundamentally only two different actions that a belief tracker needs to perform: **1)** maintain the same prediction as in the previous turn; or **2)** update the prediction given strong indication that a new slot value has been expressed. To facilitate transfer learning, the second update variant introduces additional constraints for the one-step belief state update.

2. Constrained Markovian Update This variant constrains the two matrices so that each of them contains only two different scalar values. The first one populates the diagonal elements, and the other one is replicated for all off-diagonal elements:

$$W_{curr,i,j} = \begin{cases} a_{curr}, & \text{if } i = j \\ b_{curr}, & \text{otherwise} \end{cases} \tag{5}$$

$$W_{past,i,j} = \begin{cases} a_{past}, & \text{if } i = j \\ b_{past}, & \text{otherwise} \end{cases} \tag{6}$$

where the four scalar values are learned jointly with other NBT parameters. The diagonal values learn the relative importance of propagating the previous value (a_{past}), or of accepting a newly detected value (a_{curr}). The off-diagonal elements learn how turn-level signals (b_{curr}) or past probabilities for other values (b_{past}) impact the predictions for the current belief state. The parameters acting over all slot values are in this way tied, ensuring that the model can deal with slot values unseen in training.

3 Experimental Setup

Evaluation: Data and Metrics As in prior work the DST evaluation is based on the Wizard-of-Oz (WOZ) v2.0 dataset (Wen et al., 2017; Mrkšić et al., 2017a), comprising 1,200 dialogues split into training (600 dialogues), validation (200), and test data (400). The English data were translated to German and Italian by professional translators (Mrkšić et al.,

---

slot values as part of the belief state if it has not encountered these values during training.

Model Variant	English WOZ 2.0	
	GLOVE (DIST)	PARAGRAM-SL999
Rule-Based	80.1	84.2
1. One-Step	80.8	82.1
2. Constrained	**81.8**	**84.8**

Table 1: The English DST performance (*joint goal accuracy*) with standard input word vectors (§3).

2017b). In all experiments, we report the standard DST performance measure: *joint goal accuracy*, which is defined as the proportion of dialogue turns where all the user's search goal constraints were correctly identified. Finally, all reported scores are averages over 5 NBT training runs.

Training Setup We compare three belief state update mechanisms (rule-based vs. two statistical ones) fixing all other NBT components as suggested by Mrkšić et al. (2017a): the better-performing NBT-CNN variant is used, trained by Adam (Kingma and Ba, 2015) with dropout (Srivastava et al., 2014) of 0.5, gradient clipping, batch size of 256, and 400 epochs. All model hyperparameters were tuned on the validation sets.

Word Vectors To test the model's robustness, we use a variety of standard word vectors from prior work. For English, following Mrkšić et al. (2017a) we use **1)** distributional GLOVE vectors (Pennington et al., 2014), and **2)** specialised PARAGRAM-SL999 vectors (Wieting et al., 2015), obtained by injecting similarity constraints from the Paraphrase Database (Pavlick et al., 2015) into GLOVE.

For Italian and German, we compare to the work of Vulić et al. (2017), who report state-of-the-art DST scores on the Italian and German WOZ 2.0 datasets. In this experiment, we train the models using distributional skip-gram vectors with a large vocabulary (labelled DIST in Table 2). Subsequently, we compare them to models trained using word vectors specialised using similarity constraints derived from language-specific morphological rules (labelled SPEC in Table 2).

4 Results and Discussion

Table 1 compares the two variants of the statistical update. The Constrained Markovian Update is the better of the two learned updates, despite using only four parameters to model dialogue dynamics (rather than $O(V^2)$, V being the slot value count). This shows that the ability to generalise to unseen

	Italian		German	
	DIST	spec	DIST	SPEC
Rule-Based Update	**74.2**	76.0	60.6	66.3
Learned Update	73.7	**76.1**	**61.5**	**68.1**

Table 2: DST performance on Italian and German. Only results with the better scoring learned Constrained Markovian Update are reported.

slot values matters more than the ability to model value-specific behaviour. In fact, combining the two updates led to no performance gains over the stand-alone Constrained Markovian update.

Table 2 investigates the portability of this model to other languages. The statistical update shows comparable performance to the rule-based one, outperforming it in three out of four experiments. In fact, our model trained using the specialised word vectors sets the new state-of-the-art performance for English, Italian and German WOZ 2.0 datasets. This supports our claim that eliminating the hand-tuned rule-based update makes the NBT model more stable and better suited to deployment across different dialogue domains and languages.

DST as Downstream Evaluation   All of the experiments show that the use of semantically specialised vectors benefits DST performance. The scale of these gains is robust across all experiments, regardless of language or the employed belief state update mechanism. So far, it has been hard to use the DST task as a proxy for measuring the correlation between word vectors' intrinsic performance (in tasks like SimLex-999 (Hill et al., 2015)) and their usefulness for downstream language understanding tasks. Having eliminated the rule-based update from the NBT model, we make our evaluation framework publicly available in hope that DST performance can serve as a useful tool for measuring the correlation between intrinsic and extrinsic performance of word vector collections.

5   Conclusion

This paper proposed an extension to the Neural Belief Tracking (NBT) model for Dialogue State Tracking (DST) (Mrkšić et al., 2017a). In the previous NBT model, system designers have to tune the *belief state update* mechanism manually whenever the model is deployed to new dialogue domains. On the other hand, the proposed model *learns* to update the belief state automatically, relying on no domain-specific validation sets to optimise DST performance. Our model outperforms the existing NBT model, setting the new state-of-the-art performance for the Multilingual WOZ 2.0 dataset across all three languages. We make the proposed framework publicly available in hope of providing a robust tool for exploring the DST task for the wider NLP community.

Acknowledgments

We thank the anonymous reviewers for their helpful and insightful suggestions. We are also grateful to Diarmuid Ó Séaghdha and Steve Young for many fruitful discussions.

References

Matthew Henderson, Blaise Thomson, and Steve Young. 2014a. Robust dialog state tracking using delexicalised recurrent neural networks and unsupervised adaptation. In *Proceedings of IEEE SLT*, pages 360–365.

Matthew Henderson, Blaise Thomson, and Steve Young. 2014b. Word-based dialog state tracking with recurrent neural networks. In *Proceedings of SIGDIAL*, pages 292–299.

Felix Hill, Roi Reichart, and Anna Korhonen. 2015. SimLex-999: Evaluating semantic models with (genuine) similarity estimation. *Computational Linguistics*, 41(4):665–695.

Diederik P. Kingma and Jimmy Ba. 2015. Adam: A method for stochastic optimization. In *Proceedings of ICLR (Conference Track)*.

Fei Liu and Julien Perez. 2017. Gated end-to-end memory networks. In *Proceedings of EACL*, pages 1–10.

Nikola Mrkšić, Diarmuid Ó Séaghdha, Blaise Thomson, Milica Gašić, Lina Rojas-Barahona, Pei-Hao Su, David Vandyke, Tsung-Hsien Wen, and Steve Young. 2016. Counter-fitting word vectors to linguistic constraints. In *Proceedings of NAACL-HLT*, pages 142–148.

Nikola Mrkšić, Diarmuid Ó Séaghdha, Blaise Thomson, Tsung-Hsien Wen, and Steve Young. 2017a. Neural Belief Tracker: Data-driven dialogue state tracking. In *Proceedings of ACL*, pages 1777–1788.

Nikola Mrkšić, Ivan Vulić, Diarmuid Ó Séaghdha, Ira Leviant, Roi Reichart, Milica Gašić, Anna Korhonen, and Steve Young. 2017b. Semantic specialisation of distributional word vector spaces using monolingual and cross-lingual constraints. *Transactions of the ACL*, pages 314–325.

Ellie Pavlick, Pushpendre Rastogi, Juri Ganitkevitch, Benjamin Van Durme, and Chris Callison-Burch.

2015. PPDB 2.0: Better paraphrase ranking, fine-grained entailment relations, word embeddings, and style classification. In *Proceedings of ACL*, pages 425–430.

Jeffrey Pennington, Richard Socher, and Christopher Manning. 2014. GloVe: Global vectors for word representation. In *Proceedings of EMNLP*, pages 1532–1543.

Nitish Srivastava, Geoffrey Hinton, Alex Krizhevsky, Ilya Sutskever, and Ruslan Salakhutdinov. 2014. Dropout: A simple way to prevent neural networks from overfitting. *Journal of Machine Learning Research*, 15:1929–1958.

Pei-Hao Su, Paweł Budzianowski, Stefan Ultes, Milica Gašić, and Steve Young. 2017. Sample-efficient actor-critic reinforcement learning with supervised data for dialogue management. pages 147–157.

Pei-Hao Su, Milica Gašić, Nikola Mrkšić, Lina Rojas-Barahona, Stefan Ultes, David Vandyke, Tsung-Hsien Wen, and Steve Young. 2016. On-line active reward learning for policy optimisation in spoken dialogue systems. In *Proceedings of ACL*, pages 2431–2441.

Kai Sun, Qizhe Xie, and Kai Yu. 2016. Recurrent polynomial network for dialogue state tracking. *Dialogue & Discourse*, 7(3):65–88.

Blaise Thomson and Steve Young. 2010. Bayesian update of dialogue state: A POMDP framework for spoken dialogue systems. *Computer Speech & Language*, 24(4):562–588.

Miroslav Vodolán, Rudolf Kadlec, and Jan Kleindienst. 2017. Hybrid dialog state tracker with ASR features. In *Proceedings of EACL*, pages 205–210.

Ivan Vulić, Nikola Mrkšić, Roi Reichart, Diarmuid Ó Séaghdha, Steve Young, and Anna Korhonen. 2017. Morph-fitting: Fine-tuning word vector spaces with simple language-specific rules. In *Proceedings of ACL*, pages 56–68.

Zhuoran Wang and Oliver Lemon. 2013. A Simple and Generic Belief Tracking Mechanism for the Dialog State Tracking Challenge: On the believability of observed information. In *Proceedings of SIGDIAL*.

Tsung-Hsien Wen, David Vandyke, Nikola Mrkšić, Milica Gašić, Lina M. Rojas-Barahona, Pei-Hao Su, Stefan Ultes, and Steve Young. 2017. A network-based end-to-end trainable task-oriented dialogue system. In *Proceedings of EACL*, pages 438–449.

John Wieting, Mohit Bansal, Kevin Gimpel, and Karen Livescu. 2015. From paraphrase database to compositional paraphrase model and back. *Transactions of the ACL*, 3:345–358.

Jason D. Williams, Antoine Raux, and Matthew Henderson. 2016. The Dialog State Tracking Challenge series: A review. *Dialogue & Discourse*, 7(3):4–33.

Steve Young. 2010. Cognitive user interfaces. *IEEE Signal Processing Magazine*.

Steve Young, Milica Gašić, Simon Keizer, François Mairesse, Jost Schatzmann, Blaise Thomson, and Kai Yu. 2010. The hidden information state model: A practical framework for POMDP-based spoken dialogue management. *Computer Speech & Language*, 24(2):150–174.

Some of Them Can be Guessed!
Exploring the Effect of Linguistic Context in Predicting Quantifiers

Sandro Pezzelle[*], **Shane Steinert-Threlkeld**[†], **Raffaella Bernardi**[*‡], **Jakub Szymanik**[†]
[*]CIMeC - Center for Mind/Brain Sciences, [‡]DISI, University of Trento
[†]ILLC - Institute for Logic, Language and Computation, University of Amsterdam
[*]`sandro.pezzelle@unitn.it`, [†]`s.n.m.steinert-threlkeld@uva.nl`,
[*‡]`raffaella.bernardi@unitn.it`, [†]`j.k.szymanik@uva.nl`

Abstract

We study the role of linguistic context in predicting quantifiers ('few', 'all'). We collect crowdsourced data from human participants and test various models in a *local* (single-sentence) and a *global* context (multi-sentence) condition. Models significantly out-perform humans in the former setting and are only slightly better in the latter. While human performance improves with more linguistic context (especially on proportional quantifiers), model performance suffers. Models are very effective in exploiting lexical and morpho-syntactic patterns; humans are better at genuinely understanding the meaning of the (global) context.

1 Introduction

A typical exercise used to evaluate a language learner is the cloze deletion test (Oller, 1973). In it, a word is removed and the learner must replace it. This requires the ability to understand the context and the vocabulary in order to identify the correct word. Therefore, the larger the linguistic context, the easier the test becomes. It has been recently shown that higher-ability test takers rely more on global information, with lower-ability test takers focusing more on the local context, i.e. information contained in the words immediately surrounding the gap (McCray and Brunfaut, 2018).

In this study, we explore the role of linguistic context in predicting generalized quantifiers ('few', 'some', 'most') in a cloze-test task (see Figure 1). Both human and model performance is evaluated in a *local* (single-sentence) and a *global* context (multi-sentence) condition to study the role of context and assess the cognitive plausibility of the models. The reasons we are inter-

> *<qnt> the island's breeding birds are endemic.*
>
> *The island is one of the world's most biologically diverse areas, with many endemic species.*
> *<qnt> the island's breeding birds are endemic. Other endemic species include the red-bellied lemur, the indri, and the aye-aye.*
>
> Target quantifier: ***more than half of***

Figure 1: Given a target sentence s_t, or s_t with the preceding and following sentence, the task is to predict the target quantifier replaced by $\langle \text{qnt} \rangle$.

ested in quantifiers are myriad. First, quantifiers are of central importance in linguistic semantics and its interface with cognitive science (Barwise and Cooper, 1981; Peters and Westerståhl, 2006; Szymanik, 2016). Second, the choice of quantifier depends both on local context (e.g., positive and negative quantifiers license different patterns of anaphoric reference) and global context (the degree of positivity/negativity is modulated by discourse specificity) (Paterson et al., 2009). Third and more generally, the ability of predicting *function words* in the cloze test represents a benchmark test for human linguistic competence (Smith, 1971; Hill et al., 2016).

We conjecture that human performance will be boosted by more context and that this effect will be stronger for *proportional* quantifiers (e.g. 'few', 'many', 'most') than for *logical* quantifiers (e.g. 'none', 'some', 'all') because the former are more dependent on discourse context (Moxey and Sanford, 1993; Solt, 2016). In contrast, we expect models to be very effective in exploiting the local context (Hill et al., 2016) but to suffer with a broader context, due to their reported inability to handle longer sequences (Paperno et al., 2016). Both hypotheses are confirmed. The best mod-

Proceedings of the 56th Annual Meeting of the Association for Computational Linguistics (Short Papers), pages 114–119
Melbourne, Australia, July 15 - 20, 2018. ©2018 Association for Computational Linguistics

els are very effective in the local context condition, where they significantly outperform humans. Moreover, model performance declines with more context, whereas human performance is boosted by the higher accuracy with proportional quantifiers like 'many' and 'most'. Finally, we show that best-performing models and humans make similar errors. In particuar, they tend to confound quantifiers that denote a similar 'magnitude' (Bass et al., 1974; Newstead and Collis, 1987).

Our contribution is twofold. First, we present a new task and results for training models to learn semantically-rich function words.[1] Second, we analyze the role of linguistic context in both humans and the models, with implications for cognitive plausibility and future modeling work.

2   Datasets

To test our hypotheses, we need linguistic contexts containing quantifiers. To ensure similarity in the syntactic environment of the quantifiers, we focus on partitive uses: where the quantifier is followed by the preposition 'of'. To avoid any effect of intensifiers like 'very' and 'so' and adverbs like 'only' and 'incredibly', we study only sentences in which the quantifier occurs at the beginning (see Figure 1). We experiment with a set of 9 quantifiers: 'a few', 'all', 'almost all', 'few', 'many', 'more than half', 'most', 'none', 'some'. This set strikes the best trade-off between number of quantifiers and their frequency in our *source* corpus, a large collection of written English including around 3B tokens.[2]

We build two datasets. One dataset – 1-Sent – contains datapoints that only include the sentence with the quantifier (the *target* sentence, s_t). The second – 3-Sent – contains datapoints that are 3-sentence long: the target sentence (s_t) together with both the preceding (s_p) and following one (s_f). To directly analyze the effect of the linguistic context in the task, the target sentences are exactly the same in both settings. Indeed, 1-Sent is obtained by simply extracting all target sentences $\langle s_t \rangle$ from 3-Sent ($\langle s_p, s_t, s_f \rangle$).

The 3-Sent dataset is built as follows: (1) We split our source corpus into sentences and select those starting with a '*quantifier* of' construction. Around 391K sentences of this type are found. (2)

We tokenize the sentences and replace the quantifier at the beginning of the sentence (the *target* quantifier) with the string <qnt>, to treat all target quantifiers as a single token. (3) We filter out sentences longer than 50 tokens (less than 6% of the total), yielding around 369K sentences. (4) We select all cases for which both the preceding and the following sentence are at most 50-tokens long. We also ensure that the target quantifier does not occur again in the target sentence. (5) We ensure that each datapoint $\langle s_p, s_t, s_f \rangle$ is unique. The distribution of target quantifiers across the resulting 309K datapoints ranges from 1152 cases ('more than half') to 93801 cases ('some'). To keep the dataset balanced, we randomly select 1150 points for each quantifier, resulting in a dataset of 10350 datapoints. This was split into train (80%), validation (10%), and test (10%) sets while keeping the balancing. Then, 1-Sent is obtained by extracting the target sentences $\langle s_t \rangle$ from $\langle s_p, s_t, s_f \rangle$.

3   Human Evaluation

3.1   Method

We ran two crowdsourced experiments, one per condition. In both, native English speakers were asked to pick the correct quantifier to replace <qnt> after having carefully read and understood the surrounding linguistic context. When more than one quantifier sounds correct, participants were instructed to choose the one they think best for the context. To make the results of the two surveys directly comparable, the same randomly-sampled 506 datapoints from the validation sets are used. To avoid biasing responses, the 9 quantifiers were presented in alphabetical order. The surveys were carried out via CrowdFlower.[3] Each participant was allowed to judge up to 25 points. To assess the judgments, 50 unambiguous cases per setting were manually selected by the native-English author and used as a benchmark. Overall, we collected judgments from 205 annotators in 1-Sent (avg. 7.4 judgments/annotator) and from 116 in 3-Sent (avg. 13.1). Accuracy is then computed by counting cases where at least 2 out of 3 annotators agree on the correct answer (i.e., inter-annotator agreement ≥ 0.67).

3.2   Linguistic Analysis

Overall, the task turns out to be easier in 3-Sent (131/506 correctly-guessed cases; 0.258 accu-

---

[1]Data and code are at: https://github.com/
sandropezzelle/fill-in-the-quant

[2]A concatenation of BNC, ukWaC, and a 2009-dump of Wikipedia (Baroni et al., 2014).

[3]https://www.figure-eight.com/

type	text	quantifier
meaning	<qnt> *the original station buildings survive **as they were used** as a source of materials...*	*none of*
PIs	<qnt> *these stories have **ever** been substantiated.*	*none of*
contrast Q	<qnt> *the population died out, but **a select few** with the right kind of genetic instability...*	*most of*
list	<qnt> *their major research areas are **social inequality, group dynamics, social change**...*	*some of*
quantity	<qnt> *those polled (**56%**) said that they would be willing to pay for special events...*	*more t. half of*
support Q	<qnt> *you have found this to be the case - click here for **some of** customer comments.*	*many of*
lexicalized	<qnt> ***the time**, the interest rate is set on the lender's terms...*	*most of*
syntax	<qnt> *these events **was** serious.*	*none of*

Table 1: Cues that might help human participants to predict the correct quantifier (`1-Sent`).

racy) compared to `1-Sent` (112/506; 0.221 acc.). Broader linguistic context is thus generally beneficial to the task. To gain a better understanding of the results, we analyze the correctly-predicted cases and look for linguistic cues that might be helpful for carrying out the task. Table 1 reports examples from `1-Sent` for each of these cues.

We identify 8 main types of cues and manually annotate the cases accordingly. (1) **Meaning**: the quantifier can only be guessed by understanding and reasoning about the context; (2) **PIs**: Polarity Items like 'ever', 'never', 'any' are licensed by specific quantifiers (Krifka, 1995); (3) **Contrast Q**: a contasting-magnitude quantifier embedded in an adversative clause; (4) **Support Q**: a supporting-magnitude quantifier embedded in a coordinate or subordinate clause; (5) **Quantity**: explicit quantitative information (numbers, percentages, fractions, etc.); (6) **Lexicalized**: lexicalized patterns like '*most of* the time'; (7) **List**: the text immediately following the quantifier is a list introduced by verbs like 'are' or 'include'; (8) **Syntax**: morpho-syntactic cues, e.g. agreement.

Figure 2 (left) depicts the distribution of annotated cues in correctly-guessed cases of `1-Sent`. Around 44% of these cases include cues besides meaning, suggesting that almost half of the cases can be possibly guessed by means of lexical factors such as PIs, quantity information, etc. As seen in Figure 2 (right), the role played by the meaning becomes much higher in `3-Sent`. Of the 74 cases that are correctly guessed in `3-Sent`, but not in `1-Sent`, more than 3 out of 4 do not display cues other than meaning. In the absence of lexical cues at the sentence level, the surrounding context thus plays a crucial role.

4 Models

We test several models, that we briefly describe below. All models except `FastText` are implemented in Keras and use ReLu as activation function; they are trained for 50 epochs with categorical crossentropy, initialized with frozen 300-d `word2vec` embeddings (Mikolov et al., 2013) pretrained on GoogleNews.[4] A thorough ablation study is carried out for each model to find the best configuration of parameters.[5] The best configuration is chosen based on the lowest validation loss.

BoW-conc A bag-of-words (BoW) architecture which encodes a text as the *concatenation* of the embeddings for each token. This representation is reduced by a hidden layer before softmax.

BoW-sum Same as above, but the text is encoded as the *sum* of the embeddings.

FastText Simple network for text classification that has been shown to obtain performance comparable to deep learning models (Joulin et al., 2016). `FastText` represents text as a hidden variable obtained by means of a BoW representation.

CNN Simple Convolutional Neural Network (CNN) for text classification.[6] It has two convolutional layers (`Conv1D`) each followed by `MaxPooling`. A dense layer precedes softmax.

LSTM Standard Long-Short Term Memory network (LSTM) (Hochreiter and Schmidhuber, 1997). Variable-length sequences are padded with zeros to be as long as the maximum sequence in the dataset. To avoid taking into account cells padded with zero, the 'mask zero' option is used.

bi-LSTM The Bidirectional LSTM (Schuster and Paliwal, 1997) combines information from past and future states by duplicating the first recurrent layer and then combining the two hidden states. As above, padding and mask zero are used.

---

[4] Available here: `http://bit.ly/1VxNC9t`

[5] We experiment with all possible combinations obtained by varying (a) optimizer: *adagrad, adam, nadam*; (b) hidden layers: 64 or 128 units; (c) dropout: 0.25, 0.5, 0.75.

[6] Adapted from: `http://bit.ly/2sFgOE1`

116

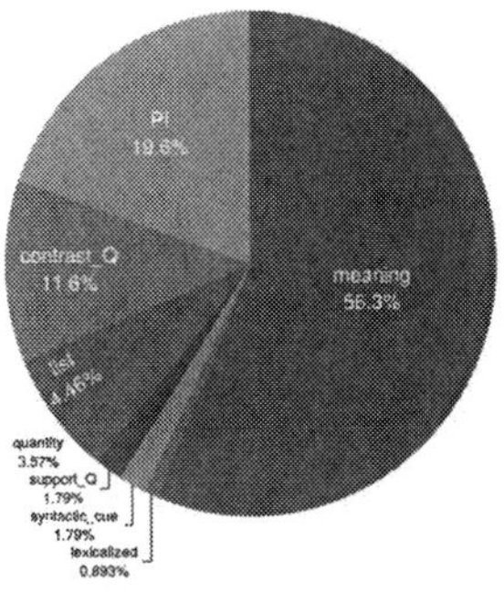 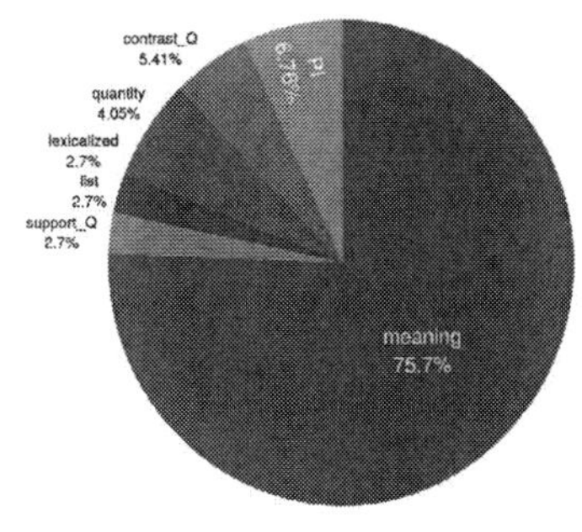

Figure 2: Left: Distribution of annotated cues across correcly-guessed cases in `1-Sent` (112 cases). Right: Distribution of cues across correctly-guessed cases in `3-Sent`, but not in `1-Sent` (74 cases).

Att-LSTM LSTM augmented with an attention mechanism (Raffel and Ellis, 2016). A feed-forward neural network computes an importance weight for each hidden state of the LSTM; the weighted sum of the hidden states according to those weights is then fed into the final classifier.

AttCon-LSTM LSTM augmented with an attention mechanism using a learned *context* vector (Yang et al., 2016). LSTM states are weighted by cosine similarity to the context vector.

5   Results

Table 2 reports the accuracy of all models and humans in both conditions. We have three main results. (1) Broader context *helps* humans to perform the task, but *hurts* model performance. This can be seen by comparing the 4-point increase of human accuracy from `1-Sent` (0.22) to `3-Sent` (0.26) with the generally worse performance of all models (e.g. `AttCon-LSTM`, from 0.34 to 0.27

	1-Sent		3-Sent	
	val	*test*	*val*	*test*
chance	0.111	0.111	0.111	0.111
BoW-conc	0.270	0.238	0.224	0.207
BoW-sum	0.308	0.290	0.267	0.245
fastText	0.305	0.271	0.297	0.245
CNN	0.310	0.304	**0.298**	0.257
LSTM	0.315	0.310	0.277	0.253
bi-LSTM	0.341	**0.337**	0.279	0.265
Att-LSTM	0.319	0.324	0.287	**0.291**
AttCon-LSTM	**0.343**	0.319	0.274	0.288
Humans	0.221*	——	0.258*	——

Table 2: Accuracy of models and humans. Values in **bold** are the highest in the column. *Note that due to an imperfect balancing of data, chance level for humans (computed as majority class) is 0.124.

in *val*). (2) All models are significantly *better* than humans in performing the task at the sentence level (`1-Sent`), whereas their performance is only slightly better than humans' in `3-Sent`. `AttCon-LSTM`, which is the best model in the former setting, achieves a significantly higher accuracy than humans' (0.34 vs 0.22). By contrast, in `3-Sent`, the performance of the best model is closer to that of humans (0.29 of `Att-LSTM` vs 0.26). It can be seen that LSTMs are overall the best-performing architectures, with `CNN` showing some potential in the handling of longer sequences (`3-Sent`). (3) As depicted in Figure 3, quantifiers that are easy/hard for humans are not necessarily easy/hard for the models. Compare 'few', 'a few', 'more than half', 'some', and 'most': while the first three are generally hard for humans but predictable by the models, the last two show the opposite pattern. Moreover, quantifiers that are guessed by humans to a larger extent in `3-Sent` compared to `1-Sent`, thus profiting from the broader linguistic context, do not experience the same boost with models. Human accuracy improves notably for 'few', 'a few', 'many', and 'most', while model performance on the same quantifiers does not.

To check whether humans and the models make similar errors, we look into the distribution of responses in `3-Sent` (*val*), which is the most comparable setting with respect to accuracy. Table 3 reports responses by humans (top) and `AttCon-LSTM` (bottom). Human errors generally involve quantifiers that display a similar magnitude as the correct one. To illustrate, 'some' is chosen in place of 'a few', and 'most' in place of either 'almost all' or 'more than half'. A similar pattern is observed in the model's predictions,

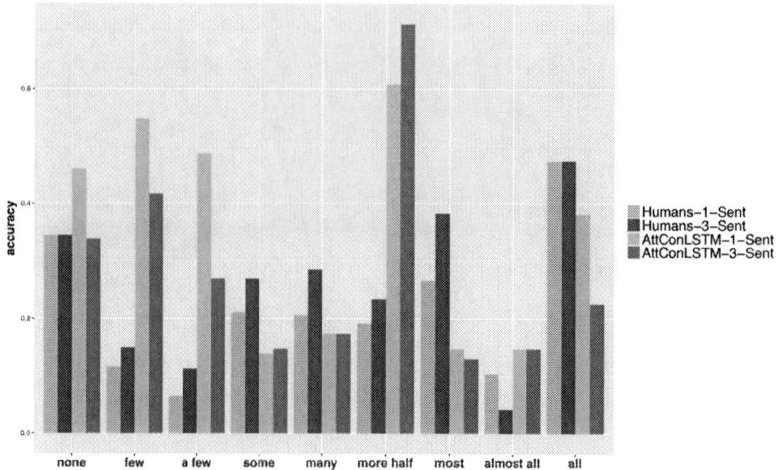

Figure 3: Human vs `AttCon-LSTM` accuracy (*val*) across quantifiers, loosely ordered by magnitude.

though we note a bias toward 'more than half'.

One last question concerns the types of linguistic cues exploited by the model (see section 3.2). We consider those cases which are correctly guessed by both humans and `AttCon-LSTM` in each setting and analyze the distribution of annotated cues. Non-semantic cues turn out to account for 41% of cases in `3-Sent` and for 50% cases in `1-Sent`. This analysis suggests that, compared to humans, the model capitalizes more on lexical, morpho-syntactic cues rather than exploiting the meaning of the context.

6 Discussion

This study explored the role of linguistic context in predicting quantifiers. For humans, the task becomes easier when a broader context is given. For the best-performing LSTMs, broader context hurts

none	**19**	1	2	0	2	0	0	0	12
few	5	**9**	2	6	5	0	3	0	2
a few	0	0	7	**17**	9	0	4	0	4
some	0	0	3	**14**	5	0	4	0	3
many	0	1	0	3	**18**	0	3	0	7
more than half	0	0	0	2	2	**11**	10	4	2
most	0	0	0	1	7	0	**23**	4	8
almost all	0	1	0	3	2	1	7	2	6
all	0	0	2	1	5	0	4	3	**28**
none	**39**	15	13	10	0	20	5	3	10
few	3	**48**	18	7	9	20	5	1	4
a few	7	13	**31**	18	5	15	12	8	6
some	5	18	16	17	16	**19**	9	5	10
many	2	18	18	15	**20**	17	10	6	9
more than half	2	7	2	3	10	**82**	2	1	6
most	8	14	14	12	12	**26**	15	5	9
almost all	5	9	15	10	8	**37**	15	6	10
all	7	12	10	15	21	13	7	4	**26**

Table 3: Responses by humans (top) and `AttCon-LSTM` (bottom) in `3-Sent` (*val*). Values in **bold** are the highest in the row.

performance. This pattern mirrors evidence that predictions by these models are mainly based on local contexts (Hill et al., 2016). Corroborating our hypotheses, *proportional* quantifiers ('few', 'many', 'most') are predicted by humans with a higher accuracy with a broader context, whereas *logical* quantifiers ('all', 'none') do not experience a similar boost. Interestingly, humans are almost always able to grasp the magnitude of the missing quantifier, even when guessing the wrong one. This finding is in line with the overlapping meaning and use of these expressions (Moxey and Sanford, 1993). It also provides indirect evidence for an ordered mental scale of quantifiers (Holyoak and Glass, 1978; Routh, 1994; Moxey and Sanford, 2000). The reason why the models fail with certain quantifiers and not others is yet not clear. It may be that part of the disadvantage in the broader context condition is due to engineering issues, as suggested by an anonymous reviewer. We leave investigating these issues to future work.

Acknowledgments

We thank Marco Baroni, Raquel Fernández, Germán Kruszewski, and Nghia The Pham for their valuable feedback. We thank the NVIDIA Corporation for the donation of GPUs used for this research, and the iV&L Net (ICT COST Action IC1307) for funding the first author's research visit. This project has received funding from the European Research Council (ERC) under the European Unions Horizon 2020 research and innovation programme (grant agreement No 716230).

References

Marco Baroni, Georgiana Dinu, and Germán Kruszewski. 2014. Don't count, predict! A systematic comparison of context-counting vs. context-predicting semantic vectors. In *Proceedings of the 52nd Annual Meeting of the Association for Computational Linguistics (Volume 1: Long Papers)*. volume 1, pages 238–247.

Jon Barwise and Robin Cooper. 1981. Generalized Quantifiers and Natural Language. *Linguistics and Philosophy* 4(2):159–219.

Bernard M Bass, Wayne F Cascio, and Edward J O'connor. 1974. Magnitude estimations of expressions of frequency and amount. *Journal of Applied Psychology* 59(3):313.

Felix Hill, Antoine Bordes, Sumit Chopra, and Jason Weston. 2016. The Goldilocks Principle: Reading Children's books with explicit memory representations. In *ICLR 2016*.

Sepp Hochreiter and Jürgen Schmidhuber. 1997. Long short-term memory. *Neural computation* 9(8):1735–1780.

Keith J Holyoak and Arnold L Glass. 1978. Recognition confusions among quantifiers. *Journal of verbal learning and verbal behavior* 17(3):249–264.

Armand Joulin, Edouard Grave, Piotr Bojanowski, and Tomas Mikolov. 2016. Bag of Tricks for Efficient Text Classification. *arXiv preprint arXiv:1607.01759* .

Manfred Krifka. 1995. The semantics and pragmatics of polarity items. *Linguistic analysis* 25(3-4):209–257.

Gareth McCray and Tineke Brunfaut. 2018. Investigating the construct measured by banked gap-fill items: Evidence from eye-tracking. *Language Testing* 35(1):51–73. https://doi.org/10.1177/0265532216677105.

Tomas Mikolov, Kai Chen, Greg Corrado, and Jeffrey Dean. 2013. Efficient estimation of word representations in vector space. *arXiv preprint arXiv:1301.3781* .

Linda M Moxey and Anthony J Sanford. 1993. *Communicating Quantities. A psychological perspective*. Lawrence Erlbaum Associates Publishers.

Linda M Moxey and Anthony J Sanford. 2000. Communicating quantities: A review of psycholinguistic evidence of how expressions determine perspectives. *Applied Cognitive Psychology* 14(3):237–255.

Stephen E Newstead and Janet M Collis. 1987. Context and the interpretation of quantifiers of frequency. *Ergonomics* 30(10):1447–1462.

John W Oller. 1973. Cloze tests of second language proficiency and what they measure. *Language learning* 23(1):105–118.

Denis Paperno, Germán Kruszewski, Angeliki Lazaridou, Quan Ngoc Pham, Raffaella Bernardi, Sandro Pezzelle, Marco Baroni, Gemma Boleda, and Raquel Fernández. 2016. The LAMBADA dataset: Word prediction requiring a broad discourse context. In *Proceedings of ACL 2016*.

Kevin B. Paterson, Ruth Filik, and Linda M. Moxey. 2009. Quantifiers and Discourse Processing. *Language and Linguistics Compass* .

Stanley Peters and Dag Westerståhl. 2006. *Quantifiers in Language and Logic*. Clarendon Press, Oxford.

Colin Raffel and Daniel P. W. Ellis. 2016. Feed-Forward Networks with Attention Can Solve Some Long-Term Memory Problems. In *International Conference of Learning Representations*. http://arxiv.org/abs/1512.08756.

David A Routh. 1994. On representations of quantifiers. *Journal of Semantics* 11(3):199–214.

Mike Schuster and Kuldip K Paliwal. 1997. Bidirectional recurrent neural networks. *IEEE Transactions on Signal Processing* 45(11):2673–2681.

Frank Smith. 1971. *Understanding reading: A psycholinguistic analysis of reading and learning to read.*. Holt, Rinehart & Winston.

Stephanie Solt. 2016. On Measurement and Quantification: The Case of most and more than half. *Language* 92:65–100.

Jakub Szymanik. 2016. *Quantifiers and Cognition. Logical and Computational Perspectives*. Studies in Linguistics and Philosophy. Springer.

Zichao Yang, Diyi Yang, Chris Dyer, Xiaodong He, Alex Smola, and Eduard Hovy. 2016. Hierarchical Attention Networks for Document Classification. In *Proceedings of NAACL-HLT 2016*. pages 1480–1489. https://doi.org/10.18653/v1/N16-1174.

A Named Entity Recognition Shootout for German

Martin Riedl and **Sebastian Padó**
Institut für Maschinelle Sprachverarbeitung
Universität Stuttgart
Pfaffenwaldring 5b, 70569 Stuttgart, Germany
{riedlmn,pado}@ims.uni-stuttgart.de,

Abstract

We ask how to practically build a model for German named entity recognition (NER) that performs at the state of the art for both contemporary and historical texts, i.e., a big-data and a small-data scenario. The two best-performing model families are pitted against each other (linear-chain CRFs and BiLSTM) to observe the trade-off between expressiveness and data requirements. BiLSTM outperforms the CRF when large datasets are available and performs inferior for the smallest dataset. BiLSTMs profit substantially from transfer learning, which enables them to be trained on multiple corpora, resulting in a new state-of-the-art model for German NER on two contemporary German corpora (CoNLL 2003 and GermEval 2014) and two historic corpora.

1 Introduction

Named entity recognition and classification (NER) is a central component in many natural language processing pipelines. High-quality NER is crucial for applications like information extraction, question answering, or entity linking.

Since the goal of NER is to recognize instances of named entities in running text, it is established practice to treat NER as a "word-by-word sequence labeling task" (Jurafsky and Martin, 2009). There are two families of sequence models that constitute promising candidates. On the one hand, linear-chain CRFs, which form the basis for many widely used systems (e.g., Finkel et al., 2005; Benikova et al., 2015), profit from hand-crafted features and can easily incorporate language- and domain-specific knowledge from dictionaries or gazetteers. On the other hand, bidirectional LSTMSs (BiL-STMs, e.g., Reimers and Gurevych, 2017) identify

informative features directly from the data, presented as word and/or character embeddings (e.g., Mikolov et al., 2013; Bojanowski et al., 2017).

When developing NER tools for new types of text, one requirement is the availability of different resources to inform features and/or embeddings. Another one is the amount of training data: linear-chain CRFs require only moderate amounts of training data compared to BiLSTM. To perform representation learning, BiLSTMs require considerably annotated data to learn proper representations (see, e.g., the impact of training size by Dernoncourt et al., 2016). This consideration becomes particularly pressing when moving to "small-data" settings such as low-resource languages, specific domains, or historical corpora. Thus, it is an open question, whether it is generally a better idea to choose different model families for different settings, or whether one model family can be optimized to perform well across settings.

This paper investigates this question empirically on a set of German corpora including two large, contemporary corpora and two small historical corpora. We pit linear-chain CRF- and BiLSTM-based systems against each other and compare to state-of-the-art models, performing three experiments. Due to these experiments, we get the following results: (a), the BiLSTM system indeed performs best on contemporary corpora, both within and across domains; (b), the BiLSTM system performs worse than the CRF systems for the smallest historical corpus due to lack of data; (c), by applying transfer learning to adduce more training data, the RNN outperform CRFs substantially for all corpora. The final BiLSTM models form a new state of the art for German NER and are freely available.

Proceedings of the 56th Annual Meeting of the Association for Computational Linguistics (Short Papers), pages 120–125
Melbourne, Australia, July 15 - 20, 2018. ©2018 Association for Computational Linguistics

2 Model Families for NER

As mentioned above, contemporary research on NER almost exclusively uses sequence classification models. Our study focuses on CRFs and BiLSTMs, the two most widely used choices.

CRF-based Systems. Linear-chain CRFs form a family of models that are well established in sequence classification. They form the basis of two widely used Named Entity recognizers.

The first one is STANFORDNER[1] (Finkel et al., 2005) which provides models for various languages. It uses a set of language-independent features, including word and character n-grams, word shapes, surrounding POS and lemmas. For German, these features are complemented by distributional clusters computed on a large German web corpus (Faruqui and Padó, 2010). The ready-to-run model is pre-trained on the German CoNLL 2003 data (Tjong Kim Sang and De Meulder, 2003).

Benikova et al. (2015) developed GERMANER[2], another CRF-based NER system. It was optimized for the GermEval 2014 NER challenge and also uses a set of standard features (word and character n-grams, POS) supplemented by a number of specific information sources (unsupervised parts of speech (Biemann, 2009), distributional semantics and topic cluster information, gazetteer lists).

BiLSTM-based Systems. Among the various deep learning architectures applied for NER, the best results have been achieved with bidirectional LSTM methods combined with a top-level CRF model (Ma and Hovy, 2016; Lample et al., 2016; Reimers and Gurevych, 2017). In this work, we use an implementation that solely uses word and character embeddings.

We train the character embeddings while training the model but use pre-trained word embeddings. To alleviate issues with out-of-vocabulary (OOV) words, we use both character- and subword-based word embeddings computed with fastText (Bojanowski et al., 2017). This method is able to retrieve embeddings for unknown words by incorporating subword information.[3]

3 Datasets

For the evaluation, we use two established datasets for NER on contemporary German and two datasets for historical German.

Contemporary German. The first large-scale German NER dataset was published as part of the CoNLL 2003 shared task (CoNLL, Tjong Kim Sang and De Meulder, 2003). It consists of about 220k tokens (for training) of annotated newspaper documents. The tagset handles locations (LOC), organizations (ORG), persons (PER) and the remaining entities as miscellaneous (MISC). The second dataset is the GermEval 2014 shared task dataset (GermEval, Benikova et al. (2014)), consisting of some 450k tokens (for training) of Wikipedia articles.[4] This dataset has two levels of annotations: outer and inner span named entities. For example, the term *Chicago Bulls* is tagged as organization in the outer span annotation. The nested term *Chicago* is annotated as location in the inner span annotation. However, there are only few inner span annotations. In addition to the standard tagsets also used in the CoNLL dataset, fine grained versions of these entities are marked with suffixes: *-deriv* marks derivations of the named entities (e.g. *German actor* – German is a derived location) and *-part* marks compounds including a named entity (e.g. in the word *Rhineshore* the compound Rhine is location). To compare to previous state-of-the-art methods, we show results on the official metric (a combination of the outer and inner spans) in Section 4. As there are only few inner span annotations, we additionally report results based on the outer spans. To be more conform with the tagsets of the CoNLL task, we focus on outer spans and remove the fine-grained tags in the follow-up experiments (see Section 5 and 6).

Historical German. We further consider two datasets based on historical texts (Neudecker, 2016)[5], extracted from the Europeana collection of historical newspapers[6], a standard resource for historical digital humanities. More specifically, our first corpus is the collection of Tyrolean periodicals and newspapers from the Dr Friedrich Temann Library (LFT), covering around 87k tokens from

---

[1] http://stanford.io/2ohopn3
[2] http://github.com/tudarmstadt-lt/GermaNER
[3] The source code and the best performing models are available online: http://www.ims.uni-stuttgart.de/forschung/ressourcen/werkzeuge/german_ner.html

[4] https://sites.google.com/site/germeval2014ner/
[5] https://github.com/KBNLresearch/europeananp-ner/
[6] www.europeana.eu/portal/de

Type	Model	Pr	R	F1
CRF	StanfordNER	80.02	62.29	70.05
CRF	GermaNER	81.31	68.00	74.06
RNN	UKP	79.54	71.10	75.09
–	ExB	78.07	74.75	76.38
RNN	BiLSTM-WikiEmb	**81.95**	**78.13**	**79.99**[*]
RNN	BiLSTM-EuroEmb	75.50	70.72	73.03

Table 1: Evaluation on GermEval data, using the official metric (metric 1) of the GermEval 2014 task that combines inner and outer chunks.

Type	Model	Pr	R	F1
CRF	StanfordNER	80.13	65.43	72.04
CRF	GermaNER	82.72	71.19	76.52
RNN	UKP	79.90	74.13	76.91
–	ExB	80.67	77.55	79.08
RNN	BiLSTM-WikiEmb	**83.07**	**80.62**	**81.83**[*]
RNN	BiLSTM-EuroEmb	76.48	73.54	74.98

Table 2: Evaluation on the test set of GermEval 2014 using the Outer Chunks evaluation schema.

Type	Model	Pr	R	F1
CRF	StanfordNER	74.18	72.50	73.33
RNN	Lample et al. (2016)	-	-	78.76
CRF	GermaNER	85.88	73.78	79.37
RNN	BiLSTM-WikiEmb	**87.67**	**78.79**	**82.99**[*]
RNN	BiLSTM-EuroEmb	79.92	72.14	75.83

Table 3: Evaluation on the test set of the German CoNLL 2003 dataset.

1926. Our second corpus is a collection of Austrian newspaper texts from the Austrian National Library (ONB), covering some 35k tokens between 1710 and 1873. These corpora give rise to a number of challenges: they are considerably smaller than the contemporary corpora from above, contain a different language variety (19th century Austrian German), and include a high rate of OCR errors since they were originally printed in Gothic typeface.[7] We use 80% of the data for training and each 10% for development and testing.

4 Experiment 1: Contemporary German

In our first experiment, we compare the NER performances on the two contemporary, large datasets. For BiLSTM, we experiment with two options for word embeddings. First, we use pre-trained embeddings computed on Wikipedia with 300 dimensions and standard parameters (WikiEmb)[8], which are presumably more appropriate for contemporary texts. Second, we compute embeddings with the same parameters from 1.5 billion tokens of historic German texts from Europeana (EuroEmb). These embeddings should be more appropriate for historical texts but may suffer from sparsity.

Table 1 shows results on GermEval using the official metric (metric 1) for the best performing systems. This measure considers both outer and inner span annotations. Within the challenge, the ExB (Hänig et al., 2015) ensemble classifier achieved the best result with an F1 score of 76.38, followed by the RNN-based method from UKP (Reimers et al., 2014) with 75.09. GermaNER achieves high precision, but cannot compete in terms of recall. Our BiLSTM with Wikipedia word embeddings, scores highest (79.99) and outperforms the shared task winner ExB significantly, based on a bootstrap resampling test (Efron and Tibshirani, 1994). Using Europeana embeddings, the performance drops to an F1 score of 73.03 – due to the difference in vocabulary. As the number of inner span annotations is marginal and hard to detect, we additionally present scores considering only outer span annotations in Table 2. Whereas the scores are slightly higher, we observe the same trend as from the previous results shown in Table 1.

On the CoNLL dataset (see Table 3) GermaNER outperforms the currently best-performing RNN-based system (Lample et al., 2016). The BiLSTM again yields the significantly best performance, matching its high precision while substantially improving recall. Again, lower F1 scores are achieved using the Europeana embeddings. In sum, we find that BiLSTM models can outperform CRF models when there is sufficient training data to profit from distributed representations.

5 Experiment 2: Cross-Corpus Performance

A potential downside of BiLSTMs is that learned models may be more text type specific, due to the high capacity of the models. Experiment 2 evaluates how well the models do when trained on one corpus and tested on another one, including historical corpora. To level the playing field, we reduce the detailed annotation of GermEval to the standard five-category set (PER, LOC, ORG, MISC, OTH). Results for these experiments are presented in

---

[7]We cleaned the corpora by correcting named entity labels and tokenization. We will make these versions available.

[8]`https://github.com/facebookresearch/fastText/blob/master/pretrained-vectors.md`

		Test data			
Model	Train	CoNLL	GermEval	LFT	ONB
Stanford NER	CoNLL	**72.12**	48.82	39.72	46.36
	GermEval	65.63	**72.09**	45.22	52.21
	LFT	35.25	35.00	**67.26**	52.77
	ONB	34.09	33.96	42.95	**72.42**
Germa NER	CoNLL	**79.37**	60.40	46.53	53.93
	GermEval	71.05	**76.37**	48.05	54.95
	LFT	44.87	45.82	**69.18**	56.38
	ONB	46.56	47.19	48.41	**73.31**
BiLSTM-WikiEmb	CoNLL	**82.99**	66.51	49.28	58.79
	GermEval	78.15	**82.93**	55.99	61.35
	LFT	57.27	53.38	**68.47**	65.53
	ONB	51.42	49.30	49.35	**70.46**
BiLSTM-EuroEmb	CoNLL	**75.83**	55.06	45.30	54.59
	GermEval	70.19	**75.24**	52.15	59.43
	LFT	43.63	43.82	**69.62**	61.10
	ONB	36.33	38.81	46.48	**67.29**

Table 4: Evaluation (F1) for two CRF-based methods and BiLSTM trained and tested on different corpora.

Table 4. Unsurprisingly, the best results are gained when testing on the same dataset as the training has been performed. GermaNER consistently outperforms StanfordNER again, highlighting the benefits of knowledge engineering when using CRFs.

Interestingly, these benefits also extend to the historical datasets for which the CRF features were presumably not optimized: overall F1-scores are only a few points lower than for the contemporary corpora, and the CRFs significantly outperform the BiLSTM models on ONB and performs comparable on the larger LFT dataset. The type of embeddings used by BiLSTM plays a minor role for the historical corpora (for contemporary corpora, Wikipedia is clearly better). In sum, we conclude that BiLSTM models run into trouble when faced with very small training datasets, while CRF-based methods are more robust (Cotterell and Duh, 2017).

6 Experiment 3: Transfer Learning

If the problems of BiLSTM from the last section are in fact due to lack of data, we might be able to obtain an improvement by combining them. A simple way of doing this is transfer learning (Lee et al., 2017): we simply start training on one corpus and at some point switch to another corpus. In our scenario, we start by training on large contemporary "source" corpora until convergence and then train additional 15 epochs on the "target" corpus from the domain on which we evaluate. The

results in Table 5 show significant improvements for the CoNLL dataset but performance drops for GermEval. Combining contemporary sources with historic target corpora yields to consistent benefits. Performance on LFT increases from 69.62 to 74.33 and on ONB from 73.31 to 78.56. Cross-domain classification scores are also improved consistently. The GermEval corpus is more appropriate as a source corpus, presumably because it is both larger and drawn from encyclopaedic text, more varied than newswire. We conclude that transfer learning is beneficial for BiLSTMs, especially when training data for the target domain is scarce. We applied the same procedure to the CRFs, but did not obtain improvements for the "target" data.

7 Data Analysis

Besides OCR errors, the lower F1 scores for the historic data are largely due to hyphens used to divide words for line breaks. The lowest F1 scores are achieved for the label organization. Evaluating on the ONB dataset, we obtain an F1 score for that label of 50.22 using GermaNER, 48.63 for the BiLSTM using Europeana embeddings and 61.48 using transfer learning. We observe a similar effect for the LFT dataset. Often, the annotations for the organization category are not entirely clear. For example, the typo "sterreichischen Außenministerlum" (should be "Außenministerium", *Austrian foreign ministry*) is manually annotated in the data but not detected by any of the models. However, "tschechoslowakischen Presse" (engl. *Czechoslovakian press*) is detected as organization by all classifiers but is not manually annotated.

8 Related Work

BiLSTMs that combine neural network architectures with CRF-based superstructures yield the highest results on English NER datasets in a number of studies (Ma and Hovy, 2016; Lample et al., 2016; Reimers and Gurevych, 2017; Lin et al., 2017). However, only few systems reported results for German NER, and restrict themselves to the "big-data" scenarios of the CoNLL 2003 (Lample et al., 2016; Reimers and Gurevych, 2017) and GermEval (Reimers et al., 2014; Christian Hnig, 2014) datasets.Sutton and McCallum (2005) showed the capability of CRFs for transfer learning by joint decoding two separately trained sequence models. Lee et al. (2017) apply transfer learning using a BiLSTM for medical NER using two similar tasks

Train	Transfer	BiLSTM-WikiEmb				BiLSTM-EuroEmb			
		CoNLL	GermEval	LFT	ONB	CoNLL	GermEval	LFT	ONB
CoNLL	GermEval	78.55	**82.93**	55.28	64.93	72.23	**75.78**	51.98	61.74
CoNLL	LFT	62.80	58.89	72.90	67.96	56.30	51.25	70.04	65.65
CoNLL	ONB	62.05	57.19	59.43	**76.17**	55.82	49.14	54.19	73.68
GermEval	CoNLL	**84.73**[†]	72.11	54.21	65.95	**78.41**	63.42	52.02	59.28
GermEval	LFT	67.77	69.09	**74.33**[†]	70.57	55.83	57.71	**72.03**	70.36
GermEval	ONB	72.15	73.18	62.52	76.06	64.05	64.20	57.12	**78.56**[†]

Table 5: Results for different test sets when using transfer learning. † marks results statistically significantly better than the ones reported in Table 4.

with different labels and show that only 60% of the data of the target domain is required to achieve good results. Crichton et al. (2017) yield improvements up to 0.8% for NER in the medical domain. Most related to our paper is the work by Ghaddar and Langlais (2017) which demonstrates the impact of transfer learning of the English CoNLL 2003 dataset with Wikipedia annotations.

9 Conclusion

Our study fills an empirical gap by considering historical datasets and performing careful comparisons of multiple models under exactly the same conditions. We have investigated the relative performance of an BiLSTM method and traditional CRFs on German NER in big- and small-data situations, asking whether it makes sense to consider different model types for different setups. We found that combining BiLSTM with a CRF as top layer, outperform CRFs with hand-coded features consistently when enough data is available. Even though RNNs struggle with small datasets, transfer learning is a simple and effective remedy to achieve state-of-the-art performance even for such datasets. In sum, modern RNNs consistently yield the best performance.In future work, we will extend the BiLSTM to other languages using cross-lingual embeddings (Ruder et al., 2017).

Acknowledgments

This study was supported by the DFG grant Oceanic Exchanges (KO 5362/2-1) and the CRETA center funded by the German Ministry for Education and Research (BMBF).

References

Darina Benikova, Chris Biemann, and Marc Reznicek. 2014. NoSta-D Named Entity Annotation for German: Guidelines and Dataset. In *Proceedings of LREC*. Reykjavik, Iceland, pages 2524–2531.

Darina Benikova, Seid Muhie Yimam, and Chris Biemann. 2015. GermaNER: Free Open German Named Entity Recognition Tool. In *Proceedings of GSCL*. Essen, Germany, pages 31–38.

Chris Biemann. 2009. Unsupervised part-of-speech tagging in the large. *Research on Language and Computation* 7(2):101–135.

Piotr Bojanowski, Edouard Grave, Armand Joulin, and Tomas Mikolov. 2017. Enriching word vectors with subword information. *Transactions of the Association for Computational Linguistics* 5:135–146.

Stefan Bordag Stefan Thomas Christian Hnig. 2014. Modular classifier ensemble architecture for named entity recognition on low resource systems. In *Proceedings of the KONVENS GermEval Shared Task on Named Entity Recognition*. Hildesheim, Germany, pages 113–116.

Ryan Cotterell and Kevin Duh. 2017. Low-resource named entity recognition with cross-lingual, character-level neural conditional random fields. In *Proceedings of IJCNLP*. Taipei, Taiwan, pages 91–96.

Gamal Crichton, Sampo Pyysalo, Billy Chiu, and Anna Korhonen. 2017. A neural network multi-task learning approach to biomedical named entity recognition. *BMC Bioinformatics* 18(1):1–14.

Franck Dernoncourt, Ji Young Lee, Ozlem Uzuner, and Peter Szolovits. 2016. De-identification of patient notes with recurrent neural networks. *Journal of the American Medical Informatics Association* 24(3):596–606.

Bradley Efron and Robert J. Tibshirani. 1994. *An Introduction to the Bootstrap*. Chapman & Hall/CRC Monographs on Statistics & Applied Probability.

Manaal Faruqui and Sebastian Padó. 2010. Training and evaluating a german named entity recognizer with semantic generalization. In *Proceedings of KONVENS*. Saarbrücken, Germany, pages 129–133.

Jenny Rose Finkel, Trond Grenager, and Christopher Manning. 2005. Incorporating non-local information into information extraction systems by gibbs sampling. In *Proceedings of ACL*. Ann Arbor, MI, USA, pages 363–370.

Abbas Ghaddar and Phillippe Langlais. 2017. WiNER: A Wikipedia Annotated Corpus for Named Entity Recognition. In *Proceedings of IJCNLP*. Taipei, Taiwan, pages 413–422.

Christian Hänig, Robert Remus, and Xose de la Puente. 2015. ExB Themis: Extensive Feature Extraction from Word Alignments for Semantic Textual Similarity. In *Proceedings of SemEval*. Denver, CO, pages 264–268.

Daniel Jurafsky and James H. Martin. 2009. *Speech and Language Processing*. Prentice Hall, 2nd edition.

Guillaume Lample, Miguel Ballesteros, Sandeep Subramanian, Kazuya Kawakami, and Chris Dyer. 2016. Neural Architectures for Named Entity Recognition. In *Proceedings of NAACL-HLT*. San Diego, CA, pages 260–270.

Ji Young Lee, Franck Dernoncourt, and Peter Szolovits. 2017. Transfer learning for named-entity recognition with neural networks. *CoRR* abs/1705.06273. http://arxiv.org/abs/1705.06273.

Bill Y. Lin, Frank Xu, Zhiyi Luo, and Kenny Zhu. 2017. Multi-channel BiLSTM-CRF Model for Emerging Named Entity Recognition in Social Media. In *Proceedings of the 3rd Workshop on Noisy User-generated Text*. Copenhagen, Denmark, pages 160–165. http://aclweb.org/anthology/W17-4421.

Xuezhe Ma and Eduard Hovy. 2016. End-to-end Sequence Labeling via Bi-directional LSTM-CNNs-CRF. In *Proceedings of ACL*. Berlin, Germany, pages 1064–1074.

Tomas Mikolov, Kai Chen, Greg Corrado, and Jeffrey Dean. 2013. Efficient Estimation of Word Representations in Vector Space. In *Proceedings of ICML*. Scottsdale, AZ, pages 1310–1318.

Clemens Neudecker. 2016. An open corpus for named entity recognition in historic newspapers. In *Proceedings of LREC*. Portoro, Slovenia, pages 4348–4352.

Nils Reimers, Judith Eckle-Kohler, Carsten Schnober, Jungi Kim, and Iryna Gurevych. 2014. Germeval-2014: Nested named entity recognition with neural networks. In *Proceedings of the KONVENS GermEval Shared Task on Named Entity Recognition*. Hildesheim, Germany, pages 117–120.

Nils Reimers and Iryna Gurevych. 2017. Reporting score distributions makes a difference: Performance study of LSTM-networks for sequence tagging. In *Proceedings of EMNLP*. Copenhagen, Denmark, pages 338–348.

Sebastian Ruder, Ivan Vuli, and Anders Sgaard. 2017. A survey of cross-lingual embedding models. *CoRR* abs/1706.04902. http://arxiv.org/abs/1706.04902.

Charles Sutton and Andrew McCallum. 2005. Composition of conditional random fields for transfer learning. In *Proceedings of HLT-EMNLP*. Vancouver, BC, pages 748–754.

Erik F. Tjong Kim Sang and Fien De Meulder. 2003. Introduction to the CoNLL-2003 Shared Task: Language-Independent Named Entity Recognition. In *Proceedings of CoNLL-2003*. Edmonton, Canada, pages 142–147.

A dataset for identifying actionable feedback
in collaborative software development

Benjamin S. Meyers[†]**, Nuthan Munaiah**[†]**, Emily Prud'hommeaux**[‡§]**, Andrew Meneely**[†]**,
Cecilia Ovesdotter Alm**[‡]**, Josephine Wolff**[‡]**, and Pradeep K. Murukannaiah**[†]

[†]Golisano College of Computing and Information Sciences, Rochester Institute of Technology
[‡]College of Liberal Arts, Rochester Institute of Technology
[§]Morrissey College of Arts and Sciences, Boston College

`bsm9339,nm6061,emilypx,axmvse,coagla,jcwgpt,pkmvse}@rit.edu`

Abstract

Software developers and testers have long struggled with how to elicit proactive responses from their coworkers when reviewing code for security vulnerabilities and errors. For a code review to be successful, it must not only identify potential problems but also elicit an active response from the colleague responsible for modifying the code. To understand the factors that contribute to this outcome, we analyze a novel dataset of more than one million code reviews for the Google Chromium project, from which we extract linguistic features of feedback that elicited responsive actions from coworkers. Using a manually-labeled subset of reviewer comments, we trained a highly accurate classifier to identify "acted-upon" comments (AUC = 0.85). Our results demonstrate the utility of our dataset, the feasibility of using NLP for this new task, and the potential of NLP to improve our understanding of how communications between colleagues can be authored to elicit positive, proactive responses.

1 Introduction

As in many other work environments, such as hospitals and law firms, employees in software development must communicate through written feedback and comments to develop functional and secure code. Developers elicit feedback from their collaborators on the code that they write through the code review process, which is an integral part of the mature software development lifecycle. Most large software development organizations, including Microsoft (Lipner, 2004) and Google (Chromium, 2017), mandate the review of all changes to the code base. Code reviews identify potential bugs or errors in software, but not all of the comments made by reviewers are acted upon by developers.

Some code reviews are taken seriously by developers and prompt significant fixes, while many others are overlooked or dismissed. In some cases, such as when code reviewers misunderstand the purpose of a proposed change or identify an unimportant issue, it may be appropriate to ignore their comments. At other times, however, the presentation and language of the reviewer's feedback may cause the problems it identifies to be overlooked. Understanding which linguistic characteristics of code reviews influence whether reviews are taken seriously can aid developers in providing effective feedback that is acted upon by their peers. In turn, this can contribute to our general understanding of how to provide meaningful written feedback in a collaborative workplace setting.

With this in mind, we present a dataset of over one million code review comments from the Chromium project (Chromium, 2017), designed with the goal of discovering the linguistic features associated with actionable developer feedback. We describe the dataset, along with an array of linguistic features capturing characteristics of complexity, content, and style, extracted from that dataset. Using a labeled subset of this large dataset, we develop a highly accurate classifier for identifying examples of actionable feedback that performs better than the keyword and sentiment features previously explored for similar tasks.

The contributions of this work are: (1) the introduction of a new NLP task: identifying actionable feedback in collaborative work conversations; (2) a large structured dataset of automatically linguistically annotated software developer conversations for feature exploration[1]; (3) a smaller manually-labeled subset of that dataset for hypothesis test-

Proceedings of the 56th Annual Meeting of the Association for Computational Linguistics (Short Papers), pages 126–131
Melbourne, Australia, July 15 - 20, 2018. ©2018 Association for Computational Linguistics

ing[1]; and (4) a demonstration of the feasibility of using NLP for this task in the form of a high-accuracy classifier of actionable feedback.

```
409      return found;
susan 2015/06/25 07:31:02
return nullptr;
william 2015/06/25 07:56:32
On 2015/06/25 07:31:02, susan wrote:
> return nullptr;
No, if line 398 breaks, |found| can be non-null.
susan 2015/06/25 08:04:40
On 2015/06/25 07:56:32, william wrote:
> On 2015/06/25 07:31:02, susan wrote:
> > return nullptr;
> No, if line 398 breaks, |found| can be non-null.
Ops. I didn't realize it.
line 398 should `return found`, instead of `break`.
william 2015/06/25 08:23:38
On 2015/06/25 08:04:40, susan wrote:
> On 2015/06/25 07:56:32, william wrote:
> > On 2015/06/25 07:31:02, susan wrote:
> > > return nullptr;
> > No, if line 398 breaks, |found| can be non-null.
> Ops. I didn't realize it.
> line 398 should `return found`, instead of `break`.
Done.
If the code doesn't break there, line 409 should
return nullptr, as the original comment suggests.
```

Figure 1: Example code review comment thread.

2 Background

A typical code review is initiated by a developer (*change-author*) who wishes to have a collection (*patchset*) of local changes (*patches*) to the source code merged into the software product. The patchset is reviewed by other developers (*reviewers*) who provide feedback to ensure that the change does not negatively impact the overall quality of the product. In response to this feedback, the change-author can submit one or more additional patchsets for further review. The process repeats until the *owner* of the source code approves the change. The Chromium project, which underlies Google's Chrome browser and Chrome OS, follows this typical code review process, requiring all changes to the source code to be reviewed before being accepted into the repository. Rietveld (The Chromium Project, 2017), an open-source tool, facilitates the code review process in Chromium.

The process of providing direct assessment of an individual's actions or performance, known as feedback intervention, has been widely studied in a number of domains (Judd, 1905; Kluger and DeNisi, 1996, 1998; Xiong et al., 2010; Xiong and Litman, 2010), but previous work applying NLP to the specific task of evaluating code review feedback is somewhat limited. Rahman et al. (2017) examined a small set of text features (e.g., reading ease, stop word ratio) in a small set of code review comments but found associations between those features and comment usefulness to be mostly insignificant. Pletea et al. (2014) examined sentiment as an indicator of comment usefulness, while Bosu et al. (2015) considered both sentiment and the presence of pre-defined keywords in feedback. While these studies offer insights into the language used by developers, they are limited to sentiment and basic lexical attributes. In contrast, we explore more subtle linguistic features that more accurately characterize actionable feedback.

3 Data

Our dataset consists of written natural language conversations among developers working to find flaws in proposed changes to software. An example is shown in Figure 1. We used Rietveld's RESTful API to retrieve, in JSON formatted documents, publicly-accessible code reviews in the Chromium project spanning eight years (2008-16). We processed the JSON documents and extracted reviews with their associated patchsets, patches, and comments, saving them to a PostgreSQL database. Of the 2,855,018 comments, 1,591,431 were posted by reviewers. We refer to this set of comments, for which we provide values for the 9 linguistic features (described in Section 4), as the **full dataset**.

With the goal of characterizing the linguistic attributes of actionable feedback, we created a **labeled dataset**, which reflects the overall distribution of actionable comments in the full dataset by including 2,994 comments automatically identified as *acted-upon* and 800 comments manually identified as *not (known-to-be) acted-upon*. We automatically identified *acted-upon* comments using the Rietveld functionality that allows change-authors to respond to feedback by clicking a link labeled "Done", which automatically posts a special comment containing only the word '*Done.*'. We consider comments by reviewers that elicit this '*Done.*' response to be *acted-upon*. Of the 1.5 million comments posted by reviewers, 690,881 (43%) were identified as *acted-upon* using the '*Done.*' metric. We independently verified a subset of 700 of these comments (Cohen's $\kappa = 0.89$) and found that in 97% of instances when a devel-

[1] `https://meyersbs.github.io/chromium-conversations/`

oper posted a comment with '*Done.*', there was an associated code change implemented.

To identify comments that were not acted upon, we manually inspected code review comments that did not terminate in a '*Done.*' comment. We randomly sampled a set of 2,047 such comments and inspected the line of code associated with a comment across all patchsets and the source code commit associated with the code review. Comments for which the authors could not find evidence that the developer acted upon the feedback were labeled as *not (known-to-be) acted-upon*. Within the sample, 800 (39.08%) were manually identified as *not (known-to-be) acted-upon*.

4 Feature Extraction

We extract nine linguistic features from the reviewer comments (examples in Table 1) that capture structure, information content, style, and tone. Before extracting features, we automatically replace all sequences of source code tokens with a single custom token. Since comments can span multiple sentences, we aggregate sentence-level features at the comment level as described below for each feature.

Syntactic complexity: Previous work (Rahman et al., 2017) attempted to measure structural complexity using readability metrics, such as Flesch reading ease (Flesch, 1948), which approximate complexity using word and sentence length. We instead evaluate the structure of comments by calculating YNGVE (Yngve, 1960) and FRAZIER (Frazier, 1987) scores, two complimentary approaches derived from constituent parses (as in Roark et al. (2011); Pakhomov et al. (2011)) that approximate the cognitive load of sentence processing (Baddeley, 2003; Sweller and Chandler, 1991). We take the maximum over all sentences in a comment for each of these scores.

Information content: We calculate both content density (C-DENSITY), which measures the content of text using the ratio of open-class to closed-class words, and propositional density (P-DENSITY), which is the ratio of propositions to the number of words in a text (Roark et al., 2011). We use an approach similar to that used by Brown et al. (2008) to detect propositions, and we aggregate both scores over the sentences in a comment.

Style and tone: We explore several features characterizing style and tone to learn whether the way reviewers choose to communicate their feedback has an influence on how their colleagues respond to that feedback.

SENTIMENT: We extract the sentiment of a code review comments using Stanford CoreNLP (Manning et al., 2014). In contrast to previous work (Bosu et al., 2015; Agarwal et al., 2011), we use only three values, merging the two *positive* classes and the two *negative* classes, and introduce a fourth class, *non-neutral*, which ignores the sentiment polarity. The sentiment at a comment level is the ratio of negative/neutral/positive/non-neutral tokens to all tokens.

FORMALITY: We use the dataset provided by Lahiri (2015) to train a logistic regression model for estimating the formality of a sentence, with precision and recall of 83%. We reduce the 7-point rating scale to a binary (formal vs. informal) scale. The features used to train the model included parts-of-speech, character n-grams, chunking tags, and other features used in predicting uncertainty Vincze (2014). For this feature and POLITENESS, we find the maximum and minimum values over all sentences in a comment.

POLITENESS: To measure politeness, we use a corpus of Wikipedia editor and Stack Exchange user conversations annotated for politeness (Danescu-Niculescu-Mizil et al., 2013). We re-implemented their logistic regression model with newer programming languages and frameworks, yielding 94% precision and 95% recall.

UNCERTAINTY: Uncertainty in natural language has been studied by Vincze (2014) and Farkas et al. (2010), who worked with Szarvas et al. (2012) to compile the Szeged Uncertainty Corpus. While Vincze (2014) trained a binary (certain vs. uncertain) model on the corpus, we trained a multi-label logistic regression model using the same features to predict the type of uncertainty exhibited by each word in a comment.

5 Results

Using the labeled dataset described in Section 3, we evaluated the association between each feature and the class labels. For continuous valued features, we used the non-parametric Mann-Whitney-Wilcoxon to test for association and Cliff's δ to assess the strength of that association. For boolean-valued features, we used the χ^2 test to test for independence between the feature and class label. Our results show that *acted-upon* code review comments were shorter, more polite, more formal,

Feature	Example Sentence from Chromium dataset
FRAZIER	Low: *This 'if' can be done more elegantly with Min(x,y)*
	High: *Please see this warning about adding things to NavigationEntry.*
YNGVE	Low: *The description is a little confusing.*
	High: *The only time we call one but not the other is in the destructor, when we don't need to call needsNewGenID, but setting two fields needlessly might be a low price to pay to ensure we never accidentally call one without the other.*
P-DENSITY	Low: *In addition to what I suggested earlier about testing for the non-existence of a third file, we could also verify that the contents of the sync database files are not nonsense.*
	High: *I tried patching this in locally and it doesn't compile.*
C-DENSITY	Low: *Slight reordering: please put system modules first, then a blank line, then local ones (PRESUBMIT).*
	High: *Please check that given user_id is child user, not currently active user is child.*
FORMALITY	Low: *But yeah, I'm just being an API astronaut*; I think that what I wrote up there is neat, but after sleeping, don't worry about it; it's too much work to go and rewrite stuff.*
	High: *Moving this elsewhere would also keep this module focused on handling the content settings / heuristics for banners, which is what it was originally intended for.*
POLITENESS	Low: *You don't actually manage the deopt table's VirtualMemory, so you shouldn't act like you do.*
	High: *Thanks for writing this test, getting there, but I think you could do this in a more principled way.*
SENTIMENT	Negative: *That's not good use of inheritance.*
	Neutral: *Are we planning on making use of this other places?*
	Positive: *It looks slightly magical.*
UNCERTAINTY	Epistemic: *This seems a bit fragile.*
	Doxastic: *I assume we added this notification purely for testing purposes?*
	Investigative: *Did you check whether it was needed?*
	Conditional: *Another possible option, if it does not cause user confusion, would be to automatically select those projects in the Files view when the dialog closes.*

Table 1: Example code review comments for a subset of the linguistic features.

Feature Set	Precision	Recall	F_1	AUC
# Tokens	0.793	0.996	0.883	0.610
# Sentences	0.792	0.999	0.884	0.584
All	0.829	0.926	0.872	0.849
Significant	0.805	0.953	0.871	0.805
Relevant	0.802	0.963	0.874	0.819

Table 2: Results of $10 \times 10-$fold cross-validation.

less uncertain, and had a lower density of propositions than those that were *not acted-upon*.

We then trained a classifier to identify code review comments that are likely to be acted upon. In training the classifier, we considered three sets of linguistic features: (1) *all* features, (2) *significant* features from association analysis, and (3) *relevant* features from recursive feature elimination. Through recursive feature elimination, we found MAX POLITENESS, P-DENSITY, MIN FORMALITY, and MAX FORMALITY to be the four most relevant features for discriminating between *acted-upon* and *not acted-upon* comments.

We trained logistic regression classifiers with these three sets of linguistic features, evaluating performance using 10x10-fold cross validation. We compare these with two baseline classifiers using only token count and sentence count. Table 2 shows the average precision, recall, F_1-measure, and AUC. The classifiers trained on the linguistic features, while performing near the baselines on the first three measures, substantially outperform the baselines on AUC, with all three yielding values over 0.8. Given these results and the imbalanced nature of the dataset, it seems that the classifiers trained on the linguistic features are able to identify both classes of comments with high accuracy, while the baseline classifiers perform only marginally better than a majority class baseline.

6 Discussion & Future work

Overall, we find that the way in which coworkers communicate feedback to each other strongly influences whether their peers will act on their advice. Remarkably, politeness and formality, two high-level discourse features, are among the most effective in distinguishing acted upon feedback. It seems that the manner in which feedback is delivered has more impact on the actions of developers than might be expected given the practical and impersonal nature of written code reviews. These results point to the critical importance of how feedback is phrased and delivered in workplace settings, beyond just the content of the feedback itself.

In our future work, we plan to explore whether these and other features can be incorporated into a code review tool like Rietveld to automatically flag feedback that is less likely to be acted upon and to encourage more effective communication strategies. We also plan to use our methods to analyze the linguistic patterns of individual reviewers to identify those with particularly effective or weak communication styles.

Our work demonstrates the potential of applying NLP to the task of identifying actionable feedback in collaborative work scenarios and the utility of our two datasets for this task. More broadly, these results speak to the importance of training code reviewers–and indeed all employees working in highly collaborative environments–not just in how to do their jobs effectively but also how to communicate their findings and feedback to their coworkers in a way that will elicit proactive responses.

References

A. Agarwal, B. Xie, I. Vovsha, O. Rambow, and R. Passonneau. 2011. Sentiment analysis of twitter data. In *Proceedings of the Workshop on Languages in Social Media*, pages 30–38.

A. Baddeley. 2003. Working memory and language: An overview. *Journal of Communication Disorders*, 36(3):189–208.

A Bosu, M Greiler, and C Bird. 2015. Characteristics of Useful Code Reviews: An Empirical Study at Microsoft. In *2015 IEEE/ACM 12th Working Conference on Mining Software Repositories*, pages 146–156.

C. Brown, T. Snodgrass, S.J. Kemper, R. Herman, and M.A. Covington. 2008. Automatic measurement of propositional idea density from part-of-speech tagging. *Behavior Research Methods*, 40(2):540–545.

Chromium. 2017. Chromium OS Developer's Guide. https://www.chromium.org/chromium-os/developer-guide. [Online; accessed 25-Aug-2017].

C. Danescu-Niculescu-Mizil, M. Sudhof, D. Jurafsky, J. Leskovec, and C. Potts. 2013. A computational approach to politeness with application to social factors. In *Proceedings of the Association for Computational Linguistics (ACL)*, pages 250–259.

R. Farkas, V. Vincze, G. Móra, J. Csirik, and G. Szarvas. 2010. The CoNLL-2010 shared task: Learning to detect hedges and their scope in natural language text. In *Proceedings of the Fourteenth Conference on Computational Natural Language Learning—Shared Task*, pages 1–12.

R. Flesch. 1948. A new readability yardstick. *Journal of Applied Psychology*, 32(3):221.

L. Frazier. 1987. Syntactic Processing: Evidence from Dutch. *Natural Language & Linguistic Theory*, 5(4):519–559.

C.H. Judd. 1905. Practice without knowledge of results. *The Psychological Review: Monograph Supplements*.

A.N. Kluger and A. DeNisi. 1996. The effects of feedback interventions on performance: a historical review, a meta-analysis and a preliminary feedback intervention theory. *Psychological Bulletin*, 119:254–284.

A.N. Kluger and A. DeNisi. 1998. Feedback interventions: Toward the understanding of a double-edged sword. *Current Directions in Psychological Science*, 7(3):67–72.

S. Lahiri. 2015. SQUINKY! A Corpus of Sentence-level Formality, Informativeness, and Implicature. *CoRR*, abs/1506.02306.

S. Lipner. 2004. The Trustworthy Computing Security Development Lifecycle. In *20th Annual Computer Security Applications Conference*, pages 2–13.

C.D. Manning, M. Surdeanu, J. Bauer, J. Finkel, S.J. Bethard, and D. McClosky. 2014. The Stanford CoreNLP Natural Language Processing Toolkit. In *Association for Computational Linguistics (ACL) System Demonstrations*, pages 55–60.

S. Pakhomov, S. Chacon, M. Wicklund, and J. Gundel. 2011. Computerized assessment of syntactic complexity in Alzheimer's disease: A case study of Iris Murdoch's writing. *Behavior Research Methods*, 43(1):136–144.

D. Pletea, B. Vasilescu, and A. Serebrenik. 2014. Security and Emotion: Sentiment Analysis of Security Discussions on GitHub. In *Proceedings of the 11th Working Conference on Mining Software Repositories*, pages 348–351.

M.M. Rahman, Chanchal K. Roy, and R.G. Kula. 2017. Predicting Usefulness of Code Review Comments Using Textual Features and Developer Experience. In *Proceedings of the 14th International Conference on Mining Software Repositories*, pages 215–226.

B. Roark, M. Mitchell, J. Hosom, K. Hollingshead, and J. Kaye. 2011. Spoken Language Derived Measures for Detecting Mild Cognitive Impairment. *Transactions on Audio, Speech, and Language Processing*, 19(7):2081–2090.

J. Sweller and P. Chandler. 1991. Evidence for cognitive load theory. *Cognition and Instruction*, 8(4):351–362.

G. Szarvas, V. Vincze, R. Farkas, G. Móra, and I. Gurevych. 2012. Cross-genre and cross-domain detection of semantic uncertainty. *Computational Linguistics*, 38(2):335–367.

The Chromium Project. 2017. Code Review — Chromium. `https://codereview.chromium.org/`. [Online; accessed 25-Aug-2017].

V. Vincze. 2014. *Uncertainty Detection in Natural Language Texts*. Ph.D. thesis, University of Szeged.

W. Xiong and D. Litman. 2010. Identifying problem localization in peer-review feedback. In *Intelligent Tutoring Systems*, pages 429–431. Springer.

W. Xiong, D.J. Litman, and C.D. Schunn. 2010. Assessing reviewers performance based on mining problem localization in peer-review data. In *Third International Conference on Educational Data Mining*, pages 211–220.

V.H. Yngve. 1960. A model and an Hypothesis for Language Structure. In *Proceedings of the American Philosophical Society*, volume 104, pages 444–466.

SNAG: Spoken Narratives and Gaze Dataset

Preethi Vaidyanathan[†‡], Emily Prud'hommeaux[‡○], Jeff B. Pelz[‡], Cecilia O. Alm[‡]
[†] LC Technologies, Inc., Fairfax, Virginia, USA
[‡] Rochester Institute of Technology, Rochester, New York, USA
[○] Boston College, Boston, Massachusetts, USA
{pxv1621,emilypx}@rit.edu, pelz@cis.rit.edu, coagla@rit.edu

Abstract

Humans rely on multiple sensory modalities when examining and reasoning over images. In this paper, we describe a new multimodal dataset that consists of gaze measurements and spoken descriptions collected in parallel during an image inspection task. The task was performed by multiple participants on 100 general-domain images showing everyday objects and activities. We demonstrate the usefulness of the dataset by applying an existing visual-linguistic data fusion framework in order to label important image regions with appropriate linguistic labels.

1 Introduction

In recent years, eye tracking has become widespread, with applications ranging from VR to assistive communication (Padmanaban et al., 2017; Holmqvist et al., 2017). Gaze data, such as fixation location and duration, can reveal crucial information about where observers look and how long they look at those locations. Researchers have used gaze measurements to understand where drivers look and to identify differences in experts' and novices' viewing behaviors in domain-specific tasks (Underwood et al., 2003; Eivazi et al., 2012). Numerous studies highlight the potential of gaze data to shed light on how humans process information, make decisions, and vary in observer behaviors (Fiedler and Glöckner, 2012; Guo et al., 2014; Hayes and Henderson, 2017; Brunyé and Gardony, 2017). Eye tracking has also long been an important tool in psycholinguistics (Cooper, 1974; Rayner, 1998; Richardson and Dale, 2005; Shao et al., 2013).

Co-collecting observers' gaze information and spoken descriptions of visual input has the potential to provide insight into how humans understand what they see. There is a need for public datasets containing both modalities. In this paper, we present the Spoken Narratives and Gaze dataset (SNAG), which contains gaze information and spoken narratives co-captured from observers as they view general domain images. We describe the data collection procedure using a high-quality eye-tracker, summary statistics of the multimodal data, and the results of applying a visual-lingustic alignment framework to automatically annotate regions of general-domain images, inspired by Vaidyanathan et al.'s (2016) work on medical images. Our main contributions are as follows:

1. We provide the language and vision communities with a unique multimodal dataset[1] comprised of co-captured gaze and audio data, and transcriptions. This dataset was collected via an image-inspection task with 100 general-domain images and American English speakers.

2. We demonstrate the usefulness of this general-domain dataset by applying an existing visual-linguistic annotation framework that successfully annotates image regions by combining gaze and language data.

2 Multimodal Data Collection

The IRB-approved data collection involved 40 university students who were native speakers of American English (10 were later removed), ranging in age from 18 to 25 years, viewing and describing 100 general-domain images. We sought out subjects who were speakers of American English in order to ensure reliable ASR output and a consistent vocabulary across subjects. Subjects consented to data release. The images

---

[1]https://mvrl-clasp.github.io/SNAG/

Proceedings of the 56th Annual Meeting of the Association for Computational Linguistics (Short Papers), pages 132–137
Melbourne, Australia, July 15 - 20, 2018. ©2018 Association for Computational Linguistics

Figure 1: Data collection set-up. The eye tracker is under the display. The observer wears a lapel microphone connected to a TASCAM recorder.

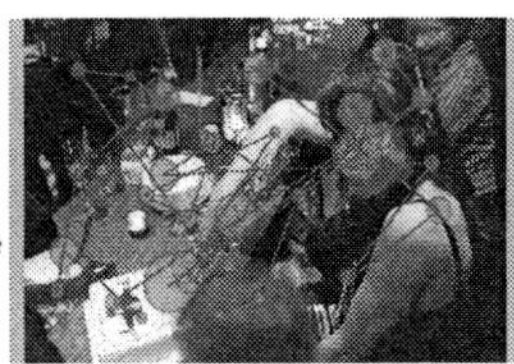

Figure 2: Example of multimodal data. *Left:* ASR transcript of a participant's spoken description. *Right:* Gaze data for the same observer overlaid on the image. Green circles show fixations, with radius representing fixation duration. Green lines connecting fixations represent saccades.

were selected from MSCOCO (Microsoft Common Objects in Context) (Lin et al., 2014), which totals over 300,000 images representing complex everyday scenes. The MSCOCO dataset was created by pooling images from sources such as Flickr and crowdsourcing them to obtain segments and captions (not used in this work). A researcher selected the images so that typically they depicted an event with at least one initiator of the event and one target of the action. Of the 100 images, 69 images clearly depict at least one event. The MSCOCO images vary in number of objects, scale, lighting, and resolution.

Gaze data was collected using a SensoMotoric Instruments (Sensomotoric Instruments, 2016) RED 250Hz eye-tracker attached under a display (Figure 1). The reported accuracy of the RED 250 eye-tracker is 0.5 degree. It is a non-intrusive and remote eye tracker that monitors the observer's gaze. Each image was presented to the observer on a 22-inch LCD monitor (1680×1050 pixels) located approximately 68 cm from the observer. We employed a double computer set-up with one computer used to present the image and the other used to run the SMI software iViewX and Experiment Center 2.3. After each stimulus, a blank gray slide was inserted to ensure that the gaze on the previous stimulus did not affect the gaze on the following stimulus. The blank gray slide was followed by a test slide with a small, visible target at the center with an invisible trigger area of interest. Using the test slide we could measure the drift between the location of the target at the center and the predicted gaze location over time that may have occurred due to the observer's movements. A validation was performed every 10 images and re-calibration was applied if the observer's validation error was more than one degree.

A TASCAM DR-100MKII recorder with a lapel microphone was used to record the spoken descriptions. To approximate the Master-Apprentice data collection method that helps in eliciting rich details (Beyer and Holtzblatt, 1997), observers were instructed to "describe the action in the images and tell the experimenter what is happening." Observers were given a mandatory break after 50 images and optional smaller breaks if needed to avoid fatigue. Observers were given a package of cookies along with a choice between entering into a raffle to win one of two \$25 gift cards or receiving course credits. Observers were cooperative and enthusiastic.

3 Fixations, Narratives, and Quality

The SMI software BeGaze 3.1.117 with default parameters and a velocity-based (I-VT) algorithm was used to detect eye-tracking events. Figure 2 shows an example of the scanpath with fixations and saccades of an observer overlaid on an image. Of the original 40 observers, we removed one observer with partial data loss and nine observers whose mean calibration and validation error was greater than two standard deviations from the mean in the horizontal or vertical direction. The mean calibration accuracy (standard deviation) for the remaining subjects was $0.67(0.25)$ and $0.74(0.27)$ degrees for the x and y directions, respectively. One degree would translate to approximately 40 pixels in our set-up, therefore our mean calibration accuracy was roughly 27 pixels. For the remainder of this work, the corpus size is 3000 multimodal instances (100 images $\times$ 30 participants), with 13 female and 17 male

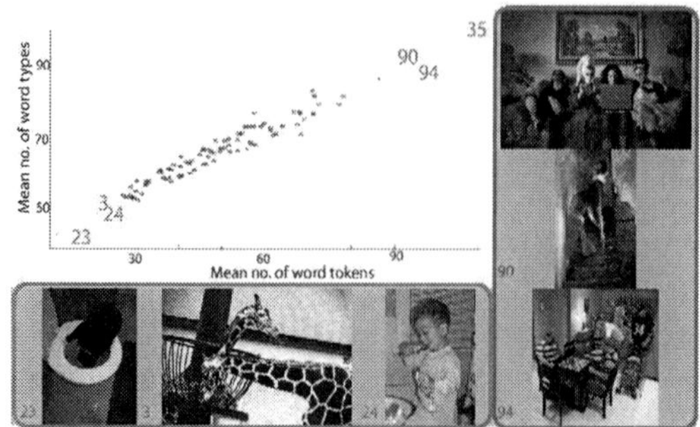

Figure 3: Scatter plot of mean word types vs. tokens per image. Example images have low (green) and high (magenta) type-token ratio.

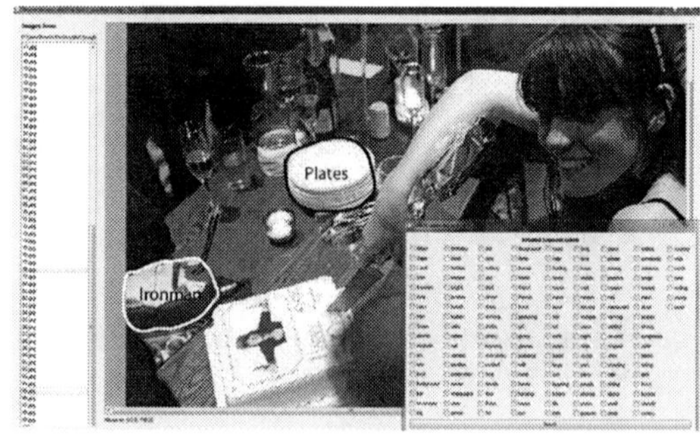

Figure 4: RegionLabeler GUI (released with dataset) used to acquire reference alignments. Annotator draws borders around regions and checks off linguistic units.

participants.

The speech recordings for the 3000 instances were machine-transcribed using the cloud-based IBM Watson Speech-to-Text service, an ASR system accessible via a Websocket connection[2]. Figure 2 (left panel) shows example ASR output, which is accurate other than the substitution of *Kate* for *cake*. IBM Watson reports timestamps for each word, and those timestamps are included in the released dataset. Additionally, all spoken descriptions for a subset of 5 images were manually corrected using Praat (Boersma, 2002) in order to verify the quality of the ASR output. We found the word error rate (WER) to be remarkably low (5%), demonstrating the viability of using ASR to automate the transcription of the narratives. The ASR and manually corrected transcriptions are included in the dataset.

A descriptive analysis of the gaze and narratives shows that the average fixation duration across the 30 participants was 250 milliseconds and the average narrative duration was about 22 seconds. The transcribed narratives were segmented into word tokens using the default NLTK word tokenizer. Various measures for the first-order analysis of the narratives were then calculated. The mean number of tokens and the average duration of narratives together indicate that on average observers uttered 2.5 words per second. The mean type-token ratio was 0.75, suggesting that there is substantial lexical diversity in the narratives, which demonstrates the richness of the dataset. Figure 3 shows a scatter plot for the mean number of word types against the mean number of word tokens for the 100 images

across 30 participants. The plot illustrates that a larger number of tokens typically results in a larger number of types. Images 23, 3, and 24, highlighted in green, have fewer mean word tokens and types than images 35, 90, and 94, highlighted in magenta. For this dataset, this may be due to the number of significant objects in the images where a significant object is defined as an object that occupies a significantly large area of the image. Images 23, 3, and 24 have on average two objects while images 35, 90, and 94 have more than two.

4   Application to Multimodal Alignment

We examine the usefulness of our general-domain dataset on image-region annotation, adapting the framework given by Vaidyanathan et al. (2016).

Linguistic units: We process the narratives in order to extract nouns and adjectives, which serve as the linguistic units. Additionally, we remove word tokens with a frequency of 1 in order to reduce the impact of speech errors and one-off ASR errors.

Visual units: To encode fixations into meaningful regions similar to Vaidyanathan et al. (2016) we apply mean shift fixation clustering (MSFC). We also use modified k-means and gradient segmentation (GSEG). Modified k-means uses the number of clusters obtained from MSFC as the value of k instead of 4 as in the original framework. GSEG uses color and texture with region merging to segment an image (Ugarriza et al., 2009). The outputs of the three clustering methods are shown in Figure 5. The rest of the alignment framework, including using the

---

[2]https://www.ibm.com/watson/services/speech-to-text/

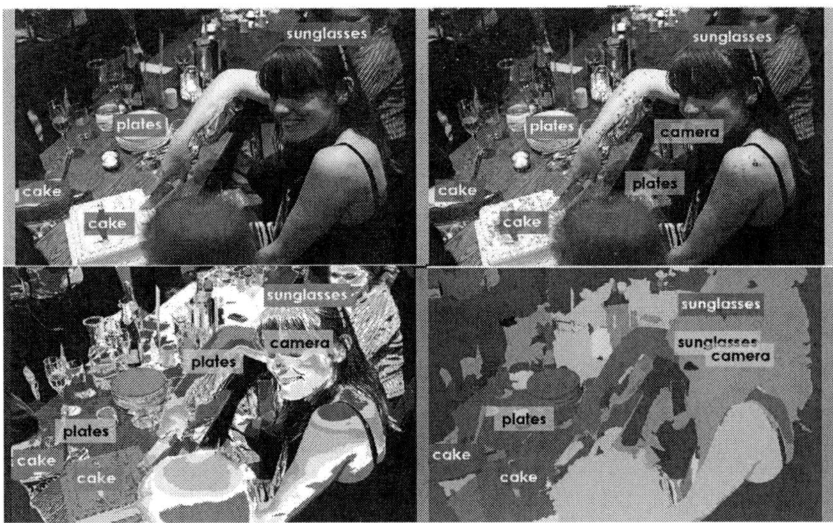

Figure 5: Example region annotations. Top-left: Reference alignments. Alignment output using: top-right: MSFC; bottom-left: modified *k*-means; and bottom-right: GSEG. Correct alignments in pink. Misalignments and labels not belonging to reference alignments in yellow.

Berkeley aligner (Liang et al., 2006), remained the same.

Reference alignments: Both SURE and POSSIBLE (Och and Ney, 2003) reference alignments were prepared using RegionLabeler, a GUI (Figure 4) to allow evaluation of the resulting multimodal alignments. With this tool, an annotator drew borders of image regions and selected the associated linguistic units.

Baseline alignments: For comparison, we use the baselines proposed by Vaidyanathan et al. (2016): *simultaneous* which assumes that the observers utter the word corresponding to a region at the exact moment their eyes fixate on that region, and *1-second delay* which assumes that there is a 1-second delay between a fixation and the utterance of the word corresponding to that region.

5 Results and Discussion

We calculated average precision, recall, and AER for alignments and compared them against the baselines following Och and Ney (2003).

The two baselines performed similarly. Table 1 shows that the alignment framework performs better than either baseline. MSFC yields the highest recall and lowest AER with an absolute improvement of 0%, 19%, and 10% for precision, recall and AER, over the 1-second delay baseline. Modified *k*-means achieves higher precision with

an absolute improvement of 6%, 14%, and 14% over baseline. GSEG performed with less success.

Figure 5 visually compares reference and obtained alignments. Most words are correctly aligned. MSFC correctly aligns labels such as *cake* and *plates*, yielding higher recall. It aligns some labels such as *plates* to incorrect regions, explaining the lower precision. All methods erroneously assign labels not grounded to any region but representing the perspective of the photographer, such as *camera*, to regions in the image, which lowers precision.

6 Related Work

There are publicly available datasets that provide gaze data with no language data (Krafka et al., 2016; Borji and Itti, 2015; Wilming et al., 2017) for tasks such as image saliency or driving. Vasudevan et al. (2018b) collected a dataset in which crowdworkers viewed objects in bounding boxes and read aloud pre-scripted phrases describing those objects. Although their dataset consists of spoken language, it lacks co-collected gaze data and uses a bounding box to highlight an object as opposed to allowing the observer to view the image freely. A more recent study describes the collection of a dataset in which crowdworkers were instructed to draw bounding boxes around objects in videos and provide written phrases describing these objects

	MSFC			Modified k-means		
	Precision	Recall	AER	Precision	Recall	AER
Simultaneous	0.42	0.30	0.65	0.49	0.17	0.74
1-second delay	**0.43**	0.31	0.64	**0.50**	0.17	0.74
Alignment framework	**0.43**	**0.50**	**0.54**	**0.56**	**0.31**	**0.60**

Table 1: Average alignment performance across images. MSFC provides the best recall and lowest AER, and modified k-means the best precision. In all cases, the alignment framework yields stronger results than either of the timing-based baselines.

(Vasudevan et al., 2018a). In a separate task, crowdworkers were asked to view those same videos and to gaze within the bounding boxes for each object while face data was recorded. The authors infer gaze using the recorded face data. None of these datasets involves simultaneous visual-linguistic capture of spoken narration or precision eye-tracking equipment during naturalistic free viewing. Ho et al. (2015) provide a dataset that consists only of gaze and speech time stamps during dyadic interactions. The closest dataset to ours is the multimodal but non-public data described by Vaidyanathan et al. (2016).

7 Conclusions

The SNAG dataset is a unique and novel resource that can provide insights into how humans view and describe scenes with common objects. In this paper, we use SNAG to demonstrate that multimodal alignment does not depend on expert observers or image type, with comparable results to Vaidyanathan et al. (2016) for dermatological images. SNAG could also serve researchers outside NLP, including psycholinguistics. Spontaneous speech coupled with eye-tracking data could be useful in answering questions about how humans produce language when engaging with visual tasks. Parallel data streams can, for example, help in investigating questions such as the effects of word complexity or frequency on language formation and production. It might also aid in studies of syntactic constructions and argument structure, and how they relate to visual perception. Qualitative analysis of our transcripts indicates that they contain some emotional information in the form of holistic comments on the overall affect of the images, which could be helpful in affective visual or linguistic computing tasks. Future work could co-collect modalities such as facial expressions, galvanic skin response, or other biophysical signals with static or dynamic visual materials.

Acknowledgments

We thank Tommy P. Keane for his assistance in developing the image annotation software.

References

Beyer, H. and Holtzblatt, K. (1997). *Contextual Design: Defining Customer-Centered Systems*. Elsevier.

Boersma, P. (2002). Praat, a system for doing phonetics by computer. *Glot International*, 5(9/10):341–345.

Borji, A. and Itti, L. (2015). Cat2000: A large scale fixation dataset for boosting saliency research. *arXiv preprint arXiv:1505.03581*.

Brunyé, T. T. and Gardony, A. L. (2017). Eye tracking measures of uncertainty during perceptual decision making. *International Journal of Psychophysiology*, 120:60–68.

Cooper, R. M. (1974). The control of eye fixation by the meaning of spoken language: A new methodology for the real-time investigation of speech perception, memory, and language processing. *Cognitive Psychology*, 6(1):84–107.

Eivazi, S., Bednarik, R., Tukiainen, M., von und zu Fraunberg, M., Leinonen, V., and Jääskeläinen, J. E. (2012). Gaze behaviour of expert and novice microneurosurgeons differs during observations of tumor removal recordings. In *Proceedings of the Symposium on Eye Tracking Research and Applications*, pages 377–380. ACM.

Fiedler, S. and Glöckner, A. (2012). The dynamics of decision making in risky choice: An eye-tracking analysis. *Frontiers in Psychology*, 3:335.

Guo, X., Li, R., Alm, C., Yu, Q., Pelz, J., Shi, P., and Haake, A. (2014). Infusing perceptual expertise and domain knowledge into a human-centered image retrieval system: A prototype application. In *Proceedings of the Symposium on Eye Tracking Research and Applications*, pages 275–278. ACM.

Hayes, T. R. and Henderson, J. M. (2017). Scan patterns during real-world scene viewing predict individual differences in cognitive capacity. *Journal of Vision*, 17(5):23–23.

Ho, S., Foulsham, T., and Kingstone, A. (2015). Speaking and listening with the eyes: Gaze signaling during dyadic interactions. *PloS One*, 10(8):e0136905.

Holmqvist, E., Thunberg, G., and Dahlstrand, M. P. (2017). Gaze-controlled communication technology for children with severe multiple disabilities: Parents and professionals perception of gains, obstacles, and prerequisites. *Assistive Technology*, 0(0):1–8. PMID: 28471273.

Krafka, K., Khosla, A., Kellnhofer, P., Kannan, H., Bhandarkar, S., Matusik, W., and Torralba, A. (2016). Eye tracking for everyone. In *IEEE Conference on Computer Vision and Pattern Recognition (CVPR)*.

Liang, P., Taskar, B., and Klein, D. (2006). Alignment by agreement. In *Proceedings of the Conference of the North American Chapter of the Association for Computational Linguistics: Human Language Technologies*, pages 104–111.

Lin, T.-Y., Maire, M., Belongie, S., Hays, J., Perona, P., Ramanan, D., Dollár, P., and Zitnick, C. L. (2014). Microsoft COCO: Common objects in context. In *Proceedings of the European Conference on Computer Vision*, pages 740–755.

Och, F. J. and Ney, H. (2003). A systematic comparison of various statistical alignment models. *Computational Linguistics*, 29(1):19–51.

Padmanaban, N., Konrad, R., Stramer, T., Cooper, E. A., and Wetzstein, G. (2017). Optimizing virtual reality for all users through gaze-contingent and adaptive focus displays. *Proceedings of the National Academy of Sciences*.

Rayner, K. (1998). Eye movements in reading and information processing: 20 years of research. *Psychological Bulletin*, 124(3):372–422.

Richardson, D. C. and Dale, R. (2005). Looking to understand: The coupling between speakers' and listeners' eye movements and its relationship to discourse comprehension. *Cognitive Science*, 29(6):1045–1060.

Sensomotoric Instruments (2016). Sensomotoric Instruments. `https://www.smivision.com/`.

Shao, Z., Roelofs, A., and Meyer, A. (2013). Predicting naming latencies for action pictures: Dutch norms. *Behavior Research Methods*, 46:274–283.

Ugarriza, L. G., Saber, E., Vantaram, S. R., Amuso, V., Shaw, M., and Bhaskar, R. (2009). Automatic image segmentation by dynamic region growth and multiresolution merging. *IEEE Transactions on Image Processing*, 18(10):2275–2288.

Underwood, G., Chapman, P., Brocklehurst, N., Underwood, J., and Crundall, D. (2003). Visual attention while driving: sequences of eye fixations made by experienced and novice drivers. *Ergonomics*, 46(6):629–646.

Vaidyanathan, P., Prud'hommeaux, E., Alm, C. O., Pelz, J. B., and Haake, A. R. (2016). Fusing eye movements and observer narratives for expert-driven image-region annotations. In *Proceedings of the Symposium on Eye Tracking Research and Applications*, pages 27–34. ACM.

Vasudevan, A. B., Dai, D., and Van Gool, L. (2018a). Object referring in videos with language and human gaze. In *Proceedings of the IEEE Conference on Computer Vision and Pattern Recognition*.

Vasudevan, A. B., Dai, D., and Van Gool, L. (2018b). Object referring in visual scene with spoken language. In *Proceedings of the IEEE Winter Conference on Applications of Computer Vision*.

Wilming, N., Onat, S., Ossandn, J. P., Acik, A., Kietzmann, T. C., Kaspar, K., Gameiro, R. R., Vormberg, A., and Knig, P. (2017). An extensive dataset of eye movements during viewing of complex images. *Scientific Data*, (4).

Analogical Reasoning on Chinese Morphological and Semantic Relations

Shen Li[1,2,♠]   Zhe Zhao[3,♣]   Renfen Hu[1,2,♠,†]   Wensi Li[1,2,♦]   Tao Liu[3,♣]   Xiaoyong Du[3,♣]

♠{shen, irishere}@mail.bnu.edu.cn
♣{helloworld, tliu, duyong}@ruc.edu.cn
♦zjklws@163.com

[1] Institute of Chinese Information Processing, Beijing Normal University
[2] UltraPower-BNU Joint Laboratory for Artificial Intelligence, Beijing Normal University
[3] School of Information, Renmin University of China

Abstract

Analogical reasoning is effective in capturing linguistic regularities. This paper proposes an analogical reasoning task on Chinese. After delving into Chinese lexical knowledge, we sketch 68 implicit morphological relations and 28 explicit semantic relations. A big and balanced dataset CA8 is then built for this task, including 17813 questions. Furthermore, we systematically explore the influences of vector representations, context features, and corpora on analogical reasoning. With the experiments, CA8 is proved to be a reliable benchmark for evaluating Chinese word embeddings.

1 Introduction

Recently, the boom of word embedding draws our attention to analogical reasoning on linguistic regularities. Given the word representations, analogy questions can be automatically solved via vector computation, e.g. *"apples - apple + car ≈ cars"* for morphological regularities and *"king - man + woman ≈ queen"* for semantic regularities (Mikolov et al., 2013). Analogical reasoning has become a reliable evaluation method for word embeddings. In addition, It can be used in inducing morphological transformations (Soricut and Och, 2015), detecting semantic relations (Herdagdelen and Baroni, 2009), and translating unknown words (Langlais and Patry, 2007).

It is well known that linguistic regularities vary a lot among different languages. For example, Chinese is a typical analytic language which lacks inflection. Figure 1 shows that function words and reduplication are used to denote grammatical and semantic information. In addition, many semantic

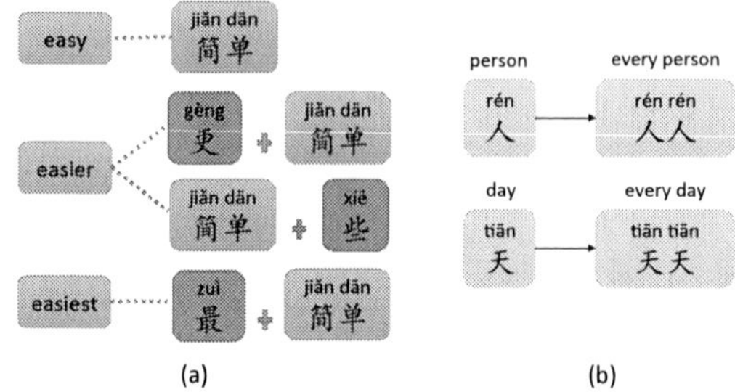

Figure 1: Examples of Chinese lexical knowledge: (a) function words (in orange boxes) are used to indicate the comparative and superlative degrees; (b) reduplication yields the meaning of *"every"*.

relations are closely related with social and cultural factors, e.g. in Chinese *"shī-xiān"* (god of poetry) refers to the poet *Li-bai* and *"shī-shèng"* (saint of poetry) refers to the poet *Du-fu*.

However, few attempts have been made in Chinese analogical reasoning. The only Chinese analogy dataset is translated from part of an English dataset (Chen et al., 2015) (denote as CA_translated). Although it has been widely used in evaluation of word embeddings (Yang and Sun, 2015; Yin et al., 2016; Su and Lee, 2017), it could not serve as a reliable benchmark since it includes only 134 unique Chinese words in three semantic relations (capital, state, and family), and morphological knowledge is not even considered.

Therefore, we would like to investigate linguistic regularities beneath Chinese. By modeling them as an analogical reasoning task, we could further examine the effects of vector offset methods in detecting Chinese morphological and semantic relations. As far as we know, this is the first study focusing on Chinese analogical reasoning. Moreover, we release a standard benchmark for evaluation of Chinese word embedding, together with 36 open-source pre-trained embeddings at

---

† Corresponding author.

Proceedings of the 56th Annual Meeting of the Association for Computational Linguistics (Short Papers), pages 138–143
Melbourne, Australia, July 15 - 20, 2018. ©2018 Association for Computational Linguistics

GitHub[1], which could serve as a solid basis for Chinese NLP tasks.

2 Morphological Relations

Morphology concerns the internal structure of words. There is a common belief that Chinese is a morphologically impoverished language since a morpheme mostly corresponds to an orthographic character, and it lacks apparent distinctions between roots and affixes. However, Packard (2000) suggests that Chinese has a different morphological system because it selects different "settings" on parameters shared by all languages. We will clarify this special system by mapping its morphological analogies into two processes: reduplication and semi-affixation.

2.1 Reduplication

Reduplication means a morpheme is repeated to form a new word, which is semantically and/or syntactically distinct from the original morpheme, e.g. the word *"tiān-tiān"(day day)* in Figure 1(b) means *"everyday"*. By analyzing all the word categories in Chinese, we find that nouns, verbs, adjectives, adverbs, and measure words have reduplication abilities. Given distinct morphemes A and B, we summarize 6 repetition patterns in Figure 2.

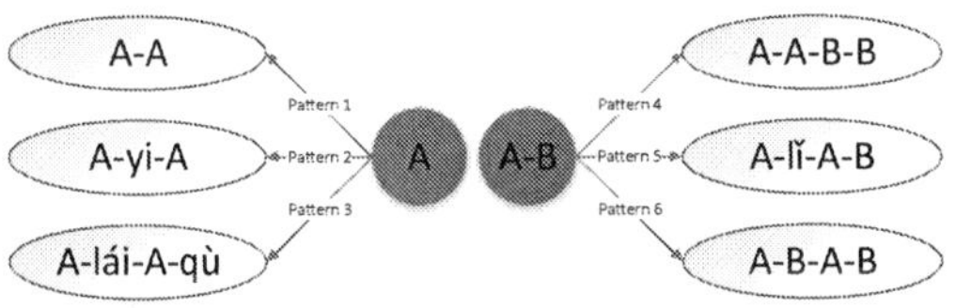

Figure 2: Reduplication patterns of A and A-B.

Each pattern may have one or more morphological functions. Taking *Pattern 1 (A→AA)* as an example, noun morphemes could form kinship terms or yield every/each meaning. For verbs, it signals doing something a little bit or things happen briefly. AA reduplication could also intensify an adjective or transform it to an adverb.

- *bà(dad)* → *bà-bà(dad)*
- *tiān(day)* → *tiān-tiān(everyday)*
- *shuō(say)* → *shuō-shuo(say a little)*
- *kàn(look)* → *kàn-kàn(have a brief look)*
- *dà(big)* → *dà-dà(very big; greatly)*
- *shēn(deep)* → *shēn-shēn(deeply)*

2.2 Semi-affixation

Affixation is a morphological process whereby a bound morpheme (an affix) is attached to roots or stems to form new language units. Chinese is a typical isolating language that has few affixes. Liu et al. (2001) points out that although affixes are rare in Chinese, there are some components behaving like affixes and can also be used as independent lexemes. They are called semi-affixes.

To model the semi-affixation process, we uncover 21 semi-prefixes and 41 semi-suffixes. These semi-suffixes can be used to denote changes of meaning or part of speech. For example, the semi-prefix *"dì-"* could be added to numerals to form ordinal numbers, and the semi-suffix *"-zi"* is able to nominalize an adjective:

- *yī(one)* → *dì-yī(first)*
  èr(two) → *dì-èr(second)*
- *pàng(fat)* → *pàng-zi(a fat man)*
  shòu(thin) → *shòu-zi(a thin man)*

3 Semantic Relations

To investigate semantic knowledge reasoning, we present 28 semantic relations in four aspects: geography, history, nature, and people. Among them we inherit a few relations from English datasets, e.g. country-capital and family members, while the rest of them are proposed originally on the basis of our observation of Chinese lexical knowledge. For example, a Chinese province may have its own abbreviation, capital city, and representative drama, which could form rich semantic analogies:

- *ān-huī* vs *zhè-jiāng* (province)
- *wǎn* vs *zhè* (abbreviation)
- *hé-féi* vs *háng-zhōu* (capital)
- *huáng-méi-xì* vs *yuè-jù* (drama)

We also address novel relations that could be used for other languages, e.g. scientists and their findings, companies and their founders.

4 Task of Chinese Analogical Reasoning

Analogical reasoning task is to retrieve the answer of the question "a is to b as c is to ?". Based on the relations discussed above, we firstly collect word pairs for each relation. Since there are no explicit word boundaries in Chinese, we take dictionaries and word segmentation specifications as references to confirm the inclusion of each word

Benchmark	Category	Type	#questions	#words	Relation
CA_translated	Semantic	Capital	506	46	capital-country
		State	175	54	city-province
		Family	272	34	family members
CA8	Morphological	Reduplication A	2554	344	A-A, A-yi-A, A-lái-A-qù
		Reduplication AB	2535	423	A-A-B-B, A-lǐ-A-B, A-B-A-B
		Semi-prefix	2553	656	21 semi-prefixes: 大, 小, 老, 第, 亚, etc.
		Semi-suffix	2535	727	41 semi-suffixes: 者, 式, 主义, 性, etc.
	Semantic	Geography	3192	305	country-capital, country-currency, province-abbreviation, province-capital, province-dramma, etc.
		History	1465	177	dynasty-emperor, dynasty-capital, title-emperor, celebrity-country
		Nature	1370	452	number, time, animal, plant, body, physics, weather, reverse, color, etc.
		People	1609	259	finding-scientist, work-writer, family members, etc.

Table 1: Comparisons of CA_translated and CA8 benchmarks. More details about the relations in CA8 can be seen in GitHub.

Window (dynamic)	Iteration	Dimension	Sub-sampling	Low-frequency threshold	Context distribution smoothing	Negative (SGNS/PPMI)	Vector offset
5	5	300	1e-5	50	0.75	5/1	3COSMUL

Table 2: Hyper-parameter details. Levy and Goldberg (2014b) unifies SGNS and PPMI in a framework, which share the same hyper-parameter settings. We exploit 3COSMUL to solve the analogical questions suggested by Levy and Goldberg (2014a).

pair. To avoid the imbalance problem addressed in English benchmarks (Gladkova et al., 2016), we set a limit of 50 word pairs at most for each relation. In this step, 1852 unique Chinese word pairs are retrieved. We then build CA8, a big, balanced dataset for Chinese analogical reasoning including 17813 questions. Compared with CA_translated (Chen et al., 2015), CA8 incorporates both morphological and semantic questions, and it brings in much more words, relation types and questions. Table 1 shows details of the two datasets. They are both used for evaluation in Experiments section.

5 Experiments

In Chinese analogical reasoning task, we aim at investigating to what extent word vectors capture the linguistic relations, and how it is affected by three important factors: vector representations (sparse and dense), context features (character, word, and ngram), and training corpora (size and domain). Table 2 shows the hyper-parameters used in this work. All the text data used in our experiments (as shown in Table 3) are preprocessed via the following steps:

- Remove the html and xml tags from the texts and set the encoding as utf-8. Digits and punctuations are remained.

- Convert traditional Chinese characters into simplified characters with Open Chinese Convert (OpenCC)[2].

- Conduct Chinese word segmentation with HanLP(v_1.5.3)[3].

5.1 Vector Representations

Existing vector representations fall into two types, dense vectors and sparse vectors. SGNS (skip-gram model with negative sampling) (Mikolov et al., 2013) and PPMI (Positive Pointwise Mutual Information) (Levy and Goldberg, 2014a) are respectively typical methods for learning dense and sparse word vectors. Table 4 lists the performance of them on CA_translated and CA8 datasets under different configurations.

We can observe that on CA8 dataset, SGNS representations perform better in analogical reasoning of morphological relations and PPMI representations show great advantages in semantic relations. This result is consistent with performance of English dense and sparse vectors on MSR (morphology-only), SemEval (semantic-only), and Google (mixed) analogy datasets (Levy and Goldberg, 2014b; Levy et al., 2015). It is

---

[2]https://github.com/BYVoid/OpenCC
[3]https://github.com/hankcs/HanLP

Corpus	Size	#tokens	$|V|$	Description
Wikipedia	1.3G	223M	2129K	Wikipedia data obtained from https://dumps.wikimedia.org/
Baidubaike	4.1G	745M	5422K	Chinese wikipedia data from https://baike.baidu.com/
People's Daily News	3.9G	668M	1664K	News data from People's Daily (1946-2017) http://data.people.com.cn/
Sogou news	3.7G	649M	1226K	News data provided by Sogou Labs http://www.sogou.com/labs/
Zhihu QA	2.1G	384M	1117K	Chinese QA data from https://www.zhihu.com/, including 32137 questions and 3239114 answers
Combination	14.8G	2668M	8175K	We build this corpus by combining the above corpora

Table 3: Detailed information of the corpora. #tokens denotes the number of tokens in corpus. $|V|$ denotes the vocabulary size.

		CA_translated			CA8									
		Cap.	Sta.	Fam.	A	AB	Pre.	Suf.	**Mor.**	Geo.	His.	Nat.	Peo.	**Sem.**
SGNS	word	.706	.966	.603	.117	.162	.181	.389	.222	.414	.345	.236	.223	.327
	word+ngram	.715	**.977**	.640	.143	.184	.197	.429	.250	.449	.308	.276	.310	.368
	word+char	.676	.966	.548	**.358**	**.540**	**.326**	**.612**	**.455**	.468	.226	.296	.305	.368
PPMI	word	.925	.920	.548	.103	.139	.138	.464	.226	.627	.501	.300	.515	.522
	word+ngram	**.943**	.960	**.658**	.102	.129	.168	.456	.230	**.680**	**.535**	**.371**	**.626**	**.586**
	word+char	.913	.886	.614	.106	.190	.173	.505	.260	.638	.502	.288	.515	.524

Table 4: Performance of word representations learned under different configurations. Baidubaike is used as the training corpus. The top 1 results are in **bold**.

probably because the reasoning on morphological relations relies more on common words in context, and the training procedure of SGNS favors frequent word pairs. Meanwhile, PPMI model is more sensitive to infrequent and specific word pairs, which are beneficial to semantic relations.

The above observation shows that CA8 is a reliable benchmark for studying the effects of dense and sparse vectors. Compared with CA_translated and existing English analogy datasets, it offers both morphological and semantic questions which are also balanced across different types [4].

5.2 Context Features

To investigate the influence of context features on analogical reasoning, we consider not only word features, but also ngram features inspired by statistical language models, and character (Hanzi) features based on the close relationship between Chinese words and their composing characters [5]. Specifically, we use word bigrams for ngram features, character unigrams and bigrams for character features.

Ngrams and Chinese characters are effective features in training word representations (Zhao et al., 2017; Chen et al., 2015; Bojanowski et al., 2016). However, Table 4 shows that there is only a slight increase on CA_translated dataset with ngram features, and the accuracies in most cases decrease after integrating character features. In contrast, on CA8 dataset, the introduction of ngram and character features brings significant and consistent improvements on almost all the categories. Furthermore, character features are especially advantageous for reasoning of morphological relations. SGNS model integrating with character features even doubles the accuracy in morphological questions.

Besides, the representations achieve surprisingly high accuracies in some categories of CA_translated, which means that there is little room for further improvement. However it is much harder for representation methods to achieve high accuracies on CA8. The best configuration only achieves 68.0%.

5.3 Corpora

We compare word representations learned upon corpora of different sizes and domains. As shown in Table 3, six corpora are used in the experiments: Chinese Wikipedia, Baidubaike, People's Daily News, Sogou News, Zhihu QA, and "Com-

---

[4]CA_translated and SemEval datasets contain only semantic questions, MSR dataset contains only morphological questions, and in Google dataset the capital:country relation constitutes 56.72% of all semantic questions.

[5]The SGNS with word and character features are implemented by fasttext toolkit, the rest are implemented by ngram2vec toolkit.

	CA_translated			CA8									
	Cap.	Sta.	Fam.	A	AB	Pre.	Suf.	**Mor.**	Geo.	His.	Nat.	Peo.	**Sem.**
Wikipedia 1.2G	.597	.771	.360	.029	.018	.152	.266	.180	.339	.125	.147	.079	.236
Baidubaike 4.3G	.706	.966	.603	.117	.162	.181	**.389**	.222	.414	**.345**	.236	**.223**	.327
People's Daily 4.2G	**.925**	**.989**	.547	.140	.158	**.213**	.355	**.226**	**.694**	.019	.206	.157	**.455**
Sogou News 4.0G	.619	.966	.496	.057	.075	.131	.176	.115	.432	.067	.150	.145	.302
Zhihu QA 2.2G	.277	.491	**.625**	**.175**	**.199**	.134	.251	.189	.146	.147	**.250**	.189	.181
Combination 15.9G	**.872**	**.994**	**.710**	**.223**	**.300**	**.234**	**.518**	**.321**	**.662**	**.293**	**.310**	**.307**	**.467**

Table 5: Performance of word representations learned upon different training corpora by SGNS with context feature of word. The top 2 results are in **bold**.

bination" which is built by combining the first five corpora together.

Table 5 shows that accuracies increase with the growth in corpus size, e.g. Baidubaike (an online Chinese encyclopedia) has a clear advantage over Wikipedia. Also, the domain of a corpus plays an important role in the experiments. We can observe that vectors trained on news data are beneficial to geography relations, especially on People's Daily which has a focus on political news. Another example is Zhihu QA, an online question-answering corpus which contains more informal data than others. It is helpful to reduplication relations since many reduplication words appear frequently in spoken language. With the largest size and varied domains, "Combination" corpus performs much better than others in both morphological and semantic relations.

Based on the above experiments, we find that vector representations, context features, and corpora all have important influences on Chinese analogical reasoning. Also, CA8 is proved to be a reliable benchmark for evaluation of Chinese word embeddings.

6 Conclusion

In this paper, we investigate the linguistic regularities beneath Chinese, and propose a Chinese analogical reasoning task based on 68 morphological relations and 28 semantic relations. In the experiments, we apply vector offset method to this task, and examine the effects of vector representations, context features, and corpora. This study offers an interesting perspective combining linguistic analysis and representation models. The benchmark and embedding sets we release could also serve as a solid basis for Chinese NLP tasks.

Acknowledgments

This work is supported by the Fundamental Research Funds for the Central Universities, National Natural Science Foundation of China with Grant (No.61472428) and Chinese Testing International Project (No.CTI2017B12).

References

Piotr Bojanowski, Edouard Grave, Armand Joulin, and Tomas Mikolov. 2016. Enriching word vectors with subword information. *arXiv preprint arXiv:1607.04606* .

Xinxiong Chen, Lei Xu, Zhiyuan Liu, Maosong Sun, and Huan-Bo Luan. 2015. Joint learning of character and word embeddings. In *IJCAI*. pages 1236–1242.

Etienne Denoual. 2007. Analogical translation of unknown words in a statistical machine translation framework. *Proceedings of Machine Translation Summit XI, Copenhagen* .

Anna Gladkova, Aleksandr Drozd, and Satoshi Matsuoka. 2016. Analogy-based detection of morphological and semantic relations with word embeddings: what works and what doesn't. In *Proceedings of the NAACL Student Research Workshop*. pages 8–15.

Amac Herdagdelen and Marco Baroni. 2009. Bagpack: A general framework to represent semantic relations. In *Proceedings of the Workshop on Geometrical Models of Natural Language Semantics*. Association for Computational Linguistics, pages 33–40.

Philippe Langlais and Alexandre Patry. 2007. Translating unknown words by analogical learning. In *EMNLP-CoNLL*. pages 877–886.

Omer Levy and Yoav Goldberg. 2014a. Linguistic regularities in sparse and explicit word representations. In *Proceedings of the eighteenth conference on computational natural language learning*. pages 171–180.

Omer Levy and Yoav Goldberg. 2014b. Neural word embedding as implicit matrix factorization. In *Advances in neural information processing systems*. pages 2177–2185.

Omer Levy, Yoav Goldberg, and Ido Dagan. 2015. Improving distributional similarity with lessons learned from word embeddings. *Transactions of the Association for Computational Linguistics* 3:211–225.

Yuehua Liu, Wenyu Pan, and Wei Gu. 2001. *Practical grammar of modern Chinese*. The Commercial Press.

Tomas Mikolov, Wen-tau Yih, and Geoffrey Zweig. 2013. Linguistic regularities in continuous space word representations. In *hlt-Naacl*. volume 13, pages 746–751.

Jerome L Packard. 2000. *The morphology of Chinese: A linguistic and cognitive approach*. Cambridge University Press.

Radu Soricut and Franz Josef Och. 2015. Unsupervised morphology induction using word embeddings. In *HLT-NAACL*. pages 1627–1637.

Tzu-ray Su and Hung-yi Lee. 2017. Learning chinese word representations from glyphs of characters. In *Proceedings of the 2017 Conference on Empirical Methods in Natural Language Processing*. pages 264–273.

Peter D Turney. 2008. A uniform approach to analogies, synonyms, antonyms, and associations. In *Proceedings of the 22nd International Conference on Computational Linguistics-Volume 1*. Association for Computational Linguistics, pages 905–912.

Liner Yang and Maosong Sun. 2015. Improved learning of chinese word embeddings with semantic knowledge. In *Chinese Computational Linguistics and Natural Language Processing Based on Naturally Annotated Big Data*, Springer, pages 15–25.

Rongchao Yin, Quan Wang, Peng Li, Rui Li, and Bin Wang. 2016. Multi-granularity chinese word embedding. In *EMNLP*. pages 981–986.

Zhe Zhao, Tao Liu, Shen Li, Bofang Li, and Xiaoyong Du. 2017. Ngram2vec: Learning improved word representations from ngram co-occurrence statistics. In *Proceedings of the 2017 Conference on Empirical Methods in Natural Language Processing*. pages 244–253.

Construction of a Chinese Corpus for the Analysis of the Emotionality of Metaphorical Expressions

Dongyu Zhang[1,2], Hongfei Lin[2], Liang Yang[2], Shaowu Zhang[2], Bo Xu[2]
[1]School of Software, Dalian University of Technology, China
[2]School of Computer Science and Technology, Dalian University of Technology, China
{zhangdongyu,hflin, liang, zhangsw}@dlut.edu.cn
xubo2011@mail.dlut.edu.cn

Abstract

Metaphors are frequently used to convey emotions. However, there is little research on the construction of metaphor corpora annotated with emotion for the analysis of emotionality of metaphorical expressions. Furthermore, most studies focus on English, and few in other languages, particularly Sino-Tibetan languages such as Chinese, for emotion analysis from metaphorical texts, although there are likely to be many differences in emotional expressions of metaphorical usages across different languages. We therefore construct a significant new corpus on metaphor, with 5,605 manually annotated sentences in Chinese. We present an annotation scheme that contains annotations of linguistic metaphors, emotional categories (joy, anger, sadness, fear, love, disgust and surprise), and intensity. The annotation agreement analyses for multiple annotators are described. We also use the corpus to explore and analyze the emotionality of metaphors. To the best of our knowledge, this is the first relatively large metaphor corpus with an annotation of emotions in Chinese.

1 Introduction

Metaphorical expressions are frequently used in human communication, and they occur on average in every third sentence of natural language, according to empirical studies (Cameron, 2003; Steen et al., 2010; Shutova and Teufel, 2010). Metaphor not only involves linguistic expressions, but also involves a cognitive process of conceptual knowledge (Lakoff and Johnson, 1980). According to Lakoff and Johnson (1980), humans use one concept in metaphors to describe another concept for reasoning and communication. For instance, in the metaphorical utterance: "experience is treasure," we use "treasure" to describe "experience" to emphasize that "experience" can be valuable. To take another metaphorical instance as an example: "he killed the engine." "An engine" is viewed as a living thing, and thus stopping its operation is related to the act of killing. Metaphor has been viewed as a mapping system that conceptualizes one domain (target) in terms of another (source).

Emotion, as an abstract and vague conception, is frequently described and conceptualized by metaphor (Goatly Musolff and Project LLE, 2007; Kövecses, 1995, 2000). There seem to be two main types of metaphors that evoke emotion. One is the metaphor in which the target domain is emotion. For example, in the instance "he was blazing at what she did," the angry, emotional self is conceptualized as "fire," and so is expressed metaphorically in terms of "blaze." The other type is metaphors that have emotional connotations. For example, in "The financial crisis has eaten up all my savings," the target domain is finances and the source domain, implied by the verb "eat up," is some sort of ravenous beast. This metaphorical sentence thus may express senses of anger and fear about a "financial crisis." From the above examples, we can see that metaphorical expressions often state or evoke emotions implicitly and indirectly. Neuroimaging studies have provided evidence that metaphorical language elicits more emotional activation of the human brain than literal language in the same context (Citron and Goldberg, 2014).

Proceedings of the 56th Annual Meeting of the Association for Computational Linguistics (Short Papers), pages 144–150
Melbourne, Australia, July 15 - 20, 2018. ©2018 Association for Computational Linguistics

The interaction between emotion and metaphor has been studied from different perspectives by scholars in many fields such as psychology (Averill, 1990; Thibodeau and Boroditsky, 2011; Fetterman et al., 2016), linguistics (Fainsilber and Ortony, 1987; Kövecses, 2010), neuroscience (Az-iz-Zadeh and Damasio, 2008; Malinowski and Horton, 2015; Jabbi et al., 2008) and natural language processing (NLP) (Mohammad, Shutova and Turney, 2016). Many approaches for sentiment analysis of metaphorical texts have been proposed in the area of NLP (Smith et al., 2007; Veale, 2012; Reyes and Rosso, 2012; Kozareva, 2013; Strzalkowski et al., 2014). In particular, along with the rapid explosion of social media applications such as Twitter and Weibo, emotional texts containing metaphorical expressions have increased considerably. It seems to be very common for Internet users to use vivid and colorful metaphorical language to express emotions on social media.

Corpora are fundamental for sound analysis of emotionality in metaphor and for high-quality automatic emotion detection in metaphor. However, many resources cover sentiment analysis (Alm et al., 2005; Dong et al., 2014; Kiritchenko et al., 2014; Mohammad et al., 2013; Strapparava and Mihalcea, 2007; Ratnadeep et al., 2013) and metaphor detection (Lönneker, 2004; Martin, 2006; Pragglejaz Group, 2007; Steen et al., 2010) separately. Moreover, although NLP has proposed approaches for sentiment analysis of metaphor, as mentioned above, an overwhelming majority of studies focus on the annotation of only positive and negative emotions rather than a range of emotions. In addition, there is limited research in NLP in languages other than English analyzing emotions in metaphors. Nevertheless there are likely to be many differences in emotional expressions of metaphorical usages in different cultures, although multiple languages share similar conceptual metaphors based on the same human cognition and physical experience (Kövecses, 1995).

According to the above account, we propose a Chinese corpus with annotations of both linguistic metaphors and emotion. Unlike the widely applied annotation of only positive and negative, we have annotated a range of emotions (joy, anger, sadness, fear, love, disgust and surprise).Based on the analysis of the corpus, our results indicate that a significant proportion of Chinese metaphorical expressions in the corpus contain emotions and the most frequent emotion is love. We also suggest potentials of the corpus contributing to automatic emotion and metaphor detection as well as further investigating mechanisms underlying emotion in metaphor from the perspectives of different cultures for future work. To the best of our knowledge, this is the first relatively large metaphor corpus with an annotation of emotions in Chinese.

2   Data Collection

With the aim of constructing a corpus in the study of emotionality of metaphorical texts in real-world Chinese, data collection took place in accordance with two principles: (1) balance, and (2) relatively abundant emotional information. Specifically, to ensure the corpus is balanced in genre, theme, and style, we selected data from a wide range of sources including books, journals, movie scripts, and networks. In addition, we focused on sources with rich emotional information such as microblogs. Table 1 presents information on corpus sources.

Sources	Characters	Words	Sentences
Books	258,9723	182,046	9,6182
Journals	52,0743	39,7065	2,1640
Scripts	168,236	108,184	11,852
Networks	124,6329	87,2210	9,5153
Total	4,525,031	1,559,505	224,827

Table 1: Information on Corpus Sources

3   Annotation Scheme

3.1   Annotation Model

We annotated metaphorical sentences with target and source domain vocabulary, emotion categories and intensity, metaphor categories (verb or noun metaphor : verb or noun used metaphorically),data sources, and metaphor devices such as 像 "like," 好似 "as," etc. as "indicators". "Indicators" can be null, while the other variables cannot. For example, if there are some terms without values, we need annotators to complete them.

The text files are organized into XML documents. The annotation model is: MetaEmotionModel=(Target, Source, EmotionCategory, Intensity, MetaphorCategory, [indicator], DataSource).The following is an example of a sentence annotation:

```
<metaphor>
  <ID>W2833</ID>
  <Sentences>他攻击了我在这个问题上的观点
   "He attacked my perspective on this problem"
  </Sentences>
  <Target>观点"perspective"</Target>
  <Source>攻击"attack"</Source>
  <EmotionCategory>ND</EmotionCategory>
  <EmotionIntensity>5</EmotionIntensity>
  <MetaphorCategory>V</MetaphorCategory>
  <Indicator> </Indicator>
  <DataSource>W</DataSource>
</metaphor>
```

3.2 Metaphor Annotation

Metaphor category. Based on our investigation of a wide range of texts, we focused on two main types of the most frequently appearing metaphorical sentences: verb metaphor, which contains a verb used metaphorically (e.g., 她怀揣着美好的梦想 "She *wove* a good dream in her mind"); noun metaphor, which contains a noun used metaphorically. Noun metaphor includes a metaphor of "A is B" (e.g., 语言就是力量 "language *is power*") and metaphor with linguistic makers such as "as" and "like" (e.g., 他像箭似的跑开了"he ran away *like an arrow*"), which is normally identified as "simile" from a linguistic perspective, but as "metaphor" in this paper, because it accords with metaphor as we define it: whenever one concept is used to describe another concept (Lakoff and Johnson, 1980). The decision to define both metaphors and similes as metaphors is based on the wish to give a fuller picture of metaphor in our study than one that does not include similes.

Literal or metaphorical. The metaphor annotation is at the relational level, which involves identification of metaphorical relations between source and target domain vocabulary. However, scholars have different opinions on the distinction between literal and metaphorical senses. Some only consider novel expressions (e.g.她为办公室注入新的活力 "She *breathed* new energy into the office") as metaphorical, whereas others consider conventional expressions as metaphors (e.g.他们赢得了这场争论 "they *won* the argument"), where they are conventionalized and fixed in form, and they are used literally by native speakers, although they have the nature of metaphor

(Nunberg, 1987). In this study, following Shutova (2017), we define metaphors as both novel and conventional, but we exclude "dead metaphors" (from which the literal sense has disappeared) from conventional metaphors. That is, conventional metaphors only include those for which the literal and metaphorical senses are clearly distinctive, and both are used contemporarily. This consideration is based on the potential application of our annotation for identification of metaphor, which focuses on word sense disambiguation rather than novel or conventional identification.

3.3 Emotion Annotation

Emotion categories. Scholars define basic emotions in numerous different ways despite research that has challenged the theories of basic emotions (Lindquist et al., 2012; De Leersnyder et al., 2015). Confucianism claims that there are seven basic human emotions (joy, anger, sadness, fear, love, disgust, and desire) (Ma et al., 2011). "七情" (Seven Emotions) is an idiomatic expression commonly used by Chinese people to describe human emotions. However, according to our study of the collected instances in the corpus, we found that "desire" does not appear widely and that "surprise" does. We therefore adopted "surprise" to replace "desire" in the Severn Emotions. The resulting classification is very close to Ekman (1992), with the only difference being the inclusion of "love" as a basic emotion. However, based on our study of the research and its wide appearance in the corpus, "love" is listed as a basic emotion in this paper.

The annotation of emotions takes place on the sentence level. The emotion contained in each metaphorical sentence was identified from one of the seven categories of emotion. We also categorized the intensity of emotion into one of five levels: 1, 3, 5, 7, or 9.

3.4 Annotation Process

Annotation setup. The annotator team comprised seven native Chinese annotators. Annotators were given standards and principles of annotation and detailed instruction for potential difficult and common problems with many annotated samples. Aside from giving them annotators detailed guidelines, we gave them a formal training lesson and a lab meeting to exchange ideas and to discuss problems about annotation once a month during the nine months of the annotation process.

The guidelines changed four times, as we added information on newly found annotation difficulties during the project period. The annotator team comprised seven students, who were not paid for their work.

These seven annotators were divided to three groups with two members for each group plus one group with one person. Using cross-validation methods for annotation, the two-member groups annotated, and the one-person group participated in the final decision when there was divergence. If there was no divergence between the members of the same group, the annotating work was complete. Otherwise another group annotated again, and the final group annotated if there was still divergence. Finally, if the three groups could not reach agreement on the annotation, everyone discussed and determined the annotation to ensure its accuracy and consistency.

Quality monitoring and control (QMC). We used a standardized operating method to achieve high-quality annotation as follows:

(1) Entry interface. On the basis of multiple manual checks and controlled information updating, we provided an interface that allowed us to enter information precisely and quickly.

(2) Error correction. We used emotional lexicon ontology [1] as a support tool to correct human errors. When there was divergence of emotion in the annotation and the sentence/word, we did not enter the annotation.

$$\text{flag} = \text{WordConsistency}(M_{emo}, W_{emo})\,\text{SentConsistency}(M_{emo}, S_{emo}). \qquad (1)$$

If the annotation result was the same as the word's emotion, we set WordConsistency(M_{emo}, W_{emo}) to 1; otherwise, we set it to 0; SentConsistency(M_{emo}, S_{emo}) followed the same logic. We entered the result when the flag was 1, while it needed checking when it was 0.

4 Annotation Agreement

Annotations of both metaphor and emotion were based on the annotators' intuition, which may be very subjective. The reliability of annotations needed to be verified, so three independent annotators annotated the same 811 sentences in the corpus to assess inter-annotator agreement.

---

[1] http://ir.dlut.edu.cn/EmotionOntologyDownload

The kappa score, κ, is widely adopted by computational linguistics to correct for agreement on the reliability of the annotation scheme by chance. We use the κ statistic to measure inter-annotator agreements (Siegel and Castellan, 1988) for emotion annotation. κ is calculated as below:

$$\kappa = \frac{P(A) - P(E)}{1 - P(E)}. \qquad (2)$$

The agreement on the identification of source and target domain words was κ=0.82, which means it is substantially reliable. Compared with noun metaphors, for verb metaphors it is relatively difficult to identify source and target words, because they are related to the assignment of levels of conventionality of metaphorical senses as discussed in 4.1.

The agreement on the choice of emotion category scored κ=0.68. For the agreement measure on emotion intensity, we classified emotion intensity into three: {1, 3}, {5, 7}, or {9}. The resulting agreement on classification of emotion intensity was κ=0.58.

5 Corpus Analysis

We annotated 4,600 sentences out of a total of 5,605 metaphorical sentences as containing emotions. That is, a significant proportion of Chinese metaphorical expressions in the corpus contain emotions. The most frequent emotion in the corpus is love. Figure 1 shows the number of sentences in the corpus of each emotion category.

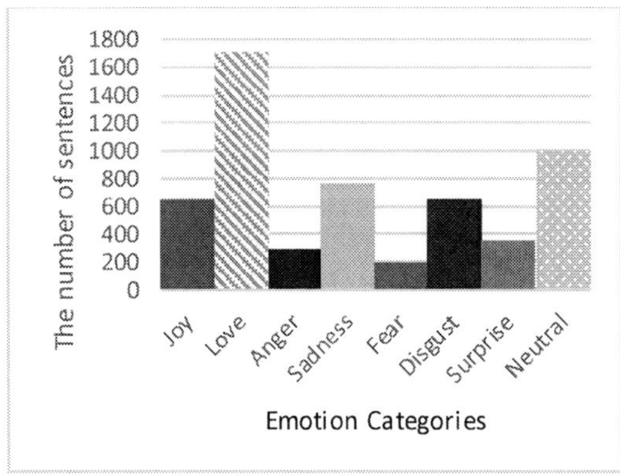

Figure 1: The number of sentences of each emotion category

We also explored the interactions between emotions and source (or target) words. We analyzed every emotional category and related it to each source or target word; we also analyzed which source or target vocabulary conveyed which emotions most frequently. Our results indicate emotions are related to some particular source or target vocabulary. These associations frequently occur together. For example, the emotion love is related to the source words 海洋"sea", 花 "flower" and 阳光"sunshine" etc.

Unlike the widely applied annotation of valence (positive-neutral-negative) in sentiment analysis, we annotated a wider range of emotions in metaphorical texts. The corpus proposed by Mohammad et al. (2016) focused on containing or not containing emotion in metaphor. We have extended their study by providing evidence that metaphorical texts can convey specific emotions such as love and joy. A simple positive/negative emotion distinction does not seem very useful for anything beyond evaluating product reviews. In addition, Mohammad et al. (2016) focus on verb metaphors, whereas we collect both verb and noun metaphors from a variety of sources. Furthermore, since both metaphor and emotion annotations are very subjective, we propose a QMC method (see above 4.4) to achieve high-quality annotation.

6   Conclusions and Future Work

With 5,605 diverse instances and 101,616 Chinese characters of metaphor, our corpus provides an important resource with relatively fine-grained sorting and annotation with both metaphors and emotion. Our study involves the Chinese language, which is very different from English, the focus of the vast majority of current research. This may encourage research into emotion analysis in other languages, particularly Sino-Tibetan languages, since there are differences in emotion between cultures (De Leersnyder, 2015).

Seven annotators spent nine months on the annotation. The manually annotated data is an important step towards automatic emotion analysis and detection of metaphorical texts, as well as metaphor detection. In addition, the application of the corpus to machine translation will be explored to improve the poor translation of metaphorical expressions (Shutova et al., 2013). Furthermore, we hope research using bilingual resources will be conducted on the datasets we have released. This may make contributions to some novel and interesting studies of the emotionality of metaphor from cross cultural perspectives as well as exploring the related, underlying mechanism.

Acknowledgements

We would like to thank our anonymous reviewers for their insightful and valuable feedback. This work is supported by NSFC Key Program (No.61632011), NSFC Programs (No.61602079; No.61702080), Ministry of Education (No. 16YJCZH141) and FRF (No. DUT17RW127).

References

Alm Cecilia Ovesdotter, Roth Dan, and Sproat Richard. 2005. Emotions from text: Machine learning for text-based emotion prediction. In *Proceedings of the Joint Conference on HLT–EMNLP*, Vancouver, BC, pages 347-354. http://dx.doi.org/10.3115/1220575.1220648.

Averill James R.. 1990. Inner feelings, works of the flesh, the beast within, diseases of the mind, driving force, and putting on a show: Six metaphors of emotion and their theoretical extensions. *Metaphors in the History of Psychology*, 1990:104-132.

Aziz-Zadeh Lisa and Damasio Antonio. 2008. Embodied semantics for actions: Findings from functional brain imaging. *Journal of Physiology–Paris*, 102(13).http://dx.doi.org/10.1016/j.jphysparis.2008.03.012.

Cameron Lynne. 2003. *Metaphor in Educational Discourse*. Continuum, London, UK.

Citron Francesca M. M. and Goldberg Adele E.. 2014. Metaphorical sentences are more emotionally engaging than their literal counterparts.*Journal of Cognitive Neuroscience*, 26(11): 2585-2595.http://dx.doi.org/10.1162/jocn_a_00654.

De Leersnyder Jozefien, Boiger Michael, and Mesquita Batja. 2015. Cultural differences in emotions. In *Emerging Trends in the Social and Behavioral Sciences: An Interdisciplinary, Searchable, and Linkable Resource*, pages 1-22.http://dx.doi.org/10.1002/9781118900772.etrds0060.

Dong Li, Wei Furu, Tan Chuanqi, Tang Duyu, Zhou Ming, and Xu Ke. 2014. Adaptive recursive neural network for target-dependent twitter sentiment classification. In *Proceedings of the 52nd Annual Meeting of the Association for Computational Linguistics*, pages 49-54.http://dx.doi.org/10.3115/v1/P14-2009.

Ekman Paul. 1992. An argument for basic emotions. *Cognition and Emotion*, 6 (3), 169–200.

Fainsilber Lynn and Ortony Andrew.1987. Metaphorical uses of language in the expression of emotions. *Metaphor and Symbolic Activity*, 2:239-250.http://dx.doi.org/10.1207/s15327868ms0204_2.

Fetterman Adam Kent, Bair Jessica L., Werth Marc, Landkammer Florian, and Robinson Michael D.. 2016. Using individual differences in metaphor usage to understand how metaphor functions. *Journal of Personality and Social Psychology*,110(3):458.

Goatly Musolff Andrew and Project LLE, Lingnan University. 2007. *Washing the Brain Metaphor and Hidden Ideology*. John Benjamins Publishing, Amsterdam. Based on *Metalude — Metaphor at Lingnan University*.(January 1, 2002). http://www.ln.edu.hk/lle/cwd/project01/web/introduction.html.

Jabbi Mbemba, Bastiaansen Jojanneke and Keysers Christian. 2008. A common anterior insula representation of disgust observation, experience and imagination shows divergent functional connectivity pathways.*PLoS ONE*, 3（8） : e2939. http://dx.doi.org/10.1371/journal.pone.0002939.

Kiritchenko Svetlana, Zhu Xiaodan, and Mohammad Saif M.. 2014. Sentiment analysis of short informal texts. *Journal of Artificial Intelligence Research*, 50:723-762.

Kövecses Zoltán. 1995. Anger: Its language, conceptualization, and physiology in the light of cross-cultural evidence. In *Language and the Cognitive Construal of the World*, ed. John R. Taylor and Robert S. Mac Laury. Mouton de Gruyter, Berlin, Germany, pages 181-196.

Kövecses Zoltán. 2000. *Metaphor and emotion: Language, culture, and body in human feeling*. Cambridge University Press, New York, NY.

Kövecses Zoltán. 2010. *Metaphor: A Practical Introduction* (2nd ed.). Oxford University Press, New York, NY.

Kozareva Zornitsa. 2013. Multilingual affect polarity and valence prediction in metaphor-rich texts. In *Proceedings of the 51st Annual Meeting of the Association for Computational Linguistics (Volume 1: Long Papers)*, Sofia, Bulgaria, August. Association for Computational Linguistics, pages 682-691.

Lakoff George and Johnson Mark. 1980. *Metaphors We Live By*. University of Chicago Press, Chicago.http://dx.doi.org/10.7208/chicago/9780226470993.001.0001.

Lindquist Kristen A., Wager Tor D., Kober Hedy, Bliss-Moreau Eliza, and Barrett Lisa Feldman. 2012. The brain basis of emotion: A meta-analytic review.*Behavioral and Brain Sciences*, 35(03):121-143.http://dx.doi.org/10.1017/S0140525X11000446.

Lönneker Birte. 2004. Lexical databases as resources for linguistic creativity: Focus on metaphor. In *Proceedings of the LREC 2004 Workshop on Language Resources for Linguistic Creativity*, Lisbon, Portugal, pages 9-16.

Ma Zuofeng, Jing Ruixue, Wang Ping and Zhang Liutong. 2011. On the "classic" in the emotional impact of ten factors. *China Journal of Basic Medicine in Traditional Chinese Medicine*, 17(11):1194-1195.

Malinowski Josie E. and Horton Caroline L.. 2015. Metaphor and hyper associativity: The imagination mechanisms behind emotion assimilation in sleep and dreaming. *Frontiers in Psychology*6:1132.

Martin, James H.. 2006. A corpus-based analysis of context effects on metaphor comprehension. *Trends in Linguistics Studies and Monographs*,171:214.

Mohammad Saif M.. 2016. Sentiment analysis: Detecting valence, emotions, and other affectual states from text. In *Emotion Measurement*,pages 201-237.http://dx.doi.org/10.1016/B978-0-08-100508-8.00009-6.

Mohammad Saif M., Kiritchenko Svetlana, and Zhu Xiaodan. 2013. NRC-Canada: Building the state-of-the-art in sentiment analysis of tweets.In *Proceedings of the International Workshop on Semantic Evaluation, SemEval '13*, Atlanta, GA, June.

Mohammad Saif M.. Shutova Ekaterina, and Turney Peter D. 2016. Metaphor as a medium for emotion: An empirical study. In *Proceedings of the Fifth Joint Conference on Lexical and Computational Semantics*, pages 23-33. http://dx.doi.org/10.18653/v1/S16-2003.

Nunberg Geoffrey. 1987. Poetic and prosaic metaphors. In *Proceedings of the 1987 workshop on Theoretical issues in natural language processing*, pages 198–201.

Pragglejaz Group. 2007. MIP: A method for identifying metaphorically used words in discourse. *Metaphor and Symbol*, 22:1-39.

Ratnadeep R., Deshmukh D., and Kirange K.. 2013. Emotion classification of news headlines using SVM. *Asian Journal of Computer Science & Information Technology*, 2(5):104-106.

Reyes Antonio and Rosso Paolo. 2012. Making objective decisions from subjective data: Detecting irony in customer reviews. *Decision Support Systems*, 53(4):754-760.http://dx.doi.org/10.1016/j.dss.2012.05.027

Shutova Ekaterina. 2017. Annotation of Linguistic and Conceptual Metaphor. *Handbook of Linguistic Annotation*. Springer, Dordrecht, pages 1073-1100.

Shutova Ekaterina and Teufel Simone. 2010. Metaphor corpus annotated for source−target domain mappings.In *Proceedings of LREC 2010*, Malta, pages 3255-3261.

Shutova Ekaterina, Teufel Simone, and Korhonen Anna. 2013. Statistical metaphor processing. *Computa-*

tional Linguistics, 39(2):301-353.http://dx.doi.org/10.1162/COLI_a_00124.

Siegel Sidney and Castellan N. John. 1988. *Nonparametric Statistics for the Behavioral Sciences*.McGraw-Hill, New York, NY.

Smith Catherine, Rumbell Tim, Barnden John, Hendley Bob, Lee Mark, and Wallington Alan. 2007. Don't worry about metaphor: Affect extraction forconversational agents. In *Proceedings of the 45th Annual Meeting of the ACL on Interactive Poster and Demonstration Sessions*, ACL '07, Association for Computational Linguistics, pages 37-40.http://dx.doi.org/10.3115/1557769.1557782.

Steen Gerard J., Dorst Aletta G., Herrmann J. Berenike, Kaal Anna A., Krennmayr Tina, and Pasma Trijntje. 2010. *A Method for Linguistic Metaphor Identification: From MIP to MIPVU.* John Benjamins, Amsterdam.http://dx.doi.org/10.1075/celcr.14

Strapparava Carlo and Mihalcea Rada. 2007. Semeval-2007 task 14: Affective text. In *Proceedings of SemEval-2007*, Prague, Czech Republic, pages 70-74. http://dx.doi.org/10.3115/1621474.1621487.

Strzalkowski Tomek, Shaikh Samira, Cho Kit, Broadwell George Aaron, Feldman Laurie, Taylor Sarah, Yamrom Boris, Liu Ting, Cases Ignacio, Peshkova Yuliya, and Elliot Kyle. 2014. Computing affectin metaphors.In *Proceedings of the Second Workshop on Metaphor in NLP*, Baltimore, MD, June. Association for Computational Linguistics pages 42-51. http://dx.doi.org/10.3115/v1/W14-2306.

Thibodeau Paul H. and Boroditsky Lera. 2011. Metaphors we think with: The role of metaphor in reasoning. *PLoS ONE*, 6(2): e16782, 02.

Veale Tony. 2012. A context-sensitive, multi-facetedmodel of lexico-conceptual affect. In *The 50th Annual Meeting of the Association for Computational Linguistics, Proceedings of the Conference*, short papers, pages 75-79.

Automatic Article Commenting: the Task and Dataset

Lianhui Qin[1]*, Lemao Liu[2], Victoria Bi[2], Yan Wang[2],
Xiaojiang Liu[2], Zhiting Hu, Hai Zhao[1], Shuming Shi[2]

Department of Computer Science and Engineering, Shanghai Jiao Tong University[1], Tencent AI Lab[2],

{lianhuiqin9,zhitinghu}@gmail.com, zhaohai@cs.sjtu.edu.cn,

{victoriabi,brandenwang,lmliu,kieranliu,shumingshi}@tencent.com

Abstract

Comments of online articles provide extended views and improve user engagement. Automatically making comments thus become a valuable functionality for online forums, intelligent chatbots, etc. This paper proposes the new task of automatic article commenting, and introduces a large-scale Chinese dataset[1] with millions of real comments and a human-annotated subset characterizing the comments' varying quality. Incorporating the human bias of comment quality, we further develop automatic metrics that generalize a broad set of popular reference-based metrics and exhibit greatly improved correlations with human evaluations.

1 Introduction

Comments of online articles and posts provide extended information and rich personal views, which could attract reader attentions and improve interactions between readers and authors (Park et al., 2016). In contrast, posts failing to receive comments can easily go unattended and buried. With the prevalence of online posting, automatic article commenting thus becomes a highly desirable tool for online discussion forums and social media platforms to increase user engagement and foster online communities. Besides, commenting on articles is one of the increasingly demanded skills of intelligent chatbot (Shum et al., 2018) to enable in-depth, content-rich conversations with humans.

Article commenting poses new challenges for machines, as it involves multiple cognitive abilities: understanding the given article, formulating opinions and arguments, and organizing natural language for expression. Compared to summarization (Hovy and Lin, 1998), a comment does not necessarily cover all salient ideas of the article; instead it is often desirable for a comment to carry additional information not explicitly presented in the articles. Article commenting also differs from making product reviews (Tang et al., 2017; Li et al., 2017), as the latter takes structured data (e.g., product attributes) as input; while the input of article commenting is in plain text format, posing a much larger input space to explore.

In this paper, we propose the new task of automatic article commenting, and release a large-scale Chinese corpus with a human-annotated subset for scientific research and evaluation. We further develop a general approach of enhancing popular automatic metrics, such as BLEU (Papineni et al., 2002) and METEOR (Banerjee and Lavie, 2005), to better fit the characteristics of the new task. In recent years, enormous efforts have been made in different contexts that analyze one or more aspects of online comments. For example, Kolhatkar and Taboada (2017) identify constructive news comments; Barker et al. (2016) study human summaries of online comment conversations. The datasets used in these works are typically not directly applicable in the context of article commenting, and are small in scale that is unable to support the unique complexity of the new task.

In contrast, our dataset consists of around 200K news articles and 4.5M human comments along with rich meta data for article categories and user votes of comments. Different from traditional text generation tasks such as machine translation (Brown et al., 1990) that has a relatively small set of gold targets, human comments on an article live in much larger space by involving diverse topics and personal views, and critically, are of vary-

---

*Work done while Lianhui interned at Tencent AI Lab

[1]The dataset is available on `http://ai.tencent.com/upload/PapersUploads/article_commenting.tgz`

Proceedings of the 56th Annual Meeting of the Association for Computational Linguistics (Short Papers), pages 151–156
Melbourne, Australia, July 15 - 20, 2018. ©2018 Association for Computational Linguistics

Title: 苹果公司iPhone 8 发布会定在9月举行 (Apple's iPhone 8 event is happening in Sept.) **Content:** 苹果公司正式向媒体发布邀请函，宣布将于9月12日召开苹果新品发布会，该公司将发布下一代iPhone，随之更新的还有苹果手表，苹果TV，和iOS软件。这次发布会将带来三款新iPhones：带OLED显示屏和3D人脸扫描技术的下一代iPhone8；是iPhone 7、iPhone 7Plus的更新版。 (Apple has sent out invites for its next big event on September 12th, where the company is expected to reveal the next iPhone, along with updates to the Apple Watch, Apple TV, and iOS software. Apple is expected to announce three new iPhones at the event: a next-generation iPhone 8 model with an OLED display and a 3D face-scanning camera; and updated versions of the iPhone 7 and 7 Plus.)	**Score Criteria**	**Example Comments**
	5 Rich in content; attractive; deep insights; new yet relevant viewpoints	还记得那年iphone 4发布后随之而来的关于iPhone 5的传闻吗？如果苹果今年也是这样我会觉得很滑稽。 (Remember a year of iPhone 5 rumors followed by the announcement of the iPhone 4S? I will be highly entertained if Apple does something similar.)
	4 Highly relevant with meaningful ideas	就说：我们相约在那个公园。 (Could have said: Meet us at the Park.)
	3 Less relevant; applied to other articles	很期待这件事！ (Looking forward to this event!)
	2 Fluent/grammatical; irrelevant	我喜欢这只猫，它很可爱！！ (I like the cat. it is so cute !)
	1 Hard to read; Broken language; Only emoji	LOL。。。！！！ (LOL... !!!)

Table 1: A data example of an article (including title and content) paired with selected comments. We also list a brief version of human judgment criteria (more details are in the supplement).

	Train	Dev	Test
#Articles	191,502	5,000	1,610
#Cmts/Articles	27	27	27
#Upvotes/Cmt	5.9	4.9	3.4

Table 2: Data statistics.

ing quality in terms of readability, relevance, argument quality, informativeness, etc (Diakopoulos, 2015; Park et al., 2016). We thus ask human annotators to manually score a subset of over 43K comments based on carefully designed criteria for comment quality. The annotated scores reflect human's cognitive bias of comment quality in the large comment space. Incorporating the scores in a broad set of automatic evaluation metrics, we obtain enhanced metrics that exhibit greatly improved correlations with human evaluations. We demonstrate the use of the introduced dataset and metrics by testing on simple retrieval and seq2seq generation models. We leave more advanced modeling of the article commenting task for future research.

2 Related Work

There is a surge of interest in natural language generation tasks, such as machine translation (Brown et al., 1990; Bahdanau et al., 2014), dialog (Williams and Young, 2007; Shum et al., 2018), text manipulation (Hu et al., 2017), visual description generation (Vinyals et al., 2015; Liang et al., 2017), and so forth. Automatic article commenting poses new challenges due to the large input and output spaces and the open-domain nature of comments.

Many efforts have been devoted to studying specific attributes of reader comments, such as constructiveness, persuasiveness, and sentiment (Wei et al., 2016; Kolhatkar and Taboada, 2017; Barker et al., 2016). We introduce the new task of generating comments, and develop a dataset that is orders-of-magnitude larger than previous related corpus. Instead of restricting to one or few specific aspects, we focus on the general comment quality aligned with human judgment, and provide over 27 gold references for each data instance to enable wide-coverage evaluation. Such setting also allows a large output space, and makes the task challenging and valuable for text generation research. Yao et al. (2017) explore defense approaches of spam or malicious reviews. We believe the proposed task and dataset can be potentially useful for the study.

Galley et al. (2015) propose ΔBLEU that weights multiple references for conversation generation evaluation. The quality weighted metrics developed in our work can be seen as a generalization of ΔBLEU to many popular reference-based metrics (e.g., METEOR, ROUGE, and CIDEr). Our human survey demonstrates the effectiveness of the generalized metrics in the article commenting task.

3 Article Commenting Dataset

The dataset is collected from Tencent News (news.qq.com), one of the most popular Chinese websites of news and opinion articles. Table 1 shows an example data instance in the dataset (For readability we also provide the English translation of the example). Each instance has a title and text content of the article, a set of reader comments, and side information (omitted in the example) including the article category assigned by editors, and the number of user upvotes of each comment.

We crawled a large volume of articles posted in Apr–Aug 2017, tokenized all text with the popular python library Jieba, and filtered out short articles with less than 30 words in content and those with less than 20 comments. The resulting corpus is split into train/dev/test sets. The selection and annotation of the test set are described shortly. Table 2 provides the key data statistics. The dataset has a vocabulary size of 1,858,452. The average lengths of the article titles and content are 15 and 554 Chinese words (not characters), respectively. The average comment length is 17 words.

Notably, the dataset contains an enormous volume of tokens, and is orders-of-magnitude larger than previous public data of article comment analysis (Wei et al., 2016; Barker et al., 2016). Moreover, each article in the dataset has on average over 27 human-written comments. Compared to other popular text generation tasks and datasets (Chen et al., 2015; Wiseman et al., 2017) which typically contain no more than 5 gold references, our dataset enables richer guidance for model training and wider coverage for evaluation, in order to fit the unique large output space of the commenting task. Each article is associated with one of 44 categories, whose distribution is shown in the supplements. The number of upvotes per comment ranges from 3.4 to 5.9 on average. Though the numbers look small, the distribution exhibits a long-tail pattern with popular comments having thousands of upvotes.

Test Set Comment Quality Annotations Real human comments are of varying quality. Selecting high-quality gold reference comments is necessary to encourage high-quality comment generation, and for faithful automatic evaluation, especially with reference-based metrics (sec.4). The upvote count of a comment is shown not to be a satisfactory indicator of its quality (Park et al., 2016; Wei et al., 2016). We thus curate a subset of data instances for human annotation of comment quality, which is also used for enhancing automatic metrics as in the next section.

Specifically, we randomly select a set of 1,610 articles such that each article has at least 30 com-

ments, each of which contains more than 5 words, and has over 200 upvotes for its comments in total. Manual inspection shows such articles and comments tend to be meaningful and receive lots of readings. We then randomly sample 27 comments for each of the articles, and ask 5 professional annotators to rate the comments. The criteria are adapted from previous journalistic criteria study (Diakopoulos, 2015) and are briefed in Table 1, right panel (More details are provided in the supplements). Each comment is randomly assigned to two annotators who are presented with the criteria and several examples for each of the quality levels. The inter-annotator agreement measured by the Cohen's κ score (Cohen, 1968) is 0.59, which indicates moderate agreement and is better or comparable to previous human studies in similar context (Lowe et al., 2017; Liu et al., 2016). The average human score of the test set comments is 3.6 with a standard deviation of 0.6, and 20% of the comments received at least one 5 grade. This shows the overall quality of the test set comments is good, though variations do exist.

4 Quality Weighted Automatic Metrics

Automatic metrics, especially the reference-based metrics such as BLEU (Papineni et al., 2002), METEOR (Banerjee and Lavie, 2005), ROUGE (Lin, 2004), CIDEr (Vedantam et al., 2015), are widely used in text generation evaluations. These metrics have assumed all references are of equal golden qualities. However, in the task of article commenting, the real human comments as references are of varying quality as shown in the above human annotations. It is thus desirable to go beyond the equality assumption, and account for the different quality scores of the references. This section introduces a series of enhanced metrics generalized from respective existing metrics, for leveraging human biases of reference quality and improving metric correlations with human evaluations.

Let **c** be a generated comment to evaluate, $\mathcal{R} = \{\mathbf{r}^j\}$ the set of references, each of which has a quality score s^j by human annotators. We assume properly normalized $s^j \in [0, 1]$. Due to space limitations, here we only present the enhanced METEOR, and defer the formulations of enhancing BLEU, ROUGE, and CIDEr to the supplements. Specifically, METEOR performs word matching through an alignment between the candidate and references. The *weighted METEOR* extends the

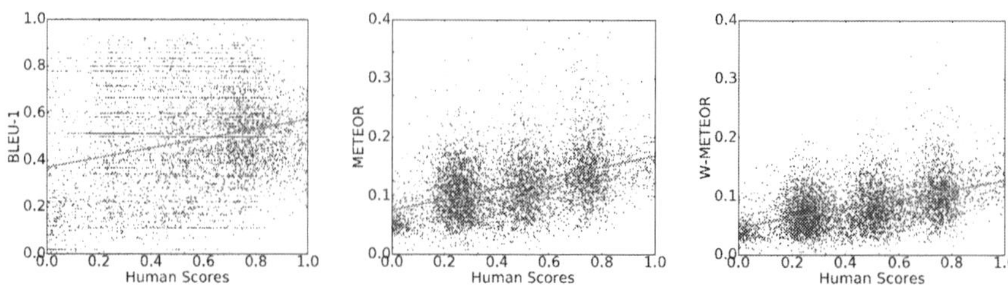

Figure 1: Scatter plots showing the correlation between metrics and human judgments. **Left:** BLEU-1; **Middle:** METEOR; **Right:** W-METEOR. Following (Lowe et al., 2017), we added Gaussian noise drawn from $\mathcal{N}(0, 0.05)$ to the integer human scores to better visualize the density of points.

original metric by weighting references with s^j:

$$\text{W-METEOR}(\mathbf{c}, \mathcal{R}) = (1 - BP) \max_j s^j F_{mean,j}, \quad (1)$$

where $F_{mean,j}$ is a harmonic mean of the precision and recall between $\mathbf{c}$ and $\mathbf{r}^j$, and BP is the penalty (Banerjee and Lavie, 2005). Note that the new metrics fall back to the respective original metrics by setting $s^j = 1$.

5 Experiments

We demonstrate the use of the dataset and metrics with simple retrieval and generation models, and show the enhanced metrics consistently improve correlations with human judgment. Note that this paper does not aim to develop solutions for the article commenting task. We leave the advanced modeling for future work.

Metric	Spearman	Pearson
METEOR	0.5595	0.5109
W-METEOR	**0.5902**	**0.5747**
Rouge_L	0.1948	0.1951
W-Rouge_L	**0.2558**	**0.2572**
CIDEr	0.3426	0.1157
W-CIDEr	**0.3539**	**0.1261**
BLEU-1	0.2145	0.1790
W-BLEU-1	0.2076	0.1604
BLEU-4	0.0983	0.0099
W-BLEU-4	**0.0998**	**0.0124**
Human	0.7803	0.7804

Table 3: Human correlation of metrics. "Human" is the results from randomly dividing human scores into two groups. All p-value < 0.01.

Setup We briefly present key setup, and defer more details to the supplements. Given an article to comment, the retrieval-based models first find a set of similar articles in the training set by TF-IDF,

and return the comments most relevant to the target article with a CNN-based relevance predictor. We use either the article title or full title/content for the article retrieval, and denote the two models with *IR-T* and *IR-TC*, respectively. The generation models are based on simple sequence-to-sequence network (Sutskever et al., 2014). The models read articles using an encoder and generate comments using a decoder with or without attentions (Bahdanau et al., 2014), which are denoted as *Seq2seq* and *Att* if only article titles are read. We also set up an attentional sequence-to-sequence model that reads full article title/content, and denote with *Att-TC*. Again, these approaches are mainly for demonstration purpose and for evaluating the metrics, and are far from solving the difficult commenting task. We discard comments with over 50 words and use a truncated vocabulary of size 30K.

Results We follow previous setting (Papineni et al., 2002; Liu et al., 2016; Lowe et al., 2017) to evaluate the metrics, by conducting human evaluations and calculating the correlation between the scores assigned by humans and the metrics. Specifically, for each article in the test set, we obtained six comments, five of which come from IR-T, IR-TC, Seq2seq, Att, and Att-TC, respectively, and one randomly drawn from real comments that are different from the reference comments. The comments were then graded by human annotators following the same procedure of test set scoring (sec.3). Meanwhile, we measure each comment with the vanilla and weighted automatic metrics based on the reference comments.

Table 3 shows the Spearman and Pearson coefficients between the comment scores assigned by humans and the metrics. The METEOR family correlates best with human judgments, and the enhanced weighted metrics improve over their vanilla versions in most cases (including BLEU-2/3 as in the supplements). E.g., the Pearson of METEOR is substantially improved from 0.51 to 0.57, and the Spearman of ROUGE_L from 0.19 to 0.26. Figure 1 visualizes the human correlation of BLEU-1, METEOR, and W-METEOR, showing that the BLEU-1 scores vary a lot given any fixed human score, appearing to be random noise, while the METEOR family exhibit strong consistency with human scores. Compared to W-METEOR, METEOR deviates from the regression line more frequently, esp. by assigning unexpectedly high scores to comments with low human grades.

Notably, the best automatic metric, W-METEOR, achieves 0.59 Spearman and 0.57 Pearson, which is higher or comparable to automatic metrics in other generation tasks (Lowe et al., 2017; Liu et al., 2016; Sharma et al., 2017; Agarwal and Lavie, 2008), indicating a good supplement to human judgment for efficient evaluation and comparison. We use the metrics to evaluate the above models in the supplements.

6 Conclusions and Future Work

We have introduced the new task and dataset for automatic article commenting, as well as developed quality-weighted automatic metrics that leverage valuable human bias on comment quality. The dataset and the study of metrics establish a testbed for the article commenting task.

We are excited to study solutions for the task in the future, by building advanced deep generative models (Goodfellow et al., 2016; Hu et al., 2018) that incorporate effective reading comprehension modules (Rajpurkar et al., 2016; Richardson et al., 2013) and rich external knowledge (Angeli et al., 2015; Hu et al., 2016).

The large dataset is also potentially useful for a variety of other tasks, such as comment ranking (Hsu et al., 2009), upvotes prediction (Rizos et al., 2016), and article headline generation (Banko et al., 2000). We encourage the use of the dataset in these context.

Acknowledgement. We would like to thank anonymous reviewers for their helpful suggestions and particularly the annotators for their contributions on the dataset. Hai Zhao was partially supported by National Key Research and Development Program of China (No. 2017YFB0304100), National Natural Science Foundation of China (No. 61672343 and No. 61733011), Key Project of National Society Science Foundation of China (No. 15-ZDA041), The Art and Science Interdisciplinary Funds of Shanghai Jiao Tong University (No. 14JCRZ04).

References

Abhaya Agarwal and Alon Lavie. 2008. METEOR, m-BLEU and m-TER: Evaluation metrics for high-correlation with human rankings of machine translation output. In *Proceedings of the Third Workshop on Statistical Machine Translation*, pages 115–118. Association for Computational Linguistics.

Gabor Angeli, Melvin Jose Johnson Premkumar, and Christopher D Manning. 2015. Leveraging linguistic structure for open domain information extraction. In *ACL*, volume 1, pages 344–354.

Dzmitry Bahdanau, Kyunghyun Cho, and Yoshua Bengio. 2014. Neural machine translation by jointly learning to align and translate. *arXiv preprint arXiv:1409.0473*.

Satanjeev Banerjee and Alon Lavie. 2005. METEOR: An automatic metric for mt evaluation with improved correlation with human judgments. In *ACL Workshop*, volume 29, pages 65–72.

Michele Banko, Vibhu O Mittal, and Michael J Witbrock. 2000. Headline generation based on statistical translation. In *ACL*, pages 318–325. Association for Computational Linguistics.

Emma Barker, Monica Lestari Paramita, Ahmet Aker, Emina Kurtic, Mark Hepple, and Robert Gaizauskas. 2016. The SENSEI annotated corpus: Human summaries of reader comment conversations in on-line news. In *Proceedings of the 17th annual meeting of the special interest group on discourse and dialogue*, pages 42–52.

Peter F Brown, John Cocke, Stephen A Della Pietra, Vincent J Della Pietra, Fredrick Jelinek, John D Lafferty, Robert L Mercer, and Paul S Roossin. 1990. A statistical approach to machine translation. *Computational linguistics*, 16(2):79–85.

Xinlei Chen, Hao Fang, Tsung-Yi Lin, Ramakrishna Vedantam, Saurabh Gupta, Piotr Dollár, and C Lawrence Zitnick. 2015. Microsoft COCO captions: Data collection and evaluation server. *arXiv preprint arXiv:1504.00325*.

Jacob Cohen. 1968. Weighted kappa: Nominal scale agreement provision for scaled disagreement or partial credit. *Psychological Bulletin*, 70(4):213.

Nicholas Diakopoulos. 2015. Picking the NYT picks: Editorial criteria and automation in the curation of online news comments. *ISOJ Journal*, 6(1):147–166.

Michel Galley, Chris Brockett, Alessandro Sordoni, Yangfeng Ji, Michael Auli, Chris Quirk, Margaret Mitchell, Jianfeng Gao, and Bill Dolan. 2015. deltaBLEU: A discriminative metric for generation tasks with intrinsically diverse targets. In *ACL*.

Ian Goodfellow, Yoshua Bengio, and Aaron Courville. 2016. *Deep Learning*. MIT Press. http://www.deeplearningbook.org.

Eduard Hovy and Chin-Yew Lin. 1998. Automated text summarization and the SUMMARIST system. In *Proceedings of a workshop on held at Baltimore, Maryland: October 13-15, 1998*, pages 197–214. Association for Computational Linguistics.

Chiao-Fang Hsu, Elham Khabiri, and James Caverlee. 2009. Ranking comments on the social web. In *Computational Science and Engineering, 2009. CSE'09. International Conference on*, volume 4, pages 90–97. IEEE.

Zhiting Hu, Xuezhe Ma, Zhengzhong Liu, Eduard Hovy, and Eric Xing. 2016. Harnessing deep neural networks with logic rules. In *ACL*.

Zhiting Hu, Zichao Yang, Xiaodan Liang, Ruslan Salakhutdinov, and Eric P Xing. 2017. Toward controlled generation of text. In *ICML*.

Zhiting Hu, Zichao Yang, Ruslan Salakhutdinov, and Eric P Xing. 2018. On unifying deep generative models. In *ICLR*.

Varada Kolhatkar and Maite Taboada. 2017. Constructive language in news comments. In *Proceedings of the First Workshop on Abusive Language Online*, pages 11–17.

Piji Li, Zihao Wang, Zhaochun Ren, Lidong Bing, and Wai Lam. 2017. Neural rating regression with abstractive tips generation for recommendation. In *SIGIR*.

Xiaodan Liang, Zhiting Hu, Hao Zhang, Chuang Gan, and Eric P Xing. 2017. Recurrent topic-transition GAN for visual paragraph generation. In *ICCV*.

Chin-Yew Lin. 2004. Rouge: A package for automatic evaluation of summaries. In *ACL workshop*, volume 8.

Chia-Wei Liu, Ryan Lowe, Iulian V Serban, Michael Noseworthy, Laurent Charlin, and Joelle Pineau. 2016. How NOT to evaluate your dialogue system: An empirical study of unsupervised evaluation metrics for dialogue response generation. *arXiv preprint arXiv:1603.08023*.

Ryan Lowe, Michael Noseworthy, Iulian V Serban, Nicolas Angelard-Gontier, Yoshua Bengio, and Joelle Pineau. 2017. Towards an automatic Turing test: Learning to evaluate dialogue responses. In *ACL*.

Kishore Papineni, Salim Roukos, Todd Ward, and Wei-Jing Zhu. 2002. BLEU: a method for automatic evaluation of machine translation. In *ACL*, pages 311–318.

Deokgun Park, Simranjit Sachar, Nicholas Diakopoulos, and Niklas Elmqvist. 2016. Supporting comment moderators in identifying high quality online news comments. In *Proceedings of the 2016 CHI Conference on Human Factors in Computing Systems*, CHI '16, pages 1114–1125, New York, NY, USA. ACM.

Pranav Rajpurkar, Jian Zhang, Konstantin Lopyrev, and Percy Liang. 2016. SQUAD: 100,000+ questions for machine comprehension of text. *arXiv preprint arXiv:1606.05250*.

Matthew Richardson, Christopher JC Burges, and Erin Renshaw. 2013. MCTest: A challenge dataset for the open-domain machine comprehension of text. In *Proceedings of the 2013 Conference on Empirical Methods in Natural Language Processing*, pages 193–203.

Georgios Rizos, Symeon Papadopoulos, and Yiannis Kompatsiaris. 2016. Predicting news popularity by mining online discussions. In *Proceedings of the 25th International Conference Companion on World Wide Web*, pages 737–742. International World Wide Web Conferences Steering Committee.

Shikhar Sharma, Layla El Asri, Hannes Schulz, and Jeremie Zumer. 2017. Relevance of unsupervised metrics in task-oriented dialogue for evaluating natural language generation. *CoRR*, abs/1706.09799.

Heung-Yeung Shum, Xiaodong He, and Di Li. 2018. From Eliza to XiaoIce: Challenges and opportunities with social chatbots. *arXiv preprint arXiv:1801.01957*.

Ilya Sutskever, Oriol Vinyals, and Quoc V Le. 2014. Sequence to sequence learning with neural networks. In *NIPS*, pages 3104–3112.

Jian Tang, Yifan Yang, Sam Carton, Ming Zhang, and Qiaozhu Mei. 2017. Context-aware natural language generation with recurrent neural networks. In *AAAI*, San Francisco, CA, USA.

Ramakrishna Vedantam, C Lawrence Zitnick, and Devi Parikh. 2015. Cider: Consensus-based image description evaluation. In *CVPR*, pages 4566–4575.

Oriol Vinyals, Alexander Toshev, Samy Bengio, and Dumitru Erhan. 2015. Show and tell: A neural image caption generator. In *CVPR*, pages 3156–3164. IEEE.

Zhongyu Wei, Yang Liu, and Yi Li. 2016. Is this post persuasive? Ranking argumentative comments in online forum. In *Proceedings of the 54th Annual Meeting of the Association for Computational Linguistics (Volume 2: Short Papers)*, volume 2, pages 195–200.

Jason D Williams and Steve Young. 2007. Partially observable Markov decision processes for spoken dialog systems. *Computer Speech & Language*, 21(2):393–422.

Sam Wiseman, Stuart M Shieber, and Alexander M Rush. 2017. Challenges in data-to-document generation. In *EMNLP*.

Yuanshun Yao, Bimal Viswanath, Jenna Cryan, Haitao Zheng, and Ben Y Zhao. 2017. Automated crowdturfing attacks and defenses in online review systems. *arXiv preprint arXiv:1708.08151*.

Improved Evaluation Framework for Complex Plagiarism Detection

Anton Belyy[1] Marina Dubova[2] Dmitry Nekrasov[1]

[1]International laboratory "Computer Technologies", ITMO University, Russia
[2]Saint Petersburg State University, Russia
{anton.belyy, marina.dubova.97, dpokrasko}@gmail.com

Abstract

Plagiarism is a major issue in science and education. It appears in various forms, starting from simple copying and ending with intelligent paraphrasing and summarization. Complex plagiarism, such as plagiarism of ideas, is hard to detect, and therefore it is especially important to track improvement of methods correctly and not to overfit to the structure of particular datasets. In this paper, we study the performance of plagdet, the main measure for Plagiarism Detection Systems evaluation, on manually paraphrased plagiarism datasets (such as PAN Summary). We reveal its fallibility under certain conditions and propose an evaluation framework with normalization of inner terms, which is resilient to the dataset imbalance. We conclude with the experimental justification of the proposed measure. The implementation of the new framework is made publicly available as a Github repository.

1 Introduction

Plagiarism is a problem of primary concern among publishers, scientists, teachers (Maurer et al., 2006). It is not only about text copying with minor revisions but also borrowing of ideas. Plagiarism appears in substantially paraphrased forms and presents conscious and unconscious appropriation of others' thoughts (Gingerich and Sullivan, 2013). This kind of borrowing has very serious consequences and can not be detected with common Plagiarism Detection Systems (PDS). That is why detection of complex plagiarism cases comes to the fore and becomes a central challenge in the field.

2 Plagiarism Detection

Most of the contributions to the plagiarism text alignment were made during the PAN annual track for plagiarism detection held from 2009 to 2015. The latest winning approach (Sanchez-Perez et al., 2014) achieved good performance on all the plagiarism types except the Summary part. Moreover, this type of plagiarism turned out to be the hardest for all the competitors.

In a brief review, Kraus emphasized (2016) that the main weakness of modern PDS is imprecision in manually paraphrased plagiarism and, as a consequence, the weak ability to deal with real-world problems. Thus, the detection of manually paraphrased plagiarism cases is a focus of recently proposed methods for plagiarism text alignment. In the most successful contributions, scientists applied genetic algorithms (Sanchez-Perez et al., 2018; Vani and Gupta, 2017), topic modeling methods (Le et al., 2016), and word embedding models (Brlek et al., 2016) to manually paraphrased plagiarism text alignment. In all of these works, authors used PAN Summary datasets to develop and evaluate their methods.

3 Task, Dataset, and Evaluation Metrics

3.1 Text Alignment

In this work we deal with an extrinsic text alignment problem. Thus, we are given pairs of suspicious documents and source candidates and try to detect all contiguous passages of borrowed information. For a review of plagiarism detection tasks, see Alzahrani et al. 2012.

3.2 Datasets

PAN corpora of datasets for plagiarism text alignment is the main resource for PDS evaluation. This collection consists of slightly or substantially different datasets used at the PAN competitions

Proceedings of the 56th Annual Meeting of the Association for Computational Linguistics (Short Papers), pages 157–162
Melbourne, Australia, July 15 - 20, 2018. ©2018 Association for Computational Linguistics

since 2009 to 2015. We used the most recent 2013 (Potthast et al., 2013) and 2014 (Potthast et al., 2014) English datasets to develop and evaluate our models and metrics. They consist of copy&paste, random, translation, and summary plagiarism types. We consider only the last part, as it exhibits the problems of plagdet framework to the greatest extent.

3.3 Evaluation Metrics

Standard evaluation framework for text alignment task is **plagdet** (Potthast et al., 2010), which consists of macro- and micro-averaged precision, recall, granularity and the overall plagdet score. In this work, we consider only the macro-averaged metrics, where **recall** can be defined as follows:

$$rec_{macro}(S, R) = \frac{1}{|S|} \sum_{s \in S} rec_{\substack{single \\ macro}}(s, R_s), \quad (1)$$

and **precision** can be defined through recall as follows:

$$prec_{macro}(S, R) = rec_{macro}(R, S), \quad (2)$$

where S and R are true plagiarism cases and system's detections, respectively.

Single case recall $rec_{\substack{single \\ macro}}(s, R_s)$ is defined as follows:

$$\frac{|s_{plg} \cap (R_s)_{plg}| + |s_{src} \cap (R_s)_{src}|}{|s_{plg}| + |s_{src}|},$$

where R_s is the union of all detections of a given case s.

4 Problem Statement

In this section, we explore problems representative to several manual plagiarism datasets (mainly, Summary part of PAN corpora), and show that the plagdet framework can fail to correctly estimate PDS quality on these datasets.

4.1 Dataset Imbalance

The PAN Summary datasets turn out to be highly imbalanced.

- Source part of each plagiarism case takes up the whole source document:

$$\forall s \in S \, \exists d_{src} \in D_{src} : s_{src} = d_{src}. \quad (3)$$

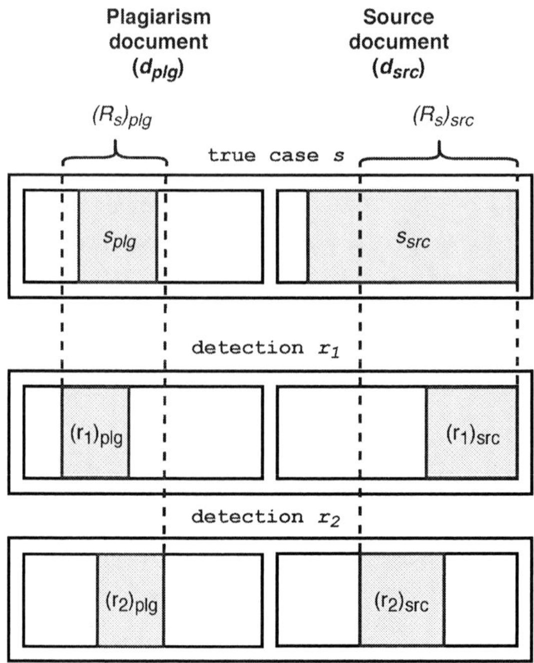

Figure 1: Single case recall computation for text alignment task. Note the imbalance in this case: plagiarism part s_{plg} is much shorter than source part s_{src}.

- For any given case, its plagiarism part is much shorter than its source part[1]:

$$\forall s \in S : |s_{plg}| << |s_{src}|. \quad (4)$$

As these datasets are publicly available, anyone can figure out these details and, therefore, construct an algorithm where statements 3 and 4 are true for detections R as well.

Let us now consider a true case s, its detections R_s and its source document d_{src}. Then single case recall for PAN Summary document will be equal to:

$$\frac{|s_{plg} \cap (R_s)_{plg}| + |d_{src}|}{|s_{plg}| + |d_{src}|} \quad (5)$$

(here we used that and $s_{src} = (R_s)_{src} = d_{src}$).

Since plagiarism part s_{plg} of the case s is much shorter than source document d_{src}, the term $|d_{src}|$ dominates numerator and denominator in eq. 5, which results in **inadequately high document-level precision and recall** on PAN Summary datasets.

---

[1]For exact lengths, see table 3

Other datasets for manual plagiarism detection display the similar properties, however, not to the PAN Summary extent. Examples include: Palkovskii15, Mashhadirajab et al. 2016, and Sochenkov et al. 2017.

Discussion

The important question is whether such dataset imbalance reflects the real-world plagiarizers' behavior.

There is an evidence that performing length unrestricted plagiarism task people tend to make texts shorter, however, not to the PAN Summary extent (Barrón-Cedeño et al., 2013). Moreover, we can find some supporting theoretical reasons. Firstly, summarization and paraphrasing are the only techniques students are taught to use for the transformation of texts. Hence, they can use summarization to plagiarize intellectually. Secondly, in the cases of inadvertent plagiarism and the plagiarism of ideas details of source texts are usually omitted or forgotten. This should also lead to smaller plagiarized texts. Though we can find some reasons, such huge imbalance does not seem to be supported enough and may be considered as a bias.

4.2 Degenerate Intersection

Lemma 4.1. *For any sets $e_1 \subseteq d$ and $e_2 \subseteq d$, their intersection length $|e_1 \cap e_2|$ is bounded by:*

$$a(e_1, e_2, d) \leqslant |e_1 \cap e_2| \leqslant b(e_1, e_2),$$

where:

$$a(e_1, e_2, d) = max(0, |e_1| + |e_2| - |d|),$$
$$b(e_1, e_2) = min(|e_1|, |e_2|).$$

Let us take a fresh look at a source part of $rec_{single \atop macro}$. We assume that $\frac{|s_{src} \cap (R_s)_{src}|}{|s_{src}|} \in [0; 1]$, and this is actually the case if:

$$0 \leqslant |s_{src} \cap (R_s)_{src}| \leqslant |s_{src}|.$$

But, according to lemma 4.1, we see that:

$$0 \leqslant a_{src} \leqslant |s_{src} \cap (R_s)_{src}| \leqslant b_{src} \leqslant |s_{src}|,$$

where:

$$a_{src} = a(s_{src}, (R_s)_{src}, d_{src}),$$
$$b_{src} = b(s_{src}, (R_s)_{src}).$$

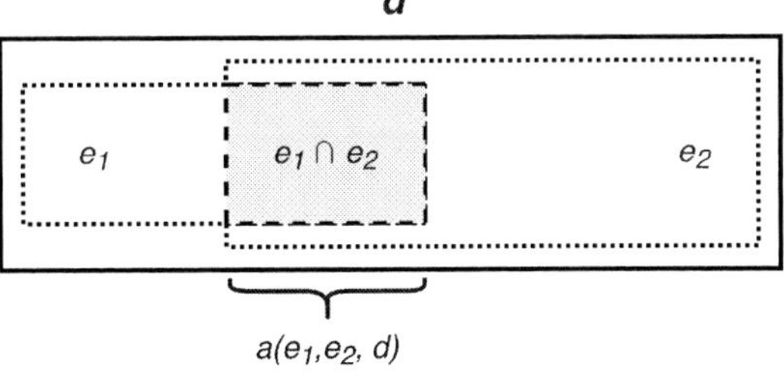

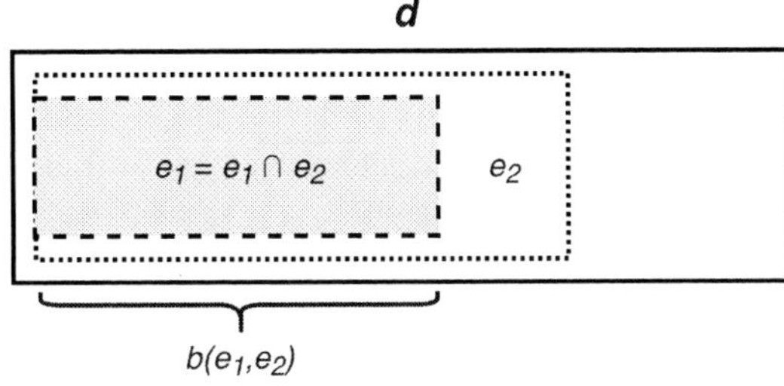

Figure 2: Degenerate intersection lemma. Intuitively, lower bound (a) is achieved when e_1 and e_2 are "farthest" away from each other in d, and upper bound (b) is achieved when $e_1 \subseteq e_2$ (or $e_2 \subseteq e_1$).

This results in a **smaller possible value range** of intersection length and, therefore, range **of precision and recall** values. Because of (3), on PAN Summary this leads to the extreme case of $a_{src} = b_{src} = |d_{src}|$, which causes precision and recall to take constant values on the source part of the dataset.

5 Proposed Metrics

5.1 Normalized Single Case Recall

To address issues of dataset imbalance (section 4.1) and degenerate intersection (section 4.2), we propose the following **normalized** version of **single case recall** $nrec_{single \atop macro}(s, R_s)$ for macro-averaged case:

$$\frac{w_{plg}(|s_{plg} \cap (R_s)_{plg}|) + w_{src}(|s_{src} \cap (R_s)_{src}|)}{w_{plg}(|s_{plg}|) + w_{src}(|s_{src}|)},$$

where:

$$w_i(x) = \frac{(x - a_i)(b_i - a_i)}{|d_i|},$$
$$a_i = a(s_i, (R_s)_i, d_i),$$
$$b_i = b(s_i, (R_s)_i),$$
$$i \in \{plg, src\}.$$

5.2 Normalized recall, precision and plagdet

The result of (1) where every $rec_{single}^{macro}(s, R_s)$ term is replaced for $nrec_{single}^{macro}(s, R_s)$ is defined as **normalized recall** $nrec_{macro}(S, R)$. **Normalized precision** $nprec_{macro}(S, R)$ can be obtained from normalized recall using eq. 2.

Normalized macro-averaged plagdet, or **normplagdet**, is defined as follows:

$$normplagdet(S, R) = \frac{F_\alpha(S, R)}{\log_2(1 + gran(S, R))},$$

where F_α is the weighted harmonic mean of $nprec_{macro}(S, R)$ and $nrec_{macro}(S, R)$, i.e. the F_α-measure, and $gran(S, R)$ is defined as in Potthast et al. 2010.

6 Adversarial models

To justify the proposed evaluation metrics, we construct two models, **M1** and **M2**, which achieve inadequately high macro-averaged precision and recall.

6.1 Preprocessing

We represent each plagiarism document d_{plg} as a sequence of sentences, where each sentence $sent_{d_{plg},i} \in d_{plg}$ is a set of tokens. Each source document d_{src} will be represented as a set of its tokens.

For each sentence $sent_{d_{plg},i}$ we also define a measure of similarity $sim_{d_{plg},d_{src},i}$ with respect to the source document as:

$$sim_{d_{plg},d_{src},i} = \frac{|sent_{d_{plg},i} \cap d_{src}|}{|sent_{d_{plg},i}|}.$$

6.2 Models

Our models are rule-based classifiers, which proceed in three steps for each pair of documents d_{plg}, d_{src}:

1. Form a candidate set according to similarity score: $cand = \left\{ i \mid sim_{d_{plg},d_{src},i} > \frac{3}{4} \right\}$.

2. Find the candidate with highest similarity score (if it exists): $best = \arg\max_i \left\{ sim_{d_{plg},d_{src},i} \mid i \in cand \right\}$.

3. **(M1)** Output sentence $best$ as a detection (if it exists).
   (M2) Output sentences $\{i \mid i \neq best\}$ as a detection (or all sentences if $best$ does not exist).

7 Results and Discussion

We evaluated our adversarial models as well as several state-of-the-art algorithms, whose source code was available to us, using plagdet and normplagdet scores on all PAN Summary datasets available to date.

In plagdet score comparison (Table 1) we included additional state-of-the-art algorithms' results (marked by $*$), borrowed from respective papers. Proposed models M1 and M2 outperform all algorithms by macro-averaged plagdet and recall measures on almost every dataset. Despite their simplicity, they show rather good results.

On the contrary, while measuring normplagdet score (Table 2), M1 and M2 exhibit poor results, while tested state-of-the-art systems evenly achieve better recall and normplagdet scores. These experimental results back up our claim that normplagdet is more resilient to dataset imbalance and degenerate intersection attacks and show that tested state-of-the-art algorithms do not exploit these properties of PAN Summary datasets.

The code for calculating normplagdet metrics, both macro- and micro-averaged, is made available as a Github repository[2]. We preserved the command line interface of plagdet framework to allow easy adaptation for existing systems.

8 Conclusion

Our paper shows that the standard evaluation framework with plagdet measure can be misused to achieve high scores on datasets for manual plagiarism detection. We constructed two primitive models that achieve state-of-the-art results for detecting plagiarism of ideas by exploiting flaws of standard plagdet. Finally, we proposed a new framework, normplagdet, that normalizes single case scores to prevent misuse of datasets such as PAN Summary, and proved its correctness experimentally. The proposed evaluation framework seems beneficial not only for plagiarism detection but for any other text alignment task with imbalance or degenerate intersection dataset properties.

Acknowledgments

This work was financially supported by Government of Russian Federation (Grant 08-08).

---

[2] https://github.com/AVBelyy/normplagdet

Table 1: Results of Summary Plagiarism Detection using Plagdet

Dataset	Model	Year	Precision	Recall	Plagdet
PAN 2013 Train	Sanchez-Perez et al.	2014	**0.9942**	0.4235	0.5761
	Brlek et al.	2016	0.9154	0.6033	0.7046
	Le et al. *	2016	0.8015	0.7722	0.7866
	Sanchez-Perez et al.	2018	0.9662	0.7407	0.8386
	Adversarial M1	2018	0.9676	0.7892	**0.8693**
	Adversarial M2	2018	0.5247	**0.8704**	0.4816
PAN 2013 Test-1	Sanchez-Perez et al.	2014	**1.0000**	0.5317	0.6703
	Brlek et al.	2016	0.9832	0.7003	0.8180
	Vani and Gupta *	2017	0.9998	0.7622	0.8149
	Sanchez-Perez et al.	2018	0.9742	0.8093	**0.8841**
	Adversarial M1	2018	0.9130	0.7641	0.8320
	Adversarial M2	2018	0.4678	**0.8925**	0.4739
PAN 2013 Test-2	Sanchez-Perez et al.	2014	**0.9991**	0.4158	0.5638
	Brlek et al.	2016	0.9055	0.6144	0.7072
	Le et al. *	2016	0.8344	0.7701	0.8010
	Vani and Gupta *	2017	0.9987	0.7212	0.8081
	Sanchez-Perez et al.	2018	0.9417	0.7226	0.8125
	Adversarial M1	2018	0.9594	0.8109	**0.8789**
	Adversarial M2	2018	0.5184	**0.8938**	0.4848

Table 2: Results of Summary Plagiarism Detection using NormPlagdet

Dataset	Model	Year	Precision	Recall	Plagdet
PAN 2013 Train	Sanchez-Perez et al.	2014	**0.9917**	0.6408	0.7551
	Brlek et al.	2016	0.8807	0.7889	0.8064
	Sanchez-Perez et al.	2018	0.8929	**0.9238**	**0.9081**
	Adversarial M1	2018	0.9673	0.1617	0.2770
	Adversarial M2	2018	0.1769	0.2984	0.1634
PAN 2013 Test-1	Sanchez-Perez et al.	2014	**0.9997**	0.7020	0.7965
	Brlek et al.	2016	0.9384	0.8254	0.8783
	Sanchez-Perez et al.	2018	0.9180	**0.9463**	**0.9319**
	Adversarial M1	2018	0.9130	0.1525	0.2614
	Adversarial M2	2018	0.1488	0.4237	0.1700
PAN 2013 Test-2	Sanchez-Perez et al.	2014	**0.9977**	0.6377	0.7470
	Brlek et al.	2016	0.8701	0.8104	0.8107
	Sanchez-Perez et al.	2018	0.8771	**0.9067**	**0.8859**
	Adversarial M1	2018	0.9585	0.1687	0.2869
	Adversarial M2	2018	0.1552	0.3299	0.1559

Table 3: Average Length of Plagiarism and Source Cases in Summary Datasets

Dataset	Plagiarism (plg)	Source (src)
PAN 2013 Train	626 ± 45	5109 ± 2431
PAN 2013 Test-1	639 ± 40	3874 ± 1427
PAN 2013 Test-2	627 ± 42	5318 ± 3310

References

Salha M Alzahrani, Naomie Salim, and Ajith Abraham. 2012. Understanding plagiarism linguistic patterns, textual features, and detection methods. *IEEE Transactions on Systems, Man, and Cybernetics, Part C (Applications and Reviews)*, 42(2):133–149.

Alberto Barrón-Cedeño, Marta Vila, M Antònia Martí, and Paolo Rosso. 2013. Plagiarism meets paraphrasing: Insights for the next generation in automatic plagiarism detection. *Computational Linguistics*, 39(4):917–947.

Arijana Brlek, Petra Franjic, and Nino Uzelac. 2016. Plagiarism detection using word2vec model. *Text Analysis and Retrieval 2016 Course Project Reports*, pages 4–7.

Amanda C Gingerich and Meaghan C Sullivan. 2013. Claiming hidden memories as one's own: a review of inadvertent plagiarism. *Journal of Cognitive Psychology*, 25(8):903–916.

Christina Kraus. 2016. Plagiarism detection-state-of-the-art systems (2016) and evaluation methods. *arXiv preprint arXiv:1603.03014*.

Huong T Le, Lam N Pham, Duy D Nguyen, Son V Nguyen, and An N Nguyen. 2016. Semantic text alignment based on topic modeling. In *Computing & Communication Technologies, Research, Innovation, and Vision for the Future (RIVF), 2016 IEEE RIVF International Conference on*, pages 67–72. IEEE.

Fatemeh Mashhadirajab, Mehrnoush Shamsfard, Razieh Adelkhah, Fatemeh Shafiee, and Chakaveh Saedi. 2016. A text alignment corpus for persian plagiarism detection. In *FIRE (Working Notes)*, pages 184–189.

Hermann A Maurer, Frank Kappe, and Bilal Zaka. 2006. Plagiarism-a survey. *J. UCS*, 12(8):1050–1084.

Martin Potthast, Matthias Hagen, Anna Beyer, Matthias Busse, Martin Tippmann, Paolo Rosso, and Benno Stein. 2014. Overview of the 6th international competition on plagiarism detection. In *CEUR Workshop Proceedings*, volume 1180, pages 845–876. CEUR Workshop Proceedings.

Martin Potthast, Matthias Hagen, Tim Gollub, Martin Tippmann, Johannes Kiesel, Paolo Rosso, Efstathios Stamatatos, and Benno Stein. 2013. Overview of the 5th international competition on plagiarism detection. In *CLEF Conference on Multilingual and Multimodal Information Access Evaluation*, pages 301–331. CELCT.

Martin Potthast, Benno Stein, Alberto Barrón-Cedeño, and Paolo Rosso. 2010. An evaluation framework for plagiarism detection. In *Proceedings of the 23rd international conference on computational linguistics: Posters*, pages 997–1005. Association for Computational Linguistics.

Miguel A Sanchez-Perez, Alexander Gelbukh, Grigori Sidorov, and Helena Gómez-Adorno. 2018. Plagiarism detection with genetic-based parameter tuning. *International Journal of Pattern Recognition and Artificial Intelligence*, 32(01):1860006.

Miguel A Sanchez-Perez, Grigori Sidorov, and Alexander F Gelbukh. 2014. A winning approach to text alignment for text reuse detection at pan 2014. In *CLEF (Working Notes)*, pages 1004–1011.

Ilya Sochenkov, Denis Zubarev, and Ivan Smirnov. 2017. The paraplag: russian dataset for paraphrased plagiarism detection. In *Proceedings of the Annual International Conference "Dialogue" 2017 (1)*, pages 284–297.

K Vani and Deepa Gupta. 2017. Detection of idea plagiarism using syntax–semantic concept extractions with genetic algorithm. *Expert Systems with Applications*, 73:11–26.

Global Encoding for Abstractive Summarization

Junyang Lin, Xu Sun, Shuming Ma, Qi Su

MOE Key Lab of Computational Linguistics, School of EECS, Peking University

School of Foreign Languages, Peking University

{linjunyang, xusun, shumingma, sukia}@pku.edu.cn

Abstract

In neural abstractive summarization, the conventional sequence-to-sequence (seq2seq) model often suffers from repetition and semantic irrelevance. To tackle the problem, we propose a global encoding framework, which controls the information flow from the encoder to the decoder based on the global information of the source context. It consists of a convolutional gated unit to perform global encoding to improve the representations of the source-side information. Evaluations on the LCSTS and the English Gigaword both demonstrate that our model outperforms the baseline models, and the analysis shows that our model is capable of generating summary of higher quality and reducing repetition[1].

1 Introduction

Abstractive summarization can be regarded as a sequence mapping task that the source text should be mapped to the target summary. Therefore, sequence-to-sequence learning can be applied to neural abstractive summarization (Kalchbrenner and Blunsom, 2013; Sutskever et al., 2014; Cho et al., 2014), whose model consists of an encoder and a decoder. Attention mechanism has been broadly used in seq2seq models where the decoder extracts information from the encoder based on the attention scores on the source-side information (Bahdanau et al., 2014; Luong et al., 2015). Many attention-based seq2seq models have been proposed for abstractive summarization (Rush et al., 2015; Chopra et al., 2016; Nallapati et al., 2016), which outperformed the conventional statistical methods.

---

[1]The code is available at https://www.github.com/lancopku/Global-Encoding

Text:	the mainstream fatah movement on monday officially chose mahmoud abbas, chairman of the palestine liberation organization (plo), as its candidate to run for the presidential election due on jan. #, ####, the official wafa news agency reported.
seq2seq:	fatah officially officially elects abbas as candidate for candidate .
Gold:	fatah officially elects abbas as candidate for presidential election

Table 1: An example of the summary of the conventional attention-based seq2seq model on the Gigaword dataset. The text highlighted indicates repetition, "#" refers to masked number.

However, recent studies show that there are salient problems in the attention mechanism. Zhou et al. (2017) pointed out that there is no obvious alignment relationship between the source text and the target summary, and the encoder outputs contain noise for the attention. For example, in the summary generated by the seq2seq in Table 1, "officially" is followed by the same word, as the attention mechanism still attends to the word with high attention score. Attention-based seq2seq model for abstractive summarization can suffer from repetition and semantic irrelevance, causing grammatical errors and insufficient reflection of the main idea of the source text.

To tackle this problem, we propose a model of global encoding for abstractive summarization. We set a convolutional gated unit to perform global encoding on the source context. The gate based on convolutional neural network (CNN) filters each encoder output based on the global context due to the parameter sharing, so that the representations at each time step are refined with consideration of the global context. We conduct experiments on LCSTS and Gigaword, two benchmark datasets for sentence summarization, which shows that our model outperforms the state-of-the-art methods with ROUGE-2 F1 score 26.8 and 17.8 respectively. Moreover, the analysis shows

Proceedings of the 56th Annual Meeting of the Association for Computational Linguistics (Short Papers), pages 163–169
Melbourne, Australia, July 15 - 20, 2018. ©2018 Association for Computational Linguistics

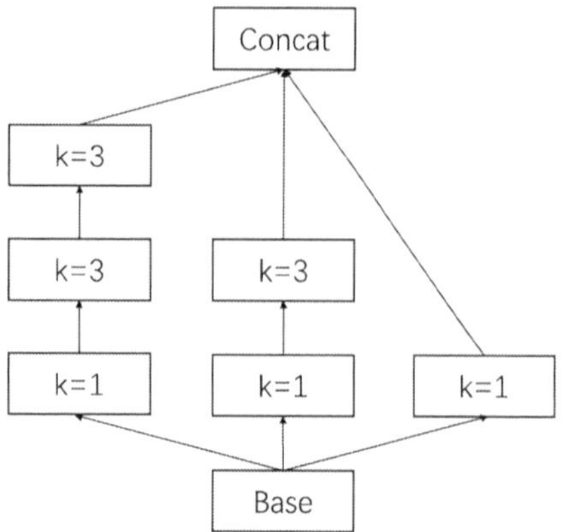

Figure 1: **Structure of our proposed Convolutional Gated Unit.** We implement 1-dimensional convolution with a structure similar to the Inception (Szegedy et al., 2015) over the outputs of the RNN encoder, where k refers to the kernel size.

that our model is capable of reducing repetition compared with the seq2seq model.

2 Global Encoding

Our model is based on the seq2seq model with attention. For the encoder, we set a convolutional gated unit for global encoding. Based on the outputs from the RNN encoder, the global encoding refines the representation of the source context with a CNN to improve the connection of the word representation with the global context. In the following, the techniques are introduced in detail .

2.1 Attention-based seq2seq

The RNN encoder receives the word embedding of each word from the source text sequentially. The final hidden state with the information of the whole source text becomes the initial hidden state of the decoder. Here our encoder is a bidirectional LSTM encoder, where the encoder outputs from both directions at each time step are concatenated $(h_i = [\overrightarrow{h_i}; \overleftarrow{h_i}])$.

We implement a unidirectional LSTM decoder to read the input words and generate summary word by word, with a fixed target vocabulary embedded in a high-dimensional space $Y \in R^{|Y| \times dim}$. At each time step, the decoder generates a summary word y_t by sampling from a distribution of the target vocabulary P_{vocab} until sampling the token representing the end of sentence. The hidden state of the decoder s_t and the en-

coders output h_i at each time step i of the encoding process are computed with a weight matrix W_a to obtain the global attention $\alpha_{t,i}$ and the context vector c_t. It is described below:

$$P_{vocab} = softmax(g([c_t; s_t])) \qquad (1)$$

$$s_t = LSTM(y_{t-1}, s_{t-1}, C_{t-1}) \qquad (2)$$

$$c_t = \sum_{i=1}^{n} \alpha_{t,i} h_i \qquad (3)$$

$$\alpha_{t,i} = \frac{exp(e_{t,i})}{\sum_{j=1}^{n} exp(e_{t,j})} \qquad (4)$$

$$e_{t,i} = s_{t-1}^{\top} W_a h_i \qquad (5)$$

where C refers to the cell state in the LSTM, and $g(\cdot)$ refers to a non-linear function.

2.2 Convolutional Gated Unit

Abstractive summarization requires the core information at each encoding time step. To reach this goal, we implement a gated unit on top of the encoder outputs at each time step, which is a CNN that convolves all the encoder outputs. The parameter sharing of the convolutional kernels enables the model to extract certain types of features, specifically n-gram features. Similar to image, language also contains local correlation, such as the internal correlation of phrase structure. The convolutional units can extract these common features in the sentence and indicate the correlation among the source annotations. Moreover, to further strengthen the global information, we implement self-attention (Vaswani et al., 2017) to mine the relationship of the annotation at a certain time step with other annotations. Therefore, the gated unit is able to find out both common n-gram features and global correlation. Based on the convolution and self-attention, the gated unit sets a gate to filter the source annotations from the RNN encoder, in order to select information relevant to the global semantic meaning. The global encoding allows the encoder output at each time step to become new representation vector with further connection to the global source side information. For convolution, we implement a structure similar to inception (Szegedy et al., 2015). We use 1-dimension convolution to extract n-gram features. Following the design principle of inception, we did not use kernel where $k = 5$ but instead used two kernels where $k = 3$ to avoid large kernel size. The details of convolution block is described below:

$$g_i = ReLU(W[h_{i-k/2}, ..., h_{i+k/2}] + b) \quad (6)$$

where $ReLU$ refers to the non-linear activation function Rectified Linear Unit (Nair and Hinton, 2010). Based on the convolution block, we implement a structure similar to inception, as shown in Figure 1.

On top of the new representations generated by the CNN module, we further implement self-attention upon these representations so as to dig out the global correlations. Vaswani et al. (2017) pointed out that self-attention encourages the model to learn long-term dependencies and does not create much computational complexity, so we implement its scaled dot-product attention for the connection between the annotation at each time step and the global information:

$$Attention(Q, K, V) = softmax(\frac{QK^T}{\sqrt{d_k}})V \quad (7)$$

where the representations, are computed through the attention mechanism with itself and packed into a matrix. To be specific, we refer Q and V to the representation matrix generated by the CNN module, while $K = W_{att}V$ where W_{att} is a learnable matrix.

A further step is to set a gate based on the generation from the CNN and self-attention module g for the source representations h' from the RNN encoder, where:

$$\tilde{h} = h \odot \sigma(g) \quad (8)$$

Since the CNN module can extract n-gram features of the whole source text and self-attention learns the long-term dependencies among the components of the input source text, the gate can perform global encoding on the encoder outputs. Based on the output of the CNN and self-attention, the logistic sigmoid function outputs a vector of value between 0 and 1 at each dimension. If the value is close to 0, the gate removes most of the information at the corresponding dimension of the source representation, and if it is close to 1, it reserves most of the information.

2.3 Training

In the following, we introduce the datasets that we conduct experiments on as well as our experimental settings.

Given the parameters θ and source text x, the models generates a summary $\tilde{y}$. The learning process is to minimize the negative log-likelihood between the generated summary $\tilde{y}$ and reference y:

$$\mathcal{L} = -\frac{1}{N}\sum_{n=1}^{N}\sum_{t=1}^{T}p(y_t^{(n)}|\tilde{y}_{<t}^{(n)}, x^{(n)}, \theta) \quad (9)$$

where the loss function is equivalent to maximizing the conditional probability of summary y given parameters θ and source sequence x.

3 Experiment Setup

In the following, we introduce the datasets that we conduct experiments on and our experiment settings as well as the baseline models that we compare with.

3.1 Datasets

LCSTS is a large-scale Chinese short text summarization dataset collected from Sina Weibo, a famous Chinese social media website (Hu et al., 2015), consisting of more than 2.4 million text-summary pairs. The original texts are shorter than 140 Chinese characters, and the summaries are created manually. We follow the previous research (Hu et al., 2015) to split the dataset for training, validation and testing, with 2.4M sentence pairs for training, 8K for validation and 0.7K for testing.

The English Gigaword is a sentence summarization dataset based on Annotated Gigaword (Napoles et al., 2012), a dataset consisting of sentence pairs, which are the first sentence of the collected news articles and the corresponding headlines. We use the data preprocessed by Rush et al. (2015) with 3.8M sentence pairs for training, 8K for validation and 2K for testing.

3.2 Experiment Settings

We implement our experiments in PyTorch on an NVIDIA 1080Ti GPU. The word embedding dimension and the number of hidden units are both 512. In both experiments, the batch size is set to 64. We use Adam optimizer (Kingma and Ba, 2014) with the default setting $\alpha = 0.001, \beta_1 = 0.9, \beta_2 = 0.999$ and $\epsilon = 1 \times 10^{-8}$. The learning rate is halved every epoch. Gradient clipping is applied with range [-10, 10].

Following the previous studies, we choose ROUGE score to evaluate the performance of our model (Lin and Hovy, 2003). ROUGE score is to

Model	R-1	R-2	R-L
RNN	21.5	8.9	18.6
RNN-context	29.9	17.4	27.2
CopyNet	34.4	21.6	31.3
SRB	33.3	20.0	30.1
DRGD	37.0	24.2	34.2
seq2seq (Our impl.)	33.8	23.1	32.5
+CGU	**39.4**	**26.9**	**36.5**

Table 2: **F-Score of ROUGE on LCSTS.**

Model	R-1	R-2	R-L
ABS	29.6	11.3	26.4
ABS+	29.8	11.9	27.0
Feats	32.7	15.6	30.6
RAS-LSTM	32.6	14.7	30.0
RAS-Elman	33.8	16.0	31.2
SEASS	36.2	17.5	33.6
DRGD	**36.3**	17.6	33.6
seq2seq (Our impl.)	33.6	16.3	31.3
+CGU	**36.3**	**18.0**	**33.8**

Table 3: **F-Score of ROUGE on Gigaword.**

calculate the degree of overlapping between generated summary and reference, including the number of n-grams. F1 scores of ROUGE-1, ROUGE-2 and ROUGE-L are used as the evaluation metrics.

3.3 Baseline Models

As we compare our results with the results of the baseline models reported in their original papers, the evaluation on the two datasets has different baselines. In the following, we introduce the baselines for LCSTS and Gigaword respectively.

Baselines for LCSTS are introduced in the following. **RNN** and **RNN-context** are the RNN-based seq2seq models (Hu et al., 2015), without and with attention mechanism respectively. **CopyNet** is the attention-based seq2seq model with the copy mechanism (Gu et al., 2016). **SRB** is a model that improves semantic relevance between source text and summary (Ma et al., 2017). **DRGD** is the conventional seq2seq with a deep recurrent generative decoder (Li et al., 2017).

As to the baselines for Gigaword, **ABS** and **ABS+** are the models with local attention and handcrafted features (Rush et al., 2015). **Feats** is a fully RNN seq2seq model with some specific methods to control the vocabulary size. **RAS-LSTM** and **RAS-Elman** are seq2seq models with a convolutional encoder and an LSTM decoder and an Elman RNN decoder respectively. **SEASS** is a seq2seq model with a selective gate mechanism. **DRGD** is also a baseline for Gigaword.

Results of our implementation of the conventional seq2seq model on both datasets are also used for the evaluation of the improvement of our proposed convolutional gated unit (CGU).

4 Analysis

In the following sections, we report the results of our experiments and analyze the performance of our model on the evaluation of repetition. Also, we provide an example to demonstrate that our model can generate summary that is more semantically consistent with the source text.

4.1 Results

In the experiments on the two datasets, our model achieves advantages of ROUGE score over the baselines, and the advantages of ROUGE score on the LCSTS are significant. Table 2 presents the results of our model and the baselines on the LCSTS, and Table 2 shows the results of models on the Gigaword. We compare the F1 scores of our model with those of the baseline models (reported in their original articles) and our own implementation of the attention-based seq2seq. Compared with the conventional seq2seq model, our model owns an advantage of ROUGE-2 score 3.7 and 1.5 on the LCSTS and Gigaword respectively.

4.2 Discussion

We show a summary generated by our model, compared with that of the baseline seq2seq model and the reference. The source text introduces a phenomenon that Starbucks, an ordinary coffee brand in the United States, becomes a brand of high class and sells coffee in a much higher price. It is apparent that the main idea of the text is about the high price of Starbucks coffee in China. However, the seq2seq model generates a summary which only contains the information of the brand and the country. In addition, it has committed a mistake of redundant repetition of the word "China". It is not semantically relevant to the source text and it is not coherent and adequate. Compared with it, the summary of our model is more coherent and more semantically relevant to the source text. Our model focuses on the information about price instead of country, and points

Source: 较早进入中国市场的星巴克，是不少小资钟情的品牌。相比在美国的平民形象，星巴克在中国就显得"高端"得多。用料并无差别的一杯中杯美式咖啡，在美国仅约合人民币12元，国内要卖21元，相当于贵了75%。第一财经日报

Starbucks, which entered Chinese market early, is a brand appealing to young people of petit bourgeoisie. Compared with its ordinary image in the United States, Starbucks seems to be of higher class in China. A Tall Americano sells about 12RMB in the United States, but 21RMB in China, which means it is 75% more expensive.

Reference: 媒体称星巴克美式咖啡售价中国比美国贵75%。

Media report that the price of Starbucks Americano in China is 75% more expensive than that in the United States.

seq2seq: 星巴克中国美式咖啡在中国。

Starbucks China Americano in China.

+CGU: 星巴克美式咖啡中国贵75%。

Starbucks Americano is 75% more expensive in China.

Table 4: An example of our summarization, compared with that of the seq2seq model and the reference.

out the price gap in its generated summary. As "China" appears twice in the source text and it is hard for the baseline model to put it in a less significant place, but for our model with CGU, it is able to filter the trivial details that are irrelevant to the core meaning of the source text and just focuses on the information that contributes most to the main idea.

As our CGU is responsible for selecting important information of the outputs from the RNN encoder to improve the quality of the attention score, it should be able to reduce repetition in the generated summary. We evaluate the degree of repetition by calculating the percentage of the duplicates at the sentence level. The evaluations on the Gigaword for duplicates of 1-gram to 4 gram prove that our model significantly reduces repetition compared to the conventional seq2seq and its repetition rate is similar to the reference's. This also shows that our model is able to generate summaries of higher diversity with less repetition.

5 Related Work

Researchers developed many statistical methods and linguistic-rule-based methods to study automatic summarization (Banko et al., 2000; Dorr et al., 2003; Zajic et al., 2004; Cohn and Lapata, 2008). With the development of Neural Network in NLP, more and more researches have appeared in abstractive summarization since it seems possible that Neural Network can help achieve the two goals. Rush et al. (2015) first applied sequence-

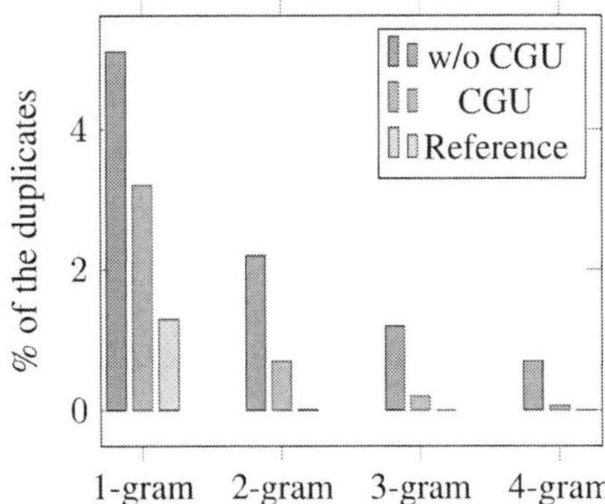

Figure 2: **Percentage of the duplicates at sentence level.** Evaluated on the Gigaword.

to-sequence model with attention mechanism to abstractive summarization and realized significant achievements. Chopra et al. (2016) changed the ABS model with an RNN decoder and Nallapati et al. (2016) changed the system to a fully-RNN sequence-to-sequence model and achieved outstanding performance. Zhou et al. (2017) proposed a selective gate mechanism to filter secondary information. Li et al. (2017) proposed a deep recurrent generative decoder to learn latent structure information. Ma et al. (2018) proposed a model that generates words by querying word embeddings.

6 Conclusion

In this paper, we propose a new model for abstractive summarization. The convolutional gated unit performs global encoding on the source side information so that the core information can be reserved and the secondary information can be filtered. Experiments on the LCSTS and Gigaword show that our model outperforms the baselines, and the analysis shows that it is able to reduce repetition in the generated summaries, and it is more robust to inputs of different lengths, compared with the conventional seq2seq model.

Acknowledgements

This work was supported in part by National Natural Science Foundation of China (No. 61673028), National High Technology Research and Development Program of China (863 Program, No. 2015AA015404), and the National Thousand Young Talents Program. Xu Sun is the corresponding author of this paper.

References

Dzmitry Bahdanau, Kyunghyun Cho, and Yoshua Bengio. 2014. Neural machine translation by jointly learning to align and translate. *CoRR*, abs/1409.0473.

Michele Banko, Vibhu O Mittal, and Michael J Witbrock. 2000. Headline generation based on statistical translation. In *Proceedings of the 38th Annual Meeting on Association for Computational Linguistics*, pages 318–325. Association for Computational Linguistics.

Kyunghyun Cho, Bart van Merrienboer, Çaglar Gülçehre, Dzmitry Bahdanau, Fethi Bougares, Holger Schwenk, and Yoshua Bengio. 2014. Learning phrase representations using RNN encoder-decoder for statistical machine translation. In *EMNLP 2014*, pages 1724–1734.

Sumit Chopra, Michael Auli, and Alexander M. Rush. 2016. Abstractive sentence summarization with attentive recurrent neural networks. In *Conference of the North American Chapter of the Association for Computational Linguistics: Human Language Technologies*, pages 93–98.

Trevor Cohn and Mirella Lapata. 2008. Sentence compression beyond word deletion. In *Proceedings of the 22nd International Conference on Computational Linguistics-Volume 1*, pages 137–144. Association for Computational Linguistics.

Bonnie Dorr, David Zajic, and Richard Schwartz. 2003. Hedge trimmer: A parse-and-trim approach to headline generation. In *Proceedings of the HLT-NAACL 03 on Text summarization workshop-Volume 5*, pages 1–8. Association for Computational Linguistics.

Jiatao Gu, Zhengdong Lu, Hang Li, and Victor O. K. Li. 2016. Incorporating copying mechanism in sequence-to-sequence learning. In *ACL 2016*.

Baotian Hu, Qingcai Chen, and Fangze Zhu. 2015. LCSTS: A large scale chinese short text summarization dataset. In *EMNLP 2015*, pages 1967–1972.

Nal Kalchbrenner and Phil Blunsom. 2013. Recurrent continuous translation models. In *EMNLP 2013*, pages 1700–1709.

Diederik P. Kingma and Jimmy Ba. 2014. Adam: A method for stochastic optimization. *CoRR*, abs/1412.6980.

Piji Li, Wai Lam, Lidong Bing, and Zihao Wang. 2017. Deep recurrent generative decoder for abstractive text summarization. In *EMNLP 2017,*, pages 2091–2100.

Chin Yew Lin and Eduard Hovy. 2003. Automatic evaluation of summaries using n-gram co-occurrence statistics. In *Conference of the North American Chapter of the Association for Computational Linguistics on Human Language Technology*, pages 71–78.

Thang Luong, Hieu Pham, and Christopher D. Manning. 2015. Effective approaches to attention-based neural machine translation. In *EMNLP 2015*, pages 1412–1421.

Shuming Ma, Xu Sun, Wei Li, Sujian Li, Wenjie Li, and Xuancheng Ren. 2018. Query and output: Generating words by querying distributed word representations for paraphrase generation. In *NAACL 2018*.

Shuming Ma, Xu Sun, Jingjing Xu, Houfeng Wang, Wenjie Li, and Qi Su. 2017. Improving semantic relevance for sequence-to-sequence learning of chinese social media text summarization. In *ACL 2017*, pages 635–640.

Vinod Nair and Geoffrey E. Hinton. 2010. Rectified linear units improve restricted boltzmann machines. In *ICML 2010*, pages 807–814.

Ramesh Nallapati, Bowen Zhou, Cícero Nogueira dos Santos, Çaglar Gülçehre, and Bing Xiang. 2016. Abstractive text summarization using sequence-to-sequence rnns and beyond. In *CoNLL 2016*, pages 280–290.

Courtney Napoles, Matthew Gormley, and Benjamin Van Durme. 2012. Annotated gigaword. In *Proceedings of the Joint Workshop on Automatic Knowledge Base Construction and Web-scale Knowledge Extraction*, pages 95–100. Association for Computational Linguistics.

Alexander M. Rush, Sumit Chopra, and Jason Weston. 2015. A neural attention model for abstractive sentence summarization. In *EMNLP 2015*, pages 379–389.

Xu Sun, Bingzhen Wei, Xuancheng Ren, and Shuming Ma. 2017. Label embedding network: Learning label representation for soft training of deep networks. *CoRR*, abs/1710.10393.

Ilya Sutskever, Oriol Vinyals, and Quoc V. Le. 2014. Sequence to sequence learning with neural networks. In *Advances in Neural Information Processing Systems 27: Annual Conference on Neural Information Processing Systems 2014*, pages 3104–3112.

Christian Szegedy, Vincent Vanhoucke, Sergey Ioffe, Jonathon Shlens, and Zbigniew Wojna. 2015. Rethinking the inception architecture for computer vision. *CoRR*, abs/1512.00567.

Sho Takase, Jun Suzuki, Naoaki Okazaki, Tsutomu Hirao, and Masaaki Nagata. 2016. Neural headline generation on abstract meaning representation. In *EMNLP 2016*, pages 1054–1059.

Ashish Vaswani, Noam Shazeer, Niki Parmar, Jakob
Uszkoreit, Llion Jones, Aidan N. Gomez, Lukasz
Kaiser, and Illia Polosukhin. 2017. Attention is all
you need. In *NIPS 2017*, pages 6000–6010.

David Zajic, Bonnie Dorr, and Richard Schwartz. 2004.
Bbn/umd at duc-2004: Topiary. In *Proceedings
of the HLT-NAACL 2004 Document Understanding
Workshop, Boston*, pages 112–119.

Qingyu Zhou, Nan Yang, Furu Wei, and Ming Zhou.
2017. Selective encoding for abstractive sentence
summarization. In *ACL 2017*, pages 1095–1104.

A Language Model based Evaluator for Sentence Compression

Yang Zhao   **Zhiyuan Luo**
The University of Tokyo
7-3-1 Hongo, Bunkyo-ku, Tokyo
{zhao,zyluo24}@is.s.u-tokyo.ac.jp

Akiko Aizawa
National Institute of Informatics
2-1-2 Hitotsubashi, Chiyoda-ku, Tokyo
aizawa@nii.ac.jp

Abstract

We herein present a language-model-based evaluator for deletion-based sentence compression, and viewed this task as a series of deletion-and-evaluation operations using the evaluator. More specifically, the evaluator is a syntactic neural language model that is first built by learning the syntactic and structural collocation among words. Subsequently, a series of trial-and-error deletion operations are conducted on the source sentences via a reinforcement learning framework to obtain the best target compression. An empirical study shows that the proposed model can effectively generate more readable compression, comparable or superior to several strong baselines. Furthermore, we introduce a 200-sentence test set for a large-scale dataset, setting a new baseline for the future research.

1 Introduction

Deletion-based sentence compression aims to delete unnecessary words from source sentence to form a short sentence (compression) while retaining grammatical and faithful to the underlying meaning of the source sentence. Previous works used either machine-learning-based approach or syntactic-tree-based approaches to yield most readable and informative compression (Jing, 2000; Knight and Marcu, 2000; Clarke and Lapata, 2006; McDonald, 2006; Clarke and Lapata, 2008; Filippova and Strube, 2008; Berg-Kirkpatrick et al., 2011; Filippova et al., 2015; Bingel and Søgaard, 2016; Andor et al., 2016; Zhao et al., 2017; Wang et al., 2017). For example, (Clarke and Lapata, 2008) proposed a syntactic-tree-based method that considers the sentence

compression task as an optimization problem by using integer linear programming, whereas (Filippova et al., 2015) viewed the sentence compression task as a sequence labeling problem using the recurrent neural network (RNN), using maximum likelihood as the objective function for optimization. The latter sets a relatively strong baseline by training the model on a large-scale parallel corpus. Although an RNN (e.g., Long short-term memory networks) can implicitly model syntactic information, it still produces ungrammatical sentences. We argue that this is because (i) the labels (or compressions) are automatically yielded by employing the syntactic-tree-pruning method. It thus contains some errors caused by syntactic tree parsing error, (ii) more importantly, the optimization objective of an RNN is the likelihood function that is based on individual words instead of readability (or informativeness) of the whole compressed sentence. A gap exists between optimization objective and evaluation. As such, we are of great interest that: (i) can we take the readability of the whole compressed sentence as a learning objective and (ii) can grammar errors be recovered through a language-model-based evaluator to yield compression with better quality?

To answer the above questions, a syntax-based neural language model is trained on large-scale datasets as a readability evaluator. The neural language model is supposed to learn the correct word collocations in terms of both syntax and semantics. Subsequently, we formulate the deletion-based sentence compression as a series of trial-and-error deletion operations through a reinforcement learning framework. The policy network performs either RETAIN or REMOVE action to form a compression, and receives a reward (e.g., readability score) to update the network.

The empirical study shows that the proposed method can produce more readable sentences that

Proceedings of the 56th Annual Meeting of the Association for Computational Linguistics (Short Papers), pages 170–175
Melbourne, Australia, July 15 - 20, 2018. ©2018 Association for Computational Linguistics

preserve the source sentences, comparable or superior to several strong baselines. In short, our contributions are two-fold: (i) an effective syntax-based evaluator is built as a post-hoc checker, yielding compression with better quality based upon the evaluation metrics; (ii) a large scale news dataset with 1.02 million sentence compression pairs are compiled for this task in addition to 200 manually created sentences. We made it publicly available.

2 Methodology

2.1 Task and Framework

Formally, deletion-based sentence compression translates word tokens, $(w_1, w_2, ..., w_n)$ into a series of ones and zeros, $(l_1, l_2, ..., l_n)$, where n refers to the length of the original sentence and $l_i \in \{0, 1\}$. Here, "1" refers to RETAIN and "0" refers to REMOVE. We first converted the word sequence into a dense vector representation through the parameter matrix E. Except for word embedding, $(e(w_1), e(w_2), ..., e(w_n))$, we also considered the part-of-speech tag and the dependency relation between w_i and its head word as extra features. Each part-of-speech tag was mapped into a vector representation, $(p(w_1), p(w_2), ..., p(w_n))$ through the parameter matrix P, while each dependency relation was mapped into a vector representation, $(d(w_1), d(w_2), ..., d(w_n))$ through the parameter matrix D. Three vector representations are concatenated, $[e(w_i); p(w_i); d(w_i)]$ as the input to the next part, policy network.

Figure 1 shows the graphical illustration of our model. The policy network is a bi-directional RNN that uses the input $[e(w_i); p(w_i); d(w_i)]$ and yields the hidden states in the forward direction, $(h_1^f, h_2^f, ..., h_n^f)$, and hidden states in the backward direction, $(h_1^b, h_2^b, ..., h_n^b)$. Then, concatenation of hidden states in both directions, $[h_i^f; h_i^b]$ are followed by a nonlinear layer to turn the output into a binary probability distribution, $y_i = \sigma(W[h_i^f; h_i^b])$ where σ is a nonlinear function $sigmoid$, and W is a parameter matrix.

The policy network continues to sample actions from the binary probability distribution above until the whole action sequence is yielded. In this task, binary actions space is {RETAIN, REMOVE}. We turn the action sequence into the predicted compression, $(w_1, w_2, ..., w_m)$, by deleting the words whose current action is REMOVE. Then

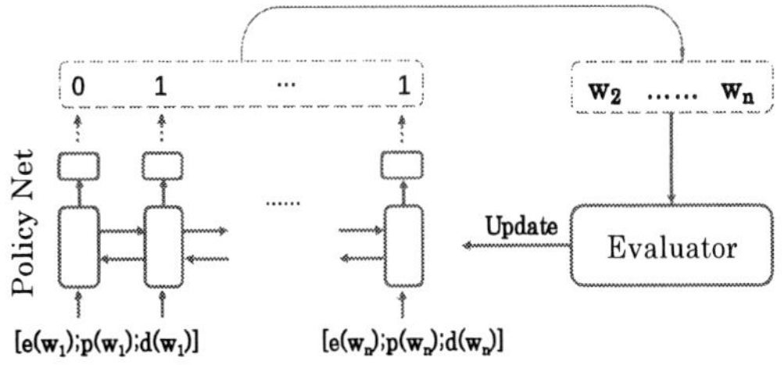

Figure 1: Graphical illustration of the framework.

the $(w_1, w_2, ..., w_m)$ is fed into a pre-trained evaluator which will be described in the next section.

2.2 Syntax-based Evaluator

The syntax-based evaluator should assess the degree to which the compressed sentence is grammatical, through being used as a reward function during the reinforcement learning phase. It needs to satisfy three conditions: (i) grammatical compressions should obtain a higher score than ungrammatical compressions, (ii) for two ungrammatical compressions, it should be able to discriminate them through the score despite the ungrammaticality, (iii) lack of important parts (such as the primary subject or verb) in the original sentence should receive a greater penalty.

We therefore considered an ad-hoc evaluator, i.e., the syntax-based language model (evaluator-SLM) for these requirements. It integrates the part-of-speech tags and the dependency relations in the input, while the output to be predicted is the next word token. We observed that the prediction of the next word could not only be based on the previous word but also the syntactic components, e.g., for the part-of-speech tag, the noun is often followed by a verb instead of an adjective or adverb and the integration of the part-of-speech tag allows the model to learn such correct word collocations. Figure 2 shows the graphical illustration of the evaluator-SLM where the input is $x_i = [e(w_i); p(w_i); d(w_i)]$, followed by a bi-directional RNN whose last layer is the Softmax layer used to represent word probability distribution. Similar to (Mousa and Schuller, 2017), we added two special tokens, <S> and </S> in the input so as to stagger the hidden vectors, thus avoiding self-prediction. Finally, we have the following formula as one part of the reward functions in the learning framework.

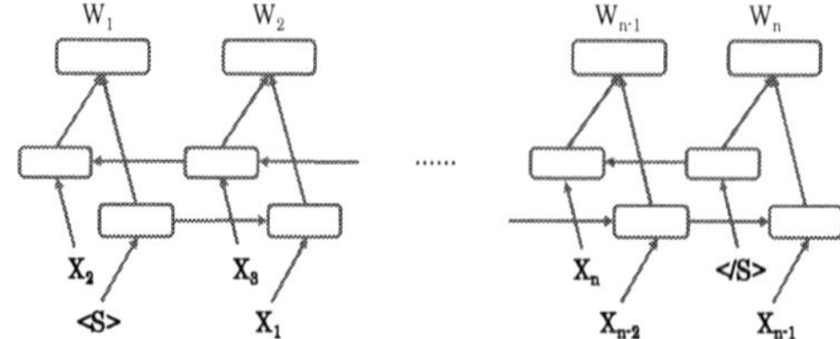

Figure 2: Graphical illustration of bi-directional recurrent neural network language model.

$$R_{SLM}(\widehat{Y}) = e^{\left(\frac{1}{|\widehat{Y}|}\sum_{t=1}^{|\widehat{Y}|} log P_{LM}(y_t|y_{0:t-1})\right)} \quad (1)$$

where $R_{SLM} \in [0,1]$ and $\widehat{Y}$ is the predicted compression by the policy network.

Further, it is noteworthy that the performance comparison should be based on a similar compression rate[1] (CR) (Napoles et al., 2011), and a smooth reward function $R_{CR} = \frac{(a+b)^{(a+b)}}{a^a b^b} x^a (1 - x)^b$ (both a, b are positive integers; e.g. $a = 2$, $b = 2$ could lead the compression rate to 0.5) is also used to attain a compressed sentence of similar length.

The total reward is $R = R_{SLM} + R_{CR}$. By using policy gradient methods (Sutton et al., 2000), the policy network is updated with the following gradient:

$$\nabla\mathcal{L}(\theta) = \sum_{t=1}^{|\widehat{Y}|} R(\widehat{Y})\nabla log \pi_\theta(a_t|S_t) \quad (2)$$

Where $a_t \in \{$RETAIN, REMOVE$\}$, is the action token by the policy network, and S_t refers to hidden state of the network, $[h_i^f; h_i^b]$ (section 2.1).

3 Experiments

3.1 Data

As neural network-based methods require a large amount of training data, we for the first time considered using Gigaword[2], a news domain corpus. More specifically, the first sentence and the headline of each article are extracted. After data cleansing, we finally compiled 1.02 million sentence and headline pairs (see details here[3]). It is noteworthy that the headline is not the extractive compression. Further, we asked two near native English speakers to create 200 extractive compressions for the first 200 sentences of this dataset; using it as the testing set, the first 1,000 sentences (excluding the testing set) is the development set, and the remainder is the training set. To assess the inter-assessor agreements, we computed Cohen 's unweighted κ. The computed unweighted κ was 0.423, reaching a moderate agreement level[4]

The second dataset we used was the Google dataset that contains 200,000 sentence compression pairs (Filippova et al., 2015). For the purpose of comparison, we used the very first 1,000 sentences as the testing set, the next 1,000 sentences as the development set, and the remainder as the training set.

3.2 Comparison Methods

We choose several strong baselines; the first one is the dependency-tree-based method that considers the sentence compression task as an optimization problem by using integer linear programming[5]. Inspired by (Filippova and Strube, 2008), (Clarke and Lapata, 2008), and (Wang et al., 2017), we defined some constrains: (1) if a word is retained in the compression, its parent should be also retained. (2) whether a word w_i is retained should partly depend on the word importance score that is the product of the TF-IDF score and headline score $h(w_i)$, $tf\text{-}idf(w_i) \cdot h(w_i)$ where $h(w_i)$ represents that whether a word (limited to nouns and verbs) is also in the headline. $h(w_i)$=5 if w_i is in the headline; $h(w_i)$=1 otherwise. (3) the dependency relations, *ROOT, dobj, nsubj, pobj*, should be retained as they are the skeletons of a sentence. (4) the sentence length should be over than α but less than β. (5) the depth of the node (word), $\lambda dep(w_i)$, in the dependency tree. (6) the word with the dependency relation *amod* is to be removed. It is noteworthy that the method is unsupervised.

The second method is the long short-term memory networks (LSTMs) which showed strong promise in sentence compression by (Filippova et al., 2015). The labels were obtained using the dependency tree pruning method (Filippova and Altun, 2013) and the LSTMs were applied in a supervised manner. Following their works, we also

---

[1]compression rate is the length of compression divided by the length of the sentence.

[2]https://catalog.ldc.upenn.edu/ldc2011t07

[3]https://github.com/code4conference/Data

[4](Landis and Koch, 1977) characterize κ values <0 as no agreement, $0 \sim 0.20$ as slight, $0.21 \sim 0.40$ as fair, $0.41 \sim 0.60$ as moderate, $0.61 \sim 0.80$ as substantial, and $0.81 \sim 1$ as almost perfect agreement.)

[5]we use http://pypi.python.org/pypi/PuLP

Gigaword Dataset	Annotator 1		Annotator 2		
	F_1	**RASP-F_1**	F_1	**RASP-F_1**	**CR**
#1 Seq2seq with attention	54.9	60.3	58.6	64.6	0.53
#2 Dependency tree+ILP	58.0	65.1	61.0	70.9	0.55
#3 LSTMs+pseudo label	60.3	64.1	64.1	69.2	0.51
#4 Evaluator-LM	64.5	67.3	66.9	72.2	0.50
#5 Evaluator-SLM	**65.0**	**69.6**	**68.2**	**73.9**	0.51

Table 1: F_1 and RASP-F_1 results for Gigaword dataset.

consider the labels yielded by our dependency-tree-based method as pseudo labels and employ LSTMs as a baseline.

Furthermore, for a comprehensive comparison, we applied the sequence-to-sequence with attention method widely used in abstractive text summarization for sentence compression. Previous works such as (Rush et al., 2015; Chopra et al., 2016) have shown promising results with this framework, although the focus was generation-based summarization rather than extractive summarization. More specifically, the source sequence of this framework is the original sentence, while the target sequence is a series of zeros and ones (zeros represents REMOVE and ones represents RETAIN). Further, we incorporated dependency labels and part-of-speech tag features in the source side of the sequence-to-sequence method.

3.3 Training

The embedding size for word, part-of-speech tag, and the dependency relation is 128. We employed the vanilla RNN with a hidden size of 512 for both the policy network and neural language model. The mini-batch size was chosen from [5, 50, 100]. Vocabulary size was 50,000. The learning rate for neural language model is 2.5e-4, and 1e-05 for the policy network. For policy learning, we used the REINFORCE algorithm (Williams, 1992) to update the parameters of the policy network and find an policy that maximizes the reward. Because starting from a random policy is impractical owing to the high variance, we pre-trained the policy network using pseudo labels in a supervised manner. For the comparison methods, the hyperparameters and were set to 0.4 and 0.7, respectively, and was set to 0.5. For reproduction, we released the source code here[6].

4 Result and Discussion

This section demonstrates the experimental results on both datasets. As the Gigaword dataset has no ground truth, we evaluated the baseline and our method on the 200-sentence test sets created by two human annotators. For the automatic evaluation, we employed F_1 and RASP-F_1 (Briscoe and Carroll, 2002) to measure the performances. The latter compares grammatical relations (such as ncsubj and dobj) found in the system compressions with those found in the gold standard, providing a means to measure the semantic aspects of the compression quality. For the human evaluation, we asked two near native English speakers to assess the quality of 50 compressed sentences out of the 200-sentence test set in terms of readability and informativeness. Here are our observations:

Gigaword	*Readability*	*Informativeness*
$1 LSTMs	3.56	3.10
$2 SLM	**4.16†**	3.16

Table 2: Human Evaluation for Gigaword dataset. †stands for significant difference with 0.95 confidence in the column.

Google Dataset	F_1	**RASP-F_1**	**CR**
&1 Seq2seq with attention	71.7	63.8	0.34
&2 LSTM (Filippova, 2015)	82.0	-	0.38
&3 LSTMs (our implement)	84.8	81.9	0.40
&4 Evaluator-LM	85.0	82.0	0.41
&5 Evaluator-SLM	85.1	82.3	0.39

Table 3: F_1 and RASP-F_1 results for Google dataset.

(1) As shown in Table 1, our Evaluator-SLM-based method yields a large improvement over the baselines, demonstrating that the language-model-based evaluator is effective as a post-hoc grammar checker for the compressed sentences. This is also validated by the significant improvement in the readability score in Table 2 ($1 vs $2). To investigate the evaluator in detail, a case study is shown in section 4.1.

---

[6]https://github.com/code4conference/code4sc

SENTENCE	The	Dalian	shipyard	has	built	two	new	huge	ships	
POS tags	*DET*	*ADJ*	*NOUN*	*VERB*	*VERB*	*NUM*	*ADJ*	*ADJ*	*NOUN*	e^{-logR}
DEP. rels	*det*	*compound*	***nsubj***	*aux*	***root***	*nummod*	*amod*	*amod*	***dobj***	
#1	The	Dalian	shipyard	has	built	two	new	huge	ships	59.8
#2	The	Dalian	shipyard	has	built	two	new	huge		140.5
#3	The	Dalian	shipyard	has		two	new	huge	ships	582.9
#4	The	Dalian		has	built	two	new	huge	ships	1313.5
#5	The	Dalian		has	built	two			ships	1244.8
#6	The			has	built	two			ships	1331.2
#7	The	Dalian	shipyard	has	built	two		huge	ships	46.9
#8	The	Dalian	shipyard	has	built	two			ships	18.2
#9	The		shipyard	has	built	two			ships	66.5

Figure 3: Case study for evaluator.

(2) by comparing annotator 1 with annotator 2 in Table 1, we observed different performances for two annotated test sets, showing that compressing a text while preserving the original sentence is subjective across the annotators.

(3) As for Google news dataset, LSTMs (LSTM+pos+dep) (&3) is a relatively strong baseline, suggesting that incorporating dependency relations and part-of-speech tags may help model learn the syntactic relations and thus make a better prediction. When further applying Evaluator-SLM, only a tiny improvement is observed (&3 vs &4), not comparable to the improvement between #3 and #5. This may be due to the difference in perplexity of the our Evaluator-SLM. For Gigaword dataset with 1.02 million instances, the perplexity of the language model is 20.3, while for the Google news dataset with 0.2 million instances, the perplexity is 76.5.

(4) To further explore the degree to which syntactic knowledge (dependency relations and part-of-speech tags) is helpful to evaluator (language model), we implemented a naive language model, i.e., Evaluator-LM, which did not include dependency relations and part-of-speech tags as input features. The results shows that small improvements are observed on two datasets (#4 vs #5; &4 vs &5), suggesting that incorporating syntactic knowledge may help evaluator to encourage more unseen but reasonable word collocations.

4.1 Evaluator Analysis

To further analyze the Evaluator-SLM performance, we used an example sentence, "The Dalian shipyard has built two new huge ships" to observe how a language model scores different word deletion operations. We converted the reward function R_{SLM} to $e^{-logR_{SLM}}$ for a better observation (sim-

ilar to "sentence perplexity", the higher the score is, the worse is the sentence). As shown in Figure 3, deleting the object(#2), verb(#3), or subject(#4) results in a significant increase in "sentence perplexity", implying that the syntax-based language model is highly sensitive to the lack of such syntactic components. Interestingly, when deleting words such as new or/and huge, the score becomes lower, suggesting that the model may prefer short sentences, with unnecessary parts such as *amod* being removed. This property makes it quite suitable for the sentence compression task aiming to shorten sentences by removing unnecessary words.

5 Conclusion

We presented a syntax-based language model for the sentence compression task. We employed unsupervised methods to yield labels to train a policy network in a supervised manner. The experimental results demonstrates that the compression could be further improved by a post-hoc language-model-based evaluator, and our evaluator-enhanced model performs better or comparable upon the evaluation metrics on two large-scale datasets.

Acknowledgments

This work was supported by JSPS KAKENHI Grant Numbers JP15H01721, JP18H03297. We are thankful for the reviewers' helpful comments and suggestions. We would also like to thank Filippova for sharing their data with us and Clarke for the Annotator Sentence Compression Instructions in his PhD dissertation.

References

Daniel Andor, Chris Alberti, David Weiss, Aliaksei Severyn, Alessandro Presta, Kuzman Ganchev, Slav Petrov, and Michael Collins. 2016. Globally normalized transition-based neural networks. In *Proceedings of the 54th Annual Meeting of the Association for Computational Linguistics (Volume 1: Long Papers)*. volume 1, pages 2442–2452.

Taylor Berg-Kirkpatrick, Dan Gillick, and Dan Klein. 2011. Jointly learning to extract and compress. In *Proceedings of the 49th Annual Meeting of the Association for Computational Linguistics: Human Language Technologies-Volume 1*. Association for Computational Linguistics, pages 481–490.

Joachim Bingel and Anders Søgaard. 2016. Text simplification as tree labeling. In *Proceedings of the 54th Annual Meeting of the Association for Computational Linguistics (Volume 2: Short Papers)*. volume 2, pages 337–343.

Ted Briscoe and John Carroll. 2002. Robust accurate statistical annotation of general text. In *Proceedings of the Third International Conference on Language Resources and Evaluation (LREC'02)*.

Sumit Chopra, Michael Auli, and Alexander M Rush. 2016. Abstractive sentence summarization with attentive recurrent neural networks. In *Proceedings of the 2016 Conference of the North American Chapter of the Association for Computational Linguistics: Human Language Technologies*. pages 93–98.

James Clarke and Mirella Lapata. 2006. Constraint-based sentence compression an integer programming approach. In *Proceedings of the COLING/ACL on Main conference poster sessions*. Association for Computational Linguistics, pages 144–151.

James Clarke and Mirella Lapata. 2008. Global inference for sentence compression: An integer linear programming approach. *Journal of Artificial Intelligence Research* 31:399–429.

Katja Filippova, Enrique Alfonseca, Carlos A Colmenares, Lukasz Kaiser, and Oriol Vinyals. 2015. Sentence compression by deletion with lstms. In *Proceedings of the 2015 Conference on Empirical Methods in Natural Language Processing*. pages 360–368.

Katja Filippova and Yasemin Altun. 2013. Overcoming the lack of parallel data in sentence compression. In *Proceedings of the 2013 Conference on Empirical Methods in Natural Language Processing*. pages 1481–1491.

Katja Filippova and Michael Strube. 2008. Dependency tree based sentence compression. *Fifth International Natural Language Generation Conference on - INLG '08* page 25.

Hongyan Jing. 2000. Sentence reduction for automatic text summarization. In *Proceedings of the sixth conference on Applied natural language processing*. Association for Computational Linguistics, pages 310–315.

Kevin Knight and Daniel Marcu. 2000. Statistics-based summarization-step one: Sentence compression. In *Proceedings of the Seventeenth National Conference on Artificial Intelligence and Twelfth Conference on Innovative Applications of Artificial Intelligence*. AAAI Press, pages 703–710.

J Richard Landis and Gary G Koch. 1977. The measurement of observer agreement for categorical data. *biometrics* pages 159–174.

Ryan McDonald. 2006. Discriminative sentence compression with soft syntactic evidence. In *11th Conference of the European Chapter of the Association for Computational Linguistics*.

Amr Mousa and Björn Schuller. 2017. Contextual bidirectional long short-term memory recurrent neural network language models: A generative approach to sentiment analysis. In *Proceedings of the 15th Conference of the European Chapter of the Association for Computational Linguistics: Volume 1, Long Papers*. volume 1, pages 1023–1032.

Courtney Napoles, Benjamin Van Durme, and Chris Callison-Burch. 2011. Evaluating sentence compression: Pitfalls and suggested remedies. In *Proceedings of the Workshop on Monolingual Text-To-Text Generation*. pages 91–97.

Alexander M Rush, Sumit Chopra, and Jason Weston. 2015. A neural attention model for abstractive sentence summarization. In *Proceedings of the 2015 Conference on Empirical Methods in Natural Language Processing*. pages 379–389.

Richard S Sutton, David A McAllester, Satinder P Singh, and Yishay Mansour. 2000. Policy gradient methods for reinforcement learning with function approximation. In *Advances in neural information processing systems*. pages 1057–1063.

Liangguo Wang, Jing Jiang, Hai Leong Chieu, Chen Hui Ong, Dandan Song, and Lejian Liao. 2017. Can syntax help? improving an lstm-based sentence compression model for new domains. In *Proceedings of the 55th Annual Meeting of the Association for Computational Linguistics (Volume 1: Long Papers)*. volume 1, pages 1385–1393.

Ronald J Williams. 1992. Simple statistical gradient-following algorithms for connectionist reinforcement learning. In *Reinforcement Learning*, Springer, pages 5–32.

Yang Zhao, Hajime Senuma, Xiaoyu Shen, and Akiko Aizawa. 2017. Gated neural network for sentence compression using linguistic knowledge. In *International Conference on Applications of Natural Language to Information Systems*. Springer, pages 480–491.

Identifying and Understanding User Reactions to Deceptive and Trusted Social News Sources

Maria Glenski   **Tim Weninger**
Computer Science and Engineering
University of Notre Dame
Notre Dame, IN 46556
{mglenski, tweninge}@nd.edu

Svitlana Volkova
Data Sciences and Analytics Group
Pacific Northwest National Laboratory
Richland, WA 99354
svitlana.volkova@pnnl.gov

Abstract

In the age of social news, it is important to understand the types of reactions that are evoked from news sources with various levels of credibility. In the present work we seek to better understand how users react to trusted and deceptive news sources across two popular, and very different, social media platforms. To that end, (1) we develop a model to classify user reactions into one of nine types, such as answer, elaboration, and question, etc, and (2) we measure the speed and the type of reaction for trusted and deceptive news sources for 10.8M Twitter posts and 6.2M Reddit comments. We show that there are significant differences in the speed and the type of reactions between trusted and deceptive news sources on Twitter, but far smaller differences on Reddit.

1 Introduction

As the reliance on social media as a source of news increases and the reliability of sources is increasingly debated, it is important to understand how users react to various sources of news. Most studies that investigate misinformation spread in social media focus on individual events and the role of the network structure in the spread (Qazvinian et al., 2011; Wu et al., 2015; Kwon et al., 2017) or detection of false information (Rath et al., 2017). These studies have found that the size and shape of misinformation cascades within a social network depends heavily on the initial reactions of the users. Other work has focused on the language of misinformation in social media (Rubin et al., 2016; Rashkin et al., 2017; Mitra et al., 2017; Wang, 2017; Karadzhov et al., 2017; Volkova et al., 2017) to detect types of deceptive news.

As an alternative to studying newsworthy events one at a time (Starbird, 2017), the current work applies linguistically-infused models to predict user reactions to deceptive and trusted news *sources*. Our analysis reveals differences in reaction types and speed across two social media platforms — Twitter and Reddit.

The first metric we report is the reaction type. Recent studies have found that 59% of bitly-URLs on Twitter are shared without ever being read (Gabielkov et al., 2016), and 73% of Reddit posts were voted on without reading the linked article (Glenski et al., 2017). Instead, users tend to rely on the commentary added to retweets or the comments section of Reddit-posts for information on the content and its credibility. Faced with this reality, we ask: what kind of reactions do users find when they browse sources of varying credibility? Discourse acts, or speech acts, can be used to identify the *use* of language within a conversation, *e.g.*, agreement, question, or answer. Recent work by Zhang et al. (2017) classified Reddit comments by their primary discourse act (*e.g.*, question, agreement, humor), and further analyzed patterns from these discussions.

The second metric we report is reaction speed. A study by Jin et al. (2013) found that trusted news *stories* spread faster than misinformation or rumor; Zeng et al. (2016) found that tweets which deny rumors had shorter delays than tweets of support. Our second goal is to determine if these trends are maintained for various types of news sources on Twitter and Reddit.

Hence, the contributions of this work are twofold: (1) we develop a linguistically-infused neural network model to classify reactions in social media posts, and (2) we apply our model to label 10.8M Twitter posts and 6.2M Reddit comments in order to evaluate the speed and type of user reactions to various news sources.

Proceedings of the 56th Annual Meeting of the Association for Computational Linguistics (Short Papers), pages 176–181
Melbourne, Australia, July 15 - 20, 2018. ©2018 Association for Computational Linguistics

2 Reaction Type Classification

In this section, we describe our approach to classify user reactions into one of eight types of discourse: agreement, answer, appreciation, disagreement, elaboration, humor, negative reaction, or question, or as none of the given labels, which we call "other", using linguistically-infused neural network models.

2.1 Reddit Data

We use a manually annotated Reddit dataset from Zhang et al. (2017) to train our reaction classification model. Annotations from 25 crowd-workers labelled the primary discourse act for 101,525 comments within 9,131 comment threads on Reddit. The Reddit IDs, but not the text content of the comments themselves, were released with the annotations. So we collected the content of Reddit posts and comments from a public archive of Reddit posts and comments.[1] Some content was deleted prior to archival, so the dataset shown in Table 1 is a subset of the original content. Despite the inability to capture all of the original dataset, Table 1 shows a similar distribution between our dataset and the original.

| | Zhang et al. | | Present work | |
Reaction Type	#	%	#	%
agreement	5,054	4.73	3,857	4.61
answer	41,281	38.63	32,561	38.94
appreciation	8,821	8.25	6,973	8.34
disagreement	3,430	3.21	2,654	3.17
elaboration	19,315	18.07	14,966	17.90
humor	2,358	2.21	1,878	2.25
negative reaction	1,901	1.78	1,473	1.76
other	1,979	1.85	1,538	1.84
question	10,568	9.89	8,194	9.80
no majority label	12,162	11.38	9532	11.40
Total	**106,869**	**100**	**83,626**	**100**

Table 1: Summary of the training data we recovered compared to the data collected by Zhang et al. (2017) reported as distributions of comments across reaction types.

2.2 Model

We develop a neural network architecture that relies on content and other linguistic signals extracted from reactions and parent posts, and takes advantage of a "late fusion" approach previously used effectively in vision tasks (Karpathy et al., 2014; Park et al., 2016). More specifically, we combine a text sequence sub-network with a vector representation sub-network as shown

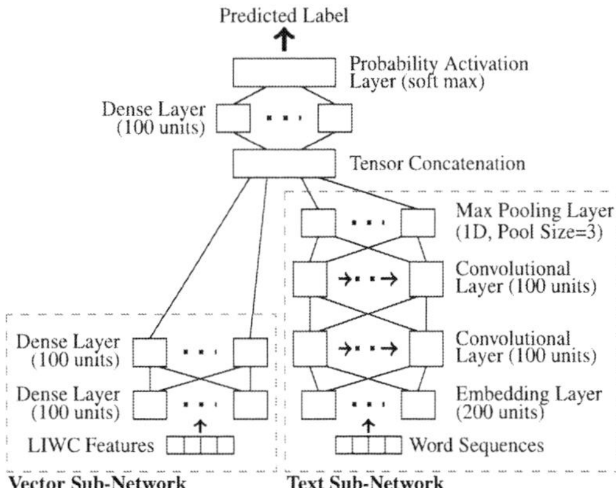

Figure 1: Architecture of neural network model used to predict reaction types.

in Figure 1. The text sequence sub-network consists of an embedding layer initialized with 200-dimensional GloVe embeddings (Pennington et al., 2014) followed by two 1-dimensional convolution layers, then a max-pooling layer followed by a dense layer. The vector representation sub-network consists of two dense layers. We incorporate information from both sub-networks through concatenated padded text sequences and vector representations of normalized Linguistic Inquiry and Word Count (LIWC) features (Pennebaker et al., 2001) for the text of each post and its parent.

2.3 Reaction Type Classification Results

As shown in Figure 2, our linguistically-infused neural network model that relies solely on the content of the reaction and its parent has comparable performance to the more-complex CRF model by Zhang et al. (2017), which relies on content as well as additional metadata like the author, thread (*e.g.,* the size of the the thread, the number of branches), structure (*e.g.,* the position within the thread), and community (*i.e.,* the subreddit in which the comment is posted).

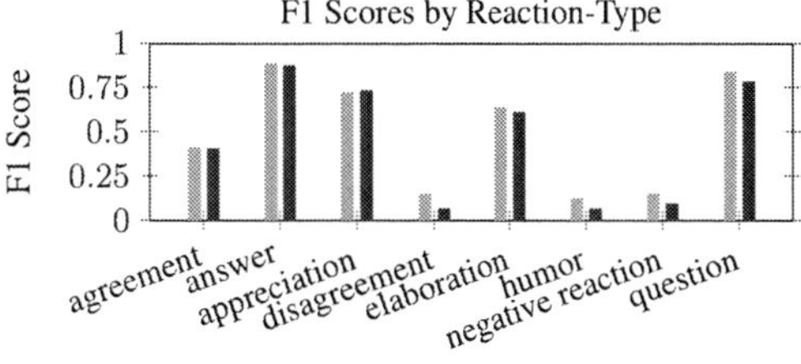

Figure 2: Comparison of our model's performance, measured using F1 score, trained only on content features, with the performance reported by Zhang et al. (2017) trained on content, author, thread, structure, and community features.

---

[1] `bigquery.cloud.google.com/dataset/`
`fh-bigquery:reddit_posts|reddit_comments`

3 Measuring Reactions to Trusted and Deceptive News Sources

In this section, we present key results of our analysis of *how often* and *how quickly* users react to content from sources of varying credibility using the reaction types predicted by our linguistically-infused neural network model.

3.1 Twitter and Reddit News Data

We focus on *trusted* news sources that provide factual information with no intent to deceive and *deceptive* news sources. Deceptive sources are ranked by their intent to deceive as follows: clickbait (attention-grabbing, misleading, or vague headlines to attract an audience), conspiracy theory (uncorroborated or unreliable information to explain events or circumstances), propaganda (intentionally misleading information to advance a social or political agenda), and disinformation (fabricated or factually incorrect information meant to intentionally deceive readers).

Trusted, clickbait, conspiracy, and propaganda sources were previously compiled by Volkova et al. (2017) through a combination of crowd-sourcing and public resources. Trusted news sources with Twitter-verified accounts were manually labeled and clickbait, conspiracy, and propaganda news sources were collected from several public resources that annotate suspicious news accounts[2]. We collected news sources identified as spreading disinformation by the European Union's East Strategic Communications Task Force from euvsdisinfo.eu. In total, there were 467 news sources: 251 trusted and 216 deceptive.

We collected reaction data for two popular platforms, Reddit and Twitter, using public APIs over the 13 month period from January 2016 through January 2017. For our Reddit dataset, we collected all Reddit posts submitted during the 13 month period that linked to domains associated with one of our labelled news sources. Then we collected all comments that directly responded to those posts. For our Twitter dataset, we collected all tweets posted in the 13 month period that explicitly @mentioned or directly retweeted content from a source and then assigned a label to each tweet based on the class of the source @mentioned

---

[2]Example resources used by Volkova et al (2017) to compile deceptive news sources: `http://www.fakenewswatch.com/`, `http://www.propornot.com/p/the-list.html` and others.

Reddit Dataset

Type	# Sources	# Comments
Trusted	169	5,429,694
Deceptive (no disinfo)	128	664,670
Deceptive	179	795,591
Total	**348**	**6,225,285**

Twitter Dataset

Type	# Sources	# Tweets
Trusted	182	6,567,002
Deceptive (no disinfo)	100	775,844
Deceptive	150	4,263,576
Total	**232**	**10,830,578**

Table 2: Summary of Twitter and Reddit datasets used to measure the speed and types of reactions to Trusted and Deceptive news sources excluding (no disinformation) or including (All) the most extreme of the deceptive sources — those identified as spreading disinformation.

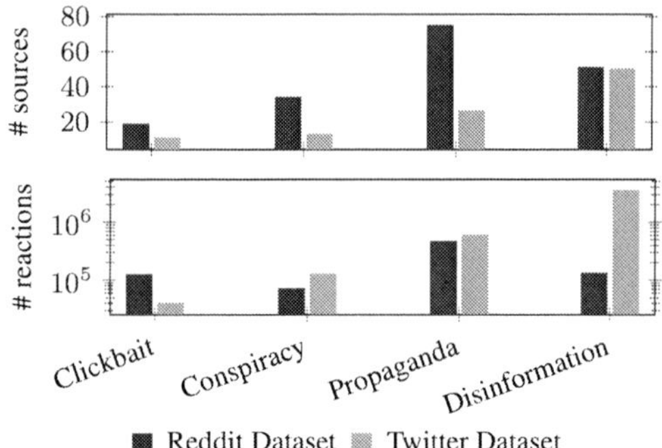

Figure 3: Distributions of Deceptive news sources and reactions to those sources (Reddit comments or tweets, respectively) for the Reddit and Twitter datasets across the four sub-categories of deceptive news sources.

or retweeted. A breakdown of each dataset by source type is shown in Table 2. Figure 3 illustrates the distribution of deceptive news sources and reactions across the four sub-categories of deceptive news sources. In our analysis, we consider the set of all deceptive sources and the set excluding the most extreme (disinformation).

3.2 Methodology

We use the linguistically-infused neural network model from Figure 1 to label the reaction type of each tweet or comment. Using these labels, we examine how often response types occur when users react to each type of news source. For clarity, we report the five most frequently occurring reaction types (expressed in at least 5% of reactions within each source type) and compare the distributions of reaction types for each type of news source.

To examine whether users react to content from trusted sources differently than from deceptive sources, we measure the reaction delay, which we define as the time elapsed between the moment the

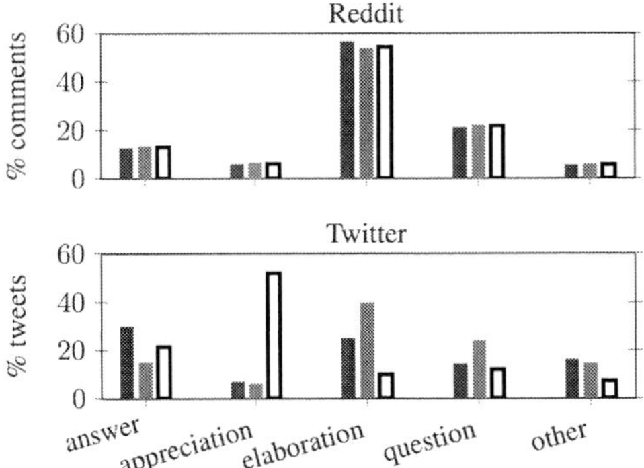

Figure 4: Distributions of five most frequently occurring reaction types within comments on Reddit and tweets on Twitter for each news source type (MWU $p < 0.01$).

link or content was posted/tweeted and the moment that the reaction comment or tweet occurred. We report the cumulative distribution functions (CDFs) for each source type and use Mann Whitney U (MWU) tests to compare whether users respond with a given reaction type with significantly different delays to news sources of different levels of credibility.

3.3 Results and Discussion

For both Twitter and Reddit datasets, we found that the primary reaction types were answer, appreciation, elaboration, question, or "other" (no label was predicted). Figure 4 illustrates the distribution of reaction types among Reddit comments (top plot) or tweets (bottom plot) responding to each type of source, as a percentage of all comments/tweets reacting to sources of the given type (*i.e.*, trusted, all deceptive, and deceptive excluding disinformation sources).

For Twitter, we report clear differences in user reactions to trusted vs. deceptive sources. *Deceptive (including disinformation) sources have a much higher rate of appreciation reactions and a lower rate of elaboration responses, compared to trusted news sources.* Differences are still significant ($p < 0.01$) but the trends reverse if we do not include disinformation sources. We also see an increase in the rate of question-reactions compared to trusted news sources if we exclude disinformation sources.

For Reddit, there appears to be a very similar distribution across reaction types for trusted and deceptive sources. However, MWU tests still found that the differences between trusted and de-

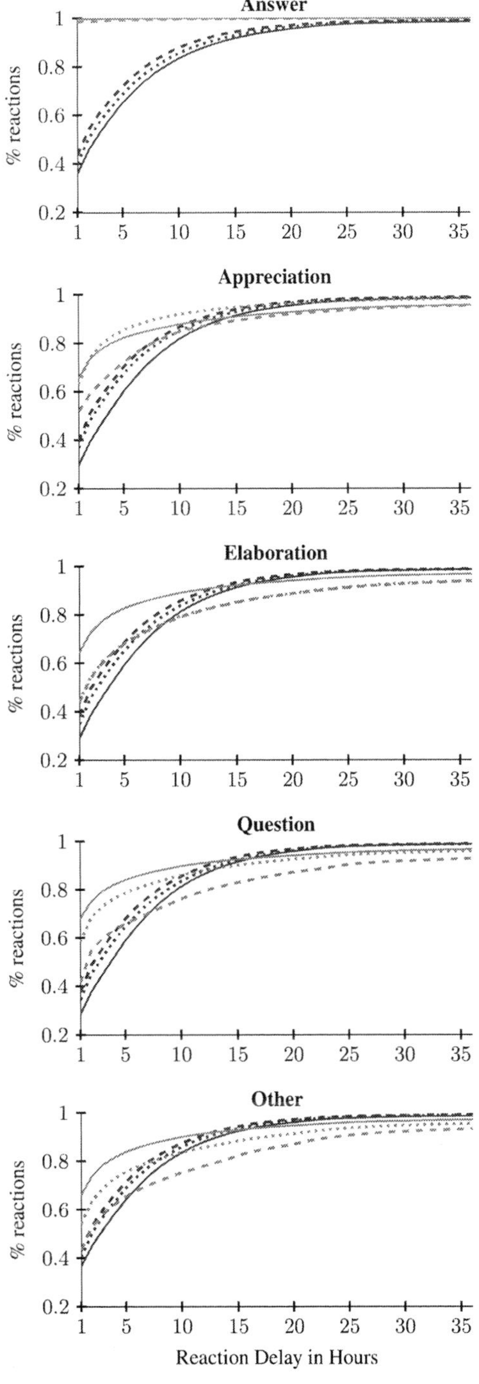

Figure 5: CDF plots of the volumes of reactions by reaction delays for the frequently occurring reactions (*i.e.*, , reactions that occur in at least 5% of comments) for each source-type, using a step size of one hour. The CDF for Elaboration-reactions to Deceptive (no disinformation) Twitter news sources is occluded by the CDF for Deceptive Twitter news sources. This figure is best viewed in color.

ceptive news sources were statistically significant ($p < 0.01$) — regardless of whether we include or exclude disinformation sources. *Posts that link to deceptive sources have higher rates of question, appreciation, and answering reactions, while posts that link to trusted sources have higher rates of elaboration, agreement, and disagreement.*

Next, we compared the speed with which users reacted to posts of sources of varying credibility. Our original hypothesis was that users react to posts of trusted sources faster than posts of deceptive sources. The CDFs for each source type and platform (solid and dashed lines represent Reddit and Twitter respectively) are shown in Figure 5. *We observe that the lifetime of direct reactions to news sources on Twitter is often more extended than for sources on Reddit. One exception is answer reactions which almost always occur within the first hour after the Twitter new source originally posted the tweet being answered.* This may be due to the different ways that users consume content on the two platforms. Users follow accounts on Twitter, whereas on Reddit users "follow" topics through their subscriptions to various subreddits. Users can view the news feeds of individual sources on Twitter and view all of the sources' posts. Reddit, on the other hand, is not designed to highlight individual users or news sources; instead new posts (regardless of the source) are viewed based on their hotness score within each subreddit.

In addition, we observe that *reactions to posts linked to trusted sources are less heavily concentrated within the first 12 to 15 hours of the post's lifetime on Reddit. The opposite is found on Twitter. Twitter sources may have a larger range of reaction delays, but they are also more heavily concentrated in the lower end of that range* ($p < 0.01$).

4 Related Work

As we noted above, most studies that examine misinformation spread focus on individual events such as natural disasters (Takahashi et al., 2015), political elections (Ferrara, 2017), or crises (Starbird et al., 2014) and examine the response to the event on social media. A recent study by Vosoughi et al. (2018) found that news stories that were fact-checked and found to be false spread faster and to more people than news items found to be true. In contrast, our methodology considers immediate reactions to news *sources* of varying credibility, so we can determine whether certain reactions or reactions to trusted or deceptive news sources evoke more or faster responses from social media users.

5 Conclusion

In the current work, we have presented a content-based model that classifies user reactions into one of nine types, such as answer, elaboration, and question, etc., and a large-scale analysis of Twitter posts and Reddit comments in response to content from news sources of varying credibility.

Our analysis of user reactions to trusted and deceptive sources on Twitter and Reddit shows significant differences in the distribution of reaction types for trusted versus deceptive news. However, due to differences in the user interface, algorithmic design, or user-base, we find that Twitter users react to trusted and deceptive sources very differently than Reddit users. For instance, Twitter users questioned disinformation sources less often and more slowly than they did trusted news sources; Twitter users also expressed appreciation towards disinformation sources more often and faster than towards trusted sources. Results from Reddit show similar, but far less pronounced, reaction results.

Future work may focus on analysis of reaction behavior from automated (*i.e.,* 'bot'), individual, or organization accounts; on additional social media platforms and languages; or between more fine-grained categories of news source credibility.

Acknowledgments

The research described in this paper is based on Twitter and Reddit data collected by the University of Notre Dame using public APIs. The research was supported by the Laboratory Directed Research and Development Program at Pacific Northwest National Laboratory, a multiprogram national laboratory operated by Battelle for the U.S. Department of Energy. This research is also supported by the Defense Advanced Research Projects Agency (DARPA), contract W911NF-17-C-0094. The U.S. Government is authorized to reproduce and distribute reprints for Governmental purposes notwithstanding any copyright annotation thereon. The views and conclusions contained herein are those of the authors and should not be interpreted as necessarily representing the official policies or endorsements, either expressed or implied, of DARPA or the U.S. Government.

References

Emilio Ferrara. 2017. Disinformation and social bot operations in the run up to the 2017 French presidential election. *First Monday* 22(8).

Maksym Gabielkov, Arthi Ramachandran, Augustin Chaintreau, and Arnaud Legout. 2016. Social clicks: What and who gets read on Twitter? In *ACM SIGMETRICS/IFIP Performance*.

Maria Glenski, Corey Pennycuff, and Tim Weninger. 2017. Consumers and curators: Browsing and voting patterns on Reddit. *IEEE Transactions on Computational Social Systems* 4(4):196–206.

Fang Jin, Edward Dougherty, Parang Saraf, Yang Cao, and Naren Ramakrishnan. 2013. Epidemiological modeling of news and rumors on Twitter. In *Proceedings of the 7th Workshop on Social Network Mining and Analysis*. page 8.

Georgi Karadzhov, Pepa Gencheva, Preslav Nakov, and Ivan Koychev. 2017. We built a fake news & clickbait filter: What happened next will blow your mind! In *Proceedings of the International Conference on Recent Advances in Natural Language Processing*.

Andrej Karpathy, George Toderici, Sanketh Shetty, Thomas Leung, Rahul Sukthankar, and Li Fei-Fei. 2014. Large-scale video classification with convolutional neural networks. In *Proceedings of CVPR*. pages 1725–1732.

Sejeong Kwon, Meeyoung Cha, and Kyomin Jung. 2017. Rumor detection over varying time windows. *PloS one* 12(1):e0168344.

Tanushree Mitra, Graham P Wright, and Eric Gilbert. 2017. A parsimonious language model of social media credibility across disparate events. In *Proceedings of the ACM Conference on Computer Supported Cooperative Work and Social Computing (CSCW)*. ACM, pages 126–145.

Eunbyung Park, Xufeng Han, Tamara L Berg, and Alexander C Berg. 2016. Combining multiple sources of knowledge in deep CNNs for action recognition. In *Proceedings of AWACV*. pages 1–8.

James W Pennebaker, Martha E Francis, and Roger J Booth. 2001. Linguistic inquiry and word count: Liwc. *Mahway: Lawrence Erlbaum Associates* .

Jeffrey Pennington, Richard Socher, and Christopher D. Manning. 2014. Glove: Global vectors for word representation. In *Proceedings of the Conference on Empirical Methods in Natural Language Processing*. pages 1532–1543.

Vahed Qazvinian, Emily Rosengren, Dragomir R Radev, and Qiaozhu Mei. 2011. Rumor has it: Identifying misinformation in microblogs. In *Proceedings of the Conference on Empirical Methods in Natural Language Processing*. pages 1589–1599.

Hannah Rashkin, Eunsol Choi, Jin Yea Jang, Svitlana Volkova, and Yejin Choi. 2017. Truth of varying shades: Analyzing language in fake news and political fact-checking. In *Proceedings of the Conference on Empirical Methods in Natural Language Processing*. pages 2921–2927.

Bhavtosh Rath, Wei Gao, Jing Ma, and Jaideep Srivastava. 2017. From retweet to believability: Utilizing trust to identify rumor spreaders on Twitter. In *Advances in Social Networks Analysis and Mining (ASONAM)*.

Victoria L Rubin, Niall J Conroy, Yimin Chen, and Sarah Cornwell. 2016. Fake news or truth? Using satirical cues to detect potentially misleading news. In *Proceedings of NAACL-HLT*. pages 7–17.

Kate Starbird. 2017. Examining the alternative media ecosystem through the production of alternative narratives of mass shooting events on Twitter. In *Proceedings of International AAAI Conference on Web and Social Media*. pages 230–239.

Kate Starbird, Jim Maddock, Mania Orand, Peg Achterman, and Robert M Mason. 2014. Rumors, false flags, and digital vigilantes: Misinformation on twitter after the 2013 boston marathon bombing. *iConference 2014 Proceedings* .

Bruno Takahashi, Edson C Tandoc, and Christine Carmichael. 2015. Communicating on twitter during a disaster: An analysis of tweets during typhoon haiyan in the philippines. *Computers in Human Behavior* 50:392–398.

Svitlana Volkova, Kyle Shaffer, Jin Yea Jang, and Nathan Hodas. 2017. Separating facts from fiction: Linguistic models to classify suspicious and trusted news posts on twitter. In *Proceedings of the 55th Annual Meeting of the Association for Computational Linguistics*. pages 647–653.

Soroush Vosoughi, Deb Roy, and Sinan Aral. 2018. The spread of true and false news online. *Science* 359(6380):1146–1151.

William Yang Wang. 2017. "Liar, liar pants on fire": A new benchmark dataset for fake news detection.

Ke Wu, Song Yang, and Kenny Q Zhu. 2015. False rumors detection on sina weibo by propagation structures. In *31st International Conference on Data Engineering (ICDE)*. IEEE, pages 651–662.

Li Zeng, Kate Starbird, and Emma S Spiro. 2016. Rumors at the speed of light? modeling the rate of rumor transmission during crisis. In *49th Hawaii International Conference on System Sciences (HICSS)*. IEEE, pages 1969–1978.

Amy Zhang, Bryan Culbertson, and Praveen Paritosh. 2017. Characterizing online discussion using coarse discourse sequences. In *Proceedings of International AAAI Conference on Web and Social Media*.

Content-based Popularity Prediction of Online Petitions Using a Deep Regression Model

Shivashankar Subramanian   **Timothy Baldwin**   **Trevor Cohn**
School of Computing and Information Systems
The University of Melbourne
shivashankar@student.unimelb.edu.au
{tbaldwin,t.cohn}@unimelb.edu.au

Abstract

Online petitions are a cost-effective way for citizens to collectively engage with policy-makers in a democracy. Predicting the popularity of a petition — commonly measured by its signature count — based on its textual content has utility for policy-makers as well as those posting the petition. In this work, we model this task using CNN regression with an auxiliary ordinal regression objective. We demonstrate the effectiveness of our proposed approach using UK and US government petition datasets.[1]

1 Introduction

A petition is a formal request for change or an action to any authority, co-signed by a group of supporters. Research has shown the impact of online petitions on the political system (Lindner and Riehm, 2011; Hansard, 2016; Bochel and Bochel, 2017). Modeling the factors that influence petition popularity — measured by the number of signatures a petition gets — can provide valuable insights to policy makers as well as those authoring petitions (Proskurnia et al., 2017).

Previous work on modeling petition popularity has focused on predicting popularity growth over time based on an initial popularity trajectory (Hale et al., 2013; Yasseri et al., 2017; Proskurnia et al., 2017), e.g. given the number of signatures a petition gets in the first x hours, prediction of the total number of signatures at the end of its lifetime. Asher et al. (2017) and Proskurnia et al. (2017) examine the effect of sharing petitions on Twitter on its overall success, as a time series regression

task. Other work has analyzed the importance of content on the success of the petition (Elnoshokaty et al., 2016). Proskurnia et al. (2017) also consider the anonymity of authors and petitions featured on the front-page of the website as additional factors. Huang et al. (2015) analyze 'power' users on petition platforms, and show their influence on other petition signers.

In general, the target authority for a petition can be political or non-political. In this work, we use petitions from the official UK and US government websites, whereby citizens can directly appeal to the government for action on an issue. In the case of UK petitions, they are guaranteed an official response at 10k signatures, and the guarantee of parliamentary debate on the topic at 100k signatures; in the case of US petitions, they are guaranteed a response from the government at 100k signatures. Political scientists refer to this as *advocacy democracy* (Dalton et al., 2003), in that people are able to engage with elected representatives directly. Our objective is to predict the popularity of a petition at the end of its lifetime, solely based on the petition text.

Elnoshokaty et al. (2016) is the closest work to this paper, whereby they target Change.org petitions and perform correlation analysis of popularity with the petition's category, target goal set,[2] and the distribution of words in General Inquirer categories (Stone et al., 1962). In our case, we are interested in the task of automatically predicting the number of signatures.

We build on the convolutional neural network (CNN) text regression model of Bitvai and Cohn (2015) to infer deep latent features. In addition, we evaluate the effect of an auxiliary ordinal regression objective, which can discriminate petitions that attract different scales of popular-

---

Proceedings of the 56th Annual Meeting of the Association for Computational Linguistics (Short Papers), pages 182–188
Melbourne, Australia, July 15 - 20, 2018. ©2018 Association for Computational Linguistics

ity (e.g., 10 signatures, the minimum count needed to not be closed vs. 10k signatures, the minimum count to receive a response from UK government).

Finally, motivated by text-based message propagation analysis work (Tan et al., 2014; Piotrkowicz et al., 2017), we hand-engineer features which capture wording effects on petition popularity, and measure the ability of the deep model to automatically infer those features.

2 Proposed Approach

Inspired by the successes of CNN for text categorization (Kim, 2014) and text regression (Bitvai and Cohn, 2015), we propose a CNN-based model for predicting the signature count. An outline of the model is provided in Figure 1. A petition has three parts: (1) title, (2) main content, and (3) (optionally) additional details.[3] We concatenate all three parts to form a single document for each petition. We have n petitions as input training examples of the form $\{a_i, y_i\}$, where a_i and y_i denote the text and signature count of petition i, respectively. Note that we log-transform the signature count, consistent with previous work (Elnoshokaty et al., 2016; Proskurnia et al., 2017).

We represent each token in the document via its pretrained GloVe embedding (Pennington et al., 2014), which we update during learning. We then apply multiple convolution filters with width one, two and three to the dense input document matrix, and apply a ReLU to each. They are then passed through a max-pooling layer with a tanh activation function, and finally a multi-layer perceptron via the exponential linear unit activation,

$$f(x) = \begin{cases} x, & \text{if } x > 0 \\ \alpha\left(\exp(x) - 1\right) & \text{otherwise}, \end{cases}$$

to obtain the final output (y_i), which is guaranteed to be positive. We train the model by minimizing mean squared error in log-space,

$$\mathcal{L}_{reg} = \frac{1}{n}\sum_{i=1}^{n} \|\hat{y}_i - y_i\|_2^2, \tag{1}$$

where $\hat{y}_i$ is the estimated signature count for petition i. We refer to this model as $\mathsf{CNN}_{regress}$.

2.1 Auxiliary Ordinal Regression Task

We augment the regression objective with an ordinal regression task, which discriminates petitions

---

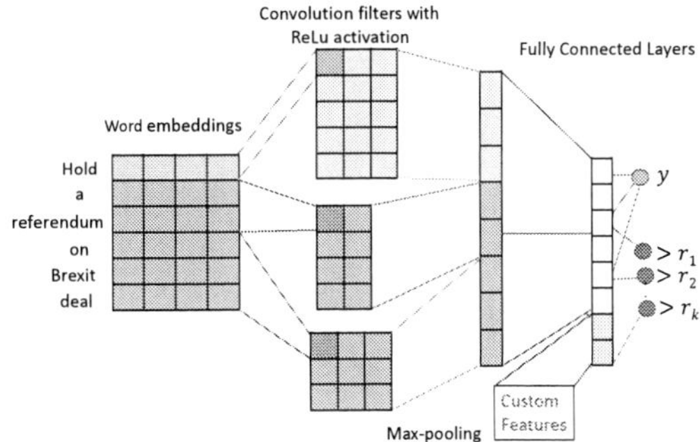

Figure 1: CNN-Regression Model. y denotes signature count. $> r_k$ is the auxiliary task that denotes p(petition attracting $> r_k$ signatures).

that achieve different scale of signatures. The intuition behind this is that there are pre-determined thresholds on signatures which trigger different events, with the most important of these being 10k (to guarantee a government response) and 100k (to trigger a parliamentary debate) for the UK petitions; and 100k (to get a government response) for the US petitions. In addition to predicting the number of signatures, we would like to be able to predict whether a petition is likely to meet these thresholds, and to this end we use the exponential ordinal scale based on the thresholds $O = \{10, 100, 1000, 10000, 100000\}$.[4] Overall this follows the exponential distribution of signature counts closely (Yasseri et al., 2017).

We transform the ordinal regression problem into a series of simpler binary classification subproblems, as proposed by Li and Lin (2007). We construct binary classification objectives for each threshold in O. For each petition i we construct an additional binary vector $\vec{o}_i$, with a 0–1 encoding for each of the ordinal classes ($\{a_i, y_i, \vec{o}_i\}$). Note that the transformation is done in a consistent way, i.e., if a petition has y signatures, then in addition to immediate lower-bound threshold in O determined by $l = \lfloor \log_{10} y \rfloor$ (for $y < 10^6$), all classes which have a lesser threshold are also set to 1 ($o_{t:t<l}$).

With this transformation, apart from the real-valued output y_i, we also learn a mapping from $\mathbf{h}_i$ with sigmoid activation for each class ($\vec{r}_i$). Finally we minimize cross-entropy loss for each binary classification task, denoted $\mathcal{L}_{aux}$.

---

[3] Applicable for the UK government petitions only.

[4] We use $O = \{1000, 10000, 100000\}$ for the US petitions, as only petitions which get a minimum of 150 signatures are published on the website.

Overall, the loss function for the joint model is:

$$\mathcal{L}_J = \mathcal{L}_{reg} + \gamma \mathcal{L}_{aux} \qquad (2)$$

where $\gamma \geq 0$ is a hyper-parameter which is tuned on the validation set. We refer to this model as $\text{CNN}_{regress+ord}$.

3 Hand-engineered Features

We hand-engineered custom features, partly based on previous work on non-petition text. This includes features from Tan et al. (2014) and Piotrkowicz et al. (2017) such as structure, syntax, bias, polarity, informativeness of title, and novelty (or freshness), in addition to novel features developed specifically for our task, such as policy category and political bias features. We provide a brief description of the features below:

- Additional Information (ADD): binary flag indicating whether the petition has additional details or not.
- Ratio of indefinite (IND) and definite (DEF) articles.
- Ratio of first-person singular pronouns (FSP), first-person plural pronouns (FPP), second-person pronouns (SPP), third-person singular pronouns (TSP), and third-person plural pronouns (TPP).
- Ratio of subjective words (SUBJ) and difference between count of positive and negative words (POL), based on General Inquirer lexicon.
- Ratio of biased words (BIAS) from the bias lexicon (Recasens et al., 2013).
- Syntactic features: number of nouns (NNC), verbs (VBC), adjectives (ADC) and adverbs (RBC).
- Number of named entities (NEC), based on the NLTK NER model (Bird et al., 2009).
- Freshness (FRE): cosine similarity with all previous petitions, inverse weighted by the difference in start date of petitions (in weeks).
- Action score of title (ACT): probability of title conveying the action requested. Predictions are obtained using an one-class SVM model built on the universal representation (Conneau et al., 2017) of titles of rejected petitions,[5] as they don't contain any action request. These rejected petitions are not part of our evaluation dataset.
- Policy category popularity score (CSC): commonality of the petition's policy issue (Subra-

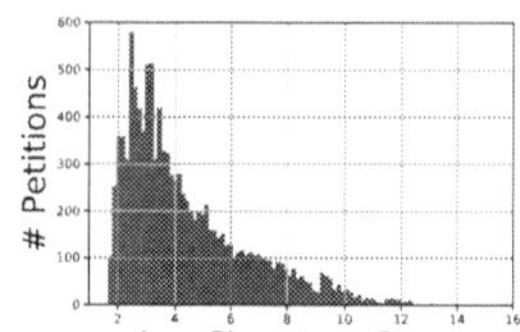

Figure 2: UK Petitions Signature Distribution.

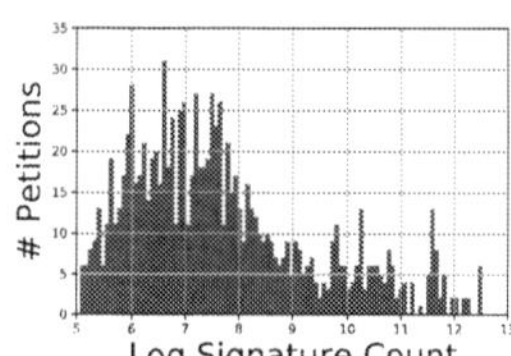

Figure 3: US Petitions Signature Distribution

manian et al., 2017), based on the recent UK/US election manifesto promises.

- Political bias and polarity: relative leaning/polarity based on: (a) $\frac{\#\text{left}+\#\text{right}}{\#\text{left}+\#\text{right}+\#\text{neutral}}$ (PBIAS) (b) $\frac{\#\text{left}-\#\text{right}}{\#\text{left}+\#\text{right}}$ (L–R). Sentence-level *left*, *right* and *neutral* classes are obtained using a model built on the CMP dataset, and the categorization given by Volkens et al. (2013).

The custom features are passed through a hidden layer with tanh activations ($\mathbf{c}_i$), and concatenated with the hidden representation learnt using the dense input document (Section 2), $\begin{bmatrix} \mathbf{h}_i \\ \mathbf{c}_i \end{bmatrix}$, before mapping to the output layer (Figure 1). We refer to this model as $\text{CNN}_{regress+ord+feat}$. We use the Adam optimizer (Kingma and Ba, 2014) to train all our models.

4 Evaluation

We collected our data from the UK[6] and US[7] government websites over the term of the 2015–17 Conservative and 2011–14 Democratic governments respectively. The UK dataset contains 10950 published petitions, with over 31m signatures in total. We removed US petitions with ≤ 150 signatures, resulting in a total of 1023 petitions, with over 12m signatures in total. We split the data chronologically into train/dev/test splits based on a 80/10/10 breakdown. Distribution over log signature counts is given in Figures 2 and 3.

To analyze the statistical significance of each feature varying across ordinal groups O, we ran

---

[5] https://petition.parliament.uk/help

[6] https://petition.parliament.uk
[7] https://petitions.whitehouse.gov/

a Kruskal-Wallis test (at $\alpha = 0.05$: Kruskal and Wallis (1952)) on the training set. The test results in the test statistic H and the corresponding p-value, with a high H indicating that there is a difference between the two groups. The analysis is given in Table 2, where $p < 0.001$, $p < 0.01$ and $p < 0.05$ are denoted as "***", "**" and "*", respectively. Note that the ordinal groups are different for the two datasets: analyzing the UK dataset with the same ordinal groups used for the US dataset ($\{1000, 10000, 100000\}$) resulted in a similarly sparse set of significance values for non-syntactic features as the US dataset.

We benchmark our proposed approach against the following baseline approaches:

Mean: average signature count in the raining set.

Linear$_{\text{BoW}}$: linear regression (Linear) model using TF-IDF weighted bag-of-words features.

Linear$_{\text{GI}}$: linear regression model based on word distributions from the General Inquirer lexicon; similar to (Elnoshokaty et al., 2016), but without the target goal set or category of the petition (neither of which is relevant to our datasets).

SVR$_{\text{BoW}}$: support vector regression (SVR) model with RBF kernel and TF-IDF weighted bag-of-words features.

SVR$_{\text{feat}}$: SVR model using the hand-engineered features from Section 3.

SVR$_{\text{BoW+feat}}$: SVR model using combined TF-IDF weighted bag-of-words and hand-engineered features.

We present the regression results for the baseline and proposed approaches based on: (1) mean absolute error (MAE), and (2) mean absolute percentage error (MAPE, similar to Proskurnia et al. (2017)), calculated as $\frac{100}{n} \sum_{i=1}^{n} \frac{|\hat{y}_i - y_i|}{y_i}$. Results are given in Table 1.

The proposed CNN models outperform all of the baselines. Comparing the CNN model with regression loss only, CNN$_{\text{regress}}$, and the joint model, CNN$_{\text{regress+ord}}$ is superior across both datasets and measures. When we add the hand-engineered features (CNN$_{\text{regress+ord+feat}}$), there is a very small improvement. In order to further understand the effect of the hand-engineering features without the ordinal regression loss, we use it only with the regression task (CNN$_{\text{regress+feat}}$), which mildly improves over CNN$_{\text{regress}}$, but is below CNN$_{\text{regress+ord+feat}}$. We also evaluate a variant of CNN$_{\text{regress+ord+feat}}$ with an additional hidden layer, given in the final row of Table 1, and find it to lead to further improvements in the regression results. Adding more hidden layers did not show further improvements.

4.1 Classification Performance

The F-score is calculated over the three classes of $[0, 10000)$, $[10000, 100000)$ and $[100000, \infty)$ (corresponding to the thresholds at which the petition leads to a government response or parliamentary debate) for the UK dataset; and $[150, 100000)$ and $[100000, \infty)$ for the US dataset, by determining if the predicted and actual signature counts are in the same bin or not. We also built an SVM-based ordinal classifier (Li and Lin, 2007) over the significant ordinal classes, as an additional baseline. The CNN models struggle to improve F-score (in large part due to the imbalanced data). For the UK dataset, CNN models with an ordinal objective (CNN$_{\text{regress+ord}}$ and CNN$_{\text{regress+ord+feat}}$) result in a macro-averaged F-score of 0.36, compared to 0.33 for all other methods. But for the US dataset, which is a binary classification task, all methods obtain a 0.49 F-score. In addition to text, considering other factors such as early signature growth (Hale et al., 2013) — which determines the timeliness to get the issue online on the US website — could be necessary.

4.2 Latent vs. Hand-engineered Features

Finally, we built a linear regression model with the estimated hidden features from CNN$_{\text{regress+ord}}$ as independent variables and hand-engineered features as dependent variables, to study their linear dependencies in a pair-wise fashion. The most significant dependencies (given by p-value, p_{hidden}) over the test set are given in Table 2. We found that the model is able to learn latent feature representations for syntactic features (NNC, VBC, ADC,[8] RBC[9]), FRE, NEC, IND and DEF,[8] but not the other features — these can be considered to provide deeper information than can be extracted automatically from the data, or else information that has no utility for the signature prediction task. From the analysis in Table 2, some of the features that vary across ordinal groups are not linearly dependent with the deep latent features. These include ADD,[8] BIAS, CSC,[8] PBIAS,[9] and L–R, where the latter ones are policy-related features. This indicates that the custom features and hidden features contain complementary signals.

---

[8]UK dataset only.
[9]US dataset only.

Approach	UK Petitions		US Petitions	
	MAE	MAPE	MAE	MAPE
Mean	4.37	159.7	2.82	44.61
$\text{Linear}_{\text{BoW}}$	1.75	57.56	2.51	37.01
$\text{Linear}_{\text{GI}}$	1.77	58.22	1.84	27.71
SVR_{BoW}	1.53	45.35	1.39	20.37
SVR_{feat}	1.54	46.96	1.40	20.48
$\text{SVR}_{\text{BoW+feat}}$	1.52	44.71	1.39	20.38
$\text{CNN}_{\text{regress}}$	1.44	36.72	1.24	14.98
$\text{CNN}_{\text{regress+ord}}$	1.42	33.86	1.22	14.68
$\text{CNN}_{\text{regress+ord+feat}}$	1.41	32.92	1.20	14.47
$\text{CNN}_{\text{regress+feat}}$	1.43	35.84	1.23	14.75
$\text{CNN}_{\text{regress+ord+feat}}$ + Additional hidden layer	**1.40**	**31.68**	**1.16**	**14.38**

Table 1: Results over UK and US Government petition datasets. Best scores are given in bold.

Feature	Description	UK Petitions			US Petitions		
		H	p	p_{hidden}	H	p	p_{hidden}
ADD	Additional details	94.59	***				
IND	Indefinite articles	14.87	*		8.56	*	*
DEF	Definite articles	34.91	***	*	3.69		
FSP	First-person singular pronouns	53.36	***		6.84	*	
FPP	First-person plural pronouns	11.26	*		6.10		
SPP	Second-person pronouns	13.80	*		3.95		
TSP	Third-person singular pronouns	5.82			9.07	*	
TPP	Third-person plural pronouns	16.13	**		5.58		
SUBJ	Subjective words	12.25	*		7.21	*	***
POL	Polarity	2.60		*	4.27		
BIAS	Biased words	11.92	*		4.56	*	
NNC	Nouns	7.34		***	1.93		**
VBC	Verbs	2.75		**	7.46	*	***
ADC	Adjectives	26.14	***	***	4.07		
RBC	Adverbs	17.09	**		2.99		*
NEC	Named entities	51.11	***	***	3.94		*
FRE	Freshness	86.97	***	*	13.86	**	*
ACT	Title's action score	3.89			3.54		
CSC	Policy category popularity	38.22	***		1.94		
PBIAS	Political bias	4.13			12.23	**	
L–R	Left–right scale	10.94	*		12.88	**	

Table 2: Dependency of hand-engineered features against the signature count (p and H) and deep hidden features (p_{hidden}). ADD is not applicable for the US government petitions dataset. $p < 0.001$, $p < 0.01$ and $p < 0.05$ are denoted as "***", "**" and "*", respectively.

Overall our proposed approach with the auxiliary loss and hand-engineered features ($\text{CNN}_{\text{regress+ord+feat}}$) provides a reduction in MAE over $\text{CNN}_{\text{regress}}$ by 2.1% and 3.2%, and SVR by 7.2% and 13.7% on the UK and US datasets, resp. Although the ordinal classification performance is not very high, it must be noted that the data is heavily skewed (only 2% of the UK test-set falls in the $[10000, 100000)$ and $[100000, \infty)$ bins put together), and we tuned the hyper-parameters wrt the regression task only.

5 Conclusion and Future Work

This paper has targeted the prediction of the popularity of petitions directed at the UK and US governments. In addition to introducing a novel task and dataset, contributions of our work include: (a) we have shown the utility of an auxiliary ordinal regression objective; and (b) determined which hand-engineered features are complementary to our deep learning model. In the future, we aim to study other factors that can influence petition popularity in conjunction with text, e.g., social media campaigns, news coverage, and early growth rates.

Acknowledgements

We thank the reviewers for their valuable comments. This work was funded in part by the Australian Government Research Training Program Scholarship, and the Australian Research Council.

References

Molly Asher, Cristina Leston Bandeira, and Viktoria Spaiser. 2017. Assessing the effectiveness of e-petitioning through Twitter conversations. *Political Studies Association (UK) Annual Conference.*

Steven Bird, Ewan Klein, and Edward Loper. 2009. *Natural Language Processing with Python.* O'Reilly Media.

Zsolt Bitvai and Trevor Cohn. 2015. Non-linear text regression with a deep convolutional neural network. In *Proceedings of the 53rd Annual Meeting of the Association for Computational Linguistics and the 7th International Joint Conference on Natural Language Processing*, pages 180–185.

Catherine Bochel and Hugh Bochel. 2017. 'Reaching in'? The potential for e-petitions in local government in the United Kingdom. *Information, Communication & Society*, 20(5):683–699.

Alexis Conneau, Douwe Kiela, Holger Schwenk, Loïc Barrault, and Antoine Bordes. 2017. Supervised learning of universal sentence representations from natural language inference data. In *Proceedings of the 2017 Conference on Empirical Methods in Natural Language Processing*, pages 670–680.

Russell J. Dalton, Susan E. Scarrow, and Bruce E. Cain. 2003. *Democracy Transformed?: Expanding Political Opportunities in Advanced Industrial Democracies.* Oxford University Press.

Ahmed Said Elnoshokaty, Shuyuan Deng, and Dong-Heon Kwak. 2016. Success factors of online petitions: Evidence from change.org. In *49th Hawaii International Conference on System Sciences*, pages 1979–1985.

Scott A. Hale, Helen Margetts, and Taha Yasseri. 2013. Petition growth and success rates on the UK No. 10 Downing Street website. In *Proceedings of the 5th Annual ACM Web Science Conference*, pages 132–138.

Hansard. 2016. *Audit of Political Engagement 13.* Hansard Society, London, UK.

Shih-Wen Huang, Minhyang Mia Suh, Benjamin Mako Hill, and Gary Hsieh. 2015. How activists are both born and made: An analysis of users on change.org. In *Proceedings of the 33rd Annual ACM Conference on Human Factors in Computing Systems*, pages 211–220.

Yoon Kim. 2014. Convolutional neural networks for sentence classification. In *Proceedings of the 2014 Conference on Empirical Methods in Natural Language Processing (EMNLP)*, pages 1746–1751.

Diederik P. Kingma and Jimmy Ba. 2014. Adam: A method for stochastic optimization. *CoRR*, abs/1412.6980.

William H. Kruskal and W. Allen Wallis. 1952. Use of ranks in one-criterion variance analysis. *Journal of the American Statistical Association*, 47(260):583–621.

Ling Li and Hsuan-Tien Lin. 2007. Ordinal regression by extended binary classification. In *Proceedings of the Advances in Neural Information Processing Systems*, pages 865–872.

Ralf Lindner and Ulrich Riehm. 2011. Broadening participation through e-petitions? An empirical study of petitions to the German parliament. *Policy & Internet*, 3(1):1–23.

Jeffrey Pennington, Richard Socher, and Christopher Manning. 2014. GloVe: Global vectors for word representation. In *Proceedings of the 2014 Conference on Empirical Methods in Natural Language Processing (EMNLP)*, pages 1532–1543.

Alicja Piotrkowicz, Vania Dimitrova, Jahna Otterbacher, and Katja Markert. 2017. Headlines matter: Using headlines to predict the popularity of news articles on Twitter and Facebook. In *Proceedings of the Eleventh International Conference on Web and Social Media*, pages 656–659.

Julia Proskurnia, Przemyslaw Grabowicz, Ryota Kobayashi, Carlos Castillo, Philippe Cudré-Mauroux, and Karl Aberer. 2017. Predicting the success of online petitions leveraging multidimensional time-series. In *Proceedings of the 26th International Conference on World Wide Web*, pages 755–764.

Marta Recasens, Cristian Danescu-Niculescu-Mizil, and Dan Jurafsky. 2013. Linguistic models for analyzing and detecting biased language. In *Proceedings of the 51st Annual Meeting of the Association for Computational Linguistics*, pages 1650–1659.

Philip J. Stone, Robert F. Bales, J. Zvi Namenwirth, and Daniel M. Ogilvie. 1962. The general inquirer: A computer system for content analysis and retrieval based on the sentence as a unit of information. *Systems Research and Behavioral Science*, 7(4):484–498.

Shivashankar Subramanian, Trevor Cohn, Timothy Baldwin, and Julian Brooke. 2017. Joint sentence-document model for manifesto text analysis. In *Proceedings of the 15th Annual Workshop of the Australasian Language Technology Association (ALTA)*, pages 25–33.

Chenhao Tan, Lillian Lee, and Bo Pang. 2014. The effect of wording on message propagation: Topic-and author-controlled natural experiments on Twitter. In *Proceedings of the 52nd Annual Meeting of the Association for Computational Linguistics*, pages 175–185.

Andrea Volkens, Judith Bara, Budge Ian, and Simon Franzmann. 2013. Understanding and validating the left-right scale (RILE). In *Mapping Policy Preferences From Texts: Statistical Solutions for Manifesto Analysts*, chapter 6. Oxford University Press.

Taha Yasseri, Scott A Hale, and Helen Z Margetts. 2017. Rapid rise and decay in petition signing. *EPJ Data Science*, 6(1):20.

Fighting Offensive Language on Social Media
with Unsupervised Text Style Transfer

Cicero Nogueira dos Santos[*]
IBM Research
T.J. Watson Research Center
cicerons@us.ibm.bom

Igor Melnyk[*]
IBM Research
T.J. Watson Research Center
igor.melnyk@ibm.com

Inkit Padhi[*]
IBM Watson
T.J. Watson Research Center
inkit.padhi@ibm.com

Abstract

We introduce a new approach to tackle the problem of offensive language in online social media. Our approach uses unsupervised text style transfer to *translate* offensive sentences into non-offensive ones. We propose a new method for training encoder-decoders using non-parallel data that combines a collaborative classifier, attention and the cycle consistency loss. Experimental results on data from Twitter and Reddit show that our method outperforms a state-of-the-art text style transfer system in two out of three quantitative metrics and produces reliable non-offensive transferred sentences.

1 Introduction

The use of offensive language is a common problem of abusive behavior on online social media networks. Various work in the past have attacked this problem by using different machine learning models to detect abusive behavior (Xiang et al., 2012; Warner and Hirschberg, 2012; Kwok and Wang, 2013; Wang et al., 2014; Nobata et al., 2016; Burnap and Williams, 2015; Davidson et al., 2017; Founta et al., 2018). Most of these work follow the assumption that it is enough to filter out the entire offensive post. However, a user that is consuming some online content may not want an entirely filtered out message but instead have it in a style that is non-offensive and still be able to comprehend it in a polite tone. On the other hand, for those users who plan to post an offensive message, if one could not only alert that a content is offensive and will be blocked, but also offer a polite version of the message that can be posted, this could encourage many users to change their mind and avoid the profanity.

In this work we introduce a new way to deal with the problem of offensive language on social media. Our approach consists on using style transfer techniques to *translate* offensive sentences into non-offensive ones. A simple encoder-decoder with attention (Bahdanau et al., 2014) would be enough to create a reasonable translator if a large parallel corpus is available. However, unlike machine translation, to the best of our knowledge, there exists no dataset of parallel data available for the case of offensive to non-offensive language. Moreover, it is important that the transferred text uses a vocabulary that is common in a particular application domain. Therefore, unsupervised methods that do not use parallel data are needed to perform this task.

We propose a method to perform text style transfer addressing two main challenges arising when using non-parallel data in the encoder-decoder framework: (a) there is no straightforward way to train the encoder-decoder because we cannot use maximum likelihood estimation on the transferred text due to lack of ground truth; (b) it is difficult to preserve content while transferring the input to a new style. We address (a) using a single collaborative classifier, as an alternative to commonly used adversarial discriminators, e.g., as in (Shen et al., 2017). We approach (b) by using the attention mechanism combined with a cycle consistency loss.

In this work we also introduce two benchmark datasets for the task of transferring offensive to non-offensive text that are based on data from two popular social media networks: Twitter and Reddit. We compare our method to the approach of Shen et al. (2017) using three quantitative metrics: classification accuracy, content preservation and perplexity. Additionally, some qualitative results are also presented with a brief error analysis.

---

[*]Equal contribution.

Proceedings of the 56th Annual Meeting of the Association for Computational Linguistics (Short Papers), pages 189–194
Melbourne, Australia, July 15 - 20, 2018. ©2018 Association for Computational Linguistics

2 Method

We assume access to a text dataset consisting of two non-parallel corpora $X = X_0 \cup X_1$ with different style values s_0 and s_1 (offensive and non-offensive) of a total of $N = m+n$ sentences, where $|X_0| = m$ and $|X_1| = n$. We denote a randomly sampled sentence k of style s_i from X as x_k^i, for $k \in 1, \dots, N$ and $i \in \{0, 1\}$. A natural approach to perform text style transfer is to use a regular encoder-decoder network. However, the training of such network would require parallel data. Since in this work we consider a problem of unsupervised style transfer on non-parallel data, we propose to extend the basic encoder-decoder by introducing a collaborative classifier and a set of specialized loss functions that enable the training on such data. Figure 1 shows an overview of the proposed style transfer approach. Note that for clarity, in Figure 1 we have used multiple boxes to show encoder, decoder and classifier, the actual model contains a single encoder and decoder, and one classifier.

As can be seen from Figure 1, the encoder (a GRU RNN, $E(x_k^i, s_i) = H_k^i$) takes as input a sentence x_k^i together with its style label s_i, and outputs H_k^i, a sequence of hidden states. The decoder/generator (also a GRU RNN, $G(H_k^i, s_j) = \hat{x}_k^{i \to j}$ for $i, j \in 0, 1$) takes as input the previously computed H_k^i and a desired style label s_j and outputs a sentence $\hat{x}_k^{i \to j}$, which is the original sentence but transferred from style s_i to style s_j. The hidden states H_k^i are used by the decoder in the attention mechanism (Bahdanau et al., 2014), and in general can improve the quality of the decoded sentence. When $i = j$, the decoded sentence $\hat{x}_k^{i \to i}$ is in its original style s_i (top part of Figure 1); for $i \neq j$, the decoded/transferred sentence $\hat{x}_k^{i \to j}$ is in a different style s_j (bottom part of Figure1). Denote all transferred sentences as $\hat{X} = \{\hat{x}_k^{i \to j} \mid i \neq j, k = 1, \dots, N\}$. The classifier (a CNN), then takes as input the decoded sentences and outputs a probability distribution over the style labels, i.e., $C(\hat{x}_k^{i \to j}) = p_C(s_j | \hat{x}_k^{i \to j})$ (see Eq. (2)). By using the collaborative classifier our goal is to produce a training signal that indicates the effectiveness of the current decoder on transferring a sentence to a given style.

Note that the top branch of Figure 1 can be considered as an auto-encoder and therefore we can enforce the closeness between $\hat{x}_k^{i \to i}$ and x_k^i by using a standard cross-entropy loss (see Eq. (1)). However, for the bottom branch, once we transferred X to $\hat{X}$ (forward-transfer step), due to the lack of parallel data, we cannot use the same approach. For this purpose, we propose to transfer $\hat{X}$ back to X (back-transfer step) and compute the reconstruction loss between $\hat{x}_k^{i \to j \to i}$ and x_k^i (see Eq. (4)). Note also that as we transfer the text forward and backward, we also control the accuracy of style transfer using the classifier (see Eqs. (2), (3) and (5)). In what follows, we present the details of the loss functions employed in training.

2.1 Forward Transfer

Reconstruction Loss. Given the encoded input sentence x_k^i and the decoded sentence $\hat{x}_k^{i \to i}$, the reconstruction loss measures how well the decoder G is able to reconstruct it:

$$\mathcal{L}_{rec} = \mathbb{E}_{x_k^i \sim X} \left[-\log p_G(x_k^i | E(x_k^i, s_i), s_i) \right]. \quad (1)$$

Classification Loss. Formulated as follows:

$$\mathcal{L}_{class\_td} = \mathbb{E}_{\hat{x}_k^{i \to j} \sim \hat{X}} \left[-\log p_C(s_j | \hat{x}_k^{i \to j}) \right]. \quad (2)$$

For the encoder-decoder this loss gives a feedback on the current generator's effectiveness on transferring sentences to a new style. For the classifier, it provides an additional training signal from generated data, enabling the classifier to be trained in a semi-supervised regime.

Classification Loss - Original Data. In order to enforce a high classification accuracy, the classifier also uses a supervised classification loss, measuring the classifier predictions on the original (supervised) instances $x_k^i \in X$:

$$\mathcal{L}_{class\_od} = \mathbb{E}_{x_k^i \sim X} \left[-\log p_C(s_i | x_k^i) \right]. \quad (3)$$

2.2 Backward Transfer

Reconstruction Loss. The *back-transfer (or cycle consistency) loss* (Zhu et al., 2017) is motivated by the difficulty of imposing constraints on the transferred sentences. Back-transfer transforms the transferred sentences $\hat{x}_k^{i \to j}$ back to the original style s_i, i.e., $\hat{x}_k^{i \to j \to i}$ and compares them to x_k^i. This also implicitly imposes the constraints on the generated sentences and improves the content preservation. The loss is formulated as follows:

$$\mathcal{L}_{back\_rec} = \mathbb{E}_{x_k^i \sim X} \left[-\log p_G(x_k^i | E(\hat{x}_k^{i \to j}, s_j), s_i) \right], \quad (4)$$

which can be thought to be similar to an auto-encoder loss in (1) but in the style domain.

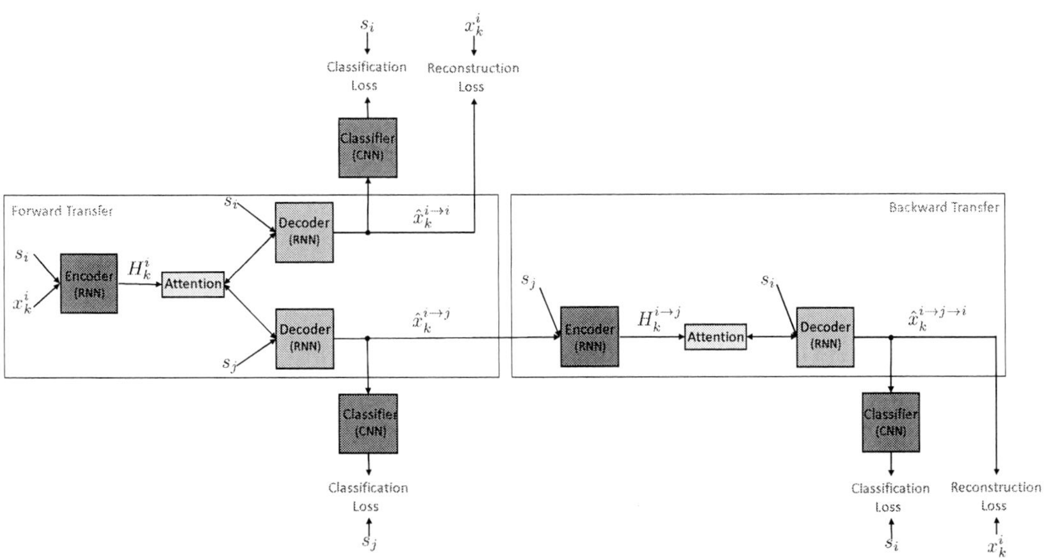

Figure 1: Proposed framework of a Neural Text Style Transfer algorithm using non-parallel data.

Classification Loss. Finally, we ensure that the back-transferred sentences $\hat{x}_k^{i\to j\to i}$ have the correct style label s_i:

$$\mathcal{L}_{class\_btd} = \mathbb{E}_{\hat{x}_k^{i\to j}\sim \hat{X}}\left[-\log p_C(s_i|G(E(\hat{x}_k^{i\to j}, s_j), s_i))\right]. \quad (5)$$

In summary, the training of the components of our architecture consists in optimizing the following loss function using SGD with back-propagation:

$$\mathcal{L}(\theta_E, \theta_G, \theta_C) = \min_{E,G,C} \mathcal{L}_{rec} + \mathcal{L}_{back\_rec}$$
$$+\mathcal{L}_{class\_od} + \mathcal{L}_{class\_td} + \mathcal{L}_{class\_btd}$$

3 Related Work

Most previous work that address the problem of offensive language on social media has focused on text classification using different machine learning methods (Xiang et al., 2012; Warner and Hirschberg, 2012; Kwok and Wang, 2013; Wang et al., 2014; Burnap and Williams, 2015; Nobata et al., 2016; Davidson et al., 2017; Founta et al., 2018). To the best of our knowledge, there is no previous work on approaching the offensive language problem using style transfer methods.

Different strategies for training encoder-decoders using non-parallel data have been proposed recently. Many of these methods borrow the idea of using an adversarial discriminator/classifier from the Generative Adversarial Networks (GANs) framework (Goodfellow et al., 2014) and/or use a cycle consistency loss. Zhu et al. (2017) proposed the pioneering use of the cycle consistency loss in GANs to perform image style transfer from non-parallel data. In the NLP area, some recent effort has been done on the use of non-parallel data for style/content transfer (Shen et al., 2017; Melnyk et al., 2017; Fu et al., 2018) and machine translation (Lample et al., 2018; Artetxe et al., 2018). Shen et al. (2017), Fu et al. (2018) and Lample et al. (2018) use adversarial classifiers as a way to force the decoder to transfer the encoded source sentence to a different style/language. Lample et al. (2018) and Artetxe et al. (2018) use the cycle consistency loss to enforce content preservation in the translated sentences. Our work differs from the previous mentioned work in different aspects: we propose a new relevant style transfer task that has not been previously explored; our proposed method combines a collaborative classifier with the cycle consistency loss, which gives more stable results. Note that a potential extension to a problem of multiple attributes transfer would still use a single classifier, while in (Shen et al., 2017; Fu et al., 2018) this may require as many discriminators as the number of attributes.

Another line of research connected to this work consists in the automatic text generation conditioned on stylistic attributes. (Hu et al., 2017) and (Ficler and Goldberg, 2017) are examples of this line of work which use labeled data during training.

4 Experiments

4.1 Datasets

We created datasets of offensive and non-offensive texts by leveraging Henderson et al. (2018)'s pre-processing of Twitter (Ritter et al., 2010) and Reddit Politics (Serban et al., 2017) corpora, which contain a large number of social media posts. Henderson et al. (2018) have used Twitter and Reddit datasets to evaluate the impact of offensive language and hate speech in neural dialogue systems.

We classified each entry in the two datasets using the offensive language and hate speech classifier from (Davidson et al., 2017). For Reddit, since the posts are long, we performed the classification at the sentence level. We note that since ground truth (parallel data) is not available, it is important to use the same classifier for data generation and evaluation so as to have a fair comparison and avoid inconsistencies. Therefore, we use the classifier from (Davidson et al., 2017) to test the performance of the compared algorithms in Sec. 4.3.

For our experiments, we used sentences/tweets with size between 2 and 15 words and removed repeated entries, which were frequent in Reddit. The final datasets have the following number of instances: Twitter - train [58,642 / 1,962,224] (offensive / non-ofensive), dev [7842] (offensive), test [7734]; Reddit - [224,319 / 7,096,473], dev [11,883], test [30,583] . In both training sets the number of non-offensive entries is much larger than of the offensive ones, which is not a problem since the objective is to have the best possible transfer to the non-offensive domain. We limited the vocabulary size by using words with frequency equal or larger than 70 (20) in Reddit (Twitter) dataset. All the other words are replaced by a placeholder token.

4.2 Experimental Setup

In all the presented experiments, we have used the same model parameters and the same configuration: the encoder/decoder is a single layer GRU RNN with 200 hidden neurons; the classifier is a single layer CNN with a set of filters of width 1, 2, 3 and 4, and size 128 (the same configuration as in the discriminators of (Shen et al., 2017)). Following (Shen et al., 2017), we have also used randomly initialized word embeddings of size 100, and trained the model using Adam optimizer with the mini-batch size of 64 and learning rate of 0.0005. The validation set has been used to select the best model

by early stopping. Our model has a quite fast convergence rate and achieves good results within just 1 epoch for the Reddit dataset and 5 epochs for the Twitter dataset.

Our baseline is the model of Shen et al. (2017)[1] and it has been used with the default hyperparameter setting proposed by the authors. We have trained the baseline neural net for three days using a K40 GPU machine, corresponding to about 13 epochs on the Twitter dataset and 5 epochs on the Reddit dataset. The validation set has also been used to select the best model by early stopping.

4.3 Results and Discussion

Although the method proposed in this paper can be used to transfer text in both directions, we are interested in transferring in the direction of offensive to non-offensive only. Therefore, all the results reported in this section correspond to this direction.

In Table 1, we compare our method with the approach of Shen et al. (2017) using three quantitative metrics: (1) *classification accuracy* (Acc.), which we compute by applying Davidson et al. (2017)'s classifier to the transferred test sentences; (2) *content preservation* (CP), a metric recently proposed by Fu et al. (2018) which uses pre-trained word embeddings to compute the content similarity between transferred and original sentences. We use Glove embeddings of size 300 (Pennington et al., 2014); (3) *perplexity* (PPL), which is computed by a word-level LSTM language model trained using the non-offensive training sentences.

Dataset	System	Acc.	CP	PPL
Reddit	[Shen17]	87.66	0.894	**93.59**
	Ours	**99.54**	**0.933**	115.75
Twitter	[Shen17]	95.36	0.891	**90.97**
	Ours	**99.63**	**0.947**	162.75

Table 1: Classification accuracy, content preservation and perplexity for two datasets.

As can be seen from the table, our proposed method achieves high accuracy on both datasets, which means that almost 100% of the time Davidson et al. (2017)'s classifier detects that the transferred sentences are non-offensive. In terms of the content preservation, for both datasets our method also produces better results (the closer to 1 the better) when compared to (Shen et al., 2017) . A

---

[1] https://github.com/shentianxiao/language-style-transfer

	Reddit	**Twitter**
Original	*for f**k sake , first world problems are the worst*	i 'm back bitc**s ! ! !
(Shen et al., 2017)	for the money , are one different countries	i 'm back ! ! !
Ours	for hell sake , first world problems are the worst	i 'm back bruh ! ! !
Original	*what a f**king circus this is .*	*lol damn imy fake as* lol*
(Shen et al., 2017)	what a this sub is bipartisan .	lol damn imy sis lol
Ours	what a big circus this is .	lol dude imy fake face lol
Original	*i hope they pay out the as* , fraudulent or no .*	*bros before hoes*
(Shen et al., 2017)	i hope the work , we out the UNK and no .	club tomorrow
Ours	i hope they pay out the state , fraudulent or no .	bros before money

Table 2: Example of offensive sentences from Reddit and Twitter and their respective transferred versions.

> what *big* century are you living in ?
> life is so *big* cheap to some people .
> you 're *big* pathetic .

Table 3: Examples of common mistakes made by our proposed model.

reason for these good results can be found by checking the examples presented in Table 2. The use of the back transfer loss and the attention mechanism makes our model good at preserving the original sentence content while being precise at replacing offensive words by the non-offensive ones. Also observe from Table 2 that, quite often, Shen et al. (2017)'s model changes many words in the original sentence, significantly modifying the content.

On the other hand, our model produces worse results in terms of perplexity values. We believe this can be due to one type of mistake that is frequent among the transferred sentences and that is illustrated in Table 3. The model uses the same non-offensive word (e.g. *big*) to replace an offensive word (e.g. *f***ing*) almost everywhere, which produces many unusual and unexpected sentences.

We have performed ablation experiments by removing some components of the proposed model. The results for the Twitter dataset are shown in Table 4. We can see that attention and back-transfer loss play important roles in the model. In particular, when both of them are removed (last row in Table 4), although the classification accuracy improves, the perplexity and the content preservation drop significantly. This behavior happens due to the trade off that the decoder has to balance when transferring a sentence from a style to another. The decoder must maintain a proper balance between transferring to the correct style and generating sentences of good quality. Each of these properties can easily be achieved on its own, e.g., copying the entire input sentence will give low perplexity and

good content preservation but low accuracy, on the other hand, outputting a single keyword can give high accuracy but high perplexity and low content preservation. While the classification loss guides the decoder to generate sentences that belong to the target style, the back transfer loss and the attention mechanism encourage the decoder to copy words from the input sentence. When both back transfer loss and attention are removed, the model is encouraged to just meet the classification requirement in the transfer step.

System	**Acc.**	**CP**	**PPL**
Full	99.63	**0.947**	**162.75**
No Attention	99.88	0.939	196.65
No Back Transfer	97.08	0.938	257.93
No Att & Back Trans	**100.0**	0.876	751.56

Table 4: Ablation results for the Twitter dataset.

It is important to note that current unsupervised text style transfer approaches can only handle well cases where the offensive language problem is lexical (such as the examples shown in Table 2), and just changing/removing few words can solve the problem. The models experimented in this work will not be effective in cases of implicit bias where ordinarily inoffensive words are used offensively.

5 Conclusions

This work is a first step in the direction of a new promising approach for fighting abusive posts on social media. Although we focus on offensive language, we believe that further improvements on the proposed methods will allow us to cope with other types of abusive behaviors.

References

Mikel Artetxe, Gorka Labaka, Eneko Agirre, and Kyunghyun Cho. 2018. Unsupervised neural machine translation. In *International Conference on Learning Representations*.

D. Bahdanau, K. Cho, and Y. Bengio. 2014. Neural machine translation by jointly learning to align and translate. In *Proceedings of the International Conference on Learning Representations*.

Pete Burnap and Matthew L. Williams. 2015. Cyber hate speech on twitter: An application of machine classification and statistical modeling for policy and decision making. *Policy & Internet* 7(2):223–242.

Thomas Davidson, Dana Warmsley, Michael Macy, and Ingmar Weber. 2017. Automated hate speech detection and the problem of offensive language. In *Proceedings of the 11th International AAAI Conference on Web and Social Media*. pages 512–515.

Jessica Ficler and Yoav Goldberg. 2017. Controlling linguistic style aspects in neural language generation. In *Workshop on Stylistic Variation*.

A.-M. Founta, D. Chatzakou, N. Kourtellis, J. Blackburn, A. Vakali, and I. Leontiadis. 2018. A unified deep learning architecture for abuse detection. *ArXiv e-prints* .

Zhenxin Fu, Xiaoye Tan, Nanyun Peng, Dongyan Zhao, and Rui Yan. 2018. Style transfer in text: Exploration and evaluation. In *Proceedings of AAAI*.

Ian Goodfellow, Jean Pouget-Abadie, Mehdi Mirza, Bing Xu, David Warde-Farley, Sherjil Ozair, Aaron Courville, and Yoshua Bengio. 2014. Generative adversarial nets. In *Advances in neural information processing systems*. pages 2672–2680.

Peter Henderson, Koustuv Sinha, Nicolas Angelard-Gontier, Nan Rosemary Ke, Genevieve Fried, Ryan Lowe, and Joelle Pineau. 2018. Ethical challenges in data-driven dialogue systems. In *Proceedings of the AAAI/ACM conference on Artificial Intelligence, Ethics, and Society*.

Zhiting Hu, Zichao Yang, Xiaodan Liang, Ruslan Salakhutdinov, and Eric P. Xing. 2017. Toward controlled generation of text. In *Proceedings of the 34th International Conference on Machine Learning*. pages 1587–1596.

Irene Kwok and Yuzhou Wang. 2013. Locate the hate: Detecting tweets against blacks. In *Proceedings of the Twenty-Seventh AAAI Conference on Artificial Intelligence*. pages 1621–1622.

Guillaume Lample, Alexis Conneau, Ludovic Denoyer, and Marc'Aurelio Ranzato. 2018. Unsupervised machine translation using monolingual corpora only. In *International Conference on Learning Representations*.

Igor Melnyk, Cicero Nogueira dos Santos, Kahini Wadhawan, Inkit Padhi, and Abhishek Kumar. 2017. Improved neural text attribute transfer with non-parallel data. In *NIPS Workshop on Learning Disentangled Representations: from Perception to Control*.

Chikashi Nobata, Joel Tetreault, Achint Thomas, Yashar Mehdad, and Yi Chang. 2016. Abusive language detection in online user content. In *Proceedings of the 25th International Conference on World Wide Web*. pages 145–153.

Jeffrey Pennington, Richard Socher, and Christopher D. Manning. 2014. Glove: Global vectors for word representation. In *Empirical Methods in Natural Language Processing (EMNLP)*. pages 1532–1543. http://www.aclweb.org/anthology/D14-1162.

Alan Ritter, Colin Cherry, and Bill Dolan. 2010. Unsupervised modeling of twitter conversations. In *The 2010 Annual Conference of the NAACL*. pages 172–180.

Iulian Vlad Serban, Chinnadhurai Sankar, Mathieu Germain, Saizheng Zhang, Zhouhan Lin, Sandeep Subramanian, Taesup Kim, Michael Pieper, Sarath Chandar, Nan Rosemary Ke, Sai Mudumba, Alexandre de Brébisson, Jose Sotelo, Dendi Suhubdy, Vincent Michalski, Alexandre Nguyen, Joelle Pineau, and Yoshua Bengio. 2017. A deep reinforcement learning chatbot. *CoRR* .

T. Shen, T. Lei, R. Barzilay, and T. Jaakkola. 2017. Style transfer from non-parallel text by cross-alignment. In *Advances in Neural Information Processing Systems*.

Wenbo Wang, Lu Chen, Krishnaprasad Thirunarayan, and Amit P. Sheth. 2014. Cursing in english on twitter. In *Proceedings of the 17th ACM Conference on Computer Supported Cooperative Work and Social Computing*. pages 415–425.

William Warner and Julia Hirschberg. 2012. Detecting hate speech on the world wide web. In *Proceedings of the Second Workshop on Language in Social Media*. pages 19–26.

Guang Xiang, Bin Fan, Ling Wang, Jason Hong, and Carolyn Rose. 2012. Detecting offensive tweets via topical feature discovery over a large scale twitter corpus. In *Proceedings of the 21st ACM International Conference on Information and Knowledge Management*. pages 1980–1984.

Jun-Yan Zhu, Taesung Park, Phillip Isola, and Alexei A Efros. 2017. Unpaired image-to-image translation using cycle-consistent adversarial networks. *arXiv preprint arXiv:1703.10593* .

Diachronic degradation of language models:
Insights from social media

Kokil Jaidka
Computer & Information Science
University of Pennsylvania
jaidka@sas.upenn.edu

Niyati Chhaya
Big Data Experience Lab
Adobe Research
nchhaya@adobe.com

Lyle H. Ungar
Computer & Information Science
University of Pennsylvania
ungar@cis.upenn.edu

Abstract

Natural languages change over time because they evolve to the needs of their users and the socio-technological environment. This study investigates the diachronic accuracy of pre-trained language models for downstream tasks in machine learning and user profiling. It asks the question: given that the social media platform and its users remain the same, how is language changing over time? How can these differences be used to track the changes in the affect around a particular topic? To our knowledge, this is the first study to show that it is possible to measure diachronic semantic drifts *within* social media and *within* the span of a few years.

1 Introduction

Natural languages are dynamic–they are constantly evolving and adapting to the needs of their users and the environment of their use (Frermann and Lapata, 2016). The arrival of large-scale collections of historic texts and online libraries and Google Books have greatly facilitated computational investigations of language change over the span of decades. Diachronic differences measure semantic drift specifically for languages over time. For instance, the meaning of the word 'follow' has changed from a reference, then to surveillance, and finally to the act of subscribing to a social media user's feed. In a quantitative analysis, diachronic differences may explain why predictive models go 'stale'. For instance, a sentiment model trained on Victorian-era language would label 'aweful' as positive sentiment; however, in contemporary usage, 'awful' is considered a negative word (Wijaya and Yeniterzi, 2011). Thus mo-

tivated, we raise the following research questions:

- How do language models trained at one point in time, perform at predicting age and gender on language from a subsequent time?
- What is the practical benefit of measuring diachronic differences on Twitter?

To our knowledge, there is no existing work which has investigated whether, and how, language models degrade over time, i.e. why predictive models trained on an older sample of language, may fail to work on contemporary language. While previous studies have explored the change in word meanings spanning decades or hundreds of years, we address a research gap by exploring finer temporal granularity and using a more accessible language corpus. Twitter's[1] discourse is rather different from traditional English writing. So far, word embeddings trained on Twitter (Kulkarni et al., 2015; Mikolov et al., 2013) have considered it a static corpus, and have not used it to study short term changes in word connotations. It contributes with the following observations:

- Diachronic differences are greater (hence, language change is faster) for younger social media users than older social media users.
- Diachronic language differences enable the measurement of the change in social attitudes (captured by word embeddings).

In order to study this phenomenon, we define the notion of *temporal cohorts* as a set of social media users who have posted on Twitter during the same time period, e.g., in the year 2011. In this study, we evaluate the linguistic differences between temporal cohorts, e.g. 20-year-olds in 2011 vs. 20-year-olds in 2015.

---

[1] https://twitter.com/

195

Proceedings of the 56th Annual Meeting of the Association for Computational Linguistics (Short Papers), pages 195–200
Melbourne, Australia, July 15 - 20, 2018. ©2018 Association for Computational Linguistics

2   Related work

A number of studies have built language models to predict users' age and gender (Sap et al., 2014), personality (Schwartz et al., 2013) and other traits (Jaidka et al., 2018a) with high accuracy from a sample of their social media posts. We offer the explanation that these language models may have 'degraded' due to the diachronic changes in language over the past few years, as compared to the predictions on their posts in 2011, which is closer to the time period for which their model was actually trained (see Figure 1).

The work by Frerman and Lapata (2016) quantified meaning change in terms of emerging meanings over many time periods, on a corpus collating documents spanning the years 1700-2010. Studies measuring semantic drift using word embedding models trained on Twitter corpora, such as Twitter GloVe and Word2Vec (Mikolov et al., 2013; Kulkarni et al., 2015), have considered microblog posts a static resource, reflective of modern language usage at a single point in time. Szymanski (2017) highlights the need to explore it in contemporary language e.g. social media. We illustrate that it is possible to measure diachronic semantic drifts *within* social media and *within* the span of a few years. Furthermore, we are arguing that year-related change affects different cohorts differently.

We use part-of-speech information about word embeddings to better understand semantic drift in terms of the adjective and affective words used to connotate everyday concepts. In doing so, we follow the approach outlined in previous work by Gart et al. (2017) and Hamilton et al. (2016a) to consider different kinds of contexts (e.g., adjectives, verbs and emotion words) to learn and compare distributional representations of target words.

3   Method

We first establish the diachronic validity of language-based models through predictive evaluations. We then use topic models and word embeddings as the quantitative lens through which to study the diachronic differences in the language of social media users, and linear methods to easily interpret the differences between standardized coefficients as diachronic differences in user trait prediction from language.

3.1   Predictive validity

We test the predictive performance of language models trained on a year's worth of social media posts from a subset of users who have provided their age and gender information.

- We train language models on the age- and gender-labeled primary dataset and evaluate their diachronic validity (Hamilton et al., 2016b), i.e. their predictive performance on subsequently collected language samples.
- We identify age groups which drift faster than others by reporting predictive performance on users, stratified by year of birth.

3.2   Language insights about diachronic differences

We use language for the following insights into diachronic drift:

- **Important changes**: For each temporal cohort, we identify the language features which have the most drift in terms of recalibrated coefficients, in regression models trained in 2011 vs. 2015. In doing so, we follow the approach described by Rieman et al. (2017) to compare the standardized coefficients of the age and gender models trained on the language samples from 2011 and 2015.
- **High drift concepts**: We use word embeddings to identify the semantic differences in the connotations around common concepts, for two sets of users who are a generation apart. Following the framework proposed by Garg et al. (2017), we calculate semantic drift as the changes in the relative normalized distance for the context words describing a set of target concepts.

Target concepts comprise a group of words representing a single idea (Garg et al., 2017), for instance, *positive emotion*, derived from the LIWC psycholinguistic dictionary (Pennebaker et al., 2007), and sexual orientation and gender expression (*LGBTQ issues*), based on a glossary on LGBTQ terms provided by the Human Rights Campaign [2]. We use the relative norm distance to identify the contextual words (mainly adjectives, adverbs and sentiment words) that are *most different* across the two word embedding models. Regular expression matching for part-of-speech, sentiment and emotion words was based on LIWC and the NRC emotion lexicon (Mohammad et al.,

---

[2]https://www.hrc.org/resources/glossary-of-terms

2013). Among a variety of distance metrics, euclidean distances provided the most interpretable results.

4 Datasets and Pre-processing

Primary data: Our primary dataset consists of the Twitter posts of adults in the United States of America who were recruited by Qualtrics (a crowdsourcing platform similar to Amazon Mechanical Turk) for an online survey, and consented to share access to their Twitter posts. This data was collected in a previous study by Preoţiuc-Pietro et al. (2017) and is available online [3]. We restrict our analysis to tweets posted between January 2011 and December 2015, by those users who indicated English as a primary language, have written at least 10 posts in their posts in each year, and have reported age and binary gender as a part of the survey. This resulted in a dataset of $N = 554$ users, who wrote a mean of 265 and a median of 156 posts per year and over 13.5 million words collectively. The mean age of the population was 33.54 years. 59% of them self-identified as male.

Decahose (Twitter 10%) dataset: For insights based on word embeddings, we used the decahose samples for the years 2011 and 2014 collected by the TrendMiner project (Preotiuc-Pietro et al., 2012), which comprises a 10% random sample of the real-time Twitter firehose using a realtime sampling algorithm. To match with our primary data, we used bounding boxes to consider only those tweets with geolocation information which were posted in the United States. In this manner, we obtained 130 and 179 million Twitter posts for 2011 and 2014 respectively.

Pre-processing: In a dataset of 554 users, the absolute vocabulary overlap may be low. By converting each users string of words into their probabilistic usage of 2000 topics, we expected to get more stable estimates than using word-based language models. We represent the language of each user as a probabilistic distribution of 2000 topics derived using Latent Dirichlet Allocation (LDA) with α set to 0.30 to favor fewer topics per document. These topics are modeled as open-ended clusters of words from actual distributions in social media over approximately 18 million Facebook updates, and are provided as an open-sourced resource in the DLATK python toolkit (Schwartz et al., 2017).

Predictive evaluation: We use Python's sklearn library to conduct a ten-fold cross-validation and train weighted linear regression models for age, and binary logistic regression models for gender, on the LDA-derived features for users in nine folds, and test on the users in the held out fold. We use feature selection, elastic-net regularization, and randomized PCA to avoid over-fitting. Although we tested other linguistic features such as n-grams, the best predictive performance was for models trained on the topic features.

Word embeddings: We separately train word embeddings on the language of the Twitter 10% sample from 2011, and the sample from 2014. We use Google's Tensorflow framework (Abadi et al., 2016) to optimize the prediction of co-occurrence relationships using an approximate objective known as skip-gram with negative sampling (Mikolov et al., 2013) with incremental initialization and optimizing our embeddings with a stochastic gradient descent. Embeddings were trained using the top-50000 words by their average frequency over the entire time period. A similar threshold has also been applied in previous papers (Hamilton et al., 2016a,b). We experimented with different window sizes and parameter settings, finally choosing a window size of 4, embeddings with 1000 dimensions, and the negative sample prior α set to $log(5)$ and the number of negative samples set to 500.[4]

5 Results

5.1 Predictive performance

In Figure 1, we report performance error in predicting age as the mean of $(actual - predicted)$ in order to better understand the model bias towards predicting younger or older ages.

We observe that the age- and gender- predictive models by Sap et al. (2014) **degrade in performance on language samples from more recent years**. They have a lower mean error in age prediction and higher accuracy in gender prediction on the a language sample from 2011 as compared to 2015; yet, our test sets are ostensibly drawn from the same corpus as the original training data. This shows that even models trained on large datasets show performance degradation if they are tested against newer language samples for the same set of users. We observe the same

---

[3]https://web.sas.upenn.edu/danielpr/resources/

[4]The trained word embedding models can be downloaded from http://www.wwbp.org/publications.html

Age (Mean Error)							Gender (Accuracy %)					
Test set	Sap et. al	2011	2012	2013	2014	2015	Sap et. al	2011	2012	2013	2014	2015
2011	2.2	0.0	0.2	1.1	1.6	1.8	83	.86	.79	.75	.75	.75
2012	3.1	0.2	-0.1	1.1	1.8	2.1	82	.78	.87	.78	.77	.74
2013	3.9	-0.2	-0.3	0.4	0.9	1.2	80	.78	.78	.87	.77	.77
2014	4.4	-1.2	-1.2	-1.1	0.0	0.7	77	.78	.78	.84	.84	.72
2015	5.0	-1.3	-1.5	-1.3	-0.4	0.0	75	.77	.78	.77	.77	.87

Figure 1: Cross-year performance for predicting (a) age (reported as $MeanError = Age_{actual} - Age_{predicted}$) and (b) gender (reported as Accuracy). The columns depict the training set for regression models: language samples posted in a particular year. The rows depict the test sets. Deeper shades of blue reflect higher underestimation errors; deeper shades of red reflect higher overestimation errors. Deeper shades of green depict higher accuracy.

trends on in-sample models trained and tested on our primary data (see Figure 1). Age and gender models perform the best when tested on a sample from the same year, but age models degrade in performance over time, with older models tending to **over-predict** the age on subsequent samples. Newer models tend to **under-predict** the age on older samples of language. Taken together, these insights suggest that the rate of change in age (1 unit per year) is less than the rate of change in language use. Gender models demonstrate an approximately 7-12% drop in accuracy for subsequent or older years.

In the next step, we attempt to understand the rate of change of language for social media users of different ages, which show larger variance as compared to gender. Figure 2 provides the results for a language model trained on the language sample of 2011 and tested to predict age from a language sample from 2011 and the subsequent years. The columns depict the birth year for users in the test set. This figure provides some important insights:

1. The first row has the smallest mean errors, which is expected since it is an in-sample prediction of a 2011-trained language model on itself.

2. The largest mean errors are seen at the bottom left, where the model is consistently **under-predicting** the age of older social media users whose language usage has little change over 5 years.

3. In the bottom-right, social media users born between 1992-1997 observe the highest **overestimation** errors as they 'sound' older than they are. Despite their annual increment in age, the model still **overpredicts** their age by approximately twice as many years.

5.2 Insights about Diachronic Differences

We want to understand performance degradation in terms of the change in the associations of linguistic features associated with higher age or with one of the genders. The age range in 2011 were [14, 41] years and in 2015 were [18, 45] years respectively. To explore diachronic differences in topic usage across two age-matched populations, we subset the population to the subjects to the age range of [18, 41] years during 2011-2015 (N=429).

Important changes: In Table 1, we compare the standardized coefficients (p < .001) of the predictors in models trained on the language of the year 2011 against those of 2015. We observe that a lot of the topics typically associated with older social media users in the 2011 model, [5] such as swearing, tiredness and sleep, changed their age bias. On the other hand, topics popular among younger social media users – for instance, topics mentioning employable skills and meetings, percolated upward as the early adopters of social media grew older. In the case of gender, topics related to business meetings, the government, computers, and money were no longer predictive of males, while topics associated with proms, relationships, and hairstyles were no longer predictive of females. [6]

Age	β_{2011}	β_{2015}
Email communication: *(send, email, message, contact)*	168.5	-53.7
Accommodation *(place, stay, found, move)*	162.2	-101.8
Sleep *(bed, lay, sleep, head, tired)*	59.6	-88.5
Swear *(wtf, damn, sh**, wth, wrong, pissed)*	38.1	-46.0
Tiredness *(i'm, sick, tired, feeling, hearing)*	33.6	-98.3
Hacking *(virus, called, open, steal, worm, system)*	-99.6	253.5
Software *(computer, error, photoshop, server, website)*	-87.2	80.7
Feeling *(feeling, weird, awkward, strange, dunno)*	-70.5.0	23.2
Meetings *(meeting, conference, student, council, board)*	-44.0	38.6
Skills *(management, business, learning, research)*	-26.4	158.0
Gender	$\beta_{2011}*$	$\beta_{2015}*$
Apple products *(iphone, apple, ipad, mac, download)*	4.1	(0)
Sports *(win, lose, game, betting, streak, change)*	3.2	(0)
Bills *(pay, money, paid, job, rent)*	2.8	(0)
Government *(government, freedom, country, democracy)*	2.8	(0)
Prom *(dress, prom, shopping, formal, homecoming)*	1.8	(0)
Hairstyles *(hair, blonde, dye, color, highlights)*	1.7	(0)
Relationships *(amazing, boyfriend, wonderful, absolutely)*	1.7	(0)
Negative emotions *(inside, deep, feel, heart, pain, empty)*	1.6	(0)

Table 1: The features whose coefficients had the biggest change and flipped sign when comparing the age and gender prediction models trained on 2011 language against those trained on 2015 language. (0) depicts that the feature was no longer significant in the 2015 model. *:(X10⁻4)

High drift concepts: We now illustrate diachronic differences in terms of the changing context around the *same* concept, in Table 2. We have

---

[5] See Schwartz et al. (2013)

[6] We also estimated feature importance through an ablation analysis, according to the difference made to the overall prediction ($\sum w_i x \beta_i$), which also yielded similar results.

Test set year	1970	1971	1972	1973	1974	1975	1976	1977	1978	1979	1980	1981	1982	1983	1984	1985	1986	1987	1988	1989	1990	1991	1992	1993	1994	1995	1996	1997
2011	4.4	4.6	4.7	5.1	3.4	1.7	1.8	1.4	0.7	0.9	-0.1	-1.0	-0.9	0.0	-3.5	-2.7	-2.0	-4.3	-4.9	-2.5	-4.0	-4.3	-3.3	-2.7	-4.8	-5.6	-3.1	-2.7
2012	6.5	5.0	6.8	6.2	4.4	3.1	3.2	3.1	1.2	2.2	-1.1	-0.8	-1.2	-2.1	-3.7	-2.9	-2.9	-5.2	-6.0	-2.9	-5.6	-2.9	-4.3	-4.7	-4.0	-7.2	-3.9	-6.1
2013	8.4	6.0	8.2	5.6	6.5	4.2	4.1	3.0	0.5	1.3	-0.4	0.2	-0.8	-1.4	-3.7	-0.8	-2.9	-4.0	-4.5	-3.7	-4.9	-3.5	-4.4	-4.8	-4.3	-8.2	-5.0	-7.0
2014	9.1	8.7	8.1	7.0	7.2	6.1	5.7	3.4	1.1	2.7	0.5	1.9	-0.1	-3.4	-2.4	-1.8	-2.3	-3.2	-4.1	-2.9	-3.8	-4.2	-4.4	-4.1	-4.7	-6.6	-4.8	-7.1
2015	10.9	8.7	10.8	6.7	8.1	6.6	6.1	4.3	3.4	2.7	2.7	2.0	0.1	-2.9	-2.9	-1.2	-3.2	-4.0	-4.5	-2.7	-4.3	-3.3	-3.8	-6.7	-5.9	-6.2	-6.2	-4.9
N	10	9	10	9	17	7	23	19	16	13	28	26	22	21	23	24	19	27	20	25	34	15	27	23	16	14	11	15

Figure 2: Cross-year performance for predicting (a) age (reported as Mean Error = $actualage - predictedage$). The rows reflect the test sets: language samples posted in the same or different year. The columns reflect users stratified according to their year of birth. Deeper shades of blue reflect higher underestimation errors; deeper shades of red reflect higher overestimation errors.

identified the words which show the largest drift between 2011-2014, in terms of their association with LGBTQ issues and positive emotion. We observe that this method of comparing the relative differences in distances, proposed by Garg et al. (2017), is able to capture social attitudes towards gender issues, as well as the emerging trends in netspeak. Specifically, in the discussions around LGBTQ issues in 2014, the words that emerge are closer to the actual experiences of the group, with words referring to 'passing' (a reference to transsexuals) and 'coping', as well as more positive emotion words ('yayy', 'harmony').

Concept	Year	Context words
LGBTQ issues	2011	strippers, conservative, pedophile, subjective, shocking
	2014	coping, passed, balance, yayy, finally, harmony
Positive emotion	2011	fagazy, bomb, totally, awesomeness, tight, fly
	2014	kickback, swag, winning, dontgiveafuck, bi*ch, thicka**

Table 2: Context words for concepts in the language of Twitter 2011 vs. 2014, selected among the words with the highest relative norm difference in distances from the concepts in the first column, between the two sets of Twitter embeddings.

6 Discussion

To summarize, our findings show that diachronic differences in language can be observed on social media and their effect differs for social media users of varying ages. In Figure 2, consider again the users of the same age at different points of time. For instance, compare the errors for 22-year old users in 2011 (born in 1989) against those for 22-year-old users in 2012 (born in 1990), and so on. The variance in error along these diagonals, are high in the right side of the table. This suggests that in every subsequent year, the language of late-teens and early-twenties is more different from the language of their contemporaries from the year before. On the other hand, compare the errors for 37-year-olds in 2011 (born in 1974) against those for 37-year-olds in 2012 (born in 1975). The errors have a low variance along the diagonals in the left of the Figure. Among social media users in their late thirties, the language of each cohort of 35-year-olds changes little over the previous year.

Next, consider the quantitative insights from Table 1. The results suggest that over time, young users from 2011 continued to use certain topics, while older users adopted newer trends. We found that if we do not use age-matched samples in this experiment, the coefficients for other topics are also flipped, but this effect is noticeably diminished with an age-matched subset. This suggests that indeed, a part of the language drift appeared because 1/5th of the population was shifting along the temporal axis, which also associates their distinct topical preferences with an older age group.

7 Conclusion & Future Work

This study offers an empirical study of how gender and age classifiers degrade over time, a qualitative study of the features whose coefficients change the most, and concepts that drift in meaning over time. The language of social media posts can be used to study semantic drift over short periods of time, even from a dataset of 554 social media users. These methods can also find application in the study of other linguistic phenomena such as polysemy (Hamilton et al., 2016b; Szymanski, 2017). However, there is a need to disentangle which differences are due to the changing use of language from the ones due to changes in topics and trends on social media.

Language models degrade over time, but it not always feasible to retrain models with new data. In future work, we plan to explore whether domain adaptation techniques can resolve diachronic performance differences, in addition to generalizing language models to other platforms (Jaidka et al., 2018b) or scaling to measure communities (Rieman et al., 2017).

References

Martín Abadi, Paul Barham, Jianmin Chen, Zhifeng Chen, Andy Davis, Jeffrey Dean, Matthieu Devin, Sanjay Ghemawat, Geoffrey Irving, Michael Isard, et al. 2016. Tensorflow: A system for large-scale machine learning. In *OSDI*. volume 16, pages 265–283.

Lea Frermann and Mirella Lapata. 2016. A bayesian model of diachronic meaning change. *Transactions of the Association for Computational Linguistics* 4:31–45.

Nikhil Garg, Londa Schiebinger, Dan Jurafsky, and James Zou. 2017. Word embeddings quantify 100 years of gender and ethnic stereotypes. *arXiv preprint arXiv:1711.08412* .

William L Hamilton, Jure Leskovec, and Dan Jurafsky. 2016a. Cultural shift or linguistic drift? comparing two computational measures of semantic change. In *Proceedings of the Conference on Empirical Methods in Natural Language Processing. Conference on Empirical Methods in Natural Language Processing*. NIH Public Access, volume 2016, page 2116.

William L Hamilton, Jure Leskovec, and Dan Jurafsky. 2016b. Diachronic word embeddings reveal statistical laws of semantic change. In *Proceedings of the 54th Annual Meeting of the Association for Computational Linguistics (Volume 1: Long Papers)*. volume 1, pages 1489–1501.

Kokil Jaidka, Anneke Buffone, Salvatore Giorgi, Johannes Eichstaedt, Masoud Rouhizadeh, and Lyle Ungar. 2018a. Modeling and visualizing locus of control with facebook language. In *Proceedings of the International AAAI Conference on Web and Social Media*.

Kokil Jaidka, Sharath Chandra Guntuku, Anneke Buffone, H. Andrew Schwartz, and Lyle Ungar. 2018b. Facebook vs. twitter: Differences in self-disclosure and trait prediction. In *Proceedings of the International AAAI Conference on Web and Social Media*.

Vivek Kulkarni, Rami Al-Rfou, Bryan Perozzi, and Steven Skiena. 2015. Statistically significant detection of linguistic change. In *Proceedings of the 24th International Conference on World Wide Web*. International World Wide Web Conferences Steering Committee, pages 625–635.

Tomas Mikolov, Ilya Sutskever, Kai Chen, Greg S Corrado, and Jeff Dean. 2013. Distributed representations of words and phrases and their compositionality. In *Advances in neural information processing systems*. pages 3111–3119.

Saif M Mohammad, Svetlana Kiritchenko, and Xiaodan Zhu. 2013. Nrc-canada: Building the state-of-the-art in sentiment analysis of tweets. *arXiv preprint arXiv:1308.6242* .

James W Pennebaker, Roger J Booth, and Martha E Francis. 2007. Linguistic inquiry and word count: Liwc [computer software]. *Austin, TX: liwc. net* .

Daniel Preoţiuc-Pietro, Ye Liu, Daniel Hopkins, and Lyle Ungar. 2017. Beyond binary labels: political ideology prediction of twitter users. In *Proceedings of the 55th Annual Meeting of the Association for Computational Linguistics (Volume 1: Long Papers)*. volume 1, pages 729–740.

Daniel Preotiuc-Pietro, Sina Samangooei, Trevor Cohn, Nicholas Gibbins, and Mahesan Niranjan. 2012. Trendminer: An architecture for real time analysis of social media text .

Daniel Rieman, Kokil Jaidka, H Andrew Schwartz, and Lyle Ungar. 2017. Domain adaptation from user-level facebook models to county-level twitter predictions. In *Proceedings of the Eighth International Joint Conference on Natural Language Processing (Volume 1: Long Papers)*. volume 1, pages 764–773.

Maarten Sap, Gregory Park, Johannes Eichstaedt, Margaret Kern, David Stillwell, Michal Kosinski, Lyle Ungar, and Hansen Andrew Schwartz. 2014. Developing age and gender predictive lexica over social media. In *Proceedings of the 2014 Conference on Empirical Methods in Natural Language Processing (EMNLP)*. pages 1146–1151.

H Andrew Schwartz, Johannes C Eichstaedt, Margaret L Kern, Lukasz Dziurzynski, Stephanie M Ramones, Megha Agrawal, Achal Shah, Michal Kosinski, David Stillwell, Martin EP Seligman, et al. 2013. Personality, gender, and age in the language of social media: The open-vocabulary approach. *PloS one* 8(9):e73791.

H Andrew Schwartz, Salvatore Giorgi, Maarten Sap, Patrick Crutchley, Lyle Ungar, and Johannes Eichstaedt. 2017. Dlatk: Differential language analysis toolkit. In *Proceedings of the 2017 Conference on Empirical Methods in Natural Language Processing: System Demonstrations*. pages 55–60.

Terrence Szymanski. 2017. Temporal word analogies: Identifying lexical replacement with diachronic word embeddings. In *Proceedings of the 55th Annual Meeting of the Association for Computational Linguistics (Volume 2: Short Papers)*. volume 2, pages 448–453.

Derry Tanti Wijaya and Reyyan Yeniterzi. 2011. Understanding semantic change of words over centuries. In *Proceedings of the 2011 international workshop on DETecting and Exploiting Cultural diversiTy on the social web*. ACM, pages 35–40.

Task-oriented Dialogue System for Automatic Diagnosis

Qianlong Liu[1], Zhongyu Wei[1*], Baolin Peng[2], Xiangying Dai[3],
Huaixiao Tou[1], Ting Chen[1], Xuanjing Huang[4], Kam-fai Wong[2,5]

[1]School of Data Science, Fudan University, China
[2]The Chinese University of Hong Kong, Hong Kong
[3]Baidu Inc., China
[4]School of Computer Science, Fudan University, China
[5]MoE Key Lab of High Confidence Software Technologies, China
{17210980040,zywei,17210980013,17210980029}@fudan.edu.cn
{blpeng, kfwong}@se.cuhk.edu.hk
daixiangying@baidu.com
xjhuang@fudan.edu.cn

Abstract

In this paper, we make a move to build a dialogue system for automatic diagnosis. We first build a dataset collected from an online medical forum by extracting symptoms from both patients' self-reports and conversational data between patients and doctors. Then we propose a task-oriented dialogue system framework to make the diagnosis for patients automatically, which can converse with patients to collect additional symptoms beyond their self-reports. Experimental results on our dataset show that additional symptoms extracted from conversation can greatly improve the accuracy for disease identification and our dialogue system is able to collect these symptoms automatically and make a better diagnosis.

1 Introduction

Automatic phenotype identification using electronic health records (EHRs) has been a rising topic in recent years (Shivade et al., 2013). Researchers explore with various machine learning approaches to identify symptoms and diseases for patients given multiple types of information (both numerical data and pure texts). Experimental results prove the effectiveness of the identification of heart failure (Jonnalagadda et al., 2017; Choi et al., 2016), type 2 diabetes (Li et al., 2015; Zheng et al., 2017), autism spectrum disorders (Doshi-Velez et al., 2014), infection detection (Tou et al., 2018) etc. Currently, most attempts focus on some

specific types of diseases and it is difficult to transfer models from one disease to another.

In general, each EHR contains multiple types of data, including personal information, admission note, diagnose tests, vital signs and medical image. And it is collected accumulatively following a diagnostic procedure in clinic, which involves interactions between patients and doctors and some complicated medical tests. Therefore, it is very expensive to collect EHRs for different diseases. How to collect the information from patient automatically remains the challenge for automatic diagnosis.

Recently, due to its promising potentials and alluring commercial values, research about task-oriented dialogue system (DS) has attracted increasing attention in different domains, including ticket booking (Li et al., 2017; Peng et al., 2017a), online shopping (Yan et al., 2017) and restaurant searching (Wen et al., 2017). We believe that applying DS in the medical domain has great potential to reduce the cost of collecting data from patients.

However, there is a gap to fill for applying DS in disease identification. There are basically two major challenges. First, the lack of annotated medical dialogue dataset. Second, no available DS framework for disease identification. By addressing these two problems, we make the first move to build a dialogue system facilitating automatic information collection and diagnosis making for medical domain. Contributions are two-fold:

- We annotate the first medical dataset for dialogue system that consists of two parts, one is self-reports from patients and the other is conversational data between patients and

---

[*]Corresponding author

Proceedings of the 56th Annual Meeting of the Association for Computational Linguistics (Short Papers), pages 201–207
Melbourne, Australia, July 15 - 20, 2018. ©2018 Association for Computational Linguistics

doctors.

- We propose a reinforcement learning based framework for medical DS. Experiment results on our dataset show that our dialogue system is able to collect symptoms from patients via conversation and improve the accuracy for automatic diagnosis.

2 Dataset for Medical DS

Our dataset is collected from the pediatric department in a Chinese online healthcare community [1]. It is a popular website for users to inquire with doctors online. Usually, a patient would provide a piece of self-report presenting his/her basic conditions. Then a doctor will initialize a conversation to collect more information and make a diagnosis based on both the self-report and the conversational data. An example is shown in Table 1. As we can see, the doctor can obtain additional symptoms during conversation beyond the self-report. For each patient, we can also obtain the final diagnosis from doctors as the label. For clarity, we term symptoms from self-reports as *explicit symptoms* while those from conversational data as *implicit symptoms*.

We choose four types of diseases for annotation, including upper respiratory infection, children functional dyspepsia, infantile diarrhea and children's bronchitis. We invite three annotators (one with medical background) to label all the symptom phrases in both self-reports and conversational data. The annotation is performed in two steps, namely symptom extraction and symptom normalization.

Symptom Extraction We follow the BIO (begin-in-out) schema for symptom identification (Figure 1). Each Chinese character is assigned a label of "B", "I" or "O". Also, each extracted symptom expression is tagged with *True* or *False* indicating whether the patient suffers from this symptom or not. In order to improve the annotation agreement between annotators, we create two guidelines for the self-report and the conversational data respectively. Each record is annotated by at least two annotators. Any inconsistency would be further judged by the third one. The Cohen's kappa coefficient between two annotators are 71% and 67% for self-reports and conversations respectively.

---

[1]http://muzhi.baidu.com

Self-report		
宝宝嗓子有痰，腹泻并伴有拉水的症状。请问要吃什么药？		
The little baby get sputum in throat and have watery diarrhea. what kind of medicine needs to be taken?		
Conversation		
......		
Doctor:	宝宝现在咳嗽拉肚子吗？	
	Does the baby have a cough or diarrhea now?	
Patient:	不咳嗽，拉肚子。	
	No cough, but diarrhea.	
Doctor:	平常呛奶吗？	
	Does the baby choking milk?	
Patient:	偶尔会吐奶。	
	He vomits milk sometimes.	
......		

Table 1: An example of a user record. Each record consists of two parts: self-report from the patient and the conversation between the doctor and the patient. Underlined phrases are symptom expressions.

Extracted symptom expression	Related concept in SNOMED CT
咳嗽(cough)	咳嗽(cough)
喷嚏(sneez)	打喷嚏(sneezing)
鼻涕(cnot)	鼻流涕(cnot)
拉肚子(have loose bowels)	腹泻(diarrhea)
温度37.5-37.7之间(body temperature between 37.5-37.7)	低热(low-grade fever)

Table 2: Examples of extracted symptom expressions and the related concepts in SNOMED CT.

Symptom Normalization After symptom expression identification, medical experts manually link each symptom expression to the most relevant concept on SNOMED CT [2] for normalization. Table 2 shows some phrases that describe symptoms in the example and some related concepts in SNOMED CT. The overview of dataset is presented in Table 3.

After symptom extraction and normalization, there are 144 unique symptoms identified. In order to reduce the size of action space of the DS, only 67 symptoms with a frequency greater than or equal to 10 are kept. Samples are then generated, called *user goal*. As we know, each user goal (see Figure 2) is derived from one real world patient record [3].

3 Proposed Framework

A task-oriented DS typically contains three components, namely Natural Language Understanding (NLU), Dialogue Manager (DM) and Natural Language Generation (NLG). NLU detects the user intent and slots with values from utterances; DM

---

[2]https://www.snomed.org/snomed-ct
[3]The dataset is available at:
www.sdspeople.fudan.edu.cn/zywei/data/acl2018-mds.zip

宝宝嗓子有痰，腹泻并伴有拉水的症状。……
O O B I I IO B I O O O B I O O O O ……
The baby get sputum in throat and have watery diarrhea. ……

Figure 1: An example utterance with annotations of symptoms in BIO format.

Disease	♯ of user goal	Ave ♯ of explicit symptoms	Ave ♯ of implicit symptoms
infantile diarrhea	200	2.15	2.71
children functional dyspepsia	150	1.70	3.20
upper respiratory infection	160	2.56	3.55
children's bronchitis	200	2.87	3.64

Table 3: Overview of the dataset. ♯ of user goal is the number of dialogue sessions of each disease, Ave ♯ of explicit symptoms and Ave ♯ of implicit symptoms are the average number of explicit and implicit symptoms among user goals respectively.

tracks the dialogue states and takes system actions; NLG generates natural language given the system actions. In this work, we focus on the DM for automatic diagnosis consisting of two sub-modules, namely, dialogue state tracker (DST) and policy learning. Both NLU and NLG are implemented with template-based models. Typically, a user simulator is designed to interact with the dialogue system (Liu et al., 2017; Peng et al., 2017b; Su et al., 2016; Schatzmann et al., 2006). We follow the same setting as Li et al. (2017) to design our medical DS. At the beginning of a dialogue session, the user simulator samples a user goal (see Figure 2), while the agent attempts to make a diagnosis for the user. The system will learn to select the best response action at each time step by maximizing a long term reward.

3.1 User Simulator

At the beginning of each dialogue session, a user simulator samples a user goal from the experiment dataset. At each turn t, the user takes an action $a_{u,t}$ according to the current user state $s_{u,t}$ and the previous agent action a_{t-1}, and transits into the next user state $s_{u,t+1}$. In practice, the user state s_u is factored into an agenda A (Schatzmann et al., 2007) and a goal G, noted as $s_u = (A, G)$. During the course of the dialogue, the goal G ensures that the user behaves in a consistent, goal-oriented manner. And the agenda contains a list of symptoms and their status (whether or not they are requested) to track the progress of the conversation.

Every dialogue session is initiated by the user

```
{
    "disease_tag": "小儿支气管炎(children's bronchitis)",
    "request_slots": {
        "disease": "unknow"
    },
    "explicit_symptoms": {
        "咳嗽(cough)": true,
        "鼻流涕(snot)": true
    },
    "implicit_symptoms": {
        "咽痛(sore throat)": true,
        "发烧(fever)": true,
        "粗糙呼吸音(harsh breath sounds)": false,
        "呕吐(emesis)": false
    }
}
```

Figure 2: An example of user goal. Each user goal consists of four parts, *disease_tag* is the disease that the user suffers; *explicit_symptoms* are symptoms extracted from the user self-report; *implicit_symptoms* are symptoms extracted from the conversational data between the patient and the doctor; *request_slots* is the *disease* slot that the user would request.

via the user action $a_{u,1}$ which consists of the requested *disease* slot and all explicit symptoms. In terms of the symptom requested by the agent during the course of the dialogue, the user will take one of the three actions including *True* (if the symptom is positive), *False* (if the symptom is negative), and *not_sure* (if the symptom is not mentioned in the user goal). If the agent informs correct disease, the dialogue session will be terminated as successful by the user. Otherwise, the dialogue session will be recognized as failed if the agent makes incorrect diagnosis or the dialogue turn reaches the maximum dialogue turn T.

3.2 Dialogue Policy Learning

Markov Decision Process Formulation for Automatic Diagnosis We cast DS as Markov Decision Process (MDP) (Young et al., 2013) and train the dialogue policy via reinforcement learning (Cuayahuitl et al., 2015). An MDP is composed of states, actions, rewards, policy, and transitions.

State S. A dialogue state s includes symptoms requested by the agent and informed by the user till the current time t, the previous action of the user, the previous action of the agent and the turn information. In terms of the representation vector of symptoms, it's dimension is equal to the number of all symptoms, whose elements for positive symptoms are 1, negative symptoms are -1, not-sure symptoms are -2 and not-mentioned symptoms are 0. Each state $s \in S$ is the concatenation of these four vectors.

Actions A. An action $a \in A$ is composed of a dialogue act (e.g., *inform, request, deny* and *confirm*) and a slot (i.e., normalized symptoms or a special slot *disease*). In addition, *thanks* and *close_dialogue* are also two actions.

Transition T. The transition from s_t to s_{t+1} is the updating of state s_t based on the agent action a_t, the previous user action $a_{u,t-1}$ and the step time t.

Reward R. The reward $r_{t+1} = R(s_t, a_t)$ is the immediate reward at step time t after taking the action a_t, also known as reinforcement.

Policy π. The policy describes the behaviors of an agent, which takes the state s_t as input and outputs the probability distribution over all possible actions $\pi(a_t|s_t)$.

Learning with DQN In this paper, the policy is parameterized with a deep Q-network (DQN) (Mnih et al., 2015), which takes the state s_t as input and outputs $Q(s_t, a; \theta)$ for all actions a. A Q-network can be trained by updating the parameters θ_i at iteration i to reduce the mean squared error between the Q-value computed from the current network $Q(s, a|\theta_i)$ and the Q-value obtained from the Bellman equation $y_i = r + \gamma \max_{a'} Q(s', a'|\theta_i^-)$, where $Q(s', a'|\theta_i^-)$ is the target network with parameters θ_i^- from some previous iteration. In practice, the behavior distribution is often selected by an ϵ-greedy policy that takes an action $a = \arg\max_{a'} Q(s_t, a'; \theta)$ with probability $1 - \epsilon$ and selects a random action with probability ϵ, which can improve the efficiency of exploration. When training the policy, we use a technique known as experience replay. We store the agent's experiences at each time-step, $e_t = (s_t, a_t, r_t, s_{t+1})$ in a fixed size, queue-like buffer D.

In a simulation epoch, the current DQN network is updated multiple times (depending on the batch size and the current size of replay buffer) with different batches drawn randomly from the buffer, while the target DQN network is fixed during the updating of current DQN network. At the end of each epoch, the target network is replaced by the current network and the current network is evaluated on training set. The buffer will be flushed if the current network performs better than all previous versions.

4 Experiments and Results

4.1 Experimental Setup

The max dialogue turn T is 22. A positive reward of $+44$ is given to the agent at the end of a success dialogue, and a -22 reward is given to a failure one. We apply a step penalty of -1 for each turn to encourage shorter dialogues. The dataset is divided into two parts: 80% for training with 568 user goals and 20% for testing with 142 user goals. The ϵ of ϵ-greedy strategy is set to 0.1 for effective action space exploration and the γ in Bellman equation is 0.9. The size of buffer D is 10000 and the batch size is 30. And the neural network of DQN is a single layer network. The learning rate is 0.001. Each simulation epoch consists of 100 dialogue sessions and the current network is evaluated on 500 dialogue sessions at the end of each epoch. Before training, the buffer is pre-filled with the experiences of the rule-based agent (see below) to warm start our dialogue system.

To evaluate the performance of the proposed framework, we compare our model with baselines in terms of three evaluation metrics following Li et al. (2017) and Peng at al. (2017a; 2017b), namely, success rate, average reward and the average number of turns per dialogue session. As for classification models, we use accuracy as the metric.

The baselines include: **(1) SVM:** This model treats the automatic diagnosis as a multi-class classification problem. It takes one-hot representation of symptoms in the user goal as input, and predicts the disease. There are two configurations: one takes both explicit and implicit symptoms as input (denoted as SVM-ex&im), and the other takes only explicit symptoms to predict the disease (denoted as SVM-ex). **(2) Random Agent:** At each turn, the random agent takes an action randomly from the action space as the response to the user's action. **(3) Rule-based Agent:** The rule-based agent takes an action based on handcrafted rules. Conditioned on the current dialogue state s_t, the agent will inform disease if all the known symptoms related are detected. If no disease can be identified, the agent will select one of the left symptoms randomly to inform. The relations between diseases and symptoms are extracted from the annotated corpus in advance. In this work, only the first $T/2.5$ [4] symptoms with high frequency are kept for each disease so that the rule-

---

[4] 2.5 is a hyper-parameter.

based agent could inform a disease within the max dialogue turn T.

Disease	SVM-ex&im	SVM-ex
Infantile diarrhea	0.91	0.89
Children functional dyspepsia	0.34	0.28
Upper respiratory infection	0.52	0.44
Children's bronchitis	0.93	0.71
Overall	0.71	0.59

Table 4: Accuracy of classification models

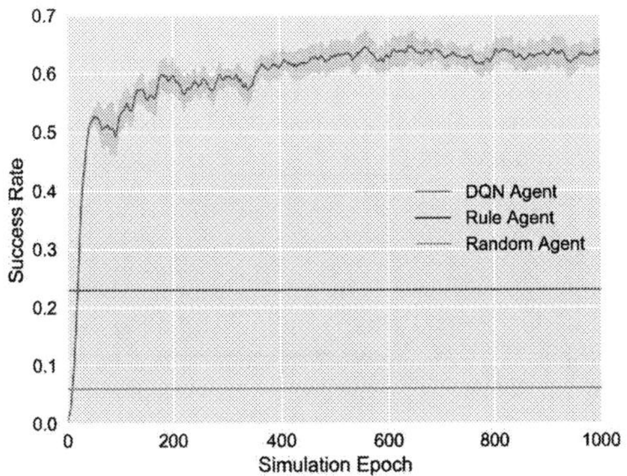

Figure 3: Learning curve of policy learning

Model	Success	Reward	Turn
Random Agent	0.06	-24.36	17.51
Rule Agent	0.23	-13.78	17.00
DQN Agent	0.65	20.51	5.11

Table 5: Performance of three dialogue systems on 5K simulated dialogues

4.2 Results

Table 4 shows the accuracy of two SVM-based models. The result shows that the implicit symptoms can greatly improve the accuracy of disease identification for all the four diseases, which demonstrates the contribution of implicit symptoms when making diagnosis for patients. Figure 3 shows the learning curve of all the three dialogue systems and Table 5 shows the performance of these agents on testing set. Due to the large action space, the random agent performs badly. The rule-based agent outperforms the random agent in a large margin. This indicates that the rule-based agent is well designed. We can also see that the RL-based DQN agent outperforms rule-based agent significantly. Moreover, DQN agent outperforms SVM-ex by collecting additional implicit symptoms via conversing with patients. However, there is still a gap between the performance of *DQN agent* and *SVM-ex&im* in terms of accuracy, which indicates that there is still rooms for the improvement of the dialogue system.

5 Related Works

In 2003, an ontology-based dialogue system that supports electronic referrals for breast cancer is proposed (Milward and Beveridge, 2003), which can deal with the informative response of users based on the medical domain ontologies. In addition, there are two works where deep reinforcement learning is applied for automatic diagnosis (Tang et al., 2016; Kao et al., 2018). However, their models need extra human resources to categorize the diseases into different groups and the data used is simulated that can not reflect the situation of the real patients.

6 Conclusions and Future Works

In this paper, we propose a reinforcement learning based framework of dialogue system for automatic diagnosis and build a dataset for training DS which is derived from the dialogue text between real patients and doctors. Experiment results on a self-constructed dataset show that our dialogue system is able to collect additional symptoms via conversation with patients and improve the accuracy for automatic diagnosis.

The relationship between diseases and symptoms is an external knowledge which is thought to be useful for the automatic diagnosis. One of our future directions is to explore models that can incorporate external knowledge for better policy learning.

Acknowledgments

We thank the anonymous reviewers for their detailed and insightful comments on this paper. The work is partially supported by National Natural Science Foundation of China (Grant No. 61702106), Shanghai Science and Technology Commission (Grant No. 17JC1420200, Grant No.17YF1427600 and Grant No. 16JC1420401). Any opinions, findings, and conclusions or recommendations expressed are those of the authors and do not necessarily reflect the views of the funding agencies.

References

Edward Choi, Andy Schuetz, Walter F Stewart, and Jimeng Sun. 2016. Using recurrent neural network models for early detection of heart failure onset. *Journal of the American Medical Informatics Association* 24(2):361–370.

Heriberto Cuayahuitl, Simon Keizer, Oliver Lemon, et al. 2015. Strategic dialogue management via deep reinforcement learning. *CoRR* .

Finale Doshi-Velez, Yaorong Ge, and Isaac Kohane. 2014. Comorbidity clusters in autism spectrum disorders: an electronic health record time-series analysis. *Pediatrics* 133(1):e54–e63.

Siddhartha R Jonnalagadda, Abhishek K Adupa, Ravi P Garg, Jessica Corona-Cox, and Sanjiv J Shah. 2017. Text mining of the electronic health record: An information extraction approach for automated identification and subphenotyping of hfpef patients for clinical trials. *Journal of cardiovascular translational research* 10(3):313–321.

Hao-Cheng Kao, Kai-Fu Tang, and Edward Y Chang. 2018. Context-aware symptom checking for disease diagnosis using hierarchical reinforcement learning .

Li Li, Wei-Yi Cheng, Benjamin S Glicksberg, Omri Gottesman, Ronald Tamler, Rong Chen, Erwin P Bottinger, and Joel T Dudley. 2015. Identification of type 2 diabetes subgroups through topological analysis of patient similarity. *Science translational medicine* 7(311):311ra174–311ra174.

Xiujun Li, Yun-Nung Chen, Lihong Li, Jianfeng Gao, and Asli Celikyilmaz. 2017. End-to-end task-completion neural dialogue systems. In *Proceedings of the Eighth International Joint Conference on Natural Language Processing (Volume 1: Long Papers)*. volume 1, pages 733–743.

Bing Liu, Gokhan Tur, Dilek Hakkani-Tur, Pararth Shah, and Larry Heck. 2017. End-to-end optimization of task-oriented dialogue model with deep reinforcement learning https://arxiv.org/abs/1711.10712.

David Milward and Martin Beveridge. 2003. Ontology-based dialogue systems. In *Proc. 3rd Workshop on Knowledge and reasoning in practical dialogue systems (IJCAI03)*. pages 9–18.

Volodymyr Mnih, Koray Kavukcuoglu, David Silver, Andrei A Rusu, Joel Veness, Marc G Bellemare, Alex Graves, Martin Riedmiller, Andreas K Fidjeland, Georg Ostrovski, et al. 2015. Human-level control through deep reinforcement learning. *Nature* 518(7540):529–533.

Baolin Peng, Xiujun Li, Jianfeng Gao, Jingjing Liu, Yun-Nung Chen, and Kam-Fai Wong. 2017a. Adversarial advantage actor-critic model for task-completion dialogue policy learning https://arxiv.org/abs/1710.11277.

Baolin Peng, Xiujun Li, Lihong Li, Jianfeng Gao, Asli Celikyilmaz, Sungjin Lee, and Kam-Fai Wong. 2017b. Composite task-completion dialogue policy learning via hierarchical deep reinforcement learning. In *Proceedings of the 2017 Conference on Empirical Methods in Natural Language Processing.* pages 2231–2240.

Jost Schatzmann, Blaise Thomson, Karl Weilhammer, Hui Ye, and Steve Young. 2007. Agenda-based user simulation for bootstrapping a pomdp dialogue system. In *Human Language Technologies 2007: The Conference of the North American Chapter of the Association for Computational Linguistics; Companion Volume, Short Papers*. Association for Computational Linguistics, pages 149–152.

Jost Schatzmann, Karl Weilhammer, Matt Stuttle, and Steve Young. 2006. A survey of statistical user simulation techniques for reinforcement-learning of dialogue management strategies. *The knowledge engineering review* 21(2):97–126.

Chaitanya Shivade, Preethi Raghavan, Eric Fosler-Lussier, Peter J Embi, Noemie Elhadad, Stephen B Johnson, and Albert M Lai. 2013. A review of approaches to identifying patient phenotype cohorts using electronic health records. *Journal of the American Medical Informatics Association* 21(2):221–230.

Pei-Hao Su, Milica Gasic, Nikola Mrksic, Lina Rojas-Barahona, Stefan Ultes, David Vandyke, Tsung-Hsien Wen, and Steve Young. 2016. Continuously learning neural dialogue management https://arxiv.org/abs/1606.02689.

Kai-Fu Tang, Hao-Cheng Kao, Chun-Nan Chou, and Edward Y Chang. 2016. Inquire and diagnose: Neural symptom checking ensemble using deep reinforcement learning. In *Proceedings of NIPS Workshop on Deep Reinforcement Learning*.

Huaixiao Tou, Lu Yao, Zhongyu Wei, Xiahai Zhuang, and Bo Zhang. 2018. Automatic infection detection based on electronic medical records. *BMC bioinformatics* 19(5):117.

TH Wen, D Vandyke, N Mrkšíc, M Gašíc, LM Rojas-Barahona, PH Su, S Ultes, and S Young. 2017. A network-based end-to-end trainable task-oriented dialogue system. In *15th Conference of the European Chapter of the Association for Computational Linguistics, EACL 2017-Proceedings of Conference.* volume 1, pages 438–449.

Zhao Yan, Nan Duan, Peng Chen, Ming Zhou, Jianshe Zhou, and Zhoujun Li. 2017. Building task-oriented dialogue systems for online shopping. In *AAAI*. pages 4618–4626.

Steve Young, Milica Gašić, Blaise Thomson, and Jason D Williams. 2013. Pomdp-based statistical spoken dialog systems: A review. *Proceedings of the IEEE* 101(5):1160–1179.

Tao Zheng, Wei Xie, Liling Xu, Xiaoying He, Ya Zhang, Mingrong You, Gong Yang, and You Chen. 2017. A machine learning-based framework to identify type 2 diabetes through electronic health records. *International journal of medical informatics* 97:120–127.

Transfer Learning for Context-Aware Question Matching in Information-seeking Conversations in E-commerce

Minghui Qiu[1], Liu Yang[2], Feng Ji[1], Wei Zhou[1], Jun Huang[1],
Haiqing Chen[1], W. Bruce Croft[2], Wei Lin[1]
[1]Alibaba Group, Hangzhou, China
[2]Center for Intelligent Information Retrieval, University of Massachusetts Amherst
`{minghui.qmh,zhongxiu.jf}@alibaba-inc.com`
`{lyang,croft}@cs.umass.edu`

Abstract

Building multi-turn information-seeking conversation systems is an important and challenging research topic. Although several advanced neural text matching models have been proposed for this task, they are generally not efficient for industrial applications. Furthermore, they rely on a large amount of labeled data, which may not be available in real-world applications. To alleviate these problems, we study transfer learning for multi-turn information seeking conversations in this paper. We first propose an efficient and effective multi-turn conversation model based on convolutional neural networks. After that, we extend our model to adapt the knowledge learned from a resource-rich domain to enhance the performance. Finally, we deployed our model in an industrial chatbot called AliMe Assist [1] and observed a significant improvement over the existing online model.

1 Introduction

With the popularity of online shopping, there is an increasing number of customers seeking information regarding their concerned items. To efficiently handle customer questions, a common approach is to build a conversational customer service system (Li et al., 2017; Yang et al., 2018). In the E-commerce environment, the information-seeking conversation system can serve millions of customer questions per day. According to the statistics from a real e-commerce website (Qiu et al., 2017), the majority of customer questions

(nearly 90%) are business-related or seeking information about logistics, coupons etc. Among these conversation sessions, 75% of them are more than one turn[2]. Hence it is important to handle multi-turn conversations or context information in these conversation systems.

Recent researches in this area have focused on deep learning and reinforcement learning (Shang et al., 2015; Yan et al., 2016; Li et al., 2016a,b; Sordoni et al., 2015; Wu et al., 2017). One of these methods is Sequential Matching Network(Wu et al., 2017), which matches a response with each utterance in the context at multiple levels of granularity and leads to state-of-the-art performance on two multi-turn conversation corpora. However, such methods suffer from at least two problems: they may not be efficient enough for industrial applications, and they rely on a large amount of labeled data which may not be available in reality.

To address the problem of efficiency, we made three major modifications to SMN to boost the efficiency of the model while preserving its effectiveness. First, we remove the RNN layers of inputs from the model; Second, SMN uses a Sentence Interaction based (SI-based) Pyramid model (Pang et al., 2016) to model each utterance and response pair. In practice, a Sentence Encoding based (SE-based) model like BCNN (Yin and Schütze, 2015) is complementary to the SI-based model. Therefore, we extend the component to incorporate an SE-based BCNN model, resulting in a hybrid CNN (hCNN) (Yu et al., 2017); Third, instead of using a RNN to model the output representations, we consider a CNN model followed by a fully-connected layer to further boost the efficiency of our model. As shown in our experiments, our final model yields comparable results

---

[1] Interested readers can access AliMe Assist through the Taobao App, or the web version via `https://consumerservice.taobao.com/online-help`

[2]According to a statistic in AliMe Assist in Alibaba Group

Proceedings of the 56th Annual Meeting of the Association for Computational Linguistics (Short Papers), pages 208–213
Melbourne, Australia, July 15 - 20, 2018. ©2018 Association for Computational Linguistics

but with higher efficiency than SMN.

To address the second problem of insufficient labeled data, we study transfer learning (TL) (Pan and Yang, 2010) to utilize a source domain with adequate labeling to help the target domain. A typical TL approach is to use a shared NN (Mou et al., 2016; Yang et al., 2017) and domain-specific NNs to derive shared and domain-specific features respectively. Recent studies (Ganin et al., 2016; Taigman et al., 2017; Chen et al., 2017; Liu et al., 2017) consider adversarial networks to learn more robust shared features across domains. Inspired by these studies, we extended our method with a Transfer Learning module to leverage information from a resource-rich domain. Similarly, our TL module consists of a shared NN and two domain-specific NNs for source and target domains. The output of the shared NN is further linked to an adversarial network as used in (Liu et al., 2017) to help learn domain invariant features. Meanwhile, we also use domain discriminators on both source and target features derived by domain-specific NNs to help learn domain-specific features. Experiments show that our TL method can further improve the model performance on a target domain with limited data.

To the best of our knowledge, our work is the first to study transfer learning for context-aware question matching in conversations. Experiments on both benchmark and commercial data sets show that our proposed model outperforms several baselines including the state-of-the-art SMN model. We have also deployed our model in an industrial bot called AliMe Assist [3] and observed a significant improvement over the existing online model.

2 Model

Our model is designed to address the following general problem. Given an input sequence of utterances $\{u_1, u_2, \ldots, u_n\}$ and a candidate question r, our task is to identify the matching degree between the utterances and the question. When the number of utterances is one, our problem is identical to paraphrase identification (PI) (Yin and Schütze, 2015) or natural language inference (NLI) (Bowman et al., 2015). Furthermore, we consider a transfer learning setting to transfer knowledge from a source domain to help a target domain.

2.1 Multi-Turn hCNN (MT-hCNN)

We present an overview of our model in Fig. 1. In a nutshell, our model first obtains a representation for each utterance and candidate question pair using hybrid CNN (hCNN), then concatenates all the representations, and feeds them into a CNN and fully-connected layer to obtain our final output.

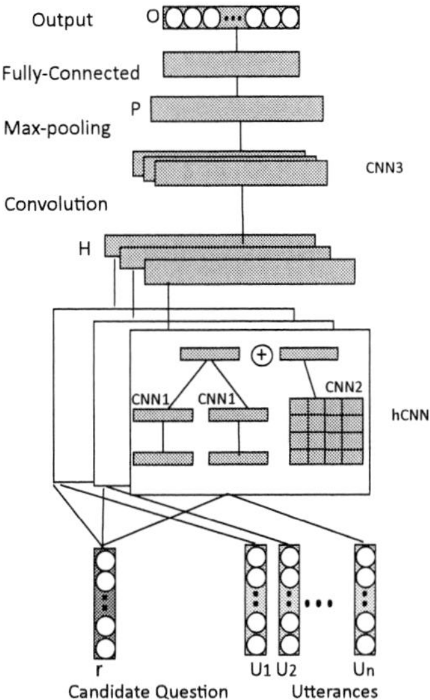

Figure 1: Our proposed multi-turn hybrid CNN.

The hybrid CNN (hCNN) model (Yu et al., 2017) is based on two models: a modified SE-based BCNN model (Yin et al., 2016) and a SI-based Pyramid model (Pang et al., 2016). The former encode the two input sentences separately with a CNN and then combines the resulting sentence embeddings as follows:

$$\mathbf{h_1} = \mathrm{CNN}_1(\mathbf{X_1}); \quad \mathbf{h_2} = \mathrm{CNN}_1(\mathbf{X_2}).$$
$$\mathbf{H_b} = \mathbf{h_1} \oplus \mathbf{h_2} \oplus (\mathbf{h_1} - \mathbf{h_2}) \oplus (\mathbf{h_1} \cdot \mathbf{h_2}).$$

where '$-$' and '$\cdot$' refer to element-wise subtraction and multiplication, and '$\oplus$' refers to concatenation.

Furthermore, we add a SI-base Pyramid component to the model, we first produce an interaction matrix $\mathbf{M} \in \mathbb{R}^{m \times m}$, where $\mathbf{M_{i,j}}$ denotes the dot-product score between the ith word in $\mathbf{X_1}$ and the jth word in $\mathbf{X_2}$. Next, we stack two 2-D convolutional layers and two 2-D max-pooling layers on it to obtain the hidden representation $\mathbf{H_p}$. Finally, we concatenate the hidden representations as output for each input sentence pair: $\mathbf{Z_{X_1,X_2}} = \mathrm{hCNN}(X_1, X_2) = \mathbf{H_b} \oplus \mathbf{H_p}$.

We now extend hCNN to handle multi-turn conversations, resulting MT-hCNN model. Let $\{u_1, u_2, u_3, \ldots, u_n\}$ be the utterances, r is the candidate question.

$$
\begin{aligned}
\mathbf{h_{u_i,r}} &= \text{hCNN}(\mathbf{u_i}, r). \quad for \quad i \in [1, n] \\
H &= [h_{u_1,r}; h_{u_2,r}; \cdots; h_{u_n,r}]. \\
P &= \text{CNN}_3(H). \\
O &= \text{Fully-Connected}(P)
\end{aligned}
$$

Note that H is obtained by stacking all the $\mathbf{h}$, CNN_3 is another CNN with a 2-D convolutional layer and a 2-D max-pooling layer, the output of CNN_3 is feed into a fully-connected layer to obtain the final representation O.

2.2 Transfer with Domain Discriminators

We further study transfer learning (TL) to learn knowledge from a source-rich domain to help our target domain, in order to reduce the dependency on a large scale labeled training data. As similar to (Liu et al., 2017), we use a shared MT-hCNN and two domain-specific MT-hCNNs to derive shared features $\mathbf{O^c}$ and domain-specific features $\mathbf{O^s}$ and $\mathbf{O^t}$. The domain specific output layers are:

$$
\hat{y}^k = \begin{cases} \sigma(\mathbf{W^{sc}O^c} + \mathbf{W^s O^s} + \mathbf{b^s}), & \text{if } k = s \\ \sigma(\mathbf{W^{tc}O^c} + \mathbf{W^t O^t} + \mathbf{b^t}), & \text{if } k = t \end{cases} \quad (1)
$$

where $\mathbf{W^{sc}}$, $\mathbf{W^{tc}}$, $\mathbf{W^s}$, and $\mathbf{W^t}$ are the weights for shared-source, shared-target, source, and target domains respectively, while $\mathbf{b^s}$ and $\mathbf{b^t}$ are the biases for source and target domains respectively.

Following (Liu et al., 2017), we use an adversarial loss L_a to encourage the shared features learned to be indiscriminate across two domains:

$$
L_a = \frac{1}{n} \sum_{i=1}^{n} \sum_{d \in s,t} p(d_i = d | \mathbf{U}, r) \log p(d_i = d | \mathbf{U}, r).
$$

where d_i is the domain label and $p(d_i|\cdot)$ is the domain probability from a domain discriminator.

Differently, to encourage the specific feature space to be discriminable between different domains, we consider applying domain discrimination losses on the two specific feature spaces. We further add two negative cross-entropy losses: L_s

for source and L_t for target domain:

$$
L_s = -\frac{1}{n_s} \sum_{i=1}^{n_s} \mathbb{I}^{d_i=s} \log p(d_i = s | \mathbf{U}^s, r^s).
$$

$$
L_t = -\frac{1}{n_t} \sum_{i=1}^{n_t} \mathbb{I}^{d_i=t} \log p(d_i = t | \mathbf{U}^t, r^t).
$$

where $\mathbb{I}^{d_i=d}$ is an indicator function set to 1 when the statement $(d_i = d)$ holds, or 0 otherwise.

Finally, we obtain a combined loss as follows:

$$
\mathcal{L} = \sum_{k \in s,t} -\frac{1}{n_k} \sum_{j=1}^{n_k} \frac{1}{2}(y_j^k - \hat{y}_j^k)^2 + \frac{\lambda_1}{2} L_a
$$

$$
+ \frac{\lambda_2}{2} L_s + \frac{\lambda_3}{2} L_t + \frac{\lambda_4}{2} ||\mathbf{\Theta}||_F^2.
$$

where $\mathbf{\Theta}$ denotes model parameters.

3 Experiments

We evaluate the efficiency and effectiveness of our base model, the transferability of the model, and the online evaluation in an industrial chatbot.

Datasets: We evaluate our methods on two multi-turn conversation corpus, namely Ubuntu Dialog Corpus (UDC) (Lowe et al., 2015) and AliMe data.

Ubuntu Dialog Corpus: The Ubuntu Dialog Corpus (UDC) (Lowe et al., 2015) contains multi-turn technical support conversation data collected from the chat logs of the Freenode Internet Relay Chat (IRC) network. We used the data copy shared by Xu et al. (Xu et al., 2016), in which numbers, urls and paths are replaced by special placeholders. It is also used in several previous related works (Wu et al., 2017). It consists of 1 million context-response pairs for training, 0.5 million pairs for validation and 0.5 million pairs for testing.

AliMe Data: We collect the chat logs between customers and a chatbot called AliMe from "2017-10-01" to "2017-10-20" in Alibaba [4]. The chatbot is built based on a question-to-question matching system (Li et al., 2017), where for each query, it finds the most similar candidate question in a QA database and return its answer as the reply. It indexes all the questions in our QA database using Lucence[5]. For each given query, it uses TF-IDF ranking algorithm to call back candidates. To form

---

[4] The textual contents related to user information are filtered.

[5] https://lucene.apache.org/core/

Table 1: Comparison of base models on Ubuntu Dialog Corpus (UDC) and an E-commerce data (AliMe).

Data	UDC					AliMeData				
Methods	MAP	R@5	R@2	R@1	Time	MAP	R@5	R@2	R@1	Time
ARC-I	0.2810	0.4887	0.1840	0.0873	16	0.7314	0.6383	0.3733	0.2171	23
ARC-II	0.5451	0.8197	0.5349	0.3498	17	0.7306	0.6595	0.3671	0.2236	24
Pyramid	0.6418	0.8324	0.6298	0.4986	17	0.8389	0.7604	0.4778	0.3114	27
Duet	0.5692	0.8272	0.5592	0.4756	20	0.7651	0.6870	0.4088	0.2433	30
MV-LSTM	0.6918	0.8982	0.7005	0.5457	1632	0.7734	0.7017	0.4105	0.2480	2495
SMN	**0.7327**	**0.9273**	0.7523	0.5948	64	0.8145	0.7271	0.4680	0.2881	91
MT-hCNN-d	0.7027	0.8992	0.7512	0.5838	20	0.8401	0.7712	0.4788	0.3238	31
MT-hCNN	0.7323	0.9172	**0.7525**	**0.5978**	24	**0.8418**	**0.7810**	**0.4796**	**0.3241**	36

our data set, we concatenated utterances within three turns [6] to form a query, and used the chatbot system to call back top 15 most similar candidate questions as candidate "responses". [7] We then asked a business analyst to annotate the candidate responses, where a "response" is labeled as positive if it matches the query, otherwise negative. In all, we have annotated 63,000 context-response pairs. This dataset is used as our *Target* data.

Furthermore, we build our *Source* data as follows. In the AliMe chatbot, if the confidence score of answering a given user query is low, i.e. the matching score is below a given threshold[8], we prompt top three related questions for users to choose. We collected the user click logs as our source data, where we treat the clicked question as positive and the others as negative. We collected 510,000 query-question pairs from the click logs in total as the source. For the source and target datasets, we use 80% for training, 10% for validation, and 10% for testing.

Compared Methods: We compared our multiturn model (MT-hCNN) with two CNN based models ARC-I and ARC-II (Hu et al., 2014), and several advanced neural matching models: MV-LSTM (Wan et al., 2016), Pyramid (Pang et al., 2016) Duet (Mitra et al., 2017), SMN (Wu et al., 2017)[9], and a degenerated version of our model that removes CNN_3 from our MT-hCNN model (MT-hCNN-d). All the methods in this paper are implemented with TensorFlow and are trained with NVIDIA Tesla K40M GPUs.

Settings: We use the same parameter settings of hCNN in (Yu et al., 2017). For the CNN_3 in our model, we set window size of convolution layer as 2, ReLU as the activation function, and the stride

of max-pooling layer as 2. The hidden node size of the Fully-Connected layer is set as 128. AdaDelta is used to train our model with an initial learning rate of 0.08. We use MAP, Recall@5, Recall@2, and Recall@1 as evaluation metrics. We set $\lambda_1 = \lambda_2 = \lambda_3 = 0.05$, and $\lambda_4 = 0.005$.

3.1 Comparison on Base Models

The comparisons on base models are shown in Table 1. First, the RNN based methods like MV-LSTM and SMN have clear advantages over the two CNN-based approaches like ARC-I and ARC-II, and are better or comparable with the state-of-the-art CNN-based models like Pyramid and Duet; Second, our MT-hCNN outperforms MT-hCNN-d, which shows the benefits of adding a convolutional layer to the output representations of all the utterances; Third, we find SMN does not perform well in AliMeData compared to UDC. One potential reason is that UDC has significantly larger data size than AliMeData (1000k vs. 51k), which can help to train a complex model like SMN; Last but not least, our proposed MT-hCNN shows the best results in terms of all the metrics in AliMeData, and the best results in terms of R@2 and R@1 in UDC, which shows the effectiveness of MT-hCNN.

We further evaluate the inference time [10] of these models. As shown in Table 1, MT-hCNN has comparable or better results when compared with SMN (the state-of-the-art multi-turn conversation model), but is much more efficient than SMN (∼60% time reduction). MT-hCNN also has similar efficiency with CNN-based methods but with better performance. As a result, our MT-hCNN module is able to support a peak QPS [11] of 40 on a cluster of 2 service instances, where each instance reserves 2 cores and 4G memory on

---

[6] Around 85% of conversations are within 3 turns.

[7] A "response" here is a question in our system.

[8] The threshold is determined by a business analyst

[9] The results are based on the TensorFlow code from authors, and with no over sampling of negative training data.

[10] The time of scoring a query and N candidate questions, where N is 10 in UDC, and 15 in AliMeData.

[11] Queries Per Second

an Intel Xeon E5-2430 machine. This shows the model is applicable to industrial bots. In all, our proposed MT-hCNN is shown to be both efficient and effective for question matching in multi-turn conversations.

3.2 Transferablity of our model

To evaluate the effectiveness of our transfer learning setting, we compare our full model with three baselines: Src-only that uses only source data, Tgt-only that uses only target data, and TL-S that uses both source and target data with the adversarial training as in (Liu et al., 2017). All the methods are evaluated on the test set of the target data.

As in Table 2, Src-only performs worse than Tgt-only. This shows the source and target domains are related but different. Despite the domain shift, TL-S is able to leverage knowledge from the source domain and boost performance; Last, our model shows better performance than TL-S, this shows the helpfulness of adding domain discriminators on both source and target domains.

Table 2: Transferablity of our model.

Data	E-commerce data (AliMeData)			
Methods	MAP	R@5	R@2	R@1
Src-only	0.7012	0.7123	0.4343	0.2846
Tgt-only	0.8418	0.7810	0.4796	0.3241
TL-S	0.8521	0.8022	0.4812	0.3255
Ours	**0.8523**	**0.8125**	**0.4881**	**0.3291**

3.3 Online Evaluations

We deployed our model online in AliMe Assist Bot. For each query, the bot uses the TF-IDF model in Lucene to return a set of candidates, then uses our model to rerank all the candidates and returns the top. We set the candidate size as 15 and context length as 3. To accelerate the computation, we bundle the 15 candidates into a mini-batch to feed into our model. We compare our method with the online model - a degenerated version of our model that only uses the current query to retrieve candidate, i.e. context length is 1. We have run 3-day A/B testing on the Click-Through-Rate (CTR) of the models. As shown in Table 3, our method consistently outperforms the online model, yielding 5% ∼ 10% improvement.

4 Related Work

Recent research in multi-turn conversation systems has focused on deep learning and reinforce-

Table 3: Comparison with the online model.

CTR	Day1	Day2	Day3
Online Model	0.214	0.194	0.221
Our Model	**0.266**	**0.291**	**0.288**

ment learning (Shang et al., 2015; Yan et al., 2016; Li et al., 2016a,b; Sordoni et al., 2015; Wu et al., 2017). The recent proposed Sequential Matching Network (SMN) (Wu et al., 2017) matches a response with each utterance in the context at multiple levels of granularity, leading to state-of-the-art performance on two multi-turn conversation corpora. Different from SMN, our model is built on CNN based modules, which yields comparable results but with better efficiency.

We study transfer learning (TL) (Pan and Yang, 2010) to help domains with limited data. TL has been extensively studied in the last decade. With the popularity of deep learning, many Neural Network (NN) based methods are proposed (Yosinski et al., 2014). A typical framework uses a shared NN to learn shared features for both source and target domains (Mou et al., 2016; Yang et al., 2017). Another approach is to use both a shared NN and domain-specific NNs to derive shared and domain-specific features (Liu et al., 2017). This is improved by some studies (Ganin et al., 2016; Taigman et al., 2017; Chen et al., 2017; Liu et al., 2017) that consider adversarial networks to learn more robust shared features across domains. Our TL model is based on (Liu et al., 2017), with enhanced source and target specific domain discrimination losses.

5 Conclusion

In this paper, we proposed a conversation model based on Multi-Turn hybrid CNN (MT-hCNN). We extended our model to adapt knowledge learned from a resource-rich domain. Extensive experiments and an online deployment in AliMe E-commerce chatbot showed the efficiency, effectiveness, and transferablity of our proposed model.

Acknowledgments

The authors would like to thank Weipeng Zhao, Juwei Ren, Zhiyu Min and other members of AliMe team for their help in deploying our model online. This work was supported in part by NSF grant IIS-1419693. We would also like to thank reviewers for their valuable comments.

References

S. R. Bowman, G. Angeli, C. Potts, and C. D. Manning. 2015. A large annotated corpus for learning natural language inference. In *EMNLP*.

Xinchi Chen, Zhan Shi, Xipeng Qiu, and Xuanjing Huang. 2017. Adversarial multi-criteria learning for chinese word segmentation. *CoRR* abs/1704.07556.

Y. Ganin, E. Ustinova, H. Ajakan, P. Germain, H. Larochelle, F. Laviolette, M. Marchand, and V. Lempitsky. 2016. Domain-adversarial training of neural networks. *Journal of Machine Learning Research* 17(59):1–35.

B. Hu, Z. Lu, H. Li, and Q. Chen. 2014. Convolutional neural network architectures for matching natural language sentences. In *NIPS '14*.

Feng-Lin Li, Minghui Qiu, Haiqing Chen, Xiongwei Wang, Xing Gao, Jun Huang, Juwei Ren, Zhongzhou Zhao, Weipeng Zhao, Lei Wang, and Guwei Jin. 2017. Alime assist: An intelligent assistant for creating an innovative e-commerce experience. In *CIKM 2017. Demo*.

J. Li, M. Galley, C. Brockett, G. P. Spithourakis, J. Gao, and W. B. Dolan. 2016a. A persona-based neural conversation model. In *ACL'16*.

J. Li, W. Monroe, A. Ritter, D. Jurafsky, M. Galley, and J. Gao. 2016b. Deep reinforcement learning for dialogue generation. In *EMNLP'16*.

P. Liu, X. Qiu, and X. Huang. 2017. Adversarial multi-task learning for text classification. In *ACL*.

R. Lowe, N. Pow, I. Serban, and J. Pineau. 2015. The ubuntu dialogue corpus: A large dataset for research in unstructured multi-turn dialogue systems. *CoRR* abs/1506.08909.

B. Mitra, F. Diaz, and N. Craswell. 2017. Learning to match using local and distributed representations of text for web search. In *WWW '17*.

L. Mou, Z. Meng, R. Yan, G. Li, Y. Xu, L. Zhang, and Z. Jin. 2016. How transferable are neural networks in nlp applications? In *EMNLP*.

S. Pan and Q. Yang. 2010. A survey on transfer learning. *IEEE Transactions on knowledge and data engineering* 22(10):1345–1359.

L. Pang, Y. Lan, J. Guo, J. Xu, S. Wan, and X. Cheng. 2016. Text matching as image recognition. In *AAAI*.

Minghui Qiu, Feng-Lin Li, Siyu Wang, Xing Gao, Yan Chen, Weipeng Zhao, Haiqing Chen, Jun Huang, and Wei Chu. 2017. Alime chat: A sequence to sequence and rerank based chatbot engine. In *ACL*.

L. Shang, Z. Lu, and H. Li. 2015. Neural responding machine for short-text conversation. In *ACL '15*.

A. Sordoni, M. Galley, M. Auli, C. Brockett, Y. Ji, M. Mitchell, J. Nie, J. Gao, and B. Dolan. 2015. A neural network approach to context-sensitive generation of conversational responses. In *NAACL '15*.

Y. Taigman, A. Polyak, and L. Wolf. 2017. Unsupervised cross-domain image generation. *ICLR* .

S. Wan, Y. Lan, J. Guo, J. Xu, L. Pang, and X. Cheng. 2016. A deep architecture for semantic matching with multiple positional sentence representations. In *AAAI '16*.

Y. Wu, W. Wu, C. Xing, M. Zhou, and Z. Li. 2017. Sequential matching network: A new architecture for multi-turn response selection in retrieval-based chatbots. In *ACL '17*.

Z. Xu, B. Liu, B. Wang, C. Sun, and X. Wang. 2016. Incorporating loose-structured knowledge into LSTM with recall gate for conversation modeling. *CoRR* .

R. Yan, Y. Song, and H. Wu. 2016. Learning to respond with deep neural networks for retrieval-based human-computer conversation system. In *SIGIR '16*.

Liu Yang, Minghui Qiu, Chen Qu, Jiafeng Guo, Yongfeng Zhang, W. Bruce Croft, Jun Huang, and Haiqing Chen. 2018. Response ranking with deep matching networks and external knowledge in information-seeking conversation systems. In *SIGIR '18*.

Z. Yang, R. Salakhutdinov, and W. W Cohen. 2017. Transfer learning for sequence tagging with hierarchical recurrent networks. *ICLR* .

W. Yin and H. Schütze. 2015. Convolutional neural network for paraphrase identification. In *NAACL-HLT* .

W. Yin, H. Schütze, B. Xiang, and B. Zhou. 2016. Abcnn: Attention-based convolutional neural network for modeling sentence pairs. *Transactions of ACL* 4:259–272.

J. Yosinski, J. Clune, Y. Bengio, and H. Lipson. 2014. How transferable are features in deep neural networks? In *NIPS*.

Jianfei Yu, Minghui Qiu, Jing Jiang, Jun Huang, Shuangyong Song, Wei Chu, and Haiqing Chen. 2017. Modelling domain relationships for transfer learning on retrieval-based question answering systems in e-commerce. *WSDM* .

A Multi-task Approach to Learning Multilingual Representations

Karan Singla[1], Dogan Can[1], Shrikanth Narayanan[1,2]
[1]Department of Computer Science
[2]Department of Electrical Engineering
University of Southern California, Los Angeles, USA
{singlak, dogancan}@usc.edu, shri@sipi.usc.edu

Abstract

We present a novel multi-task model-ing approach to learning multilingual dis-tributed representations of text. Our sys-tem learns word and sentence embeddings jointly by training a multilingual skip-gram model together with a cross-lingual sentence similarity model. Our architec-ture can transparently use both monolin-gual and sentence aligned bilingual cor-pora to learn multilingual embeddings, thus covering a vocabulary significantly larger than the vocabulary of the bilingual corpora alone. Our model shows com-petitive performance in a standard cross-lingual document classification task. We also show the effectiveness of our method in a limited resource scenario.

1 Introduction

Learning distributed representations of text, whether it be at the level of words, phrases, sentences or documents has been one of the most widely researched subjects in natural lan-guage processing in recent years (Mikolov et al., 2013; Pennington et al., 2014; Gouws et al., 2015; Socher et al., 2010; Pham et al., 2015b; Kiros et al., 2015; Conneau et al., 2017; Le and Mikolov, 2014; Chen, 2017; Wu et al., 2017). Word/sentence/document embeddings, as they are now commonly referred to, have quickly become essential ingredients of larger and more complex NLP systems looking to leverage the rich seman-tic and linguistic information present in distributed representations (Bengio et al., 2003; Maas et al., 2011; Collobert et al., 2011; Bahdanau et al., 2014; Chen and Manning, 2014).

Research that has been taking place in the con-text of distributed text representations is learn-ing multilingual text representations shared across languages (Faruqui and Dyer, 2014; Bengio and Corrado, 2015; Luong et al., 2015). Multilingual embeddings open up the possibility of transferring knowledge across languages and building complex systems even for languages with limited amount of supervised resources (Ammar et al., 2016; John-son et al., 2016). By far the most popular approach to learning multilingual embeddings is to train a multilingual word embedding model that is then used to derive representations for sentences and documents by composition (Hermann and Blun-som, 2014). These models are typically trained solely on word or sentence aligned corpora and the composition models are usually simple pre-defined functions like averages over word embed-dings (Lauly et al., 2014; Hermann and Blunsom, 2014; Mogadala and Rettinger, 2016) or paramet-ric composition models learned along with the word embeddings (Schwenk et al., 2017). For a thorough survey of cross-lingual text embedding models, please refer to (Ruder, 2017).

In this work we learn word and sentence embed-dings jointly by training a multilingual skip-gram model together with a cross-lingual sentence sim-ilarity model. Our multilingual skip-gram model is similar to (Luong et al., 2015). It transparently consumes *(word, context)* pairs constructed from monolingual as well as sentence aligned bilingual corpora. We process word embeddings with a bidirectional LSTM and then take an average of the LSTM outputs, which can be viewed as con-text dependent word embeddings, to produce sen-tence embeddings. Since our multilingual skip-gram and cross-lingual sentence similarity mod-els are trained jointly, they can inform each other through the shared word embedding layer and pro-mote the compositionality of learned word embed-dings at training time. Further, the gradients flow-ing back from the sentence similarity model can

214

Proceedings of the 56th Annual Meeting of the Association for Computational Linguistics (Short Papers), pages 214–220
Melbourne, Australia, July 15 - 20, 2018. ©2018 Association for Computational Linguistics

affect the embeddings learned for words outside the vocabulary of the parallel corpora. We hypothesize these two aspects of approach lead to more robust sentence embeddings.

The main motivation behind our approach is to learn high quality multilingual sentence and document embeddings in the low resource scenario where parallel corpus sizes are limited. The main novelty of our approach is the joint training of multilingual skip-gram and cross-lingual sentence similarity objectives with a shared word embedding layer which allows the gradients from the sentence similarity task to affect the embeddings learned for words outside the vocabulary of the parallel corpora. By jointly training these two objectives, we can transparently use monolingual and parallel data for learning multilingual sentence embeddings. Using a BiLSTM layer to contextualize word embeddings prior to averaging is orthogonal to the joint multi-task learning idea. We observed that this additional layer is beneficial in most settings and this is consistent with the observations of recent works on learning sentence and document embeddings such as (Conneau et al., 2017; Yang et al., 2016)

2 Model

Our model jointly optimizes multilingual skip-gram (Luong et al., 2015) and cross-lingual sentence similarity objectives using a shared word embedding layer in an end-to-end fashion.

Multilingual Skip-gram: Multilingual skip-gram model (Luong et al., 2015) extends the traditional skip-gram model by predicting words from both the monolingual and the cross-lingual context. The monolingual context consists of words neighboring a given word as in the case of the traditional skip-gram model. The cross-lingual context, on the other hand, consists of words neighboring the target word aligned with a given source word in a parallel sentence pair. Figure 1 shows an example alignment, where an aligned pair of words are attached to both their monolingual and bilingual contexts. For a pair of languages $L1$ and $L2$, the word embeddings are learned by optimizing the traditional skip-gram objective with *(word, context word)* pairs sampled from monolingual neighbors in $L1 \rightarrow L1$ and $L2 \rightarrow L2$ directions as well as cross-lingual neighbors in $L1 \rightarrow L2$ and $L2 \rightarrow L1$ directions. In our setup, cross-lingual pairs are sampled from parallel cor-

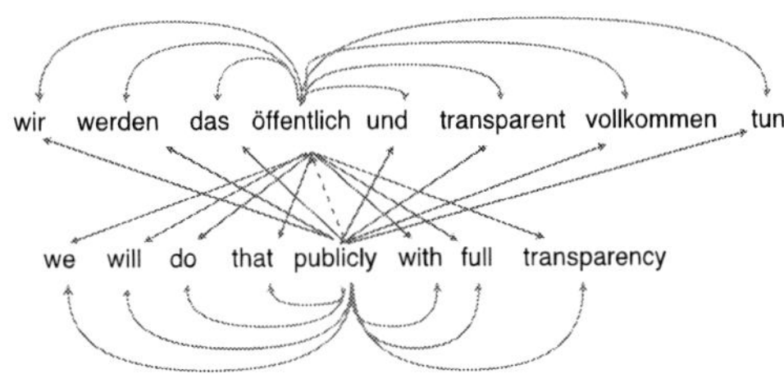

Figure 1: Example context attachments for a bilingual (en-de) skip-gram model.

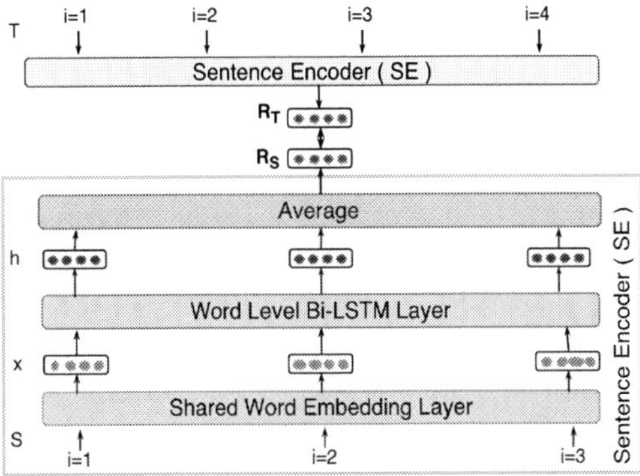

Figure 2: Overview of the architecture that we use for computing sentence representations R_S and R_T for input word sequences S and T.

pora while monolingual pairs are sampled from both parallel and monolingual corpora.

Cross-lingual Sentence Similarity: We process word embeddings with a bi-directional LSTM (Hochreiter et al., 2001; Hochreiter and Schmidhuber, 1997) and then take an average of the LSTM outputs (Figure 2). There are various implementations of LSTMs available; in this work we use an implementation based on (Zaremba et al., 2014). The LSTM outputs (hidden states) contextualize input word embeddings by encoding the history of each word into its representation. We hypothesize that this is better than averaging word embeddings as sentences generally have complex semantic structure and two sentences with different meanings can have exactly the same words. Let $R : S \rightarrow \mathbb{R}_d$ denote our sentence encoder mapping a given sequence of words S to a continuous vector in $\mathbb{R}_d$. Given a pair of parallel sentences (S, T), we define their distance as $d(S, T) = \|R_S - R_T\|^2$. For every parallel sentence pair, we randomly sample k negative sentences $\{N_i | i = 1 \ldots k\}$ and define the cross-lingual sentence similarity loss as follows:

$$l(S, T) = \sum_{i=1}^{k} \max(0, m + d(S, T) - d(S, N_i))$$

Without the LSTM layer, this loss is similar to the BiCVM loss (Hermann and Blunsom, 2014) except that we use also the reversed sample (T, S) to train the model, therefore showing each pair of sentences to the model two times per epoch.

3　Experiments

3.1　Corpora

We learn the distributed representations on the Europarl corpus v71 (Koehn, 2005). For a fair comparison with literature, we use the first 500K parallel sentences for each of the English-German (en-de), English-Spanish (en-es) and English-French (en-fr) language pairs. We keep the first 90% for training and the remaining 10% for development purposes. We also use additional 500K monolingual sentences from the Europarl corpus for each language. These sentences do not overlap with the sentences in parallel data.

Words that occur less than 5 times are replaced with the <unk> symbol. In the joint multi-task setting, the words are counted in the combined monolingual and parallel corpora. The vocabulary sizes for German (de) and English (en) are respectively 39K and 21K in the parallel corpus, 120K and 68K in the combined corpus.

We evaluate our models on the RCV1/RCV2 cross-lingual document classification task (Klementiev et al., 2012), where for each language we use 1K documents for training and 5K documents for testing.

3.2　Models

In addition to the proposed joint multi-task (JMT) model, **JMT-Sent-LSTM**, we also present ablation experiments where we omit the LSTM layer, the multilingual skip-gram objective or both. **JMT-Sent-Avg** is like the proposed model but does not include an LSTM layer. **Sent-LSTM** and **Sent-Avg** are the single-task variants of these models.

We construct document embeddings by averaging sentence representations produced by a trained sentence encoder. For a language pair $L1$-$L2$, a document classifier (single layer average perceptron) is trained on documents from $L1$, and tested

on documents from $L2$. Due to lack of supervision on the $L2$ side, this setup relies on documents from different languages with similar meaning having similar representations.

3.3　Training

The single-task models are trained with the cross-lingual sentence similarity objective end-to-end using parallel data only. We also tried training word embeddings beforehand on parallel and mono data and tuning them on the cross-lingual sentence similarity task but that did not improve the results. Those results are omitted for brevity. The multi-task models are trained by alternating between the two tasks.

Multilingual Skip-gram: We use stochastic gradient descent with a learning rate of 0.01 and exponential decay of 0.98 after 10K steps (1 step is 256 word pairs), negative sampling with 512 samples, skip-gram context window of size 5. Reducing the learning rate of the skip-gram model helps in the multi-task scenario by allowing skip-gram objective to converge in parallel with the sentence similarity objective. At every step, we sample equal number of monolingual and cross-lingual word pairs to make a mini-batch.

Cross-lingual Sentence Similarity: The batch size is 50 sentence pairs. LSTM hidden state dimension is 128 or 512. We use dropout at the embedding layer with drop probability 0.3. Hinge-loss margin m is equal to sentence embedding size. We sample 10 negative samples for the noise-contrastive loss. The model is trained using the Adam optimizer (Kingma and Ba, 2014) with a learning rate of 0.001 and an exponential decay of 0.98 after 10K steps (1 step is 50 sentence pairs).

3.4　Results

Table 1 shows the results for our models and compares them to some state-of-the-art approaches. When the sentence embedding dimension is 512, our results are close to the best results from literature. When the sentence embedding dimension is 128, our JMT-Sent-LSTM model outperforms all of the systems compared. Models with an LSTM layer (Sent-LSTM and JMT-Sent-LSTM) perform better than those without one. Joint multi-task training consistently improves the performance. The results for the data ablation experiments (*no-mono) suggest that the gains obtained in the JMT setting are partly due to the addition of monolin-

Model	en → de	de → en
500k parallel sentences, dim=128		
BiCVM-add+	86.4	74.7
BiCVM-bi+	86.1	79.0
BiSkip-UnsupAlign	88.9	77.4
Our Models		
Sent-Avg	88.2	80.0
JMT-Sent-Avg	88.5	80.5
Sent-LSTM	89.5	80.4
JMT-Sent-LSTM	**90.4**	**82.2**
JMT-Sent-Avg*no-mono	88.8	80.3
JMT-Sent-LSTM*no-mono	89.5	81.5
100k parallel sentences, dim=128		
Sent-Avg	81.6	75.2
JMT-Sent-Avg	85.3	79.1
Sent-LSTM	82.1	76.0
JMT-Sent-LSTM	87.4	80.7
JMT-Sent-LSTM*no-mono	83.4	76.5

Table 1: Results for models trained on en-de language pair. *no-mono means no monolingual data was used in training. We compare our models to: BiCVM-add+ (Hermann and Blunsom, 2014), BiCVM-bi+ (Hermann and Blunsom, 2014), BiSkip-UnsupAlign (Luong et al., 2015) and para_doc (Pham et al., 2015a).

Parallel / Mono	20K	50K	100K	500K
no-mono	60.3	68.3	82.1	89.5
20K	57.4	68.7	80.2	89.5
50K	**62.7**	69.0	83.5	89.5
100K	61.5	71.9	85.1	89.6
200K	58.1	**72.1**	85.5	90.0
500K	52.6	64.8	**87.4**	**90.4**

Table 2: Sent-LSTM vs. JMT-Sent-LSTM at different data conditions (en-de, dim=128).

Model	en-es	en-de	de-en	es-en	es-de
Sent-Avg	49.8	86.8	78.4	63.5	69.4
Sent-LSTM	53.1	89.9	77.0	67.8	65.3
JMT-Sent-Avg	51.5	87.2	75.7	60.3	**72.6**
JMT-Sent-LSTM	**57.4**	**91.0**	75.1	63.3	68.1
JMT-Sent-LSTM*	54.1	90.4	**82.2**	**68.4**	-

Table 3: Multilingual vs. bilingual* models (dim=128).

gual data and partly due to the multi-task objective.

Varying monolingual vs parallel data: The main motivation behind the multi-task architecture is to create high quality embeddings in the limited resource scenario. The bottom section of Table 1 shows the results for 128 dimensional embeddings when parallel data is limited to 100K sentences. JMT-Sent-LSTM results in this scenario are comparable to the results from the middle section of Table 1 which use 500K parallel sentences. These findings suggest that JMT-Sent-LSTM model can produce high quality embeddings even with a limited amount of parallel data by exploting additional monolingual data. Table 2 compares Sent-LSTM vs. JMT-Sent-LSTM at different data conditions. JMT-Sent-LSTM produces consistently better embeddings as long as the amount of additional monolingual data is neither too large nor too small compared to the amount of parallel data – 3-4 times parallel data size seems to be a good heuristic for choosing monolingual data size.

Multilingual vs Bilingual models: Table 3 compares multilingual models (en, es, de) to bilingual models. First four rows of Table 3 show results for multilingual systems where sentence en-

coder is trained for three languages (en,es,de) using en-es and en-de parallel data and additional monolingual data for each language. Document representations obtained from this sentence encoder are then used to train a classifier for a language pair like en-de, where the classifier is trained on en documents and then tested on de documents. In this scenario, we can build classifiers for language pairs like es-de even though we do not have access to es-de parallel data since embeddings we learn are shared between the three languages. Bottom row in Table 3 shows results for bilingual systems where we train the sentence encoder for two languages, and then use that encoder to train a document classifier for one language and test on the other. In this scenario, we cannot build classifiers for language pairs like es-de for which we do not have access to parallel data.

Multilingual models perform better than bilingual ones when English is the source language but they perform worse in the other direction. We believe this discrepancy is because Europarl documents were originally in English and later translated to other languages. The multilingual models also show promising results for es-de pair, for which there was no parallel data.

4 Linguistic analysis

As classification experiments focused on keeping semantic information in sentence level representations, we also checked if produced word embeddings still made sense. We use JMT-Sent-LSTM

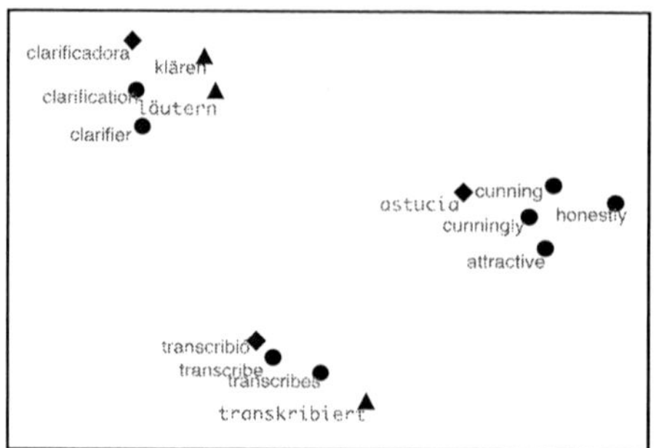

Figure 3: t-SNE projections for 3 English words (clarification, transcribe, cunningly) which are not in the parallel corpus and their four nearest neighbors. Red words are only in the monolingual corpus. Blue words exist in parallel corpus too.

model for this purpose. Figure 3 shows t-SNE projections for some sample words. Even though the model didn't use any German-Spanish parallel data it managed to map words which have similar meaning (transkribiert and transcribi) closer. Words that are antonyms but still have a similar meaning are close to each other (cunnigly (en), honestly (en) and astucia (es)). Nearest neighbors in the multilingual representation space are generally of same form across languages. It can also be observed that English words lie towards the middle of Spanish and German words which we believe is due to English being the pivot for the other two languages.

5 Conclusion

Our results suggest that joint multi-task learning of multilingual word and sentence embeddings is a promising direction. We believe that our sentence embedding model can be improved further with straightforward modifications to the sentence encoder architecture, for instance using stacked LSTMs or batch/layer normalization, and addition of sentence level auxiliary tasks such as sentiment classification or natural language inference. We plan to explore these directions and evaluate our approach on additional tasks in the future.

6 Discussion and Future Work

In our exploration of architectures for the sentence encoding model, we also tried using a self-attention layer following the intuition that not all words are equally important for the meaning of a sentence. However, we later realized that the cross lingual sentence similarity objective is at odds with what we want the attention layer to learn. When we used self attention instead of simple averaging of word embeddings, the attention layer learns to give the entire weight to a single word in both the source and the target language since that makes optimizing cross lingual sentence similarity objective easier. Another approach could be to derive high dimensional embeddings in a way similar to (Conneau et al., 2017) and using max-pooling which can allow efficient selection for each dimension to represent meaning.

Even though they are related tasks, multilingual skip-gram and cross-lingual sentence similarity models are always in a conflict to modify the shared word embeddings according to their objectives. This conflict, to some extent, can be eased by careful choice of hyper-parameters. This dependency on hyper-parameters suggests that better hyper-parameters can lead to better results in the multi-task learning scenario. We have not yet tried a full sweep of the hyper-parameters of our current models but we believe there may be easy gains to be had from such a sweep especially in the multi-task learning scenario. Other thing that remains rather unexplored is to do other levels of multi-tasking, like learning character representations or multitasking at sentence level.

References

Waleed Ammar, George Mulcaire, Miguel Ballesteros, Chris Dyer, and Noah A Smith. 2016. Many languages, one parser. *arXiv preprint arXiv:1602.01595*.

Dzmitry Bahdanau, Kyunghyun Cho, and Yoshua Bengio. 2014. Neural machine translation by jointly learning to align and translate. *arXiv preprint arXiv:1409.0473*.

Yoshua Bengio and Greg Corrado. 2015. Bilbowa: Fast bilingual distributed representations without word alignments.

Yoshua Bengio, Réjean Ducharme, Pascal Vincent, and Christian Jauvin. 2003. A neural probabilistic language model. *Journal of machine learning research*, 3(Feb):1137–1155.

Danqi Chen and Christopher D Manning. 2014. A fast and accurate dependency parser using neural networks. In *EMNLP*, pages 740–750.

Minmin Chen. 2017. Efficient vector representation for documents through corruption. *arXiv preprint arXiv:1707.02377*.

Ronan Collobert, Jason Weston, Léon Bottou, Michael Karlen, Koray Kavukcuoglu, and Pavel Kuksa. 2011. Natural language processing (almost) from scratch. *Journal of Machine Learning Research*, 12(Aug):2493–2537.

Alexis Conneau, Douwe Kiela, Holger Schwenk, Loic Barrault, and Antoine Bordes. 2017. Supervised learning of universal sentence representations from natural language inference data. *arXiv preprint arXiv:1705.02364*.

Manaal Faruqui and Chris Dyer. 2014. Improving vector space word representations using multilingual correlation. Association for Computational Linguistics.

Stephan Gouws, Yoshua Bengio, and Greg Corrado. 2015. Bilbowa: Fast bilingual distributed representations without word alignments. In *International Conference on Machine Learning*, pages 748–756.

Karl Moritz Hermann and Phil Blunsom. 2014. Multilingual models for compositional distributed semantics. *arXiv preprint arXiv:1404.4641*.

Sepp Hochreiter, Yoshua Bengio, Paolo Frasconi, and Jürgen Schmidhuber. 2001. Gradient flow in recurrent nets: the difficulty of learning long-term dependencies.

Sepp Hochreiter and Jürgen Schmidhuber. 1997. Long short-term memory. *Neural computation*, 9(8):1735–1780.

Melvin Johnson, Mike Schuster, Quoc V Le, Maxim Krikun, Yonghui Wu, Zhifeng Chen, Nikhil Thorat, Fernanda Viégas, Martin Wattenberg, Greg Corrado, et al. 2016. Google's multilingual neural machine translation system: Enabling zero-shot translation. *arXiv preprint arXiv:1611.04558*.

Diederik P Kingma and Jimmy Ba. 2014. Adam: A method for stochastic optimization. *arXiv preprint arXiv:1412.6980*.

Ryan Kiros, Yukun Zhu, Ruslan R Salakhutdinov, Richard Zemel, Raquel Urtasun, Antonio Torralba, and Sanja Fidler. 2015. Skip-thought vectors. In *Advances in neural information processing systems*, pages 3294–3302.

Alexandre Klementiev, Ivan Titov, and Binod Bhattarai. 2012. Inducing crosslingual distributed representations of words.

Philipp Koehn. 2005. Europarl: A parallel corpus for statistical machine translation. In *MT summit*, volume 5, pages 79–86.

Stanislas Lauly, Alex Boulanger, and Hugo Larochelle. 2014. Learning multilingual word representations using a bag-of-words autoencoder. *arXiv preprint arXiv:1401.1803*.

Quoc V Le and Tomas Mikolov. 2014. Distributed representations of sentences and documents. In *ICML*, volume 14, pages 1188–1196.

Thang Luong, Hieu Pham, and Christopher D Manning. 2015. Bilingual word representations with monolingual quality in mind. In *Proceedings of the 1st Workshop on Vector Space Modeling for Natural Language Processing*, pages 151–159.

Andrew L Maas, Raymond E Daly, Peter T Pham, Dan Huang, Andrew Y Ng, and Christopher Potts. 2011. Learning word vectors for sentiment analysis. In *Proceedings of the 49th Annual Meeting of the Association for Computational Linguistics: Human Language Technologies-Volume 1*, pages 142–150. Association for Computational Linguistics.

Tomas Mikolov, Ilya Sutskever, Kai Chen, Greg S Corrado, and Jeff Dean. 2013. Distributed representations of words and phrases and their compositionality. In *Advances in neural information processing systems*, pages 3111–3119.

Aditya Mogadala and Achim Rettinger. 2016. Bilingual word embeddings from parallel and nonparallel corpora for cross-language text classification. In *Proceedings of NAACL-HLT*, pages 692–702.

Jeffrey Pennington, Richard Socher, and Christopher D Manning. 2014. Glove: Global vectors for word representation. In *EMNLP*, volume 14, pages 1532–1543.

Hieu Pham, Minh-Thang Luong, and Christopher D Manning. 2015a. Learning distributed representations for multilingual text sequences. In *Proceedings of NAACL-HLT*, pages 88–94.

Nghia The Pham, Germán Kruszewski, Angeliki Lazaridou, and Marco Baroni. 2015b. Jointly optimizing word representations for lexical and sentential tasks with the c-phrase model. In *ACL (1)*, pages 971–981.

Sebastian Ruder. 2017. A survey of cross-lingual embedding models. *CoRR*, abs/1706.04902.

Holger Schwenk, Ke Tran, Orhan Firat, and Matthijs Douze. 2017. Learning joint multilingual sentence representations with neural machine translation. *arXiv preprint arXiv:1704.04154*.

Richard Socher, Christopher D Manning, and Andrew Y Ng. 2010. Learning continuous phrase representations and syntactic parsing with recursive neural networks. In *Proceedings of the NIPS-2010 Deep Learning and Unsupervised Feature Learning Workshop*, pages 1–9.

Ledell Wu, Adam Fisch, Sumit Chopra, Keith Adams, Antoine Bordes, and Jason Weston. 2017. Starspace: Embed all the things! *arXiv preprint arXiv:1709.03856*.

Zichao Yang, Diyi Yang, Chris Dyer, Xiaodong He, Alex Smola, and Eduard Hovy. 2016. Hierarchical attention networks for document classification. In *Proceedings of NAACL-HLT*, pages 1480–1489.

Wojciech Zaremba, Ilya Sutskever, and Oriol Vinyals. 2014. Recurrent neural network regularization. *arXiv preprint arXiv:1409.2329.*

Characterizing Departures from Linearity in Word Translation

Ndapa Nakashole and **Raphael Flauger**
Computer Science and Engineering
University of California, San Diego
La Jolla, CA 92093
nnakashole@eng.ucsd.edu

Abstract

We investigate the behavior of maps learned by machine translation methods. The maps translate words by projecting between word embedding spaces of different languages. We locally approximate these maps using linear maps, and find that they vary across the word embedding space. This demonstrates that the underlying maps are non-linear. Importantly, we show that the locally linear maps vary by an amount that is tightly correlated with the distance between the neighborhoods on which they are trained. Our results can be used to test non-linear methods, and to drive the design of more accurate maps for word translation.

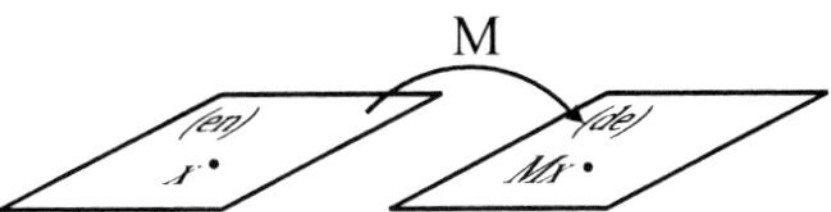
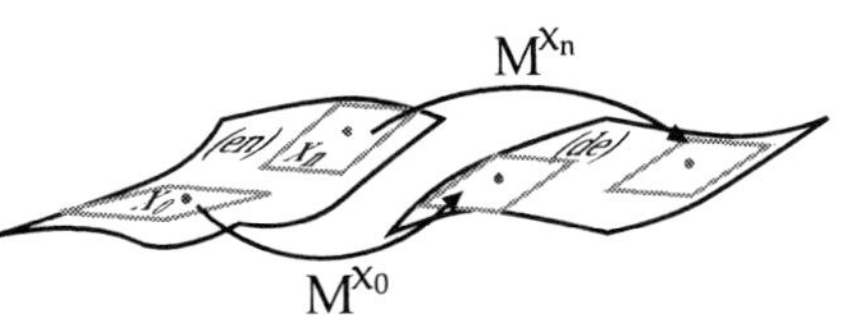

Figure 1: **Top:** Assumption of linearity implies a single linear map $\mathbf{M}$. **Bottom:** Our hypothesis is that the underlying map is expected to be non-linear but in small enough neighborhoods can be approximated by linear maps $\mathbf{M}^{x_i}$ for each neighborhood defined by $\mathbf{x}_i$.

1 Introduction

Following the success of monolingual word embeddings (Collobert et al., 2011), a number of studies have recently explored multilingual word embeddings. The goal is to learn word vectors such that similar words have similar vector representations regardless of their language (Zou et al., 2013; Upadhyay et al., 2016). Multilingual word embeddings have applications in machine translation, and hold promise for cross-lingual model transfer in NLP tasks such as parsing or part-of-speech tagging.

A class of methods has emerged whose core technique is to learn *linear* maps between vector spaces of different languages (Mikolov et al., 2013a; Faruqui and Dyer, 2014; Vulic and Korhonen, 2016; Artetxe et al., 2016; Conneau et al., 2018). These methods work as follows: For a given pair of languages, first, monolingual word vectors are learned independently for each language, and second, under the assumption that word vector spaces exhibit comparable structure across languages, a linear mapping function is learned to connect the two monolingual vector spaces. The map can then be used to translate words between the language pair.

Both seminal (Mikolov et al., 2013a), and state-of-the-art methods (Conneau et al., 2018) found linear maps to substantially outperform specific non-linear maps generated by feedforward neural networks. Advantages of linear maps include: *1)* In settings with limited training data, accurate linear maps can still be learned (Conneau et al., 2018; Zhang et al., 2017; Artetxe et al., 2017; Smith et al., 2017). For example, in unsupervised learning, (Conneau et al., 2018) found that using non-linear mapping functions made adversarial training unstable[1]. *2)* One can easily impose constraints on the linear maps at training time to ensure that the quality of the monolingual em-

---

[1] https://openreview.net/forum?id=H196sainb

Proceedings of the 56th Annual Meeting of the Association for Computational Linguistics (Short Papers), pages 221–227
Melbourne, Australia, July 15 - 20, 2018. ©2018 Association for Computational Linguistics

beddings is preserved after mapping (Xing et al.,
2015; Smith et al., 2017).

However, it is not well understood to what extent the assumption of linearity holds and how it affects performance. In this paper, we investigate the behavior of word translation maps, and show that there is clear evidence of departure from linearity.

Non-linear maps beyond those generated by feedforward neural networks have also been explored for this task (Lu et al., 2015; Shi et al., 2015; Wijaya et al., 2017; Shi et al., 2015). However, no attempt was made to characterize the resulting maps.

In this paper, we allow for an underlying mapping function that is non-linear, but assume that it can be approximated by linear maps at least in small enough neighborhoods. If the underlying map is linear, all local approximations should be identical, or, given the finite size of the training data, similar. In contrast, if the underlying map is non-linear, the locally linear approximations will depend on the neighborhood. Figure 1 illustrates the difference between the assumption of a single linear map, and our working hypothesis of locally linear approximations to a non-linear map. The variation of the linear approximations provides a characterization of the nonlinear map. We show that the local linear approximations vary across neighborhoods in the embedding space by an amount that is tightly correlated with the distance between the neighborhoods on which they are trained. The functional form of this variation can be used to test non-linear methods.

2 Review of Prior Work

To learn linear word translation maps, different loss functions have been proposed. The simplest is the regularized least squares loss, where the linear map $\mathbf{M}$ is learned as follows: $\hat{\mathbf{M}} = \arg\min_{\mathbf{M}} ||\mathbf{M}\mathbf{X} - \mathbf{Y}||_F + \lambda||\mathbf{M}||$, here $\mathbf{X}$ and $\mathbf{Y}$ are matrices that contain word embedding vectors for the source and target language (Mikolov et al., 2013a; Dinu et al., 2014; Vulic and Korhonen, 2016). The translation t of a source language word s is then given by: $t = \arg\max_t \cos(\mathbf{M}x_s, y_t)$.

(Xing et al., 2015) obtained improved results by imposing an orthogonality constraint on $\mathbf{M}$, $\mathbf{M} = ||\mathbf{M}\mathbf{W}^T - \mathbf{I}||$ where $\mathbf{I}$ is the identify matrix. Another loss function used in prior work

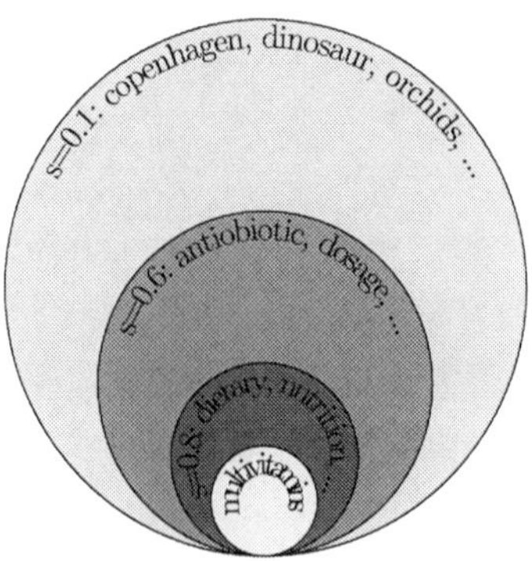

Figure 2: Neighborhoods formed around the word "multivitamins".

is the max-margin loss, which has been shown to significantly outperform the least squares loss (Lazaridou et al., 2015; Nakashole and Flauger, 2017).

Unsupervised or limited supervision methods for learning word translation maps have recently been proposed (Conneau et al., 2018; Zhang et al., 2017; Artetxe et al., 2017; Smith et al., 2017). However, the underlying methods for learning the mapping function are similar to prior work (Xing et al., 2015).

Non-linear cross-lingual mapping methods have been proposed. In (Wijaya et al., 2017) when dealing with rare words, the proposed method backs-off to a feed-forward neural network. (Shi et al., 2015) model relations across languages. (Lu et al., 2015) proposed a deep canonical correlation analysis based mapping method. Work on phrase translation has explored the use of many local maps that are individually trained (Zhao et al., 2015). In contrast to our work, these prior papers do not attempt to characterize the behavior of the resulting maps.

Our hypothesis is similar in spirit to the use of locally linear embeddings for nonlinear dimensionality reduction (Roweis and Saul, 2000).

3 Neighborhoods in Word Vector Space

In order to study the behavior of word translation maps, we begin by introducing a simple notion of neighborhoods in the embedding space. For a given language (e.g., English, en), we define a *neighborhood* of a word as follows: First, we pick a word x_i, whose corresponding vector is $x_i \in \mathbf{X}^{en}$, as an anchor. Second, we initialize a neighborhood $\mathcal{N}(x_i)$ containing a single vector x_i. We then grow the neighborhood by adding all words whose cosine similarity to x_i is $\geq s$. The resulting neighborhood is defined as: $\mathcal{N}(x_i, s) = \{ x_j \mid \cos(x_i, x_j) \geq s \}$.

Suppose we pick the word *multivitamins* as the anchor word. We can generate neighborhoods using $\mathcal{N}(x_{multivitamins}, s)$ where for each value of s we get a different neighborhood. Neighborhoods corresponding to larger values of s are subsumed by those corresponding to smaller values of s.

Figure 2 illustrates the process of generating neighborhoods around the word *multivitamins*. For large values of s (e.g., $s = 0.8$), the resulting neighborhoods only contain words that are closely related to the anchor word, such as *dietary* and *nutrition*. As s gets smaller (e.g., $s = 0.6$), the neighborhood gets larger, and includes words that are less related to the anchor, such as *antibiotic*.

Using this simple method, we can define different-sized neighborhoods around any word in the vocabulary.

4 Analysis of Map Behavior

Given the above neighborhood definition, we now seek to understand how word translation maps change as we move across neighborhoods in word embedding space.

Questions Studied. We study the following questions: [Q.1] Is there a single linear map for word translation that produces the same level of performance regardless of where in the vector space the words being translated fall? [Q.2] If there is no such single linear map, but instead multiple neighborhood-specific ones, is there a relationship between neighborhood-specific maps and the distances between their respective neighborhoods?

4.1 Experimental Setup and Data

In our first experiment we translate from English (*en*) to German (*de*). We obtained pre-trained word embeddings from FastText (Bojanowski et al., 2017). In the first experiment, we follow common practice (Mikolov et al., 2013a; Ammar et al., 2016; Nakashole and Flauger, 2017; Vulic and Korhonen, 2016), and used the Google Translate API to obtain training and test data. We make our data available for reproducibility[2]. For the second experiment, we repeat the first experiment, but instead of using Google Translate, we

---

use the recently released Facebook AI Research dictionaries [3] for training and test data. To test the generality of the findings of the first experiment, the second experiment was performed on a different language pair: English (*en*) to Swedish (*sv*).

In our all experiments, the cross-lingual maps are learned using the max-margin loss, which has been shown to perform competitively, while having fast run-times. (Lazaridou et al., 2015; Nakashole and Flauger, 2017). The max-margin loss aims to rank correct training data pairs (x_i, y_i) higher than incorrect pairs (x_i, y_j) with a margin of at least γ. The margin γ is a hyper-parameter and the incorrect labels, y_j can be selected randomly such that $j \neq i$ or in a more application specific manner. In our experiments, we set $\gamma = 0.4$ and randomly selected negative examples, one negative example for each training data point.

Given a seed dictionary as training data of the form $D^{tr} = \{x_i, y_i\}_{i=1}^{m}$, the mapping function is

$$\hat{\mathbf{W}} = \underset{\mathbf{W}}{\arg\min} \sum_{i=1}^{m} \sum_{j \neq i}^{k} \max \Big(0, \gamma$$
$$+ d(y_i, \mathbf{W}x_i) - d(y_j, \mathbf{W}x_i) \Big), \quad (1)$$

where $\hat{y}_i = \mathbf{W}x_i$ is the prediction, k is the number of incorrect examples per training instance, and $d(x, y) = (x - y)^2$ is the distance measure.

For the first experiment, we picked the following words as anchor words and obtained maps associated with each of their neighborhoods: $\mathbf{M}^{(multivitamins)}$, $\mathbf{M}^{(antibiotic)}$, $\mathbf{M}^{(disease)}$, $\mathbf{M}^{(blowflies)}$, $\mathbf{M}^{(dinosaur)}$, $\mathbf{M}^{(orchids)}$, $\mathbf{M}^{(copenhagen)}$. For each anchor word, we set $s = 0.5$, thus the neighborhoods are $\mathcal{N}(x_i, 0.5)$ where x_i is the vector of the anchor word. The training data for learning each neighborhood-specific linear map consists of vectors in $\mathcal{N}(x_i, 0.5)$ and their translations.

Table 1 shows details of the training and test data for each neighborhood. The words shown in Table 1 were picked as follows: first we picked the word *multivitamins*, then we picked the other words to have varying degrees of similarity to it. The cosine similarity of these words to the word 'multivitamins' are shown in column 3 of Table 1. It is also worth noting that there is nothing special about these words. In fact, the second experiment

---

0	1	2	3	4	5	6	7	8	9
Anchor Word	Data, $\mathcal{N}(x_i, s = 0.5)$		x_0 Similarity	Translation Accuracy				Matrix Property	
	Train	Test	$\cos(x_0, x_i)$	M	M^{x_0}	M^{x_i}	Δ	$\cos(M^{x_0}, M^{x_i})$	$||M||$
x_0:multivitamins	3,415	500	1.0	58.3	**68.2**	**68.2**	0	1.0	33.07
x_1:antibiotic	3,507	500	0.60	61.1	67.3	**72.7**	5.4 ↑	0.59	33.29
x_2:disease	2,478	500	0.45	69.3	59.2	**73.4**	14.2 ↑	0.31	35.35
x_3:blowflies	2,434	500	0.33	71.4	28.4	**73.2**	44.8 ↑	0.20	33.36
x_4:dinosaur	990	500	0.24	63.2	14.7	**77.1**	62.4 ↑	0.14	36.50
x_5:orchids	2,981	500	0.19	73.7	19.3	**78.0**	58.7 ↑	0.20	30.68
x_6:copenhagen	2,083	500	0.11	38.5	31.2	**67.4**	36.2 ↑	0.15	31.42

Table 1: The behavior of word translation maps trained on different neighborhoods (en → de translation). Highlighted columns illustrate variations in maps. Accuracy refers to precision at 10.

was carried out on different set of words, and on a different language pair.

4.2 Map Similarity Analysis

If indeed there exists a map that is the same linear map everywhere, we expect the above neighborhood-specific maps to be similar. Our analysis makes use of the following definition of matrix similarity:

$$\cos(\mathbf{M_1}, \mathbf{M_2}) = \frac{tr(\mathbf{M_1}^T \mathbf{M_2})}{\sqrt{tr(\mathbf{M_1}^T \mathbf{M_1}) tr(\mathbf{M_2}^T \mathbf{M_2})}} \quad (2)$$

Here $tr(\mathbf{M})$ denotes the trace of the matrix $\mathbf{M}$. $tr(\mathbf{M_1}^T \mathbf{M_1})$ computes the Frobenius norm $||\mathbf{M_1}||^2$, and $tr(\mathbf{M_1}^T \mathbf{M_2})$ is the Frobenius inner product. That is, $\cos(\mathbf{M_1}, \mathbf{M_2})$ computes the cosine similarity between the vectorized versions of matrices $\mathbf{M_1}$ and $\mathbf{M_2}$.

4.3 Experimental Results

The main results of our analysis are shown in Table 1.

We now analyze the results of Table 1 in detail. The *0th* column contains the anchor word, x_i, around which the neighborhood is formed. The *1st*, and *2nd* columns contain the size of the training and test data from $\mathcal{N}(x_i, s = 0.5)$ where x_i is the word vector for the anchor word.

The *3rd* column contains the cosine similarity between x_0, *multivitamins*, and x_i. For example, x_1 (*antibiotic*) is the most similar to x_0 (0.6), and x_6, *copenhagen*, is the least similar to x_0 (0.11).

The *4th* column is the translation accuracy of the single global map M, training on data from all x_i neighborhoods. The *5th* column is the translation accuracy of the map M^{x_0}, trained on the train-

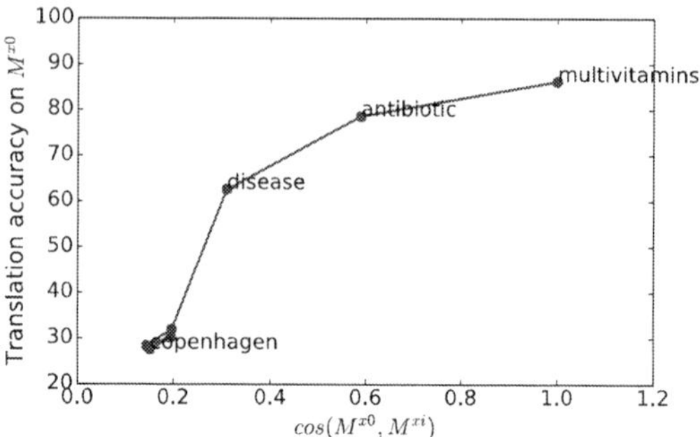

Figure 3: Correlation between the *8th* column (x-axis), map similarity $\cos(\mathbf{M^{x_0}}, \mathbf{M^{x_i}})$, and the *5th* column (y-axis), performance of map M^{x_0} on test data from the neighborhood anchored at x_i.

ing data of x_0, and tested on the test data in x_i. We use precision at top-10 as a measure of translation accuracy. Going down this column we can see that accuracy is highest on the test data from the neighborhood anchored at x_0 itself, and lowest on the test data from the neighborhood anchored at x_6, copenhagen, which is also the furthest word from x_0.

The *6th* column is translation accuracy of the map M^{x_i}, trained on the training data of the neighborhood anchored at x_i, and tested on the test data in x_i. We can see that compared to the *5th* column, in all cases performance is higher when we apply the map trained on data from the neighborhood, M^{x_i} instead of M^{x_0}. The *7th* column shows the difference in translation accuracy of the map M^{x_i} and M^{x_0}. This shows that the more dissimilar the neighborhood anchor word x_i is from x_0 according to the cosine similarity shown in the *4rd* column, the larger this difference is.

The local maps, *6th* column, M^{x_i} in all cases

0	1	2	3	4	5	6
Anchor Word	Data, $\mathcal{N}(x_i, s = 0.5)$		x_0 Similarity	Translation Accuracy		
	Train	Test	$\cos(x_0, x_i)$	M	$\mathbf{M}^{x_0}$	$\mathbf{M}^{x_i}$
x_0:species	1,765	200	1.0	58.0	**60.0**	**60.0**
x_1:genus	1,374	200	0.77	56.4	53.1	**56.0**
x_2:laticeps	1,868	200	0.60	81.0	73.4	**79.1**
x_3:femoralis	1,689	200	0.52	85.3	76.3	**83.4**
x_4:coneflower	1,077	200	0.47	39.6	31.6	**43.0**
x_5:epicauta	1,339	200	0.43	53.4	42.1	**54.2**
x_6:kristoffersen	1,227	200	0.09	24.3	10.3	**57.1**

Table 2: Different language pair (en $\rightarrow$ sv) English to Swedish, and different sets of neighborhoods. Train and test is from the FAIR/MUSE word translation lexicons. Accuracy refers to precision at 10.

outperform the global map $4th$ column.

The $8th$ column shows the similarity between maps M^{x_i} and M^{x_0} as computed by Equation 2. This column shows that the similarity between these learned maps is highly correlated with the cosine similarity or distance between the words in $3rd$ column. We also see a correlation with the translation accuracy in the $5th$ column. This correlation is visualized in Figure 3. Finally, the $9th$ column shows the magnitudes of the maps. The magnitudes vary somewhat between the maps trained on the different neighborhoods, and are significantly different from the magnitude expected for an orthogonal matrix. (For an orthogonal 300×300 matrix O the norm is $||O|| = \sqrt{300} \approx 17$).

In order to determine the generality of our results, we carried out the same experiment on a different language pair, as shown in Table 2. Crucially, we see the same trends as those observed in Table 1. This supports the generality of our findings.

4.4 Experiments Summary

Our experimental study suggests the following: i) linear maps vary across neighborhoods, implying that the assumption of a linear map does not to hold. ii) the difference between maps is tightly correlated with the distance between neighborhoods.

5 Conclusions

In this paper, we provide evidence that the assumption of linearity made by a large body of current work on cross-lingual mapping for word translation does not hold. We locally approximate the underlying non-linear map using linear maps, and show that these maps vary across neighborhoods in vector space by an amount that is tightly correlated with the distance between the neighborhoods on which they are trained. These results can be used to test non-linear methods, and we plan to use our finding to design more accurate maps in future work.

Acknowledgments

We thank the anonymous reviewers for their constructive comments. We also gratefully acknowledge Amazon for AWS Cloud Credits for Research, and Nvidia for a GPU grant.

References

Waleed Ammar, George Mulcaire, Yulia Tsvetkov, Guillaume Lample, Chris Dyer, and Noah A. Smith. 2016. Massively multilingual word embeddings. *CoRR*, abs/1602.01925.

Mikel Artetxe, Gorka Labaka, and Eneko Agirre. 2016. Learning principled bilingual mappings of word embeddings while preserving monolingual invariance. In *Proceedings of the 2016 Conference on Empirical Methods in Natural Language Processing*, pages 2289–2294.

Mikel Artetxe, Gorka Labaka, and Eneko Agirre. 2017. Learning bilingual word embeddings with (almost) no bilingual data. In *Proceedings of the 55th Annual Meeting of the Association for Computational Linguistics (Volume 1: Long Papers)*, volume 1, pages 451–462.

Phil Blunsom and Karl Moritz Hermann. 2014. Multilingual distributed representations without word alignment.

Piotr Bojanowski, Edouard Grave, Armand Joulin, and Tomas Mikolov. 2017. Enriching word vectors with subword information. *TACL*.

A. P. Sarath Chandar, Stanislas Lauly, Hugo Larochelle, Mitesh M. Khapra, Balaraman Ravindran, Vikas C. Raykar, and Amrita Saha. 2014. An autoencoder approach to learning bilingual word representations. In *NIPS*, pages 1853–1861.

Ronan Collobert, Jason Weston, Léon Bottou, Michael Karlen, Koray Kavukcuoglu, and Pavel Kuksa. 2011. Natural language processing (almost) from scratch. *Journal of Machine Learning Research*, 12(Aug):2493–2537.

Alexis Conneau, Guillaume Lample, Marc'Aurelio Ranzato, Ludovic Denoyer, and Hervé Jégou. 2018. Word translation without parallel data.

Georgiana Dinu, Angeliki Lazaridou, and Marco Baroni. 2014. Improving zero-shot learning by mitigating the hubness problem. *arXiv preprint arXiv:1412.6568*.

Manaal Faruqui and Chris Dyer. 2014. Improving vector space word representations using multilingual correlation. In *EACL*, pages 462–471.

Stephan Gouws, Yoshua Bengio, and Greg Corrado. 2015. Bilbowa: Fast bilingual distributed representations without word alignments. In *IICML*, pages 748–756.

Stephan Gouws and Anders Søgaard. 2015. Simple task-specific bilingual word embeddings. In *NAACL*, pages 1386–1390.

Aria Haghighi, Percy Liang, Taylor Berg-Kirkpatrick, and Dan Klein. 2008. Learning bilingual lexicons from monolingual corpora. In *ACL*, pages 771–779.

Alexandre Klementiev, Ivan Titov, and Binod Bhattarai. 2012. Inducing crosslingual distributed representations of words. In *COLING*, pages 1459–1474.

Tomáš Kočiský, Karl Moritz Hermann, and Phil Blunsom. 2014. Learning bilingual word representations by marginalizing alignments. *arXiv preprint arXiv:1405.0947*.

Philipp Koehn and Kevin Knight. 2002. Learning a translation lexicon from monolingual corpora. In *ACL Workshop on Unsupervised Lexical Acquisition*.

Angeliki Lazaridou, Georgiana Dinu, and Marco Baroni. 2015. Hubness and pollution: Delving into cross-space mapping for zero-shot learning. In *ACL*, pages 270–280.

Jinyu Li, Rui Zhao, Jui-Ting Huang, and Yifan Gong. 2014. Learning small-size dnn with output-distribution-based criteria. In *INTERSPEECH*, pages 1910–1914.

Ang Lu, Weiran Wang, Mohit Bansal, Kevin Gimpel, and Karen Livescu. 2015. Deep multilingual correlation for improved word embeddings. In *Proceedings of the 2015 Conference of the North American Chapter of the Association for Computational Linguistics: Human Language Technologies*, pages 250–256.

Tomas Mikolov, Quoc V. Le, and Ilya Sutskever. 2013a. Exploiting similarities among languages for machine translation. *CoRR*, abs/1309.4168.

Tomas Mikolov, Ilya Sutskever, Kai Chen, Greg S Corrado, and Jeff Dean. 2013b. Distributed representations of words and phrases and their compositionality. In *Advances in neural information processing systems*, pages 3111–3119.

Ndapandula Nakashole and Raphael Flauger. 2017. Knowledge distillation for bilingual dictionary induction. In *Proceedings of the 2017 Conference on Empirical Methods in Natural Language Processing (EMNLP)*, pages 2487–2496.

Jeffrey Pennington, Richard Socher, and Christopher Manning. 2014. Glove: Global vectors for word representation. In *Proceedings of the 2014 conference on empirical methods in natural language processing (EMNLP)*, pages 1532–1543.

Reinhard Rapp. 1999. Automatic identification of word translations from unrelated english and german corpora. In *ACL*.

Sam T Roweis and Lawrence K Saul. 2000. Nonlinear dimensionality reduction by locally linear embedding. *science*, 290(5500):2323–2326.

Tianze Shi, Zhiyuan Liu, Yang Liu, and Maosong Sun. 2015. Learning cross-lingual word embeddings via matrix co-factorization. In *Proceedings of the 53rd*

Annual Meeting of the Association for Computational Linguistics and the 7th International Joint Conference on Natural Language Processing (Volume 2: Short Papers), volume 2, pages 567–572.

Samuel L Smith, David HP Turban, Steven Hamblin, and Nils Y Hammerla. 2017. Offline bilingual word vectors, orthogonal transformations and the inverted softmax. In *ICLR*.

Anders Søgaard, Zeljko Agic, Héctor Martínez Alonso, Barbara Plank, Bernd Bohnet, and Anders Johannsen. 2015. Inverted indexing for cross-lingual NLP. In *ACL*, pages 1713–1722.

Peter D. Turney and Patrick Pantel. 2010. From frequency to meaning: Vector space models of semantics. *J. Artif. Intell. Res. (JAIR)*, 37:141–188.

Shyam Upadhyay, Manaal Faruqui, Chris Dyer, and Dan Roth. 2016. Cross-lingual models of word embeddings: An empirical comparison. In *ACL*.

Ivan Vulic and Anna Korhonen. 2016. On the role of seed lexicons in learning bilingual word embeddings. ACL.

Ivan Vulic and Marie-Francine Moens. 2015. Bilingual word embeddings from non-parallel document-aligned data applied to bilingual lexicon induction. In *ACL*, pages 719–725.

Derry Tanti Wijaya, Brendan Callahan, John Hewitt, Jie Gao, Xiao Ling, Marianna Apidianaki, and Chris Callison-Burch. 2017. Learning translations via matrix completion. In *Proceedings of the 2017 Conference on Empirical Methods in Natural Language Processing*, pages 1452–1463.

Chao Xing, Dong Wang, Chao Liu, and Yiye Lin. 2015. Normalized word embedding and orthogonal transform for bilingual word translation. In *HLT-NAACL*, pages 1006–1011.

Meng Zhang, Yang Liu, Huanbo Luan, and Maosong Sun. 2017. Adversarial training for unsupervised bilingual lexicon induction. In *Proceedings of the 55th Annual Meeting of the Association for Computational Linguistics (Volume 1: Long Papers)*, volume 1, pages 1959–1970.

Kai Zhao, Hany Hassan, and Michael Auli. 2015. Learning translation models from monolingual continuous representations. In *Proceedings of the 2015 Conference of the North American Chapter of the Association for Computational Linguistics: Human Language Technologies*, pages 1527–1536.

Will Y Zou, Richard Socher, Daniel Cer, and Christopher D Manning. 2013. Bilingual word embeddings for phrase-based machine translation. In *Proceedings of the 2013 Conference on Empirical Methods in Natural Language Processing*, pages 1393–1398.

Filtering and Mining Parallel Data in a Joint Multilingual Space

Holger Schwenk
Facebook AI Research
schwenk@dfb.com

Abstract

We learn a joint multilingual sentence embedding and use the distance between sentences in different languages to filter noisy parallel data and to mine for parallel data in large news collections. We are able to improve a competitive baseline on the WMT'14 English to German task by 0.3 BLEU by filtering out 25% of the training data. The same approach is used to mine additional bitexts for the WMT'14 system and to obtain competitive results on the BUCC shared task to identify parallel sentences in comparable corpora.

The approach is generic, it can be applied to many language pairs and it is independent of the architecture of the machine translation system.

1 Introduction

Parallel data, also called bitexts, is an important resource to train neural machine translation systems (NMT). It is usually assumed that the quality of the automatic translations increases with the amount of available training data. However, it was observed that NMT systems are more sensitive to noise than SMT systems, e.g. (Belinkov and Bisk, 2017). Well known sources of parallel data are international organizations like the European Parliament or the United Nations, or community provided translations like the TED talks. In addition, there are many texts on the Internet which are potential mutual translations, but which need to be identified and aligned. Typical examples are Wikipedia or news collections which report on the same facts in different languages. These collections are usually called comparable corpora.

In this paper we propose an unified approach to filter noisy bitexts and to mine bitexts in huge monolingual texts. The main idea is to first learn a joint multilingual sentence embedding. Then, a threshold on the distance between two sentences in this joint embedding space can be used to filter bitexts (distance between source and target sentences), or to mine for additional bitexts (pairwise distances between all source and target sentences). No additional features or classifiers are needed.

2 Related work

The problem of how to select parts of bitexts has been addressed before, but mainly from the aspect of domain adaptation (Axelrod et al., 2011; Santamaría and Axelrod, 2017). It was successfully used in many phrase-based MT systems, but it was reported to be less successful for NMT (van der Wees et al., 2017). It should be stressed that domain adaptation is different from filtering noisy training data. Data selection extracts the most relevant bitexts for the test set domain, but does not necessarily remove wrong translations, e.g. source and target sentences are both in-domain and well formed, but they are not mutual translations.

There is a huge body of research on mining bitexts, e.g. by analyzing the name of WEB pages or links (Resnik and Smith, 2003). Another direction of research is to use cross-lingual information retrieval, e.g. (Utiyama and Isahara, 2003; Munteanu and Marcu, 2005; Rauf and Schwenk, 2009). There are some works which use joint embeddings in the process of filtering or mining bitexts. For instance, Grégoire and Langlais (2017) first embed sentences into two separate spaces. Then, a classifier is learned on labeled data to decide whether sentences are parallel or not. Our approach clearly outperforms this technique on the BUCC corpus (cf. section 4). Bouamor and Sajjad (2018) use averaged multilingual word embeddings to calculate a joint embedding of all sen-

Proceedings of the 56th Annual Meeting of the Association for Computational Linguistics (Short Papers), pages 228–234
Melbourne, Australia, July 15 - 20, 2018. ©2018 Association for Computational Linguistics

tences. However, distances between all sentences are only used to extract a set of potential mutual translation. The decision is based on a different system. In Hassan et al. (2018) NMT systems for Zh $\leftrightarrow$ En are learned using a joint encoder. A sentence representation is obtained as the mean of the last encoder states. Noisy bitexts are filtered based on the distance. In all these works, embeddings are learned for two languages only, while we learn one joint embedding for up to nine languages.

3 Multilingual sentence embeddings

We are aiming at an embedding of entire sentences in different languages into one joint space, with the goal that the distance in that space reflects their semantic difference, independently of the language. There are several works on learning multilingual sentence embeddings which could be used for that purpose, i.e. (Hermann and Blunsom, 2014; Pham et al., 2015; Zhou et al., 2016; Chandar et al., 2013; Mogadala and Rettinger, 2016).

In this paper, we extend our initial approach (Schwenk and Douze, 2017). The underlying idea is to use multiple sequence encoders and decoders and to train them with N-way aligned corpora from the MT community. Instead of using one encoder for each language as in the original paper, we use a shared encoder which handles all the input languages. Joint encoders (and decoders) have already been used in NMT (Johnson et al., 2016). In contrast to that work, we do not use a special input token to indicate the target language. Our joint encoder has no information at all on the encoded language, or what will be done with sentence representation.

We trained this architecture on nine languages[1] of the Europarl corpus with about 2M sentences each. We use BPE (Sennrich et al., 2016b) to learn one 20k joint vocabulary for all the nine languages.[2] The joint encoder is a 3-layer BLSTM. The word embeddings are of size 384 and the hidden layer of the BLSTM is 512-dimensional. The 1024 dimensional sentence embedding is obtained by max-pooling over the BLSTM outputs. Dropout is set to 0.1. These settings are identical to those reported in (Schwenk and Douze, 2017), with the difference that we observe slight improvement by using a deeper network for the joint encoder. Once the system is learned, all the BLSTM

decoders are discarded and we only use the multilingual BLSTM encoder to embed the sentences into the joint space.

A very similar approach was also proposed in España-Bonet et al. (2017). A joint NMT system with attention is trained on several languages pairs, similar to (Johnson et al., 2016), including a special token to indicate the target language. After training, the sum of the encoder output states is used to obtain a fixed size sentence representation.

4 Experimental evaluation: BUCC shared task on mining bitexts

Since 2017, the workshop on Building and Using Comparable Corpora (BUCC) is organizing a shared task to evaluate the performance of approaches to mine for parallel sentences in comparable corpora (Zweigenbaum et al., 2018). Table 1 summarizes the available data, and Table 2 the official results. Roughly a 40th of the sentences are aligned. The best performing system *"VIC"* is based on the so-called STACC method which was shown to achieve state-of-the-art performance (Etchegoyhen and Azpeitia, 2016). It combines probabilistic dictionaries, search for similar sentences in both directions and a decision module which explores various features (common word prefixes, numbers, capitalized true-case tokens, etc). This STACC system was improved and adapted to the BUCC tasks with a word weighting scheme which is optimized on the monolingual corpora, and a named entity penalty. This task adaption substantially improved the generic STACC approach (Azpeitia et al., 2018). The systems RALI (Grégoire and Langlais, 2017) and H2 (Bouamor and Sajjad, 2018) have been already described in section 2. NLP2CT uses a denoising auto-encoder and a maximum-entropy classifier (Leong et al., 2018).

We applied our approach to all language pairs of the BUCC shared task (see Table 3). We used the

Lang.	Train			Test	
Pair	en	other	aligned	en	other
en-de	400k	414k	9580	397k	414k
en-fr	370k	272k	9086	373k	277k
en-ru	558k	461k	14435	566k	457k
en-zh	89k	95k	1899	90k	92k

Table 1: BUCC evaluation to mine bitexts. Number of sentences and size of the gold alignments.

---

[1] en, fr, es, it, pt, de, da, nl and fi

[2] Larger vocabularies achieve only slight improvements.

System	en-fr	en-de	en-ru	en-zh
VIC'17	79	84	-	-
RALI'17	20	-	-	-
LIMSI'17	-	-	-	43
VIC'18	81	86	81	77
H2'18	76	-	-	-
NLP2CT'18	-	-	-	56

Table 2: Official test set results of the 2017 and 2018 BUCC shared tasks (F-scores).

embeddings from (Schwenk and Douze, 2017) for ru and zh, which were trained on the UN corpus. The only task-specific adaptation is the optimization of the threshold on the distance in the multilingual joint space. Our system does not match the performance of the heavily tuned VIC system, but it is on-pair with H2 on en-fr, and outperforms all other approaches by a large margin. We would like to emphasize that our approach uses no additional features or classifiers, and that we apply the same approach to all language pairs. It is nice to see that the performance varies little for the languages.

España-Bonet et al. (2017) have also evaluated their technique on the BUCC data, but results on the official test set are not provided. Also, their joint encoder uses the *"news-commentary"* corpus during training. This is likely to add an important bias since all the parallel sentences in the BUCC corpus are from the news-commentary corpus.

Since we learn multilingual embeddings for many languages in one joint space, we can mine for parallel data for any language pair. As an example, we have mined for French/German and Chinese/Russian bitexts, respectively. There are no reference alignments to optimize the threshold for this language pair. Based on the experiments with the other languages, we chose a value of 0.55.

Task		en-fr	en-de	en-ru	en-zh
	P	81.9	82.2	79.9	76.7
Train	R	69.1	70.1	67.8	67.1
	F1	74.9	76.1	73.3	71.6
Threshold		0.58	0.50	0.57	0.64
	P	84.8	84.1	81.1	77.7
Test	R	68.6	70.7	67.6	66.4
	F1	75.8	76.9	73.8	71.6

Table 3: Results on the BUCC test set of our approach: Precision, Recall and F-measure (%). We also provide the optimal threshold.

In the annex, we provide examples of extracted parallel sentences for various values of the multilingual distance. These examples show that our approach may wrongly align sentences which are mainly an enumeration of named entities, numerical values, etc. Many of these erroneous alignments could be possibly excluded by some postprocessing, e.g. comparing the number of named entities in each sentence.

5 Experimental evaluation: improving WMT'14 En-De NMT systems

5.1 Baseline NMT systems

We have performed all our experiments with the freely available Sequence-to-Sequence PyTorch toolkit from Facebook AI Research,[3] called `fairseq-py`. It implements a convolutional model which achieves very competitive results (Gehring et al., 2017). We use this system to show the improvements obtained by filtering the standard training data and by integrating additional mined data. We will freely share this data so that it can be used to train different NMT architectures.

In this work, we focus on translating from English into German using the WMT'14 data. This task was selected for two reasons:

- it is the de-facto standard to evaluate NMT systems and many comparable results are available, e.g. (Sennrich et al., 2016b; Chunga et al., 2016; Wu et al., 2016; Gehring et al., 2017; Ashish Vaswani et al., 2017);

- only a limited amount of parallel training data is available (4.5M sentences). 2.1M are high quality human translations and 2.4M are crawled and aligned sentences (Common Crawl corpus).

As in other works, we use newstest-2014 as test set. However, in order to follow the standard WMT evaluation setting, we use `mteval-v14.pl` on untokenized hypothesis to calculate case-sensitive BLEU scores. Note that in some papers, BLEU is calculated with `multi-bleu.perl` on tokenized hypothesis. All our results are for one single system only.

We trained the `fairseq-py` system with default parameters, but a slightly different pre- and

---

[3] `https://github.com/facebookresearch/fairseq-py`

Corpus	Human only (Eparl+NC)	All WMT'14 (Eparl+NC+CC)
#sents	2.1M	4.5M
BLEU	21.87	24.75

Table 4: Our baseline results on WMT'14 en-de.

post-processing scheme. In particular, we lower-case all data and use a 40k BPE vocabulary (Sennrich et al., 2016b). Before scoring, the case of the hypothesis is restored using a recaser trained on the WMT German news data. Table 4 gives our baseline results using the provided data as it is. We distinguish results when training on human labeled data only, i.e. Europarl and News Commentary (2.1M sentences), and with all WMT'14 training data, i.e. human + Common Crawl (total of 4.5M sentences). Gehring et al. (2017) report a tokenized BLEU score of 25.16 on a slightly different version of newstest-2014 as defined in (Luong et al., 2015).[4] Please remember that the goal of this paper is not to set a new state-of-the-art in NMT on this data set, but to show relative improvement with respect to a competitive baseline.

5.2 Filtering Common Crawl

The Common Crawl corpus is provided by the organizers of WMT'14. We do not know how this corpus was produced, but like all crawled corpora, it is inherently noisy. To filter that corpus, we first embed all the sentences into the joint space and calculate the cosine distance between the English source and the provided German translation. We then extract subsets of different sizes as a function of the threshold on this distance.

All	Commas	<50 words	LID
2399k	2144k	2071k	1935k

Table 5: Pre-processing of the Common Crawl corpus before distance-based filtering.

After some initial experiments, it turned out that some additional steps are needed before calculating the distances (see Table 5): 1) remove sentences with more than 3 commas. Those are indeed often enumerations of names, cities, etc. While such sentences maybe useful to train NMT systems, the multilingual distance is not very reliable to distinguish list of named entities; 2) limit to sentences with less than 50 words; 3) perform LID on source and target sentences; These steps

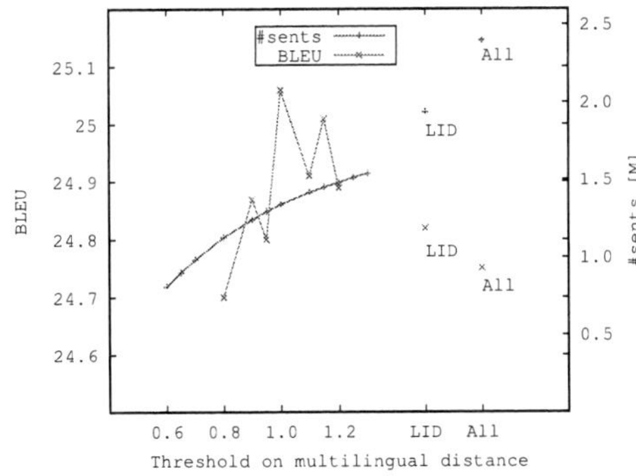

Figure 1: Filtering the Common Crawl corpus: size of corpus (pink) and BLEU scores (green).

discarded overall 19% of the data. It is surprising that almost 6% of the data seems to have the wrong source or target language.[5]

Figure 1 (pink curve) shows the amount of data as a function of the threshold on the multilingual distance. Some human inspection of the filtered corpus indicated that the translations start to be wrong for a threshold larger than 1.0. Therefore, we build NMT systems using a filtered version of Common Crawl for thresholds in the range of 0.8 to 1.2 (see Figure 1, green curve). It is good to see that the BLEU score increases when less but better data is used and then decreases again since we discard too much data. Best performance of 25.06 BLEU is achieved for a threshold of 1.0. This corresponds to a gain of 0.3 BLEU on top of a very competitive baseline (24.75→25.06), using only 3.4M instead of the original 4.5M sentence pairs. We actually discard almost half of the Common Crawl data. For comparison, we also trained an NMT system using the pre-processed Common Crawl corpus of 1.9M sentences (cf. Table 5), but without distance-based filtering. This gives a BLEU score of 24.82, a small 0.07 change.

Aiming at a compromise between speed and full convergence, we trained all systems for 55 epochs which takes less than two days on 8 NVidia GPU100s. Longer training may improve the overall results slightly.

5.3 Mining Parallel Data in WMT News

In the framework of the WMT evaluation, large news corpora are provided: 144M English and 187M German sentences (after removing sentence with more than 50 words). As in section 4, we

---

[4]This version uses a subset of 2737 out of 3003 sentences.

[5]LID itself may also commit errors, we used `https://fasttext.cc/docs/en/ language-identification.html`

embed all sentences into the joint space. For each source sentence, we search for the k-nearest sentences in the target language. We use $k = 20$ since it can happen that for the same source sentence, several possible translations are found (different news sites reporting on the same fact with different wordings). This search has a complexity of $O(N \times M)$, while filtering presumed parallel corpora is $O(N)$. In our case, $144M \times 185M$ amounts to 26 peta distance calculations. This can be quite efficiently done with the highly optimized FAISS toolkit (Johnson et al., 2017).

To start, we trained NMT systems on the extracted data only (see Table 6, 3rd column). As with the Common Crawl corpus, we discarded sentences pairs with the wrong language and many commas. By varying the threshold on the distance between two sentences in the embedding space, we can extract various amounts of data. However, the larger the threshold, the more unlikely the sentences are translations. Training on 1M mined sentences gives a modest BLEU score of 4.18, which increases up to 7.77 when 4.3M sentences are extracted. This result is well below an NMT system trained on *"real parallel data"*.

We have observed that the length distribution of the mined sentences is very different of the one of the WMT'14 training corpora (see Figure 2). The average sentence length for all the WMT training corpora is 24, while it is only 8 words for our mined texts. On one hand, it could be of course that our distance based mining approach works badly for long sentences. But on the other hand, the longer the sentences, the more unlikely it is to find perfect translation in crawled news data. If

Threshold	#Sents	BLEU		
		Mined alone	Eparl + mined	All + mined
baseline	-	-	21.87	25.06
0.25	1.0M	4.18	**22.32**	**25.07**
0.26	1.5M	5.17	22.09	-
0.27	1.9M	5.92	21.97	-
0.28	2.5M	6.48	22.29	25.03
0.29	3.3M	6.01	22.10	-
0.30	4.3M	7.77	22.24	-

Table 6: BLEU scores when training on the mined data only, adding it (at different thresholds) to the human translated training corpus (Eparl+NC) and to our best system using filtered Common Crawl.

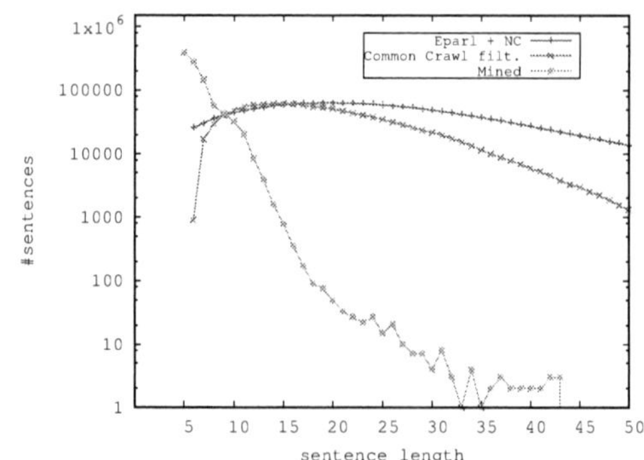

Figure 2: Number of sentences as a function of their length, for WMT'14 training corpora and the mined news texts.

we shuffle the Europarl corpus and consider it as a comparable corpus, our approach is able to extract more than 95% of the translation pairs. It is also an open question how short sentences impact the training of NMT systems. Further research in those directions is needed.

When adding our mined data to the Europarl and News Commentary corpora (2.1M sentences), we are able to achieve an improvement of 0.45 BLEU (21.87→22.32, 4th column of Table 6). However, we observe no improvement when adding the mined data to our best system which uses the filtered Common Crawl data (5th column of Table 6). It could be that some of our mined data is actually a subset of Common Crawl.

6   Conclusion

We have shown that a simple cosine distance in a joint multilingual sentence embedding space can be used to filter noisy parallel data and to mine for bitexts in large news collections. We were able to improve a competitive baseline on the WMT'14 English to German task by 0.3 BLEU by filtering out 25% of the training data. We will make the filtered and extracted data freely available, as well as a tool to filter noisy bitexts in nine languages.

There are many directions to extend this research, in particular to scale-up to larger corpora. We will apply it to the data mined by the European ParaCrawl project.[6] The proposed multilingual sentence distance could be also used in MT confidence estimation, or to filter back-translations of monolingual data (Sennrich et al., 2016a).

---

[6]http://paracrawl.eu/download.html

References

Ashish Vaswani et al. 2017. Attention is all you need. In *NIPS*.

Amittai Axelrod, Xiaodong He, and Jianfeng Gao. 2011. Domain adaptation via pseudo in-domain data selection. In *EMNLP*, pages 355–362.

Andoni Azpeitia, Thierry Etchegoyhen, and Eva Martínez Garcia. 2018. Extracting parallel sentences from comparable corpora with STACC variants. In *BUCC*.

Yonatan Belinkov and Yonatan Bisk. 2017. Synthetic and artificial noise both break neural machine translation. In *https://arxiv.org/abs/1711.02173*.

Houda Bouamor and Hassan Sajjad. 2018. H2@bucc18: Parallel sentence extraction from comparable coprora using multlingual sentence embeddings. In *BUCC*.

Sarath Chandar, Mitesh M. Khapra, Balaraman Ravindran, Vikas Raykar, and Amrita Saha. 2013. Multilingual deep learning. In *NIPS DL wshop*.

Junyoung Chunga, Kyunghyun Choa, and Yoshua Bengio. 2016. A character-level decoder without explicit segmentation for neural machine translation. In *https://arxiv.org/abs/1603.06147*.

Cristina España-Bonet, Ádám Csaba Varga, Alberto Barrón-Cedeño, and Josef van Genabith. 2017. An empirical analysis of nmt-derived interlingual embeddings and their use in parallel sentence identification. *IEEE Journal of Selected Topics in Sigmal Processing*, pages 1340–1348.

Thierry Etchegoyhen and Andoni Azpeitia. 2016. Set-theoretic alignment of comparable corpora. In *ACL*.

Jonas Gehring, Michael Auli, David Grangier, Denis Yarats, and Yann N Dauphin. 2017. Convolutional Sequence to Sequence Learning. In *ICML*.

Francis Grégoire and Philippe Langlais. 2017. Bucc 2017 shared task: a first attempt toward a deep learning framework for identifying parallel sentences in comparable corpora. In *BUCC*, pages 46–50.

Hany Hassan, Anthony Aue, Chang Chen, Vishal Chowdhary, Jonathan Clark, Christian Federmann, Xuedong Huang, Marcin Junczys-Dowmunt, William Lewis, Mu Li, Shujie Liu, Tie-Yan Liu, Renqian Luo, Arul Menezes, Tao Qin, Frank Seide, Xu Tan, Fei Tian, Lijun Wu, Shuangzhi Wu, Yingce Xia, Dongdong Zhang, Zhirui Zhang, and Ming Zhou. 2018. Achieving human parity on automatic chinese to english translation. In *https://arxiv.org/abs/1803.05567*.

Karl Moritz Hermann and Phil Blunsom. 2014. Multilingual models for compositional distributed semantics. In *ACL*, pages 58–68.

Jeff Johnson, Matthijs Douze, and Hervé Jégou. 2017. Billion-scale similarity search with gpus. *arXiv preprint arXiv:1702.08734*.

Melvin Johnson et al. 2016. Google's multilingual neural machine translation system: Enabling zero-shot translation. In *https://arxiv.org/abs/1611.04558*.

Chongman Leong, Derek F. Wong, and Lidia S. Chao. 2018. Um-paligner: Neural network-based parallel sentence identification model. In *BUCC*.

Minh-Thang Luong, Hieu Pham, and Christophe D. Manning. 2015. Effective approaches to attention-based neural machine translation. In *EMNLP*, pages 1412–1421.

Aditua Mogadala and Achim Rettinger. 2016. Bilingual word embeddings from parallel and non-parallel corpora for cross-language classification. In *NAACL*, pages 692–702.

Dragos Stefan Munteanu and Daniel Marcu. 2005. Improving machine translation performance by exploiting non-parallel corpora. *Computational Linguistics*, 31(4):477–504.

Hieu Pham, Minh-Thang Luong, and Christopher D. Manning. 2015. Learning distributed representations for multilingual text sequences. In *Workshop on Vector Space Modeling for NLP*.

Sadaf Abdul Rauf and Holger Schwenk. 2009. On the use of comparable corpora to improve SMT performance. In *EACL*, pages 16–23.

Philip Resnik and Noah A. Smith. 2003. The web as a parallel corpus. *Computational Linguistics*, 29:349–380.

Lucía Santamaría and Amittai Axelrod. 2017. Data selection with cluster-based language difference models and cynical selection. In *IWSLT*, pages 137–145.

Holger Schwenk and Matthijs Douze. 2017. Learning joint multilingual sentence representations with neural machine translation. In *ACL workshop on Representation Learning for NLP*.

Rico Sennrich, Barry Haddow, and Alexandra Birch. 2016a. Improving neural machine translation models with monolingual data. In *ACL*, pages 86–96.

Rico Sennrich, Barry Haddow, and Alexandra Birch. 2016b. Neural machine translation of rare words with subword units. In *ACL*, pages 1715–1725.

Masao Utiyama and Hitoshi Isahara. 2003. Reliable measures for aligning Japanese-English news articles and sentences. In *ACL*, pages 72–79.

Marlies van der Wees, Arianna Bisazza, and Christof Monz. 2017. Dynamic data selection for neural machine translation. In *EMNLP*, pages 1400–1410.

Yonghui Wu et al. 2016. Google's neural machine translation system: Bridging the gap between human and machine translation. In *https://arxiv.org/abs/1610.05011*.

Xinjie Zhou, Xiaojun Wan, and Jianguo Xiao. 2016. Cross-lingual sentiment classification with bilingual document representation learning. In *ACL*.

Pierre Zweigenbaum, Serge Sharoff, and Reinhard Rapp. 2018. Overview of the third bucc shared task: Spottign parallel sentences in comparable corpora. In *BUCC*, pages 60–67.

Hybrid semi-Markov CRF for Neural Sequence Labeling

Zhi-Xiu Ye
University of Science and
Technology of China
zxye@mail.ustc.edu.cn

Zhen-Hua Ling
University of Science and
Technology of China
zhling@ustc.edu.cn

Abstract

This paper proposes hybrid semi-Markov conditional random fields (SCRFs) for neural sequence labeling in natural language processing. Based on conventional conditional random fields (CRFs), SCRFs have been designed for the tasks of assigning labels to segments by extracting features from and describing transitions between segments instead of words. In this paper, we improve the existing SCRF methods by employing word-level and segment-level information simultaneously. First, word-level labels are utilized to derive the segment scores in SCRFs. Second, a CRF output layer and an SCRF output layer are integrated into an unified neural network and trained jointly. Experimental results on CoNLL 2003 named entity recognition (NER) shared task show that our model achieves state-of-the-art performance when no external knowledge is used[1].

1 Introduction

Sequence labeling, such as part-of-speech (POS) tagging, chunking, and named entity recognition (NER), is a category of fundamental tasks in natural language processing (NLP). Conditional random fields (CRFs) (Lafferty et al., 2001), as probabilistic undirected graphical models, have been widely applied to the sequence labeling tasks considering that they are able to describe the dependencies between adjacent word-level labels and to avoid illegal label combination (e.g., I-ORG can't follow B-LOC in the NER tasks using the BIOES tagging scheme). Original CRFs utilize hand-crafted features which increases the difficulty of performance tuning and domain adaptation.

[1] The code of our models is available at http://github.com/ZhixiuYe/HSCRF-pytorch

In recent years, neural networks with distributed word representations (i.e., word embeddings) (Mikolov et al., 2013; Pennington et al., 2014) have been introduced to calculate word scores automatically for CRFs (Chiu and Nichols, 2016; Huang et al., 2015).

On the other hand, semi-Markov conditional random fields (SCRFs) (Sarawagi and Cohen, 2005) have been proposed for the tasks of assigning labels to the segments of input sequences, e.g., NER. Different from CRFs, SCRFs adopt segments instead of words as the basic units for feature extraction and transition modeling. The word-level transitions within a segment are usually ignored. Some variations of SCRFs have also been studied. For example, Andrew (2006) extracted segment-level features by combining hand-crafted CRF features and modeled the Markov property between words instead of segments in SCRFs. With the development of deep learning, some models of combining neural networks and SCRFs have also been studied. Zhuo et al. (2016) and Kong et al. (2015) employed gated recursive convolutional neural networks (grConvs) and segmental recurrent neural networks (SRNNs) to calculate segment scores for SCRFs respectively.

All these existing neural sequence labeling methods using SCRFs only adopted segment-level labels for score calculation and model training. In this paper, we suppose that word-level labels can also contribute to the building of SCRFs and thus design a hybrid SCRF (HSCRF) architecture for neural sequence labeling. In an HSCRF, word-level labels are utilized to derive the segment scores. Further, a CRF output layer and an HSCRF output layer are integrated into a unified neural network and trained jointly. We evaluate our model on CoNLL 2003 English NER task (Sang and Meulder, 2003) and achieve state-of-the-art performance when no external knowledge is used.

Proceedings of the 56th Annual Meeting of the Association for Computational Linguistics (Short Papers), pages 235–240
Melbourne, Australia, July 15 - 20, 2018. ©2018 Association for Computational Linguistics

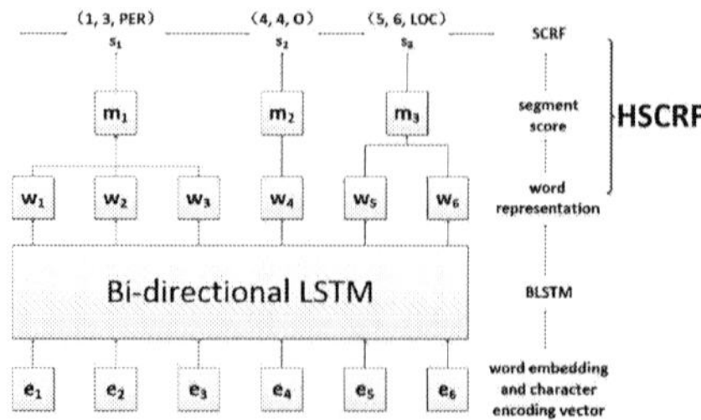

Figure 1: The diagram of a neural network with an HSCRF output layer for sequence labeling.

In summary, the contributions of this paper are: (1) we propose the HSCRF architecture which employs both word-level and segment-level labels for segment score calculation. (2) we propose a joint CRF-HSCRF training framework and a naive joint decoding algorithm for neural sequence labeling. (3) we achieve state-of-the-art performance in CoNLL 2003 NER shared task.

2 Methods

2.1 Hybrid semi-Markov CRFs

Let $\mathbf{s} = \{s_1, s_2, ..., s_p\}$ denote the segmentation of an input sentence $\mathbf{x} = \{x_1, ..., x_n\}$ and $\mathbf{w} = \{w_1, ..., w_n\}$ denote the sequence of word representations of $\mathbf{x}$ derived by a neural network as shown in Fig. 1. Each segment $s_i = (b_i, e_i, l_i)$, $0 \leq i \leq p$, is a triplet of a begin word index b_i, an end word index e_i and a segment-level label l_i, where $b_1 = 1$, $e_p = |\mathbf{x}|$, $b_{i+1} = e_i + 1$, $0 \leq e_i - b_i < L$, and L is the upperbound of the length of s_i. Correspondingly, let $\mathbf{y} = \{y_1, ..., y_n\}$ denote the word-level labels of $\mathbf{x}$. For example, if a sentence $\mathbf{x}$ in NER task is "Barack Hussein Obama and Natasha Obama", we have the corresponding $\mathbf{s} = ((1, 3, PER), (4, 4, O), (5, 6, PER))$ and $\mathbf{y} =$ (B-PER, I-PER, E-PER, O, B-PER, E-PER).

Similar to conventional SCRFs (Sarawagi and Cohen, 2005), the probability of a segmentation $\hat{\mathbf{s}}$ in an HSCRF is defined as

$$\mathrm{p}(\hat{\mathbf{s}}|\mathbf{w}) = \frac{\mathrm{score}(\hat{\mathbf{s}}, \mathbf{w})}{\sum_{\mathbf{s}' \in \mathbf{S}} \mathrm{score}(\mathbf{s}', \mathbf{w})}, \quad (1)$$

where $\mathbf{S}$ contains all possible segmentations and

$$\mathrm{score}(\mathbf{s}, \mathbf{w}) = \prod_{i=1}^{|\mathbf{s}|} \psi(l_{i-1}, l_i, \mathbf{w}, b_i, e_i). \quad (2)$$

Here, $\psi(l_{i-1}, l_i, \mathbf{w}, b_i, e_i) = exp\{m_i + b_{l_{i-1}, l_i}\}$, where $m_i = \varphi_{\mathrm{h}}(l_i, \mathbf{w}, b_i, e_i)$ is the segment score

and $b_{i,j}$ is the segment-level transition parameter from class i to class j.

Different from existing methods of utilizing SCRFs in neural sequence labeling (Zhuo et al., 2016; Kong et al., 2015), the segment score in an HSCRF is calculated using word-level labels as

$$m_i = \sum_{k=b_i}^{e_i} \varphi_{\mathrm{c}}(y_k, \mathbf{w}'_k) = \sum_{k=b_i}^{e_i} \mathbf{a}_{y_k}^{\top} \mathbf{w}'_k, \quad (3)$$

where $\mathbf{w}'_k$ is the feature vector of the k-th word, $\varphi_{\mathrm{c}}(y_k, \mathbf{w}'_k)$ calculates the score of the k-th word being classified into word-level class y_k, and $\mathbf{a}_{y_k}$ is a weight parameter vector corresponding to class y_k. For each word, $\mathbf{w}'_k$ is composed of word representation $\mathbf{w}_k$ and another two segment-level descriptions, i.e., (1) $\mathbf{w}_{e_i} - \mathbf{w}_{b_i}$ which is derived based on the assumption that word representations in the same segment (e.g., "Barack Obama") are closer to each other than otherwise (e.g., "Obama is"), and (2) $\phi(k - b_i + 1)$ which is the embedding vector of the word index in a segment. Finally, we have $\mathbf{w}'_k = [\mathbf{w}_k; \mathbf{w}_{e_i} - \mathbf{w}_{b_i}; \phi(k - b_i + 1)]$, where $b_i \leq k \leq e_i$ and $[; ;]$ is a vector concatenation operation.

The training and decoding criteria of conventional SCRFs (Sarawagi and Cohen, 2005) are followed. The negative log-likelihood (NLL), i.e., $-log\mathrm{p}(\hat{\mathbf{s}}|\mathbf{w})$, is minimized to estimate the parameters of the HSCRF layer and the lower neural network layers that derive word representations. For decoding, the Viterbi algorithm is employed to obtain the optimal segmentation as

$$\mathbf{s}^* = \underbrace{\mathrm{argmax}}_{\mathbf{s}' \in \mathbf{S}} log\mathrm{p}(\mathbf{s}'|\mathbf{m}), \quad (4)$$

where $\mathbf{S}$ contains all legitimate segmentations.

2.2 Jointly training and decoding using CRFs and HSCRFs

To further investigate the effects of word-level labels on the training of SCRFs, we integrate a CRF output layer and a HSCRF output layer into an unified neural network and train them jointly. These two output layers share the same sequence of word representations $\mathbf{w}$ which are extracted by lower neural network layers. Given both word-level and segment-level ground truth labels of training sentences, the model parameters are optimized by minimizing the summation of the loss functions of the CRF layer and the HSCRF layer with equal weights.

At decoding time, two label sequences, i.e., s_c and s_h, for an input sentence can be obtained using the CRF output layer and the HSCRF output layer respectively. A naive joint decoding algorithm is also designed to make a selection between them. Assume the NLLs of measuring s_c and s_h using the CRF and HSCRF layers are NLL_c and NLL_h respectively. Then, we exchange the models and measure the NLLs of s_c and s_h by HSCRF and CRF and obtain another two values $NLL_{c\_by\_h}$ and $NLL_{h\_by\_c}$. We just naively assign the summation of NLL_c and $NLL_{c\_by\_h}$ to s_c, and the summation of NLL_h and $NLL_{h\_by\_c}$ to s_h. Finally, we choose the one between s_c and s_h with lower NLL sum as the final result.

3 Experiments

3.1 Dataset

We evaluated our model on the CoNLL 2003 English NER dataset (Sang and Meulder, 2003). This dataset contained four labels of named entities (PER, LOC, ORG and MISC) and label O for others. The existing separation of training, development and test sets was followed in our experiments. We adopted the same word-level tagging scheme as the one used in Liu et al. (2018) (e.g., BIOES instead of BIO). For better computation efficiency, the max segment length L introduced in Section 2.1 was set to 6, which pruned less than 0.5% training sentences for building SCRFs and had no effect on the development and test sets.

3.2 Implementation

As shown in Fig. 1, the GloVe (Pennington et al., 2014) word embedding and the character encoding vector of each word in the input sentence were concatenated and fed into a bi-directional LSTM to obtain the sequence of word representations $\mathbf{w}$. Two character encoding models, LM-BLSTM (Liu et al., 2018) and CNN-BLSTM (Ma and Hovy, 2016), were adopted in our experiments. Regarding with the top classification layer, we compared our proposed HSCRF with conventional word-level CRF and grSemi-CRF (GSCRF) (Zhuo et al., 2016), which was an SCRF using only segment-level information. The descriptions of the models built in our experiments are summarized in Table 1.

For a fair comparison, we implemented all models in the same framework using PyTorch

library[2]. The hyper-parameters of the models are shown in Table 2 and they were selected according to the two baseline methods without fine-tuning. Each model in Table 1 was estimated 10 times and its mean and standard deviation of F1 score were reported considering the influence of randomness and the weak correlation between development set and test set in this task (Reimers and Gurevych, 2017).

3.3 Results

Table 1 lists the F1 score results of all built models on CoNLL 2003 NER task. Comparing model 3 with model 1/2 and model 9 with model 7/8, we can see that HSCRF performed better than CRF and GSCRF. The superiorities were significant since the p-values of t-test were smaller than 0.01. This implies the benefits of utilizing word-level labels when deriving segment scores in SCRFs. Comparing model 1 with model 4, 3 with 5, 7 with 10, and 9 with 11, we can see that the jointly training method introduced in Section 2.2 improved the performance of CRF and HSCRF significantly ($p < 0.01$ in all these four pairs). This may be attributed to that jointly training generates better word representations that can be shared by both CRF and HSCRF decoding layers. Finally, comparing model 6 with model 4/5 and model 12 with model 10/11, we can see the effectiveness of the jointly decoding algorithm introduced in Section 2.2 on improving F1 scores ($p < 0.01$ in all these four pairs). The LM-BLSTM-JNT model with jointly decoding achieved the highest F1 score among all these built models.

3.4 Comparison with existing work

Table 3 shows some recent results[3] on the CoNLL 2003 English NER task. For the convenience of comparison, we also listed the maximum F1 scores among 10 repetitions when building our models. The maximum F1 score of our re-implemented CNN-BLSTM-CRF model was slightly worse than the one originally reported in Ma and Hovy (2016), but it was similar to the one reported in Reimers and Gurevych (2017).

---

[2] http://pytorch.org/

[3] It should be noticed that the results of Liu et al. (2018) were inconsistent with the original ones reported in their paper. According to its first author's GitHub page (https://github.com/LiyuanLucasLiu/LM-LSTM-CRF), the originally reported results had errors due to some bugs. Here, we report the results after the bugs got fixed.

No.	Model Name	Word Representation	Top Layer	Decoding Layer	F1 Score ($\pm$std)
1	CNN-BLSTM-CRF	CNN-BLSTM	CRF	CRF	90.92 $\pm$ 0.08
2	CNN-BLSTM-GSCRF	CNN-BLSTM	GSCRF	GSCRF	90.96 $\pm$ 0.12
3	CNN-BLSTM-HSCRF	CNN-BLSTM	HSCRF	HSCRF	91.10 $\pm$ 0.12
4	CNN-BLSTM-JNT(CRF)	CNN-BLSTM	CRF+HSCRF	CRF	91.08 $\pm$ 0.12
5	CNN-BLSTM-JNT(HSCRF)	CNN-BLSTM	CRF+HSCRF	HSCRF	91.20 $\pm$ 0.10
6	CNN-BLSTM-JNT(JNT)	CNN-BLSTM	CRF+HSCRF	CRF+HSCRF	91.26 $\pm$ 0.10
7	LM-BLSTM-CRF	LM-BLSTM	CRF	CRF	91.17 $\pm$ 0.11
8	LM-BLSTM-GSCRF	LM-BLSTM	GSCRF	GSCRF	91.06 $\pm$ 0.05
9	LM-BLSTM-HSCRF	LM-BLSTM	HSCRF	HSCRF	91.27 $\pm$ 0.08
10	LM-BLSTM-JNT(CRF)	LM-BLSTM	CRF+HSCRF	CRF	91.24 $\pm$ 0.07
11	LM-BLSTM-JNT(HSCRF)	LM-BLSTM	CRF+HSCRF	HSCRF	91.34 $\pm$ 0.10
12	LM-BLSTM-JNT(JNT)	LM-BLSTM	CRF+HSCRF	CRF+HSCRF	91.38 $\pm$ 0.10

Table 1: Model descriptions and their performance on CoNLL 2003 NER task.

Component	Parameter	Value
word-level embedding[†‡]	dimension	100
character-level embedding[†‡]	dimension	30
character-level LSTM[†]	depth	1
	hidden size	300
highway network[†]	layer	1
word-level BLSTM[†]	depth	1
	hidden size	300
word-level BLSTM[‡]	depth	1
	hidden size	200
CNN[‡]	window size	3
	filter number	30
$\phi(\cdot)$[†‡]	dimension	10
dropout[†‡]	dropout rate	0.5
optimization[†‡]	learning rate	0.01
	batch size	10
	strategy	SGD
	gradient clip	5.0
	decay rate	1/(1+0.05t)

Table 2: Hyper-parameters of the models built in our experiments, where † indicates the ones when using LM-BLSTM for deriving word representations and ‡ indicates the ones when using CNN-BLSTM.

Model	Test Set F1 Score	
	Type	Value ($\pm$std)
Zhuo et al. (2016)	reported	88.12
Lample et al. (2016)	reported	90.94
Ma and Hovy (2016)	reported	91.21
Rei (2017)	reported	86.26
Liu et al. (2018)	mean	91.24 $\pm$ 0.12
	max	91.35
CNN-BLSTM-CRF	mean	90.92 $\pm$ 0.08
	max	91.04
LM-BLSTM-CRF	mean	91.17 $\pm$ 0.11
	max	91.30
CNN-BLSTM-JNT(JNT)	mean	91.26 $\pm$ 0.10
	max	91.41
LM-BLSTM-JNT(JNT)	mean	**91.38 $\pm$ 0.10**
	max	**91.53**
Luo et al. (2015)[*]	reported	91.2
Chiu and Nichols (2016)[*]	reported	91.62 $\pm$ 0.33
Tran et al. (2017)[*]	reported	91.66
Peters et al. (2017)[*]	reported	91.93 $\pm$ 0.19
Yang et al. (2017)[*]	reported	91.26

Table 3: Comparison with existing work on CoNLL 2003 NER task. The models labelled with * utilized external knowledge beside CoNLL 2003 training set and pre-trained word embeddings.

In the NER models listed in Table 3, Zhuo et al. (2016) employed some manual features and calculated segment scores by grConv for SCRF. Lample et al. (2016) and Ma and Hovy (2016) constructed character-level encodings using BLSTM and CNN respectively, and concatenated them with word embeddings. Then, the same BLSTM-CRF architecture was adopted in both models. Rei (2017) fed word embeddings into LSTM to obtain the word representations for CRF decoding and to predict the next word simultaneously. Similarly, Liu et al. (2018) input characters into LSTM to predict the next character and to get the character-level encoding for each word.

Some of the models listed in Table 3 utilized external knowledge beside CoNLL 2003 training set and pre-trained word embeddings. Luo et al. (2015) proposed JERL model, which was trained on both NER and entity linking tasks simultaneously. Chiu and Nichols (2016) employed lexicon features from DBpedia (Auer et al., 2007). Tran et al. (2017) and Peters et al. (2017) utilized pre-trained language models from large corpus to model word representations. Yang et al. (2017) utilized transfer learning to obtain shared information from other tasks, such as chunking and POS tagging, for word representations.

From Table 3, we can see that our CNN-BLSTM-JNT and LM-BLSTM-JNT models with

No.	Model Name	Entity Length						
		1	2	3	4	5	≥ 6	all
7	LM-BLSTM-CRF	91.68	91.88	82.64	75.81	73.68	72.73	91.17
8	LM-BLSTM-GSCRF	91.57	91.68	83.61	74.32	76.64	73.64	91.06
9	LM-BLSTM-HSCRF	91.65	91.84	82.97	76.20	78.95	74.55	91.27
12	LM-BLSTM-JNT(JNT)	**91.73**	**92.03**	**83.78**	**77.27**	**79.66**	**76.55**	**91.38**

Table 4: Model performance on CoNLL 2003 NER task for entities with different lengths.

jointly decoding both achieved state-of-the-art F1 scores among all models without using external knowledge. The maximum F1 score achieved by the LM-BLSTM-JNT model was 91.53%.

3.5 Analysis

To better understand the effectiveness of word-level and segment-level labels on the NER task, we evaluated the performance of models 7, 8, 9 and 12 in Table 3 for entities with different lengths. The mean F1 scores of 10 training repetitions are reported in Table 4. Comparing model 7 with model 8, we can see that GSCRF achieved better performance than CRF for long entities (with more than 4 words) but worse for short entities (with less than 3 words). Comparing model 7 with model 9, we can find that HSCRF outperformed CRF for recognizing long entities and meanwhile achieved comparable performance with CRF for short entities.

One possible explanation is that word-level labels may supervise models to learn word-level descriptions which tend to benefit the recognition of short entities. On the other hand, segment-level labels may guide models to capture the descriptions of combining words for whole entities which help to recognize long entities. By utilizing both labels, the LM-BLSTM-HSCRF model can achieve better overall performance of recognizing entities with different lengths. Furthermore, the LM-BLSTM-JNT(JNT) model which adopted jointly training and decoding achieved the best performance among all models shown in Table 4 for all entity lengths.

4 Conclusions

This paper proposes a hybrid semi-Markov conditional random field (HSCRF) architecture for neural sequence labeling, in which word-level labels are utilized to derive the segment scores in SCRFs. Further, the methods of training and decoding CRF and HSCRF output layers jointly are also presented. Experimental results on CoNLL 2003 English NER task demonstrated the effectiveness of the proposed HSCRF model which achieved state-of-the-art performance.

References

Galen Andrew. 2006. A hybrid Markov/semi-Markov conditional random field for sequence segmentation. In *Proceedings of the 2006 Conference on Empirical Methods in Natural Language Processing*, pages 465–472. Association for Computational Linguistics.

Sören Auer, Christian Bizer, Georgi Kobilarov, Jens Lehmann, Richard Cyganiak, and Zachary Ives. 2007. Dbpedia: A nucleus for a web of open data. In *The semantic web*, pages 722–735. Springer.

Jason Chiu and Eric Nichols. 2016. Named entity recognition with bidirectional LSTM-CNNs. *Transactions of the Association of Computational Linguistics*, 4:357–370.

Zhiheng Huang, Wei Xu, and Kai Yu. 2015. Bidirectional LSTM-CRF models for sequence tagging. *arXiv preprint arXiv:1508.01991*.

Lingpeng Kong, Chris Dyer, and Noah A Smith. 2015. Segmental recurrent neural networks. *arXiv preprint arXiv:1511.06018*.

John Lafferty, Andrew McCallum, and Fernando C-N Pereira. 2001. Conditional random fields: Probabilistic models for segmenting and labeling sequence data.

Guillaume Lample, Miguel Ballesteros, Sandeep Subramanian, Kazuya Kawakami, and Chris Dyer. 2016. Neural architectures for named entity recognition. In *Proceedings of the 2016 Conference of the North American Chapter of the Association for Computational Linguistics: Human Language Technologies*, pages 260–270. Association for Computational Linguistics.

L. Liu, J. Shang, F. Xu, X. Ren, H. Gui, J. Peng, and J. Han. 2018. Empower Sequence Labeling with Task-Aware Neural Language Model. In *AAAI*.

Gang Luo, Xiaojiang Huang, Chin-Yew Lin, and Zaiqing Nie. 2015. Joint entity recognition and disambiguation. In *Proceedings of the 2015 Conference on Empirical Methods in Natural Language Processing*, pages 879–888. Association for Computational Linguistics.

Xuezhe Ma and Eduard Hovy. 2016. End-to-end sequence labeling via bi-directional LSTM-CNNs-CRF. In *Proceedings of the 54th Annual Meeting of the Association for Computational Linguistics (Volume 1: Long Papers)*, pages 1064–1074. Association for Computational Linguistics.

Tomas Mikolov, Ilya Sutskever, Kai Chen, Greg S Corrado, and Jeff Dean. 2013. Distributed representations of words and phrases and their compositionality. In *Advances in neural information processing systems*, pages 3111–3119.

Jeffrey Pennington, Richard Socher, and Christopher Manning. 2014. GloVe: Global vectors for word representation. In *Proceedings of the 2014 Conference on Empirical Methods in Natural Language Processing (EMNLP)*, pages 1532–1543. Association for Computational Linguistics.

Matthew Peters, Waleed Ammar, Chandra Bhagavatula, and Russell Power. 2017. Semi-supervised sequence tagging with bidirectional language models. In *Proceedings of the 55th Annual Meeting of the Association for Computational Linguistics (Volume 1: Long Papers)*, pages 1756–1765. Association for Computational Linguistics.

Marek Rei. 2017. Semi-supervised multitask learning for sequence labeling. In *Proceedings of the 55th Annual Meeting of the Association for Computational Linguistics (Volume 1: Long Papers)*, pages 2121–2130. Association for Computational Linguistics.

Nils Reimers and Iryna Gurevych. 2017. Reporting score distributions makes a difference: Performance study of LSTM-networks for sequence tagging. In *Proceedings of the 2017 Conference on Empirical Methods in Natural Language Processing*, pages 338–348. Association for Computational Linguistics.

Erik F. Tjong Kim Sang and Fien De Meulder. 2003. Introduction to the CoNLL-2003 shared task: Language-independent named entity recognition. In *Proceedings of the Seventh Conference on Natural Language Learning at HLT-NAACL 2003*.

Sunita Sarawagi and William W Cohen. 2005. Semi-Markov conditional random fields for information extraction. In *Advances in neural information processing systems*, pages 1185–1192.

Quan Tran, Andrew MacKinlay, and Antonio Jimeno Yepes. 2017. Named entity recognition with stack residual LSTM and trainable bias decoding. In *Proceedings of the Eighth International Joint Conference on Natural Language Processing (Volume 1: Long Papers)*, pages 566–575. Asian Federation of Natural Language Processing.

Zhilin Yang, Ruslan Salakhutdinov, and William W Cohen. 2017. Transfer learning for sequence tagging with hierarchical recurrent networks. *arXiv preprint arXiv:1703.06345*.

Jingwei Zhuo, Yong Cao, Jun Zhu, Bo Zhang, and Zaiqing Nie. 2016. Segment-level sequence modeling using gated recursive semi-Markov conditional random fields. In *Proceedings of the 54th Annual Meeting of the Association for Computational Linguistics (Volume 1: Long Papers)*, pages 1413–1423. Association for Computational Linguistics.

A Study of the Importance of External Knowledge in the Named Entity Recognition Task

Dominic Seyler[1], Tatiana Dembelova[2], Luciano Del Corro[2],
Johannes Hoffart[2] and Gerhard Weikum[2]
[1]University of Illinois at Urbana-Champaign, IL, USA
[2]Max Planck Institute for Informatics, Saarbrücken, Germany
`dseyler2@illinois.edu`
`{tdembelo,corrogg,jhoffart,weikum}@mpi-inf.mpg.de`

Abstract

In this work, we discuss the importance of external knowledge for performing Named Entity Recognition (NER). We present a novel modular framework that divides the knowledge into four categories according to the depth of knowledge they convey. Each category consists of a set of features automatically generated from different information sources, such as a knowledge-base, a list of names, or document-specific semantic annotations. Further, we show the effects on performance when incrementally adding deeper knowledge and discuss effectiveness/efficiency trade-offs.

1 Introduction

Named Entity Recognition (NER) is the task of detecting named entity mentions in text and assigning them to their corresponding type. It is a crucial component in a wide range of natural language understanding tasks, such as named entity disambiguation (NED), question answering, etc.

Previous work (Ratinov and Roth, 2009) argued that NER is a knowledge-intensive task and used prior knowledge with outstanding results. In this work, we attempt to quantify to which extent external knowledge influences NER performance. Even though recent approaches have excelled in end-to-end neural methods, this paper aims to give transparency and user-comprehensible explainability. This is especially significant for industrial sectors (e.g., those heavily regulated) that require the use of transparent methods for which a particular decision is explainable.

We perform the study by devising a simple modular framework to exploit different sources of external knowledge. We divide the information sources into four different categories according to the depth of knowledge they convey, each one carrying more information than the previous. Each category is composed of a set of features that reflect the degree of knowledge contained in each source. Then, we feed a linear chain CRF, a transparent, widely used method used for NER.

We perform our experiments on two standard datasets by testing various combinations of knowledge categories. Our results indicate that the amount of knowledge is highly correlated with NER performance. The configurations with more external knowledge systematically outperform the more agnostic ones.

2 Knowledge Augmented NER

In the following section, we describe the four knowledge categories in detail. Table 1 gives an overview of the features on the categories that use external knowledge. The features were used to train a linear chain CRF, a simple and explainable method, proven to work well for NER (Finkel et al., 2005; Jun'ichi and Torisawa, 2007; Ratinov and Roth, 2009; Passos et al., 2014; Radford et al., 2015).

2.1 Knowledge Agnostic (A)

This category contains the "local" features, which can be extracted directly from text without any external knowledge. They are mostly of a lexical, syntactic or linguistic nature and have been well-studied in literature. We implement most of the features described in (Finkel et al., 2005):

(1) The current word and words in a window of size 2; (2) Word shapes of the current word and words in a window of size 2; (3) POS tags in a window of size 2; (4) Prefixes (length three and four) and Suffixes (length one to four); (5) Presence of the current word in a window of size 4; (6)

Proceedings of the 56th Annual Meeting of the Association for Computational Linguistics (Short Papers), pages 241–246
Melbourne, Australia, July 15 - 20, 2018. ©2018 Association for Computational Linguistics

Cat.	Feature	Description	Example
Name	**Mention tokens**	Some tokens are strongly associated to NEs	county,john,school,station,…
	POS-tag sequence	Multi-word NEs tend to share POS patterns	Organization of American States $\rightarrow$ NNP IN NNP NNP
KB	Type gazetteers	Names that are associated to types	Florida $\rightarrow$ location
	Wiki. link prob.	Tokens that are associated to NEs	"Florida" linked in Wikipedia
	Type prob.	Probability of token to type associations	Obama $\rightarrow$ person;
Entity	Doc. gazetteers	NE presence indicates other NEs	European Union $\rightarrow$ EU

Table 1: Features by category (novel features are highlighted)

Beginning of sentence.

2.2 Name-Based Knowledge (Name)

Here, the knowledge is extracted from a list of named entity names. These features attempt to identify patterns in names and exploit the fact that the set of distinct names is limited. We extracted a total of more than 20 million names from YAGO (Suchanek et al., 2007) and derived the following features:

Frequent mention tokens. Reflects the frequency of a given token in a list of entity names. We tokenized the list and computed frequencies. The feature assigns a weight to each token in the text corresponding to their normalized frequency. High weights should be assigned to tokens that indicate named entities. For instance, the top-5 tokens we found in English were "county", "john", "school", "station" and "district". All tokens without occurrences are assigned 0 weight.

Frequent POS Tag Sequences. Intends to identify POS sequences common to named entities. For example, person names tend to be described as a series of proper nouns, while organizations may have richer patterns. Both "Organization of American States" and "Union for Ethical Biotrade" share the pattern NNP-IN-NNP-NNP. We ranked the name POS tag sequences and kept the top 100. The feature is implemented by finding the longest matching sequences in the input text and marking whether the current token belongs to a frequent sequence or not.

2.3 Knowledge-Base-Based Knowledge (KB)

This category groups features extracted from a KB or an entity annotated corpus. They encode knowledge about named entities themselves or their usages. We implemented three features:

Type-infused Gazetteer Match. Finds the longest occurring token sequence in a type-specific gazetteer. It adds a binary indicator to each token, depending on whether the token is part of a sequence. We use 30 dictionaries distributed by (Ratinov and Roth, 2009) containing type-name information for English. These dictionaries can also be created automatically by mapping each dictionary to a set of KB types and extracting the corresponding names. This automatic generation is useful in multilingual settings, which we discuss in Section 3.5.

Wikipedia Link Probability. This feature measures the likelihood of a token being linked to a named entity Wikipedia page. The intuition is that tokens linked to named entity pages tend to be indicative of named entities. For instance, the token "Obama" is usually linked while "box" is not. The list of pages referring to named entities is extracted from YAGO. Given a token in the text, it is assigned the probability of being linked according to Eq. 1, where $link_d(t)$ equals 1, if token t in document d is linked to another Wikipedia document. $present_d$ equals 1 if t occurs in d.

$$P_{Wiki}(t) = \frac{\sum_{d \in D} link_d(t)}{\sum_{d \in D} present_d(t)} \qquad (1)$$

Type Probability. Encodes the likelihood of a token belonging to a given type. It captures the idea that, for instance, the token "Obama" is more likely a person than a location. Given a set of entities E in YAGO with mentions M_e and tokens T_{em} we calculate the probability of a class $c \in C$ given a token t as in Eq. 2, where $c(e) = 1$ if entity e belongs to class c and $c(e) = 0$ otherwise. For each token in the text, we create one feature per type with the respective probability as its value.

$$P(c|t) = \frac{\sum_e^E \sum_{m_e}^{M_e} \sum_{t_{em}}^{T_{em}} c(e)}{\sum_e^E \sum_{m_e}^{M_e} \sum_{t_{em}}^{T_{em}} \sum_{c_i}^{C} c_i(e)} \qquad (2)$$

Token Type Position. Reflects that tokens may appear in different positions according to the entity type. For instance, "Supreme Court of the United States", is an organization and "United" occurs at the end. In "United States", a location, it occurs at the beginning. This helps with nested named entities.

This is implemented using the BILOU (**B**egin, **I**nside, **L**ast, **O**utside, **U**nit) encoding (Ratinov and Roth, 2009), which tags each token with respect to the position in which it occurs. The number of features depends on the number of types in the dataset (4 BILU positions times n classes + O position). For each token, each feature receives the probability of a class given the token and position. The class probabilities are calculated as in Equation 2, incorporating also the token position.

As a result, for each token we now have a probability distribution over $4n + 1$ classes. Take for instance the token "Obama". We would expect it to have high probability for classes "B-Person" (i.e., last name in combination with first name) and "U-Person" (i.e., last name without first name). The probabilities for all other classes would be close to zero. In comparison, the word "box" should have high probability for class "O" and close to zero for all others, since we would not expect it to occur in many named entities.

2.4 Entity-Based Knowledge (Entity)

This category encodes document-specific knowledge about the entities found in text to exploit the association between NER and NED. Previous work showed that the flow of information between these generates significant performance improvements (Radford et al., 2015; Luo et al., 2015).

Comparatively, this module needs significantly more computational resources. It requires a first run of NED to generate document specific features, based on the disambiguated named entities. These features are used in a second run of NER.

Following (Radford et al., 2015), after the first run of NED, we create a set of document-specific gazetteers derived from the disambiguated entities. This information helps in the second round to find new named entities that were previously missed. Take the sentence "Some citizens of the European Union working in the United Kingdom do not meet visa requirements for non-EU workers after the uk leaves the bloc". We can imagine that in the first round of NED *European Union* and *United Kingdom* can be easily identified but "EU" or the wrongly capitalized "uk" might be missed. After the disambiguation, we know that both entities are organizations and have the aliases *EU* and *UK* respectively. Then, in a second round it may be easier to spot mentions "EU" and "uk".

After a first run of NER+NED, we extract all surface forms of the identified entities from YAGO. These are tokenized and assigned the type of the corresponding entity plus its BILOU position. For example, the surface form "Barack Obama" results in "Barack" and "Obama", assigned to "B-Person" and "L-Person". There are 17 binary features (BILU tags multiplied by four coarse-grained types + O tag), which fire when a token is part of a list that contains the mappings from tokens to type-BILOU pairs.

3 Evaluation

3.1 Experimental Setup

System Setup. To perform our study we use a linear chain CRF(Lafferty et al., 2001). CRFs are transparent and widely used for NER (Finkel et al., 2005; Jun'ichi and Torisawa, 2007; Ratinov and Roth, 2009; Passos et al., 2014; Radford et al., 2015; Luo et al., 2015). The entity-based component was implemented using the AIDA (Hoffart et al., 2011) entity disambiguation system.

Datasets. We evaluate on two standard NER datasets *CoNLL2003*. (Sang and Meulder, 2003), a collection of English newswires covering entities with four types (PER, ORG, LOC, MISC) and *MUC-7*, a set of New York Times articles (Chinchor and Robinson, 1997) with annotations on three types of entities (PER, ORG, LOC).

3.2 Incremental knowledge

Here we analyze the impact of incrementally adding external knowledge. Fig. 1a shows four variants. Each contains the features corresponding to a given category plus all those from the lighter categories to the left. In all cases adding knowledge boosts F_1 performance. The effect is particularly strong for MUC-7-test which registered an overall increment of almost 10 points. In both datasets, the biggest boost is registered when the KB-based features are added. As a reference point, one of the best systems to date (Chiu and Nichols, 2016) (neural-based) achieves F_1 91.62 on CoNLL2013-test, while our full-knowledge CRF reaches F_1 91.12.

Fig. 1c shows the performance for each entity type on CoNLL2003. Again, there is a boost in all cases, especially organizations. Persons also improve significantly: At first they perform similar to

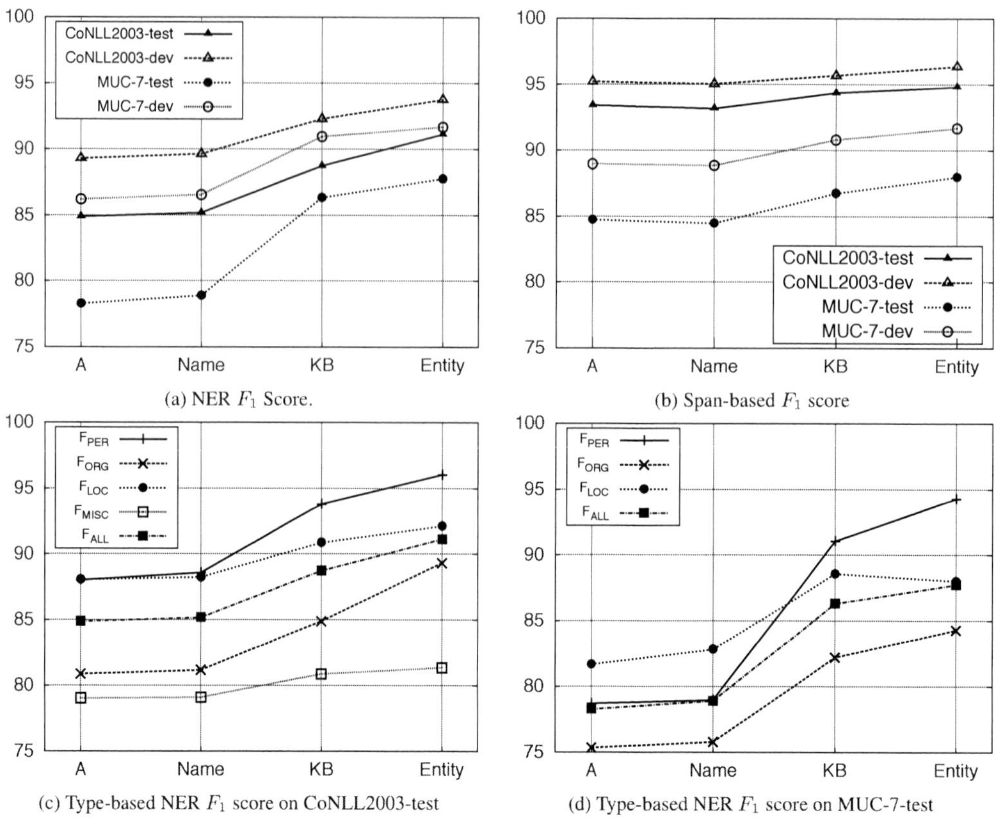

Figure 1: Evaluation results by type CoNLL2003-test and MUC-7-test.

locations, but the successive increment is sharper. F_1 for persons achieves F_1 96.03 and locations F_1 92.13. The positive effect is quite significant for organizations (F_1 80.86 to F_1 89.32), while it is moderate for miscellaneous. Fig. 1d shows results by type for MUC-7-test. The positive effect is particularly strong for persons, improving more than 15 F_1 points (78.70 to 94.28). Interestingly, locations register a slight decline between KB and Entity (0.56 F_1 points).

Finally, Fig. 1b shows the performance over span detection, which is the span where the named entity occurs without taking type information into account. This is especially important for applications such as named entity disambiguation. It drops slightly for the name-based category, but it increases again as more knowledge is added. The effect is similar on both datasets.

3.3 Ablation

Table 2 shows different combinations of knowledge categories. The relatively small improvement

from KB to Entity suggests that KB features are subsumed by the later. This is somehow expected as the entity specific information is extracted from the same KB and both rely on entity types. However, as we will see, this comes at a cost.

Feature Categories	F_1
A, Name, KB	88.73
A, Name, Entity	89.32
A, KB, Entity	91.09
All	91.12

Table 2: : Ablation study by categories on CoNLL2003-test

3.4 Timing

The Entity-based component is by far the most expensive concerning timing performance. We measure 314ms, 494ms, 693ms, and 4139ms for A, Name, KB and Entity based features, respectively (Figure 2). Since KB-based features are comparable in performance to the Entity-based features, but the latter are much more expensive, these findings allow practitioners to carefully decide whether the additional computational cost is worth the relatively small performance improvements. The modularity of our feature classes allows for optimal tuning of a system regarding effectiveness/efficiency trade-offs.

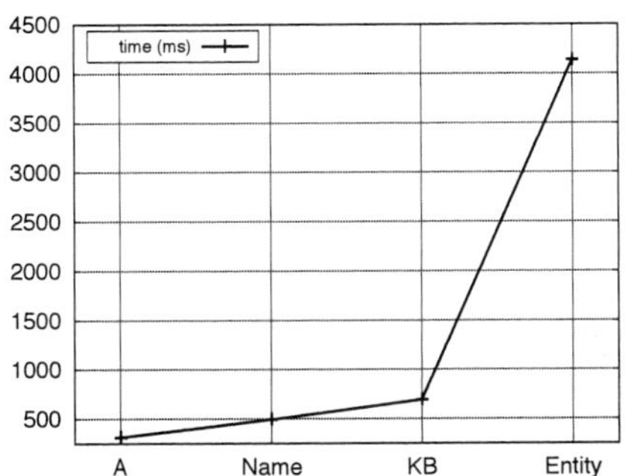

Figure 2: Timing experiments for CoNLL2003e-test in average milliseconds per document

3.5 Multilingualism

In order to demonstrate the general applicability of our approach, we implement our NER system for two additional languages, namely German and Spanish. All features for the Name, KB and Entity knowledge classes are derived from the respective language's Wikipedia. Performance is evaluated on CoNLL2003g (Sang and Meulder, 2003) for German and CoNLL2002 (Tjong Kim Sang, 2002) for Spanish. Results can be found in Figure 3. Similar to the performance on English data, we can see that adding more external knowledge improves performance. For reference, we found that performance is close to the state-of-the art in both languages. Our system lags only 1.56 F_1 points on (Lample et al., 2016) in German and 1.98 F_1 points on (Yang et al., 2016) in Spanish.

4 Related Work

NER is a widely studied problem. Most of previous work rely on the use of CRFs (Finkel et al., 2005; Jun'ichi and Torisawa, 2007; Ratinov and Roth, 2009; Passos et al., 2014; Radford et al., 2015; Luo et al., 2015). A recent trend has achieved particularly good results modeling NER as an end-to-end task using neural networks (dos Santos and Guimarães, 2015; Chiu and Nichols, 2016; Lample et al., 2016; Yang et al., 2016;

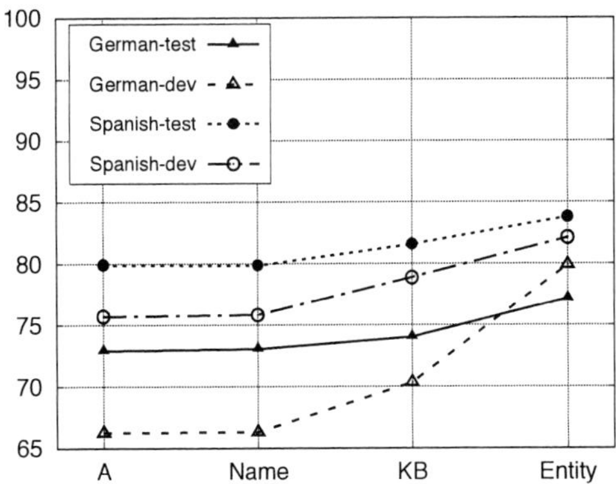

Figure 3: NER F_1 for German on CoNLL2003g dataset and Spanish on CoNLL2002 dataset.

Gillick et al., 2016). While this constitutes a big step forward, certain applications (e.g., in heavily regulated sectors) require a degree of explainability that neural approaches cannot yet provide.

Previous work has already regarded NER as a knowledge intensive task (Florian et al., 2003; Zhang and Johnson, 2003; Jun'ichi and Torisawa, 2007; Ratinov and Roth, 2009; Lin and Wu, 2009; Passos et al., 2014; Radford et al., 2015; Luo et al., 2015). Most of these works incorporate background knowledge in the form of entity-type gazetteers (Florian et al., 2003; Zhang and Johnson, 2003; Jun'ichi and Torisawa, 2007; Ratinov and Roth, 2009; Passos et al., 2014). Others, used external knowledge by exploiting the association between NER and NED (Durrett and Klein, 2014; Radford et al., 2015; Luo et al., 2015; Nguyen et al., 2016). In this study, we attempt to bring more light on the issue by quantifying the effect of different degrees of external knowledge. Our modular framework allows to test this intuition via novel feature sets that reflect the degree of knowledge contained in available knowledge sources.

5 Conclusion

We investigated the importance of external knowledge for performing Named Entity Recognition by defining four feature categories, each of which conveys a different amount of knowledge. In addition to commonly used features in existing literature, we defined four novel features that we incorporated into our category scheme. We experimentally showed that although more external knowledge leads to performance improvements, it comes at a considerable performance trade-off.

References

Nancy Chinchor and Patricia Robinson. 1997. Muc-7 named entity task definition. In *Proceedings of MUC-7*.

Jason Chiu and Eric Nichols. 2016. Named entity recognition with bidirectional lstm-cnns.

Cícero Nogueira dos Santos and Victor Guimarães. 2015. Boosting named entity recognition with neural character embeddings. *Proceedings of the Fifth Named Entity Workshop* .

Greg Durrett and Dan Klein. 2014. A joint model for entity analysis: Coreference, typing, and linking. In *TACL*.

Jenny Rose Finkel, Trond Grenager, and Christopher D. Manning. 2005. Incorporating non-local information into information extraction systems by gibbs sampling. In *Proceedings of ACL*.

Radu Florian, Abraham Ittycheriah, Hongyan Jing, and Tong Zhang. 2003. Named entity recognition through classifier combination. In *Proceedings of CoNLL*.

Dan Gillick, Cliff Brunk, Oriol Vinyals, and Amarnag Subramanya. 2016. Multilingual language processing from bytes. In *Proceedings of NAACL*.

Johannes Hoffart, Mohamed Amir Yosef, Ilaria Bordino, Hagen Fürstenau, Manfred Pinkal, Marc Spaniol, Bilyana Taneva, Stefan Thater, and Gerhard Weikum. 2011. Robust Disambiguation of Named Entities in Text. In *Proceedings of EMNLP*.

Kazama Jun'ichi and Kentaro Torisawa. 2007. Exploiting wikipedia as external knowledge for named entity recognition. In *Proceedings of EMNLP-CoNLL*.

John D. Lafferty, Andrew McCallum, and Fernando C. N. Pereira. 2001. Conditional random fields: Probabilistic models for segmenting and labeling sequence data. In *Proceedings of ICML*.

Guillaume Lample, Miguel Ballesteros, Sandeep Subramanian, Kazuya Kawakami, and Chris Dyer. 2016. Neural architectures for named entity recognition. In *Proceedings of NAACL*.

Dekang Lin and Xiaoyun Wu. 2009. Phrase clustering for discriminative learning. In *Proceedings of ACL*.

Gang Luo, Xiaojiang Huang, Chin-Yew Lin, and Zaiqing Nie. 2015. Joint entity recognition and disambiguation. In *Proceedings of EMNLP*.

Dat Ba Nguyen, Martin Theobald, and Gerhard Weikum. 2016. J-NERD: joint named entity recognition and disambiguation with rich linguistic features. *TACL* 4:215–229.

Alexandre Passos, Vineet Kumar, and Andrew McCallum. 2014. Lexicon infused phrase embeddings for named entity resolution. In *Proceedings of CoNLL*.

Will Radford, Xavier Carreras, and James Henderson. 2015. Named entity recognition with document-specific KB tag gazetteers. In *Proceedings of EMNLP*.

Lev-Arie Ratinov and Dan Roth. 2009. Design challenges and misconceptions in named entity recognition. In *Proceedings of CoNLL*.

Erik F. Tjong Kim Sang and Fien De Meulder. 2003. Introduction to the conll-2003 shared task: Language-independent named entity recognition. In *Proceedings of CoNLL*.

Fabian M. Suchanek, Gjergji Kasneci, and Gerhard Weikum. 2007. Yago: a core of semantic knowledge. In *Proceedings of WWW*.

Erik F. Tjong Kim Sang. 2002. Introduction to the conll-2002 shared task: Language-independent named entity recognition. In *Proceedings of CoNLL*.

Zhilin Yang, Ruslan Salakhutdinov, and William W. Cohen. 2016. Multi-task cross-lingual sequence tagging from scratch. *CoRR* .

Tong Zhang and David Johnson. 2003. A robust risk minimization based named entity recognition system. In *Proceedings of CoNLL*.

Improving Topic Quality by Promoting Named Entities in Topic Modeling

Katsiaryna Krasnashchok
EURA NOVA
Rue Emile Francqui, 4
1435 Mont-Saint-Guibert, Belgium
katherine.krasnoschok@euranova.eu

Salim Jouili
EURA NOVA
Rue Emile Francqui, 4
1435 Mont-Saint-Guibert, Belgium
salim.jouili@euranova.eu

Abstract

News-related content has been extensively studied in both topic modeling research and named entity recognition. However, expressive power of named entities and their potential for improving the quality of discovered topics has not received much attention. In this paper we use named entities as domain-specific terms for news-centric content and present a new weighting model for Latent Dirichlet Allocation. Our experimental results indicate that involving more named entities in topic descriptors positively influences the overall quality of topics, improving their interpretability, specificity and diversity.

1 Introduction

News-centric content conveys information about events, individuals and other entities. Analysis of news-related documents includes identifying hidden features for classifying them or summarizing the content. Topic modeling is the standard technique for such purposes, and Latent Dirichlet Allocation (LDA) (Blei et al., 2003) is the most used algorithm, which models the documents as distribution over topics and topics as distribution over words. A good topic model is characterized by its coherence: any coherent topic should contain related words belonging to the same concept. A good topic must also be distinctive enough to include domain-specific content. For news-related texts domain-specific content can be represented by named entities (NE), describing facts, events and people involved in news and discussions. It explains the need to include named entities in topic modeling process.

The main contribution of this work is improving topic quality with LDA by increasing the impor-

tance of named entities in the model. The idea is to adapt the topic model to include more domain-specific terms (NE) in the topic descriptors. We designed our model to be flexible, in order to be used in different variations of LDA. We ultimately employ a term-weighting approach for the LDA input. Our results show that: i) named entities can serve as favorable candidates for high-quality topic descriptors, and ii) weighting model based on pseudo term frequencies is able to improve overall topic quality without the need to interfere with LDA's generative process, which makes it adaptable to other LDA variations.

The paper is organized in the following manner: in Section 2 we present the related work; Section 3 describes the proposed solution and is followed by Section 4, where the details of evaluation process and results are outlined. We finish with Section 5, concluding the results and next steps.

2 Related Work

This section describes the related work in the area of topic modeling, specifically LDA.

2.1 Topic Modeling and Named Entities

Several works explored the relation between LDA and named entities in recent years. The most famous model is CorrLDA2 (Newman et al., 2006). It introduces two types of topics, general and entity, and represents word topics as a mixture of entity topics. Hu et al. (2013) reverses the concept, assuming that entities are critical for news-centric content. Their entity-centered topic model (ECTM) designs entity topics as a mixture of word topics and shows better results in entity prediction than CorrLDA2 (Hu et al., 2013). Both models, however, introduce significant changes to the LDA algorithm. In this paper we strive to incorporate named entities into LDA in a natural way, without affecting the generative algorithm, to keep it

Proceedings of the 56th Annual Meeting of the Association for Computational Linguistics (Short Papers), pages 247–253
Melbourne, Australia, July 15 - 20, 2018. ©2018 Association for Computational Linguistics

flexible and adaptable to any LDA variations.

Lau et al. (2013) study the impact of collocations on topic modeling and work with the input of LDA by replacing unigrams with collocations. Adding multiword named entities, as a special type of collocations, enhanced the topic model for the tested dataset (Lau et al., 2013). Our work follows similar tokenization process, but goes further in improving the topic model by promoting named entities in it.

2.2 Topic Modeling and Term Weighting

Traditionally, the input of LDA is a document-term matrix of term frequencies (TF), according to the bag-of-words model (BoW). However, Wilson and Chew (2010) showed that point-wise mutual information (PMI) term weighting model can be successfully applied to eliminate stop words from topic descriptors. More weighting schemes were evaluated by Truica et al. (2016) and showed promising results for clustering accuracy. Therefore, term weighting approach in LDA can be beneficial for certain tasks. In this paper we introduce unnormalized TF-based weighting scheme using pseudo frequency as a way of increasing the weight of a term.

3 Proposed model

LDA model has been criticized for favoring highly frequent, general words in topic descriptors (O'Callaghan et al., 2015). This problem can be partly solved by eliminating domain-specific stop-words from the corpus. On the other hand, instead of narrowing the corpus, it may be more efficient to promote domain-specific important words, especially if such words can be identified automatically, like named entities. In this paper we deal with the online Variational Bayes version of the LDA algorithm from Hoffman et al. (2010), as alternative to collapsed Gibbs sampling, used by Wilson and Chew (2010) and Truica et al. (2016) to incorporate weights into the LDA model. In Hoffman et al. (2010) the authors demonstrate that the objective of the optimization relies only on the counts of terms in documents, and therefore documents can be summarized by their TF values. Our proposed model takes the TF scores as initial term weights (unnormalized). To increase the weight of a named entity we add a pseudo-frequency to its TF without changing the weights of other terms. This strengthens the chances of NE to appear in

a topic descriptor, even if originally it was not mentioned often in the corpus. There are multiple ways of increasing the weights, *e.g.* we can promote all NE in the same proportion, or set their weights separately for each document in the corpus.

3.1 Independent Named Entity Promoting

NE Independent model assumes that all named entities in the corpus are α times more important than their initial weights (TF), i.e. they may not be the most important terms in the corpus, but they should weigh α times more than they do now. Therefore, for each column m_w of document-term matrix M, we apply scalar multiplication:

$$m_w = \begin{cases} \alpha * m_w & \text{if } w \text{ is NE} \\ m_w & \text{otherwise} \end{cases} \quad (1)$$

By varying α, we can set the importance of named entities in the corpus and impact the outcome of topic modeling. The value need not be an integer, since typical LDA implementation can deal with any numbers. In Section 4 we provide results for several tested values of α parameter and discuss our findings.

3.2 Document Dependent Named Entity Promoting

While we want the topics produced by LDA to include more named entities as domain-specific words, we may assume that NE, in fact, should be the most important, i.e. the most frequent, terms in each document. In order to set the weights accordingly, the maximum term-frequency per document is calculated and added to each named entity's weight in each document:

$$m_{dw} = \begin{cases} m_{dw} + \max_{w} m_{dw} & \text{if } w \text{ is NE} \\ m_{dw} & \text{otherwise} \end{cases} \quad (2)$$

This weighting scheme obliges named entities to be the "heaviest" terms in each document. At the same time, we do not change the weight of other frequent terms, so eventually they still have a high probability to make the top terms list.

4 Evaluation

We designed a series of tests to evaluate our proposed model: a) **Baseline Unigram**: basic model on the corpus consisting of single tokens (no named entities involved); b) **Baseline NE**: basic model on the corpus with named entities (the strategy of injecting NE in all tests is replacement instead of supplementation, as suggested by Lau et al., 2013); c) **NE Independent**: independent named entity promoting model described in Section 3.1; and d) **NE Document Dependent**: document dependent named entity promoting model described in Section 3.2. We evaluate the tests using the topic quality measures presented below.

4.1 Dataset And Preprocessing

Our test corpora consists of news-related publicly-available datasets: 1) 20 Newsgroups[1]: widely studied by NLP research community dataset (Aletras and Stevenson, 2013; Truica et al., 2016; Wallach et al., 2009; Röder et al., 2015; Hu et al., 2013). Contains 18846 documents with messages discussing news, people, events and other entities. 2) Reuters-2013: a set of 14595 news articles from Reuters for year 2013, obtained from Financial News Dataset[2], first compiled and used in (Ding et al., 2014). The documents in Reuters-2013 are generally longer than in 20 Newsgroups. For NE recognition we used NeuroNER[3], a tool designed by Dernoncourt et al. (2016, 2017), trained on CONLL2003 dataset and recognizing four types of NE: person, location, organization and miscellaneous. The further preprocessing pipeline consists of classic steps used in topic modeling.

4.2 Topic Coherence

The term "topic coherence" covers a set of measures describing the quality of the topics regarding interpretability by a human. Most widely used measures are based on PMI (or NPMI, normalized) and log conditional probability, both of which rely on the co-occurrence of terms (Lau et al., 2013, 2014; O'Callaghan et al., 2015; Aletras and Stevenson, 2013; Newman et al., 2010; Mimno et al., 2011; Nikolenko, 2016; Nguyen et al., 2015; Syed and Spruit, 2017). Recently a study by Röder et al. (2015) put all known coherence measures into single framework, assessed their correlation with human ratings and discovered the best performing measure - previously unknown C_v, based on cosine similarity of word vectors over a sliding window. We inferred the definition from Röder et al. (2015):

$$C_v = \frac{1}{N} \sum_{t=1...N} \frac{1}{N_t} \sum_{i=1...N_t} s_{cos}(\vec{v}_{NPMI}(w_i), \vec{v}_{NPMI}(W_t))$$

(3)

where N is the number of topics, W_t is the set of top N_t terms in topic t, the vectors are defined as:

$$\vec{v}_{NPMI}(w_i) = \left\{ NPMI(w_i, w_j) \right\}_{j \in W_t}$$

(4)

$$\vec{v}_{NPMI}(W_t) = \left\{ \sum_{w_i \in W_t} NPMI(w_i, w_j) \right\}_{w_j \in W_t}$$

(5)

and the underlying measure is NPMI with probability P_{sw} over a sliding window. C_v with sliding window of 110 words (Röder et al., 2015) is the coherence measure we use in this paper.

Majority of studies also use a reference corpus like Wikipedia for calculating word frequencies and co-occurrences (Aletras and Stevenson, 2013; O'Callaghan et al., 2015; Lau et al., 2014; Röder et al., 2015; Yang et al., 2017). In our case the need for reference corpus is particularly significant, since we change natural frequencies of named entities in the corpus, therefore coherence will definitely decline if calculated on original data. For the tests we have preprocessed the dump of English Wikipedia from 2014/06/15 with the same pipeline as used for the test corpora.

4.3 Generality Measures

Coherence measures tend to favor topics with general highly frequent terms. As a result we end up with well understandable but quite generic topics. A good topic should also be specific enough to distinguish documents (O'Callaghan et al., 2015). Moreover, averaging the coherences of all topics may produce very good coherence for a model with many repeating words across topics. For covering these aspects of the topic quality we adopt two other measures.

Exclusivity: Represents the degree of overlap between topics, based on the appearance of terms in multiple descriptors (O'Callaghan et al., 2015). We define exclusivity as $\frac{|W_u|}{|W|}$, where $|W_u|$ is the number of unique terms and $|W|$ is the total number of terms in topic descriptors.

Lift: Generally used for reranking the terms in descriptors (Taddy, 2012; Sievert and Shirley, 2014), lift is employed here as a topic quality metric. It is defined as $\frac{\beta_{ti}}{b_i}$, where β_{ti} is the weight of word i in topic t and b_i is the probability of

---

[1] http://qwone.com/~jason/20Newsgroups/
[2] https://github.com/philipperemy/financial-news-dataset
[3] https://github.com/Franck-Dernoncourt/NeuroNER

Topics	Test	20 Newsgroups			Reuters-2013		
		C_v	Lift	Excl.	C_v	Lift	Excl.
20	Baseline Unigram	0,534	3,390	0,788	0,539	3,891	0,610
	Baseline NE	0,503	3,273	0,767	0,559	4,059	0,598
	NE Independent (x1,3)	0,494	3,394	0,755	0,551	4,209	0,563
	NE Independent (x1,5)	0,527	3,464	0,770	0,552	4,308	0,618
	NE Independent (x2)	0,525	3,756	0,797	0,548	4,449	0,640
	NE Independent (x2,5)	0,539	3,779	0,765	0,550	4,661	0,635
	NE Independent (x5)	**0,543**	5,071	0,898	0,517	5,701	0,708
	NE Independent (x10)	0,486	**6,416**	**0,950**	0,511	**6,560**	**0,773**
	NE Doc. Dependent	**0,543**	4,600	0,780	**0,566**	5,749	0,625
50	Baseline Unigram	0,492	2,882	0,511	0,514	3,977	0,427
	Baseline NE	0,467	2,704	0,469	0,534	4,064	0,402
	NE Independent (x1,3)	0,476	2,825	0,487	**0,538**	4,291	0,406
	NE Independent (x1,5)	0,479	2,987	0,497	0,527	4,370	0,423
	NE Independent (x2)	0,471	3,394	0,533	0,510	4,684	0,459
	NE Independent (x2,5)	0,467	3,652	0,561	0,499	4,958	0,483
	NE Independent (x5)	0,437	5,243	0,702	0,461	5,956	0,564
	NE Independent (x10)	0,385	**6,693**	**0,787**	0,447	**6,943**	**0,641**
	NE Doc. Dependent	**0,512**	4,951	0,624	0,532	5,452	0,421
100	Baseline Unigram	**0,486**	2,457	0,325	0,503	3,692	0,286
	Baseline NE	0,478	2,248	0,282	0,525	3,775	0,253
	NE Independent (x1,3)	0,473	2,391	0,300	**0,527**	4,041	0,286
	NE Independent (x1,5)	0,467	2,499	0,315	0,520	4,126	0,295
	NE Independent (x2)	0,463	2,737	0,332	0,508	4,505	0,329
	NE Independent (x2,5)	0,453	3,108	0,374	0,491	4,705	0,339
	NE Independent (x5)	0,416	5,079	0,537	0,455	5,840	0,432
	NE Independent (x10)	0,394	**6,622**	**0,614**	0,444	**6,747**	**0,498**
	NE Doc. Dependent	0,478	4,310	0,442	0,509	5,030	0,266

Table 1: Topic quality results on the corpora

word i in the reference corpus. The overall model measure is the average of the log-lift of descriptor terms and shows the degree of presence of non-general words in topics.

4.4 Results

Table 1 depicts the results of running the experiments[4] with $N = \{20, 50, 100\}$ topics and top 10 words used for the measures. Firstly, we can observe one common outcome: NE Independent (x10) model exhibited the best exclusivity and lift values across all tests, which is logical since this model enforced the biggest number of pseudo-frequent words to be in topic descriptors. However, the same model also showed the lowest coherence in all experiments. This confirms the secondary status of lift and exclusivity: the full per-

formance of the model is decided by the combination of all three measures. From the table we can see that for 20 Newsgroups, Baseline Unigram model resulted in better coherence than Baseline NE. Previously Lau et al. (2013) showed that coherence (NPMI-based) is supposed to improve with NE replacement model. However, the goal of this work goes beyond just including named entities into LDA. We want to demonstrate that our weighting model increases the number of NE in topic descriptors, which makes them more understandable and diverse. For these purposes we use different coherence measure (Röder et al., 2015), and include additional NE type - miscellaneous, which was omitted in (Lau et al., 2013) though it contains some potentially important named entities. Hence, at the moment we do not compare our results with Lau et al. (2013). For each dataset we chose the baseline for comparison depending on

---

[4]Tests were run with *gensim*: https://radimrehurek.com/gensim/

Topic Baseline Unigram	C_v	Topic NE Doc. Dependent	C_v
game, good, year, team, player, play, think, get, time, like	0,507	game, ne_espn, ne_nhl, player, team, ne_steve, think, run, play, good	**0,565**
game, san, espn, chicago, lose, new, won, day, york, road	0,488	**ne_nhl**, ne_brown, ne_tor, ne_cal, ne_flyers, team, ne_det, ne_rangers, ne_lindros, ne_edmonton	**0,584**
year, ar, know, hockey, league, slave, new, file, list, slip	0,291		
space, launch, earth, mission, orbit, satellite, moon, planet, solar, spacecraft	0,816	ne_earth, ne_saturn, ne_pluto, ne_jupiter, **ne_nasa**, ne_venus, ne_mars, ne_galileo, ne_uranus, ne_sun	**0,902**
gun, file, control, firearm, research, crime, new, information, law, use	0,424	**ne_nra**, ne_united states, ne_congress, ne_federal, ne_code, ne_gun control, ne_senate, ne_section, ne_constitution, ne_hci	**0,530**

Table 2: Comparison of Baseline Unigram and NE Doc. Dependent topics for 20 Newsgroups

coherence: Baseline Unigram for 20 Newsgroups, and Baseline NE for Reuters-2013.

In the majority of cases NE Document Dependent ended up being the optimal model for both datasets: while it did not perform best in terms of lift or exclusivity, it achieved the best or good enough coherence values, better lift and better or the same exclusivity as baseline models. The exceptions are 20 Newsgropus with 20 topics, where NE Independent (x5) became the optimal model, and Reuters-2013 with 100 topics, where NE Independent (x1,3) performed the best for combination of all three measures. The only case where baseline model achieved superior coherence is 20 Newsgroups with $N = 100$, but we note that NE Document Dependent model came close in terms of coherence while having much better lift and exclusivity, therefore it can also be considered optimal. In general, NE Independent model showed improvement in coherence up to a certain value of α (different in each case), followed by a decline, reaching very low values for NE Independent (x10). On the other hand, NE Document Dependent model does not introduce new parameters into LDA and manages to achieve best performance in the majority of settings, thus being more stable and easy to use.

Table 2 demonstrates qualitative analysis on the individual topics from 20 Newsgroups, generated by Baseline Unigram, and their semantically closest counterparts from NE Document Dependent model. As evident from the table, baseline topics describe mostly abstract concepts of "sport", "space" and "gun control". From NE Document Dependent topics we get more specific descriptors, resulting in better coherence (as well as lift/exclusivity). It is worth particularly noting the names of the organizations (in bold), crucial to the corresponding topics, that, despite being unigrams, only appear in NE Document Dependent model, because they are not met often enough in the test corpus.

5 Conclusion

Presented results indicate that, firstly, our proposed model is capable of improving topic quality by only modifying the TF scores in the input of LDA in favor of named entities. This makes it applicable to any LDA-based models relying on the same input. Secondly, we have shown that named entities are well suited to be used as domain-specific terms and produce high-quality topics in news-related texts. Next steps in our research include experimenting with different weights for different categories of named entities, as well as adding new coherence measures, such as word2vec-based one, used by O'Callaghan et al. (2015).

Acknowledgments

The elaboration of this scientific paper was supported by the Ministry of Economy, Industry, Research, Innovation, IT, Employment and Education of the Region of Wallonia (Belgium), through the funding of the industrial research project Jericho (convention no. 7717).

References

Nikolaos Aletras and Mark Stevenson. 2013. Evaluating topic coherence using distributional semantics. In *IWCS*.

David M Blei, Andrew Y Ng, and Michael I Jordan. 2003. Latent dirichlet allocation. *Journal of machine Learning research*, 3(Jan):993–1022.

Franck Dernoncourt, Ji Young Lee, and Peter Szolovits. 2017. NeuroNER: an easy-to-use program for named-entity recognition based on neural networks. In *Proceedings of the 2017 Conference on Empirical Methods in Natural Language Processing: System Demonstrations*. Association for Computational Linguistics.

Franck Dernoncourt, Ji Young Lee, Ozlem Uzuner, and Peter Szolovits. 2016. De-identification of patient notes with recurrent neural networks. *Journal of the American Medical Informatics Association*, page ocw156.

Xiao Ding, Yue Zhang, Ting Liu, and Junwen Duan. 2014. Using structured events to predict stock price movement: An empirical investigation. In *Proceedings of the 2014 Conference on Empirical Methods in Natural Language Processing (EMNLP)*. Association for Computational Linguistics.

Matthew Hoffman, Francis R Bach, and David M Blei. 2010. Online learning for latent dirichlet allocation. In *advances in neural information processing systems*, pages 856–864.

Linmei Hu, Juanzi Li, Zhihui Li, Chao Shao, and Zhixing Li. 2013. Incorporating entities in news topic modeling. In *Communications in Computer and Information Science*, pages 139–150. Springer Berlin Heidelberg.

Jey Han Lau, Timothy Baldwin, and David Newman. 2013. On collocations and topic models. *ACM Transactions on Speech and Language Processing*, 10(3):1–14.

Jey Han Lau, David Newman, and Timothy Baldwin. 2014. Machine reading tea leaves: Automatically evaluating topic coherence and topic model quality. In *Proceedings of the 14th Conference of the European Chapter of the Association for Computational Linguistics*. Association for Computational Linguistics.

David Mimno, Hanna M Wallach, Edmund Talley, Miriam Leenders, and Andrew McCallum. 2011. Optimizing semantic coherence in topic models. In *Proceedings of the conference on empirical methods in natural language processing*, pages 262–272. Association for Computational Linguistics.

David Newman, Chaitanya Chemudugunta, and Padhraic Smyth. 2006. Statistical entity-topic models. In *Proceedings of the 12th ACM SIGKDD international conference on Knowledge discovery and data mining - KDD06*. ACM Press.

David Newman, Jey Han Lau, Karl Grieser, and Timothy Baldwin. 2010. Automatic evaluation of topic coherence. In *Human Language Technologies: The 2010 Annual Conference of the North American Chapter of the Association for Computational Linguistics*, pages 100–108. Association for Computational Linguistics.

Dat Quoc Nguyen, Kairit Sirts, and Mark Johnson. 2015. Improving topic coherence with latent feature word representations in map estimation for topic modeling. In *Proceedings of the Australasian Language Technology Association Workshop 2015*, pages 116–121.

Sergey I. Nikolenko. 2016. Topic quality metrics based on distributed word representations. In *Proceedings of the 39th International ACM SIGIR conference on Research and Development in Information Retrieval - SIGIR16*. ACM Press.

Derek O'Callaghan, Derek Greene, Joe Carthy, and Pádraig Cunningham. 2015. An analysis of the coherence of descriptors in topic modeling. *Expert Systems with Applications*, 42(13):5645–5657.

Michael Röder, Andreas Both, and Alexander Hinneburg. 2015. Exploring the space of topic coherence measures. In *Proceedings of the Eighth ACM International Conference on Web Search and Data Mining - WSDM15*. ACM Press.

Carson Sievert and Kenneth Shirley. 2014. LDAvis: A method for visualizing and interpreting topics. In *Proceedings of the Workshop on Interactive Language Learning, Visualization, and Interfaces*. Association for Computational Linguistics.

Shaheen Syed and Marco Spruit. 2017. Full-text or abstract? examining topic coherence scores using latent dirichlet allocation. In *2017 IEEE International Conference on Data Science and Advanced Analytics (DSAA)*. IEEE.

Matt Taddy. 2012. On estimation and selection for topic models. In *Artificial Intelligence and Statistics*, pages 1184–1193.

Ciprian-Octavian Truica, Florin Radulescu, and Alexandru Boicea. 2016. Comparing different term weighting schemas for topic modeling. In *2016 18th International Symposium on Symbolic and Numeric Algorithms for Scientific Computing (SYNASC)*. IEEE.

Hanna M Wallach, David M Mimno, and Andrew McCallum. 2009. Rethinking lda: Why priors matter. In *Advances in neural information processing systems*, pages 1973–1981.

Andrew T Wilson and Peter A Chew. 2010. Term weighting schemes for latent dirichlet allocation. In *human language technologies: The 2010 annual conference of the North American Chapter of the Association for Computational Linguistics*, pages 465–473. Association for Computational Linguistics.

Weiwei Yang, Jordan Boyd-Graber, and Philip Resnik. 2017. Adapting topic models using lexical associations with tree priors. In *Proceedings of the 2017 Conference on Empirical Methods in Natural Language Processing*. Association for Computational Linguistics.

Obligation and Prohibition Extraction Using Hierarchical RNNs

Ilias Chalkidis[1,2], Ion Androutsopoulos[1], and Achilleas Michos[2]

[1]Department of Informatics, Athens University of Economics and Business, Greece
[2]Cognitiv+ Ltd., London, UK

Abstract

We consider the task of detecting contractual obligations and prohibitions. We show that a self-attention mechanism improves the performance of a BILSTM classifier, the previous state of the art for this task, by allowing it to focus on indicative tokens. We also introduce a hierarchical BILSTM, which converts each sentence to an embedding, and processes the sentence embeddings to classify each sentence. Apart from being faster to train, the hierarchical BILSTM outperforms the flat one, even when the latter considers surrounding sentences, because the hierarchical model has a broader discourse view.

1 Introduction

Legal text processing (Ashley, 2017) is a growing research area, comprising tasks such as legal question answering (Kim and Goebel, 2017), contract element extraction (Chalkidis et al., 2017), and legal text generation (Alschnerd and Skougarevskiy, 2017). We consider *obligation* and *prohibition extraction* from contracts, i.e., detecting sentences (or clauses) that specify what *should* or should *not* happen (Table 1). This task is important for legal firms and legal departments, especially when they process large numbers of contracts to monitor the compliance of each party. Methods that would automatically identify (e.g., highlight) sentences (or clauses) specifying obligations and prohibitions would allow lawyers and paralegals to inspect contracts more quickly. They would also be a step towards populating databases with information extracted from contracts, along with methods that extract contractors, particular dates (e.g., start and end dates), applicable law, legislation references etc. (Chalkidis and Androutsopoulos, 2017).

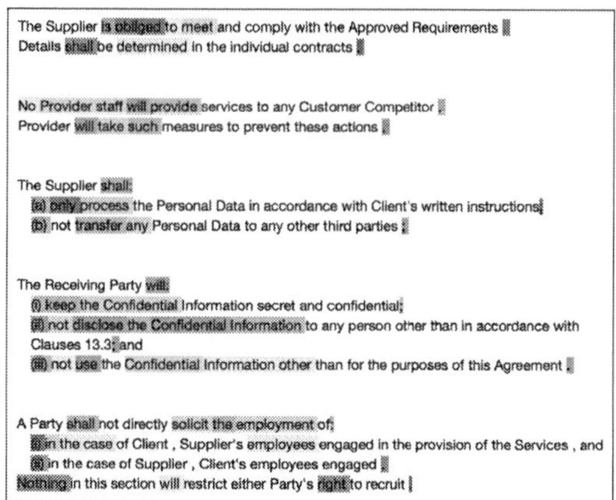

Figure 1: Heatmap visualizing the attention scores of BILSTM-ATT for some examples of Table 1.

Obligation and prohibition extraction is a kind of *deontic* sentence (or clause) classification (O'Neill et al., 2017). Different firms may use different or finer deontic classes (e.g., distinguishing between payment and delivery obligations), but obligations and prohibitions are the most common coarse deontic classes. Using similar classes, O' Neill et al. (2017) reported that a bidirectional LSTM (BILSTM) classifier (Graves et al., 2013) outperformed several others (including logistic regression, SVM, AdaBoost, Random Forests) in legal sentence classification, possibly because long-term dependencies (e.g., modal verbs or negations interacting with distant dependents) are common and crucial in legal texts, and LSTMs can cope with long-term dependencies better than methods relying on fixed-size context windows.

We improve upon the work of O' Neill et al. (2017) in four ways. First, we show that self-attention (Yang et al., 2016) improves the performance of the BILSTM classifier, by allowing the system to focus on indicative words (Fig 1). Second, we introduce a hierarchical BILSTM, where a first BILSTM processes each sentence word by

Proceedings of the 56th Annual Meeting of the Association for Computational Linguistics (Short Papers), pages 254–259
Melbourne, Australia, July 15 - 20, 2018. ©2018 Association for Computational Linguistics

No.	Gold Class	Sentences/Clauses
1	Obligation	The Supplier *is obliged to* meet and comply with the Approved Requirements.
	None	Details shall be determined in the individual contracts.
2	Prohibition	*No* Provider staff *will* provide services to any Customer Competitor.
	Obligation	Provider *will* take such measures to prevent these actions.
3	Prohibition	Provider *is not entitled* to suspend this Agreement prior to the lapse of the fifth year.
4	Oblig./Prohib. List Intro	The Supplier *shall*:
	Obligation List Item	*(a)* only process the Personal Data in accordance with Client's written instructions;
	Prohibition List Item	*(b) not* transfer any Personal Data to any other third parties;
5	Oblig./Prohib. List Intro	The Receiving Party *will*:
	Obligation List Item	*(i)* keep the Confidential Information secret and confidential;
	Prohibition List Item	*(ii) not* disclose the Confidential Information to any person other than in accordance with Clauses 13.3; and
	Prohibition List Item	*(iii) not* use the Confidential Information other than for the purposes of this Agreement.
6	Oblig./Prohib. List Intro	A Party *shall not* directly solicit the employment of:
	Prohibition List Item	*(i)* in the case of Client, Supplier's employees engaged in the provision of the Services,
	Prohibition List Item	*(ii)* in the case of Supplier, Client's employees engaged.
	None	Nothing in this section will restrict either Party's right to recruit.

Table 1: Examples of sentences and clauses, with human annotations of classes. Terms that are highly indicative of the classes are shown in bold and underlined here, but are not marked by the annotators.

Gold Class	Train	Dev	Test
None	15,401	3,905	4,141
Obligation	11,005	2,860	970
Prohibition	1,172	314	108
Obligation List Intro	828	203	70
Obligation List Item	2888	726	255
Prohibition List Item	251	28	19
Total	**31,545**	**8,036**	**5,563**

Table 2: Sentences/clauses after sentence splitting.

word producing a sentence embedding, and a second BILSTM processes the sentence embeddings to classify each sentence. The hierarchical BIL-STM is similar to Yang et al.'s (2016), but classifies sentences, not entire texts (e.g., news articles or product reviews). It outperforms a flat BILSTM that classifies each sentence independently, even when the latter considers neighbouring sentences, because the hierarchical BILSTM has a broader view of the discourse. Third, we experiment with a dataset an order of magnitude larger than the dataset of O' Neill et al. Fourth, we introduce finer classes (Tables 1–2), which fit better the target task, where nested clauses are frequent.

2 Data

We experimented with a dataset containing 6,385 training, 1,595 development, and 1,420 test sections (articles) from the main bodies (excluding introductions, covers, recitals) of 100 randomly selected English service agreements.[1] The sections

were preprocessed by a sentence splitter, which in clause lists (Examples 4–6 in Table 1) treats the introductory clause and each nested clause as separate sentences, since each nested clause may belong in a different class.[2]

The splitter produced 31,545 training, 8,036 development, and 5,563 test sentences/clauses.[3] Table 2 shows their distribution in the six gold (correct) classes. Each section was annotated by a single law student (5 students in total). All the annotations were checked and corrected by a single paralegal expert, who produces annotations of this kind on a daily basis, based on strict guidelines of the firm that provided the data.

We used pre-trained 200-dimensional word embeddings and pre-trained 25-dimensional POS tag embeddings, obtained by applying WORD2VEC (Mikolov et al., 2013) to approx. 750k and 50k English contracts, respectively, as in our previous work (Chalkidis et al., 2017). We also pre-trained 5-dimensional token shape embeddings (e.g., all capitals, first letter capital, all digits), obtained as in our previous work (Chalkidis and Androutsopoulos, 2017). Each token is represented by the concatenation of its word, POS, shape embeddings (Fig. 2, bottom). Unknown tokens are mapped to

---

[1] The splitting of the dataset into training, development, and test subsets was performed by first agglomeratively clustering all sections (articles) based on Levenshtein distance,

and then assigning entire clusters to the training, development, or test subset, to avoid having similar sections (e.g., based on boilerplate clauses) in different subsets.

[2] We use NLTK's splitter (http://www.nltk.org/), with additional post-processing based on regular expressions.

[3] There are at most 15 sentences/clauses per section in the training set. We hope to make the dataset, or a similar anonymized one, publicly available in the near future, but the dataset is currently not available due to confidentiality issues.

pre-trained POS-specific 'unk' embeddings (e.g., 'unk-n', 'unk-vb'). The dataset of Table 2 has no overlap with the corpus of contracts that was used to pre-train the embeddings.

3 Methods

BILSTM: The first classifier we considered processes a single sentence (or clause) at a time. It feeds the concatenated word, POS, shape embeddings ($e_1, \ldots, e_n \in \mathbb{R}^{230}$) of the tokens $w_1, w_2, \ldots, w_n$ of the sentence to a forward LSTM, and (in reverse order) to a backward LSTM, obtaining the forward and backward hidden states ($\overrightarrow{h}_1, \ldots, \overrightarrow{h}_n \in \mathbb{R}^{300}$ and $\overleftarrow{h}_1, \ldots \overleftarrow{h}_n \in \mathbb{R}^{300}$). The concatenation of the last states ($h = [\overrightarrow{h}_n; \overleftarrow{h}_1]$) is fed to a multinomial Logistic Regression (LR) layer, which produces a probability per class.

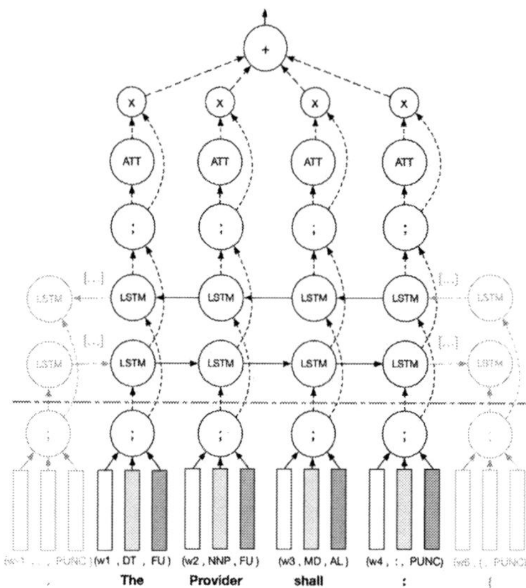

Figure 2: BILSTM with self-attention (ATT nodes) used on its own (BILSTM-ATT) or as the sentence encoder of the hierarchical BILSTM (H-BILSTM-ATT, Fig. 3). In X-BILSTM-ATT, the two LSTM chains also consider the words of surrounding sentences. The red dashed line is a drop-out layer.

BILSTM-ATT: When self-attention is added (Fig. 2), the sentence (or clause) is represented by the weighted sum (h) of the hidden states ($h_t = [\overrightarrow{h}_t; \overleftarrow{h}_t] \in \mathbb{R}^{600}$) of the BILSTM, where $a_1, \ldots, a_n \in \mathbb{R}$ are attention scores, $v \in \mathbb{R}^{600}, b \in \mathbb{R}$:

$$h = a_1 h_1 + \cdots + a_t h_t + \cdots + a_n h_n \quad (1)$$
$$a'_t = \tanh(v^T h_t + b) \quad (2)$$
$$a_t = \mathrm{softmax}(a'_t; a'_1, \ldots, a'_n) \quad (3)$$

Again, h is then fed to a multinomial LR layer. Figure 1 visualizes the attention scores ($a_1, \ldots, a_n$) of BILSTM-ATT when reading some of the sentences (or clauses) of Table 1. The attention scores are higher for modals, negations, words that indicate obligations or prohibitions (e.g., 'obliged', 'only'), and tokens indicating nested clauses (e.g., '(a)', ':', ';'), which allows BILSTM-ATT to focus more on these tokens (the corresponding states) when computing the sentence representation (h).

X-BILSTM-ATT: In an extension of BILSTM-ATT, called X-BILSTM-ATT, the BILSTM chain is fed with the token embeddings (e_t) not only of the sentence being classified, but also of the previous (and following) tokens (faded parts of Fig. 2), up to 150 previous (and 150 following) tokens, 150 being the maximum sentence length in the dataset.[4] This might allow the BILSTM chain to 'remember' key parts of the surrounding sentences (e.g., a previous clause ending with 'shall not:') when producing the context-aware embeddings (states h_t) of the current sentence. The self-attention mechanism still considers the states (h_t) of the tokens of the current sentence only, and the sentence representation (h) is still computed as in Eq. 1.

H-BILSTM-ATT: The hierarchical BILSTM classifier, H-BILSTM-ATT, considers all the sentences (or clauses) of an entire section. Each sentence (or clause) is first turned into a sentence embedding ($h \in \mathbb{R}^{600}$), as in BILSTM-ATT (Fig. 2). The sequence of sentence embeddings is then fed to a second BILSTM (Fig. 3), whose hidden states ($h_t^{(2)} = [\overrightarrow{h}_t^{(2)}; \overleftarrow{h}_t^{(2)}] \in \mathbb{R}^{600}$) are treated as context-aware sentence embeddings. The latter are passed on to a multinomial LR layer, producing a probability per class, for each sentence (or clause) of the section. We hypothesized that H-BILSTM-ATT would perform better, because it considers an entire section at a time, and salient information about a sentence or clause (e.g., that the opening clause of a list contains a negation or modal) can be 'condensed' in its sentence embedding and interact with the sentence embeddings of distant sentences or clauses (e.g., a nested clause several clauses after the opening one) in the upper BILSTM (Fig. 3).

---

[4]Memory constraints did not allow including more tokens. We used a single NVIDIA 1080 GPU. All methods were implemented using KERAS (https://keras.io/) with a TENSORFLOW backend (https://www.tensorflow.org/). We padded each sentence to the maximum length.

Gold Class	BILSTM				BILSTM-ATT				X-BILSTM-ATT				H-BILSTM-ATT			
	P	R	F1	AUC	P	R	F1	AUC	P	R	F1	AUC	P	R	F1	AUC
None	0.95	0.91	0.93	0.98	0.97	0.90	0.93	**0.99**	0.96	0.90	0.93	0.98	**0.98**	**0.96**	**0.97**	**0.99**
Obligation	0.75	0.85	0.79	0.86	0.75	0.88	0.81	0.86	0.75	0.87	0.81	0.88	**0.87**	**0.92**	**0.90**	**0.96**
Prohibition	0.67	0.62	0.64	0.75	0.74	0.75	0.74	0.80	0.65	0.75	0.70	0.74	**0.84**	**0.83**	**0.84**	**0.90**
Obl. List Begin	0.70	0.86	0.77	0.81	0.71	0.85	0.77	0.83	0.72	0.75	0.74	0.80	**0.90**	**0.89**	**0.89**	**0.93**
Obl. List Item	0.53	0.66	0.59	0.64	0.48	0.70	0.57	0.60	0.49	0.78	0.60	0.66	**0.85**	**0.94**	**0.89**	**0.94**
Proh. List Item	0.59	0.35	0.43	0.50	0.61	0.55	0.59	0.62	**0.83**	0.50	0.62	0.67	0.80	**0.84**	**0.82**	**0.92**
Macro-average	0.70	0.70	0.70	0.74	0.73	0.78	0.74	0.78	0.73	0.76	0.73	0.79	**0.87**	**0.90**	**0.89**	**0.94**
Micro-average	0.90	0.88	0.88	0.94	0.90	0.88	0.89	0.96	0.90	0.88	0.89	0.94	**0.95**	**0.95**	**0.95**	**0.98**

Table 3: Precision, recall, F1, and AUC scores, with the best results in bold and gray background.

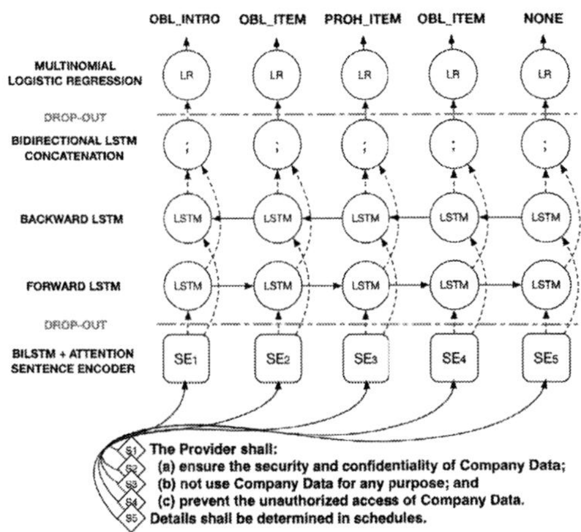

Figure 3: Upper part of the hierarchical BILSTM (H-BILSTM-ATT). The sentence embeddings (SE_i) are generated by the encoder of Fig. 2.

4 Experimental Results

Hyper-parameters were tuned by grid-searching the following sets, and selecting the values with the best validation loss: LSTM hidden units {100, 200, 300}, batch size {8, 16, 32}, drop-out rate {0.4, 0.5, 0.6}. The red dashed lines of Fig. 2–3 are drop-out layers.[5] We used categorical cross-entropy loss, Glorot initialization (Glorot and Bengio, 2010), Adam (Kingma and Ba, 2015), learning rate 0.001, and early stopping on the validation loss. Table 3 reports the precision, recall, F1 score, area under the precision-recall curve (AUC) per class, as well as micro- and macro-averages.

The self-attention mechanism (BILSTM-ATT) leads to clear overall improvements (in macro and micro F1 and AUC, Table 3) comparing to the plain BILSTM, supporting the hypothesis that self-attention allows the classifier to focus on indicative tokens. Allowing the BILSTM to consider tokens of neighboring sentences (X-BILSTM-ATT) does not lead to any clear overall improvements.

The hierarchical H-BILSTM-ATT clearly outperforms the other three methods, supporting the hypothesis that considering entire sections and allowing the sentence embeddings to interact in the upper BILSTM (Fig. 3) is beneficial.

Notice that the three flat methods (BILSTM, BILSTM-ATT, X-BILSTM-ATT) obtain particularly lower F1 and AUC scores, compared to H-BILSTM-ATT, in the classes that correspond to nested clauses (obligation list item, prohibition list item). This is due to the fact that the flat methods have no (or only limited, in the case of X-BILSTM-ATT) view of the previous sentences, which often indicate if a nested clause is an obligation or prohibition (see, for example, examples 4–6 in Table 1).

H-BILSTM-ATT is also much faster to train than BILSTM and BILSTM-ATT (Table 4), even though it has more parameters, because it converges faster (5-7 epochs vs. 12-15). X-BILSTM-ATT is particularly slow, because its BILSTM processes the same sentences multiple times, when they are classified and when they are neighboring sentences.

Network	Training Time	Parameters
BILSTM	5h 30m	1,278M
BILSTM-ATT	8h 30m	1,279M
X-BILSTM-ATT	25h 40m	1,279M
H-BILSTM-ATT	2h 30m	1,837M

Table 4: Training times and parameters to learn.

5 Related Work

As already noted, we built upon the work of O'Neill et al. (2017). The dataset of O'Neill et al. contained financial legislation, not contracts, and was an order of magnitude smaller (obligations, prohibitions, permissions had 1,297 training, 622 test sentences in total, cf. Table 2), but also included permissions, which we did not consider.

Waltl et al. (2017) classified statements from German tenancy law into 22 classes (including prohibition, permission, consequence), using active learning with Naive Bayes, LR, MLP classifiers, experimenting with 504 sentences.

---

[5]We resample the drop-out mask at each time-step.

Kiyavitskaya et al. (2008) used grammars, word lists, and heuristics to extract rights, obligations, exceptions, and other constraints from US and Italian regulations.

Asooja et al. (2015) employed SVMs with n-gram and manually crafted features to classify paragraphs of money laundering regulations into five classes (e.g., enforcement, monitoring, reporting), experimenting with 212 paragraphs.

In previous work (Chalkidis et al., 2017; Chalkidis and Androutsopoulos, 2017) we focused on extracting contract elements (e.g., contractor names, legislation references, start and end dates, amounts), a task which is similar to named entity recognition. The best results were obtained by stacked BILSTMs (Irsoy and Cardie, 2014) or stacked BILSTM-CRF models (Ma and Hovy, 2016); hierarchical BILSTMs were not considered. By contrast, in this paper we considered obligation and prohibition extraction, treating it as a sentence (or clause) classification task, and showing the benefits of employing a hierarchical BILSTM model that considers both the sequence of words in each sentence and the sequence of sentences.

Yang et al. (2016) proposed a hierarchical RNN with self-attention to classify texts. A first bidirectional RNN turns the words of each sentence to a sentence embedding, and a second one turns the sentence embeddings to a document embedding, which is fed to an LR layer. Yang et al. use self-attention in both RNNs, to assign attention scores to words and sentences. We classify sentences (or clauses), not entire texts, hence our second BILSTM does not produce a document embedding and does not use self-attention. Also, Yang et al. experimented with reviews and community question answering logs, whereas we considered legal texts.

Hierarchical RNNs have also been developed for multilingual text classification (Pappas and Popescu-Belis, 2017), language modeling (Lin et al., 2015), and dialogue breakdown detection (Xie and Ling, 2017).

6 Conclusions and Future Work

We presented the legal text analytics task of detecting contractual obligations and prohibitions. We showed that self-attention improves the performance of a BILSTM classifier, the previous state of the art in this task, by allowing the BILSTM to focus on indicative tokens. We also introduced a hierarchical BILSTM (also using attention), which converts each sentence to an embedding, and then processes the sentence embeddings to classify each sentence. Apart from being faster to train, the hierarchical BILSTM outperforms the flat one, even when the latter considers the surrounding sentences, because the hierarchical model has a broader view of the discourse.

Further performance improvements may be possible by considering deeper self-attention mechanisms (Pavlopoulos et al., 2017), stacking BILSTMs (Irsoy and Cardie, 2014), or pre-training the BILSTMs with auxiliary tasks (Ramachandran et al., 2017). The hierarchical BILSTM with attention of this paper may also be useful in other sentence, clause, or utterance classification tasks, for example in dialogue turn classification (Xie and Ling, 2017), detecting abusive user comments in on-line discussions (Pavlopoulos et al., 2017), and discourse segmentation (Hearst, 1997). We would also like to investigate replacing its BILSTMs with sequence-labeling CNNs (Bai et al., 2018), which may lead to efficiency improvements.

Acknowledgments

We are grateful to the members of AUEB's Natural Language Processing Group, for several suggestions that helped significantly improve this paper.

References

W. Alschnerd and D. Skougarevskiy. 2017. Towards an automated production of legal texts using recurrent neural networks. In *Proceeding of the 16th International Conference on Artificial Intelligence and Law*, pages 159–168, London, UK.

K.D. Ashley. 2017. *Artificial Intelligence and Legal Analytics: New Tools for Law Practice in the Digital Age*. Cambridge University Press.

K. Asooja, G. Bordea, G. Vulcu, L. O'Brien, A. Espinoza, E. Abi-Lahoud, P. Buitelaar, and T. Butler. 2015. Semantic annotation of finance regulatory text using multilabel classification. In *Proceedings of the International Workshop on Legal Domain and Semantic Web Applications*, Portoroz, Slovenia.

S. Bai, J.Z. Kolter, and V. Koltun. 2018. An empirical evaluation of generic convolutional and recurrent networks for sequence modeling. *CoRR*, abs/1803.01271.

I. Chalkidis and I. Androutsopoulos. 2017. A deep learning approach to contract element extraction. In *Proceedings of the 30th International Conference on Legal Knowledge and Information Systems*, pages 155–164, Luxembourg.

I. Chalkidis, I. Androutsopoulos, and A. Michos. 2017. Extracting contract elements. In *Proceedings of the 16th International Conference on Artificial Intelligence and Law*, pages 19–28, London, UK.

X. Glorot and Y. Bengio. 2010. Understanding the difficulty of training deep feedforward neural networks. In *Proceedings of the International Conference on Artificial Intelligence and Statistics*, pages 249–256, Sardinia, Italy.

A. Graves, N. Jaitly, and A. Mohamed. 2013. Hybrid speech recognition with deep bidirectional LSTM. In *IEEE Workshop on Automatic Speech Recognition and Understanding*, pages 273–278, Olomouc, Czech Republic.

Marti A. Hearst. 1997. Texttiling: Segmenting text into multi-paragraph subtopic passages. *Computational Linguistics*, 23(1):33–64.

O. Irsoy and C. Cardie. 2014. Deep recursive neural networks for compositionality in language. In *Proceedings of the 27th International Conference on Neural Information Processing Systems*, pages 2096–2104, Montreal, Canada.

M.Y. Kim and R. Goebel. 2017. Two-step cascaded textual entailment for legal bar exam question answering. In *Proceedings of the 4th Competition on Legal Information Extraction/Entailment*, London, UK.

D. P. Kingma and J. Ba. 2015. Adam: A method for stochastic optimization. In *Proceedings of the 5th International Conference on Learning Representations*, San Diego, CA, USA.

N. Kiyavitskaya, N. Zeni, Travis D. Breaux, Annie I. Antón, James R. Cordy, L. Mich, and J. Mylopoulos. 2008. Automating the extraction of rights and obligations for regulatory compliance. In *Proceedings of the 27th International Conference on Conceptual Modeling*, pages 154–168, Barcelona, Spain.

R. Lin, S. Liu, M. Yang, M. Li, M. Zhou, and S. Li. 2015. Hierarchical recurrent neural network for document modeling. In *Proceedings of the Conference on Empirical Methods in Natural Language Processing*, pages 899–907, Lisbon, Portugal.

X. Ma and E. Hovy. 2016. End-to-end sequence labeling via bi-directional LSTM-CNNs-CRF. In *Proceedings of the 54th Annual Meeting of the ACL*, pages 1064–1074, Berlin, Germany.

T. Mikolov, I. Sutskever, K. Chen, G. Corrado, and J. Dean. 2013. Distributed Representations of Words and Phrases and their Compositionality. In *Proceedings of the 26th International Conference on Neural Information Processing Systems*, Stateline, NV.

J. O'Neill, P. Buitelaar, C. Robin, and L. O' Brien. 2017. Classifying Sentential Modality in Legal Language: A Use Case in Financial Regulations, Acts and Directives. In *Proceedings of the 16th International Conference on Artificial Intelligence and Law*, pages 159–168, London, UK.

N. Pappas and A. Popescu-Belis. 2017. Multilingual hierarchical attention networks for document classification. In *Proceedings of the 8th International Joint Conference on Natural Language Processing*, Tapei, Taiwan.

J. Pavlopoulos, P. Malakasiotis, and I. Androutsopoulos. 2017. Deeper attention to abusive user content moderation. In *Proceedings of the Conference on Empirical Methods in Natural Language Processing*, pages 1125–1135, Copenhagen, Denmark.

P. Ramachandran, P.r J. Liu, and Q. V. Le. 2017. Unsupervised pretraining for sequence to sequence learning. In *Proceedings of the Conference on Empirical Methods in Natural Language Processing*, pages 383–391, Copenhagen, Denmark.

B. Waltl, J. Muhr, I. Glaser, G. Bonczek, E. Scepankova, and F. Matthes. 2017. Classifying legal norms with active machine learning. In *Proceedings of the 30th International Conference on Legal Knowledge and Information Systems*, pages 11–20, Luxembourg City Luxembourg.

Z. Xie and G. Ling. 2017. Dialogue breakdown detection using hierarchical bi-directional LSTMs. In *Proceedings of the 6th Dialog System Technology Challenges (Track 3: Dialog Breakdown Detection)*, Long Beach, USA.

Z. Yang, D. Yang, C. Dyer, X. He, A. Smola, and E. Hovy. 2016. Hierarchical attention networks for document classification. In *Proceedings of the 15th Conference of the North American Chapter of the Association for Computational Linguistics: Human Language Technologies*, pages 1480–1489, San Diego, CA, USA.

Paper Abstract Writing through Editing Mechanism

Qingyun Wang[1*], Zhihao Zhou[1*], Lifu Huang[1], Spencer Whitehead[1],
Boliang Zhang[1], Heng Ji[1], Kevin Knight[2]

[1] Rensselaer Polytechnic Institute
jih@rpi.edu
[2] University of Southern California
knight@isi.edu

Abstract

We present a paper abstract writing system based on an attentive neural sequence-to-sequence model that can take a title as input and automatically generate an abstract. We design a novel Writing-editing Network that can attend to both the title and the previously generated abstract drafts and then iteratively revise and polish the abstract. With two series of Turing tests, where the human judges are asked to distinguish the system-generated abstracts from human-written ones, our system passes Turing tests by junior domain experts at a rate up to 30% and by non-expert at a rate up to 80%.[1]

1 Introduction

Routine writing, such as writing scientific papers or patents, is a very common exercise. It can be traced back to the *"Eight legged essay"*, an austere writing style in the Ming-Qing dynasty.[2] We explore automated routine writing, with paper abstract writing as a case study. Given a title, we aim to automatically generate a paper abstract. We hope our approach can serve as an assistive technology for human to write paper abstracts more efficiently and professionally, by generating an initial draft for humans further editing, correction and enrichment.

A scientific paper abstract should always **focus on the topics** specified in the title. However, a typical recurrent neural network (RNN) based approach easily loses focus. Given the title *"An effective method of using **Web based information** for **Relation Extraction**"* from Keong and Su (2008), we compare the human written abstract and system generated abstracts in Table 1. The *LSTM_LM* baseline generated abstract misses the key term *"Web"* mentioned in the paper title. We introduce a title attention (Bahdanau et al., 2015; Luong et al., 2015) into a sequence-to-sequence model (Sutskever et al., 2014; Cho et al., 2014) to guide the generation process so the abstract is topically relevant to the given title, as shown in the "Seq2seq with attention" row of Table 1.

Previous work usually models natural language generation as a one-way decision problem, where models generate a sequence of tokens as output and then moves on, never coming back to modify or improve the output. However, human writers usually start with a draft and keep polishing and revising it. As C. J. Cherryh once said, "it is perfectly okay to write garbage - as long as you edit brilliantly." [3] We model abstract generation as a conditioned, iterative text generation problem and design a new **Writing-editing Network** with an **Attentive Revision Gate** to iteratively examine, improve, and edit the abstract with guidance from the paper title as well as the previously generated abstract. A result of the Writing-editing Network is shown in Table 1, where we can see that the initial draft contains more topically relevant and richer concepts than the title, such as the term *'IE'*. By adding this initial draft as feedback and guidance, it eases the next generation iteration, allowing the model to focus on a more limited learning space, and generate more concise and coherent abstracts.

---

*Qingyun Wang and Zhihao Zhou contributed equally to this work.

[1]The datasets and programs are publicly available for research purpose `https://github.com/EagleW/Writing-editing-Network`

[2]https://en.wikipedia.org/wiki/Eight-legged_essay

[3]https://www.goodreads.com/quotes/398754-it-is-perfectly-okay-to-write-garbage--as-long-as-you

Proceedings of the 56th Annual Meeting of the Association for Computational Linguistics (Short Papers), pages 260–265
Melbourne, Australia, July 15 - 20, 2018. ©2018 Association for Computational Linguistics

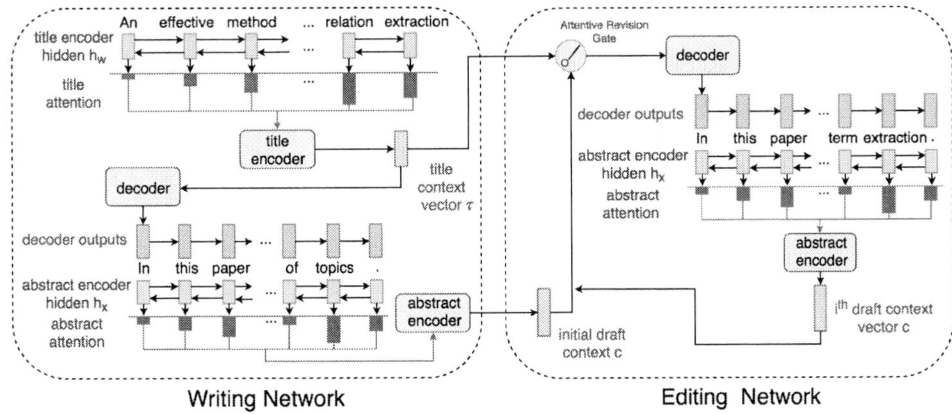

Figure 1: Writing-editing Network architecture overview.

Title	An effective method of using **Web** based **information** for **Relation Extraction (Keong and Su, 2008)**
Human written abstract	*We propose a method that incorporates paraphrase **information** from the **Web** to boost the performance of a supervised **relation extraction** system. Contextual **information** is extracted from the **Web** using a semi-supervised process, and summarized by skip-bigram overlap measures over the entire **extract**. This allows the capture of local contextual **information** as well as more distant associations. We observe a statistically significant boost in **relation extraction** performance.*
LSTM_LM	*This paper proposes a method for automatic **extraction** of salient **information** from an original text. Our method shows promising results in which a noun clustering is employed. The **relation** is then be applied to the **relation extraction** task.*
Seq2seq with attention (Initial Draft)	*In this paper we focus on the task of **extracting** the most commonly used **Web** pages in named entity recognition (IE) **information** from a large corpus of news articles. In particular, we propose a new kernel method that can be applied to a large collection of **Web** pages by automatic detection of labeled and unlabeled data. Our method is very simple and because the related method of using the data to be used as a guide as a source of **information** for the topic detection and classification can be applied, but often fail at improving the performance by combining **relations** and previous methods. In this method, the co-occurrence counts and the occurrences of each **relation** are not statistically significant, but also that it is possible to contribute to entity **relations** with a term in a variety of topics.*
Writing-editing Networks (Final Draft)	*In this paper we focus on the task of identifying the most commonly relevant features of **Web** documents. In particular, we propose a generic, automated IE algorithm that can be applied to a large collection of **Web** pages containing full large documents. This is a first step in helping a wide range of collaborative works for **relation extraction**. We show that it is possible to eliminate a good number of errors in **relation extraction** from a variety of documents, but that it is difficult to define a problem of term **extraction**.*

Table 1: Human and system generated abstracts for the same title.

2 Approach

In this section, we describe our "Writing-editing Network" (Figure 1). The writing network takes a title as input and generates the first abstract draft. The editing network takes both the title and previous draft as input to iteratively proof-read, improve, and generate new versions.

2.1 Writing Network

Our Writing Network is based on an attentive sequence-to-sequence model. We use a bi-directional gated recurrent unit (GRU) (Cho et al., 2014) as an encoder, which takes a title $\mathcal{T} = \{w_1, \ldots, w_K\}$ as input. For each token, w_k, the encoder produces a hidden state, h_{w_k}.

We employ a GRU as our decoder to generate the draft abstract $X^{(0)} = \{x_1^{(0)}, \ldots, x_N^{(0)}\}$. To capture the correlation between the title, $\mathcal{T}$, and the abstract draft, $X^{(0)}$, we adopt a soft-alignment attention mechanism (Bahdanau et al., 2015), which enables the decoder to focus on the most relevant words from the title. At the nth decoder step, we apply the soft attention to the encoder hidden states to obtain an attentive title context vector, τ_n:

$$\tau_n = \sum_{k=1}^{K} \alpha_{n,k} h_{w_k}$$
$$\alpha_{n,k} = \text{softmax}\left(f\left(s_{n-1}, h_{w_k}\right)\right) \tag{1}$$

where s_{n-1} is the $n-1^{th}$ hidden state, $s_0 = h_{w_K}$ which is the last hidden state of the encoder, f is a function that measures the relatedness of word w_k in the title and word $x_{n-1}^{(0)}$ in the output abstract.

The decoder then generates the nth hidden state, s_n, which is given by:

$$s_n = \text{GRU}(x_{n-1}^{(0)}, s_{n-1}, \tau_n)$$
$$p(x_n^{(0)}|x_{1:n-1}^{(0)}, w_{1:K}) = g(x_{n-1}^{(0)}, s_n, \tau_n) \quad (2)$$

where the function g is a softmax classifier, which is used to find the next word, $x_n^{(0)}$, by selecting the word of maximum probability.

2.2 Editing Network

The concepts contained in the titles are usually limited, so the learning space for the generator is huge, which hinders the quality of the generated abstract. Compared to the title, the generated abstracts contain more topically relevant concepts, and can provide better guidance. Therefore, we design an Editing Network, which, besides the title, also takes the previously generated abstract as input and iteratively refines the generated abstract. The Editing Network follows an architecture similar to the Writing Network.

Given an initial draft, $X^{(0)}$, from the Writing Network, we use a separate bi-directional GRU encoder, to encode each $x_n^{(0)} \in X^{(0)}$ into a new representation, $h_{x_n^{(0)}}$. As in the Writing Network, we use $s_0 = h_{w_K}$ as the initial decoder hidden state of the Editing Network decoder, which shares weights with the Writing Network decoder.

At the nth decoder step, we compute an attentive draft context vector, c_t, by applying the same soft attention function from Eq. (1) to the encoded draft representations, $\{h_{x_1^{(0)}}, \ldots, h_{x_N^{(0)}}\}$, using decoder state s_{n-1}.[4] We also recompute the attentive title context vector, τ_n, with the same soft attention, though these attentions do not share weights. Intuitively, this attention mechanism allows the model to proofread the previously generated abstract and improve it by better capturing long-term dependency and relevance to the title. We incorporate c_t into the model through a novel **Attentive Revision Gate** that adaptively attends to the title and the previous draft at each generation step:

$$r_n = \sigma\left(W_{r,c}c_n + W_{r,\tau}\tau_n + b_r\right) \quad (3)$$
$$z_n = \sigma\left(W_{z,c}c_n + W_{z,\tau}\tau_n + b_z\right) \quad (4)$$
$$\rho_n = \tanh\left(W_{\rho,c}c_n + z_n \odot \left(W_{\rho,\tau}\tau_n + b_\rho\right)\right) \quad (5)$$
$$a_n = r_n \odot c_n + (1 - r_n) \odot \rho_n \quad (6)$$

where all W and b are learned parameters. With the attention vector, a_n, we compute the nth token with the same decoder as in section 2.1, yielding another draft $X^{(1)} = \{x_1^{(1)}, \ldots, x_T^{(1)}\}$. We repeat this process for d iterations. In our experiments, we set d to 2 and found it to work best.

3 Experiments

3.1 Data and Hyperparameters

We select NLP as our test domain because we have easy access to data and domain experts for human judges. We collected a data set of 10,874 paper title and abstract pairs[5] from the ACL Anthology Network[6] (until 2016) for our experiments. We randomly dividing them into training (80%), validation (10%), and testing (10%) sets. On average, each title and abstract include 9 and 116 words, respectively. Our model has 512 dimensional word embeddings, 512 encoder hidden units, and 1,024 decoder hidden units.

3.2 Method Comparison

Method	METEOR	ROUGE-L	HUMAN PREFERENCE
LSTM-LM	8.7	15.1	0
Seq2seq	13.5	19.2	22
ED(1)	13.3	**20.3**	30
ED(2)	**14.0**	19.8	**48**

Table 2: Method Comparison (%).

n	1	2	3	4	5	6
System	100	94.4	67.3	35.0	15.9	6.6
Human	98.2	78.5	42.2	17.9	7.7	4.1

Table 3: Plagiarism Check: Percentage (%) of n-grams in test abstracts generated by system/human which appeared in training data.

We include an LSTM Language Model (Sundermeyer et al., 2012) (*LSTM-LM*) and a Seq2seq with Attention (*Seq2seq*) model as our baselines and compare them with the first (*ED(1)*) and second revised draft (*ED(2)*) produced by the Writing-editing Network.

Table 2 presents METEOR (Denkowski and Lavie, 2014) and ROUGE-L (Lin, 2004) scores for each method, where we can see score gains on

---

[4]The indices are changed since the generated sequence lengths from the writing and editing networks may differ.

[5]https://github.com/EagleW/ACL_titles_abstracts_dataset

[6]http://clair.eecs.umich.edu/aan/index.php

	# Tests	# Choices per Test	Non-expert		NLP Expert	
			Non-CS	CS	Junior	Senior
Different Titles	50	2	30%	15%	12%	0%
	20	5	60%	20%	30%	20%
	10	10	80%	30%	30%	20%
Same Title	50	2	54%	10%	4%	0%
	20	5	75%	25%	5%	5%

Table 4: Turing Test Passing Rates.

both metrics from the Editing Mechanism. Additionally, 10 NLP researchers manually assess the quality of each method. We randomly selected 50 titles and applied each model to generate an abstract. We then asked human judges to choose the best generated abstract for each title and computed the overall percentage of each model being preferred by human, which we record as *Human Preference*. The criteria the human judges adopt include topical relevance, logical coherence, and conciseness. Table 2 shows that the human judges strongly favor the abstracts from our ED(2) method.

We also conduct a plagiarism check in Table 3, which shows that 93.4% of 6-grams generated by ED(2) did not appear in the training data, indicating that our model is not simply copying. The 6-grams borrowed by both our model and human include *"word sense disambiguation (wsd)"*, *"support vector machines (svm)"*, *"show that our approach is feasible"*, and *"we present a machine learning approach"*. However, human writing is still more creative. The uni-grams and bi-grams that appear in human written test abstracts but not in the training set include *"android"*, *"ascii"*, *'p2p'*, *"embellish"*, *"supervision bottleneck"*, *"medical image"*, *"online behaviors"*, and *"1,000 languages"*.

3.3 Impact of Editing Mechanism

n	1	2	3	4	5	6
METEOR	13.3	**14.0**	13.6	13.9	13.8	13.5
ROUGE-L	**20.3**	19.8	18.6	19.2	18.9	18.8

Table 5: Iteration comparison (%)

We trained and evaluated our editing approach with 1-6 iterations and the experimental results (Table 5) showed that the second iteration produced the best results. The reason may be as follows. The attentive revision gate incorporates the knowledge from the paper title and the previous generated abstract. As the editing process iterates,

the knowledge pool will diverge since in each iteration the generated abstract may introduce some irrelevant information. Empirically the second iteration achieved a good trade-off between good quality of generated abstract and relevance with topics in the title.

3.4 Turing Test

We carried out two series of Turing tests, where the human judges were asked to distinguish the fake (system-generated) abstracts from the real (human-written) ones. (1)**Abstracts for different titles**. We asked the human judges to identify the fake abstract from a set of $N - 1$ real ones (i.e., N choose 1 question). A test is passed when a human judge mistakenly chooses a real abstract. (2) **Abstracts for the same title**. We asked the human judges to choose the real abstract from a set of $N - 1$ fake ones. A test is passed when a human judge mistakenly chooses a fake abstract.

As expected, Table 4 shows that people with less domain knowledge are more easily deceived. Specifically, non-CS human judges fail at more than half of the 1-to-1 sets for the same titles, which suggests that most of our system generated abstracts follow correct grammar and consistent writing style. Domain experts fail on 1 or 2 sets, mostly because the human written abstracts in those sets don't seem very topically relevant. Additionally, the more abstracts that we provided to human judges, the easier it is to conceal the system generated abstract amongst human generated ones.

A human is still more intelligent than the machine on this task from many reasons: (1) Machines lack knowledge of the deep connections among scientific knowledge elements and thus produce some fluent but scientifically incorrect concepts like *"...a translation system to generate a parallel corpus..."* and *"...automatic generation of English verbs..."*. (2) Humans know better about what terms are more important than others in a title. For example, if a language name appears in the title, it must appear in the abstract. We have an automatic term labeling approach, but, unfortunately, its performance (75% F-score) is not good enough to help the abstract generation. (3) Human written abstracts are generally more specific, concise, and engaging, often containing specific lab names, author names (e.g., *"Collins proposed..."*), system abbreviations, and terminologies (e.g., *"Italian complex nominals (cns) of the type n+p+n"*). In contrast, our system occasionally generates too general descriptions like *"Topic modeling is a research topic in Natural Language Processing."* (4) Machines lack common sense knowledge, so a system generated abstract may mention three areas/steps, but only outline two of them. (5) Machines lack logical coherence. A system generated abstract may contain *"The two languages..."* and not state which languages. (6) We are not asking the system to perform scientific experiments, and thus the system generated "experimental results" are often invalid, such as *"Our system ranked first out of the participating teams in the field of providing such a distribution."*.

4   Related work

Deep neural networks are widely applied to text generation tasks such as poetry creation (Greene et al., 2010; Ghazvininejad et al., 2016; Zhang et al., 2017), recipe generation (Kiddon et al., 2016), abstractive summarization (Gu et al., 2016; Wang and Ling, 2016; See et al., 2017), and biography generation (Lebret et al., 2016; Liu et al., 2018). We introduce a new task of generating paper abstracts from the given titles. We design a Writing-editing Network which shares ideas with Curriculum Learning (Bengio et al., 2009), where training on a data point from coarse to fine-grained can lead to better convergence (Krueger and Dayan, 2009). Our model is different from previous theme-rewriting (Polozov et al., 2015; Koncel-Kedziorski et al., 2016) approach which has been applied to math word problems but more similar to the Feedback Network (Zamir et al., 2017) by using previous generated outputs as feedback to guide subsequent generation. Moreover, our Writing-editing Network treats previous drafts as independent observations and does not propagate errors to previous draft generation stages. This property is vital for training feedback architectures for discrete data. Another similar approach is the deliberation network used for Ma-

chine Translation (Xia et al., 2017). Instead of directly concatenating the output of the encoder and writing network, we use the learnable Attentive Revision Gate to control their integration.

5   Conclusions and Future Work

We propose a new paper abstract generation task, present a novel Writing-editing Network architecture based on an Editing Mechanism, and demonstrate its effectiveness through both automatic and human evaluations. In the future we plan to extend the scope to generate a full paper by taking additional knowledge bases as input.

References

Dzmitry Bahdanau, Kyunghyun Cho, and Yoshua Bengio. 2015. Neural machine translation by jointly learning to align and translate. In *International Conference on Learning Representations*.

Yoshua Bengio, Jérôme Louradour, Ronan Collobert, and Jason Weston. 2009. Curriculum learning. In *Proceedings of the 26th Annual International Conference on Machine Learning*.

Kyunghyun Cho, Bart Van Merriënboer, Caglar Gulcehre, Dzmitry Bahdanau, Fethi Bougares, Holger Schwenk, and Yoshua Bengio. 2014. Learning phrase representations using rnn encoder-decoder for statistical machine translation. In *Proceedings of the 2014 Conference on Empirical Methods in Natural Language Processing*.

Michael Denkowski and Alon Lavie. 2014. Meteor universal: Language specific translation evaluation for any target language. In *Proceedings of the Ninth Workshop on Statistical Machine Translation*.

Marjan Ghazvininejad, Xing Shi, Yejin Choi, and Kevin Knight. 2016. Generating topical poetry. In *Proceedings of the 2016 Conference on Empirical Methods in Natural Language Processing*.

Erica Greene, Tugba Bodrumlu, and Kevin Knight. 2010. Automatic analysis of rhythmic poetry with applications to generation and translation. In *Proceedings of the 2010 Conference on Empirical Methods in Natural Language Processing*.

Jiatao Gu, Zhengdong Lu, Hang Li, and Victor O.K. Li. 2016. Incorporating copying mechanism in sequence-to-sequence learning. In *Proceedings of the 54th Annual Meeting of the Association for Computational Linguistics*.

Stanley Yong Wai Keong and Jian Su. 2008. An effective method of using web based information for relation extraction. In *Proceedings of the Third International Joint Conference on Natural Language Processing*.

Chloé Kiddon, Luke Zettlemoyer, and Yejin Choi. 2016. Globally coherent text generation with neural checklist models. In *Proceedings of the 2016 Conference on Empirical Methods in Natural Language Processing*.

Rik Koncel-Kedziorski, Ioannis Konstas, Luke Zettlemoyer, and Hannaneh Hajishirzi. 2016. A theme-rewriting approach for generating algebra word problems. In *Proceedings of the 2016 Conference on Empirical Methods in Natural Language Processing*.

Kai A Krueger and Peter Dayan. 2009. Flexible shaping: How learning in small steps helps. *Cognition*, 110(3):380–394.

Rémi Lebret, David Grangier, and Michael Auli. 2016. Neural text generation from structured data with application to the biography domain. In *Proceedings of the 2016 Conference on Empirical Methods in Natural Language Processing*.

Chin-Yew Lin. 2004. Rouge: A package for automatic evaluation of summaries. In *Proceedings of Text Summarization Branches Out*.

Tianyu Liu, Kexiang Wang, Lei Sha, Baobao Chang, and Zhifang Sui. 2018. Table-to-text generation by structure-aware seq2seq learning. In *Proceedings of the 32nd AAAI Conference on Artificial Intelligence*.

Minh-Thang Luong, Hieu Pham, and Christopher D Manning. 2015. Effective approaches to attention-based neural machine translation. In *Proceedings of the 2015 Conference on Empirical Methods in Natural Language Processing*.

Oleksandr Polozov, Eleanor O'Rourke, Adam M. Smith, Luke Zettlemoyer, Sumit Gulwani, and Zoran Popovic. 2015. Personalized mathematical word problem generation. In *Proceedings of the 25th International Joint Conference on Artificial Intelligence*.

Abigail See, Peter J. Liu, and Christopher D. Manning. 2017. Get to the point: Summarization with pointer-generator networks. In *Proceedings of the 55th Annual Meeting of the Association for Computational Linguistics*.

Martin Sundermeyer, Ralf Schlüter, and Hermann Ney. 2012. Lstm neural networks for language modeling. In *Proceedings of Thirteenth Annual Conference of the International Speech Communication Association*.

Ilya Sutskever, Oriol Vinyals, and Quoc V Le. 2014. Sequence to sequence learning with neural networks. In *Advances in Neural Information Processing systems*.

Lu Wang and Wang Ling. 2016. Neural network-based abstract generation for opinions and arguments. In *Proceedings of the 2016 Conference of the North American Chapter of the Association for Computational Linguistics: Human Language Technologies*.

Yingce Xia, Fei Tian, Lijun Wu, Jianxin Lin, Tao Qin, Nenghai Yu, and Tie-Yan Liu. 2017. Deliberation networks: Sequence generation beyond one-pass decoding. In *Advances in Neural Information Processing Systems 30*.

Amir R. Zamir, Te-Lin Wu, Lin Sun, William B. Shen, Bertram E. Shi, Jitendra Malik, and Silvio Savarese. 2017. Feedback networks. In *Proceedings of the IEEE Conference on Computer Vision and Pattern Recognition*.

Jiyuan Zhang, Yang Feng, Dong Wang, Yang Wang, Andrew Abel, Shiyue Zhang, and Andi Zhang. 2017. Flexible and creative chinese poetry generation using neural memory. In *Proceedings of the 55th Annual Meeting of the Association for Computational Linguistics*.

Conditional Generators of Words Definitions

Artyom Gadetsky
National Research University
Higher School of Economics
artygadetsky@yandex.ru

Ilya Yakubovskiy
Joom
yakubovskiy@joom.com

Dmitry Vetrov
National Research University
Higher School of Economics
Samsung-HSE Laboratory
vetrovd@yandex.ru

Abstract

We explore recently introduced definition modeling technique that provided the
tool for evaluation of different distributed
vector representations of words through
modeling dictionary definitions of words.
In this work, we study the problem of
word ambiguities in definition modeling
and propose a possible solution by employing latent variable modeling and soft
attention mechanisms. Our quantitative
and qualitative evaluation and analysis of
the model shows that taking into account
words ambiguity and polysemy leads to
performance improvement.

1 Introduction

Continuous representations of words are used in
many natural language processing (NLP) applications. Using pre-trained high-quality word embeddings are most effective if not millions of
training examples are available, which is true for
most tasks in NLP (Kumar et al., 2016; Karpathy and Fei-Fei, 2015). Recently, several unsupervised methods were introduced to learn word
vectors from large corpora of texts (Mikolov et al.,
2013; Pennington et al., 2014; Joulin et al., 2016).
Learned vector representations have been shown
to have useful and interesting properties. For example, Mikolov et al. (2013) showed that vector operations such as subtraction or addition reflect semantic relations between words. Despite
all these properties it is hard to precisely evaluate embeddings because analogy relation or word
similarity tasks measure learned information indirectly.

Quite recently Noraset et al. (2017) introduced
a more direct way for word embeddings evaluation. Authors suggested considering definition

modeling as the evaluation task. In definition
modeling vector representations of words are used
for conditional generation of corresponding word
definitions. The primary motivation is that high-
quality word embedding should contain all useful
information to reconstruct the definition. The important drawback of Noraset et al. (2017) definition models is that they cannot take into account
words with several different meanings. These
problems are related to word disambiguation task,
which is a common problem in natural language
processing. Such examples of polysemantic words
as "bank" or "spring" whose meanings can only
be disambiguated using their contexts. In such
cases, proposed models tend to generate definitions based on the most frequent meaning of the
corresponding word. Therefore, building models
that incorporate word sense disambiguation is an
important research direction in natural language
processing.

In this work, we study the problem of word
ambiguity in definition modeling task. We propose several models which can be possible solutions to it. One of them is based on recently
proposed Adaptive Skip Gram model (Bartunov
et al., 2016), the generalized version of the original SkipGram Word2Vec, which can differ word
meanings using word context. The second one
is the attention-based model that uses the context
of a word being defined to determine components
of embedding referring to relevant word meaning.
Our contributions are as follows: (1) we introduce two models based on recurrent neural network (RNN) language models, (2) we collect new
dataset of definitions, which is larger in number
of unique words than proposed in Noraset et al.
(2017) and also supplement it with examples of the
word usage (3) finally, in the experiment section
we show that our models outperform previously
proposed models and have the ability to generate

Proceedings of the 56th Annual Meeting of the Association for Computational Linguistics (Short Papers), pages 266–271
Melbourne, Australia, July 15 - 20, 2018. ©2018 Association for Computational Linguistics

definitions depending on the meaning of words.

2 Related Work

2.1 Constructing Embeddings Using Dictionary Definitions

Several works utilize word definitions to learn embeddings. For example, Hill et al. (2016) use definitions to construct sentence embeddings. Authors propose to train recurrent neural network producing an embedding of the dictionary definition that is close to an embedding of the corresponding word. The model is evaluated with the reverse dictionary task. Bahdanau et al. (2017) suggest using definitions to compute embeddings for out-of-vocabulary words. In comparison to Hill et al. (2016) work, dictionary reader network is trained end-to-end for a specific task.

2.2 Definition Modeling

Definition modeling was introduced in Noraset et al. (2017) work. The goal of the definition model $p(D|w^*)$ is to predict the probability of words in the definition $D = \{w_1, \ldots, w_T\}$ given the word being defined w^*. The joint probability is decomposed into separate conditional probabilities, each of which is modeled using the recurrent neural network with soft-max activation, applied to its logits.

$$p(D|w^*) = \prod_{t=1}^{T} p(w_t|w_{i<t}, w^*) \qquad (1)$$

Authors of definition modeling consider following conditional models and their combinations: *Seed (S)* - providing word being defined at the first step of the RNN, *Input (I)* - concatenation of embedding for word being defined with embedding of word on corresponding time step of the RNN, *Gated (G)*, which is the modification of GRU cell. Authors use a character-level convolutional neural network (CNN) to provide character-level information about the word being defined, this feature vector is denoted as *(CH)*. One more type of conditioning referred to as *(HE)*, is hypernym relations between words, extracted using Hearst-like patterns.

3 Word Embeddings

Many natural language processing applications treat words as atomic units and represent them as continuous vectors for further use in machine learning models. Therefore, learning high-quality vector representations is the important task.

3.1 Skip-gram

One of the most popular and frequently used vector representations is Skip-gram model. The original Skip-gram model consists of grouped word prediction tasks. Each task is formulated as a prediction of the word v given word w using their input and output representations:

$$p(v|w, \theta) = \frac{exp(in_w^T out_v)}{\sum_{v'=1}^{V} \exp(in_w^T out_{v'})} \qquad (2)$$

where θ and V stand for the set of input and output word representations, and dictionary size respectively. These individual prediction tasks are grouped in a way to independently predict all adjacent (with some sliding window) words $y = \{y_1, \ldots y_C\}$ given the central word x:

$$p(y|x, \theta) = \prod_{j} p(y_j|x, \theta) \qquad (3)$$

The joint probability of the model is written as follows:

$$p(Y|X, \theta) = \prod_{i=1}^{N} p(y_i|x_i, \theta) \qquad (4)$$

where $(X, Y) = \{x_i, y_i\}_{i=1}^{N}$ are training pairs of words and corresponding contexts and θ stands for trainable parameters.

Also, optimization of the original Skip-gram objective can be changed to a negative sampling procedure as described in the original paper or hierarchical soft-max prediction model (Mnih and Hinton, 2009) can be used instead of (2) to deal with computational costs of the denominator. After training, the input representations are treated as word vectors.

3.2 Adaptive Skip-gram

Skip-gram model maintains only one vector representation per word that leads to mixing of meanings for polysemantic words. Bartunov et al. (2016) propose a solution to the described problem using latent variable modeling. They extend Skip-gram to Adaptive Skip-gram (AdaGram) in a way to automatically learn the required number of vector representations for each word using Bayesian nonparametric approach. In comparison with Skip-gram AdaGram assumes several meanings for each word and therefore keeps several vectors representations for each word. They introduce latent variable z that encodes the index of meaning and extend (2) to $p(v|z, w, \theta)$. They use hierarchical soft-max approach rather than negative sampling to overcome computing denominator.

$$p(v|z = k, w, \theta) = \prod_{n \in path(v)} \sigma(ch(n) in_{wk}^T out_n)$$

(5)

Here in_{wk} stands for input representation of word w with meaning index k and output representations are associated with nodes in a binary tree, where leaves are all possible words in model vocabulary with unique paths from the root to the corresponding leaf. $ch(n)$ is a function which returns 1 or -1 to each node in the $path(\cdot)$ depending on whether n is a left or a right child of the previous node in the path. Huffman tree is often used for computational efficiency.

To automatically determine the number of meanings for each word authors use the constructive definition of Dirichlet process via stick-breaking representation ($p(z = k|w, \beta)$), which is commonly used prior distribution on discrete latent variables when the number of possible values is unknown (e.g. infinite mixtures).

$$p(z = k|w, \beta) = \beta_{wk} \prod_{r=1}^{k-1} (1 - \beta_{wr})$$

$$p(\beta_{wk}|\alpha) = Beta(\beta_{wk}|1, \alpha)$$

(6)

This model assumes that an infinite number of meanings for each word may exist. Providing that we have a finite amount of data, it can be shown that only several meanings for each word will have non-zero prior probabilities.

Finally, the joint probability of all variables in AdaGram model has the following form:

$$p(Y, Z, \beta|X, \alpha, \theta) = \prod_{w=1}^{V} \prod_{k=1}^{\infty} p(\beta_{wk}|\alpha) \cdot$$

$$\cdot \prod_{i=1}^{N} [p(z_i|x_i, \beta) \prod_{j=1}^{C} p(y_{ij}|z_i, x_i, \theta)]$$

(7)

Model is trained by optimizing Evidence Lower Bound using stochastic variational inference (Hoffman et al., 2013) with fully factorized variational approximation of the posterior distribution $p(Z, \beta|X, Y, \alpha, \theta) \approx q(Z)q(\beta)$.

One important property of the model is an ability to disambiguate words using context. More formally, after training on data $D = \{x_i, y_i\}_{i=1}^{N}$ we may compute the posterior probability of word meaning given context and take the word vector with the highest probability.:

$$p(z = k|x, y, \theta) \propto$$

$$\propto p(y|x, z = k, \theta) \int p(z = k|\beta, x)q(\beta)d\beta$$

(8)

This knowledge about word meaning will be further utilized in one of our models as $disambiguation(x|y)$.

4 Models

In this section, we describe our extension to original definition model. The goal of the extended definition model is to predict the probability of a definition $D = \{w_1, \ldots, w_T\}$ given a word being defined w^* and its context $C = \{c_1, \ldots, c_m\}$ (e.g. example of use of this word). As it was motivated earlier, the context will provide proper information about word meaning. The joint probability is also decomposed in the conditional probabilities, each of which is provided with the information about context:

$$p(D|w^*, C) = \prod_{t=1}^{T} p(w_t|w_{i<t}, w^*, C)$$

(9)

4.1 AdaGram based

Our first model is based on original *Input (I)* conditioned on Adaptive Skip-gram vector representations. To determine which word embedding to provide as *Input (I)* we disambiguate word being defined using its context words C. More formally our *Input (I)* conditioning is turning in:

$$h_t = g([v^*; v_t], h_{t-1})$$

$$v^* = disambiguation(w^*|C)$$

(10)

where g is the recurrent cell, $[a; b]$ denotes vector concatenation, v^* and v_t are embedding of word being defined w and embedding of word w_t respectively. We refer to this model as *Input Adaptive (I-Adaptive)*.

4.2 Attention based

Adaptive Skip-gram model is very sensitive to the choice of concentration parameter in Dirichlet process. The improper setting will cause many similar vectors representations with smoothed meanings due to theoretical guarantees on a number of learned components. To overcome this problem and to get rid of careful tuning of this hyper-parameter we introduce following model:

$$h_t = g([a^*; v_t], h_{t-1})$$
$$a^* = v^* \odot mask$$
$$mask = \sigma(W \frac{\sum_{i=1}^m ANN(c_i)}{m} + b) \quad (11)$$

where $\odot$ is an element-wise product, σ is a logistic sigmoid function and ANN is attention neural network, which is a feed-forward neural network. We motivate these updates by the fact, that after learning Skip-gram model on a large corpus, vector representation for each word will absorb information about every meaning of the word. Using soft binary mask dependent on word context we extract components of word embedding relevant to corresponding meaning. We refer to this model as *Input Attention (I-Attention)*.

4.3 Attention SkipGram

For attention-based model, we use different embeddings for context words. Because of that, we pre-train attention block containing embeddings, attention neural network and linear layer weights by optimizing a negative sampling loss function in the same manner as the original Skip-gram model:

$$\log \sigma(v_{w_O}'^T v_{w_I})$$
$$+ \sum_{i=1}^k \mathbb{E}_{w_i \sim P_n(w)}[\log \sigma(-v_{w_i}'^T v_{w_I})] \quad (12)$$

where v_{w_O}', v_{w_I} and v_{w_i}' are vector representation of "positive" example, anchor word and negative example respectively. Vector v_{w_I} is computed using embedding of w_I and attention mechanism proposed in previous section.

5 Experiments

5.1 Data

We collected new dataset of definitions using OxfordDictionaries.com (2018) API. Each entry is a triplet, containing the word, its definition and example of the use of this word in the given meaning. It is important to note that in our data set words can have one or more meanings, depending on the corresponding entry in the Oxford Dictionary. Table 1 shows basic statistics of the new dataset.

Split	train	val	test
#Words	33,128	8,867	8,850
#Entries	97,855	12,232	12,232
#Tokens	1,078,828	134,486	133,987
Avg length	11.03	10.99	10.95

Table 1: Statistics of new dataset

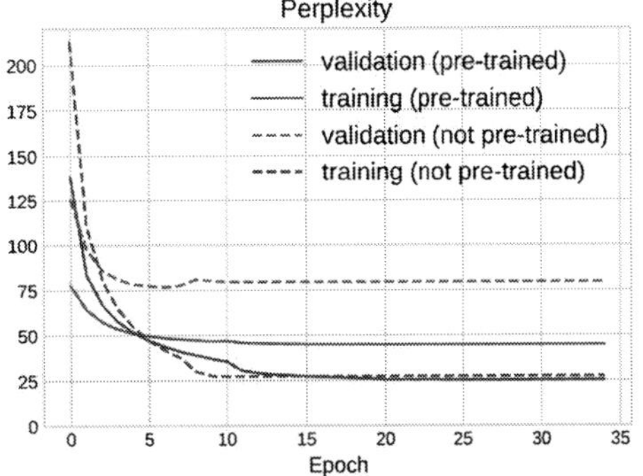

Figure 1: Perplexities of *S+I Attention* model for the case of pre-training (solid lines) and for the case when the model is trained from scratch (dashed lines).

5.2 Pre-training

It is well-known that good language model can often improve metrics such as BLEU for a particular NLP task (Jozefowicz et al., 2016). According to this, we decided to pre-train our models. For this purpose, WikiText-103 dataset (Merity et al., 2016) was chosen. During pre-training we set v^* (eq. 10) to zero vector to make our models purely unconditional. Embeddings for these language models were initialized by Google Word2Vec vectors[1] and were fine-tuned. Figure 1 shows that this procedure helps to decrease perplexity and prevents over-fitting. Attention Skip-gram vectors were also trained on the WikiText-103.

5.3 Results

Both our models are LSTM networks (Hochreiter and Schmidhuber, 1997) with an embedding layer. The attention-based model has own embedding layer, mapping context words to vector representations. Firstly, we pre-train our models using the procedure, described above. Then, we train them on the collected dataset maximizing log-likelihood objective using Adam (Kingma and Ba, 2014). Also, we anneal learning rate by

---

[1] https://code.google.com/archive/p/word2vec/

Word	Context	Definition
star	she got star treatment	a person who is very important
star	bright star in the sky	a small circle of a celestial object or planet that is seen in a circle
sentence	sentence in prison	an act of restraining someone or something
sentence	write up the sentence	a piece of text written to be printed
head	the head of a man	the upper part of a human body
head	he will be the head of the office	the chief part of an organization, institution, etc
reprint	they never reprinted the famous treatise	a written or printed version of a book or other publication
rape	the woman was raped on her way home at night	the act of killing
invisible	he pushed the string through an inconspicuous hole	not able to be seen
shake	my faith has been shaken	cause to be unable to think clearly
nickname	the nickname for the u.s. constitution is 'old ironsides '	a name for a person or thing that is not genuine

Table 2: Examples of definitions generated by *S + I-Attention* model for the words and contexts from the test set.

Model	PPL	BLEU
S+G+CH+HE (1)	45.62	11.62 ± 0.05
S+G+CH+HE (2)	46.12	-
S+G+CH+HE (3)	46.80	-
S + I-Adaptive (2)	46.08	11.53 ± 0.03
S + I-Adaptive (3)	46.93	-
S + I-Attention (2)	**43.54**	**12.08 ± 0.02**
S + I-Attention (3)	44.9	-

Table 3: Performance comparison between best model proposed by Noraset et al. (2017) and our models on the test set. Number in brackets means number of LSTM layers. BLEU is averaged across 3 trials.

a factor of 10 if validation loss doesn't decrease per epochs. We use original Adaptive Skip-gram vectors as inputs to *S+I-Adaptive*, which were obtained from the official repository[2]. We compare different models using perplexity and BLEU score on the test set. BLEU score is computed only for models with the lowest perplexity and only on the test words that have multiple meanings. The results are presented in Table 3. We see that both models that utilize knowledge about meaning of the word have better performance than the competing one. We generated definitions using *S + I-Attention* model with simple temperature sampling

algorithm ($\tau = 0.1$). Table 2 shows the examples. The source code and dataset will be freely available [3].

6 Conclusion

In the paper, we proposed two definition models which can work with polysemantic words. We evaluate them using perplexity and measure the definition generation accuracy with BLEU score. Obtained results show that incorporating information about word senses leads to improved metrics. Moreover, generated definitions show that even implicit word context can help to differ word meanings. In future work, we plan to explore individual components of word embedding and the mask produced by our attention-based model to get a deeper understanding of vectors representations of words.

Acknowledgments

This work was partly supported by Samsung Research, Samsung Electronics, Sberbank AI Lab and the Russian Science Foundation grant 17-71-20072.

---

[2]https://github.com/sbos/AdaGram.jl

[3]https://github.com/agadetsky/pytorch-definitions

References

Dzmitry Bahdanau, Tom Bosc, Stanislaw Jastrzebski, Edward Grefenstette, Pascal Vincent, and Yoshua Bengio. 2017. Learning to compute word embeddings on the fly. *arXiv preprint arXiv:1706.00286*.

Sergey Bartunov, Dmitry Kondrashkin, Anton Osokin, and Dmitry Vetrov. 2016. Breaking sticks and ambiguities with adaptive skip-gram. In *Artificial Intelligence and Statistics*, pages 130–138.

Felix Hill, KyungHyun Cho, Anna Korhonen, and Yoshua Bengio. 2016. Learning to understand phrases by embedding the dictionary. *Transactions of the Association for Computational Linguistics*, 4:17–30.

Sepp Hochreiter and Jürgen Schmidhuber. 1997. Long short-term memory. *Neural Comput.*, 9(8):1735–1780.

Matthew D. Hoffman, David M. Blei, Chong Wang, and John Paisley. 2013. Stochastic variational inference. *Journal of Machine Learning Research*, 14:1303–1347.

Armand Joulin, Edouard Grave, Piotr Bojanowski, Matthijs Douze, Hérve Jégou, and Tomas Mikolov. 2016. Fasttext.zip: Compressing text classification models. *arXiv preprint arXiv:1612.03651*.

Rafal Jozefowicz, Oriol Vinyals, Mike Schuster, Noam Shazeer, and Yonghui Wu. 2016. Exploring the limits of language modeling. *arXiv preprint arXiv:1602.02410*.

Andrej Karpathy and Li Fei-Fei. 2015. Deep visual-semantic alignments for generating image descriptions. In *Proceedings of the IEEE conference on computer vision and pattern recognition*, pages 3128–3137.

Diederik P. Kingma and Jimmy Ba. 2014. Adam: A method for stochastic optimization. *CoRR*, abs/1412.6980.

Ankit Kumar, Ozan Irsoy, Peter Ondruska, Mohit Iyyer, James Bradbury, Ishaan Gulrajani, Victor Zhong, Romain Paulus, and Richard Socher. 2016. Ask me anything: Dynamic memory networks for natural language processing. In *Proceedings of The 33rd International Conference on Machine Learning*, volume 48 of *Proceedings of Machine Learning Research*, pages 1378–1387. PMLR.

Stephen Merity, Caiming Xiong, James Bradbury, and Richard Socher. 2016. Pointer sentinel mixture models. *arXiv preprint arXiv:1609.07843*.

Tomas Mikolov, Ilya Sutskever, Kai Chen, Greg S Corrado, and Jeff Dean. 2013. Distributed representations of words and phrases and their compositionality. In C. J. C. Burges, L. Bottou, M. Welling, Z. Ghahramani, and K. Q. Weinberger, editors, *Advances in Neural Information Processing Systems 26*, pages 3111–3119. Curran Associates, Inc.

Andriy Mnih and Geoffrey E Hinton. 2009. A scalable hierarchical distributed language model. In *Advances in Neural Information Processing Systems 21*, pages 1081–1088. Curran Associates, Inc.

Thanapon Noraset, Chen Liang, Larry Birnbaum, and Doug Downey. 2017. Definition modeling: Learning to define word embeddings in natural language. In *31st AAAI Conference on Artificial Intelligence, AAAI 2017*, pages 3259–3266. AAAI press.

OxfordDictionaries.com. 2018. Oxford University Press.

Jeffrey Pennington, Richard Socher, and Christopher Manning. 2014. Glove: Global vectors for word representation. In *Proceedings of the 2014 conference on empirical methods in natural language processing (EMNLP)*, pages 1532–1543.

CNN for Text-Based Multiple Choice Question Answering

Akshay Chaturvedi[†] **Onkar Pandit**[‡] **Utpal Garain**[†]

[†]Computer Vision & Pattern Recognition Unit, Indian Statistical Institute,
203, B. T. Road, Kolkata-700108, India
[‡]INRIA,40 Avenue Halley, Villeneuve-d'Ascq 59650, Lille, France
{akshay91.isi,oapandit}@gmail.com, utpal@isical.ac.in

Abstract

The task of Question Answering is at the very core of machine comprehension. In this paper, we propose a Convolutional Neural Network (CNN) model for text-based multiple choice question answering where questions are based on a particular article. Given an article and a multiple choice question, our model assigns a score to each question-option tuple and chooses the final option accordingly. We test our model on Textbook Question Answering (TQA) and SciQ dataset. Our model outperforms several LSTM-based baseline models on the two datasets.

1 Introduction

Answering questions based on a particular text requires a diverse skill set. It requires look-up ability, ability to deduce, ability to perform simple mathematical operations (e.g. to answer questions like how many times did the following word occur?), ability to merge information contained in multiple sentences. This diverse skill set makes question answering a challenging task.

Question Answering (QA) has seen a great surge of more challenging datasets and novel architectures in recent times. Question Answering task may require the system to reason over few sentences (Weston et al., 2015), table (Pasupat and Liang, 2015), Wikipedia passage (Rajpurkar et al., 2016; Yang et al., 2015), lesson (Kembhavi et al., 2017). Increase in the size of the datasets has allowed researchers to explore different neural network architectures (Chen et al., 2016; Cui et al., 2016; Xiong et al., 2016; Trischler et al., 2016) for this task. Given a question based on a text, the model needs to attend to a specific portion of the text in order to answer the question. Hence,

the use of attention mechanism (Bahdanau et al., 2014) is common in these architectures.

Convolutional Neural Networks (CNN) have been shown to be effective for various natural language processing tasks such as sentiment analysis, question classification etc. (Kim, 2014). However for the task of question answering, Long Short Term Memory (LSTM) (Hochreiter and Schmidhuber, 1997) based methods are the most common. In this paper we build a CNN based model for multiple choice question answering[1]. We show the effectiveness of the proposed model by comparing it with several LSTM-based baselines.

The main contributions of this paper are (i) The proposed CNN model performs comparatively or better than LSTM-based baselines on two different datasets. (Kembhavi et al., 2017; Welbl et al., 2017) (ii) Our model takes question-option tuple to generate a score for the concerned option. We argue that this is a better strategy than considering questions and options separately for multiple choice question answering. For example, consider the question "The color of the ball is" with three options: red, green and yellow. If the model generates a vector which is to be compared with the three option embeddings, then this might lead to error since the three option embeddings are close to each other. (iii) We have devised a simple but effective strategy to deal with questions having options like none of the above, two of the above, all of the above, both (a) and (b) etc. which was not done before. (iv) Instead of attending on words present in the text, our model attends at sentence level. This helps the model for answering look-up questions since the necessary information required to answer such questions will often be contained in a single sentence.

---

[1]The code is available at https://github.com/akshay107/CNN-QA

Proceedings of the 56th Annual Meeting of the Association for Computational Linguistics (Short Papers), pages 272–277
Melbourne, Australia, July 15 - 20, 2018. ©2018 Association for Computational Linguistics

2 Method

Given a question based on an article, usually a small portion of article is needed to answer the concerned question. Hence it is not fruitful to give the entire article as input to the neural network. To select the most relevant paragraph in the article, we take both the question and the options into consideration instead of taking just the question into account for the same. The rationale behind this approach is to get the most relevant paragraphs in cases where the question is very general in nature. For example, consider that the article is about the topic *carbon* and the question is "Which of the following statements is true about carbon?". In such a scenario, it is not possible to choose the most relevant paragraph by just looking at the question. We select the most relevant paragraph by word2vec based query expansion (Kuzi et al., 2016) followed by tf-idf score (Foundation, 2011).

2.1 Neural Network Architecture

We use word embeddings (Mikolov et al., 2013) to encode the words present in question, option and the most relevant paragraph. As a result, each word is assigned a fixed d-dimensional representation. The proposed model architecture is shown in Figure 1. Let q, o_i denote the word embeddings of words present in the question and the ith option respectively. Thus, $q \in \mathbb{R}^{d \times l_q}$ and $o_i \in \mathbb{R}^{d \times l_o}$ where l_q and l_o represent the number of words in the question and option respectively. The question-option tuple (q, o_i) is embedded using Convolutional Neural Network (CNN) with a convolution layer followed average pooling. The convolution layer has three types of filters of sizes $f_j \times d \ \forall j = 1, 2, 3$ with size of output channel of k. Each filter type j produces a feature map of shape $(l_q + l_o - f_j + 1) \times k$ which is average pooled to generate a k-dimensional vector. The three k-dimensional vectors are concatenated to form $3k$-dimensional vector. Note that Kim (2014) used max pooling but we use average pooling to ensure different embedding for different question-option tuples. Hence,

$$h_i = CNN([q; o_i]) \quad \forall i = 1, 2, .., n_q \quad (1)$$

where n_q is the number of options, h_i is the output of CNN and $[q; o_i]$ denotes the concatenation of q and o_i i.e. $[q; o_i] \in \mathbb{R}^{d \times (l_q + l_o)}$. The sentences in the most relevant paragraph are embedded using the same CNN. Let s_j denote the word embeddings of words present in the jth sentence i.e. $s_j \in \mathbb{R}^{d \times l_s}$ where l_s is the number of words in the sentence. Then,

$$d_j = CNN(s_j) \quad \forall j = 1, 2, .., n_{sents} \quad (2)$$

where n_{sents} is the number of sentences in the most relevant paragraph and d_j is the output of CNN. The rationale behind using the same CNN for embedding question-option tuple and sentences in the most relevant paragraph is to ensure similar embeddings for similar question-option tuple and sentences. Next, we use h_i to attend on the sentence embeddings. Formally,

$$a_{ij} = \frac{h_i \cdot d_j}{||h_i|| \cdot ||d_j||} \quad (3)$$

$$r_{ij} = \frac{exp(a_{ij})}{\sum\limits_{j=1}^{n_{sents}} exp(a_{ij})} \quad (4)$$

$$m_i = \sum\limits_{j=1}^{n_{sents}} r_{ij} d_j \quad (5)$$

where $||.||$ signifies the l^2 norm, $exp(x) = e^x$ and $h_i \cdot d_j$ is the dot product between the two vectors. Since a_{ij} is the cosine similarity between h_i and d_j, the attention weights r_{ij} give more weighting to those sentences which are more relevant to the question. The attended vector m_i can be thought of as the *evidence* in favor of the ith option. Hence, to give a score to the ith option, we take the cosine similarity between h_i and m_i i.e.

$$score_i = \frac{h_i \cdot m_i}{||h_i|| \cdot ||m_i||} \quad (6)$$

Finally, the scores are normalized using softmax to get the final probability distribution.

$$p_i = \frac{exp(score_i)}{\sum\limits_{i=1}^{n_q} exp(score_i)} \quad (7)$$

where p_i denotes the probability for the ith option.

2.2 Dealing with forbidden options

We refer to options like none of the above, two of the above, all of the above, both (a) and (b) as *forbidden options*. During training, the questions

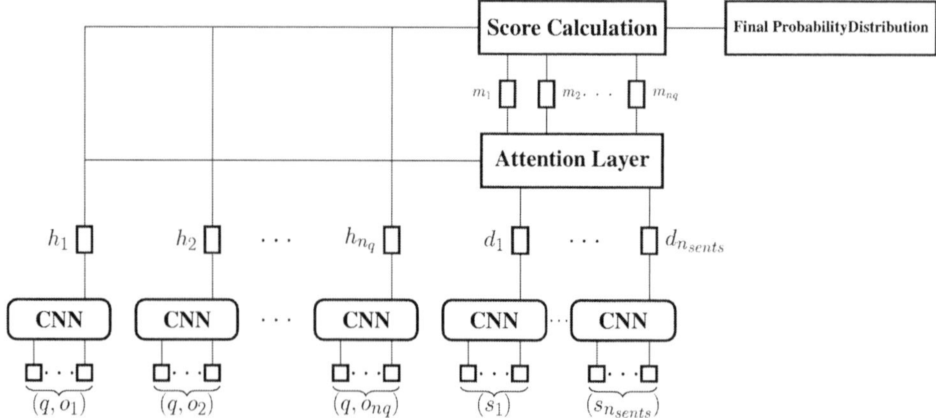

Figure 1: Architecture of our proposed model. Attention layer attends on sentence embeddings d_j's using question-option tuple embeddings h_i's. Score Calculation layer calculates the cosine similarity between m_i and h_i which is passed through softmax to get the final probability distribution.

having a forbidden option as the correct option were not considered. Furthermore, if a question had a forbidden option, that particular question-option tuple was not taken into consideration. Let $S = [score_i \; \forall i \mid i^{th}$ option not in forbidden options] and $|S| = k$. During prediction, the questions having one of the forbidden options as an option are dealt with as follows:

1. **Questions with none of the above/ all of the above option**: If the $max(S) - min(S) < threshold$ then the final option is the concerned forbidden option. Else, the final option is $argmax(p_i)$.

2. **Questions with two of the above option**: If the $S_{(k)} - S_{(k-1)} < threshold$ where $S_{(n)}$ denotes the nth order statistic, then the final option is the concerned forbidden option. Else, the final option is $argmax(p_i)$.

3. **Questions with both (a) and (b) type option**: For these type of questions, let the corresponding scores for the two options be $score_{i_1}$ and $score_{i_2}$. If the $|score_{i_1} - score_{i_2}| < threshold$ then the final option is the concerned forbidden option. Else, the final option is $argmax(p_i)$.

4. **Questions with any of the above option**: Very few questions had this option. In this case, we always choose the concerned forbidden option.

We tried different $threshold$ values ranging from 0.0 to 1.0. Finally, the $threshold$ was set to a value gave the highest accuracy on the training set for these kind of questions.

2.3 Training Details

We tried two different CNN models, one having f_j's equal to 3,4,5 and other having f_j's equal to 2,3,4. We refer to two models as $CNN_{3,4,5}$ and $CNN_{2,3,4}$ respectively. The values of hyperparameters used are: $d = 300, k = 100$. The other hyperparamters vary from dataset to dataset. Since the number of options vary from question to question, our model generates the probability distribution over the set of available options. Similarly, the number of sentences in the most relevant paragraph can vary from question to question, so we set $a_{ij} = -\infty$ whenever d_j was a zero vector. Cross entropy loss function was minimized during training.

3 Results and Discussion

The accuracy of our proposed model on validation set of TQA and SciQ dataset (Kembhavi et al., 2017; Welbl et al., 2017) is given in Table 1 and Table 2. GRU_{bl} refers to the model where CNN is replaced by Gated Recurrent Unit (GRU) (Cho et al., 2014) to embed question-option tuples and the sentences. The size of GRU cell was 100.

For SciQ dataset, we used the associated passage provided with the question. AS Reader (Kadlec et al., 2016) which models the question and the paragraph using GRU followed by attention mechanism got 74.1% accuracy on the SciQ test set. However, for a question, they used a different corpus to extract the text passage. Hence it is not judicious to compare the two models. As

Model	True-False (Correct/Total)	Multiple Choice (Correct/Total)
GRU_{bl}	536/994 (53.9%)	529/1530 (34.6%)
$CNN_{3,4,5}$	531/994 (52.4%)	531/1530 (34.7%)
$CNN_{2,3,4}$	537/994 (54.0%)	543/1530 (35.5%)

Table 1: Accuracy for true-false and multiple choice questions on validation set of TQA dataset.

can be seen from the Tables 1 and 2, $CNN_{2,3,4}$ gives the best performance on the validation set of both the datasets so we evaluate it on the test sets. Note that GRU_{bl} highly overfits on the SciQ dataset which shows that CNN-based models work better for those datasets where long-term dependency is not a major concern. This rationale is also supported by the fact that $CNN_{2,3,4}$ performed better than $CNN_{3,4,5}$ on the two datasets.

Model	Accuracy
GRU_{bl}	68.2%
$CNN_{3,4,5}$	87.1%
$CNN_{2,3,4}$	87.8%
$CNN_{2,3,4}$	84.7% (test-set)

Table 2: Accuracy of the models on SciQ dataset. The first three accuarcies are on validation set. The last accuracy is of $CNN_{2,3,4}$ model on the test set.

Baselines for TQA dataset: Three baselines models are mentioned in Kembhavi (2017) . These baseline models rely on word-level attention and encoding question and options separately. The baseline models are random model, Text-Only model and BIDAF Model (Seo et al., 2016). Text-Only model is a variant of Memory network (Weston et al., 2014) where the paragraph, question and options are embedded separately using LSTM followed by attention mechanism. In BIDAF Model, character and word level embedding is used to encode the question and the text followed by bidirectional attention mechanism. This model predicts the subtext within the text containing the answer. Hence, the predicted subtext is compared with each of the options to select the final option.

Note that the result of the baseline models given in Kembhavi (2017) were on test set but the authors had used a different data split than the publicly released split. As per the suggestion of the authors, we evaluate $CNN_{2,3,4}$ model by combin-

ing validation and test set. The comparison with the baseline models is given in Table 3.

Model	True-False	Multiple Choice
Random*	50.0	22.7
Text-Only*	50.2	32.9
BIDAF*	50.4	32.2
$CNN_{2,3,4}$	**53.7**	**35.8**

Table 3: Accuracy of different models for true-false and multiple choice questions. Results marked with (*) are taken from Kembhavi (2017) and are on test set obtained using a different data split. Result of our proposed model is on publicly released validation and test set combined.

As can be seen from Table 3, $CNN_{2,3,4}$ model shows significant improvement over the baseline models. We argue that our proposed model outperforms the Text-Only model because of three reasons (i) sentence level attention, (ii) question-option tuple as input, and (iii) ability to tackle forbidden options. Sentence level attention leads to better attention weights, especially in cases where a single sentence suffices to answer the question. If question is given as input to the model, then the model has to extract the embedding of the answer whereas giving question-option tuple as input simplifies the task to comparison between the two embeddings.

SciQ dataset didn't have any questions with forbidden options. However, in the validation set of TQA, 433 out of 1530 multiple choice questions had forbidden options. Using the proposed threshold strategy for tackling forbidden options, $CNN_{2,3,4}$ gets 188 out of 433 questions correct. Without using this strategy and giving every question-option tuple as input, $CNN_{2,3,4}$ gets 109 out of 433 questions correct.

4 Conclusions and Future Work

In this paper, we proposed a CNN based model for multiple choice question answering and showed its effectiveness in comparison with several LSTM-based baselines. We also proposed a strategy for dealing with forbidden options. Using question-option tuple as input gave significant advantage to our model. However, there is a lot of scope for future work. Our proposed model doesn't work well in cases where complex deductive reasoning is needed to answer the question. For example, suppose the question is "How much percent of parent isotope remains after two half-lives?" and the lesson is on carbon dating which contains the definition of *half-life*. Answering this question using the definition requires understanding the definition and transforming the question into a numerical problem. Our proposed model lacks such skills and will have near random performance for such questions.

References

Dzmitry Bahdanau, Kyunghyun Cho, and Yoshua Bengio. 2014. Neural machine translation by jointly learning to align and translate. *CoRR* abs/1409.0473. http://arxiv.org/abs/1409.0473.

Danqi Chen, Jason Bolton, and Christopher D. Manning. 2016. A thorough examination of the cnn/daily mail reading comprehension task. In *Association for Computational Linguistics (ACL)*. https://www.aclweb.org/anthology/P16-1223.

Kyunghyun Cho, Bart van Merriënboer, Çalar Gülçehre, Dzmitry Bahdanau, Fethi Bougares, Holger Schwenk, and Yoshua Bengio. 2014. Learning phrase representations using rnn encoder–decoder for statistical machine translation. In *Proceedings of the 2014 Conference on Empirical Methods in Natural Language Processing (EMNLP)*. Association for Computational Linguistics, Doha, Qatar, pages 1724–1734. http://www.aclweb.org/anthology/D14-1179.

Yiming Cui, Zhipeng Chen, Si Wei, Shijin Wang, Ting Liu, and Guoping Hu. 2016. Attention-over-attention neural networks for reading comprehension. *CoRR* abs/1607.04423. http://arxiv.org/abs/1607.04423.

Apache Software Foundation. 2011. Apache lucene - scoring. Letzter Zugriff: 20. Oktober 2011. https://lucene.apache.org/core/.

Sepp Hochreiter and Jürgen Schmidhuber. 1997. Long short-term memory. *Neural computation* 9(8):1735–1780. http://www.bioinf.jku.at/publications/older/2604.pdf.

Rudolf Kadlec, Martin Schmid, Ondrej Bajgar, and Jan Kleindienst. 2016. Text understanding with the attention sum reader network. In *Proceedings of the 54th Annual Meeting of the Association for Computational Linguistics, ACL 2016, August 7-12, 2016, Berlin, Germany, Volume 1: Long Papers*. http://aclweb.org/anthology/P/P16/P16-1086.pdf.

Aniruddha Kembhavi, Minjoon Seo, Dustin Schwenk, Jonghyun Choi, Ali Farhadi, and Hannaneh Hajishirzi. 2017. Are you smarter than a sixth grader? textbook question answering for multimodal machine comprehension. In *Conference on Computer Vision and Pattern Recognition (CVPR)*.

Yoon Kim. 2014. Convolutional neural networks for sentence classification. In *Proceedings of the 2014 Conference on Empirical Methods in Natural Language Processing, EMNLP 2014, October 25-29, 2014, Doha, Qatar, A meeting of SIGDAT, a Special Interest Group of the ACL*. pages 1746–1751. http://aclweb.org/anthology/D/D14/D14-1181.pdf.

Saar Kuzi, Anna Shtok, and Oren Kurland. 2016. Query expansion using word embeddings. In *Proceedings of the 25th ACM International on Conference on Information and Knowledge Management*. ACM, New York, NY, USA, CIKM '16, pages 1929–1932. https://doi.org/10.1145/2983323.2983876.

Tomas Mikolov, Kai Chen, Greg Corrado, and Jeffrey Dean. 2013. Efficient estimation of word representations in vector space. *CoRR* abs/1301.3781. http://arxiv.org/abs/1301.3781.

Panupong Pasupat and Percy Liang. 2015. Compositional semantic parsing on semi-structured tables. In *Proceedings of the 53rd Annual Meeting of the Association for Computational Linguistics and the 7th International Joint Conference on Natural Language Processing of the Asian Federation of Natural Language Processing, ACL 2015, July 26-31, 2015, Beijing, China, Volume 1: Long Papers*. pages 1470–1480. http://aclweb.org/anthology/P/P15/P15-1142.pdf.

Pranav Rajpurkar, Jian Zhang, Konstantin Lopyrev, and Percy Liang. 2016. Squad: 100, 000+ questions for machine comprehension of text. In *Proceedings of the 2016 Conference on Empirical Methods in Natural Language Processing, EMNLP 2016, Austin, Texas, USA, November 1-4, 2016*. pages 2383–2392. http://aclweb.org/anthology/D/D16/D16-1264.pdf.

Min Joon Seo, Aniruddha Kembhavi, Ali Farhadi, and Hannaneh Hajishirzi. 2016. Bidirectional attention flow for machine comprehension. *CoRR* abs/1611.01603. http://arxiv.org/abs/1611.01603.

Adam Trischler, Zheng Ye, Xingdi Yuan, Philip Bachman, Alessandro Sordoni, and Kaheer Suleman. 2016. Natural language comprehension with the epireader. In *Proceedings of the 2016 Conference on Empirical Methods in Natural Language Processing, EMNLP 2016, Austin, Texas, USA, November 1-4, 2016*. pages 128–137. http://aclweb.org/anthology/D/D16/D16-1013.pdf.

Johannes Welbl, Nelson F. Liu, and Matt Gardner. 2017. Crowdsourcing multiple choice science questions. *CoRR* abs/1707.06209. http://arxiv.org/abs/1707.06209.

Jason Weston, Antoine Bordes, Sumit Chopra, and Tomas Mikolov. 2015. Towards ai-complete question answering: A set of prerequisite toy tasks. *CoRR* abs/1502.05698. http://arxiv.org/abs/1502.05698.

Jason Weston, Sumit Chopra, and Antoine Bordes. 2014. Memory networks. *CoRR* abs/1410.3916. http://arxiv.org/abs/1410.3916.

Caiming Xiong, Victor Zhong, and Richard Socher. 2016. Dynamic coattention networks for question answering. *CoRR* abs/1611.01604. http://arxiv.org/abs/1611.01604.

Yi Yang, Scott Wen-tau Yih, and Chris Meek. 2015. Wikiqa: A challenge dataset for open-domain question answering. ACL Association for Computational Linguistics. https://www.microsoft.com/en-us/research/publication/wikiqa-a-challenge-dataset-for-open-domain-question-answering/.

Narrative Modeling with Memory Chains and Semantic Supervision

Fei Liu   **Trevor Cohn**   **Timothy Baldwin**
School of Computing and Information Systems
The University of Melbourne
Victoria, Australia
`fliu3@student.unimelb.edu.au`
`t.cohn@unimelb.edu.au  tb@ldwin.net`

Abstract

Story comprehension requires a deep semantic understanding of the narrative, making it a challenging task. Inspired by previous studies on ROC Story Cloze Test, we propose a novel method, tracking various semantic aspects with external neural memory chains while encouraging each to focus on a particular semantic aspect. Evaluated on the task of story ending prediction, our model demonstrates superior performance to a collection of competitive baselines, setting a new state of the art. [1]

1 Introduction

Story narrative comprehension has been a long-standing challenge in artificial intelligence (Winograd, 1972; Turner, 1994; Schubert and Hwang, 2000). The difficulties of this task arise from the necessity for understanding not only narratives, but also commonsense and normative social behaviour (Charniak, 1972). Of particular interest in this paper is the work by Mostafazadeh et al. (2016) on understanding commonsense stories in the form of a Story Cloze Test: given a short story, we must predict the most coherent sentential ending from two options (e.g. see Figure 1).

Many attempts have been made to solve this problem, based either on linear classifiers with handcrafted features (Schwartz et al., 2017; Chaturvedi et al., 2017), or representation learning via deep learning models (Mihaylov and Frank, 2017; Bugert et al., 2017; Mostafazadeh et al., 2017). Another widely used component of competitive systems is language model-based features, which require training on large corpora in the story domain.

---

[1] Code available at `http://github.com/liufly/narrative-modeling`.

> **Context**: Sam loved his old belt. He matched it with everything. Unfortunately he gained too much weight. It became too small.
> **Coherent Ending**: Sam went on a diet.
> **Incoherent Ending**: Sam was happy.

Figure 1: Story Cloze Test example.

The current state-of-the-art approach of Chaturvedi et al. (2017) is based on understanding the context from three perspectives: (1) event sequence, (2) sentiment trajectory, and (3) topic consistency. Chaturvedi et al. (2017) adopt external tools to recognise relevant aspect-triggering words, and manually design features to incorporate them into the classifier. While identifying triggers has been made easy by the use of various linguistic resources, crafting such features is time consuming and requires domain-specific knowledge along with repeated experimentation.

Inspired by the argument for tracking the dynamics of events, sentiment and topic, we propose to address the issues identified above with multiple external memory chains, each responsible for a single aspect. Building on Recurrent Entity Networks (`EntNets`), a superior framework to `LSTMs` demonstrated by Henaff et al. (2017) for reasoning-focused question answering and cloze-style reading comprehension, we introduce a novel multi-task learning objective, encouraging each chain to focus on a particular aspect. While still making use of external linguistic resources, we do not extract or design features from them but rather utilise such tools to generate labels. The generated labels are then used to guide training so that each chain focuses on tracking a particular aspect. At test time, our model is free of feature engineering such that, once trained, it can be easily deployed to unseen data without preprocessing. Moreover, our

278

Proceedings of the 56th Annual Meeting of the Association for Computational Linguistics (Short Papers), pages 278–284
Melbourne, Australia, July 15 - 20, 2018. ©2018 Association for Computational Linguistics

approach also differs in the lack of a ROC Stories language model component, eliminating the need for large, domain-specific training corpora.

Evaluated on the task of Story Cloze Test, our model outperforms a collection of competitive baselines, achieving state-of-the-art performance under more modest data requirements.

2 Methodology

In the story cloze test, given a story of length L, consisting of a sequence of context sentences $\mathbf{c} = \{c_1, c_2, \ldots, c_L\}$, we are interested in predicting the coherent ending to the story out of two ending options o_1 and o_2. Following previous studies (Schwartz et al., 2017), we frame this problem as a binary classification task. Assuming o_1 and o_2 are the logical and inconsistent endings respectively with their associated labels being y_1 and y_2, we assign $y_1 = 1$ and $y_2 = 0$. At test time, given a pair of possible endings, the system returns the one with the higher score as the prediction. In this section, we first describe the model architecture and then detail how we identify aspect-triggering words in text and incorporate them in training.

2.1 Proposed Model

First, to take neighbouring contexts into account, we process context sentences and ending options at the word level with a bi-directional gated recurrent unit ("Bi-GRU": Chung et al. (2014)): $\overrightarrow{h}_i = \overrightarrow{\text{GRU}}(w_i, \overrightarrow{h}_{i-1})$ where w_i is the embedding of the i-th word in the story or ending option. The backward hidden representation $\overleftarrow{h}_i$ is computed analogously but with a different set of GRU parameters. We simply take the sum $h_i = \overrightarrow{h}_i + \overleftarrow{h}_i$ as the representation at time i. An ending option, denoted o, is represented by taking the sum of final states of the same Bi-GRU over the ending option word sequence.

This representation is then taken as input to a Recurrent Entity Network ("EntNet": Henaff et al. (2017)), capable of tracking the state of the world with external memory. Developed in the context of machine reading comprehension, EntNet maintains a number of "memory chains" — one for each entity — and dynamically updates the representations of them as it progresses through a story. Here, we borrow the concept of "entity" and use each chain to track a unique aspect. An illustration of EntNet is provided in Figure 2.

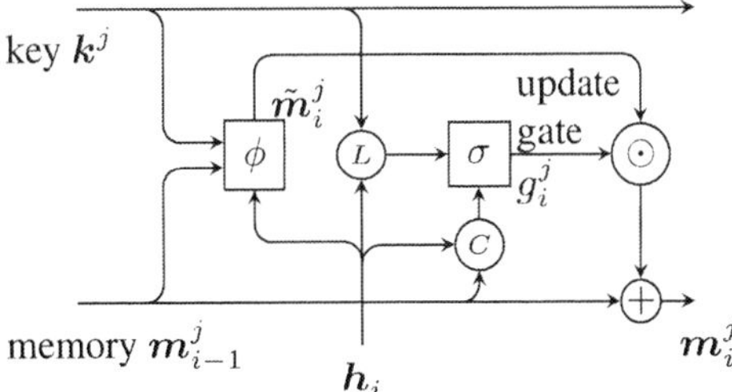

Figure 2: Illustration of EntNet with a single memory chain at time i. ϕ and σ represent Equations 1 and 2, while circled nodes L, C, $\odot$ and $+$ depict the location, content terms, Hadamard product, and addition, resp.

Memory update candidate. At every time step i, the internal memory update candidate $\overrightarrow{\tilde{m}}_i^j$ for the j-th memory chain is computed as:

$$\overrightarrow{\tilde{m}}_i^j = \phi(\overrightarrow{U}\,\overrightarrow{m}_{i-1}^j + \overrightarrow{V}k^j + \overrightarrow{W}h_i) \qquad (1)$$

where k^j is the embedding for the j-th entity (key), $\overrightarrow{U}$, $\overrightarrow{V}$ and $\overrightarrow{W}$ are trainable parameters, and ϕ is the parametric ReLU (He et al., 2015).

Memory update. The update of each memory chain is controlled by a gating mechanism:

$$\overrightarrow{g}_i^j = \sigma(h_i \cdot k^j + h_i \cdot \overrightarrow{m}_{i-1}^j) \qquad (2)$$

$$\overrightarrow{\tilde{m}}_i^j = \overrightarrow{m}_{i-1}^j + \overrightarrow{g}_i^j \odot \overrightarrow{\tilde{m}}_i^j \qquad (3)$$

where $\odot$ denotes Hadamard product (resulting in the unnormalised memory representation $\overrightarrow{\tilde{m}}_i^j$), and σ is the sigmoid function. The gate $\overrightarrow{g}_i^j$ controls how much the memory chain should be updated, a decision factoring in two elements: (1) the "location" term, quantifying how related the current input h_i (the output of the Bi-GRU at time i) is to the key k^j of the entity being tracked; and (2) the "content" term, measuring the similarity between the input and the current state $\overrightarrow{m}_{i-1}^j$ of the entity tracked by the j-th memory chain.

Normalisation. We normalise each memory representation: $\overrightarrow{m}_i^j = \overrightarrow{\tilde{m}}_i^j / \|\overrightarrow{\tilde{m}}_i^j\|$ where $\|\overrightarrow{\tilde{m}}_i^j\|$ denotes the Euclidean norm of $\overrightarrow{\tilde{m}}_i^j$. In doing so, we allow the model to forget in the sense that, as $\overrightarrow{m}_i^j$ is constrained to be lying on the surface of the unit sphere, adding new information carried by $\overrightarrow{\tilde{m}}_i^j$ and then performing normalisation inevitably causes forgetting in that the cosine distance between the original and updated memory decreases.

Bi-directionality. In contrast to `EntNet`, we apply the above steps in both directions, scanning a story both forward and backward, with arrows denoting the processing direction. $\overleftarrow{m}_i^j$ is computed analogously to $\overrightarrow{m}_i^j$ but with a different set of parameters, and $m_i^j = \overrightarrow{m}_i^j + \overleftarrow{m}_i^j$. We further define g_i^j to be the average of the gate values of both directions at time i for the j-th chain:

$$g_i^j = (\overrightarrow{g}_i^j + \overleftarrow{g}_i^j)/2 \qquad (4)$$

which will be used for semantic supervision.

Final classifier. The final prediction $\hat{y}$ to an ending option given its context story is performed by incorporating the last states of all memory chains in the form of a weighted sum u:

$$p^j = \text{softmax}((k^j)^\top W_{att} o) \qquad (5)$$
$$u = \sum_j p^j m_T^j \qquad (6)$$

where T denotes the total number of words in a story and W_{att} is a trainable weight matrix. We then transform u to get the final prediction:

$$\hat{y} = \sigma(R\phi(Hu + o)) \qquad (7)$$

where R and H are trainable weight matrices.

2.2 Semantically Motivated Memory Chains

In order to encourage each chain to focus on a particular aspect, we supervise the activation of each update gate (Equation 2) with binary labels. Intuitively, for the sentiment chain, a sentiment-bearing word (e.g. *amazing*) receives a label of 1, allowing the model to open the gate and therefore change the internal state relevant to this aspect, while a neutral one (e.g. *school*) should not trigger the activation with an assigned label of 0. To achieve this, we use three memory chains to independently track each of: (1) event sequence, (2) sentiment trajectory, and (3) topical consistency. To supervise the memory update gates of these chains, we design three sequences of binary labels: $l^j = \{l_1^j, l_2^j, \ldots, l_T^j\}$ for $j \in [1, 3]$ representing event, sentiment, and topic, and $l_i^j \in \{0, 1\}$. The label at time i for the j-th aspect is only assigned a value of 1 if the word is a trigger for that particular aspect: $l_i^j = 1$; otherwise $l_i^j = 0$. During training, we utilise such sequences of binary labels to supervise the memory update gate activations of each chain. Specifically, each chain is encouraged

	Ricky	fell	while	hiking	in	the	woods
l^{Event}	0	1	0	1	0	0	1
$l^{Sentiment}$	0	1	0	0	0	0	0
l^{Topic}	1	1	0	1	0	0	1

Table 1: An example of the linguistically motivated memory chain supervision binary labels.

to open its gate only when it sees a trigger bearing information semantically sensitive to that particular aspect. Note that at test time, we do not apply such supervision. This effectively becomes a binary tagging task for each memory chain independently and results in individual memory chains being sensitive to only a specific set of triggers bearing one of the three types of signals.

While largely inspired by Chaturvedi et al. (2017), our approach differs in how we extract and use such features. Also note that, while still making use of external linguistic resources to detect trigger words, our approach lets the memory chains decide how such words should influence the final prediction, as opposed to the handcrafted conditional probability features of Chaturvedi et al. (2017).

To identify the trigger words, we use external linguistic tools, and mark trigger words for each aspect with a label of 1. An example is presented in Table 1, noting that the same word can act as trigger for multiple aspects.

Event sequence. We parse each sentence into its FrameNet representation with `SEMAFOR` (Das et al., 2010), and identify each frame target (word or phrase tokens evoking a frame).

Sentiment trajectory. Following Chaturvedi et al. (2017), we utilise a pre-compiled list of sentiment words (Liu et al., 2005). To take negation into account, we parse each sentence with the `Stanford Core NLP` dependency parser (Manning et al., 2014; Chen and Manning, 2014) and include negation words as trigger words.

Topical consistency. We process each sentence with the `Stanford Core NLP` POS tagger and identify nouns and verbs, following Chaturvedi et al. (2017).

2.3 Training Loss

In addition to the cross entropy loss of the final prediction of right/wrong endings, we also take into account the memory update gate supervision of each chain by adding the second term. More formally, the model is trained to minimise the loss:

$$\mathcal{L} = \text{XEntropy}(y, \hat{y}) + \alpha \sum_{i,j} \text{XEntropy}(l_i^j, g_i^j)$$

where $\hat{y}$ and g_i^j are defined in Equations 7 and 4 respectively, y is the gold label for the current ending option o, and l_i^j is the semantic supervision binary label at time i for the j-th memory chain. In our experiments, we empirically set α to 0.5 based on development data.

3 Experiments

3.1 Experimental Setup

Dataset. To test the effectiveness of our model, we employ the Story Cloze Test dataset of Mostafazadeh et al. (2016). The development and test set each consist of 1,871 4-sentence stories, each with a pair of ending options. Consistent with previous studies, we split the development set into a training and validation set (for early stopping), resulting in 1,683 and 188 in each set, resp. Note that while most current approaches make use of the much larger training set, comprised of 100K 5-sentence ROC stories (with coherent endings only, also released as part of the dataset) to train a language model, we make no use of this data.

Model configuration. We initialise our model with `word2vec` embeddings (300-D, pre-trained on 100B Google News articles, not updated during training: Mikolov et al. (2013a,b)). In addition to the three supervised chains, we also add a "free" chain, unconstrained to any semantic aspect.

Training is carried out over 200 epochs with the FTRL optimiser (McMahan et al., 2013) and a batch size of 128 and learning rate of 0.1. We use the following hyper-parameters for weight matrices in both directions: $R \in \mathbb{R}^{300 \times 1}$, H, U, V, W are all matrices of size $\mathbb{R}^{300 \times 300}$, and hidden size of the `Bi-GRU` is 300. Dropout is applied to the output of ϕ in the final classifier (Equation 7) with a rate of 0.2. Moreover, we employ the technique introduced by Gal and Ghahramani (2016) where the same dropout mask is applied at every step to the input w_i to the `Bi-GRU` and the input h_i to the memory chains with rates of 0.5 and 0.2 respectively. Lastly, to curb overfitting, we regularise the last layer (Equation 7) with an L_2 penalty on its weights: $\lambda \|R\|$ where $\lambda = 0.001$.

Model	Acc.	SD
DSSM	58.5	—
TBMIHAYLOV	72.8	—
MSAP	75.2	—
HCM	77.6	—
EntNet †	77.6	±0.5
Our model†	**78.5**	±0.5

Table 2: Performance on the Story Cloze test set. **Bold** = best performance, † = ave. accuracy over 5 runs, SD = standard deviation, "—" = not reported.

Evaluation. Following previous studies, we evaluate the performance in terms of coherent ending prediction accuracy: $\frac{\#\text{correct}}{\#\text{total}}$. Here, we report the average accuracy over 5 runs with different random seeds. Echoing Melis et al. (2018), we also observe some variance in model performance even if training is carried out with the same random seed, which is largely due to the non-deterministic ordering of floating-point operations in our environment (`Tensorflow` (Abadi et al., 2015) with a single GPU). Therefore, to account for the randomness, we further train our model 5 times for each random seed and select the model with the best validation performance.

We benchmark against a collection of strong baselines, including the top-3 systems of the 2017 LSDSem workshop shared task (Mostafazadeh et al., 2017): MSAP (Schwartz et al., 2017), HCM (Chaturvedi et al., 2017)[2], and TBMIHAYLOV (Mihaylov and Frank, 2017). The first two primarily rely on a simple logistic regression classifier, both taking linguistic and probability features from a ROC Stories domain-specific neural language model. TBMIHAYLOV is LSTM-based; we also include DSSM (Mostafazadeh et al., 2016). We additionally implement a bi-directional EntNet (Henaff et al., 2017) with the same hyper-parameter settings as our model and no semantic supervision.[3]

3.2 Results and Discussion

The experimental results are shown in Table 2.

State-of-the-art results. Our model outperforms a collection of strong baselines, setting a new state of the art. Note that this is achieved with-

---

[2]We take the performance reported in a subsequent paper, 3.2% better than the original submission to the shared task.

[3]`EntNet` is also subject to the same model selection criterion described above.

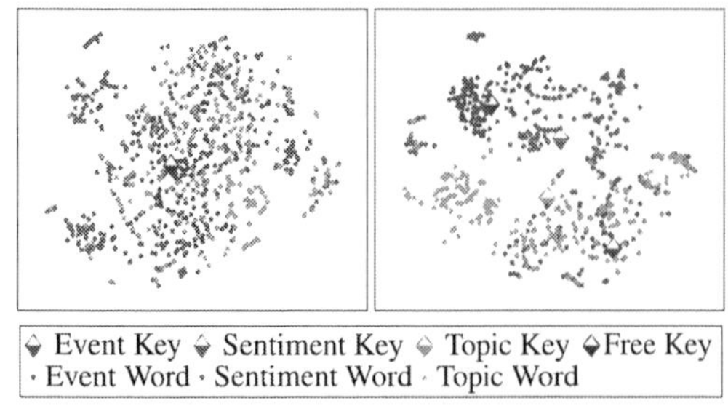

Figure 3: t-SNE scatter plot of aspect-triggering words (output representations h_i by Bi-GRU, 500 randomly sampled from each aspect) and the learned keys. EntNet (left) vs. our model (right). Best viewed in colour.

Model	Acc.	SD
Our model	78.5	±0.5
—bi-directionality	77.8	±0.7
—all semantic supervision	77.6	±0.5
—event sequence	**78.7**	±0.2
—sentiment trajectory	75.9	±0.4
—topical consistency	77.3	±0.4
—free chain	77.0	±0.4

Table 3: Ablation study. Average accuracy over 5 runs on the Story Cloze test set (all subject to the same model selection criterion as our model). **Bold**: best performance. SD: standard deviation.

out any external linguistic resources at test time or domain-specific language model-based probability features, highlighting the effectiveness of the proposed model.

EntNet vs. our model. We see clear improvements of the proposed method over EntNet, an absolute gain of 0.9% in accuracy. This validates the hypothesis that encouraging each memory chain to focus on a unique, well-defined aspect is beneficial.

Discussion. To better understand the benefits of the proposed method, we visualise the learned word representations (output representation of the Bi-GRU, h_i) and keys between EntNet and our model in Figure 3. With EntNet, while sentiment words form a loose cluster, words bearing event and topic signal are placed in close proximity and are largely indistinguishable. With our model, on the other hand, the degree of separation is much clearer. The intersection of a small portion of the event and topic groups is largely due to the fact that both aspects include verbs. Another interesting perspective is the location of the automatically learned keys (displayed as diamonds): while all the keys with EntNet end up overlapping, indicating little difference among them, the keys learned by our method demonstrate semantic diversity, with each placed within its respective cluster. Note that the free key is learned to complement the event key, a difficult challenge given the two disjoint clusters.

Ablation study. We further perform a ablation study to analyse the utility of each component in Table 3. The uni-directional variant, with its performance down to 77.8, is inferior to its bi-directional cousin. Removing all semantic supervision (resulting in 4 free memory chains) is also damaging to the accuracy (dropping to 77.6). Among the different types of semantic supervision, we see various degrees of performance degradation, with removing sentiment trajectory being the most detrimental, reflecting its value to the task. Interestingly, we observe improvement when removing event sequence supervision from consideration. We suspect that this is mainly due to the noise introduced by the rather inaccurate FrameNet representation output of SEMAFOR ($F_1 = 61.4\%$ in frame identification as reported in Das et al. (2010)). While it is possible that replacing SEMAFOR with the SemLM approach (with the extended frame definition to include explicit discourse markers, e.g. *but*) in Peng and Roth (2016) and Chaturvedi et al. (2017) may potentially reduce the amount of noise, we leave this exercise for future work.

4 Conclusion

In this paper, we have proposed a novel model for tracking various semantic aspects with external memory chains. While requiring less domain-specific training data, our model achieves state-of-the-art performance on the task of ROC Story Cloze ending prediction, beating a collection of strong baselines.

Acknowledgments

We thank the anonymous reviewers for their valuable feedback, and gratefully acknowledge the support of Australian Government Research Training Program Scholarship. This work was also supported in part by the Australian Research Council.

References

Martín Abadi, Ashish Agarwal, Paul Barham, Eugene Brevdo, Zhifeng Chen, Craig Citro, Greg S. Corrado, Andy Davis, Jeffrey Dean, Matthieu Devin, Sanjay Ghemawat, Ian Goodfellow, Andrew Harp, Geoffrey Irving, Michael Isard, Yangqing Jia, Rafal Jozefowicz, Lukasz Kaiser, Manjunath Kudlur, Josh Levenberg, Dandelion Mané, Rajat Monga, Sherry Moore, Derek Murray, Chris Olah, Mike Schuster, Jonathon Shlens, Benoit Steiner, Ilya Sutskever, Kunal Talwar, Paul Tucker, Vincent Vanhoucke, Vijay Vasudevan, Fernanda Viégas, Oriol Vinyals, Pete Warden, Martin Wattenberg, Martin Wicke, Yuan Yu, and Xiaoqiang Zheng. 2015. TensorFlow: Large-scale machine learning on heterogeneous systems. Software available from tensorflow.org.

Michael Bugert, Yevgeniy Puzikov, Andreas Rücklé, Judith Eckle-Kohler, Teresa Martin, Eugenio Martínez-Cámara, Daniil Sorokin, Maxime Peyrard, and Iryna Gurevych. 2017. LSDSem 2017: Exploring data generation methods for the story cloze test. In *Proceedings of the 2nd Workshop on Linking Models of Lexical, Sentential and Discourse-level Semantics (LSDSem 2017)*, pages 56–61, Valencia, Spain.

Eugene Charniak. 1972. Toward a model of children"s story comprehension. Technical report, Massachusetts Institute of Technology, Cambridge, USA.

Snigdha Chaturvedi, Haoruo Peng, and Dan Roth. 2017. Story comprehension for predicting what happens next. In *Proceedings of the 2017 Conference on Empirical Methods in Natural Language Processing (EMNLP 2017)*, pages 1603–1614, Copenhagen, Denmark.

Danqi Chen and Christopher Manning. 2014. A fast and accurate dependency parser using neural networks. In *Proceedings of the 2014 Conference on Empirical Methods in Natural Language Processing (EMNLP 2014)*, pages 740–750, Doha, Qatar.

Junyoung Chung, Caglar Gulcehre, KyungHyun Cho, and Yoshua Bengio. 2014. Empirical evaluation of gated recurrent neural networks on sequence modeling. In *Proceedings of the NIPS 2014 Deep Learning and Representation Learning Workshop*.

Dipanjan Das, Nathan Schneider, Desai Chen, and Noah A. Smith. 2010. Probabilistic frame-semantic parsing. In *Human Language Technologies: The 2010 Annual Conference of the North American Chapter of the Association for Computational Linguistics (NAACL-HLT 2010)*, pages 948–956, Los Angeles, USA.

Yarin Gal and Zoubin Ghahramani. 2016. A theoretically grounded application of dropout in recurrent neural networks. In *Proceedings of Advances in Neural Information Processing Systems (NIPS 2016)*, pages 1027–1035, Barcelona, Spain.

Kaiming He, Xiangyu Zhang, Shaoqing Ren, and Jian Sun. 2015. Delving deep into rectifiers: Surpassing human-level performance on ImageNet classification. In *Proceedings of the 2015 IEEE International Conference on Computer Vision (ICCV 2015)*, pages 1026–1034, Washington, DC, USA.

Mikael Henaff, Jason Weston, Arthur Szlam, Antoine Bordes, and Yann LeCun. 2017. Tracking the world state with recurrent entity networks. In *Proceedings of the 5th International Conference on Learning Representations (ICLR 2017)*, Toulon, France.

Bing Liu, Minqing Hu, and Junsheng Cheng. 2005. Opinion observer: analyzing and comparing opinions on the web. In *Proceedings of the 14th International Conference on World Wide Web (WWW 2005)*, pages 342–351, Chiba, Japan.

Christopher D. Manning, Mihai Surdeanu, John Bauer, Jenny Finkel, Steven J. Bethard, and David McClosky. 2014. The Stanford CoreNLP natural language processing toolkit. In *Association for Computational Linguistics (ACL) System Demonstrations*, pages 55–60.

H. Brendan McMahan, Gary Holt, David Sculley, Michael Young, Dietmar Ebner, Julian Grady, Lan Nie, Todd Phillips, Eugene Davydov, Daniel Golovin, et al. 2013. Ad click prediction: A view from the trenches. In *Proceedings of the 19th ACM SIGKDD International Conference on Knowledge Discovery and Data Mining (KDD 2013)*, pages 1222–1230, Chicago, USA.

Gábor Melis, Chris Dyer, and Phil Blunsom. 2018. On the state of the art of evaluation in neural language models. In *Proceedings of the 6th International Conference on Learning Representations (ICLR 2018)*, Vancouver, Canada.

Todor Mihaylov and Anette Frank. 2017. Story cloze ending selection baselines and data examination. In *Proceedings of the 2nd Workshop on Linking Models of Lexical, Sentential and Discourse-level Semantics (LSDSem 2017)*, pages 87–92, Valencia, Spain.

Tomas Mikolov, Kai Chen, Greg Corrado, and Jeffrey Dean. 2013a. Efficient estimation of word representations in vector space. In *Proceedings of the 1st International Conference on Learning Representations (ICLR 2013)*, Scottsdale, USA.

Tomas Mikolov, Ilya Sutskever, Kai Chen, Greg Corrado, and Jeff Dean. 2013b. Distributed representations of words and phrases and their compositionality. In *Proceedings of the 27th Annual Conference on Neural Information Processing Systems (NIPS 2013)*, pages 3111–3119, Stateline, USA.

Nasrin Mostafazadeh, Nathanael Chambers, Xiaodong He, Devi Parikh, Dhruv Batra, Lucy Vanderwende, Pushmeet Kohli, and James Allen. 2016. A corpus and cloze evaluation for deeper understanding of commonsense stories. In *Proceedings of the 2016*

Conference of the North American Chapter of the Association for Computational Linguistics: Human Language Technologies (NAACL-HLT 2016), pages 839–849, San Diego, USA.

Nasrin Mostafazadeh, Michael Roth, Annie Louis, Nathanael Chambers, and James Allen. 2017. LS-DSem 2017 shared task: The story cloze test. In *Proceedings of the 2nd Workshop on Linking Models of Lexical, Sentential and Discourse-level Semantics (LSDSem 2017)*, pages 46–51, Valencia, Spain.

Haoruo Peng and Dan Roth. 2016. Two discourse driven language models for semantics. In *Proceedings of the 54th Annual Meeting of the Association for Computational Linguistics (ACL 2016)*, pages 290–300, Berlin, Germany.

Lenhart K. Schubert and Chung Hee Hwang. 2000. Episodic logic meets little red riding hood: A comprehensive, natural representation for language understanding. In Lucja Iwanska and Stuart C. Shapiro, editors, *Natural Language Processing and Knowledge Representation: Language for Knowledge and Knowledge for Language*, pages 111–174. MIT/AAAI Press, Menlo Park, USA.

Roy Schwartz, Maarten Sap, Ioannis Konstas, Leila Zilles, Yejin Choi, and Noah A. Smith. 2017. The effect of different writing tasks on linguistic style: A case study of the ROC story cloze task. In *Proceedings of the 21st Conference on Computational Natural Language Learning (CoNLL 2017)*, pages 15–25, Vancouver, Canada.

Scott R. Turner. 1994. *The Creative Process: A Computer Model of Storytelling and Creativity.* Lawrence Erlbaum, Hillsdale, USA.

Terry Winograd. 1972. Understanding natural language. *Cognitive Psychology*, 3(1):1–191.

Injecting Relational Structural Representation in Neural Networks for Question Similarity

Antonio Uva[†] and **Daniele Bonadiman**[†] and **Alessandro Moschitti**
[†]DISI, University of Trento, 38123 Povo (TN), Italy
Amazon, Manhattan Beach, CA, USA, 90266
`{antonio.uva, d.bonadiman}@unitn.it`
`amosch@amazon.com`

Abstract

Effectively using full syntactic parsing information in Neural Networks (NNs) to solve relational tasks, e.g., question similarity, is still an open problem. In this paper, we propose to inject structural representations in NNs by (*i*) learning an SVM model using Tree Kernels (TKs) on relatively few pairs of questions (few thousands) as gold standard (GS) training data is typically scarce, (*ii*) predicting labels on a very large corpus of question pairs, and (*iii*) pre-training NNs on such large corpus. The results on Quora and SemEval question similarity datasets show that NNs trained with our approach can learn more accurate models, especially after fine tuning on GS.

1 Introduction

Recent years have seen an exponential growth and use of web forums, where users can exchange and find information just asking questions in natural language. Clearly, the possibility of reusing previously asked questions makes forums much more useful. Thus, many tasks have been proposed to build automatic systems for detecting duplicate questions. These were both organized in academia, e.g., SemEval (Nakov et al., 2016, 2017), or companies, e.g., Quora [1]. An interesting outcome of the SemEval challenge was that syntactic information is essential to achieve high accuracy in question reranking tasks. Indeed, the top-systems were built using Support Vector Machines (SVMs) trained with Tree Kernels (TKs), which were applied to a syntactic representation of question text (Filice et al., 2016, 2017; Barrón-Cedeño et al., 2016).

In contrast, NNs-based models struggled to get good accuracy as (*i*) large training sets are typically not available [2], and (*ii*) effectively exploiting full-syntactic parse information in NNs is still an open issue. Indeed, despite Das et al. (2016) showed that NNs are very effective to manage lexical variability, no neural model encoding syntactic information has shown a clear improvement. Indeed, also NNs directly exploiting syntactic information, such as the Recursive Neural Networks by Socher et al. (2013) or the Tree-LSTM by Tai et al. (2015), have been shown to be outperformed by well-trained sequential models (Li et al., 2015).

Finally, such tree-based approaches depend on sentence structure, thus are difficult to optimize and parallelize. This is a shame as NNs are very flexible in general and enable an easy system deployment in real applications, while TK models require syntactic parsing and longer testing time.

In this paper, we propose an approach that aims at injecting syntactic information in NNs, still keeping them simple. It consists of the following steps: (*i*) train a TK-based model on a few thousands training examples; (*ii*) apply such classifier to a much larger set of unlabeled training examples to generate automatic annotation; (*iii*) pre-train NNs on the automatic data; and (*iv*) fine-tune NNs on the smaller GS data.

Our experiments on two different datasets, i.e., Quora and Qatar Living (QL) from SemEval, show that (*i*) when NNs are pre-trained on the predicted data, they achieve accuracy higher than the one of TK models and (*ii*) NNs can be further boosted by fine-tuning them on the available GS data. This suggests that the TK properties are captured by NNs, which can exploit syntactic information even more effectively, thanks to their well-known generalization ability.

---

[1] https://www.kaggle.com/c/quora-question-pairs

[2] SQuAD by Rajpurkar et al. (2016) is an exception, also possible because dealing with a simpler factoid QA task

Proceedings of the 56th Annual Meeting of the Association for Computational Linguistics (Short Papers), pages 285–291
Melbourne, Australia, July 15 - 20, 2018. ©2018 Association for Computational Linguistics

In contrast to other semi-supervised approaches, e.g., self-training, we show that the improvement of our approach is obtained only when a very different classifier, i.e., TK-based, is used to label a large portion of the data. Indeed, using the same NNs in a self-training fashion (or another NN in a co-training approach) to label the semi-supervised data does not provide any improvement. Similarly, when SVMs using standard similarity lexical features are applied to label data, no improvement is observed in NNs.

One evident consideration is the fact that TKs-based models mainly exploit syntactic information to classify data. Although, assessing that NNs specifically learn such syntax should require further investigation, our results show that only the transfer from TKs produces improvement: this is a significant evidence that makes it worth to further investigate the main claim of our paper. In any case, our approach increases the accuracy of NNs, when small datasets are available to learn high-level semantic task such as question similarity. It consists in (*i*) using heavier syntactic/semantic models, e.g., based on TKs, to produce training data; and (*ii*) exploit the latter to learn a neural model, which can then be fine-tuned on the small available GS data.

2   Tasks and Baseline Models

We introduce our question similarity tasks along with two of the most competitive models for their solutions.

2.1   Question Matching and Ranking

Question similarity in forums can be set in different ways, e.g., detecting if two questions are semantically similar or ranking a set of retrieved questions in terms of their similarity with the original question. We describe the two methods below:

The Quora task regards detecting if two questions are duplicate or not, or, in other words, if they have the same intent. The associated dataset (Wang et al., 2017) contains over $404,348$ pairs of questions, posted by users on the Quora website, labelled as duplicate pair or not. For example, *How do you start a bakery?* and *How can one start a bakery business?* are duplicated while *What are natural numbers?* and *What is a least natural number?* are not. The ground-truth labels contain some amount of noise.

In the QL task at SemEval-2016 (Nakov et al., 2016) users were provided with a new (original) question q_o and a set of related questions $(q_1, q_2, ...q_n)$ from the QL forum[3] retrieved by a search engine, i.e., Google. The goal is to rank question candidates, q_i, by their similarity with respect to q_o. q_i were manually annotated as *Perfect-Match*, *Relevant* or *Irrelevant*, depending on their similarity with q_o. *PerfectMatch* and *Relevant* are considered as relevant. A question is composed of a subject, a body and a unique identifier.

2.2   Support Vector machines

A top-performing model in the SemEval challenge is built with SVMs, which learn a classification function, $f : Q \times Q \rightarrow \{0, 1\}$, on the relevant vs. irrelevant questions belonging to the question set, Q. The classifier score is used to rerank a set of candidate questions q_i provided in the dataset with respect to an original question q_o. Three main representations were proposed: (*i*) vectors of similarity features derived between two questions; (*ii*) a TK function applied to the syntactic structure of question pairs; or (*iii*) a combination of both.

Feature Vectors (FV) are built for question pairs, (q_1, q_2), using a set of *text similarity* features that capture the relations between two questions. More specifically, we compute 20 similarities $sim(q_1, q_2)$ using word n-grams ($n = [1, \ldots, 4]$), after stopword removal, greedy string tiling (Wise, 1996), longest common subsequences (Allison and Dix, 1986), Jaccard coefficient (Jaccard, 1901), word containment (Lyon et al., 2001), and cosine similarity.

Tree Kernels (TKs) measure the similarity between the syntactic structures of two questions. Following (Filice et al., 2016), we build two macro-trees, one for each question in the pair, containing the syntactic trees of the sentences composing a question. In addition, we link two macro-trees by connecting the phrases, e.g., NP, VP, PP, etc., when there is a lexical match between the phrases of two questions. We apply the following kernel to two pairs of question trees: $K(\langle q_1, q_2 \rangle, \langle q_1', q_2' \rangle) = TK(t(q_1, q_2), t(q_1', q_2')) + TK(t(q_2, q_1), t(q_2', q_1'))$, where $t(x, y)$ extracts the syntactic tree from the text x, enriching it with relational tags (REL) derived by matching the lexical between x and y.

---

[3]http://www.qatarliving.com/forum

3 Injecting Structures in NNs

We inject TK knowledge in two well-known and state-of-the-art networks for question similarity, enriching them with relational information.

3.1 NNs for question similarity

We implemented the Convolutional NN (CNN) model proposed by (Severyn and Moschitti, 2016). This learns f, using two separate sentence encoders $f_{q_1} : Q \rightarrow \mathbb{R}^n$ and $f_{q_2} : Q \rightarrow \mathbb{R}^n$, which map each question into a fixed size dense vector of dimension n. The resulting vectors are concatenated and passed to a Multi Layer Perceptron that performs the final classification. Each question is encoded into a fixed size vector using an embedding layer, a convolution operation and a global max pooling function. The embedding layer transforms the input question, i.e., a sequence of token, $X_q = [x_{q_1}, ..., x_{q_i}, ..., x_{q_n}]$, into a sentence matrix, $S_q \in R^{m \times n}$, by concatenating the word embeddings w_i corresponding to the tokens x_{q_i} in the input sentence.

Additionally, we implemented a Bidirectional (BiLSTM), using the standard LSTM by Hochreiter and Schmidhuber (1997). An LSTM iterates over the sentence one word at the time by creating a new word representation h_i by composing the representation of the previews word and the current word vector $h_i = LSTM(w_i, h_{i-1})$. A BiLSTM iterates over the sentence in both directions and the final representation is a concatenation of the hidden representations, h_N, obtained after processing the whole sentence. We apply two sentence models (with different weights), one for each question, then we concatenate the two fixed-size representations and fed them to a Multi-Layer Perceptron.

3.2 Relational Information

Severyn and Moschitti (2016) showed that relational information encoded in terms of overlapping words between two pairs of text can highly improve accuracy. Thus, for both networks above, we mark each word with a binary feature indicating if a word from a question appears in the other pair question. This feature is encoded with a fixed size vector (in the same way it is done for words).

3.3 Learning NNs with structure

To inject structured information in the network, we use a weak supervision technique: (*i*) an SVM with TK is trained on the GS data; (*ii*) this model classifies an additional unlabelled dataset, creating automatic data; and (*iii*) a neural network is trained on the latter data.

The pre-trained network can be fine-tuned on the GS data, using a smaller learning rate γ. This prevents catastrophic forgetting (Goodfellow et al., 2013), which may occur with a larger learning rate.

4 Experiments

We experiment with two datasets comparing models trained on gold and automatic data and their combination, before and after fine tuning.

4.1 Data

Quora dataset contains $384,358$ pairs in the training set and $10,000$ pairs both in the dev. and test sets. The latter two contain the same number of positive and negative examples.

QL dataset contains $3,869$ question pairs divided in $2,669$, 500 and 700 pairs in the training, dev. and test sets. We created 93k[4] unlabelled pairs from the QL dump, retrieving 10 candidates with Lucene for $9,300$ query questions.

4.2 NN setup

We pre-initialize our word embeddings with skip-gram embeddings of dimensionality 50 jointly trained on the English Wikipedia dump (Mikolov et al., 2013) and the jacana corpus[5]. The input sentences are encoded with fixed-sized vectors using a CNN with the following parameters: a window of size 5, an output of 100 dimensions, followed by a global max pooling. We use a single non-linear hidden layer, whose size is equal to the size of the sentence embeddings, i.e., 100. The word overlap embeddings is set to 5 dimensions. The activation function for both convolution and hidden layers is ReLU. During training the model optimizes the binary cross-entropy loss. We used SGD with Adam update rule, setting the learning rate to γ to 10^{-4} and 10^{-5} for the pre-training and fine tuning phases, respectively.

4.3 Results on Quora

Table 1 reports our different models, FV, TK, CNN and LSTM described in the previous section, where the suffix, -10k or -5k, indicates the amount of GS data used to train them, and the name in

---

[4]Note that we will release the 400k automatically labelled pairs from Quora as well as the new 93k pairs of QL along with their automatic labels for research purposes.

[5]Embeddings are available in the repository: `https://github.com/aseveryn/deep-qa`

Model	Automatic data	GS data	DEV	TEST
FV-10k	–	10k	0.7046	0.7023
TK-10k	–	10k	0.7405	0.7337
CNN-10k	–	10k	0.7646	0.7569
LSTM-10k	–	10k	0.7521	0.7450
CNN(CNN-10k)	50k	–	0.7666	0.7619
CNN(CNN-10k)*	50k	10k	0.7601	0.7598
CNN(FV-10k)	50k	–	0.6960	0.6931
CNN(FV-10k)*	50k	10k	0.7681	0.7565
CNN(TK-10k)	50k	–	0.7446	0.7370
CNN(TK-10k)*	50k	10k	0.7748	0.7652
LSTM(TK-10k)	50k	–	0.7478	0.7371
LSTM(TK-10k)*	50k	10k	0.7706	0.7505
TK-5k	–	5k	0.6859	0.6774
CNN-5k	–	5k	0.7532	0.7450
CNN(TK-5k)	50k	–	0.7239	0.7208
CNN(TK-5k)*	50k	5k	0.7574	0.7493
CNN(TK-10k)	375k	–	0.7524	0.7471
CNN(TK-10k)*	375k	10k	**0.7796**	**0.7728**
Voting(TK+CNN)	–	10k	0.7838	0.7792

Table 1: Accuracy on the Quora dataset.

parenthesis indicates the model used for generating automatic data, e.g., CNN(TK-10k) means that a CNN has been pre-trained with the data labelled by a TK model trained on 10k GS data. The amount of automatic data for pre-training is in the second column, while the amount of GS data for training or fine tuning (indicated by *) is in the third column. Finally, the results on the dev. and test sets are in the fourth and fifth columns.

We note that: first, NNs trained on 10k of GS data obtain higher accuracy than FV and TK on both dev. and test sets (see the first four lines);

Second, CNNs pre-trained with the data generated by FV or in a self-training setting, i.e., CNN(CNN-10k), and also fine-tuned do not improve[6] on the baseline model, i.e., CNN-10K, (see the second part of the table).

Third, when CNNs and LSTMs are trained on the data labelled by the TK model, match the TK model accuracy (third part of the table). Most importantly, when they are fine-tuned on GS data, they obtain better results than the original models trained on the same amount of data, e.g., 1% accuracy over CNN-10k.

Next, the fourth part of the table shows that the improvement given by our method is still present when training TK (and fine tuning the NNs) on

less GS data, i.e., only 5k.

Additionally, the fifth section of the table shows a high improvement by training NNs on all available Quora data annotated by TK-10k (trained on just 10k). This suggests that NNs require more data to learn complex relational syntactic patterns expressed by TKs. However, the plot in Figure 1 shows that the improvement reaches a plateau around 100k examples.

Finally, in the last row of the table, we report the result of a voting approach using a combination of the normalized scores of TK-10k and CNN-10k. The accuracy is almost the same than CNN(TK-10k)*. This shows that NNs completely learn the combination of a TK model, mainly exploiting syntax, and a CNN, only using lexical information. Note that the voting model is heavy to deploy as it uses syntactic parsing and the kernel algorithm, which has a time complexity quadratic in the number of support vectors.

4.4 Results on Qatar Living

Table 2 reports the results when applying our technique to a smaller and different dataset such as QL. Here, CNNs have lower performance than TK models as 2,669 pairs are not enough to train their parameters, and the text is also noisy, i.e., there are a lot of spelling errors. Despite this problem, the results show that CNNs can approximate the

---

[6]The improvement of 0.5 is not statistically significant.

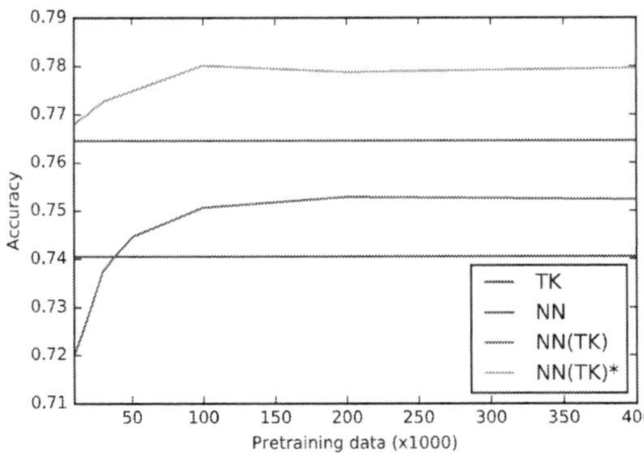

Figure 1: Impact of the pre-training data.

Model	Automatic Data	Dev	Test
CNN		0.7000	0.7514
TK		0.7340	0.7686
CNN(TK)	50k	0.5580	0.5428
CNN(TK)*	50k	0.7160	**0.7814**
CNN(TK)	93k	0.7000	0.6957
CNN(TK)*	93k	**0.7380**	0.7614

Table 2: Accuracy on QL using all available GS data.

TK models well, when using a large set of automatic data. For example, the CNN trained on 93k automatically annotated examples and then fine tuned exhibits 0.4% accuracy improvement on the dev. set and almost 3% on the test set over TK models. On the other hand, using too much automatically labeled data may hurt the performance on the test set. This may be due to the fact the quality of information contained in the gold labeled data deteriorates. In other words, using the right amount of weekly-supervision is an important hyper-parameter that needs to be carefully chosen.

5 Related Work

Determining question similarity is one of the main challenges in building systems that answer real user questions (Agichtein et al., 2015, 2016) in community QA, thus different approaches have been proposed. Jeon et al. (2005) used a language model based on word translation table to compute the probability of generating a query question, given a target/related question. Zhou et al. (2011) showed the effectiveness of phrase-based translation models on Yahoo! Answers. Cao et al. (2009); Duan et al. (2008) proposed a similarity between two questions based on a language model that exploits the category structure of Yahoo! Answers. Wang et al. (2009) proposed a model to find semantically related questions by computing similarity between syntactic trees representing questions. Ji et al. (2012) and Zhang et al. (2014) used latent semantic topics that generate question/answer pairs.

Regarding the use of automatically labelled data, Blum and Mitchell (1998) applied semi-supervised approaches, such as self-training and co-training to non-neural models. The main point of our paper is the use standard weakly-supervised methods to inject syntactic information in NNs.

Hu et al. (2016) tried to combine symbolic representations with NNs by transferring structured information of logic rules into the weights of NNs. Our work is rather different as we inject syntactic, and not logic, information in NNs.

The work most similar to our is the one by Croce et al. (2017), who use Nystrom methods to compact the TK representation in embedding vectors and use the latter to train a feed forward NNs. In contrast, we present a simpler approach, where NNs learn syntactic properties directly from data.

To our knowledge, ours is the first work trying to use NNs to learn structural information from data labelled by TK-based models. Finally, no systems of the SemEval challenges used NNs trained on syntactic information.

6 Conclusion

In this work, we have trained TK-based models, which make use of structural information, on relatively small data and applied them to new data to produce a much larger automatically labeled dataset. Our experiments show that NNs trained on the automatic data improve their accuracy. We may speculate that NNs learn relational structural information as (*i*) TK models mainly use syntactic structures to label data and (*ii*) other advanced models based on similarity feature vectors do not produce any improvement. Indeed, the latter only exploit lexical similarity measures, which are typically also generated by NNs. However, even if our conjecture were wrong, the bottom line would be that, thanks to our approach, we can have NN models comparable to TK-based approaches, by also avoiding to use syntactic parsing and expensive TK processing at deployment time.

References

Eugene Agichtein, David Carmel, Dan Pelleg, Yuval Pinter, and Donna Harman. 2015. Overview of the TREC 2015 LiveQA Track. In *TREC*.

Eugene Agichtein, David Carmel, Dan Pelleg, Yuval Pinter, and Donna K. Harman. 2016. Overview of the TREC 2016 LiveQA Track. In *TREC*.

Lloyd Allison and Trevor Dix. 1986. A bit-string longest-common-subsequence algorithm. *Information Processing Letters*, 23(6):305–310.

Alberto Barrón-Cedeño, Daniele Bonadiman, Giovanni Da San Martino, Shafiq Joty, Alessandro Moschitti, Fahad A Al Obaidli, Salvatore Romeo, Kateryna Tymoshenko, and Antonio Uva. 2016. ConvKN at SemEval-2016 Task 3: Answer and question selection for question answering on Arabic and English fora. *Proceedings of SemEval*, pages 896–903.

Avrim Blum and Tom Mitchell. 1998. Combining labeled and unlabeled data with co-training. In *Proceedings of the eleventh annual conference on Computational learning theory*, pages 92–100. ACM.

Xin Cao, Gao Cong, Bin Cui, Christian Søndergaard Jensen, and Ce Zhang. 2009. The use of categorization information in language models for question retrieval. In *Proceedings of the 18th ACM conference on Information and knowledge management*, pages 265–274. ACM.

Danilo Croce, Simone Filice, Giuseppe Castellucci, and Roberto Basili. 2017. Deep learning in semantic kernel spaces. In *Proceedings of the 55th Annual Meeting of the Association for Computational Linguistics (Volume 1: Long Papers)*, volume 1, pages 345–354.

Arpita Das, Harish Yenala, Manoj Chinnakotla, and Manish Shrivastava. 2016. Together we stand: Siamese networks for similar question retrieval. In *Proceedings of the 54th Annual Meeting of the Association for Computational Linguistics (Volume 1: Long Papers)*, pages 378–387, Berlin, Germany. Association for Computational Linguistics.

Huizhong Duan, Yunbo Cao, Chin-Yew Lin, and Yong Yu. 2008. Searching questions by identifying question topic and question focus. In *Proceedings of ACL-08: HLT*, pages 156–164, Columbus, Ohio. Association for Computational Linguistics.

Simone Filice, Danilo Croce, Alessandro Moschitti, and Roberto Basili. 2016. KeLP at SemEval-2016 Task 3: Learning Semantic Relations between Questions and Answers. In *Proceedings of the 10th International Workshop on Semantic Evaluation (SemEval-2016)*, pages 1116–1123. Association for Computational Linguistics.

Simone Filice, Giovanni Da San Martino, and Alessandro Moschitti. 2017. KeLP at SemEval-2017 Task 3: Learning Pairwise Patterns in Community Question Answering. In *Proceedings of the 11th International Workshop on Semantic Evaluation (SemEval-2017)*, pages 326–333. Association for Computational Linguistics.

Ian J. Goodfellow, Mehdi Mirza, Da Xiao, Aaron Courville, and Yoshua Bengio. 2013. An empirical investigation of catastrophic forgetting in gradient-based neural networks. *arXiv preprint arXiv:1312.6211*.

Sepp Hochreiter and Jürgen Schmidhuber. 1997. Long Short-Term Memory. *Neural computation*, 9(8):1735–1780.

Zhiting Hu, Xuezhe Ma, Zhengzhong Liu, Eduard Hovy, and Eric Xing. 2016. Harnessing deep neural networks with logic rules. In *Proceedings of the 54th Annual Meeting of the Association for Computational Linguistics (Volume 1: Long Papers)*, pages 2410–2420. Association for Computational Linguistics.

Paul Jaccard. 1901. Étude comparative de la distribution florale dans une portion des Alpes et des Jura. *Bulletin del la Société Vaudoise des Sciences Naturelles*.

Jiwoon Jeon, W Bruce Croft, and Joon Ho Lee. 2005. Finding similar questions in large question and answer archives. In *Proceedings of the 14th ACM international conference on Information and knowledge management*, pages 84–90. ACM.

Zongcheng Ji, Fei Xu, Bin Wang, and Ben He. 2012. Question-answer topic model for question retrieval in community question answering. In *Proceedings of the 21st ACM international conference on Information and knowledge management*, pages 2471–2474. ACM.

Jiwei Li, Minh-Thang Luong, Dan Jurafsky, and Eudard Hovy. 2015. When are tree structures necessary for deep learning of representations? *arXiv preprint arXiv:1503.00185*.

Caroline Lyon, James Malcolm, and Bob Dickerson. 2001. Detecting short passages of similar text in large document collections. In *Proceedings of the 2001 Conference on Empirical Methods in Natural Language Processing*, EMNLP, pages 118–125, Pittsburgh, PA, USA.

Tomas Mikolov, Ilya Sutskever, Kai Chen, Greg S Corrado, and Jeff Dean. 2013. Distributed representations of words and phrases and their compositionality. In *Advances in Neural Information Processing Systems 26*.

Preslav Nakov, Doris Hoogeveen, Lluís Màrquez, Alessandro Moschitti, Hamdy Mubarak, Timothy Baldwin, and Karin Verspoor. 2017. Semeval-2017 task 3: Community question answering. In *Proceedings of the 11th International Workshop on Semantic Evaluation (SemEval-2017)*, pages 27–48. Association for Computational Linguistics.

Preslav Nakov, Lluís Màrquez, Alessandro Moschitti, Walid Magdy, Hamdy Mubarak, abed Alhakim Freihat, Jim Glass, and Bilal Randeree. 2016. Semeval-2016 task 3: Community question answering. In *Proceedings of the 10th International Workshop on Semantic Evaluation (SemEval-2016)*, pages 525–545. Association for Computational Linguistics.

Pranav Rajpurkar, Jian Zhang, Konstantin Lopyrev, and Percy Liang. 2016. Squad: 100,000+ questions for machine comprehension of text. In *Proceedings of the 2016 Conference on Empirical Methods in Natural Language Processing*, pages 2383–2392. Association for Computational Linguistics.

Aliaksei Severyn and Alessandro Moschitti. 2016. Modeling relational information in question-answer pairs with convolutional neural networks. *arXiv preprint arXiv:1604.01178*.

Richard Socher, Alex Perelygin, Jean Wu, Jason Chuang, Christopher D Manning, Andrew Ng, and Christopher Potts. 2013. Recursive deep models for semantic compositionality over a sentiment treebank. In *Proceedings of the 2013 conference on empirical methods in natural language processing*, pages 1631–1642.

Kai Sheng Tai, Richard Socher, and Christopher D Manning. 2015. Improved semantic representations from tree-structured long short-term memory networks. *arXiv preprint arXiv:1503.00075*.

Kai Wang, Zhaoyan Ming, and Tat-Seng Chua. 2009. A syntactic tree matching approach to finding similar questions in community-based QA services. In *Proceedings of the 32nd international ACM SIGIR conference on Research and development in information retrieval*, pages 187–194. ACM.

Zhiguo Wang, Wael Hamza, and Radu Florian. 2017. Bilateral multi-perspective matching for natural language sentences. *arXiv preprint arXiv:1702.03814*.

Michael J. Wise. 1996. YAP3: Improved detection of similarities in computer program and other texts. In *ACM SIGCSE Bulletin*, volume 28, pages 130–134. ACM.

Kai Zhang, Wei Wu, Haocheng Wu, Zhoujun Li, and Ming Zhou. 2014. Question retrieval with high quality answers in community question answering. In *Proceedings of the 23rd ACM International Conference on Conference on Information and Knowledge Management*, pages 371–380. ACM.

Guangyou Zhou, Li Cai, Jun Zhao, and Kang Liu. 2011. Phrase-based translation model for question retrieval in community question answer archives. In *Proceedings of the 49th Annual Meeting of the Association for Computational Linguistics: Human Language Technologies-Volume 1*, pages 653–662. Association for Computational Linguistics.

A Simple and Effective Approach to Coverage-Aware Neural Machine Translation

Yanyang Li[1], Tong Xiao[1], Yinqiao Li[1], Qiang Wang[1],
Changming Xu[1] and Xueqiang Lu[2]
[1]Natural Language Processing Lab., Northeastern University
[2]Beijing Key Laboratory of Internet Culture and Digital Dissemination Research
blamedrlee@outlook.com, xiaotong@mail.neu.edu.cn,
li.yin.qiao.2012@hotmail.com, wangqiangneu@gmail.com,
changmingxu@neuq.edu.cn, lxq@bistu.edu.cn

Abstract

We offer a simple and effective method to seek a better balance between model confidence and length preference for Neural Machine Translation (NMT). Unlike the popular length normalization and coverage models, our model does not require training nor reranking the limited n-best outputs. Moreover, it is robust to large beam sizes, which is not well studied in previous work. On the Chinese-English and English-German translation tasks, our approach yields $+0.4 \sim 1.5$ BLEU improvements over the state-of-the-art baselines.

1 Introduction

In the past few years, Neural Machine Translation (NMT) has achieved state-of-the-art performance in many translation tasks. It models the translation problem using neural networks with no assumption of the hidden structures between two languages, and learns the model parameters from bilingual texts in an end-to-end fashion (Kalchbrenner and Blunsom, 2013; Sutskever et al., 2014; Cho et al., 2014). In such systems, target words are generated over a sequence of time steps. The model score is simply defined as the sum of the log-scale word probabilities:

$$\log P(\mathbf{y}|\mathbf{x}) = \sum_{j=1}^{|\mathbf{y}|} \log P(y_j|y_{<j}, \mathbf{x}) \qquad (1)$$

where $\mathbf{x}$ and $\mathbf{y}$ are the source and target sentences, and $P(y_j|y_{<j}, \mathbf{x})$ is the probability of generating the j-th word y_j given the previously-generated words $y_{<j}$ and the source sentence $\mathbf{x}$.

However, the straightforward implementation of this model suffers from many problems, the most obvious one being the bias that the system tends to choose shorter translations because the log-probability is added over time steps. The situation is worse when we use beam search where the shorter translations have more chances to beat the longer ones. It is in general to normalize the model score by translation length (say length normalization) to eliminate this system bias (Wu et al., 2016).

Though widely used, length normalization is not a perfect solution. NMT systems still have under-translation and over-translation problem even with a normalized model. It is due to the lack of the *coverage model* that indicates the degree a source word is translated. As an extreme case, a source word might be translated for several times, which results in many duplicated target words. Several research groups have proposed solutions to this bad case (Tu et al., 2016; Mi et al., 2016). E.g., Tu et al. (2016) developed a coverage-based model to measure the fractional count that a source word is translated during decoding. It can be jointly learned with the NMT model. Alternatively, one can rerank the n-best outputs by coverage-sensitive models, but this method just affects the final output list which has a very limited scope (Wu et al., 2016).

In this paper we present a simple and effective approach by introducing a coverage-based feature into NMT. Unlike previous studies, we do not resort to developing extra models nor reranking the limited n-best translations. Instead, we develop a coverage score and apply it to each decoding step. Our approach has several benefits,

- Our approach does not require to train a huge neural network and is easy to implement.

- Our approach works on beam search for each target position and thus can access more translation hypotheses.

- Our approach works consistently well under different sized beam search and sentence lengths contrary to what is observed in other systems (Koehn and Knowles, 2017).

Proceedings of the 56th Annual Meeting of the Association for Computational Linguistics (Short Papers), pages 292–297
Melbourne, Australia, July 15 - 20, 2018. ©2018 Association for Computational Linguistics

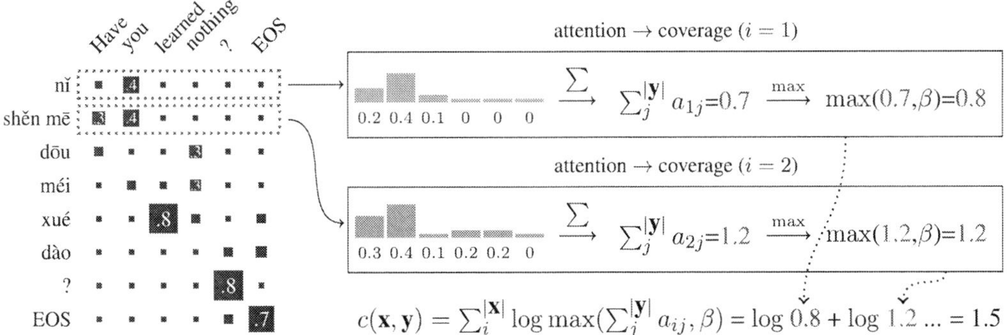

Figure 1: The coverage score for a running example (Chinese pinyin-English and $\beta = 0.8$).

We test our approach on the NIST Chinese-English and WMT English-German translation tasks, and it outperforms several state-of-the-art baselines by 0.4~1.5 BLEU points.

2 The Coverage Score

Given a word sequence, a coverage vector indicates whether the word of each position is translated. This is trivial for statistical machine translation (Koehn, 2009) because there is no overlap between the translation units of a hypothesis, i.e., we have a 0-1 coverage vector.

However, it is not the case for NMT where the coverage is modeled in a soft way. In NMT, no explicit translation units or rules are used. The attention mechanism is used instead to model the correspondence between a source position and a target position (Bahdanau et al., 2015). For a given target position j, the attention-based NMT computes attention score a_{ij} for each source position i. a_{ij} can be regarded as the measure of the correspondent strength between i and j, and is normalized over all source positions (i.e., $\sum_i^{|\mathbf{x}|} a_{ij} = 1$) [1].

Here, we present a coverage score (CS) to describe to what extent the source words are translated. In principle, the coverage score should be high if the translation covers most words in source sentence, and low if it covers only a few of them. Given a source position i, we define its *coverage* as the sum of the past attention probabilities $c_i = \sum_j^{|\mathbf{y}|} a_{ij}$ (Wu et al., 2016; Tu et al., 2016). Then, the coverage score of the sentence pair $(\mathbf{x},\mathbf{y})$ is defined as the sum of the truncated coverage over all positions (See Figure 1 for an illustration):

$$c(\mathbf{x},\mathbf{y}) = \sum_i^{|\mathbf{x}|} \log \max(\sum_j^{|\mathbf{y}|} a_{ij},\beta) \qquad (2)$$

where β is a parameter that can be tuned on a development set. This model has two properties:

- **Non-linearity** Eq. (2) is a log-linear model. It is desirable because this model does not benefit too much from the received attention when the coverage of a source word is high. This can prevent the cases that the system puts too much attention on a few words while others only receive a little attention to have relatively high scores. Beyond this, the log-scale scoring fits into the NMT model where word probabilities are represented in the logarithm manner (See Eq. (1)).

- **Truncation** At the early stage of decoding, the coverage of the most source words is close to 0. This may result in a negative infinity value after the logarithm function, and discard hypotheses with sharp attention distributions, which is not necessarily bad. The truncation with the lowest value β can ensure that the coverage score has a reasonable value. Here β is similar to model warm-up, which makes the model easy to run in the first few decoding steps. Note that our way of truncation is different from Wu et al. (2016)'s, where they clip the coverage into [0, 1] and ignore the fact that a source word may be translated into multiple target words and its coverage should be of a value larger than 1.

For decoding, we incorporate the coverage score into beam search via linear combination with the NMT model score as below,

---

[1] As the discussion of the attention mechanism is out of the scope of this work, we refer the reader to Bahdanau et al. (2015); Luong et al. (2015) for more details.

$$s(\mathbf{x}, \mathbf{y}) = (1 - \alpha) \cdot \log \mathrm{P}(\mathbf{y}|\mathbf{x}) + \alpha \cdot c(\mathbf{x}, \mathbf{y}) \quad (3)$$

where $\mathbf{y}$ is a partial translation generated during decoding, $\log \mathrm{P}(\mathbf{y}|\mathbf{x})$ is the model score, and α is the coefficient for linear interpolation.

In standard implementation of NMT systems, once a hypothesis is finished, it is removed from the beam and the beam shrinks accordingly. Here we choose a different decoding strategy. We keep the finished hypotheses in the beam until the decoding completes, which means that we compare the finished hypotheses with partial translations at each step. This method helps because it can dynamically determine whether a finished hypothesis is kept in beam through the entire decoding process, and thus reduce search errors. It enables the decoder to throw away finished hypotheses if they have very low coverage but are of high likelihood values.

3 Experiments

3.1 Setup

We evaluated our approach on Chinese-English and German-English translation tasks. We used 1.8M sentence Chinese-English bitext provided within NIST12 OpenMT[2] and 4.5M sentence German-English bitext provided within WMT16. For Chinese-English translation, we chose the evaluation data of NIST MT06 as the development set, and MT08 as the test set. All Chinese sentences were word segmented using the tool provided within NiuTrans (Xiao et al., 2012). For German-English translation, we chose newstest2013 as the development set and newstest2014 as the test set.

Our baseline systems were based on the open-source implementation of the NMT model presented in Luong et al. (2017). The model was consisted of a 4-layer bi-directional LSTM encoder and a 4-layer LSTM decoder. The size of the embedding and hidden layers was set to 1024. We applied the additive attention model on top of the multi-layer LSTMs (Bahdanau et al., 2015). For training, we used the Adam optimizer (Kingma and Ba, 2015) where the learning rate and batch size were set to 0.001 and 128. We selected the top

---

[2]LDC2000T46, LDC2000T47, LDC2000T50, LDC2003E14, LDC2005T10, LDC2002E18, LDC2007T09, LDC2004T08

Entry		Zh-En		En-De	
		dev	test	dev	test
b=10	base	37.55	30.91	23.72	23.36
	LN	38.85	32.32	23.96	22.93
	CP	38.68	31.84	23.92	23.27
	CP†	35.93	29.98	23.67	23.53
	LN+CP	39.07	32.47	23.98	23.26
	CS	39.13	32.24	24.13	**23.62**
	CS†	38.76	32.18	24.18	23.30
	LN+CS	39.59	32.73	24.24	23.32
	LN+CP+CS	**39.62**	**32.75**	**24.27**	23.30
b=100	base	35.17	28.48	23.54	23.50
	LN	38.60	31.97	24.04	23.14
	CP	37.64	30.82	23.77	23.65
	CP†	34.77	27.45	23.69	23.63
	LN+CP	38.93	32.39	23.95	23.60
	CS	39.60	32.71	24.01	**23.84**
	CS†	37.79	31.57	23.99	23.75
	LN+CS	39.88	33.20	24.22	23.60
	LN+CP+CS	**39.90**	**33.23**	**24.24**	23.65
b=500	base	23.40	17.95	23.15	23.24
	LN	37.60	30.81	23.95	23.16
	CP	34.81	28.82	23.43	23.46
	CP†	32.23	25.09	23.65	23.61
	LN+CP	37.88	31.46	23.77	23.64
	CS	39.50	32.77	23.96	**23.85**
	CS†	35.89	29.92	23.75	23.70
	LN+CS	**39.77**	**32.89**	**24.17**	23.57
	LN+CP+CS	39.73	32.85	24.17	23.69

Table 1: BLEU results of NMT systems. `base` = base system, `LN` = length normalization, `CP` = coverage penalty, and `CS` = our coverage score.

30k entries for both source and target vocabularies. For the English-German task, BPE (Sennrich et al., 2016) was used for better performance.

For comparison, we re-implemented the length normalization (LN) and coverage penalty (CP) methods (Wu et al., 2016). We used grid search to tune all hyperparameters on the development set as Wu et al. (2016). Specifically, weights for both CP and our CS are evaluated in interval $[0, 1]$ with step 0.1, while the weight for LN is in interval $[0.5, 1.5]$. We found that the settings determined with beam size 10 can be reliably applied to larger beam sizes in the preliminary experiments and thus we tuned all systems with beam size 10. For Chinese-English translation, we used a weight of 1.0 for both LN and CP, and set $\alpha = 0.6$ and $\beta = 0.4$. For English-German translation, we set the weights of LN and CP to 1.5 and 0.3, and set $\alpha = 0.3$ and $\beta = 0.2$. More details can be found in the Appendix.

3.2 Results

Table 1 shows the BLEU scores of the systems under different beam sizes (10, 100, and 500). We see, first of all, that our method outperforms

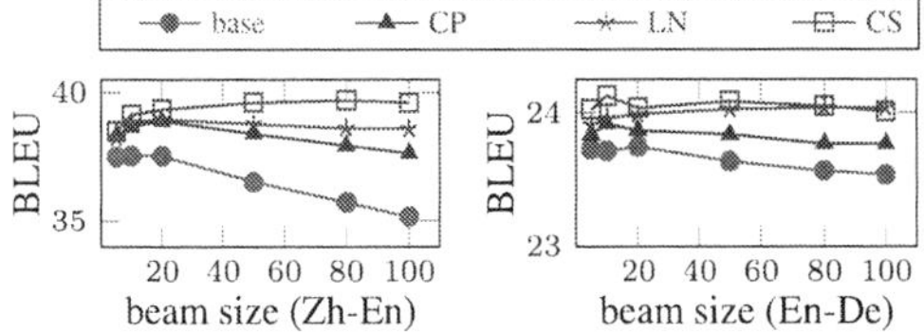

Figure 2: BLEU against beam size.

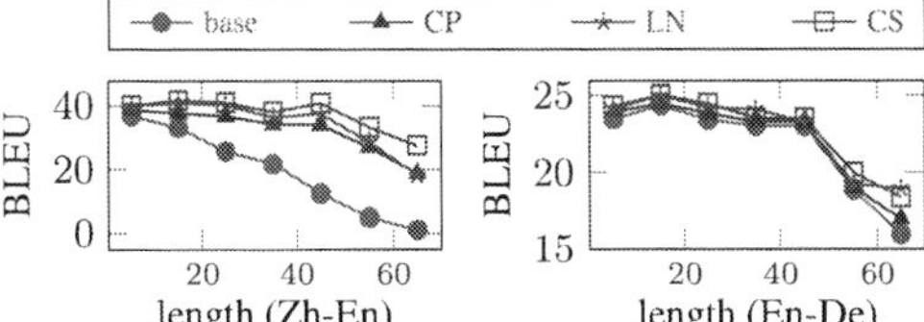

Figure 3: BLEU against sentence length.

Entry		Zh-En			En-De		
		Len	Diff	LR	Len	Diff	LR
b=50	base	22.71	3.68	0.86	19.90	2.02	0.94
	CS	25.19	1.82	0.94	20.09	1.88	0.95
b=500	base	15.88	10.12	0.61	19.53	2.32	0.92
	CS	25.20	1.86	0.94	20.04	1.91	0.94

Table 2: Length statistics. Len = average length of translations, Diff = average length difference between translations and shortest references, LR = translation length ratio.

	$\beta = 0.0$	$\beta = 0.2$	$\beta = 0.4$	$\beta = 0.6$
$\alpha = 0.1$	36.2 / 23.7	37.8 / 24.0	37.8 / 24.0	37.7 / 23.9
$\alpha = 0.3$	30.8 / 18.9	38.2 / **24.1**	38.2 / 24.0	37.8 / 23.9
$\alpha = 0.6$	22.5 / 13.4	37.6 / 23.8	**39.1** / 23.9	38.6 / 23.8
$\alpha = 0.9$	13.0 / 7.03	26.6 / 17.2	35.1 / 21.6	35.4 / 21.7

Table 3: BLEU against α and β (zh-en/en-de)

four of the baselines, and the improvement is the largest when the beam size is 500. For a clear presentation, we plotted the BLEU curves by varying beam size. Figure 2 shows that our method has a consistent improvement as the beam size becomes larger, while others start to decline when the beam size is around 50, which indicates that integrating our coverage score into decoding is beneficial to prune out undesirable hypotheses when we search in a larger hypothesis space. We also see that the model gives even better results (+0.5 BLEU) after combining all these methods, which implies that our method doesn't overlap with the others. More interestingly, it is observed that the improvement on the En-De task is smaller than that on the Zh-En task. A possible reason is that there are relatively good word correspondences between English and German, and it is not so difficult for the base model to learn word deletions and insertions in En-De translation. Hence, the baseline system generates translations with proper lengths and does not benefit too much from the coverage model.

An interesting phenomenon in Table 1 is that using large beam size 100 rather than standard beam size (around 10) could give considerable improvements, e.g., 0.5 BLEU for Zh-En and 0.2 for En-De, yet the extremely large beam size 500 does not help much. This might result from the fact that our method is applied to each decoding step, thus helps model to search in a larger space and select better hypotheses, while a much larger beam size does not provide more benefits because the model already generates sufficiently good translations with a small beam size.

We also compared CP with our method by ap-plying CP to each decoding step (Line CP[†]) and our method only to reranking (Line CS[†]) in Table 1. We noted that model performance dropped in most cases when CP was applied to each decoding step, and our method was helpful in reranking and obtained even better results as well when it is employed by beam search. This implies that the way of truncation is essential to enable the effective utilization of coverage inside beam search to achieve more significant improvements.

Then, Figure 3 shows that our method has a relatively better ability to handle longer sentences. It obtains a significant improvement over the baselines when we translate sentences of more than 50 words. This is expectable because the coverage provides rich information from the past, which helps to address the long term dependency issue.

Another interesting question is whether the N-MT systems can generate translations with appropriate lengths. To seek its answer, we studied the length difference between the MT output and the shortest reference. Table 2 shows that our method helps on both tasks. It generates translations whose lengths are closer to those of their references, which agrees with the BLEU results in Table 1. This is reasonable because our method encourages the hypotheses with higher coverage scores and thus higher recall. It means that our method can help the model to preserve the meaning of source words, which alleviates the under-translation problem.

Sensitivity analysis on α and β in Table 3 shows that the two tasks have different optimal choices of these values, which might be due to the natural need of length preference for different languages.

4 Related Work

The length preference and coverage problems have been discussed for years since the rise of statistical machine translation (Koehn, 2009). In NMT, several good methods have been developed. The simplest of these is length normalization which penalizes short translations in decoding (Wu et al., 2016). More sophisticated methods focus on modeling the coverage problem with extra sub-modules in NMT and require a training process (Tu et al., 2016; Mi et al., 2016).

Perhaps the most related work to this paper is Wu et al. (2016). In their work, the coverage problem can be interpreted in a probability story. However, it fails to account for the cases that one source word is translated into multiple target words and is thus of a total attention score > 1. To address this issue, we remove the probability constraint and make the coverage score interpretable for different cases. Another difference lies in that our coverage model is applied to every beam search step, while Wu et al. (2016)'s model affects only a small number of translation outputs.

Previous work have pointed out that BLEU scores of NMT systems drop as beam size increases (Britz et al., 2017; Tu et al., 2017; Koehn and Knowles, 2017), and the existing length normalization and coverage models can alleviate this problem to some extent. In this work we show that our method can do this much better. Almost no BLEU drop is observed even when beam size is set to 500.

5 Conclusion

We have described a coverage score and integrated it into a state-of-the-art NMT system. Our method is easy to implement and does not need training for additional models. Also, it performs well in searching with large beam sizes. On Chinese-English and English-German translation tasks, it outperforms several baselines significantly.

Acknowledgments

This work was supported in part by the National Science Foundation of China (61672138, 61432013 and 61671070), the Opening Project of Beijing Key Laboratory of Internet Culture and Digital Dissemination Research and the Fundamental Research Funds for the Central Universities. The authors would like to thank anonymous reviewers, Chunliang Zhang, Quan Du and Jingbo Zhu for their comments.

References

Dzmitry Bahdanau, Kyunghyun Cho, and Yoshua Bengio. 2015. Neural machine translation by jointly learning to align and translate. *International Conference on Learning Representations*.

Denny Britz, Anna Goldie, Minh-Thang Luong, and Quoc V. Le. 2017. Massive exploration of neural machine translation architectures. *CoRR*, abs/1703.03906.

Kyunghyun Cho, Bart van Merrienboer, Caglar Gulcehre, Dzmitry Bahdanau, Fethi Bougares, Holger Schwenk, and Yoshua Bengio. 2014. Learning phrase representations using rnn encoder–decoder for statistical machine translation. In *Proceedings of the 2014 Conference on Empirical Methods in Natural Language Processing (EMNLP)*, pages 1724–1734, Doha, Qatar. Association for Computational Linguistics.

Nal Kalchbrenner and Phil Blunsom. 2013. Recurrent continuous translation models. In *Proceedings of the 2013 Conference on Empirical Methods in Natural Language Processing*, pages 1700–1709, Seattle, Washington, USA. Association for Computational Linguistics.

Diederik P Kingma and Jimmy Lei Ba. 2015. Adam: A method for stochastic optimization. *International Conference on Learning Representations*.

Philip Koehn. 2009. *Statistical Machine Translation*. Cambridge University Press, Cambridge, UK.

Philipp Koehn and Rebecca Knowles. 2017. Six challenges for neural machine translation. In *Proceedings of the First Workshop on Neural Machine Translation, NMT@ACL 2017, Vancouver, Canada, August 4, 2017*, pages 28–39.

Minh-Thang Luong, Eugene Brevdo, and Rui Zhao. 2017. Neural machine translation (seq2seq) tutorial. *https://github.com/tensorflow/nmt*.

Thang Luong, Hieu Pham, and Christopher D. Manning. 2015. Effective approaches to attention-based neural machine translation. In *Proceedings of the 2015 Conference on Empirical Methods in Natural Language Processing*, pages 1412–1421, Lisbon, Portugal. Association for Computational Linguistics.

Haitao Mi, Baskaran Sankaran, Zhiguo Wang, and Abe Ittycheriah. 2016. Coverage embedding models for neural machine translation. In *Proceedings of the 2016 Conference on Empirical Methods in Natural Language Processing*, pages 955–960, Austin, Texas. Association for Computational Linguistics.

Rico Sennrich, Barry Haddow, and Alexandra Birch. 2016. Neural machine translation of rare words with subword units. In *Proceedings of the 54th Annual Meeting of the Association for Computational Linguistics (Volume 1: Long Papers)*, pages 1715–1725, Berlin, Germany. Association for Computational Linguistics.

Ilya Sutskever, Oriol Vinyals, and Quoc V Le. 2014. Sequence to sequence learning with neural networks. In *Advances in Neural Information Processing Systems 27*, pages 3104–3112. Curran Associates, Inc.

Zhaopeng Tu, Yang Liu, Lifeng Shang, Xiaohua Liu, and Hang Li. 2017. Neural machine translation with reconstruction. In *Proceedings of the Thirty-First AAAI Conference on Artificial Intelligence, February 4-9, 2017, San Francisco, California, USA.*, pages 3097–3103.

Zhaopeng Tu, Zhengdong Lu, Yang Liu, Xiaohua Liu, and Hang Li. 2016. Modeling coverage for neural machine translation. In *Proceedings of the 54th Annual Meeting of the Association for Computational Linguistics (Volume 1: Long Papers)*, pages 76–85, Berlin, Germany. Association for Computational Linguistics.

Yonghui Wu, Mike Schuster, Zhifeng Chen, Quoc V. Le, Mohammad Norouzi, Wolfgang Macherey, Maxim Krikun, Yuan Cao, Qin Gao, Klaus Macherey, Jeff Klingner, Apurva Shah, Melvin Johnson, Xiaobing Liu, Lukasz Kaiser, Stephan Gouws, Yoshikiyo Kato, Taku Kudo, Hideto Kazawa, Keith Stevens, George Kurian, Nishant Patil, Wei Wang, Cliff Young, Jason Smith, Jason Riesa, Alex Rudnick, Oriol Vinyals, Greg Corrado, Macduff Hughes, and Jeffrey Dean. 2016. Google's neural machine translation system: Bridging the gap between human and machine translation. *CoRR*, abs/1609.08144.

Tong Xiao, Jingbo Zhu, Hao Zhang, and Qiang Li. 2012. Niutrans: An open source toolkit for phrase-based and syntax-based machine translation. In *Proceedings of the ACL 2012 System Demonstrations*, pages 19–24, Jeju Island, Korea. Association for Computational Linguistics.

Dynamic Sentence Sampling for Efficient Training of Neural Machine Translation

Rui Wang, Masao Utiyama, and Eiichiro Sumita

National Institute of Information and Communications Technology (NICT)

3-5 Hikari-dai, Seika-cho, Soraku-gun, Kyoto, Japan

`{wangrui, mutiyama, eiichiro.sumita}@nict.go.jp`

Abstract

Traditional Neural machine translation (NMT) involves a fixed training procedure where each sentence is sampled once during each epoch. In reality, some sentences are well-learned during the initial few epochs; however, using this approach, the well-learned sentences would continue to be trained along with those sentences that were not well learned for 10-30 epochs, which results in a wastage of time. Here, we propose an efficient method to dynamically sample the sentences in order to accelerate the NMT training. In this approach, a weight is assigned to each sentence based on the measured difference between the training costs of two iterations. Further, in each epoch, a certain percentage of sentences are dynamically sampled according to their weights. Empirical results based on the NIST Chinese-to-English and the WMT English-to-German tasks show that the proposed method can significantly accelerate the NMT training and improve the NMT performance.

1 Introduction

Recently neural machine translation (NMT) has been prominently used to perform various translation tasks (Luong and Manning, 2015; Bojar et al., 2017). However, NMT is much more time-consuming than traditional phrase-based statistical machine translation (PBSMT) due to its deep neural network structure. To improve the efficiency of NMT training, most of the studies focus on reducing the number of parameters in the model (See et al., 2016; Crego et al., 2016; Hubara et al., 2016) and implementing parallelism

in the data or in the model (Wu et al., 2016; Kalchbrenner et al., 2016; Gehring et al., 2017; Vaswani et al., 2017).

Although these technologies have been adopted, deep networks have to be improved to achieve state-of-the-art performance in order to handle very large datasets and several training iterations. Therefore, some researchers have proposed to accelerate the NMT training by resampling a smaller subset of the data that makes a relatively high contribution, to improve the training efficiency of NMT. Specifically, Kocmi and Bojar (2017) empirically investigated curriculum learning based on the sentence length and word rank. Wang et al. (2017a) proposed a static sentence-selection method for domain adaptation using the internal sentence embedding of NMT. They also proposed a sentence weighting method with dynamic weight adjustment (Wang et al., 2017b). Wees et al. (2017) used domain-based cross-entropy as a criterion to gradually fine-tune the NMT training in a dynamical manner. All of these criteria (Wang et al., 2017a,b; Wees et al., 2017) are calculated before performing the NMT training based on the domain information and are fixed while performing the complete procedure. Zhang et al. (2017) adopted the sentence-level training cost as a dynamic criterion to gradually fine-tune the NMT training. This approach was developed based on the idea that the training cost is a useful measure to determine the translation quality of a sentence. However, some of the sentences that can be potentially improved by training may be deleted using this method. In addition, all of the above works primarily focused on NMT translation performance, instead of training efficiency.

In this study, we propose a method of dynamic sentence sampling (DSS) to improve the NMT training efficiency. First, the differences between

Proceedings of the 56th Annual Meeting of the Association for Computational Linguistics (Short Papers), pages 298–304

Melbourne, Australia, July 15 - 20, 2018. ©2018 Association for Computational Linguistics

the training costs of two iterations, which is a measure of whether the translation quality of a sentence can be potentially improved, is measured to be the criterion. We further proposed two sentence resampling strategies, i.e., weighted sampling and review mechanism to help NMT focus on the not well-learned sentences as well as remember the knowledge from the well-learned sentences.

The remainder of this paper is organized as follows. In Section 2, we introduce the dynamic sentence sampling method. Experiments are described and analyzed in Section 3. We discussed some other effects of the proposed methods in Section 4. We conclude our paper in the last section.

2 Dynamic Sentence Sampling (DSS)

2.1 NMT Background

An attention-based NMT system uses a bidirectional RNN as an encoder and a decoder that emulates the search through a source sentence during the decoding process (Bahdanau et al., 2015; Luong et al., 2015). The training objective function to be minimized can be formulated as:

$$J = \sum_{\langle x,y \rangle \in D} -\log P(y|x, \boldsymbol{\theta}), \tag{1}$$

where $\langle x, y \rangle$ is the parallel sentence pair from the training corpus D, $P(y|x)$ is the translation probability, and $\boldsymbol{\theta}$ is the neural network parameters.

2.2 Criteria

The key to perform sentence sampling is to measure the criteria. As we know, the NMT system continually alters throughout the training procedure. However, most of the criteria described in the introduction remain constant during the NMT training process. Zhang et al. (2017) adopted the sentence-level training cost to be a dynamic criterion; further, the training cost of a sentence pair $\langle x, y \rangle$ during the ith iteration can be calculated as:

$$cost^i_{\langle x,y \rangle} = -\log P(y|x, \boldsymbol{\theta}). \tag{2}$$

Directly adopting training cost as the criterion to select the top-ranked sentences that represent the largest training costs has two drawbacks: 1) The translation qualities of sentences with

small training costs may be further improved during the succeeding epochs. 2) If the training corpus become smaller after each iteration, the knowledge associated with the removed sentences may be lost over the course of the NMT process.

Therefore, we adopt the ratio of differences (dif) between training costs of two training iterations to be the criterion,

$$dif^i_{\langle x,y \rangle} = \frac{cost^{i-1}_{\langle x,y \rangle} - cost^i_{\langle x,y \rangle}}{cost^{i-1}_{\langle x,y \rangle}}. \tag{3}$$

It should be noted that some of $dif_{\langle x,y \rangle}$ are negative. That is, the costs of some sentence pairs even increase after one epoch training. Therefore, the difference is normalized into [0, 1] as the final criterion:

$$criterion^i_{\langle x,y \rangle} = \frac{dif^i_{\langle x,y \rangle} - min(dif^i)}{max(dif^i) - min(dif^i)}. \tag{4}$$

This criterion indicates the likelihood of a sentence to be further improved in the next iteration; low values indicate that the training cost of a sentence is unlikely to change and that it would not significantly contribute to the NMT training even if the sentence was trained further.

2.3 Dynamic Sampling

As we know, the NMT performance improves significantly during the initial several epochs and less significantly thereafter. This is partially because that some of the sentences have been learned sufficiently (i.e., low $criterion^i_{\langle x,y \rangle}$ values). However, they are kept further training with the ones which have not been learned enough (i.e., high $criterion^i_{\langle x,y \rangle}$ values). Therefore, in this approach, these sentences are deleted for the subsequent iterations. To ensure that knowledge from the deleted sentences is retained, we propose two mechanisms for dynamic sampling, which are described in the succeeding sections.

2.3.1 Weighted Sampling (WS)

We assign a normalized weight to each sentence according to the criterion that can be given as:

$$weight^i_{\langle x,y \rangle} = \frac{criterion^i_{\langle x,y \rangle}}{\sum_{\langle x,y \rangle \in D} criterion^i_{\langle x,y \rangle}}. \tag{5}$$

Further, weighted sampling without any replacement was used to select a small subset, such as 80%[1] of the entire corpus, as the corpus D_{ws}^{i+1} to perform the subsequent iteration. The updated objective function using weighted sampling J_{ws} can be formulated as follows:

$$J_{ws} = \sum_{\langle x,y \rangle \in D_{ws}} -\log P(y|x, \boldsymbol{\theta}). \tag{6}$$

Thus only 80% of the entire corpus is used to perform the NMT training during each iteration (for the first two iteration, all of the sentences should be sampled). Because the criterion continually changes, the sentence selection procedure also changes during the NMT training. Those that are not selected in an epoch still have a chance to be selected in the subsequent epoch[2].

2.3.2 Review Mechanism (RM)

We further propose an alternate sentence sampling mechanism. After performing an iteration during training, 80% of the top-ranked sentences are selected to act as the training data for the subsequent iteration. Each sentence that is not selected is classified into the low-criterion group D_{low} and does not have a chance to be sampled again. In this case, the D_{low} will become larger and larger, and D_{high} will becomes smaller and smaller. To prevent the loss of the knowledge that was obtained from the D_{low} group during NMT, a small percentage λ, such as 10%, of the D_{low} group is sampled as the knowledge to be reviewed. The updated NMT objective function is formalized as follows,

$$J_{rm} = \sum_{\langle x,y \rangle \in D_{high}} -\log P(y|x, \boldsymbol{\theta}) + \sum_{\langle x,y \rangle \in \lambda D_{low}} -\log P(y|x, \boldsymbol{\theta}). \tag{7}$$

3 Experiments

3.1 Datasets

The proposed methods were applied to perform 1) the NIST Chinese (ZH) to English (EN) translation task that contained a training dataset of 1.42 million bilingual sentence pairs from LDC

corpora[3]. The NIST02 and NIST03-08 datasets were used as the development and test datasets, respectively. 2) the WMT English to German (DE) translation task for which 4.43 million bilingual sentence pairs from the WMT-14 dataset[4] was used as the training data. The newstest2012 and newstest2013-2015 datasets were used as development and test datasets, respectively.

3.2 Baselines and Settings

Beside the PBSMT (Koehn et al., 2007) and vanilla NMT, three typical existing approaches described in the introduction were empirically compared: 1) Curriculum learning using the source sentence length as the criterion (Kocmi and Bojar, 2017). 2) Gradual fine-tuning using language model-based cross-entropy (Wees et al., 2017)[5]. 3) NMT boosting method by eliminating 20% of the training data with the lowest training cost after performing every iteration (Zhang et al., 2017).

For the proposed DSS method, we adopted one epoch as one iteration for the EN-DE task and three epochs as one iteration for the ZH-EN task, because the corpus size of the EN-DE task is approximately three times larger than that of the ZH-EN task.

3.3 NMT Systems

The proposed method was implemented in Nematus (Sennrich et al., 2017) with the following default settings: the word embedding dimension was 620, the size of each hidden layer was 1,000, the batch size was 80, the maximum sequence length was 50, and the beam size for the decoding was 10. A 30K-word vocabulary was created and data was shuffled before each epoch. Training was conducted on a single Tesla P100 GPU using default dropout and the ADADELTA optimizer (Zeiler, 2012) with default learning rate 0.0001. All of the systems were trained for 500K batches which took approximately 7 days.

---

[1]Zhang et al. (2017) adopted 80% as the selection threshold and we follow their settings for fair comparison. Due to limited space, we will empirically investigate the effect of the thresholds as our future work.

[2]For those 20% sentences who are not selected, their $criterion_{\langle x,y \rangle}^{i+1} = criterion_{\langle x,y \rangle}^{i}$.

[3]LDC2002E18, LDC2003E07, LDC2003E14, Hansards portion of LDC2004T07, LDC2004T08, and LDC2005T06.

[4]https://nlp.stanford.edu/projects/nmt/data/wmt14.en-de/

[5]Wees et al. (2017) also proposed a weighted sampling method; however, its performance was worse than that of the gradual fine-tuning. The method originally adopted by Wees et al. was based on the cross-entropy differences between two domains. Because no domain information is available for this task; the development data was used as the in-domain data by that method. In the method proposed in this study, the development data is not required.

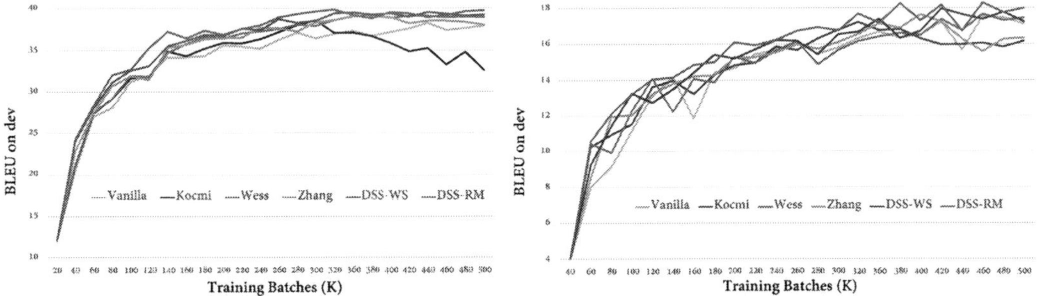

Figure 1: Learning curves. Left: NIST ZH-to-EN; Right EN-to-DE.

Table 1: Results from the NIST ZH-to-EN translation task.

Methods	Dev (NIST02)	NIST03	NIST04	NIST05	NIST06	NIST08	Test (all)
PBSMT	33.15	31.02	33.78	30.33	29.62	23.53	29.66
Vanilla NMT	38.48	37.53	39.95	35.24	33.86	27.23	35.08
Random Sampling	38.35	36.45	40.01	34.27	33.70	26.37	34.62
Kocmi and Bojar (2017)	38.51	37.60	39.87	35.43	33.76	27.37	35.19
Wees et al. (2017)	**39.16**	38.09	40.30	**35.59**	**34.14**	27.46	**35.62**
Zhang et al. (2017)	39.08	**38.27**	**40.37**	35.32	33.57	**27.87**	35.57
DSS-WS	39.54+	39.23++	**40.84+**	**35.98+**	34.91++	28.42+	36.85++
DSS-RM	**39.89++**	**39.90++**	40.60	35.77+	**35.45++**	**29.30++**	**37.33++**

Table 2: Results from the WMT EN-to-DE translation task.

Methods	Dev (newstest2012)	newstest2013	newstest2014	newstest2015	Test (all)
PBSMT	14.89	16.75	15.19	16.84	16.35
Vanilla NMT	17.55	20.92	19.16	20.01	20.06
Random Sampling	17.39	20.32	18.36	20.30	19.61
Kocmi and Bojar (2017)	17.63	20.63	19.21	**20.47**	20.18
Wees et al. (2017)	**17.69**	**20.81**	19.21	20.24	20.19
Zhang et al. (2017)	17.67	20.80	**19.37**	20.42	**20.30**
DSS-WS	17.99	21.11	19.89+	**21.20+**	20.96+
DSS-RM	**18.34+**	**21.76++**	**20.04++**	21.02+	**21.22++**

Note: The translation performance was measured using the case-insensitive BLEU (Papineni et al., 2002) scores. Marks after the scores indicate that the proposed methods significantly (Koehn, 2004) outperformed the existing optimal baselines in bold ("++"denotes better at a significance level of $\alpha = 0.01$, whereas "+"denotes better at a significance level of $\alpha = 0.05$.).

3.4 Results and Analyses

3.4.1 Training Efficiency

The learning curve is depicted in Figure 1.

1) The BLEU score (ZH-EN as example) of vanilla NMT increased from 0 to 35 using approximately 200K training batches. Further, the BLEU increased from 35 to 38 using around 200K additional training batches. This is consistent with our hypothesis that the improvement in NMT shows decreasing significance as the training progresses.

2) For the baselines, the method developed by Kocmi and Bojar (2017) did not provide significant improvement in speed. The method proposed by Wees et al. (2017) and Zhang et al. (2017) slightly accelerated the NMT training.

3) The proposed DSS methods significantly accelerated the NMT training. The BLEU score (ZH-EN as example) reached 35 after using approximately 140K training batches; further, the BLEU score reached 38 after using approximately additional 120K training batches. This may be caused due to the fact that the amount of well-learned became larger and larger as the training kept going. If these sentences were continually trained, the performance would not increase significantly. In comparison, DSS methods eliminated these well-learned sentences; therefore, the performance kept improving significantly until all of the sentences become well-learned.

4) The performances of Kocmi and Bojar

(2017) and Zhang et al. (2017) decreased significantly after reaching the highest BLEU. This is consistent with the hypothesis that NMT may forget the learned knowledge by directly removing corresponding sentences. In comparison, the performances of the proposed DSS methods did not decrease significantly, because the removed sentences still have chances to be sampled.

3.4.2 Translation Performance

For fair comparison, we evaluated the best performed (on dev data) model during 500K training batches on the test data. The results are shown in Tables 1 and 2.

1) The methods proposed by Wees et al. (2017) and Zhang et al. (2017) slightly improved performances. On Test(all), the proposed DSS methods significantly improved the BLEU score by approximately 1.2~2.2 as compared to the vanilla NMT and by 0.9~1.7 to the best performing baselines. As the well-learned sentences increases during NMT training, it did not only slow down NMT training, but also prevent NMT from learning knowledge from the sentences which were not well learned and cause the improvement stagnate.

2) Within the DSS methods, the review mechanism appears to be a slightly better mechanism than weighted sampling. This indicates that the review mechanism retained the learned knowledge in a better manner than the learned knowledge of the weighted sampling.

4 Discussions

During the response period, the comments and suggestions of reviewers inspired us a lot. Due to the limited time and space, we briefly discussed these suggestions in this paper. We will show the empirical results in our future work.

4.1 Effect on Extreme Large Data

For the large corpus, we have tested the WMT EN-FR task, which containing approximately 12M sentences. The NMT trained from large-scale corpus still gained slight BLEU improvement after several-epoch training. After 6 epochs training (1M batches), the proposed dynamic sentence sampling method outperformed the baseline by approximately 0.6 BLEU.

For the web-scale corpora which may be converged within one epoch, in our opinion, if a sentence pair is not well-learned enough, it is necessary to learn it once more. To accelerate this judging processing, we can adopt the sentence similarities between the untrained sentence with small-sized trained sentences as the criteria for sentence sampling.

4.2 Effect on Long-time Training

Similarly, for the WMT EN-DE and NIST ZH-EN, if we keep training for more than 1M batches which takes 2-3 weeks, the BLEU would increase by 1.0-1.5 and differences between baseline and the proposed method would slightly decrease by 0.5-0.7 BLEU. Because 7-10 days is a reasonable time for NMT training, we reported 500K batches training results in this paper.

4.3 Effect on Noisy Data

We added 20% noisy data, which is wrongly aligned, to the NIST ZH-EN corpus. Empirical result shows that the training cost of these noise data did not decrease significantly and even increase sometimes during the training processing. After the first-time time dynamic sampling training by the proposed method, the noise data ratio decreased from 20% to 13%. After the second-time dynamic sampling training, the noise data ratio decreased from 13% to 7%. This indicates that the proposed method can also detect the noisy data.

5 Conclusion

In this study, the sentences for which training costs of two iterations do not show any significant variation are defined as well-learned sentences. Using a dynamic sentence sampling method, these well-learned sentences are assigned a lower probability of being sampled during the subsequent epoch. The empirical results illustrated that the proposed method can significantly accelerate the NMT training and improve the NMT performances.

Acknowledgments

Thanks a lot for the helpful discussions of Kehai Chen, Zhisong Zhang, and three anonymous reviewers. This work is partially supported by the program "Promotion of Global Communications Plan: Research, Development, and Social Demonstration of Multilingual Speech Translation Technology" of MIC, Japan.

References

Dzmitry Bahdanau, Kyunghyun Cho, and Yoshua Bengio. 2015. Neural machine translation by jointly learning to align and translate. In *International Conference on Learning Representations*, San Diego.

Ondřej Bojar, Rajen Chatterjee, Christian Federmann, Yvette Graham, Barry Haddow, Shujian Huang, Matthias Huck, Philipp Koehn, Qun Liu, Varvara Logacheva, Christof Monz, Matteo Negri, Matt Post, Raphael Rubino, Lucia Specia, and Marco Turchi. 2017. Findings of the 2017 conference on machine translation (WMT17). In *Proceedings of the Second Conference on Machine Translation*, pages 169–214, Copenhagen, Denmark. Association for Computational Linguistics.

Josep Maria Crego, Jungi Kim, Guillaume Klein, Anabel Rebollo, Kathy Yang, Jean Senellart, Egor Akhanov, Patrice Brunelle, Aurelien Coquard, Yongchao Deng, Satoshi Enoue, Chiyo Geiss, Joshua Johanson, Ardas Khalsa, Raoum Khiari, Byeongil Ko, Catherine Kobus, Jean Lorieux, Leidiana Martins, Dang-Chuan Nguyen, Alexandra Priori, Thomas Riccardi, Natalia Segal, Christophe Servan, Cyril Tiquet, Bo Wang, Jin Yang, Dakun Zhang, Jing Zhou, and Peter Zoldan. 2016. Systran's pure neural machine translation systems. *CoRR*, abs/1610.05540.

Jonas Gehring, Michael Auli, David Grangier, Denis Yarats, and Yann N. Dauphin. 2017. Convolutional sequence to sequence learning. *CoRR*, abs/1705.03122.

Itay Hubara, Matthieu Courbariaux, Daniel Soudry, Ran El-Yaniv, and Yoshua Bengio. 2016. Quantized neural networks: Training neural networks with low precision weights and activations. *CoRR*, abs/1609.07061.

Nal Kalchbrenner, Lasse Espeholt, Karen Simonyan, Aäron van den Oord, Alex Graves, and Koray Kavukcuoglu. 2016. Neural machine translation in linear time. *CoRR*, abs/1610.10099.

Tom Kocmi and Ondrej Bojar. 2017. Curriculum learning and minibatch bucketing in neural machine translation. *CoRR*, abs/1707.09533.

Philipp Koehn. 2004. Statistical significance tests for machine translation evaluation. In *Proceedings of the 2004 Conference on Empirical Methods in Natural Language Processing*, pages 388–395, Barcelona, Spain.

Philipp Koehn, Hieu Hoang, Alexandra Birch, Chris Callison-Burch, Marcello Federico, Nicola Bertoldi, Brooke Cowan, Wade Shen, Christine Moran, Richard Zens, Chris Dyer, Ondrej Bojar, Alexandra Constantin, and Evan Herbst. 2007. Moses: Open source toolkit for statistical machine translation. In *Proceedings of the 45th Annual Meeting of the Association for Computational Linguistics Companion Volume Proceedings of the Demo and Poster Sessions*, pages 177–180, Prague, Czech Republic.

Minh-Thang Luong and Christopher D Manning. 2015. Stanford neural machine translation systems for spoken language domains. In *Proceedings of the International Workshop on Spoken Language Translation*, pages 76–79, Da Nang, Vietnam.

Thang Luong, Hieu Pham, and Christopher D. Manning. 2015. Effective approaches to attention-based neural machine translation. In *Proceedings of the 2015 Conference on Empirical Methods in Natural Language Processing*, pages 1412–1421, Lisbon, Portugal.

Kishore Papineni, Salim Roukos, Todd Ward, and Wei-Jing Zhu. 2002. BLEU: a method for automatic evaluation of machine translation. In *Proceedings of the 40th Annual Meeting on Association for Computational Linguistics*, pages 311–318, Philadelphia, Pennsylvania.

Abigail See, Minh-Thang Luong, and Christopher D. Manning. 2016. Compression of neural machine translation models via pruning. *CoRR*, abs/1606.09274.

Rico Sennrich, Orhan Firat, Kyunghyun Cho, Alexandra Birch, Barry Haddow, Julian Hitschler, Marcin Junczys-Dowmunt, Samuel Läubli, Antonio Valerio Miceli Barone, Jozef Mokry, and Maria Nadejde. 2017. Nematus: a toolkit for neural machine translation. In *Proceedings of the Software Demonstrations of the 15th Conference of the European Chapter of the Association for Computational Linguistics*, pages 65–68, Valencia, Spain.

Ashish Vaswani, Noam Shazeer, Niki Parmar, Jakob Uszkoreit, Llion Jones, Aidan N. Gomez, Lukasz Kaiser, and Illia Polosukhin. 2017. Attention is all you need. *CoRR*, abs/1706.03762.

Rui Wang, Andrew Finch, Masao Utiyama, and Eiichiro Sumita. 2017a. Sentence embedding for neural machine translation domain adaptation. In *Proceedings of the 55th Annual Meeting of the Association for Computational Linguistics (Volume 2: Short Papers)*, pages 560–566, Vancouver, Canada.

Rui Wang, Masao Utiyama, Lemao Liu, Kehai Chen, and Eiichiro Sumita. 2017b. Instance weighting for neural machine translation domain adaptation. In *Proceedings of the 2017 Conference on Empirical Methods in Natural Language Processing*, pages 1483–1489, Copenhagen, Denmark.

Marlies Wees, Arianna Bisazza, and Christof Monz. 2017. Dynamic data selection for neural machine translation. In *Proceedings of the 2017 Conference on Empirical Methods in Natural Language Processing*, pages 1411–1421, Copenhagen, Denmark.

Yonghui Wu, Mike Schuster, Zhifeng Chen, Quoc V. Le, Mohammad Norouzi, Wolfgang Macherey, Maxim Krikun, Yuan Cao, Qin Gao, Klaus Macherey, Jeff Klingner, Apurva Shah, Melvin Johnson, Xiaobing Liu, Lukasz Kaiser, Stephan Gouws, Yoshikiyo Kato, Taku Kudo, Hideto Kazawa, Keith Stevens, George Kurian, Nishant Patil, Wei Wang, Cliff Young, Jason Smith, Jason Riesa, Alex Rudnick, Oriol Vinyals, Greg Corrado, Macduff Hughes, and Jeffrey Dean. 2016. Google's neural machine translation system: Bridging the gap between human and machine translation. *CoRR*, abs/1609.08144.

Matthew D Zeiler. 2012. ADADELTA: an adaptive learning rate method. *arXiv preprint arXiv:1212.5701.*

Dakun Zhang, Jungi Kim, Josep Crego, and Jean Senellart. 2017. Boosting neural machine translation. In *Proceedings of the Eighth International Joint Conference on Natural Language Processing (Volume 2: Short Papers)*, pages 271–276, Taipei, Taiwan.

Compositional Representation of Morphologically-Rich Input for Neural Machine Translation

Duygu Ataman
FBK, Trento, Italy
University of Trento, Italy
ataman@fbk.eu

Marcello Federico
MMT Srl, Trento, Italy
FBK, Trento, Italy
federico@fbk.eu

Abstract

Neural machine translation (NMT) models are typically trained with fixed-size input and output vocabularies, which creates an important bottleneck on their accuracy and generalization capability. As a solution, various studies proposed segmenting words into sub-word units and performing translation at the sub-lexical level. However, statistical word segmentation methods have recently shown to be prone to morphological errors, which can lead to inaccurate translations. In this paper, we propose to overcome this problem by replacing the source-language embedding layer of NMT with a bi-directional recurrent neural network that generates compositional representations of the input at any desired level of granularity. We test our approach in a low-resource setting with five languages from different morphological typologies, and under different composition assumptions. By training NMT to compose word representations from character trigrams, our approach consistently outperforms (from 1.71 to 2.48 BLEU points) NMT learning embeddings of statistically generated sub-word units.

1 Introduction

An important problem in neural machine translation (NMT) is translating infrequent or unseen words. The reasons are twofold: the necessity of observing many examples of a word until its input representation (embedding) becomes reliable, and the computational requirement of limiting the input and output vocabularies to few tens of thousands of words. These requirements eventually lead to coverage issues when dealing with low-resource and/or morphologically-rich languages, due to their high lexical sparseness. To cope with this well-known problem, several approaches have been proposed redefining the model vocabulary in terms of interior orthographic units compounding the words, ranging from character n-grams (Ling et al., 2015b; Costa-jussà and Fonollosa, 2016; Lee et al., 2017; Luong and Manning, 2016) to statistically-learned sub-word units (Sennrich et al., 2016; Wu et al., 2016; Ataman et al., 2017). While the former provide an ideal open vocabulary solution, they mostly failed to achieve competitive results. This might be related to the semantic ambiguity caused by solely relying on input representations based on character n-grams which are generally learned by disregarding any morphological information. In fact, the second approach is now prominent and has established a pre-processing step for constructing a vocabulary of sub-word units before training the NMT model. However, several studies have shown that segmenting words into sub-word units without preserving morpheme boundaries can lead to loss of semantic and syntactic information and, thus, inaccurate translations (Niehues et al., 2016; Ataman et al., 2017; Pinnis et al., 2017; Huck et al., 2017; Tamchyna et al., 2017).

In this paper, we propose to improve the quality of input (source language) representations of rare words in NMT by augmenting its *embedding layer* with a *bi-directional recurrent neural network* (bi-RNN), which can learn compositional input representations at different levels of granularity. Compositional word embeddings have recently been applied in language modeling and obtained successful results (Vania and Lopez, 2017). The apparent advantage of our approach is that by feeding NMT with simple character n-grams, our bi-RNN can potentially learn the morphology necessary to create word-level representations of the in-

Proceedings of the 56th Annual Meeting of the Association for Computational Linguistics (Short Papers), pages 305–311
Melbourne, Australia, July 15 - 20, 2018. ©2018 Association for Computational Linguistics

put language directly at training time, thus, avoiding the burden of a separate and sub-optimal word segmentation step. We compare our approach against conventional embedding-based representations learned from statistical word segmentation in a public evaluation benchmark, which provides low-resource training conditions by pairing English with five morphologically-rich languages: Arabic, Czech, German, Italian and Turkish, where each language represents a distinct morphological typology and language family. The experimental results show that our compositional input representations lead to significantly and consistently better translation quality in all language directions.

2   Neural Machine Translation

In this paper, we use the NMT model of Bahdanau et al. (2014). The model essentially estimates the conditional probability of translating a source sequence $x = (x_1, x_2, \ldots x_m)$ into a target sequence $y = (y_1, y_2, \ldots y_l)$, using the decomposition

$$p(y|x) = \prod_{i=1}^{l} p(y_j | y_{i-1}, .., y_0, x_{m-1}, .., x_1) \quad (1)$$

The model is trained by maximizing the log-likelihood of a parallel training set via stochastic gradient descent (Bottou, 2010) and the backpropagation through time (Werbos, 1990) algorithms.

The inputs of the network are *one-hot* vectors, which are binary vectors with a single bit set to 1 to identify a specific word in the vocabulary. Each one-hot vector is then mapped to an *embedding*, a distributed representation of the word in a lower dimension but a more dense continuous space. From this input, a representation of the whole input sequence is learned using a bi-RNN, the *encoder*, which maps x into m dense sentence vectors corresponding to its hidden states. Next, another RNN, the *decoder*, predicts each target token y_i by sampling from a distribution computed from the previous target token y_{i-1}, the previous decoder hidden state, and the *context vector*. The latter is a linear combination of the encoder hidden states, whose weights are dynamically computed by a feed-forward neural network called *attention model* (Bahdanau et al., 2014). The probability of generating each target word y_j is normalized via a softmax function.

Both the source and target vocabulary sizes play an important role in terms of defining the complexity of the model. In a standard architecture, like ours, the source and target embedding matrices actually account for the vast majority of the network parameters. The vocabulary size also plays an important role when translating from and to low-resource and morphologically-rich languages, due to the sparseness of the lexical distribution. Therefore, a conventional approach has now become to compose both the source and target vocabularies of sub-word units generated through statistical segmentation methods (Sennrich et al., 2016; Wu et al., 2016; Ataman et al., 2017), and performing NMT by directly learning embeddings of subword units. A popular one of these is the Byte-Pair Encoding (BPE) method (Gage, 1994; Sennrich et al., 2016), which finds the optimal description of a corpus vocabulary by iteratively merging the most frequent character sequences. A more recent approach is the Linguistically-Motivated Vocabulary Reduction (LMVR) method (Ataman et al., 2017), which similarly generates a new vocabulary by segmenting words into sub-lexical units based on their likeliness of being morphemes and their morphological categories. A drawback of these methods is that, as pre-processing steps to NMT, they are not optimized for the translation task. Moreover, they can suffer from morphological errors at different levels, which can lead to loss of semantic or syntactic information.

3   Learning Compositional Input Representations via bi-RNNs

In this paper, we propose to perform NMT from input representations learned by composing smaller symbols, such as character n-grams (Ling et al., 2015a), that can easily fit in the model vocabulary. This composition is essentially a function which can establish a mapping between combinations of ortographic units and lexical meaning, that is learned using the bilingual context so that it can produce representations that are optimized for machine translation.

In our model (Figure 1), the one-hot vectors, after being fed into the embedding layer, are processed by an additional *composition layer*, which computes the final input representations passed to the encoder to generate translations. For learning the composition function, we employ a bi-RNN. Hence, by encoding each interior unit inside the word, we hope to capture important cues about their functional role, *i.e.* semantic or syn-

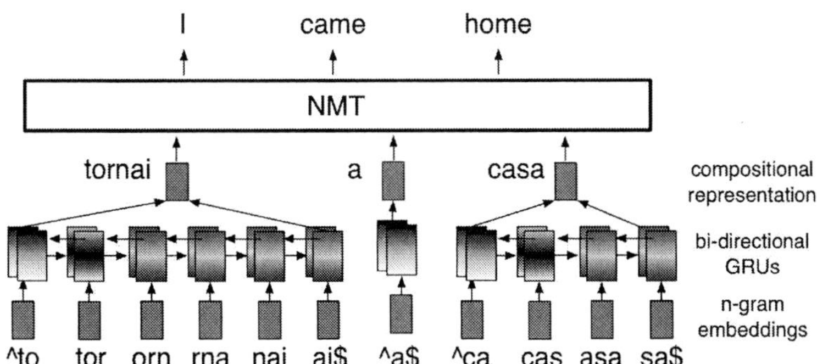

Figure 1: Translation of the Italian sentence *tornai a casa* (*I came home*) with a word-level representation composed from character trigrams.

tactic contribution to the word. We implement the network using gated recurrent units (GRUs) (Cho et al., 2014), which have shown comparable performance to long-short-term-memory units (Hochreiter and Schmidhuber, 1997), whereas they provide much faster computation. As a minimal set of input symbols required to cope with contextual ambiguities, we opt to use intersecting sequences of character trigrams, as recently suggested by Vania and Lopez (2017).

Given a bi-RNN with a forward (f) and backward (b) layer, the input representation $\mathbf{w}$ of a token of t characters is computed from the hidden states $\mathbf{h}_t^f$ and $\mathbf{h}_b^0$, *i.e.* the final outputs of the forward and backward RNNs, as follows:

$$\mathbf{w} = \mathbf{W}_f \mathbf{h}_f^t + \mathbf{W}_b \mathbf{h}_b^0 + \mathbf{b} \qquad (2)$$

where $\mathbf{W}_f$ and $\mathbf{W}_b$ are weight matrices associated to each RNN and $\mathbf{b}$ is a bias vector (Ling et al., 2015a). These parameters are jointly learned together with the internal parameters of the GRUs and the input token embedding matrix while training the NMT model. For an input of m tokens, our implementation increases the computational complexity of the network by $O(Kt_{\max}m)$, where K is the bi-RNN cost and $t_{\max}$ is the maximum number of symbols per word. However, since computation of each input representation is independent, a parallelised implementation could cut the overhead down to $O(Kt_{\max})$.

4 Experiments

We test our approach along with statistical word segmentation based open vocabulary NMT methods in an evaluation benchmark simulating a low-resource translation setting pairing English (*En*) with five languages from different language families and morphological typologies: Arabic (*Ar*), Czech (*Cs*), German (*De*), Italian (*It*) and Turk-

ish (*TR*). The characteristics of each language are given in Table 1, whereas Table 2 presents the statistical properties of the training data. We train our NMT models using the TED Talks corpora (Cettolo et al., 2012) and test them on the official data sets of IWSLT[1] (Mauro et al., 2017).

Language	Morphological Typology	Morphological Complexity
Turkish	*Agglutinative*	*High*
Arabic	*Templatic*	*High*
Czech	*Fusional, Agglutinative*	*High*
German	*Fusional*	*Medium*
Italian	*Fusional*	*Low*

Table 1: The languages evaluated in our study and their morphological characteristics.

Language Pair	# tokens		# types	
	Src	Tgt	Src	Tgt
Tr - En	2,7M	2,0M	171K	53K
Ar - En	3,9M	4,9M	220K	120K
Cs - En	2,0M	2,3M	118K	50K
De - En	4,0M	4,3M	144K	69K
It - En	3,5M	3,8M	95K	63K

Table 2: Sizes of the training sets and vocabularies in the TED Talks benchmark. Development and test sets are on average 50K to 100K tokens. (*M*: Million, *K*: Thousand.)

The *simple* NMT model constitutes the baseline in our study and performs translation directly at the level of sub-word units, which can be of four different types: characters, character trigrams, BPE sub-word units, and LMVR sub-word units.

---

[1] The International Workshop on Spoken Language Translation with shared tasks organized between 2003-2017.

The *compositional* model, on the other hand, performs NMT with input representations composed from sub-lexical vocabulary units. In our study, we evaluate representations composed from character trigrams, BPE, and LMVR units. In order to choose the segmentation method to apply on the English side (the output of NMT decoder), we compare BPE and LMVR sub-word units by carrying out an evaluation on the official data sets of Morpho Challenge 2010[2](Kurimo et al., 2010). The results of this evaluation, as given in Table 3, suggest that LMVR seems to provide a segmentation that is more consistent with morpheme boundaries, which motivates us to use sub-word tokens generated by LMVR for the target side. This choice aids us in evaluating the morphological knowledge contained in input representations in terms of the translation accuracy in NMT.

The compositional bi-RNN layer is implemented in Theano (Team et al., 2016) and integrated into the Nematus NMT toolkit (Sennrich et al., 2017). In our experiments, we use a compositional bi-RNN with 256 hidden units, an NMT model with a one-layer bi-directional GRU encoder and one-layer GRU decoder of 512 hidden units, and an embedding dimension of 256 for both models. We use a highly restricted dictionary size of 30,000 for both source and target languages, and train the segmentation models (BPE and LMVR) to generate sub-word vocabularies of the same size. We train the NMT models using the Adagrad (Duchi et al., 2011) optimizer with a mini-batch size of 50, a learning rate of 0.01, and a dropout rate of 0.1 (in all layers and embeddings). In order to prevent over-fitting, we stop training if the perplexity on the validation does not decrease for 5 epochs, and use the best model to translate the test set. The model outputs are evaluated using the (case-sensitive) BLEU (Papineni et al., 2002) metric and the Multeval (Clark et al., 2011) significance test.

Method	Precision	Recall	F_1 Score
BPE	52.87	24.44	33.43
LMVR	**70.22**	**55.66**	**62.10**

Table 3: The performance of different segmentation models trained on the English portion of our benchmark in the Morpho Challenge shared task.

5 Results

The performance of NMT models in translating each language using different vocabulary units and encoder input representations can be seen in Table 4. With the simple model, LMVR based units achieve the best accuracy in translating all languages, with improvements over BPE by **0.85** to **1.09** BLEU points in languages with high morphological complexity (Arabic, Czech and Turkish) and **0.32** to **0.53** BLEU points in languages with low to medium complexity (Italian and German). This confirms our previous results in (Ataman and Federico, 2018). Moreover, simple models using character trigrams as vocabulary units reach much higher translation accuracy compared to models using characters, indicating their superior performance in handling contextual ambiguity. In the Italian to English translation direction, the performance of simple models using character trigrams and BPE sub-word units as input representations are almost comparable, showing that character trigrams can even be sufficient as the standalone vocabulary units in languages with low lexical sparseness. These findings suggest that each type of sub-word unit used in the simple model is specifically convenient for a given morphological typology.

Using our compositional model improves the quality of input representations for each type of vocabulary unit, nevertheless, the best performance is obtained by using character trigrams as input symbols and words as input representations. The higher quality of these input representations compared to those obtained from subword units generated with LMVR suggest that our compositional model can learn morphology better than LMVR, which was found to provide comparable performance to morphological analyzers in Turkish to English NMT (Ataman et al., 2017). Moreover, sample outputs from both models show that the compositional model is also able to better capture syntactic information of input sentences. Figure 5 illustrates two example translations from Italian and Turkish. In Italian, the simple model fails to understand the common subject of different verbs in the sentence due to the repetition of the same inflective suffix after segmentation. In Turkish, the genitive case "yerlerin fotoğraflarının" (*the photographs of places*) and the complex predicate "birleştirilmesiyle meydana geldi" (*is composed of*) are both incorrectly

Model	Vocabulary	Input	BLEU				
	Units	Representations	Tr-En	Ar-En	Cs-En	De-En	It-En
Simple	Characters	Characters	12.29	8.95	13.42	21.32	22.88
	Char Trigrams	Char Trigrams	16.13	11.91	20.87	25.01	26.68
	Subwords (BPE)	Subwords (BPE)	16.79	11.14	21.99	26.61	27.02
	Subwords (LMVR)	Subwords (LMVR)	17.82	12.23	22.84	27.18	27.34
Composi-	Char Trigrams	Subwords (BPE)	15.40	11.50	21.67	27.05	27.80
tional	Char Trigrams	Subwords (LMVR)	16.63	13.29	23.07	26.86	26.84
	Char Trigrams	Words	**19.53**	**14.22**	**25.16**	**29.09**	**29.82**
	Subwords (BPE)	Words	12.64	11.51	23.13	27.10	27.96
	Subwords (LMVR)	Words	18.90	13.55	24.31	28.07	28.83

Table 4: Experiment results. Best scores for each translation direction are in bold font. All improvements over the baseline (simple model with BPE) are statistically significant (*p-value* < 0.05).

Input (Simple Model)	e comunque, em@@ ig@@ *riamo* , circol@@ *iamo* e mescol@@ *iamo* così tanto che non esiste più l' isolamento necessario affinché avvenga un' evoluzione .
NMT Output (Simple Model)	and anyway , *we* repair, and *we* mix so much that there 's no longer the isolation that *we* need to happen to make an evolution .
Input (Compositional Model)	e comunque, emigriamo, circoliamo e mescoliamo così tanto che non esiste più l' isolamento necessario affinché avvenga un' evoluzione.
NMT Output (Compositional Model)	and anyway , *we* migrate , circle and mix so much that there 's no longer the isolation necessary to become evolutionary .
Reference	and by the way , *we* immigrate and circulate and intermix so much that you can 't any longer have the isolation that is necessary for evolution to take place .

Input (Simple Model)	ama aslında bu resim tamamen , farklı *yerlerin fotoğraf@@ larının* **birleştir@@ il@@ mesiyle meydana geldi** .
NMT Output (Simple Model)	but in fact , this picture **came up with** a completely different *place of photographs* .
Input (Compositional Model)	ama aslında bu resim tamamen , farklı *yerlerin fotoğraflarının* **birleştirilmesiyle meydana geldi** .
NMT Output (Compositional Model)	but in fact , this picture **came from collecting** *pictures of* different *places* .
Reference	but this image **is** actually entirely **composed of** *photographs from* different *locations* .

Table 5: Example translations with different approaches in *Italian* (above) and *Turkish* (below).

translated by the simple model. On the other hand, the compositional model is able to capture the correct sentence semantics and syntax in either case. These findings suggest that maintaining translation at the lexical level apparently aids the attention mechanism and provides more semantically and syntactically consistent translations. The overall improvements obtained with this model over the best performing simple model are **1.99** BLEU points in Arabic, **2.32** BLEU points in Czech, **1.91** BLEU points in German, **2.48** BLEU points in Italian and **1.71** BLEU points in Turkish to English translation directions. As evident from the significant and consistent improvements across all languages, our approach provides a more promising and generic solution to the data sparseness problem in NMT.

6 Conclusion

In this paper, we addressed the problem of translating infrequent words in NMT and proposed to solve it by replacing the conventional sub-word embeddings with input representations compositionally learned from character n-grams using a bi-RNN. Our approach showed significant and consistent improvements over a variety of languages, making it a competitive solution for NMT of low-resource and morphologically-rich languages. In the future, we plan to optimize our implementation and to test its scalability on larger data sets.

Acknowledgments

The authors would like to thank NVIDIA for their computational support that aided this research.

References

Duygu Ataman and Marcello Federico. 2018. An Evaluation of Two Vocabulary Reduction Methods for Neural Machine Translation. In *Proceedings of the 13th Conference of The Association for Machine Translation in the Americas*, pages 97–110.

Duygu Ataman, Matteo Negri, Marco Turchi, and Marcello Federico. 2017. Linguistically Motivated Vocabulary Reduction for Neural Machine Translation from Turkish to English. In *The Prague Bulletin of Mathematical Linguistics*, volume 108, pages 331–342.

Dzmitry Bahdanau, Kyunghyun Cho, and Yoshua Bengio. 2014. Neural Machine Translation by Jointly Learning to Align and Translate. In *arXiv preprint arXiv:1409.0473*.

Léon Bottou. 2010. Large-Scale Machine Learning with Stochastic Gradient Descent. In *Proceedings of 19th International Conference on Computational Statistics (COMPSTAT)*, pages 177–186. Springer.

Mauro Cettolo, Christian Girardi, and Marcello Federico. 2012. Wit3: Web Inventory of Transcribed and Translated Talks. In *Proceedings of the 16th Conference of the European Association for Machine Translation (EAMT)*, pages 261–268.

Kyunghyun Cho, Bart van Merrienboer, Dzmitry Bahdanau, and Yoshua Bengio. 2014. On the properties of neural machine translation: Encoder–decoder approaches. In *Proceedings of 8th Workshop on Syntax, Semantics and Structure in Statistical Translation (SSST)*, pages 103–111.

Jonathan H. Clark, Chris Dyer, Alon Lavie, and Noah A. Smith. 2011. Better Hypothesis Testing for Statistical Machine Translation: Controlling for Optimizer Instability. In *Proceedings of the 49th Annual Meeting of the Association for Computational Linguistics (ACL)*, pages 176–181.

Marta R Costa-jussà and José AR Fonollosa. 2016. Character-based neural machine translation. In *Proceedings of the 54th Annual Meeting of the Association for Computational Linguistics (ACL)*, volume 2, pages 357–361.

John Duchi, Elad Hazan, and Yoram Singer. 2011. Adaptive Subgradient Methods for Online Learning and Stochastic Optimization. In *Journal of Machine Learning Research*, volume 12, pages 2121–2159.

Philip Gage. 1994. A New Algorithm for Data Compression. In *The C Users Journal*, volume 12, pages 23–38.

Sepp Hochreiter and Jürgen Schmidhuber. 1997. Long short-term memory. In *Neural computation*, volume 9, pages 1735–1780. MIT Press.

Matthias Huck, Simon Riess, and Alexander Fraser. 2017. Target-Side Word Segmentation Strategies for Neural Machine Translation. In *Proceedings of the 2nd Conference on Machine Translation (WMT)*, pages 56–67.

Mikko Kurimo, Sami Virpioja, Ville Turunen, and Krista Lagus. 2010. Morpho challenge competition 2005–2010: evaluations and results. In *Proceedings of the 11th Meeting of the ACL Special Interest Group on Computational Morphology and Phonology*, pages 87–95. Association for Computational Linguistics.

Jason Lee, Kyunghyun Cho, and Thomas Hofmann. 2017. Fully character-Level Neural Machine Translation without Explicit Segmentation. In *Transactions of the Association for Computational Linguistics (TACL)*, volume 5, pages 365–378.

Wang Ling, Chris Dyer, Alan W Black, Isabel Trancoso, Ramon Fermandez, Silvio Amir, Luis Marujo, and Tiago Luis. 2015a. Finding function in form: Compositional character models for open vocabulary word representation. In *Proceedings of the 2015 Conference on Empirical Methods in Natural Language Processing (EMNLP)*, pages 1520–1530.

Wang Ling, Isabel Trancoso, Chris Dyer, and Alan W Black. 2015b. Character-based Neural Machine Translation. In *arXiv preprint arXiv:1511.04586*.

Minh-Thang Luong and Christopher D Manning. 2016. Achieving Open Vocabulary Neural Machine Translation with Hybrid Word-Character Models. In *Proceedings of the 54th Annual Meeting of the Association for Computational Linguistics (ACL)*, pages 1054–1063.

Cettolo Mauro, Federico Marcello, Bentivogli Luisa, Niehues Jan, Stüker Sebastian, Sudoh Katsuitho, Yoshino Koichiro, and Federmann Christian. 2017. Overview of the iwslt 2017 evaluation campaign. In *International Workshop on Spoken Language Translation*, pages 2–14.

Jan Niehues, Eunah Cho, Thanh-Le Ha, and Alex Waibel. 2016. Pre-translation for Neural Machine Translation. In *Proceedings of The 26th International Conference on Computational Linguistics (COLING)*, pages 1828–1836.

Kishore Papineni, Salim Roukos, Todd Ward, and Wei-Jing Zhu. 2002. BLEU: a Method for Automatic Evaluation of Machine Translation. In *Proceedings of the 40th Annual Meeting of the Association for Computational Linguistics (ACL)*, pages 311–318.

Mārcis Pinnis, Rihards Krišlauks, Daiga Deksne, and Toms Miks. 2017. Neural Machine Translation for Morphologically Rich Languages with Improved Subword Units and Synthetic Data. In *Proceedings of the International Conference on Text, Speech, and Dialogue (TSD)*, pages 237–245.

Rico Sennrich, Orhan Firat, Kyunghyun Cho, Alexandra Birch, Barry Haddow, Julian Hitschler, Marcin

Junczys-Dowmunt, Samuel Läubli, Antonio Valerio Miceli Barone, Jozef Mokry, et al. 2017. Nematus: a toolkit for Neural Machine Translation. In *Proceedings of the 15th Annual Meeting of the European Chapter of the Association for Computational Linguistics (EACL)*, pages 65–68.

Rico Sennrich, Barry Haddow, and Alexandra Birch. 2016. Neural Machine Translation of Rare Words with Subword Units. In *Proceedings of the 54th Annual Meeting of the Association for Computational Linguistics (ACL)*, pages 1715–1725.

Aleš Tamchyna, Marion Weller-Di Marco, and Alexander Fraser. 2017. Modeling Target-Side Inflection in Neural Machine Translation. In *Proceedings of the 2nd Conference on Machine Translation (WMT)*, pages 32–42.

The Theano Development Team, Rami Al-Rfou, Guillaume Alain, Amjad Almahairi, Christof Angermueller, Dzmitry Bahdanau, Nicolas Ballas, Frédéric Bastien, Justin Bayer, Anatoly Belikov, et al. 2016. Theano: A python framework for fast computation of mathematical expressions. In *arXiv preprint arXiv:1605.02688*.

Clara Vania and Adam Lopez. 2017. From characters to words to in between: Do we capture morphology? In *Proceedings of the 55th Annual Meeting of the Association for Computational Linguistics (ACL)*, volume 1, pages 2016–2027.

Paul J Werbos. 1990. Backpropagation Through Time: What it does and How to do it. In *Proceedings of the Institute of Electrical and Electronics Engineers (IEEE)*, volume 78, pages 1550–1560.

Yonghui Wu, Mike Schuster, Zhifeng Chen, Quoc V Le, Mohammad Norouzi, Wolfgang Macherey, Maxim Krikun, Yuan Cao, Qin Gao, Klaus Macherey, et al. 2016. Googles neural machine translation system: Bridging the gap between human and machine translation. In *arXiv preprint arXiv:1609.08144*.

Extreme Adaptation for Personalized Neural Machine Translation

Paul Michel
Language Technologies Institute
Carnegie Mellon University
pmichel1@cs.cmu.edu

Graham Neubig
Language Technologies Institute
Carnegie Mellon University
gneubig@cs.cmu.edu

Abstract

Every person speaks or writes their own flavor of their native language, influenced by a number of factors: the content they tend to talk about, their gender, their social status, or their geographical origin. When attempting to perform Machine Translation (MT), these variations have a significant effect on how the system should perform translation, but this is not captured well by standard one-size-fits-all models. In this paper, we propose a simple and parameter-efficient adaptation technique that only requires adapting the bias of the output softmax to each particular user of the MT system, either directly or through a factored approximation. Experiments on TED talks in three languages demonstrate improvements in translation accuracy, and better reflection of speaker traits in the target text.

1 Introduction

The production of language varies depending on the speaker or author, be it to reflect personal traits (*e.g.* job, gender, role, dialect) or the topics that tend to be discussed (*e.g.* technology, law, religion). Current Neural Machine Translation (NMT) systems do not incorporate any explicit information about the speaker, and this forces the model to learn these traits implicitly. This is a difficult and indirect way to capture inter-personal variations, and in some cases it is impossible without external context (Table 1, Mirkin et al. (2015)).

Recent work has incorporated side information about the author such as personality (Mirkin et al., 2015), gender (Rabinovich et al., 2017) or politeness (Sennrich et al., 2016a), but these methods can only handle phenomena where there are ex-

Source	Translation
I went home	[Man]: Je suis rentré à la maison [Woman]: Je suis rentrée à la maison
I do drug testing	[Doctor]: Je teste des médicaments [Police]: Je dépiste des drogues

Table 1: Examples where speaker information influences English-French translation.

plicit labels for the traits. Our work investigates how we can efficiently model speaker-related variations to improve NMT models.

In particular, we are interested in improving our NMT system given few training examples for any particular speaker. We propose to approach this task as a domain adaptation problem with an extremely large number of domains and little data for each domain, a setting where we may expect traditional approaches to domain adaptation that adjust all model parameters to be sub-optimal (§2). Our proposed solution involves modeling the speaker-specific variations as an additional bias vector in the softmax layer, where we either learn this bias directly, or through a factored model that treats each user as a mixture of a few prototypical bias vectors (§3).

We construct a new dataset of Speaker Annotated TED talks (SATED, §4) to validate our approach. Adaptation experiments (§5) show that explicitly incorporating speaker information into the model improves translation quality and accuracy with respect to speaker traits.[1]

2 Problem Formulation and Baselines

In the rest of this paper, we refer to the person producing the source sentence (speaker, author,

---

[1] Data/code publicly available at
http://www.cs.cmu.edu/~pmichel1/
sated/ and https://github.com/neulab/
extreme-adaptation-for-personalized-translation
respectively.

Proceedings of the 56th Annual Meeting of the Association for Computational Linguistics (Short Papers), pages 312–318
Melbourne, Australia, July 15 - 20, 2018. ©2018 Association for Computational Linguistics

etc...) generically as the *speaker*. We denote as $\mathcal{S}$ the set of all speakers.

The usual objective of NMT is to find parameters θ of the conditional distribution $p(y \mid x; \theta)$ to maximize the empirical likelihood. We argue that personal variations in language warrant decomposing the empirical distribution into $|\mathcal{S}|$ speaker specific domains $\mathcal{D}_s$ and learning a different set of parameters θ_s for each. This setting exhibits specific traits that set it apart from common domain adaptation settings:

1. The number of speakers is very large. Our particular setting deals with $|\mathcal{S}| \approx 1800$ but our approaches should be able to accommodate orders of magnitude more speakers.

2. There is very little data (even monolingual, let alone bilingual or parallel) for each speaker, compared to millions of sentences usually used in NMT.

3. As a consequence of 1, we can assume that many speakers share similar characteristics such as gender, social status, and as such may have similar associated domains.[2]

2.1 Baseline NMT model

All of our experiments are based on a standard neural sequence to sequence model. We use one layer LSTMs as the encoder and decoder and the *concat* attention mechanism described in Luong and Manning (2015). We share the parameters in the embedding and softmax matrix of the decoder as proposed in Press and Wolf (2017). All the layers have dimension 512 except for the attention layer (dimension 256). To make our baseline competitive, we apply several regularization techniques such as dropout (Srivastava et al., 2014) in the output layer and within the LSTM (using the variant presented in Gal and Ghahramani, 2016). We also drop words in the target sentence with probability 0.1 according to Iyyer et al. (2015) and implement label smoothing as proposed in Szegedy et al. (2016) with coefficient 0.1. Appendix A provides a more thorough description of the baseline model.

2.2 Baseline adaptation strategy

As mentioned in §2, our goal is to learn a separate conditional distribution $p(y \mid x, s)$ and

parametrization θ_s to improve translation for speaker s. The usual way of adapting from general domain parameters θ to θ_s is to retrain the full model on the domain specific data (Luong and Manning, 2015). Naively applying this approach in the context of personalizing a model for each speaker however has two main drawbacks:

Parameter cost Maintaining a set of model parameters for each speaker is expensive. For example, the model in §2.1 has $\approx$47M parameters when the vocabulary size is 40k, as is the case in our experiments in §5. Assuming each parameter is stored as a 32bit float, every speaker-specific model costs $\approx$188MB. In a production environment with thousands to billions of speakers, this is impractical.

Overfitting Training each speaker model with very little data is a challenge, necessitating careful and heavy regularization (Miceli Barone et al., 2017) and an early stopping procedure.

2.3 Domain Token

A more efficient domain adaptation technique is the *domain token* idea used in Sennrich et al. (2016a); Chu et al. (2017): introduce an additional token marking the domain in the source and/or the target sentence. In experiments, we add a token indicating the speaker at the start of the target sentence for each speaker. We refer to this method as the spk_token method in the following.

Note that in this case there is now only an embedding vector (of dimension 512 in our experiments) for each speaker. However, the resulting domain embedding are non-trivial to interpret (i.e. it is not clear what they tell us about the domain or speaker itself).

3 Speaker-specific Vocabulary Bias

In NMT models, the final choice of which word to use in the next step t of translation is generally performed by the following softmax equation

$$p_t = \text{softmax}(E_T o_t + b_T) \tag{1}$$

where o_t is predicted in a context-sensitive manner by the NMT system and E_T and b_T are the weight matrix and bias vector parameters respectively. Importantly, b_T governs the overall likelihood that the NMT model will choose particular vocabulary. In this section, we describe our proposed methods for making this bias term speaker-

---

[2] Note that the speakers are still unique, and many might use very specific words (*e.g.* the name of their company or of a specific medical procedure that they are an expert on).

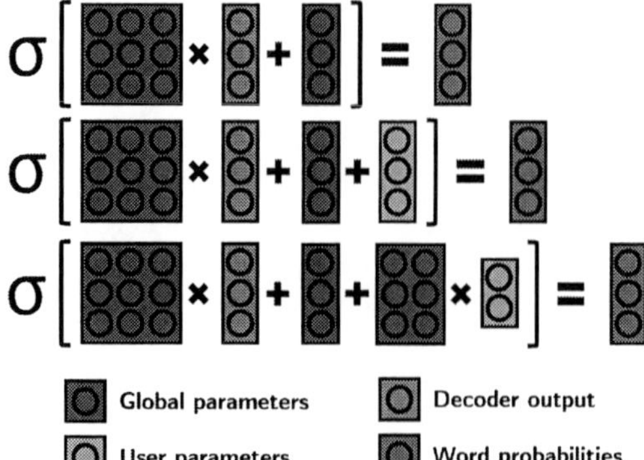

Figure 1: Graphical representation of our different adaptation models for the softmax layer. From top to bottom is the base softmax, the full_bias softmax and the fact_bias softmax

specific, which provides an efficient way to allow for speaker-specific vocabulary choice.[3]

3.1 Full speaker bias

We first propose to learn speaker-specific parameters for the bias term in the output softmax only. This means changing Eq. 1 to

$$p_t = \text{softmax}(E_T o_t + b_T + b_s) \qquad (2)$$

for speaker s. This only requires learning and storing a vector equal to the size of the vocabulary, which is a mere 0.09% of the parameters in the full model in our experiments. In effect, this greatly reducing the parameter cost and concerns of overfitting cited in §2.2. This model is also easy to interpret as each coordinate of the bias vector corresponds to a log-probability on the target vocabulary. We refer to this variant as full_bias.

3.2 Factored speaker bias

The biases for a set of speakers $\mathcal{S}$ on a vocabulary $\mathcal{V}$ can be represented as a matrix:

$$B \in \mathbb{R}^{|\mathcal{S}| \times |\mathcal{V}|} \qquad (3)$$

where each row of B is one speaker bias b_s. In this formulation, the $|\mathcal{S}|$ rows are still linearly independent, meaning that B is high rank. In practical terms, this means that we cannot share information among users about how their vocabulary

	en-fr	en-es	en-de
#talks	1,887	1,922	1,670
#train	177,743	182,582	156,134
#dev	3,774	3,844	3,340
#test	3,774	3,844	3,340
avg. sent/talk	94,2	95.0	93,5
std dev	57,6	57.8	60,3

Table 2: Dataset statistics

selection co-varies, which is likely sub-ideal given that speakers share common characteristics.

Thus, we propose another parametrization of the speaker bias, fact_bias, where the B matrix is factored according to:

$$B = S\tilde{B}$$
$$S \in \mathbb{R}^{|\mathcal{S}| \times r}, \qquad (4)$$
$$\tilde{B} \in \mathbb{R}^{r \times |\mathcal{V}|}$$

where S is a matrix of speaker vectors of low dimension r and $\tilde{B}$ is a matrix of r speaker independent biases. Here, the bias for each speaker is a mixture of r "centroid" biases $\tilde{B}$ with r speaker "weights". This reduces the total number of parameters allocated to speaker adaptation from $|\mathcal{S}||\mathcal{V}|$ to $r(|\mathcal{S}| + |\mathcal{V}|)$. In our experiments, this corresponds to using between 99.38 and 99.45% fewer parameters than the full_bias model depending on the language pair, with r parameters per speaker. In this work, we will use $r = 10$.

We provide a graphical summary of our proposed approaches in figure 1.

4   Speaker Annotated TED Talks Dataset

In order to evaluate the effectiveness of our proposed methods, we construct a new dataset, Speaker Annotated TED (SATED) based on TED talks,[4] with three language pairs, English-French (en-fr), English-German (en-de) and English-Spanish (en-es) and speaker annotation.

The dataset consists of transcripts directly collected from https://www.ted.com/talks, and contains roughly 271K sentences in each language distributed among 2324 talks. We pre-process the data by removing sentences that don't have any translation or are longer than 60 words, lowercasing, and tokenizing (using the Moses tokenizer (Koehn et al., 2007)).

---

[3]Notably, while this limits the model to only handling word choice and does not explicitly allow it to model syntactic variations, favoring certain words over others can indirectly favor certain phenomena (*e.g.* favoring passive speech by increasing the probability of auxiliaries).

[4]https://www.ted.com

Some talks are partially or not translated in some of the languages (in particular there are fewer translations in German than in French or Spanish), we therefore remove any talk with less than 10 translated sentences in each language pair.

The data is then partitioned into training, validation and test sets. We split the corpus such that the test and validation split each contain 2 sentence pairs from each talk, thus ensuring that all talks are present in every split. Each sentence pair is annotated with the name of the talk and the speaker. Table 2 lists statistics on the three language pairs.

This data is made available under the Creative Commons license, Attribution-Non Commercial-No Derivatives (or the CC BY-NC-ND 4.0 International, `https://creativecommons.org/licenses/by-nc-nd/4.0/legalcode`), all credit for the content goes to the TED organization and the respective authors of the talks. The data itself can be found at `http://www.cs.cmu.edu/~pmichel1/sated/`.

5 Experiments

We run a set of experiments to validate the ability of our proposed approach to model speaker-induced variations in translation.

5.1 Experimental setup

We test three models base (a baseline ignoring speaker labels), `full_bias` and `fact_bias`. During training, we limit our vocabulary to the 40,000 most frequent words. Additionally, we discard any word appearing less than 2 times. Any word that doesn't satisfy those conditions is replaced with an UNK token.[5]

All our models are implemented with the DyNet (Neubig et al., 2017) framework, and unless specified we use the default settings therein. We refer to appendix B for a detailed explanation of the training process. We translate the test set using beam search with beam size 5.

5.2 Does explicitly modeling speaker-related variation improve translation quality?

Table 3 shows final test scores for each model with statistical significance measured with paired boot-

	en-fr	en-es	en-de
base	38.05	39.89	26.46
spk_token	**38.85**	40.04	26.52
full_bias	**38.54**	**40.30**	**27.20**
fact_bias	**39.01**	39.88	**26.94**

Table 3: Test BLEU. Scores significantly ($p < 0.05$) better than the baseline are written in bold

strap resampling (Koehn, 2004). As shown in the table, both proposed methods give significant improvements in BLEU score, with the biggest gains in English to French ($+0.99$) and smaller gains in German and Spanish ($+0.74$ and $+0.40$ respectively). Reducing the number of parameters with `fact_bias` gives slightly better (en-fr) or worse (en-de) BLEU score, but in those cases the results are still significantly better than the baseline.

However, BLEU is not a perfect evaluation metric. In particular, we are interested in evaluating how much of the personal traits of each speaker our models capture. To gain more insight into this aspect of the MT results, we devise a simple experiment. For every language pair, we train a classifier (continuous bag-of-n-grams; details in Appendix C) to predict the author of each sentence on the target language part of the training set. We then evaluate the classifier on the ground truth and the outputs from our 3 models (base, `full_bias` and `fact_bias`).

The results are reported in Figure 2. As can be seen from the figure, it is easier to predict the author of a sentence from the output of speaker-specific models than from the baseline. This demonstrates that explicitly incorporating information about the author of a sentence allows for better transfer of personal traits during translations, although the difference from the ground truth demonstrates that this problem is still far from solved. Appendix D shows qualitative examples of our model improving over the baseline.

5.3 Further experiments on the Europarl corpus

One of the quirks of the TED talks is that the speaker annotation correlates with the topic of their talk to a high degree. Although the topics that a speaker talks about can be considered as a manifestation of speaker traits, we also perform a control experiment on a different dataset to verify that our model is indeed learning more than just topical

---

[5]Recent NMT systems also commonly use sub-word units (Sennrich et al., 2016b). This may influence on the result, either negatively (less direct control over high-frequency words) or positively (more capacity to adapt to high-frequency words). We leave a careful examination of these effects for future work.

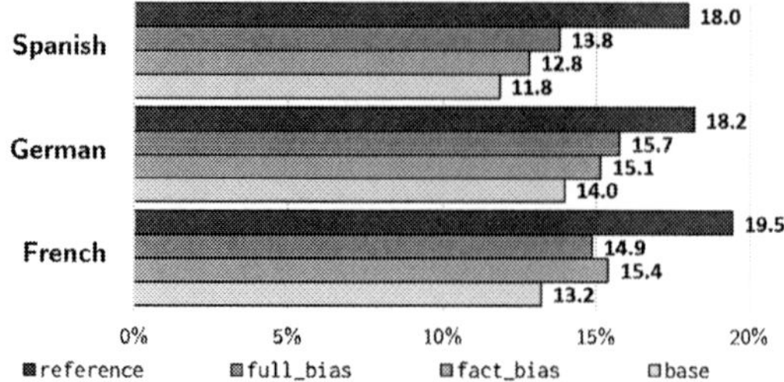

Figure 2: Speaker classification accuracy of our continuous bag-of-n-grams model.

	en-de
base	26.04
spk_token	26.49
full_bias	26.44
fact_bias	**26.87**

Table 4: Test BLEU on the Europarl corpus. Scores significantly ($p < 0.05$) better than the baseline are written in bold

information. Specifically, we train our models on a speaker annotated version of the Europarl corpus (Rabinovich et al., 2017), on the en-de language pair[6].

We use roughly the same training procedure as the one described in §5.1, with a random train/dev/test split since none is provided in the original dataset. Note that in this case, the number of speakers is much lower (747) whereas the total size of the dataset is bigger ($\approx$300k).

We report the results in table 4. Although the difference is less salient than in the case of SATED, our factored bias model still performs significantly better than the baseline (+0.83 BLEU). This suggests that even outside the context of TED talks, our proposed method is capable of improvements over a speaker-agnostic model.

6 Related work

Domain adaptation techniques for MT often rely on data selection (Moore and Lewis, 2010; Li et al., 2010; Chen et al., 2017; Wang et al., 2017), tuning (Luong and Manning, 2015; Miceli Barone et al., 2017), or adding domain tags to NMT input (Chu et al., 2017). There are also methods that fine-tune parameters of the model on each sentence in the test set (Li et al., 2016), and methods that adapt based on human post-edits (Turchi et al., 2017), although these follow our baseline adaptation strategy of tuning all parameters. There are also partial update methods for transfer learning, albeit for the very different task of transfer between language pairs (Zoph et al., 2016).

Pioneering work by Mima et al. (1997) introduced ways to incorporate information about speaker role, rank, gender, and dialog domain for rule based MT systems. In the context of data-driven systems, previous work has treated specific traits such as politeness or gender as a "domain" in domain adaptation models and applied adaptation techniques such as adding a "politeness tag" to moderate politeness (Sennrich et al., 2016a), or doing data selection to create gender-specific corpora for training (Rabinovich et al., 2017). The aforementioned methods differ from ours in that they require explicit signal (gender, politeness...) for which labeling (manual or automatic) is needed, and also handle a limited number of "domains" (≈ 2), where our method only requires annotation of the speaker, and must scale to a much larger number of "domains" ($\approx 1,800$).

7 Conclusion

In this paper, we have explained and motivated the challenge of modeling the speaker explicitly in NMT systems, then proposed two models to do so in a parameter-efficient way. We cast this problem as an extreme form of domain adaptation and showed that, even when adapting a small proportion of parameters (the softmax bias, $< 0.1\%$ of all parameters), allowed the model to better reflect personal linguistic variations through translation.

We further showed that the number of parameters specific to any person could be reduced to as low as 10 while still retaining better scores than a baseline for some language pairs, making it viable in a real world application with potentially millions of different users.

Acknowledgements

The authors give their thanks the anonymous reviewers for their useful feedback which helped make this paper what it is, as well as the members of Neulab who helped proof read this paper and provided constructive criticism. This work was supported by a Google Faculty Research Award 2016 on Machine Translation.

---

[6]available here: https://www.kaggle.com/ellarabi/
europarl-annotated-for-speaker-gender-and-age/
version/1

References

Boxing Chen, Colin Cherry, George Foster, and Samuel Larkin. 2017. Cost weighting for neural machine translation domain adaptation. In *Proceedings of the First Workshop on Neural Machine Translation*. Association for Computational Linguistics, Vancouver, pages 40–46. http://www.aclweb.org/anthology/W17-3205.

Chenhui Chu, Raj Dabre, and Sadao Kurohashi. 2017. An empirical comparison of domain adaptation methods for neural machine translation. In *Proceedings of the 55th Annual Meeting of the Association for Computational Linguistics (Volume 2: Short Papers)*. Association for Computational Linguistics, Vancouver, Canada, pages 385–391. http://aclweb.org/anthology/P17-2061.

Michael Denkowski and Graham Neubig. 2017. Stronger baselines for trustable results in neural machine translation. *arXiv preprint arXiv:1706.09733* .

Yarin Gal and Zoubin Ghahramani. 2016. A theoretically grounded application of dropout in recurrent neural networks. In *Advances in neural information processing systems*. pages 1019–1027.

Mohit Iyyer, Varun Manjunatha, Jordan Boyd-Graber, and Hal Daumé III. 2015. Deep unordered composition rivals syntactic methods for text classification. In *Proceedings of the 53rd Annual Meeting of the Association for Computational Linguistics and the 7th International Joint Conference on Natural Language Processing (Volume 1: Long Papers)*. Association for Computational Linguistics, Beijing, China, pages 1681–1691. http://www.aclweb.org/anthology/P15-1162.

Diederik P. Kingma and Jimmy Ba. 2014. Adam: A method for stochastic optimization. In *ICLR*.

Philipp Koehn. 2004. Statistical significance tests for machine translation evaluation. In Dekang Lin and Dekai Wu, editors, *Proceedings of EMNLP 2004*. Association for Computational Linguistics, Barcelona, Spain, pages 388–395.

Philipp Koehn, Hieu Hoang, Alexandra Birch, Chris Callison-Burch, Marcello Federico, Nicola Bertoldi, Brooke Cowan, Wade Shen, Christine Moran, Richard Zens, Chris Dyer, Ondřej Bojar, Alexandra Constantin, and Evan Herbst. 2007. Moses: Open source toolkit for statistical machine translation. In *Proceedings of the 45th Annual Meeting of the ACL on Interactive Poster and Demonstration Sessions*. Association for Computational Linguistics, Stroudsburg, PA, USA, ACL '07, pages 177–180. http://dl.acm.org/citation.cfm?id=1557769.1557821.

Mu Li, Yinggong Zhao, Dongdong Zhang, and Ming Zhou. 2010. Adaptive development data selection for log-linear model in statistical machine translation. In *Proceedings of the 23rd International Conference on Computational Linguistics (Coling 2010)*. Coling 2010 Organizing Committee, Beijing, China, pages 662–670. http://www.aclweb.org/anthology/C10-1075.

Xiaoqing Li, Jiajun Zhang, and Chengqing Zong. 2016. One sentence one model for neural machine translation. *arXiv preprint arXiv:1609.06490* .

Minh-Thang Luong and Christopher D Manning. 2015. Stanford neural machine translation systems for spoken language domains. In *Proceedings of the International Workshop on Spoken Language Translation*.

Antonio Valerio Miceli Barone, Barry Haddow, Ulrich Germann, and Rico Sennrich. 2017. Regularization techniques for fine-tuning in neural machine translation. In *Proceedings of the 2017 Conference on Empirical Methods in Natural Language Processing*. Association for Computational Linguistics, Copenhagen, Denmark, pages 1490–1495. https://www.aclweb.org/anthology/D17-1156.

Hideki Mima, Osamu Furuse, and Hitoshi Iida. 1997. Improving performance of transfer-driven machine translation with extra-linguistic informatioon from context, situation and environment. In *IJCAI (2)*. pages 983–989.

Shachar Mirkin, Scott Nowson, Caroline Brun, and Julien Perez. 2015. Motivating personality-aware machine translation. In *Proceedings of the 2015 Conference on Empirical Methods in Natural Language Processing*. Association for Computational Linguistics, Lisbon, Portugal, pages 1102–1108. http://aclweb.org/anthology/D15-1130.

Robert C. Moore and William Lewis. 2010. Intelligent selection of language model training data. In *Proceedings of the ACL 2010 Conference Short Papers*. Association for Computational Linguistics, Uppsala, Sweden, pages 220–224. http://www.aclweb.org/anthology/P10-2041.

Graham Neubig, Chris Dyer, Yoav Goldberg, Austin Matthews, Waleed Ammar, Antonios Anastasopoulos, Miguel Ballesteros, David Chiang, Daniel Clothiaux, Trevor Cohn, et al. 2017. Dynet: The dynamic neural network toolkit. *arXiv preprint arXiv:1701.03980* .

Ofir Press and Lior Wolf. 2017. Using the output embedding to improve language models. In *Proceedings of the 15th Conference of the European Chapter of the Association for Computational Linguistics: Volume 2, Short Papers*. Association for Computational Linguistics, Valencia, Spain, pages 157–163. http://www.aclweb.org/anthology/E17-2025.

Ella Rabinovich, Raj Nath Patel, Shachar Mirkin, Lucia Specia, and Shuly Wintner. 2017. Personalized machine translation: Preserving original author traits. In *Proceedings of the 15th Conference of the European Chapter of the Association for Computational Linguistics: Volume*

1, Long Papers. Association for Computational Linguistics, Valencia, Spain, pages 1074–1084. http://www.aclweb.org/anthology/E17-1101.

Rico Sennrich, Barry Haddow, and Alexandra Birch. 2016a. Controlling politeness in neural machine translation via side constraints. In *Proceedings of the 2016 Conference of the North American Chapter of the Association for Computational Linguistics: Human Language Technologies*. Association for Computational Linguistics, San Diego, California, pages 35–40. http://www.aclweb.org/anthology/N16-1005.

Rico Sennrich, Barry Haddow, and Alexandra Birch. 2016b. Neural machine translation of rare words with subword units. In *Proceedings of the 54th Annual Meeting of the Association for Computational Linguistics (Volume 1: Long Papers)*. Association for Computational Linguistics, Berlin, Germany, pages 1715–1725. http://www.aclweb.org/anthology/P16-1162.

Nitish Srivastava, Geoffrey E Hinton, Alex Krizhevsky, Ilya Sutskever, and Ruslan Salakhutdinov. 2014. Dropout: a simple way to prevent neural networks from overfitting. *Journal of machine learning research* 15(1):1929–1958.

Christian Szegedy, Vincent Vanhoucke, Sergey Ioffe, Jon Shlens, and Zbigniew Wojna. 2016. Rethinking the inception architecture for computer vision. In *Proceedings of the IEEE Conference on Computer Vision and Pattern Recognition*. pages 2818–2826.

Marco Turchi, Matteo Negri, M Amin Farajian, and Marcello Federico. 2017. Continuous learning from human post-edits for neural machine translation. *The Prague Bulletin of Mathematical Linguistics* 108(1):233–244.

Rui Wang, Masao Utiyama, Lemao Liu, Kehai Chen, and Eiichiro Sumita. 2017. Instance weighting for neural machine translation domain adaptation. In *Proceedings of the 2017 Conference on Empirical Methods in Natural Language Processing*. Association for Computational Linguistics, Copenhagen, Denmark, pages 1483–1489. https://www.aclweb.org/anthology/D17-1155.

Barret Zoph, Deniz Yuret, Jonathan May, and Kevin Knight. 2016. Transfer learning for low-resource neural machine translation. In *Proceedings of the 2016 Conference on Empirical Methods in Natural Language Processing*. Association for Computational Linguistics, Austin, Texas, pages 1568–1575. https://aclweb.org/anthology/D16-1163.

Multi-representation Ensembles and Delayed SGD Updates
Improve Syntax-based NMT

Danielle Saunders[†] and **Felix Stahlberg**[†] and **Adrià de Gispert**[‡†] and **Bill Byrne**[‡†]

[†]Department of Engineering, University of Cambridge, UK

[‡]SDL Research, Cambridge, UK

Abstract

We explore strategies for incorporating target syntax into Neural Machine Translation. We specifically focus on syntax in ensembles containing multiple sentence representations. We formulate beam search over such ensembles using WFSTs, and describe a delayed SGD update training procedure that is especially effective for long representations like linearized syntax. Our approach gives state-of-the-art performance on a difficult Japanese-English task.

1 Introduction

Ensembles of multiple NMT models consistently and significantly improve over single models (Garmash and Monz, 2016). Previous work has observed that NMT models trained to generate target syntax can exhibit improved sentence structure (Aharoni and Goldberg, 2017; Eriguchi et al., 2017) relative to those trained on plain-text, while plain-text models produce shorter sequences and so may encode lexical information more easily (Nadejde et al., 2017). We hypothesize that an NMT ensemble would be strengthened if its component models were complementary in this way.

However, ensembling often requires component models to make predictions relating to the same output sequence position at each time step. Models producing different sentence representations are necessarily synchronized to enable this. We propose an approach to decoding ensembles of models generating different representations, focusing on models generating syntax.

As part of our investigation we suggest strategies for practical NMT with very long target sequences. These long sequences may arise through the use of linearized constituency trees and can be much longer than their plain byte pair encoded (BPE) equivalent representations (Table 1). Long sequences make training more difficult (Bahdanau et al., 2015), which we address with an adjusted training procedure for the Transformer architecture (Vaswani et al., 2017), using delayed SGD updates which accumulate gradients over multiple batches. We also suggest a syntax representation which results in much shorter sequences.

1.1 Related Work

Nadejde et al. (2017) perform NMT with syntax annotation in the form of Combinatory Categorial Grammar (CCG) supertags. Aharoni and Goldberg (2017) translate from source BPE into target linearized parse trees,

Proceedings of the 56th Annual Meeting of the Association for Computational Linguistics (Short Papers), pages 319–325
Melbourne, Australia, July 15 - 20, 2018. ©2018 Association for Computational Linguistics

but omit POS tags to reduce sequence length. They demonstrate improved target language reordering when producing syntax. Eriguchi et al. (2017) combine recurrent neural network grammar (RNNG) models (Dyer et al., 2016) with attention-based models to produce well-formed dependency trees. Wu et al. (2017) similarly produce both words and arc-standard algorithm actions (Nivre, 2004).

Previous approaches to ensembling diverse models focus on model inputs. Hokamp (2017) shows improvements in the quality estimation task using ensembles of NMT models with multiple input representations which share an output representation. Garmash and Monz (2016) show translation improvements with multi-source-language NMT ensembles.

2 Ensembles of Syntax Models

We wish to ensemble using models which generate linearized constituency trees but these representations can be very long and difficult to model. We therefore propose a derivation-based representation which is much more compact than a linearized parse tree (examples in Table 1). Our linearized derivation representation ((4) in Table 1) consists of the derivation's right-hand side tokens with an end-of-rule marker, </R> , marking the last non-terminal in each rule. The original tree can be directly reproduced from the sequence, so that structure information is maintained. We map words to subwords as described in Section 3.

2.1 Delayed SGD Update Training for Long Sequences

We suggest a training strategy for the Transformer model (Vaswani et al., 2017) which gives improved performance for long sequences, like syntax representations, without requiring additional GPU memory. The Tensor2Tensor framework (Vaswani et al., 2018) defines batch size as the number of tokens per batch, so batches will contain fewer sequences if their average length increases. During NMT training, by default, the gradients used to update model parameters are calculated over individual batches. A possible consequence is that batches containing fewer sequences per update may have 'noisier' estimated gradients than batches with more sequences.

Previous research has used very large batches to improve training convergence while requiring fewer model updates (Smith et al., 2017; Neishi et al., 2017). However, with such large batches the model size may exceed available GPU memory. Training on multiple GPUs is one way to increase the amount of data used to estimate gradients, but it requires significant resources. Our strategy avoids this problem by using delayed SGD updates. We accumulate gradients over a fixed number of batches before using the accumulated gradients to update the model[1]. This lets us effectively use very large batch sizes without requiring multiple GPUs.

2.2 Ensembling Representations

Table 1 shows several different representations of the same hypothesis. To formulate an ensembling decoder over pairs of these representations, we assume we have a transducer T that maps from one representation to the other representation. The complexity of the transduction depends on the representations. Mapping from word to BPE representations is straightforward, and mapping from (linearized) syntax to plain-text simply deletes non-terminals. Let $\mathcal{P}$ be the paths in T leading from the start state to any final state. A path

---

[1] https://github.com/fstahlberg/tensor2tensor

Representation	Sample	Mean length
(1) Plain-text	No complications occurred	27.5
(2) Linearized tree	(ROOT (S (NP (DT No) (NNS complications)) (VP (VBD occurred))))	120.0
(3) Derivation	ROOT→S ; S→NP VP ; NP→DT NNS ; DT→No ; NNS→complications ; VP→VBD ; VBD→occurred	-
(4) Linearized derivation	S</R> NP VP</R> DT NNS</R> No complications VBD</R> occurred	73.8
(5) POS/plain-text	DT No NNS complications VBD occurred	53.3

Table 1: Examples for proposed representations. Lengths are for the first 1M WAT English training sentences with BPE subwords (Sennrich et al., 2016).

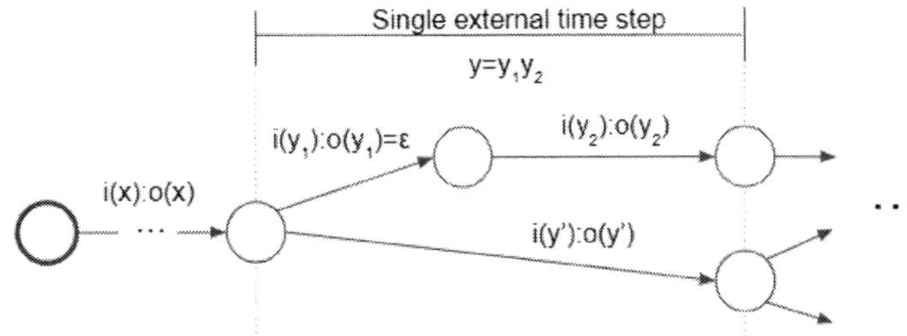

Figure 1: Transducer mapping internal to external representations. A partial hypothesis might be $o(xy_2)$ in the external representation and $i(xy_1y_2)$ in the internal representation.

$p \in \mathcal{P}$ maps an *internal representation* $i(p)$ to an *external representation* $o(p)$.

The ensembling decoder produces external representations. Two NMT systems are trained, one for each representation, giving models P_i and P_o. An ideal equal-weight ensembling of P_i and P_o yields

$$p^* = \underset{p \in \mathcal{P}}{\mathrm{argmax}}\ P_i(i(p))\, P_o(o(p)) \qquad (1)$$

with $o(p^*)$ as the external representation of the translation.

In practice, beam decoding is performed in the external representation, i.e. over projections of paths in $\mathcal{P}$ [2]. Let $h = h_1 \dots h_j$ be a partial hypothesis in the output representation. The set of partial paths yielding h are:

$$M(h) = \qquad (2)$$
$$\{(x,y)|xyz \in \mathcal{P}, o(x) = h_{<j}, o(xy) = h\}$$

Here z is the path suffix. The ensembled score of h is then:

$$P(h_j|h_{<j}) = P_o(h_j|h_{<j}) \times \qquad (3)$$
$$\max_{(x,y) \in M(h)} P_i(i(y)|i(x))$$

The max performed for each partial hypothesis h is itself approximated by a beam search. This leads to an outer beam search over external representations with inner beam searches for the best matching internal representations. As search proceeds, each model score is updated separately with its appropriate representation. Symbols in the internal representation are consumed as needed to stay synchronized with the external representation, as illustrated in Figure 1; epsilons are consumed with a probability of 1.

---

[2] See the `tokenization` wrappers in `https://github.com/ucam-smt/sgnmt`

Reference	low - energy electron microscope (LEEM) and photoelectron microscope (PEEM) were attracted attention as new surface electron microscope .
Plain BPE	low energy electron microscope (LEEM) and photoelectron microscope (PEEM) are noticed as new surface electron microscope .
Linearized derivation	low-energy electron microscopy (LEEM) and photoelectron microscopy (PEEM) are attracting attention as new surface electron microscopes .

Table 2: Sample generated translations from individual models

3 Experiments

We first explore the effect of our delayed SGD update training scheme on single models, contrasting updates every batch with accumulated updates every 8 batches. To compare target representations we train Transformer models with target representations (1), (2), (4) and (5) shown in Table 1, using delayed SGD updates every 8 batches. We decode with individual models and two-model ensembles, comparing results for single-representation and multi-representation ensembles. Each multi-representation ensemble consists of the plain BPE model and one other individual model.

All Transformer architectures are Tensor2Tensor's base Transformer model (Vaswani et al., 2018) with a batch size of 4096. In all cases we decode using SGNMT (Stahlberg et al., 2017) with beam size 4, using the average of the final 20 checkpoints. For comparison with earlier target syntax work, we also train two RNN attention-based seq2seq models (Bahdanau et al., 2015) with normal SGD to produce plain BPE sequences and linearized derivations. For these models we use embedding size 400, a single BiLSTM layer of size 750, and batch size 80.

We report all experiments for Japanese-English, using the first 1M training sentences of the Japanese-English ASPEC data (Nakazawa et al., 2016). All models use plain BPE Japanese source sentences. English constituency trees are obtained using CKYlark (Oda et al., 2015), with words replaced by BPE subwords. We train separate Japanese (lowercased) and English (cased) BPE vocabularies on the plain-text, with 30K merges each. Non-terminals are included as separate tokens. The linearized derivation uses additional tokens for non-terminals with </R> .

3.1 Results and Discussion

Our first results in Table 3 show that large batch training can significantly improve the performance of single Transformers, particularly when trained to produce longer sequences. Accumulating the gradient over 8 batches of size 4096 gives a 3 BLEU improvement for the linear derivation model. It has been suggested that decaying the learning rate can have a similar effect to large batch training (Smith et al., 2017), but reducing the initial learning rate by a factor of 8 alone did not give the same improvements.

Representation	Batches / update	Learning rate	Test BLEU
Plain BPE	1	0.025	27.5
	1	0.2	27.2
	8	0.2	28.9
Linearized derivation	1	0.025	25.6
	1	0.2	25.6
	8	0.2	28.7

Table 3: Single Transformers trained to convergence on 1M WAT Ja-En, batch size 4096

Our plain BPE baseline (Table 4) outperforms the current best system on WAT Ja-En, an 8-model ensemble (Morishita et al., 2017). Our syntax models achieve similar results despite producing much longer sequences. Table

Architecture	Representation	Dev BLEU	Test BLEU
Seq2seq (8-model ensemble)	Best WAT17 result (Morishita et al., 2017)	-	28.4
Seq2seq	Plain BPE	21.6	21.2
	Linearized derivation	21.9	21.2
Transformer	Plain BPE	28.0	28.9
	Linearized tree	28.2	28.4
	Linearized derivation	28.5	28.7
	POS/BPE	28.5	29.1

Table 4: Single models on Ja-En. Previous evaluation result included for comparison.

External representation	Internal representation	Test BLEU
Plain BPE	Plain BPE	29.2
Linearized derivation	Linearized derivation	28.8
Linearized tree	Plain BPE	28.9
Plain BPE	Linearized derivation	28.8
Linearized derivation	Plain BPE	29.4†
POS/BPE	Plain BPE	29.3†
Plain BPE	POS/BPE	29.4†

Table 5: Ja-En Transformer ensembles: † marks significant improvement on plain BPE baseline shown in Table 4 ($p < 0.05$ using bootstrap resampling (Koehn et al., 2007)).

3 indicates that large batch training is instrumental in this.

We find that RNN-based syntax models can equal plain BPE models as in Aharoni and Goldberg (2017); Eriguchi et al. (2017) use syntax for a 1 BLEU improvement on this dataset, but over a much lower baseline. Our plain BPE Transformer outperforms all syntax models except POS/BPE. More compact syntax representations perform better, with POS/BPE outperforming linearized derivations, which outperform linearized trees.

Ensembles of two identical models trained with different seeds only slightly improve over the single model (Table 5). However, an ensemble of models producing plain BPE and linearized derivations improves by 0.5 BLEU over the plain BPE baseline.

By ensembling syntax and plain-text we hope to benefit from their complementary strengths. To highlight these, we examine hypotheses generated by the plain BPE and linearized derivation models. We find that the syntax model is often more grammatical, even when the plain BPE model may share more vocabulary with the reference (Table 2).

In ensembling plain-text with a syntax external representation we observed that in a small proportion of cases non-terminals were over-generated, due to the mismatch in target sequence lengths. Our solution was to penalise scores of non-terminals under the syntax model by a constant factor.

It is also possible to constrain decoding of linearized trees and derivations to well-formed outputs. However, we found that this gives little improvement in BLEU over unconstrained decoding although it remains an interesting line of research.

4 Conclusions

We report strong performance with individual models that meets or improves over the recent best WAT Ja-En ensemble results. We train these models using a delayed SGD update training procedure that is especially effective for the long representations that arise from including target language syntactic information in the output. We further improve on the individual results via a decoding strategy allowing ensembling of models producing different output representations, such as subword units and syntax. We propose these techniques as practical approaches to including target syntax in NMT.

Acknowledgments

This work was supported by EPSRC grant EP/L027623/1.

References

Roee Aharoni and Yoav Goldberg. 2017. Towards string-to-tree neural machine translation. In *Proceedings of the 55th Annual Meeting of the Association for Computational Linguistics (Volume 2: Short Papers)*, volume 2, pages 132–140.

Dzmitry Bahdanau, Kyunghyun Cho, and Yoshua Bengio. 2015. Neural machine translation by jointly learning to align and translate. In *ICLR*.

Chris Dyer, Adhiguna Kuncoro, Miguel Ballesteros, and Noah A Smith. 2016. Recurrent neural network grammars. In *Proceedings of NAACL-HLT*, pages 199–209.

Akiko Eriguchi, Yoshimasa Tsuruoka, and Kyunghyun Cho. 2017. Learning to parse and translate improves neural machine translation. In *Proceedings of the 55th Annual Meeting of the Association for Computational Linguistics (Volume 2: Short Papers)*, volume 2, pages 72–78.

Ekaterina Garmash and Christof Monz. 2016. Ensemble learning for multi-source neural machine translation. In *Proceedings of COLING 2016, the 26th International Conference on Computational Linguistics: Technical Papers*, pages 1409–1418.

Chris Hokamp. 2017. Ensembling factored neural machine translation models for automatic post-editing and quality estimation. In *Proceedings of the Second Conference on Machine Translation*, pages 647–654.

Philipp Koehn, Hieu Hoang, Alexandra Birch, Chris Callison-Burch, Marcello Federico, Nicola Bertoldi, Brooke Cowan, Wade Shen, Christine Moran, Richard Zens, et al. 2007. Moses: Open source toolkit for statistical machine translation. In *Proceedings of the 45th annual meeting of the ACL on interactive poster and demonstration sessions*, pages 177–180. Association for Computational Linguistics.

Makoto Morishita, Jun Suzuki, and Masaaki Nagata. 2017. NTT neural machine translation systems at WAT 2017. In *Proceedings of the 4th Workshop on Asian Translation (WAT2017)*, pages 89–94.

Maria Nadejde, Siva Reddy, Rico Sennrich, Tomasz Dwojak, Marcin Junczys-Dowmunt, Philipp Koehn, and Alexandra Birch. 2017. Predicting target language CCG supertags improves neural machine translation. In *Proceedings of the Second Conference on Machine Translation*, pages 68–79.

Toshiaki Nakazawa, Manabu Yaguchi, Kiyotaka Uchimoto, Masao Utiyama, Eiichiro Sumita, Sadao Kurohashi, and Hitoshi Isahara. 2016. ASPEC: Asian scientific paper excerpt corpus. In *Proceedings of the Ninth International Conference on Language Resources and Evaluation (LREC)*, pages 2204–2208. European Language Resources Association (ELRA).

Masato Neishi, Jin Sakuma, Satoshi Tohda, Shonosuke Ishiwatari, Naoki Yoshinaga, and Masashi Toyoda. 2017. A bag of useful tricks for practical neural machine translation: Embedding layer initialization and large batch size. In *Proceedings of the 4th Workshop on Asian Translation (WAT2017)*, pages 99–109.

Joakim Nivre. 2004. Incrementality in deterministic dependency parsing. In *Proceedings of the Workshop on Incremental Parsing: Bringing Engineering and Cognition Together*, pages 50–57. Association for Computational Linguistics.

Yusuke Oda, Graham Neubig, Sakriani Sakti, Tomoki Toda, and Satoshi Nakamura. 2015. Ckylark: A more robust PCFG-LA parser. In *Proceedings of the 2015 Conference of the North American Chapter of the Association for Computational Linguistics: Demonstrations*, pages 41–45.

Rico Sennrich, Barry Haddow, and Alexandra Birch. 2016. Neural machine translation of rare words with subword units. In *Proceedings of the 54th Annual Meeting of the Association for Computational Linguistics (Volume 1: Long Papers)*, volume 1, pages 1715–1725.

Samuel L Smith, Pieter-Jan Kindermans, and Quoc V Le. 2017. Don't decay the learning rate, increase the batch size. *arXiv preprint arXiv:1711.00489*.

Felix Stahlberg, Eva Hasler, Danielle Saunders, and Bill Byrne. 2017. SGNMT–a flexible NMT decoding platform for quick prototyping of new models and search strategies. In *Proceedings of the 2017 Conference on Empirical Methods in Natural Language Processing: System Demonstrations*, pages 25–30.

Ashish Vaswani, Samy Bengio, Eugene Brevdo, Francois Chollet, Aidan N. Gomez, Stephan Gouws, Llion Jones, Łukasz Kaiser, Nal Kalchbrenner, Niki Parmar, Ryan Sepassi, Noam Shazeer, and Jakob Uszkoreit. 2018. Tensor2tensor for neural machine translation. *CoRR*, abs/1803.07416.

Ashish Vaswani, Noam Shazeer, Niki Parmar, Jakob Uszkoreit, Llion Jones, Aidan N Gomez, Łukasz Kaiser, and Illia Polosukhin. 2017. Attention is all you need. In *Advances in Neural Information Processing Systems*, pages 6000–6010.

Shuangzhi Wu, Dongdong Zhang, Nan Yang, Mu Li, and Ming Zhou. 2017. Sequence-to-dependency neural machine translation. In *Proceedings of the 55th Annual Meeting of the Association for Computational Linguistics (Volume 1: Long Papers)*, volume 1, pages 698–707.

Learning from Chunk-based Feedback in Neural Machine Translation

Pavel Petrushkov and **Shahram Khadivi** and **Evgeny Matusov**
eBay Inc.
Kasernenstr. 25
52064 Aachen, Germany
{ppetrushkov, skhadivi, ematusov}@ebay.com

Abstract

We empirically investigate learning from partial feedback in neural machine translation (NMT), when partial feedback is collected by asking users to highlight a correct chunk of a translation. We propose a simple and effective way of utilizing such feedback in NMT training. We demonstrate how the common machine translation problem of domain mismatch between training and deployment can be reduced solely based on chunk-level user feedback. We conduct a series of simulation experiments to test the effectiveness of the proposed method. Our results show that chunk-level feedback outperforms sentence based feedback by up to 2.61% BLEU absolute.

1 Introduction

In recent years, machine translation (MT) quality improved rapidly, especially because of advances in neural machine translation (NMT). Most of remaining MT errors arguably come from domain, style, or terminology mismatch between the data on which the MT was trained on and data which it has to translate. It is hard to alleviate this mismatch since usually only limited amounts of relevant training data are available. Yet MT systems deployed on-line in e.g. e-commerce websites or social networks can benefit from user feedback for overcoming this mismatch. Whereas MT users are usually not bilingual, they likely have a good command of the target language and are able to spot severe MT errors in a given translated sentence, sometimes with the help of e.g. an accompanying image, video, or simply prior knowledge.

A common approach to get user feedback for MT is explicit ratings of translations on an n-point Likert scale. The main problem of such methods is that users are not qualified enough to provide reliable feedback for the whole sentence. Since different users do not adhere to a single set of guidelines, their ratings may be influenced by various factors, such as user expectations, user knowledge, or user satisfaction with the platform. In (Kreutzer et al., 2018), the authors investigate the reliability and validity of real user ratings by re-evaluating five-star ratings by three independent human annotators, however the inter-annotator agreement between experts was relatively low and no correlation to the averaged user rating was found.

Instead of providing a rating, a user might be asked to correct the generated translation, in a process called post-editing. Using corrected sentences for training an NMT system brings larger improvements, but this method requires significant effort and expertise from the user.

Alternatively, feedback can be collected by asking users to mark correct parts (chunks) of the translation (Marie and Max, 2015). It can be seen as the middle ground between quick sentence level rating and more expensive post-editing. We hypothesize that collecting feedback in this form implicitly forces guidelines on the user, making it less susceptible to various user-dependent factors. We expect marking of correct chunks in a translation to be simple enough for non-experts to do quickly and precisely and also be more intuitive than providing a numerical rating.

In this paper, we investigate the empirical hypothesis that NMT is able to learn from the good chunks of a noisy sentence and describe a simple way of utilizing such chunk-level feedback in NMT training. To the best of our knowledge, no dataset with human feedback recorded in this form is available, therefore we experiment with user feedback that was artificially created from parallel data.

Proceedings of the 56th Annual Meeting of the Association for Computational Linguistics (Short Papers), pages 326–331
Melbourne, Australia, July 15 - 20, 2018. ©2018 Association for Computational Linguistics

The rest of this paper is structured as follows. In Section 2 we review related work. We describe our partial feedback approach in Section 3. Next we present our experimental results in Section 4, followed by the conclusion in Section 5.

2 Related work

Integrating user ratings in NMT has been studied in (Kreutzer et al., 2017), who view this as a bandit structured prediction task. They demonstrate how the user feedback can be integrated into NMT training and perform a series of experiments using GLEU (Wu et al., 2016) to simulate user feedback. Nguyen et al. (2017) have also studied this problem and adapted an actor-critic approach (Mnih et al., 2016) which has shown to be robust to skewed, high variance feedback from real users.

(Lam et al., 2018) extended the work of (Nguyen et al., 2017) by asking users to provide feedback for partial hypotheses to iteratively generate the translation, their goal is to minimize the required human involvement. They performed simulated experiments using chrF (Popovic, 2015) as simulated feedback.

In all previous works feedback needs to be generated on-line during the training process, however in this paper we focus on the case where there might be a significant time lag between generation of translation and acquiring of the feedback. Lawrence et al. (2017) have proposed a method to leverage user feedback that is available only for logged translated data for a phrase-based statistical machine translation system.

(Kreutzer et al., 2018) have experimented with sentence level star ratings collected from real users of an e-commerce site for logged translation data, but found the feedback to be too noisy to gain improvements. They also proposed using implicit word level task feedback based on query matching in an e-commerce application to improve both translation quality and task specific metrics.

Marie and Max (2015) have proposed an interactive framework which iteratively improves translation generated by the phrase-based system by asking users to select correct parts. Domingo et al. (2016) extended this idea to also include word deletions and substitutions with the goal of reducing human effort in translation.

Grangier and Auli (2017) have studied the task of paraphrasing an already generated translation by excluding words that the user has marked as incorrect. They modify NMT model to also accept the marked target sentence as input and train it to produce similar sentences that do not contain marked words.

(Chen et al., 2017; Wang et al., 2017) have proposed sentence level weighting method for domain adaptation in NMT.

3 Method

In this work we use the encoder-decoder NMT architecture with attention, proposed by (Bahdanau et al., 2014; Sutskever et al., 2014). NMT model is trained to maximize the conditional likelihood of a target sentence $e_1^I : e_1, \ldots, e_I$ given a source sentence $f_1^J : f_1, \ldots, f_J$ from a parallel dataset D:

$$\mathcal{L} = \sum_{f_1^J, e_1^I \in D} \sum_{i=1}^{I} \log p(e_i | e_1^{i-1}, f_1^J). \quad (1)$$

Training objective (1) is appropriate when the target sentence e_1^I comes from real data. However, we would like to benefit from model-generated sentences $\tilde{e}_1^I$ by introducing partial feedback.

We assume that partial feedback for a sentence $\tilde{e}_1^I$ is given as a sequence of binary values $w_1^I : w_1, \ldots, w_I$, such that $w_i = 1$ if the word $\tilde{e}_i$ is marked as correct, $w_i = 0$ if it is unrated or incorrect. We propose a simple modification to the loss in Equation (1):

$$\mathcal{L}_{PF} = \sum_{f_1^J, \tilde{e}_1^I, w_1^I \in D} \sum_{i=1}^{I} w_i \log p(\tilde{e}_i | \tilde{e}_1^{i-1}, f_1^J) \quad (2)$$

Considering the definition of the binary partial feedback, the model would be trained to predict correct target words, while ignoring unrated and incorrect ones. However, incorrect words are still used as inputs to the model and influence the prediction context of correct words.

While partial feedback is gathered in a binary form (selected/not selected), word weights w_i can take any real value, depending on the weight assignment scheme.

Our training objective can be seen as a generalization of sentence level weighting method (Chen et al., 2017; Wang et al., 2017). The special case of sentence level weight can be expressed as $w_i = w, \forall i$, where w is the weight for sentence $\tilde{e}_1^I$.

We differentiate between two practical methods of obtaining the partial feedback data. First, gathering the feedback from humans, by presenting them with translations and asking to highlight correct words. This method is expected to produce high quality feedback, but is relatively expensive and, to the best of our knowledge, no such dataset is publicly available.

Another method is to generate partial feedback automatically using heuristics or statistical models. This type of feedback would be cheap to obtain, but is unlikely to be of high quality.

In this paper, to show the effectiveness of high quality chunk feedback, we generate artificial feedback by comparing model predictions to reference translations using heuristic methods. This approach is cheap, produces high quality feedback, but is not practically useful, because it requires access to reference human translation.

We have experimented with several methods of extracting artificial feedback. A simple matching method assigns $w_i = 1$ if predicted word $\tilde{e}_i$ is present in reference translation at any position, and $w_i = 0$ otherwise. A slightly more sophisticated method is to find the longest common substring (LCS) between the predicted and reference translations and set the weights for words which belong to the LCS to 1, and to 0 otherwise. In our experiments we have found the latter method to perform slightly better.

4 Experiments

In this section, we conduct a series of experiments to study how well an NMT system is able to learn only from partial user feedback when this feedback is given for in-domain translations, whereas the baseline system is trained on out-of-domain data.

4.1 Datasets

We report results on two datasets: WMT 2017 German to English news translation task (Bojar et al., 2017) and an in-house English to Spanish dataset in the e-commerce domain. On all data we apply byte-pair encoding (Sennrich et al., 2016) with 40,000 merge operations learned separately for each language.

For each dataset we separate the larger out-of-domain and smaller in-domain training data. For De-En we use 1.8M sentence pairs randomly sampled from available parallel corpora as out-of-domain data and 800K sentence pairs sampled from back-translated monolingual and unused parallel corpora as in-domain data. For En-Es we have 2.7M out-of-domain and 1.5M in-domain sentence pairs. We evaluate our models on *newstest2016* (2999 sentence pairs) for the De-En task and an in-house test set of 1000 sentence pairs for the En-Es task using case-insensitive BLEU (Papineni et al., 2002) and TER (Snover et al., 2006).

We have implemented our NMT model using TensorFlow (Abadi et al., 2015) library. Our encoder is a bidirectional LSTM with a layer size of 512; our decoder is an LSTM with 2 layers of the same size. We also use embedding size of 512 and MLP attention layer. We train our networks using SGD with a learning rate schedule that starts gradually decaying to 0.01 after the initial 4 epochs. As regularization we use dropout on the RNN inputs with dropping probability of 0.2.

4.2 Results

We pre-train baseline NMT models on parallel out-of-domain data for 15 epochs. We then use the pre-trained model to generate translations from the source side of parallel in-domain corpus. Using heuristics described in Section 3 and the reference target side of the in-domain corpus we generate artificial partial feedback to simulate real user input. Then we continue training with a small learning rate for another 10 epochs on in-domain data with or without user feedback.

In Table 1, we show the effect of different types of feedback on translation performance. First, we see that even using no feedback slightly improves the model due to self-training on automatically translated in-domain data.

Introducing sentence level feedback improves De-En and En-Es models by at most 0.2% and 0.6% absolute BLEU, respectively. Sentence level feedback is artificially generated from parallel corpora using heuristics, similar to the ones described in Section 3, but $w_i, \forall i$ are set to the same sentence weight w. For example, we have tried using sentence BLEU (sBLEU) and a binary rule, which outputs 1 if more than 33% of predicted words were marked as correct, and 0 otherwise (binary). We have also experimented with other heuristics, but did not achieve better results.

Finally, chunk-based feedback approach based on LCS improves on top of sentence level feedback by another 0.7% and 2.6% BLEU for De-

	De-En		En-Es	
	BLEU [%]	TER [%]	BLEU [%]	TER [%]
Baseline	30.6	49.6	32.7	52.6
+self-training	31.4	48.1	35.6	49.1
+sent-sBLEU	31.4	48.1	36.0	48.4
+sent-binary	31.6	47.8	36.2	47.6
+chunk-match	32.2	47.0	37.9	45.4
+chunk-lcs	**32.3**	**46.5**	**38.8**	**44.5**

Table 1: Chunk-level feedback compared to sentence-level feedback. *Self-training* is equivalent to having no feedback or setting all $w_i = 1, \forall i$ in the training objective in Eq. (2). *sent-sBLEU* and *sent-binary* are sentence-level methods with sentence BLEU and binary weighting rules, defined as in Section 4.2. *chunk-match* and *chunk-lcs*-level feedback refers to assigning w_i using simple matching or LCS method described in Section 3.

En and En-Es, respectively. We also note a significant improvement of 1.3% and 3.1% in TER. Chunk-based approach based on simple matching also outperforms sentence level methods, but not by as much as lcs-based, which suggests that this method benefits more from consecutive segments, rather than single correct words.

We believe that the success of the partial feedback approach can be explained by the fact that often a sentence can be split into chunks which can be translated independently of the context. Reinforcement of the correct translation of such a chunk in one training example seems to positively affect translations of such chunks in other, different sentences. By focusing on the good and masking out erroneous chunks, partial feedback acts as a precise noise reduction method.

We have also trained the models using fine-tuning (Luong and Manning, 2015) on the reference target in-domain data, which further improved translation by 2% and 3.8% BLEU on De-En and En-Es compared to using chunk-based feedback. We note that by using partial feedback we are able to recover between 30% and 45% of improvements that come from in-domain adaptation.

4.3 Robustness

The proposed artificially generated partial feedback is very precise as it does not introduce any

#		De-En		En-Es	
		BLEU [%]	TER [%]	BLEU [%]	TER [%]
1	Chunk-level feedback	32.3	46.5	38.8	44.5
	Under selection ratio:				
2	25%	32.2	47.0	38.9	45.0
3	50%	31.9	47.4	38.1	45.6
4	75%	31.4	47.9	36.7	46.7
	Incorrect selection ratio:				
5	10%	32.0	47.2	38.1	44.9
6	25%	31.5	47.9	37.2	46.9
7	50%	30.9	48.8	35.6	50.0
8	#2 + #5	31.6	47.7	38.1	45.5

Table 2: Impact of user errors on the translation performance. *Under selection ratio%* indicates on average what percentage of words in a correct chunk have not been selected in user simulation, but all selected words are correct. *Incorrect selection ratio%* indicates what percentage of words are incorrectly selected, here the total number of marked words is the same as in chunk-level feedback. In the last row, 10% of marked words are actually incorrect and the total number of marked words is 25% less compared to system in row 1.

type of noise in marking of good chunks. For example, on the En-Es dataset artificial methods mark 40% of all words as correct. However, a user might not mark all the correct words in a sentence, but select only a few.

Furthermore, artificially generated partial feedback does not contain noise, given that the reference translation is adequate. However, users may make mistakes in selection. We differentiate two types of errors that a user can make: under selection, when a correct word was not marked; and incorrect selection, when an incorrect word was marked as correct.

To anticipate the impact of these mistakes we experiment with deliberately impairing the feedback in Table 2. We see that randomly dropping 25% of the selection has very little effect on the model, while dropping 50% and more decreases the translation performance significantly, yet still performing at the same level or better than self-training system.

When selection contains noise, the impact already becomes noticeable at 10%. Increasing the amount of noise up to 25% decreases the performance by 1.6% BLEU in En-Es task. At 50% noise level, which is similar to random selection, there is no improvement from using feedback at all. While we expect users to provide mostly clean feedback, this result indicates the necessity of cleaning user feedback data, e.g. by aggregating feedback from multiple users.

We have also experimented with replacing unselected words by random noise and saw only small decrease in translation performance, which suggests that our approach is able to benefit from very poor translations, as long as the selected chunk is correct.

4.4 Example

An example where the NMT system with chunk-based feedback yields a better translation in comparison to other systems is the German sentence "Die Krise ist vorüber." ("The crisis is over."). The German word "vorüber" is rare and ambiguous, especially after the BPE-based splitting. The system with self-training translates the sentence as "The crisis is above all.", whereas the system with chunk-based feedback exactly matches the reference translation. We have analyzed the feedback training set: in that data, out of nine occurrences of the word "vorüber" with the reference translation "over", the baseline system got it right three times, getting rewards for the chunks "is over ...", "is over", "is over ."

5 Conclusion and future work

In this work, we have proposed a simple way to integrate partial chunk-based feedback into NMT training. We have experimented with artificially created partial feedback and shown that using partial feedback results in significant improvements of MT quality in terms of BLEU and TER. We have shown that chunk-level feedback can be used more effectively than sentence-level feedback. We have studied the robustness of our approach and observed that our model is robust against a moderate amount of noise.

We argue that collecting partial feedback by asking users to highlight correct parts of a translation is more intuitive for users than sentence level ratings and leads to less variation and errors.

In the future, we plan to investigate how to integrate negative partial user feedback, as well as automatic feedback generation methods which do not rely on existing parallel data.

References

Martín Abadi, Ashish Agarwal, Paul Barham, Eugene Brevdo, Zhifeng Chen, Craig Citro, Greg S. Corrado, Andy Davis, Jeffrey Dean, Matthieu Devin, Sanjay Ghemawat, Ian Goodfellow, Andrew Harp, Geoffrey Irving, Michael Isard, Yangqing Jia, Rafal Jozefowicz, Lukasz Kaiser, Manjunath Kudlur, Josh Levenberg, Dan Mané, Rajat Monga, Sherry Moore, Derek Murray, Chris Olah, Mike Schuster, Jonathon Shlens, Benoit Steiner, Ilya Sutskever, Kunal Talwar, Paul Tucker, Vincent Vanhoucke, Vijay Vasudevan, Fernanda Viégas, Oriol Vinyals, Pete Warden, Martin Wattenberg, Martin Wicke, Yuan Yu, and Xiaoqiang Zheng. 2015. TensorFlow: Large-scale machine learning on heterogeneous systems. Software available from tensorflow.org.

Dzmitry Bahdanau, Kyunghyun Cho, and Yoshua Bengio. 2014. Neural machine translation by jointly learning to align and translate. *CoRR*, abs/1409.0473.

Ondřej Bojar, Rajen Chatterjee, Christian Federmann, Yvette Graham, Barry Haddow, Shujian Huang, Matthias Huck, Philipp Koehn, Qun Liu, Varvara Logacheva, Christof Monz, Matteo Negri, Matt Post, Raphael Rubino, Lucia Specia, and Marco Turchi. 2017. Findings of the 2017 conference on machine translation (wmt17). In *Proceedings of the Second Conference on Machine Translation, Volume 2: Shared Task Papers*, pages 169–214, Copenhagen, Denmark. Association for Computational Linguistics.

Boxing Chen, Colin Cherry, George Foster, and Samuel Larkin. 2017. Cost weighting for neural machine translation domain adaptation. In *Proceedings of the First Workshop on Neural Machine Translation*, pages 40–46. Association for Computational Linguistics.

Miguel Domingo, Alvaro Peris, and Francisco Casacuberta. 2016. Interactive-predictive translation based on multiple word-segments. In *Proceedings of the 19th Annual Conference of the European Association for Machine Translation*, pages 282–291.

David Grangier and Michael Auli. 2017. Quickedit: Editing text & translations via simple delete actions. *CoRR*, abs/1711.04805.

Julia Kreutzer, Shahram Khadivi, Evgeny Matusov, and Stefan Riezler. 2018. Can neural machine translation be improved with user feedback? *CoRR*, abs/1804.05958.

Julia Kreutzer, Artem Sokolov, and Stefan Riezler. 2017. Bandit structured prediction for neural sequence-to-sequence learning. In *Proceedings of the 55th Annual Meeting of the Association for Computational Linguistics, ACL 2017, Vancouver, Canada, July 30 - August 4, Volume 1: Long Papers*, pages 1503–1513.

Tsz Kin Lam, Julia Kreutzer, and Stefan Riezler. 2018. A Reinforcement Learning Approach to Interactive-Predictive Neural Machine Translation. ArXiv:1805.01553v1.

Carolin Lawrence, Artem Sokolov, and Stefan Riezler. 2017. Counterfactual learning from bandit feedback under deterministic logging : A case study in statistical machine translation. In *Proceedings of the 2017 Conference on Empirical Methods in Natural Language Processing, EMNLP 2017, Copenhagen, Denmark, September 9-11, 2017*, pages 2566–2576.

Minh-Thang Luong and Christopher D. Manning. 2015. Stanford neural machine translation systems for spoken language domains. In *Proceedings of the International Workshop on Spoken Language Translation : December 3-4, 2015, Da Nang, Vietnam / Edited by Marcello Federico, Sebastian Stker, Jan Niehues*.

Benjamin Marie and Aurélien Max. 2015. Touch-based pre-post-editing of machine translation output. In *Proceedings of the 2015 Conference on Empirical Methods in Natural Language Processing*, pages 1040–1045, Lisbon, Portugal. Association for Computational Linguistics.

Volodymyr Mnih, Adria Puigdomenech Badia, Mehdi Mirza, Alex Graves, Timothy Lillicrap, Tim Harley, David Silver, and Koray Kavukcuoglu. 2016. Asynchronous methods for deep reinforcement learning. In *Proceedings of The 33rd International Conference on Machine Learning*, volume 48 of *Proceedings of Machine Learning Research*, pages 1928–1937, New York, New York, USA. PMLR.

Khanh Nguyen, Hal Daumé III, and Jordan L. Boyd-Graber. 2017. Reinforcement learning for bandit neural machine translation with simulated human feedback. In *Proceedings of the 2017 Conference on Empirical Methods in Natural Language Processing, EMNLP 2017, Copenhagen, Denmark, September 9-11, 2017*, pages 1464–1474.

Kishore Papineni, Salim Roukos, Todd Ward, and Wei-Jing Zhu. 2002. Bleu: A method for automatic evaluation of machine translation. In *Proceedings of the 40th Annual Meeting on Association for Computational Linguistics*, ACL '02, pages 311–318, Stroudsburg, PA, USA. Association for Computational Linguistics.

Maja Popovic. 2015. chrf: character n-gram f-score for automatic MT evaluation. In *Proceedings of the Tenth Workshop on Statistical Machine Translation, WMT@EMNLP 2015, 17-18 September 2015, Lisbon, Portugal*, pages 392–395. The Association for Computer Linguistics.

Rico Sennrich, Barry Haddow, and Alexandra Birch. 2016. Neural machine translation of rare words with subword units. In *Proceedings of the 54th Annual Meeting of the Association for Computational Linguistics, ACL 2016, August 7-12, 2016, Berlin, Germany, Volume 1: Long Papers*.

Matthew Snover, Bonnie Dorr, Richard Schwartz, Linnea Micciulla, and John Makhoul. 2006. A study of translation edit rate with targeted human annotation. In *In Proceedings of Association for Machine Translation in the Americas*, pages 223–231.

Ilya Sutskever, Oriol Vinyals, and Quoc V. Le. 2014. Sequence to sequence learning with neural networks. In *Proceedings of the 27th International Conference on Neural Information Processing Systems - Volume 2*, NIPS'14, pages 3104–3112, Cambridge, MA, USA. MIT Press.

Rui Wang, Masao Utiyama, Lemao Liu, Kehai Chen, and Eiichiro Sumita. 2017. Instance weighting for neural machine translation domain adaptation. In *Proceedings of the 2017 Conference on Empirical Methods in Natural Language Processing*, pages 1482–1488. Association for Computational Linguistics.

Yonghui Wu, Mike Schuster, Zhifeng Chen, Quoc V. Le, Mohammad Norouzi, Wolfgang Macherey, Maxim Krikun, Yuan Cao, Qin Gao, Klaus Macherey, Jeff Klingner, Apurva Shah, Melvin Johnson, Xiaobing Liu, ukasz Kaiser, Stephan Gouws, Yoshikiyo Kato, Taku Kudo, Hideto Kazawa, Keith Stevens, George Kurian, Nishant Patil, Wei Wang, Cliff Young, Jason Smith, Jason Riesa, Alex Rudnick, Oriol Vinyals, Greg Corrado, Macduff Hughes, and Jeffrey Dean. 2016. Google's neural machine translation system: Bridging the gap between human and machine translation. *CoRR*, abs/1609.08144.

Bag-of-Words as Target for Neural Machine Translation

Shuming Ma[1], Xu Sun[1,2], Yizhong Wang[1], Junyang Lin[3]
[1]MOE Key Lab of Computational Linguistics, School of EECS, Peking University
[2]Deep Learning Lab, Beijing Institute of Big Data Research, Peking University
[3]School of Foreign Languages, Peking University
{shumingma, xusun, yizhong, linjunyang}@pku.edu.cn

Abstract

A sentence can be translated into more than one correct sentences. However, most of the existing neural machine translation models only use one of the correct translations as the targets, and the other correct sentences are punished as the incorrect sentences in the training stage. Since most of the correct translations for one sentence share the similar bag-of-words, it is possible to distinguish the correct translations from the incorrect ones by the bag-of-words. In this paper, we propose an approach that uses both the sentences and the bag-of-words as targets in the training stage, in order to encourage the model to generate the potentially correct sentences that are not appeared in the training set. We evaluate our model on a Chinese-English translation dataset, and experiments show our model outperforms the strong baselines by the BLEU score of 4.55.[1]

1 Introduction

Neural Machine Translation (NMT) has achieve success in generating coherent and reasonable translations. Most of the existing neural machine translation systems are based on the sequence-to-sequence model (Sutskever et al., 2014). The sequence-to-sequence model (Seq2Seq) regards the translation problem as the mapping from the source sequences to the target sequences. The encoder of Seq2Seq compresses the source sentences into the latent representation, and the decoder of Seq2Seq generates the target sentences from the source representations. The cross-entropy loss,

---

[1]The code is available at https://github.com/lancopku/bag-of-words

Source: 今年前两月广东高新技术产品出口37.6亿美元。
Reference: Export of high - tech products in guangdong in first two months this year reached 3.76 billion us dollars .
Translation 1: Guangdong 's export of new high technology products amounts to us $3.76 billion in first two months of this year .
Translation 2: Export of high - tech products has frequently been in the spotlight , making a significant contribution to the growth of foreign trade in guangdong .

Table 1: An example of two generated translations. Although Translation 1 is much more reasonable, it is punished more severely than Translation 2 by Seq2Seq.

which measures the distance of the generated distribution and the target distribution, is minimized in the training stage, so that the generated sentences are as similar as the target sentences.

Due to the limitation of the training set, most of the existing neural machine translation models only have one reference sentences as the targets. However, a sentence can be translated into more than one correct sentences, which have different syntax structures and expressions but share the same meaning. The correct translations that are not appeared in the training set will be punished as the incorrect translation by Seq2Seq, which is a potential harm to the model. Table 1 shows an example of two generated translations from Chinese to English. Translation 1 is apparently more proper as the translation of the source sentence than Translation 2, but it is punished even more severely than Translation 2 by Seq2Seq.

Because most of the correct translations for one source sentence share the similar bag-of-words, it

Proceedings of the 56th Annual Meeting of the Association for Computational Linguistics (Short Papers), pages 332–338
Melbourne, Australia, July 15 - 20, 2018. ©2018 Association for Computational Linguistics

is possible to distinguish the correct translations from the incorrect ones by the bag-of-words in most cases. In this paper, we propose an approach that uses both sentences and bag-of-words as the targets. In this way, the generated sentences which cover more words in the bag-of-words (e.g. Translation 1 in Table 1) are encouraged, while the incorrect sentences (e.g. Translation 2) are punished more severely. We perform experiments on a popular Chinese-English translation dataset. Experiments show our model outperforms the strong baselines by the BLEU score of 4.55.

2 Bag-of-Words as Target

In this section, we describe the proposed approach in detail.

2.1 Notation

Given a translation dataset that consists of N data samples, the i-th data sample (x^i, y^i) contains a source sentence x^i, and a target sentence y^i. The bag-of-words of y^i is denoted as b^i. The source sentence x^i, the target sentence y^i, and the bag-of-words b^i are all sequences of words:

$$x^i = \{x^i_1, x^i_2, ..., x^i_{L_i}\}$$

$$y^i = \{y^i_1, y^i_2, ..., y^i_{M_i}\}$$

$$b^i = \{b^i_1, b^i_2, ..., b^i_{K_i}\}$$

where L_i, M_i, and K_i denote the number of words in x^i, y^i, and b^i, respectively.

The target of our model is to generate both the target sequence y^i and the corresponding bag-of-words b^i. For the purpose of simplicity, (x, y, b) is used to denote each data pair in the rest of this section.

2.2 Bag-of-Words Generation

We regard the bag-of-words generation as the multi-label classification problem. We first perform the encoding and decoding to obtain the scores of words at each position of the generated sentence. Then, we sum the scores of all positions as the sentence-level score. Finally, the sentence-level score is used for multi-label classification, which identifies whether the word appears in the translation.

In our model, the encoder is a bi-directional Long Short-term Memory Network (BiL-STM), which produces the representation

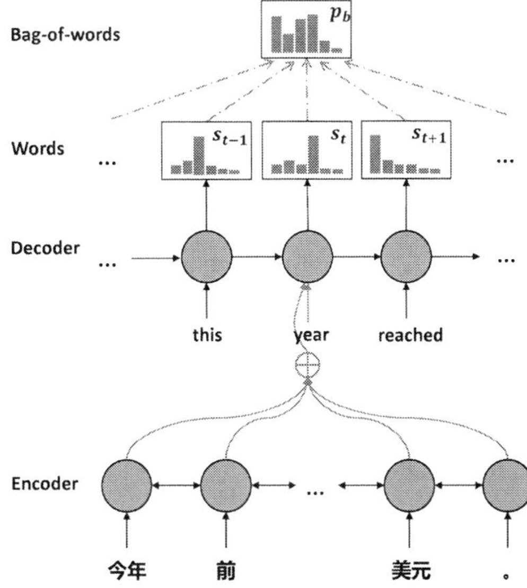

Figure 1: The overview of our model. The encoder inputs the source sentence, and the decoder outputs the word distribution at each position. The distribution of all position is summed up to a sentence-level score, which can be used to generate the bag-of-words.

$h = \{h_1, h_2, ..., h_L\}$ from the source text x:

$$\vec{h}_t = \vec{f}(x_t, \vec{h}_{t-1}) \tag{1}$$

$$\overleftarrow{h}_t = \overleftarrow{f}(x_t, \overleftarrow{h}_{t+1}) \tag{2}$$

$$h_t = \vec{h}_t + \overleftarrow{h}_t \tag{3}$$

where $\vec{f}$ and $\overleftarrow{f}$ are the forward and the backward functions of LSTM for one time step, $\vec{h}_t$ and $\overleftarrow{h}_t$ are the forward and the backward hidden outputs respectively, x_t is the input at the t-th time step, and L is the number of words in sequence x.

The decoder consists of a uni-directional LSTM, with an attention, and a word generator. The LSTM generates the hidden output q_t:

$$q_t = f(y_{t-1}, q_{t-1}) \tag{4}$$

where f is the function of LSTM for one time step, and y_{t-1} is the last generated words at t-th time step. The attention mechanism (Luong and Manning, 2015) is used to capture the source information:

$$v_t = \sum_{i=1}^{N} \alpha_{ti} h_i \tag{5}$$

$$\alpha_{ti} = \frac{e^{g(q_t,h_i)}}{\sum_{j=1}^{N} e^{g(q_t,h_j)}} \qquad (6)$$

$$g(q_t, h_i) = \tanh\left(q_t^T W_t h_i\right) \qquad (7)$$

where W_t is a trainable parameter matrix. Then, the word generator is used to compute the probability of each output word at t-th time step:

$$p_{w_t} = softmax(s_t) \qquad (8)$$

$$s_t = W_g v_t + b_g \qquad (9)$$

where W_g and b_g are parameters of the generator.

To get a sentence-level score for the generated sentence, we generate a sequence of word-level score vectors s_t at all positions with the output layer of decoder, and then we sum up the word-level score vectors to obtain a sentence-level score vector. Each value in the vector represents the sentence-level score of the corresponding word, and the index of the value is the index of the word in the dictionary. After normalizing the sentence-level score with sigmoid function, we get the probability for each word, which represents how possible the word appears in the generated sentence regardless of the position in the sentence. Compared with the word-level probability p_{w_t}, the sentence-level probability p_b of each word is independent of the position in the sentence.

More specifically, the sentence-level probability of the generated bag-of-words p_b can be written as:

$$p_b = sigmoid(\sum_{t=1}^{M} s_t) \qquad (10)$$

where M is the number of words in the target sentence.

2.3 Targets and Loss Function

We have two targets at the training stage: the reference translation (appears in the training set) and the bag-of-words. The bag-of-words is used as the approximate representation of the correct translations that do not appear in the training set. For the targets, we have two parts of loss functions:

$$l_1 = -\sum_{t=1}^{M} y_t \log p_{w_t}(y_t) \qquad (11)$$

$$l_2 = -\sum_{i=1}^{K} b_i \log p_b(b_i) \qquad (12)$$

The total loss function can be written as:

$$l = l_1 + \lambda_i l_2 \qquad (13)$$

where λ_i is the coefficient to balance two loss functions at i-th epoch. Since the bag-of-words generation module is built on the top of the word generation, we assign a small weight for the bag-of-words training at the initial time, and gradually increase the weight until a certain value λ:

$$\lambda_i = min(\lambda, k + \alpha i) \qquad (14)$$

In our experiments, we set the $\lambda = 1.0$, $k = 0.1$, and $\alpha = 0.1$, based on the performance on the validation set.

3 Experiments

This section introduces the details of our experiments, including datasets, setups, baseline models as well as results.

3.1 Datasets

We evaluated our proposed model on the NIST translation task for Chinese-English translation and provided the analysis on the same task. We trained our model on 1.25M sentence pairs extracted from LDC corpora [2], with 27.9M Chinese words and 34.5M English words. We validated our model on the dataset for the NIST 2002 translation task and tested our model on that for the NIST 2003, 2004, 2005, 2006, 2008 translation tasks. We used the most frequent 50,000 words for both the Chinese vocabulary and the English vocabulary. The evaluation metric is BLEU (Papineni et al., 2002).

3.2 Setting

We implement the models using *PyTorch*, and the experiments are conducted on an *NVIDIA 1080Ti* GPU. Both the size of word embedding and hidden size are 512, and the batch size is 64. We use Adam optimizer (Kingma and Ba, 2014) to train the model with the default setting $\beta_1 = 0.9$, $\beta_2 = 0.999$ and $\epsilon = 1 \times 10^{-8}$, and we initialize the learning rate to 0.0003.

Based on the performance on the development sets, we use a 3-layer LSTM as the encoder and a 2-layer LSTM as the decoder. We clip the gradients (Pascanu et al., 2013) to the maximum norm

---

[2]The corpora include LDC2002E18, LDC2003E07, LDC2003E14, Hansards portion of LDC2004T07, LDC2004T08 and LDC2005T06.

Model	MT-02	MT-03	MT-04	MT-05	MT-06	MT-08	All
Moses (Su et al., 2016)	33.19	32.43	34.14	31.47	30.81	23.85	31.04
RNNSearch (Su et al., 2016)	34.68	33.08	35.32	31.42	31.61	23.58	31.76
Lattice (Su et al., 2016)	35.94	34.32	36.50	32.40	32.77	24.84	32.95
CPR (Zhang et al., 2017)	33.84	31.18	33.26	30.67	29.63	22.38	29.72
POSTREG (Zhang et al., 2017)	34.37	31.42	34.18	30.99	29.90	22.87	30.20
PKI (Zhang et al., 2017)	36.10	33.64	36.48	33.08	32.90	24.63	32.51
Bi-Tree-LSTM (Chen et al., 2017)	36.57	35.64	36.63	34.35	30.57	-	-
Mixed RNN (Li et al., 2017)	37.70	34.90	38.60	35.50	35.60	-	-
Seq2Seq+Attn (our implementation)	34.71	33.15	35.26	32.36	32.45	23.96	31.96
+Bag-of-Words (this paper)	**39.77**	**38.91**	**40.02**	**36.82**	**35.93**	**27.61**	**36.51**

Table 2: Results of our model and the baselines (directly reported in the referred articles) on the Chinese-English translation. "-" means that the studies did not test the models on the corresponding datasets.

of 10.0. Dropout is used with the dropout rate set to 0.2. Following Xiong et al. (2017), we use beam search with a beam width of 10 to generate translation for the evaluation and test, and we normalize the log-likelihood scores by sentence length.

3.3 Baselines

We compare our model with several NMT systems, and the results are directly reported in their articles.

- **Moses** is an open source phrase-based translation system with default configurations and a 4-gram language model trained on the training data for the target language.

- **RNNSearch** (Bahdanau et al., 2014) is a bidirectional GRU based model with the attention mechanism. The results of Moses, and RNNSearch come from Su et al. (2016).

- **Lattice** (Su et al., 2016) is a Seq2Seq model which encodes the sentences with multiple tokenizations.

- **Bi-Tree-LSTM** (Chen et al., 2017) is a tree-structured model which models source-side syntax.

- **Mixed RNN** (Li et al., 2017) extends RNNSearch with a mixed RNN as the encoder.

- **CPR** (Wu et al., 2016) extends RNNSearch with a coverage penalty.

- **POSTREG** (Ganchev et al., 2010) extends RNNSearch with posterior regularization with a constrained posterior set. The results of CPR, and POSTREG come from Zhang et al. (2017).

- **PKI** (Zhang et al., 2017) extends RNNSearch with posterior regularization to integrate prior knowledge.

3.4 Results

Table 2 shows the overall results of the systems on the Chinese-English translation task. We compare our model with our implementation of Seq2Seq+Attention model. For fair comparison, the experimental setting of Seq2Seq+Attention is the same as BAT, so that we can regard it as our proposed model removing the bag-of-words target. The results show that our model achieves the BLEU score of 36.51 on the total test sets, which outperforms the Seq2Seq baseline by the BLEU of 4.55.

In order to further evaluate the performance of our model, we compare our model with the recent NMT systems which have been evaluated on the same training set and the test sets as ours. Their results are directly reported in the referred articles. As shown in Table 2, our model achieves high BLEU scores on all of the NIST Machine Translation test sets, which demonstrates the efficiency of our model.

We also give two translation examples of our model. As shown in Table 3, The translations of Seq2Seq+Attn omit some words, such as "*of*", "*committee*", and "*protection*", and contain some redundant words, like "*human chromosome*" and "*<unk>*". Compared with Seq2Seq, the translations of our model is more informative and ade-

Source: 人类共有二十三对染色体。
Reference: Humans have a total of 23 pairs of chromosomes .
Seq2Seq+Attn: Humans have 23 pairs chromosomes in human chromosome .
+Bag-of-Words: There are 23 pairs of chromosomes in mankind .
Source: 一名奥林匹克筹备委员会官员说:「这项倡议代表筹委会对环保的敏感性。」
Reference: An official from the olympics organization committee said : " this proposal represents the committee 's sensitivity to environmental protection . "
Seq2Seq+Attn: An official of the olympic preparatory committee said : " this proposal represents the <unk> of environmental sensitivity . "
+Bag-of-Words: An official of the olympic preparatory committee said : " this proposal represents the sensitivity of the preparatory committee on environmental protection . "

Table 3: Two translation examples of our model, compared with the Seq2Seq+Attn baseline.

quate, with a better coverage of the bag-of-words of the references.

4 Related Work

The studies of encoder-decoder framework (Kalchbrenner and Blunsom, 2013; Cho et al., 2014; Sutskever et al., 2014) for this task launched the Neural Machine Translation. To improve the focus on the information in the encoder, Bahdanau et al. (2014) proposed the attention mechanism, which greatly improved the performance of the Seq2Seq model on NMT. Most of the existing NMT systems are based on the Seq2Seq model and the attention mechanism. Some of them have variant architectures to capture more information from the inputs (Su et al., 2016; Xiong et al., 2017; Tu et al., 2016), and some improve the attention mechanism (Luong et al., 2015; Meng et al., 2016; Mi et al., 2016; Jean et al., 2015; Feng et al., 2016; Calixto et al., 2017), which also enhanced the performance of the NMT model.

There are also some effective neural networks other RNN. Gehring et al. (2017) turned the RNN-based model into CNN-based model, which greatly improves the computation speed. Vaswani et al. (2017) only used attention mechanism to build the model and showed outstanding performance. Also, some researches incorporated external knowledge and also achieved obvious improvement (Li et al., 2017; Chen et al., 2017).

There is also a study (Zhao et al., 2017) shares a similar name with this work, i.e. bag-of-word loss, our work has significant difference with this study. First, the methods are very different. The previous work uses the bag-of-word to constrain the latent variable, and the latent variable is the output of the encoder. However, we use the bag-of-word to supervise the distribution of the generated words, which is the output of the decoder. Compared with the previous work, our method directly supervises the predicted distribution to improve the whole model, including the encoder, the decoder and the output layer. On the contrary, the previous work only supervises the output of the encoder, and only the encoder is trained. Second, the motivations are quite different. The bag-of-word loss in the previous work is an assistant component, while the bag of word in this paper is a direct target. For example, in the paper you mentioned, the bag-of-word loss is a component of variational autoencoder to tackle the vanishing latent variable problem. In our paper, the bag of word is the representation of the unseen correct translations to tackle the data sparseness problem.

5 Conclusions and Future Work

We propose a method that regard both the reference translation (appears in the training set) and the bag-of-words as the targets of Seq2Seq at the training stage. Experimental results show that our model obtains better performance than the strong baseline models on a popular Chinese-English translation dataset. In the future, we will explore how to apply our method to other language pairs, especially the morphologically richer languages than English, and the low-resources languages.

Acknowledgements

This work was supported in part by National Natural Science Foundation of China (No. 61673028), National High Technology Research and Development Program of China (863 Program, No. 2015AA015404), and the National Thousand Young Talents Program. Xu Sun is the corresponding author of this paper.

References

Dzmitry Bahdanau, Kyunghyun Cho, and Yoshua Bengio. 2014. Neural machine translation by jointly learning to align and translate. *CoRR*, abs/1409.0473.

Iacer Calixto, Qun Liu, and Nick Campbell. 2017. Doubly-attentive decoder for multi-modal neural machine translation. In *Proceedings of the 55th Annual Meeting of the Association for Computational Linguistics, ACL 2017, Vancouver, Canada, July 30 - August 4, Volume 1: Long Papers*, pages 1913–1924.

Huadong Chen, Shujian Huang, David Chiang, and Jiajun Chen. 2017. Improved neural machine translation with a syntax-aware encoder and decoder. In *ACL 2017*, pages 1936–1945.

Jianpeng Cheng and Mirella Lapata. 2016. Neural summarization by extracting sentences and words. In *Proceedings of the 54th Annual Meeting of the Association for Computational Linguistics, ACL 2016, August 7-12, 2016, Berlin, Germany, Volume 1: Long Papers*.

Kyunghyun Cho, Bart van Merrienboer, Çaglar Gülçehre, Dzmitry Bahdanau, Fethi Bougares, Holger Schwenk, and Yoshua Bengio. 2014. Learning phrase representations using RNN encoder-decoder for statistical machine translation. In *EMNLP 2014*, pages 1724–1734.

Shi Feng, Shujie Liu, Nan Yang, Mu Li, Ming Zhou, and Kenny Q. Zhu. 2016. Improving attention modeling with implicit distortion and fertility for machine translation. In *COLING 2016*, pages 3082–3092.

Kuzman Ganchev, Jennifer Gillenwater, Ben Taskar, et al. 2010. Posterior regularization for structured latent variable models. *Journal of Machine Learning Research*, 11(Jul):2001–2049.

Jonas Gehring, Michael Auli, David Grangier, Denis Yarats, and Yann N. Dauphin. 2017. Convolutional sequence to sequence learning. In *ICML 2017*, pages 1243–1252.

Sébastien Jean, KyungHyun Cho, Roland Memisevic, and Yoshua Bengio. 2015. On using very large target vocabulary for neural machine translation. In *ACL 2015*, pages 1–10.

Nal Kalchbrenner and Phil Blunsom. 2013. Recurrent continuous translation models. In *EMNLP 2013*, pages 1700–1709.

Diederik P. Kingma and Jimmy Ba. 2014. Adam: A method for stochastic optimization. *CoRR*, abs/1412.6980.

Junhui Li, Deyi Xiong, Zhaopeng Tu, Muhua Zhu, Min Zhang, and Guodong Zhou. 2017. Modeling source syntax for neural machine translation. In *ACL 2017*, pages 688–697.

Junyang Lin, Shuming Ma, Qi Su, and Xu Sun. 2018. Decoding-history-based adaptive control of attention for neural machine translation. *CoRR*, abs/1802.01812.

Minh-Thang Luong and Christopher D Manning. 2015. Stanford neural machine translation systems for spoken language domains. In *Proceedings of the International Workshop on Spoken Language Translation*.

Thang Luong, Hieu Pham, and Christopher D. Manning. 2015. Effective approaches to attention-based neural machine translation. In *EMNLP 2015*, pages 1412–1421.

Shuming Ma, Xu Sun, Wei Li, Sujian Li, Wenjie Li, and Xuancheng Ren. 2018. Query and output: Generating words by querying distributed word representations for paraphrase generation. In *NAACL 2018*.

Fandong Meng, Zhengdong Lu, Hang Li, and Qun Liu. 2016. Interactive attention for neural machine translation. In *COLING 2016*, pages 2174–2185.

Haitao Mi, Zhiguo Wang, and Abe Ittycheriah. 2016. Supervised attentions for neural machine translation. In *EMNLP 2016*, pages 2283–2288.

Kishore Papineni, Salim Roukos, Todd Ward, and Wei-Jing Zhu. 2002. Bleu: a method for automatic evaluation of machine translation. In *ACL, 2002*, pages 311–318.

Razvan Pascanu, Tomas Mikolov, and Yoshua Bengio. 2013. On the difficulty of training recurrent neural networks. In *Proceedings of the 30th International Conference on Machine Learning, ICML 2013, Atlanta, GA, USA, 16-21 June 2013*, pages 1310–1318.

Jinsong Su, Zhixing Tan, Deyi Xiong, and Yang Liu. 2016. Lattice-based recurrent neural network encoders for neural machine translation. *CoRR*, abs/1609.07730.

Xu Sun, Xuancheng Ren, Shuming Ma, and Houfeng Wang. 2017a. meprop: Sparsified back propagation for accelerated deep learning with reduced overfitting. In *ICML 2017*, pages 3299–3308.

Xu Sun, Bingzhen Wei, Xuancheng Ren, and Shuming Ma. 2017b. Label embedding network: Learning label representation for soft training of deep networks. *CoRR*, abs/1710.10393.

Ilya Sutskever, Oriol Vinyals, and Quoc V. Le. 2014. Sequence to sequence learning with neural networks. In *NIPS, 2014*, pages 3104–3112.

Sho Takase, Jun Suzuki, Naoaki Okazaki, Tsutomu Hirao, and Masaaki Nagata. 2016. Neural headline generation on abstract meaning representation. In *Proceedings of the 2016 Conference on Empirical Methods in Natural Language Processing, EMNLP 2016, Austin, Texas, USA, November 1-4, 2016*, pages 1054–1059.

Zhaopeng Tu, Zhengdong Lu, Yang Liu, Xiaohua Liu, and Hang Li. 2016. Modeling coverage for neural machine translation. In *ACL 2016*.

Ashish Vaswani, Noam Shazeer, Niki Parmar, Jakob Uszkoreit, Llion Jones, Aidan N. Gomez, Lukasz Kaiser, and Illia Polosukhin. 2017. Attention is all you need. *CoRR*, abs/1706.03762.

Yonghui Wu, Mike Schuster, Zhifeng Chen, Quoc V. Le, Mohammad Norouzi, Wolfgang Macherey, Maxim Krikun, Yuan Cao, Qin Gao, Klaus Macherey, Jeff Klingner, Apurva Shah, Melvin Johnson, Xiaobing Liu, Lukasz Kaiser, Stephan Gouws, Yoshikiyo Kato, Taku Kudo, Hideto Kazawa, Keith Stevens, George Kurian, Nishant Patil, Wei Wang, Cliff Young, Jason Smith, Jason Riesa, Alex Rudnick, Oriol Vinyals, Greg Corrado, Macduff Hughes, and Jeffrey Dean. 2016. Google's neural machine translation system: Bridging the gap between human and machine translation. *CoRR*, abs/1609.08144.

Hao Xiong, Zhongjun He, Xiaoguang Hu, and Hua Wu. 2017. Multi-channel encoder for neural machine translation. *CoRR*, abs/1712.02109.

Jingjing Xu, Xu Sun, Xuancheng Ren, Junyang Lin, Binzhen Wei, and Wei Li. 2018a. Dp-gan: Diversity-promoting generative adversarial network for generating informative and diversified text. *CoRR*, abs/1802.01345.

Jingjing Xu, Xu Sun, Qi Zeng, Xiaodong Zhang, Xuancheng Ren, Houfeng Wang, and Wenjie Li. 2018b. Unpaired sentiment-to-sentiment translation: A cycled reinforcement learning approach. In *ACL 2018*.

Jiacheng Zhang, Yang Liu, Huanbo Luan, Jingfang Xu, and Maosong Sun. 2017. Prior knowledge integration for neural machine translation using posterior regularization. In *ACL 2017*, pages 1514–1523.

Tiancheng Zhao, Ran Zhao, and Maxine Eskénazi. 2017. Learning discourse-level diversity for neural dialog models using conditional variational autoencoders. In *Proceedings of the 55th Annual Meeting of the Association for Computational Linguistics, ACL 2017, Vancouver, Canada, July 30 - August 4, Volume 1: Long Papers*, pages 654–664.

Improving Beam Search by Removing Monotonic Constraint for Neural Machine Translation

Raphael Shu
The University of Tokyo
shu@nlab.ci.i.u-tokyo.ac.jp

Hideki Nakayama
The University of Tokyo
nakayama@ci.i.u-tokyo.ac.jp

Abstract

To achieve high translation performance, neural machine translation models usually rely on the beam search algorithm for decoding sentences. The beam search finds good candidate translations by considering multiple hypotheses of translations simultaneously. However, as the algorithm searches in a monotonic left-to-right order, a hypothesis can not be revisited once it is discarded. We found such monotonicity forces the algorithm to sacrifice some decoding paths to explore new paths. As a result, the overall quality of the hypotheses selected by the algorithm is lower than expected. To mitigate this problem, we relax the monotonic constraint of the beam search by maintaining all found hypotheses in a single priority queue and using a universal score function for hypothesis selection. The proposed algorithm allows discarded hypotheses to be recovered in a later step. Despite its simplicity, we show that the proposed decoding algorithm enhances the quality of selected hypotheses and improve the translations even for high-performance models in English-Japanese translation task.

1 Introduction

Machine translation models composed of end-to-end neural networks (Sutskever et al., 2014; Bahdanau et al., 2014; Shazeer et al., 2017; Gehring et al., 2017) are starting to become mainstream. Essentially, neural machine translation (NMT) models define a probabilistic distribution $p(y_t|y_1, ..., y_{t-1}, X)$ to generate translations. During translation phase, new words are sampled from this distribution.

As the search space of possible outputs is incredibly large, we can only afford to explore a limited number of search paths. In practice, NMT models use the beam search algorithm to generate output sequences in a limited time budget (Graves, 2012; Sutskever et al., 2014). Beam search limits the search space by considering only a fixed number of hypotheses (i.e., partial translations) in each step, and predicting next output words only for the selected hypotheses. The fixed number B is referred to as *beam size*. Beam search keeps decoding until B finished translations that end with an end-of-sequence token "⟨/s⟩" are found.

Comparing to the greedy search that only considers the best hypothesis in each step, beam search can find a good candidate translation that suffers in a middle step. Generally, using beam search can improve the quality of outputs over the greedy search. However, we found that the hard restriction of hypothesis selection imposed by the beam search affects the quality of the decoding paths negatively.

We can think the decoding process of an NMT model as solving a pathfinding problem, where we search for an optimal path starts from "⟨s⟩" and ends at "⟨/s⟩". For any pathfinding algorithm, a certain amount of exploration is crucial for making sure that the algorithm is following a right path. For beam search, since the beam size is fixed, it must give up some currently searching paths in order to explore new paths. The problem has a similar flavor as the exploration-exploitation dilemma in reinforcement learning. As the beam search decodes in left-to-right order monotonically, a discarded decoding path can not be recovered later.

As the decoding algorithm is essentially driven by a language model, an output with high probability (local score) is not guaranteed to have high scores for future predictions. Beam search can be trapped by such a high-confidence output. This is-

Proceedings of the 56th Annual Meeting of the Association for Computational Linguistics (Short Papers), pages 339–344
Melbourne, Australia, July 15 - 20, 2018. ©2018 Association for Computational Linguistics

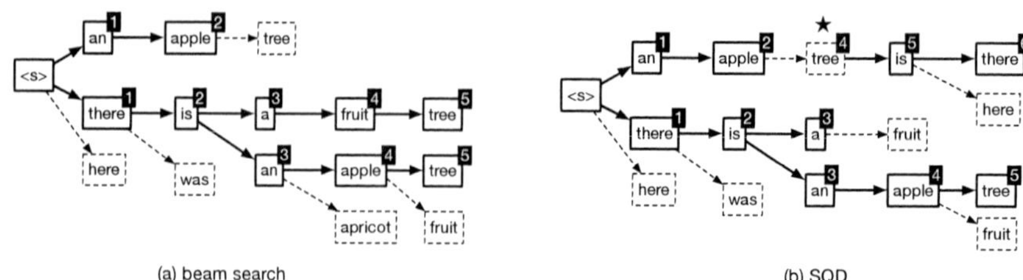

(a) beam search   (b) SQD

Figure 1: An intuitive comparison between beam search and single-queue decoding (SQD) with a beam size of 2. In each step, two selected hypotheses (solid boxes) and one immediately discarded hypothesis (dashed boxes) are shown in the figure. In the top right of selected hypotheses, the step numbers when they are selected are marked. The hypothesis *"an apple tree"* is discarded in step 3 in both algorithms. Comparing to beam search, SQD is able to recover this hypothesis in step 4 when other hypotheses have worse scores.

sue is more severe for language pairs that are not well aligned. One solution is to predict the expected future scores, which is considerably difficult. Another workaround for this problem is to enable the algorithm to revisit a previous hypothesis when the quality of current ones degrades.

In this work, we extend the beam search to introduce more flexibility. We manage all found hypotheses in a single priority queue so that they can be selected later when necessary. Based on a universal score function, the hypotheses with highest scores are selected to be expanded. The proposed algorithm is referred to as *single-queue decoding* (SQD) in this paper.

As the priority queue can contain massive hypotheses, we design two auxiliary score functions to help the algorithm select proper candidates. Experiments show that the proposed algorithm is able to improve the quality of selected hypotheses and thus results in better performance in English-Japanese translation task.

2   Related Work

To improve the quality of the score function in beam search, Wiseman and Rush (2016) propose to run beam search in the forward pass of training, then apply a new objective function to ensure the gold output does not fall outside the beam. An alternative approach is to correct the scores with reinforcement learning (Li et al., 2017). Diverse decoding (Li et al., 2016; Li and Jurafsky, 2016) modifies the score function for increase the diversity of hypotheses. In contrast, this work focuses on removing the constraint of beam search rather than improving the score function.

Hu et al. (2015) also describes a priority queue integrated with the standard beam search but has a different mechanism and purpose. The priority queue in their work contains top-1 hypotheses from different hypothesis stacks. In each step, only one hypothesis from the queue is allowed to be considered. Their purpose is to use the priority queue to speed up beam search at the cost of slight performance loss, which is different to this work.

As the proposed algorithm is a best-first searching algorithm, which has a flavor similar to A^* search (Hart et al., 1968). Typical implementations of A^* search also use a priority queue (heap) to maintain visited paths.

3   Deficiency of Beam Search

Since the beam size is fixed, when the algorithm attempts to explore multiple new decoding paths for a hypothesis, it has to discard some existing decoding paths. However, the new decoding paths may lead to bad hypotheses in the near future. As past hypotheses can not be revisited again, the beam search has to decode the hypotheses with degraded qualities continually. This phenomenon is illustrated in Fig. 1 (a), where the graph depicts the decoding process of a sentence. The correct output is supposed to be *"an apple tree is there"* or *"there is an apple tree"*. In step 3, as the algorithm explores two new hypotheses in the bottom branch, the hypothesis *"an apple tree"* is discarded. In the next step, it realized that the hypothesis *"there is a"* leads to a wrong path. However, as the algorithm can not return to a discarded hypothesis, the beam search has to keep searching in the hopeless path. In this case, the candidate *"an apple tree is there"* can never be reached.

Algorithm 1 Single-queue decoding

Initialize:
    $B \leftarrow$ beam size
    $H \leftarrow$ empty hypothesis queue
    $T \leftarrow$ max steps
for $t \leftarrow 1$ to T **do**
    $S \leftarrow$ pop best B unfinished hyps from H
    $S' \leftarrow$ expand S to get $B \times K$ new hyps
    Evaluate scores of hyps in S' with Eq. 1
    Push S' into H
    if $\#(\text{finished hyps in } H) \geq B$ **then**
        break
$\hat{y} \leftarrow$ best finished hyp in H
output $\hat{y}$

---

4 Single-Queue Decoding

In this section, we introduce an extended decoding algorithm of the beam search, which maintains a single priority queue that contains all visited hypotheses. In contrast to the standard beam search, which only considers hypotheses with the same length in each step, the proposed algorithm selected arbitrary hypotheses from the queue that may differ in length. Therefore, a hypothesis discarded in one step can be recovered in a later step.

An intuitive illustration of the proposed algorithm can be found in Fig. 1 (b). In step 4, the proposed algorithm is able to recover the hypothesis *"an apple tree"* from the queue which is discarded a previous step.

The pseudo code of the *single-queue decoding* algorithm is given in Alg. 1. Let B be the beam size. The algorithm will keep decoding until finding B finished translation candidates. The proposed decoding algorithm relies on a universal score function $\text{score}(y)$ to evaluate a hypothesis y. In each step, the hypotheses with highest scores are removed from the queue to predict next words for them. New expanded hypotheses are pushed back into the queue after scoring.

In hypothesis expansion, we collect $B \times K$ (but not $B \times |V|$) hypotheses that have highest local scores (word probability). This simple filtering is essential to avoid spending to much time computing the score function. In practice, we set $K = B$.

4.1 Universal Score Function

In the proposed algorithm, a score function is required to fairly evaluate hypotheses with different lengths, which has the following form:

$$\text{score}(y) = \frac{1}{|y|^\lambda} \log p(y|X) + \alpha \, \text{PG}(y) + \beta \, \text{LMP}(y). \tag{1}$$

The first part of the equation is the log probability with length-normalization, where λ is a hyperparameter that is similar to the definition of length penalty in Wu et al. (2016). We found simply utilizing this score function will sometimes cause the algorithm decode for infinite steps. To help the algorithm select proper candidates from the large queue, we designed two auxiliary penalties.

Progress Penalty: The second part of Eq. 1 is a progress penalty, which encourages the algorithm to select longer hypotheses:

$$\text{PG}(y) = \begin{cases} 0 & \text{if } y \text{ finished} \\ \frac{|y|^\gamma}{|X|^\gamma} & \text{otherwise} \end{cases} \tag{2}$$

where γ are is weight that control the strength of this function. The progress penalty encourages the algorithm to select longer hypotheses.

Length Matching Penalty: The last part of Eq. 1 is a *length matching penalty*. It filters out the hypotheses that tend to produce a final translation much shorter or longer than expected.

To achieve this, we predict two Gaussian distributions. One distribution p_x^l predicts the expected length of a correct translation. Another Gaussian p_y^l predicts the expected final length if decoding a particular hypothesis. The parameters of the distributions (μ_x, σ_x and μ_y, σ_y) are predicted by an additional simple neural network, which is trained separately from the NMT model. Then we compute the cross-entropy of the two Gaussians to measure whether the expected length of translation tends to match the correct length as:

$$H(p_x^l, p_y^l) = \frac{1}{2} \log(2\pi\sigma_y{}^2) + \frac{\sigma_x{}^2 + (\mu_y - \mu_x)^2}{2\sigma_y{}^2}. \tag{3}$$

We penalize a hypothesis if the cross entropy exceeds a threshold τ as:

$$\text{LMP}(y) = \begin{cases} 0 & \text{if } y \text{ finished} \\ \mathbf{I}(H(p_x^l, p_y^l) > \tau) & \text{otherwise} \end{cases} \tag{4}$$

where $I(\cdot)$ is an indicator function.

5 Experiments

5.1 Experimental Settings

We evaluate the proposed decoding algorithm mainly with an off-the-shelf NMT model (Bahdanau et al., 2014), which has a bi-directional LSTM encoder and a single-layer LSTM decoder. The embeddings and LSTM layers have a size of 1000. We evaluate the algorithms on AS-PEC English-Japanese translation task (Nakazawa et al., 2016). The vocabulary contains 80k words for English side and 40k words for the Japanese side. We report BLEU score based on a standard post-processing procedure [1].

All NMT models in this work are trained with Nesterov's accelerated gradient (Nesterov, 1983) with an initial learning rate of 0.25. The learning rate is decreased by a factor of 10 if no improvement is observed in 20k iterations. The training ends after the learning rate is annealed for three times. The models are trained on 4 GPUs; each GPU computes the gradient of a mini-batch. The gradients are averaged and distributed to each GPU using the nccl framework.

The hyperparameters of the decoding algorithms are tuned by Bayesian optimization (Snoek et al., 2012) on a small validation set composed of 500 sentences. We utilize the "bayes_opt" package for Bayesian optimization. We use the default acquisition function "ucb" with a κ value of 5. We first explore 50 initial points, then optimize for another 50 iterations.

We allow the decoding algorithms to run for a maximum of 150 steps. If the algorithm fails to find a finished translation in the limited steps, an empty translation is outputted.

5.2 Main Results

The main evaluation results are shown in Table 1, which uses a beam size of 5 as such a small beam size is more useful in a production system. The results show that the proposed single-queue decoding (SQD) algorithm significantly improves the quality of translations. With the length matching penalty (LMP), SQD outperforms the beam search with length-normalization by 1.14 BLEU on the test set. Without the progress penalty (PG), the scores are much worse.

Since SQD computes B hypotheses in batch mode at each step just like beam search, the com-

	BLEU(%)		#step	time (ms)
	valid	test		
vanilla beam search	29.61	32.87	30.3	199
w/ length-normalization	37.16	34.29	30.3	208
SQD w/o PG	38.09	34.62	36.1	238
SQD w/ PG	38.50	35.03	33.8	225
SQD w/ PG, LMP	**38.93**	**35.43**	35.0	260

Table 1: Evaluation results using a baseline model with a beam size of 5

	Test BLEU(%)			
	BS=3	BS=5	BS=8	BS=12
beam search w/ LN	37.69	37.93	38.26	38.38
SQD w/ PG	38.18	38.68	**38.98**	**39.02**
SQD w/ PG, LMP	**38.37**	**38.73**	38.89	38.98

Table 2: Evaluation results using a large NMT model with different beam sizes (BS). The scores of the beam search with length-normalization (LN) are reported as the baselines.

putational cost inside the loop of Alg. 1 remains the same. The factor affecting the decoding time is the actual number of time steps. To clarify that SQD does not improve the performance by significantly increasing the number of steps, we also report the average number of steps and the decoding time for translating one sentence. We can see that it is effective applying *length matching penaltiy*. However, it slows down the algorithm as extra computation is required.

5.3 Experiments with a Large NMT Model

In order to see whether the performance gain can be generalized to deeper models, we train a large NMT model with two layers of LSTM decoders. We apply residual connection (He et al., 2016) to the decoder states. Before the softmax layer, an additional fully-connected layer with 600 hidden units is applied. For the attention mechanism, we use a variant of the key-value attention (Miller et al., 2016), where the keys are computed by a linear transformation of the encoder states, the queries of the attention are the sum of the feedback word embeddings and the LSTM states of the first decoder. Dropout (Srivastava et al., 2014) is applied everywhere after non-recurrent layers with a dropping rate of 0.2. To further enhance the model performance, we use byte pair encoding (Sennrich et al., 2016) with a coding size of 40k to segment the sentences of the training data into subwords. The experiment results are shown in Table 2.

By applying various techniques, the NMT model achieves high single-model BLEU scores. The results indicate that SQD is still effective with a high-performance NMT model. The proposed algorithm is more effective with a small beam size. For this model, the contribution of *length matching penalty* is only beneficial when the beam size is smaller than 8, which may be a side-effect of applying byte pair encoding (BPE). As it is more difficult to correctly predict the number of output tokens in sub-word level.

6 Discussion

The proposed algorithm requires a block of GPU memory for storing the states of LSTM decoders for all stored hypotheses in the priority queue. The increased memory usage does not cause a problem unless a large beam size is used.

Although all hypotheses are expected to be evaluated fairly, we found only averagely 2 discarded hypotheses are recovered when decoding each sentence. The reason is that longer hypotheses tend to have higher local scores in general, which makes it difficult for the algorithm to select a short hypothesis. As a future work, a better score function is required to fully exploit the flexibility of the proposed algorithm.

7 Conclusion

In this paper, we present a novel decoding algorithm that removes the constraint imposed by the monotonicity of beam search, so that a discarded hypothesis can be revisited in a later step.

The proposed algorithm maintains all reusable hypotheses in a single priority queue. In each step, the algorithm selects hypotheses from the queue with highest scores evaluated by a universal score function. We design two auxiliary scores to help selecting proper hypotheses from a large queue.

Acknowledgments

This work is supported by JSPS KAKENHI Grant Number 16H05872.

References

Dzmitry Bahdanau, Kyunghyun Cho, and Yoshua Bengio. 2014. Neural machine translation by jointly learning to align and translate. *arXiv preprint arXiv:1409.0473*.

Jonas Gehring, Michael Auli, David Grangier, Denis Yarats, and Yann Dauphin. 2017. Convolutional sequence to sequence learning. *CoRR*, abs/1705.03122.

Alex Graves. 2012. Sequence transduction with recurrent neural networks. *CoRR*, abs/1211.3711.

Peter E. Hart, Nils J. Nilsson, and Bertram Raphael. 1968. Correction to "a formal basis for the heuristic determination of minimum cost paths". *SIGART Newsletter*, 37:28–29.

Kaiming He, Xiangyu Zhang, Shaoqing Ren, and Jian Sun. 2016. Deep residual learning for image recognition. *2016 IEEE Conference on Computer Vision and Pattern Recognition (CVPR)*, pages 770–778.

Xiaoguang Hu, Wei Li, Xiang Lan, Hua Wu, and Haifeng Wang. 2015. Improved beam search with constrained softmax for nmt. *Proceedings of MT Summit XV*, page 297.

Jiwei Li and Daniel Jurafsky. 2016. Mutual information and diverse decoding improve neural machine translation. *CoRR*, abs/1601.00372.

Jiwei Li, Will Monroe, and Dan Jurafsky. 2017. Learning to decode for future success. *arXiv preprint arXiv:1701.06549*.

Jiwei Li, Will Monroe, and Daniel Jurafsky. 2016. A simple, fast diverse decoding algorithm for neural generation. *CoRR*, abs/1611.08562.

Alexander H. Miller, Adam Fisch, Jesse Dodge, Amir-Hossein Karimi, Antoine Bordes, and Jason Weston. 2016. Key-value memory networks for directly reading documents. In *EMNLP*.

Toshiaki Nakazawa, Manabu Yaguchi, Kiyotaka Uchimoto, Masao Utiyama, Eiichiro Sumita, Sadao Kurohashi, and Hitoshi Isahara. 2016. Aspec: Asian scientific paper excerpt corpus. In *LREC*.

Yurii Nesterov. 1983. A method for unconstrained convex minimization problem with the rate of convergence o (1/k2). In *Doklady an SSSR*, volume 269, pages 543–547.

Rico Sennrich, Barry Haddow, and Alexandra Birch. 2016. Neural machine translation of rare words with subword units. *CoRR*, abs/1508.07909.

Noam Shazeer, Azalia Mirhoseini, Krzysztof Maziarz, Andy Davis, Quoc V. Le, Geoffrey E. Hinton, and Jeff Dean. 2017. Outrageously large neural networks: The sparsely-gated mixture-of-experts layer. *CoRR*, abs/1701.06538.

Jasper Snoek, Hugo Larochelle, and Ryan P. Adams. 2012. Practical bayesian optimization of machine learning algorithms. In *NIPS*.

Nitish Srivastava, Geoffrey E. Hinton, Alex Krizhevsky, Ilya Sutskever, and Ruslan Salakhutdinov. 2014. Dropout: a simple way to prevent neural networks from overfitting. *Journal of Machine Learning Research*, 15:1929–1958.

Ilya Sutskever, Oriol Vinyals, and Quoc VV Le. 2014. Sequence to sequence learning with neural networks. In *NIPS*.

Sam Wiseman and Alexander M. Rush. 2016. Sequence-to-sequence learning as beam-search optimization. In *EMNLP*.

Yonghui Wu, Mike Schuster, Zhifeng Chen, Quoc V Le, Mohammad Norouzi, Wolfgang Macherey, Maxim Krikun, Yuan Cao, Qin Gao, Klaus Macherey, et al. 2016. Google's neural machine translation system: Bridging the gap between human and machine translation. *arXiv preprint arXiv:1609.08144*.

Leveraging distributed representations and lexico-syntactic fixedness for token-level prediction of the idiomaticity of English verb–noun combinations

Milton King and **Paul Cook**

Faculty of Computer Science, University of New Brunswick
Fredericton, NB E3B 5A3 Canada
`milton.king@unb.ca, paul.cook@unb.ca`

Abstract

Verb–noun combinations (VNCs) — e.g., *blow the whistle*, *hit the roof*, and *see stars* — are a common type of English idiom that are ambiguous with literal usages. In this paper we propose and evaluate models for classifying VNC usages as idiomatic or literal, based on a variety of approaches to forming distributed representations. Our results show that a model based on averaging word embeddings performs on par with, or better than, a previously-proposed approach based on skip-thoughts. Idiomatic usages of VNCs are known to exhibit lexico-syntactic fixedness. We further incorporate this information into our models, demonstrating that this rich linguistic knowledge is complementary to the information carried by distributed representations.

1 Introduction

Multiword expressions (MWEs) are combinations of multiple words that exhibit some degree of idiomaticity (Baldwin and Kim, 2010). Verb–noun combinations (VNCs), consisting of a verb with a noun in its direct object position, are a common type of semantically-idiomatic MWE in English and cross-lingually (Fazly et al., 2009). Many VNCs are ambiguous between MWEs and literal combinations, as in the following examples of *see stars*, in which 1 is an idiomatic usage (i.e., an MWE), while 2 is a literal combination.[1]

1. Hereford United were <u>seeing stars</u> at Gillingham after letting in 2 early goals

2. Look into the night sky to <u>see</u> the <u>stars</u>

[1] These examples, and idiomaticity judgements, are taken from the VNC-Tokens dataset (Cook et al., 2008).

MWE identification is the task of automatically determining which word combinations at the token-level form MWEs (Baldwin and Kim, 2010), and must be able to make such distinctions. This is particularly important for applications such as machine translation (Sag et al., 2002), where the appropriate meaning of word combinations in context must be preserved for accurate translation.

In this paper, following prior work (e.g., Salton et al., 2016), we frame token-level identification of VNCs as a supervised binary classification problem, i.e., idiomatic vs. literal. We consider a range of approaches to forming distributed representations of the context in which a VNC occurs, including word embeddings (Mikolov et al., 2013), word embeddings tailored to representing sentences (Kenter et al., 2016), and skip-thoughts sentence embeddings (Kiros et al., 2015). We then train a support vector machine (SVM) on these representations to classify unseen VNC instances. Surprisingly, we find that an approach based on representing sentences as the average of their word embeddings performs comparably to, or better than, the skip-thoughts based approach previously proposed by Salton et al. (2016).

VNCs exhibit lexico-syntactic fixedness. For example, the idiomatic interpretation in example 1 above is typically only accessible when the verb *see* has active voice, the determiner is null, and the noun *star* is in plural form, as in *see stars* or *seeing stars*. Usages with a determiner (as in example 2), a singular noun (e.g., *see a star*), or passive voice (e.g., *stars were seen*) typically only have the literal interpretation.

In this paper we further incorporate knowledge of the lexico-syntactic fixedness of VNCs — automatically acquired from corpora using the method of Fazly et al. (2009) — into our various embedding-based approaches. Our experimental results show that this leads to substantial improve-

Proceedings of the 56th Annual Meeting of the Association for Computational Linguistics (Short Papers), pages 345–350
Melbourne, Australia, July 15 - 20, 2018. ©2018 Association for Computational Linguistics

ments, indicating that this rich linguistic knowledge is complementary to that available in distributed representations.

2 Related work

Much research on MWE identification has focused on specific kinds of MWEs (e.g., Patrick and Fletcher, 2005; Uchiyama et al., 2005), including English VNCs (e.g., Fazly et al., 2009; Salton et al., 2016), although some recent work has considered the identification of a broad range of kinds of MWEs (e.g., Schneider et al., 2014; Brooke et al., 2014; Savary et al., 2017).

Work on MWE identification has leveraged rich linguistic knowledge of the constructions under consideration (e.g., Fazly et al., 2009; Fothergill and Baldwin, 2012), treated literal and idiomatic as two senses of an expression and applied approaches similar to word-sense disambiguation (e.g., Birke and Sarkar, 2006; Hashimoto and Kawahara, 2008), incorporated topic models (e.g., Li et al., 2010), and made use of distributed representations of words (Gharbieh et al., 2016).

In the most closely related work to ours, Salton et al. (2016) represent token instances of VNCs by embedding the sentence that they occur in using skip-thoughts (Kiros et al., 2015) — an encoder–decoder model that can be viewed as a sentence-level counterpart to the word2vec (Mikolov et al., 2013) skip-gram model. During training the target sentence is encoded using a recurrent neural network, and is used to predict the previous and next sentences. Salton et al. then use these sentence embeddings, representing VNC token instances, as features in a supervised classifier. We treat this skip-thoughts based approach as a strong baseline to compare against.

Fazly et al. (2009) formed a set of eleven lexico-syntactic patterns for VNC instances capturing the voice of the verb (active or passive), determiner (e.g., *a*, *the*), and number of the noun (singular or plural). They then determine the canonical form, $C(v, n)$, for a given VNC as follows:[2]

$$C(v, n) = \{pt_k \in P | z(v, n, pt_k) > T_z\} \quad (1)$$

where P is the set of patterns, T_z is a predetermined threshold, which is set to 1, and $z(v, n, pt_k)$ is calculated as follows:

$$z(v, n, pt_k) = \frac{f(v, n, pt_k) - \overline{f}}{s} \quad (2)$$

where $f(\cdot)$ is the frequency of a VNC occurring in a given pattern in a corpus,[3] and $\overline{f}$ and s are the mean and standard deviations for all patterns for the given VNC, respectively.

Fazly et al. (2009) showed that idiomatic usages of a VNC tend to occur in that expression's canonical form, while literal usages do not. This approach provides a strong, linguistically-informed, unsupervised baseline, referred to as CForm, for predicting whether VNC instances are idiomatic or literal. In this paper we incorporate knowledge of canonical forms into embedding-based approaches to VNC token classification, and show that this linguistic knowledge can be leveraged to improve such approaches.

3 Models

We describe the models used to represent VNC token instances below. For each model, a linear SVM classifier is trained on these representations.

3.1 Word2vec

We trained word2vec's skip-gram model (Mikolov et al., 2013) on a snapshot of Wikipedia from September 2015, which consists of approximately 2.6 billion tokens. We used a window size of ± 8 and 300 dimensions. We ignore all words that occur less than fifteen times in the training corpus, and did not set a maximum vocabulary size. We perform negative sampling and set the number of training epochs to five. We used batch processing with approximately $10k$ words in each batch.

To embed a given a sentence containing a VNC token instance, we average the word embeddings for each word in the sentence, including stopwords.[4] Prior to averaging, we normalize each embedding to have unit length.

3.2 Siamese CBOW

The Siamese CBOW model (Kenter et al., 2016) learns word embeddings that are better able to represent a sentence through averaging than conventional word embeddings such as skip-gram or CBOW. We use a Siamese CBOW model that was pretrained on a snapshot of Wikipedia from November 2012 using randomly initialized word

---

[2]In a small number of cases a VNC is found to have a small number of canonical forms, as opposed to just one.

[3]Fazly et al. (2009) used the British National Corpus (Burnard, 2000).

[4]Preliminary experiments showed that models performed better when stopword removal was not applied.

embeddings.[5] Similarly to the word2vec model, to embed a given sentence containing a VNC instance, we average the word embeddings for each word in the sentence.

3.3 Skip-thoughts

We use a publicly-available skip-thoughts model, that was pre-trained on a corpus of books.[6] We represent a given sentence containing a VNC instance using the skip-thoughts encoder. Note that this approach is our re-implementation of the skip-thoughts based method of Salton et al. (2016), and we use it as a strong baseline for comparison.

4 Data and evaluation

In this section, we discuss the dataset used in our experiments, and the evaluation of our models.

4.1 Dataset

We use the VNC-Tokens dataset (Cook et al., 2008) — the same dataset used by Fazly et al. (2009) and Salton et al. (2016) — to train and evaluate our models. This dataset consists of sentences containing VNC usages drawn from the British National Corpus (Burnard, 2000),[7] along with a label indicating whether the VNC is an idiomatic or literal usage (or whether this cannot be determined, in which case it is labelled "unknown").

VNC-Tokens is divided into DEV and TEST sets that each include fourteen VNC types and a total of roughly six hundred instances of these types annotated as literal or idiomatic. Following Salton et al. (2016), we use DEV and TEST, and ignore all token instances annotated as "unknown".

Fazly et al. (2009) and Salton et al. (2016) structured their experiments differently. Fazly et al. report results over DEV and TEST separately. In this setup TEST consists of expressions that were not seen during model development (done on DEV). Salton et al., on the other hand, merge DEV and TEST, and create new training and testing sets, such that each expression is present in the training and testing data, and the ratio of idiomatic to literal usages of each expression in the training data is roughly equal to that in the testing data.

We borrowed ideas from both of these approaches in structuring our experiments. We retain

Model	Penalty cost				
	0.01	0.1	1	10	100
Word2vec	0.619	0.654	0.818	**0.830**	0.807
Siamese CBOW	0.619	0.621	0.665	0.729	**0.763**
Skip-thoughts	0.661	0.784	**0.803**	0.800	0.798

Table 1: Accuracy on DEV while tuning the penalty cost for the SVM for each model. The highest accuracy for each model is shown in boldface.

the type-level division of Fazly et al. (2009) into DEV and TEST. We then divide each of these into training and testing sets, using the same ratios of idiomatic to literal usages for each expression as Salton et al. (2016). This allows us to develop and tune a model on DEV, and then determine whether, when retrained on instances of unseen VNCs in (the training portion of) TEST, that model is able to generalize to new VNCs without further tuning to the specific expressions in TEST.

4.2 Evaluation

The proportion of idiomatic usages in the testing portions of both DEV and TEST is 63%. We therefore use accuracy to evaluate our models following Fazly et al. (2009) because the classes are roughly balanced. We randomly divide both DEV and TEST into training and testing portions ten times, following Salton et al. (2016). For each of the ten runs, we compute the accuracy for each expression, and then compute the average accuracy over the expressions. We then report the average accuracy over the ten runs.

5 Experimental results

In this section we first consider the effect of tuning the cost parameter of the SVM for each model on DEV, and then report results on DEV and TEST using the tuned models.

5.1 Parameter tuning

We tune the SVM for each model on DEV by carrying out a linear search for the penalty cost from 0.01–100, increasing by a factor of ten each time. Results for this parameter tuning are shown in Table 1. These results highlight the importance of choosing an appropriate setting for the penalty cost. For example, the accuracy of the word2vec model ranges from 0.619–0.830 depending on the cost setting. In subsequent experiments, for each

Model	DEV		TEST	
	−CF	+CF	−CF	+CF
CForm	-	0.721	-	0.749
Word2vec	**0.830**	**0.854**	**0.804**	**0.852**
Siamese CBOW	0.763	0.774	0.717	0.779
Skip-thoughts	0.803	0.827	0.786	0.842

Table 2: Accuracy on DEV and TEST for each model, without (−CF) and with (+CF) the canonical form feature. The highest accuracy for each setting on each dataset is shown in boldface.

model, we use the penalty cost that achieves the highest accuracy in Table 1.

5.2 DEV and TEST results

In Table 2 we report results on DEV and TEST for each model, as well as the unsupervised CForm model of Fazly et al. (2009), which simply labels a VNC as idiomatic if it occurs in its canonical form, and as literal otherwise. We further consider each model (other than CForm) in two setups. −CF corresponds to the models as described in Section 3. +CF further incorporates lexico-syntactic knowledge of canonical forms into each model by concatenating the embedding representing each VNC token instance with a one-dimensional vector which is one if the VNC occurs in its canonical form, and zero otherwise.

We first consider results for the −CF setup. On both DEV and TEST, the accuracy achieved by each supervised model is higher than that of the unsupervised CForm approach, except for Siamese CBOW on TEST. The word2vec model achieves the highest accuracy on DEV and TEST of 0.830 and 0.804, respectively. The difference between the word2vec model and the next-best model, skip-thoughts, is significant using a bootstrap test (Berg-Kirkpatrick et al., 2012) with $10k$ repetitions for DEV ($p = 0.006$), but not for TEST ($p = 0.051$). Nevertheless, it is remarkable that the relatively simple approach to averaging word embeddings used by word2vec performs as well as, or better than, the much more complex skip-thoughts model used by Salton et al. (2016).[8]

Turning to the +CF setup, we observe that, for both DEV and TEST, each model achieves higher accuracy than in the −CF setup.[9] All of these differences are significant using a bootstrap test ($p < 0.002$ in each case). In addition, each method outperforms the unsupervised CForm approach on both DEV and TEST. These findings demonstrate that the linguistically-motivated, lexico-syntactic knowledge encoded by the canonical form feature is complementary to the information from a wide range of types of distributed representations. In the +CF setup, the word2vec model again achieves the highest accuracy on both DEV and TEST of 0.854 and 0.852, respectively.[10] The difference between the word2vec model and the next-best model, again skip-thoughts, is significant for both DEV and TEST using a bootstrap test ($p < 0.05$ in each case).

To better understand the impact of the canonical form feature when combined with the word2vec model, we compute the average precision, recall, and F1 score for each MWE for both the positive (idiomatic) and negative (literal) classes, for each run on TEST.[11] For a given run, we then compute the average precision, recall, and F1 score across all MWEs, and then the average over all ten runs. We do this using CForm, and the word2vec model with and without the canonical form feature. Results are shown in Table 3. In line with the findings of Fazly et al. (2009), CForm achieves higher precision and recall on idiomatic usages than literal ones. In particular, the relatively low recall for the literal class indicates that many literal usages occur in a canonical form. Comparing the word2vec model with and without the canonical form feature, we see that, when this feature is used, there is a relatively larger increase in precision and recall (and F1 score) for the literal class, than for the idiomatic class. This indicates that, although the

---

⁸The word2vec and skip-thoughts models were trained on different corpora, which could contribute to the differences in results for these models. We therefore carried out an additional experiment in which we trained word2vec on Book-Corpus, the corpus on which skip-thoughts was trained. This new word2vec model achieved accuracies of 0.825 and 0.809, on DEV and TEST, respectively, which are also higher accu-

racies than those obtained by the skip-thoughts model.

⁹In order to determine that this improvement is due to the information about canonical forms carried by the additional feature in the +CF setup, and not due to the increase in number of dimensions, we performed additional experiments in which we concatenated the embedding representations with a random binary feature, and with a randomly chosen value between 0 and 1. For each model, neither of these approaches outperformed that model using the +CF setup.

¹⁰In the +CF setup, the word2vec model using embeddings that were trained on the same corpus as skip-thoughts achieved accuracies of 0.846 and 0.851, on DEV and TEST, respectively. These are again higher accuracies than the corresponding setup for the skip-thoughts model.

¹¹We carried out the same analysis on DEV. The findings were similar.

Model	Idiomatic			Literal			Ave. F
	P	R	F	P	R	F	
CForm	0.766	0.901	0.794	0.668	0.587	0.576	0.685
Word2vec −CF	0.815	0.879	0.830	0.627	0.542	0.556	0.693
Word2vec +CF	0.830	0.892	0.848	0.758	0.676	0.691	0.770

Table 3: Precision (P), recall (R), and F1 score (F), for the idiomatic and literal classes, as well as average F1 score (Ave. F), for TEST.

canonical form feature itself performs relatively poorly on literal usages, it provides information that enables the word2vec model to better identify literal usages.

6 Conclusions

Determining whether a usage of a VNC is idiomatic or literal is important for applications such as machine translation, where it is vital to preserve the meanings of word combinations. In this paper we proposed two approaches to the task of classifying VNC token instances as idiomatic or literal based on word2vec embeddings and Siamese CBOW. We compared these approaches against a linguistically-informed unsupervised baseline, and a model based on skip-thoughts previously applied to this task (Salton et al., 2016). Our experimental results show that a comparatively simple approach based on averaging word embeddings performs at least as well as, or better than, the approach based on skip-thoughts. We further proposed methods to combine linguistic knowledge of the lexico-syntactic fixedness of VNCs — so-called "canonical forms", which can be automatically acquired from corpora via statistical methods — with the embedding based approaches. Our findings indicate that this rich linguistic knowledge is complementary to that available in distributed representations.

Alternative approaches to embedding sentences containing VNC instances could also be considered, for example, FastSent (Hill et al., 2016). However, all of the models we used represent the context of a VNC by the sentence in which it occurs. In future work we therefore also intend to consider approaches such as context2vec (Melamud et al., 2016) which explicitly encode the context in which a token occurs. Finally, one known challenge of VNC token classification is to develop models that are able to generalize to VNC types that were not seen during training (Gharbieh et al., 2016). In future work we plan to explore this experimental setup.

References

Timothy Baldwin and Su Nam Kim. 2010. Multiword expressions. In Nitin Indurkhya and Fred J. Damerau, editors, *Handbook of Natural Language Processing*, CRC Press, Boca Raton, USA. 2nd edition.

Taylor Berg-Kirkpatrick, David Burkett, and Dan Klein. 2012. An empirical investigation of statistical significance in NLP. In *Proceedings of the 2012 Joint Conference on Empirical Methods in Natural Language Processing and Computational Natural Language Learning*. Association for Computational Linguistics, pages 995–1005. http://www.aclweb.org/anthology/D12-1091.

Julia Birke and Anoop Sarkar. 2006. A clustering approach for nearly unsupervised recognition of non-literal language. In *Proceedings of the 11th Conference of the European Chapter of the Association for Computational Linguistics (EACL-2006)*. Trento, Italy, pages 329–336. http://aclweb.org/anthology/E/E06/E06-1042.pdf.

Julian Brooke, Vivian Tsang, Graeme Hirst, and Fraser Shein. 2014. Unsupervised multiword segmentation of large corpora using prediction-driven decomposition of n-grams. In *Proceedings of COLING 2014, the 25th International Conference on Computational Linguistics: Technical Papers*. Dublin, Ireland, pages 753–761.

Lou Burnard. 2000. *The British National Corpus Users Reference Guide*. Oxford University Computing Services.

Paul Cook, Afsaneh Fazly, and Suzanne Stevenson. 2008. The VNC-Tokens Dataset. In *Proceedings of the LREC Workshop on Towards a Shared Task for Multiword Expressions (MWE 2008)*. Marrakech, Morocco, pages 19–22. http://www.lrec-conf.org/proceedings/lrec2008/workshops/W20_Proceedings.pdf.

Afsaneh Fazly, Paul Cook, and Suzanne Stevenson. 2009. Unsupervised type and token identification of idiomatic expressions. *Computational Linguistics* 35(1):61–103. http://dx.doi.org/10.1162/coli.08-010-R1-07-048.

Richard Fothergill and Timothy Baldwin. 2012. Combining resources for mwe-token classification. In *SEM 2012: The First Joint Conference on Lexical and Computational Semantics – Volume 1: Proceedings of the main conference and the shared task, and Volume 2: Proceedings of the Sixth International Workshop on Semantic Evaluation (SemEval 2012)*. Montréal, Canada, pages 100–104. http://www.aclweb.org/anthology/S12-1017.

Waseem Gharbieh, Virendra C Bhavsar, and Paul Cook. 2016. A word embedding approach to identifying verb–noun idiomatic combinations. In *Proceedings of the 12th Workshop on Multiword Expressions (MWE 2016)*. Association for Computational Linguistics, Berlin, Germany, pages 112–118. http://aclweb.org/anthology/W/W16/W16-1817.pdf.

Chikara Hashimoto and Daisuke Kawahara. 2008. Construction of an idiom corpus and its application to idiom identification based on WSD incorporating idiom-specific features. In *Proceedings of the 2008 Conference on Empirical Methods in Natural Language Processing*. Honolulu, Hawaii, pages 992–1001.

Felix Hill, Kyunghyun Cho, and Anna Korhonen. 2016. Learning distributed representations of sentences from unlabelled data. In *Proceedings of the 2016 Conference of the North American Chapter of the Association for Computational Linguistics: Human Language Technologies*. Association for Computational Linguistics, San Diego, California, pages 1367–1377. http://www.aclweb.org/anthology/N16-1162.

Tom Kenter, Alexey Borisov, and Maarten de Rijke. 2016. Siamese cbow: Optimizing word embeddings for sentence representations. In *Proceedings of the 54th Annual Meeting of the Association for Computational Linguistics (Volume 1: Long Papers)*. Association for Computational Linguistics, Berlin, Germany, pages 941–951. http://www.aclweb.org/anthology/P16-1089.

Ryan Kiros, Yukun Zhu, Ruslan Salakhutdinov, Richard S. Zemel, Antonio Torralba, Raquel Urtasun, and Sanja Fidler. 2015. Skip-thought vectors. In C. Cortes, N. D. Lawrence, D. D. Lee, M. Sugiyama, and R. Garnett, editors, *Advances in Neural Information Processing Systems 28*, Curran Associates, Inc., pages 3276–3284.

Linlin Li, Benjamin Roth, and Caroline Sporleder. 2010. Topic models for word sense disambiguation and token-based idiom detection. In *Proceedings of the 48th Annual Meeting of the Association for Computational Linguistics*. Uppsala, Sweden, pages 1138–1147.

Oren Melamud, Jacob Goldberger, and Ido Dagan. 2016. context2vec: Learning generic context embedding with bidirectional lstm. In *Proceedings of The 20th SIGNLL Conference on Computational Natural Language Learning*. pages 51–61. http://www.aclweb.org/anthology/K16-1006.

Tomas Mikolov, Kai Chen, Greg Corrado, and Jeffrey Dean. 2013. Efficient estimation of word representations in vector space. In *Proceedings of Workshop at the International Conference on Learning Representations, 2013*. Scottsdale, USA. https://arxiv.org/abs/1301.3781.

Jon Patrick and Jeremy Fletcher. 2005. Classifying verb-particle constructions by verb arguments. In *Proceedings of the Second ACL-SIGSEM Workshop on the Linguistic Dimensions of Prepositions and their use in Computational Linguistics Formalisms and Applications*. Colchester, UK, pages 200–209.

Ivan A. Sag, Timothy Baldwin, Francis Bond, Ann Copestake, and Dan Flickinger. 2002. Multiword expressions: A pain in the neck for NLP. In *Proceedings of the Third International Conference on Intelligent Text Processing and Computational Linguistics (CICLING 2002)*. pages 1–15. http://dl.acm.org/citation.cfm?id=647344.724004.

Giancarlo Salton, Robert Ross, and John Kelleher. 2016. Idiom token classification using sentential distributed semantics. In *Proceedings of the 54th Annual Meeting of the Association for Computational Linguistics (Volume 1: Long Papers)*. Association for Computational Linguistics, Berlin, Germany, pages 194–204. http://www.aclweb.org/anthology/P16-1019.

Agata Savary, Carlos Ramisch, Silvio Cordeiro, Federico Sangati, Veronika Vincze, Behrang Qasemi-Zadeh, Marie Candito, Fabienne Cap, Voula Giouli, Ivelina Stoyanova, and Antoine Doucet. 2017. The parseme shared task on automatic identification of verbal multiword expressions. In *Proceedings of the 13th Workshop on Multiword Expressions (MWE 2017)*. Association for Computational Linguistics, Valencia, Spain, pages 31–47. http://www.aclweb.org/anthology/W17-1704.

Nathan Schneider, Emily Danchik, Chris Dyer, and Noah A. Smith. 2014. Discriminative lexical semantic segmentation with gaps: Running the mwe gamut. *Transactions of the Association of Computational Linguistics* 2:193–206.

Kiyoko Uchiyama, Timothy Baldwin, and Shun Ishizaki. 2005. Disambiguating Japanese compound verbs. *Computer Speech and Language, Special Issue on Multiword Expressions* 19(4):497–512.

Using pseudo-senses for improving the extraction of synonyms from word embeddings

Olivier Ferret

CEA, LIST, Vision and Content Engineering Laboratory,
Gif-sur-Yvette, F-91191 France.
`olivier.ferret@cea.fr`

Abstract

The methods proposed recently for specializing word embeddings according to a particular perspective generally rely on external knowledge. In this article, we propose *Pseudofit*, a new method for specializing word embeddings according to semantic similarity without any external knowledge. *Pseudofit* exploits the notion of pseudo-sense for building several representations for each word and uses these representations for making the initial embeddings more generic. We illustrate the interest of *Pseudofit* for acquiring synonyms and study several variants of *Pseudofit* according to this perspective.

1 Introduction

The interest aroused by word embeddings in Natural Language Processing, especially for neural models, has led to propose methods for creating them from texts (Mikolov et al., 2013; Pennington et al., 2014) but also for specializing them according to a particular viewpoint. This viewpoint generally comes in the form of set of lexical relations. For instance, Kiela et al. (2015) specialize word embeddings towards semantic similarity or relatedness by relying either on synonyms or free lexical associations. Methods such as Retrofitting (Faruqui et al., 2015), Counterfitting (Mrkšić et al., 2016) or PARAGRAM (Wieting et al., 2015) fall within the same framework.

The specialization of word embeddings can also come from the way they are built. For instance, Levy and Goldberg (2014) bring word embeddings towards similarity rather than relatedness by using dependency-based distributional contexts rather than linear bag-of-word contexts. Finally, some methods aim at improving word embeddings

but without a clearly defined orientation, such as the All-but-the-Top method (Mu, 2018), which focuses on dimensionality reduction, or (Vulić et al., 2017), which exploits morphological relations.

In this article, we propose *Pseudofit*, a method that improves word embeddings without external knowledge and focuses on semantic similarity and synonym extraction. The principle of *Pseudofit* is to exploit the notion of pseudo-sense coming from word sense disambiguation for building representations accounting for distributional variability and to create better word embeddings by bringing these representations closer together. We show the interest of *Pseudofit* and its variants through both intrinsic and extrinsic evaluations.

2 Method

The distributional representation of a word varies from one corpus to another. Without even taking into account the plurality of meanings of a word, this variability also exists inside any corpus C, even if it is quite homogeneous: the distributional representations of a word built from each half of C, C_1 and C_2, are not identical. However, from the more general viewpoint of its meaning, they should be identical, or at least very close, and their differences be considered as incidental. Following this perspective, a representation resulting from the convergence of the representations built from C_1 and C_2 should be more generic and show better semantic similarity properties.

The method we propose, *Pseudofit*, formalizes this approach through the notion of pseudo-sense. This notion is related to the notion of pseudo-word introduced in the field of word sense disambiguation by Gale et al. (1992) and Schütze (1992). A pseudo-word is an artificial word resulting from the clustering of two or more different words, each of them being considered as one pseudo-sense of

351

Proceedings of the 56th Annual Meeting of the Association for Computational Linguistics (Short Papers), pages 351–357
Melbourne, Australia, July 15 - 20, 2018. ©2018 Association for Computational Linguistics

the pseudo-word. *Pseudofit* adopts the opposite viewpoint. For each word w, more precisely nouns in our case, it splits arbitrarily its occurrences into two sets: the occurrences of one set are labeled as pseudo-sense w_1 while the occurrences of the other set are labeled as pseudo-sense w_2. A distributional representation is built for w, w_1 and w_2 under the same conditions, with a neural model in our case. The second stage of *Pseudofit* adapts *a posteriori* the representation of w according to the convergence of the representations of w_1 and w_2. This adaptation is performed by exploiting the similarity relations between w, w_1 and w_2 in the context of a word embedding specialization method. By considering simultaneously w, w_1 and w_2, *Pseudofit* benefits from both the variations between the representations of w_1 and w_2 and the quality of the representation of w, since it is built from the whole C while the two others are built from half of it.

2.1 Building of Word Embeddings

The first stage of *Pseudofit* consists in building a distributional representation of each word w and its two pseudo-senses w_1 and w_2. The starting point of this process is the generation of a set of distributional contexts for each occurrence of w. Classically, this generation is based on a linear fixed-size window centered on the considered occurrence. The specificity of *Pseudofit* is that contexts are generated both for the target word and one of its pseudo-sense. The pseudo-sense changes from one occurrence of w to the following, leading to the same frequency for w_1 and w_2. The generation of such contexts with a window of 3 words (before and after the target word *policeman*) is illustrated here for the following sentence:

A *policeman*$_1$ was arrested by another *policeman*$_2$.

TARGET	CONTEXTS
policeman	{a, be, arrest (2), by (2), another}
policeman$_1$	{a, be, arrest, by}
policeman$_2$	{another, by, arrest}

This sentence, which is voluntarily artificial, shows how three different contexts are built for a word in a corpus: one context (first line) is built from all the occurrences of the target word; a second one (second line) is built from half of the occurrences of the target word, representing its first pseudo-sense, while the third context (last line) is built from the other half of the occurrences of the target word, representing its second pseudo-sense.

The generated contexts are then used for building word embeddings. More precisely, we adopt the variant of the Skip-gram model (Mikolov et al., 2013) proposed by Levy and Goldberg (2014), which can take as input arbitrary contexts.

2.2 Convergence of Word Representations

The second stage of *Pseudofit* brings the representations of each target word w and its pseudo-senses w_1 and w_2 closer together. This convergence aims at producing a more general representation of w by erasing the differences between the representations of w, w_1 and w_2, which are assumed to be incidental since these representations refer by nature to the same object.

The implementation of this convergence process relies on the PARAGRAM algorithm, which takes as inputs word embeddings and a set of binary lexical relations accounting for semantic similarity. PARAGRAM gradually modifies the input embeddings for bringing closer together the vectors of the words that are part of similarity relations. This adaptation is controlled by a kind of regularization that tends to preserve the input embeddings. This twofold objective consists more formally in minimizing the following objective function by stochastic gradient descent:

$$
\sum_{(x_1, x_2)\, \in \mathcal{L}_i} \max\left(0, \delta + \mathbf{x}_1 \mathbf{t}_1 - \mathbf{x}_1 \mathbf{x}_2\right) +
$$
$$
\max\left(0, \delta + \mathbf{x}_2 \mathbf{t}_2 - \mathbf{x}_1 \mathbf{x}_2\right) + \lambda \sum_{\mathbf{x}_i\, \in V(\mathcal{L}_i)} \left\|\mathbf{x}_i^{init} - \mathbf{x}_i\right\|^2 \tag{1}
$$

where the first sum expresses the convergence of the vectors according to the similarity relations while the second sum, modulated by the λ parameter, corresponds to the regularization term.

The specificity of PARAGRAM, compared to methods such as Retrofitting, lies in its adaptation term. While it logically tends to bring closer together the vectors of the words that are part of similarity relations (attracting term $\mathbf{x}_1 \mathbf{x}_2$), it also pushes them away from the vectors of the words that are not part these relations (repelling terms $\mathbf{x}_1 \mathbf{t}_1$ and $\mathbf{x}_2 \mathbf{t}_2$). More precisely, the relations are split into a set of mini-batches $\mathcal{L}_i$. For each word (vector $\mathbf{x}_i$) of a relation, a word (vector $\mathbf{t}_j$) outside the relation is selected among the words of the mini-batch of the current relation in such a way that $\mathbf{t}_j$ is the closest word to $\mathbf{x}_i$ according to the *Cosine* measure, which represents the most discriminative option. δ is the margin between the attracting and repelling terms.

	INITIAL	Pseudofit	Retrofit.	Counter-fit.
SimLex-999	49.5	51.2	49.6	49.5
MEN	78.3	79.9	77.4	77.2
MTurk 771	65.6	68.0	65.0	64.9

Table 1: Intrinsic evaluation of *Pseudofit* ($\times 100$)

The application of PARAGRAM to the embeddings resulting from the first stage of *Pseudofit* exploits the fact that a word and its pseudo-words are supposed to be similar. Hence, for each word w, three similarity relations are defined and used by PARAGRAM for adapting the initial embeddings: (w, w_1), (w, w_2) et (w_1, w_2). Finally, only the representations of words w are exploited since they are built from a corpus that is twice as large as the corpus used for pseudo-words.

3 Experiments

3.1 Experimental Setup

For implementing *Pseudofit*, we randomly select at the level of sentences a 1 billion word subpart of the Annotated English Gigaword corpus (Napoles et al., 2012). This corpus is made of news articles in English processed by the Stanford CoreNLP toolkit (Manning et al., 2014). We use this corpus under its lemmatized form. The building of the embeddings are performed with *word2vecf*, the adaptation of *word2vec* from (Levy and Goldberg, 2014), with the best parameter values from (Baroni et al., 2014): minimal count=5, vector size=300, window size=5, 10 negative examples and 10^{-5} for the subsampling probability of the most frequent words. For PARAGRAM, we adopt most of the parameter values from (Vulić et al., 2017): $\delta = 0.6$ and $\lambda = 10^{-9}$, with the AdaGrad optimizer (Duchi et al., 2011) and 50 epochs[1]. Retrofitting and Counter-fitting are used with the parameter values specified respectively in (Faruqui et al., 2015) and (Mrkšić et al., 2016).

3.2 Evaluation of *Pseudofit*

Our first evaluation of *Pseudofit* at word level is a classical intrinsic evaluation consisting in measuring for a set of word pairs the Spearman's rank correlation between human judgments and the similarity of these words computed from their embeddings by the *Cosine* measure. This evaluation is performed for the nouns of three large enough reference datasets: SimLex-999 (Hill et al., 2015),

method	$R_{prec.}$	MAP	P@1	P@2	P@5
INITIAL	13.0	15.2	18.3	13.1	7.7
Pseudofit	+2.5	+3.3	+3.0	+2.5	+1.8
Retrofitting	−0.5	−0.6	−0.6	−0.2[†]	−0.3
Counter-fitting	−0.6	−0.8	−0.6	−0.5	−0.4

Table 2: Evaluation of *Pseudofit* for synonym extraction (differences / INITIAL, $\times 100$)

MEN (Bruni et al., 2014) and MTurk-771 (Halawi et al., 2012). Table 1 clearly shows that *Pseudofit* significantly[2] improves the initial embeddings for the three datasets. By contrast, it also shows that replacing PARAGRAM with Retrofitting or Counter-fitting, two other reference methods for specializing embeddings, does not lead to comparable improvements and can even degrade results.

Our second evaluation, which is our main focus, is a more extrinsic task consisting in extracting synonyms[3]. This extraction is performed by ranking a set of candidate synonyms for each target word according to the similarity, computed here by the *Cosine* measure, of their embeddings. We evaluate the relevance of this ranking as in Information Retrieval with R-precision ($R_{prec.}$), MAP (Mean Average Precision) and precisions at various ranks (P@r). Our reference is made up of the synonyms of WordNet (Miller, 1990) while both our target words and candidate synonyms are made up of the nouns with more than ten occurrences in each half of our corpus, which represents 20,813 nouns.

Table 2 gives the result of this second evaluation for 11,481 nouns with synonyms in WordNet among our 20,813 targets. As in the first evaluation, *Pseudofit* significantly[4] outperforms the initial embeddings. Moreover, replacing PARAGRAM with Retrofitting or Counter-fitting leads to a systematic decrease of results, which emphasizes the importance of the repelling term of PARAGRAM. This term probably prevents the representation of a word from being changed too much by its pseudosenses, which are interesting variants in terms of representations but were built from half of the corpus only.

---

[1]We used the implementation of PARAGRAM provided by https://github.com/nmrksic/attract-repel.

[2]The statistical significance of differences are judged according to a two-tailed Steiger's test with p-value < 0.01 with the R package *cocor* (Diedenhofen and Musch, 2015).

[3]The TOEFL test, which is close to our task, is considered sometimes as extrinsic and sometimes as intrinsic.

[4]The significance of differences are judged according to a paired Wilcoxon test with the following notation: nothing if $p <= 0.01$, † if $0.01 < p \leq 0.05$ and ‡ if $p > 0.05$.

method	$R_{prec.}$	MAP	P@1	P@2	P@5
INITIAL$_{high}$	15.4	17.7	22.6	16.4	9.7
INITIAL$_{low}$	9.4	11.5	11.8	8.1	4.7
Pseudofit$_{high}$	+0.7	+1.1	+0.3‡	+0.8	0.9
Pseudofit$_{low}$	+5.3	+6.7	+7.0	+5.2	+3.1

Table 3: Evaluation of *Pseudofit* for synonym extraction according to the frequency (*high* or *low*) of the target words (differences / INITIAL, ×100)

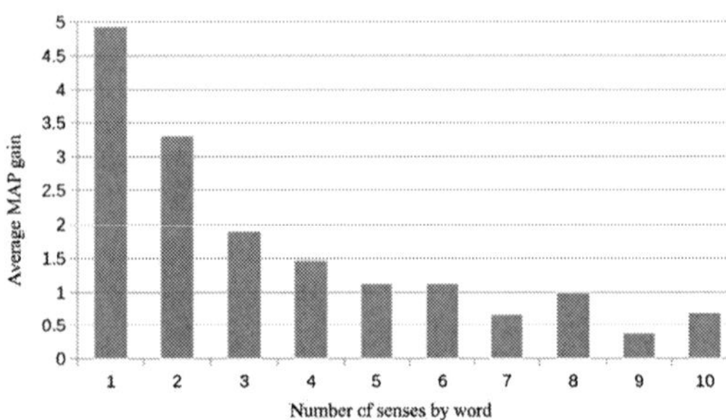

Figure 1: Gain brought by *Pseudofit* for MAP according to the ambiguity of the target word

Finally, we performed a finer analysis of these results according to the frequency and the degree of ambiguity of the target words. Concerning frequency, Table 3 shows that *Pseudofit* is particularly efficient for the lower half of the target words in terms of frequency, with a large increase of 5.3 points for R-precision, 6.7 points for MAP, 7.0 points for P@1 and 5.2 points for P@2 while the largest increase for the higher half of the target words is equal to 1.1 points for MAP.

One possible explanation of this gap between high and low frequency words is linked to the degree of ambiguity of words: high frequency words are more likely to be polysemous and *Pseudofit* does not take into account the polysemy of words. Figure 1 tends to confirm this hypothesis by showing that the improvement brought by *Pseudofit* for a word is inversely proportional to its ambiguity as estimated by its number of senses in WordNet[5].

3.3 Variants of *Pseudofit*

We defined and tested several variants of *Pseudofit*. The first one, *Pseudofit max*, focuses on the strategy for selecting $\{t_j\}$ in PARAGRAM. The results of Table 1, as those of (Mrkšić et al., 2017), are obtained with a setting where half of $\{t_j\}$ are selected randomly. In *Pseudofit max*, all $\{t_j\}$ are

---

[5]Words with at most 10 senses cover 98.9% of the nouns of our evaluation.

Variant	$R_{prec.}$	MAP	P@1	P@2	P@5
Pseudofit	15.5	18.5	21.3	15.6	9.5
max	+0.2‡	+0.3	+0.3†	+0.2†	+0.1
3 pseudo-senses	+0.2‡	+0.2	+0.4†	+0.2‡	+0.0‡
context	+0.4†	+0.3‡	+0.5†	+0.2‡	+0.0‡
fus-average	+0.2†	+0.3	+0.4	+0.2†	+0.1
fus-add	+0.0‡	+0.0	+0.2‡	+0.1‡	+0.1†
fus-max-pool	+0.2‡	+0.3	+0.4	+0.2	+0.2
max+fus-max-pool	+0.4	+0.5	+0.5	+0.4	+0.2

Table 4: Evaluation of *Pseudofit*'s variants (differences / *Pseudofit*, ×100)

selected according to their similarity with $\{x_i\}$.

The second variant, *Pseudofit 3 pseudo-senses*, aims at determining if increasing the number of pseudo-senses, from two to three at first, can have a positive impact on results.

The third variant, *Pseudofit context*, tests the interest of defining pseudo-senses for the words of distributional contexts. In this configuration, pseudo-senses are defined for all nouns, verbs and adjectives with more than 21 occurrences in the corpus, which corresponds to a minimal frequency of 10 in each half of the corpus.

Finally, similarly to the second variant, the last variant, *Pseudofit fus-**, adds a supplementary representation of the target word. However, this representation is not an additional pseudo-sense but an aggregation of its already existing pseudo-senses, which can be viewed as another global representation of the target word. Three aggregation methods are considered: *Pseudofit fus-addition* performs an elementwise addition of the embeddings of pseudo-senses, *Pseudofit fus-average* computes their mean while *Pseudofit fus-max-pooling* takes their maximal value.

Each presented variant outperforms the base version of *Pseudofit* but Table 4 also shows that not all variants are of equal interest. From the viewpoint of both the absolute level of their results and the significance of their difference with *Pseudofit*, *Pseudofit max* and *Pseudofit fus-max-pooling* are clearly the most interesting variants. Their combination, *Pseudofit max+fus-max-pooling*, leads to our best results and significantly outperforms *Pseudofit* for all measures. Among the *Pseudofit fus-** variants, *Pseudofit fus-max-pooling* and *Pseudofit fus-average* are close to each other and clearly exceeds *Pseudofit fus-addition*. The results of *Pseudofit 3 pseudo-senses* show that using more than two pseudo-senses by word faces the problem of having too few occurrences for each pseudo-sense. The same frequency effect, at the level of contexts, probably explains the very limited impact of the introduction of pseudo-senses in contexts in the case of *Pseudofit context*.

3.4 Sentence Similarity

Our final evaluation, which is fully extrinsic, examines the impact of *Pseudofit* on the identification of semantic similarity between sentences. More precisely, we adopt the STS Benchmark dataset on semantic textual similarity (Cer et al., 2017). The overall principle of this task is similar to the word similarity task of our first evaluation but at the level of sentences: the similarity of a set of sentence pairs is computed by the system to evaluate and compared with a correlation measure, the Pearson correlation coefficient, against a gold standard produced by human annotators.

This framework is interesting for the evaluation of *Pseudofit* because the computation of the similarity of a pair of sentences can be achieved by unsupervised approaches based on word embeddings in a very competitive way, as demonstrated by (Hill et al., 2016). More precisely, the approach we adopt is a classical baseline that composes the embeddings of the plain words of each sentence to compare by elementwise addition and computes the *Cosine* measure between the two resulting vectors. For building the representation of a sentence, we compare the use of our initial embeddings with that of the embeddings produced by *Pseudofit max+fus-max-pooling*, the best variant of *Pseudofit*. For this experiment, pseudo-senses are distinguished not only for nouns but more generally for all nouns, verbs and adjectives with more than 21 occurrences in the corpus.

Table 5 shows the result of this evaluation for the 1,379 sentence pairs of the test part of the STS Benchmark dataset. As for the two previous evaluations, the use of the embeddings modified by *Pseudofit* leads to a significant improvement of results[6] compared to the initial embeddings, which demonstrates that the improvement at word level can be transposed at a larger scale. Table 5 also shows four reference results from (Cer et al., 2017): the lowest and the best baselines based on averaged word embeddings (Skip-gram

---

[6]With the same evaluation of statistical significance as for word similarity.

method	$\rho \times 100$
INITIAL	63.2
Pseudofit max+fus-max-pooling	66.0
(Cer et al., 2017)	
Best baseline (averaged embeddings)	56.5
Lowest baseline (averaged embeddings)	40.6
Best unsupervised system	75.8
Lowest unsupervised system	59.2

Table 5: Evaluation of *Pseudofit* for identifying sentence similarity

and GloVe respectively), which are very close to our approach, and the best (Conneau et al., 2017) and the lowest (Duma and Menzel, 2017) unsupervised systems. Although our goal is not to compete with the best systems, it is interesting to note that our results are in line with the state of the art since they significantly outperform the two baselines and the lowest unsupervised system as well as other unsupervised systems mentioned in (Cer et al., 2017).

4 Conclusion and Perspectives

In this article, we presented *Pseudofit*, a method that specializes word embeddings towards semantic similarity without external knowledge by exploiting the variability of distributional contexts. This method can be described as hybrid since it operates both before and after the building of word embeddings. A set of intrinsic and extrinsic evaluations demonstrates the interest of the word embeddings produced by *Pseudofit* and its variants, with a particular emphasis on the extraction of synonyms.

In the presented work, the principles underlying *Pseudofit*, in particular the generation and convergence of different representations of a word, were tested only within the same corpus. In conjunction with the work about word meta-embeddings (Yin and Schütze, 2016), it would be interesting to apply these principles to representations built from several corpora, like (Mrkšić et al., 2017) for different languages.

Acknowledgments

This work has been partially funded by French National Research Agency (ANR) under project ADDICTE (ANR-17-CE23-0001). The author thanks the anonymous reviewers for their valuable comments.

References

Marco Baroni, Georgiana Dinu, and Germán Kruszewski. 2014. Don't count, predict! A systematic comparison of context-counting vs. context-predicting semantic vectors. In *52nd Annual Meeting of the Association for Computational Linguistics (ACL 2014)*, pages 238–247, Baltimore, Maryland.

Elia Bruni, N Tram, Marco Baroni, et al. 2014. Multimodal distributional semantics. *Journal of Artificial Intelligence Research*, 49:1–47.

Daniel Cer, Mona Diab, Eneko Agirre, Inigo Lopez-Gazpio, and Lucia Specia. 2017. SemEval-2017 Task 1: Semantic Textual Similarity Multilingual and Crosslingual Focused Evaluation. In *11th International Workshop on Semantic Evaluation (SemEval-2017)*, pages 1–14, Vancouver, Canada.

Alexis Conneau, Douwe Kiela, Holger Schwenk, Loïc Barrault, and Antoine Bordes. 2017. Supervised Learning of Universal Sentence Representations from Natural Language Inference Data. In *2017 Conference on Empirical Methods in Natural Language Processing (EMNLP 2017)*, pages 670–680, Copenhagen, Denmark.

Birk Diedenhofen and Jochen Musch. 2015. cocor: A Comprehensive Solution for the Statistical Comparison of Correlations. *PLOS ONE*, 10(4):1–12.

John Duchi, Elad Hazan, and Yoram Singer. 2011. Adaptive Subgradient Methods for Online Learning and Stochastic Optimization. *Journal of Machine Learning Research*, 12:2121–2159.

Mirela-Stefania Duma and Wolfgang Menzel. 2017. SEF@UHH at SemEval-2017 Task 1: Unsupervised Knowledge-Free Semantic Textual Similarity via Paragraph Vector. In *11th International Workshop on Semantic Evaluation (SemEval-2017)*, pages 170–174, Vancouver, Canada.

Manaal Faruqui, Jesse Dodge, Sujay Kumar Jauhar, Chris Dyer, Eduard Hovy, and Noah A. Smith. 2015. Retrofitting Word Vectors to Semantic Lexicons. In *2015 Conference of the North American Chapter of the Association for Computational Linguistics: Human Language Technologies (NAACL HLT 2015)*, pages 1606–1615, Denver, Colorado.

William A Gale, Kenneth W Church, and David Yarowsky. 1992. Work on statistical methods for word sense disambiguation. In *AAAI Fall Symposium on Probabilistic Approaches to Natural Language*, pages 54–60.

Guy Halawi, Gideon Dror, Evgeniy Gabrilovich, and Yehuda Koren. 2012. Large-scale Learning of Word Relatedness with Constraints. In *18th ACM SIGKDD International Conference on Knowledge Discovery and Data Mining (KDD'12)*, pages 1406–1414. ACM.

Felix Hill, Kyunghyun Cho, and Anna Korhonen. 2016. Learning Distributed Representations of Sentences from Unlabelled Data. In *2016 Conference of the North American Chapter of the Association for Computational Linguistics: Human Language Technologies (NAACL HLT 2016)*, pages 1367–1377, San Diego, California.

Felix Hill, Roi Reichart, and Anna Korhonen. 2015. Simlex-999: Evaluating semantic models with (genuine) similarity estimation. *Computational Linguistics*, 41(4):665–695.

Douwe Kiela, Felix Hill, and Stephen Clark. 2015. Specializing Word Embeddings for Similarity or Relatedness. In *2015 Conference on Empirical Methods in Natural Language Processing (EMNLP 2015)*, pages 2044–2048, Lisbon, Portugal.

Omer Levy and Yoav Goldberg. 2014. Dependency-Based Word Embeddings. In *52nd Annual Meeting of the Association for Computational Linguistics (ACL 2014)*, pages 302–308, Baltimore, Maryland.

Christopher D. Manning, Mihai Surdeanu, John Bauer, Jenny Finkel, Steven J. Bethard, and David McClosky. 2014. The Stanford CoreNLP Natural Language Processing Toolkit. In *52nd Annual Meeting of the Association for Computational Linguistics (ACL 2014), system demonstrations*, pages 55–60.

Tomas Mikolov, Kai Chen, Greg Corrado, and Jeffrey Dean. 2013. Efficient estimation of word representations in vector space. In *ICLR 2013, workshop track*.

George A. Miller. 1990. WordNet: An On-Line Lexical Database. *International Journal of Lexicography*, 3(4).

Nikola Mrkšić, Diarmuid Ó Séaghdha, Blaise Thomson, Milica Gašić, Lina M. Rojas-Barahona, Pei-Hao Su, David Vandyke, Tsung-Hsien Wen, and Steve Young. 2016. Counter-fitting Word Vectors to Linguistic Constraints. In *2016 Conference of the North American Chapter of the Association for Computational Linguistics: Human Language Technologies (NAACL HLT 2016)*, pages 142–148, San Diego, California.

Nikola Mrkšić, Ivan Vulić, Diarmuid Ó Séaghdha, Ira Leviant, Roi Reichart, Gašić Milica, Anna Korhonen, and Steve Young. 2017. Semantic Specialization of Distributional Word Vector Spaces using Monolingual and Cross-Lingual Constraints. *Transactions of the Association for Computational Linguistics*, 5:309–324.

Jiaqi Mu. 2018. All-but-the-Top: Simple and Effective Postprocessing for Word Representations. In *Sixth International Conference on Learning Representations (ICLR 2018), poster session*, Vancouver, Canada.

Courtney Napoles, Matthew R. Gormley, and Benjamin Van Durme. 2012. Annotated Gigaword. In *NAACL Joint Workshop on Automatic Knowledge Base Construction and Web-scale Knowledge Extraction (AKBC-WEKEX)*, pages 95–100, Montréal, Canada.

Jeffrey Pennington, Richard Socher, and Christopher D. Manning. 2014. GloVe: Global Vectors for Word Representation. In *2014 Conference on Empirical Methods in Natural Language Processing (EMNLP 2014)*, pages 1532–1543, Doha, Qatar.

Hinrich Schütze. 1992. Dimensions of meaning. In *1992 ACM/IEEE conference on Supercomputing*, pages 787–796. IEEE Computer Society Press.

Ivan Vulić, Nikola Mrkšić, Roi Reichart, Diarmuid Ó Séaghdha, Steve Young, and Anna Korhonen. 2017. Morph-fitting: Fine-Tuning Word Vector Spaces with Simple Language-Specific Rules. In *55th Annual Meeting of the Association for Computational Linguistics (ACL 2017)*, pages 56–68, Vancouver, Canada.

John Wieting, Mohit Bansal, Kevin Gimpel, and Karen Livescu. 2015. From Paraphrase Database to Compositional Paraphrase Model and Back. *Transactions of the Association for Computational Linguistics*, 3:345–358.

Wenpeng Yin and Hinrich Schütze. 2016. Learning Word Meta-Embeddings. In *54th Annual Meeting of the Association for Computational Linguistics (ACL 2016)*, pages 1351–1360, Berlin, Germany.

Hearst Patterns Revisited:
Automatic Hypernym Detection from Large Text Corpora

Stephen Roller, Douwe Kiela, and Maximilian Nickel
Facebook AI Research
`{roller,dkiela,maxn}@fb.com`

Abstract

Methods for unsupervised hypernym detection may broadly be categorized according to two paradigms: pattern-based and distributional methods. In this paper, we study the performance of both approaches on several hypernymy tasks and find that simple pattern-based methods consistently outperform distributional methods on common benchmark datasets. Our results show that pattern-based models provide important contextual constraints which are not yet captured in distributional methods.

1 Introduction

Hierarchical relationships play a central role in knowledge representation and reasoning. Hypernym detection, i.e., the modeling of word-level hierarchies, has long been an important task in natural language processing. Starting with Hearst (1992), pattern-based methods have been one of the most influential approaches to this problem. Their key idea is to exploit certain *lexico-syntactic patterns* to detect *is-a* relations in text. For instance, patterns like "NP_y *such as* NP_x", or "NP_x *and other* NP_y" often indicate hypernymy relations of the form x *is-a* y. Such patterns may be predefined, or they may be learned automatically (Snow et al., 2004; Shwartz et al., 2016). However, a well-known problem of Hearst-like patterns is their extreme sparsity: words must co-occur in exactly the right configuration, or else no relation can be detected.

To alleviate the sparsity issue, the focus in hypernymy detection has recently shifted to distributional representations, wherein words are represented as vectors based on their distribution across large corpora. Such methods offer rich representations of lexical meaning, alleviating the sparsity problem, but require specialized similarity measures to distinguish different lexical relationships. The most successful measures to date are generally inspired by the Distributional Inclusion Hypothesis (DIH) (Zhitomirsky-Geffet and Dagan, 2005), which states roughly that contexts in which a narrow term x may appear ("cat") should be a subset of the contexts in which a broader term y ("animal") may appear. Intuitively, the DIH states that we should be able to replace any occurrence of "cat" with "animal" and still have a valid utterance. An important insight from work on distributional methods is that the definition of context is often critical to the success of a system (Shwartz et al., 2017). Some distributional representations, like positional or dependency-based contexts, may even capture crude Hearst pattern-like features (Levy et al., 2015; Roller and Erk, 2016).

While both approaches for hypernym detection rely on co-occurrences within certain contexts, they differ in their context selection strategy: pattern-based methods use predefined manually-curated patterns to generate high-precision extractions while DIH methods rely on unconstrained word co-occurrences in large corpora.

Here, we revisit the idea of using pattern-based methods for hypernym detection. We evaluate several pattern-based models on modern, large corpora and compare them to methods based on the DIH. We find that simple pattern-based methods consistently outperform specialized DIH methods on several difficult hypernymy tasks, including detection, direction prediction, and graded entailment ranking. Moreover, we find that taking low-rank embeddings of pattern-based models substantially improves performance by remedying the sparsity issue. Overall, our results show that Hearst patterns provide high-quality and robust predictions on large corpora by capturing important contextual constraints, which are not yet modeled in distributional methods.

358

Proceedings of the 56th Annual Meeting of the Association for Computational Linguistics (Short Papers), pages 358–363
Melbourne, Australia, July 15 - 20, 2018. ©2018 Association for Computational Linguistics

2 Models

In the following, we discuss pattern-based and distributional methods to detect hypernymy relations. We explicitly consider only relatively simple pattern-based approaches that allow us to directly compare their performance to DIH-based methods.

2.1 Pattern-based Hypernym Detection

First, let $\mathcal{P} = \{(x, y)\}_{i=1}^{n}$ denote the set of hypernymy relations that have been extracted via Hearst patterns from a text corpus $\mathcal{T}$. Furthermore let $w(x, y)$ denote the count of how often (x, y) has been extracted and let $W = \sum_{(x,y)\in\mathcal{P}} w(x, y)$ denote the total number extractions. In the first, most direct application of Hearst patterns, we then simply use the counts $w(x, y)$ or, equivalently, the extraction probability

$$p(x, y) = \frac{w(x, y)}{W} \qquad (1)$$

to predict hypernymy relations from $\mathcal{T}$.

However, simple extraction probabilities as in Equation (1) are skewed by the occurrence probabilities of their constituent words. For instance, it is more likely that we extract *(France, country)* over *(France, republic)*, just because the word *country* is more likely to occur than *republic*. This skew in word distributions is well-known for natural language and also translates to Hearst patterns (see also Figure 1). For this reason, we also consider predicting hypernymy relations based on the Pointwise Mutual Information of Hearst patterns: First, let $p^-(x) = \sum_{(x,y)\in\mathcal{P}} w(x, y)/W$ and $p^+(x) = \sum_{(y,x)\in\mathcal{P}} w(y, x)/W$ denote the probability that x occurs as a hyponym and hypernym, respectively. We then define the Positive Pointwise Mutual Information for (x, y) as

$$\text{ppmi}(x, y) = \max\left(0, \log\frac{p(x, y)}{p^-(x)p^+(y)}\right). \qquad (2)$$

While Equation (2) can correct for different word occurrence probabilities, it cannot handle missing data. However, sparsity is one of the main issues when using Hearst patterns, as a necessarily incomplete set of extraction rules will lead inevitably to missing extractions. For this purpose, we also study low-rank embeddings of the PPMI matrix, which allow us to make predictions for unseen pairs. In particular, let $m = |\{x : (x, y) \in \mathcal{P} \vee (y, x) \in \mathcal{P}\}|$ denote the number of unique terms in $\mathcal{P}$. Furthermore, let $X \in \mathbb{R}^{m \times m}$ be the PPMI matrix with

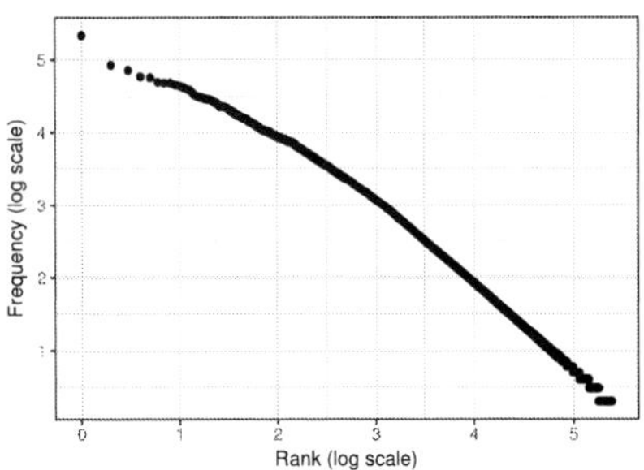

Figure 1: Frequency distribution of words appearing in Hearst patterns.

entries $M_{xy} = \text{ppmi}(x, y)$ and let $M = U\Sigma V^\top$ be its *Singular Value Decomposition* (SVD). We can then predict hypernymy relations based on the truncated SVD of M via

$$\text{spmi}(x, y) = \mathbf{u}_x^\top \Sigma_r \mathbf{v}_y \qquad (3)$$

where $\mathbf{u}_x$, $\mathbf{v}_y$ denote the x-th and y-th row of U and V, respectively, and where Σ_r is the diagonal matrix of truncated singular values (in which all but the r largest singular values are set to zero).

Equation (3) can be interpreted as a smoothed version of the observed PPMI matrix. Due to the truncation of singular values, Equation (3) computes a low-rank embedding of M where similar words (in terms of their Hearst patterns) have similar representations. Since Equation (3) is defined for all pairs (x, y), it allows us to make hypernymy predictions based on the similarity of words. We also consider factorizing a matrix that is constructed from occurrence probabilities as in Equation (1), denoted by $\text{sp}(x, y)$. This approach is then closely related to the method of Cederberg and Widdows (2003), which has been proposed to improve precision and recall for hypernymy detection from Hearst patterns.

2.2 Distributional Hypernym Detection

Most unsupervised distributional approaches for hypernymy detection are based on variants of the Distributional Inclusion Hypothesis (Weeds et al., 2004; Kotlerman et al., 2010; Santus et al., 2014; Lenci and Benotto, 2012; Shwartz et al., 2017). Here, we compare to two methods with strong empirical results. As with most DIH measures, they are only defined for large, sparse, positively-valued distributional spaces. First, we consider *WeedsPrec* (Weeds et al., 2004) which captures the features of x which are *included* in the set of a broader term's features, **y**:

$$\text{WeedsPrec}(\mathbf{x}, \mathbf{y}) = \frac{\sum_{i=1}^{n} x_i * \mathbb{1}_{y_i > 0}}{\sum_{i=1}^{n} x_i}$$

Second, we consider *invCL* (Lenci and Benotto, 2012) which introduces a notion of distributional *exclusion* by also measuring the degree to which the broader term contains contexts *not* used by the narrower term. In particular, let

$$\text{CL}(\mathbf{x}, \mathbf{y}) = \frac{\sum_{i=1}^{n} \min(x_i, y_i)}{\sum_{i=1}^{n} x_i}$$

denote the degree of inclusion of x in y as proposed by Clarke (2009). To measure both the inclusion of x in y and the non-inclusion of y in x, *invCL* is then defined as

$$\text{invCL}(\mathbf{x}, \mathbf{y}) = \sqrt{\text{CL}(\mathbf{x}, \mathbf{y}) * (1 - \text{CL}(\mathbf{y}, \mathbf{x}))}$$

Although most unsupervised distributional approaches are based on the DIH, we also consider the distributional SLQS model based on an alternative *informativeness* hypothesis (Santus et al., 2014; Shwartz et al., 2017). Intuitively, the SLQS model presupposes that general words appear mostly in uninformative contexts, as measured by entropy. Specifically, SLQS depends on the median entropy of a term's top N contexts, defined as

$$E_x = \text{median}_{i=1}^{N} \left[H(c_i) \right],$$

where $H(c_i)$ is the Shannon entropy of context c_i across all terms, and N is chosen in hyperparameter selection. Finally, SLQS is defined using the ratio between the two terms:

$$\text{SLQS}(x, y) = 1 - \frac{E_x}{E_y}.$$

Since the SLQS model only compares the relative generality of two terms, but does not make judgment about the terms' relatedness, we report SLQS-cos, which multiplies the SLQS measure by cosine similarity of x and y (Santus et al., 2014).

For completeness, we also include cosine similarity as a baseline in our evaluation.

3 Evaluation

To evaluate the relative performance of pattern-based and distributional models, we apply them to several challenging hypernymy tasks.

Pattern
X which is a (example|class|kind|…) of Y
X (and|or) (any|some) other Y
X which is called Y
X is JJS (most)? Y
X a special case of Y
X is an Y that
X is a !(member|part|given) Y
!(features|properties) Y such as X_1, X_2, …
(Unlike|like) (most|all|any|other) Y, X
Y including X_1, X_2, …

Table 1: Hearst patterns used in this study. Patterns are lemmatized, but listed as inflected for clarity.

3.1 Tasks

Detection: In hypernymy detection, the task is to classify whether pairs of words are in a hypernymy relation. For this task, we evaluate all models on five benchmark datasets: First, we employ the noun-noun subset of BLESS, which contains hypernymy annotations for 200 concrete, mostly unambiguous nouns. Negative pairs contain a mixture of co-hyponymy, meronymy, and random pairs. This version contains 14,542 total pairs with 1,337 positive examples. Second, we evaluate on LEDS (Baroni et al., 2012), which consists of 2,770 noun pairs balanced between positive hypernymy examples, and randomly shuffled negative pairs. We also consider EVAL (Santus et al., 2015), containing 7,378 pairs in a mixture of hypernymy, synonymy, antonymy, meronymy, and adjectival relations. EVAL is notable for its absence of random pairs. The largest dataset is SHWARTZ (Shwartz et al., 2016), which was collected from a mixture of WordNet, DBPedia, and other resources. We limit ourselves to a 52,578 pair subset excluding multiword expressions. Finally, we evaluate on WBLESS (Weeds et al., 2014), a 1,668 pair subset of BLESS, with negative pairs being selected from co-hyponymy, random, and hyponymy relations. Previous work has used different metrics for evaluating on BLESS (Lenci and Benotto, 2012; Levy et al., 2015; Roller and Erk, 2016). We chose to evaluate the global ranking using Average Precision. This allowed us to use the same metric on all detection benchmarks, and is consistent with evaluations in Shwartz et al. (2017).

Direction: In direction prediction, the task is to identify which term is broader in a given pair of words. For this task, we evaluate all models on three datasets described by Kiela et al. (2015): On BLESS, the task is to predict the direction for all 1337 positive pairs in the dataset. Pairs are only counted correct if the hypernymy direction scores higher than the reverse direction, i.e. $\text{score}(x, y) > \text{score}(y, x)$. We reserve 10% of the data for validation, and test on the remaining 90%. On WBLESS, we follow prior work (Nguyen et al., 2017; Vulić and Mrkšić, 2017) and perform 1000 random iterations in which 2% of the data is used as a validation set to learn a classification threshold, and test on the remainder of the data. We report average accuracy across all iterations. Finally, we evaluate on BIBLESS (Kiela et al., 2015), a variant of WBLESS with hypernymy and hyponymy pairs explicitly annotated for their direction. Since this task requires three-way classification (hypernymy, hyponymy, and other), we perform two-stage classification. First, a threshold is tuned using 2% of the data, identifying whether a pair exhibits hypernymy in either direction. Second, the relative comparison of scores determines which direction is predicted. As with WBLESS, we report the average accuracy over 1000 iterations.

Graded Entailment: In graded entailment, the task is to quantify the *degree* to which a hypernymy relation holds. For this task, we follow prior work (Nickel and Kiela, 2017; Vulić and Mrkšić, 2017) and use the noun part of HYPER-LEX (Vulić et al., 2017), consisting of 2,163 noun pairs which are annotated to what degree x *is-a* y holds on a scale of $[0, 6]$. For all models, we report Spearman's rank correlation ρ. We handle out-of-vocabulary (OOV) words by assigning the median of the scores (computed across the training set) to pairs with OOV words.

3.2 Experimental Setup

Pattern-based models: We extract Hearst patterns from the concatenation of Gigaword and Wikipedia, and prepare our corpus by tokenizing, lemmatizing, and POS tagging using CoreNLP 3.8.0. The full set of Hearst patterns is provided in Table 1. Our selected patterns match prototypical Hearst patterns, like "animals such as cats," but also include broader patterns like "New Year is the most important holiday." Leading and following noun phrases are allowed to match limited modifiers (compound nouns, adjectives, etc.), in which case we also generate a hit for the head of the noun phrase. Dur-

ing postprocessing, we remove pairs which were not extracted by at least two distinct patterns. We also remove any pair (y, x) if $p(y, x) < p(x, y)$. The final corpus contains roughly 4.5M matched pairs, 431K unique pairs, and 243K unique terms. For SVD-based models, we select the rank from $r \in \{5, 10, 15, 20, 25, 50, 100, 150, 200, 250, 300, 500, 1000\}$ on the validation set. The other pattern-based models do not have any hyperparameters.

Distributional models: For the distributional baselines, we employ the large, sparse distributional space of Shwartz et al. (2017), which is computed from UkWaC and Wikipedia, and is known to have strong performance on several of the detection tasks. The corpus was POS tagged and dependency parsed. Distributional contexts were constructed from adjacent words in dependency parses (Padó and Lapata, 2007; Levy and Goldberg, 2014). Targets and contexts which appeared fewer than 100 times in the corpus were filtered, and the resulting co-occurrence matrix was PPMI transformed.[1] The resulting space contains representations for 218K words over 732K context dimensions. For the SLQS model, we selected the number of contexts N from the same set of options as the SVD rank in pattern-based models.

3.3 Results

Table 2 shows the results from all three experimental settings. In nearly all cases, we find that pattern-based approaches substantially outperform all three distributional models. Particularly strong improvements can be observed on BLESS (0.76 average precision vs 0.19) and WBLESS (0.96 vs. 0.69) for the detection tasks and on all directionality tasks. For directionality prediction on BLESS, the SVD models surpass even the state-of-the-art *supervised* model of Vulić and Mrkšić (2017). Moreover, both SVD models perform generally better than their sparse counterparts on all tasks and datasets except on HYPERLEX. We performed a posthoc analysis of the validation sets comparing the ppmi and spmi models, and found that the truncated SVD improved recall via its matrix completion properties. We also found that the spmi model downweighted

---

[1]In addition, we also experimented with further distributional spaces and weighting schemes from Shwartz et al. (2017). We also experimented with distributional spaces using the same corpora and preprocessing as the Hearst patterns (i.e., Wikipedia and Gigaword). We found that the reported setting generally performed best, and omit others for brevity.

	Detection (AP)					Direction (Acc.)			Graded (ρ_s)
	BLESS	EVAL	LEDS	SHWARTZ	WBLESS	BLESS	WBLESS	BIBLESS	HYPERLEX
Cosine	.12	.29	.71	.31	.53	.00	.54	.52	.14
WeedsPrec	.19	.39	.87	.43	.68	.63	.59	.45	.43
invCL	.18	.37	**.89**	.38	.66	.64	.60	.47	.43
SLQS	.15	.35	.60	.38	.69	.75	.67	.51	.16
p(x, y)	.49	.38	.71	.29	.74	.46	.69	.62	**.62**
ppmi(x, y)	.45	.36	.70	.28	.72	.46	.68	.61	.60
sp(x, y)	.66	.45	.81	.41	.91	**.96**	.84	.80	.51
spmi(x, y)	**.76**	**.48**	.84	**.44**	**.96**	**.96**	**.87**	**.85**	.53

Table 2: Experimental results comparing distributional and pattern-based methods in all settings.

many high-scoring outlier pairs composed of rare terms.

When comparing the $p(x, y)$ and ppmi models to distributional models, we observe mixed results. The SHWARTZ dataset is difficult for sparse models due to its very long tail of low frequency words that are hard to cover using Hearst patterns. On EVAL, Hearst-pattern based methods get penalized by OOV words, due to the large number of verbs and adjectives in the dataset, which are not captured by our patterns. However, in 7 of the 9 datasets, at least one of the sparse models outperforms all distributional measures, showing that Hearst patterns can provide strong performance on large corpora.

4 Conclusion

We studied the relative performance of Hearst pattern-based methods and DIH-based methods for hypernym detection. Our results show that the pattern-based methods substantially outperform DIH-based methods on several challenging benchmarks. We find that embedding methods alleviate sparsity concerns of pattern-based approaches and substantially improve coverage. We conclude that Hearst patterns provide important contexts for the detection of hypernymy relations that are not yet captured in DIH models. Our code is available at `https://github.com/facebookresearch/hypernymysuite`.

Acknowledgments

We would like to thank the anonymous reviewers for their helpful suggestions. We also thank Vered Shwartz, Enrico Santus, and Dominik Schlechtweg for providing us with their distributional spaces and baseline implementations.

References

Marco Baroni, Raffaella Bernardi, Ngoc-Quynh Do, and Chung-chieh Shan. 2012. Entailment above the word level in distributional semantics. In *Proceedings of the 2012 Conference of the European Chapter of the Association for Computational Linguists*, pages 23–32, Avignon, France.

Scott Cederberg and Dominic Widdows. 2003. Using lsa and noun coordination information to improve the recall and precision of automatic hyponymy extraction. In *Proceedings of the Seventh Conference on Natural Language Learning at HLT-NAACL 2003*.

Daoud Clarke. 2009. Context-theoretic semantics for natural language: An overview. In *Proceedings of the 2011 Workshop on GEometrical Models of Natural Language Semantics*, pages 112–119, Athens, Greece. Association for Computational Linguistics.

Marti A. Hearst. 1992. Automatic acquisition of hyponyms from large text corpora. In *Proceedings of the 1992 Conference on Computational Linguistics*, pages 539–545, Nantes, France.

Douwe Kiela, Laura Rimell, Ivan Vulić, and Stephen Clark. 2015. Exploiting image generality for lexical entailment detection. In *Proceedings of the 53rd Annual Meeting of the Association for Computational Linguistics and the 7th International Joint Conference on Natural Language Processing (Volume 2: Short Papers)*, pages 119–124, Beijing, China. Association for Computational Linguistics.

Lili Kotlerman, Ido Dagan, Idan Szpektor, and Maayan Zhitomirsky-Geffet. 2010. Directional distributional similarity for lexical inference. *Natural Language Engineering*, 16:359–389.

Alessandro Lenci and Giulia Benotto. 2012. Identifying hypernyms in distributional semantic spaces. In *Proceedings of the First Joint Conference on Lexical and Computational Semantics*, pages 75–79, Montréal, Canada. Association for Computational Linguistics.

Omer Levy and Yoav Goldberg. 2014. Dependency-based word embeddings. In *Proceedings of the 52nd Annual Meeting of the Association for Computational Linguistics*, pages 302–308, Baltimore, Maryland. Association for Computational Linguistics.

Omer Levy, Steffen Remus, Chris Biemann, and Ido Dagan. 2015. Do supervised distributional methods really learn lexical inference relations? In *Proceedings of the 2015 North American Chapter of the Association for Computational Linguistics: Human Language Technologies*, pages 970–976, Denver, Colorado.

Kim Anh Nguyen, Maximilian Keper, Sabine Schulte im Walde, and Ngoc Thang Vu. 2017. Hierarchical Embeddings for Hypernymy Detection and Directionality. In *Proceedings of the Conference on Empirical Methods in Natural Language Processing*, pages 233–243, Copenhagen, Denmark.

Maximillian Nickel and Douwe Kiela. 2017. Poincaré embeddings for learning hierarchical representations. In I. Guyon, U. V. Luxburg, S. Bengio, H. Wallach, R. Fergus, S. Vishwanathan, and R. Garnett, editors, *Advances in Neural Information Processing Systems 30*, pages 6338–6347. Curran Associates, Inc.

Sebastian Padó and Mirella Lapata. 2007. Dependency-based construction of semantic space models. *Computational Linguistics*, 33(2):161–199.

Stephen Roller and Katrin Erk. 2016. Relations such as hypernymy: Identifying and exploiting hearst patterns in distributional vectors for lexical entailment. In *Proceedings of the 2016 Conference on Empirical Methods in Natural Language Processing*, Austin, Texas, USA. Association for Computational Linguistics.

Enrico Santus, Alessandro Lenci, Qin Lu, and Sabine Schulte im Walde. 2014. Chasing hypernyms in vector spaces with entropy. In *Proceedings of the 14th Conference of the European Chapter of the Association for Computational Linguistics, volume 2: Short Papers*, pages 38–42, Gothenburg, Sweden. Association for Computational Linguistics.

Enrico Santus, Frances Yung, Alessandro Lenci, and Chu-Ren Huang. 2015. EVALution 1.0: An evolving semantic dataset for training and evaluation of distributional semantic models. In *Proceedings of the Fourth Workshop on Linked Data in Linguistics: Resources and Applications*, pages 64–69, Beijing, China. Association for Computational Linguistics.

Vered Shwartz, Yoav Goldberg, and Ido Dagan. 2016. Improving hypernymy detection with an integrated path-based and distributional method. In *Proceedings of the 54th Annual Meeting of the Association for Computational Linguistics*, pages 2389–2398, Berlin, Germany. Association for Computational Linguistics.

Vered Shwartz, Enrico Santus, and Dominik Schlechtweg. 2017. Hypernyms under siege: Linguistically-motivated artillery for hypernymy detection. In *Proceedings of the 15th Conference of the European Chapter of the Association for Computational Linguistics: Volume 1, Long Papers*, pages 65–75, Valencia, Spain. Association for Computational Linguistics.

Rion Snow, Daniel Jurafsky, and Andrew Y. Ng. 2004. Learning syntactic patterns for automatic hypernym discovery. In L. K. Saul, Y. Weiss, and L. Bottou, editors, *Advances in Neural Information Processing Systems 17*, pages 1297–1304. MIT Press.

Ivan Vulić, Daniela Gerz, Douwe Kiela, Felix Hill, and Anna Korhonen. 2017. Hyperlex: A large-scale evaluation of graded lexical entailment. *Computational Linguistics*, 43(4):781–835.

Ivan Vulić and Nikola Mrkšić. 2017. Specialising word vectors for lexical entailment. *CoRR*, abs/1710.06371.

Julie Weeds, Daoud Clarke, Jeremy Reffin, David Weir, and Bill Keller. 2014. Learning to distinguish hypernyms and co-hyponyms. In *Proceedings of the 2014 International Conference on Computational Linguistics*, pages 2249–2259, Dublin, Ireland.

Julie Weeds, David Weir, and Diana McCarthy. 2004. Characterising measures of lexical distributional similarity. In *Proceedings of the 2004 International Conference on Computational Linguistics*, pages 1015–1021, Geneva, Switzerland.

Maayan Zhitomirsky-Geffet and Ido Dagan. 2005. The distributional inclusion hypotheses and lexical entailment. In *Proceedings of the 2005 Annual Meeting of the Association for Computational Linguistics*, pages 107–114, Ann Arbor, Michigan.

Jointly Predicting Predicates and Arguments
in Neural Semantic Role Labeling

Luheng He   Kenton Lee   Omer Levy   Luke Zettlemoyer
Paul G. Allen School of Computer Science & Engineering
University of Washington, Seattle WA
`{luheng, kentonl, omerlevy, lsz}@cs.washington.edu`

Abstract

Recent BIO-tagging-based neural semantic role labeling models are very high performing, but assume gold predicates as part of the input and cannot incorporate span-level features. We propose an end-to-end approach for jointly predicting all predicates, arguments spans, and the relations between them. The model makes independent decisions about what relationship, if any, holds between every possible word-span pair, and learns contextualized span representations that provide rich, shared input features for each decision. Experiments demonstrate that this approach sets a new state of the art on PropBank SRL without gold predicates.[1]

1 Introduction

Semantic role labeling (SRL) captures predicate-argument relations, such as "who did what to whom." Recent high-performing SRL models (He et al., 2017; Marcheggiani et al., 2017; Tan et al., 2018) are BIO-taggers, labeling argument spans for a single predicate at a time (as shown in Figure 1). They are typically only evaluated with gold predicates, and must be pipelined with error-prone predicate identification models for deployment.

We propose an end-to-end approach for predicting all the predicates and their argument spans in one forward pass. Our model builds on a recent coreference resolution model (Lee et al., 2017), by making central use of learned, contextualized span representations. We use these representations to predict SRL graphs directly over text spans. Each edge is identified by independently predicting which role, if any, holds between every possible pair of text spans, while using aggressive beam

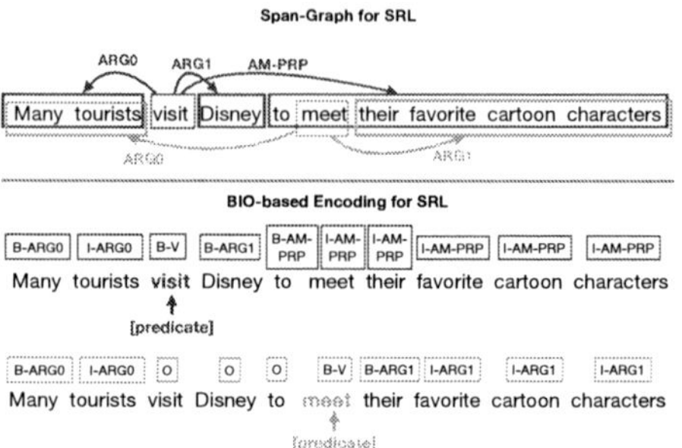

Figure 1: A comparison of our span-graph structure (top) versus BIO-based SRL (bottom).

pruning for efficiency. The final graph is simply the union of predicted SRL roles (edges) and their associated text spans (nodes).

Our span-graph formulation overcomes a key limitation of semi-markov and BIO-based models (Kong et al., 2016; Zhou and Xu, 2015; Yang and Mitchell, 2017; He et al., 2017; Tan et al., 2018): it can model overlapping spans across different predicates in the same output structure (see Figure 1). The span representations also generalize the token-level representations in BIO-based models, letting the model dynamically decide which spans and roles to include, without using previously standard syntactic features (Punyakanok et al., 2008; FitzGerald et al., 2015).

To the best of our knowledge, this is the first span-based SRL model that does not assume that predicates are given. In this more realistic setting, where the predicate must be predicted, our model achieves state-of-the-art performance on PropBank. It also reinforces the strong performance of similar span embedding methods for coreference (Lee et al., 2017), suggesting that this style of models could be used for other span-span relation tasks, such as syntactic parsing (Stern et al., 2017), relation extraction (Miwa and Bansal, 2016), and QA-SRL (FitzGerald et al., 2018).

---

[1]Code and models: https://github.com/luheng/lsgn

364

Proceedings of the 56th Annual Meeting of the Association for Computational Linguistics (Short Papers), pages 364–369
Melbourne, Australia, July 15 - 20, 2018. ©2018 Association for Computational Linguistics

2 Model

We consider the space of possible predicates to be all the tokens in the input sentence, and the space of arguments to be all continuous spans. Our model decides what relation exists between each predicate-argument pair (including *no relation*).

Formally, given a sequence $X = w_1, \ldots, w_n$, we wish to predict a set of labeled predicate-argument relations $Y \subseteq \mathcal{P} \times \mathcal{A} \times \mathcal{L}$, where $\mathcal{P} = \{w_1, \ldots, w_n\}$ is the set of all tokens (predicates), $\mathcal{A} = \{(w_i, \ldots, w_j) \mid 1 \leq i \leq j \leq n\}$ contains all the spans (arguments), and $\mathcal{L}$ is the space of semantic role labels, including a null label ϵ indicating no relation. The final SRL output would be all the non-empty relations $\{(p, a, l) \in Y \mid l \neq \epsilon\}$.

We then define a set of random variables, where each random variable $y_{p,a}$ corresponds to a predicate $p \in \mathcal{P}$ and an argument $a \in \mathcal{A}$, taking value from the discrete label space $\mathcal{L}$. The random variables $y_{p,a}$ are conditionally independent of each other given the input X:

$$P(Y \mid X) = \prod_{p \in \mathcal{P}, a \in \mathcal{A}} P(y_{p,a} \mid X) \quad (1)$$

$$P(y_{p,a} = l \mid X) = \frac{\exp(\phi(p, a, l))}{\sum_{l' \in \mathcal{L}} \exp(\phi(p, a, l'))} \quad (2)$$

Where $\phi(p, a, l)$ is a scoring function for a possible (predicate, argument, label) combination. ϕ is decomposed into two unary scores on the predicate and the argument (defined in Section 3), as well as a label-specific score for the relation:

$$\phi(p, a, l) = \Phi_{\mathrm{a}}(a) + \Phi_{\mathrm{p}}(p) + \Phi_{\mathrm{rel}}^{(l)}(a, p) \quad (3)$$

The score for the *null* label is set to a constant: $\phi(p, a, \epsilon) = 0$, similar to logistic regression.

Learning For each input X, we minimize the negative log likelihood of the gold structure Y^*:

$$\mathcal{J}(X) = -\log P(Y^* \mid X) \quad (4)$$

Beam pruning As our model deals with $O(n^2)$ possible argument spans and $O(n)$ possible predicates, it needs to consider $O(n^3 |\mathcal{L}|)$ possible relations, which is computationally impractical. To overcome this issue, we define two beams B_{a} and B_{p} for storing the candidate arguments and predicates, respectively. The candidates in each beam are ranked by their unary score (Φ_{a} or Φ_{p}). The sizes of the beams are limited by $\lambda_{\mathrm{a}} n$ and $\lambda_{\mathrm{p}} n$. Elements that fall out of the beam do not participate in computing the edge factors $\Phi_{\mathrm{rel}}^{(l)}$, reducing the overall number of relational factors evaluated by the model to $O(n^2 |\mathcal{L}|)$. We also limit the maximum width of spans to a fixed number W (e.g. $W = 30$), further reducing the number of computed unary factors to $O(n)$.

3 Neural Architecture

Our model builds contextualized representations for argument spans a and predicate words p based on BiLSTM outputs (Figure 2) and uses feedforward networks to compute the factor scores in $\phi(p, a, l)$ described in Section 2 (Figure 3).

Word-level contexts The bottom layer consists of pre-trained word embeddings concatenated with character-based representations, i.e. for each token w_i, we have $\mathbf{x}_i = [\mathrm{WORDEMB}(w_i); \mathrm{CHARCNN}(w_i)]$. We then contextualize each $\mathbf{x}_i$ using an m-layered bidirectional LSTM with highway connections (Zhang et al., 2016), which we denote as $\bar{\mathbf{x}}_i$.

Argument and predicate representation We build contextualized representations for all candidate arguments $a \in \mathcal{A}$ and predicates $p \in \mathcal{P}$. The argument representation contains the following: end points from the BiLSTM outputs $(\bar{\mathbf{x}}_{\mathrm{START}(a)}, \bar{\mathbf{x}}_{\mathrm{END}(a)})$, a soft head word $\mathbf{x}_{\mathrm{h}}(a)$, and embedded span width features $\mathbf{f}(a)$, similar to Lee et al. (2017). The predicate representation is simply the BiLSTM output at the position $\mathrm{INDEX}(p)$.

$$\mathbf{g}(a) = [\bar{\mathbf{x}}_{\mathrm{START}(a)}; \bar{\mathbf{x}}_{\mathrm{END}(a)}; \mathbf{x}_{\mathrm{h}}(a); \mathbf{f}(a)] \quad (5)$$

$$\mathbf{g}(p) = \bar{\mathbf{x}}_{\mathrm{INDEX}(p)} \quad (6)$$

The soft head representation $\mathbf{x}_{\mathrm{h}}(a)$ is an attention mechanism over word inputs $\mathbf{x}$ in the argument span, where the weights $\mathbf{e}(a)$ are computed via a linear layer over the BiLSTM outputs $\bar{\mathbf{x}}$.

$$\mathbf{x}_{\mathrm{h}}(a) = \mathbf{x}_{\mathrm{START}(a):\mathrm{END}(a)} \mathbf{e}(s)^{\mathsf{T}} \quad (7)$$

$$\mathbf{e}(a) = \mathrm{SOFTMAX}(\mathbf{w}_{\mathrm{e}}^{\mathsf{T}} \bar{\mathbf{x}}_{\mathrm{START}(a):\mathrm{END}(a)}) \quad (8)$$

$\mathbf{x}_{\mathrm{START}(a):\mathrm{END}(a)}$ is a shorthand for stacking a list of vectors $\mathbf{x}_t$, where $\mathrm{START}(a) \leq t \leq \mathrm{END}(a)$.

Scoring The scoring functions Φ are implemented with feed-forward networks based on the predicate and argument representations $\mathbf{g}$:

$$\Phi_{\mathrm{a}}(a) = \mathbf{w}_{\mathrm{a}}^{\mathsf{T}} \mathrm{MLP}_{\mathrm{a}}(\mathbf{g}(a)) \quad (9)$$

$$\Phi_{\mathrm{p}}(p) = \mathbf{w}_{\mathrm{p}}^{\mathsf{T}} \mathrm{MLP}_{\mathrm{p}}(\mathbf{g}(p)) \quad (10)$$

$$\Phi_{\mathrm{rel}}^{(l)}(a, p) = \mathbf{w}_{\mathrm{r}}^{(l)\mathsf{T}} \mathrm{MLP}_{\mathrm{r}}([\mathbf{g}(a); \mathbf{g}(p)]) \quad (11)$$

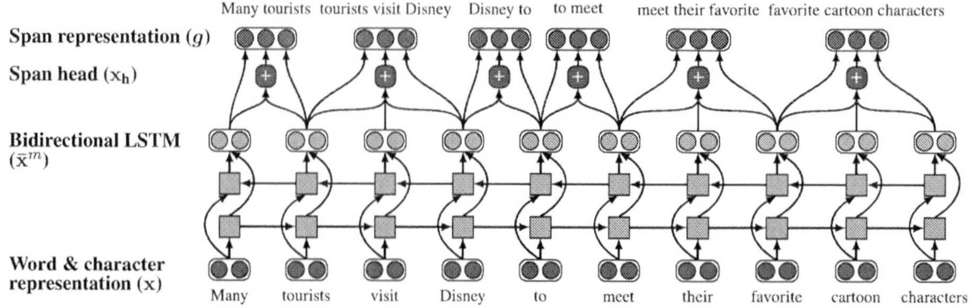

Figure 2: Building the argument span representations $\mathbf{g}(a)$ from BiLSTM outputs. For clarity, we only show one BiLSTM layer and a small subset of the arguments.

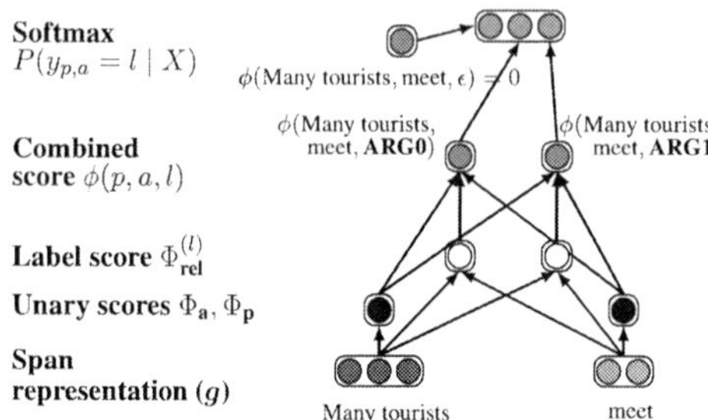

Figure 3: The span-pair classifier takes in predicate and argument representations as inputs, and computes a softmax over the label space $\mathcal{L}$.

4 Experiments

We experiment on the CoNLL 2005 (Carreras and Màrquez, 2005) and CoNLL 2012 (OntoNotes 5.0, (Pradhan et al., 2013)) benchmarks, using two SRL setups: *end-to-end* and *gold predicates*. In the *end-to-end* setup, a system takes a tokenized sentence as input, and predicts all the predicates and their arguments. Systems are evaluated on the micro-averaged F1 for correctly predicting (predicate, argument span, label) tuples. For comparison with previous systems, we also report results with *gold predicates*, in which the complete set of predicates in the input sentence is given as well. Other experimental setups and hyperparameteres are listed in Appendix A.1.

ELMo embeddings To further improve performance, we also add ELMo word representations (Peters et al., 2018) to the BiLSTM input (in the +ELMo rows). Since the contextualized representations ELMo provides can be applied to most previous neural systems, the improvement is orthogonal to our contribution. In Table 1 and 2, we organize all the results into two categories: the comparable single model systems, and the mod-

els augmented with ELMo or ensembling (in the PoE rows).

End-to-end results As shown in Table 1,[2] our joint model outperforms the previous best pipeline system (He et al., 2017) by an F1 difference of anywhere between 1.3 and 6.0 in every setting. The improvement is larger on the Brown test set, which is out-of-domain, and the CoNLL 2012 test set, which contains nominal predicates. On all datasets, our model is able to predict over 40% of the sentences completely correctly.

Results with gold predicates To compare with additional previous systems, we also conduct experiments with gold predicates by constraining our predicate beam to be gold predicates only. As shown in Table 2, our model significantly out-performs He et al. (2017), but falls short of Tan et al. (2018), a very recent attention-based (Vaswani et al., 2017) BIO-tagging model that was developed concurrently with our work. By adding the contextualized ELMo representations, we are able to out-perform all previous systems, including Peters et al. (2018), which applies ELMo to the SRL model introduced in He et al. (2017).

5 Analysis

Our model's architecture differs significantly from previous BIO systems in terms of both input and decision space. To better understand our model's strengths and weaknesses, we perform three analyses following Lee et al. (2017) and He et al. (2017), studying (1) the effectiveness of beam

---

[2]For the end-to-end setting on CoNLL 2012, we used a subset of the train/dev data from previous work due to noise in the dataset; the dev result is not directly comparable. See Appendix A.2 for detailed explanation.

End-to-End	CoNLL 05 In-domain (WSJ)				Out-of-domain (Brown)			CoNLL 2012 (OntoNotes)			
	Dev. F1	P	R	F1	P	R	F1	Dev. F1	P	R	F1
Ours+ELMo	**85.3**	**84.8**	**87.2**	**86.0**	**73.9**	**78.4**	**76.1**	**83.0**	**81.9**	**84.0**	**82.9**
He et al. (2017)[PoE]	81.5	82.0	83.4	82.7	69.7	70.5	70.1	77.2	80.2	76.6	78.4
Ours	**81.6**	**81.2**	**83.9**	**82.5**	**69.7**	**71.9**	**70.8**	**79.4**	79.4	**80.1**	**79.8**
He et al. (2017)	80.3	80.2	82.3	81.2	67.6	69.6	68.5	75.5	78.6	75.1	76.8

Table 1: End-to-end SRL results for CoNLL 2005 and CoNLL 2012, compared to previous systems. CoNLL 05 contains two test sets: WSJ (in-domain) and Brown (out-of-domain).

	WSJ	Brown	OntoNotes
Ours+ELMo	**87.4**	**80.4**	**85.5**
Peters et al. (2018)+ELMo	-	-	84.6
Tan et al. (2018)[PoE]	86.1	74.8	83.9
He et al. (2017)[PoE]	84.6	73.6	83.4
FitzGerald et al. (2015)[PoE]	80.3	72.2	80.1
Ours	83.9	73.7	82.1
Tan et al. (2018)	**84.8**	**74.1**	**82.7**
He et al. (2017)	83.1	72.1	81.7
Yang and Mitchell (2017)	81.9	72.0	-
Zhou and Xu (2015)	82.8	69.4	81.1

Table 2: Experiment results with gold predicates.

Arg. Beam	Φ_a	Pred. Beam	Φ_p
by ambulance	2.5	says	0.1
her mother ... ambulance	2.2	transported	0.0
her mother	2.2	ambulance	-8.3
Priscilla	1.9	been	-11.3
should	1.8		
transported by ambulance	-0.3		
Priscilla says .... ambulance	-2.2		
ambulance	-3.2		

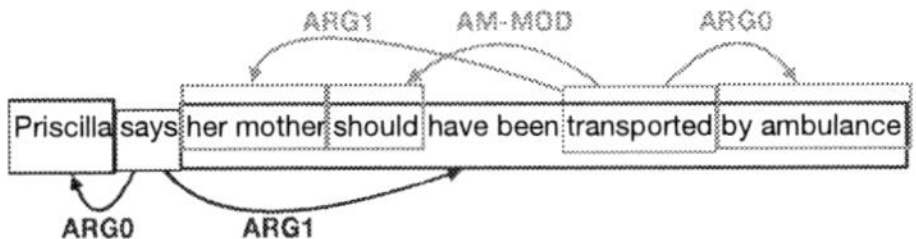

Figure 4: Top: The candidate arguments and predicates in the argument beam B_a and predicate beam B_p after pruning, along with their unary scores. Bottom: Predicted SRL relations with two identified predicates and their arguments.

pruning, (2) the ability to capture long-range dependencies, (3) agreement with syntactic spans, and (4) the ability to predict globally consistent SRL structures. The analyses are performed on the development sets without using ELMo embeddings. [3]

Effectiveness of beam pruning   Figure 4 shows the predicate and argument spans kept in the beam, sorted with their unary scores. Our model efficiently prunes unlikely argument spans and predicates, significantly reduces the number of edges it needs to consider. Figure 5 shows the recall of predicate words on the CoNLL 2012 development set. By retaining $\lambda_p = 0.4$ predicates per word, we are able to keep over 99.7% argument-bearing predicates. Compared to having a part-of-speech tagger (POS:X in Figure 5), our joint beam pruning allowing the model to have a soft trade-off between efficiency and recall.[4]

Long-distance dependencies   Figure 6 shows the performance breakdown by binned distance between arguments to the given predicates. Our model is better at accurately predicting arguments that are farther away from the predicates, even

compared to an ensemble model (He et al., 2017) that has a higher overall F1. This is very likely due to architectural differences; in a BIO tagger, predicate information passes through many LSTM timesteps before reaching a long-distance argument, whereas our architecture enables direct connections between all predicates-arguments pairs.

Agreement with syntax   As mentioned in He et al. (2017), their BIO-based SRL system has good agreement with gold syntactic span boundaries (94.3%) but falls short of previous syntax-based systems (Punyakanok et al., 2004). By directly modeling span information, our model achieves comparable syntactic agreement (95.0%) to Punyakanok et al. (2004) without explicitly modeling syntax.

Global consistency   On the other hand, our model suffers from global consistency issues. For example, on the CoNLL 2005 test set, our model has lower complete-predicate accuracy (62.6%) than the BIO systems (He et al., 2017; Tan et al., 2018) (64.3%-66.4%). Table 3 shows its viola-

---

[3]For comparability with prior work, analyses (2)-(4) are performed on the CoNLL 05 dev set with gold predicates.

[4]The predicate ID accuracy of our model is not comparable with that reported in He et al. (2017), since our model does not predict non-argument-bearing predicates.

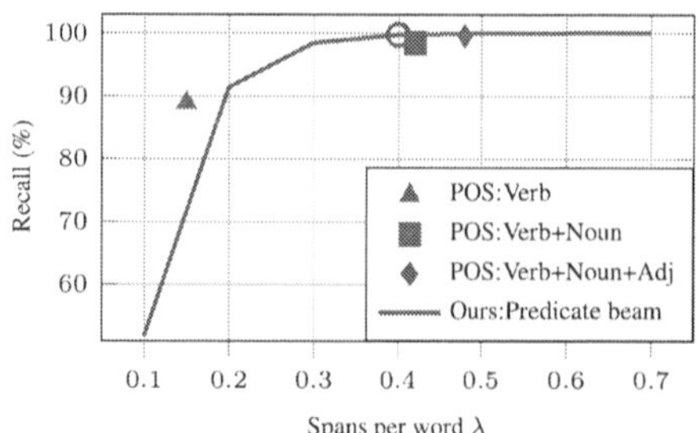

Figure 5: Recall of gold argument-bearing predicates on the CoNLL 2012 development data as we increase the number of predicates kept per word. POS:X shows the gold predicate recall from using certain pos-tags identified by the NLTK part-of-speech tagger (Bird, 2006).

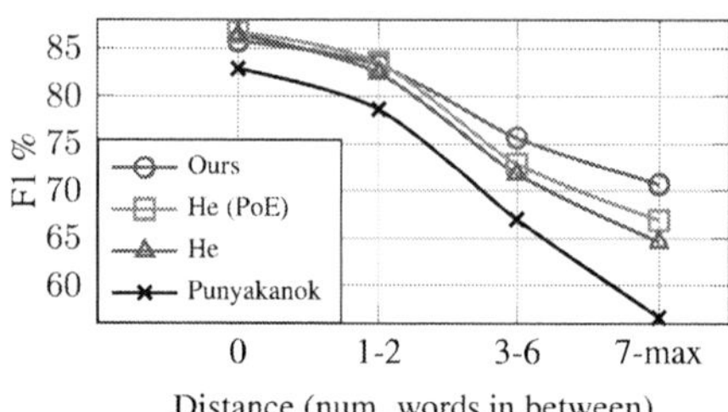

Figure 6: F1 by surface distance between predicates and arguments, showing degrading performance on long-range arguments.

tions of global structural constraints[5] compared to previous systems. Our model made more constraint violations compared to previous systems. For example, our model predicts duplicate core arguments[6] (shown in the U column in Table 3) more often than previous work. This is due to the fact that our model uses independent classifiers to label each predicate-argument pair, making it difficult for them to implicitly track the decisions made for several arguments with the same predicate.

The *Ours+decode* row in Table 3 shows SRL performance after enforcing the U-constraint using dynamic programming (Täckström et al., 2015) at decoding time. Constrained decoding at test time is effective at eliminating all the core-role inconsistencies (shown in the U-column), but did not bring significant gain on the end result (shown

---

[5]Punyakanok et al. (2008) described a list of global constraints for SRL systems, e.g., there can be at most one core argument of each type for each predicate.

[6]Arguments with labels ARG0,ARG1,…,ARG5 and AA.

| | | | SRL-Violations | | |
Model/Oracle	SRL F1	Syn %	U	C	R
Gold	100.0	98.7	24	0	61
Ours+decode	82.4	95.1	0	8	104
Ours	82.3	95.0	69	7	105
He (PoE)	82.7	94.3	37	3	68
He	81.6	94.0	48	4	73
Punyakanok	77.4	95.3	0	0	0

Table 3: Comparison on the CoNLL 05 development set against previous systems in terms of unlabeled agreement with gold constituency (Syn%) and each type of SRL-constraints violations (**U**nique core roles, **C**ontinuation roles and **R**eference roles).

in SRL F1), which only evaluates the piece-wise predicate-argument structures.

6 Conclusion and Future Work

We proposed a new SRL model that is able to jointly predict all predicates and argument spans, generalized from a recent coreference system (Lee et al., 2017). Compared to previous BIO systems, our new model supports joint predicate identification and is able to incorporate span-level features. Empirically, the model does better at long-range dependencies and agreement with syntactic boundaries, but is weaker at global consistency, due to our strong independence assumption.

In the future, we could incorporate higher-order inference methods (Lee et al., 2018) to relax this assumption. It would also be interesting to combine our span-based architecture with the self-attention layers (Tan et al., 2018; Strubell et al., 2018) for more effective contextualization.

Acknowledgments

This research was supported in part by the ARO (W911NF-16-1-0121), the NSF (IIS-1252835, IIS-1562364), a gift from Tencent, and an Allen Distinguished Investigator Award. We thank Eunsol Choi, Dipanjan Das, Nicholas Fitzgerald, Ariel Holtzman, Julian Michael, Noah Smith, Swabha Swayamdipta, and our anonymous reviewers for helpful feedback.

References

Steven Bird. 2006. Nltk: the natural language toolkit. In *ACL*.

Xavier Carreras and Lluís Màrquez. 2005. Introduction to the conll-2005 shared task: Semantic role labeling. In *CoNLL*.

Nicholas FitzGerald, Julian Michael, Luheng He, and Luke Zettlemoyer. 2018. Large-scale qa-srl parsing. In *ACL*.

Nicholas FitzGerald, Oscar Täckström, Kuzman Ganchev, and Dipanjan Das. 2015. Semantic role labeling with neural network factors. In *EMNLP*.

Luheng He, Kenton Lee, Mike Lewis, and Luke S. Zettlemoyer. 2017. Deep semantic role labeling: What works and what's next. In *ACL*.

Lingpeng Kong, Chris Dyer, and Noah A Smith. 2016. Segmental recurrent neural networks. In *ICLR*.

Kenton Lee, Luheng He, Mike Lewis, and Luke S. Zettlemoyer. 2017. End-to-end neural coreference resolution. In *EMNLP*.

Kenton Lee, Luheng He, and Luke Zettlemoyer. 2018. Higher-order coreference resolution with coarse-to-fine inference. In *NAACL*.

Diego Marcheggiani, Anton Frolov, and Ivan Titov. 2017. A simple and accurate syntax-agnostic neural model for dependency-based semantic role labeling. In *CoNLL*.

Makoto Miwa and Mohit Bansal. 2016. End-to-end relation extraction using lstms on sequences and tree structures. In *ACL*.

Matthew E. Peters, Mark Neumann, Mohit Iyyer, Matt Gardner, Christopher Clark, Kenton Lee, and Luke Zettlemoyer. 2018. Deep contextualized word representations. In *NAACL*.

Sameer Pradhan, Alessandro Moschitti, Nianwen Xue, Hwee Tou Ng, Anders Björkelund, Olga Uryupina, Yuchen Zhang, and Zhi Zhong. 2013. Towards robust linguistic analysis using ontonotes. In *CoNLL*.

Vasin Punyakanok, Dan Roth, Wen tau Yih, Dav Zimak, and Yuancheng Tu. 2004. Semantic role labeling via generalized inference over classifiers. In *CoNLL*.

Vasin Punyakanok, Dan Roth, and Wen-tau Yih. 2008. The importance of syntactic parsing and inference in semantic role labeling. *Computational Linguistics*.

Mitchell Stern, Jacob Andreas, and Dan Klein. 2017. A minimal span-based neural constituency parser. In *ACL*.

Emma Strubell, Patrick Verga, Daniel Andor, David Weiss, and Andrew McCallum. 2018. Linguistically-Informed Self-Attention for Semantic Role Labeling. *arXiv preprint*.

Oscar Täckström, Kuzman Ganchev, and Dipanjan Das. 2015. Efficient inference and structured learning for semantic role labeling. *Transactions of the Association for Computational Linguistics*.

Zhixing Tan, Mingxuan Wang, Jun Xie, Yidong Chen, and Xiaodong Shi. 2018. Deep semantic role labeling with self-attention. In *AAAI*.

Ashish Vaswani, Noam Shazeer, Niki Parmar, Jakob Uszkoreit, Llion Jones, Aidan N Gomez, Łukasz Kaiser, and Illia Polosukhin. 2017. Attention is all you need. In *NIPS*.

Bishan Yang and Tom M. Mitchell. 2017. A joint sequential and relational model for frame-semantic parsing. In *EMNLP*.

Yu Zhang, Guoguo Chen, Dong Yu, Kaisheng Yaco, Sanjeev Khudanpur, and James Glass. 2016. Highway long short-term memory rnns for distant speech recognition. In *ICASSP*.

Jie Zhou and Wei Xu. 2015. End-to-end learning of semantic role labeling using recurrent neural networks. In *ACL*.

Sparse and Constrained Attention for Neural Machine Translation

Chaitanya Malaviya[*]
Language Technologies Institute
Carnegie Mellon University
cmalaviy@cs.cmu.edu

Pedro Ferreira
Instituto Superior Técnico
Universidade de Lisboa
Lisbon, Portugal
pedro.miguel.ferreira
@tecnico.ulisboa.pt

André F. T. Martins
Unbabel
& Instituto de Telecomunicações
Lisbon, Portugal
andre.martins
@unbabel.com

Abstract

In NMT, words are sometimes dropped from the source or generated repeatedly in the translation. We explore novel strategies to address the coverage problem that change only the attention transformation. Our approach allocates fertilities to source words, used to bound the attention each word can receive. We experiment with various sparse and constrained attention transformations and propose a new one, constrained sparsemax, shown to be differentiable and sparse. Empirical evaluation is provided in three languages pairs.

1 Introduction

Neural machine translation (NMT) emerged in the last few years as a very successful paradigm (Sutskever et al., 2014; Bahdanau et al., 2014; Gehring et al., 2017; Vaswani et al., 2017). While NMT is generally more fluent than previous statistical systems, adequacy is still a major concern (Koehn and Knowles, 2017): common mistakes include dropping source words and repeating words in the generated translation.

Previous work has attempted to mitigate this problem in various ways. Wu et al. (2016) incorporate coverage and length penalties during beam search—a simple yet limited solution, since it only affects the scores of translation hypotheses that are already in the beam. Other approaches involve architectural changes: providing coverage vectors to track the attention history (Mi et al., 2016; Tu et al., 2016), using gating architectures and adaptive attention to control the amount of source context provided (Tu et al., 2017a; Li and Zhu, 2017), or adding a reconstruction loss (Tu et al., 2017b). Feng et al. (2016) also use the notion of fertility

implicitly in their proposed model. Their fertility conditioned decoder uses a coverage vector and an extract gate which are incorporated in the decoding recurrent unit, increasing the number of parameters.

In this paper, we propose a different solution that does not change the overall architecture, but only the **attention transformation**. Namely, we replace the traditional softmax by other recently proposed transformations that either promote attention sparsity (Martins and Astudillo, 2016) or upper bound the amount of attention a word can receive (Martins and Kreutzer, 2017). The bounds are determined by the fertility values of the source words. While these transformations have given encouraging results in various NLP problems, they have never been applied to NMT, to the best of our knowledge. Furthermore, we combine these two ideas and propose a novel attention transformation, **constrained sparsemax**, which produces *both* sparse and bounded attention weights, yielding a compact and interpretable set of alignments. While being in-between soft and hard alignments (Figure 2), the constrained sparsemax transformation is end-to-end differentiable, hence amenable for training with gradient backpropagation.

To sum up, our contributions are as follows:[1]

- We formulate constrained sparsemax and derive efficient linear and sublinear-time algorithms for running forward and backward propagation. This transformation has two levels of sparsity: over time steps, and over the attended words at each step.

- We provide a detailed empirical comparison of various attention transformations, including softmax (Bahdanau et al., 2014), sparse-

---

[*]Work done during an internship at Unbabel.

[1]Our software code is available at the OpenNMT fork www.github.com/Unbabel/OpenNMT-py/tree/dev and the running scripts at www.github.com/Unbabel/sparse_constrained_attention.

Proceedings of the 56th Annual Meeting of the Association for Computational Linguistics (Short Papers), pages 370–376
Melbourne, Australia, July 15 - 20, 2018. ©2018 Association for Computational Linguistics

max (Martins and Astudillo, 2016), constrained softmax (Martins and Kreutzer, 2017), and our newly proposed constrained sparsemax. We provide error analysis including two new metrics targeted at detecting coverage problems.

2 Preliminaries

Our underlying model architecture is a standard attentional encoder-decoder (Bahdanau et al., 2014). Let $x := x_{1:J}$ and $y := y_{1:T}$ denote the source and target sentences, respectively. We use a Bi-LSTM encoder to represent the source words as a matrix $H := [h_1, \ldots, h_J] \in \mathbb{R}^{2D \times J}$. The conditional probability of the target sentence is given as

$$p(y \mid x) := \prod_{t=1}^{T} p(y_t \mid y_{1:(t-1)}, x), \quad (1)$$

where $p(y_t \mid y_{1:(t-1)}, x)$ is computed by a softmax output layer that receives a decoder state s_t as input. This state is updated by an auto-regressive LSTM, $s_t = \text{RNN}(\text{embed}(y_{t-1}), s_{t-1}, c_t)$, where c_t is an input context vector. This vector is computed as $c_t := H\alpha_t$, where α_t is a probability distribution that represents the attention over the source words, commonly obtained as

$$\alpha_t = \text{softmax}(z_t), \quad (2)$$

where $z_t \in \mathbb{R}^J$ is a vector of scores. We follow Luong et al. (2015) and define $z_{t,j} := s_{t-1}^\top W h_j$ as a bilinear transformation of encoder and decoder states, where W is a model parameter.[2]

3 Sparse and Constrained Attention

In this work, we consider alternatives to Eq. 2. Since the softmax is strictly positive, it forces all words in the source to receive *some* probability mass in the resulting attention distribution, which can be wasteful. Moreover, it may happen that the decoder attends repeatedly to the same source words across time steps, causing repetitions in the generated translation, as Tu et al. (2016) observed.

With this in mind, we replace Eq. 2 by $\alpha_t = \rho(z_t, u_t)$, where ρ is a transformation that may depend both on the scores $z_t \in \mathbb{R}^J$ and on **upper bounds** $u_t \in \mathbb{R}^J$ that limit the amount of attention that each word can receive. We consider three alternatives to softmax, described next.

---

[2]This is the default implementation in the OpenNMT package. In preliminary experiments, feedforward attention (Bahdanau et al., 2014) did not show improvements.

Sparsemax. The sparsemax transformation (Martins and Astudillo, 2016) is defined as:

$$\text{sparsemax}(z) := \underset{\alpha \in \Delta^J}{\arg\min} \|\alpha - z\|^2, \quad (3)$$

where $\Delta^J := \{\alpha \in \mathbb{R}^J \mid \alpha \geq 0, \sum_j \alpha_j = 1\}$. In words, it is the Euclidean projection of the scores z onto the probability simplex. These projections tend to hit the boundary of the simplex, yielding a sparse probability distribution. This allows the decoder to attend only to a few words in the source, assigning zero probability mass to all other words. Martins and Astudillo (2016) have shown that the sparsemax can be evaluated in $O(J)$ time (same asymptotic cost as softmax) and gradient backpropagation takes sublinear time (faster than softmax), by exploiting the sparsity of the solution.

Constrained softmax. The constrained softmax transformation was recently proposed by Martins and Kreutzer (2017) in the context of easy-first sequence tagging, being defined as follows:

$$\text{csoftmax}(z; u) := \underset{\alpha \in \Delta^J}{\arg\min} \, \text{KL}(\alpha \| \text{softmax}(z))$$
$$\text{s.t.} \quad \alpha \leq u, \quad (4)$$

where u is a vector of upper bounds, and $\text{KL}(.\|.)$ is the Kullback-Leibler divergence. In other words, it returns the distribution closest to $\text{softmax}(z)$ whose attention probabilities are bounded by u. Martins and Kreutzer (2017) have shown that this transformation can be evaluated in $O(J \log J)$ time and its gradients backpropagated in $O(J)$ time.

To use this transformation in the attention mechanism, we make use of the idea of **fertility** (Brown et al., 1993). Namely, let $\beta_{t-1} := \sum_{\tau=1}^{t-1} \alpha_\tau$ denote the **cumulative attention** that each source word has received up to time step t, and let $f := (f_j)_{j=1}^J$ be a vector containing fertility upper bounds for each source word. The attention at step t is computed as

$$\alpha_t = \text{csoftmax}(z_t, f - \beta_{t-1}). \quad (5)$$

Intuitively, each source word j gets a credit of f_j units of attention, which are consumed along the decoding process. If all the credit is exhausted, it receives zero attention from then on. Unlike the sparsemax transformation, which places sparse attention over the source words, the constrained softmax leads to sparsity over time steps.

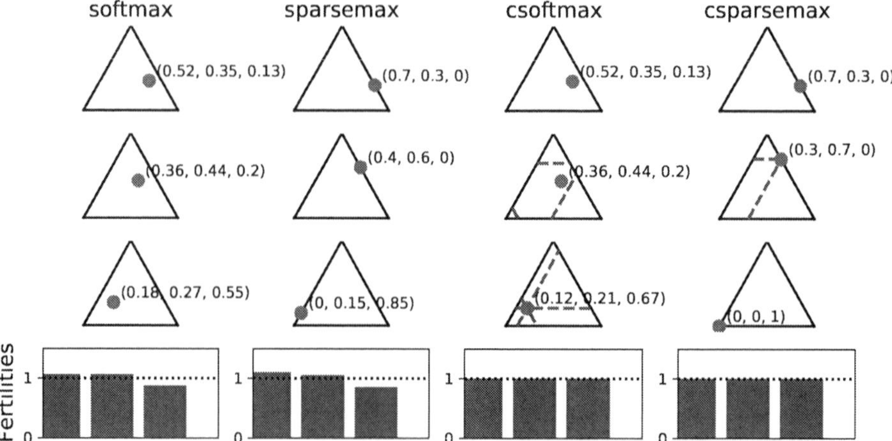

Figure 1: Illustration of the different attention transformations for a toy example with three source words. We show the attention values on the probability simplex. In the first row we assume scores $z = (1.2, 0.8, -0.2)$, and in the second and third rows $z = (0.7, 0.9, 0.1)$ and $z = (-0.2, 0.2, 0.9)$, respectively. For constrained softmax/sparsemax, we set unit fertilities to every word; for each row the upper bounds (represented as green dashed lines) are set as the difference between these fertilities and the cumulative attention each word has received. The last row illustrates the cumulative attention for the three words after all rounds.

Constrained sparsemax. In this work, we propose a novel transformation which shares the two properties above: it provides *both* sparse and bounded probabilities. It is defined as:

$$\text{csparsemax}(z; u) := \underset{\alpha \in \Delta^J}{\arg\min} \, \|\alpha - z\|^2$$
$$\text{s.t.} \quad \alpha \leq u. \quad (6)$$

The following result, whose detailed proof we include as supplementary material (Appendix A), is key for enabling the use of the constrained sparsemax transformation in neural networks.

Proposition 1 *Let* $\alpha^\star = \text{csparsemax}(z; u)$ *be the solution of Eq. 6, and define the sets* $\mathcal{A} = \{j \in [J] \mid 0 < \alpha_j^\star < u_j\}$, $\mathcal{A}_L = \{j \in [J] \mid \alpha_j^\star = 0\}$, *and* $\mathcal{A}_R = \{j \in [J] \mid \alpha_j^\star = u_j\}$. *Then:*

- **Forward propagation.** $\alpha^\star$ *can be computed in* $O(J)$ *time with the algorithm of Pardalos and Kovoor (1990) (Alg. 1 in Appendix A). The solution takes the form* $\alpha_j^\star = \max\{0, \min\{u_j, z_j - \tau\}\}$, *where* τ *is a normalization constant.*

- **Gradient backpropagation.** *Backpropagation takes sublinear time* $O(|\mathcal{A}| + |\mathcal{A}_R|)$. *Let* $L(\theta)$

be a loss function, $d\alpha = \nabla_\alpha L(\theta)$ *be the output gradient, and* $dz = \nabla_z L(\theta)$ *and* $du = \nabla_u L(\theta)$ *be the input gradients. Then, we have:*

$$dz_j = \mathbb{1}(j \in \mathcal{A})(d\alpha_j - m) \quad (7)$$
$$du_j = \mathbb{1}(j \in \mathcal{A}_R)(d\alpha_j - m), \quad (8)$$

where $m = \frac{1}{|\mathcal{A}|} \sum_{j \in \mathcal{A}} d\alpha_j$.

4 Fertility Bounds

We experiment with three ways of setting the fertility of the source words: CONSTANT, GUIDED, and PREDICTED. With CONSTANT, we set the fertilities of all source words to a fixed integer value f. With GUIDED, we train a word aligner based on IBM Model 2 (we used `fast_align` in our experiments, Dyer et al. (2013)) and, for each word in the vocabulary, we set the fertilities to the maximal observed value in the training data (or 1 if no alignment was observed). With the PREDICTED strategy, we train a separate fertility predictor model using a bi-LSTM tagger.[3] At training time, we provide as supervision the fertility estimated by `fast_align`. Since our model works

---

[3] A similar strategy was recently used by Gu et al. (2018) as a component of their non-autoregressive NMT model.

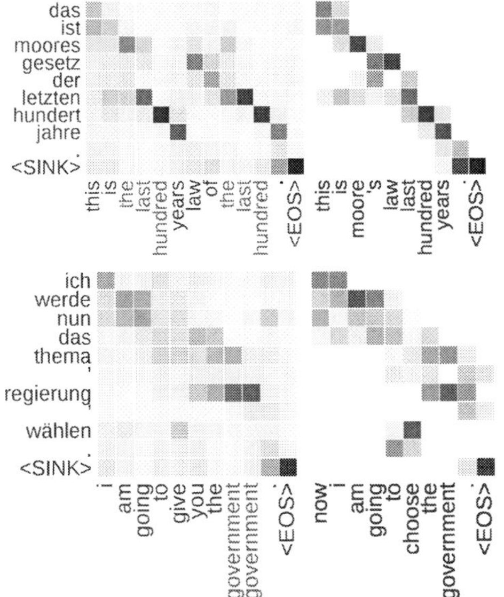

Figure 2: Attention maps for softmax and csparsemax for two DE-EN sentence pairs (white means zero attention). Repeated words are highlighted. The reference translations are *"This is Moore's law over the last hundred years"* and *"I am going to go ahead and select government."*

with fertility *upper bounds* and the word aligner may miss some word pairs, we found it beneficial to add a constant to this number (1 in our experiments). At test time, we use the expected fertilities according to our model.

Sink token. We append an additional <SINK> token to the end of the source sentence, to which we assign unbounded fertility ($f_{J+1} = \infty$). The token is akin to the null alignment in IBM models. The reason we add this token is the following: without the sink token, the length of the generated target sentence can never exceed $\sum_j f_j$ words if we use constrained softmax/sparsemax. At training time this may be problematic, since the target length is fixed and the problems in Eqs. 4–6 can become infeasible. By adding the sink token we guarantee $\sum_j f_j = \infty$, eliminating the problem.

Exhaustion strategies. To avoid missing source words, we implemented a simple strategy to encourage more attention to words with larger credit: we redefine the pre-attention word scores as $z'_t = z_t + cu_t$, where c is a constant ($c = 0.2$ in our experiments). This increases the score of words which have not yet exhausted their fertility (we may regard it as a "soft" lower bound in Eqs. 4–6).

5 Experiments

We evaluated our attention transformations on three language pairs. We focused on small datasets, as they are the most affected by coverage mistakes. We use the IWSLT 2014 corpus for DE-EN, the KFTT corpus for JA-EN (Neubig, 2011), and the WMT 2016 dataset for RO-EN. The training sets have 153,326, 329,882, and 560,767 parallel sentences, respectively. Our reason to prefer smaller datasets is that this regime is what brings more adequacy issues and demands more structural biases, hence it is a good test bed for our methods. We tokenized the data using the Moses scripts and preprocessed it with subword units (Sennrich et al., 2016) with a joint vocabulary and 32k merge operations. Our implementation was done on a fork of the OpenNMT-py toolkit (Klein et al., 2017) with the default parameters [4]. We used a validation set to tune hyperparameters introduced by our model. Even though our attention implementations are CPU-based using NumPy (unlike the rest of the computation which is done on the GPU), we did not observe any noticeable slowdown using multiple devices.

As baselines, we use softmax attention, as well as two recently proposed coverage models:

- COVPENALTY (Wu et al., 2016, §7). At test time, the hypotheses in the beam are rescored with a global score that includes a length and a coverage penalty.[5] We tuned α and β with grid search on $\{0.2k\}_{k=0}^{5}$, as in Wu et al. (2016).

- COVVECTOR (Tu et al., 2016). At training and test time, coverage vectors β and additional parameters v are used to condition the next attention step. We adapted this to our bilinear attention by defining $z_{t,j} = s_{t-1}^{\top}(\boldsymbol{W}\boldsymbol{h}_j + \boldsymbol{v}\beta_{t-1,j})$. We also experimented combining the strategies above with the sparsemax transformation.

As evaluation metrics, we report tokenized BLEU, METEOR (Denkowski and Lavie (2014), as well as two new metrics that we describe next to account for over and under-translation.[6]

---

[4]We used a 2-layer LSTM, embedding and hidden size of 500, dropout 0.3, and the SGD optimizer for 13 epochs.

[5]Since our sparse attention can become 0 for some words, we extended the original coverage penalty by adding another parameter ϵ, set to 0.1: $\mathrm{cp}(x;y) := \beta \sum_{j=1}^{J} \log \max\{\epsilon, \min\{1, \sum_{t=1}^{|y|} \alpha_{jt}\}\}$.

[6]Both evaluation metrics are included in our software package at www.github.com/Unbabel/sparse_constrained_attention.

	De-En				Ja-En				Ro-En			
	BLEU	METEOR	REP	DROP	BLEU	METEOR	REP	DROP	BLEU	METEOR	REP	DROP
softmax	29.51	31.43	3.37	5.89	20.36	23.83	13.48	23.30	29.67	32.05	2.45	5.59
softmax + CovPenalty	29.69	31.53	3.47	5.74	20.70	24.12	14.12	22.79	29.81	32.15	2.48	5.49
softmax + CovVector	29.63	31.54	2.93	5.65	21.53	24.50	11.07	22.18	**30.08**	**32.22**	2.42	5.47
sparsemax	29.73	31.54	3.18	5.90	21.28	24.25	13.09	22.40	29.97	32.12	2.19	5.60
sparsemax + CovPenalty	29.83	31.60	3.24	5.79	**21.64**	24.49	13.36	21.91	30.07	32.20	2.20	5.47
sparsemax + CovVector	29.22	31.18	3.13	6.15	21.35	**24.74**	**10.11**	**21.25**	29.30	31.84	2.18	5.87
csoftmax ($c = 0.2$)	29.39	31.33	3.29	5.86	20.71	24.00	12.38	22.73	29.39	31.83	2.37	5.64
csparsemax ($c = 0.2$)	**29.85**	**31.76**	**2.67**	**5.23**	21.31	24.51	11.40	21.59	29.77	32.10	**1.98**	**5.44**

Table 1: BLEU, METEOR, REP and DROP scores on the test sets for different attention transformations.

	BLEU	METEOR
CONSTANT, $f = 2$	29.66	31.60
CONSTANT, $f = 3$	29.64	31.56
GUIDED,	29.56	31.45
PREDICTED, $c = 0$	29.78	31.60
PREDICTED, $c = 0.2$	**29.85**	**31.76**

Table 2: Impact of various fertility strategies for the csparsemax attention model (DE-EN).

REP-score: a new metric to count repetitions. Formally, given an n-gram $s \in V^n$, let $t(s)$ and $r(s)$ be the its frequency in the model translation and reference. We first compute a sentence-level score

$$\sigma(t,r) \;=\; \lambda_1 \sum_{s \in V^n,\, t(s) \geq 2} \max\{0, t(s) - r(s)\} \;+\; \lambda_2 \sum_{w \in V} \max\{0, t(ww) - r(ww)\}.$$

The REP-score is then given by summing $\sigma(t,r)$ over sentences, normalizing by the number of words on the reference corpus, and multiplying by 100. We used $n = 2$, $\lambda_1 = 1$ and $\lambda_2 = 2$.

DROP-score: a new metric that accounts for possibly dropped words. To compute it, we first compute two sets of word alignments: from source to reference translation, and from source to the predicted translation. In our experiments, the alignments were obtained with `fast_align` (Dyer et al., 2013), trained on the training partition of the data. Then, the DROP-score computes the percentage of source words that aligned with some word from the reference translation, but not with any word from the predicted translation.

Table 1 shows the results. We can see that on average, the sparse models (csparsemax as well as sparsemax combined with coverage models) have higher scores on both BLEU and METEOR. Generally, they also obtain better REP and DROP scores than csoftmax and softmax, which suggests that sparse attention alleviates the problem of coverage to some extent.

To compare different fertility strategies, we ran experiments on the DE-EN for the csparsemax transformation (Table 2). We see that the PRE-DICTED strategy outperforms the others both in terms of BLEU and METEOR, albeit slightly.

Figure 2 shows examples of sentences for which the csparsemax fixed repetitions, along with the corresponding attention maps. We see that in the case of softmax repetitions, the decoder attends repeatedly to the same portion of the source sentence (the expression *"letzten hundert"* in the first sentence and *"regierung"* in the second sentence). Not only did csparsemax avoid repetitions, but it also yielded a sparse set of alignments, as expected. Appendix B provides more examples of translations from all models in discussion.

6 Conclusions

We proposed a new approach to address the coverage problem in NMT, by replacing the softmax attentional transformation by sparse and constrained alternatives: sparsemax, constrained softmax, and the newly proposed constrained sparsemax. For the latter, we derived efficient forward and backward propagation algorithms. By incorporating a model for fertility prediction, our attention transformations led to sparse alignments, avoiding repeated words in the translation.

Acknowledgments

We thank the Unbabel AI Research team for numerous discussions, and the three anonymous reviewers for their insightful comments. This work was supported by the European Research Council (ERC StG DeepSPIN 758969) and by the Fundação para a Ciência e Tecnologia through contracts UID/EEA/50008/2013, PTDC/EEI-SII/7092/2014 (LearnBig), and CMU-PERI/TIC/0046/2014 (GoLocal).

References

Miguel B. Almeida and André F. T. Martins. 2013. Fast and Robust Compressive Summarization with Dual Decomposition and Multi-Task Learning. In *Proc. of the Annual Meeting of the Association for Computational Linguistics*.

Dzmitry Bahdanau, Kyunghyun Cho, and Yoshua Bengio. 2014. Neural machine translation by jointly learning to align and translate. *arXiv preprint arXiv:1409.0473* .

Manuel Blum, Robert W Floyd, Vaughan Pratt, Ronald L Rivest, and Robert E Tarjan. 1973. Time bounds for selection. *Journal of Computer and System Sciences* 7(4):448–461.

Peter F Brown, Vincent J Della Pietra, Stephen A Della Pietra, and Robert L Mercer. 1993. The mathematics of statistical machine translation: Parameter estimation. *Computational linguistics* 19(2):263–311.

Michael Denkowski and Alon Lavie. 2014. Meteor universal: Language specific translation evaluation for any target language. In *Proceedings of the EACL 2014 Workshop on Statistical Machine Translation*.

Chris Dyer, Victor Chahuneau, and Noah A Smith. 2013. A simple, fast, and effective reparameterization of ibm model 2. Association for Computational Linguistics.

Shi Feng, Shujie Liu, Nan Yang, Mu Li, Ming Zhou, and Kenny Q. Zhu. 2016. Improving attention modeling with implicit distortion and fertility for machine translation. In *Proceedings of COLING 2016, the 26th International Conference on Computational Linguistics: Technical Papers*. The COLING 2016 Organizing Committee, Osaka, Japan, pages 3082–3092.

Jonas Gehring, Michael Auli, David Grangier, and Yann Dauphin. 2017. A convolutional encoder model for neural machine translation. In *Proceedings of the 55th Annual Meeting of the Association for Computational Linguistics (Volume 1: Long Papers)*. volume 1, pages 123–135.

Jiatao Gu, James Bradbury, Caiming Xiong, Victor OK Li, and Richard Socher. 2018. Non-autoregressive neural machine translation. In *Proc. of International Conference on Learning Representations*.

Guillaume Klein, Yoon Kim, Yuntian Deng, Jean Senellart, and Alexander M. Rush. 2017. Opennmt: Open-source toolkit for neural machine translation. In *Proceedings of the 55th Annual Meeting of the Association for Computational Linguistics, ACL 2017, Vancouver, Canada, July 30 - August 4, System Demonstrations*. pages 67–72.

Philipp Koehn and Rebecca Knowles. 2017. Six challenges for neural machine translation. In *Proceedings of the First Workshop on Neural Machine Translation*. Association for Computational Linguistics, Vancouver, pages 28–39.

Junhui Li and Muhua Zhu. 2017. Learning when to attend for neural machine translation. *arXiv preprint arXiv:1705.11160* .

Thang Luong, Hieu Pham, and Christopher D Manning. 2015. Effective approaches to attention-based neural machine translation. In *Proceedings of the 2015 Conference on Empirical Methods in Natural Language Processing*. pages 1412–1421.

Andre Martins and Ramon Astudillo. 2016. From softmax to sparsemax: A sparse model of attention and multi-label classification. In *International Conference on Machine Learning*. pages 1614–1623.

André FT Martins and Julia Kreutzer. 2017. Learning what's easy: Fully differentiable neural easy-first taggers. In *Proceedings of the 2017 Conference on Empirical Methods in Natural Language Processing*. pages 349–362.

Haitao Mi, Baskaran Sankaran, Zhiguo Wang, and Abe Ittycheriah. 2016. Coverage embedding models for neural machine translation. In *Proceedings of the 2016 Conference on Empirical Methods in Natural Language Processing, EMNLP 2016, Austin, Texas, USA, November 1-4, 2016*. pages 955–960.

Graham Neubig. 2011. The Kyoto free translation task. http://www.phontron.com/kftt.

Panos M. Pardalos and Naina Kovoor. 1990. An algorithm for a singly constrained class of quadratic programs subject to upper and lower bounds. *Mathematical Programming* 46(1):321–328.

Rico Sennrich, Barry Haddow, and Alexandra Birch. 2016. Neural machine translation of rare words with subword units. In *Proceedings of the 54th Annual Meeting of the Association for Computational Linguistics, ACL 2016, August 7-12, 2016, Berlin, Germany, Volume 1: Long Papers*.

Ilya Sutskever, Oriol Vinyals, and Quoc V Le. 2014. Sequence to sequence learning with neural networks. In *Advances in neural information processing systems*. pages 3104–3112.

Zhaopeng Tu, Yang Liu, Zhengdong Lu, Xiaohua Liu, and Hang Li. 2017a. Context gates for neural machine translation .

Zhaopeng Tu, Yang Liu, Lifeng Shang, Xiaohua Liu, and Hang Li. 2017b. Neural machine translation with reconstruction. In *AAAI*. pages 3097–3103.

Zhaopeng Tu, Zhengdong Lu, Yang Liu, Xiaohua Liu, and Hang Li. 2016. Modeling coverage for neural machine translation. In *Proceedings of the 54th Annual Meeting of the Association for Computational Linguistics*.

Ashish Vaswani, Noam Shazeer, Niki Parmar, Jakob Uszkoreit, Llion Jones, Aidan N Gomez, Łukasz Kaiser, and Illia Polosukhin. 2017. Attention is all you need. In *Advances in Neural Information Processing Systems*. pages 6000–6010.

Yonghui Wu, Mike Schuster, Zhifeng Chen, Quoc V
Le, Mohammad Norouzi, Wolfgang Macherey,
Maxim Krikun, Yuan Cao, Qin Gao, Klaus
Macherey, et al. 2016. Google's neural machine translation system: Bridging the gap between
human and machine translation. *arXiv preprint
arXiv:1609.08144* .

Neural Hidden Markov Model for Machine Translation

Weiyue Wang, Derui Zhu, Tamer Alkhouli, Zixuan Gan, Hermann Ney
Human Language Technology and Pattern Recognition, Computer Science Department
RWTH Aachen University, 52056 Aachen, Germany
<surname>@i6.informatik.rwth-aachen.de

Abstract

This work aims to investigate alternative neural machine translation (NMT) approaches and thus proposes a neural hidden Markov model (HMM) consisting of neural network-based alignment and lexicon models. The neural models make use of encoder and decoder components, but drop the attention component. The training is end-to-end and the standalone decoder is able to provide comparable performance with the state-of-the-art attention-based models on three different translation tasks.

1 Introduction

Attention-based neural translation models (Bahdanau et al., 2015; Luong et al., 2015) attend to specific positions on the source side to generate translation. Using the attention component provides significant improvements over the pure encoder-decoder sequence-to-sequence approach (Sutskever et al., 2014) that uses no such attention mechanism. In this work, we aim to compare the performance of attention-based models to another baseline, namely, neural hidden Markov models.

The neural HMM has been successfully applied in the literature on top of conventional phrase-based systems (Wang et al., 2017). In this work, our purpose is to explore its application in standalone decoding, i.e. the model is used to generate and score candidates without assistance from a phrase-based system. Because translation is done standalone using only neural models, we still refer to this as NMT. In addition, while Wang et al. (2017) applied feedforward networks to model alignment and translation, the recurrent structures proposed in this work surpass the feedforward variants by up to 1.3% in BLEU.

By comparing neural HMM and attention-based NMT, we shed light on the role of the attention component. To this end, we use an alignment-based model that has a recurrent bidirectional encoder and a recurrent decoder, but use no attention component. We replace the attention mechanism by a first-order HMM alignment model. Attention levels are deterministic normalized similarity scores part of the architecture design of an otherwise fully supervised classifier. HMM-style alignments on the other hand are discrete random variables and (unlike attention levels) must be marginalized. Once alignments are marginalized, which is tractable for a first-order HMM, parameters can be estimated to attain a local optimum of log-likelihood of observations as usual.

2 Motivation

In attention-based approaches, the alignment distribution is used to select the positions in the source sentence that the decoder attends to during translation. Thus the alignment model can be considered as an implicit part of the translation model. On the other hand, separating the alignment model from the lexicon model has its own advantages: First of all, this leads to more flexibility in modeling and training: The models can not only be trained separately, but they can also have different model types, such as neural models, count-based models, etc. Second, the separation avoids propagating errors from one model to another. In attention-based systems, the translation score is based on the alignment distribution, in which errors can be propagated from the alignment part to the translation part. Third, probabilistic treatment to alignments in NMT typically implies an extended degree of interpretability (e.g. one can inspect posteriors) and control over the model (e.g. one can impose priors over alignments

Proceedings of the 56th Annual Meeting of the Association for Computational Linguistics (Short Papers), pages 377–382
Melbourne, Australia, July 15 - 20, 2018. ©2018 Association for Computational Linguistics

and lexical distributions).

3   Neural Hidden Markov Model

Given a source sentence $f_1^J = f_1...f_j...f_J$ and a target sentence $e_1^I = e_1...e_i...e_I$, where $j = b_i$ is the source position aligned to the target position i, we model translation using an alignment model and a lexicon model:

$$p(e_1^I|f_1^J) = \sum_{b_1^I} p(e_1^I, b_1^I|f_1^J) \tag{1}$$

$$:= \sum_{b_1^I} \prod_{i=1}^I \underbrace{p(e_i|b_1^i, e_0^{i-1}, f_1^J)}_{\text{lexicon model}} \cdot \underbrace{p(b_i|b_1^{i-1}, e_0^{i-1}, f_1^J)}_{\text{alignment model}} \tag{2}$$

Instead of predicting the absolute source position b_i, we use an alignment model $p(\Delta_i|b_1^{i-1}, e_0^{i-1}, f_1^J)$ that predicts the jump $\Delta_i = b_i - b_{i-1}$.

Wang et al. (2017) applied feedforward neural networks for modeling the lexicon and alignment probabilities. In this work, we would like to model these distributions using recurrent neural networks (RNN). RNNs have been shown to outperform feedforward variants in language and translation modeling. This is mainly due to that RNN can handle arbitrary input lengths and thus include unbounded context information. Unfortunately, the recurrent hidden layer cannot be easily applied for the neural hidden Markov model, since it will significantly complicate the computation of forward-backward messages when running Baum-Welch. Nevertheless, we can apply long short-term memory (LSTM) (Hochreiter and Schmidhuber, 1997) structure for source and target words embedding. With this technique we can take the essence of LSTM RNN and do not break any sequential generative model assumptions.

Our models are close in structure to the model proposed in Luong et al. (2015), where we have a component that encodes the source sentence, and another that encodes the target sentence. As shown in Figure 1, we use a source side bidirectional LSTM embedding $h_j = \overrightarrow{h}_j + \overleftarrow{h}_j$, where $\overrightarrow{h}_j = \text{LSTM}(W, f_j, \overrightarrow{h}_{j-1})$ and $\overleftarrow{h}_j = \text{LSTM}(V, f_j, \overleftarrow{h}_{j+1})$, as well as a target side LSTM embedding $s_{i-1} = \text{LSTM}(U, e_{i-1}, s_{i-2})$. h_j, $\overrightarrow{h}_j$, $\overleftarrow{h}_j$ and s_{i-1}, s_{i-2} are vectors, W, V and U are weight matrices. Before the non-linear hidden layers, there is a projection layer which

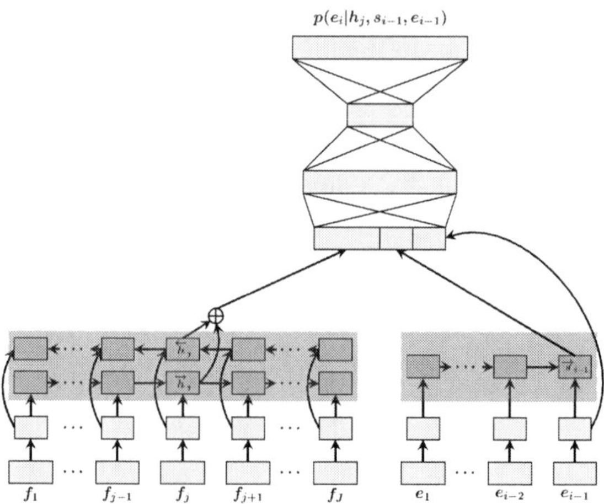

Figure 1: The architecture of our neural networks with LSTM RNN on source and target side.

concatenates h_j, s_{i-1} and e_{i-1}. Then the neural network-based lexicon model is given by

$$p(e_i|b_1^i, e_0^{i-1}, f_1^J) := p(e_i|h_j, s_{i-1}, e_{i-1}) \tag{3}$$

and the neural network-based alignment model

$$p(b_i|b_1^{i-1}, e_0^{i-1}, f_1^J) := p(\Delta_i|h_{j'}, s_{i-1}, e_{i-1}) \tag{4}$$

where $j' = b_{i-1}$.

The training criterion is the logarithm of sentence posterior probabilities over training sentence pairs $(F_r, E_r), r = 1, ..., R$:

$$\arg\max_\theta \left\{ \sum_r \log p_\theta(E_r|F_r) \right\} \tag{5}$$

The derivative for a single sentence pair $(F, E) = (f_1^J, e_1^I)$ is:

$$\frac{\partial}{\partial\theta} \log p_\theta(E|F)$$
$$= \sum_{j',j} \sum_i p_i(j', j|f_1^J, e_1^I; \theta)$$
$$\cdot \frac{\partial}{\partial\theta} \log p(j, e_i|j', e_0^{i-1}, f_1^J; \theta) \tag{6}$$

with HMM posterior weights $p_i(j', j|f_1^J, e_1^I; \theta)$, which can be computed using the forward-backward algorithm.

The entire training procedure can be summarized as *backpropagation in an EM framework*:

1. compute:
   - the posterior HMM weights
   - the local gradients (backpropagation)

2. update neural network weights

4 Decoding

In the decoding stage we still calculate the sum over alignments and apply a target-synchronous beam search for the target string.

The auxiliary quantity for each unknown partial string e_0^i is specified as $Q(i, j; e_0^i)$. During search, the partial hypothesis is extended from e_0^{i-1} to e_0^i:

$$
\begin{aligned}
&Q(i, j; e_0^i) \\
&= \sum_{j'} \left[p(j, e_i | j', e_0^{i-1}, f_1^J) \cdot Q(i-1, j'; e_0^{i-1}) \right]
\end{aligned}
$$

$$(7)$$

The decoder is shown in Algorithm 1. In the innermost loop (line 11-13), alignments are hypothesized and used to calculate the auxiliary quantity $Q(i, j; e_0^i)$. Then for each source position j, the lexical distribution over the full target vocabulary is computed (line 14). The distributions are accumulated ($Q(i; e_0^i) = \sum_j Q(i, j; e_0^i)$, line 16), then sorted (line 18) and the best candidate translations ($\arg\max_{e_i} Q(i; e_0^i)$) lying within the beam are used to expand the partial hypotheses (line 19-23). `cache` is a two-dimensional list of size $J \times |V_{\text{src}}|$ (source vocabulary size), which is used to cache the current quantities.

Whenever a partial hypothesis in the beam ends with the sentence end symbol (<EOF>), the counter will be increased by 1 (line 26-28). The translation is terminated if the counter reaches the beam size or hypothesis sentence length reaches three times the source sentence length (line 6). If a hypothesis stops but its score is worse than other hypotheses, it is eliminated from the beam, but it still contests non-terminated hypotheses. During comparison the scores are normalized by hypothesis sentence length. Note that we have no explicit coverage constraints. This means that a source position can be revisited many times, whereby creating one-to-many alignment cases. This also allows unaligned source words.

In the neural HMM decoder, word alignments are estimated and scored according to the distribution calculated by the neural network alignment model, leading alignment decisions to become part of the beam search. The search space consists of both alignment and translation decisions. In contrast, the search space in attention-based decoding consists only of translation decisions.

The decoding complexity is $\mathcal{O}(J^2 \cdot I)$ (J = source sentence length, I = target sentence length)

Algorithm 1 Neural HMM Decoder

```
 1: function TRANSLATE(f_1^J, beam_size)
 2:     count = 0
 3:     i = 1
 4:     hyps = {e_0}
 5:     new_hyps = {}
 6:     while count < beam_size and i < 3 · J do
 7:         for hyp in hyps do
 8:             sum_dist = [0] * |V|_src
 9:             for j from 1 to J do
10:                 sum = 0
11:                 for j' from 1 to J do
12:                     sum = sum + SCORES(hyp, j')
                                ·p_align(f_j', j − j')
13:                 end for
14:                 cache[j] = sum · lex_dist(f_j)
15:                 #Element wise addition
16:                 sum_dist = sum_dist ⊕ cache[j]
17:             end for
18:             dist = SORT(sum_dist, beam_size)
19:             for word in dist[:beam_size] do
20:                 new_hyp = EXTEND(hyp, word)
21:                 SETSCORES(new_hyp, cache)
22:                 new_hyps.INSERT(new_hyp)
23:             end for
24:         end for
25:         PRUNE(new_hyps, beam_size)
26:         for <EOF> in new_hyps do
27:             count = count + 1
28:         end for
29:         hyps = new_hyps
30:         i = i + 1
31:     end while
32:     return GETBEST(hyps)
33: end function
```

compared to $\mathcal{O}(J \cdot I)$ for attention-based models. These are theoretical complexities of decoding on a CPU only considering source and target sentence lengths. In practice, the size of the neural network must also be taken into account, and there are some optimized matrix multiplications for decoding on a GPU. In general, the decoding speed of our model is about 3 times slower than that of a standard attention model (1.07 sentences per second vs. 3.00 sentences per second) on a single GPU. This is still an initial decoder and we did not spend much time on accelerating its decoding yet. The optimization of our decoder would be a promising future work.

5 Experiments

The experiments are conducted on the WMT 2017 German↔English and Chinese→English translation tasks, which consist of $5M$ and $23M$ parallel sentence pairs respectively. Translation quality is measured with the case sensitive BLEU (Papineni et al., 2002) and TER (Snover et al., 2006) metric on `newstests` 2017, which contain 3004 (German↔English) and 2001 (Chinese→English) sentence pairs.

For German and English preprocessing, we use the *Moses* tokenizer with hyphen splitting, and perform truecasing with *Moses* scripts (Koehn et al., 2007). For German↔English subword segmentation (Sennrich et al., 2016), we use $20K$ joint BPE operations. For the Chinese data, we segment it using the *Jieba*[1] segmenter. We then learn a BPE model on the segmented Chinese, also using $20K$ merge operations. During training, sentences with a length greater than 50 subwords are filtered out.

5.1 Attention-Based System

The attention-based systems are trained with *Sockeye* (Hieber et al., 2017), which implement an attentional encoder-decoder with small modifications to the model in Bahdanau et al. (2015). The encoder and decoder word embeddings are of size 620. The encoder consists of a bidirectional layer with 1000 LSTMs with peephole connections to encode the source side. We use *Adam* (Kingma and Ba, 2015) as optimizer with a learning rate of 0.001, and a batch size of 50. The network is trained with 30% dropout for up to $500K$ iterations and evaluated every $10K$ iterations on the development set with BLEU. Decoding is done using beam search with a beam size of 12. In the end the four best models are averaged as described in

[1] https://github.com/fxsjy/jieba

the beginning of Junczys-Dowmunt et al. (2016).

5.2 Neural Hidden Markov Model

The entire neural hidden Markov model is implemented in *TensorFlow* (Abadi et al., 2016). The feedforward models have three hidden layers of sizes 1000, 1000 and 500 respectively, with a 5-word source window and a 3-gram target history. 200 nodes are used for word embeddings.

The output layer of the neural lexicon model consists of around $25K$ nodes for all subword units, while the neural alignment model has a small output layer with 201 nodes, which reflects that the aligned position can jump within the scope from -100 to 100.

Apart from the basic projection layer, we also applied LSTM layers for the source and target words embedding. The embedding layers have 350 nodes and the size of the projection layer is 800 ($400 + 200 + 200$, Figure 1). We use *Adam* as optimizer with a learning rate of 0.001. Neural lexicon and alignment models are trained with 30% dropout and the norm of the gradient is clipped with a threshold 1 (Pascanu et al., 2014). In decoding we use a beam size of 12 and the element-wise average of all weights of the four best models also results in better performance.

5.3 Results

We compare the neural HMM approach (Subsection 5.2) with the state-of-the-art attention-based approach (Subsection 5.1) on different translation tasks. The results are presented in Table 1. Compare to the model presented in Wang et al. (2017), switching to LSTM models has a clear advantage, which improves the FFNN-based system by up to 1.3% BLEU and 1.8% TER. It seems that the HMM model benefits from richer features, such as LSTM states, which are very similar to what an attention mechanism would require. We actually

WMT 2017	# free parameters	German→English		English→German		Chinese→English	
		BLEU[%]	TER[%]	BLEU[%]	TER[%]	BLEU[%]	TER[%]
FFNN-based neural HMM [1]	33M	28.3	51.4	23.4	58.8	19.3	64.8
LSTM-based neural HMM [2]	52M	**29.6**	**50.5**	24.6	**57.0**	**20.2**	**63.7**
Attention-based neural network [3]	77M	29.5	50.8	**24.7**	57.4	**20.2**	63.8

Table 1: Experimental results on WMT 2017 German↔English and Chinese→English test sets. All models are trained without synthetic data. Single model is used for decoding.
[1] (Wang et al., 2017) but applied in decoding instead of rescoring
[2] This work
[3] (Bahdanau et al., 2015) with small modifications (Section 5.1)

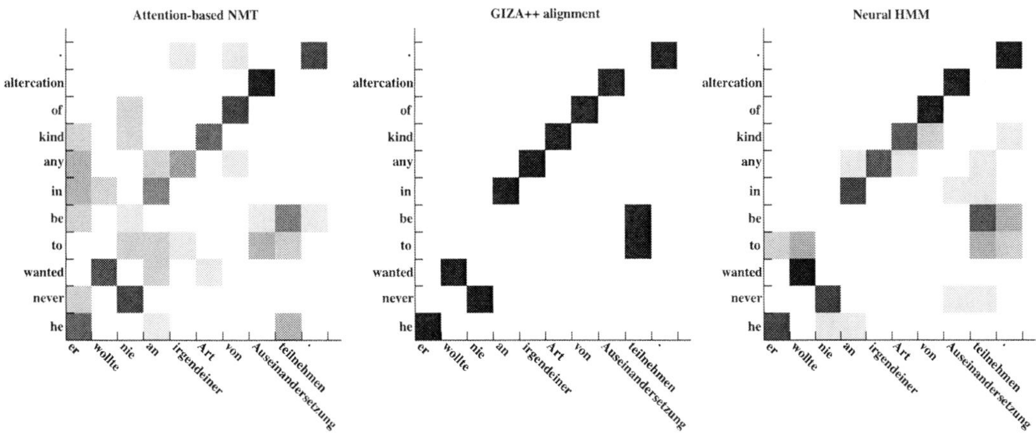

Figure 2: Attention weight and alignment matrices visualized in heat map form. Generated by the attention NMT baseline, GIZA++ and the neural hidden Markov model.

expected it to do with less, the reason being that alignment distributions get refined a posteriori and so they do not have to be as strong a priori. We can also observe that the performance of our approach is comparable with the state-of-the-art attention-based system with $25M$ more parameters on all three tasks.

5.4 Alignment Analysis

We show an example from the German→English `newstest` 2017 in Figure 2, along with the attention and alignment matrices. We can observe that the neural network-based HMM could generate a more clear alignment path compared to the attention weights. In this example, it can exactly estimate the alignment positions for words `wanted` and `of`.

6 Discussion

We described a novel formulation for a neural network-based machine translation system, which applied neural networks to the conventional hidden Markov model. The training is end-to-end, the model is monolithic and can be used as a standalone decoder. This results in a more modern and efficient way to use HMM in machine translation and enables neural networks to benefit from HMMs.

Experiments show that replacing attention with alignment does not improve the translation performance of NMT significantly. One possible reason is that alignment may fail to capture relevant contexts as attention does. While alignment aims to identify translation equivalents between two languages, attention is designed to find relevant context for predicting the next target word. Source words with high attention weights are not necessarily translation equivalents of the target word. Although using alignment does not lead to significant improvements in terms of BLEU over attention, we think alignment-based NMT models are still useful for automatic post editing and developing coverage-based models. These might be interesting future directions to explore.

Acknowledgments

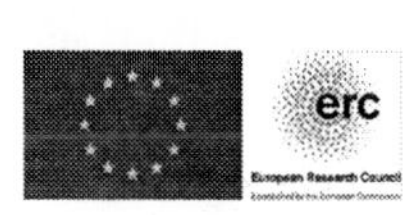

This project has received funding from the European Union's Horizon 2020 research and innovation programme under grant agreement n° 645452 (QT21), and from the European Research Council (ERC) under the European Unions Horizon 2020 research and innovation programme, grant agreement n° 694537 (SEQCLAS). The work reflects only the authors' views and neither the European Research Council Executive Agency nor the European Commission is responsible for any use that may be made of the information it contains. The GPU cluster used for the experiments was partially funded by Deutsche Forschungsgemeinschaft (DFG) Grant INST 222/1168-1. Tamer Alkhouli was partly funded by the 2016 Google PhD Fellowship for North America, Europe and the Middle East.

References

Martín Abadi, Ashish Agarwal, and Paul Barham et al. 2016. TensorFlow: Large-Scale Machine Learning on Heterogeneous Distributed Systems. *CoRR* abs/1603.04467.

Dzmitry Bahdanau, Kyunghyun Cho, and Yoshua Bengio. 2015. Neural Machine Translation by Jointly Learning to Align and Translate. In *Proceedings of the 3rd International Conference on Learning Representations*. San Diego, CA, USA.

Felix Hieber, Tobias Domhan, Michael Denkowski, David Vilar, Artem Sokolov, Ann Clifton, and Matt Post. 2017. Sockeye: A Toolkit for Neural Machine Translation. *ArXiv e-prints* https://arxiv.org/abs/1712.05690.

Sepp Hochreiter and Jürgen Schmidhuber. 1997. Long Short-Term Memory. *Neural Computation* 9(8):1735–1780.

Marcin Junczys-Dowmunt, Tomasz Dwojak, and Rico Sennrich. 2016. The AMU-UEDIN Submission to the WMT16 News Translation Task: Attention-based NMT Models as Feature Functions in Phrase-based SMT. In *Proceedings of the First Conference on Machine Translation, Volume 2: Shared Task Papers*. Berlin, Germany, pages 319–325.

Diederik P. Kingma and Jimmy Lei Ba. 2015. Adam: A method for stochastic optimization. In *Proceedings of the Third International Conference on Learning Representations*. San Diego, CA, USA.

Philipp Koehn, Hieu Hoang, Alexandra Birch, Chris Callison-Burch, Marcello Federico, Nicola Bertoldi, Brooke Cowan, Wade Shen, Christine Moran, Richard Zens, Chris Dyer, Ondrej Bojar, Alexandra Constantin, and Evan Herbst. 2007. Moses: Open Source Toolkit for Statistical Machine Translation. In *Proceedings of the 45th Annual Meeting of the Association for Computational Linguistics Companion Volume Proceedings of the Demo and Poster Sessions*. Prague, Czech Republic, pages 177–180.

Minh-Thang Luong, Hieu Pham, and Christopher D. Manning. 2015. Effective approaches to attention-based neural machine translation. In *Conference on Empirical Methods in Natural Language Processing*. Lisbon, Portugal, pages 1412–1421.

Kishore Papineni, Salim Roukos, Todd Ward, and Wei-Jing Zhu. 2002. BLEU: A Method for Automatic Evaluation of Machine Translation. In *Proceedings of the 40th Annual Meeting on Association for Computational Linguistics*. Philadelphia, PA, USA, pages 311–318.

Razvan Pascanu, Caglar Gulcehre, Kyunghyun Cho, and Yoshua Bengio. 2014. How to Construct Deep Recurrent Neural Networks. In *Proceedings of the Second International Conference on Learning Representations*. Banff, Canada.

Rico Sennrich, Barry Haddow, and Alexandra Birch. 2016. Neural Machine Translation of Rare Words with Subword Units. In *Proceedings of the 54th Annual Meeting of the Association for Computational Linguistics*. Berlin, Germany, pages 1715–1725.

Matthew Snover, Bonnie Dorr, Richard Schwartz, Linnea Micciulla, and John Makhoul. 2006. A study of translation edit rate with targeted human annotation. In *Proceedings of the Conference of the Association for Machine Translation in the Americas*. Cambridge, MA, USA, pages 223–231.

Ilya Sutskever, Oriol Vinyals, and Quoc V. Le. 2014. Sequence to Sequence Learning with Neural Networks. In *Proceedings of the Advances in Neural Information Processing Systems 27*. Montréal, Canada, pages 3104–3112.

Weiyue Wang, Tamer Alkhouli, Derui Zhu, and Hermann Ney. 2017. Hybrid Neural Network Alignment and Lexicon Model in Direct HMM for Statistical Machine Translation. In *Proceedings of the 55th Annual Meeting of the Association for Computational Linguistics*. Vancouver, Canada, pages 125–131.

Bleaching Text: Abstract Features for Cross-lingual Gender Prediction

Rob van der Goot[♡]   Nikola Ljubešić[♠]   Ian Matroos[♡]   Malvina Nissim[♡]   Barbara Plank[♡♣]
[♡] Center for Language and Cognition, University of Groningen, The Netherlands
[♠] Department of Knowledge Technologies, Jozef Stefan Institute, Ljubljana, Slovenia
[♣] IT University of Copenhagen, Copenhagen, Denmark
`{r.van.der.goot,i.matroos,m.nissim}@rug.nl,nljubesi@gmail.com,bplank@itu.dk`

Abstract

Gender prediction has typically focused on lexical and social network features, yielding good performance, but making systems highly language-, topic-, and platform-dependent. Cross-lingual embeddings circumvent some of these limitations, but capture gender-specific style less. We propose an alternative: *bleaching text*, i.e., transforming lexical strings into more abstract features. This study provides evidence that such features allow for better transfer across languages. Moreover, we present a first study on the ability of humans to perform *cross-lingual* gender prediction. We find that human predictive power proves similar to that of our bleached models, and both perform better than lexical models.

1 Introduction

Author profiling is the task of discovering latent user attributes disclosed through text, such as gender, age, personality, income, location and occupation (Rao et al., 2010; Burger et al., 2011; Feng et al., 2012; Jurgens, 2013; Bamman et al., 2014; Plank and Hovy, 2015; Flekova et al., 2016). It is of interest to several applications including personalized machine translation, forensics, and marketing (Mirkin et al., 2015; Rangel et al., 2015).

Early approaches to gender prediction (Koppel et al., 2002; Schler et al., 2006, e.g.) are inspired by pioneering work on authorship attribution (Mosteller and Wallace, 1964). Such stylometric models typically rely on carefully hand-selected sets of content-independent features to capture style beyond topic. Recently, *open vocabulary* approaches (Schwartz et al., 2013), where the entire linguistic production of an author is used, yielded substantial performance gains in on-line user-attribute prediction (Nguyen et al., 2014; Preoţiuc-Pietro et al., 2015; Emmery et al., 2017). Indeed, the best performing gender prediction models exploit chiefly lexical information (Rangel et al., 2017; Basile et al., 2017).

Relying heavily on the lexicon though has its limitations, as it results in models with limited portability. Moreover, performance might be overly optimistic due to topic bias (Sarawgi et al., 2011). Recent work on cross-lingual author profiling has proposed the use of solely language-independent features (Ljubešić et al., 2017), e.g., specific textual elements (percentage of emojis, URLs, etc) and users' meta-data/network (number of followers, etc), but this information is not always available.

We propose a novel approach where the actual text is still used, but bleached out and transformed into more abstract, and potentially better transferable features. One could view this as a method in between the open vocabulary strategy and the stylometric approach. It has the advantage of fading out content in favor of more shallow patterns still based on the original text, without introducing additional processing such as part-of-speech tagging. In particular, we investigate to what extent gender prediction can rely on generic non-lexical features (**RQ1**), and how predictive such models are when transferred to other languages (**RQ2**). We also glean insights from human judgments, and investigate how well people can perform cross-lingual gender prediction (**RQ3**). We focus on gender prediction for Twitter, motivated by data availability.

Contributions In this work i) we are the first to study cross-lingual gender prediction without relying on users' meta-data; ii) we propose a novel simple abstract feature representation which is surprisingly effective; and iii) we gauge human ability to perform cross-lingual gender detection, an angle of analysis which has not been studied thus far.

383

Proceedings of the 56th Annual Meeting of the Association for Computational Linguistics (Short Papers), pages 383–389
Melbourne, Australia, July 15 - 20, 2018. ©2018 Association for Computational Linguistics

Original	a	bag	of	Doritos	for	lunch!	🍟🍟🍟🍟
Frequency	4	2	4	0	4	1	0
Length	01	03	02	07	03	06	04
PunctC	W	W	W	W	W	W!	🍟🍟🍟🍟
PunctA	W	W	W	W	W	WP	JJJJ
Shape	L	LL	LL	ULL	LL	LLX	XX
Vowels	V	CVC	VC	CVCVCVC	CVC	CVCCCO	OOOO

Table 1: Abstract features example transformation.

2 Profiling with Abstract Features

Can we recover the gender of an author from bleached text, i.e., transformed text were the raw lexical strings are converted into abstract features? We investigate this question by building a series of predictive models to infer the gender of a Twitter user, in absence of additional user-specific metadata. Our approach can be seen as taking advantage of elements from a data-driven open-vocabulary approach, while trying to capture gender-specific style in text beyond topic.

To represent utterances in a more language agnostic way, we propose to simply transform the text into alternative textual representations, which deviate from the lexical form to allow for abstraction. We propose the following transformations, exemplified in Table 1. They are mostly motivated by intuition and inspired by prior work, like the use of shape features from NER and parsing (Petrov and Klein, 2007; Schnabel and Schütze, 2014; Plank et al., 2016; Limsopatham and Collier, 2016):

- **Frequency** Each word is presented as its binned frequency in the training data; bins are sized by orders of magnitude.

- **Length** Number of characters (prefixed by 0 to avoid collision with the next transformation).

- **PunctC** Merges all consecutive alphanumeric characters to one 'W' and leaves all other characters as they are (C for conservative).

- **PunctA** Generalization of PunctC (A for aggressive), converting different types of punctuation to classes: emoticons[1] to 'E' and emojis[2] to 'J', other punctuation to 'P'.

- **Shape** Transforms uppercase characters to 'U', lowercase characters to 'L', digits to 'D' and all other characters to 'X'. Repetitions

of transformed characters are condensed to a maximum of 2 for greater generalization.

- **Vowel-Consonant** To approximate vowels, while being able to generalize over (Indo-European) languages, we convert any of the 'aeiou' characters to 'V', other alphabetic character to 'C', and all other characters to 'O'.

- **AllAbs** A combination (concatenation) of all previously described features.

3 Experiments

In order to test whether abstract features are effective and transfer across languages, we set up experiments for gender prediction comparing lexicalized and bleached models for both in- and cross-language experiments. We compare them to a model using multilingual embeddings (Ruder, 2017). Finally, we elicit human judgments both within language and across language. The latter is to check whether a person with no prior knowledge of (the lexicon of) a given language can predict the gender of a user, and how that compares to an in-language setup and the machine. If humans can predict gender cross-lingually, they are likely to rely on aspects beyond lexical information.

Data We obtain data from the TwiSty corpus (Verhoeven et al., 2016), a multi-lingual collection of Twitter users, for the languages with 500+ users, namely Dutch, French, Portuguese, and Spanish. We complement them with English, using data from a predecessor of TwiSty (Plank and Hovy, 2015). All datasets contain manually annotated gender information. To simplify interpretation for the cross-language experiments, we balance gender in all datasets by downsampling to the minority class. The datasets' final sizes are given in Table 2. We use 200 tweets per user, as done by previous work (Verhoeven et al., 2016). We leave the data untokenized to exclude any language-dependent processing, because original tokenization could preserve some signal. Apart from mapping usernames to 'USER' and urls to 'URL' we do not perform any further data pre-processing.

3.1 Lexical vs Bleached Models

We use the `scikit-learn` (Pedregosa et al., 2011) implementation of a linear SVM with default parameters (e.g., L2 regularization). We use 10-fold cross validation for all in-language experiments. For the cross-lingual experiments, we train

---

[1] Using the NLTK tokenizer http://www.nltk.org/_modules/nltk/tokenize/casual.html

[2] https://pypi.python.org/pypi/emoji/

Test	Users	IN-LANGUAGE		CROSS-LANGUAGE				
		Lexical	Abstract	Lex Avg	Lex All	Embeds	Abs Avg	Abs All
EN	850	69.3	66.1	51.8	50.5	61.6	55.3	59.8
NL	894	81.3	71.8	52.3	50.0	56.8	59.5	69.2
FR	1,008	80.8	68.3	53.4	53.8	50.0	58.7	65.4
PT	3,066	86.0	68.1	55.3	63.8	59.5	59.3	58.9
ES	8,112	85.3	69.8	55.6	63.5	71.3	56.6	66.0

Table 2: Number of users per language and results for gender prediction (accuracy). IN-LANGUAGE: 10-fold cross-validation. CROSS-LANGUAGE: Testing on all test data in two setups: averages over single source models (AVG) or training a single model on all languages except the target (ALL). Comparison of lexical n-gram models (LEX), bleached models (ABS) and multilingual embeddings model (EMBEDS).

on all available source language data and test on all target language data.

For the lexicalized experiments, we adopt the features from the best performing system at the latest PAN evaluation campaign[3] (Basile et al., 2017) (word 1-2 grams and character 3-6 grams).

For the multilingual embeddings model we use the mean embedding representation from the system of (Plank, 2017) and add max, std and coverage features. We create multilingual embeddings by projecting monolingual embeddings to a single multilingual space for all five languages using a recently proposed SVD-based projection method with a pseudo-dictionary (Smith et al., 2017). The monolingual embeddings are trained on large amounts of in-house Twitter data (as much data as we had access to, i.e., ranging from 30M tweets for French to 1,500M tweets in Dutch, with a word type coverage between 63 and 77%). This results in an embedding space with a vocabulary size of 16M word types. All code is available at `https://github.com/bplank/bleaching-text`.

For the bleached experiments, we ran models with each feature set separately. In this paper, we report results for the model where all features are combined, as it proved to be the most robust across languages. We tuned the n-gram size of this model through in-language cross-validation, finding that $n = 5$ performs best.

When testing across languages, we report accuracy for two setups: average accuracy over each single-language model (AVG), and accuracy obtained when training on the concatenation of all languages but the target one (ALL). The latter setting is also used for the embeddings model. We report accuracy for all experiments.

	Test $\rightarrow$	EN	NL	FR	PT	ES
Train	EN		52.8	48.0	51.6	50.4
	NL	51.1		50.3	50.0	50.2
	FR	55.2	50.0		58.3	57.1
	PT	50.2	56.4	59.6		64.8
	ES	50.8	50.1	55.6	61.2	
	Avg	51.8	52.3	53.4	55.3	55.6

Table 3: Pair-wise results for lexicalized models.

Results and Analysis Table 2 shows results for both the cross-language and in-language experiments in the lexical and abstract-feature setting.

Within language, the lexical features unsurprisingly work the best, achieving an average accuracy of 80.5% over all languages. The abstract features lose some information and score on average 11.8% lower, still beating the majority baseline (50%) by a large margin (68.7%). If we go across language, the lexical approaches break down (overall to 53.7% for LEX AVG/56.3% for ALL), except for Portuguese and Spanish, thanks to their similarities (see Table 3 for pair-wise results). The closely-related-language effect is also observed when training on all languages, as scores go up when the classifier has access to the related language. The same holds for the multilingual embeddings model. On average it reaches an accuracy of 59.8%.

The closeness effect for Portuguese and Spanish can also be observed in language-to-language experiments, where scores for ES↦PT and PT↦ES are the highest. Results for the lexical models are generally lower on English, which might be due to smaller amounts of data (see first column in Table 2 providing number of users per language).

The abstract features fare surprisingly well and

[3] `http://pan.webis.de`

	Male	Female
1	W W W W "W"	USER E W W W
2	W W W W ?	3 5 1 5 2
3	2 5 0 5 2	W W W W ♥
4	5 4 4 5 4	E W W W W
5	W W, W W W?	LL LL LL LL LX
6	4 4 2 1 4	LL LL LL LL LUU
7	PP W W W W	W W W W *-*
8	5 5 2 2 5	W W W W JJJ
9	02 02 05 02 06	W W W W &W;W
10	5 0 5 5 2	J W W W W

Table 4: Ten most predictive features of the ABS model across all five languages. Features are ranked by how often they were in the top-ranked features for each language. Those prefixed with 0 (line 9) are length features. The prefix is used to avoid clashes with the frequency features.

tweets/user:	Human	Mach. LEX		Mach. ABS	
	20	20	200	20	200
NL↦NL	70.5	69.0	81.0	49.5	72.0
NL↦PT	58.7	49.5	50.5	57.0	61.5
FR↦NL	60.3	50.0	50.0	50.5	62.0

Table 5: Accuracy human versus machine.

work a lot better across languages. The performance is on average 6% higher across all languages (57.9% for AVG, 63.9% for ALL) in comparison to their lexicalized counterparts, where ABS ALL results in the overall best model. For Spanish, the multilingual embedding model clearly outperforms ABS. However, the approach requires large Twitter-specific embeddings.[4]

For our ABS model, if we investigate predictive features over all languages, cf. Table 4, we can see that the use of an emoji (like ♥) and shape-based features are predictive of female users. Quotes, question marks and length features, for example, appear to be more predictive of male users.

3.2 Human Evaluation

We experimented with three different conditions, one within language and two across language. For the latter, we set up an experiment where native speakers of Dutch were presented with tweets written in Portuguese and were asked to guess the poster's gender. In the other experiment, we asked speakers of French to identify the gender of the writer when reading Dutch tweets. In both cases, the participants declared to have no prior knowledge of the target language. For the in-language experiment, we asked Dutch speakers to identify the gender of a user writing Dutch tweets. The

Dutch speakers who participated in the two experiments are distinct individuals. Participants were informed of the experiment's goal. Their identity is anonymized in the data.

We selected a random sample of 200 users from the Dutch and Portuguese data, preserving a 50/50 gender distribution. Each user was represented by twenty tweets. The answer key (F/M) order was randomized. For each of the three experiments we had six judges, balanced for gender, and obtained three annotations per target user.

Results and Analysis Inter-annotator agreement for the tasks was measured via Fleiss kappa ($n = 3, N = 200$), and was higher for the in-language experiment ($K = 0.40$) than for the cross-language tasks (NL↦PT: $K = 0.25$; FR↦NL: $K = 0.28$). Table 5 shows accuracy against the gold labels, comparing humans (average accuracy over three annotators) to lexical and bleached models on the exact same subset of 200 users. Systems were tested under two different conditions regarding the number of tweets per user for the target language: machine and human saw the exact same twenty tweets, or the full set of tweets (200) per user, as done during training (Section 3.1).

First of all, our results indicate that in-language performance of humans is 70.5%, which is quite in line with the findings of Flekova et al. (2016), who report an accuracy of 75% on English. Within language, lexicalized models are superior to humans if exposed to enough information (200 tweets setup). One explanation for this might lie in an observation by Flekova et al. (2016), according to which people tend to rely too much on stereotypical lexical indicators when assigning gender to the poster of a tweet, while machines model less evident patterns. Lexicalized models are also superior to the bleached ones, as already seen on the full datasets (Table 2).

We can also observe that the amount of information available to represent a user influences system's performance. Training on 200 tweets per

<hr>

[4]We tested the approach with more generic (from Wikipedia) but smaller (in terms of vocabulary size) Polyglot embeddings resulting in inferior multilingual embeddings for our task.

user, but testing on 20 tweets only, decreases performance by 12 percentage points. This is likely due to the fact that inputs are sparser, especially since the bleached model is trained on 5-grams.[5] The bleached model, when given 200 tweets per user, yields a performance that is slightly higher than human accuracy.

In the cross-language setting, the picture is very different. Here, human performance is superior to the lexicalized models, independently of the amount of tweets per user at testing time. This seems to indicate that if humans cannot rely on the lexicon, they might be exploiting some other signal when guessing the gender of a user who tweets in a language unknown to them. Interestingly, the bleached models, which rely on non-lexical features, not only outperform the lexicalized ones in the cross-language experiments, but also neatly match the human scores.

4 Related Work

Most existing work on gender prediction exploits shallow lexical information based on the linguistic production of the users. Few studies investigate deeper syntactic information (Koppel et al., 2002; Feng et al., 2012) or non-linguistic input, e.g., language-independent clues such as visual (Alowibdi et al., 2013) or network information (Jurgens, 2013; Plank and Hovy, 2015; Ljubešić et al., 2017). A related angle is cross-genre profiling. In both settings lexical models have limited portability due to their bias towards the language/genre they have been trained on (Rangel et al., 2016; Busger op Vollenbroek et al., 2016; Medvedeva et al., 2017).

Lexical bias has been shown to affect in-language human gender prediction, too. Flekova et al. (2016) found that people tend to rely too much on stereotypical lexical indicators, while Nguyen et al. (2014) show that more than 10% of the Twitter users do actually not employ words that the crowd associates with their biological sex. Our features abstract away from such lexical cues while retaining predictive signal.

5 Conclusions

Bleaching text into abstract features is surprisingly effective for predicting gender, though lexical infor-

mation is still more useful within language (**RQ1**). However, models based on lexical clues fail when transferred to other languages, or require large amounts of unlabeled data from a similar domain as our experiments with the multilingual embedding model indicate. Instead, our bleached models clearly capture some signal beyond the lexicon, and perform well in a cross-lingual setting (**RQ2**). We are well aware that we are testing our cross-language bleached models in the context of closely related languages. While some features (such as PunctA, or Frequency) might carry over to genetically more distant languages, other features (such as Vowels and Shape) would probably be meaningless. Future work on this will require a sensible setting from a language typology perspective for choosing and testing adequate features.

In our novel study on human proficiency for cross-lingual gender prediction, we discovered that people are also abstracting away from the lexicon. Indeed, we observe that they are able to detect gender by looking at tweets in a language they do not know (**RQ3**) with an accuracy of 60% on average.

Acknowledgments

We would like to thank the three anonymous reviewers and our colleagues for their useful feedback on earlier versions of this paper. Furthermore, we are grateful to Chloé Braud for helping with the French human evaluation part. We would like to thank all of our human participants.

References

Jalal S. Alowibdi, Ugo A. Buy, and Philip Yu. 2013. Language independent gender classification on twitter. In *Proceedings of the 2013 IEEE/ACM International Conference on Advances in Social Networks Analysis and Mining*, ASONAM '13, pages 739–743, New York, NY, USA. ACM.

David Bamman, Jacob Eisenstein, and Tyler Schnoebelen. 2014. Gender identity and lexical variation in social media. *Journal of Sociolinguistics*, 18(2):135–160.

Angelo Basile, Gareth Dwyer, Maria Medvedeva, Josine Rawee, Hessel Haagsma, and Malvina Nissim. 2017. N-gram: New groningen author-profiling model. In *Proceedings of the CLEF 2017 Evaluation Labs and Workshop – Working Notes Papers, 11-14 September, Dublin, Ireland (Sept. 2017)*.

John D. Burger, John Henderson, George Kim, and Guido Zarrella. 2011. Discriminating Gender on Twitter. In *Proceedings of the 2011 Conference on*

---

[5]We experimented with training on 20 tweets rather than 200, and with different n-gram sizes (e.g., 1–4). Despite slightly better results, we decided to use the trained models as they were to employ the same settings across all experiments (200 tweets per users, $n = 5$), with no further tuning.

Empirical Methods in Natural Language Processing, pages 1301–1309, Edinburgh, Scotland, UK. Association for Computational Linguistics.

Chris Emmery, Grzegorz Chrupała, and Walter Daelemans. 2017. Simple queries as distant labels for predicting gender on twitter. In *Proceedings of the 3rd Workshop on Noisy User-generated Text*, pages 50–55, Copenhagen, Denmark. Association for Computational Linguistics.

Song Feng, Ritwik Banerjee, and Yejin Choi. 2012. Characterizing stylistic elements in syntactic structure. In *Proceedings of the 2012 Joint Conference on Empirical Methods in Natural Language Processing and Computational Natural Language Learning*, pages 1522–1533. Association for Computational Linguistics.

Lucie Flekova, Jordan Carpenter, Salvatore Giorgi, Lyle Ungar, and Daniel Preoţiuc-Pietro. 2016. Analyzing biases in human perception of user age and gender from text. In *Proceedings of the 54th Annual Meeting of the Association for Computational Linguistics (Volume 1: Long Papers)*, pages 843–854, Berlin, Germany. Association for Computational Linguistics.

David Jurgens. 2013. That's what friends are for: Inferring location in online social media platforms based on social relationships. *ICWSM*, 13(13):273–282.

Moshe Koppel, Shlomo Argamon, and Anat Rachel Shimoni. 2002. Automatically categorizing written texts by author gender. *Literary and Linguistic Computing*, 17:401–412.

Nut Limsopatham and Nigel Collier. 2016. Bidirectional lstm for named entity recognition in twitter messages. In *Proceedings of the 2nd Workshop on Noisy User-generated Text (WNUT)*, pages 145–152, Osaka, Japan. The COLING 2016 Organizing Committee.

Nikola Ljubešić, Darja Fišer, and Tomaž Erjavec. 2017. Language-independent gender prediction on twitter. In *Proceedings of the Second Workshop on NLP and Computational Social Science*, pages 1–6, Vancouver, Canada. Association for Computational Linguistics.

Maria Medvedeva, Hessel Haagsma, and Malvina Nissim. 2017. An analysis of cross-genre and in-genre performance for author profiling in social media. In *Experimental IR Meets Multilinguality, Multimodality, and Interaction - 8th International Conference of the CLEF Association, CLEF 2017, Dublin, Ireland, September 11-14, 2017, Proceedings*, pages 211–223.

Shachar Mirkin, Scott Nowson, Caroline Brun, and Julien Perez. 2015. Motivating personality-aware machine translation. In *Proceedings of the 2015 Conference on Empirical Methods in Natural Language Processing*, pages 1102–1108.

Frederick Mosteller and David Wallace. 1964. Inference and disputed authorship: The federalist.

Dong Nguyen, Dolf Trieschnigg, A Seza Doğruöz, Rilana Gravel, Mariët Theune, Theo Meder, and Franciska De Jong. 2014. Why gender and age prediction from tweets is hard: Lessons from a crowdsourcing experiment. In *Proceedings of COLING 2014, the 25th International Conference on Computational Linguistics: Technical Papers*, pages 1950–1961.

F. Pedregosa, G. Varoquaux, A. Gramfort, V. Michel, B. Thirion, O. Grisel, M. Blondel, P. Prettenhofer, R. Weiss, V. Dubourg, J. Vanderplas, A. Passos, D. Cournapeau, M. Brucher, M. Perrot, and E. Duchesnay. 2011. Scikit-learn: Machine learning in Python. *Journal of Machine Learning Research*, 12:2825–2830.

Slav Petrov and Dan Klein. 2007. Improved inference for unlexicalized parsing. In *Human Language Technologies 2007: The Conference of the North American Chapter of the Association for Computational Linguistics; Proceedings of the Main Conference*, pages 404–411, Rochester, New York. Association for Computational Linguistics.

Barbara Plank. 2017. All-in-1 at ijcnlp-2017 task 4: Short text classification with one model for all languages. *Proceedings of the IJCNLP 2017, Shared Tasks*, pages 143–148.

Barbara Plank and Dirk Hovy. 2015. Personality traits on twitter—or—how to get 1,500 personality tests in a week. In *Proceedings of the 6th Workshop on Computational Approaches to Subjectivity, Sentiment and Social Media Analysis*, pages 92–98, Lisboa, Portugal. Association for Computational Linguistics.

Barbara Plank, Anders Søgaard, and Yoav Goldberg. 2016. Multilingual Part-of-Speech Tagging with Bidirectional Long Short-Term Memory Models and Auxiliary Loss. In *Proceedings of the 54th Annual Meeting of the Association for Computational Linguistics*.

Daniel Preoţiuc-Pietro, Vasileios Lampos, and Nikolaos Aletras. 2015. An analysis of the user occupational class through twitter content. In *Proceedings of the 53rd Annual Meeting of the Association for Computational Linguistics and the 7th International Joint Conference on Natural Language Processing (Volume 1: Long Papers)*, volume 1, pages 1754–1764.

Francisco Rangel, Paolo Rosso, Martin Potthast, and Benno Stein. 2017. Overview of the 5th author profiling task at pan 2017: Gender and language variety identification in twitter. *Working Notes Papers of the CLEF*.

Francisco Rangel, Paolo Rosso, Martin Potthast, Benno Stein, and Walter Daelemans. 2015. Overview of the 3rd author profiling task at pan 2015. In *CLEF*, page 2015. sn.

Francisco Rangel, Paolo Rosso, Ben Verhoeven, Walter Daelemans, Martin Potthast, and Benno Stein. 2016. Overview of the 4th Author Profiling Task at PAN 2016: Cross-genre Evaluations. In *Working Notes Papers of the CLEF 2016 Evaluation Labs. CEUR Workshop Proceedings*. CLEF and CEUR-WS.org.

Delip Rao, David Yarowsky, Abhishek Shreevats, and Manaswi Gupta. 2010. Classifying latent user attributes in twitter. In *Proceedings of the 2nd international workshop on Search and mining user-generated contents*, pages 37–44. ACM.

Sebastian Ruder. 2017. A survey of cross-lingual embedding models. *arXiv preprint arXiv:1706.04902*.

Ruchita Sarawgi, Kailash Gajulapalli, and Yejin Choi. 2011. Gender attribution: tracing stylometric evidence beyond topic and genre. In *Proceedings of the Fifteenth Conference on Computational Natural Language Learning*, pages 78–86. Association for Computational Linguistics.

Jonathan Schler, Moshe Koppel, Shlomo Argamon, and James W. Pennebaker. 2006. Effects of Age and Gender on Blogging. In *AAAI Spring Symposium: Computational Approaches to Analyzing Weblogs*, pages 199–205. AAAI.

Tobias Schnabel and Hinrich Schütze. 2014. Flors: Fast and simple domain adaptation for part-of-speech tagging. *Transactions of the ACL*, 2:15–26.

H Andrew Schwartz, Johannes C Eichstaedt, Margaret L Kern, Lukasz Dziurzynski, Stephanie M Ramones, Megha Agrawal, Achal Shah, Michal Kosinski, David Stillwell, Martin EP Seligman, et al. 2013. Personality, gender, and age in the language of social media: The open-vocabulary approach. *PloS one*, 8(9):e73791.

Samuel L Smith, David HP Turban, Steven Hamblin, and Nils Y Hammerla. 2017. Offline bilingual word vectors, orthogonal transformations and the inverted softmax. *arXiv preprint arXiv:1702.03859*.

Ben Verhoeven, Walter Daelemans, and Barbara Plank. 2016. Twisty: A multilingual twitter stylometry corpus for gender and personality profiling. In *Proceedings of the Tenth International Conference on Language Resources and Evaluation (LREC 2016)*, Paris, France. European Language Resources Association (ELRA).

M. Busger op Vollenbroek, T. Carlotto, T. Kreutz, M. Medvedeva, C. Pool, J. Bjerva, H. Haagsma, and M. Nissim. 2016. Gronup: Groningen user profiling notebook for PAN at CLEF. In *CLEF 2016 Evaluation Labs and Workshop – Working Notes Papers*.

Orthographic Features for Bilingual Lexicon Induction

Parker Riley and **Daniel Gildea**
Department of Computer Science
University of Rochester
Rochester, NY 14627

Abstract

Recent embedding-based methods in bilingual lexicon induction show good results, but do not take advantage of orthographic features, such as edit distance, which can be helpful for pairs of related languages. This work extends embedding-based methods to incorporate these features, resulting in significant accuracy gains for related languages.

1 Introduction

Over the past few years, new methods for bilingual lexicon induction have been proposed that are applicable to low-resource language pairs, for which very little sentence-aligned parallel data is available. Parallel data can be very expensive to create, so methods that require less of it or that can utilize more readily available data are desirable.

One prevalent strategy involves creating multilingual word embeddings, where each language's vocabulary is embedded in the same latent space (Vulić and Moens, 2013; Mikolov et al., 2013a; Artetxe et al., 2016); however, many of these methods still require a strong cross-lingual signal in the form of a large seed dictionary.

More recent work has focused on reducing that constraint. Vulić and Moens (2016) and Vulic and Korhonen (2016) use document-aligned data to learn bilingual embeddings instead of a seed dictionary. Artetxe et al. (2017) use a very small, automatically-generated seed lexicon of identical numerals as the initialization in an iterative self-learning framework to learn a linear mapping between monolingual embedding spaces; Zhang et al. (2017) use an adversarial training method to learn a similar mapping. Lample et al. (2018a) use a series of techniques to align monolingual embedding spaces in a completely unsupervised way; their method is used by Lample et al. (2018b) as the initialization for a completely unsupervised machine translation system.

These recent advances in unsupervised bilingual lexicon induction show promise for use in low-resource contexts. However, none of them make use of linguistic features of the languages themselves (with the arguable exception of syntactic/semantic information encoded in the word embeddings). This is in contrast to work that predates many of these embedding-based methods that leveraged linguistic features such as edit distance and orthographic similarity: Dyer et al. (2011) and Berg-Kirkpatrick et al. (2010) investigate using linguistic features for word alignment, and Haghighi et al. (2008) use linguistic features for unsupervised bilingual lexicon induction. These features can help identify words with common ancestry (such as the English-Italian pair *agile-agile*) and borrowed words (*macaroni-maccheroni*).

The addition of linguistic features led to increased performance in these earlier models, especially for related languages, yet these features have not been applied to more modern methods. In this work, we extend the modern embedding-based approach of Artetxe et al. (2017) with orthographic information in order to leverage similarities between related languages for increased accuracy in bilingual lexicon induction.

2 Background

This work is directly based on the work of Artetxe et al. (2017). Following their work, let $X \in \mathbb{R}^{|V_s| \times d}$ and $Z \in \mathbb{R}^{|V_t| \times d}$ be the word embedding matrices of two distinct languages, referred to respectively as the source and target, such that each row corresponds to the d-dimensional embedding of a single word. We refer to the ith row of one of

390

Proceedings of the 56th Annual Meeting of the Association for Computational Linguistics (Short Papers), pages 390–394
Melbourne, Australia, July 15 - 20, 2018. ©2018 Association for Computational Linguistics

these matrices as X_{i*} or Z_{i*}. The vocabularies for each language are V_s and V_t, respectively. Also let $D \in \{0,1\}^{|V_s| \times |V_t|}$ be a binary matrix representing a dictionary such that $D_{ij} = 1$ if the ith word in the source language is aligned with the jth word in the target language. We wish to find a mapping matrix $W \in \mathbb{R}^{d \times d}$ that maps source embeddings onto their aligned target embeddings. Artetxe et al. (2017) define the optimal mapping matrix W^* with the following equation,

$$W^* = \arg\min_W \sum_i \sum_j D_{ij} \|X_{i*}W - Z_{j*}\|^2$$

which minimizes the sum of the squared Euclidean distances between mapped source embeddings and their aligned target embeddings.

By normalizing and mean-centering X and Z, and enforcing that W be an orthogonal matrix ($W^T W = I$), the above formulation becomes equivalent to maximizing the dot product between the mapped source embeddings and target embeddings, such that

$$W^* = \arg\max_W \operatorname{Tr}(XWZ^TD^T)$$

where $\operatorname{Tr}(\cdot)$ is the trace operator, the sum of all diagonal entries. The optimal solution to this equation is $W^* = UV^T$, where $X^T DZ = U\Sigma V^T$ is the singular value decomposition of $X^T DZ$.

This formulation requires a seed dictionary. To reduce the need for a large seed dictionary, Artetxe et al. (2017) propose an iterative, self-learning framework that determines W as above, uses it to calculate a new dictionary D, and then iterates until convergence. In the dictionary induction step, they set $D_{ij} = 1$ if $j = \arg\max_k (X_{i*}W) \cdot Z_{k*}$ and $D_{ij} = 0$ otherwise.

We propose two methods for extending this system using orthographic information, described in the following two sections.

3 Orthographic Extension of Word Embeddings

This method augments the embeddings for all words in both languages before using them in the self-learning framework of Artetxe et al. (2017). To do this, we append to each word's embedding a vector of length equal to the size of the union of the two languages' alphabets. Each position in this vector corresponds to a single letter, and its value is set to the count of that letter within the spelling of the word. This letter count vector is then scaled by a constant before being appended to the base word embedding. After appending, the resulting augmented vector is normalized to have magnitude 1.

Mathematically, let A be an ordered set of characters (an alphabet), containing all characters appearing in both language's alphabets:

$$A = A_{source} \cup A_{target}$$

Let O_{source} and O_{target} be the orthographic extension matrices for each language, containing counts of the characters appearing in each word w_i, scaled by a constant factor c_e:

$$O_{ij} = c_e \cdot \operatorname{count}(A_j, w_i), O \in \{O_{source}, O_{target}\}$$

Then, we concatenate the embedding matrices and extension matrices:

$$X' = [X; O_{source}], \quad Z' = [Z; O_{target}]$$

Finally, in the normalized embedding matrices X'' and Z'', each row has magnitude 1:

$$X''_{i*} = \frac{X'_{i*}}{\|X'_{i*}\|}, \quad Z''_{i*} = \frac{Z'_{i*}}{\|Z'_{i*}\|}$$

These new matrices are used in place of X and Z in the self-learning process.

4 Orthographic Similarity Adjustment

This method modifies the similarity score for each word pair during the dictionary induction phase of the self-learning framework of Artetxe et al. (2017), which uses the dot product of two words' embeddings to quantify similarity. We modify this similarity score by adding a measure of orthographic similarity, which is a function of the normalized string edit distance of the two words.

The normalized edit distance is defined as the Levenshtein distance ($\mathrm{L}(\cdot, \cdot)$) (Levenshtein, 1966) divided by the length of the longer word. The Levenshtein distance represents the minimum number of insertions, deletions, and substitutions required to transform one word into the other. The normalized edit distance function is denoted as $\mathrm{NL}(\cdot, \cdot)$.

$$\mathrm{NL}(w_1, w_2) = \frac{\mathrm{L}(w_1, w_2)}{\max(|w_1|, |w_2|)}$$

We define the orthographic similarity of two words w_1 and w_2 as $\log(2.0 - \mathrm{NL}(w_1, w_2))$. These

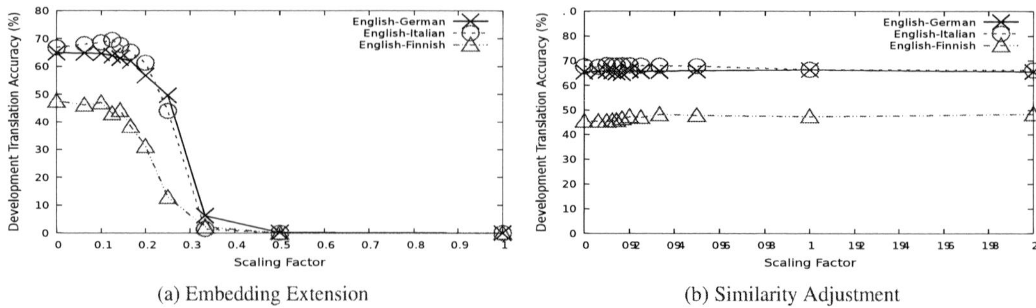

(a) Embedding Extension   (b) Similarity Adjustment

Figure 1: Performance on development data vs. scaling factors c_e and c_s. The lowest tested value for both was 10^{-6}.

similarity scores are used to form an orthographic similarity matrix S, where each entry corresponds to a source-target word pair. Each entry is first scaled by a constant factor c_s. This matrix is added to the standard similarity matrix, XWZ^T.

$$S_{ij} = c_s \cdot \log(2.0 - \mathrm{NL}(w_i, w_j)), w_i \in V_s, w_j \in V_t$$

The vocabulary for each language is 200,000 words, so computing a similarity score for each pair would involve 40 billion edit distance calculations. Also, the vast majority of word pairs are orthographically very dissimilar, resulting in a normalized edit distance close to 1 and an orthographic similarity close to 0, having little to no effect on the overall estimated similarity. Therefore, we only calculate the edit distance for a subset of possible word pairs.

Thus, the actual orthographic similarity matrix that we use is as follows:

$$S'_{ij} = \begin{cases} S_{ij} & \langle w_i, w_j \rangle \in \mathtt{symDelete}\,(V_t, V_s, k) \\ 0 & \text{otherwise} \end{cases}$$

This subset of word pairs was chosen using an adaptation of the Symmetric Delete spelling correction algorithm described by Garbe (2012), which we denote as $\mathtt{symDelete}(\cdot, \cdot, \cdot)$. This algorithm takes as arguments the target vocabulary, source vocabulary, and a constant k, and identifies all source-target word pairs that are identical after k or fewer deletions from each word; that is, all pairs where each is reachable from the other with no more than k insertions and k deletions. For example, the Italian-English pair *moderno-modern* will be identified with $k = 1$, and the pair *tollerante-tolerant* will be identified with $k = 2$.

The algorithm works by computing all strings formed by k or fewer deletions from each target

word, stores them in a hash table, then does the same for each source word and generates source-target pairs that share an entry in the hash table. The complexity of this algorithm can be expressed as $O(|V|l^k)$, where $V = V_t \cup V_s$ is the combined vocabulary and l is the length of the longest word in V. This is linear with respect to the vocabulary size, as opposed to the quadratic complexity required for computing the entire matrix. However, the algorithm is sensitive to both word length and the choice of k. In our experiments, we found that ignoring all words of length greater than 30 allowed the algorithm to complete very quickly while skipping less than 0.1% of the data. We also used small values of k ($0 < k < 4$), and used $k = 1$ for our final results, finding no significant benefit from using a larger value.

5 Experiments

We use the datasets used by Artetxe et al. (2017), consisting of three language pairs: English-Italian, English-German, and English-Finnish. The English-Italian dataset was introduced in Dinu and Baroni (2014); the other datasets were created by Artetxe et al. (2017). Each dataset includes monolingual word embeddings (trained with word2vec (Mikolov et al., 2013b)) for both languages and a bilingual dictionary, separated into a training and test set. We do not use the training set as the input dictionary to the system, instead using an automatically-generated dictionary consisting only of numeral identity translations (such as 2-2, 3-3, et cetera) as in Artetxe et al. (2017).[1] However, because the methods presented in this work feature tunable hyperparameters, we use a portion of the training set as devel-

---

[1] https://github.com/artetxem/vecmap

392

Method	English-German	English-Italian	English-Finnish
Artetxe et al. (2017)	40.27	39.40	26.47
Artetxe et al. (2017) + identity	51.73	44.07	42.63
Embedding extension, $c_e = \frac{1}{8}$	50.33	48.40	29.63
Embedding extension + identity, $c_e = \frac{1}{8}$	55.40	47.13	**43.54**
Similarity adjustment, $c_s = 1$	43.73	39.93	28.16
Similarity adjustment + identity, $c_s = 1$	52.20	44.27	41.99
Combined, $c_e = \frac{1}{8}, c_s = 1$	53.53	**49.13**	32.51
Combined + identity, $c_e = \frac{1}{8}, c_s = 1$	**55.53**	46.27	41.78

Table 1: Comparison of methods on test data. Scaling constants c_e and c_s were selected based on performance on development data over all three language pairs. The last two rows report the results of using both methods together.

Source Word	Our Prediction (Language)	Incorrect Baseline Prediction (Translation)
caesium	*cäsium* (German)	*isotope* (*isotope*)
unevenly	*ungleichmäßig* (German)	*gleichmäßig* (*evenly*)
Ethiopians	*Äthiopier* (German)	*Afrikaner* (*Africans*)
autumn	*autunno* (Italian)	*primavera* (*spring*)
Brueghel	*Bruegel* (Italian)	*Dürer* (*Dürer*)
Latvians	*latvialaiset* (Finnish)	*ukrainalaiset* (*Ukrainians*)

Table 2: Examples of pairs correctly identified by our embedding extension method that were incorrectly translated by the system of Artetxe et al. (2017). Our system can disambiguate semantic clusters created by word2vec.

opment data.[2] In all experiments, a single target word is predicted for each source word, and full points are awarded if it is one of the listed correct translations. On average, the number of translations for each source (non-English) word was 1.2 for English-Italian, 1.3 for English-German, and 1.4 for English-Finnish.

6   Results and Discussion

For our experiments with orthographic extension of word embeddings, each embedding was extended by the size of the union of the alphabets of both languages. The size of this union was 199 for English-Italian, 200 for English-German, and 287 for English-Finnish.

These numbers are perhaps unintuitively high. However, the corpora include many other characters, including diacritical markings and various symbols (%, [, !, etc.) that are an indication that tokenization of the data could be improved. We did not filter these characters in this work.

For our experiments with orthographic similarity adjustment, the heuristic identified approximately 2 million word pairs for each language pair out of a possible 40 billion, resulting in significant computation savings.

Figure 1 shows the results on the development data. Based on these results, we selected $c_e = \frac{1}{8}$ and $c_s = 1$ as our hyperparameters. The local optima were not identical for all three languages, but we felt that these values struck the best compromise among them.

Table 1 compares our methods against the system of Artetxe et al. (2017), using scaling factors selected based on development data results. Because approximately 20% of source-target pairs in the dictionary were identical, we also extended all systems to guess the identity translation if the source word appeared in the target vocabulary. This improved accuracy in most cases, with some exceptions for English-Italian. We also experimented with both methods together, and found that this was the best of the settings that did not include the identity translation component; with the identity component included, however, the embedding extension method alone was best for English-Finnish. The fact that Finnish is the only language here that is not in the Indo-European family (and has fewer words borrowed from English or its ancestors) may explain why the performance trends for English-Finnish were different than those of the other two language pairs.

In addition to identifying orthographically similar words, the extension method is capable of

---

[2]We use all source-target pairs containing one of 1,000 randomly-selected target words.

learning a mapping between source and target *letters*, which could partially explain its improved performance over our edit distance method.

Table 2 shows some correct translations from our system that were missed by the baseline.

7 Conclusion and Future Work

In this work, we presented two techniques (which can be combined) for improving embedding-based bilingual lexicon induction for related languages using orthographic information and no parallel data, allowing their use with low-resource language pairs. These methods increased accuracy in our experiments, with both the combined and embedding extension methods providing significant gains over the baseline system.

In the future, we want to extend this work to related languages with different alphabets (experimenting with transliteration or phonetic transcription) and to extend other unsupervised bilingual lexicon induction systems, such as that of Lample et al. (2018a).

Acknowledgments We are grateful to the anonymous reviewers for suggesting useful additions. This research was supported by NSF grant number 1449828.

References

Mikel Artetxe, Gorka Labaka, and Eneko Agirre. 2016. Learning principled bilingual mappings of word embeddings while preserving monolingual invariance. In *Proceedings of the 2016 Conference on Empirical Methods in Natural Language Processing (EMNLP-16)*, pages 2289–2294, Austin, Texas.

Mikel Artetxe, Gorka Labaka, and Eneko Agirre. 2017. Learning bilingual word embeddings with (almost) no bilingual data. In *Proceedings of the 55th Annual Meeting of the Association for Computational Linguistics (ACL-17)*, pages 451–462, Vancouver, Canada.

Taylor Berg-Kirkpatrick, Alexandre Bouchard-Côté, John DeNero, and Dan Klein. 2010. Painless unsupervised learning with features. In *Proceedings of the 2010 Meeting of the North American chapter of the Association for Computational Linguistics (NAACL-10)*, pages 582–590.

Georgiana Dinu and Marco Baroni. 2014. Improving zero-shot learning by mitigating the hubness problem. *CoRR*, abs/1412.6568.

Chris Dyer, Jonathan Clark, Alon Lavie, and Noah A Smith. 2011. Unsupervised word alignment with arbitrary features. In *Proceedings of the 49th Annual Meeting of the Association for Computational Linguistics (ACL-11)*, pages 409–419.

Wolf Garbe. 2012. 1000x faster spelling correction algorithm. `http://blog.faroo.com/2012/06/07/improved-edit-distance-based-spelling-correction/`. Accessed: 2018-02-12.

Aria Haghighi, Taylor Berg-Kirkpatrick, and Dan Klein. 2008. Learning bilingual lexicons from monolingual corpora. In *Proceedings of the 46th Annual Meeting of the Association for Computational Linguistics (ACL-08)*, pages 771–779.

Guillaume Lample, Alexis Conneau, Marc'Aurelio Ranzato, Ludovic Denoyer, and Hervé Jégou. 2018a. Word translation without parallel data. In *International Conference on Learning Representations (ICLR)*.

Guillaume Lample, Ludovic Denoyer, and Marc'Aurelio Ranzato. 2018b. Unsupervised machine translation using monolingual corpora only. In *International Conference on Learning Representations (ICLR)*.

V. I. Levenshtein. 1966. Binary codes capable of correcting deletions, insertions, and reversals. *Cybernetics and Control Theory*, 10(8):707–710. Original in *Doklady Akademii Nauk SSSR* 163(4): 845–848 (1965).

Tomas Mikolov, Quoc V Le, and Ilya Sutskever. 2013a. Exploiting similarities among languages for machine translation. *arXiv preprint arXiv:1309.4168*.

Tomas Mikolov, Ilya Sutskever, Kai Chen, Greg S Corrado, and Jeff Dean. 2013b. Distributed representations of words and phrases and their compositionality. In *Advances in Neural Information Processing Systems*, pages 3111–3119.

Ivan Vulic and Anna Korhonen. 2016. On the role of seed lexicons in learning bilingual word embeddings. In *Proceedings of the 54th Annual Meeting of the Association for Computational Linguistics (ACL-16)*, pages 247–257, Berlin, Germany.

Ivan Vulić and Marie-Francine Moens. 2013. A study on bootstrapping bilingual vector spaces from non-parallel data (and nothing else). In *Proceedings of the 2013 Conference on Empirical Methods in Natural Language Processing (EMNLP-13)*, pages 1613–1624, Seattle, Washington, USA.

Ivan Vulić and Marie-Francine Moens. 2016. Bilingual distributed word representations from document-aligned comparable data. *J. Artif. Int. Res.*, 55(1):953–994.

Meng Zhang, Yang Liu, Huanbo Luan, and Maosong Sun. 2017. Adversarial training for unsupervised bilingual lexicon induction. In *Proceedings of the 55th Annual Meeting of the Association for Computational Linguistics (ACL-17)*, pages 1959–1970, Vancouver, Canada.

Neural Cross-Lingual Coreference Resolution And Its Application To Entity Linking

Gourab Kundu and **Avirup Sil** and **Radu Florian** and **Wael Hamza**
IBM Research
1101 Kitchawan Road
Yorktown Heights, NY 10598
{gkundu, avi, raduf, whamza}@us.ibm.com

Abstract

We propose an entity-centric neural cross-lingual coreference model that builds on multi-lingual embeddings and language-independent features. We perform both intrinsic and extrinsic evaluations of our model. In the intrinsic evaluation, we show that our model, when trained on English and tested on Chinese and Spanish, achieves competitive results to the models trained directly on Chinese and Spanish respectively. In the extrinsic evaluation, we show that our English model helps achieve superior entity linking accuracy on Chinese and Spanish test sets than the top 2015 TAC system without using any annotated data from Chinese or Spanish.

1 Introduction

Cross-lingual models for NLP tasks are important since they can be used on data from a new language without requiring annotation from the new language (Ji et al., 2014, 2015). This paper investigates the use of multi-lingual embeddings (Faruqui and Dyer, 2014; Upadhyay et al., 2016) for building cross-lingual models for the task of coreference resolution (Ng and Cardie, 2002; Pradhan et al., 2012). Consider the following text from a Spanish news article:

"Tormenta de nieve afecta a 100 millones de personas en EEUU. Unos 100 millones de personas enfrentaban el sábado nuevas dificultades tras la enorme tormenta de nieve de hace días en la costa este de Estados Unidos."

The mentions "EEUU" ("US" in English) and "Estados Unidos" ("United States" in English) are coreferent. A coreference model trained on English data is unlikely to coreference these two

mentions in Spanish since these mentions did not appear in English data and a regular English style abbreviation of "Estados Unidos" will be "EU" instead of "EEUU". But in the bilingual English-Spanish word embedding space, the word embedding of "EEUU" sits close to the word embedding of "US" and the sum of word embeddings of "Estados Unidos" sit close to the sum of word embeddings of "United States". Therefore, a coreference model trained using English-Spanish bilingual word embeddings on English data has the potential to make the correct coreference decision between "EEUU" and "Estados Unidos" without ever encountering these mentions in training data.

The contributions of this paper are two-fold. Firstly, we propose an entity-centric neural cross-lingual coreference model. This model, when trained on English and tested on Chinese and Spanish from the TAC 2015 Trilingual Entity Discovery and Linking (EDL) Task (Ji et al., 2015), achieves competitive results to models trained directly on Chinese and Spanish respectively. Secondly, a pipeline consisting of this coreference model and an Entity Linking (henceforth EL) model can achieve superior linking accuracy than the official top ranking system in 2015 on Chinese and Spanish test sets, without using any supervision in Chinese or Spanish.

Although most of the active coreference research is on solving the problem of noun phrase coreference resolution in the Ontonotes data set, invigorated by the 2011 and 2012 CoNLL shared task (Pradhan et al., 2011, 2012), there are many important applications/end tasks where the mentions of interest are not noun phrases. Consider the sentence,

"(U.S. president Barack Obama who started ((his) political career) in (Illinois)), was born in (Hawaii)."

The bracketing represents the Ontonotes style

Proceedings of the 56th Annual Meeting of the Association for Computational Linguistics (Short Papers), pages 395–400
Melbourne, Australia, July 15 - 20, 2018. ©2018 Association for Computational Linguistics

noun phrases and underlines represent the phrases that should be linked to Wikipedia by an EL system. Note that mentions like "U.S." and "Barack Obama" do not align with any noun phrase. Therefore, in this work, we focus on coreference on mentions that arise in our end task of entity linking and conduct experiments on TAC TriLingual 2015 data sets consisting of English, Chinese and Spanish.

2 Coreference Model

Each mention has a *mention* type (m_type) of either name or nominal and an *entity* type (e_type) of Person (PER) / Location (LOC) / GPE / facility (FAC) / organization (ORG) (following standard TAC (Ji et al., 2015) notations).

The objective of our model is to compute a function that can decide whether two partially constructed entities should be coreferenced or not. We gradually merge the mentions in the given document to form entities. Mentions are considered in the order of names and then nominals and within each group, mentions are arranged in the order they appear in the document. Suppose, the sorted order of mentions are $m_1, \ldots, m_{N_1}, m_{N_1+1}, \ldots, m_{N_1+N_2}$ where N_1 and N_2 are respectively the number of the named and nominal mentions. A singleton entity is created from each mention. Let the order of entities be $e_1, \ldots, e_{N_1}, e_{N_1+1}, \ldots, e_{N_1+N_2}$.
We merge the named entities with other named entities, then nominal entities with named entities in the same sentence and finally we merge nominal entities across sentences as follows:

Step 1: For each *named* entity e_i ($1 \leq i \leq N_1$), antecedents are all entities e_j ($1 \leq j \leq i - 1$) such that e_j and e_i have same e_type. Training examples are triplets of the form (e_i, e_j, y_{ij}). If e_i and e_j are coreferent (meaning, y_{ij}=1), they are merged.

Step 2: For each nominal entity e_i ($N_1 + 1 \leq i \leq N_1 + N_2$), we consider antecedents e_j such that e_i and e_j have the same e_type and e_j has some mention that appears in the *same sentence* as some mention in e_i. Training examples are generated and entities are merged as in the previous step.

Step 3: This is similar to previous step, except e_i and e_j have *no* sentence restriction.

Features: For each training triplet (e_1, e_2, y_{12}), the network takes the entity pair (e_1, e_2) as input and tries to predict y_{12} as output. Since each entity represents a set of mentions, the entity-pair embedding is obtained from the embeddings of mention pairs generated from the cross product of the entity pair. Let $M(e_1, e_2)$ be the set $\{(m_i, m_j) \mid (m_i, m_j) \in e_1 \times e_2\}$. For each $(m_i, m_j) \in M(e_1, e_2)$, a feature vector ϕ_{m_i, m_j} is computed. Then, every feature in ϕ_{m_i, m_j} is embedded as a vector in the real space. Let v_{m_i, m_j} dentote the concatenation of embeddings of all features in ϕ_{m_i, m_j}. Embeddings of all features except the words are learned in the training process. Word embeddings are pre-trained. v_{m_i, m_j} includes the following language independent features:

String match: whether m_i is a substring or exact match of m_j and vice versa (e.g. m_i = "Barack Obama" and m_j = "Obama")

Distance: word distance and sentence distance between m_i and m_j discretized into bins

m_type: concatenation of m_types for m_i and m_j

e_type: concatenation of e_types for m_i and m_j

Acronym: whether m_i is an acronym of m_j or vice versa (e.g. m_i = "United States" and m_j = "US")

First name mismatch: whether m_i and m_j belong to e_type of PERSON with the same last name but different first name (e.g. m_i="Barack Obama" and m_j = "Michelle Obama")

Speaker detection: whether m_i and m_j both occur in the context of words indicating speech e.g. "say", "said"

In addition, v_{m_i, m_j} includes the average of the word embeddings of m_i and average of the word embeddings of m_j.

2.1 Network Architecture

The network architecture from the input to the output is shown in figure 1.

Embedding Layer: For each training triplet (e_1, e_2, y), a sequence of vectors v_{m_i, m_j} (for each $((m_i, m_j) \in M(e_1, e_2))$) is given as input to the network.

Relu Layer: $v_{m_i, m_j}^r = max(0, W^{(1)} v_{m_i, m_j})$

Attention Layer: To generate the entity-pair embedding, we need to combine the embeddings of mention pairs generated from the entity-pair. Consider two entities e_1 = (President[1], Obama)} and e_2 = {(President[2], Clinton)}. Here the superscripts are used to indicate two different mentions with the same surface form. Since the named mention pair (Obama, Clinton) has no string overlap, e_1 and e_2 should not be coreferenced even though the

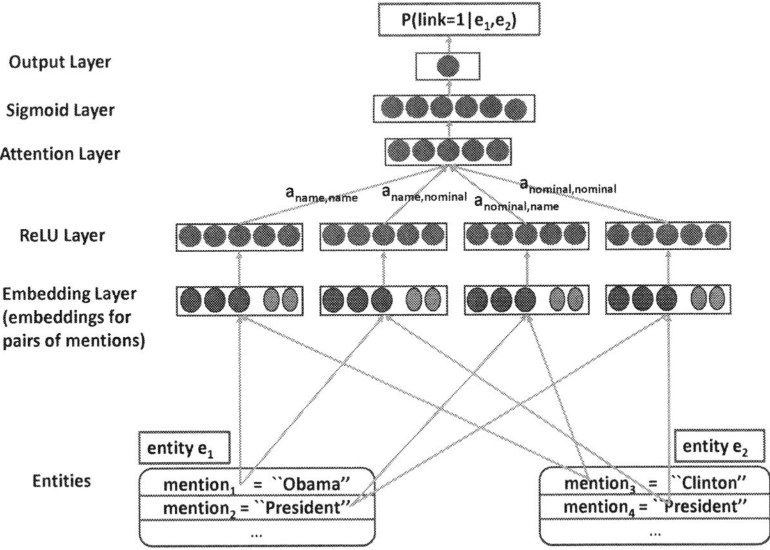

Figure 1: Network architecture for our coreference system. Blue circles in mention-pair embeddings layer represent embeddings of features. Green circles represent word embeddings.

nominal mention pair (President[1], President[2]) has full string overlap. So, while combining the embeddings for the mention pairs, mention pairs with m_type (name, name) should get higher weight than mention pairs with m_type (nominal, nominal). The entity pair embedding is the weighted sum of the mention-pair embeddings. We introduce 4 parameters $a_{name,name}$, $a_{name,nominal}$, $a_{nominal,nominal}$ and $a_{nominal,name}$ as weights for mention pair embeddings with m_types of (name, name), (name, nominal), (nominal, nominal) and (nominal, name) respectively. The entity pair embedding is computed as follows:

$$v^a_{e_1,e_2} = \sum_{(m_i,m_j)\in M(e_1,e_2)} \frac{a_{m\_type(m_i),m\_type(m_j)}}{N} v^r_{m_i,m_j}$$

Here N is a normalizing constant given by:

$$N = \sqrt{\sum_{(m_i,m_j)\in M(e_1,e_2)} a^2_{m\_type(m_i),m\_type(m_j)}}$$

This layer represents attention over the mention pair embeddings where attention weights are based on the m_types of the mention pairs.

Sigmoid Layer: $v^s_{e_1,e_2} = \sigma(W^{(2)} v^a_{e_1,e_2})$

Output Layer:

$$P(y_{12} = 1|e_1, e_2) = \frac{1}{1 + e^{-w^s \cdot v^s_{e_1,e_2}}}$$

The training objective is to maximize L.

$$L = \prod_{d\in D} \prod_{(e_1,e_2,y_{12})\in S_d} P(y_{12}|e_1, e_2; W^{(1)}, W^{(2)}, a, w^s)$$

(1)

Here D is the corpus and S_d is the training triplets generated from document d.

Decoding proceeds similarly to training algorithm, except at each of the three steps, for each entity e_i, the highest scoring antecdent e_j is selected and if the score is above a threshold, e_i and e_j are merged.

3 A Zero-shot Entity Linking model

We use our recently proposed cross-lingual EL model, described in (Sil et al., 2018), where our target is to perform "zero shot learning" (Socher et al., 2013; Palatucci et al., 2009). We train an EL model on English and use it to decode on any other language, provided that we have access to multi-lingual embeddings from English and the target language. We briefly describe our techniques here and direct the interested readers to the paper. The EL model computes several similarity/coherence *scores S* in a "feature abstraction layer" which computes several measures of similarity between the context of the mention m in the query document and the context of the candidate link's Wikipedia page which are fed to a feed-forward neural layer which acts as a binary classifier to predict the correct link for m. Specifically, the feature abstraction layer computes cosine similarities (Sil and Florian, 2016) between the representations of the source query document and the target Wikipedia pages over various granularities. These representations are computed by performing CNNs and LSTMs over the context of the entities. Then these similarities are fed into a Multi-perspective Binning layer which maps each similarity into a higher dimensional vector. We also train fine-grained similarities and dissimilarities between the query and candidate document from multiple perspectives, combined with convolution and tensor networks.

The model achieves state-of-the-art (SOTA) results on English benchmark EL datasets and also performs surprisingly well on Spanish and Chinese. However, although the EL model is "zeroshot", the within-document coreference resolution in the system is a language-dependent SOTA coreference system that has won multiple TAC-KBP (Ji et al., 2015; Sil et al., 2015) evaluations but is trained on the target language. Hence, our aim is to apply our proposed coreference model to the EL system to perform an extrinsic evaluation of our proposed algorithm.

4 Experiments

We evaluate cross-lingual transfer of coreference models on the TAC 2015 Tri-Lingual EL datasets. It contains mentions annotated with their grounded Freebase [1] links (if such links exist) or corpus-wide clustering information for 3 languages: English (henceforth, En), Chinese (henceforth, Zh) and Spanish (henceforth, Es). Table 1 shows the size of the training and test sets for the three languages. The documents come from two genres of newswire and discussion forums. The mentions in this dataset are either named entities or nominals that belong to five types: PER, ORG, GPE, LOC and FAC.

Hyperparameters: Every feature is embedded in a 50 dimensional space except the words which reside in a 300 dimensional space. The Relu and Sigmoid layers have 100 and 500 neurons respectively. We use SGD for optimization with an initial learning rate of 0.05 which is linearly reduced to

	En	Es	Zh
Train	168	129	147
Test	167	167	166

Table 1: No of documents for the TAC 2015 Tri-Lingual EL Dataset

	MUC	B^3	CEAF	CoNLL
This work	87.8	86.8	80.9	**85.2**
C&M16	83.6	78.7	69.2	77.2

Table 2: Coreference results on the En test set of TAC 15 competition. Our model significantly outperforms C&M16.

0.0001. Our mini batch size is 32 and we train for 50 epochs and keep the best model based on dev set.

Coreference Results: For each language, we follow the official train-test splits made in the TAC 2015 competition. Except, a small portion of the training set is held out as development set for tuning the models. All experimental results on all languages reported in this paper were obtained on the official test sets. We used the official CoNLL 2012 evaluation script and report MUC, B^3 and CEAF scores and their average (CONLL score). See Pradhan et al. (2011, 2012).

To test the competitiveness of our model with other SOTA models, we train the publicly available system of Clark and Manning (2016) (henceforth, C&M16) on the TAC 15 En training set and test on the TAC 15 En test set. The C&M16 system normally outputs both noun phrase mentions and their coreference and is trained on Ontonotes. To ensure a fair comparison, we changed the configuration of the system to accept gold mention boundaries both during training and testing. Since the system was unable to deal with partially overlapping mentions, we excluded such mentions in the evaluation. Table 2 shows that our model outperforms C&M16 by 8 points.

For cross-lingual experiments, we build monolingual embeddings for En, Zh and Es using the widely used CBOW word2vec model (Mikolov et al., 2013a). Recently Canonical Correlation Analysis (CCA) (Faruqui and Dyer, 2014), Multi-CCA (Ammar et al., 2016) and Weighted Regression (Mikolov et al., 2013b) have been proposed for building the multi-lingual embedding space from monolingual embedding. In our prelimi-

---

[1]TAC uses BaseKB, which is a snapshot of Freebase. Sɪʟ18 links entities to Wikipedia and in-turn links them to BaseKB.

	MUC	B^3	CEAF	CoNLL
Es Test Set				
En model	89.5	91.2	87.2	89.3
Es Model	90	91.4	88	**89.8**
Zh Test Set				
En model	95.5	93.3	88.7	92.5
Zh Model	96	92.8	89.6	**92.8**

Table 3: Coreference results on the Es and Zh test sets of TAC 15. En model performs competitively to the models trained on target language data.

Systems	Train on Target Lang	Acc. on Es	Acc. on Zh
EL - Coref	No	78.1	81.3
EL + En Coref	**No**	**81.1**	**83.9**
TAC Rank 1	Yes	80.4	83.1
SIL18	Yes	82.3	84.4

Table 4: Performance comparison on the TAC 2015 Es and Zh datasets. EL + En Coref outperforms the best 2015 TAC system (Rank 1) without requiring any Es or Zh coreference data.

nary experiments, the technique of Mikolov et al. (2013b) performed the best and so we used it to project the embeddings of Zh and Es onto En.

In Table 3, "En Model" refers to the model that was trained on the En training set of TAC 15 using *multi-lingual* embeddings and tested on the Es and Zh testing set of TAC 15. "Es Model" refers to the model trained on Es training set of TAC 15 using Es embeddings. "Zh Model" refers to the model trained on the Zh training set of TAC 15 using Zh embeddings. The En model performs 0.5 point below the Es model on the Es test set. On the Zh test set, the En model performs only 0.3 point below the Zh model. Hence, we show that without using any target language training data, the En model with multi-lingual embeddings gives comparable results to models trained on the target language.

EL Results: We replace the in-document coreference system (trained on the target language) of SIL18 with our En model to investigate the performance of our proposed algorithm on an extrinsic task. Table 4 shows the EL results on Es and Zh test sets respectively. "EL - Coref" refers to the case where the first step of coreference is not used and EL is used to link the mentions directly to Freebase. "EL + En Coref" refers to the case where the neural english coreference model is first used on Zh or Es data followed by the EL model. The former is 3 points below the latter on Es and 2.6 points below Zh, implying coreference is a vital task for EL. Our "EL + En Coref" outperforms the 2015 TAC best system by 0.7 points on Es and 0.8 points on Zh, without requiring any training data for coreference on Es and Zh respectively. Finally, we show the SOTA results on these two data sets recently reported by SIL18. Although their EL model does not use any supervision from Es or Zh, their coreference resolution model is trained on a large internal data set on the same language as

the test set .Without using any in-language training data, our results are competitive to their results (1.2% below on Es and 0.5% below on Zh).

5   Related Work

Rule based (Raghunathan et al., 2010) and statistical coreference models (Bengtson and Roth, 2008; Rahman and Ng, 2009; Fernandes et al., 2012; Durrett et al., 2013; Clark and Manning, 2015; Martschat and Strube, 2015; Björkelund and Kuhn, 2014) are hard to transfer across languages due to their use of lexical features or patterns in the rules. Neural coreference is promising since it allows cross-lingual transfer using multilingual embedding. However, most of the recent neural coreference models (Wiseman et al., 2015, 2016; Clark and Manning, 2015, 2016; Lee et al., 2017) have focused on training and testing on the same language. In contrast, our model performs cross-lingual coreference. There have been some recent promising results regarding such cross-lingual models for other tasks, most notably mention detection(Ni et al., 2017) and EL (Tsai and Roth, 2016; Sil and Florian, 2016). In this work, we show that such promise exists for coreference also.

The tasks of EL and coreference are intrinsically related, prompting joint models (Durrett and Klein, 2014; Hajishirzi et al., 2013). However, the recent SOTA was obtained using pipeline models of coreference and EL (Sil et al., 2018). Compared to a joint model, pipeline models are easier to implement, improve and adapt to a new domain.

6   Conclusion

The proposed cross-lingual coreference model was found to be empirically strong in both intrinsic and extrinsic evaluations in the context of an entity linking task.

References

Waleed Ammar, George Mulcaire, Yulia Tsvetkov, Guillaume Lample, Chris Dyer, and Noah A Smith. 2016. Massively multilingual word embeddings. *arXiv preprint arXiv:1602.01925*.

Eric Bengtson and Dan Roth. 2008. Understanding the value of features for coreference resolution. In *EMNLP*.

Anders Björkelund and Jonas Kuhn. 2014. Learning structured perceptrons for coreference resolution with latent antecedents and non-local features. In *ACL*.

Kevin Clark and Christopher D Manning. 2015. Entity-centric coreference resolution with model stacking. In *ACL*.

Kevin Clark and Christopher D Manning. 2016. Improving coreference resolution by learning entity-level distributed representations. In *ACL*.

Greg Durrett, David Leo Wright Hall, and Dan Klein. 2013. Decentralized entity-level modeling for coreference resolution. In *ACL*.

Greg Durrett and Dan Klein. 2014. A joint model for entity analysis: Coreference, typing, and linking. *Transactions of the Association for Computational Linguistics*, 2.

Manaal Faruqui and Chris Dyer. 2014. Improving vector space word representations using multilingual correlation. In *EACL*.

Eraldo Rezende Fernandes, Cícero Nogueira Dos Santos, and Ruy Luiz Milidiú. 2012. Latent structure perceptron with feature induction for unrestricted coreference resolution. In *EMNLP-CoNLL*.

Hannaneh Hajishirzi, Leila Zilles, Daniel S Weld, and Luke Zettlemoyer. 2013. Joint coreference resolution and named-entity linking with multi-pass sieves. In *EMNLP*.

Heng Ji, Joel Nothman, Ben Hachey, and Radu Florian. 2015. Overview of tac-kbp2015 tri-lingual entity discovery and linking. In *TAC*.

Heng Ji, Joel Nothman, Ben Hachey, et al. 2014. Overview of tac-kbp2014 entity discovery and linking tasks. In *TAC*.

Kenton Lee, Luheng He, Mike Lewis, and Luke Zettlemoyer. 2017. End-to-end neural coreference resolution. *arXiv preprint arXiv:1707.07045*.

Sebastian Martschat and Michael Strube. 2015. Latent structures for coreference resolution. *Transactions of the Association for Computational Linguistics*, 3:405–418.

Tomas Mikolov, Kai Chen, Greg Corrado, and Jeffrey Dean. 2013a. Efficient estimation of word representations in vector space. *arXiv preprint arXiv:1301.3781*.

Tomas Mikolov, Quoc V Le, and Ilya Sutskever. 2013b. Exploiting similarities among languages for machine translation. *arXiv preprint arXiv:1309.4168*.

Vincent Ng and Claire Cardie. 2002. Improving machine learning approaches to coreference resolution. In *ACL*.

Jian Ni, Georgiana Dinu, and Radu Florian. 2017. Weakly supervised cross-lingual named entity recognition via effective annotation and representation projection. In *ACL*.

Mark Palatucci, Dean Pomerleau, Geoffrey E Hinton, and Tom M Mitchell. 2009. Zero-shot learning with semantic output codes. In *NIPS*.

Sameer Pradhan, Alessandro Moschitti, Nianwen Xue, Olga Uryupina, and Yuchen Zhang. 2012. Conll-2012 shared task: Modeling multilingual unrestricted coreference in ontonotes. In *EMNLP-CoNLL*.

Sameer Pradhan, Lance Ramshaw, Mitchell Marcus, Martha Palmer, Ralph Weischedel, and Nianwen Xue. 2011. Conll-2011 shared task: Modeling unrestricted coreference in ontonotes. In *CoNLL*.

Karthik Raghunathan, Heeyoung Lee, Sudarshan Rangarajan, Nathanael Chambers, Mihai Surdeanu, Dan Jurafsky, and Christopher Manning. 2010. A multipass sieve for coreference resolution. In *EMNLP*.

Altaf Rahman and Vincent Ng. 2009. Supervised models for coreference resolution. In *EMNLP*.

Avirup Sil, Georgiana Dinu, and Radu Florian. 2015. The ibm systems for trilingual entity discovery and linking at tac 2015. In *TAC*.

Avirup Sil and Radu Florian. 2016. One for all: Towards language independent named entity linking. In *ACL*.

Avirup Sil, Gourab Kundu, Radu Florian, and Wael Hamza. 2018. Neural cross-lingual entity linking. In *AAAI*.

Richard Socher, Milind Ganjoo, Christopher D Manning, and Andrew Ng. 2013. Zero-shot learning through cross-modal transfer. In *NIPS*.

Chen-Tse Tsai and Dan Roth. 2016. Cross-lingual wikification using multilingual embeddings. In *HLT-NAACL*.

Shyam Upadhyay, Manaal Faruqui, Chris Dyer, and Dan Roth. 2016. Cross-lingual models of word embeddings: An empirical comparison. In *ACL*.

Sam Wiseman, Alexander M Rush, and Stuart M Shieber. 2016. Learning global features for coreference resolution. In *NAACL*.

Sam Joshua Wiseman, Alexander Matthew Rush, Stuart Merrill Shieber, and Jason Weston. 2015. Learning anaphoricity and antecedent ranking features for coreference resolution. In *ACL*.

Judicious Selection of Training Data in Assisting Language for Multilingual Neural NER

Rudra Murthy V[†], Anoop Kunchukuttan[‡,*], Pushpak Bhattacharyya[†]
[†] Center for Indian Language Technology (CFILT)
Department of Computer Science and Engineering
IIT Bombay, India.
[‡]Microsoft AI & Research, Hyderabad, India.
{rudra,pb}@cse.iitb.ac.in, ankunchu@microsoft.com

Abstract

Multilingual learning for Neural Named Entity Recognition (NNER) involves jointly training a neural network for multiple languages. Typically, the goal is improving the NER performance of one of the languages (the primary language) using the other assisting languages. We show that the divergence in the tag distributions of the common named entities between the primary and assisting languages can reduce the effectiveness of multilingual learning. To alleviate this problem, we propose a metric based on symmetric KL divergence to filter out the highly divergent training instances in the assisting language. We empirically show that our data selection strategy improves NER performance in many languages, including those with very limited training data.

1 Introduction

Neural NER trains a deep neural network for the NER task and has become quite popular as they minimize the need for hand-crafted features and, learn feature representations from the training data itself. Recently, multilingual learning has been shown to benefit Neural NER in a resource-rich language setting (Gillick et al., 2016; Yang et al., 2017). Multilingual learning aims to improve the NER performance on the language under consideration (primary language) by adding training data from one or more assisting languages. The neural network is trained on the combined data of the primary (D_P) and the assisting languages (D_A). The neural network has a combination of language-dependent and language-independent layers, and, the network learns better cross-lingual features via these language-independent layers.

This work began when the second author was a research scholar at IIT Bombay

Existing approaches add all training sentences from the assisting language to the primary language and train the neural network on the combined data. However, data from assisting languages can introduce a drift in the tag distribution for named entities, since the common named entities from the two languages may have vastly divergent tag distributions. For example, the entity *China* appears in training split of Spanish (primary) and English (assisting) (Tjong Kim Sang, 2002; Tjong Kim Sang and De Meulder, 2003) with the corresponding tag frequencies, Spanish = { *Loc* : 20, *Org* : 49, *Misc* : 1 } and English = { *Loc* : 91, *Org* : 7 }. By adding English data to Spanish, the tag distribution of *China* is skewed towards *Location* entity in Spanish. This leads to a drop in named entity recognition performance. In this work, we address this problem of drift in tag distribution owing to adding training data from a supporting language.

The problem is similar to the problem of data selection for domain adaptation of various NLP tasks, except that additional complexity is introduced due to the multilingual nature of the learning task. For domain adaptation in various NLP tasks, several approaches have been proposed to address drift in data distribution (Moore and Lewis, 2010; Axelrod et al., 2011; Ruder and Plank, 2017). For instance, in machine translation, sentences from out-of-domain data are selected based on a suitably defined metric (Moore and Lewis, 2010; Axelrod et al., 2011). The metric attempts to capture similarity of the out-of-domain sentences with the in-domain data. Out-of-domain sentences most similar to the in-domain data are added.

Like the domain adaptation techniques summarized above, we propose to judiciously add sentences from the assisting language to the primary language data based on the divergence between the tag distributions of named entities in the train-

Proceedings of the 56th Annual Meeting of the Association for Computational Linguistics (Short Papers), pages 401–406
Melbourne, Australia, July 15 - 20, 2018. ©2018 Association for Computational Linguistics

Language	Source	Train (#Tokens)	Test (#Tokens)	Word Embeddings
English	Tjong Kim Sang and De Meulder (2003)	204,567	46,666	Dhillon et al. (2015) (Spectral embeddings)
Spanish	Tjong Kim Sang (2002)	264,715	51,533	
Dutch	Tjong Kim Sang (2002)	202,931	68,994	
Italian	Speranza (2009)	149,651	86,420	
German	Faruqui and Padó (2010)	74,907	20,696	
Hindi	Lalitha Devi et al. (2014)	81,817	23,696	Bojanowski et al. (2017) (fastText embeddings)
Marathi	In-house	71,299	36,581	
Tamil	Lalitha Devi et al. (2014)	66,143	18,646	
Bengali	Lalitha Devi et al. (2014)	34,387	7,614	
Malayalam	Lalitha Devi et al. (2014)	26,295	8,275	

Table 1: Dataset Statistics

ing instances. Adding assisting language sentences with lower divergence reduces the possibility of entity drift enabling the multilingual model to learn better cross-lingual features.

Following are the contributions of the paper: (a) We present a simple approach to select assisting language sentences based on symmetric KL-Divergence of overlapping entities (b) We demonstrate the benefits of multilingual Neural NER on low-resource languages. We compare the proposed data selection approach with monolingual Neural NER system, and the multilingual Neural NER system trained using all assisting language sentences. To the best of our knowledge, ours is the first work for judiciously selecting a subset of sentences from an assisting language for multilingual Neural NER.

2 Judicious Selection of Assisting Language Sentences

For every assisting language sentence, we calculate the sentence score based on the average symmetric KL-Divergence score of overlapping entities present in that sentence. By overlapping entities, we mean entities whose surface form appears in both the languages' training data. The symmetric KL-Divergence $SKL(x)$, of a named entity x, is defined as follows,

$$SKL(x) = \big[\, KL(\, P_p(x) \,||\, P_a(x)\,) \\ + KL(\, P_a(x) \,||\, P_p(x)\,)\, \big]/2 \quad (1)$$

where $P_p(x)$ and $P_a(x)$ are the probability distributions for entity x in the primary (p) and the assisting (a) languages respectively. KL refers to the standard KL-Divergence score between the two probability distributions.

KL-Divergence calculates the distance between the two probability distributions. Lower the KL-Divergence score, higher is the tag agreement for an entity in both the languages thereby, reducing the possibility of entity drift in multilingual learning. Assisting language sentences with the sentence score below a threshold value are added to the primary language data for multilingual learning. If an assisting language sentence contains no overlapping entities, the corresponding sentence score is zero resulting in its selection.

Network Architecture

Several deep learning models (Collobert et al., 2011; Ma and Hovy, 2016; Murthy and Bhattacharyya, 2016; Lample et al., 2016; Yang et al., 2017) have been proposed for monolingual NER in the literature. Apart from the model by Collobert et al. (2011), remaining approaches extract sub-word features using either Convolution Neural Networks (CNNs) or Bi-LSTMs. The proposed data selection strategy for multilingual Neural NER can be used with any of the existing models. We choose the model by Murthy and Bhattacharyya (2016)[1] in our experiments.

Multilingual Learning

We consider two parameter sharing configurations for multilingual learning (i) sub-word feature extractors shared across languages (Yang et al., 2017) (*Sub-word*) (ii) the entire network trained in a language independent way (*All*). As Murthy and Bhattacharyya (2016) use CNNs to extract sub-word features, only the character-level CNNs are shared for the *Sub-word* configuration.

---

[1]The code is available here: `https://github.com/murthyrudra/NeuralNER`

Primary Language	Assisting Language	Layers Shared	Data Selection		Primary Language	Assisting Language	Layers Shared	Data Selection	
			All	SKL				All	SKL
German	Monolingual	None	87.64	-	Italian	Monolingual	None	75.98	-
	English	All	89.08	**89.46**		English	All	76.22	**76.91**†
		Sub-word	88.76	**89.10**			Sub-word	79.44	79.44
	Spanish	All	89.02	**91.61**†		Spanish	All	74.94	**76.92**†
		Sub-word	88.37	**89.10**†			Sub-word	76.99	**77.45**†
	Dutch	All	89.66	**90.85**†		Dutch	All	75.59	**77.29**†
		Sub-word	89.94	**90.11**			Sub-word	77.38	**77.56**

Table 2: F-Score for German and Italian Test data using Monolingual and Multilingual learning strategies. † indicates that the *SKL* results are statistically significant compared to adding all assisting language data with p-value < 0.05 using two-sided Welch t-test.

3 Experimental Setup

In this section we list the datasets used and the network configurations used in our experiments.

3.1 Datasets

The Table 1 lists the datasets used in our experiments along with pre-trained word embeddings used and other dataset statistics. For German NER, we use *ep-96-04-16.conll* to create train and development splits, and use *ep-96-04-15.conll* as test split. As Italian has a different tag set compared to English, Spanish and Dutch, we do not share output layer for *All* configuration in multilingual experiments involving Italian. Even though the languages considered are resource-rich languages, we consider German and Italian as primary languages due to their relatively lower number of train tokens. The German NER data followed *IO* notation and for all experiments involving German, we converted other language data to *IO* notation. Similarly, the Italian NER data followed *IOBES* notation and for all experiments involving Italian, we converted other language data to *IOBES* notation.

For low-resource language setup, we consider the following Indian languages: Hindi, Marathi[2], Bengali, Tamil and Malayalam. Except for Hindi all are low-resource languages. We consider only *Person, Location* and *Organization* tags. Though the scripts of these languages are different, they share the same set of phonemes making script mapping across languages easier. We convert Tamil, Bengali and Malayalam data to the Devanagari script using the *Indic NLP li-*

brary[3] (Kunchukuttan et al., 2015) thereby, allowing sharing of sub-word features across the Indian languages. For Indian languages, the annotated data followed the *IOB* format.

3.2 Network Hyper-parameters

With the exception of English, Spanish and Dutch, remaining language datasets did not have official train and development splits provided. We randomly select 70% of the train split for training the model and remaining as development split. The threshold for sentence score *SKL*, is selected based on cross-validation for every language pair. The dimensions of the Bi-LSTM hidden layer are 200 and 400 for the monolingual and multilingual experiments respectively. We extract 20 features per convolution filter, with width varying from 1 to 9. The initial learning rate is 0.4 and multiplied by 0.7 when validation error increases. The training is stopped when the learning rate drops below 0.002. We assign a weight of 0.1 to assisting language sentences and oversample primary language sentences to match the assisting language sentence count in all multilingual experiments.

For European languages, we have performed hyper-parameter tuning for both the monolingual and multilingual learning (with all assisting language sentences) configurations. The best hyper-parameter values for the language pair involved were observed to be within similar range. Hence, we chose the same set of hyper-parameter values for all languages.

---

[2]Data is available here: http://www.cfilt.iitb.ac.in/ner/annotated_corpus/

[3]https://github.com/anoopkunchukuttan/indic_nlp_library

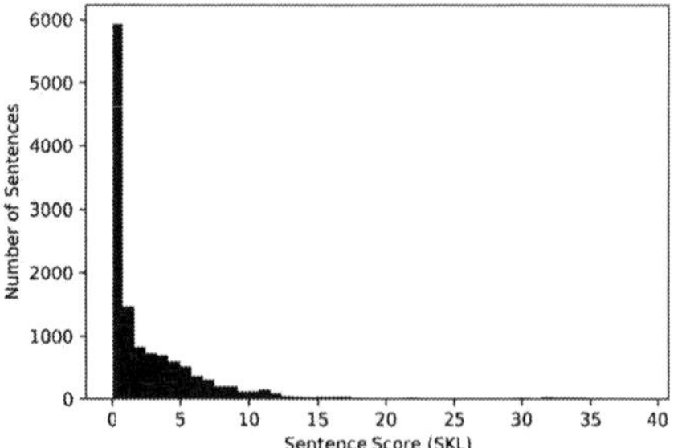

(a) English-Italian: Histogram of English Sentences

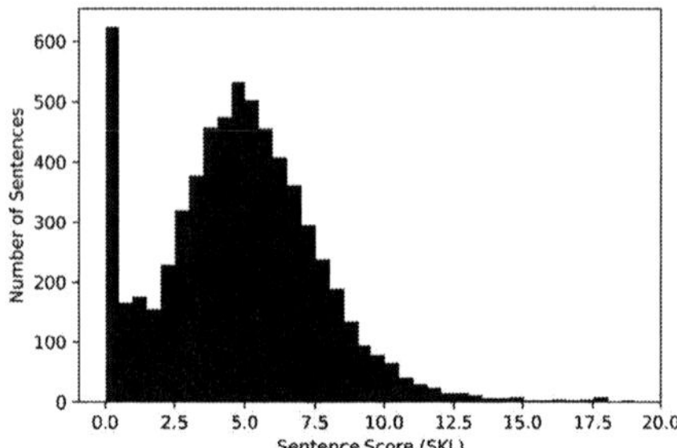

(b) Spanish-Italian: Histogram of Spanish Sentences

Figure 1: Histogram of assisting language sentences ranked by their sentence scores

4 Results

We now present the results on both resource-rich and resource-poor languages.

4.1 Resource-Rich Languages

Table 2 presents the results for German and Italian NER. We consistently observe improvements for German and Italian NER using our data selection strategy, irrespective of whether only sub-word features are shared (*Sub-word*) or the entire network (*All*) is shared across languages.

Adding all Spanish/Dutch sentences to Italian data leads to drop in Italian NER performance when all layers are shared. Label drift from overlapping entities is one of the reasons for the poor results. This can be observed by comparing the histograms of English and Spanish sentences ranked by the SKL scores for Italian multilingual learning (Figure 1). Most English sentences have lower SKL scores indicating higher tag agreement for overlapping entities and lower drift in tag distribution. Hence, adding all English sentences improves Italian NER accuracy. In contrast, most Spanish sentences have larger SKL

scores and adding these sentences adversely impacts Italian NER performance. By judiciously selecting assisting language sentences, we eliminate sentences which are responsible for drift occurring during multilingual learning.

To understand how overlapping entities impact the NER performance, we study the statistics of overlapping named entities between Italian-English and Italian-Spanish pairs. 911 and 916 unique entities out of 4061 unique Italian entities appear in the English and Spanish data respectively. We had hypothesized that entities with divergent tag distribution are responsible for hindering the performance in multilingual learning. If we sort the common entities based on their SKL divergence value. We observe that 484 out of 911 common entities in English and 535 out of 916 common entities in Spanish have an SKL score greater than 1.0. 162 out of 484 common entities in English-Italian data having SKL divergence value greater than 1.0 also appear more than 10 times in the English corpus. Similarly, 123 out of 535 common entities in Spanish-Italian data having SKL divergence value greater than 1.0 also appear more than 10 times in the Spanish corpus. However, these common 162 entities have a combined frequency of 12893 in English, meanwhile the 123 common entities have a combined frequency of 34945 in Spanish. To summarize, although the number of overlapping entities is comparable in English and Spanish sentences, entities with larger SKL divergence score appears more frequently in Spanish sentences compared to English sentences. As a consequence, adding all Spanish sentences leads to significant drop in Italian NER performance which is not the case when all English sentences are added.

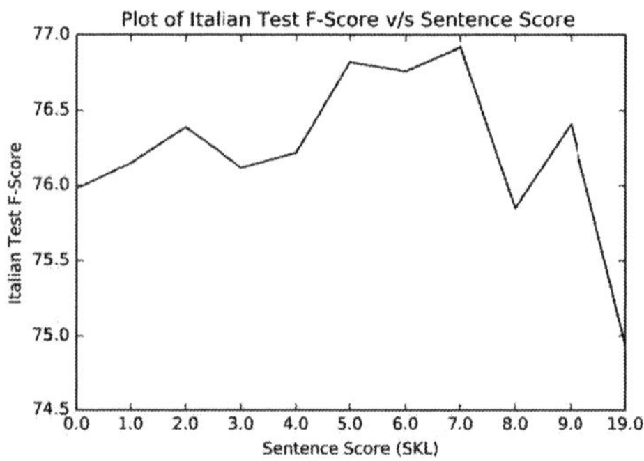

Figure 2: Spanish-Italian Multilingual Learning: Influence of Sentence score (SKL) on Italian NER

Primary Language	Assisting Language									
	Hindi		Marathi		Bengali		Malayalam		Tamil	
	ALL	SKL	ALL	SKL	ALL	SKL	ALL	SKL	ALL	SKL
Hindi	64.93	-	59.30	**66.33**	58.51	59.30	58.21	59.13	56.75	58.75
Marathi	54.46	**63.30**	61.46	-	47.67	61.28	50.13	61.05	59.04	58.62
Bengali	44.34	**51.05**†	41.28	**55.77**†	40.02	-	48.79	**49.84**†	38.38	**44.14**†
Malayalam	59.74	**64.00**†	65.88	**66.42**†	58.01	**63.65**†	57.94	-	58.25	**58.92**
Tamil	60.13	**61.51**†	60.54	**61.67**†	53.27	**60.32**†	61.03	**61.45**	53.13	-

Table 3: Test set F-Score from monolingual and multilingual learning on Indian languages. Result from monolingual training on the primary language is underlined. † indicates *SKL* results statistically significant compared to adding all assisting language data with p-value < 0.05 using two-sided Welch t-test.

4.2 Resource-Poor Languages

As Indian languages exhibit high lexical overlap (Kunchukuttan and Bhattacharyya, 2016) and syntactic relatedness (V Subbārāo, 2012), we share all layers of the network across languages. Table 3 presents the results. Bengali, Malayalam, and Tamil (low-resource languages) benefits from our data selection strategy. Hindi and Marathi NER performance improves when the other is used as assisting language.

Bengali, Malayalam, and Tamil have weaker baselines compared to Hindi and Marathi, and are benefited from our approach irrespective of the assisting language chosen. However, Hindi and Marathi are not benefited from multilingual learning with Bengali, Malayalam and Tamil. Malayalam and Tamil being morphologically rich have low entity overlap (surface level) with Hindi and Marathi. As a result, only 2-3% of Malayalam and Tamil sentences are eliminated from our approach, leading to no gains from multilingual learning. Hindi and Marathi are negatively impacted by noisy Bengali data. Bengali has less training sentences compared to other languages and, choosing a low SKL threshold results in selecting very few Bengali sentences for multilingual learning.

4.3 Influence of SKL Threshold

Here, we study the influence of SKL score threshold on the NER performance. We run experiments for Italian NER by adding Spanish training sentences and sharing all layers except for output layer across languages. We vary the threshold value from 1.0 to 9.0 in steps of 1, and select sentences with score less than the threshold. A threshold of 0.0 indicates monolingual training and threshold greater than 9.0 indicates all assist-

ing language sentences considered. The plot of Italian test F-Score against SKL score is shown in the Figure 2. Italian test F-Score increases initially as we add more and more Spanish sentences and then drops due to influence of drift becoming significant. Finding the right SKL threshold is important, hence we use a validation set to tune the SKL threshold.

5 Conclusion

In this paper, we address the problem of divergence in tag distribution between primary and assisting languages for multilingual Neural NER. We show that filtering out the assisting language sentences exhibiting significant divergence in the tag distribution can improve NER accuracy. We propose to use the symmetric KL-Divergence metric to measure the tag distribution divergence. We observe consistent improvements in multilingual Neural NER performance using our data selection strategy. The strategy shows benefits for extremely low resource primary languages too.

This problem of drift in data distribution may not be unique to multilingual NER, and we plan to study the influence of data selection for multilingual learning on other NLP tasks like sentiment analysis, question answering, neural machine translation, *etc*. We also plan to explore more metrics for multilingual learning, specifically for morphologically rich languages.

Acknowledgements

We thank Gajanan Rane and Geetanjali Rane for annotating the Marathi data, which was created as part of the CLIA project.

References

Amittai Axelrod, Xiaodong He, and Jianfeng Gao. 2011. Domain adaptation via pseudo in-domain data selection. In *Proceedings of the 2011 Conference on Empirical Methods in Natural Language Processing*, Edinburgh, United Kingdom.

Piotr Bojanowski, Edouard Grave, Armand Joulin, and Tomas Mikolov. 2017. Enriching word vectors with subword information. *Transactions of the Association for Computational Linguistics*.

Ronan Collobert, Jason Weston, Léon Bottou, Michael Karlen, Koray Kavukcuoglu, and Pavel Kuksa. 2011. Natural language processing (almost) from scratch. *Journal of Machine Learning Research*.

Paramveer S. Dhillon, Dean P. Foster, and Lyle H. Ungar. 2015. Eigenwords: Spectral word embeddings. *Journal of Machine Learning Research*.

Manaal Faruqui and Sebastian Padó. 2010. Training and evaluating a German Named Entity Recognizer with semantic generalization. In *Proceedings of KONVENS*.

Dan Gillick, Cliff Brunk, Oriol Vinyals, and Amarnag Subramanya. 2016. Multilingual language processing from bytes. In *Proceedings of the 2016 Conference of the North American Chapter of the Association for Computational Linguistics*, San Diego, US.

Anoop Kunchukuttan and Pushpak Bhattacharyya. 2016. Orthographic syllable as basic unit for SMT between related languages. In *Proceedings of the 2016 Conference on Empirical Methods in Natural Language Processing*, Texas, USA.

Anoop Kunchukuttan, Ratish Puduppully, and Pushpak Bhattacharyya. 2015. Brahmi-net: A transliteration and script conversion system for languages of the Indian subcontinent. In *Proceedings of the 2015 Conference of the North American Chapter of the Association for Computational Linguistics: Demonstrations*, Colorado, USA.

Shobha Lalitha Devi, Pattabhi RK Rao, Malarkodi C.S, and R Vijay Sundar Ram. 2014. Indian language NER annotated FIRE 2014 corpus (FIRE 2014 NER Corpus). In *Named-Entity Recognition Indian Languages FIRE 2014 Evaluation Track*.

Guillaume Lample, Miguel Ballesteros, Kazuya Kawakami, Sandeep Subramanian, and Chris Dyer. 2016. Neural architectures for Named Entity Recognition. In *Proceedings of the 2016 Conference of the North American Chapter of the Association for Computational Linguistics*, San Diego, US.

Xuezhe Ma and Eduard Hovy. 2016. End-to-end sequence labeling via Bi-directional LSTM-CNNs-CRF. In *Proceedings of the 54th Annual Meeting of the Association for Computational Linguistics*, Berlin, Germany.

Robert C. Moore and William Lewis. 2010. Intelligent selection of language model training data. In *Proceedings of the 48th Annual Meeting of the Association for Computational Linguistics*, Uppsala, Sweden.

Rudra V. Murthy and Pushpak Bhattacharyya. 2016. A deep learning solution to Named Entity Recognition. In *CICLing*, Konya, Turkey.

Sebastian Ruder and Barbara Plank. 2017. Learning to select data for transfer learning with Bayesian Optimization. In *Proceedings of the 2017 Conference on Empirical Methods in Natural Language Processing*, Copenhagen, Denmark.

Manuela Speranza. 2009. The Named Entity Recognition task at EVALITA 2009. In *Proceedings of the Workshop Evalita*.

Erik F. Tjong Kim Sang. 2002. Introduction to the conll-2002 shared task: Language-independent Named Entity Recognition. In *Proceedings of the 6th Conference on Natural Language Learning at COLING-02*, Taipei, Taiwan.

Erik F. Tjong Kim Sang and Fien De Meulder. 2003. Introduction to the conll-2003 shared task: Language-independent Named Entity Recognition. In *Proceedings of the Seventh Conference on Natural Language Learning at HLT-NAACL 2003*, Edmonton, Canada.

Kārumūri V Subbārāo. 2012. *South Asian Languages: A Syntactic Typology*. Cambridge University Press.

Zhilin Yang, Ruslan Salakhutdinov, and William Cohen. 2017. Multi-task cross-lingual sequence tagging from scratch. In *International Conference on Learning Representations*, Toulon, France.

Neural Open Information Extraction

Lei Cui, **Furu Wei**, and **Ming Zhou**

Microsoft Research Asia
{lecu,fuwei,mingzhou}@microsoft.com

Abstract

Conventional Open Information Extraction (Open IE) systems are usually built on hand-crafted patterns from other NLP tools such as syntactic parsing, yet they face problems of error propagation. In this paper, we propose a neural Open IE approach with an encoder-decoder framework. Distinct from existing methods, the neural Open IE approach learns highly confident arguments and relation tuples bootstrapped from a state-of-the-art Open IE system. An empirical study on a large benchmark dataset shows that the neural Open IE system significantly outperforms several baselines, while maintaining comparable computational efficiency.

1 Introduction

Open Information Extraction (Open IE) involves generating a structured representation of information in text, usually in the form of triples or n-ary propositions. An Open IE system not only extracts arguments but also relation phrases from the given text, which does not rely on pre-defined ontology schema. For instance, given the sentence *"deep learning is a subfield of machine learning"*, the triple (*deep learning*; *is a subfield of*; *machine learning*) can be extracted, where the relation phrase *"is a subfield of"* indicates the semantic relationship between two arguments. Open IE plays a key role in natural language understanding and fosters many downstream NLP applications such as knowledge base construction, question answering, text comprehension, and others.

The Open IE system was first introduced by TEXTRUNNER (Banko et al., 2007), followed by several popular systems such as REVERB (Fader et al., 2011), OLLIE (Mausam et al., 2012), ClausIE (Del Corro and Gemulla, 2013) Stanford OPENIE (Angeli et al., 2015), PropS (Stanovsky et al., 2016) and most recently OPENIE4[1] (Mausam, 2016) and OPENIE5[2]. Although these systems have been widely used in a variety of applications, most of them were built on hand-crafted patterns from syntactic parsing, which causes errors in propagation and compounding at each stage (Banko et al., 2007; Gashteovski et al., 2017; Schneider et al., 2017). Therefore, it is essential to solve the problems of cascading errors to alleviate extracting incorrect tuples.

To this end, we propose a neural Open IE approach with an encoder-decoder framework. The encoder-decoder framework is a text generation technique and has been successfully applied to many tasks, such as machine translation (Cho et al., 2014; Bahdanau et al., 2014; Sutskever et al., 2014; Wu et al., 2016; Gehring et al., 2017; Vaswani et al., 2017), image caption (Vinyals et al., 2014), abstractive summarization (Rush et al., 2015; Nallapati et al., 2016; See et al., 2017) and recently keyphrase extraction (Meng et al., 2017). Generally, the encoder encodes the input sequence to an internal representation called 'context vector' which is used by the decoder to generate the output sequence. The lengths of input and output sequences can be different, as there is no one on one relation between the input and output sequences. In this work, Open IE is cast as a sequence-to-sequence generation problem, where the input sequence is the sentence and the output sequence is the tuples with special placeholders. For instance, given the input sequence *"deep learning is a subfield of machine learning"*, the output sequence will be "⟨arg1⟩ deep learning ⟨/arg1⟩ ⟨rel⟩ is a subfield of ⟨/rel⟩ ⟨arg2⟩ machine

---

[1] https://github.com/allenai/openie-standalone
[2] https://github.com/dair-iitd/OpenIE-standalone

407

Proceedings of the 56th Annual Meeting of the Association for Computational Linguistics (Short Papers), pages 407–413
Melbourne, Australia, July 15 - 20, 2018. ©2018 Association for Computational Linguistics

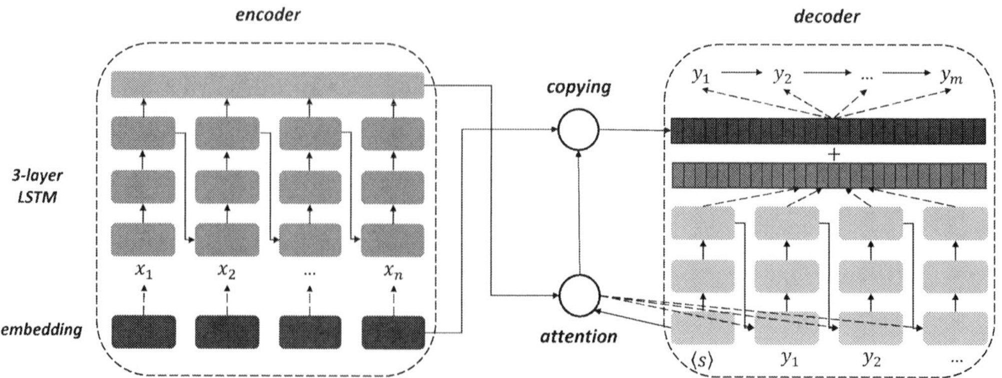

Figure 1: The encoder-decoder model architecture for the neural Open IE system

learning $\langle$/arg2$\rangle$". We obtain the input and output sequence pairs from highly confident tuples bootstrapped from a state-of-the-art Open IE system. Experiment results on a large benchmark dataset illustrate that the neural Open IE approach is significantly better than others in precision and recall, while also reducing the dependencies on other NLP tools.

The contributions of this paper are three-fold. First, the encoder-decoder framework learns the sequence-to-sequence task directly, bypassing other hand-crafted patterns and alleviating error propagation. Second, a large number of high-quality training examples can be bootstrapped from state-of-the-art Open IE systems, which is released for future research. Third, we conduct comprehensive experiments on a large benchmark dataset to compare different Open IE systems to show the neural approach's promising potential.

2 Methodology

2.1 Problem Definition

Let (X, Y) be a sentence and tuples pair, where $X = (x_1, x_2, ..., x_m)$ is the word sequence and $Y = (y_1, y_2, ..., y_n)$ is the tuple sequence extracted from X. The conditional probability of $P(Y|X)$ can be decomposed as:

$$P(Y|X) = P(Y|x_1, x_2, ..., x_m)$$
$$= \prod_{i=1}^{n} p(y_i|y_1, y_2, ..., y_{i-1}; x_1, x_2, ...x_m) \tag{1}$$

In this work, we only consider the binary extractions from sentences, leaving n-ary extractions and

nested extractions for future research. In addition, we ensure that both the argument and relation phrases are sub-spans of the input sequence. Therefore, the output vocabulary equals the input vocabulary plus the placeholder symbols.

2.2 Encoder-Decoder Model Architecture

The encoder-decoder framework takes a variable length input sequence to a compressed representation vector that is used by the decoder to generate the output sequence. In this work, both the encoder and decoder are implemented using Recurrent Neural Networks (RNN) and the model architecture is shown in Figure 1.

The encoder uses a 3-layer stacked Long Short-Term Memory (LSTM) (Hochreiter and Schmidhuber, 1997) network to covert the input sequence $X = (x_1, x_2, ...x_m)$ into a set of hidden representations $\mathbf{h} = (h_1, h_2, ..., h_m)$, where each hidden state is obtained iteratively as follows:

$$h_t = \mathbf{LSTM}(x_t, h_{t-1}) \tag{2}$$

The decoder also uses a 3-layer LSTM network to accept the encoder's output and generate a variable-length sequence Y as follows:

$$s_t = \mathbf{LSTM}(y_{t-1}, s_{t-1}, c)$$
$$p(y_t) = \mathbf{softmax}(y_{t-1}, s_t, c) \tag{3}$$

where s_t is the hidden state of the decoder LSTM at time t, c is the context vector that is introduced later. We use the softmax layer to calculate the output probability of y_t and select the word with the largest probability.

An attention mechanism is vital for the encoder-decoder framework, especially for our neural

Open IE system. Both the arguments and relations are sub-spans that correspond to the input sequence. We leverage the attention method proposed by Bahdanau et al. to calculate the context vector c as follows:

$$c_i = \sum_{j=1}^{n} \alpha_{ij} h_j$$

$$\alpha_{ij} = \frac{\exp(e_{ij})}{\sum_{k=1}^{n} \exp(e_{ik})} \quad (4)$$

$$e_{ij} = a(s_{i-1}, h_j)$$

where a is an alignment model that scores how well the inputs around position j and the output at position i match, which is measured by the encoder hidden state h_j and the decoder hidden state s_{i-1}. The encoder and decoder are jointly optimized to maximize the log probability of the output sequence conditioned on the input sequence.

2.3 Copying Mechanism

Since most encoder-decoder methods maintain a fixed vocabulary of frequent words and convert a large number of long-tail words into a special symbol "$\langle unk \rangle$", the copying mechanism (Gu et al., 2016; Gulcehre et al., 2016; See et al., 2017; Meng et al., 2017) is designed to copy words from the input sequence to the output sequence, thus enlarging the vocabulary and reducing the proportion of generated unknown words. For the neural Open IE task, the copying mechanism is more important because the output vocabulary is directly from the input vocabulary except for the placeholder symbols. We simplify the copying method in (See et al., 2017), the probability of generating the word y_t comes from two parts as follows:

$$p(y_t) = \begin{cases} p(y_t|y_1, y_2, ..., y_{t-1}; X) & \text{if } y_t \in V \\ \sum_{i:x_i=y_t} a_i^t & \text{otherwise} \end{cases}$$
$$(5)$$

where V is the target vocabulary. We combine the sequence-to-sequence generation and attention-based copying together to derive the final output.

3 Experiments

3.1 Data

For the training data, we used Wikipedia dump 20180101[3] and extracted all the sentences that are 40 words or less. OPENIE4 is used to analyze the sentences and extract all the tuples

with binary relations. To further obtain high-quality tuples, we only kept the tuples whose confidence score is at least 0.9. Finally, there are a total of 36,247,584 $\langle$sentence, tuple$\rangle$ pairs extracted. The training data is released for public use at `https://1drv.ms/u/s!ApPZx_ TWwibImH149ZBwxOU0ktHv`.

For the test data, we used a large benchmark dataset (Stanovsky and Dagan, 2016) that contains 3,200 sentences with 10,359 extractions[4]. We compared with several state-of-the-art baselines including OLLIE, ClausIE, Stanford OPENIE, PropS and OPENIE4. The evaluation metrics are precision and recall.

3.2 Parameter Settings

We implemented the neural Open IE model using OpenNMT (Klein et al., 2017), which is an open source encoder-decoder framework. We used 4 M60 GPUs for parallel training, which takes 3 days. The encoder is a 3-layer bidirectional LSTM and the decoder is another 3-layer LSTM. Our model has 256-dimensional hidden states and 256-dimensional word embeddings. A vocabulary of 50k words is used for both the source and target sides. We optimized the model with SGD and the initial learning rate is set to 1. We trained the model for 40 epochs and started learning rate decay from the 11th epoch with a decay rate 0.7. The dropout rate is set to 0.3. We split the data into 20 partitions and used data sampling in OpenNMT to train the model. This reduces the length of the epochs for more frequent learning rate updates and validation perplexity computation.

3.3 Results

We used the script in (Stanovsky and Dagan, 2016)[5] to evaluate the precision and recall of different baseline systems as well as the neural Open IE system. The precision-recall curve is shown in Figure 2. It is observed that the neural Open IE system performs best among all tested systems. Furthermore, we also calculated the Area under Precision-Recall Curve (AUC) for each system. The neural Open IE system with top-5 outputs achieves the best AUC score 0.473, which is significantly better than other systems. Although the

---

[3]https://dumps.wikimedia.org/enwiki/20180101/

[4]`https://github.com/gabrielStanovsky/ oie-benchmark`

[5]The absolute scores are different from the original paper because the authors changed the matching function in their GitHub Repo, but did not change the relative performance.

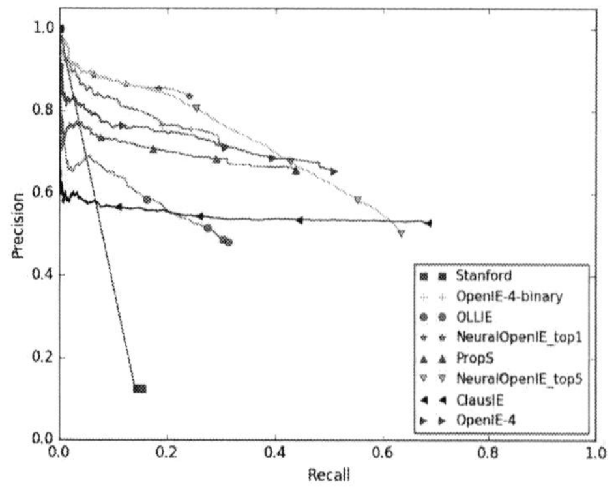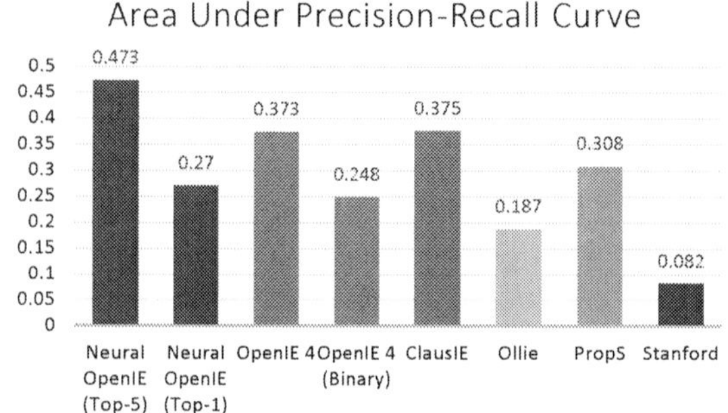

Figure 2: The Precision-Recall (P-R) curve and Area under P-R curve (AUC) of Open IE systems

neural Open IE is learned from the bootstrapped outputs of OPENIE4's extractions, only 11.4% of the extractions from neural Open IE agree with the OPENIE4's extractions, while the AUC score is even better than OPENIE4's result. We believe this is because the neural approach learns arguments and relations across a large number of highly confident training instances. This also indicates that the generalization capability of the neural approach is better than previous methods. We observed many cases in which the neural Open IE is able to correctly identify the boundary of arguments but OpenIE4 cannot, for instance:

Input	Instead , much of numerical analysis is concerned with obtaining approximate solutions while maintaining reasonable bounds on errors .
Gold	much of numerical analysis ||| concerned ||| with obtaining approximate solutions **while maintaining reasonable bounds on errors**
OpenIE4	much of numerical analysis ||| is concerned with ||| obtaining approximate solutions
Neural Open IE	much of numerical analysis ||| is concerned ||| with obtaining approximate solutions **while maintaining reasonable bounds on errors**

This case illustrates that the neural approach reduces the limitation of hand-crafted patterns from other NLP tools. Therefore, it reduces the error propagation effect and performs better than other systems especially for long sentences.

We also investigated the computational cost of different systems. For the baseline systems, we obtained the Open IE extractions using a Xeon 2.4 GHz CPU. For the neural Open IE, we evaluated performance based on an M60 GPU. The

running time was calculated by extracting Open IE tuples from the test dataset that contains a total of 3,200 sentences. The results are shown in Table 1. Among the aforementioned conventional systems, Ollie is the most efficient approach which takes around 160s to finish the extraction. By using GPU, the neural approach takes 172s to extract the tuples from the test data, which is comparable with conventional approaches. As the neural approach does not depend on other NLP tools, we can further optimize the computational cost in future research efforts.

System	Device	Time
Stanford	CPU	234s
Ollie	CPU	160s
ClausIE	CPU	960s
PropS	CPU	432s
OpenIE4	CPU	181s
Neural Open IE	GPU	172s

Table 1: Running time of different systems

4   Related Work

The development of Open IE systems has witnessed rapid growth during the past decade (Mausam, 2016). The Open IE system was introduced by TEXTRUNNER (Banko et al., 2007) as the first generation. It casts the argument and relation extraction task as a sequential labeling problem. The system is highly scalable and extracts facts from large scale web content. REVERB (Fader et al., 2011) improved over TEXTRUNNER with syntactic and lexical constraints on binary relations expressed by verbs, which more than doubles the area under the precision-recall curve. Following these efforts, the second generation known as R2A2 (Etzioni et al., 2011) was developed based on REVERB and an argument identifier, ARGLEARNER, to better extract the arguments for the relation phrases. The first and second generation Open IE systems extract only relations that are mediated by verbs and ignore contexts. To alleviate these limitations, the third generation OLLIE (Mausam et al., 2012) was developed, which achieves better performance by extracting relations mediated by nouns, adjectives, and more. In addition, contextual information is also leveraged to improve the precision of extractions. All the three generations only consider binary extractions from the text, while binary extractions are not always enough for their semantics representations. Therefore, SRLIE (Christensen et al., 2010) was developed to include an attribute context with a tuple when it is available. OPENIE4 was built on SRLIE with a rule-based extraction system RELNOUN (Pal and Mausam, 2016) for extracting noun-mediated relations. Recently, OPENIE5 improved upon extractions from numerical sentences (Saha et al., 2017) and broke conjunctions in arguments to generate multiple extractions. During this period, there were also some other Open IE systems emerged and successfully applied in different scenarios, such as ClausIE (Del Corro and Gemulla, 2013) Stanford OPENIE (Angeli et al., 2015), PropS (Stanovsky et al., 2016), and more.

The encoder-decoder framework was introduced by Cho et al. and Sutskever et al., where a multi-layered LSTM/GRU is used to map the input sequence to a vector of a fixed dimensionality, and then another deep LSTM/GRU to decode the target sequence from the vector. Bahdanau et al. and Luong et al. further improved the encoder-decoder framework by integrating an attention mechanism so that the model can automatically find parts of a source sentence that are relevant to predicting a target word. To improve the parallelization of model training, convolutional sequence-to-sequence (ConvS2S) framework (Gehring et al., 2016, 2017) was proposed to fully parallelize the training since the number of non-linearities is fixed and independent of the input length. Recently, the transformer framework (Vaswani et al., 2017) further improved over the vanilla S2S model and ConvS2S in both accuracy and training time.

In this paper, we use the LSTM-based S2S approach to obtain binary extractions for the Open IE task. To the best of our knowledge, this is the first time that the Open IE task is addressed using an end-to-end neural approach, bypassing the hand-crafted patterns and alleviating error propagation.

5 Conclusion and Future Work

We proposed a neural Open IE approach using an encoder-decoder framework. The neural Open IE model is trained with highly confident binary extractions bootstrapped from a state-of-the-art Open IE system, therefore it can generate high-quality tuples without any hand-crafted patterns from other NLP tools. Experiments show that our approach achieves very promising results on a large benchmark dataset.

For future research, we will further investigate how to generate more complex tuples such as n-ary extractions and nested extractions with the neural approach. Moreover, other frameworks such as convolutional sequence-to-sequence and transformer models could apply to achieve better performance.

Acknowledgments

We are grateful to the anonymous reviewers for their insightful comments and suggestions.

References

Gabor Angeli, Melvin Jose Johnson Premkumar, and Christopher D. Manning. 2015. Leveraging linguistic structure for open domain information extraction. In *Proceedings of the 53rd Annual Meeting of the Association for Computational Linguistics and the 7th International Joint Conference on Natural Language Processing (Volume 1: Long Papers)*. Association for Computational Linguistics, Beijing, China, pages 344–354. http://www.aclweb.org/anthology/P15-1034.

Dzmitry Bahdanau, Kyunghyun Cho, and Yoshua Bengio. 2014. Neural machine translation by jointly learning to align and translate. *CoRR* abs/1409.0473. http://arxiv.org/abs/1409.0473.

Michele Banko, Michael J. Cafarella, Stephen Soderland, Matt Broadhead, and Oren Etzioni. 2007. Open information extraction from the web. In *Proceedings of the 20th International Joint Conference on Artifical Intelligence*. Morgan Kaufmann Publishers Inc., San Francisco, CA, USA, IJCAI'07, pages 2670–2676. http://dl.acm.org/citation.cfm?id=1625275.1625705.

Kyunghyun Cho, Bart van Merrienboer, Caglar Gulcehre, Dzmitry Bahdanau, Fethi Bougares, Holger Schwenk, and Yoshua Bengio. 2014. Learning phrase representations using rnn encoder–decoder for statistical machine translation. In *Proceedings of the 2014 Conference on Empirical Methods in Natural Language Processing (EMNLP)*. Association for Computational Linguistics, Doha, Qatar, pages 1724–1734. http://www.aclweb.org/anthology/D14-1179.

Janara Christensen, Mausam, Stephen Soderland, and Oren Etzioni. 2010. Semantic role labeling for open information extraction. In *Proceedings of the NAACL HLT 2010 First International Workshop on Formalisms and Methodology for Learning by Reading*. Association for Computational Linguistics, Los Angeles, California, pages 52–60. http://www.aclweb.org/anthology/W10-0907.

Luciano Del Corro and Rainer Gemulla. 2013. Clausie: Clause-based open information extraction. In *Proceedings of the 22Nd International Conference on World Wide Web*. ACM, New York, NY, USA, WWW '13, pages 355–366. https://doi.org/10.1145/2488388.2488420.

Oren Etzioni, Anthony Fader, Janara Christensen, Stephen Soderland, and Mausam Mausam. 2011. Open information extraction: The second generation. In *Proceedings of the Twenty-Second International Joint Conference on Artificial Intelligence - Volume Volume One*. AAAI Press, IJCAI'11, pages 3–10. https://doi.org/10.5591/978-1-57735-516-8/IJCAI11-012.

Anthony Fader, Stephen Soderland, and Oren Etzioni. 2011. Identifying relations for open information extraction. In *Proceedings of the Conference of Empirical Methods in Natural Language Processing (EMNLP '11)*. Edinburgh, Scotland, UK.

Kiril Gashteovski, Rainer Gemulla, and Luciano Del Corro. 2017. Minie: Minimizing facts in open information extraction. In *Proceedings of the 2017 Conference on Empirical Methods in Natural Language Processing*. Association for Computational Linguistics, Copenhagen, Denmark, pages 2630–2640. https://www.aclweb.org/anthology/D17-1278.

Jonas Gehring, Michael Auli, David Grangier, and Yann N Dauphin. 2016. A Convolutional Encoder Model for Neural Machine Translation. *ArXiv e-prints* .

Jonas Gehring, Michael Auli, David Grangier, Denis Yarats, and Yann N Dauphin. 2017. Convolutional Sequence to Sequence Learning. *ArXiv e-prints* .

Jiatao Gu, Zhengdong Lu, Hang Li, and Victor O.K. Li. 2016. Incorporating copying mechanism in sequence-to-sequence learning. In *Proceedings of the 54th Annual Meeting of the Association for Computational Linguistics (Volume 1: Long Papers)*. Association for Computational Linguistics, Berlin, Germany, pages 1631–1640. http://www.aclweb.org/anthology/P16-1154.

Caglar Gulcehre, Sungjin Ahn, Ramesh Nallapati, Bowen Zhou, and Yoshua Bengio. 2016. Pointing the unknown words. In *Proceedings of the 54th Annual Meeting of the Association for Computational Linguistics (Volume 1: Long Papers)*. Association for Computational Linguistics, Berlin, Germany, pages 140–149. http://www.aclweb.org/anthology/P16-1014.

Sepp Hochreiter and Jürgen Schmidhuber. 1997. Long short-term memory. *Neural Comput.* 9(8):1735–1780. https://doi.org/10.1162/neco.1997.9.8.1735.

Guillaume Klein, Yoon Kim, Yuntian Deng, Jean Senellart, and Alexander M. Rush. 2017. Opennmt: Open-source toolkit for neural machine translation. *CoRR* abs/1701.02810. http://arxiv.org/abs/1701.02810.

Thang Luong, Hieu Pham, and Christopher D. Manning. 2015. Effective approaches to attention-based neural machine translation. In *Proceedings of the 2015 Conference on Empirical Methods in Natural Language Processing*. Association for Computational Linguistics, Lisbon, Portugal, pages 1412–1421. http://aclweb.org/anthology/D15-1166.

Mausam. 2016. Open information extraction systems and downstream applications. In *Proceedings of the Twenty-Fifth International Joint Conference on Artificial Intelligence*. AAAI Press, IJCAI'16, pages 4074–4077. http://dl.acm.org/citation.cfm?id=3061053.3061220.

Mausam, Michael Schmitz, Robert Bart, Stephen Soderland, and Oren Etzioni. 2012. Open language learning for information extraction. In *Proceedings of Conference on Empirical Methods in Natural Language Processing and Computational Natural Language Learning (EMNLP-CONLL)*.

Rui Meng, Sanqiang Zhao, Shuguang Han, Daqing He, Peter Brusilovsky, and Yu Chi. 2017. Deep keyphrase generation. In *Proceedings of the 55th Annual Meeting of the Association for Computational Linguistics (Volume 1: Long Papers)*. Association for Computational Linguistics, Vancouver, Canada, pages 582–592. http://aclweb.org/anthology/P17-1054.

Ramesh Nallapati, Bowen Zhou, Cícero Nogueira dos Santos, aglar Gülehre, and Bing Xiang. 2016. Abstractive text summarization using sequence-to-sequence rnns and beyond. In *CoNLL*.

Harinder Pal and Mausam. 2016. Demonyms and compound relational nouns in nominal open ie. In *Proceedings of the 5th Workshop on Automated Knowledge Base Construction*. Association for Computational Linguistics, San Diego, CA, pages 35–39. http://www.aclweb.org/anthology/W16-1307.

Alexander M. Rush, Sumit Chopra, and Jason Weston. 2015. A neural attention model for abstractive sentence summarization. In *Proceedings of the 2015 Conference on Empirical Methods in Natural Language Processing*. Association for Computational Linguistics, Lisbon, Portugal, pages 379–389. http://aclweb.org/anthology/D15-1044.

Swarnadeep Saha, Harinder Pal, and Mausam. 2017. Bootstrapping for numerical open ie. In *Proceedings of the 55th Annual Meeting of the Association for Computational Linguistics (Volume 2: Short Papers)*. Association for Computational Linguistics, Vancouver, Canada, pages 317–323. http://aclweb.org/anthology/P17-2050.

Rudolf Schneider, Tom Oberhauser, Tobias Klatt, Felix A. Gers, and Alexander Löser. 2017. Analysing errors of open information extraction systems. In *Proceedings of the First Workshop on Building Linguistically Generalizable NLP Systems*. Association for Computational Linguistics, Copenhagen, Denmark, pages 11–18. http://www.aclweb.org/anthology/W17-5402.

Abigail See, Peter J. Liu, and Christopher D. Manning. 2017. Get to the point: Summarization with pointer-generator networks. In *Proceedings of the 55th Annual Meeting of the Association for Computational Linguistics (Volume 1: Long Papers)*. Association for Computational Linguistics, Vancouver, Canada, pages 1073–1083. http://aclweb.org/anthology/P17-1099.

Gabriel Stanovsky and Ido Dagan. 2016. Creating a large benchmark for open information extraction. In *Proceedings of the 2016 Conference on Empirical Methods in Natural Language Processing*. Association for Computational Linguistics, Austin, Texas, pages 2300–2305. https://aclweb.org/anthology/D16-1252.

Gabriel Stanovsky, Jessica Ficler, Ido Dagan, and Yoav Goldberg. 2016. Getting more out of syntax with props. *CoRR* abs/1603.01648. http://arxiv.org/abs/1603.01648.

Ilya Sutskever, Oriol Vinyals, and Quoc V. Le. 2014. Sequence to sequence learning with neural networks. *CoRR* abs/1409.3215. http://arxiv.org/abs/1409.3215.

Ashish Vaswani, Noam Shazeer, Niki Parmar, Jakob Uszkoreit, Llion Jones, Aidan N Gomez, Ł ukasz Kaiser, and Illia Polosukhin. 2017. Attention is all you need. In I. Guyon, U. V. Luxburg, S. Bengio, H. Wallach, R. Fergus, S. Vishwanathan, and R. Garnett, editors, *Advances in Neural Information Processing Systems 30*, Curran Associates, Inc., pages 5998–6008. http://papers.nips.cc/paper/7181-attention-is-all-you-need.pdf.

Oriol Vinyals, Alexander Toshev, Samy Bengio, and Dumitru Erhan. 2014. Show and tell: A neural image caption generator. *CoRR* abs/1411.4555. http://arxiv.org/abs/1411.4555.

Yonghui Wu, Mike Schuster, Zhifeng Chen, Quoc V. Le, Mohammad Norouzi, Wolfgang Macherey, Maxim Krikun, Yuan Cao, Qin Gao, Klaus Macherey, Jeff Klingner, Apurva Shah, Melvin Johnson, Xiaobing Liu, Lukasz Kaiser, Stephan Gouws, Yoshikiyo Kato, Taku Kudo, Hideto Kazawa, Keith Stevens, George Kurian, Nishant Patil, Wei Wang, Cliff Young, Jason Smith, Jason Riesa, Alex Rudnick, Oriol Vinyals, Greg Corrado, Macduff Hughes, and Jeffrey Dean. 2016. Google's neural machine translation system: Bridging the gap between human and machine translation. *CoRR* abs/1609.08144. http://arxiv.org/abs/1609.08144.

Document Embedding Enhanced Event Detection with Hierarchical and Supervised Attention

Yue Zhao, Xiaolong Jin, Yuanzhuo Wang, Xueqi Cheng

CAS Key Laboratory of Network Data Science and Technology,
Institute of Computing Technology, Chinese Academy of Science (CAS);
School of Computer and Control Engineering, The University of CAS

`zhaoyue@software.ict.ac.cn;`
`{jinxiaolong, wangyuanzhuo, cxq}@ict.ac.cn`

Abstract

Document-level information is very important for event detection even at sentence level. In this paper, we propose a novel Document Embedding Enhanced Bi-RNN model, called DEEB-RNN, to detect events in sentences. This model first learns event detection oriented embeddings of documents through a hierarchical and supervised attention based RNN, which pays word-level attention to event triggers and sentence-level attention to those sentences containing events. It then uses the learned document embedding to enhance another bidirectional RNN model to identify event triggers and their types in sentences. Through experiments on the ACE-2005 dataset, we demonstrate the effectiveness and merits of the proposed DEEB-RNN model via comparison with state-of-the-art methods.

1 Introduction

Event Detection (ED) is an important subtask of event extraction. It extracts event triggers from individual sentences and further identifies the type of the corresponding events. For instance, according to the ACE-2005 annotation guideline, in the sentence "Jane and John are married", an ED system should be able to identify the word "*married*" as a trigger of the event "*Marry*". However, it may be difficult to identify events from isolated sentences, because the same event trigger might represent different event types in different contexts.

Existing ED methods can mainly be categorized into two classes, namely, feature-based methods (e.g., (McClosky et al., 2011; Hong et al., 2011; Li et al., 2014)) and representation-based methods (e.g., (Nguyen and Grishman, 2015; Chen et al.,

2015; Liu et al., 2016a; Chen et al., 2017)). The former mainly rely on a set of hand-designed features, while the latter employ distributed representation to capture meaningful semantic information. In general, most of these existing methods mainly exploit sentence-level contextual information. However, document-level information is also important for ED, because the sentences in the same document, although they may contain different types of events, are often correlated with respect to the theme of the document. For example, there are the following sentences in ACE-2005:

... I knew it was time to *leave*. Isn't that a great argument for term limits? ...

If we only examine the first sentence, it is hard to determine whether the trigger "*leave*" indicates a "*Transport*" event meaning that he wants to leave the current place, or an "*End-Position*" event indicating that he will stop working for his current organization. However, if we can capture the contextual information of this sentence, it is more confident for us to label "*leave*" as the trigger of an "*End-Position*" event. Upon such observation, there have been some feature-based studies (Ji and Grishman, 2008; Liao and Grishman, 2010; Huang and Riloff, 2012) that construct rules to capture document-level information for improving sentence-level ED. However, they suffer from two major limitations. First, the features used therein often need to be manually designed and may involve error propagation due to natural language processing; Second, they discover inter-event information at document level by constructing inference rules, which is time-consuming and is hard to make the rule set as complete as possible. Besides, a representation-based study has been presented in (Duan et al., 2017), which employs the PV-DM model to train document embeddings and further uses it in a RNN-based event classifier. However, as being limited by the unsupervised training

414

Proceedings of the 56th Annual Meeting of the Association for Computational Linguistics (Short Papers), pages 414–419
Melbourne, Australia, July 15 - 20, 2018. ©2018 Association for Computational Linguistics

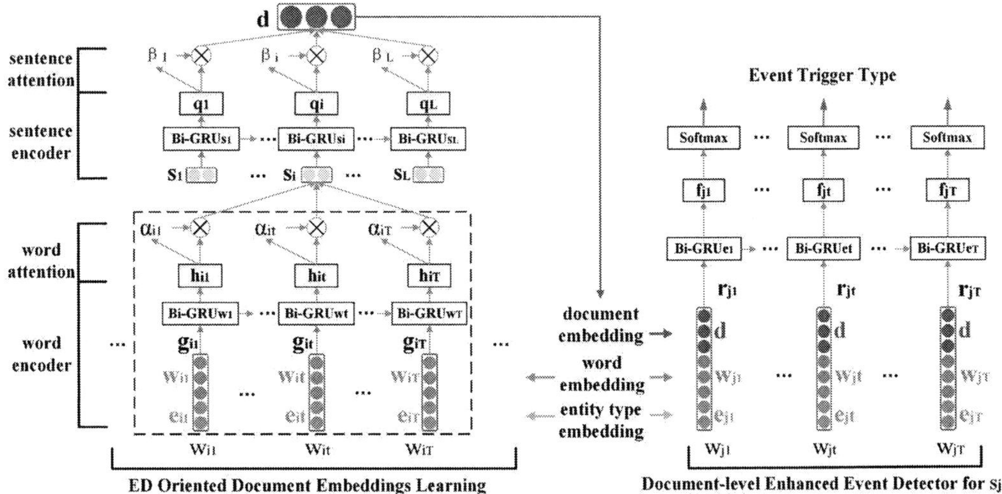

Figure 1: The schematic diagram of the DEEB-RNN model for ED at sentence level.

process, the document-level representation cannot specifically capture event-related information.

In this paper, we propose a novel Document Embedding Enhanced Bi-RNN model, called DEEB-RNN, for ED at sentence level. This model first learns ED oriented embeddings of documents through a hierarchical and supervised attention based bidirectional RNN, which pays word-level attention to event triggers and sentence-level attention to those sentences containing events. It then uses the learned document embeddings to facilitate another bidirectional RNN model to identify event triggers and their types in individual sentences. This learning process is guided by a general loss function where the loss corresponding to attention at both word and sentence levels and that of event type identification are integrated. It should be mentioned that although the attention mechanism has recently been applied effectively in various tasks, including machine translation (Zhang et al., 2017), question answering (Hao et al., 2017), document summarization (Tan et al., 2017), etc., this is the first study, to the best of our knowledge, which adopts a hierarchical and supervised attention mechanism to learn ED oriented embeddings of documents.

We evaluate the developed DEEB-RNN model on the benchmark dataset, ACE-2005, and systematically investigate the impacts of different supervised attention strategies on its performance. Experimental results show that the DEEB-RNN model outperforms both feature-based and representation-based state-of-the-art methods in terms of recall and F1-measure.

2 The Proposed Model

We formalize ED as a multi-class classification problem. Given a sentence, we treat every word in it as a trigger candidate, and classify each candidate to a certain event type. In the ACE-2005 dataset, there are 8 event types, further being divided into 33 subtypes, and a "Not Applicable (NA)" type. Without loss of generality, in this paper we regard the 33 subtypes as 33 event types. Figure 1 presents the schematic diagram of the proposed DEEB-RNN model, which contains two main modules:

1. The ED Oriented Document Embedding Learning (EDODEL) module, which learns the distributed representations of documents from both word and sentence levels via the well-designed hierarchical and supervised attention mechanism.

2. The Document-level Enhanced Event Detector (DEED) module, which tags each trigger candidate with an event type based on the learned embedding of documents.

2.1 The EDODEL Module

To learn the ED oriented embedding of a document, we apply the hierarchical and supervised attention network presented in Figure 1, which consists of a word-level Bi-GRU (Schuster and Paliwal, 2002) encoder with attention on event triggers

415

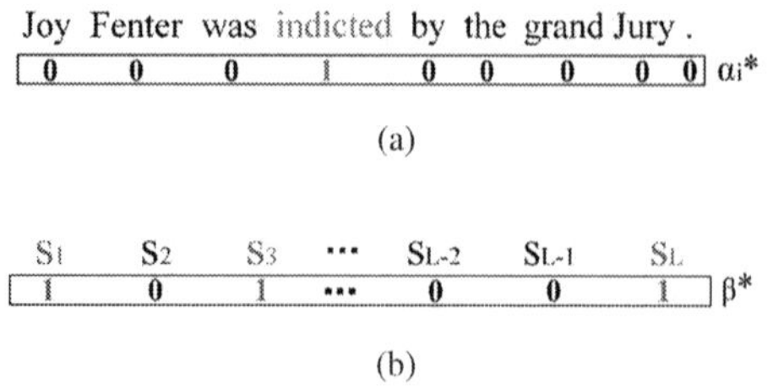

0	0	0	1	0	0	0	0	0	α_i*

(a)

S_1	S_2	S_3	$\cdots$	S_{L-2}	S_{L-1}	S_L	
1	0	1	$\cdots$	0	0	1	β*

(b)

Figure 2: Examples of the gold word- and sentence-level attention without normalization. (a) Word-level attention. *"Indicated"* is a candidate trigger; (b) Sentence-level attention. The sentences in purple contain trigger words.

and a sentence-level Bi-GRU encoder with attention on sentences with events. Given a document with L sentences, DEEB-RNN learns its embedding for detecting events in all sentences.

Word-level embeddings Given a sentence s_i $(i = 1, 2, ..., L)$ consisting of words $\{w_{it}|t = 1, 2, ..., T\}$. For each word w_{it}, we first concatenate its embedding w_{it} and its entity type embedding[1] e_{it} (Nguyen and Grishman, 2015) as the input g_{it} of a Bi-GRU and thus obtain the bidirectional hidden state h_{it}:

$$h_{it} = [\overrightarrow{\text{GRU}}_w(g_{it}), \overleftarrow{\text{GRU}}_w(g_{it})]. \quad (1)$$

We then feed h_{it} to a perceptron with no bias to get $u_{it} = \tanh(W_w h_{it})$ as a hidden representation of h_{it} and also obtain an attention weight $\alpha_{it} = u_{it}^{\mathrm{T}} c_w$, which should be normalized through a softmax function. Here, similar to that in (Yang et al., 2016), c_w is a vector representing the word-level context of w_{it}, which is initialized at random. Finally, the embedding of the sentence s_i can be obtained by summing up h_{it} with their weights:

$$s_i = \sum_{t=1}^{T} \alpha_{it} h_{it}. \quad (2)$$

To pay more attention to trigger words than other words, we construct the *gold word-level attention signals* α_i^* for the sentence s_i, as illustrated in Figure 2a. We can then take the square error as the general loss of the attention at word level to supervise the learning process:

$$E_w(\alpha^*, \alpha) = \sum_{i=1}^{L} \sum_{t=1}^{T} (\alpha_{it}^* - \alpha_{it})^2. \quad (3)$$

[1] The words in the ACE-2005 dataset are annotated with their entity types (annotated as "NA" if they are not an entity).

Sentence-level embeddings Given the sentence embeddings $\{s_i|i = 1, 2, ..., L\}$, we first get the hidden state q_i via a Bi-GRU:

$$q_i = [\overrightarrow{\text{GRU}}_s(s_i), \overleftarrow{\text{GRU}}_s(s_i)]. \quad (4)$$

Then we feed q_i to a perceptron with no bias to get the hidden representation $t_i = \tanh(W_s q_i)$ and also obtain an attention weight $\beta_i = t_i^{\mathrm{T}} c_s$ to be normalized via softmax. Similarly, c_s represents the sentence-level context of s_i to be randomly initialized. We eventually obtain the document embedding d as:

$$d = \sum_{i=1}^{L} \beta_i s_i. \quad (5)$$

We also think that the sentences containing event should obtain more attention than other ones. Therefore, similar to the case at word level, we construct the *gold sentence-level attention signals* β^* for the document d, as illustrated in Figure 2b, and further take the square error as the general loss of the attention at sentence level to supervise the learning process:

$$E_s(\beta^*, \beta) = \sum_{i=1}^{L} (\beta_i^* - \beta_i)^2. \quad (6)$$

2.2 The DEED Module

We employ another Bi-GRU encoder and a softmax output layer to model the ED task, which can handle event triggers with multiple words. Specifically, given a sentence s_j $(j = 1, 2, ..., L)$ in document d, for each of its word w_{jt} $(t = 1, 2, ..., T)$, we concatenate its word embedding w_{jt} and entity type embedding e_{jt} with the corresponding document embedding d as the input r_{jt} of the Bi-GRU and thus obtain the hidden state f_{jt}:

$$f_{jt} = [\overrightarrow{\text{GRU}}_e(r_{jt}), \overleftarrow{\text{GRU}}_e(r_{jt})]. \quad (7)$$

Finally, we get the probability vector o_{jt} with K dimensions through a softmax layer for w_{jt}, where the k-th element, $o_{jt}^{(k)}$, of o_{jt} indicates the probability of classifying w_{jt} to the k-th event type. The loss function, $J(y, o)$, can thus be defined in terms of the cross-entropy error of the real event type y_{jt} and the predicted probability $o_{jt}^{(k)}$ as follows:

$$J(y, o) = -\sum_{j=1}^{L} \sum_{t=1}^{T} \sum_{k=1}^{K} \mathrm{I}(y_{jt} = k) \log o_{jt}^{(k)}, \quad (8)$$

where $I(\cdot)$ is the indicator function.

416

2.3 Joint Training of the DEEB-RNN model

In the DEEB-RNN model, the above two modules are jointly trained. For this purpose, we define the joint loss function in the training process upon the losses specified for different modules as follows:

$$\mathbb{J}(\theta) = \sum_{\forall d \in \phi} (J(\boldsymbol{y}, \boldsymbol{o}) + \lambda E_w(\boldsymbol{\alpha}^*, \boldsymbol{\alpha}) + \mu E_s(\boldsymbol{\beta}^*, \boldsymbol{\beta})), \tag{9}$$

where θ denotes, as a whole, the parameters used in DEEB-RNN, ϕ is the training document set, and λ and μ are hyper-parameters for striking a balance among $J(\boldsymbol{y}, \boldsymbol{o})$, $E_w(\boldsymbol{\alpha}^*, \boldsymbol{\alpha})$ and $E_s(\boldsymbol{\beta}^*, \boldsymbol{\beta})$.

3 Experiments

3.1 Datasets and Settings

We validate the proposed model through comparison with state-of-the-art methods on the ACE-2005 dataset. In the experiments, the validation set has 30 documents from different genres, the test set has 40 documents and the training set contains the remaining 529 documents. All the data preprocessing and evaluation criteria follow those in (Ghaeini et al., 2016).

Hyper-parameters are tuned on the validation set. We set the dimension of the hidden layers corresponding to GRU_w, GRU_s, and GRU_e to 300, 200, and 300, respectively, the output size of W_w and W_s to 600 and 400, respectively, the dimension of entity type embeddings to 50, the batch size to 25, the dropout rate to 0.5. In addition, we utilize the pre-trained word embeddings with 300 dimensions from (Mikolov et al., 2013) for initialization. For entity types, their embeddings are randomly initialized. We train the model using Stochastic Gradient Descent (SGD) over shuffled mini-batches and using dropout (Krizhevsky et al., 2012) for regularization.

3.2 Baseline Models

In order to validate the proposed DEEB-RNN model through experimental comparison, we choose the following typical models as the baselines.

Sentence-level is a feature-based model proposed in (Hong et al., 2011), which regards entity-type consistency as a key feature to predict event mentions.

Joint Local is a feature-based model developed in (Li et al., 2013), which incorporates such features that explicitly capture the dependency among multiple triggers and arguments.

Methods	λ	μ	P	R	F_1
Bi-GRU	-	-	66.2	72.3	69.1
DEEB-RNN	0	0	69.3	75.2	72.1
DEEB-RNN1	1	0	70.9	76.7	73.7
DEEB-RNN2	0	1	72.3	74.5	73.4
DEEB-RNN3	1	1	72.3	75.8	74.0

Table 1: Experimental results with different attention strategies.

JRNN is a representation-based model proposed in (Nguyen et al., 2016), which exploits the inter-dependency between event triggers and argument roles via discrete structures.

Skip-CNN is a representation-based model presented in (Nguyen and Grishman, 2016), which proposes a novel convolution to exploit non-consecutive k-grams for event detection.

ANN-S2 is a representation-based model developed in (Liu et al., 2017), which explicitly exploits argument information for event detection via supervised attention mechanisms.

Cross-event is a feature-based model proposed in (Liao and Grishman, 2010), which learns relations among event types from training corpus and futher helps predict the occurrence of events.

PSL is a feature-based model developed in (Liu et al., 2016b), which encodes global information such as event-event association in the form of logic using the probabilistic soft logic model.

DLRNN is a representation-based model proposed in (Duan et al., 2017), which automatically extracts cross-sentence clues to improve sentence-level event detection.

3.3 Impacts of Different Attention Strategies

In this section, we conduct experiments on the ACE-2005 dataset to demonstrate the effectiveness of different attention strategies.

Bi-GRU is the basic ED model, which does not employ document-level embeddings.

DEEB-RNN uses the document embeddings and computes attentions without supervision, in which hyper-parameters λ and μ are set to 0.

DEEB-RNN1/2/3 means they uses the gold attention signals as supervision information. Specifically, DEEB-RNN1 uses only the gold word-level attention signal ($\lambda = 1$ and $\mu = 0$), DEEB-RNN2 uses only the gold sentence-level attention signal ($\lambda = 0$ and $\mu = 1$), whilst DEEB-RNN3 employs the gold attention signals at both word and sen-

Methods	P	R	F_1
Sentence-level (2011)	67.6	53.5	59.7
Joint Local (2013)	73.7	59.3	65.7
JRNN (2016)	66.0	73.0	69.3
Skip-CNN (2016)	N/A	N/A	71.3
ANN-S2 (2017)	78.0	66.3	71.7
Cross-event (2010)†	68.7	68.9	68.8
PSL (2016)†	75.3	64.4	69.4
DLRNN (2017)†	77.2	64.9	70.5
DEEB-RNN1†	70.9	76.7	73.7
DEEB-RNN2†	72.3	74.5	73.4
DEEB-RNN3†	72.3	75.8	74.0

Table 2: Comparison between different methods. † indicates that the corresponding ED method uses information at both sentence and document levels.

tence levels ($\lambda = 1$ and $\mu = 1$).

Table 1 compares these methods, where we can observe that the methods with document embeddings (i.e., the last four) significantly outperform the pure Bi-GRU method, which suggests that document-level information is very beneficial for ED. An interesting phenomenon is that, as compared to DEEB-RNN, DEEB-RNN2 changes the precision-recall balance. This is because of the following reasons. On one hand, as compared to DEEB-RNN, DEEB-RNN2 uses the gold sentence-level attention signal, indicating that it pays special attention to the sentences containing events with event triggers. In this way, the Bi-RNN model for learning document embeddings will filter out the sentences containing events but without explicit event triggers. That means the events detected by DEEB-RNN2 are basically the ones with explicit event triggers. Therefore, as compared to DEEB-RNN, the precision of DEEB-RNN2 is improved; On the other hand, the above strategy may result in less learning of words, which are event triggers but do not appear in the training dataset. Therefore, those sentences with such event triggers cannot be detected. The recall of DEEB-RNN2 is thus lowered, as compared to DEEB-RNN. Moreover, DEEB-RNN3 shows the best performance, indicating that the gold attention signals at both word and sentence levels are useful for ED.

3.4 Performance Comparison

Table 2 presents the overall performance of all methods on ACE-2005. We can see that different versions of DEEB-RNN consistently out-perform the existing state-of-the-art methods in terms of both recall and F1-measure, while their precision is comparable to that of others. The better performance of DEEB-RNN can be explained by the following reasons: (1) Compared with feature-based methods, including *Sentence-level*, *Joint Local*, and representation-based methods, including *JRNN*, *Skip-CNN* and *ANN-S2*, our method exploits document-level information (i.e., the ED oriented document embeddings) from both word and sentence levels in a document by the supervised attention mechanism, which enhance the ability of identifying trigger words; (2) Compared with feature-based methods using document-level information, such as *Cross-event*, *PSL*, our method can automatically capture event types in documents via a end-to-end Bi-RNN based model without manually designed rules; (3) Compared with representation-based methods using document-level information, such as *DLRNN*, our method can learn event detection oriented embeddings of documents through the hierarchical and supervised attention based Bi-RNN network.

4 Conclusions and Future Work

In this study, we proposed a hierarchical and supervised attention based and document embedding enhanced Bi-RNN method, called DEEB-RNN, for event detection. We explored different strategies to construct gold word- and sentence-level attentions to focus on event information. Experiments on the ACE-2005 dataset demonstrate that DEEB-RNN achieves better performance as compared to the state-of-the-art methods in terms of both recall and F1-measure. In this paper, we can strike a balance between sentence and document embeddings by adjusting their dimensions. In the future, we may improve the DEEB-RNN model to automatically determine the weights of sentence and document embeddings.

Acknowledgments

This work is supported by National Key Research and Development Program of China under grants 2016YFB1000902 and 2017YFC0820404, and National Natural Science Foundation of China under grants 61772501, 61572473, 61572469, and 91646120. We are grateful to Dr. Liu Kang of the Institute of Automation, Chinese Academy of Sciences for very helpful discussion on event detection.

References

Yubo Chen, Shulin Liu, Xiang Zhang, Kang Liu, and Jun Zhao. 2017. Automatically labeled data generation for large scale event extraction. In *Association for Computational Linguistics*, pages 409–419.

Yubo Chen, Liheng Xu, Kang Liu, daojian zeng, and jun zhao. 2015. Event extraction via dynamic multipooling convolutional neural networks. In *Association for Computational Linguistics*, pages 167–176.

Shaoyang Duan, Ruifang He, and Wenli Zhao. 2017. Exploiting document level information to improve event detection via recurrent neural networks. In *Proceedings of the Eighth International Joint Conference on Natural Language Processing - Volume 1)*, pages 352–361.

Reza Ghaeini, Xiaoli Fern, Liang Huang, and Prasad Tadepalli. 2016. Event nugget detection with forward-backward recurrent neural networks. In *Association for Computational Linguistics*, pages 369–373.

Yanchao Hao, Yuanzhe Zhang, Kang Liu, Shizhu He, Zhanyi Liu, Hua Wu, and Jun Zhao. 2017. An end-to-end model for question answering over knowledge base with cross-attention combining global knowledge. In *Association for Computational Linguistics*, pages 221–231.

Yu Hong, Jianfeng Zhang, Bin Ma, Jianmin Yao, Guodong Zhou, and Qiaoming Zhu. 2011. Using cross-entity inference to improve event extraction. In *Association for Computational Linguistics*, pages 1127–1136.

Ruihong Huang and Ellen Riloff. 2012. Modeling textual cohesion for event extraction. In *AAAI*, pages 1664–1670.

Heng Ji and Ralph Grishman. 2008. Refining event extraction through cross-document inference. In *Association for Computational Linguistics*, pages 254–262.

Alex Krizhevsky, Ilya Sutskever, and Geoffrey E. Hinton. 2012. Imagenet classification with deep convolutional neural networks. In *Proceedings of the 25th International Conference on Neural Information Processing Systems - Volume 1*, pages 1097–1105.

Qi Li, Heng Ji, Yu Hong, and Sujian Li. 2014. Constructing information networks using one single model. In *Empirical Methods in Natural Language Processing*, pages 1846–1851.

Qi Li, Heng Ji, and Liang Huang. 2013. Joint event extraction via structured prediction with global features. In *Association for Computational Linguistics*, pages 73–82.

Shasha Liao and Ralph Grishman. 2010. Using document level cross-event inference to improve event extraction. In *Association for Computational Linguistics*, pages 789–797.

Shulin Liu, Yubo Chen, Shizhu He, Kang Liu, and Jun Zhao. 2016a. Leveraging framenet to improve automatic event detection. In *Association for Computational Linguistics*, pages 2134–2143.

Shulin Liu, Yubo Chen, Kang Liu, and Jun Zhao. 2017. Exploiting argument information to improve event detection via supervised attention mechanisms. In *Association for Computational Linguistics*, pages 1789–1798.

Shulin Liu, Kang Liu, Shizhu He, and Jun Zhao. 2016b. A probabilistic soft logic based approach to exploiting latent and global information in event classification. In *Proceedings of the Thirtieth AAAI Conference on Artificial Intelligence*, pages 2993–2999.

David McClosky, Mihai Surdeanu, and Christopher D. Manning. 2011. Event extraction as dependency parsing for bionlp 2011. In *Association for Computational Linguistics*, pages 41–45.

Tomas Mikolov, Ilya Sutskever, Kai Chen, Greg Corrado, and Jeffrey Dean. 2013. Distributed representations of words and phrases and their compositionality. In *Proceedings of the 26th International Conference on Neural Information Processing Systems - Volume 2*, pages 3111–3119.

Thien Nguyen, Kyunghyun Cho, and Ralph Grishman. 2016. Joint event extraction via recurrent neural networks. In *NAACL*, pages 300–309.

Thien Nguyen and Ralph Grishman. 2015. Event detection and domain adaptation with convolutional neural networks. In *IJCNLP*, pages 365–371.

Thien Nguyen and Ralph Grishman. 2016. Modeling skip-grams for event detection with convolutional neural networks. In *Empirical Methods in Natural Language Processing*, pages 886–891.

M. Schuster and K.K. Paliwal. 2002. Bidirectional recurrent neural networks. *IEEE Transactions on Signal Processing*, 45:2673–2681.

Jiwei Tan, Xiaojun Wan, and Jianguo Xiao. 2017. Abstractive document summarization with a graph-based attentional neural model. In *Association for Computational Linguistics*, pages 1171–1181.

Zichao Yang, Diyi Yang, Chris Dyer, Xiaodong He, Alex Smola, and Eduard Hovy. 2016. Hierarchical attention networks for document classification. In *NAACL*, pages 1480–1489.

Jinchao Zhang, Mingxuan Wang, Qun Liu, and Jie Zhou. 2017. Incorporating word reordering knowledge into attention-based neural machine translation. In *Association for Computational Linguistics*, pages 1524–1534.

Learning Matching Models with Weak Supervision for Response Selection in Retrieval-based Chatbots

Yu Wu[†], Wei Wu[‡], Zhoujun Li[†*], Ming Zhou[◇]

[†]State Key Lab of Software Development Environment, Beihang University, Beijing, China
[†] Authors are supported by AdeptMind Scholarship
[◇]Microsoft Research, Beijing, China
[‡] Microsoft Corporation, Beijing, China
{wuyu,lizj}@buaa.edu.cn {wuwei,mingzhou}@microsoft.com

Abstract

We propose a method that can leverage unlabeled data to learn a matching model for response selection in retrieval-based chatbots. The method employs a sequence-to-sequence architecture (Seq2Seq) model as a weak annotator to judge the matching degree of unlabeled pairs, and then performs learning with both the weak signals and the unlabeled data. Experimental results on two public data sets indicate that matching models get significant improvements when they are learned with the proposed method.

1 Introduction

Recently, more and more attention from both academia and industry is paying to building non-task-oriented chatbots that can naturally converse with humans on any open domain topics. Existing approaches can be categorized into generation-based methods (Shang et al., 2015; Vinyals and Le, 2015; Serban et al., 2016; Sordoni et al., 2015; Xing et al., 2017; Serban et al., 2017; Xing et al., 2018) which synthesize a response with natural language generation techniques, and retrieval-based methods (Hu et al., 2014; Lowe et al., 2015; Yan et al., 2016; Zhou et al., 2016; Wu et al., 2017) which select a response from a pre-built index. In this work, we study response selection for retrieval-based chatbots, not only because retrieval-based methods can return fluent and informative responses, but also because they have been successfully applied to many real products such as the social-bot XiaoIce from Microsoft (Shum et al., 2018) and the E-commerce assistant AliMe Assist from Alibaba Group (Li et al., 2017).

A key step to response selection is measuring the matching degree between a response candidate and an input which is either a single message (Hu et al., 2014) or a conversational context consisting of multiple utterances (Wu et al., 2017). While existing research focuses on how to define a matching model with neural networks, little attention has been paid to how to learn such a model when few labeled data are available. In practice, because human labeling is expensive and exhausting, one cannot have large scale labeled data for model training. Thus, a common practice is to transform the matching problem to a classification problem with human responses as positive examples and randomly sampled ones as negative examples. This strategy, however, oversimplifies the learning problem, as most of the randomly sampled responses are either far from the semantics of the messages or the contexts, or they are false negatives which pollute the training data as noise. As a result, there often exists a significant gap between the performance of a model in training and the same model in practice (Wang et al., 2015; Wu et al., 2017).[1]

We propose a new method that can effectively leverage unlabeled data for learning matching models. To simulate the real scenario of a retrieval-based chatbot, we construct an unlabeled data set by retrieving response candidates from an index. Then, we employ a weak annotator to provide matching signals for the unlabeled input-response pairs, and leverage the signals to supervise the learning of matching models. The weak annotator is pre-trained from large scale human-human conversations without any annotations, and thus a Seq2Seq model becomes a natural choice. Our approach is compatible with any matching models, and falls in a teacher-student framework

---

[*] Corresponding Author

[1]The model performs well on randomly sampled data, but badly on human labeled data.

Proceedings of the 56th Annual Meeting of the Association for Computational Linguistics (Short Papers), pages 420–425
Melbourne, Australia, July 15 - 20, 2018. ©2018 Association for Computational Linguistics

(Hinton et al., 2015) where the Seq2Seq model transfers the knowledge from human-human conversations to the learning process of the matching models. Broadly speaking, both of (Hinton et al., 2015) and our work let a neural network supervise the learning of another network. An advantage of our method is that it turns the hard zero-one labels in the existing learning paradigm to soft (weak) matching scores. Hence, the model can learn a large margin between a true response with a true negative example, and the semantic distance between a true response and a false negative example is short. Furthermore, due to the simulation of real scenario, harder examples can been seen in the training phase that makes the model more robust in the testing.

We conduct experiments on two public data sets, and experimental results on both data sets indicate that models learned with our method can significantly outperform their counterparts learned with the random sampling strategy.

Our contributions include: (1) proposal of a new method that can leverage unlabeled data to learn matching models for retrieval-based chatbots; and (2) empirical verification of the effectiveness of the method on public data sets.

2 Approach

2.1 The Existing Learning Approach

Given a data set $\mathcal{D} = \{x_i, (y_{i,1}, \ldots, y_{i,n})\}_{i=1}^{N}$ with x_i a message or a conversational context and $y_{i,j}$ a response candidate of x_i, we aim to learn a matching model $\mathcal{M}(\cdot, \cdot)$ from $\mathcal{D}$. Thus, for any new pair (x, y), $\mathcal{M}(x, y)$ measures the matching degree between x and y.

To obtain a matching model, one has to deal with two problems: (1) how to define $\mathcal{M}(\cdot, \cdot)$; and (2) how to perform learning. Existing work focuses on Problem (1) where state-of-the-art methods include dual LSTM (Lowe et al., 2015), Multi-View LSTM (Zhou et al., 2016), CNN (Yan et al., 2016), and Sequential Matching Network (Wu et al., 2017), but adopts a simple strategy for Problem (2): $\forall x_i$, a human response is designated as $y_{i,1}$ with a label 1, and some randomly sampled responses are treated as $(y_{i,2}, \ldots, y_{i,n})$ with labels 0. $\mathcal{M}(\cdot, \cdot)$ is then learned by maximizing the following objective:

$$\sum_{i=1}^{N} \sum_{j=1}^{n} [r_{i,j} \log(\mathcal{M}(x_i, y_{i,j})) + (1 - r_{i,j}) \log(1 - \mathcal{M}(x_i, y_{i,j}))],$$
$$(1)$$

where $r_{i,j} \in \{0, 1\}$ is a label. While matching accuracy can be improved by carefully designing $\mathcal{M}(\cdot, \cdot)$ (Wu et al., 2017), the bottleneck becomes the learning approach which suffers obvious problems: most of the randomly sampled $y_{i,j}$ are semantically far from x_i which may cause an undesired decision boundary at the end of optimization; some $y_{i,j}$ are false negatives. As hard zero-one labels are adopted in Equation (1), these false negatives may mislead the learning algorithm. The problems remind us that besides good architectures of matching models, we also need a good approach to learn such models from data.

2.2 A New Learning Method

As human labeling is infeasible when training complicated neural networks, we propose a new method that can leverage unlabeled data to learn a matching model. Specifically, instead of random sampling, we construct $\mathcal{D}$ by retrieving $(y_{i,2}, \ldots, y_{i,n})$ from an index ($y_{i,1}$ is the human response of x_i). By this means, some $y_{i,j}$ are true positives, and some are negatives but semantically close to x_i. After that, we employ a weak annotator $G(\cdot, \cdot)$ to indicate the matching degree of every $(x_i, y_{i,j})$ in $\mathcal{D}$ as weak supervision signals. Let $s_{ij} = G(x_i, y_{i,j})$, then the learning approach can be formulated as:

$$\underset{\mathcal{M}(\cdot, \cdot)}{\arg\min} \sum_{i=1}^{N} \sum_{j=1}^{n} \max(0, \mathcal{M}(x_i, y_{i,j}) - \mathcal{M}(x_i, y_{i,1}) + s'_{i,j}),$$
$$(2)$$

where s'_{ij} is a normalized weak signal defined as $max(0, \frac{s_{i,j}}{s_{i,1}} - 1)$. The normalization here eliminates bias from different x_i.

Objective (2) encourages a large margin between the matching of an input and its human response and the matching of the input and a negative response judged by $G(\cdot, \cdot)$ (as will be seen later, $\frac{s_{i,j}}{s_{i,1}} > 1$). The learning approach simulates how we build a matching model in a retrieval-based chatbot: given $\{x_i\}$, some response candidates are first retrieved from an index. Then human annotators are hired to judge the matching degree of each pair. Finally, both the data and the human labels are fed to an optimization program for model training. Here, we replace the expensive human labels with cheap judgment from $G(\cdot, \cdot)$.

We define $G(\cdot, \cdot)$ as a sequence-to-sequence architecture (Vinyals and Le, 2015) with an attention mechanism (Bahdanau et al., 2015), and pre-train it with large amounts of human-human conversation data. The Seq2Seq model can capture the semantic correspondence between an input and a response, and then transfer the knowledge to the learning of a matching model in the optimization of (2). s_{ij} is then defined as the likelihood of generating $y_{i,j}$ from x_i:

$$s_{ij} = \sum_k \log[p(w_{y_{i,j},k}, |x_i, w_{y_{i,j},l<k})], \qquad (3)$$

where $w_{y_{i,j},k}$ is the k-th word of $y_{i,j}$ and $w_{y_{i,j},l<k}$ is the word sequence before $w_{y_{i,j},k}$.

Since negative examples are retrieved by a search engine, the oversimplification problem of the negative sampling approach can be partially mitigated. We leverage a weak annotator to assign a score for each example to distinguish false negative examples and true negative examples. Equation (2) turns the hard zero-one labels in Equation (1) to soft matching degrees, and thus our method encourages the model to be more confident to classify a response with a high $s_{i,j}$ score as a negative one. In this way, we can avoid false negative examples and true negative examples are treated equally during training, and update the model toward a correct direction.

It is noteworthy that although our approach also involves an interaction between a generator and a discriminator, it is different from the GANs (Goodfellow et al., 2014) in principle. GANs try to learn a better generator via an adversarial process, while our approach aims to improve the discriminator with supervision from the generator, which also differentiates it from the recent work on transferring knowledge from a discriminator to a generative visual dialog model (Lu et al., 2017). Our approach is also different from those semi-supervised approaches in the teacher-student framework (Dehghani et al., 2017a,b), as there are no labeled data in learning.

3 Experiment

We conduct experiments on two public data sets: STC data set (Wang et al., 2013) for single-turn response selection and Douban Conversation Corpus (Wu et al., 2017) for multi-turn response selection. Note that we do not test the proposed approach on Ubuntu Corpus (Lowe et al., 2015), because both training and test data in the corpus are constructed by random sampling.

3.1 Implementation Details

We implement our approach with TensorFlow. In both experiments, the same Seq2Seq model is exploited which is trained with 3.3 million input-response pairs extracted from the training set of the Douban data. Each input is a concatenation of consecutive utterances in a context, and the response is the next turn ($\{u_{<i}\}, u_i$). We set the vocabulary size as $30,000$, the hidden vector size as 1024, and the embedding size as 620. Optimization is conducted with stochastic gradient descent (Bottou, 2010), and is terminated when perplexity on a validation set (170k pairs) does not decrease in 3 consecutive epochs. In optimization of Objective (2), we initialize $\mathcal{M}(\cdot, \cdot)$ with a model trained under Objective (1) with the (random) negative sampling strategy, and fix word embeddings throughout training. This can stabilize the learning process. The learning rate is fixed as 0.1.

3.2 Single-turn Response Selection

Experiment settings: in the STC (stands for Short Text Conversation) data set, the task is to select a proper response for a post in Weibo[2]. The training set contains 4.8 million post-response (true response) pairs. The test set consists of 422 posts with each one associated with around 30 responses labeled by human annotators in "good" and "bad". In total, there are $12,402$ labeled pairs in the test data. Following (Wang et al., 2013, 2015), we combine the score from a matching model with TF-IDF based cosine similarity using RankSVM whose parameters are chosen by 5-fold cross validation. Precision at position 1 (P@1) is employed as an evaluation metric. In addition to the models compared on the data in the existing literatures, we also implement dual LSTM (Lowe et al., 2015) as a baseline. As case studies, we learn a dual LSTM and an CNN (Hu et al., 2014) with the proposed approach, and denote them as LSTM+WS (Weak Supervision) and CNN+WS, respectively. When constructing $\mathcal{D}$, we build an index with the training data using Lucene[3] and retrieve 9 candidates (i.e., $\{y_{i,2}, \ldots, y_{i,n}\}$) for each post with the inline algorithm of the index. We form a validation set by randomly sampling 10 thousand posts associated with the responses from $\mathcal{D}$ (human response is positive and others are treated as negative).

Results: Table 1 reports the results. We can see

[2]http://weibo.sina.com
[3]https://lucenenet.apache.org/

	P@1
TFIDF (Wang et al., 2013)	0.574
+Translation (Wang et al., 2013)	0.587
+WordEmbedding	0.579
+DeepMatch$_{topic}$ (Lu and Li, 2013)	0.587
+DeepMatch$_{tree}$ (Wang et al., 2015)	0.608
+LSTM (Lowe et al., 2015)	0.592
+LSTM+WS	0.616
+CNN (Hu et al., 2014)	0.585
+CNN+WS	0.604

Table 1: Results on STC

that CNN and LSTM consistently get improved when learned with the proposed approach, and the improvements over the models learned with random sampling are statistically significant (t-test with p-value < 0.01). LSTM+WS even surpasses the best performing model, DeepMatch$_{tree}$, reported on this data. These results indicate the usefulness of the proposed approach in practice. One can expect improvements to models like DeepMatch$_{tree}$ with the new learning method. We leave the verification as future work.

3.3 Multi-turn Response Selection

Experiment settings: Douban Conversation Corpus contains 0.5 million context-response (true response) pairs for training and 1000 contexts for test. In the test set, every context has 10 response candidates, and each of the response has a label "good" or "bad" judged by human annotators. Mean average precision (MAP) (Baeza-Yates et al., 1999), mean reciprocal rank (MRR) (Voorhees, 1999), and precision at position 1 (P@1) are employed as evaluation metrics. We copy the numbers reported in (Wu et al., 2017) for the baseline models, and learn LSTM, Multi-View, and SMN with the proposed approach. We build an index with the training data, and retrieve 9 candidates with the method in (Wu et al., 2017) for each context when constructing $\mathcal{D}$. 10 thousand pairs are sampled from $\mathcal{D}$ as a validation set.

Results: Table 2 reports the results. Consistent with the results on the STC data, every model (+WS one) gets improved with the new learning approach, and the improvements are statistically significant (t-test with p-value < 0.01).

3.4 Discussion

Ablation studies: we first replace the weak supervision $s'_{i,j}$ in Equation (2) with a constant ϵ selected from $\{0.1, 0.2, \ldots, 0.9\}$ on validation, and denote the models as model+const. Then, we keep

	MAP	MRR	P@1
TFIDF	0.331	0.359	0.180
RNN	0.390	0.422	0.208
CNN	0.417	0.440	0.226
BiLSTM	0.479	0.514	0.313
DL2R (Yan et al., 2016)	0.488	0.527	0.330
LSTM (Lowe et al., 2015)	0.485	0.527	0.320
LSTM+WS	0.519	0.559	0.359
Multi-View (Zhou et al., 2016)	0.505	0.543	0.342
Multi-View+WS	0.534	0.575	0.378
SMN (Wu et al., 2017)	0.526	0.571	0.393
SMN+WS	0.565	0.609	0.421

Table 2: Results on Douban Conversation Corpus

	STC	Douban		
	P@1	MAP	MRR	P@1
CNN+WSrand	0.590	-	-	-
CNN+const	0.598	-	-	-
CNN+WS	0.604	-	-	-
LSTM+WSrand	0.598	0.501	0.532	0.323
LSTM+const	0.607	0.510	0.545	0.331
LSTM+WS	0.616	0.519	0.559	0.359
Multi-View+WSrand	-	0.515	0.549	0.357
Multi-View+const	-	0.528	0.564	0.370
Multi-View+WS	-	0.534	0.575	0.378
SMN+WSrand	-	0.536	0.574	0.377
SMN+const	-	0.558	0.603	0.417
SMN+WS	-	0.565	0.609	0.421

Table 3: Ablation results.

everything the same as our approach but replace $\mathcal{D}$ with a set constructed by random sampling, denoted as model+WSrand. Table 3 reports the results. We can conclude that both the weak supervision and the strategy of training data construction are important to the success of the proposed learning approach. Training data construction plays a more crucial role, because it involves more true positives and negatives with different semantic distances to the positives into learning.

Does updating the Seq2Seq model help? It is well known that Seq2Seq models suffer from the "safe response" (Li et al., 2016a) problem, which may bias the weak supervision signals to high-frequency responses. Therefore, we attempt to iteratively optimize the Seq2Seq model and the matching model and check if the matching model can be further improved. Specifically, we update the Seq2Seq model every 20 mini-batches with the policy-based reinforcement learning approach proposed in (Li et al., 2016b). The reward is defined as the matching score of a context and a response given by the matching model. Unfortunately, we do not observe significant improvement on the matching model. The result is attributed to two factors: (1) it is difficult to significantly improve the Seq2Seq model with a policy gradient based method; and (2) eliminating "safe response" for Seq2Seq model cannot help a matching model to learn a better decision boundary.

How the number of response candidates affects learning: we vary the number of $\{y_{i,j}\}_{j=1}^n$ in $\mathcal{D}$ in $\{2, 5, 10, 20\}$ and study how the hyperparameter influences learning. We study with LSTM on the STC data and SMN on the Douban data. Table 4 reports the results. We can see that as the number of candidates increases, the performance of the the learned models becomes better. Even with 2 candidates (one from human and the other from retrieval), our approach can still improve the peformance of matching models.

	LSTM$_2$	LSTM$_5$	LSTM$_{10}$	LSTM$_{20}$
P@1	0.603	0.608	0.615	0.616
	SMN$_2$	SMN$_5$	SMN$_{10}$	SMN$_{20}$
MAP	0.542	0.556	0.565	0.567
MRR	0.588	0.594	0.609	0.609
P@1	0.408	0.412	0.421	0.423

Table 4: The effect of instance number

4 Conclusion and Future Work

Previous studies focus on architecture design for retrieval-based chatbots, but neglect the problems brought by random negative sampling in the learning process. In this paper, we propose leveraging a Seq2Seq model as a weak annotator on unlabeled data to learn a matching model for response selection. By this means, we can mine hard instances for matching model and give them scores with a weak annotator. Experimental results on public data sets verify the effectiveness of the new learning approach. In the future, we will investigate how to remove bias from the weak supervisors, and further improve the matching model performance with a semi-supervised approach.

Acknowledgment

Yu Wu is supported by Microsoft Fellowship Scholarship and AdeptMind Scholarship. This work is supported by the National Natural Science Foundation of China (Grand Nos. 61672081,U1636211,61370126), Beijing Advanced Innovation Center for Imaging Technology (No.BAICIT-2016001).

References

Ricardo Baeza-Yates, Berthier Ribeiro-Neto, et al. 1999. *Modern information retrieval*, volume 463. ACM press New York.

Dzmitry Bahdanau, Kyunghyun Cho, and Yoshua Bengio. 2015. Neural machine translation by jointly learning to align and translate. *ICLR* .

Léon Bottou. 2010. Large-scale machine learning with stochastic gradient descent. In *Proceedings of COMPSTAT'2010*, Springer, pages 177–186.

Mostafa Dehghani, Arash Mehrjou, Stephan Gouws, Jaap Kamps, and Bernhard Schölkopf. 2017a. Fidelity-weighted learning. *arXiv preprint arXiv:1711.02799* .

Mostafa Dehghani, Aliaksei Severyn, Sascha Rothe, and Jaap Kamps. 2017b. Avoiding your teacher's mistakes: Training neural networks with controlled weak supervision. *arXiv preprint arXiv:1711.00313* .

Ian Goodfellow, Jean Pouget-Abadie, Mehdi Mirza, Bing Xu, David Warde-Farley, Sherjil Ozair, Aaron Courville, and Yoshua Bengio. 2014. Generative adversarial nets. In *Advances in neural information processing systems*. pages 2672–2680.

Geoffrey Hinton, Oriol Vinyals, and Jeff Dean. 2015. Distilling the knowledge in a neural network. *arXiv preprint arXiv:1503.02531* .

Baotian Hu, Zhengdong Lu, Hang Li, and Qingcai Chen. 2014. Convolutional neural network architectures for matching natural language sentences. In *Advances in Neural Information Processing Systems*. pages 2042–2050.

Feng-Lin Li, Minghui Qiu, Haiqing Chen, Xiongwei Wang, Xing Gao, Jun Huang, Juwei Ren, Zhongzhou Zhao, Weipeng Zhao, Lei Wang, et al. 2017. Alime assist: An intelligent assistant for creating an innovative e-commerce experience. In *Proceedings of the 2017 ACM on Conference on Information and Knowledge Management*. ACM, pages 2495–2498.

Jiwei Li, Michel Galley, Chris Brockett, Jianfeng Gao, and Bill Dolan. 2016a. A diversity-promoting objective function for neural conversation models. In *NAACL HLT 2016, The 2016 Conference of the North American Chapter of the Association for Computational Linguistics: Human Language Technologies, San Diego California, USA, June 12-17, 2016*. pages 110–119.

Jiwei Li, Will Monroe, Alan Ritter, Dan Jurafsky, Michel Galley, and Jianfeng Gao. 2016b. Deep reinforcement learning for dialogue generation. In *Proceedings of the 2016 Conference on Empirical Methods in Natural Language Processing, EMNLP 2016, Austin, Texas, USA, November 1-4, 2016*. pages 1192–1202.

Ryan Lowe, Nissan Pow, Iulian Serban, and Joelle Pineau. 2015. The ubuntu dialogue corpus: A large dataset for research in unstructured multi-turn dialogue systems. *SIGDIAL* .

Jiasen Lu, Anitha Kannan, Jianwei Yang, Devi Parikh, and Dhruv Batra. 2017. Best of both worlds: Transferring knowledge from discriminative learning to a generative visual dialog model. In *Advances in Neural Information Processing Systems*. pages 313–323.

Zhengdong Lu and Hang Li. 2013. A deep architecture for matching short texts. In *Advances in Neural Information Processing Systems*. pages 1367–1375.

Iulian Vlad Serban, Alessandro Sordoni, Yoshua Bengio, Aaron C. Courville, and Joelle Pineau. 2016. End-to-end dialogue systems using generative hierarchical neural network models. In *Proceedings of the Thirtieth AAAI Conference on Artificial Intelligence, February 12-17, 2016, Phoenix, Arizona, USA.*. pages 3776–3784.

Iulian Vlad Serban, Alessandro Sordoni, Ryan Lowe, Laurent Charlin, Joelle Pineau, Aaron C Courville, and Yoshua Bengio. 2017. A hierarchical latent variable encoder-decoder model for generating dialogues. In *AAAI*. pages 3295–3301.

Lifeng Shang, Zhengdong Lu, and Hang Li. 2015. Neural responding machine for short-text conversation. In *ACL 2015, July 26-31, 2015, Beijing, China, Volume 1: Long Papers*. pages 1577–1586.

Heung-Yeung Shum, Xiaodong He, and Di Li. 2018. From eliza to xiaoice: Challenges and opportunities with social chatbots. *arXiv preprint arXiv:1801.01957* .

Alessandro Sordoni, Michel Galley, Michael Auli, Chris Brockett, Yangfeng Ji, Margaret Mitchell, Jian-Yun Nie, Jianfeng Gao, and Bill Dolan. 2015. A neural network approach to context-sensitive generation of conversational responses. In *NAACL HLT 2015, The 2015 Conference of the North American Chapter of the Association for Computational Linguistics: Human Language Technologies, Denver, Colorado, USA, May 31 - June 5, 2015*. pages 196–205.

Oriol Vinyals and Quoc Le. 2015. A neural conversational model. *arXiv preprint arXiv:1506.05869* .

Ellen M. Voorhees. 1999. The TREC-8 question answering track report. In *Proceedings of The Eighth Text REtrieval Conference, TREC 1999, Gaithersburg, Maryland, USA, November 17-19, 1999*.

Hao Wang, Zhengdong Lu, Hang Li, and Enhong Chen. 2013. A dataset for research on short-text conversations. In *Proceedings of the 2013 Conference on Empirical Methods in Natural Language Processing, EMNLP 2013, 18-21 October 2013, Grand Hyatt Seattle, Seattle, Washington, USA, A meeting of SIGDAT, a Special Interest Group of the ACL*. pages 935–945.

Mingxuan Wang, Zhengdong Lu, Hang Li, and Qun Liu. 2015. Syntax-based deep matching of short texts. In *Twenty-Fourth International Joint Conference on Artificial Intelligence*.

Yu Wu, Wei Wu, Chen Xing, Ming Zhou, and Zhoujun Li. 2017. Sequential matching network: A new architecture for multi-turn response selection in retrieval-based chatbots. In *Proceedings of the 55th Annual Meeting of the Association for Computational Linguistics (Volume 1: Long Papers)*. volume 1, pages 496–505.

Chen Xing, Wei Wu, Yu Wu, Jie Liu, Yalou Huang, Ming Zhou, and Wei-Ying Ma. 2017. Topic aware neural response generation. In *AAAI 2017*. pages 3351–3357.

Chen Xing, Wei Wu, Yu Wu, Ming Zhou, Yalou Huang, and Wei-Ying Ma. 2018. Hierarchical recurrent attention network for response generation. *AAAI-18*

.

Rui Yan, Yiping Song, and Hua Wu. 2016. Learning to respond with deep neural networks for retrieval-based human-computer conversation system. In *Proceedings of the 39th International ACM SIGIR conference on Research and Development in Information Retrieval, SIGIR 2016, Pisa, Italy, July 17-21, 2016*. pages 55–64.

Xiangyang Zhou, Daxiang Dong, Hua Wu, Shiqi Zhao, Dianhai Yu, Hao Tian, Xuan Liu, and Rui Yan. 2016. Multi-view response selection for human-computer conversation. In *Proceedings of the 2016 Conference on Empirical Methods in Natural Language Processing, EMNLP 2016, Austin, Texas, USA, November 1-4, 2016*. pages 372–381.

Improving Slot Filling in Spoken Language Understanding with Joint Pointer and Attention

Lin Zhao and **Zhe Feng**
Bosch Research and Technology Center
Sunnyvale, CA 94085, USA
{lin.zhao, zhe.feng2}@us.bosch.com

Abstract

We present a generative neural network model for slot filling based on a sequence-to-sequence (Seq2Seq) model together with a pointer network, in the situation where only sentence-level slot annotations are available in the spoken dialogue data. This model predicts slot values by jointly learning to copy a word which may be out-of-vocabulary (OOV) from an input utterance through a pointer network, or generate a word within the vocabulary through an attentional Seq2Seq model. Experimental results show the effectiveness of our slot filling model, especially at addressing the OOV problem. Additionally, we integrate the proposed model into a spoken language understanding system and achieve the state-of-the-art performance on the benchmark data.

1 Introduction

Slot filling is a key component in spoken language understanding (SLU), which is usually treated as a sequence labeling problem and solved using methods such as conditional random fields (CRFs) (Raymond and Riccardi, 2007) or recurrent neural networks (RNNs) (Yao et al., 2013; Mesnil et al., 2015).

Although these models have achieved good results, they are learned on the datasets with word-level annotations, e.g., with the BIO tagging schema as in ATIS (Hemphill et al., 1990). Manual annotations at word level require big effort and some corpora has only sentence-level annotations available, e.g., the utterance *"... moderately priced restaurant"* has a slot-value pair annotation of *"pricerange=moderate"*. As such datasets lack explicit alignment between the annotations and the

input words, some systems rely on handcrafted rules to find the alignments in order to automatically create word-level labels to learn the sequence model (Zhou and He, 2011; Henderson, 2015), but finding such alignments is non-trivial. For example, it was shown in (Henderson, 2015) that when applying the manually created word aliases to the speech recognition hypotheses, only around 73% of alignments can be found due to the noise, and a CRF model trained on such noisy data performs particularly worse than some other methods. In addition it is time-consuming to adapt the manual rules or aliases to new domains.

Some other work avoids this issue by regarding slot filling as a classification task (Henderson et al., 2012; Williams, 2014; Barahona et al., 2016), where an utterance is classified into one or more slot-value pairs. This, however, brings other challenges. One is that some types of slots may have a large or even unlimited number of possible values, so the classifiers may suffer from the data sparsity problem when the training data is limited. Another is the OOV problem caused by unknown slot values (e.g., restaurant name, street name), which is impossible to predefine and is very common in real-world spoken dialogue applications.

To address these challenges, we present a neural generative model for slot filling on unaligned dialog data, specifically for slot value prediction as it has more challenges caused by OOV. The model uses Seq2Seq learning to predict a sequence of slot values from an utterance. Inspired by the ability of pointer network (Ptr-Net) (Vinyals et al., 2015) at addressing OOV problems, we incorporate Ptr-Net into a standard Seq2Seq attentional model to handle OOV slots. It can predict slot values by either generating one from a fixed vocabulary or selecting a word from the utterance. The final model is a weighted combination of the two operations.

To summarize, our main contributions are:

Proceedings of the 56th Annual Meeting of the Association for Computational Linguistics (Short Papers), pages 426–431
Melbourne, Australia, July 15 - 20, 2018. ©2018 Association for Computational Linguistics

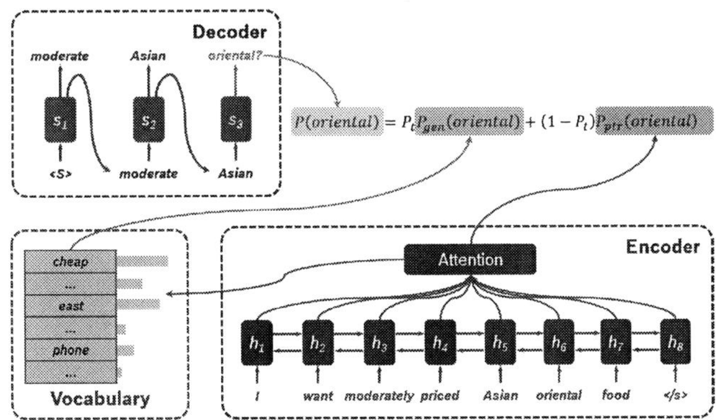

Figure 1: Our model for slot value prediction based on Seq2Seq learning with attention and Ptr-Net.

- We use a neural generative model for slot filling on the data without word-level annotations which has received less attention.

- We adopt the pointer network to handle the OOV problem in slot value prediction, which achieves good performance without any manually-designed rules or features.

2 Background of Pointer Network

Ptr-Net is a variation of the standard Seq2Seq model with attention. At each decoding step, it selects a position from the input sequence based on the attention distribution instead of generating a token from the target vocabulary. Given the input $X = \{x_1, ..., x_T\}$, the output y_t at time step t is predicted by:

$$P_{ptr}(y_t = w | y_1^{t-1}, X) = \sum_{i:x_i=w} a_i^t \qquad (1)$$

where a_i^t is the attention weight of position i at step t. The advantage of Ptr-Net is that it can make better predictions on unknown or rare words. It has been successfully applied to tasks such as abstractive summarization (See et al., 2017), question answering (He et al., 2017), reading comprehension (Wang and Jiang, 2016), and chunking (Zhai et al., 2017).

3 Model for Slot Value Prediction

Our model for slot value prediction is a hybrid of a Seq2Seq attentional model and a Ptr-Net, similar as the one in See et al. (2017). The input is a sequence of words in an utterance, and the output is a sequence of slot values whose tokens may or may not appear in the input.

The hybrid model, illustrated in Figure 1, allows us to both generate a slot value from a fixed vocabulary and pick a value from the input via pointing. The two components (*Seq2Seq* and *Ptr-Net*) share the same encoder-decoder architecture and attention scores. We adopt a single-layer bidirectional GRU (Cho et al., 2014) for the encoder, and a single-layer unidirectional GRU for the decoder. The attention is calculated as in Bahdanau et al. (2014).

The slot vocabulary is set to contain only the values of enumerable slots, but not those of non-enumerable slots (e.g., values of *"restaurant name"*) as we assume these are not known in advance in the real scenarios.

We use the term "extended vocabulary" to denote the union of the slot vocabulary and all words from the input utterances. The probability distribution over the extended vocabulary is calculated as:

$$P(w) = p_t P_{gen} + (1 - p_t) P_{ptr} \qquad (2)$$

That is, the model makes the final predictions using a weighted combination of the predictions from two individual components. At the decoding step t, the Seq2Seq component produces the probability distribution P_{gen} for the next slot value within the vocabulary, while Ptr-Net produces the probability distribution P_{ptr} over the input positions. $p_t \in [0, 1]$ is a parameter to balance the two components. It is learned at each time step based on the decoder input d_t, decoder state s_t and the context vector c_t as follows:

$$p_t = \sigma(w_c c_t + w_s s_t + w_d d_t + b) \qquad (3)$$

where σ is a sigmoid function. w_c, w_s and w_d are all trainable weights.

Model	P	R	F
CNN	**93.3**	76.3	84.0
Seq2Seq w/ attention	86.6	**81.9**	84.2
Our model	88.8	81.3	**84.9**

Table 1: Results of slot value prediction.

4 Experiments

In this section, we present our experimental results on DSTC2 (Dialog State Tracking Challenge) (Henderson et al., 2014), including the results of slot value prediction solely and a complete SLU system. Our models are implemented using Keras[1] with TensorFlow as backend. In all the experiments, the dimension of hidden states is 128, dimension of word embeddings is 100, dropout rate is 0.5, and batch size is 32. Word embeddings are not pre-trained but learned from scratch during training. Teacher forcing is used during training, with Adam optimizer (Kingma and Ba, 2014). All training consists of 10 epochs with early stopping on the development set.

4.1 Data

DSTC2 consists of multi-turn dialogues between users and a dialog system, in the restaurant search domain. Each utterance is annotated with semantics including dialog-acts and slot-value pairs. For an utterance, both its transcription and 10-best hypotheses are provided. We use the top hypothesis as input throughout our experiments. The corpus has been separated into training, development and testing, containing 11,677, 3,934 and 9,890 utterances respectively.

4.2 A Complete SLU System

For better evaluation and comparison, we integrated our model of slot value prediction into a complete SLU system, which uses a CNN classifier to obtain dialog-acts and slot types respectively after slot value prediction. For dialog act prediction, the input to the CNN model is the utterance and the output is one or more dialog acts (some utterances can have more than one dialog acts). For slot type prediction, the input is each predicted slot value together with the utterance, and the output is one of the predefined slot types. Given the limited numbers of various dialog-acts and slot types for classification, a standard CNN model is expected to achieve good performance.

[1]https://keras.io

| Training size | 5% | 10% | 15% | 20% |
OOV ratio	(16%)	(12%)	(4%)	(2%)
CNN P	91.6	93.0	92.7	93.4
CNN R	61.7	62.5	65.8	69.2
CNN F	73.7	74.8	77.0	79.5
Seq2Seq w/ attention P	81.3	83.6	84.1	85.3
Seq2Seq w/ attention R	69.6	74.7	74.9	76.5
Seq2Seq w/ attention F	75.0	78.9	79.2	80.7
Our model P	86.9	86.4	85.7	85.9
Our model R	73.2	75.3	77.0	77.4
Our model F	**79.5**	**80.5**	**81.1**	**81.4**

Table 2: Results of slot value prediction with varying training size and OOV ratio.

Note that we can adopt other SLU frameworks as well (e.g., some joint frameworks), but given our focus in this work is to explore the hybrid Seq2Seq solutions for slot filling, we do not explore much on the SLU architecture, nor do we use any extra information (e.g., dialogue context). Despite the simplicity of our SLU system, it outperforms the prior state-of-the-art. In the whole process, neither manually designed features nor domain-specific rules are employed.

4.3 Baselines

We compare the overall SLU performance of our system against two existing baselines on DSTC2. One baseline (Williams, 2014) uses binary SVM classifiers to predict the existence of each slot-value pair and dialog act. The other (Barahona et al., 2016) uses CNN and LSTM jointly for classification.

For slot value prediction, since it is a sub-task of SLU and not reported in the prior work, we implemented another two models for it. One adopts CNN to classify an utterance into one or more slot values. The other uses the basic Seq2Seq attentional model (without Ptr-Net). Note that when learning this basic model, the target vocabulary is set to contain all the slot values in the training set.

4.4 Results of Slot Value Prediction

We first report the results on slot value prediction only. We compare the results of our proposed model and our own implemented baselines in Table 1, using precision, recall and F1.

We can see that the proposed hybrid model achieves the best F1 score. Although CNN has a high precision, it suffers from the low recall. By looking into the results for each slot type, it is ob-

Model	P	R	F
SLU1 (Williams, 2014)	84.6	76.2	80.2
SLU2 (Williams, 2014)	87.0	77.7	82.1
CNN+LSTM_w4 (Barahona et al., 2016)	-	-	83.6
CNN	**93.5**	78.5	85.3
Seq2Seq w/ attention	87.5	82.7	85.0
Our model	89.0	**82.8**	**85.8**

Table 3: Overall SLU performance.

Training Size		5%	10%	15%	20%
	P	91.6	92.0	92.3	93.0
CNN	R	67.5	70.4	71.7	72.7
	F	77.8	79.8	80.7	81.6
Seq2Seq w/ attention	P	82.8	87.2	86.4	87.9
	R	74.3	75.1	78.0	78.4
	F	78.3	80.7	82.0	82.9
Our model	P	84.9	86.3	88.4	88.0
	R	76.8	77.9	79.0	79.9
	F	**80.6**	**81.9**	**83.4**	**83.8**

Table 4: SLU results with varying training size.

served that CNN performs much poorer on non-enumerable types of slots such as *"food"* due to its high cardinality. While both our model and the basic Seq2Seq model have higher recall.

Since our assumption is that the proposed model can better handle the OOV problem, we analyze the OOV rate in the corpus to obtain more insight. By checking the percentage of slot values in the testing set that do not exist in the training, we find that the OOV problem in DSTC2 is not that severe, with a OOV ratio less than 0.1%. This could be a reason why our model does not obtain larger gain on the complete dataset. We therefore design more experiments in the next section to assess the model when the OOV problem is more severe.

4.5 OOV Slot Prediction

We create specific datasets by re-sampling from the original corpus. In particular, let group A denote all the training utterances that contain non-enumerable slots, and group B denote the rest of the training utterances. We randomly select 5%, 10%, 15%, and 20% of group A, plus the whole set of group B. In this way, we can create training data with less non-enumerable slot values thus resulting in a higher OOV ratio. The testing set is same as before. We compare the proposed model with the baselines on these four specific datasets with different OOV ratios (Table 2).

Input: **danish** food in the **centre** of town
Output: danish centre | spanish centre | centre
Input: i would like **singaporean** food
Output: singaporean | korean | None
Input: what about chiquito (**portuguese**)
Output: chiquito | portuguese | None
Input: an **expensive** restaurant serving **cantonese** food
Output: cantonese | portuguese expensive | expensive

Table 5: Examples of predicted slot values. Output is from the proposed model, Seq2Seq w/ attn, and CNN respectively (split by "|"). **Bold** denotes gold standard and "None" denotes empty result.

As shown in each column, on all the specific datasets, our model achieves the best performance. The CNN model performs much poorer than before in terms of the recall. We can see that by reducing the training size, the OOV ratio (indicated in the first row in the brackets) goes up, and the performance of all models decreases in general. While CNN and the basic Seq2Seq model decline 10.3% and 9.2% in F1 respectively using the smallest training set compared to using the complete one, our model is the most stable one with the least performance drop of 5.4%. The gain of our model over the other two becomes more significant with the larger OOV rate. This shows the capability of the Ptr-Net to correctly predict the OOV slots.

Overall, the results in Section 4.4 and 4.5 demonstrate the effectiveness of the proposed hybrid model for slot value prediction, especially when the training set is small and the OOV ratio is large.

4.6 SLU Results

Table 3 compares the results of the overall SLU task by our systems (incorporated with different slot value prediction models) and prior arts. All our systems outperform the prior work, and among them the one with the proposed hybrid model achieves the best F1 score.

We also conduct the similar OOV experiments as in Section 4.5 for SLU (Table 4). Similar trend is observed as discussed before. The performance of the proposed model with 20% training data already reaches that of the best system reported in the literature with 100% training data.

4.7 Case Study and Error Analysis

Table 5 gives some examples of slot values predicted by the proposed model and baselines. We can see that for the less frequent slots, our model can still predict the values correctly, while without the Ptr-Net, the basic Seq2Seq model tends to generate words not appearing in the input, and CNN outputs nothing in many cases, which aligns with our assumption. We analyze the cases where Ptr-Net does not perform well and find several major types of errors: 1) partial prediction (e.g., detect only *"oriental"* for *"asian oriental food"*; 2) the prediction contains repetition of correct values; 3) speech recognition error although the prediction is proper if we look at the hypothesis itself (the third example). There are also cases where all the models fail to give a completely correct prediction, yet with different behaviors (the last example).

5 Conclusion

We adopt an attentional Seq2Seq model with Ptr-Net to predict slot values on dialogue data when only sentence-level semantic annotations are available. By switching between copying and generating words, this solution can bypass the need of word-level annotations and overcome the OOV issue which is very common in real-world spoken dialogue applications. It does not require any domain specific rules or dictionaries, and therefore can be easily adapted to new domains. Our model has achieved the state-of-the-art performance for both slot value prediction and SLU on the benchmark even with less training data.

Acknowledgments

We would like to thank Yifan He for helpful discussions and proofreading, and the anonymous reviewers for their valuable feedback.

References

Dzmitry Bahdanau, Kyunghyun Cho, and Yoshua Bengio. 2014. Neural machine translation by jointly learning to align and translate. *arXiv preprint arXiv:1409.0473*.

Lina M Rojas Barahona, Milica Gasic, Nikola Mrkšić, Pei-Hao Su, Stefan Ultes, Tsung-Hsien Wen, and Steve Young. 2016. Exploiting sentence and context representations in deep neural models for spoken language understanding. In *Proceedings of COLING 2016*, pages 258–267.

Kyunghyun Cho, Bart Van Merriënboer, Caglar Gulcehre, Dzmitry Bahdanau, Fethi Bougares, Holger Schwenk, and Yoshua Bengio. 2014. Learning phrase representations using RNN encoder-decoder for statistical machine translation. In *Proceedings of the 2014 Conference on Empirical Methods in Natural Language Processing (EMNLP)*, pages 1724–1734.

Shizhu He, Cao Liu, Kang Liu, and Jun Zhao. 2017. Generating natural answers by incorporating copying and retrieving mechanisms in sequence-to-sequence learning. In *Proceedings of the 55th Annual Meeting of the Association for Computational Linguistics (Volume 1: Long Papers)*, volume 1, pages 199–208.

Charles T Hemphill, John J Godfrey, George R Doddington, et al. 1990. The atis spoken language systems pilot corpus. In *Proceedings of the DARPA speech and natural language workshop*, pages 96–101.

Matthew Henderson, Milica Gašić, Blaise Thomson, Pirros Tsiakoulis, Kai Yu, and Steve Young. 2012. Discriminative spoken language understanding using word confusion networks. In *Spoken Language Technology Workshop (SLT), 2012 IEEE*, pages 176–181. IEEE.

Matthew Henderson, Blaise Thomson, and Jason D Williams. 2014. The second dialog state tracking challenge. In *SIGDIAL Conference*, pages 263–272.

Matthew S Henderson. 2015. *Discriminative methods for statistical spoken dialogue systems*. Ph.D. thesis, University of Cambridge.

Diederik P Kingma and Jimmy Ba. 2014. Adam: A method for stochastic optimization. *arXiv preprint arXiv:1412.6980*.

Grégoire Mesnil, Yann Dauphin, Kaisheng Yao, Yoshua Bengio, Li Deng, Dilek Hakkani-Tur, Xiaodong He, Larry Heck, Gokhan Tur, Dong Yu, et al. 2015. Using recurrent neural networks for slot filling in spoken language understanding. *IEEE/ACM Transactions on Audio, Speech and Language Processing (TASLP)*, 23(3):530–539.

Christian Raymond and Giuseppe Riccardi. 2007. Generative and discriminative algorithms for spoken language understanding. In *Eighth Annual Conference of the International Speech Communication Association*.

Abigail See, Peter J Liu, and Christopher D Manning. 2017. Get to the point: Summarization with pointer-generator networks. In *Proceedings of the 55th Annual Meeting of the Association for Computational Linguistics (Volume 1: Long Papers)*, pages 1073–1083.

Oriol Vinyals, Meire Fortunato, and Navdeep Jaitly. 2015. Pointer networks. In *Advances in Neural Information Processing Systems*, pages 2692–2700.

Shuohang Wang and Jing Jiang. 2016. Machine comprehension using match-LSTM and answer pointer. *arXiv preprint arXiv:1608.07905*.

Jason D Williams. 2014. Web-style ranking and slu combination for dialog state tracking. In *SIGDIAL Conference*, pages 282–291.

Kaisheng Yao, Geoffrey Zweig, Mei-Yuh Hwang, Yangyang Shi, and Dong Yu. 2013. Recurrent neural networks for language understanding. In *Interspeech*, pages 2524–2528.

Feifei Zhai, Saloni Potdar, Bing Xiang, and Bowen Zhou. 2017. Neural models for sequence chunking. In *AAAI*, pages 3365–3371.

Deyu Zhou and Yulan He. 2011. Learning conditional random fields from unaligned data for natural language understanding. *Advances in Information Retrieval*, pages 283–288.

Large-Scale Multi-Domain Belief Tracking with Knowledge Sharing

Osman Ramadan, Paweł Budzianowski, Milica Gašić
Department of Engineering,
University of Cambridge, U.K.
{oior2,pfb30,mg436}@cam.ac.uk

Abstract

Robust dialogue belief tracking is a key component in maintaining good quality dialogue systems. The tasks that dialogue systems are trying to solve are becoming increasingly complex, requiring scalability to multi-domain, semantically rich dialogues. However, most current approaches have difficulty scaling up with domains because of the dependency of the model parameters on the dialogue ontology. In this paper, a novel approach is introduced that fully utilizes semantic similarity between dialogue utterances and the ontology terms, allowing the information to be shared across domains. The evaluation is performed on a recently collected multi-domain dialogues dataset, one order of magnitude larger than currently available corpora. Our model demonstrates great capability in handling multi-domain dialogues, simultaneously outperforming existing state-of-the-art models in single-domain dialogue tracking tasks.

1 Introduction

Spoken Dialogue Systems (SDS) are computer programs that can hold a conversation with a human. These can be task-based systems that help the user achieve specific goals, e.g. finding and booking hotels or restaurants. In order for the SDS to infer the user goals/intentions during the conversation, its *Belief Tracking* (BT) component maintains a distribution of states, called a *belief state*, across dialogue turns (Young et al., 2010). The belief state is used by the system to take actions in each turn until the conversation is concluded and the user goal is achieved. In order to extract these belief states from the conversation, traditional approaches use a Spoken Language Understanding (SLU) unit that utilizes a semantic dictionary to hold all the key terms, rephrasings and alternative mentions of a belief state. The SLU then *delexicalises* each turn using this semantic dictionary, before it passes it to the BT component (Wang and Lemon, 2013; Henderson et al., 2014b; Williams, 2014; Zilka and Jurcicek, 2015; Perez and Liu, 2016; Rastogi et al., 2017). However, this approach is not scalable to multi-domain dialogues because of the effort required to define a semantic dictionary for each domain. More advanced approaches, such as the Neural Belief Tracker (NBT), use word embeddings to alleviate the need for *delexicalisation* and combine the SLU and BT into one unit, mapping directly from turns to belief states (Mrkšić et al., 2017). Nevertheless, the NBT model does not tackle the problem of mixing different domains in a conversation. Moreover, as each slot is trained independently without sharing information between different slots, scaling such approaches to large multi-domain systems is greatly hindered.

In this paper, we propose a model that jointly identifies the domain and tracks the belief states corresponding to that domain. It uses semantic similarity between ontology terms and turn utterances to allow for parameter sharing between different slots across domains and within a single domain. In addition, the model parameters are independent of the ontology/belief states, thus the dimensionality of the parameters does not increase with the size of the ontology, making the model practically feasible to deploy in multi-domain environments without any modifications. Finally, we introduce a new, large-scale corpora of natural, human-human conversations providing new possibilities to train complex, neural-based models. Our model systematically improves upon state-of-the-art neural approaches both in single and multi-domain conversations.

Proceedings of the 56th Annual Meeting of the Association for Computational Linguistics (Short Papers), pages 432–437
Melbourne, Australia, July 15 - 20, 2018. ©2018 Association for Computational Linguistics

2 Background

The belief states of the BT are defined based on an ontology - the structured representation of the database which contains entities the system can talk about. The ontology defines the terms over which the distribution is to be tracked in the dialogue. This ontology is constructed in terms of slots and values in a single domain setting. Or, alternatively, in terms of domains, slots and values in a multi-domain environment. Each domain consists of multiple slots and each slot contains several values, e.g. `domain=hotel`, `slot=price`, `value=expensive`. In each turn, the BT fits a distribution over the values of each slot in each domain, and a *none* value is added to each slot to indicate if the slot is not mentioned so that the distribution sums up to 1. The BT then passes these states to the Policy Optimization unit as full probability distributions to take actions. This allows robustness to noisy environments (Young et al., 2010). The larger the ontology, the more flexible and multi-purposed the system is, but the harder it is to train and maintain a good quality BT.

3 Related Work

In recent years, a plethora of research has been generated on belief tracking (Williams et al., 2016). For the purposes of this paper, two previously proposed models are particularly relevant.

3.1 Neural Belief Tracker (NBT)

The main idea behind the NBT (Mrkšić et al., 2017) is to use semantically specialized pre-trained word embeddings to encode the user utterance, the system act and the candidate slots and values taken from the ontology. These are fed to semantic decoding and context modeling modules that apply a *three-way* gating mechanism and pass the output to a non-linear classifier layer to produce a distribution over the values for each slot. It uses a simple update rule, $p(s_t) = \beta p(s_{t-1}) + \lambda y$, where $p(s_t)$ is the belief state at time step t, y is the output of the binary decision maker of the NBT and β and λ are tunable parameters.

The NBT leverages semantic information from the word embeddings to resolve lexical/morphological ambiguity and maximize the shared parameters across the values of each slot. However, it only applies to a single domain and does not share parameters across slots.

3.2 Multi-domain Dialogue State Tracking

Recently, Rastogi et al. (2017) proposed a multi-domain approach using *delexicalized* utterances fed to a two layer stacked bi-directional GRU network to extract features from the user and the system utterances. These, combined with the candidate slots and values, are passed to a feed-forward neural network with a softmax in the last layer. The candidate set fed to the network consists of the selected candidates from the previous turn and candidates from the ontology to a limit K, which restricts the maximum size of the chosen set. Consequently, the model does not need an ad-hoc belief state update mechanism like in the NBT.

The parameters of the GRU network are defined for the domain, whereas the parameters of the feed-forward network are defined per slot, allowing transfer learning across different domains. However, the model relies on *delexicalization* to extract the features, which limits the performance of the BT, as it does not scale to the rich variety of the language. Moreover, the number of parameters increases with the number of slots.

4 Method

The core idea is to leverage semantic similarities between the utterances and ontology terms to compute the belief state distribution. In this way, the model parameters only learn to model the interactions between turn utterances and ontology terms in the semantic space, rather than the mapping from utterances to states. Consequently, information is shared between both slots and across domains. Additionally, the number of parameters does not increase with the ontology size. Domain tracking is considered as a separate task but is learned jointly with the belief state tracking of the slots and values. The proposed model uses semantically specialized pre-trained word embeddings (Wieting et al., 2015). To encode the user and system utterances, we employed 7 independent bi-directional LSTMs (Graves and Schmidhuber, 2005). Three of them are used to encode the system utterance for domain, slot and value tracking respectively. Similarly, three Bi-LSTMs encode the user utterance while and the last one is used to track the user affirmation. A variant of the CNNs as a feature extractor, similar to the one used in the NBT-CNN (Mrkšić et al., 2017) is also employed.

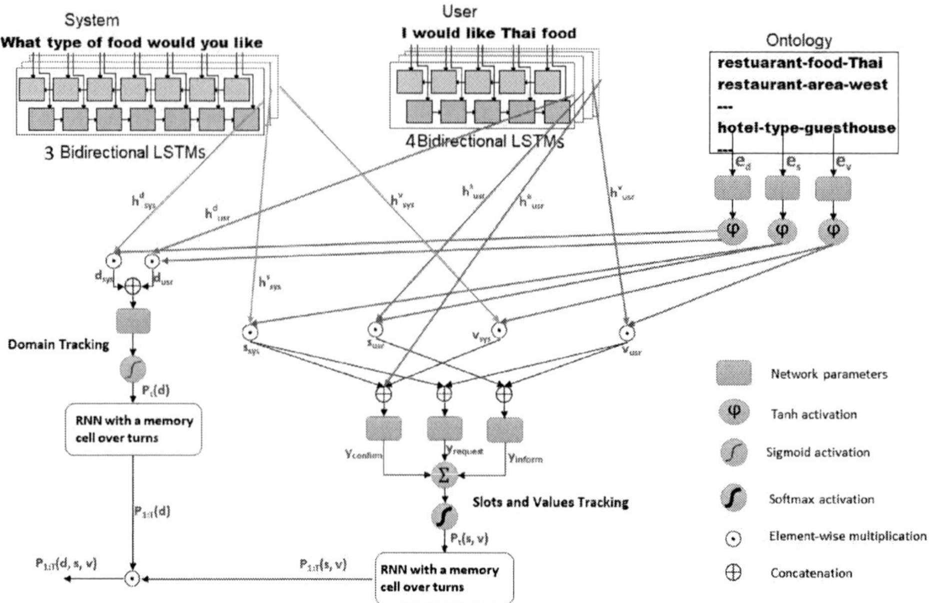

Figure 1: The proposed model architecture, using Bi-LSTMs as encoders. Other variants of the model use CNNs as feature extractors (Kim, 2014; Kalchbrenner et al., 2014).

4.1 Domain Tracking

Figure 1 presents the system architecture with two bi-directional LSTM networks as information encoders running over the word embeddings of the user and system utterances. The last hidden states of the forward and backward layers are concatenated to produce $\mathbf{h}_{usr}^d$, $\mathbf{h}_{sys}^d$ of size L for the user and system utterances respectively. In the second variant of the model, CNNs are used to produce these vectors (Kim, 2014; Kalchbrenner et al., 2014). To detect the presence of the domain in the dialogue turn, element-wise multiplication is used as a similarity metric between the hidden states and the ontology embeddings of the domain:

$$\mathbf{d}_k = \mathbf{h}_k^d \odot \tanh(\mathbf{W}_d\,\mathbf{e}_d + \mathbf{b}_d),$$

where $k \in \{usr, sys\}$, $\mathbf{e}_d$ is the embedding vector of the domain and $\mathbf{W}_d \in \mathcal{R}^{L \times D}$ transforms the domain word embeddings of dimension D to the hidden representation. The information about semantic similarity is held by $\mathbf{d}_{usr}$ and $\mathbf{d}_{sys}$, which are fed to a non-linear layer to output a binary decision:

$$\mathcal{P}_t(d) = \sigma(\mathbf{w}_d\,\{\mathbf{d}_{usr} \oplus \mathbf{d}_{sys}\} + b_d),$$

where $\mathbf{w}_d \in \mathcal{R}^{2L}$ and b_d are learnable parameters that map the semantic similarity to a belief state probability $\mathcal{P}_t(d)$ of a domain d at a turn t.

4.2 Candidate Slots and Values Tracking

Slots and values are tracked using a similar architecture as for domain tracking (Figure 1). However, to correctly model the context of the system-user dialogue at each turn, three different cases are considered when computing the similarity vectors:

1. **Inform:** The user is informing the system about his/her goal, e.g. *'I am looking for a restaurant that serves Turkish food'*.

2. **Request:** The system is requesting information by asking the user about the value of a specific slot. If the system utterance is: *'When do you want the taxi to arrive?'* and the user answers with *'19:30'*.

3. **Confirm:** The system wants to confirm information about the value of a specific slot. If the system asked: *'Would you like free parking?'*, the user can either affirm positively or negatively. The model detects the user affirmation, using a separate bi-directional LSTM or CNN to output $\mathbf{h}_{usr}^a$.

The three cases are modelled as following:

$$y_{inf}^{s,v} = \mathbf{w}_{inf}\,\{\mathbf{s}_{usr} \oplus \mathbf{v}_{usr}\} + b_{inf},$$
$$y_{req}^{s,v} = \mathbf{w}_{req}\,\{\mathbf{s}_{sys} \oplus \mathbf{v}_{usr}\} + b_{req},$$
$$y_{af}^{s,v} = \mathbf{w}_{af}\,\{\mathbf{s}_{sys} \oplus \mathbf{v}_{sys} \oplus \mathbf{h}_{usr}^a\} + b_{af},$$

434

where $\mathbf{s}_k, \mathbf{v}_k$ for $k \in \{usr, sys\}$ represent semantic similarity between the user and system utterances and the ontology slot and value terms respectively computed as shown in Figure 1, and $\mathbf{w}$ and b are learnable parameters.

The distribution over the values of slot s in domain d at turn t can be computed by summing the unscaled states, y_{inf}, y_{req} and y_{af} for each value v in s, and applying a softmax to normalize the distribution:

$$\mathcal{P}_t(s, v) = \text{softmax}(y_{inf}^{s,v} + y_{req}^{s,v} + y_{af}^{s,v}).$$

4.3 Belief State Update

Since dialogue systems in the real-world operate in noisy environments, a robust BT should utilize the flow of the conversation to reduce the uncertainty in the belief state distribution. This can be achieved by passing the output of the decision maker, at each turn, as an input to an RNN that runs over the dialogue turns as shown in Figure 1, which allows the gradients to be propagated across turns. This alleviates the problem of tuning hyper-parameters for rule-based updates. To avoid the vanishing gradient problem, three networks were tested: a simple RNN, an RNN with a memory cell (Henderson et al., 2014a) and a LSTM. The RNN with a memory cell proved to give the best results. In addition to the fact that it reduces the vanishing gradient problem, this variant is less complex than an LSTM, which makes training easier. Furthermore, a variant of RNN used for domain tracking has all its weights of the form: $\mathbf{W}_i = \alpha_i \mathbf{I}$, where α_i is a distinct learnable parameter for hidden, memory and previous state layers and $\mathbf{I}$ is the identity matrix. Similarly, weights of the RNN used to track the slots and values is of the form: $\mathbf{W}_j = \gamma_j \mathbf{I} + \lambda_j (\mathbf{1} - \mathbf{I})$, where γ_j and λ_j are the learnable parameters. These two variants of RNN are a combination of Henderson et al. (2014a) and Mrkvsić and Vulić (2018) previous works. The output is $\mathcal{P}_{1:T}(\mathbf{d})$ and $\mathcal{P}_{1:T}(\mathbf{s}, \mathbf{v})$, which represents the joint probability distribution of the domains and slots and values respectively over the complete dialogue. Combining these together produces the full belief state distribution of the dialogue:

$$\mathcal{P}_{1:T}(\mathbf{d}, \mathbf{s}, \mathbf{v}) = \mathcal{P}_{1:T}(\mathbf{d})\mathcal{P}_{1:T}(\mathbf{s}, \mathbf{v}).$$

4.4 Training Criteria

Domain tracking and slots and values tracking are trained disjointly. Belief state labels for each turn are split into domains and slots and values. Thanks to the disjoint training, the learning of slot and value belief states are not restricted to a specific domain. Therefore, the model shares the knowledge of slots and values across different domains. The loss function for the domain tracking is:

$$\mathcal{L}_d = - \sum_{n=1}^{N} \sum_{\mathbf{d} \in \mathcal{D}} t^n(\mathbf{d})\log\mathcal{P}_{1:T}^n(\mathbf{d}),$$

where $\mathbf{d}$ is a vector of domains over the dialogue, $t^n(\mathbf{d})$ is the domain label for the dialogue n and N is the number of dialogues. Similarly, the loss function for the slots and values tracking is:

$$\mathcal{L}_{s,v} = - \sum_{n=1}^{N} \sum_{\mathbf{s}, \mathbf{v} \in \mathcal{S}, \mathcal{V}} t^n(\mathbf{s}, \mathbf{v})\log\mathcal{P}_{1:T}^n(\mathbf{s}, \mathbf{v}),$$

where $\mathbf{s}$ and $\mathbf{v}$ are vectors of slots and values over the dialogue and $t^n(\mathbf{s}, \mathbf{v})$ is the joint label vector for the dialogue n.

5 Datasets and Baselines

Neural approaches to statistical dialogue development, especially in a task-oriented paradigm, are greatly hindered by the lack of large scale datasets. That is why, following the Wizard-of-Oz (WOZ) approach (Kelley, 1984; Wen et al., 2017), we ran text-based multi-domain corpus data collection scheme through Amazon MTurk. The main goal of the data collection was to acquire human-human conversations between a tourist visiting a city and a clerk from an information center. At the beginning of each dialogue the user (visitor) was given explicit instructions about the goal to fulfill, which often spanned multiple domains. The task of the system (wizard) is to assist a visitor having an access to databases over domains. The WOZ paradigm allowed us to obtain natural and semantically rich multi-topic dialogues spanning over multiple domains such as hotels, attractions, restaurants, booking trains or taxis. The dialogues cover from 1 up to 5 domains per dialogue greatly varying in length and complexity.

5.1 Data Structure

The data consists of 2480 single-domain dialogues and 7375 multi-domain dialogues usually spanning from 2 up to 5 domains. Some domains consists also of sub-domains like booking. The average sentence lengths are 11.63 and 15.01 for users

	WOZ 2.0			New WOZ (only restaurants)		
Slot	**NBT-CNN**	**Bi-LSTM**	**CNN**	**NBT-CNN**	**Bi-LSTM**	**CNN**
Food	88.9	96.1	**96.4**	78.3	84.7	**85.3**
Price range	93.7	**98.0**	97.9	92.6	**95.6**	93.6
Area	94.3	97.8	**98.1**	78.3	82.6	**86.4**
Joint goals	84.2	85.1	**85.5**	57.7	59.9	**63.7**

Table 1: WOZ 2.0 and new dataset test set accuracies of the NBT-CNN and the two variants of the proposed model, for slots *food, price range, area* and *joint goals*.

and wizards respectively. The combined ontology consists of 5 domains, 27 slots and 663 values making it significantly larger than observed in other datasets. To enforce reproducibility of results, we distribute the corpus with a pre-specified train/test/development random split. The test and development sets contain 1k examples each. Each dialogues consists of a goal, user and system utterances and a belief state per turn. The data and model is publicly available.[1]

5.2 Evaluation

We also used the extended WOZ 2.0 dataset (Wen et al., 2017).[2] WOZ2 dataset consists of 1200 single topic dialogues constrained to the restaurant domain. All the weights were initialised using normal distribution of zero mean and unit variance and biases were initialised to zero. ADAM optimizer (Kingma and Ba, 2014) (with 64 batch size) is used to train all the models for 600 epochs. Dropout (Srivastava et al., 2014) was used for regularisation (50% dropout rate on all the intermediate representations). For each of the two datasets we compare our proposed architecture (using either Bi-LSTM or CNN as encoders) to the NBT model[3] (Mrkšić et al., 2017).

6 Results

Table 1 shows the performance of our model in tracking the belief state of single-domain dialogues, compared to the NBT-CNN variant of the NBT discussed in Section 3.1. Our model outperforms NBT in all the three slots and the joint goals for the two datasets. NBT previously achieved state-of-the-art results (Mrkšić et al., 2017). Moreover, the performance of all models is worse on the new dataset for restaurant compared to WOZ 2.0.

New WOZ (multi-domain)		
Model	**F1 score**	**Accuracy %**
Uniform Sampling	0.108	10.8
Bi-LSTM	0.876	**93.7**
CNN	**0.878**	93.2

Table 2: The overall F1 score and accuracy for the multi-domain dialogues test set.[4]

This is because the dialogues in the new dataset are richer and more noisier, as a closer resemblance to real environment dialogues.

Table 2 presents the results on multi-domain dialogues from the new dataset described in Section 5. To demonstrate the difficulty of the multi-domain belief tracking problem, values of a theoretical baseline that samples the belief state uniformly at random are also presented. Our model gracefully handles such a difficult task. In most of the cases, CNNs demonstrate better performance than Bi-LSTMs. We hypothesize that this comes from the effectiveness of extracting local and position-invariant features, which are crucial for semantic similarities (Yin et al., 2017).

7 Conclusions

In this paper, we proposed a new approach that tackles the issue of multi-domain belief tracking, such as model parameter scalability with the ontology size. Our model shows improved performance in single-domain tasks compared to the state-of-the-art NBT method. By exploiting semantic similarities between dialogue utterances and ontology terms, the model alleviates the need for ontology-dependent parameters and maximizes the amount of information shared between slots and across domains. In future, we intend to investigate introducing new domains and ontology terms without further training thus performing zero-shot learning.

---

[1] http://dialogue.mi.eng.cam.ac.uk/index.php/corpus/

[2] Publicly available at `https://mi.eng.cam.ac.uk/~nm480/woz_2.0.zip`.

[3] Publicly available at `https://github.com/nmrksic/neural-belief-tracker`.

[4] F1-score is computed by considering all the values in each slot of each domain as positive and the "none" state of the slot as negative.

Acknowledgments

The authors would like to thank Nikola Mrkšić, Jacquie Rowe, the Cambridge Dialogue Systems Group and the ACL reviewers for their constructive feedback. Paweł Budzianowski is supported by EPSRC Council and Toshiba Research Europe Ltd, Cambridge Research Laboratory. The data collection was funded through Google Faculty Award.

References

Alex Graves and Jürgen Schmidhuber. 2005. Framewise phoneme classification with bidirectional lstm and other neural network architectures. *Neural Networks* 18(5-6):602–610.

Matthew Henderson, Blaise Thomson, and Steve Young. 2014a. Robust dialog state tracking using delexicalised recurrent neural networks and unsupervised adaptation. In *Spoken Language Technology Workshop (SLT), 2014 IEEE*. IEEE, pages 360–365.

Matthew Henderson, Blaise Thomson, and Steve Young. 2014b. Word-based dialog state tracking with recurrent neural networks. In *Proceedings of the 15th Annual Meeting of the Special Interest Group on Discourse and Dialogue (SIGDIAL)*. pages 292–299.

Nal Kalchbrenner, Edward Grefenstette, and Phil Blunsom. 2014. A convolutional neural network for modelling sentences. *In Proceedings of ACL* .

John F Kelley. 1984. An iterative design methodology for user-friendly natural language office information applications. *ACM Transactions on Information Systems (TOIS)* 2(1):26–41.

Yoon Kim. 2014. Convolutional neural networks for sentence classification. *In Proceedings of EMNLP* .

Diederik P Kingma and Jimmy Ba. 2014. Adam: A method for stochastic optimization. *ICLR* .

Nikola Mrkšić, Diarmuid Ó Séaghdha, Tsung-Hsien Wen, Blaise Thomson, and Steve Young. 2017. Neural belief tracker: Data-driven dialogue state tracking. In *Proceedings of the 55th Annual Meeting of the Association for Computational Linguistics (Volume 1: Long Papers)*. volume 1, pages 1777–1788.

Nikola Mrkvsić and Ivan Vulić. 2018. Fully statistical neural belief tracking. In *Proceedings of ACL*.

Julien Perez and Fei Liu. 2016. Dialog state tracking, a machine reading approach using memory network. *arXiv preprint arXiv:1606.04052* .

Abhinav Rastogi, Dilek Hakkani-Tur, and Larry Heck. 2017. Scalable multi-domain dialogue state tracking. *arXiv preprint arXiv:1712.10224* .

Nitish Srivastava, Geoffrey Hinton, Alex Krizhevsky, Ilya Sutskever, and Ruslan Salakhutdinov. 2014. Dropout: A simple way to prevent neural networks from overfitting. *Journal of Machine Learning Research* 15:1929–1958.

Zhuoran Wang and Oliver Lemon. 2013. A simple and generic belief tracking mechanism for the dialog state tracking challenge: On the believability of observed information. In *Proceedings of the SIGDIAL 2013 Conference*. pages 423–432.

Tsung-Hsien Wen, Milica Gašić, Nikola Mrkšić, Lina M. Rojas-Barahona, Pei-Hao Su, Stefan Ultes, David Vandyke, and Steve Young. 2017. A network-based end-to-end trainable task-oriented dialogue system. *In Proceedings on EACL* .

John Wieting, Mohit Bansal, Kevin Gimpel, Karen Livescu, and Dan Roth. 2015. From paraphrase database to compositional paraphrase model and back. *Transactions of the Association for Computational Linguistics* 3:345–358.

Jason Williams, Antoine Raux, and Matthew Henderson. 2016. The dialog state tracking challenge series: A review. *Dialogue & Discourse* 7(3):4–33.

Jason D Williams. 2014. Web-style ranking and slu combination for dialog state tracking. In *Proceedings of the 15th Annual Meeting of the Special Interest Group on Discourse and Dialogue (SIGDIAL)*. pages 282–291.

Wenpeng Yin, Katharina Kann, Mo Yu, and Hinrich Schütze. 2017. Comparative study of cnn and rnn for natural language processing. *arXiv preprint arXiv:1702.01923* .

Steve Young, Milica Gašić, Simon Keizer, François Mairesse, Jost Schatzmann, Blaise Thomson, and Kai Yu. 2010. The hidden information state model: A practical framework for pomdp-based spoken dialogue management. *Computer Speech & Language* 24(2):150–174.

Lukas Zilka and Filip Jurcicek. 2015. Incremental lstm-based dialog state tracker. In *Automatic Speech Recognition and Understanding (ASRU), 2015 IEEE Workshop on*. IEEE, pages 757–762.

Modeling Discourse Cohesion for Discourse Parsing via Memory Network

Yanyan Jia, Yuan Ye, Yansong Feng, Yuxuan Lai, Rui Yan and **Dongyan Zhao**
Institute of Computer Science and Technology, Peking University
The MOE Key Laboratory of Computational Linguistics, Peking University
{jiayanyan,pkuyeyuan,fengyansong,erutan,ruiyan,zhaody}@pku.edu.cn

Abstract

Identifying long-span dependencies between discourse units is crucial to improve discourse parsing performance. Most existing approaches design sophisticated features or exploit various off-the-shelf tools, but achieve little success. In this paper, we propose a new transition-based discourse parser that makes use of memory networks to take discourse cohesion into account. The automatically captured discourse cohesion benefits discourse parsing, especially for long span scenarios. Experiments on the RST discourse treebank show that our method outperforms traditional featured based methods, and the memory based discourse cohesion can improve the overall parsing performance significantly [1].

1 Introduction

Discourse parsing aims to identify the structure and relationship between different element discourse units (EDUs). As a fundamental topic in natural language processing, discourse parsing can assist many down-stream applications such as summarization (Louis et al., 2010), sentiment analysis (Polanyi and van den Berg, 2011) and question-answering (Ferrucci et al., 2010). However, the performance of discourse parsing is still far from perfect, especially for EDUs that are distant to each other in the discourse. In fact, as found in (Jia et al., 2018), the discourse parsing performance drops quickly as the dependency span increases. The reason may be twofold:

Firstly, as discussed in previous works (Joty et al., 2013), it is important to address discourse structure characteristics, e.g., through modeling lexical chains in a discourse, for discourse parsing, especially in dealing with long span scenarios. However, most existing approaches mainly focus on studying the semantic and syntactic aspects of EDU pairs, in a more local view. Discourse cohesion reflects the syntactic or semantic relationship between words or phrases in a discourse, and, to some extent, can indicate the topic changing or threads in a discourse. Discourse cohesion includes five situations, including reference, substitution, ellipsis, conjunction and lexical cohesion (Halliday and Hasan, 1989). Here, lexical cohesion reflects the semantic relationship of words, and can be modeled as the recurrence of words, synonym and contextual words.

However, previous works do not well model the discourse cohesion within the discourse parsing task, or do not even take this issue into account. Morris and Hirst (1991) proposes to utilize Roget thesauri to form lexical chains (sequences of semantically related words that can reflect the topic shifts within a discourse), which are used to extract features to characterize discourse structures. (Joty et al., 2013) uses lexical chain feature to model multi-sentential relation. Actually, these simplified cohesion features can already improve parsing performance, especially in long spans.

Secondly, in modern neural network methods, modeling discourse cohesion as part of the networks is not a trivial task. One can still use off-the-shell tools to obtain lexical chains, but these tools can not be jointly optimized with the main neural network parser. We argue that characterizing discourse cohesion implicitly within a unified framework would be more

---

[1] Code for replicating our experiments is available at https://github.com/PKUYeYuan/ACL2018_CFDP.

438

Proceedings of the 56th Annual Meeting of the Association for Computational Linguistics (Short Papers), pages 438–443
Melbourne, Australia, July 15 - 20, 2018. ©2018 Association for Computational Linguistics

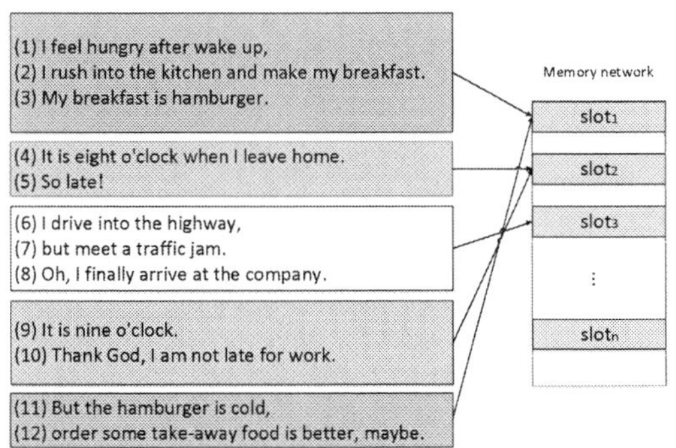

Figure 1: An illustration for modelling discourse cohesion with memory network. The example discourse includes 12 EDUs and talks about 3 different threads (food, time and traffic), which are colored by blue, gray and white, respectively.

straightforward and effective for our neural network based parser. As shown in Figure 1, the 12 EDUs in the given discourse talk about different topics, marked with 3 different colors, which could be captured by a memory network that maintains several memory slots. In discourse parsing, such an architecture may help to cluster topically similar or related EDUs into the same memory slot, and each slot could be considered as a representation that maintains a specific topic or thread within the current discourse. Intuitively, we could also treat such a mechanism as a way to capture the cohesion characteristics of the discourse, just like the lexical chain features used in previous works, but without relying on external tools or resources.

In this paper, we investigate how to exploit discourse cohesion to improve discourse parsing. Our contribution includes: 1) we design a memory network method to capture discourse cohesion implicitly in order to improve discourse parsing. 2) We choose bidirectional long-short term memory (LSTM) (Hochreiter and Schmidhuber, 1997) with an attention mechanism to represent EDUs directly from embeddings, and use simple position features to capture shallow discourse structures, without relying on off-the-shelf tools or resources. Experiments on the RST corpus show that the memory based discourse cohesion model can help better capture discourse structure information and lead to significant improvement over traditional feature based discourse parsing methods.

2 Model overview

Our parser is an arc-eager style transition system (Nivre, 2003) with 2 stacks and a queue as shown in Figure 2, which is similar in spirit with (Dyer et al., 2015; Ballesteros et al., 2015). We follow the conventional data structures in transition-based dependency parsing, i.e., a queue (B) of EDUs to be processed, a stack (S) to store the partially constructed discourse trees, and a stack (A) to represent the history of transitions (actions combined with discourse relations).

In our parser, the transition actions include *Shift*, *Reduce*, *Left-arc* and *Right-arc*. At each step, the parser chooses to take one of the four actions and pushes the selected transition into A. *Shift* pushes the first EDU in queue B to the top of the stack S, while *Reduce* pops the top item of S. *Left-arc* connects the first EDU (head) in B to the top EDU (dependent) in S and then pops the top item of S, while *Right-arc* connects the top EDU (head) of S to the first EDU (dependent) in B and then pushes B's first EDU to the top of S. A parse tree can be finally constructed until B is empty and S only contains a complete discourse tree. For more details, please refer to (Nivre, 2003).

As shown in Figure 2, at time t, we characterize the current parsing process by preserving the top two elements in B, top three elements in A and the root EDU in the partially constructed tree at the top of S. We first concatenate the embeddings of the preserved elements in each data structure to obtain the embeddings of S, B and A. We then append the three representations with the $position_2$ features (introduced in Section 2.1), respectively. We pass them through one ReLU layer and two fully connected layers with ReLU as their activation functions to obtain the final state representation p_t at time t, which will be used to determine the best transition to take at t.

Next, we apply an affine transformation to p_t and feed it to a softmax layer to get the distribution over all possible decisions (actions combined with discourse relations). We train our model using the automatically generated oracle action sequences as the gold-standard annotations, and utilize cross entropy as the loss function. We perform greedy search during decoding.

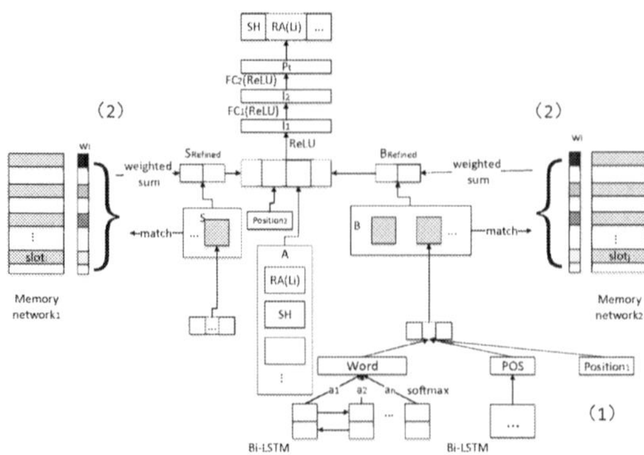

Figure 2: Our discourse parsing framework: (1) Basic EDU representation module; (2) Memory networks to capture the discourse cohesion so as to obtain the refined representations of S and B. RA(Li) means that the chosen action is *Right-arc* and its relation is *List*. SH means *Shift*. a_1 to a_n are weights for the attention mechanism of the bidirectional LSTM.

2.1 Discourse Structures

As mentioned in previous work (Jia et al., 2018), when the top EDUs in S and B are far from each other in the discourse, i.e., with a long span, the parser will be prone to making wrong decisions. To deal with these long-span cases, one should take discourse structures into account, e.g., extracting features from the structure of a long discourse or analyzing and characterizing different topics discussed in the discourse.

We, therefore, choose two kinds of position features to reflect the structure information, which can be viewed as a shallow form of discourse cohesion. The first one describes the position of an EDU alone, while the second represents the spatial relationship between the top EDUs of S and B. (1) $Position_1$: the positions of the EDU in the sentence, paragraph and discourse, respectively. (2) $Position_2$: whether the top EDUs of S and B are in the same sentence/paragraph or not, and the distance between them.

3 Memory based Discourse Cohesion

Basic EDU representation: In our model, the EDUs in both S and B follow the same representation method, and we take an EDU in B as an example as shown in Figure 2. The basic representation for an EDU is built by concatenating three components, i.e., *word*, *POS* and $Position_1$. Regarding *word*, we feed the

sequence of words in the EDU to a bi-directional Long Short Term Memory (LSTM) with attention mechanism and obtain the final *word* representation by concatenating the two final outputs from both directions. Here, we use pre-trained Glove (Pennington et al., 2014) as the word embeddings. We get the POS tags from Stanford CoreNLP toolkit (Manning et al., 2014), and similarly, send the POS tag sequence of the EDU to a bi-directional LSTM with attention mechanism to obtain the final *POS* representation. For concise, we omit the bi-directional LSTM network structure for *POS* in Figure 2, which is the same as the one for *word*. The $Position_1$ feature vectors are randomly initialized and we expect them to work as a proxy to capture the shallow discourse structure information.

Memory Refined Representation: Besides the shallow structure features, we design a memory network component to cluster EDUs with similar topics to the same memory slot to alleviate the long span issues, as illustrated in Figure 1. We expect these memory slots can work as lexical chains, which can maintain different threads within the discourse. Such a memory mechanism has the advantage that it can perform the clustering automatically and does not rely on extra tools or resources to train.

Concretely, we match the representations of S and B with their corresponding memory networks, respectively, to get their discourse cohesion clues, which are used to improve the original representations. Take B as an example, we first compute the similarity between the representation of B (V_b) and each memory slot m_i in B's memory. We adopt the cosine similarity as our metric as below:

$$Sim[x, y] = \frac{x \cdot y}{\|x\| \cdot \|y\|} \quad (1)$$

Then, we use this cosine similarity to produce a normalized weight w_i for each memory slot. We introduce a strength factor λ to improve the focus.

$$w_i = \frac{\exp(\lambda Sim[V_b, m_i])}{\sum_j \exp(\lambda Sim[V_b, m_j])} \quad (2)$$

Finally, we get the discourse cohesion clue of B (denoted by B_{Coh}) from its memory according to the weighted sum of m_i.

$$B_{Coh} = \sum_i w_i m_i \quad (3)$$

We concatenate B_{Coh} (the discourse cohesion clue of B) and the original embedding of B to get the refined representation $B_{refined}$ for B. Similarly, we concatenate S_{Coh} and the embedding of S to get the refined representation $S_{refined}$ for S, as shown in Figure 2. In our experiments, each memory contains 20 slots, which are randomly initialized and optimized during training.

4 Evaluation and Results

Dataset: We use the RST Discourse Treebank (Carlson et al., 2001) with the same split as in (Li et al., 2014), i.e., 312 for training, 30 for development and 38 for testing. We experiment with two set of relations, the 111 types of fine-grained relations and the 19 types of coarse-grained relations, respectively.

Evaluation Metrics: In the Rhetorical Structure Theory (RST) (Mann and Thompson, 1988), *head* is the core of a discourse, and a *dependent* gives supporting evidence to its head with certain relationship. We adopt unlabeled accuracy UAS (the ratio of EDUs that correctly identify their heads) and labeled accuracy LAS (the ratio of EDUs that have both correct heads and relations) as our evaluation metrics.

Baselines: We compare our method with the following baselines and models: (1) **Perceptron**: We re-implement the perceptron based arc-eager style dependency discourse parser as mentioned in (Jia et al., 2018) with coarse-grained relation. The **Perceptron** model chooses words, POS tags, positions and length features, totally 100 feature templates, with the *early update* strategy (Collins and Roark, 2004). (2) **Jia18**: Jia et al. (2018) implement a transition-based discourse parser with stacked LSTM, where they choose a two-layer LSTM to represent EDUs by encoding four kinds of features including words, POS tags, positions and length features. (3) Basic EDU representation (**Basic**): Our discourse parser with the basic EDU representation method mentioned in Section 3. (4) Memory refined representation (**Refined**): Our full parser equipped with the basic EDU representation method and the memory networks to capture the discourse cohesion mentioned in Section 3. (5) **MST-full** (Li et al., 2014): a graph-based dependency discourse parser with carefully selected 6 sets of features including words, POS tags, positions,

length, syntactic and semantic similarity features, which achieves the state-of-art performance on the RST Treebank.

4.1 Results

We list the overall discourse parsing performance in Table 1. Here, **Jia18**, a stack LSTM based method (Jia et al., 2018), outperforms the traditional **Perceptron** method, but falls behind our **Basic** model with *word*, *POS* tags and *Position* features. The reason may be that representing EDUs directly from the sequence of word/POS embeddings could probably capture the semantic meaning of EDUs, which is especially useful for taking into account synonyms or paraphrases that often confuse traditional feature-based methods. We can also see that **Basic**(word+pos+position) significantly outperforms **Basic**(word+pos), as the *Position* features may play a crucial role in providing useful structural clues to our parser. Such position information can also be considered as a shallow treatment to capture the discourse cohesion, especially for long span scenarios. When using the memory network, our **Refined** method achieves better performance than the **Basic**(word+pos+position) in both UAS and LAS. The reason may come from the ability of the memory networks in simulating the lexical chains within a discourse, where the memory networks can model the discourse cohesion so as to provide topical or structural clues to our parser. We use SIGF V2 (Padó, 2006) to perform significance test for the discussed models. We find that the **Basic**(word+pos+position) method significantly outperforms (Jia et al., 2018), and our **Refined** model performs significantly better than **Basic**(word+pos+position) (with $p < 0.1$).

However, when compared with **MST-full** (Li et al., 2014), our models still fall behind this state-of-the-art method. The main reason might be that **MST-full** follows a global graph-based dependency parsing framework, where their high order methods (in cubic time complexity) can directly analyze the relationship between any EDUs pairs in the discourse, while, we choose the transition-based local method with linear time complexity, which can only investigate the top EDUs in S and B according to the selected actions, thus usually has a lower performance than the global graph-based methods, but with a lower (linear) time complexity. On the other hand, the neural network components help us maintain much fewer features than **MST-full**, which carefully selects 6 different sets of features that are usually obtained using extra tools and resources. And, the neural network design is flexible enough to incorporate various clues into a uniform framework, just like how we introduce the memory networks as a proxy to capture discourse cohesion.

In the RST corpus, when the distance between two EDUs is larger, there are usually fewer numbers of such EDU pairs, but the parsing performance for those long span cases drops more significantly. For example, the LAS is even lower than 5% for those dependencies that have a range of 6 EDUs. We take a detailed look at the parsing performance for dependencies at different lengths (from 1 to 6 as an example) using coarse-grained relations. As shown in Table 2, compared with the **Basic** method, both UAS and LAS of the **Refined** method are improved significantly in almost all spans, where we observe more prominent improvement for the UAS in larger spans such as **span 5** and *span 6*, with about 8.70% and 6.38%, respectively.

Method	UAS	LAS (Fine)	LAS (Coarse)
Perceptron	0.5422	0.3231	0.3777
Jia18	0.5852	0.3286	0.4037
Basic (word+pos)	0.5588	0.367	0.3985
Basic (word+pos+position)	0.5933	0.3832	0.4305
Refined (20 slots)	0.6197	0.3947	0.4445
MST-full	0.7331	0.4309	0.4851

Table 1: Overall discourse parsing performance in the RST dataset.

span (count)	Basic(word+pos+position)		Refined (20)	
	UAS	LAS	UAS	LAS
1(1225)	0.7796	0.618	**0.8261**	**0.6261**
2 (405)	**0.6198**	0.4	0.6025	**0.4124**
3 (212)	0.434	0.2217	**0.4576**	**0.2642**
4 (125)	0.256	0.112	**0.296**	**0.128**
5 (69)	0.1739	0.0725	**0.2609**	**0.1015**
6 (47)	0.1064	0.0426	**0.1702**	**0.0638**

Table 2: Performance in different discourse spans.

Finally, let us take a detailed comparison between **Refined** and **Basic** to investigate the advantages of capturing discourse cohesion. Note that, our **Refined** method wins **Basic** in almost all relations. Here, we discuss one typical relation *List*, which often indicates a long span dependency between a pair of EDUs. In the test set of RST, the average span for *List* is 7.55, with the max span of 69. Our **Refined** can successfully identify 55 of them, with an average span of 9.02 and the largest one of 63, while, the **Basic** method can only identify 41 edges labeled with *List*, which are mostly shorter cases, with an average span of 1.32 and the largest one of 5. More detailedly, there are 18 edges that are correctly identified by our **Refined** but missed by the **Basic** method. The average span of those dependencies is 25.39. It is easy to find that without further considerations in discourse structures, the **Basic** method has limited ability in correctly identifying longer span dependencies. And those comparisons prove again that our **Refined** can take better advantage of modeling discourse cohesion, which enables our model to perform better in long span scenarios.

5 Conclusions

In this paper, we propose to utilize memory networks to model discourse cohesion automatically. By doing so we could capture the topic change or threads within a discourse, which can further improve the discourse parsing performance, especially for long span scenarios. Experimental results on the RST Discourse Treebank show that our proposed method can characterize the discourse cohesion efficiently and archive significant improvement over traditional feature based discourse parsing methods.

Acknowledgments

We would like to thank our anonymous reviewers, Bingfeng Luo, and Sujian Li for their helpful comments and suggestions, which greatly improved our work. This work is supported by National High Technology R&D Program of China (Grant No.2015AA015403), and Natural Science Foundation of China (Grant No. 61672057, 61672058). For any correspondence, please contact Yansong Feng.

References

Miguel Ballesteros, Chris Dyer, and Noah A. Smith. 2015. Improved transition-based parsing by modeling characters instead of words with lstms. In *Proceedings of the 2015 Conference on Empirical Methods in Natural Language Processing, EMNLP 2015, Lisbon,*

Portugal, September 17-21, 2015. pages 349–359. http://aclweb.org/anthology/D/D15/D15-1041.pdf.

Lynn Carlson, Daniel Marcu, and Mary Ellen Okurovsky. 2001. Building a discourse-tagged corpus in the framework of rhetorical structure theory. In *Proceedings of the SIGDIAL 2001 Workshop, The 2nd Annual Meeting of the Special Interest Group on Discourse and Dialogue, Saturday, September 1, 2001 to Sunday, September 2, 2001, Aalborg, Denmark.* http://aclweb.org/anthology/W/W01/W01-1605.pdf.

Michael Collins and Brian Roark. 2004. Incremental parsing with the perceptron algorithm. In *Proceedings of the 42nd Annual Meeting of the Association for Computational Linguistics, 21-26 July, 2004, Barcelona, Spain..* pages 111–118. http://aclweb.org/anthology/P/P04/P04-1015.pdf.

Chris Dyer, Miguel Ballesteros, Wang Ling, Austin Matthews, and Noah A. Smith. 2015. Transition-based dependency parsing with stack long short-term memory. In *Proceedings of the 53rd Annual Meeting of the Association for Computational Linguistics and the 7th International Joint Conference on Natural Language Processing of the Asian Federation of Natural Language Processing, ACL 2015, July 26-31, 2015, Beijing, China, Volume 1: Long Papers.* pages 334–343. http://aclweb.org/anthology/P/P15/P15-1033.pdf.

David A. Ferrucci, Eric W. Brown, Jennifer Chu-Carroll, James Fan, David Gondek, Aditya Kalyanpur, Adam Lally, J. William Murdock, Eric Nyberg, John M. Prager, Nico Schlaefer, and Christopher A. Welty. 2010. Building watson: An overview of the deepqa project. *AI Magazine* 31(3):59–79. http://www.aaai.org/ojs/index.php/aimagazine/article/view/2303.

M.A.K. Halliday and Ruqaiya Hasan. 1989. *Language, Context, and Text: Aspects of Language in a Social-Semiotic Perspective.*

Sepp Hochreiter and Jürgen Schmidhuber. 1997. Long short-term memory. *Neural Computation* 9(8):1735–1780. https://doi.org/10.1162/neco.1997.9.8.1735.

Yanyan Jia, Yansong Feng, Yuan Ye, Chao Lv, Chongde Shi, and Dongyan Zhao. 2018. Improved discourse parsing with two-step neural transition-based model. *ACM Trans. Asian & Low-Resource Lang. Inf. Process.* 17(2):11:1–11:21. https://doi.org/10.1145/3152537.

Shafiq R. Joty, Giuseppe Carenini, Raymond T. Ng, and Yashar Mehdad. 2013. Combining intra- and multi-sentential rhetorical parsing for document-level discourse analysis. In *Proceedings of the 51st Annual Meeting of the Association for Computational Linguistics,*

ACL 2013, 4-9 August 2013, Sofia, Bulgaria, Volume 1: Long Papers. pages 486–496. http://aclweb.org/anthology/P/P13/P13-1048.pdf.

Sujian Li, Liang Wang, Ziqiang Cao, and Wenjie Li. 2014. Text-level discourse dependency parsing. In *Proceedings of the 52nd Annual Meeting of the Association for Computational Linguistics, ACL 2014, June 22-27, 2014, Baltimore, MD, USA, Volume 1: Long Papers.* pages 25–35. http://aclweb.org/anthology/P/P14/P14-1003.pdf.

Annie Louis, Aravind K. Joshi, and Ani Nenkova. 2010. Discourse indicators for content selection in summarization. In *Proceedings of the SIGDIAL 2010 Conference, The 11th Annual Meeting of the Special Interest Group on Discourse and Dialogue, 24-15 September 2010, Tokyo, Japan.* pages 147–156. http://www.aclweb.org/anthology/W10-4327.

William C. Mann and Sandra A. Thompson. 1988. Rhetorical structure theory: Toward a functional theory of text organization. *Text - Interdisciplinary Journal for the Study of Discourse* 8(3):243–281.

Christopher D. Manning, Mihai Surdeanu, John Bauer, Jenny Rose Finkel, Steven Bethard, and David McClosky. 2014. The stanford corenlp natural language processing toolkit. In *Proceedings of the 52nd Annual Meeting of the Association for Computational Linguistics, ACL 2014, June 22-27, 2014, Baltimore, MD, USA, System Demonstrations.* pages 55–60. http://aclweb.org/anthology/P/P14/P14-5010.pdf.

Jane Morris and Graeme Hirst. 1991. Lexical cohesion computed by thesaural relations as an indicator of the structure of text. *Computational Linguistics* 17(1):21–48.

J Nivre. 2003. An efficient algorithm for projective dependency parsing. In *Iwpt-2003 : International Workshop on Parsing Technology.* pages 149–160.

Sebastian Padó. 2006. *User's guide to `sigf`: Significance testing by approximate randomisation.*

Jeffrey Pennington, Richard Socher, and Christopher D. Manning. 2014. Glove: Global vectors for word representation. In *Proceedings of the 2014 Conference on Empirical Methods in Natural Language Processing, EMNLP 2014, October 25-29, 2014, Doha, Qatar, A meeting of SIGDAT, a Special Interest Group of the ACL.* pages 1532–1543. http://aclweb.org/anthology/D/D14/D14-1162.pdf.

Livia Polanyi and Martin van den Berg. 2011. Discourse structure and sentiment. In *Data Mining Workshops (ICDMW), 2011 IEEE 11th International Conference on, Vancouver, BC, Canada, December 11, 2011.* pages 97–102. https://doi.org/10.1109/ICDMW.2011.67.

SciDTB: Discourse Dependency TreeBank for Scientific Abstracts

An Yang   **Sujian Li**[*]

Key Laboratory of Computational Linguistics, Peking University, MOE, China

{yangan, lisujian}@pku.edu.cn

Abstract

Annotation corpus for discourse relations benefits NLP tasks such as machine translation and question answering. In this paper, we present SciDTB, a domain-specific discourse treebank annotated on scientific articles. Different from widely-used RST-DT and PDTB, SciDTB uses dependency trees to represent discourse structure, which is flexible and simplified to some extent but do not sacrifice structural integrity. We discuss the labeling framework, annotation workflow and some statistics about SciDTB. Furthermore, our treebank is made as a benchmark for evaluating discourse dependency parsers, on which we provide several baselines as fundamental work.

1 Introduction

Discourse relation depicts how the text spans in a text relate to each other. These relations can be categorized into different types according to semantics, logic or writer's intention. Annotations of such discourse relations can benefit many down-stream NLP tasks including machine translation (Guzmán et al., 2014; Joty et al., 2014) and automatic summarization (Gerani et al., 2014).

Several discourse corpora have been proposed in previous work, grounded with various discourse theories. Among them Rhetorical Structure Theory TreeBank (RST-DT) (Carlson et al., 2003) and Penn Discourse TreeBank (PDTB) (Prasad et al., 2007) are the most widely-used resources. PDTB focuses on shallow discourse relations between two arguments and ignores the whole organization. RST-DT based on Rhetorical Structure Theory (RST) (Mann and Thompson, 1988) represents a text into a hierarchical discourse tree. Though RST-DT provides more comprehensive discourse information, its limitations including the introduction of intermediate nodes and absence of non-projective structures bring the annotation and parsing complexity.

Li et al. (2014) and Yoshida et al. (2014) both realized the problems of RST-DT and introduced dependency structures into discourse representation. Stede et al. (2016) adopted dependency tree format to compare RST structure and Segmented Discourse Representation Theory(SDRT) (Lascarides and Asher, 2008) structure for a corpus of short texts. Their discourse dependency framework is adapted from syntactic dependency structure (Hudson, 1984; Böhmová et al., 2003), with words replaced by elementary discourse units (EDUs). Binary discourse relations are represented from dominant EDU (called "head") to subordinate EDU (called "dependent"), which makes non-projective structure possible. However, Li et al. (2014) and Yoshida et al. (2014) mainly focused on the definition of discourse dependency structure and directly transformed constituency trees in RST-DT into dependency trees. On the one hand, they only simply treated the transformation ambiguity, while constituency structures and dependency structures did not correspond one-to-one. On the other hand, the transformed corpus still did not contain non-projective dependency trees, though "crossed dependencies" actually exist in the real flexible discourse structures (Wolf and Gibson, 2005). In such case, it is essential to construct a discourse dependency treebank from scratch instead of through automatically converting from the constituency structures.

In this paper, we construct the discourse dependency corpus SciDTB[1]. based on scientific abstracts, with the reference to the discourse de-

---

[1]The treebank is available at https://github.com/PKU-TANGENT/SciDTB

Proceedings of the 56th Annual Meeting of the Association for Computational Linguistics (Short Papers), pages 444–449
Melbourne, Australia, July 15 - 20, 2018. ©2018 Association for Computational Linguistics

pendency representation in Li et al. (2014). We choose scientific abstracts as the corpus for two reasons. First, we observe that when long news articles in RST-DT have several paragraphs, the discourse relations between paragraphs are very loose and their annotations are not so meaningful. Thus, short texts with obvious logics become our preference. Here, we choose scientific abstracts from ACL Anthology[2] which are usually composed of one passage and have strong logics. Second, we prefer to conduct domain-specific discourse annotation. RST-DT and PDTB are both constructed on news articles, which are unspecific in domain coverage. We choose the scientific domain that is more specific and can benefit further academic applications such as automatic summarization and translation. Furthermore, our treebank SciDTB can be made as a benchmark for evaluating discourse parsers. Three baselines are provided as fundamental work.

2 Annotation Framework

In this section, we describe two key aspects of our annotation framework, including elementary discourse units (EDU) and discourse relations.

2.1 Elementary Discourse Units

We first need to divide a passage into non-overlapping text spans, which are named elementary discourse units (EDUs). We follow the criterion of Polanyi (1988) and Irmer (2011) which treats clauses as EDUs.

However, since a discourse unit is a semantic concept but a clause is defined syntactically, in some cases segmentation by clauses is still not the most proper strategy. In practice, we refer to the guidelines defined by (Carlson and Marcu, 2001). For example, subjective clauses, objective clauses of non-attributive verbs and verb complement clauses are not segmented. Nominal postmodifiers with predicates are treated as EDUs. Strong discourse cues such as *"despite"* and *"because of"* starts a new EDU no matter they are followed by a clause or a phrase. We give an EDU segmentation example as follows.

1. *[Despite bilingual embeddings success,][**the contextual information**][which is of critical*

	Coarse	Fine
1.	ROOT	ROOT
2.	Attribution	Attribution
3.	Background	Related, Goal, General
4.	Cause-effect	Cause, Result
5.	Comparison	Comparison
6.	Condition	Condition
7.	Contrast	Contrast
8.	Elaboration	Addition, Aspect, Process-step, Definition, Enumerate, Example
9.	Enablement	Enablement
10.	Evaluation	Evaluation
11.	Explain	Evidence, Reason
12.	Joint	Joint
13.	Manner-means	Manner-means
14.	Progression	Progression
15.	Same-unit	Same-unit
16.	Summary	Summary
17.	Temporal	Temporal

Table 1: Discourse relation category of SciDTB.

*importance to translation quality,][**was ignored in previous work.**]*

It is noted, as in Example 1, there are EDUs which are broken into two parts (in bold) by relative clauses or nominal postmodifiers. Like RST, we connect the two parts by a pseudo-relation type *Same-unit* to represent their integrity.

2.2 Discourse Relations

A discourse relation is defined as tri-tuple (h, d, r), where h means the head EDU, d is the dependent EDU, and r defines the relation category between h and d. For a discourse relation, head EDU is defined as the unit with essential information and dependent EDU with supportive content. Here, we follow Carlson and Marcu (2001) to adopt deletion test in the determination of head and dependent. If one unit in a binary relation pair is deleted but the whole meaning can still be almost understood from the other unit, the deleted unit is treated as dependent and the other one as the head.

For the relation categories, we mainly refer to the work of (Carlson and Marcu, 2001) and (Bunt and Prasad, 2016). Table 1 presents the discourse relation set of SciDTB, which are not explained detailedly one by one due to space limitation. Through investigation of scientific abstracts, we define 17 coarse-grained relation types and 26 fine-grained relations for SciDTB.

It is noted that we make some modifications to adapt to the scientific domain. For example, In SciDTB, *Background* relation is divided into three

[2] http://www.aclweb.org/anthology/. SciDTB follows the same CC BY-NC-SA 3.0 and CC BY 4.0 licenses as ACL Anthology.

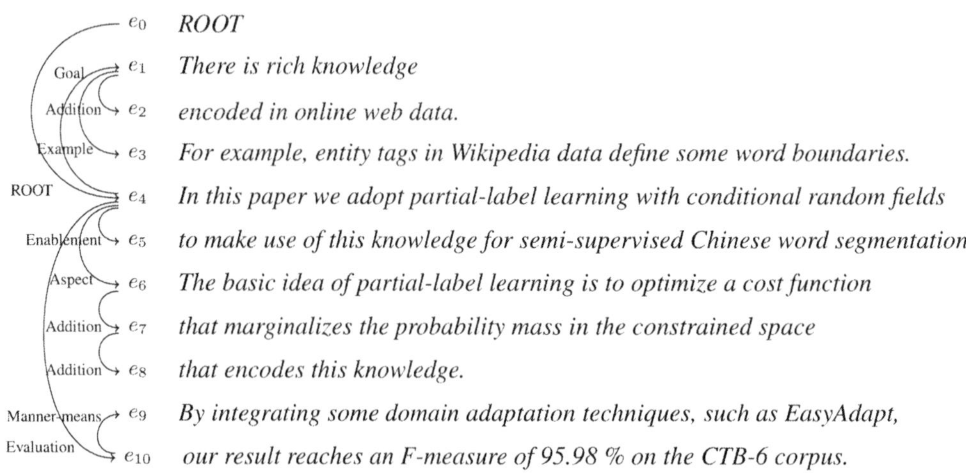

Figure 1: An example discourse dependency tree for an abstract in SciDTB.

subtypes: *Related*, *Goal* and *General*, because the background description in scientific abstracts usually has more different intents. Meanwhile, for *attribution* relation we treat the attributive content rather than act as head, which is contrary to that defined in (Carlson and Marcu, 2001), because scientific facts or research arguments mentioned in attributive content are more important in abstracts. For some symmetric discourse relations such as *joint* and *comparison*, where two connected EDUs are equally important and have interchangeable semantic roles, we follow the strategy as (Li et al., 2014) and treat the preceding EDU as the head.

Another issue on coherence relations is about polynary relations which involve more than two EDUs. The first scenario is that one EDU dominates a set of posterior EDUs as its member. In this case, we annotate binary relations from head EDU to each member EDU with the same relation. The second scenario is that several EDUs are of equal importance in a polynary relation. For this case, we link each former EDU to its neighboring EDU with the same relation, forming a relation chain similar to "right-heavy" binarization transformation in (Morey et al., 2017).

By assuring that each EDU has one and only one head EDU, we can obtain a dependency tree for each scientific abstract. An example of dependency annotation is shown in Figure 1.

3 Corpus Construction

Following the annotation framework, we collected 798 abstracts from ACL anthology and constructed the SciDTB corpus. The construction details are introduced as follows.

Annotator Recruitment To select annotators, we put forward two requirements to ensure the annotation quality. First, we required the candidates to have linguistic knowledge. Second, each candidate was asked to join a test annotation of 20 abstracts, whose quality was evaluated by experts. After the judgement, 5 annotators were qualified to participate in our work.

EDU Segmentation We performed EDU segmentation in a semi-automatic way. First, we did sentence tokenization on raw texts using NLTK 3.2 (Bird and Loper, 2004). Then we used SPADE (Soricut and Marcu, 2003), a pre-trained EDU segmenter relying on Charniak's syntactic parser (Charniak, 2000), to automatically cut sentences into EDUs. Then, we manually checked each segmented abstract to ensure the segmentation quality. Two annotators conducted the checking task, with one proofreading the output of SPADE, and the other reviewing the proofreading. The checking process was recorded for statistical analysis.

Tree Annotation Labeling dependency trees was the most labor-intensive work in the corpus construction. 798 segmented abstracts were labeled by 5 annotators in 6 months. 506 abstracts were annotated more than twice separately by different annotators, with the purpose of analysing annotation consistency and providing human performance as an upper bound. The annotated trees were stored in JSON format. For convenience, we developed an online tool[3] for annotating and visualising discourse dependency trees.

4 Corpus Statistics

SciDTB contains 798 unique abstracts with 63% labeled more than once and 18,978 discourse relations in total. Table 2 compares the size of SciDTB with RST-DT and another PDTB-style domain-specific corpus BioDRB (Prasad et al., 2011), we can see SciDTB has a comparable size with RST-DT. Moreover, it is relatively easy for SciDTB to augment its size since the dependency structure simplifies the annotation to some extent. Compared with BioDRB, SciDTB has larger size and passage-level representations.

Corpus	#Doc.	#Doc. (unique)	#Relation
SciDTB	1355	798	18978
RST-DT	438	385	23611
BioDRB	24	24	5859

Table 2: Size of SciDTB and other discourse relation banks.

4.1 Annotation Consistency

EDU Segmentation We use 214 abstracts for analysis. After the proofreading of the first annotator, the abstracts are composed of totally 2,772 EDUs. Among these EDUs, only 28 (1.01%) EDUs are disagreed and revised by the second annotator, which means a very high consensus between annotators on EDU segmentation.

Annotator	#Doc.	UAS	LAS	Kappa score
1 & 2	93	0.811	0.644	0.763
1 & 3	147	0.800	0.628	0.761
1 & 4	42	0.772	0.609	0.767
3 & 4	46	0.806	0.639	0.772
4 & 5	44	0.753	0.550	0.699

Table 3: Relation annotation consistency.

Tree Labeling Here, we evaluate the consistency of two annotators on labeling discourse relations using 3 metrics from different aspects. When labeling a discourse relation, each non-root EDU must choose its head with a specific relation type. Thus, the annotation disagreement mainly comes from selecting head or determining relation type. Similar to syntactic dependency parsing, unlabeled and labeled attachment scores (**UAS** and

Distance	#Relations	Percentage/%
0 EDU	10576	61.64
1 EDU	2208	12.87
2 EDUs	1231	7.17
3-5 EDUs	1626	9.48
6-10 EDUs	1146	6.68
11-15 EDUs	304	1.77
>15 EDUs	67	0.39
Total	17158	100.00

Table 4: Distribution of dependency distance.

LAS) are employed to measure the labeling correspondence. UAS calculates the proportion of EDUs which are assigned the same head in two annotations, while LAS considers the uniformity of both head and relation label. **Cohen's Kappa score** evaluates the agreement of labeling relation types under the premise of knowing the correct heads.

Table 3 shows the agreement results between two annotators. We can see that most of the **LAS** values between annotators exceed 0.60. The agreement on tree structure reflected by **UAS** all reaches 0.75. The **Kappa** values for relation types agreement keep equal to or greater than 0.7.

4.2 Structural Characteristics

Non-projection in Treebank One advantage of dependency trees is that they can represent non-projective structures. In SciDTB, we annotated 39 non-projective dependency trees, which account for about 3% of the whole corpus. This phenomenon in our treebank is not so frequent as (Wolf and Gibson, 2005). We think this may be because scientific abstracts are much shorter and scientific expressions are relatively restricted.

Dependency Distance Here we investigate the distance of two EDUs involved in a discourse relation. The distance is defined as the number of EDUs between head and dependent. We present the distance distribution of all the relations in SciDTB, as shown in Table 4. It should be noted that *ROOT* and *Same-unit* relations are omitted in this analysis. From Table 4, we find most relations connect near EDUs. Most relations (61.6%) occur between neighboring EDUs and about 75% relations occur with at most one intermediate EDU.

Although most dependency relations function intra-sentence, there exist long-range dependency relations in the treebank. On average, the distance of 8.8% relations is greater than 5. We summarize that the most frequent 5 fine-grained rela-

---

[3] http://123.56.88.210/demo/depannotate/

tion types of these long-distance relations belong to *Evaluation*, *Aspect*, *Addition*, *Process-step* and *Goal*, which tend to appear on higher level in dependency trees.

5 Benchmark for Discourse Parsers

We further apply SciDTB as a benchmark for comparing and evaluating discourse dependency parsers. For the 798 unique abstracts in SciDTB, 154 are used for development set and 152 for test set. The remaining 492 abstracts are used for training. We implement two transition-based parsers and a graph-based parser as baselines.

Vanilla Transition-based Parser We adopt the transition-based method for dependency parsing by Nivre (2003). The action set of arc-standard system (Nivre et al., 2004) is employed. We build an SVM classifier to predict most possible transition action for given configuration. We adopt the N-gram features, positional features, length features and dependency features for top-2 EDUs in the stack and top EDU in the buffer, which can be referred from (Li et al., 2014; Wang et al., 2017)

Two-stage Transition-based Parser We implement a two-stage transition-based dependency parser following (Wang et al., 2017). First, an unlabeled tree is produced by vanilla transition-based approach. Then we train a separate SVM classifier to predict relation types on the tree in pre-order. For the 2nd-stage, apart from features in the 1st-stage, two kinds of features are added, including depth of head and dependent in the tree and the predicted relation between the head and its head.

Graph-based Parser We implement a graph-based parser as in (Li et al., 2014). For simplicity, we use averaged perceptron rather than MIRA to train weights. N-gram, positional, length and dependency features between head and dependent labeled with relation type are considered.

Hyper-parameters During training, the hyper-parameters of these models are tuned using development set. For vanilla transition-based parser, we take linear kernel for the SVM classifier. The penalty parameter C is set to 1.5. For two-stage parser, the 1st-stage classifier follows the same setting as the vanilla parser. For 2nd-stage, we use the linear kernel and set C to 0.5. The averaged perceptron in graph-based parser is trained for 10 epochs on the training set. Weights of features are

	Dev set		Test set	
	UAS	LAS	UAS	LAS
Vanilla transition	**0.730**	0.557	**0.702**	0.535
Two-stage transition	**0.730**	**0.577**	**0.702**	**0.545**
Graph-based	0.607	0.455	0.576	0.425
Human	0.806	0.627	0.802	0.622

Table 5: Performance of baseline parsers.

initialized to be 0 and trained with fixed learning rate.

Results Table 5 shows the performance of these parsers on development and test data. We also measure parsing accuracy with UAS and LAS. The human agreement is presented for comparison. With the addition of tree structural features in relation type prediction, the two-stage dependency parser gets better performance on LAS than vanilla system on both development and test set. Compared with graph-based model, the two transition-based baselines achieve higher accuracy with regard to UAS and LAS. Using more effective training strategies like MIRA may improve graph-based models. We can also see that human performance is still much higher than the three parsers, meaning there is large space for improvement in future work.

6 Conclusions

In this paper, we propose to construct a discourse dependency treebank SciDTB for scientific abstracts. It represents passages with dependency tree structure, which is simpler and more flexible for analysis. We have presented our annotation framework, construction workflow and statistics of SciDTB, which can provide annotation experience for extending to other domains. Moreover, this treebank can serve as an evaluating benchmark of discourse parsers.

In the future, we will enlarge our annotation scale to cover more domains and longer passages, and explore how to use SciDTB in some downstreaming applications.

Acknowledgments

We thank the anonymous reviewers for their insightful comments on this paper. We especially thank Liang Wang for developing the online annotation tool. This work was partially supported by National Natural Science Foundation of China (61572049 and 61333018). The correspondence author of this paper is Sujian Li.

References

Steven Bird and Edward Loper. 2004. Nltk: the natural language toolkit. In *Proceedings of the ACL 2004 on Interactive poster and demonstration sessions*. Association for Computational Linguistics, page 31.

Alena Böhmová, Jan Hajič, Eva Hajičová, and Barbora Hladká. 2003. The prague dependency treebank. In *Treebanks*, Springer, pages 103–127.

Harry Bunt and Rashmi Prasad. 2016. Iso dr-core (iso 24617-8): Core concepts for the annotation of discourse relations. In *Proceedings 12th Joint ACL-ISO Workshop on Interoperable Semantic Annotation (ISA-12)*. pages 45–54.

Lynn Carlson and Daniel Marcu. 2001. Discourse tagging reference manual. *ISI Technical Report ISI-TR-545* 54:56.

Lynn Carlson, Daniel Marcu, and Mary Ellen Okurowski. 2003. Building a discourse-tagged corpus in the framework of rhetorical structure theory. In *Current and new directions in discourse and dialogue*, Springer, pages 85–112.

Eugene Charniak. 2000. A maximum-entropy-inspired parser. In *Proceedings of the 1st North American chapter of the Association for Computational Linguistics conference*. Association for Computational Linguistics, pages 132–139.

Shima Gerani, Yashar Mehdad, Giuseppe Carenini, Raymond T Ng, and Bita Nejat. 2014. Abstractive summarization of product reviews using discourse structure. In *EMNLP*. volume 14, pages 1602–1613.

Francisco Guzmán, Shafiq Joty, Lluís Màrquez, and Preslav Nakov. 2014. Using discourse structure improves machine translation evaluation. In *Proceedings of the 52nd Annual Meeting of the Association for Computational Linguistics (Volume 1: Long Papers)*. volume 1, pages 687–698.

Richard A Hudson. 1984. *Word grammar*. Blackwell Oxford.

Matthias Irmer. 2011. *Bridging inferences: Constraining and resolving underspecification in discourse interpretation*, volume 11. Walter de Gruyter.

Shafiq Joty, Francisco Guzmán, Lluís Màrquez, and Preslav Nakov. 2014. Discotk: Using discourse structure for machine translation evaluation. In *Proceedings of the Ninth Workshop on Statistical Machine Translation*. pages 402–408.

Alex Lascarides and Nicholas Asher. 2008. Segmented discourse representation theory: Dynamic semantics with discourse structure. In *Computing meaning*, Springer, pages 87–124.

Sujian Li, Liang Wang, Ziqiang Cao, and Wenjie Li. 2014. Text-level discourse dependency parsing. In *Proceedings of the 52nd Annual Meeting of the Association for Computational Linguistics (Volume 1: Long Papers)*. volume 1, pages 25–35.

William C Mann and Sandra A Thompson. 1988. Rhetorical structure theory: Toward a functional theory of text organization. *Text-Interdisciplinary Journal for the Study of Discourse* 8(3):243–281.

Mathieu Morey, Philippe Muller, and Nicholas Asher. 2017. How much progress have we made on rst discourse parsing? a replication study of recent results on the rst-dt. In *Proceedings of the 2017 Conference on Empirical Methods in Natural Language Processing*. pages 1319–1324.

Joakim Nivre. 2003. An efficient algorithm for projective dependency parsing. In *Proceedings of the 8th International Workshop on Parsing Technologies (IWPT*. Citeseer.

Joakim Nivre, Johan Hall, and Jens Nilsson. 2004. Memory-based dependency parsing. In *Proceedings of the Eighth Conference on Computational Natural Language Learning (CoNLL-2004) at HLT-NAACL 2004*.

Livia Polanyi. 1988. A formal model of the structure of discourse. *Journal of pragmatics* 12(5-6):601–638.

Rashmi Prasad, Susan McRoy, Nadya Frid, Aravind Joshi, and Hong Yu. 2011. The biomedical discourse relation bank. *BMC bioinformatics* 12(1):188.

Rashmi Prasad, Eleni Miltsakaki, Nikhil Dinesh, Alan Lee, Aravind Joshi, Livio Robaldo, and Bonnie L Webber. 2007. The penn discourse treebank 2.0 annotation manual .

Radu Soricut and Daniel Marcu. 2003. Sentence level discourse parsing using syntactic and lexical information. In *Proceedings of the 2003 Conference of the North American Chapter of the Association for Computational Linguistics on Human Language Technology-Volume 1*. Association for Computational Linguistics, pages 149–156.

Manfred Stede, Stergos D Afantenos, Andreas Peldszus, Nicholas Asher, and Jérémy Perret. 2016. Parallel discourse annotations on a corpus of short texts. In *LREC*.

Yizhong Wang, Sujian Li, and Houfeng Wang. 2017. A two-stage parsing method for text-level discourse analysis. In *Proceedings of the 55th Annual Meeting of the Association for Computational Linguistics (Volume 2: Short Papers)*. volume 2, pages 184–188.

Florian Wolf and Edward Gibson. 2005. Representing discourse coherence: A corpus-based study. *Computational Linguistics* 31(2):249–287.

Yasuhisa Yoshida, Jun Suzuki, Tsutomu Hirao, and Masaaki Nagata. 2014. Dependency-based discourse parser for single-document summarization. In *Proceedings of the 2014 Conference on Empirical Methods in Natural Language Processing (EMNLP)*. pages 1834–1839.

Predicting accuracy on large datasets from smaller pilot data

Mark Johnson
Macquarie University
Mark.Johnson@MQ.edu.au

Peter Anderson
Australian National University
Peter.Anderson@ANU.edu.au

Mark Dras
Macquarie University
Mark.Dras@MQ.edu.au

Mark Steedman
University of Edinburgh
steedman@inf.ed.ac.uk

Abstract

Because obtaining training data is often the most difficult part of an NLP or ML project, we develop methods for predicting how much data is required to achieve a desired test accuracy by extrapolating results from systems trained on a small pilot training dataset. We model how accuracy varies as a function of training size on subsets of the pilot data, and use that model to predict how much training data would be required to achieve the desired accuracy. We introduce a new performance extrapolation task to evaluate how well different extrapolations predict system accuracy on larger training sets. We show that details of hyperparameter optimisation and the extrapolation models can have dramatic effects in a document classification task. We believe this is an important first step in developing methods for estimating the resources required to meet specific engineering performance targets.

1 Introduction

An engineering discipline should be able to predict the cost of a project before the project is started. Because training data is often the most expensive part of an NLP or ML project, it is important to estimate how much training data required for a system to achieve a target accuracy. Unfortunately our field only offers fairly impractical advice, e.g., that more data increases accuracy (Banko and Brill, 2001); we currently have no practical methods for estimating how much data or what quality of data is required to achieve a target accuracy goal. Imagine if bridge construction was planned the way we build our systems!

Our long-term goal is to develop practical methods for designing systems that achieve target performance specifications, including identifying the amount of training data that the system will require. This paper starts to address this goal by introducing an extrapolation methodology that predicts a system's accuracy on a larger dataset from its performance on subsets of much smaller pilot data. These extrapolations allow us to estimate how much training data a system will require to achieve a target accuracy. We focus on a specific task (document classification) using a specific system (the fastText classifier of Joulin et al. (2016)), and leave to future work to determine if our approach and results generalise to other tasks and systems.

We introduce an *accuracy extrapolation task* that can be used to evaluate different extrapolation models. We describe three well-known extrapolation models and evaluate them on a *document classification dataset*. On our development data the biased power-law method with binomial item weighting performs best, so we propose it should be a baseline for future research. We demonstrate the importance of hyperparameter optimisation on each different-sized data subset (rather than just optimising on the largest data subset) and item weighting, and show that these can have a dramatic impact on extrapolation, especially from small pilot data sets. The data and code for all experiments in this paper, including the R code for the graphics, is available from http://web.science.mq.edu.au/~mjohnson.

2 Related work

Power analysis (Cohen, 1992) is widely-used statistical technique (e.g., in biomedical trials) for predicting the number of measurements required in an experimental design; we aim to develop sim-

Proceedings of the 56th Annual Meeting of the Association for Computational Linguistics (Short Papers), pages 450–455
Melbourne, Australia, July 15 - 20, 2018. ©2018 Association for Computational Linguistics

ilar techniques for NLP and ML systems. There is a large body of research on the relationship between training data size and system performance. Geman et al. (1992) decompose the squared error of a model into a *bias term* (due to model errors) and a *variance term* (due to statistical noise). Bias does not vary with training data size n, but the error due to variance should decrease as $O(1/\sqrt{n})$ if the training observations are independent (Domingos, 2000a,b). The power-law models used in this paper have been investigated many times in prior literature (Haussler et al., 1996; Mukherjee et al., 2003; Figueroa et al., 2012; Beleites et al., 2013; Hajian-Tilaki, 2014; Cho et al., 2015). Sun et al. (2017), Barone et al. (2017) and the concurrent unpublished work by Hestness et al. (2017) point out that these power-law models describe modern ML and NLP systems quite well, including complex deep-learning systems, so we expect our results to generalise to these systems.

This paper differs from prior work in that we explicitly focus on the task of extrapolating system performance from small pilot data. We introduce a new evaluation task to compare the effectiveness of different models for this extrapolation, and demonstrate the importance of per-subset hyperparameter optimisation and item weighting, which prior work did not investigate.

3 Models for extrapolating pilot data

We are given a system whose accuracy on a large dataset we wish to predict, but only a smaller pilot dataset is available. We train the system on different-sized subsets of the pilot dataset, and use the results of those training runs to estimate how the system's accuracy varies as a function of training data size.

We focus on predicting the minimum error rate $e(n)$ that the system can achieve on a dataset of size n after hyperparameter optimisation (where the error rate is $1-$accuracy for a classifier) given a pilot dataset of size $m \ll n$ (in the task below, $m = n/2$ or $m = n/10$). We investigate three different extrapolation models of $e(n)$ in this paper:

- *Power law:* $\hat{e}(n) = bn^c$
- *Inverse square-root:* $\hat{e}(n) = a + bn^{-1/2}$
- *Biased power law:* $\hat{e}(n) = a + bn^c$

Here $\hat{e}(n)$ is the estimate of $e(n)$, and a, b and c are adjustable parameters that are estimated based on the system's performance on the pilot dataset.

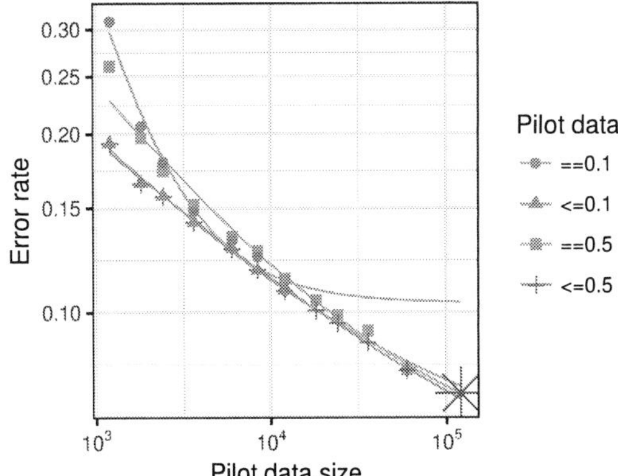

Figure 1: An extrapolation run from pilot data consisting of either 0.1 or 0.5 of the ag_news corpus. The x-axis is the size of the subset of pilot data, while the y-axis is the classification error rate. The shapes/colors show the maximum fraction of the corpus used in the pilot data, and whether hyperparameters were optimised only once on all of the pilot data (e.g., = 0.1 and = 0.5) or at each smaller subset of the pilot data (e.g., ≤ 0.1 and ≤ 0.5). The lines are least-squares fits of biased power-law models ($\hat{e}(n) = a + bn^c$) to the corresponding pilot data. The red star shows minimum error rate when all the training data is used to train the classifier (this is the value we are trying to predict).

The inverse square-root curve is what one would expect if the error is distributed according to a Bias-Variance decomposition (Geman et al., 1992) with a constant bias term a and a variance term that asymptotically follows the Central Limit Theorem. We fit these models using *weighted least squares regression*. Each data point or *item* in the regression is the result of a run of the system on a subset of the pilot dataset.

Assuming that the underlying system has adjustable hyperparameters, the question arises: how should the hyperparameters be set? The computationally least demanding approach is to optimise the system's hyperparameters on the full pilot dataset, and use these hyperparameters for all the runs on subsets of the pilot dataset. An alternative, computationally more demanding approach is to optimise the system's hyperparameters separately on each of the subsets of the pilot dataset. Figure 1 shows an example where optimising the hyperparameters just on the full pilot dataset is clearly inferior to optimising the hyperparameters on each subset of the pilot dataset. We show below that the more demanding approach of optimising on each subset is superior, especially when extrapolating from small pilot datasets.

We also investigate how details of the regression fit affect the regression accuracy $\hat{e}(n)$. We experimented with several link functions (we used the default Gaussian link here), but found that these had less impact than adjusting the *item weights* in the regression. Runs with smaller training sets presumably have higher variance, and since our goal is to extrapolate to larger datasets, it is reasonable to place more weight on items corresponding to larger datasets. We investigated three item weighting functions in regression:

- constant weights (1),
- linear weights (n), and
- binomial weights ($n/e(1-e)$)

Linear weights are motivated by the assumption that the item variance follows the Central Limit Theorem, while the binomial weights are motivated by the assumption that item variance follows a binomial distribution (see the Supplemental Materials for further discussion). As Figure 2 makes clear, linear weights and binomial weights generally produce more accurate extrapolations than constant weights, so we use binomial weights in our evaluation in Table 2.

4   A performance extrapolation task

We used the fastText document classifier and the document classification corpora distributed with it; see Joulin et al. (2016) for full details. FastText's speed and evaluation scripts make it easy to do the experiments described below. We fitted our extrapolation models to the fastText document classifier results on the 8 corpora distributed with the fastText classifier. These corpora contain labelled documents for a document classification task, and come randomised and divided into training and test sections. All our results are on these test sections.

The corpora were divided into development and evaluation corpora (each with train and test splits) as shown in table 1.   We use the amazon_review_polarity, sogou_news, yahoo_answers and yelp_review_full corpora as our test set (so these are only used in the final evaluation), while the ag_news, dbpedia, amazon_review_full and yelp_review_polarity were used as development corpora. The development and evaluation sets contain document collections of roughly similar sizes and complexities, but no attempt was made to accurately "balance" the development and evaluation corpora.

We trained the fastText classifier on 13 differently-sized prefixes of each training set that are approximately logarithmically spaced over two orders of magnitude (i.e., varying from $1/100$ to all of the training corpus). To explore the effect of hyperparameter tuning on extrapolation, for each prefix of each training set we trained a classifier on each of 1,079 different hyperparameter settings, varying the n-gram length, learning rate, dimensionality of the hidden units and the loss function (the fastText classifier crashed on 17 hyperparameter combinations; we did not investigate why). We re-ran the entire process 8 times on randomly-shuffled versions of each training corpus.

As expected, the minimum error configuration invariably requires the full training data. When extrapolating from subsets of a smaller pilot set (we explored pilot sets consisting of 0.1 and 0.5 of the full training data) there are two plausible ways of performing hyperparameter optimisation. Ideally, one would optimise the hyperparameters for each subset of the pilot data considered (we selected the best-performing hyperparameters using grid search). However, if one is not working with computationally efficient algorithms like fastText, one might be tempted to only optimise the hyperparameters once on all the pilot data, and use the hyperparameters optimised on all the pilot data when calculating the error rate on subsets of that pilot data. As figure 2 and table 2 make clear, selecting the optimal hyperparameters for each subset of the pilot data generally produces better extrapolation results. Figure 1 shows how different ways of choosing hyperparameters can affect extrapolation. As that figure shows, hyperparameters optimised on 50% of the training data perform very badly on 1% of the training data. As figure 2 shows, this can lead simpler extrapolation models such as the power-law to dramatically underestimate the error on the full dataset. Interestingly, more complex extrapolation models, such as the extended power-law model, often do much better.

Based on the development corpora results presented in Figures 1 and 2, we choose the biased power law model ($\hat{e}(n) = a + bn^c$) with binomial

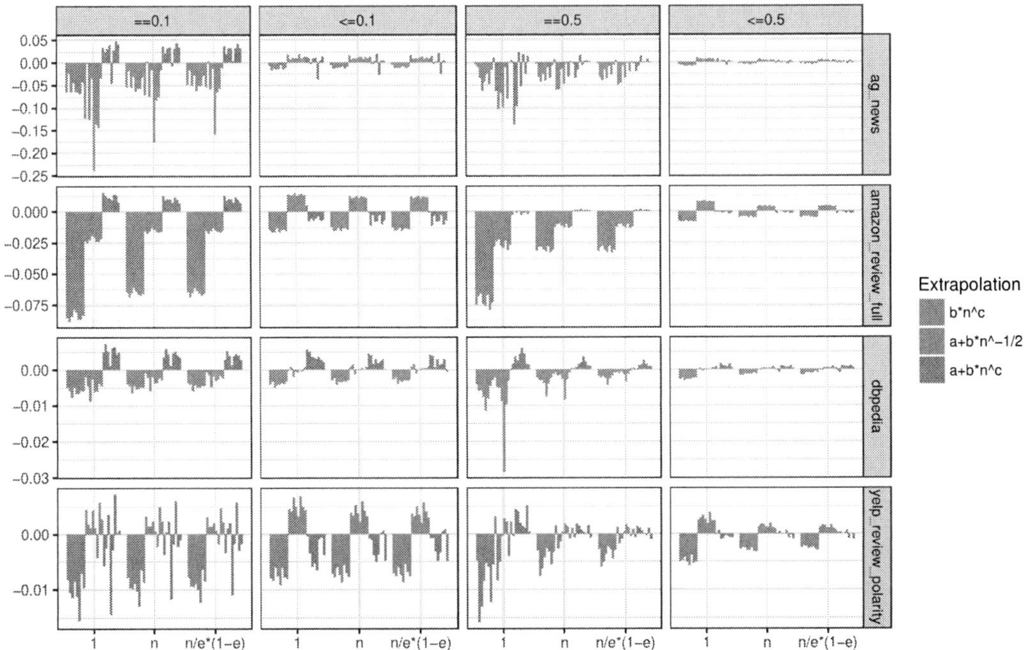

Figure 2: Residuals on 8 runs when extrapolating from pilot data consisting of 0.1 or 0.5 of each development training corpus. The y-axis shows the residual error (the difference between the predicted error and the minimum error when the classifier is trained on all the training data), and the x-axis indicates the weight function used in extrapolation. Colours indicate the model fitted, (i.e., power-law ($\hat{e}(n) = bn^c$), inverse square-root ($\hat{e}(n) = a + bn^{-1/2}$), or biased power-law ($\hat{e}(n) = a + bn^c$) models). Facets indicate the development corpus used, and whether hyperparameters were optimised only once on all of the pilot data (e.g., = 0.5 and = 0.1) or on each subset of the pilot data (e.g., $\leq$ 0.5 and $\leq$ 0.1).

Corpus	Labels	Train (K)	Test (K)
ag_news	4	120	7.6
dbpedia	14	560	70
amazon_review_full	5	3,000	650
yelp_review_polarity	2	560	38
amazon_review_polarity	2	3,600	400
sogou_news	5	450	60
yahoo_answers	10	1,400	60
yelp_review_full	5	650	50

Table 1: Summary statistics of the development corpora (above line) and evaluation corpora (below line).

Pilot data	amazon review polarity	sogou news	yahoo answers	yelp review full	**Overall**
= 0.1	0.1016	0.2752	0.0519	0.0496	0.1510
$\leq$ 0.1	**0.0209**	**0.1900**	**0.0264**	**0.0406**	**0.0986**
= 0.5	0.0338	0.0438	0.0254	0.0160	0.0315
$\leq$ 0.5	**0.0049**	**0.0390**	**0.0053**	**0.0046**	**0.0200**

Table 2: RMS relative residuals ($\hat{e}/e - 1$) on the four evaluation corpora over all runs for the biased power law model ($\hat{e}(n) = a + bn^c$) with binomial item weights ($n/e(1 - e)$). Lower scores are better.

item weights ($n/e(1 - e)$) as the model to evaluate on the evaluation corpora.

We evaluate an extrapolation by calculating the root-mean-square (RMS) of the relative residuals $\hat{e}/e - 1$, where e is the minimum error achieved by the classifier with any hyperparameter setting when trained on the full training set, and $\hat{e}$ is the predicted error made by the extrapolation model

from the pilot dataset.[1]

Unsurprisingly, Table 2 shows that extrapolation is more accurate from larger pilot datasets; increasing the size of the pilot dataset 5 times re-

---

[1]We use relative residuals because the residuals themselves vary greatly from corpus to corpus, and we use RMS to penalise large extrapolation errors. We admit that RMS relative residuals is probably not a close approximation to the extrapolation loss in real applications, and we hope future work will develop more realistic loss functions.

duces the RMS relative residuals by a factor of 10. It also clearly shows that it valuable to perform hyperparameter optimisation on all subsets of the pilot dataset, not just on the whole pilot data. Interestingly, Table 2 shows that the RMS difference between the two approaches to hyperparameter setting is greater when the pilot data is larger. This makes sense; the hyperparameters that are optimal on a large pilot dataset may be far from optimal on a very small subset (this is clearly visible in Figure 1, where the items deviating most are those for the = 0.5 pilot data and hyperparameter choice).

5   Conclusions and Future Work

This paper introduced an extrapolation methodology for predicting accuracy on large dataset from a small pilot dataset, applied it to a document classification system, and identified the biased power-law model with binomial weights as a good baseline extrapolation model. This only scratches the surface of performance extrapolation tasks. We hope that teams with greater computational resources will study the extrapolation task for computationally more-demanding systems, including popular deep learning models. The power-law models should be considered baselines for more sophisticated extrapolation models, which might exploit more information than just accuracy on subsets of the pilot data.

We hope this work will spur the development of better methods for estimating the resources needed to build an NLP or ML system to meet a specification, as we believe this is essential for any mature engineering field.

Acknowledgments

We would like to thank the anonymous reviewers for their insightful comments and suggestions. This research was supported by a Google award through the Natural Language Understanding Focused Program, and under the Australian Research Council's Discovery Projects funding scheme (project number DP160102156).

References

M. Banko and Eric Brill. 2001. Mitigating the paucity-of-data problem: Exploring the effect of training corpus size on classifier performance for natural language processing. In *Human Language Technology Conference : Proceedings of HLT 2001 : First International Conference on Human Language Technology Research*. Morgan Kaufmann.

Antonio Valerio Miceli Barone, Barry Haddow, Ulrich Germann, and Rico Sennrich. 2017. Regularization techniques for fine-tuning in neural machine translation. *CoRR* abs/1707.09920.

Claudia Beleites, Ute Neugebauer, Thomas Bocklitz, Christoph Krafft, and Jürgen Popp. 2013. Sample size planning for classification models. *Analytica chimica acta* 760:25–33.

J. Cho, K. Lee, E. Shin, G. Choy, and S. Do. 2015. How much data is needed to train a medical image deep learning system to achieve necessary high accuracy? *arXiv:1511.06348* .

Jacob Cohen. 1992. A power primer. *Psychological bulletin* 112(1):155.

Pedro Domingos. 2000a. A unified bias-variance decomposition. In *Proceedings of 17th International Conference on Machine Learning*. pages 231–238.

Pedro Domingos. 2000b. A unified bias-variance decomposition for zero-one and squared loss. *AAAI/IAAI* 2000:564–569.

Rosa L Figueroa, Qing Zeng-Treitler, Sasikiran Kandula, and Long H Ngo. 2012. Predicting sample size required for classification performance. *BMC medical informatics and decision making* 12(1):8.

Stuart Geman, Elie Bienenstock, and René Doursat. 1992. Neural networks and the bias/variance dilemma. *Neural Computation* 4:1–58.

Karimollah Hajian-Tilaki. 2014. Sample size estimation in diagnostic test studies of biomedical informatics. *Journal of biomedical informatics* 48:193–204.

David Haussler, Michael Kearns, H. Sebastian Seung, and Naftali Tishby. 1996. Rigorous learning curve bounds from statistical mechanics. *Machine Learning* 25(2).

Joel Hestness, Sharan Narang, Newsha Ardalani, Gregory Diamos, Heewoo Jun, Hassan Kianinejad, Md. Mostofa Ali Patwary, Yang Yang, and Yanqi Zhou. 2017. Deep learning scaling is predictable, empirically. *arXiv:1712.00409* .

Armand Joulin, Edouard Grave, Piotr Bojanowski, and Tomas Mikolov. 2016. Bag of tricks for efficient text classification. *arXiv:1607.01759* .

Sayan Mukherjee, Pablo Tamayo, Simon Rogers, Ryan Rifkin, Anna Engle, Colin Campbell, Todd R Golub, and Jill P Mesirov. 2003. Estimating dataset size requirements for classifying DNA microarray data. *Journal of computational biology* 10(2):119–142.

Chen Sun, Abhinav Shrivastava, Saurabh Singh, and Abhinav Gupta. 2017. Revisiting unreasonable effectiveness of data in deep learning era. *arXiv:1707.02968* .

The Influence of Context on Sentence Acceptability Judgements

Jean-Philippe Bernardy
University of Gothenburg
jean-philippe.bernardy@gu.se

Shalom Lappin
University of Gothenburg
shalom.lappin@gu.se

Jey Han Lau
IBM Research Australia
jeyhan.lau@gmail.com

Abstract

We investigate the influence that document context exerts on human acceptability judgements for English sentences, via two sets of experiments. The first compares ratings for sentences presented on their own with ratings for the same set of sentences given in their document contexts. The second assesses the accuracy with which two types of neural models — one that incorporates context during training and one that does not — predict these judgements. Our results indicate that: (1) context improves acceptability ratings for ill-formed sentences, but also reduces them for well-formed sentences; and (2) context helps unsupervised systems to model acceptability.[1]

1 Introduction

Sentence acceptability is defined as the extent to which a sentence is well formed or natural to native speakers of a language. It encompasses semantic, syntactic and pragmatic plausibility and other non-linguistic factors such as memory limitation. Grammaticality, by contrast, is the syntactic well-formedness of a sentence. Grammaticality as characterised by formal linguists is a theoretical concept that is difficult to elicit from non-expert assessors. In the research presented here we are interested in predicting acceptability judgements.[2]

Lau et al. (2015, 2016) present unsupervised probabilistic methods to predict sentence acceptability, where sentences were judged independently of context. In this paper we extend this

research to investigate the impact of context on human acceptability judgements, where context is defined as the full document environment surrounding a sentence. We also test the accuracy of more sophisticated language models — one which incorporates document context during training — to predict human acceptability judgements.

We believe that understanding how context influences acceptability is crucial to success in modelling human acceptability judgements. It has implications for tasks such as style/coherence assessment and language generation. Showing a strong correlation between unsupervised language model sentence probability and acceptability supports the view that linguistic knowledge can be represented as a probabilistic system. This result addresses foundational questions concerning the nature of grammatical knowledge (Lau et al., 2016).

Our work is guided by 3 hypotheses:

H_1: Document context boosts sentence acceptability judgements.

H_2: Document context helps language models to model acceptability.

H_3: A language model predicts acceptability more accurately when it is tested on sentences within document context than when it is tested on the sentences alone.

We sample sentences and their document contexts from English Wikipedia articles. We perform round-trip machine translation to generate sentences of varying degrees of well-formedness and ask crowdsourced workers to judge the acceptability of these sentences, presenting the sentences with and without their document environments. We describe this experiment and address H_1 in Section 2.

In Section 3, we experiment with two types of language models to predict acceptability: a standard language model and a topically-driven model. The latter extends the language model by incorporating document context as a conditioning

---

[1]Annotated data (with acceptability ratings) is available at: https://github.com/GU-CLASP/BLL2018.

[2]See Lau et al. (2016) for a detailed discussion of the relationship between acceptability and grammaticality. They provide motivation for measuring acceptability rather than grammaticality in their crowd source surveys and modelling experiments.

Proceedings of the 56th Annual Meeting of the Association for Computational Linguistics (Short Papers), pages 456–461
Melbourne, Australia, July 15 - 20, 2018. ©2018 Association for Computational Linguistics

variable. The model comparison allows us to understand the impact of incorporating context during training for acceptability prediction. We also experiment with adding context as input at test time for both models. These experiments collectively address H_2, by investigating the impact of using context during training and testing for modelling acceptability. We evaluate the models against crowd-sourced annotated sentences judged both in context and out of context. This tests H_3.

In Section 4 we briefly consider related work. We indicate the issues to be addressed in future research and summarise our conclusions in Section 5.

2 The Influence of Document Context on Acceptability Ratings

Our goal is to construct a dataset of sentences annotated with acceptability ratings, judged with and without document context. To obtain sentences and their document context, we extracted 100 random articles from the English Wikipedia and sampled a sentence from each article. To generate a set of sentences with varying degrees of acceptability we used the Moses MT system (Koehn et al., 2007) to translate each sentence from English to 4 target languages — Czech, Spanish, German and French — and then back to English.[3] We chose these 4 languages because preliminary experiments found that they produce sentences with different sorts of grammatical, semantic, and lexical infelicities. Note that we only translate the sentences; the document context is not modified.

To gather acceptability judgements we used Amazon Mechanical Turk and asked workers to judge acceptability using a 4-point scale.[4] We ran the annotation task twice: first where we presented sentences without context, and second within their document context. For the in-context experiment, the target sentence was highlighted in boldface, with one preceding and one succeeding sentence included as additional context. Workers had the option of revealing the full document context by clicking on the preceding and succeeding sentences. We did not check whether subjects viewed the full context when recording their ratings.

Henceforth human judgements made without context are denoted as h^- and judgements with context as h^+. We collected 20 judgements per sentence, giving us a total of a 20,000 annotations (100 sentences $\times$ 5 languages $\times$ 2 presentations $\times$ 20 judgements).

To ensure annotation reliability, sentences were presented in groups of five, one from the original English set, and four from the round-trip translations, one per target language, with no sentence type (English original or its translated variant) appearing more than once in a HIT.[5] We assume that the original English sentences are generally acceptable, and we filtered out workers who fail to consistently rate these sentences as such.[6] Postfiltering, we aggregate the multiple ratings and compute the mean.

We first look at the correlation between without-context (h^-) and with-context (h^+) mean ratings. Figure 1 is a scatter plot of this relation. We found a strong correlation of Pearson's $r = 0.80$ between the two sets of ratings.

We see that adding context generally improves acceptability (evidenced by points above the diagonal), but the pattern reverses as acceptability increases, suggesting that context boosts sentence ratings most for ill-formed sentences. The trend persists throughout the whole range of acceptability, so that for the most acceptable sentences, adding context actually diminishes their rated acceptability. We can see this trend clearly in Figure 1, where the average difference between h^- and h^+ is represented by the distance between the linear regression and the diagonal. These lines cross at $h^+ = h^- = 3.28$, the point where context no longer boosts acceptability.

To understand the spread of individual judgements on a sentence, we compute the standard deviation of ratings for each sentence and then take the mean over all sentences. We found a small difference: 0.71 for h^- and 0.76 for h^+. We also calculate one-vs-rest correlation, where for each

---

[3]We use the pre-trained Moses models for translation: `http://www.statmt.org/moses/RELEASE-4.0/models/`.

[4]We ask workers to judge how "natural" they find a sentence. For more details on the AMT protocol and our use of a four category naturalness rating system, see Lau et al. (2015, 2016).

[5]A HIT is a "human intelligence task". It constitutes a unit of work for crowdworkers.

[6]Control sentence rating threshold $= 3$. Minimum accuracy for control sentences $= 0.70$. To prevent workers from gaming this system (by giving all perfect ratings), we also removed workers whose average rating ≥ 3.5. Using these rules we filtered out on average, for each sentence, 7.5125 answers for h^+ and 3.9725 for h^-. This gave us approximately 13 and 16 annotators for each h^+ and h^- sentence respectively.

Language	Sentence	h^-	h^+
—	david acker, harry's son, became the president of sleepy's in 2001.	3.47	3.38
Czech	david acker harry' with son has become president of the sleepy' with in 2001.	1.75	2.08
German	david field, harry' the son was the president of '' in 2001.	1.63	3.00
Spanish	david acker, harry' his son, became president of the sleeping' in 2001.	2.19	2.62
French	david acker, harry' son, the president of the sleepy' in 2001.	1.47	2.46

Table 1: A sample of sentences with their without-context (h^-) and with-context (h^+) ratings. The "Language" column denotes the intermediate translation language. The original English sentence is marked with "—".

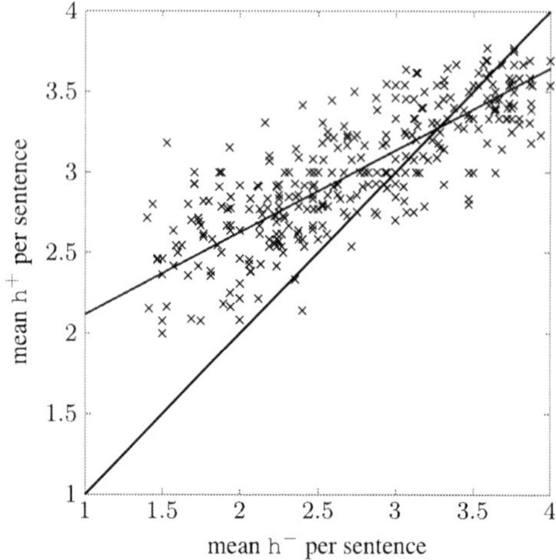

Figure 1: With-context (h^+) against without-context (h^-) ratings. Points above the full diagonal represent sentences which are judged more acceptable when presented with context. The total least-square linear regression is shown as the second line.

sentence we randomly single out an annotator rating and compute the Pearson correlation between these judgements against the mean ratings for the rest of the annotators.[7] This number can be interpreted as a performance upper bound on a single annotator for predicting the mean acceptability of a group of annotators.

We found a big gap in the one-vs-rest correlations: 0.628 for h^- and 0.293 for h^+. We were initially surprised as to why the correlation is so different, even though the standard deviation is similar. Further investigation reveals that this difference is explained by the pattern shown in Figure 1. Adding context "compressess" the distribution of (mean) ratings, pushing the extremes to the middle (i.e. very ill/well-formed sentences are now less ill/well-formed). The net effect is that it lowers correlation, as the good and bad sentences are now less separable.

One possible explanation for this compression is that workers focus more on global semantic and pragmatic coherence when context is supplied. If this is the case, then the syntactic mistakes introduced by MT have less effect on ratings than for the out-of-context sentences, where global coherence is not a factor.

To give a sense how context influences ratings, we present a sample of sentences with their without-context (h^-) and with-context (h^+) ratings in Table 1.

3   Modelling Sentence Acceptability with Enriched LMs

Lau et al. (2015, 2016) explored a number of unsupervised models for predicting acceptability, including n-gram language models, Bayesian HMMs, LDA-based models, and a simple recurrent network language model. They found that the neural model outperforms the others consistently over multiple domains, in several languages. In light of this, we experiment with neural models in this paper. We use: (1) a LSTM language model (`lstm`: Hochreiter and Schmidhuber (1997); Mikolov et al. (2010)), and (2) a topically driven neural language model (`tdlm`: Lau et al. (2017)).[8]

`lstm` is a standard LSTM language model, trained over a corpus to predict word sequences.

---

[7]Trials are repeated 1000 times and the average correlation is computed, to insure that we obtain robust results and avoid outlier ratings skewing our Pearson coefficient value. See Lau et al. (2016) for the details of this and an alternative method for simulating an individual annotator.

[8]We use the following `tdlm` implementation: `https://github.com/jhlau/topically-driven-language-model`.

Acc. Measure	Equation
LogProb	$\log P_m(s,c)$
Mean LP	$\dfrac{\log P_m(s,c)}{\|s\|}$
Norm LP (Div)	$-\dfrac{\log P_m(s,c)}{\log P_u(s)}$
Norm LP (Sub)	$\log P_m(s,c) - \log P_u(s)$
SLOR	$\dfrac{\log P_m(s,c) - \log P_u(s)}{\|s\|}$

Table 2: Acceptability measures for predicting the acceptability of a sentence. s is the sentence ($\|s\|$ is the sentence length); c is the document context (only used by $\texttt{lstm}^+$ and $\texttt{tdlm}^+$); $P_m(s,c)$ is the probability of the sentence given by a model; $P_u(s)$ is the unigram probability of the sentence.

Rtg	Model	*LP*	*Mean*	*NrmD*	*NrmS*	*SLOR*
h^-	$\texttt{lstm}^-$	0.151	0.487	**0.586**	0.342	0.584
	$\texttt{lstm}^+$	0.161	0.529	0.618	0.351	**0.633**
	$\texttt{tdlm}^-$	0.147	0.515	0.634	0.359	**0.640**
	$\texttt{tdlm}^+$	0.165	0.541	0.645	0.373	**0.653**
h^+	$\texttt{lstm}^-$	0.153	0.421	0.494	0.293	**0.503**
	$\texttt{lstm}^+$	0.168	0.459	0.522	0.310	**0.546**
	$\texttt{tdlm}^-$	0.153	0.450	0.541	0.313	**0.557**
	$\texttt{tdlm}^+$	0.169	0.473	0.552	0.325	**0.568**

Table 3: Pearson's r of acceptability measures and human ratings. "Rtg" = "Rating", "LP" = *LogProb*, "Mean" = *Mean LP*, "NrmD" = *Norm LP (Div)* and "NrmS" = *Norm LP (Sub)*. Boldface indicates optimal performance in each row.

$\texttt{tdlm}$ is a joint model of topic and language. The topic model component produces topics by processing documents through a convolutional layer and aligning it with trainable topic embeddings. The language model component incorporates context by combining its topic vector (produced by the topic model component) with the LSTM's hidden state, to generate the probability distribution for the next word.

After training, given a sentence both $\texttt{lstm}$ and $\texttt{tdlm}$ produce a sentence probability (aggregated using the sequence of conditional word probabilities). In our case, we also have the document context, information which both models can leverage. Therefore we have 4 variants at **test time**: models that use only the sentence as input, $\texttt{lstm}^-$ and $\texttt{tdlm}^-$, and models that use both sentence and context, $\texttt{lstm}^+$ and $\texttt{tdlm}^+$.[9] $\texttt{lstm}^+$ incorporates context by feeding it to the LSTM network and taking its final state[10] as the initial state for the current sentence. $\texttt{tdlm}^-$ ignores the context by converting the topic vector into a vector of zeros.

To map sentence probability to acceptability, we compute several *acceptability measures* (Lau et al., 2016), which are designed to normalise sentence length and word frequency. These are given in Table 2.

We train $\texttt{tdlm}$ and $\texttt{lstm}$ on a sample of 100K English Wikipedia articles, which has no over-lap with the 100 documents used for the annotation described in Section 2. The training data has approximately 40M tokens and a vocabulary size of 66K.[11] Training details and all model hyper-parameter settings are detailed in the supplementary material.

To assess the performance of the acceptability measures, we compute Pearson's r against mean human ratings (Table 3). We also experimented with Spearman's rank correlation, but found similar trends and so present only the Pearson results.

The first observation is that we replicate the performance of the original experiment setting (Lau et al., 2015). We achieved a correlation of 0.584 when we compared $\texttt{lstm}^-$ against h^-, which is similar to the previously reported performance (0.570).[12] *SLOR* outperforms all other measures, which is consistent with the findings in Lau et al. (2015). We will focus on *SLOR* for the remainder of the discussion.

Across all models ($\texttt{lstm}$ and $\texttt{tdlm}$) and human ratings (h^- and h^+), using context at test time improves model performance. This suggests that taking context into account helps in modelling acceptability, regardless of whether it is tested against judgements made with (h^+) or without context (h^-).[13] We also see that $\texttt{tdlm}$ consis-

---

[9] There are only two trained models: $\texttt{lstm}$ and $\texttt{tdlm}$. The four variants are generated by varying the type of input provided at test time when computing the sentence probability.

[10] The final state is the hidden state produced by the last word of the context.

[11] We filter word types that occur less than 10 times, lowercase all words, and use a special unkown token to represent unseen words.

[12] We note two differences. First, we use a different set of Wikipedia training and testing articles. Second, we employ a LSTM instead of a simple RNN for the language model.

[13] We believe incorporating context at test time for $\texttt{lstm}$ improves performance because context puts the starting state of the current sentence in the right "semantic" space when predicting its words. Without context, the initial state for the current sentence is defaulted to a vector of zeros, and the

tently outperforms `lstm` over both types of human ratings and test input variants, showing that `tdlm` is a better model at predicting acceptability. In fact, if we look at `tdlm`$^-$ vs. `lstm`$^+$ (h^-: 0.640 vs. 0.633; h^+: 0.557 vs. 0.546), `tdlm` still performs better without context than `lstm` with context. These observations confirm that context helps in the modelling of acceptability, whether it is incorporated during training (`lstm` vs. `tdlm`) or at test time (`lstm`$^-$/`tdlm`$^-$ vs. `lstm`$^+$/`tdlm`$^+$).

Interestingly, we see a lower correlation when we are predicting sentence acceptability that is judged with context. The *SLOR* correlation of `lstm`$^+$/`tdlm`$^+$ vs. h^+ (0.546/568) is lower than that of `lstm`$^-$/`tdlm`$^-$ vs. h^- (0.584/0.640). This result corresponds to the low one-vs-rest human performance of h^+ compared to h^- (0.299 vs. 0.636, see Section 2). It suggests that h^+ ratings are more difficult to predict than h^-. With human performance taken into account, both models substantially outperform the average single-annotator correlation, which is encouraging for the prospect of accurate model prediction on this task.

4   Related Work

Nagata (1988) reports a small scale experiment with 12 Japanese speakers on the effect of repetition of sentences, and embedding them in context. He notes that both repetition and context cause acceptability judgements for ill formed sentences to be more lenient. Gradience in acceptability judgements are studied in the works of Sorace and Keller (2005) and Sprouse (2007).

There is an extensive literature on automatic detection of grammatical errors (Atwell, 1987; Chodorow and Leacock, 2000; Bigert and Knutsson, 2002; Sjöbergh, 2005; Wagner et al., 2007), but limited work on acceptability prediction. Heilman et al. (2014) trained a linear regression model that uses features such as spelling errors, sentence scores from n-gram models and parsers. Lau et al. (2015, 2016) experimented with unsupervised learners and found that a simple RNN was the best performing model. Both works predict acceptability independently of any contextual factors outside the target sentence.

---

model has no information as to what words will be relevant.

5   Future Work and Conclusions

We found that (i) context positively influences acceptability, particularly for ill-formed sentences, but it also has the reverse effect for well-formed sentences (H_1); (ii) incorporating context (during training or testing) when modelling acceptability improves model performance (H_2); and (iii) prediction performance declines when tested on judgements collected with context, overturning our original hypothesis (H_3). We discovered that human agreement decreases when context is introduced, suggesting that ratings are less predictable in this case.

While it is intuitive that context should improve acceptability for ill-formed sentences, it is less obvious why it reduces acceptability for well-formed sentences. We will investigate this question in future work. We will also experiment with a wider range of models, including sentence embedding methodologies such as Skip-Thought (Kiros et al., 2015).

Acknowledgments

We are grateful to the anonymous ACL reviewers for their helpful comments. Versions of this paper were presented to the Queen Mary University of London NLP Seminar in March 2018, and the Saarland University SFB Language Sciences Colloquium in May 2018. We are grateful to the audiences of both forums, and to colleagues at CLASP for useful discussion of the ideas presented here.

The research of the first two authors was supported by grant 2014-39 from the Swedish Research Council, which funds the Centre for Linguistic Theory and Studies in Probability in FLoV at the University of Gothenburg.

References

E.S. Atwell. 1987. How to detect grammatical errors in a text without parsing it. In *Proceedings of the third conference on European chapter of the Association for Computational Linguistics*. Association for Computational Linguistics Morristown, NJ, USA, pages 38–45.

J. Bigert and O. Knutsson. 2002. Robust error detection: A hybrid approach combining unsupervised error detection and linguistic knowledge. In *Proc. 2nd Workshop Robust Methods in Analysis of Natural language Data (ROMAND'02), Frascati, Italy*. pages 10–19.

M. Chodorow and C. Leacock. 2000. An unsupervised method for detecting grammatical errors. In *Proceedings of the 1st North American chapter of the Association for Computational Linguistics conference*. Morgan Kaufmann Publishers Inc. San Francisco, CA, USA, pages 140–147.

Michael Heilman, Aoife Cahill, Nitin Madnani, Melissa Lopez, Matthew Mulholland, and Joel Tetreault. 2014. Predicting grammaticality on an ordinal scale. In *Proceedings of the 52nd Annual Meeting of the Association for Computational Linguistics (Volume 2: Short Papers)*. Baltimore, Maryland, pages 174–180.

Sepp Hochreiter and Jürgen Schmidhuber. 1997. Long short-term memory. *Neural Computation* 9:1735–1780.

Ryan Kiros, Yukun Zhu, Ruslan Salakhutdinov, Richard S. Zemel, Antionio Torralba, Raquel Urtasun, and Sanja Fidler. 2015. Skip-thought vectors. Montreal, Canada, pages 3294–3302.

Philipp Koehn, Hieu Hoang, Alexandra Birch, Chris Callison-Burch, Marcello Federico, Nicola Bertoldi, Brooke Cowan, Wade Shen, Christine Moran, Richard Zens, Chris Dyer, Ondrej Bojar, Alexandra Constantin, and Evan Herbst. 2007. Moses: Open source toolkit for statistical machine translation. In *Proceedings of the 45th Annual Meeting of the Association for Computational Linguistics Companion Volume Proceedings of the Demo and Poster Sessions*. Prague, Czech Republic, pages 177–180.

Jey Han Lau, Timothy Baldwin, and Trevor Cohn. 2017. Topically driven neural language model. In *Proceedings of the 55th Annual Meeting of the Association for Computational Linguistics (Volume 1: Long Papers)*. Vancouver, Canada, pages 355–365.

Jey Han Lau, Alexander Clark, and Shalom Lappin. 2015. Unsupervised prediction of acceptability judgements. In *Proceedings of the 53rd Annual Meeting of the Association for Computational Linguistics and the 7th International Joint Conference on Natural Language Processing (Volume 1: Long Papers)*. Association for Computational Linguistics, Beijing, China, pages 1618–1628.

Jey Han Lau, Alexander Clark, and Shalom Lappin. 2016. Grammaticality, acceptability, and probability: A probabilistic view of linguistic knowledge. *Cognitive Science* pages 1–40.

Tomas Mikolov, Martin Karafiát, Lukas Burget, Jan Cernockỳ, and Sanjeev Khudanpur. 2010. Recurrent neural network based language model. Makuhari, Japan, pages 1045–1048.

Hiroshi Nagata. 1988. The relativity of linguistic intuition: The effect of repetition on grammaticality. *Journal of Psycholinguistic Research* 17:1–17.

J. Sjöbergh. 2005. Chunking: an unsupervised method to find errors in text. *NODALIDA2005* page 180.

A. Sorace and F. Keller. 2005. Gradience in linguistic data. *Lingua* 115(11):1497–1524.

J. Sprouse. 2007. Continuous acceptability, categorical grammaticality, and experimental syntax. *Biolinguistics* 1:123–134.

J. Wagner, J. Foster, and J. Van Genabith. 2007. A comparative evaluation of deep and shallow approaches to the automatic detection of common grammatical errors. *Proceedings of EMNLP-CoNLL-2007* .

Do Neural Network Cross-Modal Mappings Really Bridge Modalities?

Guillem Collell
Department of Computer Science
KU Leuven
gcollell@kuleuven.be

Marie-Francine Moens
Department of Computer Science
KU Leuven
sien.moens@cs.kuleuven.be

Abstract

Feed-forward networks are widely used in cross-modal applications to bridge modalities by mapping distributed vectors of one modality to the other, or to a shared space. The predicted vectors are then used to perform e.g., retrieval or labeling. Thus, the success of the whole system relies on the ability of the mapping to make the neighborhood structure (i.e., the pairwise similarities) of the predicted vectors akin to that of the target vectors. However, whether this is achieved has not been investigated yet. Here, we propose a new similarity measure and two ad hoc experiments to shed light on this issue. In three cross-modal benchmarks we learn a large number of language-to-vision and vision-to-language neural network mappings (up to five layers) using a rich diversity of image and text features and loss functions. Our results reveal that, surprisingly, the neighborhood structure of the predicted vectors consistently resembles more that of the input vectors than that of the target vectors. In a second experiment, we further show that untrained nets do not significantly disrupt the neighborhood (i.e., semantic) structure of the input vectors.

1 Introduction

Neural network mappings are widely used to bridge modalities or spaces in cross-modal retrieval (Qiao et al., 2017; Wang et al., 2016; Zhang et al., 2016), zero-shot learning (Lazaridou et al., 2015b, 2014; Socher et al., 2013) in building multimodal representations (Collell et al., 2017) or in word translation (Lazaridou et al., 2015a), to name a few. Typically, a neural network is firstly trained to predict the distributed vectors of one modality (or space) from the other. At test time, some operation such as retrieval or labeling is performed based on the nearest neighbors of the predicted (mapped) vectors. For instance, in zero-shot image classification, image features are mapped to the text space and the label of the nearest neighbor word is assigned. Thus, the success of such systems relies entirely on the ability of the map to make the predicted vectors similar to the target vectors in terms of semantic or neighborhood structure.[1] However, whether neural nets achieve this goal in general has not been investigated yet. In fact, recent work evidences that considerable information about the input modality propagates into the predicted modality (Collell et al., 2017; Lazaridou et al., 2015b; Frome et al., 2013).

To shed light on these questions, we first introduce the (to the best of our knowledge) first existing measure to quantify *similarity between the neighborhood structures of two sets of vectors*. Second, we perform extensive experiments in three benchmarks where we learn image-to-text and text-to-image neural net mappings using a rich variety of state-of-the-art text and image features and loss functions. Our results reveal that, contrary to expectation, the semantic structure of the mapped vectors consistently resembles more that of the input vectors than that of the target vectors of interest. In a second experiment, by using six concept similarity tasks we show that the semantic structure of the input vectors is preserved after mapping them with an untrained network, further evidencing that feed-forward nets naturally preserve semantic information about the input. Overall, we uncover and rise awareness of a largely

---

[1] We indistinctly use the terms *semantic structure*, *neighborhood structure* and *similarity structure*. They refer to all pairwise similarities of a set of N vectors, for some similarity measure (e.g., Euclidean or cosine).

Proceedings of the 56th Annual Meeting of the Association for Computational Linguistics (Short Papers), pages 462–468
Melbourne, Australia, July 15 - 20, 2018. ©2018 Association for Computational Linguistics

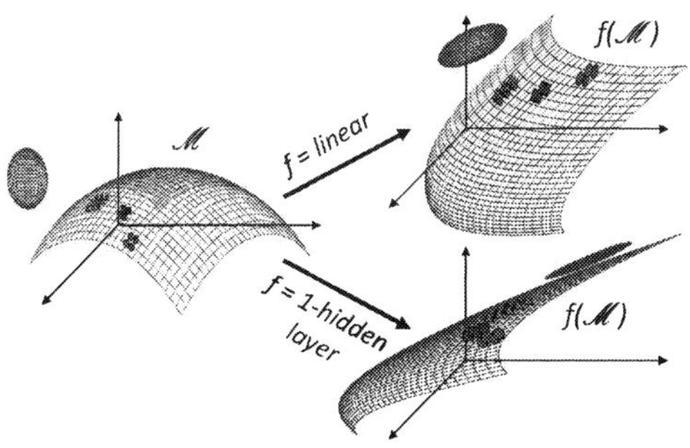

Figure 1: Effect of applying a mapping f to a (disconnected) manifold $\mathcal{M}$ with three hypothetical classes (■, ▲ and ●).

ignored phenomenon relevant to a wide range of cross-modal / cross-space applications such as retrieval, zero-shot learning or image annotation.

Ultimately, this paper aims at: (1) Encouraging the development of better architectures to bridge modalities / spaces; (2) Advocating for the use of semantic-based criteria to evaluate the quality of predicted vectors such as the neighborhood-based measure proposed here, instead of purely geometric measures such as mean squared error (MSE).

2   Related Work and Motivation

Neural network and linear mappings are popular tools to bridge modalities in *cross-modal retrieval* systems. Lazaridou et al. (2015b) leverage a text-to-image linear mapping to retrieve images given text queries. Weston et al. (2011) map label and image features into a shared space with a linear mapping to perform *image annotation*. Alternatively, Frome et al. (2013), Lazaridou et al. (2014) and Socher et al. (2013) perform *zero-shot* image classification with an image-to-text neural network mapping. Instead of mapping to latent features, Collell et al. (2018) use a 2-layer feedforward network to map word embeddings directly to image pixels in order to *visualize* spatial arrangements of objects. Neural networks are also popular in other cross-space applications such as *cross-lingual* tasks. Lazaridou et al. (2015a) learn a linear map from language A to language B and then translate new words by returning the nearest neighbor of the mapped vector in the B space.

In the context of zero-shot learning, shortcomings of cross-space neural mappings have also been identified. For instance, "hubness" (Radovanović et al., 2010) and "pollu-

tion" (Lazaridou et al., 2015a) relate to the high-dimensionality of the feature spaces and to overfitting respectively. Crucially, we do not assume that our cross-modal problem has any class labels, and we study the similarity between input and mapped vectors and between output and mapped vectors.

Recent work evidences that the predicted vectors of cross-modal neural net mappings are still largely informative about the input vectors. Lazaridou et al. (2015b) qualitatively observe that abstract textual concepts are grounded with the visual input modality. Counterintuitively, Collell et al. (2017) find that the vectors "imagined" from a language-to-vision neural map, outperform the original visual vectors in concept similarity tasks. The paper argued that the reconstructed visual vectors become grounded with language because the map preserves topological properties of the input. Here, we go one step further and show that the mapped vectors often resemble the input vectors more than the target vectors in semantic terms, which goes against the goal of a cross-modal map.

Well-known theoretical work shows that networks with as few as one hidden layer are able to approximate any function (Hornik et al., 1989). However, this result does not reveal much neither about test performance nor about the semantic structure of the mapped vectors. Instead, the phenomenon described is more closely tied to other properties of neural networks. In particular, continuity guarantees that topological properties of the input, such as connectedness, are preserved (Armstrong, 2013). Furthermore, continuity in a topology induced by a metric also ensures that points that are close together are mapped close together. As a toy example, Fig. 1 illustrates the distortion of a manifold after being mapped by a neural net.[2]

In a noiseless world with fully statistically dependent modalities, the vectors of one modality could be perfectly predicted from those of the other. However, in real-world problems this is unrealistic given the noise of the features and the fact that modalities encode complementary information (Collell and Moens, 2016). Such unpredictability combined with continuity and topology-preserving properties of neural nets propel the phenomenon identified, namely mapped vectors resembling more the input than the target vectors, in nearest neighbors terms.

---

[2]Parameters of these mappings were generated at random.

3 Proposed Approach

To bridge modalities $\mathcal{X}$ and $\mathcal{Y}$, we consider two popular cross-modal mappings $f : \mathcal{X} \to \mathcal{Y}$.

(i) **Linear** mapping (***lin***):

$$f(x) = W_0 x + b_0$$

with $W_0 \in \mathbb{R}^{d_y \times d_x}$, $b_0 \in \mathbb{R}^{d_y}$, where d_x and d_y are the input and output dimensions respectively.

(ii) Feed-forward **neural network** (***nn***):

$$f(x) = W_1 \sigma(W_0 x + b_0) + b_1$$

with $W_1 \in \mathbb{R}^{d_y \times d_h}$, $W_0 \in \mathbb{R}^{d_h \times d_x}$, $b_0 \in \mathbb{R}^{d_h}$, $b_1 \in \mathbb{R}^{d_y}$ where d_h is the number of hidden units and $\sigma()$ the non-linearity (e.g., tanh or sigmoid). Although single hidden layer networks are already universal approximators (Hornik et al., 1989), we explored whether deeper nets with **3 and 5 hidden layers** could improve the fit (see Supplement).

Loss: Our primary choice is the *MSE*: $\frac{1}{2}\|f(x) - y\|^2$, where y is the target vector. We also tested other losses such as the *cosine*: $1 - \cos(f(x), y)$ and the *max-margin*: $\max\{0, \gamma + \|f(x) - y\| - \|f(\tilde{x}) - y\|\}$, where $\tilde{x}$ belongs to a different class than (x, y), and γ is the margin. As in Lazaridou et al. (2015a) and Weston et al. (2011), we choose the first $\tilde{x}$ that violates the constraint. Notice that losses that do not require class labels such as *MSE* are suitable for a wider, more general set of tasks than discriminative losses (e.g., cross-entropy). In fact, cross-modal retrieval tasks often do not exhibit any class labels. Additionally, our research question concerns the cross-space mapping problem in isolation (independently of class labels).

Let us denote a set of N input and output vectors by $X \in \mathbb{R}^{N \times d_x}$ and $Y \in \mathbb{R}^{N \times d_y}$ respectively. Each input vector x_i is paired to the output vector y_i of the same index ($i = 1, \cdots, N$). Let us henceforth denote the mapped input vectors by $f(X) \in \mathbb{R}^{N \times d_y}$. In order to explore the similarity between $f(X)$ and X, and between $f(X)$ and Y, we propose two *ad hoc* settings below.

3.1 Neighborhood Structure of Mapped Vectors (Experiment 1)

To measure the similarity between the neighborhood structure of two sets of *paired* vectors V and Z, we propose the *mean nearest neighbor overlap* measure (***mNNO***$^K(V, Z)$). We define the *nearest neighbor overlap* ***NNO***$^K(v_i, z_i)$ as the *number of K nearest neighbors that two paired vectors v_i, z_i share in their respective spaces*. E.g., if the 3 ($= K$) nearest neighbors of v_{cat} in V are $\{v_{dog}, v_{tiger}, v_{lion}\}$ and those of z_{cat} in Z are $\{z_{mouse}, z_{tiger}, z_{lion}\}$, the ***NNO***$^3(v_{cat}, z_{cat})$ is 2.

Definition 1 *Let* $V = \{v_i\}_{i=1}^N$ *and* $Z = \{z_i\}_{i=1}^N$ *be two sets of N paired vectors. We define:*

$$\textbf{\textit{mNNO}}^K(V, Z) = \frac{1}{KN} \sum_{i=1}^{N} NNO^K(v_i, z_i) \quad (1)$$

with ***NNO***$^K(v_i, z_i) = |NN^K(v_i) \cap NN^K(z_i)|$, *where* $NN^K(v_i)$ *and* $NN^K(z_i)$ *are the indexes of the K nearest neighbors of v_i and z_i, respectively.*

The normalizing constant K simply scales $mNNO^K(V, Z)$ between 0 and 1, making it independent of the choice of K. Thus, a $mNNO^K(V, Z) = 0.7$ means that the vectors in V and Z share, on average, 70% of their nearest neighbors. Notice that *mNNO* implicitly performs retrieval for some similarity measure (e.g., Euclidean or cosine), and quantifies how semantically similar two sets of paired vectors are.

3.2 Mapping with Untrained Networks (Experiment 2)

To complement the setting above (Sect. 3.1), it is instructive to consider the limit case of an untrained network. Concept similarity tasks provide a suitable setting to study the semantic structure of distributed representations (Pennington et al., 2014). That is, semantically similar concepts should ideally be close together. In particular, our interest is in comparing X with its projection $f(X)$ through a mapping with random parameters, to understand the extent to which the mapping may disrupt or preserve the semantic structure of X.

4 Experimental Setup

4.1 Experiment 1

4.1.1 Datasets

To test the generality of our claims, we select a rich diversity of cross-modal tasks involving texts at three levels: *word* level (ImageNet), *sentence* level (IAPR TC-12), and *document* level (Wiki). **ImageNet** (Russakovsky et al., 2015). Consists of $\sim$14M images, covering $\sim$22K WordNet synsets (or meanings). Following Collell et al. (2017), we take the most relevant word for each synset and keep only synsets with more than 50 images. This yields 9,251 different words (or instances).

IAPR TC-12 (Grubinger et al., 2006). Contains 20K images (18K train / 2K test) annotated with 255 labels. Each image is accompanied with a short description of one to three sentences.

Wikipedia (Pereira et al., 2014). Has 2,866 samples (2,173 train / 693 test). Each sample is a section of a Wikipedia article paired with one image.

4.1.2 Hyperparameters and Implementation

See the Supplement (Sect. 1) for details.

4.1.3 Image and Text Features

To ensure that results are independent of the choice of image and text features, we use 5 (2 image + 3 text) features of varied dimensionality (64-d, 128-d, 300-d, 2,048-d) and two directions, text-to-image ($T \to I$) and image-to-text ($I \to T$). We make our extracted features publicly available.[3]

Text. In *ImageNet* we use 300-dimensional GloVe[4] (Pennington et al., 2014) and 300-d word2vec (Mikolov et al., 2013) word embeddings. In *IAPR TC-12* and *Wiki*, we employ state-of-the-art bidirectional gated recurrent unit (bi-GRU) features (Cho et al., 2014) that we learn with a classification task (see Sect. 2 of Supplement).

Image. For *ImageNet*, we use the publicly available[5] VGG-128 (Chatfield et al., 2014) and ResNet (He et al., 2015) visual features from Collell et al. (2017), where we obtained 128-dimensional VGG-128 and 2,048-d ResNet features from the last layer (before the softmax) of the forward pass of each image. The final representation for a word is the average feature vector (centroid) of all available images for this word. In *IAPR TC-12* and *Wiki*, features for individual images are obtained similarly from the last layer of a ResNet and a VGG-128 model.

4.2 Experiment 2

4.2.1 Datasets

We include six benchmarks, comprising three types of concept similarity: **(i) Semantic similarity**: *SemSim* (Silberer and Lapata, 2014), *Simlex999* (Hill et al., 2015) and *SimVerb-3500* (Gerz et al., 2016); **(ii) Relatedness**: *MEN* (Bruni et al.,

2014) and *WordSim-353* (Finkelstein et al., 2001); **(iii) Visual similarity**: *VisSim* (Silberer and Lapata, 2014) which includes the same word pairs as *SemSim*, rated for visual similarity instead of semantic. All six test sets contain human ratings of similarity for word pairs, e.g., ('cat','dog').

4.2.2 Hyperparameters and Implementation

The parameters in W_0, W_1 are drawn from a random uniform distribution $[-1, 1]$ and b_0, b_1 are set to zero. We use a tanh activation $\sigma()$.[6] The output dimension d_y is set to 2,048 for all embeddings.

4.2.3 Image and Text Features

Textual and visual features are the same as described in Sect. 4.1.3 for the *ImageNet* dataset.

4.2.4 Similarity Predictions

We compute the prediction of similarity between two vectors z_1, z_2 with both the cosine $\frac{z_1 z_2}{\|z_1\|\|z_2\|}$ and the Euclidean similarity $\frac{1}{1+\|z_1-z_2\|}$.[7]

4.2.5 Performance Metrics

As is common practice, we evaluate the predictions of similarity of the embeddings (Sect. 4.2.4) against the human similarity ratings with the *Spearman correlation* ρ. We report the average of 10 sets of randomly generated parameters.

5 Results and Discussion

We test statistical significance with a two-sided Wilcoxon rank sum test adjusted with Bonferroni. The null hypothesis is that a compared pair is equal. In Tab. 1, * indicates that $mNNO(X, f(X))$ differs from $mNNO(Y, f(X))$ (p < 0.001) on the same mapping, embedding and direction. In Tab. 2, * indicates that performance of mapped and input vectors differs (p < 0.05) in the 10 runs.

5.1 Experiment 1

Results below are with cosine neighbors and $K = 10$. Euclidean neighbors yield similar results and are thus left to the Supplement. Similarly, results in ImageNet with GloVe embeddings are shown below and word2vec results in the Supplement. The choice of $K = \{5, 10, 30\}$ had no visible effect on results. Results with *3- and 5-layer* nets did not show big differences with the results below (see Supplement). The ***cosine*** and ***max-margin*** losses

---

[3]http://liir.cs.kuleuven.be/software.html
[4]http://nlp.stanford.edu/projects/glove
[5]http://liir.cs.kuleuven.be/software.html

[6]We find that sigmoid and ReLu yield similar results.
[7]Notice that papers generally use only cosine similarity (Lazaridou et al., 2015b; Pennington et al., 2014).

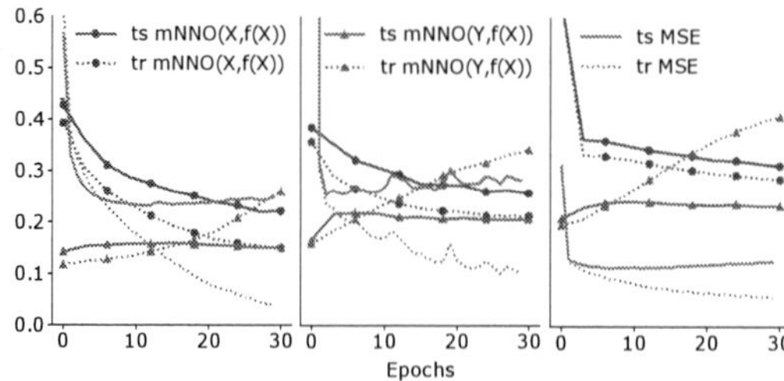

Figure 2: Learning a **nn** model in **Wiki** (left), **IAPR TC-12** (middle) and **ImageNet** (right).

performed slightly worse than *MSE* (see Supplement). Although Lazaridou et al. (2015a) and Weston et al. (2011) find that *max-margin* performs the best in their tasks, we do not find our result entirely surprising given that max-margin focuses on inter-class differences while we look also at intra-class neighbors (in fact, we do not require classes).

Tab. 1 shows our core finding, namely that the semantic structure of $f(X)$ resembles more that of X than that of Y, for both *lin* and *nn* maps.

			ResNet		VGG-128	
			$X, f(X)$	$Y, f(X)$	$X, f(X)$	$Y, f(X)$
ImageNet	$I \to T$	*lin*	**0.681**[*]	0.262	**0.723**[*]	0.236
		nn	**0.622**[*]	0.273	**0.682**[*]	0.246
	$T \to I$	*lin*	**0.379**[*]	0.241	**0.339**[*]	0.229
		nn	**0.354**[*]	0.27	**0.326**[*]	0.256
IAPR TC-12	$I \to T$	*lin*	**0.358**[*]	0.214	**0.382**[*]	0.163
		nn	**0.336**[*]	0.219	**0.331**[*]	0.18
	$T \to I$	*lin*	**0.48**[*]	0.2	**0.419**[*]	0.167
		nn	**0.413**[*]	0.225	**0.372**[*]	0.182
Wikipedia	$I \to T$	*lin*	**0.235**[*]	0.156	**0.235**[*]	0.143
		nn	**0.269**[*]	0.161	**0.282**[*]	0.148
	$T \to I$	*lin*	**0.574**[*]	0.156	**0.6**[*]	0.148
		nn	**0.521**[*]	0.156	**0.511**[*]	0.151

Table 1: Test mean nearest neighbor overlap. Boldface indicates the largest score at each $mNNO^{10}(X, f(X))$ and $mNNO^{10}(Y, f(X))$ pair, which are abbreviated by $X, f(X)$ and $Y, f(X)$.

Fig. 2 is particularly revealing. If we would only look at *train* performance (and allow train MSE to reach 0) then $f(X) = Y$ and clearly train $mNNO(f(X), Y) = 1$ while $mNNO(f(X), X)$ can only be smaller than 1. However, the interest is always on *test* samples, and (near-)perfect *test* prediction is unrealistic. Notice in fact in Fig. 2 that even if we look at *train* fit, MSE needs to be close to 0 for $mNNO(f(X), Y)$ to be reasonably large. In all the combinations from Tab. 1, the *test mNNO*$(f(X), Y)$ never surpasses *test mNNO*$(f(X), X)$ for any number of epochs, even with an oracle (not shown).

5.2 Experiment 2

Tab. 2 shows that untrained linear (f_{lin}) and neural net (f_{nn}) mappings preserve the semantic structure of the input X, complementing thus the findings of Experiment 1. Experiment 1 concerns learning, while, by "ablating" the learning part and randomizing weights, Experiment 2 is revealing about the natural tendency of neural nets to preserve semantic information about the input, regardless of the choice of the target vectors and loss function.

	WS-353		Men		SemSim	
	Cos	Eucl	Cos	Eucl	Cos	Eucl
f_{nn}(GloVe)	**0.632**	**0.634**[*]	0.795	**0.791**[*]	0.75[*]	**0.744**[*]
f_{lin}(GloVe)	0.63	0.606	0.798	0.781	0.763	0.712
GloVe	**0.632**	0.601	**0.801**	0.782	**0.768**	0.716
f_{nn}(ResNet)	0.402	0.408[*]	0.556	**0.554**[*]	0.512	0.513
f_{lin}(ResNet)	**0.425**	0.449	0.566	0.534	0.533	0.514
ResNet	0.423	**0.457**	**0.567**	0.535	**0.534**	**0.516**

	VisSim		SimLex		SimVerb	
	Cos	Eucl	Cos	Eucl	Cos	Eucl
f_{nn}(GloVe)	0.594[*]	**0.59**[*]	0.369	**0.363**[*]	0.313	**0.301**[*]
f_{lin}(GloVe)	0.602[*]	0.576	0.369	0.341	**0.326**	0.23
GloVe	**0.606**	0.58	**0.371**	0.34	0.32	0.235
f_{nn}(ResNet)	0.527[*]	**0.526**[*]	0.405	**0.406**	0.178	0.169
f_{lin}(ResNet)	0.541	0.498	**0.409**	0.404	0.198	0.182
ResNet	**0.543**	0.501	**0.409**	0.403	**0.211**	**0.199**

Table 2: Spearman correlations between human ratings and the similarities (cosine or Euclidean) predicted from the embeddings. Boldface denotes best performance per input embedding type.

6 Conclusions

Overall, we uncovered a phenomenon neglected so far, namely that neural net cross-modal mappings can produce mapped vectors more akin to the input vectors than the target vectors, in terms of semantic structure. Such finding has been possible thanks to the proposed measure that explicitly quantifies similarity between the neighborhood structure of two sets of vectors. While other measures such as mean squared error can be misleading, our measure provides a more realistic estimate of the semantic similarity between predicted and target vectors. In fact, it is the semantic structure (or pairwise similarities) what ultimately matters in cross-modal applications.

Acknowledgments

This work has been supported by the CHIST-ERA EU project MUSTER[8] and by the KU Leuven grant RUN/15/005.

References

Mark Anthony Armstrong. 2013. *Basic topology*. Springer Science & Business Media.

Elia Bruni, Nam-Khanh Tran, and Marco Baroni. 2014. Multimodal distributional semantics. *JAIR* 49(1-47).

Ken Chatfield, Karen Simonyan, Andrea Vedaldi, and Andrew Zisserman. 2014. Return of the devil in the details: Delving deep into convolutional nets. In *BMVC*.

Kyunghyun Cho, Bart Van Merriënboer, Caglar Gulcehre, Dzmitry Bahdanau, Fethi Bougares, Holger Schwenk, and Yoshua Bengio. 2014. Learning phrase representations using rnn encoder-decoder for statistical machine translation. *arXiv preprint arXiv:1406.1078* .

Guillem Collell and Marie-Francine Moens. 2016. Is an Image Worth More than a Thousand Words? On the Fine-Grain Semantic Differences between Visual and Linguistic Representations. In *COLING*. ACL, pages 2807–2817.

Guillem Collell, Luc Van Gool, and Marie-Francine Moens. 2018. Acquiring Common Sense Spatial Knowledge through Implicit Spatial Templates. In *AAAI*. AAAI.

Guillem Collell, Teddy Zhang, and Marie-Francine Moens. 2017. Imagined Visual Representations as Multimodal Embeddings. In *AAAI*. AAAI, pages 4378–4384.

Lev Finkelstein, Evgeniy Gabrilovich, Yossi Matias, Ehud Rivlin, Zach Solan, Gadi Wolfman, and Eytan Ruppin. 2001. Placing search in context: The concept revisited. In *WWW*. ACM, pages 406–414.

Andrea Frome, Greg S Corrado, Jon Shlens, Samy Bengio, Jeff Dean, Tomas Mikolov, et al. 2013. Devise: A deep visual-semantic embedding model. In *NIPS*. pages 2121–2129.

Daniela Gerz, Ivan Vulić, Felix Hill, Roi Reichart, and Anna Korhonen. 2016. Simverb-3500: A large-scale evaluation set of verb similarity. *arXiv preprint arXiv:1608.00869* .

Michael Grubinger, Paul Clough, Henning Müller, and Thomas Deselaers. 2006. The iapr tc-12 benchmark: A new evaluation resource for visual information systems. In *International workshop ontoImage*. volume 5, page 10.

Kaiming He, Xiangyu Zhang, Shaoqing Ren, and Jian Sun. 2015. Deep residual learning for image recognition. *arXiv preprint arXiv:1512.03385* .

Felix Hill, Roi Reichart, and Anna Korhonen. 2015. Simlex-999: Evaluating semantic models with (genuine) similarity estimation. *Computational Linguistics* 41(4):665–695.

Kurt Hornik, Maxwell Stinchcombe, and Halbert White. 1989. Multilayer feedforward networks are universal approximators. *Neural networks* 2(5):359–366.

Angeliki Lazaridou, Elia Bruni, and Marco Baroni. 2014. Is this a wampimuk? cross-modal mapping between distributional semantics and the visual world. In *ACL*. pages 1403–1414.

Angeliki Lazaridou, Georgiana Dinu, and Marco Baroni. 2015a. Hubness and pollution: Delving into cross-space mapping for zero-shot learning. In *ACL*. volume 1, pages 270–280.

Angeliki Lazaridou, Nghia The Pham, and Marco Baroni. 2015b. Combining language and vision with a multimodal skip-gram model. *arXiv preprint arXiv:1501.02598* .

Tomas Mikolov, Ilya Sutskever, Kai Chen, Gregory S. Corrado, and Jeffrey Dean. 2013. Distributed representations of words and phrases and their compositionality. In *NIPS*. pages 3111–3119.

Jeffrey Pennington, Richard Socher, and Christopher D Manning. 2014. Glove: Global vectors for word representation. In *EMNLP*. volume 14, pages 1532–1543.

Jose Costa Pereira, Emanuele Coviello, Gabriel Doyle, Nikhil Rasiwasia, Gert RG Lanckriet, Roger Levy, and Nuno Vasconcelos. 2014. On the role of correlation and abstraction in cross-modal multimedia retrieval. *TPAMI* 36(3):521–535.

Ruizhi Qiao, Lingqiao Liu, Chunhua Shen, and Anton van den Hengel. 2017. Visually aligned word embeddings for improving zero-shot learning. *arXiv preprint arXiv:1707.05427* .

Milos Radovanović, Alexandros Nanopoulos, and Mirjana Ivanović. 2010. On the existence of obstinate results in vector space models. In *SIGIR*. ACM, pages 186–193.

Olga Russakovsky, Jia Deng, Hao Su, Jonathan Krause, Sanjeev Satheesh, Sean Ma, Zhiheng Huang, Andrej Karpathy, Aditya Khosla, Michael Bernstein, et al. 2015. Imagenet large scale visual recognition challenge. *IJCV* 115(3):211–252.

Carina Silberer and Mirella Lapata. 2014. Learning grounded meaning representations with autoencoders. In *ACL*. pages 721–732.

[8]http://www.chistera.eu/projects/muster

Richard Socher, Milind Ganjoo, Christopher D Manning, and Andrew Ng. 2013. Zero-shot learning through cross-modal transfer. In *NIPS*. pages 935–943.

Kaiye Wang, Qiyue Yin, Wei Wang, Shu Wu, and Liang Wang. 2016. A comprehensive survey on cross-modal retrieval. *arXiv preprint arXiv:1607.06215* .

Jason Weston, Samy Bengio, and Nicolas Usunier. 2011. Wsabie: Scaling up to large vocabulary image annotation. In *IJCAI*. volume 11, pages 2764–2770.

Yang Zhang, Boqing Gong, and Mubarak Shah. 2016. Fast zero-shot image tagging. In *CVPR*. IEEE, pages 5985–5994.

Policy Gradient as a Proxy for
Dynamic Oracles in Constituency Parsing

Daniel Fried and **Dan Klein**
Computer Science Division
University of California, Berkeley
{dfried,klein}@cs.berkeley.edu

Abstract

Dynamic oracles provide strong supervision for training constituency parsers with exploration, but must be custom defined for a given parser's transition system. We explore using a policy gradient method as a parser-agnostic alternative. In addition to directly optimizing for a tree-level metric such as F1, policy gradient has the potential to reduce exposure bias by allowing exploration during training; moreover, it does not require a dynamic oracle for supervision. On four constituency parsers in three languages, the method substantially outperforms static oracle likelihood training in almost all settings. For parsers where a dynamic oracle is available (including a novel oracle which we define for the transition system of Dyer et al. (2016)), policy gradient typically recaptures a substantial fraction of the performance gain afforded by the dynamic oracle.

1 Introduction

Many recent state-of-the-art models for constituency parsing are transition based, decomposing production of each parse tree into a sequence of action decisions (Dyer et al., 2016; Cross and Huang, 2016; Liu and Zhang, 2017; Stern et al., 2017), building on a long line of work in transition-based parsing (Nivre, 2003; Yamada and Matsumoto, 2003; Henderson, 2004; Zhang and Clark, 2011; Chen and Manning, 2014; Andor et al., 2016; Kiperwasser and Goldberg, 2016).

However, models of this type, which decompose structure prediction into sequential decisions, can be prone to two issues (Ranzato et al., 2016; Wiseman and Rush, 2016). The first is *exposure bias*: if, at training time, the model only observes states resulting from correct past decisions, it will not be prepared to recover from its own mistakes during prediction. Second is the *loss mismatch* between the action-level loss used at training and any structure-level evaluation metric, for example F1.

A large family of techniques address the exposure bias problem by allowing the model to make mistakes and explore incorrect states during training, supervising actions at the resulting states using an expert policy (Daumé III et al., 2009; Ross et al., 2011; Choi and Palmer, 2011; Chang et al., 2015); these expert policies are typically referred to as *dynamic oracles* in parsing (Goldberg and Nivre, 2012; Ballesteros et al., 2016). While dynamic oracles have produced substantial improvements in constituency parsing performance (Coavoux and Crabbé, 2016; Cross and Huang, 2016; Stern et al., 2017; González and Gómez-Rodríguez, 2018), they must be custom designed for each transition system.

To address the loss mismatch problem, another line of work has directly optimized for structure-level cost functions (Goodman, 1996; Och, 2003). Recent methods applied to models that produce output sequentially commonly use policy gradient (Auli and Gao, 2014; Ranzato et al., 2016; Shen et al., 2016) or beam search (Xu et al., 2016; Wiseman and Rush, 2016; Edunov et al., 2017) at training time to minimize a structured cost. These methods also reduce exposure bias through exploration but do not require an expert policy for supervision.

In this work, we apply a simple policy gradient method to train four different state-of-the-art transition-based constituency parsers to maximize expected F1. We compare against training with a dynamic oracle (both to supervise exploration and provide loss-augmentation) where one is available, including a novel dynamic oracle that we define for the top-down transition system of

Proceedings of the 56th Annual Meeting of the Association for Computational Linguistics (Short Papers), pages 469–476
Melbourne, Australia, July 15 - 20, 2018. ©2018 Association for Computational Linguistics

Dyer et al. (2016).

We find that while policy gradient usually outperforms standard likelihood training, it typically underperforms the dynamic oracle-based methods – which provide direct, model-aware supervision about which actions are best to take from arbitrary parser states. However, a substantial fraction of each dynamic oracle's performance gain is often recovered using the model-agnostic policy gradient method. In the process, we obtain new state-of-the-art results for single-model discriminative transition-based parsers trained on the English PTB (92.6 F1), French Treebank (83.5 F1), and Penn Chinese Treebank Version 5.1 (87.0 F1).

2 Models

The transition-based parsers we use all decompose production of a parse tree $\mathbf{y}$ for a sentence $\mathbf{x}$ into a sequence of actions $(a_1, \ldots a_T)$ and resulting states $(s_1, \ldots s_{T+1})$. Actions a_t are predicted sequentially, conditioned on a representation of the parser's current state s_t and parameters θ:

$$p(\mathbf{y}|\mathbf{x}; \theta) = \prod_{t=1}^{T} p(a_t \mid s_t; \theta) \qquad (1)$$

We investigate four parsers with varying transition systems and methods of encoding the current state and sentence: (1) the discriminative Recurrent Neural Network Grammars (RNNG) parser of Dyer et al. (2016), (2) the In-Order parser of Liu and Zhang (2017), (3) the Span-Based parser of Cross and Huang (2016), and (4) the Top-Down parser of Stern et al. (2017).[1] We refer to the original papers for descriptions of the transition systems and model parameterizations.

3 Training Procedures

Likelihood training without exploration maximizes Eq. 1 for trees in the training corpus, but may be prone to exposure bias and loss mismatch (Section 1). Dynamic oracle methods are known to improve on this training procedure for a variety of parsers (Coavoux and Crabbé, 2016; Cross and Huang, 2016; Stern et al., 2017; González and Gómez-Rodríguez, 2018), supervising exploration

---

[1]Stern et al. (2017) trained their model using a non-probabilistic, max-margin objective. For comparison to the other models and to allow training with policy gradient, we create a locally-normalized probabilistic variant of their model by applying a softmax function to the predicted scores for each action.

during training by providing the parser with the best action to take at each explored state. We describe how policy gradient can be applied as an oracle-free alternative. We then compare to several variants of dynamic oracle training which focus on addressing exposure bias, loss mismatch, or both.

3.1 Policy Gradient

Given an arbitrary cost function Δ comparing structured outputs (e.g. negative labeled F1, for trees), we use the *risk objective*:

$$\mathcal{R}(\theta) = \sum_{i=1}^{N} \sum_{\mathbf{y}} p(\mathbf{y} \mid \mathbf{x}^{(i)}; \theta) \Delta(\mathbf{y}, \mathbf{y}^{(i)})$$

which measures the model's expected cost over possible outputs $\mathbf{y}$ for each of the training examples $(\mathbf{x}^{(1)}, \mathbf{y}^{(1)}), \ldots, (\mathbf{x}^{(N)}, \mathbf{y}^{(N)})$.

Minimizing a risk objective has a long history in structured prediction (Povey and Woodland, 2002; Smith and Eisner, 2006; Li and Eisner, 2009; Gimpel and Smith, 2010) but often relies on the cost function decomposing according to the output structure. However, we can avoid any restrictions on the cost using reinforcement learning-style approaches (Xu et al., 2016; Shen et al., 2016; Edunov et al., 2017) where cost is ascribed to the entire output structure – albeit at the expense of introducing a potentially difficult credit assignment problem.

The policy gradient method we apply is a simple variant of REINFORCE (Williams, 1992). We perform mini-batch gradient descent on the gradient of the risk objective:

$$\nabla \mathcal{R}(\theta) = \sum_{i=1}^{N} \sum_{\mathbf{y}} p(\mathbf{y}|\mathbf{x}^{(i)}) \Delta(\mathbf{y}, \mathbf{y}^{(i)}) \nabla \log p(\mathbf{y}|\mathbf{x}^{(i)}; \theta)$$

$$\approx \sum_{i=1}^{N} \sum_{\mathbf{y} \in \mathcal{Y}(\mathbf{x}^{(i)})} \Delta(\mathbf{y}, \mathbf{y}^{(i)}) \nabla \log p(\mathbf{y}|\mathbf{x}^{(i)}; \theta)$$

where $\mathcal{Y}(\mathbf{x}^{(i)})$ is a set of k candidate trees obtained by sampling from the model's distribution for sentence $\mathbf{x}^{(i)}$. We use negative labeled F1 for Δ.

To reduce the variance of the gradient estimates, we standardize Δ using its running mean and standard deviation across all candidates used so far throughout training. Following Shen et al. (2016), we also found better performance when including the gold tree $\mathbf{y}^{(i)}$ in the set of k candidates $\mathcal{Y}(\mathbf{x}^{(i)})$, and do so for all experiments reported here.[2]

---

[2]Including the gold tree in the set of candidates does bias

3.2 Dynamic Oracle Supervision

For a given parser state s_t, a dynamic oracle defines an action $a^*(s_t)$ which should be taken to incrementally produce the best tree still reachable from that state.[3]

Dynamic oracles provide strong supervision for training with exploration, but require custom design for a given transition system. Cross and Huang (2016) and Stern et al. (2017) defined optimal (with respect to F1) dynamic oracles for their respective transition systems, and below we define a novel dynamic oracle for the top-down system of RNNG.

In RNNG, tree production occurs in a stack-based, top-down traversal which produces a left-to-right linearized representation of the tree using three actions: OPEN a labeled constituent (which fixes the constituent's span to begin at the next word in the sentence which has not been shifted), SHIFT the next word in the sentence to add it to the current constituent, or CLOSE the current constituent (which fixes its span to end after the last word that has been shifted). The parser stores opened constituents on the stack, and must therefore close them in the reverse of the order that they were opened.

At a given parser state, our oracle does the following:

1. If there are any open constituents on the stack which can be closed (i.e. have had a word shifted since being opened), check the topmost of these (the one that has been opened most recently). If closing it would produce a constituent from the the gold tree that has not yet been produced (which is determined by the constituent's label, span beginning position, and the number of words currently shifted), or if the constituent could not be closed at a later position in the sentence to produce a constituent in the gold tree, return CLOSE.

2. Otherwise, if there are constituents in the gold tree which have not yet been opened in the parser state, with span beginning at the next unshifted word, OPEN the outermost of these.

3. Otherwise, SHIFT the next word.

While we do not claim that this dynamic oracle is optimal with respect to F1, we find that it still helps substantially in supervising exploration (Section 5).

Likelihood Training with Exploration Past work has differed on how to use dynamic oracles to guide exploration during oracle training (Ballesteros et al., 2016; Cross and Huang, 2016; Stern et al., 2017). We use the same sample-based method of generating candidate sets $\mathcal{Y}$ as for policy gradient, which allows us to control the dynamic oracle and policy gradient methods to perform an equal amount of exploration. Likelihood training with exploration then maximizes the sum of the log probabilities for the oracle actions for all states composing the candidate trees:

$$\mathcal{L}_E(\theta) = \sum_{i=1}^{N} \sum_{\mathbf{y} \in \mathcal{Y}(\mathbf{x}^{(i)})} \sum_{s \in \mathbf{y}} \log p(a^*(s) \mid s)$$

where $a^*(s)$ is the dynamic oracle's action for state s.

Softmax Margin Softmax margin loss (Gimpel and Smith, 2010; Auli and Lopez, 2011) addresses loss mismatch by incorporating task cost into the training loss. Since trees are decomposed into a sequence of local action predictions, we cannot use a global cost, such as F1, directly. As a proxy, we rely on the dynamic oracles' action-level supervision.

In all models we consider, action probabilities (Eq. 1) are parameterized by a softmax function

$$p_{ML}(a \mid s_t; \theta) \propto \exp(z(a, s_t, \theta))$$

for some state–action scoring function z. The softmax-margin objective replaces this by

$$p_{SMM}(a \mid s_t; \theta) \propto \exp(z(a, s_t, \theta) + \Delta(a, a_t^*)) \tag{2}$$

We use $\Delta(a, a_t^*) = 0$ if $a = a_t^*$ and 1 otherwise. This can be viewed as a "soft" version of the max-margin objective used by Stern et al. (2017) for training without exploration, but retains a locally-normalized model that we can use for sampling-based exploration.

---

the estimate of the risk objective's gradient; however since in the parsing tasks we consider, the gold tree has constant and minimal cost, augmenting with the gold is equivalent to jointly optimizing the standard likelihood and risk objectives, using an adaptive scaling factor for each objective that is dependent on the cost for the trees that have been sampled from the model. We found that including the gold candidate in this manner outperformed initial experiments that first trained a model using likelihood training and then fine-tuned using unbiased policy gradient.

[3]More generally, an oracle can return a set of such actions that could be taken from the current state, but the oracles we use select a single canonical action.

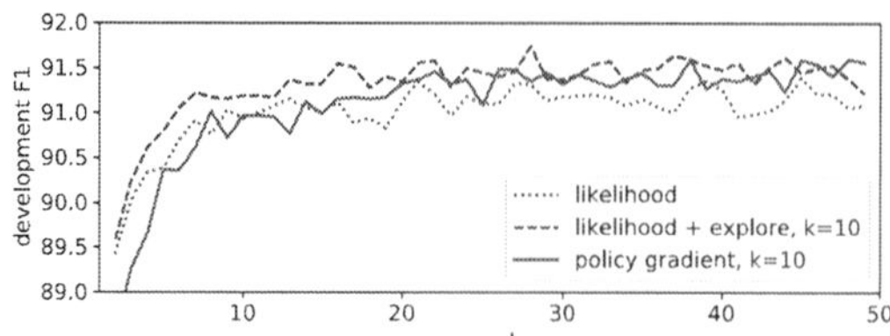

Figure 1: English development set F1 by training epoch, comparing likelihood training with two exploration variants for the Top-Down parser.

Softmax Margin with Exploration Finally, we train using a combination of softmax margin loss augmentation and exploration. We perform the same sample-based candidate generation as for policy gradient and likelihood training with exploration, but use Eq. 2 to compute the training loss for candidate states. For those parsers that have a dynamic oracle, this provides a means of training that more directly provides both exploration and cost-aware losses.

4   Experiments

We compare the constituency parsers listed in Section 2 using the above training methods. Our experiments use the English PTB (Marcus et al., 1993), French Treebank (Abeillé et al., 2003), and Penn Chinese Treebank (CTB) Version 5.1 (Xue et al., 2005).

Training To compare the training procedures as closely as possible, we train all models for a given parser in a given language from the same randomly-initialized parameter values.

We train two different versions of the RNNG model: one model using size 128 for the LSTMs and hidden states (following the original work), and a larger model with size 256. We perform evaluation using greedy search in the Span-Based and Top-Down parsers, and beam search with beam size 10 for the RNNG and In-Order parsers. We found that beam search improved performance for these two parsers by around 0.1-0.3 F1 on the development sets, and use it at inference time in every setting for these two parsers.

In our experiments, policy gradient typically requires more epochs of training to reach performance comparable to either of the dynamic oracle-based exploration methods. Figure 1 gives a typical learning curve, for the Top-Down parser on English. We found that policy gradient is also more sensitive to the number of candidates sampled per

sentence than either of the other exploration methods, with best performance on the development set usually obtained with $k = 10$ for $k \in \{2, 5, 10\}$ (where k also counts the sentence's gold tree, included in the candidate set). See Appendix A in the supplemental material for the values of k used.

Tags, Embeddings, and Morphology We largely follow previous work for each parser in our use of predicted part-of-speech tags, pretrained word embeddings, and morphological features.

All parsers use predicted part-of-speech tags as part of their sentence representations. For English and Chinese, we follow the setup of Cross and Huang (2016): training the Stanford tagger (Toutanova et al., 2003) on the training set of each parsing corpus to predict development and test set tags, and using 10-way jackknifing to predict tags for the training set.

For French, we use the predicted tags and morphological features provided with the SPMRL dataset (Seddah et al., 2014). We modified the publicly released code for all parsers to use predicted morphological features for French. We follow the approach outlined by Cross and Huang (2016) and Stern et al. (2017) for representing morphological features as learned embeddings, and use the same dimensions for these embeddings as in their papers. For RNNG and In-Order, we similarly use 10-dimensional learned embeddings for each morphological feature, feeding them as LSTM inputs for each word alongside the word and part-of-speech tag embeddings.

For RNNG and the In-Order parser, we use the same word embeddings as the original papers for English and Chinese, and train 100-dimensional word embeddings for French using the structured skip-gram method of Ling et al. (2015) on French Wikipedia.

5   Results and Discussion

Table 1 compares parser F1 by training procedure for each language. Policy gradient improves upon likelihood training in 14 out of 15 cases, with improvements of up to 1.5 F1. One of the three dynamic oracle-based training methods – either likelihood with exploration, softmax margin (SMM), or softmax margin with exploration – obtains better performance than policy gradient in 10 out of 12 cases. This is perhaps unsurprising given the strong supervision provided by the dynamic oracles and the credit assignment problem faced by

training	English	French	Chinese
Span-Based (Cross and Huang, 2016)			
C&H[*]	91.3	83.3	—
likelihood	91.0	81.5	83.3
policy gradient	91.4 (+0.4)	81.4 (-0.1)	83.5 (+0.2)
likelihood+explore[*]	91.3 (+0.3)	81.2 (-0.3)	83.5 (+0.2)
SMM[*]	91.3 (+0.3)	81.5 (+0.0)	83.7 (+0.4)
SMM+explore[*]	**91.5 (+0.5)**	**81.7 (+0.2)**	**84.0 (+0.7)**
Top-Down (Stern et al., 2017)			
Stern et al.[*†]	91.8	82.2	—
likelihood	91.2	80.7	83.9
policy gradient	**91.4 (+0.2)**	81.4 (+0.7)	84.7 (+0.8)
likelihood+explore[*]	91.3 (+0.1)	81.5 (+0.8)	**85.3 (+1.4)**
SMM[*]	91.1 (-0.1)	81.2 (+0.5)	84.5 (+0.6)
SMM+explore[*]	**91.4 (+0.2)**	**81.9 (+1.2)**	84.8 (+0.9)
RNNG Discriminative, Size 128 (Dyer et al., 2016)			
Dyer et al.	91.7	—	84.6
likelihood	91.4	83.2	84.5
policy gradient	91.6 (+0.2)	83.3 (+0.1)	84.7 (+0.2)
likelihood+explore[*]	**92.1 (+0.7)**	83.0 (-0.2)	**85.5 (+1.0)**
SMM[*]	91.5 (+0.1)	82.8 (-0.4)	83.6 (-0.9)
SMM+explore[*]	**92.1 (+0.7)**	**83.5 (+0.3)**	85.0 (+0.5)
RNNG Discriminative, Size 256			
likelihood	91.7	83.1	84.5
policy gradient	92.3 (+0.7)	**83.2 (+0.1)**	85.6 (+1.1)
likelihood+explore	**92.6 (+0.9)**	82.9 (-0.2)	**86.0 (+1.5)**
In-Order (Liu and Zhang, 2017)			
L&Z	91.8	—	86.1
likelihood	91.6	82.7	85.5
policy gradient	**92.2 (+0.6)**	**83.3 (+0.6)**	**87.0 (+1.5)**

Table 1: Test set F1 by training procedure, and in comparison to past work using the same models. Improvements over likelihood training are indicated in parentheses, with the highest results among the training procedures compared here in bold. [*]: training uses a dynamic oracle; [†]: past work using a global scoring model (all models we train here are locally-normalized).

policy gradient. However, a substantial fraction of this performance gain is recaptured by policy gradient in most cases.

While likelihood training with exploration using a dynamic oracle more directly addresses exploration bias, and softmax margin training more directly addresses loss mismatch, these two phenomena are still entangled, and the best dynamic oracle-based method to use varies. The effectiveness of the oracle method is also likely to be influenced by the nature of the dynamic oracle available for the parser. For example, the oracle for RNNG lacks F1 optimality guarantees, and softmax margin without exploration often underperforms likelihood for this parser. However, exploration improves softmax margin training across all parsers and conditions.

Although results from likelihood training are mostly comparable between RNNG-128 and the larger model RNNG-256 across languages, policy gradient and likelihood training with exploration both typically yield larger improvements in the larger models, obtaining 92.6 F1 for English and 86.0 for Chinese (using likelihood training with exploration), although results are slightly higher for the policy gradient and dynamic oracle-based methods for the smaller model on French (including 83.5 with softmax margin with exploration). Finally, we observe that policy gradient also provides large improvements for the In-Order parser, where a dynamic oracle has not been defined.

We note that although some of these results (92.6 for English, 83.5 for French, 87.0 for Chinese) are state-of-the-art for single model, discriminative transition-based parsers, other work on constituency parsing achieves better performance through other methods. Techniques that combine multiple models or add semi-supervised data (Vinyals et al., 2015; Dyer et al., 2016; Choe and Charniak, 2016; Kuncoro et al., 2017; Liu and Zhang, 2017; Fried et al., 2017) are orthogonal to, and could be combined with, the single-model, fixed training data methods we explore. Other recent work (Gaddy et al., 2018; Kitaev and Klein, 2018) obtains comparable or stronger performance with global chart decoders, where training uses loss augmentation provided by an oracle. By performing model-optimal global inference, these parsers likely avoid the exposure bias problem of the sequential transition-based parsers we investigate, at the cost of requiring a chart decoding procedure for inference.

Overall, we find that although optimizing for F1 in a model-agnostic fashion with policy gradient typically underperforms the model-aware expert supervision given by the dynamic oracle training methods, it provides a simple method for consistently improving upon static oracle likelihood training, at the expense of increased training costs.

Acknowledgments

DF is supported by a Huawei / Berkeley AI fellowship. This research used the Savio computational cluster provided by the Berkeley Research Computing program at the University of California, Berkeley.

References

Anne Abeillé, Lionel Clément, and François Toussenel. 2003. *Building a Treebank for French*. Springer Netherlands, Dordrecht.

Daniel Andor, Chris Alberti, David Weiss, Aliaksei Severyn, Alessandro Presta, Kuzman Ganchev, Slav Petrov, and Michael Collins. 2016. Globally normalized transition-based neural networks. In *Proceedings of the 54th Annual Meeting of the Association for Computational Linguistics (Volume 1: Long Papers)*, pages 2442–2452, Berlin, Germany. Association for Computational Linguistics.

Michael Auli and Jianfeng Gao. 2014. Decoder integration and expected BLEU training for recurrent neural network language models. In *Proceedings of the 52nd Annual Meeting of the Association for Computational Linguistics (Volume 2: Short Papers)*, volume 2, pages 136–142.

Michael Auli and Adam Lopez. 2011. Training a log-linear parser with loss functions via softmax-margin. In *Proceedings of the Conference on Empirical Methods in Natural Language Processing*, EMNLP '11, pages 333–343, Stroudsburg, PA, USA. Association for Computational Linguistics.

Miguel Ballesteros, Yoav Goldberg, Chris Dyer, and Noah A. Smith. 2016. Training with exploration improves a greedy stack lstm parser. In *Proceedings of the 2016 Conference on Empirical Methods in Natural Language Processing*, pages 2005–2010, Austin, Texas. Association for Computational Linguistics.

Kai-Wei Chang, Akshay Krishnamurthy, Alekh Agarwal, Hal Daumé III, and John Langford. 2015. Learning to search better than your teacher. In *International Conference on Machine Learning*.

Danqi Chen and Christopher Manning. 2014. A fast and accurate dependency parser using neural networks. In *Proceedings of the 2014 conference on empirical methods in natural language processing (EMNLP)*, pages 740–750.

Do Kook Choe and Eugene Charniak. 2016. Parsing as language modeling. In *Empirical Methods in Natural Language Processing*.

Jinho D. Choi and Martha Palmer. 2011. Getting the most out of transition-based dependency parsing. In *Proceedings of the 49th Annual Meeting of the Association for Computational Linguistics: Human Language Technologies: Short Papers - Volume 2*, HLT '11, pages 687–692, Stroudsburg, PA, USA. Association for Computational Linguistics.

Maximin Coavoux and Benoit Crabbé. 2016. Neural greedy constituent parsing with dynamic oracles. In *Proceedings of the 54th Annual Meeting of the Association for Computational Linguistics (Volume 1: Long Papers)*, pages 172–182, Berlin, Germany. Association for Computational Linguistics.

James Cross and Liang Huang. 2016. Span-based constituency parsing with a structure-label system and provably optimal dynamic oracles. In *Proceedings of the 2016 Conference on Empirical Methods in Natural Language Processing*, pages 1–11, Austin, Texas. Association for Computational Linguistics.

Hal Daumé III, John Langford, and Daniel Marcu. 2009. Search-based structured prediction. *Machine learning*, 75(3):297–325.

Chris Dyer, Adhiguna Kuncoro, Miguel Ballesteros, and Noah A. Smith. 2016. Recurrent neural network grammars. In *Proceedings of the 2016 Conference of the North American Chapter of the Association for Computational Linguistics: Human Language Technologies*, pages 199–209, San Diego, California. Association for Computational Linguistics.

Sergey Edunov, Myle Ott, Michael Auli, David Grangier, and Marc'Aurelio Ranzato. 2017. Classical structured prediction losses for sequence to sequence learning. *arXiv preprint arXiv:1711.04956*.

Daniel Fried, Mitchell Stern, and Dan Klein. 2017. Improving neural parsing by disentangling model combination and reranking effects. In *Proceedings of ACL*.

David Gaddy, Mitchell Stern, and Dan Klein. 2018. What's going on in neural constituency parsers? an analysis. In *Proceedings of NAACL*.

Kevin Gimpel and Noah A. Smith. 2010. Softmax-margin crfs: Training log-linear models with cost functions. In *Human Language Technologies: The 2010 Annual Conference of the North American Chapter of the Association for Computational Linguistics*, pages 733–736, Los Angeles, California. Association for Computational Linguistics.

Yoav Goldberg and Joakim Nivre. 2012. A dynamic oracle for arc-eager dependency parsing. In *Proceedings of COLING 2012*, pages 959–976, Mumbai, India. The COLING 2012 Organizing Committee.

Daniel Fernández González and Carlos Gómez-Rodríguez. 2018. Faster shift-reduce constituent parsing with a non-binary, bottom-up strategy. *arXiv preprint*, 1804.07961.

Joshua Goodman. 1996. Parsing algorithms and metrics. In *Proceedings of the 34th Annual Meeting of the Association for Computational Linguistics*, pages 177–183, Santa Cruz, California, USA. Association for Computational Linguistics.

James Henderson. 2004. Discriminative training of a neural network statistical parser. In *Proceedings of the 42Nd Annual Meeting on Association for Computational Linguistics*, ACL '04, Stroudsburg, PA, USA. Association for Computational Linguistics.

Eliyahu Kiperwasser and Yoav Goldberg. 2016. Simple and accurate dependency parsing using bidirectional lstm feature representations. *Transactions of the Association for Computational Linguistics*, 4:313–327.

Nikita Kitaev and Dan Klein. 2018. Constituency parsing with a self-attentive encoder. *arXiv preprint arXiv:1805.01052*.

Adhiguna Kuncoro, Miguel Ballesteros, Lingpeng Kong, Chris Dyer, Graham Neubig, and Noah A. Smith. 2017. What do recurrent neural network grammars learn about syntax? In *Proceedings of the 15th Conference of the European Chapter of the Association for Computational Linguistics: Volume 1, Long Papers*, pages 1249–1258, Valencia, Spain. Association for Computational Linguistics.

Zhifei Li and Jason Eisner. 2009. First- and second-order expectation semirings with applications to minimum-risk training on translation forests. In *Proceedings of the 2009 Conference on Empirical Methods in Natural Language Processing: Volume 1 - Volume 1*, EMNLP '09, pages 40–51, Stroudsburg, PA, USA. Association for Computational Linguistics.

Wang Ling, Chris Dyer, Alan W Black, and Isabel Trancoso. 2015. Two/too simple adaptations of word2vec for syntax problems. In *Proceedings of the 2015 Conference of the North American Chapter of the Association for Computational Linguistics: Human Language Technologies*, pages 1299–1304. Association for Computational Linguistics.

Jiangming Liu and Yue Zhang. 2017. In-order transition-based constituent parsing. *Transactions of the Association for Computational Linguistics*, 5:413–424.

Mitchell P Marcus, Mary Ann Marcinkiewicz, and Beatrice Santorini. 1993. Building a large annotated corpus of English: The Penn treebank. *Computational Linguistics*, 19(2):313–330.

Joakim Nivre. 2003. An efficient algorithm for projective dependency parsing. In *Proceedings of the 8th International Workshop on Parsing Technologies (IWPT)*.

Franz Josef Och. 2003. Minimum error rate training in statistical machine translation. In *Proceedings of the 41st Annual Meeting of the Association for Computational Linguistics*, pages 160–167, Sapporo, Japan. Association for Computational Linguistics.

Daniel Povey and Philip C Woodland. 2002. Minimum phone error and i-smoothing for improved discriminative training. In *Acoustics, Speech, and Signal Processing (ICASSP), 2002 IEEE International Conference on*, volume 1, pages I–105. IEEE.

Marc'Aurelio Ranzato, Sumit Chopra, Michael Auli, and Wojciech Zaremba. 2016. Sequence level training with recurrent neural networks. *International Conference on Learning Representations*.

Stéphane Ross, Geoffrey Gordon, and Drew Bagnell. 2011. A reduction of imitation learning and structured prediction to no-regret online learning. In *Proceedings of the fourteenth international conference on artificial intelligence and statistics*, pages 627–635.

Djamé Seddah, Sandra Kübler, and Reut Tsarfaty. 2014. Introducing the spmrl 2014 shared task on parsing morphologically-rich languages. In *Proceedings of the First Joint Workshop on Statistical Parsing of Morphologically Rich Languages and Syntactic Analysis of Non-Canonical Languages*, pages 103–109, Dublin, Ireland. Dublin City University.

Shiqi Shen, Yong Cheng, Zhongjun He, Wei He, Hua Wu, Maosong Sun, and Yang Liu. 2016. Minimum risk training for neural machine translation. In *Proceedings of the 54th Annual Meeting of the Association for Computational Linguistics (Volume 1: Long Papers)*, pages 1683–1692, Berlin, Germany. Association for Computational Linguistics.

David A. Smith and Jason Eisner. 2006. Minimum risk annealing for training log-linear models. In *Proceedings of the COLING/ACL 2006 Main Conference Poster Sessions*, pages 787–794, Sydney, Australia. Association for Computational Linguistics.

Mitchell Stern, Jacob Andreas, and Dan Klein. 2017. A minimal span-based neural constituency parser. In *Proceedings of ACL*.

Kristina Toutanova, Dan Klein, Christopher D. Manning, and Yoram Singer. 2003. Feature-rich part-of-speech tagging with a cyclic dependency network. In *Proceedings of the 2003 Conference of the North American Chapter of the Association for Computational Linguistics on Human Language Technology - Volume 1*, NAACL '03, pages 173–180, Stroudsburg, PA, USA. Association for Computational Linguistics.

Oriol Vinyals, Łukasz Kaiser, Terry Koo, Slav Petrov, Ilya Sutskever, and Geoffrey Hinton. 2015. Grammar as a foreign language. In *Proceedings of NIPS*, pages 2773–2781.

Ronald J Williams. 1992. Simple statistical gradient-following algorithms for connectionist reinforcement learning. In *Reinforcement Learning*, pages 5–32. Springer.

Sam Wiseman and Alexander M. Rush. 2016. Sequence-to-sequence learning as beam-search optimization. In *Proceedings of the 2016 Conference on Empirical Methods in Natural Language Processing*, pages 1296–1306, Austin, Texas. Association for Computational Linguistics.

Wenduan Xu, Michael Auli, and Stephen Christopher Clark. 2016. Expected f-measure training for shift-reduce parsing with recurrent neural networks. In *Proceedings of the 2016 Conference of the North*

American Chapter of the Association for Computational Linguistics on Human Language Technology. Association for Computational Linguistics.

Naiwen Xue, Fei Xia, Fu-dong Chiou, and Marta Palmer. 2005. The penn chinese treebank: Phrase structure annotation of a large corpus. *Nat. Lang. Eng.*, 11(2):207–238.

Hiroyasu Yamada and Yuji Matsumoto. 2003. Statistical dependency analysis with support vector machines. In *Proceedings of the 8th International Workshop on Parsing Technologies (IWPT)*.

Yue Zhang and Stephen Clark. 2011. Syntactic processing using the generalized perceptron and beam search. *Computational linguistics*, 37(1):105–151.

Linear-Time Constituency Parsing with RNNs
and Dynamic Programming

Juneki Hong [1]
[1]School of EECS
Oregon State University, Corvallis, OR

Liang Huang [1,2]
[2]Silicon Valley AI Lab
Baidu Research, Sunnyvale, CA

{juneki.hong, liang.huang.sh}@gmail.com

Abstract

Recently, span-based constituency parsing has achieved competitive accuracies with extremely simple models by using bidirectional RNNs to model "spans". However, the minimal span parser of Stern et al. (2017a) which holds the current state of the art accuracy is a chart parser running in cubic time, $O(n^3)$, which is too slow for longer sentences and for applications beyond sentence boundaries such as end-to-end discourse parsing and joint sentence boundary detection and parsing. We propose a linear-time constituency parser with RNNs and dynamic programming using graph-structured stack and beam search, which runs in time $O(nb^2)$ where b is the beam size. We further speed this up to $O(nb \log b)$ by integrating cube pruning. Compared with chart parsing baselines, this linear-time parser is substantially faster for long sentences on the Penn Treebank and orders of magnitude faster for discourse parsing, and achieves the highest F1 accuracy on the Penn Treebank among single model end-to-end systems.

1 Introduction

Span-based neural constituency parsing (Cross and Huang, 2016; Stern et al., 2017a) has attracted attention due to its high accuracy and extreme simplicity. Compared with other recent neural constituency parsers (Dyer et al., 2016; Liu and Zhang, 2016; Durrett and Klein, 2015) which use neural networks to model tree structures, the span-based framework is considerably simpler, only using bidirectional RNNs to model the *input sequence* and not the *output tree*. Because of this factorization, the output space is decomposable

which enables efficient dynamic programming algorithm such as CKY. But existing span-based parsers suffer from a crucial limitation in terms of search: on the one hand, a greedy span parser (Cross and Huang, 2016) is fast (linear-time) but only explores one single path in the exponentially large search space, and on the other hand, a chart-based span parser (Stern et al., 2017a) performs exact search and achieves state-of-the-art accuracy, but in cubic time, which is too slow for longer sentences and for applications that go beyond sentence boundaries such as end-to-end discourse parsing (Hernault et al., 2010; Zhao and Huang, 2017) and integrated sentence boundary detection and parsing (Björkelund et al., 2016).

We propose to combine the merits of both greedy and chart-based approaches and design a linear-time span-based neural parser that searches over exponentially large space. Following Huang and Sagae (2010), we perform left-to-right dynamic programming in an action-synchronous style, with $(2n - 1)$ actions (i.e., steps) for a sentence of n words. While previous non-neural work in this area requires sophisticated features (Huang and Sagae, 2010; Mi and Huang, 2015) and thus high time complexity such as $O(n^{11})$, our states are as simple as $\ell : (i, j)$ where ℓ is the step index and (i, j) is the span, modeled using bidirectional RNNs without any syntactic features. This gives a running time of $O(n^4)$, with the extra $O(n)$ for step index. We further employ beam search to have a practical runtime of $O(nb^2)$ at the cost of exact search where b is the beam size. However, on the Penn Treebank, most sentences are less than 40 words ($n < 40$), and even with a small beam size of $b = 10$, the *observed* complexity of an $O(nb^2)$ parser is *not* exactly linear in n (see Experiments). To solve this problem, we apply cube pruning (Chiang, 2007; Huang and Chiang, 2007) to improve the runtime to $O(nb \log b)$ which

Proceedings of the 56th Annual Meeting of the Association for Computational Linguistics (Short Papers), pages 477–483
Melbourne, Australia, July 15 - 20, 2018. ©2018 Association for Computational Linguistics

renders an observed complexity that is linear in n (with minor extra inexactness).

We make the following contributions:

- We design the first neural parser that is both linear time and capable of searching over exponentially large space.[1]

- We are the first to apply cube pruning to incremental parsing, and achieves, for the first time, the complexity of $O(nb \log b)$, i.e., linear in sentence length and (almost) linear in beam size. This leads to an observed complexity strictly linear in sentence length n.

- We devise a novel loss function which penalizes wrong spans that cross gold-tree spans, and employ max-violation update (Huang et al., 2012) to train this parser with structured SVM and beam search.

- Compared with chart parsing baselines, our parser is substantially faster for long sentences on the Penn Treebank, and orders of magnitude faster for end-to-end discourse parsing. It also achieves the highest F1 score on the Penn Treebank among single model end-to-end systems.

- We devise a new formulation of graph-structured stack (Tomita, 1991) which requires no extra bookkeeping, proving a new theorem that gives deep insight into GSS.

2 Preliminaries

2.1 Span-Based Shift-Reduce Parsing

A span-based shift-reduce constituency parser (Cross and Huang, 2016) maintains a stack of spans (i, j), and progressively adds a new span each time it takes a shift or reduce action. With (i, j) on top of the stack, the parser can either *shift* to push the next singleton span $(j, j + 1)$ on the stack, or it can *reduce* to combine the top two spans, (k, i) and (i, j), forming the larger span (k, j). After each shift/reduce action, the top-most span is labeled as either a constituent or with a *null* label $\varnothing$, which means that the subsequence is not a subtree in the final decoded parse. Parsing initializes with an empty stack and continues until $(0, n)$ is formed, representing the entire sentence.

input	$w_0 \ldots w_{n-1}$
state	$\ell : \langle i, j \rangle : (c, v)$
init	$0 : \langle 0, 0 \rangle : (0, 0)$
goal	$2n - 1 : \langle 0, n \rangle : (c, c)$

$$\textbf{shift} \quad \frac{\ell : \langle \_, j \rangle : (c, \_)}{\ell + 1 : \langle j, j+1 \rangle : (c + \xi, \xi)} \quad j < n$$

$$\textbf{reduce} \quad \frac{\ell' : \langle k, i \rangle : (c', v') \quad \ell : \langle i, j \rangle : (\_, v)}{\ell + 1 : \langle k, j \rangle : (c' + v + \sigma, v' + v + \sigma)}$$

Figure 1: Our shift-reduce deductive system. Here ℓ is the step index, c and v are prefix and inside scores. Unlike Huang and Sagae (2010) and Cross and Huang (2016), ξ and σ are not shift/reduce scores; instead, they are the (best) label scores of the resulting span: $\xi = \max_X s(j, j+1, X)$ and $\sigma = \max_X s(k, j, X)$ where X is a nonterminal symbol (could be $\varnothing$). Here $\ell' = \ell - 2(j - i) + 1$.

2.2 Bi-LSTM features

To get the feature representation of a span (i, j), we use the output sequence of a bi-directional LSTM (Cross and Huang, 2016; Stern et al., 2017a). The LSTM produces $\mathbf{f}_0, ..., \mathbf{f}_n$ forwards and $\mathbf{b}_n, ..., \mathbf{b}_0$ backwards outputs, which we concatenate the differences of $(\mathbf{f}_j - \mathbf{f}_i)$ and $(\mathbf{b}_i - \mathbf{b}_j)$ as the representation for span (i, j). This eliminates the need for complex feature engineering, and can be stored for efficient querying during decoding.

3 Dynamic Programming

3.1 Score Decomposition

Like Stern et al. (2017a), we also decompose the score of a tree t to be the sum of the span scores:

$$s(t) = \sum_{(i,j,X) \in t} s(i, j, X) \tag{1}$$

$$= \sum_{(i,j) \in t} \max_X s((\mathbf{f}_j - \mathbf{f}_i; \mathbf{b}_i - \mathbf{b}_j), X) \tag{2}$$

Note that X is a nonterminal label, a unary chain (e.g., S-VP), or null label $\varnothing$.[2] In a shift-reduce setting, there are $2n - 1$ steps (n shifts and $n - 1$ reduces) and after each step we take the best label for the resulting span; therefore there are exactly

$2n - 1$ such (labeled) spans (i, j, X) in tree t. Also note that the choice of the label for any span (i, j) is only dependent on (i, j) itself (and not depending on any subtree information), thus the max over label X is independent of other spans, which is a nice property of span-based parsing (Cross and Huang, 2016; Stern et al., 2017a).

3.2 Graph-Struct. Stack w/o Bookkeeping

We now reformulate this DP parser in the above section as a shift-reduce parser. We maintain a step index ℓ in order to perform action-synchronous beam search (see below). Figure 1 shows how to represent a parsing stack using only the top span (i, j). If the top span (i, j) shifts, it produces $(j, j + 1)$, but if it reduces, it needs to know the second last span on the stack, (k, i), which is *not* represented in the current state. This problem can be solved by graph-structure stack (Tomita, 1991; Huang and Sagae, 2010), which maintains, for each state p, a set of predecessor states $\pi(p)$ that p can combine with on the left.

This is the way our actual code works ($\pi(p)$ is implemented as a list of pointers, or "left pointers"), but here for simplicity of presentation we devise a novel but easier-to-understand formulation in Fig. 1, where we explicitly represent the set of predecessor states that state $\ell : (i, j)$ can combine with as $\ell' : (k, i)$ where $\ell' = \ell - 2(j - i) + 1$, i.e., (i, j) at step ℓ can combine with any (k, i) for any k at step ℓ'. The rationale behind this new formulation is the following theorem:

Theorem 1 *The predecessor states $\pi(\ell : (i, j))$ are all in the same step $\ell' = \ell - 2(j - i) + 1$.*

Proof. By induction.

This Theorem bring new and deep insights and suggests an alternative implementation that does not require any extra bookkeeping. The time complexity of this algorithm is $O(n^4)$ with the extra $O(n)$ due to step index.[3]

3.3 Action-Synchronous Beam Search

The incremental nature of our parser allows us to further lower the runtime complexity at the cost of inexact search. At each time step, we maintain the top b parsing states, pruning off the rest. Thus, a candidate parse that made it to the end of decoding had to survive within the top b at every step.

With $O(n)$ parsing actions our time complexity becomes linear in the length of the sentence.

3.4 Cube Pruning

However, Theorem 1 suggests that a parsing state p can have up to b predecessor states ("left pointers"), i.e., $|\pi(p)| \leq b$ because $\pi(p)$ are all in the same step, a reduce action can produce up to b subsequent new reduced states. With b items on a beam and $O(n)$ actions to take, this gives us an overall complexity of $O(nb^2)$. Even though b^2 is a constant, even modest values of b can make b^2 dominate the length of the sentence. [4]

To improve this at the cost of additional inexactness, we introduce cube pruning to our beam search, where we put candidate actions into a heap and retrieve the top b states to be considered in the next time-step. We heapify the top b shift-merged states and the top b reduced states. To avoid inserting all b^2 reduced states from the previous beam, we only consider each state's highest scoring left pointer,[5] and whenever we pop a reduced state from the heap, we iterate down its left pointers to insert the next non-duplicate reduced state back into the heap. This process finishes when we pop b items from the heap. The initialization of the heap takes $O(b)$ and popping b items takes $O(b \log b)$, giving us an overall improved runtime of $O(nb \log b)$.

4 Training

We use a Structured SVM approach for training (Stern et al., 2017a; Shi et al., 2017). We want the model to score the gold tree t^* higher than any other tree t by at least a margin $\Delta(t, t^*)$:

$$\forall t, s(t^*) - s(t) \geq \Delta(t, t^*).$$

Note that $\Delta(t, t) = 0$ for any t and $\Delta(t, t^*) > 0$ for any $t \neq t^*$. At training time we perform loss-augmented decoding:

$$\hat{t} = \arg\max_t s_\Delta(t) = \arg\max_t s(t) + \Delta(t, t^*).$$

---

[3]The word-synchronous alternative does not need the step index ℓ and enjoys a cubic time complexity, being almost identical to CKY. However, beam search becomes very tricky.

[4]The average length of a sentence in the Penn Treebank training set is about 24. Even with a beam size of 10, we already have $b^2 = 100$, which would be a significant factor in our runtime. In practice, each parsing state will rarely have the maximum b left pointers so this ends up being a loose upper-bound. Nevertheless, the beam search should be performed with the input length in mind, or else as b increases we risk losing a linear runtime.

[5]If each previous beam is sorted, and if the beam search is conducted by going top-to-bottom, then each state's left pointers will implicitly be kept in sorted order.

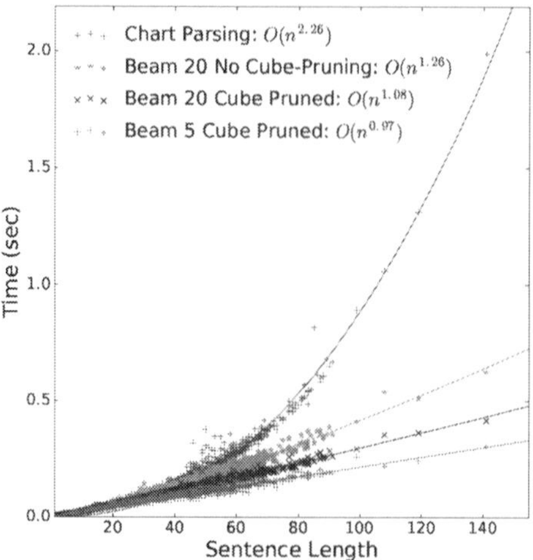

Figure 2: Runtime plots of decoding on the training set of the Penn Treebank. The differences between the different algorithms become evident after sentences of length 40. The regression curves have been empirically fitted.

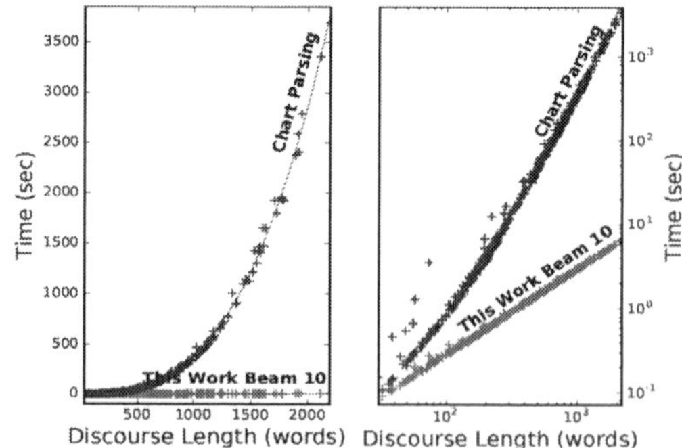

Figure 3: Runtime plot of decoding the discourse treebank training set. The log-log plot on the right shows the cubic complexity of baseline chart parsing. Whereas beam search decoding maintains linear time even for sequences of thousands of words.

where $s_\Delta(\cdot)$ is the loss-augmented score. If $\hat{t} = t^*$, then all constraints are satisfied (which implies $\arg\max_t s(t) = t^*$), otherwise we perform an update by backpropagating from $s_\Delta(\hat{t}) - s(t^*)$.

4.1 Cross-Span Loss

The baseline loss function from Stern et al. (2017a) counts the incorrect labels (i, j, X) in the predicted tree:

$$\Delta_{base}(t, t^*) = \sum_{(i,j,X)\in t} \mathbb{1}\left(X \neq t^*_{(i,j)}\right).$$

Note that X can be null $\varnothing$, and $t^*_{(i,j)}$ denotes the gold label for span (i, j), which could also be $\varnothing$.[6] However, there are two cases where $t^*_{(i,j)} = \varnothing$: a subspan (i, j) due to binarization (e.g., a span combining the first two subtrees in a ternary branching node), or an invalid span in t that crosses a gold span in t^*. In the baseline function above, these two cases are treated equivalently; for example, a span $(3, 5, \varnothing) \in t$ is not penalized even if there is a gold span $(4, 6, \text{VP}) \in t^*$. So we revise our loss function as:

$$\Delta_{new}(t, t^*) = \sum_{(i,j,X)\in t} \mathbb{1}\Big(X \neq t^*_{(i,j)}$$
$$\vee \operatorname{cross}(i, j, t^*)\Big)$$

where $\operatorname{cross}(i, j, t^*) = \exists (k, l) \in t^*$, and $i < k < j < l$ or $k < i < l < j$.

4.2 Max Violation Updates

Given that we maintain loss-augmented scores even for partial trees, we can perform a training update on a given example sentence by choosing to take the loss where it is the greatest along the parse trajectory. At each parsing time-step ℓ, the *violation* is the difference between the highest augmented-scoring parse trajectory up to that point and the gold trajectory (Huang et al., 2012; Yu et al., 2013). Note that computing the violation gives us the max-margin loss described above. Taking the largest violation from all time-steps gives us the max-violation loss.

5 Experiments

We present experiments on the Penn Treebank (Marcus et al., 1993) and the PTB-RST discourse treebank (Zhao and Huang, 2017). In both cases, the training set is shuffled before each epoch, and dropout (Hinton et al., 2012) is employed with probability 0.4 to the recurrent outputs for regularization. Updates with minibatches of size 10 and 1 are used for PTB and the PTB-RST respectively. We use Adam (Kingma and Ba, 2014) with default settings to schedule learning rates for all the weights. To address unknown words during training, we adopt the strategy described by Kiperwasser and Goldberg (Kiperwasser and Goldberg, 2016); words in the training set are replaced with the unknown word symbol UNK with probability $p_{unk} = \frac{1}{1+f(w)}$, with $f(w)$ being the number of

---

[6] Note that the predicted tree t has exactly $2n - 1$ spans but t^* has much fewer spans (only labeled spans without $\varnothing$).

	Development Set 22 (F1)		Time
	Baseline	+cross-span	
This Work Beam 1	89.41	89.93	0.042
This Work Beam 5	91.27	91.91	0.050
This Work Beam 10	91.56	92.09	0.058
This Work Beam 15	91.74	92.16	0.062
This Work Beam 20	91.65	92.20	0.066
Chart	92.02	92.21	0.076

Table 1: Comparison of PTB development set results, with the time measured in seconds-per-sentence. The baseline chart parser is from Stern et al. (2017b), with null-label scores unconstrained to be nonzero, replicating their paper.

End-to-End & Single Model	Test Set 23		
	LR	LP	F1
Socher et al. (2013)			90.4
Durrett and Klein (2015)			91.1
Cross and Huang (2016)	90.5	92.1	91.3
Liu and Zhang (2016)	91.3	92.1	91.7
Dyer et al. (2016) (discrim.)			91.7
Stern et al. (2017a)	90.63	92.98	91.79
Stern et al. (2017a) +cross-span	91.67	91.94	91.81
Stern et al. (2017b)	91.35	92.38	91.86
This Work Beam 10	91.44	91.91	91.67
This Work Beam 15	91.64	92.04	91.84
This Work Beam 20	91.49	92.45	**91.97**
Reranking/Ensemble/Separate Decoding			
Vinyals et al. (2015) (ensem)			90.5
Dyer et al. (2016) (gen., rerank)			93.3
Choe and Charniak (2016) (rerank)			93.8
Stern et al. (2017c) (sep. decoding)	92.57	92.56	92.56
Fried et al. (2017) (ensem/rerank)			94.25

Table 2: Final PTB Test Results. We compare our models with other (neural) single-model end-to-end trained systems.

occurrences of word w in the training corpus. Our system is implemented in Python using the DyNet neural network library (Neubig et al., 2017).

5.1 Penn Treebank

We use the Wall Street Journal portion of the Penn Treebank, with the standard split of sections 2-21 for training, 22 for development, and 23 for testing. Tags are provided using the Stanford tagger with 10-way jackknifing.

Table 1 shows our development results and overall speeds, while Table 2 compares our test results. We show that a beam size of 20 can be fast while still achieving state-of-the-art performances.

5.2 Discourse Parsing

To measure the tractability of parsing on longer sequences, we also consider experiments on the

	LR	LP	F1
Zhao and Huang (2017)	81.6	83.5	82.5
This Work Beam 10	80.47	80.61	80.54
This Work Beam 20	80.86	80.73	80.79
This Work Beam 200	81.51	80.84	81.18
This Work Beam 500*	81.50	80.81	81.16
This Work Beam 1000*	81.55	80.85	81.20

Table 3: Overall test accuracies for PTB-RST discourse treebank. Starred* rows indicate a run that was decoded from the beam 200 model.

	segment	structure	+nuclearity	+relation
Bach et al. (2012)	95.1	-	-	-
Hernault et al. (2010)	94.0	72.3	59.1	47.3
Zhao and Huang (2017)	95.4	78.8	65.0	52.2
This Work Beam 200	91.20	73.36	58.87	46.38
This Work Beam 500*	93.52	74.93	60.16	47.03
This Work Beam 1000*	94.06	75.60	60.61	47.37

Table 4: F1 scores comparing discourse systems. Results correspond to the accuracies in Table 3, broken down to focus on the discourse labels.

PTB-RST discourse Treebank, a joint discourse and constituency dataset with a combined representation, allowing for parsing at either level (Zhao and Huang, 2017). We compare our runtimes out-of-the-box in Figure 3. Without any pre-processing, and by treating discourse examples as constituency trees with thousands of words, our trained models represent end-to-end discourse parsing systems.

For our overall constituency results in Table 3, and for discourse results in Table 4, we adapt the split-point feature described in (Zhao and Huang, 2017) in addition to the base parser. We find that larger beamsizes are required to achieve good discourse scores.

6 Conclusions

We have developed a new neural parser that maintains linear time, while still searching over an exponentially large space. We also use cube pruning to further improve the runtime to $O(nb \log b)$. For training, we introduce a new loss function, and achieve state-of-the-art results among single-model end-to-end systems.

Acknowledgments

We thank Dezhong Deng who contributed greatly to Secs. 3.2 and 4 (he deserves co-authorship), and Mitchell Stern for releasing his code and and suggestions. This work was supported in part by NSF IIS-1656051 and DARPA N66001-17-2-4030.

References

Ngo Xuan Bach, Nguyen Le Minh, and Akira Shimazu. 2012. A reranking model for discourse segmentation using subtree features. In *Proceedings of the 13th Annual Meeting of the Special Interest Group on Discourse and Dialogue*. Association for Computational Linguistics, pages 160–168.

Anders Björkelund, Agnieszka Faleńska, Wolfgang Seeker, and Jonas Kuhn. 2016. How to train dependency parsers with inexact search for joint sentence boundary detection and parsing of entire documents. In *Proceedings of the 54th Annual Meeting of the Association for Computational Linguistics (Volume 1: Long Papers)*. volume 1, pages 1924–1934.

David Chiang. 2007. Hierarchical phrase-based translation. *Computational Linguistics* 33(2):201–208.

Do Kook Choe and Eugene Charniak. 2016. Parsing as language modeling. In *Proceedings of the Conference on Empirical Methods in Natural Language Processing*. pages 2331–2336.

James Cross and Liang Huang. 2016. Span-based constituency parsing with a structure-label system and provably optimal dynamic oracles. In *Proceedings of the 2016 Conference on Empirical Methods in Natural Language Processing*. Association for Computational Linguistics, Austin, Texas, pages 1–11. https://aclweb.org/anthology/D16-1001.

Greg Durrett and Dan Klein. 2015. Neural CRF parsing. *arXiv preprint arXiv:1507.03641* .

Chris Dyer, Adhiguna Kuncoro, Miguel Ballesteros, and Noah A Smith. 2016. Recurrent neural network grammars. *arXiv preprint arXiv:1602.07776* .

Daniel Fried, Mitchell Stern, and Dan Klein. 2017. Improving neural parsing by disentangling model combination and reranking effects. In *Proceedings of the Association for Computational Linguistics*.

Hugo Hernault, Helmut Prendinger, David A DuVerle, Mitsuru Ishizuka, and Tim Paek. 2010. Hilda: a discourse parser using support vector machine classification. *Dialogue and Discourse* 1(3):1–33.

Geoffrey E Hinton, Nitish Srivastava, Alex Krizhevsky, Ilya Sutskever, and Ruslan R Salakhutdinov. 2012. Improving neural networks by preventing co-adaptation of feature detectors. *arXiv preprint arXiv:1207.0580* .

Liang Huang and David Chiang. 2007. Forest rescoring: Fast decoding with integrated language models. In *Proceedings of ACL 2007*. Prague, Czech Rep.

Liang Huang, Suphan Fayong, and Yang Guo. 2012. Structured perceptron with inexact search. In *Proceedings of NAACL*. http://www.isi.edu/ lhuang/perc-inexact.pdf.

Liang Huang and Kenji Sagae. 2010. Dynamic programming for linear-time incremental parsing. In *Proceedings of ACL 2010*. Uppsala, Sweden.

Diederik P Kingma and Jimmy Ba. 2014. Adam: A method for stochastic optimization. *arXiv preprint arXiv:1412.6980* .

Eliyahu Kiperwasser and Yoav Goldberg. 2016. Simple and accurate dependency parsing using bidirectional LSTM feature representations. *CoRR* abs/1603.04351. http://arxiv.org/abs/1603.04351.

Jiangming Liu and Yue Zhang. 2016. Shift-reduce constituent parsing with neural lookahead features. *arXiv preprint arXiv:1612.00567* .

Mitchell P Marcus, Mary Ann Marcinkiewicz, and Beatrice Santorini. 1993. Building a large annotated corpus of english: The penn treebank. *Computational linguistics* 19(2):313–330.

Haitao Mi and Liang Huang. 2015. Shift-reduce constituency parsing with dynamic programming and pos tag lattice. In *Proceedings of NAACL 2015.*

Graham Neubig, Chris Dyer, Yoav Goldberg, Austin Matthews, Waleed Ammar, Antonios Anastasopoulos, Miguel Ballesteros, David Chiang, Daniel Clothiaux, Trevor Cohn, Kevin Duh, Manaal Faruqui, Cynthia Gan, Dan Garrette, Yangfeng Ji, Lingpeng Kong, Adhiguna Kuncoro, Gaurav Kumar, Chaitanya Malaviya, Paul Michel, Yusuke Oda, Matthew Richardson, Naomi Saphra, Swabha Swayamdipta, and Pengcheng Yin. 2017. Dynet: The dynamic neural network toolkit. *arXiv preprint arXiv:1701.03980* .

Tianze Shi, Liang Huang, and Lillian Lee. 2017. Fast(er) exact decoding and global training for transition-based dependency parsing via a minimal feature set. In *Proceedings of EMNLP 2017 (to appear).*

Richard Socher, John Bauer, Christopher D Manning, and Andrew Y Ng. 2013. Parsing with compositional vector grammars. In *Proceedings of the Association for Computational Linguistics*. Association for Computational Linguistics, volume 1, pages 455–465.

Mitchell Stern, Jacob Andreas, and Dan Klein. 2017a. A minimal span-based neural constituency parser. In *Proceedings of the Association for Computational Linguistics*.

Mitchell Stern, Jacob Andreas, and Dan Klein. 2017b. A minimal span-based neural constituency parser (code base). https://github.com/mitchellstern/minimal-span-parser.

Mitchell Stern, Daniel Fried, and Dan Klein. 2017c. Effective inference for generative neural parsing. In *Proceedings of Empirical Methods in Natural Language Processing*. pages 1695–1700.

Masaru Tomita, editor. 1991. *Generalized LR Parsing*. Kluwer Academic Publishers.

Oriol Vinyals, Łukasz Kaiser, Terry Koo, Slav Petrov, Ilya Sutskever, and Geoffrey Hinton. 2015. Grammar as a foreign language. In *Advances in Neural Information Processing Systems*. pages 2773–2781.

Heng Yu, Liang Huang, Haitao Mi, and Kai Zhao. 2013. Max-violation perceptron and forced decoding for scalable mt training. In *Proceedings of EMNLP 2013*.

Kai Zhao and Liang Huang. 2017. Joint syntacto-discourse parsing and the syntacto-discourse treebank. In *Proceedings of the 2017 Conference on Empirical Methods in Natural Language Processing*. pages 2117–2123.

Simpler but More Accurate Semantic Dependency Parsing

Timothy Dozat
Stanford University
`tdozat@stanford.edu`

Christopher D. Manning
Stanford University
`manning@stanford.edu`

Abstract

While syntactic dependency annotations concentrate on the surface or functional structure of a sentence, semantic dependency annotations aim to capture between-word relationships that are more closely related to the meaning of a sentence, using graph-structured representations. We extend the LSTM-based syntactic parser of Dozat and Manning (2017) to train on and generate these graph structures. The resulting system on its own achieves state-of-the-art performance, beating the previous, substantially more complex state-of-the-art system by 0.6% labeled F1. Adding linguistically richer input representations pushes the margin even higher, allowing us to beat it by 1.9% labeled F1.

1 Introduction

Syntactic dependency parsing is arguably the most popular method for automatically extracting the low-level relationships between words in a sentence for use in natural language understanding tasks. However, typical syntactic dependency frameworks are limited in the number and types of relationships that can be captured. For example, in the sentence *Mary wants to buy a book*, the word *Mary* is the subject of both *want* and *buy*—either or both relationships could be useful in a downstream task, but a tree-structured representation of this sentence (as in Figure 1a) can only represent one of them.[1]

The 2014 SemEval shared task on Broad-Coverage Semantic Dependency Parsing (Oepen et al., 2014) introduced three new dependency representations that do away with the assumption of strict tree structure in favor of a richer graph-structured representation, allowing them to capture more linguistic information about a sentence. This opens up the possibility of providing more useful information to downstream tasks (Reddy et al., 2017; Schuster et al., 2017), but increases the difficulty of automatically extracting that information, since most previous work on parsing has focused on generating trees.

Dozat and Manning (2017) developed a successful syntactic dependency parsing system with few task-specific sources of complexity. In this paper, we extend that system so that it can train on and produce the graph-structured data of semantic dependency schemes. We also consider straightforward extensions of the system that are likely to increase performance over the straightforward baseline, including giving the system access to lemma embeddings and building in a character-level word embedding model. Finally, we briefly examine some of the design choices of that architecture, in order to assess which components are necessary for achieving the highest accuracy and which have little impact on final performance.

2 Background

2.1 Semantic dependencies

The 2014 SemEval (Oepen et al., 2014, 2015) shared task introduced three new semantic dependency formalisms, applied to the Penn Treebank (shown in Figure 1, compared to Universal Dependencies (Nivre et al., 2016)): DELPH-IN MRS, or DM (Flickinger et al., 2012; Oepen and Lønning, 2006); Predicate-Argument Structures, or PAS (Miyao and Tsujii, 2004); and Prague Semantic Dependencies, or PSD (Hajic et al., 2012). Whereas syntactic dependencies generally annotate functional relationships between words—such as *subject* and *object*—semantic dependencies aim

---

[1]Though efforts have been made to address this limitation; seeDe Marneffe et al. (2006); Nivre et al. (2016); Schuster and Manning (2016); Candito et al. (2017) for examples.

Proceedings of the 56th Annual Meeting of the Association for Computational Linguistics (Short Papers), pages 484–490
Melbourne, Australia, July 15 - 20, 2018. ©2018 Association for Computational Linguistics

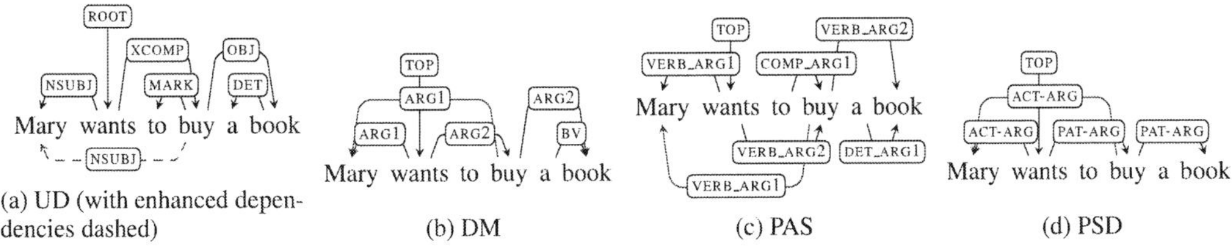

Figure 1: Comparison between syntactic and semantic dependency schemes

to reflect semantic relationships—such as *agent* and *patient* (cf. semantic role labeling (Gildea and Jurafsky, 2002)). The SemEval semantic dependency schemes are also directed acyclic graphs (DAGs) rather than trees, allowing them to annotate function words as being heads without lengthening paths between content words (as in 1b).

2.2 Related work

Our approach to semantic dependency parsing is primarily inspired by the success of Dozat and Manning (2017) and Dozat et al. (2017) at syntactic dependency parsing and Peng et al. (2017) at semantic dependency parsing. In Dozat and Manning (2017) and Peng et al. (2017), parsing involves first using a multilayer bidirectional LSTM over word and part-of-speech tag embeddings. Parsing is then done using directly-optimized self-attention over recurrent states to attend to each word's head (or heads), and labeling is done with an analgous multi-class classifier.

Peng et al.'s (2017) system uses a max-margin classifer on top of a BiLSTM, with the score for each graph coming from several sources. First, it scores each word as either taking dependents or not. For each ordered pair of words, it scores the arc from the first word to the second. Lastly, it scores each possible labeled arc between the two words. The graph that maximizes these scores may not be consistent, with an edge coming from a non-predicate, for example, so they enforce hard constraints in order to prune away invalid semantic graphs. Decisions are not independent, so in order to find the highest-scoring graph that follows these constraints, they use the AD³ decoding algorithm (Martins et al., 2011).

Dozat and Manning's (2017) approach to syntactic dependency parsing is similar, but avoids the possibility of generating invalid trees by fully factorizing the system. Rather than summing the scores from multiple modules and then finding the valid structure that maximizes that sum, the sys-

tem makes parsing and labeling decisions sequentially, choosing the labels for each edge only after the edges in the tree have been finalized by an MST algorithm.

Wang et al. (2018) take a different approach in their recent work, using a transition-based parser built on stack-LSTMs (Dyer et al., 2015). They extend Choi and McCallum's (2013) transition system for producing non-projective trees so that it can produce arbitrary DAGs and they modify the stack-LSTM architecture slightly to make the network more powerful.

3 Approach

3.1 Basic approach

We can formulate the semantic dependency parsing task as labeling each edge in a directed graph, with *null* being the label given to pairs with no edge between them. Using only one module that labels each edge in this way would be an *unfactorized* approach. We can, however, factorize it into two modules: one that predicts whether or not a directed edge (w_j, w_i) exists between two words, and another that predicts the best label for each potential edge.

Our approach closely follows that of Dozat and Manning (2017). As with many successful recent parsers, we concatenate word and POS tag[2] embeddings, and feed them into a multilayer bidirectional LSTM to get contextualized word representations.[3]

$$\mathbf{x}_i = \mathbf{e}_i^{(\text{word})} \oplus \mathbf{e}_i^{(\text{tag})} \qquad (1)$$

$$R = \text{BiLSTM}(X) \qquad (2)$$

---

[2]We use the POS tags (and later, lemmas) provided with each dataset.

[3]We follow the convention of representing scalars in lowercase italics a, vectors in lowercase bold $\mathbf{a}$, matrices in uppercase italics A, and tensors in uppercase bold $\mathbf{A}$. We maintain this convention when indexing and stacking, so $\mathbf{a}_i$ is row i of matrix A and A contains the sequence of vectors $(\mathbf{a}_1, \ldots, \mathbf{a}_n)$.

For each of the two modules, we use single-layer feedforward networks (FNN) to split the top recurrent states into two parts—a *head* representation, as in Eq. (5, 6) and a *dependent* representation, as in Eq. (7, 8). This allows us to reduce the recurrent size to avoid overfitting in the classifer without weakening the LSTM's capacity. We can then use bilinear or biaffine classifiers in Eq. (3, 4)—which are generalizations of linear classifiers to include multiplicative interactions between two vectors—to predict edges and labels.[4]

$$\text{Bilin}(\mathbf{x}_1, \mathbf{x}_2) = \mathbf{x}_1^\top \mathbf{U} \mathbf{x}_2 \tag{3}$$

$$\text{Biaff}(\mathbf{x}_1, \mathbf{x}_2) = \mathbf{x}_1^\top \mathbf{U} \mathbf{x}_2 + W(\mathbf{x}_1 \oplus \mathbf{x}_2) + \mathbf{b} \tag{4}$$

$$\mathbf{h}_i^{(\text{edge-head})} = \text{FNN}^{(\text{edge-head})}(\mathbf{r}_i) \tag{5}$$

$$\mathbf{h}_i^{(\text{label-head})} = \text{FNN}^{(\text{label-head})}(\mathbf{r}_i) \tag{6}$$

$$\mathbf{h}_i^{(\text{edge-dep})} = \text{FNN}^{(\text{edge-dep})}(\mathbf{r}_i) \tag{7}$$

$$\mathbf{h}_i^{(\text{label-dep})} = \text{FNN}^{(\text{label-dep})}(\mathbf{r}_i) \tag{8}$$

$$s_{i,j}^{(\text{edge})} = \text{Biaff}^{(\text{edge})}\left(\mathbf{h}_i^{(\text{edge-dep})}, \mathbf{h}_j^{(\text{edge-head})}\right) \tag{9}$$

$$\mathbf{s}_{i,j}^{(\text{label})} = \text{Biaff}^{(\text{label})}\left(\mathbf{h}_i^{(\text{label-dep})}, \mathbf{h}_j^{(\text{label-head})}\right) \tag{10}$$

$$y_{i,j}'^{(\text{edge})} = \{s_{i,j} \geq 0\} \tag{11}$$

$$y_{i,j}'^{(\text{label})} = \arg\max \mathbf{s}_{i,j} \tag{12}$$

The tensor $\mathbf{U}$ can optionally be diagonal (such that $u_{i,k,j} = 0$ wherever $i \neq j$) to conserve parameters. The unlabeled parser scores every edge between pairs of words in the sentence—these scores can be decoded into a graph by keeping only edges that received a positive score. The labeler scores every label for each pair of words, so we simply assign each predicted edge its highest-scoring label and discard the rest. We can train the system by summing the losses from the two modules, backpropagating error to the labeler only through edges with a non-*null* gold label. This system is shown graphically in Figure 2. We find that sometimes the loss for one module overwhelms the loss for the other, causing the system to underfit. Thus we add a tunable interpolation constant $\lambda \in (0, 1)$ to even out the two losses.

$$\ell = \lambda \ell^{(\text{label})} + (1 - \lambda)\ell^{(\text{edge})} \tag{13}$$

Worth noting is that the removal of the maximum spanning tree algorithm and change from softmax cross-entropy to sigmoid cross-entropy in

---

[4]For the labeled parser, $\mathbf{U}$ will be $(d \times c \times d)$-dimensional, where c is the number of labels. For the unlabeled parser, $\mathbf{U}$ will be $(d \times 1 \times d)$-dimensional, so that $s_{i,j}$ will be a single score.

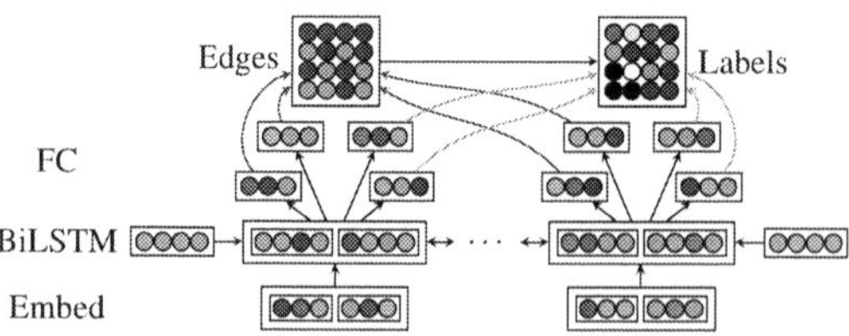

Figure 2: The basic architecture of our factorized system. Labels are only assigned to word pairs with an edge between them.

the unlabeled parser represent the only changes needed to allow the original syntactic parser to generate fully graph-structured semantic dependency output. Note also that this system is general enough that it could be used for any graph-structured dependency scheme, including the enhanced dependencies of the Universal Dependencies formalism (which allows cyclic graphs).

3.2 Augmentations

Ballesteros et al. (2016), Dozat et al. (2017), and Ma et al. (2018) find that character-level word embedding models improve performance for syntactic dependency parsing, so we also want to explore the impact it has on semantic dependency parsing. Dozat et al. (2017) confirm that their syntactic parser performs better with POS tags, which leads us to examine whether word lemmas—another form of low-level lexical information—might also improve dependency parsing performance.

4 Results

4.1 Hyperparameters

We tuned the hyperparameters for our basic system (with no character embeddings or lemmas) fairly extensively on the DM development data. The hyperparameter configuration for our final system is given in Table 2. All input embeddings (word, pretrained, POS, etc.) were concatenated. We used 100-dimensional pretrained GloVe embeddings (Pennington et al., 2014), but linearly transformed them to be 125-dimensional. Only words or lemmas that occurred 7 times or more were included in the word and lemma embedding matrix—including less frequent words appeared to facilitate overfitting. Character-level word embeddings were generated using a one-layer unidirectional LSTM that convolved over three character embeddings at a time, whose end state was linearly transformed to be 100-dimensional. The core BiL-

	DM		PAS		PSD		Avg	
	ID	OOD	ID	OOD	ID	OOD	ID	OOD
(Du et al., 2015)	89.1	81.8	91.3	87.2	75.7	73.3	85.3	80.8
(Almeida and Martins, 2015)	88.2	81.8	90.9	86.9	76.4	74.8	85.2	81.2
WCGL18	90.3	84.9	91.7	87.6	78.6	75.9	86.9	82.8
PTS17: Basic	89.4	84.5	92.2	88.3	77.6	75.3	87.4	83.6
PTS17: Freda3	90.4	85.3	92.7	89.0	78.5	76.4	88.0	84.4
Ours: Basic	91.4	86.9	93.9	**90.8**	79.1	77.5	88.1	85.0
Ours: +Char	92.7	87.8	**94.0**	90.6	80.5	78.6	89.1	85.7
Ours: +Lemma	93.3	88.8	93.9	90.5	80.3	78.7	89.1	86.0
Ours: +Char +Lemma	**93.7**	**88.9**	93.9	90.6	**81.0**	**79.4**	**89.5**	**86.3**

Table 1: Comparison between our system and the previous state of the art on in-domain (WSJ) and out-of-domain (Brown corpus) data, according to labeled F1 (LF1).

Hidden Sizes

Word/Glove/POS/ Lemma/Char	100
GloVe linear	125
Char LSTM	1 @ 400
Char linear	100
BiLSTM	3 @ 600
Arc/Label	600

Dropout Rates (drop prob)

Word/GloVe/ POS/Lemma	20%
Char LSTM (FF/recur)	33%
Char linear	33%
BiLSTM (FF/recur)	45%/25%
Arc/Label	25%/33%

Loss & Optimizer

Interpolation (λ)	.025
L_2 regularization	$3e^{-9}$
Learning rate	$1e^{-3}$
Adam β_1	0
Adam β_2	.95

Table 2: Final hyperparameter configuration.

STM was three layers deep. The different types of word embeddings—word, GloVe, and character-level—were dropped simultaneously, but independently from POS and lemma embeddings (which were dropped independently from each other). Dropped embeddings were replaced with learned <DROP> tokens. LSTMs used same-mask recurrent dropout (Gal and Ghahramani, 2016). The systems were trained with batch sizes of 3000 tokens for up to 75,000 training steps, terminating early after 10,000 steps pass with no improve-

ment in validation accuracy. The L_2 regularization penalty was so small that it likely had little impact.

4.2 Performance

We use biaffine classifiers, with no nonlinearities, and a diagonal tensor in the label classifier but not the edge classifier. The system trains at a speed of about 300 sequences/second on an nVidia Titan X and parses about 1,000 sequences/second. Du et al. (2015) and Almeida and Martins (2015) are the systems that won the 2015 shared task (closed track). *PTS17: Basic* represents the single-task versions of Peng et al. (2017), which they make multitask across the three datasets in Freda3 by adding *frustratingly easy domain adaptation* (Daumé III, 2007; Kim et al., 2016) and a third-order decoding mechanism. WCGL18 is Wang et al.'s (2018) transition-based system. Table 1 compares our performance with these systems. Our fully factorized basic system already substantially outperforms Peng et al.'s single-task baseline and also beats out their much more complex multi-task approach. Simply adding in either a character-level word embedding model (similar to Dozat et al.'s (2017)) or a lemma embedding matrix likewise improves performance quite a bit, and including both together generally pushes performance even higher. Many infrequent words were excluded from the frequent token embedding matrix, so it makes sense that the system should improve when provided more lexical information that's harder to overfit on.

Surprisingly, the PAS dataset seems not to benefit substantially from lemma or character embeddings. It has been noted that PAS is the easiest of the three datasets to achieve good performance for;

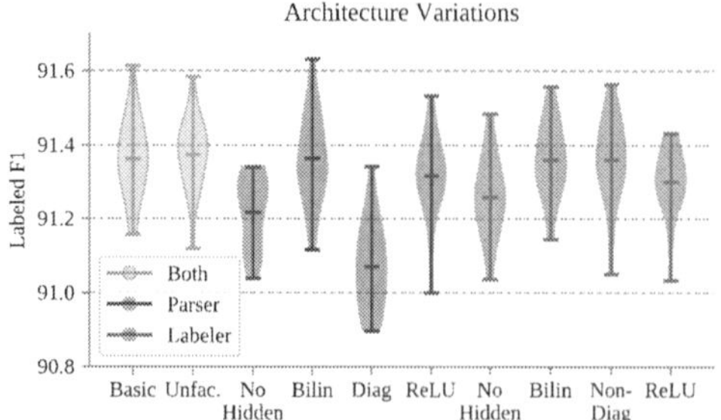

Figure 3: Performance of architecture variations: our basic system; unfactorized (labeler-only); ommitting the hidden layers (Eqs. 7–6); with bilinear classifiers (Eq. 3); with nondiagonal tensors in the labeler or diagonal tensors in the parser; with the ReLU nonlinearity.

so one possible explanation is that 94% LF1 may simply be near the ceiling of what can be achieved for the dataset. Alternatively, the main difference bewteen PAS as DM/PSD is that PAS includes semantically vacuous function words in its representation. Because function words are extremely frequent, it's possible that they are being disproportionately represented in the loss or LF1 score. Using a hinge loss (like Peng et al. (2017)) instead of a cross-entropy loss might help, since the system would stop focusing on potentially "easy" functional predicates once it learned to predict their argument structures confidently, allowing it to put more resources into modeling more challenging phenomena.

4.3 Variations

We also consider the impact that slight variations on basic architecture have on final performance in Figure 3. We train twenty models on the DM treebank for each variation we consider, reducing the number of training steps but keeping all other hyperparameters constant. Rank-sum tests (Lehmann et al., 1975) reveal that the basic system outperforms variants with no hidden layers in the edge classifier ($W=339; p<.001$) or the label classifier ($W=307; p<.01$). Using a diagonal tensor $\mathbf{U}$ in the unlabeled parser also significantly hurts performance ($W=388; p<.001$), likely being too underpowered. While the other variations (especially the unfactorized and ReLU systems) appeared to make a difference during hyperparameter tuning, they were not significant here.

The improved performance of deeper systems (replicating Dozat and Manning (2017)) likely justifies the added complexity. On the other hand, the choice between biaffine and bilinear classifiers comes down largely to aesthetics. This is perhaps unsurprising since the change from biaffine to bilinear represents only a small decrease in overall power. Unusually, using no nonlinearity in the hidden layers in Eqs. (7–6) works as well as ReLU—in fact, using ReLU in the unlabeled parser marginally reduced performance ($W=269; p=.063$). Overall, the parser displayed considerable invariance to architecture changes. Since our system is significantly larger and more heavily regularized than the systems we compare against, this suggests that unglamorous, low-level hyperparameters—such as hidden sizes and dropout rates—are more critical to system performance than high-level architecture enhancements.

5 Discussion

We minimally extended a simple syntactic dependency parser to produce graph-structured dependencies. Without any further augmentations, our carefully-tuned system achieves state-of-the-art performance, highlighting the importance of finding the best hyperparameter configuration (and by extension, building fast systems that can be trained quickly). Additionally, we can see that a multitask system relying on a complex decoding algorithm to prune away invalid graph structures isn't necessary for achieving the level of parsing performance a simple system can achieve (though it could push performance even higher). We also find easier or independently motivated ways to improve accuracy—taking advantage of provided lemma or subtoken information provides a boost comparable to one found by drastically increasing system complexity.

Further, we observe a high-performing graph-based parser can be adapted to different types of dependency graphs (projective tree, nonprojective tree, directed graph) with only small changes without obviously hurting accuracy. By contrast, transition-based parsers—which were originally designed for parsing projective constituency trees (Nivre, 2003; Aho and Ullman, 1972)—require whole new transition sets or even data structures to generate arbitrary graphs. We feel that this points to graph-based parsers being the most natural way to produce dependency graphs with different structural restrictions.

References

Alfred V Aho and Jeffrey D Ullman. 1972. *The theory of parsing, translation, and compiling*, volume 1. Prentice Hall.

Mariana SC Almeida and André FT Martins. 2015. Lisbon: Evaluating turbosemanticparser on multiple languages and out-of-domain data. In *Proceedings of the 9th International Workshop on Semantic Evaluation (SemEval 2015)*. pages 970–973.

Miguel Ballesteros, Yoav Goldberg, Chris Dyer, and Noah A Smith. 2016. Training with exploration improves a greedy stack-LSTM parser. *Proceedings of the conference on empirical methods in natural language processing* .

Marie Candito, Bruno Guillaume, Guy Perrier, and Djamé Seddah. 2017. Enhanced ud dependencies with neutralized diathesis alternation. In *Depling 2017-Fourth International Conference on Dependency Linguistics*.

Jinho D Choi and Andrew McCallum. 2013. Transition-based dependency parsing with selectional branching. In *Proceedings of the 51st Annual Meeting of the Association for Computational Linguistics (Volume 1: Long Papers)*. volume 1, pages 1052–1062.

Hal Daumé III. 2007. Frustratingly easy domain adaptation. *ACL 2007* page 256.

Marie-Catherine De Marneffe, Bill MacCartney, Christopher D Manning, et al. 2006. Generating typed dependency parses from phrase structure parses. In *Proceedings of LREC*. volume 6, pages 449–454.

Timothy Dozat and Christopher D. Manning. 2017. Deep biaffine attention for neural dependency parsing. *ICLR 2017* .

Timothy Dozat, Peng Qi, and Christopher D Manning. 2017. Stanford's graph-based neural dependency parser at the conll 2017 shared task. *CoNLL* pages 20–30.

Yantao Du, Fan Zhang, Xun Zhang, Weiwei Sun, and Xiaojun Wan. 2015. Peking: Building semantic dependency graphs with a hybrid parser. In *Proceedings of the 9th International Workshop on Semantic Evaluation (SemEval 2015)*. pages 927–931.

Chris Dyer, Miguel Ballesteros, Wang Ling, Austin Matthews, and Noah A Smith. 2015. Transition-based dependency parsing with stack long short-term memory. *Proceedings of the conference on empirical methods in natural language processing* .

Dan Flickinger, Yi Zhang, and Valia Kordoni. 2012. Deepbank. a dynamically annotated treebank of the wall street journal. In *Proceedings of the 11th International Workshop on Treebanks and Linguistic Theories*. pages 85–96.

Yarin Gal and Zoubin Ghahramani. 2016. Dropout as a bayesian approximation: Representing model uncertainty in deep learning. *International Conference on Machine Learning* .

Daniel Gildea and Daniel Jurafsky. 2002. Automatic labeling of semantic roles. *Computational linguistics* 28(3):245–288.

Jan Hajic, Eva Hajicová, Jarmila Panevová, Petr Sgall, Ondrej Bojar, Silvie Cinková, Eva Fucíková, Marie Mikulová, Petr Pajas, Jan Popelka, et al. 2012. Announcing prague czech-english dependency treebank 2.0. In *LREC*. pages 3153–3160.

Young-Bum Kim, Karl Stratos, and Ruhi Sarikaya. 2016. Frustratingly easy neural domain adaptation. In *Proceedings of COLING 2016, the 26th International Conference on Computational Linguistics: Technical Papers*. pages 387–396.

Erich Leo Lehmann, HJM D'Abrera, et al. 1975. *Nonparametrics*. Holden-Day.

Xuezhe Ma, Zecong Hu, Jingzhou Liu, Nanyun Peng, Graham Neubig, and Eduard Hovy. 2018. Stack-pointer networks for dependency parsing. *ACL* .

André FT Martins, Noah A Smith, Pedro MQ Aguiar, and Mário AT Figueiredo. 2011. Dual decomposition with many overlapping components. In *Proceedings of the Conference on Empirical Methods in Natural Language Processing*. Association for Computational Linguistics, pages 238–249.

Yusuke Miyao and Jun'ichi Tsujii. 2004. Deep linguistic analysis for the accurate identification of predicate-argument relations. In *Proceedings of the 20th international conference on Computational Linguistics*. Association for Computational Linguistics, page 1392.

Joakim Nivre. 2003. An efficient algorithm for projective dependency parsing. In *Proceedings of the 8th International Workshop on Parsing Technologies (IWPT*. Citeseer.

Joakim Nivre, Marie-Catherine de Marneffe, Filip Ginter, Yoav Goldberg, Jan Hajic, Christopher D Manning, Ryan McDonald, Slav Petrov, Sampo Pyysalo, Natalia Silveira, et al. 2016. Universal dependencies v1: A multilingual treebank collection. In *Proceedings of the 10th International Conference on Language Resources and Evaluation (LREC 2016)*.

Stephan Oepen, Marco Kuhlmann, Yusuke Miyao, Daniel Zeman, Silvie Cinková, Dan Flickinger, Jan Hajic, and Zdenka Uresova. 2015. Semeval 2015 task 18: Broad-coverage semantic dependency parsing. In *Proceedings of the 9th International Workshop on Semantic Evaluation*. pages 915–926.

Stephan Oepen, Marco Kuhlmann, Yusuke Miyao, Daniel Zeman, Dan Flickinger, Jan Hajic, Angelina Ivanova, and Yi Zhang. 2014. Semeval 2014 task 8: Broad-coverage semantic dependency parsing. In

Proceedings of the 8th International Workshop on Semantic Evaluation. pages 63–72.

Stephan Oepen and Jan Tore Lønning. 2006. Discriminant-based mrs banking. In *Proceedings of the 5th International Conference on Language Resources and Evaluation.* pages 1250–1255.

Hao Peng, Sam Thomson, and Noah A Smith. 2017. Deep multitask learning for semantic dependency parsing. In *ACL.* volume 1, pages 2037–2048.

Jeffrey Pennington, Richard Socher, and Christopher D Manning. 2014. Glove: Global vectors for word representation. *Proceedings of the Empiricial Methods in Natural Language Processing (EMNLP 2014)* 12.

Siva Reddy, Oscar Täckström, Slav Petrov, Mark Steedman, and Mirella Lapata. 2017. Universal semantic parsing. *arXiv preprint arXiv:1702.03196* .

Sebastian Schuster and Christopher D. Manning. 2016. Enhanced English Universal Dependencies: An improved representation for natural language understanding tasks. In *Proceedings of the Tenth International Conference on Language Resources and Evaluation (LREC 2016).*

Sebastian Schuster, Éric Villemonte de la Clergerie, Marie Candito, Benoît Sagot, Christopher D. Manning, and Djamé Seddah. 2017. Paris and Stanford at EPE 2017: Downstream evaluation of graph-based dependency representations. In *Proceedings of the 2017 Shared Task on Extrinsic Parser Evaluation (EPE 2017).*

Yuxuan Wang, Wanxiang Che, Jiang Guo, and Ting Liu. 2018. A neural transition-based approach for semantic dependency graph parsing. *AAAI* .

Simplified Abugidas

Chenchen Ding, Masao Utiyama, and Eiichiro Sumita
Advanced Translation Technology Laboratory,
Advanced Speech Translation Research and Development Promotion Center,
National Institute of Information and Communications Technology
3-5 Hikaridai, Seika-cho, Soraku-gun, Kyoto, 619-0289, Japan
{chenchen.ding, mutiyama, eiichiro.sumita}@nict.go.jp

Abstract

An abugida is a writing system where the consonant letters represent syllables with a default vowel and other vowels are denoted by diacritics. We investigate the feasibility of recovering the original text written in an abugida after omitting subordinate diacritics and merging consonant letters with similar phonetic values. This is crucial for developing more efficient input methods by reducing the complexity in abugidas. Four abugidas in the southern Brahmic family, i.e., Thai, Burmese, Khmer, and Lao, were studied using a newswire $20,000$-sentence dataset. We compared the recovery performance of a support vector machine and an LSTM-based recurrent neural network, finding that the abugida graphemes could be recovered with $94\% - 97\%$ accuracy at the top-1 level and $98\% - 99\%$ at the top-4 level, even after omitting most diacritics ($10 - 30$ types) and merging the remaining $30 - 50$ characters into 21 graphemes.

1 Introduction

Writing systems are used to record utterances in a wide range of languages and can be organized into the hierarchy shown in Fig. 1. The symbols in a writing system generally represent either speech sounds (phonograms) or semantic units (logograms). Phonograms can be either segmental or syllabic, with segmental systems being more phonetic because they use separate symbols (i.e., letters) to represent consonants and vowels. Segmental systems can be further subdivided depending on their representation of vowels. Alphabets (e.g., the Latin, Cyrillic, and Greek scripts) are the most common and treat vowel and consonant let-

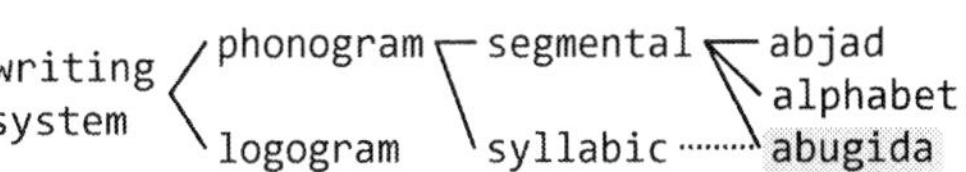

Figure 1: Hierarchy of writing systems.

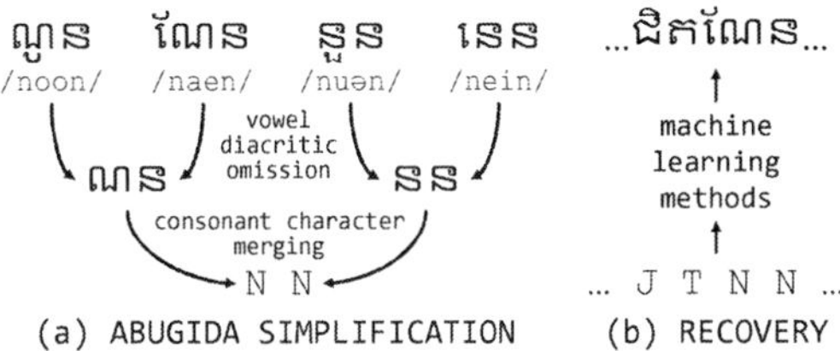

(a) ABUGIDA SIMPLIFICATION (b) RECOVERY

Figure 2: Overview of the approach in this study.

ters equally. In contrast, abjads (e.g., the Arabic and Hebrew scripts) do not write most vowels explicitly. The third type, abugidas, also called alphasyllabary, includes features from both segmental and syllabic systems. In abugidas, consonant letters represent syllables with a default vowel, and other vowels are denoted by diacritics. Abugidas thus denote vowels less explicitly than alphabets but more explicitly than abjads, while being less phonetic than alphabets, but more phonetic than syllabaries. Since abugidas combine segmental and syllabic systems, they typically have more symbols than conventional alphabets.

In this study, we investigate how to simplify and recover abugidas, with the aim of developing a more efficient method of encoding abugidas for input. Alphabets generally do not have a large set of symbols, making them easy to map to a traditional keyboard, and logogram and syllabic systems need specially designed input methods because of their large variety of symbols. Traditional input methods for abugidas are similar to those for alphabets, mapping two or three different symbols onto each key and requiring users to type each character and diacritic exactly. In contrast, we are able to substantially simplify inputting abugidas by encoding them in a *lossy* (or "*fuzzy*") way.

491

Proceedings of the 56th Annual Meeting of the Association for Computational Linguistics (Short Papers), pages 491–495
Melbourne, Australia, July 15 - 20, 2018. ©2018 Association for Computational Linguistics

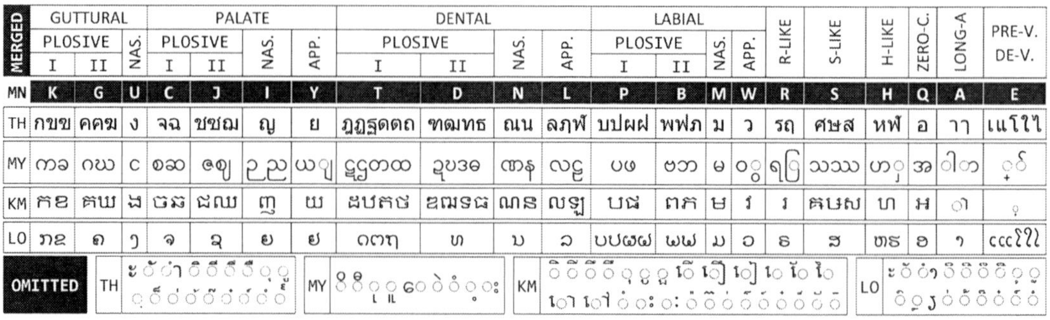

Figure 3: Merging and omission for Thai (TH), Burmese (MY), Khmer (KM), and Lao (LO) scripts. The MN row lists the mnemonics assigned to graphemes in our experiment. In this study, the mnemonics can be assigned arbitrarily, and we selected Latin letters related to the real pronunciation wherever possible.

Fig. 2 gives an overview of this study, showing examples in Khmer. We simplify abugidas by omitting vowel diacritics and merging consonant letters with identical or similar phonetic values, as shown in (a). This simplification is intuitive, both orthographically and phonetically. To resolve the ambiguities introduced by the simplification, we use data-driven methods to recover the original texts, as shown in (b). We conducted experiments on four southern Brahmic scripts, i.e., Thai, Burmese, Khmer, and Lao scripts, with a unified framework, using data from the Asian Language Treebank (ALT) (Riza et al., 2016). The experiments show that the abugidas can be recovered satisfactorily by a recurrent neural network (RNN) using long short-term memory (LSTM) units, even when nearly all of the diacritics (10 – 30 types) have been omitted and the remaining 30 – 50 characters have been merged into 21 graphemes. Thai gave the best performance, with 97% top-1 accuracy for graphemes and over 99% top-4 accuracy. Lao, which gave the worst performance, still achieved the top-1 and top-4 accuracies of around 94% and 98%, respectively. The Burmese and Khmer results, which lay in-between the other two, were also investigated by manual evaluation.

2 Related Work

Some optimized keyboard layout have been proposed for specific abugidas (Ouk et al., 2008). Most studies on input methods have focused on Chinese and Japanese characters, where thousands of symbols need to be encoded and recovered. For Chinese characters, Chen and Lee (2000) made an early attempt to apply statistical methods to sentence-level processing, using a hidden Markov model. Others have examined max-entropy models, support vector machines (SVMs), conditional random fields (CRFs), and machine translation techniques (Wang et al., 2006; Jiang et al., 2007; Li et al., 2009; Yang et al., 2012). Similar methods have also been developed for character conversion in Japanese (Tokunaga et al., 2011). This study takes a similar approach to the research on Chinese and Japanese, transforming a less informative encoding into strings in a natural and redundant writing system. Furthermore, our study can be considered as a specific lossy compression scheme on abugida textual data. Unlike images or audio, the lossy text compression has received little attention as it may cause difficulties with reading (Witten et al., 1994). However, we handle this issue within an input method framework, where the simplified encoding is not read directly.

3 Simplified Abugidas

We designed simplification schemes for several different scripts within a unified framework based on phonetics and conventional usages, without considering many language specific features. Our primary aim was to investigate the feasibility of reducing the complexity of abugidas and to establish methods of recovering the texts. We will consider language-specific optimization in a future work, via both data- and user-driven studies.

The simplification scheme is shown in Fig. 3.[1] Generally, the merges are based on the common distribution of consonant phonemes in most natural languages, as well as the etymology of the characters in each abugida. Specifically, three or four

[1] Each script also includes native punctuation marks, digit notes, and standalone vowel characters that are not represented by diacritics. These characters were kept in the experimental texts but not evaluated in the final results, as the usage of these characters is trivial. In addition, white spaces, Latin letters, Arabic digits, and non-native punctuation marks were normalized into placeholders in the experiments, and were also excluded from evaluation.

graphemes are preserved for the different articulation locations (i.e., guttural, palate, dental, and labial), that two for plosives, one for nasal (`NAS.`), and one for approximant (`APP.`) if present. Additional consonants such as trills (`R-LIKE`), fricatives (`S-/H-LIKE`), and empty (`ZERO-C.`) are also assigned their own graphemes. Although the simplification omits most diacritics, three types are retained, i.e., one basic mark common to nearly all Brahmic abugidas (`LONG-A`), the pre-posed vowels in Thai and Lao (`PRE-V.`), and the vowel-depressors (and/or consonant-stackers) in Burmese and Khmer (`DE-V.`). We assigned graphemes to these because we found they informed the spelling and were intuitive when typing. The net result was the omission of 18 types of diacritics in Thai, 9 in Burmese, 27 in Khmer, and 18 in Lao, and the merging of the remaining 53 types of characters in Thai, 43 in Burmese, 37 in Khmer, and 33 in Lao, into a unified set of 21 graphemes. The simplification thus substantially reduces the number of graphemes, and represents a straightforward benchmark for further language-specific refinement to build on.

4   Recovery Methods

The recovery process can be formalized as a sequential labeling task, that takes the simplified encoding as input, and outputs the writing units, composed of merged and omitted character(s) in the original abugidas, corresponding to each simplified grapheme. Although structured learning methods such as CRF (Lafferty et al., 2001) have been widely used, we found that searching for the label sequences in the output space was too costly, because of the number of labels to be recovered.[2] Instead, we adopted non-structured point-wise prediction methods using a linear SVM (Cortes and Vapnik, 1995) and an LSTM-based RNN (Hochreiter and Schmidhuber, 1997).

Fig. 4 shows the overall structure of the RNN. After many experimentations, a general "shallow and broad" configuration was adopted. Specifically, simplified grapheme bi-grams are first embedded into 128-dimensional vectors[3] and then encoded in one layer of a bi-directional LSTM,

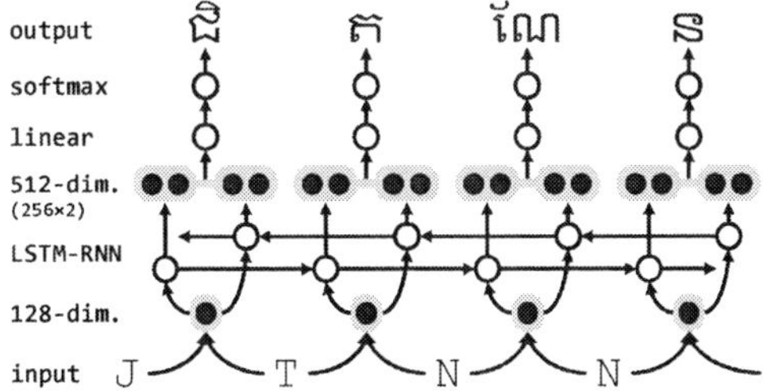

Figure 4: Structure of the RNN used in this study.

resulting in a final representation consisting of a 512-dimensional vector that concatenates two 256-dimensional vectors from the two directions. The number of dimensions used here is large because we found that higher-dimensional vectors were more effective than the deeper structures for this task, as memory capacity was more important than classification ability. For the same reason, the representations obtained from the LSTM layer are transformed linearly before the softmax function is applied, as we found that non-linear transformations, which are commonly used for final classification, did not help for this task.

5   Experiments and Evaluation

We used raw textual data from the ALT,[4] comprising around 20,000 sentences translated from English. The data were divided into training, development, and test sets as specified by the project.[5]

For the SVM experiments, we used the off-the-shelf `LIBLINEAR` library (Fan et al., 2008) wrapped by the `KyTea` toolkit.[6] Table 1 gives the recovery accuracies, demonstrating that recovery is not a difficult classification task, given well represented contextual features. In general, using up to 5-gram features before/after the simplified grapheme yielded the best results for the baseline, except with Burmese, where 7-gram features brought a small additional improvement. Because Burmese texts use relatively more spaces than the other three scripts, longer contexts help more. Meanwhile, Lao produced the worst results, possibly because the omission and merging process was harsh: Lao is the most phonetic of the four scripts, with the least redundant spellings.

The LSTM-based RNN was implemented using `DyNet` (Neubig et al., 2017), and it was trained using `Adam` (Kingma and Ba, 2014) with an initial

---

[2] One consonant character can be modified by multiple diacritics. In the ALT data used in this study, there are around 600 – 900 types of writing units in each script, and there could be over 1,000 on larger textual data.

[3] Directly embedding uni-grams (single graphemes) did not give good performance in our preliminary experiments.

[4] http://www2.nict.go.jp/astrec-att/member/mutiyama/ALT/

[5] Around 18,000, 1,000, and 1,000 sentences, resp.

[6] http://www.phontron.com/kytea/

learning rate of 10^{-3}. If the accuracy decreased on the development set, the learning rate was halved, and learning was terminated when there was no improvement on the development set for three iterations. We did not use dropout (Srivastava et al., 2014) but instead a voting ensemble over a set of differently initialized models trained in parallel, which is both more effective and faster.

As shown in Table 2, the RNN outperformed SVM on all scripts in terms of top-1 accuracy. A more lenient evaluation, i.e., top-n accuracy, showed a satisfactory coverage of around 98% (Khmer and Lao) to 99% (Thai and Burmese) considering only the top four results. Fig. 5 shows the effect of changing the size of the training dataset by repeatedly halving it until it was one-eighth of its original size, demonstrating that the RNN outperformed SVM regardless of training data size. The LSTM-based RNN should thus be a substantially better solution than the SVM for this task.

We also investigated Burmese and Khmer further using manual evaluation. The results of $\text{RNN}^{@1}_{\oplus16}$ in Table 2 were evaluated by native speakers, who examined the output writing units corresponding to each input simplified grapheme and classified the errors using four levels: 0) acceptable, i.e., alternative spelling, 1) clear and easy to identify the correct result, 2) confusing but possible to identify the correct result, and 3) incomprehensible. Table 3 shows the error distribution. For Burmese, most of the errors are at levels 1 and 2, and Khmer has a wider distribution. For both scripts, around 50% of the errors are serious (level 2 or 3), but the distributions suggest that they have different characteristics. We are currently conducting a case study on these errors for further language-specific improvements.

6 Conclusion and Future Work

In this study, a scheme was used to substantially simplify four abugidas, omitting most diacritics and merging the remaining characters. An SVM and an LSTM-based RNN were then used to recover the original texts, showing that the simplified abugidas could be recovered well. This illustrates the feasibility of encoding abugidas less redundantly, which could help with the development of more efficient input methods.

As for the future work, we are planning to include language-specific optimizations in the design of the simplification scheme and to improve

	Thai	Burmese	Khmer	Lao
$\text{Dev}_{\pm3}$	96.1%	94.0%	94.6%	91.5%
$\text{Dev}_{\pm5}$	**97.1%**	96.0%	**95.7%**	**93.1%**
$\text{Dev}_{\pm7}$	97.0%	**96.3%**	**95.7%**	93.0%
Test	97.2%	96.1%	95.2%	93.1%
Leng.	76.0%	74.0%	77.6%	72.8%

Table 1: Top-1 recovery accuracy for the SVM. Here, "$\text{Dev}_{\pm m}$" represents the results for the development set when using N-gram ($N \in [1, m]$) features within m-grapheme windows of the simplified encodings, and "Test" represents the test set results when using the feature set that gave the best development set results. "Leng." shows the ratio of the number of characters in the simplified encodings compared with the original strings.

	Thai	Burmese	Khmer	Lao
SVM	97.2%	96.1%	95.2%	93.1%
$\text{RNN}^{@1}_{\oplus4}$	97.2%	96.3%‡	95.5%‡	93.3%‡
$\text{RNN}^{@1}_{\oplus8}$	97.3%†	96.4%‡	**95.6%‡**	**93.6%‡**
$\text{RNN}^{@1}_{\oplus16}$	**97.4%‡**	**96.5%‡**	**95.6%‡**	**93.6%‡**
$\text{RNN}^{@2}_{\oplus16}$	98.8%	98.4%	97.5%	96.6%
$\text{RNN}^{@4}_{\oplus16}$	99.2%	98.8%	98.1%	97.7%
$\text{RNN}^{@8}_{\oplus16}$	99.2%	98.9%	98.4%	97.9%

Table 2: Top-n accuracy on the test set for the LSTM-based RNN with an m-model ensemble ($\text{RNN}^{@n}_{\oplus m}$). Here, † and ‡ mean the RNN outperformed the SVM with statistical significance at $p < 10^{-2}$ and $p < 10^{-3}$ level, respectively, measured by bootstrap re-sampling.

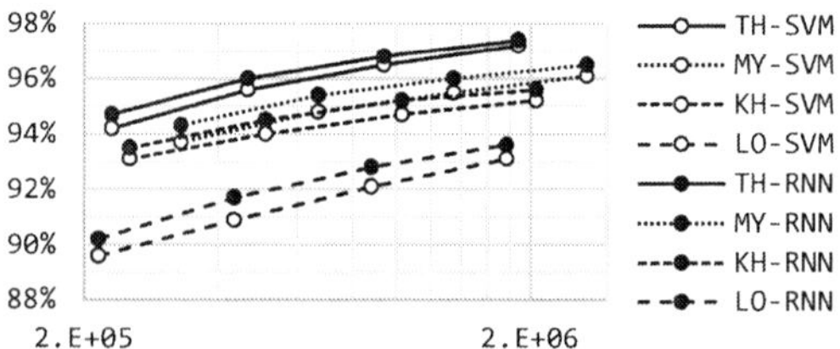

Figure 5: Top-1 accuracy on the test set (y-axis) for different training data sizes (x-axis, number of graphemes after simplification, logarithmic).

Level	0	1	2	3
Burmese	4.5%	51.0%	42.2%	2.2%
Khmer	22.5%	28.5%	16.3%	32.8%

Table 3: Recovery error distribution.

the LSTM-based RNN by integrating dictionaries and increasing the amount of training data.

Acknowledgments

The experimental results of Burmese were evaluated by Dr. Win Pa Pa and Ms. Aye Myat Mon from *University of Computer Studies, Yangon*, Myanmar. The experimental resutls of Khmer were evaluated by Mr. Vichet Chea, Mr. Hour Kaing, Mr. Kamthong Ley, Mr. Vanna Chuon, and Mr. Saly Keo from *National Institute of Posts, Telecommunications and ICT*, Cambodia. We are grateful for their collaboration. We would like to thank Dr. Atsushi Fujita for his helpful comments.

References

Zheng Chen and Kai-Fu Lee. 2000. A new statistical approach to Chinese pinyin input. In *Proc. of ACL.* pages 241–247.

Corinna Cortes and Vladimir Vapnik. 1995. Support-vector networks. *Machine learning* 20(3):273–297.

Rong-En Fan, Kai-Wei Chang, Cho-Jui Hsieh, Xiang-Rui Wang, and Chih-Jen Lin. 2008. LIBLINEAR: A library for large linear classification. *Journal of machine learning research* 9(Aug):1871–1874.

Sepp Hochreiter and Jürgen Schmidhuber. 1997. Long short-term memory. *Neural computation* 9(8):1735–1780.

Wei Jiang, Yi Guan, Xiaolong Wang, and Bingquan Liu. 2007. Pinyin-to-character conversion model based on support vector machines. *Journal of Chinese information processing* 21(2):100–105.

Diederik Kingma and Jimmy Ba. 2014. Adam: A method for stochastic optimization. *arXiv preprint.*

John Lafferty, Andrew McCallum, and Fernando C. N. Pereira. 2001. Conditional random fields: Probabilistic models for segmenting and labeling sequence data. In *Proc. of ICML.* pages 282–289.

Lu Li, Xuan Wang, Xiaolong Wang, and Yanbing Yu. 2009. A conditional random fields approach to Chinese pinyin-to-character conversion. *Journal of Communication and Computer* 6(4):25–31.

Graham Neubig, Chris Dyer, Yoav Goldberg, Austin Matthews, Waleed Ammar, Antonios Anastasopoulos, Miguel Ballesteros, David Chiang, Daniel Clothiaux, Trevor Cohn, Kevin Duh, Manaal Faruqui, Cynthia Gan, Dan Garrette, Yangfeng Ji, Lingpeng Kong, Adhiguna Kuncoro, Gaurav Kumar, Chaitanya Malaviya, Paul Michel, Yusuke Oda, Matthew Richardson, Naomi Saphra, Swabha Swayamdipta, and Pengcheng Yin. 2017. DyNet: The dynamic neural network toolkit. *arXiv preprint.*

Phavy Ouk, Ye Kyaw Thu, Mitsuji Matsumoto, and Yoshiyori Urano. 2008. The design of Khmer word-based predictive non-QWERTY soft keyboard for stylus-based devices. In *Proc. of VL/HCC.* pages 225–232.

Hammam Riza, Michael Purwoadi, Gunarso, Teduh Uliniansyah, Aw Ai Ti, Sharifah Mahani Aljunied, Luong Chi Mai, Vu Tat Thang, Nguyen Phuong Thai, Rapid Sun, Vichet Chea, Khin Mar Soe, Khin Thandar Nwet, Masao Utiyama, and Chenchen Ding. 2016. Introduction of the Asian language treebank. In *Proc. of O-COCOSDA.* pages 1–6.

Nitish Srivastava, Geoffrey E. Hinton, Alex Krizhevsky, Ilya Sutskever, and Ruslan Salakhutdinov. 2014. Dropout: A simple way to prevent neural networks from overfitting. *Journal of machine learning research* 15(1):1929–1958.

Hiroyuki Tokunaga, Daisuke Okanohara, and Shinsuke Mori. 2011. Discriminative method for Japanese kana-kanji input method. In *Proc. of WTIM.* pages 10–18.

Xuan Wang, Lu Li, Lin Yao, and Waqas Anwar. 2006. A maximum entropy approach to Chinese pinyin-to-character conversion. In *Proc. of SMC.* pages 2956–2959.

Ian H. Witten, Timothy C. Bell, Alistair Moffat, Craig G. Nevill-Manning, Tony C. Smith, and Harold Thimbleby. 1994. Semantic and generative models for lossy text compression. *The Computer Journal* 37(2):83–87.

Shaohua Yang, Hai Zhao, and Baoliang Lu. 2012. A machine translation approach for Chinese whole-sentence pinyin-to-character conversion. In *Proc. of PACLIC.* pages 333–342.

Automatic Academic Paper Rating Based on Modularized Hierarchical Convolutional Neural Network

Pengcheng Yang[2], Xu Sun[1,2], Wei Li[1], Shuming Ma[1]

[1]MOE Key Lab of Computational Linguistics, School of EECS, Peking University
[2]Deep Learning Lab, Beijing Institute of Big Data Research, Peking University
{yang_pc, xusun, liweitj47, shumingma}@pku.edu.cn

Abstract

As more and more academic papers are being submitted to conferences and journals, evaluating all these papers by professionals is time-consuming and can cause inequality due to the personal factors of the reviewers. In this paper, in order to assist professionals in evaluating academic papers, we propose a novel task: automatic academic paper rating (AAPR), which automatically determine whether to accept academic papers. We build a new dataset for this task and propose a novel modularized hierarchical convolutional neural network to achieve automatic academic paper rating. Evaluation results show that the proposed model outperforms the baselines by a large margin. The dataset and code are available at https://github.com/lancopku/AAPR

1 Introduction

Every year there are thousands of academic papers submitted to conferences and journals. Rating all these papers can be exhausting, and sometimes rating scores can be affected by the personal factors of the reviewers, leading to inequality problem. Therefore, there is a great need for rating academic papers automatically. In this paper, we explore how to automatically rate the academic papers based on their LaTeX source file and meta information, which we call the task of automatic academic paper rating (AAPR).

A task that is similar to the AAPR is automatic essay scoring (AES). AES has been studied for a long time. Project Essay Grade (Page, 1967, 1968) is one of the earliest attempts to solve the AES task by predicting the score using linear regression over expert crafted textual features. Much of the following work applied similar methods by using various classifiers with more sophisticated features including grammar, vocabulary and style (Rudner and Liang, 2002; Attali and Burstein, 2004). These traditional methods can work almost as well as human raters. However, they all demand a large amount of feature engineering, which requires a lot of expertise.

Recent studies turn to use deep neural networks, claiming that deep learning models can relieve the system from heavy feature engineering. Alikaniotis et al. (2016) proposed to use long short term memory network (Hochreiter and Schmidhuber, 1997) with a linear regression output layer to predict the score. They added a score prediction loss to the original C&W embedding (Collobert and Weston, 2008; Collobert et al., 2011), so that the word embeddings are related to the quality of the essay. Taghipour and Ng (2016) also applied recurrent neural networks to process the essay, except that they put a convolutional layer ahead of the recurrent layer to extract local features. Dong and Zhang (2016) proposed to apply a two-layer convolutional neural network (CNN) to model the essay. The first layer is responsible for encoding the sentence and the second layer is to encode the whole essay. Dong et al. (2017) further proposed to add attention mechanism to the pooling layer to automatically decide which part is more important in determining the quality of the essay.

Although there has been a lot of work dealing with AES task, researchers have not attempted the AAPR task. Different from the essay in language capability tests, academic papers are much longer with much more information, and the overall quality is affected by a variety of factors besides the writing. Therefore, we propose a model that considers the overall information of one academic paper, including the title, authors, abstract and the main content of the LaTeX source file of the paper.

Proceedings of the 56th Annual Meeting of the Association for Computational Linguistics (Short Papers), pages 496–502
Melbourne, Australia, July 15 - 20, 2018. ©2018 Association for Computational Linguistics

Our main contributions are listed as follows:

- We propose the task of automatically rating academic papers and build a new dataset for this task.

- We propose a modularized hierarchical convolutional neural network model that considers the overall information of the source paper. Experimental results show that the proposed method outperforms the baselines by a large margin.

2 Proposed Method

A source paper usually consists of several modules, such as *abstract*[1], *title* and so on. There is also a hierarchical structure from word-level to sentence-level in each module. The structure information is likely to be helpful to make more accurate predictions. Besides, the model can be improved by considering the difference in contributions of various parts of the source paper. Based on this observation, we propose a modularized hierarchical CNN. An overview of our model is shown in Figure 1. We assume that a source paper has l modules, with m words and the filter size is h (detailed explanations can be referred to Section 2.1 and Section 2.2). l, m and h are set to be 3, 3, 2, respectively in the Figure 1 for simplicity.

2.1 Modularized Hierarchical CNN

Given a complete source paper r, represented by a sequence of tokens, we first divide it into several modules $(r_1, r_2, \cdots, r_l)$ based on the general structure of the source paper (*abstract, title, authors, introduction, related work, methods and conclusion*). For each module, the one-hot representation of the i-th word w_i is embedded to a dense vector x_i through an embedding matrix. For the following modules (*abstract, introduction, related work, methods, conclusion*), we use the attention-based CNN (illustrated in Section 2.2) in word-level to get the representation s_i of the i-th sentence. Another attention-based CNN layer is applied to encode the sentence-level representations into the representation m_i of the i-th module.

There is only one sentence in the title of the source paper, so it is reasonable to get the module-level representation of *title* only using attention-based CNN in word-level. Besides, the weighted

---

[1] Italicized words represent modules of the source paper.

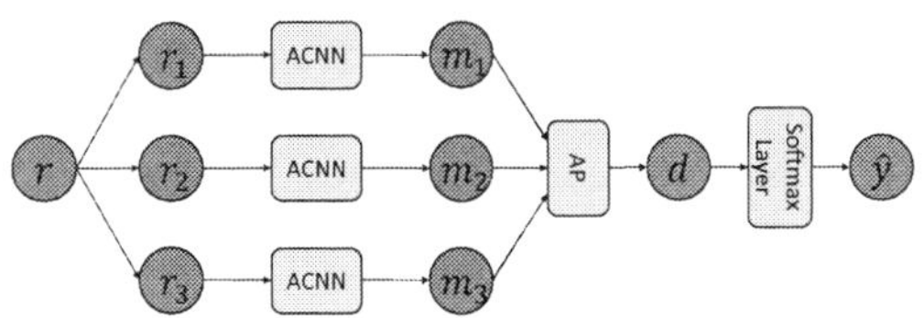

(a) Modularized hierarchical convolutional neural network.

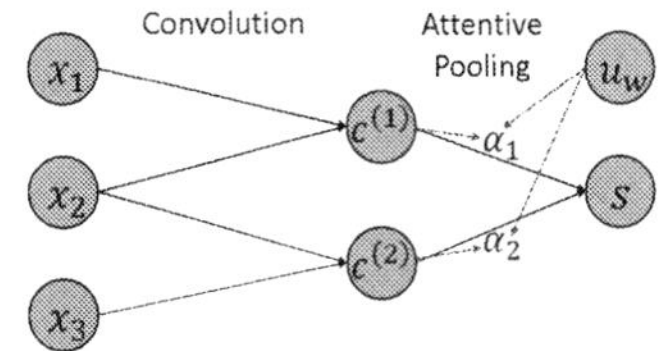

(b) Attention-based convolutional neural network.

Figure 1: The overview of our model. ACNN denotes attention-based CNN, whose basic structure is shown in (b). AP denotes attentive pooling.

average method is applied to obtain the module-level representation of *authors* by Equation (1) because the authors are independent of each other.

$$m_{authors} = \sum_{i=1}^{A} \gamma_i a_i \tag{1}$$

where $\gamma = (\gamma_1, \ldots, \gamma_A)^T$ is the weight parameter. a_i is the embedding vector of the i-th author in the source paper, which is randomly initialized and can be learned at the training stage. A is the maximum length of the author sequence.

Representations $m_1, m_2, \cdots, m_l$ of all modules are aggregated to form the paper-level representation d of the source paper with an attentive pooling layer. A $softmax$ layer is used to take d as input and predict the probability of being accepted. At the training stage, the cross entropy loss function is optimized as objective function, which is widely used in various classification tasks.

$$\hat{y} = softmax(W_d d + b_d) \tag{2}$$

2.2 Details of Attention-Based CNN

Attention-based CNN consists of a convolution layer and an attentive pooling layer. The convolution layer is used to capture local features and attentive pooling layer can automatically decide the relative weights of words, sentences, and modules.

Convolution layer: A sequence of vectors of length m is represented as the row concatenation of m k-dimensional vectors: $X = [x_1; x_2; \cdots; x_m]$. A filter $W_x \in \mathbb{R}^{h \times k}$ convolves with the window vectors at each position to generate a feature map $c \in \mathbb{R}^{m-h+1}$. Each element c_j of the feature map is calculated as follows:

$$c_j = f(\boldsymbol{W}_x \circ [\boldsymbol{x}_j : \boldsymbol{x}_{j+h-1}] + b_x) \qquad (3)$$

where $\circ$ is element-wise multiplication, $b_x \in \mathbb{R}$ is a bias term, and f is a non-linear activation function. Here we choose f to be ReLU (Nair and Hinton, 2010). n different filters can be used to extract multiple feature maps $\boldsymbol{c}_1, \boldsymbol{c}_2, \cdots, \boldsymbol{c}_n$. We get new feature representations $C \in \mathbb{R}^{(m-h+1) \times n}$ as the column concatenation of feature maps $C = [\boldsymbol{c}_1, \boldsymbol{c}_2, \cdots, \boldsymbol{c}_n]$. The i-th row $\boldsymbol{c}^{(i)}$ of C is the new feature representation generated at position i.

Attentive pooling layer: Given a sequence $\boldsymbol{c}^{(1)}, \boldsymbol{c}^{(2)}, \cdots, \boldsymbol{c}^{(q)}$, which are q n-dimensional vectors, the attentive pooling is applied to aggregate the representations of the sequence by measuring the contribution of each vector to form the high-level representation $\boldsymbol{s}$ of the whole sequence. Formally, we have

$$\boldsymbol{z}_i = \tanh(\boldsymbol{W}_c \boldsymbol{c}^{(i)} + \boldsymbol{b}_c) \qquad (4)$$

$$\alpha_i = \frac{\boldsymbol{z}_i^T \boldsymbol{u}_w}{\sum_k \exp(\boldsymbol{z}_k^T \boldsymbol{u}_w)} \qquad (5)$$

$$\boldsymbol{s} = \sum_i \alpha_i \boldsymbol{z}_i \qquad (6)$$

where $\boldsymbol{W}_c$ and $\boldsymbol{b}_c$ are weight matrix and bias vector, respectively. $\boldsymbol{u}_w$ is a randomly initialized vector, which can be learned at the training stage.

3 Experiments

In this section, we evaluate our model on the dataset we build for this task. We first introduce the dataset, evaluation metric, and experimental details. Then, we compare our model with baselines. Finally, we provide the analysis and the discussion of experimental results.

3.1 Dataset

Arxiv Academic Paper Dataset: As there is no existing dataset that can be used directly, we create a dataset by collecting data on academic papers in the field of artificial intelligence from the website[2]. The dataset consists of 19,218 academic papers. The information of each source paper consists of the venue which marks whether the paper is accepted, and the source LaTeX file. We divide the dataset into training, validation, and test parts. The details are shown in Table 1.

[2] https://arxiv.org/

Dataset	#Total	#Positive	#Negative
Training set	17,218	8,889	8,329
Validation set	1,000	507	493
Test set	1,000	504	496

Table 1: Statistical information of Arxiv academic paper dataset. **Positive** and **Negative** denote whether the source paper is accepted.

3.2 Experimental Details

We use accuracy as our evaluation metric instead of the F-score, precision, and recall because the positive and negative examples in our dataset are well balanced.

Since the author names are different from the common scientific words in the paper, we separately build up vocabulary for authors and text words of source papers with the size of 20,000 and 50,000, respectively.

We use the training strategies mentioned in Zhang and Wallace (2015) for CNN classifier to tune the hyper-parameters based on the accuracy on the validation set. The word or author embedding is randomly initialized and can be learned during training. The size of word embedding or author embedding is 128 and the batch size is 32. Adam optimizer (Kingma and Ba, 2014) is used to minimize cross entropy loss function. We apply dropout regularization (Srivastava et al., 2014) to avoid overfitting and clip the gradients (Pascanu et al., 2013) to the maximum norm of 5.0.

During training, we train the model for a fixed number of epochs and monitor its performance on the validation set after every 50 updates. Once training is finished, we select the model with the highest accuracy on the validation set as our final model and evaluate its performance on the testing set.

3.3 Baselines

We compare our model with the following baselines:

- **Randomly predict (RP):** We randomly decide whether the source paper can be accepted. In other words, the probability of acceptance of every source paper is always 0.5 using this strategy.

- **Traditional machine learning algorithms:** We use various machine learning classifiers

Models	Accuracy	Models	Accuracy
RP	50.0%	Logistic	60.0%
CART	58.6%	KNN	60.3%
MNB	58.3%	GNB	58.5%
SVM	61.6%	AdaBoost	58.9%
Bagging	59.4%	LSTM	60.5%
CNN	61.3%	C-LSTM	60.8%
MHCNN	**67.7%**		

Table 2: Comparison between our proposed model and the baselines on the test set. Our proposed model is denoted as **MHCNN**.

- to predict the labels based on the tf-idf features of the text.

- **Neural networks models:** We apply three representative neural network models: CNN (Kim, 2014), LSTM (Hochreiter and Schmidhuber, 1997), and C-LSTM (Zhou et al., 2015). We concatenate all modules of the source paper into a long text sequence as the input to the neural network models.

3.4 Results

In this subsection, we present the results of evaluation by comparing our proposed method with the baselines. Table 2 reports experimental results of various models. As is shown in Table 2, the proposed MHCNN outperforms all the above mentioned baselines. The best baseline model SVM achieves the accuracy of 61.6%, while the proposed model achieves the accuracy of 67.7%. In addition, our MHCNN outperforms other representative deep-learning models by a large margin. For instance, the proposed MHCNN achieves an improvement of 6.4% accuracy over the traditional CNN. This shows that our MHCNN can learn better representation by considering modularized hierarchical structure in the source paper. Our proposed MHCNN aims to divide a long text into several modules and using attention mechanism to aggregate the representations of each module to form a final high-level representation of a complete source paper. By incorporating knowledge of the structure of the source paper and automatically selecting the most informative words, the model is capable of making more accurate predictions.

4 Analysis and Discussions

Here we perform further analysis on the model and experiment results.

Models	Accuracy	Decline
MHCNN	67.7%	— —
w/o Attention	66.8%*	↓0.9%
w/o Module	61.3%*	↓6.4%

Table 3: Ablation Study. The symbol * indicates that the difference compared to MHCNN is significant with $p \leq 0.05$ under t-test.

4.1 Exploration on Internal Structure of the Model

As is shown in Table 2, our MHCNN model outperforms all baselines by a large margin. Compared with the basic CNN model, the proposed model has a modularized hierarchical structure and uses multiple attention mechanisms. In order to explore the impact of internal structure of the model, we remove the modularized hierarchical structure and attention mechanisms in turn. The performance is shown in Table 3. "w/o Attention" means that we still use modularized hierarchical structure while do not use any attention mechanism. "w/o Module" means that we do not use both attention mechanism and modularized hierarchical structure, which is the same as the CNN model in the baselines.

As is shown in Table 3, the accuracy of the model drops by 0.9% when the attention mechanism is removed from the model. This shows that there are differences in the contribution of textual content. For instance, the *abstract* of a source paper is more important than its *title*. Attention mechanism can automatically decide the relative weights of modules, which makes model predictions more accurate. However, the accuracy of the model drops by 6.4% when we remove the modularized hierarchical structure, which is much larger than 0.9%. It shows that the modularized hierarchical structure of the model is of great help to obtain better representations by incorporating knowledge of the structure of the source paper.

4.2 The Impact of Modules of the Source Paper

One interesting issue is which part of the source paper best determines whether it can be accepted. To explore this issue, we subtract each module from complete source papers in turn and observe the change in the performance of the model. The experimental result is shown in Table 4.

As is shown in Table 4, the performance of the

Contexts	Accuracy	Decline
Full data	67.7%	— —
w/o *Title*	66.6%*	↓1.1%
w/o *Abstract*	65.5%*	↓2.2%
w/o *Authors*	64.6%*	↓3.1%
w/o *Introduction*	65.7%*	↓2.0%
w/o *Related work*	66.0%*	↓1.7%
w/o *Methods*	66.2%*	↓1.5%
w/o *Conclusion*	65.0%*	↓2.7%

Table 4: Ablation Study. The symbol * indicates that the difference compared to full data is significant with $p \leq 0.05$ under t-test.

model shows different degrees of decline when we remove different modules of the source paper. This shows that there are differences in the contribution of different modules of the source paper to its acceptance, which further illustrates the reasonableness of our use of modularized hierarchical structure and attention mechanism. All the declines are significant with $p \leq 0.05$ under the t-test.

When we remove *authors* module, the accuracy drops by 3.1%, which is the largest decline. This shows that the authors of the source paper largely determines whether it can be accepted. Obviously, a source paper written by a proficient scholar tends to be good work, which has a higher probability of being accepted. Except for *authors*, the two most significant modules affecting the probability of being accepted are *conclusions* and *abstract*. Because they are the essence of the entire source paper, which can directly reflect the quality of the source paper. However, the *methods* module of the source paper has little effect on the probability of being accepted according to Table 4. The reason may be that the *methods* of different source papers vary widely, which means that there exists high variance in this module. Therefore, our model may not do well in capturing a unified internal pattern to make prediction. The impact of the *title* is the smallest and the accuracy of the model drops by only 1.1% when *title* is removed from the source paper.

5   Related Work

The most relevant task for our work is automatic essay scoring (AES). There are two main types of methods for the AES task: traditional machine learning algorithms and neural network models.

Most traditional methods for the AES task use supervised learning algorithms, including classification (Larkey, 1998; Rudner and Liang, 2002; Yannakoudakis et al., 2011; Chen and He, 2013), regression (Attali and Burstein, 2004; Phandi et al., 2015; Zesch et al., 2015) and so on. However, they all require lots of manual features, for instance, bag of words, spelling errors, or lengths, which can be time-consuming and requires a large amount of expertise.

In recent years, some neural network models have also been used for the AES task, which have achieved great success. Alikaniotis et al. (2016) proposed to use the LSTM model with a linear regression output layer to predict the score. Taghipour and Ng (2016) applied the CNN model followed by a recurrent layer to extract local features and model sequence dependencies. A two-layer CNN model was proposed by Dong and Zhang (2016) to cover more high-level and abstract information. Dong et al. (2017) further proposed to add attention mechanism to the pooling layer to automatically decide which part is more important in determining the quality of the essay. Song et al. (2017) proposed a multi-label neural sequence labeling approach for discourse mode identification and showed that features extracted by this method can further improve the AES task.

6   Conclusions

In this paper, we propose the task of automatic academic paper rating (AAPR), which aims to automatically determine whether to accept academic papers. We propose a novel modularized hierarchical CNN for this task to make use of the structure of a source paper. Experimental results show that the proposed model outperforms various baselines by a large margin. In addition, we find that the conclusion and abstract parts have the most influence on whether the source paper can be accepted when setting aside the factor of authors.

7   Acknowledgements

This work is supported in part by National Natural Science Foundation of China (No. 61673028), National High Technology Research and Development Program of China (863 Program, No. 2015AA015404), and the National Thousand Young Talents Program. Xu Sun is the corresponding author of this paper.

References

Dimitrios Alikaniotis, Helen Yannakoudakis, and Marek Rei. 2016. Automatic text scoring using neural networks. *arXiv preprint arXiv:1606.04289*.

Yigal Attali and Jill Burstein. 2004. Automated essay scoring with e-rater v. 2.0. *ETS Research Report Series*, 2004(2).

Chengyao Chen, Zhitao Wang, Wenjie Li, and Xu Sun. 2018. Modeling scientific influence for research trending topic prediction. In *Proceedings of the Thirty-Second AAAI Conference on Artificial Intelligence, New Orleans, Louisiana, USA, February 2-7, 2018*.

Hongbo Chen and Ben He. 2013. Automated essay scoring by maximizing human-machine agreement. In *Proceedings of the 2013 Conference on Empirical Methods in Natural Language Processing*, pages 1741–1752.

Ronan Collobert and Jason Weston. 2008. A unified architecture for natural language processing: Deep neural networks with multitask learning. In *Proceedings of the 25th international conference on Machine learning*, pages 160–167. ACM.

Ronan Collobert, Jason Weston, Léon Bottou, Michael Karlen, Koray Kavukcuoglu, and Pavel Kuksa. 2011. Natural language processing (almost) from scratch. *Journal of Machine Learning Research*, 12(Aug):2493–2537.

Fei Dong and Yue Zhang. 2016. Automatic features for essay scoring – an empirical study. In *Proceedings of the 2016 Conference on Empirical Methods in Natural Language Processing*, pages 1072–1077.

Fei Dong, Yue Zhang, and Jie Yang. 2017. Attention-based recurrent convolutional neural network for automatic essay scoring. In *Proceedings of the 21st Conference on Computational Natural Language Learning (CoNLL 2017)*, pages 153–162.

Sepp Hochreiter and Jürgen Schmidhuber. 1997. Long short-term memory. *Neural computation*, 9(8):1735–1780.

Yoon Kim. 2014. Convolutional neural networks for sentence classification. In *Proceedings of the 2014 Conference on Empirical Methods in Natural Language Processing, EMNLP 2014, October 25-29, 2014, Doha, Qatar, A meeting of SIGDAT, a Special Interest Group of the ACL*, pages 1746–1751.

Diederik P. Kingma and Jimmy Ba. 2014. Adam: A method for stochastic optimization. *CoRR*, abs/1412.6980.

Leah S Larkey. 1998. Automatic essay grading using text categorization techniques. In *Proceedings of the 21st annual international ACM SIGIR conference on Research and development in information retrieval*, pages 90–95. ACM.

Dehong Ma, Sujian Li, Xiaodong Zhang, Houfeng Wang, and Xu Sun. 2017. Cascading multiway attentions for document-level sentiment classification. In *Proceedings of the Eighth International Joint Conference on Natural Language Processing (Volume 1: Long Papers)*, volume 1, pages 634–643.

Fanqi Meng, Dehong Gao, Wenjie Li, Xu Sun, and Yuexian Hou. 2013. A unified graph model for personalized query-oriented reference paper recommendation. In *Proceedings of the 22nd ACM international conference on Information & Knowledge Management*, pages 1509–1512. ACM.

Vinod Nair and Geoffrey E Hinton. 2010. Rectified linear units improve restricted boltzmann machines. In *Proceedings of the 27th international conference on machine learning (ICML-10)*, pages 807–814.

Ellis B Page. 1967. Grading essays by computer: Progress report. In *Proceedings of the invitational Conference on Testing Problems*.

Ellis B Page. 1968. The use of the computer in analyzing student essays. *International review of education*, 14(2):210–225.

Razvan Pascanu, Tomas Mikolov, and Yoshua Bengio. 2013. On the difficulty of training recurrent neural networks. In *International Conference on Machine Learning*, pages 1310–1318.

Peter Phandi, Kian Ming A Chai, and Hwee Tou Ng. 2015. Flexible domain adaptation for automated essay scoring using correlated linear regression. In *Proceedings of the 2015 Conference on Empirical Methods in Natural Language Processing*, pages 431–439.

Lawrence M Rudner and Tahung Liang. 2002. Automated essay scoring using bayes' theorem. *The Journal of Technology, Learning and Assessment*, 1(2).

Wei Song, Dong Wang, Ruiji Fu, Lizhen Liu, Ting Liu, and Guoping Hu. 2017. Discourse mode identification in essays. In *Proceedings of the 55th Annual Meeting of the Association for Computational Linguistics (Volume 1: Long Papers)*, volume 1, pages 112–122.

Nitish Srivastava, Geoffrey E. Hinton, Alex Krizhevsky, Ilya Sutskever, and Ruslan Salakhutdinov. 2014. Dropout: a simple way to prevent neural networks from overfitting. *Journal of Machine Learning Research*, 15(1):1929–1958.

Kaveh Taghipour and Hwee Tou Ng. 2016. A neural approach to automated essay scoring. In *Proceedings of the 2016 Conference on Empirical Methods in Natural Language Processing*, pages 1882–1891.

Bingzhen Wei, Xu Sun, Xuancheng Ren, and Jingjing Xu. 2017. Minimal effort back propagation for convolutional neural networks. *arXiv preprint arXiv:1709.05804*.

Helen Yannakoudakis, Ted Briscoe, and Ben Medlock. 2011. A new dataset and method for automatically grading esol texts. In *Proceedings of the 49th Annual Meeting of the Association for Computational Linguistics: Human Language Technologies-Volume 1*, pages 180–189. Association for Computational Linguistics.

Torsten Zesch, Michael Wojatzki, and Dirk Scholten-Akoun. 2015. Task-independent features for automated essay grading. In *Proceedings of the Tenth Workshop on Innovative Use of NLP for Building Educational Applications*, pages 224–232.

Ye Zhang and Byron C. Wallace. 2015. A sensitivity analysis of (and practitioners' guide to) convolutional neural networks for sentence classification. *CoRR*, abs/1510.03820.

Chunting Zhou, Chonglin Sun, Zhiyuan Liu, and Francis C. M. Lau. 2015. A C-LSTM neural network for text classification. *CoRR*, abs/1511.08630.

Automated essay scoring with string kernels and word embeddings

Mădălina Cozma and **Andrei M. Butnaru** and **Radu Tudor Ionescu**
University of Bucharest
Department of Computer Science
14 Academiei, Bucharest, Romania
`butnaruandreimadalin@gmail.com`
`raducu.ionescu@gmail.com`

Abstract

In this work, we present an approach based on combining string kernels and word embeddings for automatic essay scoring. String kernels capture the similarity among strings based on counting common character n-grams, which are a low-level yet powerful type of feature, demonstrating state-of-the-art results in various text classification tasks such as Arabic dialect identification or native language identification. To our best knowledge, we are the first to apply string kernels to automatically score essays. We are also the first to combine them with a high-level semantic feature representation, namely the bag-of-super-word-embeddings. We report the best performance on the Automated Student Assessment Prize data set, in both in-domain and cross-domain settings, surpassing recent state-of-the-art deep learning approaches.

1 Introduction

Automatic essay scoring (AES) is the task of assigning grades to essays written in an educational setting, using a computer-based system with natural language processing capabilities. The aim of designing such systems is to reduce the involvement of human graders as far as possible. AES is a challenging task as it relies on grammar as well as semantics, pragmatics and discourse (Song et al., 2017). Although traditional AES methods typically rely on handcrafted features (Larkey, 1998; Foltz et al., 1999; Attali and Burstein, 2006; Dikli, 2006; Wang and Brown, 2008; Chen and He, 2013; Somasundaran et al., 2014; Yannakoudakis et al., 2014; Phandi et al., 2015), recent results indicate that state-of-the-art deep learning methods reach better performance (Alikaniotis et al., 2016; Dong and Zhang, 2016; Taghipour and Ng, 2016; Dong et al., 2017; Song et al., 2017; Tay et al., 2018), perhaps because these methods are able to

capture subtle and complex information that is relevant to the task (Dong and Zhang, 2016).

In this paper, we propose to combine string kernels (low-level character n-gram features) and word embeddings (high-level semantic features) to obtain state-of-the-art AES results. Since recent methods based on string kernels have demonstrated remarkable performance in various text classification tasks ranging from authorship identification (Popescu and Grozea, 2012) and sentiment analysis (Giménez-Pérez et al., 2017; Popescu et al., 2017) to native language identification (Popescu and Ionescu, 2013; Ionescu et al., 2014; Ionescu, 2015; Ionescu et al., 2016; Ionescu and Popescu, 2017) and dialect identification (Ionescu and Popescu, 2016; Ionescu and Butnaru, 2017), we believe that string kernels can reach equally good results in AES. To the best of our knowledge, string kernels have never been used for this task. As string kernels are a simple approach that relies solely on character n-grams as features, it is fairly obvious that such an approach will not to cover several aspects (e.g.: semantics, discourse) required for the AES task. To solve this problem, we propose to combine string kernels with a recent approach based on word embeddings, namely the bag-of-super-word-embeddings (BOSWE) (Butnaru and Ionescu, 2017). To our knowledge, this is the first successful attempt to combine string kernels and word embeddings. We evaluate our approach on the Automated Student Assessment Prize data set, in both in-domain and cross-domain settings. The empirical results indicate that our approach yields a better performance than state-of-the-art approaches (Phandi et al., 2015; Dong and Zhang, 2016; Dong et al., 2017; Tay et al., 2018).

2 Method

String kernels. Kernel functions (Shawe-Taylor and Cristianini, 2004) capture the intuitive notion of similarity between objects in a specific do-

Proceedings of the 56th Annual Meeting of the Association for Computational Linguistics (Short Papers), pages 503–509
Melbourne, Australia, July 15 - 20, 2018. ©2018 Association for Computational Linguistics

main. For example, in text mining, string kernels can be used to measure the pairwise similarity between text samples, simply based on character n-grams. Various string kernel functions have been proposed to date (Lodhi et al., 2002; Shawe-Taylor and Cristianini, 2004; Ionescu et al., 2014). One of the most recent string kernels is the *histogram intersection string kernel* (HISK) (Ionescu et al., 2014). For two strings over an alphabet Σ, $x, y \in \Sigma^*$, the intersection string kernel is formally defined as follows:

$$k^\cap(x, y) = \sum_{v \in \Sigma^n} \min\{\text{num}_v(x), \text{num}_v(y)\}, \quad (1)$$

where $\text{num}_v(x)$ is the number of occurrences of n-gram v as a substring in x, and n is the length of v. In our AES experiments, we use the intersection string kernel based on a range of character n-grams. We approach AES as a regression task, and employ ν-Support Vector Regression (ν-SVR) (Suykens and Vandewalle, 1999; Shawe-Taylor and Cristianini, 2004) for training.

Bag-of-super-word-embeddings. Word embeddings are long known in the NLP community (Bengio et al., 2003; Collobert and Weston, 2008), but they have recently become more popular due to the *word2vec* (Mikolov et al., 2013) framework that enables the building of efficient vector representations from words. On top of the word embeddings, Butnaru and Ionescu (2017) developed an approach termed *bag-of-super-word-embeddings* (BOSWE) by adapting an efficient computer vision technique, the bag-of-visual-words model (Csurka et al., 2004), for natural language processing tasks. The adaptation consists of replacing the image descriptors (Lowe, 2004) useful for recognizing object patterns in images with word embeddings (Mikolov et al., 2013) useful for recognizing semantic patterns in text documents.

The BOSWE representation is computed as follows. First, each word in the collection of training documents is represented as word vector using a pre-trained word embeddings model. Based on the fact that word embeddings carry semantic information by projecting semantically related words in the same region of the embedding space, the next step is to cluster the word vectors in order to obtain relevant semantic clusters of words. As in the standard bag-of-visual-words model, the clustering is done by k-means (Leung and Malik, 2001), and the formed centroids are stored in a randomized forest of k-d trees (Philbin et al., 2007) to reduce search cost. The centroid of each cluster is interpreted as a *super word embedding* or *super word vector* that embodies all the semantically related word vectors in a small region of the embedding space. Every embedded word in the collection of documents is then assigned to the nearest cluster centroid (the nearest super word vector). Put together, the super word vectors generate a vocabulary (codebook) that can further be used to describe each document as a *bag-of-super-word-embeddings*. To obtain the BOSWE represenation for a document, we just have to compute the occurrence count of each super word embedding in the respective document. After building the representation, we employ a kernel method to train the BOSWE model for our specific task. To be consistent with the string kernel approach, we choose the histogram intersection kernel and the same regression method, namely ν-SVR.

Model fusion. In the primal form, a linear classifier takes as input a feature matrix X of r samples (rows) with m features (columns) and optimizes a set of weights in order to reproduce the r training labels. In the dual form, the linear classifier takes as input a kernel matrix K of $r \times r$ components, where each component k_{ij} is the similarity between examples x_i and x_j. Kernel methods work by embedding the data in a Hilbert space and by searching for linear relations in that space, using a learning algorithm. The embedding can be performed either (i) implicitly, by directly specifying the similarity function between each pair of samples, or (ii) explicitly, by first giving the embedding map ϕ and by computing the inner product between each pair of samples embedded in the Hilbert space. For the linear kernel, the associated embedding map is $\phi(x) = x$ and options (i) or (ii) are equivalent, i.e. the similarity function is the inner product. Hence, the linear kernel matrix K can be obtained as $K = X \cdot X'$, where X' is the transpose of X. For other kernels, e.g. the histogram intersection kernel, it is not possible to explicitly define the embedding map (Shawe-Taylor and Cristianini, 2004), and the only solution is to adopt option (i) and compute the corresponding kernel matrix directly. Therefore, we combine HISK and BOSWE in the dual (kernel) form, by simply summing up the two corresponding kernel matrices. However, summing up kernel matrices is equivalent to feature vector concatenation in the primal Hilbert space. To better explain

Prompt	Number of Essays	Score Range
1	1783	2-12
2	1800	1-6
3	1726	0-3
4	1726	0-3
5	1772	0-4
6	1805	0-4
6	1569	0-30
6	723	0-60

Table 1: The number of essays and the score ranges for the 8 different prompts in the Automated Student Assessment Prize (ASAP) data set.

this statement, let us suppose that we can define the embedding map of the histogram intersection kernel and, consequently, we can obtain the corresponding feature matrix of HISK with $r \times m_1$ components denoted by X_1 and the corresponding feature matrix of BOSWE with $r \times m_2$ components denoted by X_2. We can now combine HISK and BOSWE in two ways. One way is to compute the corresponding kernel matrices $K_1 = X_1 \cdot X_1'$ and $K_2 = X_2 \cdot X_2'$, and to sum the matrices into a single kernel matrix $K_+ = K_1 + K_2$. The other way is to first concatenate the feature matrices into a single feature matrix $X_+ = [X_1 X_2]$ of $r \times (m_1 + m_2)$ components, and to compute the final kernel matrix using the inner product, i.e. $K_+ = X_+ \cdot X_+'$. Either way, the two approaches, HISK and BOSWE, are fused before the learning stage. As a consequence of kernel summation, the search space of linear patterns grows, which should help the kernel classifier, in our case ν-SVR, to find a better regression function.

3 Experiments

Data set. To evaluate our approach, we use the Automated Student Assessment Prize (ASAP) [1] data set from Kaggle. The ASAP data set contains 8 prompts of different genres. The number of essays per prompt along with the score ranges are presented in Table 1. Since the official test data of the ASAP competition is not released to the public, we, as well as others before us (Phandi et al., 2015; Dong and Zhang, 2016; Dong et al., 2017; Tay et al., 2018), use only the training data in our experiments.

Evaluation procedure. As Dong and Zhang (2016), we scaled the essay scores into the range

0-1. We closely followed the same settings for data preparation as (Phandi et al., 2015; Dong and Zhang, 2016). For the in-domain experiments, we use 5-fold cross-validation. The 5-fold cross-validation procedure is repeated for 10 times and the results were averaged to reduce the accuracy variation introduced by randomly selecting the folds. We note that the standard deviation in all cases in below 0.2%.

For the cross-domain experiments, we use the same source→target domain pairs as (Phandi et al., 2015; Dong and Zhang, 2016), namely, 1→2, 3→4, 5→6 and 7→8. All essays in the source domain are used as training data. Target domain samples are randomly divided into 5 folds, where one fold is used as test data, and the other 4 folds are collected together to sub-sample target domain train data. The sub-sample sizes are $n_t = \{10, 25, 50, 100\}$. The sub-sampling is repeated for 5 times as in (Phandi et al., 2015; Dong and Zhang, 2016) to reduce bias. As our approach performs very well in the cross-domain setting, we also present experiments *without* sub-sampling data from the target domain, i.e. when the sub-sample size is $n_t = 0$. As evaluation metric, we use the quadratic weighted kappa (QWK).

Baselines. We compare our approach with state-of-the-art methods based on handcrafted features (Phandi et al., 2015), as well as deep features (Dong and Zhang, 2016; Dong et al., 2017; Tay et al., 2018). We note that results for the cross-domain setting are reported only in some of these recent works (Phandi et al., 2015; Dong and Zhang, 2016).

Implementation choices. For the string kernels approach, we used the histogram intersection string kernel (HISK) based on the blended range of character n-grams from 1 to 15. To compute the intersection string kernel, we used the open-source code provided by Ionescu et al. (2014). For the BOSWE approach, we used the pre-trained word embeddings computed by the *word2vec* toolkit (Mikolov et al., 2013) on the Google News data set using the Skip-gram model, which produces 300-dimensional vectors for 3 million words and phrases. We used functions from the VLFeat library (Vedaldi and Fulkerson, 2008) for the other steps involved in the BOSWE approach, such as the k-means clustering and the randomized forest of k-d trees. We set the number of clusters (dimension of the vocabulary) to $k = 500$. After

---

[1] https://www.kaggle.com/c/asap-aes/data

Method	1	2	3	4	5	6	7	8	Overall
Human	0.721	0.814	0.769	0.851	0.753	0.776	0.721	0.629	0.754
(Phandi et al., 2015)	0.761	0.606	0.621	0.742	0.784	0.775	0.730	0.617	0.705
(Dong and Zhang, 2016)	-	-	-	-	-	-	-	-	0.734
(Dong et al., 2017)	0.822	0.682	0.672	0.814	0.803	0.811	0.801	0.705	0.764
(Tay et al., 2018)	0.832	0.684	**0.695**	0.788	0.815	0.810	0.800	0.697	0.764
HISK and ν-SVR	0.836	0.724	0.677	0.821	0.830	0.828	0.801	0.726	0.780
BOSWE and ν-SVR	0.788	0.689	0.667	0.809	0.824	0.824	0.766	0.679	0.756
HISK+BOSWE and ν-SVR	**0.845**	**0.729**	0.684	**0.829**	**0.833**	**0.830**	**0.804**	**0.729**	**0.785**

Table 2: In-domain automatic essay scoring results of our approach versus several state-of-the-art methods (Phandi et al., 2015; Dong and Zhang, 2016; Dong et al., 2017; Tay et al., 2018). Results are reported in terms of the quadratic weighted kappa (QWK) measure, using 5-fold cross-validation. The best QWK score (among the machine learning systems) for each prompt is highlighted in bold.

computing the BOSWE representation, we apply the L_1-normalized intersection kernel. We combine HISK and BOSWE in the dual form by summing up the two corresponding matrices. For the learning phase, we employ the dual implementation of ν-SVR available in LibSVM (Chang and Lin, 2011). We set its regularization parameter to $c = 10^3$ and $\nu = 10^{-1}$ in all our experiments.

In-domain results. The results for the in-domain automatic essay scoring task are presented in Table 2. In our empirical study, we also include feature ablation results. We report the QWK measure on each prompt as well as the overall average. We first note that the histogram intersection string kernel alone reaches better overall performance (0.780) than all previous works (Phandi et al., 2015; Dong and Zhang, 2016; Dong et al., 2017; Tay et al., 2018). Remarkably, the overall performance of the HISK is also higher than the inter-human agreement (0.754). Although the BOSWE model can be regarded as a shallow approach, its overall results are comparable to those of deep learning approaches (Dong and Zhang, 2016; Dong et al., 2017; Tay et al., 2018). When we combine the two models (HISK and BOSWE), we obtain even better results. Indeed, the combination of string kernels and word embeddings attains the best performance on 7 out of 8 prompts. The average QWK score of HISK and BOSWE (0.785) is more than 2% better the average scores of the best-performing state-of-the-art approaches (Dong et al., 2017; Tay et al., 2018).

Cross-domain results. The results for the cross-domain automatic essay scoring task are presented in Table 3. For each and every source→target pair, we report better results than both state-of-the-art methods (Phandi et al., 2015; Dong and Zhang, 2016). We observe that the difference between our best QWK scores and the other approaches are sometimes much higher in the cross-domain setting than in the in-domain setting. We particularly notice that the difference from (Phandi et al., 2015) when $n_t = 0$ is always higher than 10%. Our highest improvement (more than 54%, from 0.187 to 0.728) over (Phandi et al., 2015) is recorded for the pair 5→6, when $n_t = 0$. Our score in this case (0.728) is even higher than both scores of Phandi et al. (2015) and Dong and Zhang (2016) when they use $n_t = 50$. Different from the in-domain setting, we note that the combination of string kernels and word embeddings does not always provide better results than string kernels alone, particularly when the number of target samples (n_t) added into the training set is less or equal to 25.

Discussion. It is worth noting that in a set of preliminary experiments (not included in the paper), we actually considered another approach based on word embeddings. We tried to obtain a document embedding by averaging the word vectors for each document. We computed the average as well as the standard deviation for each component of the word vectors, resulting in a total of 600 features, since the word vectors are 300-dimensional. We applied this method in the in-domain setting and we obtained a surprisingly low overall QWK score, around 0.251. We concluded that this simple approach is not useful, and decided to use BOSWE (Butnaru and Ionescu, 2017) instead.

It would have been interesting to present an error analysis based on the discriminant features weighted higher by the ν-SVR method. Unfortu-

Source→Target	Method	$n_t = 0$	$n_t = 10$	$n_t = 25$	$n_t = 50$	$n_t = 100$
1→2	(Phandi et al., 2015)	0.434	0.463	0.457	0.492	0.510
	(Dong and Zhang, 2016)	-	0.546	0.569	0.563	0.559
	HISK and ν-SVR	0.440	**0.586**	**0.637**	0.652	0.657
	BOSWE and ν-SVR	0.398	0.474	0.478	0.492	0.506
	HISK+BOSWE and ν-SVR	**0.542**	0.584	0.632	**0.657**	**0.661**
3→4	(Phandi et al., 2015)	0.522	0.593	0.609	0.618	0.646
	(Dong and Zhang, 2016)	-	0.628	0.656	0.659	0.662
	HISK and ν-SVR	**0.703**	**0.716**	0.724	0.742	0.751
	BOSWE and ν-SVR	0.615	0.640	0.716	0.728	0.727
	HISK+BOSWE and ν-SVR	0.701	0.713	**0.737**	**0.754**	**0.779**
5→6	(Phandi et al., 2015)	0.187	0.539	0.662	0.680	0.713
	(Dong and Zhang, 2016)	-	0.647	0.700	0.714	0.750
	HISK and ν-SVR	0.715	0.726	0.754	0.757	0.781
	BOSWE and ν-SVR	0.617	0.623	0.644	0.650	0.692
	HISK+BOSWE and ν-SVR	**0.728**	**0.734**	**0.764**	**0.771**	**0.788**
7→8	(Phandi et al., 2015)	0.171	0.586	0.607	0.613	0.621
	(Dong and Zhang, 2016)	-	0.570	0.590	0.568	0.587
	HISK and ν-SVR	0.486	0.604	0.617	0.626	0.639
	BOSWE and ν-SVR	0.419	0.526	0.577	0.582	0.591
	HISK+BOSWE and ν-SVR	**0.522**	**0.606**	**0.637**	**0.638**	**0.649**

Table 3: Corss-domain automatic essay scoring results of our approach versus two state-of-the-art methods (Phandi et al., 2015; Dong and Zhang, 2016). Results are reported in terms of the quadratic weighted kappa (QWK) measure, using the same evaluation procedure as (Phandi et al., 2015; Dong and Zhang, 2016). The best QWK scores for each source→target domain pair are highlighted in bold.

nately, this is not possible because our approach works in the dual space and we cannot transform the dual weights into primal weights, as long as the histogram intersection kernel does not have an explicit embedding map associated to it. In future work, however, we aim to replace the histogram intersection kernel with the presence bits kernel, which will enable us to perform an error analysis based on the overused or underused patterns, as described by Ionescu et al. (2016).

4 Conclusion

In this paper, we described an approach based on combining string kernels and word embeddings for automatic essay scoring. We compared our approach on the Automated Student Assessment Prize data set, in both in-domain and cross-domain settings, with several state-of-the-art approaches (Phandi et al., 2015; Dong and Zhang, 2016; Dong et al., 2017; Tay et al., 2018). Overall, the in-domain and the cross-domain comparative studies indicate that string kernels, both alone and in combination with word embeddings, attain the best performance on the automatic essay scoring task. Using a shallow approach, we report better results compared to recent deep learning approaches (Dong and Zhang, 2016; Dong et al., 2017; Tay et al., 2018).

Acknowledgments

We thank the reviewers for their useful comments. The work of Radu Tudor Ionescu was partially supported through project grant PN-III-P1-1.1-PD-2016-0787.

References

Dimitrios Alikaniotis, Helen Yannakoudakis, and Marek Rei. 2016. Automatic text scoring using neural networks. In *Proceedings of ACL*. pages 715–725.

Yigal Attali and Jill Burstein. 2006. Automated essay scoring with e-rater v. 2.0. *Journal of Technology, Learning, and Assessment* 4(3):1–30.

Yoshua Bengio, Réjean Ducharme, Pascal Vincent, and Christian Janvin. 2003. A Neural Probabilistic Language Model. *Journal of Machine Learning Research* 3:1137–1155.

Andrei Butnaru and Radu Tudor Ionescu. 2017. From Image to Text Classification: A Novel Approach based on Clustering Word Embeddings. In *Proceedings of KES*. page 17841793.

Chih-Chung Chang and Chih-Jen Lin. 2011. LibSVM: A Library for Support Vector Machines. *ACM Transactions on Intelligent Systems and Technology* 2:27:1–27:27. Software available at http://www.csie.ntu.edu.tw/~cjlin/libsvm.

Hongbo Chen and Ben He. 2013. Automated essay scoring by maximizing human-machine agreement. In *Proceedings of EMNLP*. pages 1741–1752.

Ronan Collobert and Jason Weston. 2008. A Unified Architecture for Natural Language Processing: Deep Neural Networks with Multitask Learning. In *Proceedings of ICML*. pages 160–167.

Gabriella Csurka, Christopher R. Dance, Lixin Fan, Jutta Willamowski, and Cdric Bray. 2004. Visual categorization with bags of keypoints. *In Workshop on Statistical Learning in Computer Vision, ECCV* pages 1–22.

Semire Dikli. 2006. An Overview of Automated Scoring of Essays. *Journal of Technology, Learning, and Assessment* 5(1):1–35.

Fei Dong and Yue Zhang. 2016. Automatic Features for Essay Scoring – An Empirical Study. In *Proceedings of EMNLP*. pages 1072–1077.

Fei Dong, Yue Zhang, and Jie Yang. 2017. Attention-based Recurrent Convolutional Neural Network for Automatic Essay Scoring. In *Proceedings of CONLL*. pages 153–162.

Peter W. Foltz, Darrell Laham, and Thomas K Landauer. 1999. Automated essay scoring: Applications to educational technology. In *Proceedings of EdMedia*. pages 40–64.

Rosa M. Giménez-Pérez, Marc Franco-Salvador, and Paolo Rosso. 2017. Single and Cross-domain Polarity Classification using String Kernels. In *Proceedings of EACL*. pages 558–563.

Radu Tudor Ionescu. 2015. A Fast Algorithm for Local Rank Distance: Application to Arabic Native Language Identification. In *Proceedings of ICONIP*. volume 9490, pages 390–400.

Radu Tudor Ionescu and Andrei Butnaru. 2017. Learning to Identify Arabic and German Dialects using Multiple Kernels. In *Proceedings of VarDial Workshop of EACL*. pages 200–209.

Radu Tudor Ionescu and Marius Popescu. 2016. UnibucKernel: An Approach for Arabic Dialect Identification based on Multiple String Kernels. In *Proceedings of VarDial Workshop of COLING*. pages 135–144.

Radu Tudor Ionescu and Marius Popescu. 2017. Can string kernels pass the test of time in native language identification? In *Proceedings of the 12th Workshop on Innovative Use of NLP for Building Educational Applications*. pages 224–234.

Radu Tudor Ionescu, Marius Popescu, and Aoife Cahill. 2014. Can characters reveal your native language? a language-independent approach to native language identification. In *Proceedings of EMNLP*. pages 1363–1373.

Radu Tudor Ionescu, Marius Popescu, and Aoife Cahill. 2016. String kernels for native language identification: Insights from behind the curtains. *Computational Linguistics* 42(3):491–525.

Leah S. Larkey. 1998. Automatic essay grading using text categorization techniques. In *Proceedings of SIGIR*. pages 90–95.

Thomas Leung and Jitendra Malik. 2001. Representing and Recognizing the Visual Appearance of Materials using Three-dimensional Textons. *International Journal of Computer Vision* 43(1):29–44.

Huma Lodhi, Craig Saunders, John Shawe-Taylor, Nello Cristianini, and Christopher J. C. H. Watkins. 2002. Text classification using string kernels. *Journal of Machine Learning Research* 2:419–444.

David G. Lowe. 2004. Distinctive Image Features from Scale-Invariant Keypoints. *International Journal of Computer Vision* 60(2):91–110.

Tomas Mikolov, Ilya Sutskever, Kai Chen, Gregory S. Corrado, and Jeffrey Dean. 2013. Distributed Representations of Words and Phrases and their Compositionality. In *Proceedings of NIPS*. pages 3111–3119.

Peter Phandi, Kian Ming A. Chai, and Hwee Tou Ng. 2015. Flexible Domain Adaptation for Automated Essay Scoring Using Correlated Linear Regression. In *Proceedings of EMNLP*. pages 431–439.

James Philbin, Ondrej Chum, Michael Isard, Josef Sivic, and Andrew Zisserman. 2007. Object retrieval with large vocabularies and fast spatial matching. In *Proceedings of CVPR*. pages 1–8.

Marius Popescu and Cristian Grozea. 2012. Kernel methods and string kernels for authorship analysis. In *Proceedings of CLEF (Online Working Notes/Labs/Workshop)*.

Marius Popescu, Cristian Grozea, and Radu Tudor Ionescu. 2017. HASKER: An efficient algorithm for string kernels. Application to polarity classification in various languages. In *Proceedings of KES*. pages 1755–1763.

Marius Popescu and Radu Tudor Ionescu. 2013. The Story of the Characters, the DNA and the Native Language. *Proceedings of the Eighth Workshop on Innovative Use of NLP for Building Educational Applications* pages 270–278.

John Shawe-Taylor and Nello Cristianini. 2004. *Kernel Methods for Pattern Analysis*. Cambridge University Press.

Swapna Somasundaran, Jill Burstein, and Martin Chodorow. 2014. Lexical Chaining for Measuring Discourse Coherence Quality in Test-taker Essays. In *Proceedings of COLING*. pages 950–961.

Wei Song, Dong Wang, Ruiji Fu, Lizhen Liu, Ting Liu, and Guoping Hu. 2017. Discourse Mode Identification in Essays. In *Proceedings of ACL*. pages 112–122.

J. A. K. Suykens and J. Vandewalle. 1999. Least Squares Support Vector Machine Classifiers. *Neural Processing Letters* 9(3):293–300.

Kaveh Taghipour and Hwee Tou Ng. 2016. A neural approach to automated essay scoring. In *Proceedings of EMNLP*. pages 1882–1891.

Yi Tay, Minh C. Phan, Luu Anh Tuan, and Siu Cheung Hui. 2018. SkipFlow: Incorporating Neural Coherence Features for End-to-End Automatic Text Scoring. In *Proceedings of AAAI*. pages 1–8.

Andrea Vedaldi and B. Fulkerson. 2008. VLFeat: An Open and Portable Library of Computer Vision Algorithms. http://www.vlfeat.org/.

Jinhao Wang and Michelle Stallone Brown. 2008. Automated essay scoring versus human scoring: A correlational study. *Contemporary Issues in Technology and Teacher Education* 8(4):310–325.

Helen Yannakoudakis, Ted Briscoe, and Ben Medlock. 2014. A New Dataset and Method for Automatically Grading ESOL Texts. In *Proceedings of ACL*. pages 180–189.

Party Matters: Enhancing Legislative Embeddings with Author Attributes for Vote Prediction

Anastassia Kornilova   **Daniel Argyle**   **Vlad Eidelman**
FiscalNote
{anastassia.kornilova,daniel,vlad}@fiscalnote.com

Abstract

Predicting how Congressional legislators will vote is important for understanding their past and future behavior. However, previous work on roll-call prediction has been limited to single session settings, thus did not consider generalization across sessions. In this paper, we show that metadata is crucial for modeling voting outcomes in new contexts, as changes between sessions lead to changes in the underlying data generation process. We show how augmenting bill text with the sponsors' ideologies in a neural network model can achieve an average of a 4% boost in accuracy over the previous state-of-the-art.

1   Introduction

Quantitative analysis of the voting behavior of legislators has long been a problem of interest in political science, and recently in NLP as well (Gerrish and Blei, 2011; Kraft et al., 2016). One of the most popular techniques in political science for modeling legislator behavior is the application of spatial, or ideal point, models built from voting records (Poole and Rosenthal, 1985; Clinton et al., 2004), that are often used to represent uni-dimensional or multi-dimensional ideological stances. While *roll call votes* (i.e Congressional voting records) provide explanatory power about a legislators position with respect to previously voted-on bills, these models are limited to in-sample analysis, and are thus incapable of predicting votes on new bills.

To address this limitation, recent work has introduced methods that take advantage the text of the bill, along with the voting records, to model Congressional voting behavior (Gerrish and Blei, 2011; Nguyen et al., 2015; Kraft et al., 2016). This work is related to a long line of studies on using political text to model behavior, ranging over political books, Supreme Court decisions, speeches and Twitter (Mosteller and Wallace, 1963; Thomas et al., 2006; Yu et al., 2008; Sim et al., 2016; Iyyer et al., 2014a; Sim et al., 2013; Preoţiuc-Pietro et al., 2017).

In addition to enabling prediction, associating text with ideology allows for a further degree of interpretability. However, all previous work incorporating text into roll call prediction have limited their evaluation to in-session training and testing.[1]

As legislators typically serve for multiple sessions, and similar bills are proposed across sessions, we want to be able to leverage this data across sessions to inform our model. However, the generalizability of previous methods to a cross-session setting is unknown.

In this work, we explore the problem of roll call prediction across sessions. We show that previous methods are unable to generalize across sessions, thus suggesting that current text representations are not sufficient for modeling voting outcomes in new contexts. We hypothesize that each session has a different underlying data generation process, wherein the ideological position of the observed bills varies depending on the controlling party. This is supported by the observation that about 75% of bills up for a vote in a given session have a sponsor in the party in power.

As noted in Linder et al. (2018), the policy area, or topic, of the bill, and the ideological position, are two separate dimensions underlying the text. Since legislators tend to sponsor bills that are ideologically aligned with them, a model trained on a single session will mostly be exposed to bills with a specific ideology on each topic. Thus, a

---

[1]A session is a 2-year period of legislative business.

510

Proceedings of the 56th Annual Meeting of the Association for Computational Linguistics (Short Papers), pages 510–515
Melbourne, Australia, July 15 - 20, 2018. ©2018 Association for Computational Linguistics

single session model may get the ideology information as an implicit prior without needing to explicitly capture it. This challenge was not obvious in previous studies that were limited to a single session. Across sessions, however, the ideological prior on a given topic changes, resulting in variations in voting patterns that are not captured by current text modeling methodologies alone.

In applications where the text may contain an insufficient signal, researchers may turn to additional metadata features. This technique has previously been used in various contexts, such as incorporating sponsor and committee features for predicting bill committee survival (Yano et al., 2012), and enhancing tweet recommendations with location data (Xing and Paul, 2017).

We propose a neural architecture that directly models the ideological variation across sessions using metadata about the bill sponsors, and show that this can strongly improve performance with little overhead to complexity and training time.

2 Model

Spatial voting models assume that a legislator has a numeric *ideal point* which represents their ideology. They make voting decisions on bills, which also have a numeric representation. While the details of the implementation vary,[2] spatial voting models share the idea that the closer a bill's representation is to a legislator's ideal point the more likely the legislator is to vote *yes*.

Following this framework, we model the core vote prediction problem as follows: Given a legislator, L, and a bill, B, predict their vote y, with possible outcomes: *yes* or *no*.

Using these inputs, let v_L be an embedding representing the legislator, and v_B be the bill embedding. First, v_B is projected into the legislator embedding space:

$$v_{BL} = \mathbf{W_B} v_B + \mathbf{b_B} \quad (1)$$

where $\mathbf{W_B}$ and $\mathbf{b_B}$ are a weight matrix and a bias vector, respectively. Then, we measure the alignment between the two vectors. Previous work used a dot-product for this step, instead, we express the comparison as follows:

$$\mathbf{W_v}(v_{BL} \odot v_L) + \mathbf{b_v} \quad (2)$$

where $\odot$ represents element-wise multiplication, and $\mathbf{W_v}$ is a weight vector of the same dimensions as v_L. Finally, we apply a sigmoid activation function to get the vote prediction:

$$p(y = yes|B, L) = \sigma(\mathbf{W_v}(v_{BL} \odot v_L) + \mathbf{b_v}) \quad (3)$$

Using this architecture, we develop several novel bill representations. First, we consider different text-only representations, then we show how to incorporate metadata.

2.1 Text Model

Previous work incorporating text has primarily been based on topic models (Gerrish and Blei, 2011; Lauderdale and Clark, 2014; Nguyen et al., 2015) and embeddings (Kraft et al., 2016). As the embedding framework achieved superior performance, we adopt a similar architecture. While Kraft et al. (2016) represented the text using a mean word embedding (MWE) representation, we replace it with a Convolutional Neural Network (CNN) representation (Kim, 2014), which has achieved superior performance on recent text classification tasks (Dauphin et al., 2016; Wen et al., 2016; Yang et al., 2016). Our CNN uses 4-grams and 400 filter maps.

2.2 Sponsor Metadata

We posit that a legislator's voting behavior is influenced both by the topic and the ideology of a bill. A legislator may be more liberal on one issue and more conservative on another. Thus, we need to capture both aspects. While previous work has shown that text alone contains ideological information (Iyyer et al., 2014b), the metadata of the bill may be a stronger source, especially for ideology. This approach has had success in the related problem of bill committee survival,[3] where signals about the sponsors, committee and chamber were used in conjunction with text models (Yano et al., 2012).

We use this idea to improve our bill representations. One particularly strong signal is the author of the bill, because of their ideological motives. For simplicity, we represent the bill's authorship as the percentage of Republican and Democrat sponsors (p_r and p_d). We propose that the Republican and Democratic sponsors influence the text

---

[2]For example, Poole and Rosenthal represent bills as cutpoints that divide legislators into yes and no groups (Poole and Rosenthal, 1985) and later work based on item response theory conceptualizes bills as "discrimination" vectors that are mutiplied by an ideal point vector.

---

[3]Congressional bills, first, are voted on in a committee, before moving to the floor.

of the bill in different ways. To obtain the overall ideological position of the bill, we combine the versions of the bill influenced by each party. The final bill can thus be represented as follows:

$$v_B = ((\mathbf{a}_r p_r) \cdot T_r) + ((\mathbf{a}_d p_d) \cdot T_d) \qquad (4)$$

where T_r and T_d are the Republican and Democratic copies of the text representation (e.g MWE or CNN); p_r and p_d are the scalars representing the percentage of sponsors from each party (e.g 0.7 and 0.3); and $\mathbf{a_r}$ and $\mathbf{a_p}$ are vectors representing how the percentages should influence each dimension of the text embedding.

The larger p_r or p_d is, the stronger the influence of that party on the bill.

We test two text representations for T_r and T_d: one using MWEs and one using CNNs. The underlying word embeddings are initialized with 50d GloVE vectors (Pennington et al., 2014) and are non-static during training.

The rest of the model weights are initialized randomly with the *glorot uniform* distribution (Glorot and Bengio, 2010). The length of v_L is set to 25. All models are trained using binary cross-entropy loss and optimized with the *AdaMax* algorithm (Kingma and Ba, 2014). The models are trained for 50 epochs, using mini-batches of size 50.

3 Dataset

Our dataset was collected from GovTrack,[4] and consists of nonunanimous roll call votes and texts of resolutions and bills introduced in the 106th to 111th Congressional sessions.[5] We also collect the bill summaries written by the Congressional Research Service[6] (a non-partisan organization), that provide shorter descriptions of the key actions in each bill. All text is preprocessed by lowercasing and removing stop-words.

As bills are often much longer than the typical document encountered in other NLP tasks, with an average of 2683 words per bill, and some bills having hundreds of pages, with correspondingly

---

[4] https://theunitedstates.io/

[5] We exclude bills with unanimous votes because these are typically associated with routine matters (for example, the naming a post office or an official commendation) that do not contain ideological motivation. We consider bills where less than 1% of legislators voted 'no' to be unanimous; about 42% of bills fall into this category.

[6] https://www.congress.gov/help/legislative-glossary/

Session	Total Bills	Total Votes	% Yes Votes
2005-2012	1718	685,091	68.4%
2013-2014	360	136,807	66.4%
2015-2016	382	153,605	61.8%

Table 1: Count of Bills and Votes

Session	House Majority	Senate Majority
2005-2006	R	R
2007-2008	D	D
2009-2010	D	D
2011-2012	R	D
2013-2014	R	D
2015-2016	R	R

Table 2: Party in power by session

lengthy summaries, this poses a problem for our compositional neural architecture. To address this, we limit the length of each full-text and summary to N words, where N is empirically set to the 80th percentile of the collection. For summaries $N=400$, and for full-text $N=2000$.

4 Experiments

As described earlier, the experimental framework in previous work treated each session individually. To evaluate the ability of our model to generalize across sessions, we perform several sets of experiments. In the first set, in-session, we perform 5 fold cross-validation over the 2005-2012 sessions. In the second, out-of-session, we train on multiple sessions, 2005-2012, and evaluate on sessions not included during training, the 2013-2014 and 2015-2016 sessions. During testing, we only include legislators present in the training data.

The overall statistics for our dataset are presented in Tables 1 and 2.

5 Results

To understand how sponsor parties and text interact in the input, and how our predictive power changes when testing on in-session bills and out-of-session bills. We test the following models:

- MWE: mean word embedding text model as described in Kraft et al. (2016) using summaries;

- MWE+FT: MWE model using full bill text;

- CNN: text model from Section 2.1 over summaries;

- MWE+Meta: MWE representation combined with metadata as described in Section 2.2;

- CNN+Meta: like MWE+Meta but using a CNN instead of averaging;

- MWE+Meta+FT: As above using full bill text;

- Meta-Only: A variation on MWE+Meta that uses the same, random "dummy" text for all the bills, only changing the metadata (p_r and p_d).

Each model is first evaluated in-session, where both train and test bills come from the same set of sessions, and thus same distribution, and then out-of-session, where training bills are from one set of sessions and the model is evaluated on a different set. All results are presented in Table 3.

5.1 In-session Results

We evaluate our models with accuracy on 5-fold cross-validation. All three models combining text with metadata perform significantly better than the others, showing that the text and meta information have complimentary predictive power, and that our models' sponsor-augmented text representation is able to capture the ideological preference. The CNN+Meta achieves the highest accuracy of 86.21, followed by MWE+Meta at 85.96, showing that the CNN learns a somewhat better text representation than MWE. Compare this to the baseline MWE model without meta information, which achieves an accuracy of 81.10, only slightly better than the Meta-Only model at 80.27. Contrary to our hypothesis, MWE achieves higher accuracy than Meta-Only. However, it remains unclear whether this signal is related to ideology or other contextual information. The performance on the out-of-session setting will determine whether this signal is akin to ideology.

5.2 Out-of-session Results

In this setting, on both test sessions, text with meta information achieves the best performance as well. On the 2013-2014 session, the CNN+Meta model does the best at 83.59. Unlike the in-session setting, Meta-only does better than the text-only

	in-session	out-of-session	
	2005-2012	2013-2014	2015-2016
Guess Yes	68.31	65.92	61.07
MWE	81.10	77.57	69.80
MWE + FT	81.46	68.33	57.94
CNN	83.24	77.49	69.63
Meta-Only	80.87	82.28	67.10
MWE + Meta	85.96	82.73	**71.90**
MWE+Meta+FT	85.14	82.43	69.86
CNN + Meta	**86.21**	**83.59**	70.99

Table 3: Accuracy Results

models (MWE, CNN). This supports the theory that within the sessions we are able to capture contextual ideology from the text, but once we move to a new session the text models no longer contain an accurate representation of the Congressional ideology.

While in other experiments we are able to achieve at least a 17% improvement over the Guess Yes baseline, on 2015-2016, the best model, MWE+Meta, is only able to achieve a 10% gain. During this session divisions arose within the Republican party in the House of Representatives that disrupted the typical voting dynamics.[7] Unlike 2013-2014, the Meta-Only model does worse than the text ones; however, the gap between them is much smaller.

5.3 Overall Analysis

These experiments provide several interesting insights. First, because using both text and metadata (MWE+Meta or CNN+Meta) results in the strongest model in every case, we confirm that legislators vote based on both the topic and the ideology of the bill.

Second, the text-only models do significantly worse on the out-of-session tests than the in-session ones. This confirms our theory that session-specific contextual information is implicitly captured by the previous single-session models, but that context is not accurate in new sessions. If we were capturing ideology from the text, then the text only model should have performed well out-of-session.

____

[7]A conservative bloc of the Republican Party (the Freedom Caucus) began to assert influence over party leadership, eventually resulting in the ouster of John Boehner as Speaker (Lizza, 2017).

Third, to further examine whether a neural model was the best technique for modeling text with metadata, we trained a SVM model over the bag-of-words representation of the summary, indicator variables for the legislators and the percent of bill sponsors in each party (e.g p_d). This model did not perform as well as either MWE or Meta-Only, showing that the embedding approach is better at representing this combination of features.

Finally, the models that embed the full text (+FT) generally perform worse than embedding the summaries. While this confirms that the summary contains sufficient information about the topics and the actions in the bill, we did not fully explore the bill text.

6 Future Work

While Congress introduces close to $20,000$ bills every session, very few of them receive a vote, limiting the dataset. We would like to explore various bootstrapping techniques that would allow us to expand the dataset size with artificial votes.

Furthermore, while our text representations are sufficient for modeling shorter text, i.e. summaries, we would like to test more sophisticated representations in the future, in particular, those designed to handle longer texts.

7 Conclusion

In this paper, we developed a neural network architecture to predict legislators votes that augments bill text with sponsor metadata. We introduced a new evaluation setting for this task: out-of-session performance; which allows us to examine the generalizability of our proposed model, and was not considered in past studies. Finally, we showed that the introduction of metadata to bias the text representations outperforms the existing text-based methods in all experimental settings.

References

Joshua Clinton, Simon Jackman, and Douglas Rivers. 2004. The statistical analysis of roll call data. *American Political Science Review*, 98(2).

Yann N. Dauphin, Angela Fan, Michael Auli, and David Grangier. 2016. Language modeling with gated convolutional networks. *CoRR*, abs/1612.08083.

Sean Gerrish and David M Blei. 2011. Predicting legislative roll calls from text. In *Proceedings of ICML*.

Xavier Glorot and Yoshua Bengio. 2010. Understanding the difficulty of training deep feedforward neural networks. In *Proceedings of AISTATS*.

Mohit Iyyer, Peter Enns, Jordan Boyd-Graber, and Philip Resnik. 2014a. Political ideology detection using recursive neural networks. In *Proceedings of ACL*, volume 1, pages 1113–1122.

Mohit Iyyer, Peter Enns, Jordan Boyd-Graber, and Philip Resnik. 2014b. Political ideology detection using recursive neural networks. In *Association for Computational Linguistics*.

Yoon Kim. 2014. Convolutional neural networks for sentence classification. *arXiv:1408.5882*.

Diederik P. Kingma and Jimmy Ba. 2014. Adam: A method for stochastic optimization. *CoRR*, abs/1412.6980.

Peter Kraft, Hirsh Jain, and Alexander M Rush. 2016. An embedding model for predicting roll-call votes. In *Proceedings of EMNLP*.

Benjamin E. Lauderdale and Tom S. Clark. 2014. Scaling politically meaningful dimensions using texts and votes. *American Journal of Political Science*, 58(3):754–771.

Fridolin Linder, Bruce A. Desmarais, Matthew Burgess, and Eugenia Giraudy. 2018. Text as policy: Measuring policy similarity through bill text reuse. *SSRN/2812607*.

Ryan Lizza. 2017. The war inside the republican party.

Frederick Mosteller and David L Wallace. 1963. Inference in an authorship problem: A comparative study of discrimination methods applied to the authorship of the disputed federalist papers. *Journal of the American Statistical Association*, 58(302):275–309.

Viet-An Nguyen, Jordan L. Boyd-Graber, Philip Resnik, and Kristina Miler. 2015. Tea party in the house: A hierarchical ideal point topic model and its application to republican legislators in the 112th congress. In *Proceedings of ACL*.

Jeffrey Pennington, Richard Socher, and Christopher Manning. 2014. Glove: Global vectors for word representation. In *Proceedings of EMNLP*, pages 1532–1543.

Keith T Poole and Howard Rosenthal. 1985. A spatial model for legislative roll call analysis. *American Journal of Political Science*, pages 357–384.

Daniel Preoţiuc-Pietro, Ye Liu, Daniel Hopkins, and Lyle Ungar. 2017. Beyond binary labels: political ideology prediction of twitter users. In *Proceedings of ACL*.

Yanchuan Sim, Brice DL Acree, Justin H Gross, and Noah A Smith. 2013. Measuring ideological proportions in political speeches. In *Proceedings of EMNLP*.

Yanchuan Sim, Bryan R. Routledge, and Noah A. Smith. 2016. Friends with motives: Using text to infer influence on scotus. In *Proceedings of EMNLP*.

Matt Thomas, Bo Pang, and Lillian Lee. 2006. Get out the vote: Determining support or opposition from congressional floor-debate transcripts. *CoRR*, abs/cs/0607062.

Ying Wen, Weinan Zhang, Rui Luo, and Jun Wang. 2016. Learning text representation using recurrent convolutional neural network with highway layers. *CoRR*, abs/1606.06905.

Linzi Xing and Michael J Paul. 2017. Incorporating metadata into content-based user embeddings. In *Proceedings of the 3rd Workshop on Noisy User-generated Text*, pages 45–49.

Xiao Yang, Craig MacDonald, and Iadh Ounis. 2016. Using word embeddings in twitter election classification. *CoRR*, abs/1606.07006.

Tae Yano, Noah A Smith, and John D Wilkerson. 2012. Textual predictors of bill survival in congressional committees. In *Proceedings of NAACL*. Association for Computational Linguistics.

Bei Yu, Stefan Kaufmann, and Daniel Diermeier. 2008. Classifying party affiliation from political speech. *Journal of Information Technology & Politics*, 5(1):33–48.

Dynamic and Static Topic Model
for Analyzing Time-Series Document Collections

Rem Hida[†]   **Naoya Takeishi**[‡†]   **Takehisa Yairi**[†]   **Koichi Hori**[†]

[†]Department of Aeronautics and Astronautics, The University of Tokyo
{hida,yairi,hori}@ailab.t.u-tokyo.ac.jp
[‡]RIKEN Center for Advanced Intelligence Project, Tokyo, Japan
naoya.takeishi@riken.jp

Abstract

For extracting meaningful topics from texts, their structures should be considered properly. In this paper, we aim to analyze structured time-series documents such as a collection of news articles and a series of scientific papers, wherein topics evolve along time depending on multiple topics in the past, and are also related to each other at each time. To this end, we propose a *dynamic and static topic model*, which simultaneously considers the dynamic structures of the temporal topic evolution and the static structures of the topic hierarchy at each time. We show the results of experiments on collections of scientific papers, in which the proposed method outperformed conventional models. Moreover, we show an example of extracted topic structures, which we found helpful for analyzing research activities.

1 Introduction

Probabilistic topic models such as latent Dirichlet allocation (LDA) (Blei et al., 2003) have been utilized for analyzing a wide variety of datasets such as document collections, images, and genes. Although vanilla LDA has been favored partly due to its simplicity, one of its limitations is that the output is not necessarily very understandable because the priors on the topics are independent. Consequently, there has been a lot of research aimed at improving probabilistic topic models by utilizing the inherent *structures* of datasets in their modeling (see, e.g., Blei and Lafferty (2006); Li and McCallum (2006); see Section 2 for other models).

In this work, we aimed to leverage the dynamic and static structures of topics for improving the modeling capability and the understandability of topic models. These two types of structures, which we instantiate below, are essential in many types of datasets, and in fact, each of them has been considered separately in several previous studies. In this paper, we propose a topic model that is aware of both of these structures, namely *dynamic and static topic model* (DSTM).

The underlying motivation of DSTM is twofold. First, a collection of documents often has *dynamic structures*; i.e., topics evolve along time influencing each other. For example, topics in papers are related to topics in past papers. We may want to extract such dynamic structures of topics from collections of scientific papers for summarizing research activities. Second, there are also *static structures* of topics such as correlation and hierarchy. For instance, in a collection of news articles, the "sports" topic must have the "baseball" topic and the "football" topic as its subtopic. This kind of static structure of topics helps us understand the relationship among them.

The remainder of this paper is organized as follows. In Section 2, we briefly review related work. In Section 3, the generative model and the inference/learning procedures of DSTM are presented. In Section 4, the results of the experiments are shown. This paper is concluded in Section 5.

2 Related Work

Researchers have proposed several variants of topic models that consider the dynamic or static structure. Approaches focusing on the dynamic structure include dynamic topic model (DTM) (Blei and Lafferty, 2006), topic over time (TOT) (Wang and McCallum, 2006), multiscale dynamic topic model (MDTM) (Iwata et al., 2010), dependent Dirichlet processes mixture model (D-DPMM) (Lin et al., 2010), and infinite dynamic topic model (iDTM) (Ahmed and Xing, 2010).

516

Proceedings of the 56th Annual Meeting of the Association for Computational Linguistics (Short Papers), pages 516–520
Melbourne, Australia, July 15 - 20, 2018. ©2018 Association for Computational Linguistics

D^t	number of documents at epoch t
n_d^t	number of words in the d-th doc. at epoch t
$w_{d,i}^t$	the i-th word in the d-th doc. at epoch t
K	total number of subtopics
S	number of supertopics
$y_{d,i}^t$	supertopic of $w_{d,i}^t$
$z_{d,i}^t$	subtopic of $w_{d,i}^t$
$^1\theta_d^t$	multinomial distribution over supertopics for the d-th doc. at epoch t
$^2\theta_{d,s}^t$	multinomial distribution over subtopics for the d-th doc. in s-th supertopic at epoch t
ϕ_k^t	multinomial distribution over words for the k-th subtopic at epoch t
$^2\alpha_s^t$	static structure weight (prior of $^2\theta_{d,s}^t$)
β^t	dynamic structure weight between topics at time $t-1$ and those at epoch t

Table 1: Notations in the proposed model.

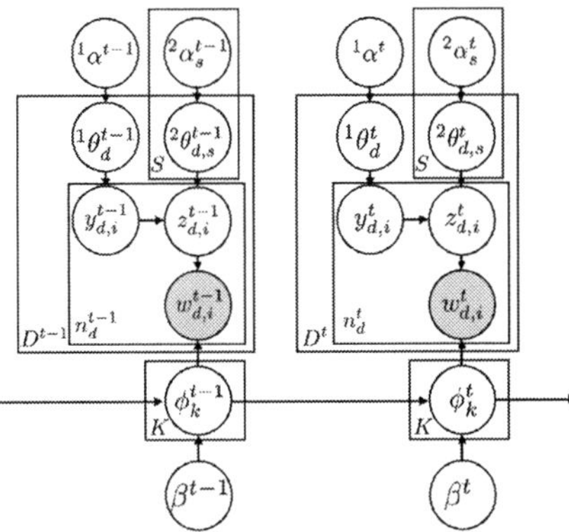

Figure 1: Graphical model of the proposed model for epochs $t-1$ and t.

These methods have been successfully applied to a temporal collection of documents, but none of them take temporal dependencies between multiple topics into account; i.e., in these models, only a single topic contributes to a topic in the future.

For the static structure, several models including correlated topic model (CTM) (Lafferty and Blei, 2006), pachinko allocation model (PAM) (Li and McCallum, 2006), and segmented topic model (STM) (Du et al., 2010) have been proposed. CTM models the correlation between topics using the normal distribution as the prior, PAM introduces the hierarchical structure to topics, and STM uses paragraphs or sentences as the hierarchical structure. These models can consider the static structure such as correlation and hierarchy between topics. However, most of them lack the dynamic structure in their model; i.e., they do not premise temporal collections of documents.

One of the existing methods that is most related to the proposed model is the hierarchical topic evolution model (HTEM) (Song et al., 2016). HTEM captures the relation between evolving topics using a nested distance-dependent Chinese restaurant process. It has been successfully applied to a temporal collection of documents for extracting structure but does not take multiple topics dependencies into account either.

In this work, we built a new model to overcome the limitation of the existing models, i.e., to examine both the dynamic and static structures simultaneously. We expect that the proposed model can be applied to various applications such as topic trend analysis and text summarization.

3 Dynamic and Static Topic Model

In this section, we state the generative model of the proposed method, DSTM. Afterward, the procedure for inference and learning is presented. Our notations are summarized in Table 1.

3.1 Generative Model

In the proposed model, DSTM, the dynamic and static structures are modeled as follows.

Dynamic Structure We model the temporal evolution of topic-word distribution by making it proportional to a weighted sum of topic-word distributions at the previous time (epoch), i.e.,

$$\phi_k^t \sim \text{Dirichlet}\left(\sum_{k'=1}^{K} \beta_{k,k'}^t \phi_{k'}^{t-1}\right), \quad (1)$$

where ϕ_k^t denotes the word distribution of the k-th topic at the t-th time-epoch, and $\beta_{k,k'}^t$ is a weight that determines the dependency between the k-th topic at epoch t and the k'-th topic at epoch $t-1$.

Static Structure We model the static structure as a hierarchy of topics at each epoch. We utilize the supertopic-subtopic structure as in PAM (Li and McCallum, 2006), where the priors of topics (subtopics) are determined by their supertopic.

Generative Process In summary, the generative process at epoch t is as follows.
1. For each subtopic $k = 1, .., K$,
   (a) Draw a topic-word distribution
       $\phi_k^t \sim \text{Dirichlet}(\sum_{k'} \beta_{k,k'}^t \phi_{k'}^{t-1})$.
2. For each document $d = 1, ..., D^t$,
   (a) Draw a supertopic distribution
       $^1\theta_d^t \sim \text{Dirichlet}(^1\alpha^t)$.

(b) For each supertopic $s = 1, ..., S$,

    i. Draw a subtopic distribution
$${}^2\theta^t_{d,s} \sim \text{Dirichlet}({}^2\alpha^t_s).$$

(c) For each word $i = 1, ..., n^t_d$,

    i. Draw a supertopic-word assignment
$$y^t_{d,i} \sim \text{Multinomial}({}^1\theta^t_d).$$

    ii. Draw a subtopic-word assignment
$$z^t_{d,i} \sim \text{Multinomial}({}^2\theta^t_{d,y^t_{d,i}}).$$

    iii. Draw a word-observation
$$w^t_{d,i} \sim \text{Multinomial}(\phi^t_{z^t_{d,i}}).$$

Note that the above process should be repeated for every epoch t. The corresponding graphical model is presented in Figure 1.

3.2 Inference and Learning

Since analytical inference for DSTM is intractable, we resort to a stochastic EM algorithm (Andrieu et al., 2003) with the collapsed Gibbs sampling (Griffiths and Steyvers, 2004). However, such a strategy is still much costly due to the temporal dependencies of ϕ. Therefore, we introduce a further approximation; we surrogate $\phi^{t-1}_{k'}$ in Eq. (1) by its expectation $\hat{\phi}^{t-1}_{k'} = \mathbb{E}[\phi^{t-1}_{k'}]$. This compromise enables us to run the EM algorithm *for each* epoch in sequence from $t = 1$ to $t = T$ without any backward inference. In fact, such approximation technique is also utilized in the inference of MDTM (Iwata et al., 2010).

Note that the proposed model has a moderate number of hyperparameters to be set manually, and that they can be tuned according to the existing know-how of topic modeling. This feature makes the proposed model appealing in terms of inference and learning.

E-step In E-step, the supertopic/subtopic assignments are sampled. Given the current state of all variables except $y^t_{d,i}$ and $z^t_{d,i}$, new values for them should be sampled according to

$$p(y^t_{d,i} = s, z^t_{d,i} = k \mid w^t, y^t, z^t, \Phi^{t-1}, {}^1\alpha^t, {}^2\alpha^t, \beta^t)$$

$$\propto \frac{n^t_{d,s\backslash i} + {}^1\alpha^t_s}{n^t_{d\backslash i} + \sum_{s=1}^{S} {}^1\alpha^t_s} \cdot \frac{n^t_{d,s,k\backslash i} + {}^2\alpha^t_{s,k}}{n^t_{d,s\backslash i} + \sum_{k=1}^{K} {}^2\alpha^t_{s,k}} \quad (2)$$

$$\cdot \frac{n^t_{k,v\backslash i} + \sum_{k'=1}^{K} \beta^t_{k,k'}\hat{\phi}^{t-1}_{k',v}}{n^t_{k\backslash i} + \sum_{k'=1}^{K} \beta^t_{k,k'}},$$

where $n^t_{k,v}$ denotes the number of tokens assigned to topic k for word v at epoch t, $n^t_k = \sum_v n^t_{k,v}$, and $n^t_{d,s}$ and $n^t_{d,s,k}$ denote the number of tokens in document d assigned to supertopic s and subtopic

	NIPS	Drone
Date	1987–1999	2009–2016
# Documents	1,740	1,035
# Vocabulary	11,443	3,442
# Tokens	2,271,087	68,305

Table 2: Summary of the datasets.

k (via s), at epoch t respectively. Moreover, $n^t_{\cdot\backslash i}$ denotes the count yielded excluding the i-th token.

M-step In M-step, ${}^2\alpha^t$ and β^t are updated using the fixed-point iteration (Minka, 2000).

$$({}^2\alpha^t_{s,k})^* = {}^2\alpha^t_{s,k} \frac{\sum_{d=1}^{D^t} \Psi(n^t_{d,s,k} + {}^2\alpha^t_{s,k}) - \Psi({}^2\alpha^t_{s,k})}{\sum_{d=1}^{D^t} \Psi(n^t_{d,s} + {}^2\alpha^t_s) - \Psi({}^2\alpha^t_s)}, \quad (3)$$

$$(\beta^t_{k,k'})^* = \beta^t_{k,k'} \frac{\sum_v \hat{\phi}^{t-1}_{k',v} B^t_{k',v}}{\Psi(n^t_k + \sum_{k'} \beta^t_{k,k'}) - \Psi(\sum_{k'} \beta^t_{k,k'})}. \quad (4)$$

Here, Ψ is the digamma function, ${}^2\alpha^t_s = \sum_k {}^2\alpha^t_{s,k}$, and

$$B^t_{k',v} = \Psi\left(n^t_{k,v} + \sum_{k'} \beta^t_{k,k'}\hat{\phi}^{t-1}_{k',v}\right) - \Psi\left(\sum_{k'} \beta^t_{k,k'}\hat{\phi}^{t-1}_{k',v}\right).$$

Overall Procedure The EM algorithm is run for each epoch in sequence; at epoch t, after running the EM until convergence, $\hat{\phi}^t_{k,v}$ is computed by

$$\hat{\phi}^t_{k,v} = \frac{n^t_{k,v} + \sum_{k'} \beta^t_{k,k'}\hat{\phi}^{t-1}_{k',v}}{n^t_k + \sum_{k'} \beta^t_{k,k'}},$$

and then this value is used for the EM at the next epoch $t + 1$. Moreover, see Supplementary A for the computation of the statistics of the other variables.

4 Experiments

4.1 Datasets

We used two datasets comprising technical papers: **NIPS** (Perrone et al., 2016) and **Drone** (Liew et al., 2017). **NIPS** is a collection of the papers that appeared in NIPS conferences. **Drone** is a collection of abstracts of papers on unmanned aerial vehicles (UAVs) and was collected from related conferences and journals for surveying recent developments in UAVs. The characteristics of those datasets are summarized in Table 2. See Supplementary B for the details of data preprocessing.

	static	dynamic	NIPS			Drone		
			K30 (S15)	K40 (S20)	K50 (S25)	K15 (S3)	K20 (S3)	K25 (S3)
LDA	-	-	1455.6 (16.7)	1407.3 (15.9)	1374.6 (16.8)	1624.3 (191.1)	1634.8 (189.1)	1644.7 (193.0)
PAM	✓	-	1455.1 (18.2)	1407.0 (17.5)	1376.9 (16.7)	1587.4 (185.1)	1589.9 (191.4)	1590.8 (186.8)
DRTM	-	✓	1380.7 (18.5)	1308.6 (17.5)	1253.9 (17.9)	1212.5 (153.2)	1206.1 (148.0)	1201.2 (143.5)
DSTM	✓	✓	**1378.7 (16.5)**	**1301.0 (17.9)**	**1247.3 (17.2)**	**1194.2 (148.2)**	**1180.0 (147.0)**	**1171.6 (141.4)**

Table 3: Means (and standard deviations) of PPLs averaged over all epochs for each dataset with different values of K and S. The proposed method, DSTM, achieved the smallest PPL.

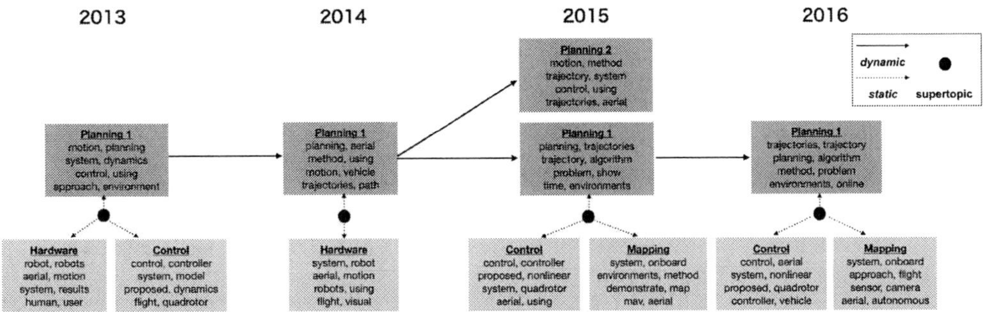

Figure 2: Part of the topic structure extracted from **Drone** dataset using the proposed method. The solid arrows denote the temporal evolution of "planning" topics. The dotted arrows mean that "planning" topics are related to "hardware", "control", and "mapping" topics via some supertopics (filled circles).

4.2 Evaluation by Perplexity

First, we evaluate the performance of the proposed method quantitatively using perplexity (PPL):

$$\text{PPL} = \exp\left(-\frac{\sum_{d=1}^{D} \sum_{w_d^{\text{test}}} \log p(w_{d,i}|\mathcal{M})}{\sum_{d=1}^{D} n_d^{\text{test}}} \right).$$

For each epoch, we used 90% of tokens in each document for training and calculated the PPL using the remaining 10% of tokens. We randomly created 10 train-test pairs and evaluated the means of the PPLs over those random trials. We compared the performance of DSTM to three baselines: LDA (Blei et al., 2003), PAM (Li and McCallum, 2006), and the proposed model without the static structure, which we term DRTM. See Supplementary C on their hyperparameter setting.

The means of the PPLs averaged over all epochs for each dataset with different values K are shown in Table 3. In both datasets with every setting of K, the proposed model, DSTM, achieved the smallest PPL, which implies its effectiveness for modeling a collection of technical papers. For clarity, we conducted paired t-tests between the perplexities of the proposed method and those of the baselines. On the differences between DSTM and DRTM, the p-values were 4.2×10^{-2} ($K = 30$), 7.9×10^{-5} ($K = 40$), and 6.4×10^{-7} ($K = 50$) for the **NIPS** dataset, and 1.3×10^{-4} ($K = 15$), 8.8×10^{-5} ($K = 20$), and 4.9×10^{-6} ($K = 25$) for the **Drone** dataset, respectively. It is also noteworthy that DRTM shows more significant improvement relative to LDA than PAM does. This suggests that the dynamic structure with multiple-topic dependencies is essential for datasets of this kind.

4.3 Analysis of Extracted Structure

We examined the topic structures extracted from the **Drone** dataset using DSTM. In Figure 2, we show a part of the extracted structure regarding planning of the UAV's path and/or movement. We identified "planning" topics by looking for keywords such as "trajectory" and "motion." In Figure 2, each node is labeled with eight most probable keywords. Moreover, solid arrows (dynamic relations) are drawn if the corresponding $\beta_{k,k'}^{t}$ is larger than 200, and dotted arrows (static relations) are drawn between a supertopic and subtopics with the two or three largest values of $^{2}\alpha_{s,k}^{t}$.

Looking at the dynamic structure, we may see how research interest regarding planning has changed. For example, word "online" first emerges in the "planning" topic in 2016. This is possibly due to the increasing interest in real-time planning problems, which is becoming feasible due to the recent development of on-board computers. In regard to the static structures, for example, the "planning" topic is related to the "hardware" and "control" topics in 2013 and 2014, whereas it is also related to the "mapping" topic in 2015 and 2016. Looking at these static structures, we may anticipate how research areas are related to each other in each year. In this case, we can anticipate that planning problems are combined with mapping problems well in recent years. Note that we cannot obtain these results unless the dynamic and static structures are considered simultaneously.

5 Conclusion

In this work, we developed a topic model with dynamic and static structures. We confirmed the superiority of the proposed model to the conventional topic models in terms of perplexity and analyzed the topic structures of a collection of papers. Possible future directions of research include automatic inference of the number of topics and application to topic trend analysis in various domains.

Acknowledgments

We thank Chun Fui Liew for sharing his dataset with us and advice.

References

Amr Ahmed and Eric P. Xing. 2010. Timeline: A dynamic hierarchical Dirichlet process model for recovering birth/death and evolution of topics in text stream. In *Proceedings of the 26th Conference on Uncertainty in Artificial Intelligence*, pages 20–29.

Christophe Andrieu, Nando de Freitas, Arnaud Doucet, and Michael I. Jordan. 2003. An introduction to MCMC for machine learning. *Machine Learning*, 50(1):5–43.

David M. Blei and John D. Lafferty. 2006. Dynamic topic models. In *Proceedings of the 23rd International Conference on Machine Learning*, pages 113–120.

David M. Blei, Andrew Y. Ng, and Michael I. Jordan. 2003. Latent Dirichlet allocation. *Journal of Machine Learning Research*, 3(Jan):993–1022.

Lan Du, Wray Buntine, and Huidong Jin. 2010. A segmented topic model based on the two-parameter Poisson-Dirichlet process. *Machine Learning*, 81(1):5–19.

Thomas L. Griffiths and Mark Steyvers. 2004. Finding scientific topics. In *Proceedings of the National Academy of Sciences of the United States of America*, volume 101, pages 5228–5235.

Tomoharu Iwata, Takeshi Yamada, Yasushi Sakurai, and Naonori Ueda. 2010. Online multiscale dynamic topic models. In *Proceedings of the 16th ACM SIGKDD International Conference on Knowledge Discovery and Data Mining*, pages 663–672.

John D. Lafferty and David M. Blei. 2006. Correlated topic models. In *Advances in Neural Information Processing Systems*, volume 18, pages 147–154.

Wei Li and Andrew McCallum. 2006. Pachinko allocation: DAG-structured mixture models of topic correlations. In *Proceedings of the 23rd International Conference on Machine Learning*, pages 577–584.

Chun Fui Liew, Danielle DeLatte, Naoya Takeishi, and Takehisa Yairi. 2017. Recent developments in aerial robotics: A survey and prototypes overview. arXiv:1711.10085.

Dahua Lin, Eric Grimson, and John W. Fisher. 2010. Construction of dependent Dirichlet processes based on Poisson processes. In *Advances in Neural Information Processing Systems*, volume 23, pages 1396–1404.

Thomas Minka. 2000. Estimating a Dirichlet distribution. Technical report, MIT.

Valerio Perrone, Paul A. Jenkins, Dario Spano, and Yee Whye Teh. 2016. Poisson random fields for dynamic feature models. arXiv:1611.07460.

Jun Song, Yu Huang, Xiang Qi, Yuheng Li, Feng Li, Kun Fu, and Tinglei Huang. 2016. Discovering hierarchical topic evolution in time-stamped documents. *Journal of the Association for Information Science and Technology*, 67(4):915–927.

Xuerui Wang and Andrew McCallum. 2006. Topics over time: A non-Markov continuous-time model of topical trends. In *Proceedings of the 12th ACM SIGKDD International Conference on Knowledge Discovery and Data Mining*, pages 424–433.

PhraseCTM: Correlated Topic Modeling on Phrases within Markov Random Fields

Weijing Huang[1], Tengjiao Wang[1], Wei Chen[1], Siyuan Jiang[2], Kam-Fai Wong[1,3]

[1] Key Lab of High Confidence Software Technologies (MOE),
School of EECS, Peking University, Beijing, China

[2] Department of Computer Science and Engineering, University of Notre Dame, USA

[3] Department of Systems Engineering and Engineering Management,
The Chinese University of Hong Kong, Hong Kong

`{huangweijing,tjwang,pekingchenwei}@pku.edu.cn,`
`sjiang1@nd.edu, kfwong@se.cuhk.edu.hk`

Abstract

Recent emerged phrase-level topic models are able to provide topics of phrases, which are easy to read for humans. But these models are lack of the ability to capture the correlation structure among the discovered numerous topics. We propose a novel topic model PhraseCTM and a two-stage method to find out the correlated topics at phrase level. In the first stage, we train PhraseCTM, which models the generation of words and phrases simultaneously by linking the phrases and component words within Markov Random Fields when they are semantically coherent. In the second stage, we generate the correlation of topics from PhraseCTM. We evaluate our method by a quantitative experiment and a human study, showing the correlated topic modeling on phrases is a good and practical way to interpret the underlying themes of a corpus.

1 Introduction

In recent years, topic modeling on phrases has been developed for providing more interpretable topics (El-Kishky et al., 2014; Kawamae, 2014; He, 2016). They represent each topic as a list of phrases, which are easy to read for humans. For example, the topic represented in *"grounding conductor, grounding wire, aluminum wiring, neutral ground, ..."* is easier to read than the topic with words *"ground, wire, use, power, cable, wires, ...",* although they are both about the topic of *household electricity.*

But when the number of topics grows, it's hard to review all the topics, even they are represented in phrases. The correlation structure is introduced by CTM (Blei and Lafferty, 2005) to figure out the

correlated relationship between topics and group the similar topics together. And the correlated topics mined from the scientific papers (Blei and Lafferty, 2007), news corpus (He et al., 2017), and social science data (Roberts et al., 2016), showed their practical utility on grasping the semantic meaning of text documents.

However, it's nontrivial to apply CTM directly on phrases. The reasons are mainly due to two facts: (1) phrases are much less than words in each document; (2) similar to LDA (Tang et al., 2014), CTM doesn't perform well on short documents. Therefore, CTM needs more contextual information to build a good enough model, rather than only using the extracted phrases.

To find out the correlated topics at phrase level, we take full advantage of contextual information about the phrases. Firstly, the topic of a phrase in a document is highly related to the topics of other words and phrases in the same document. Secondly, some phrases' meaning can be implied from their component words. Taking a document in Figure 1 as an example, the phrase *"orbital vehicle"* shares the same topic as the word *"DC-X"* (a reusable spaceship), as well as its component words *"orbital",* and *"vehicle",* which are all about the topic of *space exploration.* The assumption that the words within the same phrase tend to have the same latent topic is directly used by PhraseLDA (El-Kishky et al., 2014). Note that not all the phrases always have the same topic as their component words (*e.g.,* the newspaper *Boston Globe*) (Mikolov et al., 2013). It's difficult to distinguish the *"orbital vehicle"* type phrases from *"Boston Globe"* type phrases, but we can use the data-driven method to find out the semantically coherent ones by the NPMI metric (Bouma, 2009), and put them in Markov Random Fields (Kindermann and Snell, 1980) to align the topics of phrases and their component words.

Proceedings of the 56th Annual Meeting of the Association for Computational Linguistics (Short Papers), pages 521–526
Melbourne, Australia, July 15 - 20, 2018. ©2018 Association for Computational Linguistics

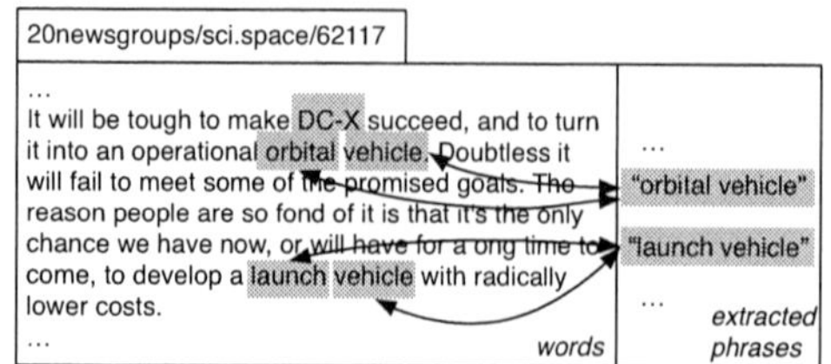

Figure 1: An example of phrases' contextual information. The phrases and words marked gray are about the same topic. The arrows show the topics of the phrases and their component words tend to be same, which tendency are modeled within Markov Random Field.

Based on these two kinds of contextual information, we propose a novel topic model PhraseCTM and a two-stage method. In the first stage, we train PhraseCTM, which (1) double counts the phrases as two parts, one as the phrase itself, the other as the component words; (2) models the generation of words and phrases simultaneously by linking the phrases and component words within Markov Random Fields when they are semantically coherent; (3) uses the logistic normal distribution to represent the correlation among the topics, like a previous method CTM. In the second stage, we generate the correlation of topics from PhraseCTM.

We evaluate our method on five datasets by a quantitative experiment and a human study, showing that the correlated topic modeling on phrases is a good way to interpret the underlying themes of a corpus.

2   Related Works

There are two orthogonal lines of research studies related to our work. (1) With the development of phrase extraction techniques (El-Kishky et al., 2014; Liu et al., 2015; Shang et al., 2018), several topic models based on extracted phrases are proposed to provide high-quality phrase-level topics, such as PhraseLDA (El-Kishky et al., 2014), and TPM (He, 2016). Because of the quality of extracted phrases, PhraseLDA performs better than previous n-gram method TNG (Wang et al., 2007), which combines phrase extraction and topic modeling together. (2) CTM (Blei and Lafferty, 2005) uses the logistic normal distribution (Aitchison, 1982) to replace the Dirichlet prior, so it can capture the correlated structure of topics. And the experiments in the further works (Chen et al., 2013; Roberts et al., 2016; He et al., 2017) showed its usefulness in exploring the text corpus by using

the correlated word-level topics. Note that our work is not a simple combination of these two methods, because the existing topic models on phrases lack the ability to capture the correlation structure while CTM cannot be directly applied on phrases due to the sparseness of phrases in each document. And as we used Markov Random Fields (Kindermann and Snell, 1980), our work is different from previous ones (Daume III, 2009; Sun et al., 2009; Xie et al., 2015) because we don't put all links into Markov Random Fields but only choose the semantic coherent links.

3   The proposed method

By preparing data as described in the subsection 3.1, our method is carried out in two stages, shown in the subsection 3.2, and 3.3 respectively.

3.1   Semantically Coherent Links for MRF

Given the input data in the form of raw text documents, we transform each document into the format as "words, phrases, semantically coherent links between phrases and component words". Extracting words is trivial, and extracting phrases can be conducted by using an existing tool, *e.g.*, AutoPhrase (Shang et al., 2018). In this process, each extracted phrase is counted twice, one as the phrase itself (represented in the phrase vocabulary), the other is divided into component words (represented in the word vocabulary).

In a given document, we denote the i-th phrase as $w_i^{(\mathcal{P})}$, and its component words as $\boldsymbol{w}_{l(i)}$. We use the Equation (1) to determine the semantic coherent score between $w_i^{(\mathcal{P})}$ and $\boldsymbol{w}_{l(i)}$ by utilizing NPMI (Bouma, 2009) . The NPMI metric is defined upon two word types as $\text{NPMI}(x, y) = \log \frac{p(x,y)}{p(x)p(y)} / (-\log p(x, y))$, where $p(x)$ is estimated by the document frequency $\frac{|d(x)|}{D}$, and $p(x, y) = \frac{|d(x) \cap d(y)|}{D}$.

$$s(w_i^{(\mathcal{P})}, \boldsymbol{w}_{l(i)}) = \min_{j,k \in l(i)} \{\text{NPMI}(w_j, w_k)\} \quad (1)$$

Bouma (2009) pointed out that NPMI has the advantage that it ranges within the fixed interval. Inherited from NPMI, the semantic coherent score also ranges from -1 to 1. A negative semantic coherent score means the phrase does not share the same topic with its component words in the corpus level (*e.g.*, *long run*, the newspaper *Boston Globe*). A positive score means the opposite, and the score

1 suggests that the phrase and its component words should be aligned to the same topic in whole corpus. By a reasonable threshold τ, we can add the semantically coherent link for $w_i^{(\mathcal{P})}$ and $\boldsymbol{w}_{l(i)}$, if $s(w_i^{(\mathcal{P})}, \boldsymbol{w}_{l(i)}) > \tau$. In practice, we set τ to 0.4.

Assuming the topic of the phrase $w_i^{(\mathcal{P})}$ is $z_i^{(\mathcal{P})}$ and the topics of words $\boldsymbol{w}_{l(i)}$ are $\boldsymbol{z}_{l(i)}$, when they have the above mentioned semantically coherent link, we put $z_i^{(\mathcal{P})}$ and $\boldsymbol{z}_{l(i)}$ in a Markov Random Field. More specifically, for $z_i^{(\mathcal{P})}$ and z_j, $j \in l(i)$, there's the edge potential function $\exp\{\kappa \cdot \mathbb{I}(z_i^{(\mathcal{P})} = z_j)/|l(i)|\}$, where κ is the weight to adjust how much the link is introduced to constraint the topics to be same. In the following experiment, κ is set to be 10^{-3}.

3.2 PhraseCTM

In the first stage, when given the prepared data as described in subsection 3.1, we are going to train better correlated phrase-level topics $\boldsymbol{\beta}^{(\mathcal{P})}$. The contextual information of phrases include (i) words in the same document, and (ii) their component words within semantically coherent links. Part (ii) has been modeled in the previous subsection. For part (i), we let the phrases and words in a same document d share the topic parameter η_d, which is a K-dimension vector sampled from a Gaussian distribution $\mathcal{N}(\mu, \Sigma)$. Like CTM, Σ is the covariance matrix, modeling the correlation between topics.

As a part of MRF, the unary potential on the topic node $z_{d,i}^{(\mathcal{P})}$ or $z_{d,j}$ is defined by a logistic-normal distribution like CTM $p(z_{d,j} = k|\eta_d) = \exp \eta_{d,k} / \sum_k \exp \eta_{d,k}$. Therefore, the joint distribution of topics over the phrases and the words in document d are defined as the following equation, where $A_d(\eta_d)$ is used for normalization, and N_{L_d} is the number of semantically coherent links in document d.

$$p(z_d, z_d^{(\mathcal{P})}|\eta_d) = \frac{1}{A_d(\eta_d)} \prod_{m=1}^{N_d} p(z_{d,m}|\eta_d)$$

$$\cdot \prod_{i=1}^{N_d^{(\mathcal{P})}} p(z_{d,i}^{(\mathcal{P})}|\eta_d) \cdot \exp\{\sum_{i=1}^{N_{L_d}} (\frac{\kappa}{|l(d,i)|} \sum_{j \in l(d,i)} \mathbb{I}(z_{d,i}^{(\mathcal{P})} = z_{d,j}))\}$$

The whole generation process is illustrated in Figure 2(a). We train PhraseCTM by variational inference like CTM. The different part lies in the phrases and component words which are in semantically coherent links. For these phrases, we use

Eq. (2) to update the variational parameters $\phi_{d,i}^{(\mathcal{P})}$ for the latent topic $z_{d,i}^{(\mathcal{P})}$ of the phrase $w_{d,i}^{(\mathcal{P})}$. For the phrases that are not in semantically coherent links, we use the Eq. (3), which is same as the original CTM's variational inference. In Eqs. (2) and (3), λ_d is the variational parameter for η_d such that $\eta_{d,k} \sim \mathcal{N}(\lambda_{d,k}, \nu_{d,k}^2)$.

$$\hat{\phi}_{d,i,k}^{(\mathcal{P})} \propto \beta_{k,w_i}^{(\mathcal{P})} \exp(\lambda_{d,k} + \frac{\kappa}{|l(d,i)|} \sum_{j \in l(d,i)} \phi_{d,j,k}) \quad (2)$$

$$\hat{\phi}_{d,i,k}^{(\mathcal{P})} \propto \beta_{k,w_i}^{(\mathcal{P})} \exp(\lambda_{d,k}) \quad (3)$$

Similarly, the variational parameters for the component words in semantically coherent links are updated by Eq. (4), while other words are updated by Eq. (5). In this way, PhraseCTM introduces the impact from words and phrases on each other by Markov Random Fields.

$$\hat{\phi}_{d,i,k} \propto \beta_{k,w_i} \exp(\lambda_{d,k} + \frac{\kappa}{|l(d,j)|} \phi_{d,j,k}^{(\mathcal{P})}), \ i \in l(d,j) \quad (4)$$

$$\hat{\phi}_{d,i,k} \propto \beta_{k,w_i} \exp(\lambda_{d,k}) \quad (5)$$

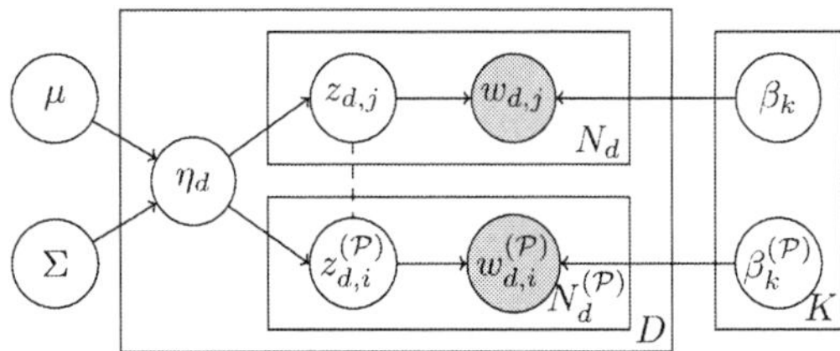

(a) The first stage: training on our proposed model PhraseCTM. When observed words W and phrases $W^{(\mathcal{P})}$, we learn word topics $\boldsymbol{\beta}$, and phrase topics $\boldsymbol{\beta}^{(\mathcal{P})}$.

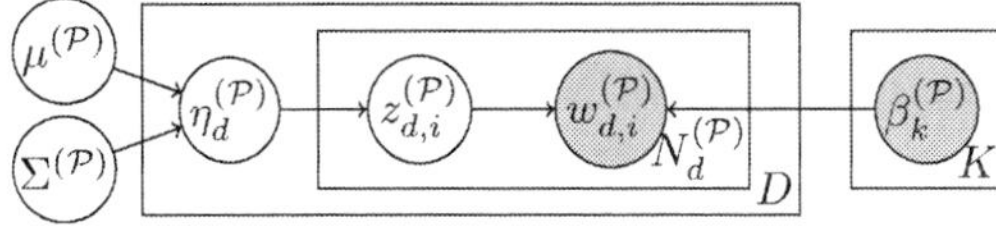

(b) The second stage: inferring the phrase topics' correlation. When given the phrases $W^{(\mathcal{P})}$, and the phrase topics $\boldsymbol{\beta}^{(\mathcal{P})}$ learned from the first stage, we infer the phrase-level topics' covariance $\Sigma^{(\mathcal{P})}$ as the correlation result.

Figure 2: Illustration of two stages of our method

3.3 Generation of Phrase Topics' Correlation

In the second stage, we aim to get the correlation for $\boldsymbol{\beta}^{(\mathcal{P})}$. It cannot be directly derived from Σ, which has also been learned in the first stage, because Σ consists the impact from word topics. Thus, given $W^{(\mathcal{P})}$ and $\boldsymbol{\beta}^{(\mathcal{P})}$, we use the variational inference again to learn $\Sigma^{(\mathcal{P})}$ as the illustration of Figure 2(b). Finally, the correlation matrix can be computed by $corr^{(\mathcal{P})}(i, j) = \frac{\Sigma_{i,j}^{(\mathcal{P})}}{\sqrt{\Sigma_{i,i}^{(\mathcal{P})} \Sigma_{j,j}^{(\mathcal{P})}}}$.

	$|V|$	$|V^{(\mathcal{P})}|$	$|W|$	$|W^{(\mathcal{P})}|$	$|D|$	$|W|/|D|$	$|W^{(\mathcal{P})}|/|D|$
20 Newsgroup	22,787	4,245	1,361,843	51,024	18,828	72.3	2.7
Argentina@Wiki	20,847	5,505	1,052,674	98,502	8,617	122.2	11.4
Mathematics@Wiki	43,779	27,371	6,062,815	594,704	27,947	216.9	21.3
Chemistry@Wiki	76,265	67,979	11,346,781	1,546,088	60,375	187.9	25.6
PubMed Abstracts	34,125	24,233	11,274,350	968,928	99,214	113.6	9.8

Table 1: The statistics of the datasets. In average, phrases appear more sparse than words. Phrases are extracted by AutoPhrase (Shang et al., 2018).

4 Experiments

PhraseCTM is supposed to get benefits from two aspects: (1) generating high-quality phrase-level topics; (2) providing the correlation among phrase topics to help users to understand the underlying themes of a corpus. To check the first claim, we compare PhraseCTM with existing topic models on phrases. To evaluate the second claim, we design a user study to compare PhraseCTM with standard CTM that runs only on words.

Datasets. We choose several public text corpora, including *20Newsgroups* (Lang, 1995), subsets of *English Wikipedia*, a subset of *PubMed Abstracts* (Varmus et al., 1999). Due to efficiency problem, we do not test on the whole Wikipedia corpus. We construct the *Mathematics*, *Chemistry*, and *Argentina* subsets of English Wikipedia as (Huang et al., 2017). For each corpus, we extract the phrases by the implementation[1] of AutoPhrase (Shang et al., 2018), and build the semantically coherent links as subsection 3.1. More specifically, in phrase extraction process, we set the minimum support as 5, and leave other parameters in AutoPhrase as its suggestion. In average, each document of the resulted *20Newsgroups* only contains 2.7 phrases while 72.3 words, showing that phrases are much less than words. More statistics about the datasets are shown in Table 1.

4.1 Quantitative Result

Baselines. We compare with PhraseLDA (El-Kishky et al., 2014), the state-of-the-art model on phrases. Besides that, we run plain LDA and plain CTM[2] directly on the extracted phrases (without considering the impact of words). To check the effectiveness of MRF, we run a variant version PhraseCTM(-) by removing all the semantically coherent links from PhraseCTM. We also run a n-gram based topic model TNG (Wang et al., 2007),

which has already been implemented in Mallet[3]. All the topic numbers are set to be 100. For plain LDA and PhraseLDA, we set $\beta = 0.005$. For plain CTM and TNG, we use the default settings in their existing implementations. Since TNG combines phrase extraction and topic modeling together, we run it on the raw datasets.

We use the NPMI metric (Bouma, 2009) to evaluate the semantic coherence of top-10 phrases in each topic (K=100), by taking the entire English Wikipedia as the reference corpus. Roder (2015) has shown that the NPMI metric is highly correlated to human topic coherence ratings, so it's natural to use it to show how PhraseCTM improves the quality of topics. Although we have already used NPMI in the semantic coherent score for finding semantically coherent links, it does not influence the rationality of the metric used for topic evaluation, because the semantic coherent score is defined upon two word types while the NPMI score on topics is defined upon two phrase types.

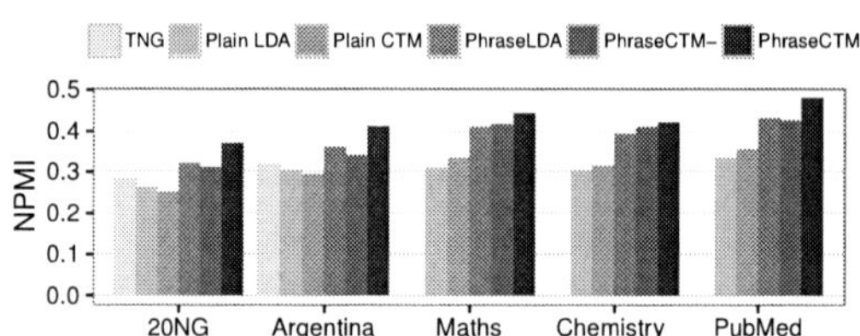

Figure 3: The quality of the learned topics.

The result is shown in Figure 3. Due to the computational costs, TNG cannot scale up to large datasets. Plain LDA and plain CTM performs not well on the datasets because of the sparsity of phrases in each document, while TNG performs better than them as it can utilize more words as its contextual information. PhraseCTM(-) is comparable to PhraseLDA in the experiment. PhraseLDA also utilizes all the contextual information with the assumption that the words in a phrase have the same topic. But this assumption

---

[1] `https://github.com/shangjingbo1226/AutoPhrase`

[2] `https://github.com/blei-lab/ctm-c`

[3] `http://mallet.cs.umass.edu/`

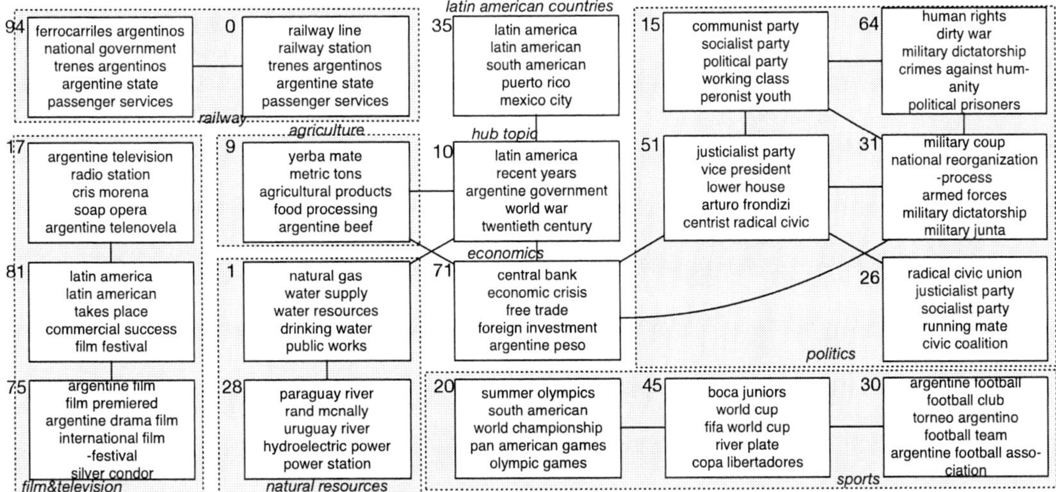

Figure 4: A part of the topic graph (K=100) generated by our method on the Argentina-related Wikipedia pages, where each node shows the top-5 phrases in each topic, and edges connect correlated topics. The left-aligned numbers in the graph represent the topic ID.

is too strong, which can be adjusted by our introduced semantically coherent links in MRF. This experiment demonstrates that our method has generated high-quality phrase-level topics.

4.2 Human Study

To compare the correlated topics at different level, we directly run CTM on words. Trained on *Argentina@Wiki* and *Maths@Wiki* by CTM and PhraseCTM respectively, we outputted the topics with top-10 words/phrases in each topic and the correlation of topics for 10 human annotators, and asked them to label the topics. The duration of consuming time for topic labeling is a quite useful metric to check whether the topics are easy to understand for human annotators. It's based on our following observation in the human study: the confused topic may consume more time to give it an appropriate label, while the good one is easy to understand for human and consumes less time.

There are 2 groups of annotators. The annotators in Group A got the CTM result on *Maths@Wiki* and PhraseCTM's on *Argentina@Wiki*. The annotators in Group B got the results in the opposite setting. The labeling process was logged to calculate the accumulated time. The labeling time to reach 50 accurate topics' labels on PhraseCTM is much less than the labeling time on CTM. In average, the annotators spent 7.1 minutes on PhraseCTM while 13.2 minutes on the others, which is listed in Table 2. In Figure 3, it's easy to label the topics in top right corner as *poli-*

	CTM		PhraseCTM	
	Maths	Argentina	Maths	Argentina
Group A	12.4	-	-	7.5
Group B	-	14.0	6.7	-
In Average		13.2		7.1

Table 2: Human time consumption on topic labeling for correlated topics generated by CTM and PhraseCTM, measured in minutes.

tics. And the edges in the figure illustrate the correlation between topics. As an example, the edge between the topic 71 and the topic 31 represents that the economics and the politics in Argentina is related, helping users to understand the corpus.

5 Conclusion

We provide a new topic model PhraseCTM to make the Correlated Topic Modeling available for phrase-level topics. PhraseCTM utilizes more contextual information of phrases, and put them within Markov Random Fields, so it can provide high-quality correlated topics at phrase level. The experiments show that the correlated topic modeling on phrases is a practical tool to interpret the underlying themes of a corpus. In future, we will optimize the efficiency of PhraseCTM to scale it up to large datasets.

Acknowledgments

This research is supported by the Natural Science Foundation of China (Grant No.61572043) and National Key Research and Development Program (Project Number: 2016YFB1000704).

References

John Aitchison. 1982. The statistical analysis of compositional data. *Journal of the Royal Statistical Society. Series B (Methodological)*, 44(2):139–177.

David M. Blei and John D. Lafferty. 2005. Correlated topic models. In *Proceedings of the 18th International Conference on Neural Information Processing Systems*, NIPS'05, pages 147–154. MIT Press.

David M. Blei and John D. Lafferty. 2007. A correlated topic model of science. *The Annals of Applied Statistics*, 1(1):17–35.

Gerlof Bouma. 2009. Normalized (pointwise) mutual information in collocation extraction. In *Proceedings of the German Society for Computational Linguistics & Language Technology*, pages 31–40.

Jianfei Chen, Jun Zhu, Zi Wang, Xun Zheng, and Bo Zhang. 2013. Scalable inference for logistic-normal topic models. In *Advances in Neural Information Processing Systems 26*, pages 2445–2453.

Hal Daume III. 2009. Markov random topic fields. In *Proceedings of the ACL-IJCNLP 2009 Conference Short Papers*, pages 293–296. Association for Computational Linguistics.

Ahmed El-Kishky, Yanglei Song, Chi Wang, Clare R. Voss, and Jiawei Han. 2014. Scalable topical phrase mining from text corpora. In *Proceedings of the VLDB Endowment*, volume 8, pages 305–316. VLDB Endowment.

Junxian He, Zhiting Hu, Taylor Berg-Kirkpatrick, Ying Huang, and Eric P. Xing. 2017. Efficient correlated topic modeling with topic embedding. In *Proceedings of the 23rd ACM SIGKDD International Conference on Knowledge Discovery and Data Mining*, KDD'17, pages 225–233. ACM.

Yulan He. 2016. Extracting topical phrases from clinical documents. In *Proceedings of the Thirtieth AAAI Conference on Artificial Intelligence*, AAAI'16, pages 2957–2963. AAAI Press.

Weijing Huang, Tengjiao Wang, Wei Chen, and Yazhou Wang. 2017. Category-level transfer learning from knowledge base to microblog stream for accurate event detection. In *International Conference on Database Systems for Advanced Applications*, DASFAA'17, pages 50–67. Springer.

Noriaki Kawamae. 2014. Supervised n-gram topic model. In *Proceedings of the 7th ACM International Conference on Web Search and Data Mining*, WSDM '14, pages 473–482. ACM.

Ross Kindermann and J Laurie Snell. 1980. *Markov random fields and their applications*, volume 1. American Mathematical Society.

Ken Lang. 1995. Newsweeder: Learning to filter netnews. In *Proceedings of the 12th International Conference on Machine Learning*, pages 331–339.

Jialu Liu, Jingbo Shang, Chi Wang, Xiang Ren, and Jiawei Han. 2015. Mining quality phrases from massive text corpora. In *Proceedings of the 2015 ACM SIGMOD International Conference on Management of Data*, SIGMOD '15, pages 1729–1744. ACM.

Tomas Mikolov, Ilya Sutskever, Kai Chen, Greg S Corrado, and Jeff Dean. 2013. Distributed representations of words and phrases and their compositionality. In *Advances in Neural Information Processing Systems 26*, pages 3111–3119.

Margaret E. Roberts, Brandon M. Stewart, and Edoardo M. Airoldi. 2016. A model of text for experimentation in the social sciences. *Journal of the American Statistical Association*, 111(515):988–1003.

Michael Röder, Andreas Both, and Alexander Hinneburg. 2015. Exploring the space of topic coherence measures. In *Proceedings of the Eighth ACM International Conference on Web Search and Data Mining*, WSDM '15, pages 399–408. ACM.

Jingbo Shang, Jialu Liu, Meng Jiang, Xiang Ren, Clare R Voss, and Jiawei Han. 2018. Automated phrase mining from massive text corpora. *IEEE Transactions on Knowledge and Data Engineering*.

Yizhou Sun, Jiawei Han, Jing Gao, and Yintao Yu. 2009. itopicmodel: Information network-integrated topic modeling. In *Ninth IEEE International Conference on Data Mining*, pages 493–502. IEEE.

Jian Tang, Zhaoshi Meng, Xuanlong Nguyen, Qiaozhu Mei, and Ming Zhang. 2014. Understanding the limiting factors of topic modeling via posterior contraction analysis. In *Proceedings of the 31st International Conference on Machine Learning*, pages 190–198.

Harold Varmus, David Lipman, and Patrick Brown. 1999. Pubmed central: an nih-operated site for electronic distribution of life sciences research reports.

Xuerui Wang, Andrew McCallum, and Xing Wei. 2007. Topical n-grams: Phrase and topic discovery, with an application to information retrieval. In *Proceedings of the 2007 Seventh IEEE International Conference on Data Mining*, ICDM '07, pages 697–702. IEEE.

Pengtao Xie, Diyi Yang, and Eric Xing. 2015. Incorporating word correlation knowledge into topic modeling. In *Proceedings of the 2015 Conference of the North American Chapter of the Association for Computational Linguistics: Human Language Technologies*, pages 725–734. Association for Computational Linguistics.

A Document Descriptor using Covariance of Word Vectors

Marwan Torki
Alexandria University, Egypt
`mtorki@alexu.edu.eg`

Abstract

In this paper, we address the problem of finding a novel document descriptor based on the covariance matrix of the word vectors of a document. Our descriptor has a fixed length, which makes it easy to use in many supervised and unsupervised applications. We tested our novel descriptor in different tasks including supervised and unsupervised settings. Our evaluation shows that our document covariance descriptor fits different tasks with competitive performance against state-of-the-art methods.

1 Introduction

Retrieving documents that are similar to a query using vectors has a long history. Earlier methods modeled documents and queries using vector space models via bag-of-words (BOW) representation (Salton and Buckley, 1988). Other representations include latent semantic indexing (LSI) (Deerwester et al., 1990), which can be used to define dense vector representation for documents and/or queries. The past few years have witnessed a big interest in distributed representation for words, sentences, paragraphs and documents. This was achieved by leveraging deep learning methods that learn word vector representation. Introduction of neural language models (Bengio et al., 2003) using deep learning allowed to learn word vector representation (word embedding for simplicity). The seminal work of Mikolov et al. introduced an efficient way to compute dense vectorized representation of words (Mikolov et al., 2013a,b). A more recent step was taken to move beyond distributed representation of words. This is to find a distributed representation for sentences, paragraphs and documents. Most of the presented works study the interrelationship between words in a text snip-

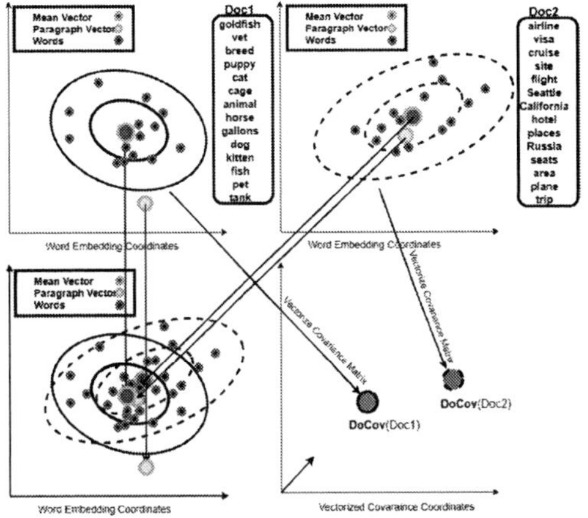

Figure 1: Doc1 is about "pets" and Doc2 is about "travel". **Top:** The first two dimensions of a word embedding for each document. **Bottom Left:** The embedding of the words of the two documents. The Mean vectors and the paragraph vectors are shown. Covariance matrices are shown via the confidence ellipses. **Bottom Right:** Corresponding covariance matrices are represented as points in a new space.

pet (Hill et al., 2016; Kiros et al., 2015; Le and Mikolov, 2014) in an unsupervised fashion. Other methods build a task specific representation (Kim, 2014; Collobert et al., 2011).

In this paper we propose to use the covariance matrix of the word vectors in some document to define a novel descriptor for a document. We call our representation DoCoV descriptor. Our descriptor obtains a fixed-length representation of the paragraph which captures the interrelationship between the dimensions of the word embedding via the covariance matrix elements. This makes our work distinguished from to the work of (Le and Mikolov, 2014; Hill et al., 2016; Kiros et al., 2015) where they study the interrelationship of words in the text

Proceedings of the 56th Annual Meeting of the Association for Computational Linguistics (Short Papers), pages 527–532
Melbourne, Australia, July 15 - 20, 2018. ©2018 Association for Computational Linguistics

snippet.

1.1 Toy Example

We show a toy example to highlight the differences between DoCoV vector, the Mean vector and paragraph vector (Le and Mikolov, 2014). First, we used Gensim library[1] to generate word vectors and paragraph vectors using a dummy training corpus. Next, we formed two hypothetical documents; first document contains words about "pets" and second document contains words about "travel". In figure 1 we show on the top part the first two dimensions of a word embedding for each document separately. On the bottom Left, we show embedding of the two documents' words in the same space. We also show the Mean vectors and the paragraph vectors. In the word embedding space the covariance matrices are represented via the confidence ellipses. On the bottom right we show the corresponding covariance matrices as points in a new space after vectorization step.

1.2 Motivation and Contributions

Below we describe our motivation towards the proposal of our novel representation:
(1) Some neural-based paragraph representations such as paragraph vectors (Le and Mikolov, 2014) , FastSent (Hill et al., 2016) use a shared space between the words and paragraphs. This is counter intuitive, as the paragraph is a different entity other than the words. Figure 1 illustrates that point, we do not see a clear interpretation of why the paragraph vectors (Le and Mikolov, 2014) are positioned in the space as in figure 1.
(2) The covariance matrix represents the second order summary statistic of multivariate data. This distinguishes the covariance matrix from the mean vector. In figure 1 we visualize the covariance matrix using confidence ellipse representation.We see that the covariance encodes the shape of the density composed of the words of interest. In the earlier example the Mean vectors of two dissimilar documents are put close by the word embedding. On the other hand, the covariance matrices capture the distinctness of the two documents.
(3) The use of the covariance as a spatial descriptor for multivariate data has a great success in different domains like computer vision (Tuzel et al., 2006; Hussein et al., 2013; Sharaf et al., 2015) and brain signal analysis (Barachant et al., 2013). With this global success of this representation, we believe this method can be useful for text-related tasks.
(4) The computation of the covariance descriptor is known to be fast and highly parallelizable. Moreover, there is no inference steps involved while computing the covariance matrix given its observations. This is an advantage compared to existing methods for generating paragraph vectors, such as (Le and Mikolov, 2014; Hill et al., 2016).

Our contribution in this work is two-fold:
(1) We propose the Document-Covariance descriptor (**DoCoV**) to represent every document as the covariance of the word embedding of its words. To the best of our knowledge, we are the first to explicitly compute covariance descriptors on word embedding such as word2vec (Mikolov et al., 2013b) or similar word vectors.
(2) We empirically show the effectiveness of our novel descriptor in comparison to the state-of-the-art methods in various unsupervised and supervised classification tasks. Our results show that our descriptor can attain comparable accuracy to state-of-the-art methods in a diverse set of tasks.

1.3 Related Work

We can see the word embedding at the core of recent state-of-art methods for solving many tasks like semantic textual similarity, sentiment analysis and more. Among the approaches of finding word embedding are (Pennington et al., 2014; Levy and Goldberg, 2014; Mikolov et al., 2013b). These alternatives share the same objective of finding a fixed-length vectorized representation for words to capture the semantic and syntactic regularities between words.

These efforts paved the way for many researchers to judge document similarity based on word embedding. Some efforts aimed at finding a global representation of a text snippet using a paragraph-level representation such as paragraph vectors (Le and Mikolov, 2014). Recently other neural-based sentence and paragraph level representations appeared to provide a fixed length representation like Skip-Thought Vectors (Kiros et al., 2015) and FastSent (Hill et al., 2016). Some efforts focused on defining a Word Mover Distance(WMD) based on word level representation (Kusner et al., 2015).

Prior to this work, we proposed earlier trials for using covariance features in community question answering (Malhas et al., 2016b,a; Torki et al.,

---

[1] https://radimrehurek.com/gensim/

2017). In these trials we used the covariance features in combination with lexical and semantic features. Close to our work is (Nikolentzos et al., 2017), they build an implicit representation of documents using multidimensional Gaussian distribution. Then they compute a similarity kernel to be used in document classification task. Our work is distinguished from (Nikolentzos et al., 2017) as we compute an explicit descriptor for any document. Moreover, we use linear models which scale much better than non-linear kernels as introduced in (Nikolentzos et al., 2017).

2 Document Covariance Descriptor

We present our DoCoV descriptor. First, we define a document observation matrix. Second, we show how to extract our DoCoV descriptor.

Document Observation Matrix

Given a d-dimensional word embedding model and an n-terms document. We can define a document observation matrix $O \in \mathbb{R}^{n \times d}$. In the matrix O, a row represents a term in the document and columns represent the d-dimensional word embedding representation for that term.

Assume that we have observed n terms of a d-dimensional random variable; we have a data matrix $O(n \times d)$:

$$O = \begin{pmatrix} x_{11} & \cdots & x_{1d} \\ x_{21} & \cdots & x_{2d} \\ \vdots & \ddots & \vdots \\ x_{n1} & \cdots & x_{nd} \end{pmatrix} \quad (1)$$

The rows $x_i = \begin{bmatrix} x_1 & x_2 & \cdots & x_d \end{bmatrix}^T \in R^d$, denote the i-th observation of a d-dimensional random variable $X \in R^d$. The "sample mean vector" of the n observations $\in R^d$ is given by the vector $\bar{x}$ of the means $\bar{x}_j$ of the d variables:

$$\bar{x} = \begin{bmatrix} \bar{x}_1 & \bar{x}_2 & \cdots & \bar{x}_d \end{bmatrix}^T \in R^d \quad (2)$$

From hereafter, when we mention the Mean vector we mean the sample Mean Vector $\bar{x}$.

Document-Covariance Descriptor (DoCoV)

Given an observation matrix O for a document, we compute the covariance matrix entriesfor every pair of dimensions (X, Y).

$$\sigma_{X,Y} = \frac{\sum_{i=1}^{N} (x_i - \bar{x})(y_i - \bar{y})}{N} \quad (3)$$

The matrix $C \in \mathbb{R}^{d \times d}$ is a symmetric matrix and is defined as

$$C = \begin{pmatrix} \sigma_{X_1}^2 & \sigma_{X_1 X_2} & \cdots & \sigma_{X_1 X_d} \\ \sigma_{X_1 X_2} & \sigma_{X_2}^2 & \cdots & \sigma_{X_2 X_d} \\ \vdots & \vdots & \ddots & \vdots \\ \sigma_{X_1 X_d} & \sigma_{X_2 X_d} & \cdots & \sigma_{X_d}^2 \end{pmatrix} (4)$$

We Compute a vectorized representation of the matrix C as the stacking of the upper triangular part of matrix C as in eq. 5. This process produces a vector $v \in \mathbb{R}^{d(d+1)/2}$. The Euclidean distance between vectorized matrices is equivalent to the Frobenius norm of the original covariance matrices.

$$v = \textbf{vect}(C) = \begin{cases} \sqrt{2} C_{p,q} & \text{if } p < q \\ C_{p,q} & \text{if } p = q \end{cases} \quad (5)$$

3 Experimental Evaluation

We show an extensive comparative evaluation for unsupervised paragraph representation approaches. We test the *unsupervised* semantic textual similarity task. Next, we show a comparative evaluation for text classification benchmarks.

3.1 Effect of Word Embedding Source and Dimensionality on Classification Results

We evaluate classification performance over the IMDB movie reviews dataset using error rate as the evaluation measure. We report our results using a linear SVM classifier.We chose the default parameters for Linear SVM classifier in scikit-learn library[2].

The IMDB movie review dataset was first proposed by Maas et al. (Maas et al., 2011) as a benchmark for sentiment analysis. The dataset consists of 100K IMDB movie reviews and each review has several sentences. The 100K reviews are divided into three datasets: 25K labelled training instances, 25K labelled test instances and 50K unlabelled training instances. Each review has one label representing the sentiment of it: Positive or Negative. These labels are balanced in both the training and the test set.

The objective is to show that theDoCoV descriptor can be used with different alternatives for word representations. Also, the experiment shows that pre-trained models are giving the best results, namely the word2vec model built on Google news. This alleviates the need of computing a problem

---

[2] http://scikit-learn.org/

specific word embedding. In some cases there is no available data to construct the word embedding. To illustrate that we tried different alternatives for word representation.

(1) We computed our own skipgram models using Gensim Library. We used the Training and unlabelled subsets of IMDB dataset to obtain different embedding by setting number of dimensions to 100, 200 and 300.

(2) We used pre-trained GloVe models trained on wikipedia2014 and Gigaword5. We tested the available different dimensionality 100, 200 and 300. We also used the 300 dimensions GloVe model that used commoncrawl with 42 Billion tokens We call the last one *Lrg*. This model provides word vectors of 300 dimensions for each word.

(3) We used pre-trained word2vec model trained on Google news. We call it *Gnews*. This model provides word vectors of 300 dimensions for each word. Table 1 shows the results when using DoCoV computed at different dimensions of word embedding in classification. The table also compares classification performance when using DoCoV to the performance when using the Mean of word embedding as a baseline. Also, we show the effect of fusing DoCoV with other feature sets. We mainly experiment with the following sets: DoCoV, Mean, and bag-of-words (BOW). We use the mean and DoCoV features.

Observations

From the results we can observe the following
(1) We observe that the DoCoV is consistently outperforming the **Mean** vector for different dimensionality of the word embedding regardless of the embedding source.
(3) The best performing feature concatenation is DoCoV+BOW. This ensures that the concatenation in fact is benefiting from both representations.
(3) In general the best results are achieved using the available 300-dimensions *Gnews* word embedding. In the subsequent experiments we will use that embedding such that we do not need to build a different word embedding for every task on hand.

Unsupervised Semantic Textual Similarity

We conduct a comparative evaluation against the state-of-the-art approaches in unsupervised paragraph representation. We follow the setup used in (Hill et al., 2016).

Datasets and Baselines

We contrast our results against the methods reported in (Hill et al., 2016). The competing methods are the paragraph vectors (Le and Mikolov, 2014), skip-thought vectors (Kiros et al., 2015), Fastsent (Hill et al., 2016), Sequential (Denoising) Autoencoders (SDAE) (Hill et al., 2016). The Mean vector baseline is also implemented. Also, we use the sum of the similarities generated by the DoCoV and the mean vectors. All of our results are reported using the freely available *Gnews* word2vec of $dim = 300$. We use same evaluation measures (Hill et al., 2016). We use the Pearson correlation and Spearman correlation with the manual relatedness judgements.

The semantic sentence relatedness datasets used in the comparative evaluation the SICK dataset (Marelli et al., 2014) consists of 10,000 pairs of sentences and relatedness judgements and the STS 2014 dataset (Agirre et al., 2014) consists of 3,750 pairs and ratings from six linguistic domains.

Results and Discussion

We show the correlation values between the similarities computed via DoCoV and the human judgements. We contrast the performance of other representations in table 2.

We observe that DoCoV representation outperforms other representations in this task. Other models such as skipthought vectors (Kiros et al., 2015) and SDAE (Hill et al., 2016) requires building an encoder-decoder model which takes time[3] to learn. For other models like paragraph vectors (Le and Mikolov, 2014) and Fastsent vectors (Hill et al., 2016), they require a gradient descent inference step to compute the paragraph/sentence vectors. Using the DoCoV, we just require a pre-trained word embedding model and we do not need any additional training like encoder-decoder models or inference steps via gradient descent.

Text Classification Benchmarks

The datasets used in this experiment form a text-classification benchmark for sentence and paragraph classification. Towards the end of this section we can clearly identify the value of the DoCoV descriptor as a generic descriptor for text classification tasks.

Datasets and Baselines

We contrast our results against the same methods of unsupervised paragraph representations. In addition to the results of DoCoV we examined concatenation of BoW with tf-idf weighting and Mean vectors with our DoCoV descriptors. We use linear

---

[3]Up to weeks.

Table 1: Error-Rate performance when changing word vectors dimensionality.

Model/Dim					
BOW	9.66%				
Gensim	Mean	DoCoV	DoCoV +Mean	DoCoV Bow	DoCoV +Mean+Bow
d=100	14.13%	11.64%	11.16%	9.39%	9.44%
d=200	12.86%	11.08%	10.80%	9.39%	9.58%
d=300	12.83%	11.08%	10.85%	9.41%	9.47%
Glove	Mean	DoCoV	DoCoV +Mean	DoCoV Bow	DoCoV +Mean+Bow
d=100	20%	13.07%	12.88%	9.63%	9.62%
d=200	16.95%	12.36%	12.22%	9.64%	9.65%
d=300	16.29%	12.00%	11.91%	9.63%	9.66%
d=300.*Lrg*	14.94%	11.70%	11.56%	9.5%	9.6%
Gnews	Mean	DoCoV	DoCoV +Mean	DoCoV Bow	DoCoV +Mean+Bow
d=300	14.03%	11.11%	10.75%	**9.32%**	9.6%

Table 2: Spearman/Pearson correlations on *unsupervised* (relatedness) evaluations.

Model	STS-2014							SICK
	News	Forums	Wordnet	Twitter	Images	Headlines	All	
P2vec (Le and Mikolov, 2014)	0.42/0.46	0.33/0.34	0.51/0.48	0.54/0.57	0.32/0.30	0.46/0.47	0.44/0.44	0.44/0.46
FastSent (Hill et al., 2016)	0.44/0.45	0.14/0.15	0.39/0.34	0.42/0.43	0.55/0.60	0.43/0.44	0.27/0.29	0.57/0.60
FastSent+AE (Hill et al., 2016)	**0.58/0.59**	**0.41/0.36**	**0.74/0.70**	0.63/0.66	**0.74/0.78**	0.57/0.59	**0.63/0.64**	**0.61/0.72**
Skip-Thought (Kiros et al., 2015)	0.56/**0.59**	**0.41/0.40**	0.69/0.64	**0.70/0.74**	0.63/0.65	**0.58/0.60**	0.62/0.62	0.60/0.65
SAE (Hill et al., 2016)	0.17/0.16	0.12/0.12	0.30/0.23	0.28/0.22	0.49/0.46	0.13/0.11	0.12/0.13	0.32/0.31
SAE+embs (Hill et al., 2016)	0.52/0.54	0.22/0.23	0.60/0.55	0.60/0.60	0.64/0.64	0.41/0.41	0.42/0.43	0.47/0.49
SDAE (Hill et al., 2016)	.07/0.04	0.11/0.13	0.33/0.24	0.44/0.42	0.44/0.38	0.36/0.36	0.17/0.15	0.46/0.46
SDAE+embs (Hill et al., 2016)	0.51/0.54	0.29/0.29	0.56/0.50	0.57/0.58	0.59/0.59	0.43/0.44	0.37/0.38	0.46/0.46
Mean	**0.65/0.68**	0.46/0.45	0.75/0.78	**0.71/0.75**	0.76/0.78	0.59/0.64	0.64/0.66	**0.63/0.73**
DoCoV	0.62/0.68	0.50/**0.51**	0.77/**0.79**	0.69/0.75	**0.78/0.80**	0.60/0.63	**0.67/0.70**	0.61/0.69
DoCoV+Mean	0.64/**0.70**	**0.51/0.51**	**0.79/0.78**	**0.71/0.76**	**0.78/0.81**	**0.61/0.65**	**0.67/0.70**	0.62/0.71

Table 3: Accuracy of sentence representation models on text classification benchmarks.

Representation \ Dataset	MR	CR	Trec	Subj	Overall
Mean	77.4	79.2	80	91.3	81.98
BOW +tf-idf weights	77.1	78.5	89.3	89.3	83.55
P2vec (Le and Mikolov, 2014)	74.8	78.1	91.8	90.5	83.8
Skip-uni (Kiros et al., 2015)	75.5	79.3	91.4	92.1	84.58
bi-skip (Kiros et al., 2015)	73.9	77.9	89.4	92.5	84.43
comb-skip (Kiros et al., 2015)	**76.5**	**80.1**	**92.2**	**93.6**	**85.6**
FastSent (Hill et al., 2016)	70.8	78.4	76.8	88.7	78.68
FastSentAE (Hill et al., 2016)	71.8	76.7	80.4	88.8	79.43
SAE (Hill et al., 2016)	62.6	68	80.2	86.1	74.23
SAE+embs (Hill et al., 2016)	73.2	75.3	80.4	89.8	79.68
SDAE (Hill et al., 2016)	67.6	74	77.6	89.3	77.13
SDAE+embs (Hill et al., 2016)	74.6	78	78.4	90.8	80.45
COV	79.7	79.4	89.5	92.8	85.35
COV+Mean	80.2	80.1	90.3	93.1	85.93
COV+Bow	80.7	80.5	**91.8**	**93.3**	86.58
COV+Mean+BOW	**81.1**	**81.5**	91.6	93.2	*86.85*

SVM for all the tasks. All of our results are reported using the freely available *Gnews* word2vec of $dim = 300$. We use classification accuracy as the evaluation measure for this experiment as (Hill et al., 2016).

The subsets used in comparative benchmark evaluation are: Movie Reviews **MR** (Pang and Lee, 2005), Subjectivity **Subj** (Pang and Lee, 2004),Customer Reviews **CR** (Hu and Liu, 2004) and TREC Question **TREC** (Li and Roth, 2002).

Results and Discussion

Table 3 shows the results of our variants against state-of-art algorithms that use unsupervised paragraph representation.

We observe that DoCoV is consistently better than the Mean vector and BOW with tf-idf weights. Also, DoCoV is improving consistently when concatenated with baselines such as Mean vector and BOW vectors. This means each feature is capturing different discriminating information. This justifies the choice of concatenating DoCoV with other features. We further observe that DoCoV is consistently better than the paragraph vectors (Le and Mikolov, 2014), Fastsent and SDAE (Hill et al., 2016). The overall accuracy of DoCoV is highlighted and it outperforms other methods on the text classification benchmark.

4 Conclusion

We presented a novel descriptor to represent text on any level such as sentences, paragraphs or documents. Our representation is generic which makes it useful for different supervised and unsupervised tasks. It has fixed-length property which makes it useful for different learning algorithms. Also, our descriptor requires minimal training. We do not require a encoder-decoder model or a gradient descent iterations to be computed.

Empirically we showed the effectiveness of the descriptor in different tasks. We showed better performance against other state-of-the-art methods in supervised and unsupervised settings.

References

Eneko Agirre, Carmen Banea, Claire Cardie, Daniel Cer, Mona Diab, Aitor Gonzalez-Agirre, Weiwei Guo, Rada Mihalcea, German Rigau, and Janyce Wiebe. 2014. Semeval-2014 task 10: Multilingual semantic textual similarity. In *SemEval*.

Alexandre Barachant, Stéphane Bonnet, Marco Congedo, and Christian Jutten. 2013. Classification of covariance matrices using a riemannian-based kernel for bci applications. *Neurocomputing*.

Yoshua Bengio, Réjean Ducharme, Pascal Vincent, and Christian Janvin. 2003. A neural probabilistic language model. *J. Mach. Learn. Res.*

Ronan Collobert, Jason Weston, Léon Bottou, Michael Karlen, Koray Kavukcuoglu, and Pavel Kuksa. 2011. Natural language processing (almost) from scratch. *JMLR*.

Scott Deerwester, Susan T Dumais, George W Furnas, Thomas K Landauer, and Richard Harshman. 1990. Indexing by latent semantic analysis. *Journal of the American society for information science*.

Felix Hill, Kyunghyun Cho, and Anna Korhonen. 2016. Learning distributed representations of sentences from unlabelled data. In *NAACL*.

Minqing Hu and Bing Liu. 2004. Mining and summarizing customer reviews. In *SIGKDD*.

Mohamed E Hussein, Marwan Torki, Mohammad Abdelaziz Gowayyed, and Motaz El-Saban. 2013. Human action recognition using a temporal hierarchy of covariance descriptors on 3d joint locations. In *IJCAI*.

Yoon Kim. 2014. Convolutional neural networks for sentence classification. *arXiv preprint arXiv:1408.5882*.

Ryan Kiros, Yukun Zhu, Ruslan R Salakhutdinov, Richard Zemel, Raquel Urtasun, Antonio Torralba, and Sanja Fidler. 2015. Skip-thought vectors. In *NIPS*.

Matt J Kusner, Yu Sun, Nicholas I Kolkin, Kilian Q Weinberger, et al. 2015. From word embeddings to document distances. In *ICML*.

Quoc V Le and Tomas Mikolov. 2014. Distributed representations of sentences and documents. In *ICML*.

Omer Levy and Yoav Goldberg. 2014. Neural word embedding as implicit matrix factorization. In *NIPS*.

Xin Li and Dan Roth. 2002. Learning question classifiers. In *ACL*.

Andrew L Maas, Raymond E Daly, Peter T Pham, Dan Huang, Andrew Y Ng, and Christopher Potts. 2011. Learning word vectors for sentiment analysis. In *ACL-HLT*.

Rana Malhas, Marwan Torki, Rahma Ali, Tamer Elsayed, and Evi Yulianti. 2016a. Real, live, and concise: Answering open-domain questions with word embedding and summarization. In *TREC*.

Rana Malhas, Marwan Torki, and Tamer Elsayed. 2016b. Qu-ir at semeval 2016 task 3: Learning to rank on arabic community question answering forums with word embedding. In *SemEval*.

Marco Marelli, Stefano Menini, Marco Baroni, Luisa Bentivogli, Raffaella Bernardi, and Roberto Zamparelli. 2014. A sick cure for the evaluation of compositional distributional semantic models. In *LREC*.

Tomas Mikolov, Kai Chen, Greg Corrado, and Jeffrey Dean. 2013a. Efficient estimation of word representations in vector space. *arXiv preprint arXiv:1301.3781*.

Tomas Mikolov, Ilya Sutskever, Kai Chen, Greg S Corrado, and Jeff Dean. 2013b. Distributed representations of words and phrases and their compositionality. In *NIPS*.

Giannis Nikolentzos, Polykarpos Meladianos, François Rousseau, Yannis Stavrakas, and Michalis Vazirgiannis. 2017. Multivariate gaussian document representation from word embeddings for text categorization. In *EACL*.

Bo Pang and Lillian Lee. 2004. A sentimental education: Sentiment analysis using subjectivity summarization based on minimum cuts. In *ACL*.

Bo Pang and Lillian Lee. 2005. Seeing stars: Exploiting class relationships for sentiment categorization with respect to rating scales. In *ACL*.

Jeffrey Pennington, Richard Socher, and Christopher D. Manning. 2014. Glove: Global vectors for word representation. In *EMNLP*.

Gerard Salton and Christopher Buckley. 1988. Term-weighting approaches in automatic text retrieval. *Information processing & management*.

Amr Sharaf, Marwan Torki, Mohamed E Hussein, and Motaz El-Saban. 2015. Real-time multi-scale action detection from 3d skeleton data. In *WACV*.

Marwan Torki, Maram Hasanain, and Tamer Elsayed. 2017. Qu-bigir at semeval 2017 task 3: Using similarity features for arabic community question answering forums. In *SemEval*.

Oncel Tuzel, Fatih Porikli, and Peter Meer. 2006. Region covariance: A fast descriptor for detection and classification. In *Computer Vision–ECCV 2006*.

Learning with Structured Representations for Negation Scope Extraction

Hao Li and **Wei Lu**
Singapore University of Technology and Design
8 Somapah Road, Singapore, 487372
`hao_li@mymail.sutd.edu.sg, luwei@sutd.edu.sg`

Abstract

We report an empirical study on the task of negation scope extraction given the negation cue. Our key observation is that certain useful information such as features related to negation cue, long distance dependencies as well as some latent structural information can be exploited for such a task. We design approaches based on conditional random fields (CRF), semi-Markov CRF, as well as latent-variable CRF models to capture such information. Extensive experiments on several standard datasets demonstrate that our approaches are able to achieve better results than existing approaches reported in the literature.

1 Introduction

Negation is an important linguistic phenomenon (Morante and Sporleder, 2012), which reverts the assertion associated with a proposition. Broadly speaking, the part of the sentence being negated is called *negation scope* (Huddleston et al., 2002). Automatic negation scope detection is a vital but challenging task that has various applications in areas such as text mining (Szarvas et al., 2008), and sentiment analysis (Wiegand et al., 2010; Councill et al., 2010). Negation scope detection task commonly involves a negation cue which can be one of the following 3 types – either a single word (e.g., *not*), affixes (e.g., *im-, -less*) or multiple words (e.g., *no longer*) expressing negation. Figure 1 presents two real examples for such a task, where the first example involves discontinuous negation scope of an affix cue. The second example shows a discontinuous negation cue and its corresponding discontinuous negation scope.

Most existing approaches tackled the negation scope detection problem from a boundary detection perspective, aiming to identify whether each word token in the sentence belongs to the negation scope or not. To perform sequence labeling, various approaches have been proposed based on models such as support vector machines (SVMs) (with heuristic rules) (Read et al., 2012; de Albornoz et al., 2012; Packard et al., 2014), conditional random fields (CRF) (Lapponi et al., 2012; Chowdhury and Mahbub, 2012; White, 2012; Zou et al., 2015) and neural networks (Fancellu et al., 2016; Qian et al., 2016). These models typically either make use of external resources for extracting complex syntax and grammar features, or are based on neural architectures such as long short-term memory networks (LSTM) and convolutional neural networks (CNNs) to extract automatic features.

We observe that there are some useful features that can be explicitly and implicitly captured and modelled in the learning process for negation scope extraction. We use the term partial scope to refer to a continuous text span that is part of discontinuous scope, and use the term gap to refer to the text span between two pieces of partial scope.

From the first example in Figure 1 we can observe that, with the negation cue as a prefix in a word, the partial scope *before, after* and *in the middle* of the negation cue differ in terms of composition of words and their associated syntactic roles in the sentence. Furthermore, the type of cue

He declares that he heard cries but is **unable** to state from what direction they came .

There is **neither** money **nor** credit in it , and yet one would wish to tidy it up .

Figure 1: Two examples with negation cues in bold blue and negation scope in red.

Proceedings of the 56th Annual Meeting of the Association for Computational Linguistics (Short Papers), pages 533–539
Melbourne, Australia, July 15 - 20, 2018. ©2018 Association for Computational Linguistics

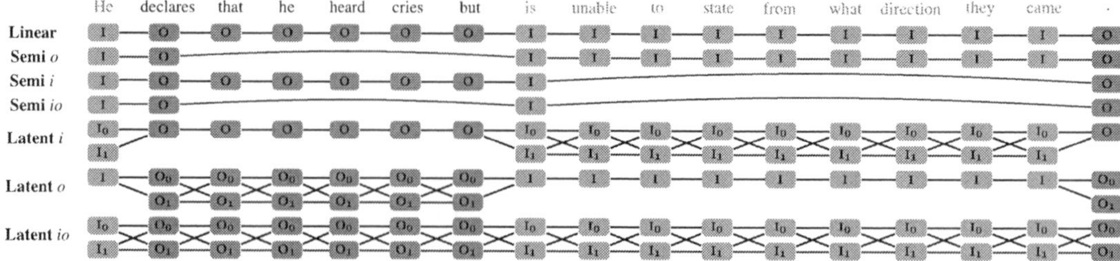

Figure 2: Label assignments of model variants for the first example mentioned in Figure 1.

as we mentioned earlier may also reveal crucial information for this task. Moreover, two pieces of partial scope separated by a gap might have some long distance dependencies. For instance, in the first sentence of Figure 1, "*He*" as the first partial scope is the subject phrase of the token "*is*" which is the first word of the second partial scope with a long gap in between.

Similarly, the second example shows that a discontinuous negation cue involves multiple words, *neither* and *nor*, which shows the importance of cue features and some long distance dependencies among text spans.

Furthermore, besides explicit features that we are able to define, we believe there exist some implicit linguistic patterns within the scope for a given negation cue. While it is possible to manually design linguistic features to extract such patterns, approaches that can automatically capture such implicit patterns in a domain and language independent manner can be more attractive. How to design models that can effectively capture such features mentioned above remains a research question to be answered.

In the paper, we design different models to capture such useful features based on the above motivations, and report our empirical findings through extensive experiments. We release our code at `http://statnlp.org/research/st`.

2 Approaches

Based on the observations described earlier, we aim to capture three types of features by designing different models based on CRF.

Negation Cue

The linear CRF (Lafferty et al., 2001) model (which we refer to as **Linear** in this paper), as illustrated in Figure 2 , is used to capture negation cue related features. The probability of predicting a possible output $\mathbf{y}$, the label sequence capturing negation scope, given an input sentence $\mathbf{x}$ is:

$$p(\mathbf{y}|\mathbf{x}) = \frac{\exp\left(\mathbf{w}^T\mathbf{f}(\mathbf{x}, \mathbf{y})\right)}{\sum_{\mathbf{y}'\in\mathcal{Y}(\mathbf{x})}\exp(\mathbf{w}^T\mathbf{f}(\mathbf{x}, \mathbf{y}'))}$$

where $\mathbf{f}(\mathbf{x}, \mathbf{y})$ is a feature function defined over the $(\mathbf{x}, \mathbf{y})$ pair. The negation cue related features mainly involve cue type, position of the cue, as well as relative positions of each partial scope. For example, the cue type refers to the string form of the cue, which could be a single word, an affix (prefix or suffix), or a multi-word expression.

We follow a standard approach to assign tags to words. Specifically, $\mathbf{O}$ and $\mathbf{I}$ are used to indicate whether a word appears outside or inside the negation scope respectively.

Long Distance Dependencies

We use the semi-CRF (Sarawagi and Cohen, 2004) model (referred to as **Semi**) to capture long distance dependencies. The semi-CRF is an extension to the linear-CRF. The difference is that the output $\mathbf{y}$ may not be a sequence of individual words. Rather, it is now a sequence of spans, where each span consists of one or more words. The semi-CRF model is more expressive than the linear-CRF model as such a model is able to capture features that are defined at the span level, allowing longer-range dependencies to be captured.

Since the **Semi** approach is capable of modeling a span (which can be a gap or partial scope), we are able to model the features between two separate text spans. We propose three variants for the **Semi** model, as illustrated in Figure 2, to capture different types of long distance features. The **Semi** *i* model regards a piece of partial scope as a span in order to capture long distance dependencies between two gaps. The **Semi** *o* model treats a gap as a span to capture long distance dependencies between two pieces of partial scope. The **Semi** *io* model regards both partial scope and gaps as spans to capture both types of long distance dependencies mentioned above.

Implicit Patterns

The latent variable CRF model, denoted as **Latent**, is used to model implicit patterns. The probability of predicting a possible output $\mathbf{y}$, which is the label sequence capturing negation scope information, given an input sentence $\mathbf{x}$ is defined as:

$$p(\mathbf{y}|\mathbf{x}) = \frac{\sum_{\mathbf{h}} \exp\left(\mathbf{w}^T \mathbf{f}(\mathbf{x}, \mathbf{y}, \mathbf{h})\right)}{\sum_{\mathbf{y}' \in \mathcal{Y}(\mathbf{x})} \sum_{\mathbf{h}'} \exp(\mathbf{w}^T \mathbf{f}(\mathbf{x}, \mathbf{y}', \mathbf{h}'))}$$

where $\mathbf{h}$ is a latent variable encoding the implicit pattern.

We believe such latent pattern information can be learned from data without any linguistic guidance. The **Latent** model is capable of capturing this type of implicit signals. For example, as illustrated as **Latent** *io* in Figure 2, each position has $\mathbf{O_0}$, $\mathbf{O_1}$, $\mathbf{I_0}$ and $\mathbf{I_1}$ as latent tags. This way, we can construct features of forms such as "*He*/$\mathbf{O}_i$-*declares*/$\mathbf{I}_j$" that capture the underlying interactions between the words and the latent tag patterns.

In order to investigate the relation between latent variables and tags, we proposed another two latent models. The **Latent** *i* only considers latent variables on **I** tags (for partial scope), while **Latent** *o* only takes latent variables on **O** tags (for gaps).

3 Experimental Setup

CDS-CO	Train	Dev	Test
#Sentence	847	144	235
#Instance	983	173	264

Table 1: Statistics of the *CDS-CO* corpus.

We mainly conducted our experiments on the *CDS-CO* corpus released from the *SEM2012 shared task (Morante and Blanco, 2012). The negation cue and corresponding negation scope are annotated. For each word token, the corresponding POS tag and the syntax tree information are provided. If the sentence contains multiple negation cues, each of them is annotated separately. The corpus statistics is listed in Table 1. During training and testing, following prior works (Fancellu et al., 2016), only instances with at least one negation cue will be selected. For the sentence containing multiple negation cues, we create as many copies as the number of instances,

System	Token-Level			Scope-Level (Exact Scope Match)					
	$P.$	$R.$	F_1	$P_A.$	$R_A.$	F_{1A}	$P_B.$	$R_B.$	F_{1B}
Read et al. (2012)	-	-	-	98.8	64.3	77.9	-	-	-
Packard et al. (2014)	86.1	**90.4**	88.2	98.8	65.5	78.7	-	-	-
Fancellu et al. (2016)	92.6	85.1	88.7	99.4	63.9	77.8	-	-	-
Linear (*-c -r*)	84.7	73.9	78.6	99.2	49.4	65.6	51.5	49.4	50.4
Linear (*-r*)	90.6	78.4	84.1	100	60.6	75.5	61.4	60.6	61.0
Linear (*-c*)	91.0	78.9	84.5	99.3	56.6	72.1	60.0	56.6	58.3
Linear	94.4	82.6	88.1	100	67.9	80.9	69.3	67.9	68.6
Semi *i*	95.0	84.1	89.2	100	67.5	80.6	69.4	67.5	68.4
Semi *o*	94.0	85.3	**89.4**	100	69.1	81.7	**71.1**	69.1	**70.1**
Semi *io*	94.5	84.1	89.0	100	68.3	81.2	70.3	68.3	69.3
Latent *i*	94.4	83.4	88.6	99.4	67.9	80.7	69.6	67.9	68.7
Latent *o*	90.4	83.9	87.1	99.4	65.5	78.9	66.3	65.5	65.9
Latent *io*	**94.8**	83.2	88.6	100	**69.5**	**82.0**	70.6	**69.5**	70.0

Table 2: Main results on *CDS-CO* data

each of which has only one negation cue and its corresponding negation scope.

The L_2 regularization hyper-parameter λ is set to 0.1 based on the development set. We conduct evaluations of negation scope extraction based on metrics at token-level evaluations and scope-level evaluations. There are two versions of evaluation metrics, referred to as version A and version B[1], defined at the scope-level that can be used to measure the performance according to *SEM2012 shared task (Morante and Blanco, 2012).

Moreover, to understand the model robustness, we also conducted additional experiments on BioScope (Szarvas et al., 2008) and CNeSP (Zou et al., 2015).

4 Results and Discussion

4.1 Main Results

The main results on the *CDS-CO* corpus are shown in Table 2. $P_A.$, $R_A.$ and $F_{1A}.$ are precision, recall and F_1 measure under version A, while $P_B.$, $R_B.$, $F_{1B}.$ are for version B. Note that none of the prior works reported results under version B. Moreover, *c* refers to the cue type features, *r* refers to relative position of partial scope with respect to the cue.

We focus on **Linear** models first, where **Linear** (*-c -r*) is the baseline without features *c* and *r* for comparisons. By adding *c*, the **Linear** (*-r*) model improves the performance by 9.9 and 10.6 in terms of F_1 scores for both versions of evaluation methods at the scope level respectively. By adding *r* solely, the **Linear** (*-c*) model increases the performance by 6.5 and 7.9 on F_1 scores of both versions. By adding both *c* and *r*, the **Linear** model increases the performance by 15.3 and 18.2 on F_1 scores at the scope level, outperforming previous

---

[1]The official evaluation contains both two versions. We explain the differences between two versions of evaluation in the supplementary material.

Figure 3: Examples showing incorrect instances in the **Linear** model but correct in **Semi** o model (The incorrect predictions by Linear model are underlined).

works. These improvements demonstrate the importance of the negation cue features.

Compared with the **Linear** model, **Semi** models achieve better results. Specifically, **Semi** o model achieves the best result on F_{1B} at the scope level among all the models and achieves the highest result on F_1 at the token level.

The **Latent** io model outperforms all the other models in terms of F_{1A} at scope level and a competitive result in terms of F_{1B}.

4.2 Analysis

By analyzing predictions that are incorrect in **Linear** model that are correct in the **Semi** models, we have some interesting observations explaining why **Semi** models work better. The first type of observation is that the **Semi** models tend to predict more correct scope tokens, which improves results at scope level and token level. The second type is that **Semi** models recover some missing remote partial scope, which shows the importance of capturing long distance dependencies. For instance, in the first example of Figure 3, the **Semi** models recover the subject phrase "*This person*" as the first partial scope. The third type happens on discontinuous cues as well as multiple short gaps as shown in the second example in Figure 3. The **Linear** model fails to predict "*Mr. Waren ,*" and "*I ,*" as two pieces of partial scope between three cue words which are also gaps. These observations indicate that **Semi** models are capable of capturing long distance features and can correct some wrong predictions made by the **Linear** model.

Similarly, by analyzing predictions that are incorrect in **Linear** model that are correct in the **Latent** models, we observe that **Latent** models tend to make more accurate predictions. We found that there is only 1 incorrect prediction from the **Latent** io that is corrected by the **Linear** model. This indicates that the **Latent** io model is able to fix er-

System	Abstract			Full Paper			Clinical		
	F_{1T}	F_{1A}	PCS	F_{1T}	F_{1A}	PCS	F_{1T}	F_{1A}	PCS
Li et al. (2010)	-	-	81.8	-	-	**64.0**	-	-	89.8
Velldal et al. (2012)	-	74.4	-	-	70.2	-	-	90.7	-
Zou et al. (2013)	-	-	76.9	-	-	61.2	-	-	85.3
Qian et al. (2016)	89.9	-	77.1	**83.5**	-	55.3	94.4	-	89.7
Linear	90.3	90.3	82.3	80.8	74.0	58.8	96.4	96.6	93.3
Semi io	**92.1**	**91.3**	**84.1**	**83.1**	**75.1**	60.1	**97.5**	**97.1**	**94.4**
Latent io	91.5	90.8	83.2	79.5	71.0	55.1	97.3	97.0	94.1

Table 3: Results on BioScope datasets.

rors for the **Linear** model without producing other wrong predictions. This analysis implies that the **Latent** models are able to capture some latent patterns to some extent. The performance of the **Latent** o model is lower than the performance of **Latent** io and **Latent** i, indicating that latent variables on tag I captures more information.

Let us focus on the token-level performance of our model. We obtained satisfactory precision scores, but comparatively low recall scores. Meanwhile, at the scope level, our precision scores are comparable to the previous works, but our recall scores are consistently better, indicating our models are capable of successfully recovering more gold scope information from the test data. Our further analysis shows that our models tend to predict negation scope that is significantly shorter than the gold scope for those instances that involve some long negation scope. We find that around 1/3 of the word tokens appearing inside any negation scope come from such instances. These facts make token-level recall of our models comparatively low.

In addition, we inspect the top 200 features with highest feature weights, and we find that around 45% of them are related to POS tags with label transition (the string form concatenating current tag and next tag), indicating POS tag features play an important role in the learning process for our models.

4.3 Experiments on Model Robustness

To understand the robustness of our model, we additionally conducted two sets of experiments.

BioScope

The BioScope corpus (Szarvas et al., 2008) contains three data collections from medical domains: *Abstract*, *Full Paper* and *Clinical*. NLTK (Bird and Loper, 2004) is used to perform tokenization and POS tagging for preprocessing. Following (Morante and Daelemans, 2009; Qian et al., 2016), we perform 10-fold cross validation on *Ab-*

System	Product Review			
	F_{1T}	F_{1A}	F_{1B}	PCS
(Zou et al., 2015)	-	-	-	60.93
Linear	89.60	81.86	69.39	69.39
Semi *io*	**90.78**	83.49	71.69	71.69
Latent *io*	90.60	**83.95**	**72.43**	**72.43**

Table 4: Results on *Product Review* from CNeSP.

stract, whereas the results on *Full Paper* and *Clinical* are obtained by training on the full *Abstract* dataset and testing on *Full Paper* and *Clinical* respectively. The latter experiment can help us understand the robustness of the model by applying the learned model to different types of text within the same domain.

The **Semi** *io* model mostly outperforms the other models. Comparing against all the prior works, our models are able to achieve better results on *Abstract* under both token-level and scope-level F_1 as well as PCS [2]. Moreover, we also obtain significantly higher results in terms of scope-level F_1 on *Full Paper* and *Clinical*, indicating the good robustness of our approaches. Note that the PCS score on *Full Paper* is not as satisfactory as on *Clinical*. This is largely because the model is trained on *Abstract*, but *Full Paper* contains much longer sentences with longer negation scope, which presents a challenge for our model as discussed in the previous sections. On the other hand, the baseline systems (Li et al., 2010; Velldal et al., 2012) adopt features from syntactic trees, which allow them to capture long-distance syntactic dependencies.

CNeSP

To understand how well our model works on another language other than English, we also conducted an experiment on the *Product Review* collection from the CNeSP corpus (Zou et al., 2015). We used Jieba (Sun, 2012) and Stanford tagger (Toutanova and Manning, 2000) to perform Chinese word segmentation and POS tagging. Following the data splitting scheme described in (Zou et al., 2015), we performed 10-fold cross-validation and the results are shown in Table 4. Our model obtains a significantly higher PCS score than the model reported in (Zou et al., 2015). The results further confirm the robustness of our model, showing it is language independent.

---

[2] PCS is defined as percentage of correct scope which is the same as the recall score.

5 Related Work

The negation scope extraction task has been studied within the NLP community through the BioScope corpus (Szarvas et al., 2008) in biomedical domain, usually together with the negation cue detection task. The negation scope detection task has mostly been regarded as a boundary detection task. Morante et al. (2008) and Morante and Daelemans (2009) tackled the task by building classifiers based on k-nearest neighbors algorithm (Cover and Hart, 1967), SVM (Cortes and Vapnik, 1995) as well as CRF (Lafferty et al., 2001) on each token to determine if it is inside the scope. Li et al. (2010) incorporated more syntactic features such as parse tree information by adopting shallow semantic parsing (Gildea and Palmer, 2002; Punyakanok et al., 2005) for building an SVM classifier. With similar motivation, Apostolova et al. (2011) proposed a rule-based method to extract lexico-syntactic patterns to identify the scope boundaries. To further investigate the syntactic features, Zou et al. (2013) extracted more syntactic information from constituency and dependency trees obtained from parsers to feed into the SVM classifier. Qian et al. (2016) adopted a convolutional neural network based approach (LeCun et al., 1989) to extract position features and syntactic path features encoding the path from the cue to the candidate token along the constituency trees. They also captured relative position information between the words in the scope and the cue as features in their model.

In order to resolve the corpus scarcity issue in different languages for the negation scope extraction task, Zou et al. (2015) constructed a Chinese corpus CNeSP analogous to the BioScope corpus. They again tackled the negation scope extraction task using CRF with rich syntactic features extracted from constituency and dependency trees.

6 Conclusion

We explored several approaches based on CRF to capture some useful features for solving the task of extracting negation scope based on a given negation cue in a sentence. We conducted extensive experiments on a standard dataset, and the results show that our models are able to achieve significantly better results than various previous approaches. We also demonstrated the robustness of our approaches through extensive analysis as well as additional experiments on other datasets.

Acknowledgments

We would like to thank the anonymous reviewers for their constructive comments on this work. We would also like to thank Bowei Zou for answering our questions. This work is supported by Singapore Ministry of Education Academic Research Fund (AcRF) Tier 2 Project MOE2017-T2-1-156.

References

Emilia Apostolova, Noriko Tomuro, and Dina Demner-Fushman. 2011. Automatic extraction of lexico-syntactic patterns for detection of negation and speculation scopes. In *Proc. of ACL*. http://www.aclweb.org/anthology/P11-2049.

Steven Bird and Edward Loper. 2004. Nltk: The natural language toolkit. In *Proc. of ACL*. https://doi.org/10.3115/1219044.1219075.

Md Chowdhury and Faisal Mahbub. 2012. Fbk: Exploiting phrasal and contextual clues for negation scope detection. In *Proc. of *SEM2012*. http://www.aclweb.org/anthology/S12-1045.

Corinna Cortes and Vladimir Vapnik. 1995. Support-vector networks. *Machine learning* https://link.springer.com/content/pdf//10.1007/BF00994018.pdf.

Isaac G Councill, Ryan McDonald, and Leonid Velikovich. 2010. What's great and what's not: learning to classify the scope of negation for improved sentiment analysis. In *Proc. of NeSp-NLP*. https://aclanthology.info/pdf/W/W10/W10-3110.pdf.

Thomas Cover and Peter Hart. 1967. Nearest neighbor pattern classification. *IEEE transactions on information theory* https://ieeexplore.ieee.org/document/1053964.

Jorge Carrillo de Albornoz, Laura Plaza, Alberto Díaz, and Miguel Ballesteros. 2012. Ucm-i: A rule-based syntactic approach for resolving the scope of negation. In *Proc. of *SEM2012*. http://www.aclweb.org/anthology/S12-1037.

Federico Fancellu, Adam Lopez, and Bonnie L Webber. 2016. Neural networks for negation scope detection. In *Proc. of ACL*. https://doi.org/10.18653/v1/p16-1047.

Daniel Gildea and Martha Palmer. 2002. The necessity of parsing for predicate argument recognition. In *Proc. of ACL*. https://doi.org/10.3115/1073083.1073124.

Rodney Huddleston, Geoffrey K Pullum, et al. 2002. The cambridge grammar of english. *Language. Cambridge: Cambridge University Press* http://www.academia.edu/download/37907813//2001025630.pdf.

John Lafferty, Andrew McCallum, and Fernando CN Pereira. 2001. Conditional random fields: Probabilistic models for segmenting and labeling sequence data. In *Proc. of ICML*. http://repository.upenn.edu/cis_papers/159.

Emanuele Lapponi, Erik Velldal, Lilja Øvrelid, and Jonathon Read. 2012. Uio 2: sequence-labeling negation using dependency features. In *Proc. of *SEM2012*. http://www.aclweb.org/anthology/S12-1042.

Yann LeCun, Bernhard Boser, John S Denker, Donnie Henderson, Richard E Howard, Wayne Hubbard, and Lawrence D Jackel. 1989. Backpropagation applied to handwritten zip code recognition. *Neural Computation* https://doi.org/10.1162/neco.1989.1.4.541.

Junhui Li, Guodong Zhou, Hongling Wang, and Qiaoming Zhu. 2010. Learning the scope of negation via shallow semantic parsing. In *Proc. of COLING*. http://www.aclweb.org/anthology/C10-1076.

Roser Morante and Eduardo Blanco. 2012. *sem 2012 shared task: Resolving the scope and focus of negation. In *Proc. of *SEM 2012*. http://www.aclweb.org/anthology/S12-1035.

Roser Morante and Walter Daelemans. 2009. A metalearning approach to processing the scope of negation. In *Proc. of CoNLL*. http://www.aclweb.org/anthology/W09-1105.

Roser Morante, Anthony Liekens, and Walter Daelemans. 2008. Learning the scope of negation in biomedical texts. In *Proc. of ACL*. https://doi.org/10.3115/1613715.1613805.

Roser Morante and Caroline Sporleder. 2012. Modality and negation: An introduction to the special issue. *Computational linguistics* 38(2):223–260. https://doi.org/10.1162/COLI_a_00095.

Woodley Packard, Emily M Bender, Jonathon Read, Stephan Oepen, and Rebecca Dridan. 2014. Simple negation scope resolution through deep parsing: A semantic solution to a semantic problem. In *Proc. of ACL*. https://doi.org/10.3115/v1/p14-1007.

Vasin Punyakanok, Dan Roth, and Wen-tau Yih. 2005. The necessity of syntactic parsing for semantic role labeling. In *Proc. of IJCAI*. http://www.ijcai.org/Proceedings/05/Papers/1672.pdf.

Zhong Qian, Peifeng Li, Qiaoming Zhu, Guodong Zhou, Zhunchen Luo, and Wei Luo. 2016. Speculation and negation scope detection via convolutional neural networks. In *Proc. of EMNLP*. https://doi.org/10.18653/v1/d16-1078.

Jonathon Read, Erik Velldal, Lilja Øvrelid, and Stephan Oepen. 2012. Uio 1: Constituent-based discriminative ranking for negation resolution. In *Proc. of *SEM2012*. http://www.aclweb.org/anthology/S12-1041.

Sunita Sarawagi and William W Cohen. 2004. Semi-markov conditional random fields for information extraction. In *Advances in neural information processing systems*. pages 1185–1192. http://papers.nips.cc/paper/2648-semi-markov-conditional-random-fields-for-information-extraction.pdf.

J Sun. 2012. Jieba chinese word segmentation tool. https://github.com/fxsjy/jieba.

György Szarvas, Veronika Vincze, Richárd Farkas, and János Csirik. 2008. The bioscope corpus: annotation for negation, uncertainty and their scope in biomedical texts. In *Proc. of the Workshop on Current Trends in Biomedical Natural Language Processing*. https://aclanthology.info/pdf/W/W08/W08-0606.pdf.

Kristina Toutanova and Christopher D Manning. 2000. Enriching the knowledge sources used in a maximum entropy part-of-speech tagger. In *Proc. of EMNLP*. https://doi.org/10.3115/1117794.1117802.

Erik Velldal, Lilja Øvrelid, Jonathon Read, and Stephan Oepen. 2012. Speculation and negation: Rules, rankers, and the role of syntax. *Computational linguistics* 38(2):369–410. https://doi.org/10.1162/COLI_a_00126.

James Paul White. 2012. Uwashington: Negation resolution using machine learning methods. In *Proc. of *SEM2012*. http://www.aclweb.org/anthology/S12-1044.

Michael Wiegand, Alexandra Balahur, Benjamin Roth, Dietrich Klakow, and Andrés Montoyo. 2010. A survey on the role of negation in sentiment analysis. In *Proc. of the workshop on negation and speculation in natural language processing*. https://aclanthology.info/pdf/W/W10/W10-3111.pdf.

Bowei Zou, Guodong Zhou, and Qiaoming Zhu. 2013. Tree kernel-based negation and speculation scope detection with structured syntactic parse features. In *Proc. of EMNLP*. http://www.aclweb.org/anthology/D13-1099.

Bowei Zou, Qiaoming Zhu, and Guodong Zhou. 2015. Negation and speculation identification in chinese language. In *Proc. of ACL*. https://doi.org/10.3115/v1/p15-1064.

End-Task Oriented Textual Entailment
via Deep Explorations of Inter-Sentence Interactions

Wenpeng Yin,[1] Hinrich Schütze,[2] Dan Roth[1]
[1]Dept. of Computer Science, University of Pennsylvania, USA
[2]CIS, LMU Munich, Germany
{wenpeng,danroth}@seas.upenn.edu

Abstract

This work deals with SCITAIL, a natural entailment challenge derived from a multi-choice question answering problem. The premises and hypotheses in SCITAIL were generated with no awareness of each other, and did not specifically aim at the entailment task. This makes it more challenging than other entailment data sets and more directly useful to the end-task – question answering. We propose DEISTE (**d**eep **e**xplorations of **i**nter-sentence interactions for textual **e**ntailment) for this entailment task. Given word-to-word interactions between the premise-hypothesis pair (P, H), DEISTE consists of: (i) a *parameter-dynamic convolution* to make important words in P and H play a dominant role in learnt representations; and (ii) a *position-aware attentive convolution* to encode the representation and position information of the aligned word pairs. Experiments show that DEISTE gets $\approx 5\%$ improvement over prior state of the art and that the pretrained DEISTE on SCITAIL generalizes well on RTE-5.[1]

1 Introduction

Textual entailment (TE) is a fundamental problem in natural language understanding and has been studied intensively recently using multiple benchmarks – PASCAL RTE challenges (Dagan et al., 2006, 2013), Paragraph-Headline (Burger and Ferro, 2005), SICK (Marelli et al., 2014) and SNLI (Bowman et al., 2015). In particular, SNLI – while much easier than earlier datasets

Premise P	
Pluto rotates once on its axis every 6.39 Earth days.	0
Once per day, the earth rotates about its axis.	1
It rotates on its axis once every 60 Earth days.	0
Earth orbits Sun, and rotates once per day about axis.	1

Table 1: Examples of four premises for the hypothesis "Earth rotates on its axis once times in one day" in SCITAIL dataset. Right column (label): "1" means *entail*, "0" otherwise.

– has generated much work based on deep neural networks due to its large size. However, these benchmarks were mostly derived independently of any NLP problems.[2] Therefore, the premise-hypothesis pairs were composed under the constraint of predefined rules and the language skills of humans. As a result, while top-performing systems push forward the state-of-the-art, they do not necessarily learn to support language inferences that emerge commonly and naturally in real NLP problems.

In this work, we study SCITAIL (Khot et al., 2018), an end-task oriented challenging entailment benchmark. SCITAIL is reformatted from a multi-choice question answering problem. All hypotheses H were obtained by rewriting (question, correct answer) pairs; all premises P are relevant web sentences collected by an Information retrieval (IR) method; then (P, H) pairs are annotated via crowdsourcing. Table 1 shows examples. *By this construction, a substantial performance gain on* SCITAIL *can be turned into better QA performance* (Khot et al., 2018). Khot et al. (2018) report that SCITAIL challenges neural entailment models that show outstanding performance on SNLI, e.g., Decomposable Attention Model (Parikh et al., 2016) and Enhanced LSTM (Chen et al., 2017).

We propose DEISTE for SCITAIL. Given word-to-word inter-sentence interactions between

---

[1]https://github.com/yinwenpeng/SciTail

[2]RTE-{5,6,7} is an exception to this rule.

Proceedings of the 56th Annual Meeting of the Association for Computational Linguistics (Short Papers), pages 540–545
Melbourne, Australia, July 15 - 20, 2018. ©2018 Association for Computational Linguistics

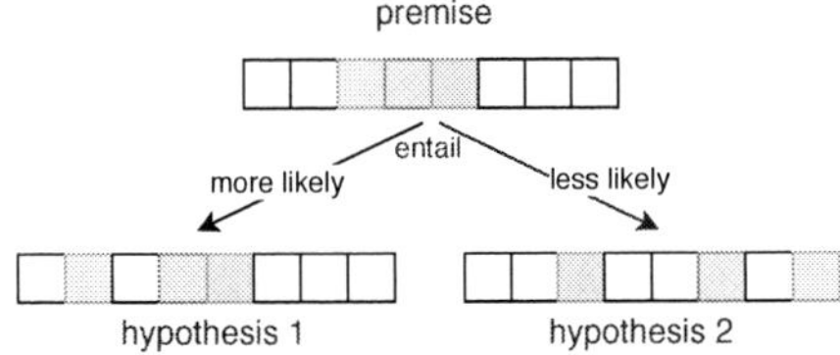

Figure 1: The motivation of considering alignment positions in TE. The same color in (premise, hypothesis) means the two words are best aligned.

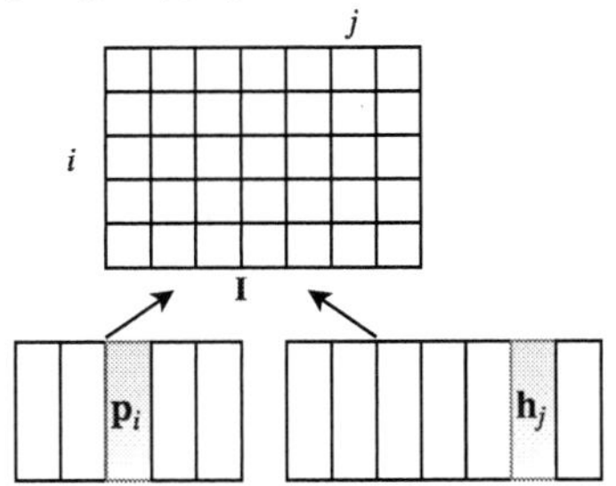

Given : $\mathbf{I}$ = interactions$(\mathbf{P}, \mathbf{H})$
Learn :

(1) $\dfrac{1.0}{1.0 + \max(\mathbf{I}[i,:])}$: importance of $\mathbf{p}_i$

(2) $\mathbf{H} \cdot \mathrm{softmax}(\mathbf{I}[i,:])$: soft best match of $\mathbf{p}_i$

(3) $\mathrm{argmax}(\mathbf{I}[i,:])$: hard location of best match of $\mathbf{p}_i$

Figure 2: The basic principles of DEISTE in modeling the pair (P, H)

the pair (P, H), DEISTE pursues three deep exploration strategies of these interactions. (a) How to express the importance of a word, and let it play a dominant role in learnt representations. (b) For any word in one of (P, H), how to find the best aligned word in the other sentence, so that we know their connection is indicative of the final decision. (c) For a window of words in P or H, whether the locations of their best aligned words in the other sentence provides clues. As Figure 1 illustrates, the premise "in this incident, the cop (C) shot (S) the thief (T)" is more likely to entail the hypothesis "$\hat{C} \ldots \hat{S} \ldots \hat{T}$" than "$\hat{T} \ldots \hat{S} \ldots \hat{C}$" where $\hat{X}$ is the word that best matches X.

Our model DEISTE is implemented in convolutional neural architecture (LeCun et al., 1998). Specifically, DEISTE consists of (i) a parameter-dynamic convolution for exploration strategy (a) given above; and (ii) a position-aware attentive convolution for exploration strategies (b) and (c). In experiments, DEISTE outperforms prior top systems by $\approx 5\%$. Perhaps even more interestingly, the pretrained model over SCI-TAIL generalizes well on RTE-5.

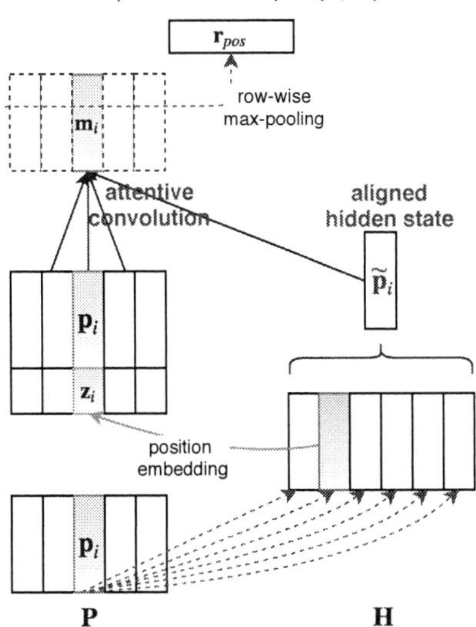

Figure 3: Position-aware attentive convolution in modeling the pair (P, H)

2 Method

To start, a sentence S ($S \in \{P, H\}$) is represented as a sequence of n_s hidden states, e.g., $\mathbf{p}_i, \mathbf{h}_i \in \mathbb{R}^d$ ($i = 1, 2, \ldots, |n_{p/h}|$), forming a feature map $\mathbf{S} \in \mathbb{R}^{d \times |n_s|}$, where d is the dimensionality of hidden states. Figure 2 depicts the basic principle of DEISTE in modeling premise-hypothesis pair (P, H) with feature maps $\mathbf{P}$ and $\mathbf{H}$, respectively.

First, $\mathbf{P}$ and $\mathbf{H}$ have fine-grained interactions $\mathbf{I} \in \mathbb{R}^{n_p \times n_h}$ by comparing any pair of $(\mathbf{p}_i, \mathbf{h}_j)$:

$$\mathbf{I}[i, j] = \mathrm{cosine}(\mathbf{p}_i, \mathbf{h}_j) \tag{1}$$

We now elaborate DEISTE's exploration strategies (a), (b) and (c) of the interaction results $\mathbf{I}$.

2.1 Parameter-dynamic convolution

Intuitively, important words should be expressed more intensively than other words in the learnt representation of a sentence. However, the importance of words within a specific sentence might not depend on the sentence itself. E.g., Yin and Schütze (2017b) found that in question-aware answer sentence selection, words well matched are more important; while in textual entailment, words hardly matched are more important.

In this work, we try to make the semantics of those important words dominate in the output representations of a convolution encoder.

Given a local window of hidden states in the feature map $\mathbf{P}$, e.g., three adjacent ones $\mathbf{p}_{i-1}$, $\mathbf{p}_i$ and $\mathbf{p}_{i+1}$, a conventional convolution learns a higher-level representation $\mathbf{r}$ for this trigram:

$$\mathbf{r} = \tanh(\mathbf{W} \cdot [\mathbf{p}_{i-1}, \mathbf{p}_i, \mathbf{p}_{i+1}] + \mathbf{b}) \qquad (2)$$

where $\mathbf{W} \in \mathbb{R}^{d \times 3d}$ and $\mathbf{b} \in \mathbb{R}^d$.

For simplicity, we neglect the bias term $\mathbf{b}$ and split the multiplication of big matrices – $\mathbf{W} \cdot [\mathbf{p}_{i-1}, \mathbf{p}_i, \mathbf{p}_{i+1}]$ – into three parts, then $\mathbf{r}$ can be formulated as:

$$\begin{aligned}
\mathbf{r} &= \tanh(\mathbf{W}^{-1} \cdot \mathbf{p}_{i-1} \oplus \mathbf{W}^0 \cdot \mathbf{p}_i \oplus \mathbf{W}^{+1} \cdot \mathbf{p}_{i+1}) \\
&= \tanh(\hat{\mathbf{p}}_{i-1} \oplus \hat{\mathbf{p}}_i \oplus \hat{\mathbf{p}}_{i+1})
\end{aligned}$$

where $\oplus$ means element-wise addition; $\mathbf{W}^{-1}$, $\mathbf{W}^0$, $\mathbf{W}^{+1} \in \mathbf{R}^{d \times d}$, and their concatenation equals to the $\mathbf{W}$ in Equation 2; $\hat{\mathbf{p}}_i$ is set to be $\mathbf{W}^0 \cdot \mathbf{p}_i$, so $\hat{\mathbf{p}}_i$ can be seen as the projection of $\mathbf{p}_i$ in a new space by parameters $\mathbf{W}^0$; finally the three projected outputs contribute equally in the addition: $\hat{\mathbf{p}}_{i-1} \oplus \hat{\mathbf{p}}_i \oplus \hat{\mathbf{p}}_{i+1}$.

The convolution encoder shares parameters $[\mathbf{W}^{-1}, \mathbf{W}^0, \mathbf{W}^{+1}]$ in all trigrams, so we cannot expect those parameters to express the importance of $\hat{\mathbf{p}}_{i-1}$, $\hat{\mathbf{p}}_i$ or $\hat{\mathbf{p}}_{i+1}$ in the output representation $\mathbf{r}$. Instead, we formulate the idea as follows:

$$\mathbf{m}_i = \tanh(\alpha_{i-1}\hat{\mathbf{p}}_{i-1} \oplus \alpha_i\hat{\mathbf{p}}_i \oplus \alpha_{i+1}\hat{\mathbf{p}}_{i+1})$$

in which the three scalars α_{i-1}, α_i and α_{i+1} indicate the importance scores of $\hat{\mathbf{p}}_{i-1}$, $\hat{\mathbf{p}}_i$ and $\hat{\mathbf{p}}_{i+1}$ respectively. In our work, we adopt:

$$\alpha_i = \frac{1.0}{1.0 + \max(\mathbf{I}[i, :])} \qquad (3)$$

Since $\alpha_i\hat{\mathbf{p}}_i = \alpha_i\mathbf{W}^0 \cdot \mathbf{p}_i = \mathbf{W}^{0,i} \cdot \mathbf{p}_i$, we notice that the original shared parameter $\mathbf{W}^0$ is mapped to a dynamic parameter $\mathbf{W}^{0,i}$, which is specific to the input $\mathbf{p}_i$. We refer to this as *parameter-dynamic convolution*, which enables our system DEISTE to highlight important words in higher-level representations.

Finally, a max-pooling layer is stacked over $\{\mathbf{m}_i\}$ to get the representation for the pair (P, H), denoted as $\mathbf{r}_{dyn}$.

2.2 Position-aware attentive convolution

Our position-aware attentive convolution, shown in Figure 3, aims to encode the representations as well as the positions of the best word alignments.

Representation. Given the interaction scores in $\mathbf{I}$, the representation $\tilde{\mathbf{p}}_i$ of all soft matches for hidden state $\mathbf{p}_i$ in P is the weighted average of all hidden states in H:

$$\tilde{\mathbf{p}}_i = \sum_j \mathrm{softmax}(\mathbf{I}[i, :])_j \cdot \mathbf{h}_j \qquad (4)$$

methods	dev	test
Majority Class	50.4	60.4
Hypothesis only	66.9	65.1
Premise only	72.6	73.4
NGram model	65.0	70.6
ESIM-600D	70.5	70.6
Decomp-Att	75.4	72.3
DGEM	79.6	77.3
AttentiveConvNet	79.3	78.1
DEISTE	**82.4**	**82.1**
w/o dyn-conv	80.2	79.1
w/o representation	76.3	74.9
w/o position	82.1	81.3

Table 2: DEISTE vs. baselines on SCITAIL

Position. For a trigram $[\mathbf{p}_{i-1}, \mathbf{p}_i, \mathbf{p}_{i+1}]$ in P, knowing where its best-matched words are located in H is helpful in TE, as discussed in Section 1.

For $\mathbf{p}_i$, we first retrieve the index x_i of the best-matched word in H by:

$$x_i = \mathrm{argmax}(\mathbf{I}[i, :]) \qquad (5)$$

then embed the concrete $\{x_i\}$ into randomly-initialized continuous space:

$$\mathbf{z}_i = \mathbf{M}[x_i] \qquad (6)$$

where $\mathbf{M} \in \mathbb{R}^{n_h \times d_m}$; n_h is the length of H; d_m is the dimensionality of position embeddings.

Now, the three positions $[i - 1, i, i + 1]$ in P concatenate vector-wisely original hidden states $[\mathbf{p}_{i-1}, \mathbf{p}_i, \mathbf{p}_{i+1}]$ with position embeddings $[\mathbf{z}_{i-1}, \mathbf{z}_i, \mathbf{z}_{i+1}]$, getting a new sequence of hidden states: $[\mathbf{c}_{i-1}, \mathbf{c}_i, \mathbf{c}_{i+1}]$. As a result, a position i in P has hidden state $\mathbf{c}_i$, left context $\mathbf{c}_{i-1}$, right context $\mathbf{c}_{i+1}$ and the representation of soft-aligned words in H, i.e., $\tilde{\mathbf{p}}_i$. Then a convolution works at position i in P as:

$$\mathbf{n}_i = \tanh(\mathbf{W} \cdot [\mathbf{c}_{i-1}, \mathbf{c}_i, \mathbf{c}_{i+1}, \tilde{\mathbf{p}}_i] + \mathbf{b}) \qquad (7)$$

As Figure 3 shows, the position-aware attentive convolution finally stacks a standard max-pooling layer over $\{\mathbf{n}_i\}$ to get the representation for the pair (P, H), denoted as $\mathbf{r}_{pos}$.

Overall, our DEISTE will generate a representation $\mathbf{r}_{dyn}$ through the parameter-dynamic convolution, and generate a representation $\mathbf{r}_{pos}$ through the position-aware attentive convolution. Finally the concatenation – $[\mathbf{r}_{dyn}, \mathbf{r}_{pos}]$ – is fed to a logistic regression classifier.

methods	acc.
Majority Class	34.3
Premise only	33.5
Hypothesis only	68.7
ESIM	86.7
Decomp-Att	86.8
AttentiveConvNet	86.3
DEISTE$_{\text{SCITAIL}}$	84.7
DEISTE$_{tune}$	87.1
State-of-the-art	88.7

Table 3: DEISTE vs. baselines on SNLI. DEISTE$_{\text{SCITAIL}}$ has exactly the same system layout and hyperparameters as the one reported on SCITAIL in Table 2; DEISTE$_{tune}$: tune hyperparameters on SNLI dev. State-of-the-art refers to (Peters et al., 2018). Ensemble results are not considered.

3 Experiments

Dataset. SCITAIL[3] (Khot et al., 2018) is for textual entailment in binary classification: entailment or neutral. Accuracy is reported.

Training setup. All words are initialized by 300D Word2Vec (Mikolov et al., 2013) embeddings, and are fine-tuned during training. The whole system is trained by AdaGrad (Duchi et al., 2011). Other hyperparameter values include: learning rate 0.01, d_m=50 for position embeddings M, hidden size 300, batch size 50, filter width 3.

Baselines. (i) Decomposable Attention Model (Decomp-Att) (Parikh et al., 2016): Develop attention mechanisms to decompose the problem into subproblems to solve in parallel. (ii) Enhanced LSTM (ESIM) (Chen et al., 2017): Enhance LSTM by encoding syntax and semantics from parsing information. (iii) Ngram Overlap: An overlap baseline, considering unigrams, one-skip bigrams and one-skip trigrams. (iv) DGEM (Khot et al., 2018): A decomposed graph entailment model, the current state-of-the-art. (v) AttentiveConvNet (Yin and Schütze, 2017a): Our top-performing textual entailment system on SNLI dataset, equipped with RNN-style attention mechanism in convolution.[4]

In addition, to check if SCITAIL can be easily resolved by features from only premises or hypotheses (like the problem of SNLI shown by Gururangan et al. (2018)), we put a vanilla CNN (convolution&max-pooling) over merely hypothesis or premise to derive the pair label.

Table 2 presents **results** on SCITAIL. (i) Our model DEISTE has a big improvement ($\sim$ 5%) over DGEM, the best baseline. Interestingly, AttentiveConvNet performs very competitively, surpassing DGEM by 0.8% on test. These two results show the effectiveness of attentive convolution. DEISTE, equipped with a parameter-dynamic convolution and a more advanced position-aware attentive convolution, clearly gets a big plus. (ii) The ablation shows that all three aspects we explore from the inter-sentence interactions contribute; "position" encoding is less important than "dyn-conv" and "representation". Without "representation", the system performs much worse. This is in line with the result of AttentiveConvNet baseline.

To further study the systems and datasets, Table 3 gives performance of DEISTE and baselines on SNLI. We see that DEISTE gets competitive performance on SNLI.

Comparing Tables 2 and 3, the baselines "hypothesis only" and "premise only" show analogous while different phenomena between SCITAIL and SNLI. On one hand, both SNLI and SCITAIL can get a relatively high number by looking at only one of {premise, hypothesis} – "premise only" gets 73.4% accuracy on SCITAIL, even higher than two more complicated baselines (ESIM-600D and Decomp-Att), and "hypothesis only" gets 68.7% accuracy on SNLI which is more than 30% higher than the "majority" and "premise only" baselines. Notice the contrast: SNLI "prefers" hypothesis, SCITAIL "prefers" premise. For SNLI, this is not surprising as the crowd-workers tend to construct the hypotheses in SNLI by some regular rules (Gururangan et al., 2018). The phenomenon in SCITAIL is left to explore in future work.

Error Analysis. Table 4 gives examples of errors. We explain them as follows.

Language conventions: The pair #1 uses dash "–" to indicate a definition sentence for "Front"; The pair #2 has "A (or B)" to denote the equivalence between A and B. This challenge is expected to be handled by rules.

Ambiguity: The pair #3 looks like having a similar challenge with the pair #2. We guess the annotators treat "$\cdots$ a vertebral column or backbone" and "$\cdots$ the backbone (or vertebral column)" as the same convention, which may be debatable.

Complex discourse relation: The premise in

---

[3]Please refer to (Khot et al., 2018) for more details.

[4]https://github.com/yinwenpeng/Attentive_Convolution

#	(Premise P, Hypothesis H) Pair	G/P	Challenge
1	(P) Front – The boundary between two different air masses. (H) In weather terms, the boundary between two air masses is called front.	1/0	language conventions
2	(P) … the notochord forms the backbone (or vertebral column). (H) Backbone is another name for the vertebral column.	1/0	language conventions
3	(P) ⋯ animals with a vertebral column or backbone and animals without one. (H) Backbone is another name for the vertebral column.	1/0	ambiguity
4	(P) Heterotrophs get energy and carbon from living plants or animals (consumers) or from dead organic matter (decomposers). (H) Mushrooms get their energy from decomposing dead organisms.	0/1	discourse relation
5	(P) Ethane is a simple hydrocarbon, a molecule made of two carbon and six hydrogen atoms. (H) Hydrocarbons are made of one carbon and four hydrogen atoms.	0/1	discourse relation
6	(P) … the SI unit… for force is the Newton (N) and is defined as (kg·m/s^{-2}). (H) Newton (N) is the SI unit for weight.	0/1	beyond text

Table 4: Error cases of DEISTE in SCITAIL. "⋯": truncated text. "G/P": gold/predicted label.

	dev	test
Majority baseline	50.0	50.0
State-of-the-art	–	73.5
training data		
SNLI	47.1	46.0
SCITAIL	60.5	60.2

Table 5: Train on different TE datasets, test accuracy on two-way RTE-5. State-of-the-art refers to (Iftene and Moruz, 2009)

the pair #4 has an "or" structure. In the pair #5, "a molecule made of ⋯" defines the concept "Ethane" instead of the "hydrocarbon". Both cases require the model to be able to comprehend the discourse relation.

Knowledge beyond text: The main challenge in the pair #6 is to distinguish between "weight" and "force", which requires more physical knowledge that is beyond the text described here and beyond the expressivity of word embeddings.

Transfer to RTE-5. One main motivation of exploring this SCITAIL problem is that this is an end-task oriented TE task. A natural question thus is how well the trained model can be transferred to other end-task oriented TE tasks. In Table 5, we take the models pretrained on SCITAIL and SNLI and test them on RTE-5. Clearly, the model pretrained on SNLI has not learned anything useful for RTE-5 – its performance of 46.0% is even worse than the majority baseline. The model pretrained on SCITAIL, in contrast, demonstrates much more promising generalization performance: 60.2% vs. 46.0%.

4 Related Work

Learning automatically inter-sentence word-to-word interactions or alignments was first studied in recurrent neural networks (Elman, 1990).

Rocktäschel et al. (2016) employ neural word-to-word attention for SNLI task. Wang and Jiang (2016) propose match-LSTM, an extension of the attention mechanism in (Rocktäschel et al., 2016), by more fine-grained matching and accumulation. Cheng et al. (2016) present a new LSTM equipped with a memory tape. Other work following this attentive matching idea includes Bilateral Multi-Perspective Matching model (Wang et al., 2017), Enhanced LSTM (Chen et al., 2016) etc.

In addition, convolutional neural networks (Le-Cun et al., 1998), equipped with attention mechanisms, also perform competitively in TE. Yin et al. (2016) implement the attention *in pooling phase* so that important hidden states will be pooled with higher probabilities. Yin and Schütze (2017a) further develop the attention idea in CNNs, so that a RNN-style attention mechanism is integrated into the convolution filters. This is similar with our position-aware attentive convolution. We instead explored a way to make use of position information of alignments to do reasoning.

Attention mechanisms in both RNNs and CNNs make use of sentence interactions. Our work achieves a deep exploration of those interactions, in order to guide representation learning in TE.

5 Summary

This work proposed DEISTE to deal with an end-task oriented textual entailment task – SCITAIL. Our model enables a comprehensive utilization of inter-sentence interactions. DEISTE outperforms competitive systems by big margins.

Acknowledgments. We thank all the reviewers for insightful comments. This research is supported in part by DARPA under agreement number FA8750-13-2-0008, and by a gift from Google.

References

Samuel R. Bowman, Gabor Angeli, Christopher Potts, and Christopher D. Manning. 2015. A large annotated corpus for learning natural language inference. In *Proceedings of EMNLP*. pages 632–642.

John Burger and Lisa Ferro. 2005. Generating an entailment corpus from news headlines. In *Proceedings of the ACL Workshop on Empirical Modeling of Semantic Equivalence and Entailment*. pages 49–54.

Qian Chen, Xiaodan Zhu, Zhen-Hua Ling, Si Wei, and Hui Jiang. 2016. Enhancing and combining sequential and tree LSTM for natural language inference. *CoRR* abs/1609.06038.

Qian Chen, Xiaodan Zhu, Zhen-Hua Ling, Si Wei, Hui Jiang, and Diana Inkpen. 2017. Enhanced LSTM for natural language inference. In *Proceedings of ACL*. pages 1657–1668.

Jianpeng Cheng, Li Dong, and Mirella Lapata. 2016. Long short-term memory-networks for machine reading. In *Proceedings of EMNLP*. pages 551–561.

Ido Dagan, Oren Glickman, and Bernardo Magnini. 2006. The PASCAL recognising textual entailment challenge. In *Machine Learning Challenges, Evaluating Predictive Uncertainty, Visual Object Classification and Recognizing Textual Entailment, First PASCAL Machine Learning Challenges Workshop*. pages 177–190.

Ido Dagan, Dan Roth, Mark Sammons, and Fabio Massimo Zanzoto. 2013. *Recognizing Textual Entailment: Models and Applications*. Morgan and Claypool.

John Duchi, Elad Hazan, and Yoram Singer. 2011. Adaptive subgradient methods for online learning and stochastic optimization. *JMLR* 12:2121–2159.

Jeffrey L. Elman. 1990. Finding structure in time. *Cognitive Science* 14(2):179–211.

Suchin Gururangan, Swabha Swayamdipta, Omer Levy, Roy Schwartz, Samuel R. Bowman, and Noah A. Smith. 2018. Annotation artifacts in natural language inference data. In *Proceedings of NAACL*.

Adrian Iftene and Mihai Alex Moruz. 2009. UAIC participation at RTE5. In *Proceedings of TAC*.

Tushar Khot, Ashish Sabharwal, and Peter Clark. 2018. SciTail: A textual entailment dataset from science question answering. In *Proceedings of AAAI*.

Yann LeCun, Léon Bottou, Yoshua Bengio, and Patrick Haffner. 1998. Gradient-based learning applied to document recognition. In *Proceedings of the IEEE*. pages 2278–2324.

Marco Marelli, Stefano Menini, Marco Baroni, Luisa Bentivogli, Raffaella Bernardi, and Roberto Zamparelli. 2014. A SICK cure for the evaluation of compositional distributional semantic models. In *Proceedings of LREC*. pages 216–223.

Tomas Mikolov, Ilya Sutskever, Kai Chen, Greg S Corrado, and Jeff Dean. 2013. Distributed representations of words and phrases and their compositionality. In *Proceedings of NIPS*. pages 3111–3119.

Ankur P. Parikh, Oscar Täckström, Dipanjan Das, and Jakob Uszkoreit. 2016. A decomposable attention model for natural language inference. In *Proceedings of EMNLP*. pages 2249–2255.

Matthew E. Peters, Mark Neumann, Mohit Iyyer, Matt Gardner, Christopher Clark, Kenton Lee, and Luke Zettlemoyer. 2018. Deep contextualized word representations. *CoRR* abs/1802.05365.

Tim Rocktäschel, Edward Grefenstette, Karl Moritz Hermann, Tomáš Kočiský, and Phil Blunsom. 2016. Reasoning about entailment with neural attention. In *Proceedings of ICLR*.

Shuohang Wang and Jing Jiang. 2016. Learning natural language inference with LSTM. In *Proceedings of NAACL*. pages 1442–1451.

Zhiguo Wang, Wael Hamza, and Radu Florian. 2017. Bilateral multi-perspective matching for natural language sentences. In *Proceedings of IJCAI*. pages 4144–4150.

Wenpeng Yin and Hinrich Schütze. 2017a. Attentive convolution. *CoRR* abs/1710.00519.

Wenpeng Yin and Hinrich Schütze. 2017b. Task-specific attentive pooling of phrase alignments contributes to sentence matching. In *Proceedings of EACL*. pages 699–709.

Wenpeng Yin, Hinrich Schütze, Bing Xiang, and Bowen Zhou. 2016. ABCNN: attention-based convolutional neural network for modeling sentence pairs. *TACL* 4:259–272.

Sense-Aware Neural Models for Pun Location in Texts

Yitao Cai and **Yin Li** and **Xiaojun Wan**
Institute of Computer Science and Technology, Peking University
The MOE Key Laboratory of Computational Linguistics, Peking University
{caiyitao,xyz1305121,wanxiaojun}@pku.edu.cn

Abstract

A homographic pun is a form of wordplay in which one signifier (usually a word) suggests two or more meanings by exploiting polysemy for an intended humorous or rhetorical effect. In this paper, we focus on the task of pun location, which aims to identify the pun word in a given short text. We propose a sense-aware neural model to address this challenging task. Our model first obtains several WSD results for the text, and then leverages a bidirectional LSTM network to model each sequence of word senses. The outputs at each time step for different LSTM networks are then concatenated for prediction. Evaluation results on the benchmark SemEval 2017 dataset demonstrate the efficacy of our proposed model.

1 Introduction

There exists a class of language constructs known as puns in natural language utterances and texts, and the speaker or writer intends for a certain word or other lexical item to be interpreted as simultaneously carrying two or more separate meanings. Though puns are an important feature in many discourse types, they have attracted relatively little attention in the area of natural language processing.

A pun is a form of wordplay in which a word suggests two or more meanings by exploiting polysemy, homonymy, or phonological similarity to another word, for an intended humorous or rhetorical effect (Miller et al., 2017). Puns where the two meanings share the same pronunciation are known as homographic puns, which are the focus of this study. For example, the following punning joke exploits contrasting meanings of the word "interest" and it is a homographic pun.

I used to be a banker but I lost interest.

Since the pun word plays the key role in forming a pun, it is very important and meaningful to identify the pun word in a given text. The task of identifying the pun word is known as pun location, which is defined in SemEval 2017 Task 7[1]. In order to address this special task, various approaches have been attempted, including rule based approach (Vechtomova, 2017), knowledge-based approach (Indurthi and Oota, 2017; Xiu et al., 2017) and supervised approach (Pramanick and Das, 2017; Mikhalkova and Karyakin, 2017). However, these approaches do not achieve good results, and the best F1 score for homographic pun location is just 0.6631, which is achieved by the Idiom Savant system with a knowledge based approach (Doogan et al., 2017). The results demonstrate that pun location is a very challenging task.

In order to address this challenging task and improve the state-of-the-art results, we propose a sense-aware neural model in this study. Our model first obtains several WSD (Word Sense Disambiguation) results for the text, and leverages a bidirectional LSTM network to model each sequence of word senses. The outputs at each time step for different LSTM networks are then concatenated for pun word prediction. Evaluation results of cross-validation on the benchmark SemEval 2017 dataset demonstrate the efficacy of our proposed model.

The contributions of this paper are summarized as follows:

- We propose a novel sense-aware neural model to address the pun location task.

- Our proposed model outperforms several baseline neural models and achieves the state-of-the-art performance.

---

[1]http://alt.qcri.org/semeval2017/task7/

Proceedings of the 56th Annual Meeting of the Association for Computational Linguistics (Short Papers), pages 546–551
Melbourne, Australia, July 15 - 20, 2018. ©2018 Association for Computational Linguistics

2   Related Work

Pun detection aims to determine whether a given short text contains a pun (Miller et al., 2017). Various methods have been proposed to address this task, including WSD based methods (Pedersen, 2017), PMI-based methods (Sevgili et al., 2017) supervised methods (Xiu et al., 2017; Indurthi and Oota, 2017; Pramanick and Das, 2017; Mikhalkova and Karyakin, 2017; Vadehra, 2017). More specifically, the bi-directional RNN has been used in (Indurthi and Oota, 2017), and vote-based ensemble classifier is used by (Vadehra, 2017).

Pun location is a more challenging task than pun detection, because it aims to find the actual pun word in the given text. Previous works find some clues about puns in the texts. For example, pun is more likely appeared towards the end of sentences (Pedersen, 2017; Miller and Turković, 2016). Many puns have a particularly strong associations with other words in the contexts (Sevgili et al., 2017). A variety of methods have been proposed to locate the pun words. For example, UWaterloo system constructs a rule-based pun locator that scores candidate words according to eleven simple heuristics (Vechtomova, 2017). BuzzSaw system attempts to locate the pun in a sentence by selecting the polysemous word with the two most dissimilar senses (Oele and Evang, 2017). Duluth system identifies the last word which changed senses between different word sense disambiguation results (Pedersen, 2017). Fermi system uses Bi-directional RNN to learn a classification model (Indurthi and Oota, 2017). Idiom Savant system uses n-grams features, and only content words including nouns, verbs, adverbs and adjectives are considered as candidate words (Doogan et al., 2017). Pun interpretation is considered a subsequent step for pun location, and it aims to annotate the two meanings of the given pun by reference to WordNet sense keys. In the work of (Miller and Gurevych, 2015), traditional language-agnostic WSD approaches are adapted to "disambiguate" puns, and rather to identify their double meanings.

Word Sense Disambiguation (WSD) is also related to our work. Some prior works compute overlaps of glosses between the target word and its context (Lesk, 1986). These approaches derive information from some lexicon thesauruses for WSD, including WordNet (Fellbaum, 1998) and BabelNet (Navigli and Ponzetto, 2012). Supervised models, including neural models, have been successfully applied to WSD (Yuan et al., 2016; Raganato et al., 2017).

3   Baseline Neural Model (BM)

The task of pun location needs to locate the exact pun word in each short text or sentence. We regard pun location as a word-level classification task, and attempt to train a model that can predict whether a word in a sentence is a pun or not. A word will be regarded as a pun word with high probability when it is a noun, verb, adjective or adverb, therefore, we only try to make prediction of one word when it has one of the four kinds of parts of speech tags.

Our baseline model for pun word prediction is similar to (Indurthi and Oota, 2017) and it adopts a bi-directional LSTM network to accomplish this task. The neural network architecture of the model is shown in Figure 1. The input to the network is the embeddings of words, and we use the pre-trained word embeddings by using word2vec (Mikolov et al., 2013) on the Wikipedia corpus whose size is over 11G. The hidden state of the forward LSTM and the hidden state of the backward LSTM are concatenated at each time step (word), and we get the concatenated hidden vectors for all words: $h_1, ..., h_n$. The vector h_i for each word having one of the four kinds of POS tags is then sent to a two-layer feed-forward neural network with $tanh$ as activation function, and the output is a real number o_i. We then use the sigmoid function σ on o_i to make prediction. Since in the experimental data there is only one pun word in each sentence, we will take the k-th word as pun word if and only if o_k is the largest number out of all $o_i, i = 1, ..., n$, and $\sigma(o_k) > 0.5$. We use the cross-entropy loss in this model.

4   Sense-Aware Neural Model (SAM)

The baseline neural model is built on the word level and the word senses can only be implicitly captured by the model. Moreover, a pun word usually has two senses in the sentence, while the baseline neural model cannot disambiguate them. In order to improve the prediction performance, we propose a sense-award neural model which is built on WSD results. Two or more WSD results are obtained by using different WSD algorithms or different configurations, and the WSD results may be different. The sequence of word senses corresponding to each WSD result is modeled by a

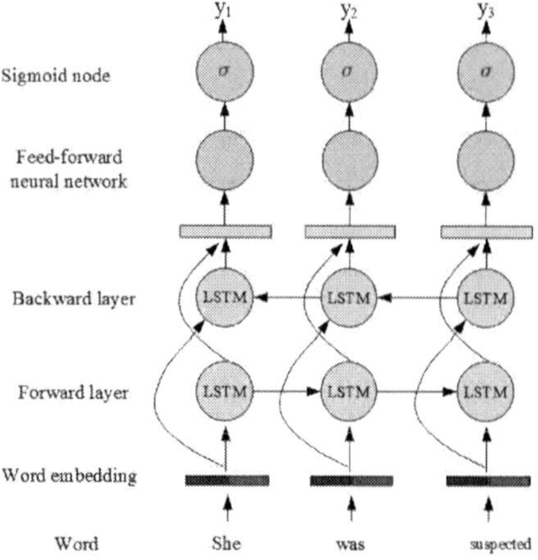

Figure 1: Baseline neural model with bidirectional LSTMs

bi-directional LSTM network and the outputs of different LSTM networks are then concatenated for prediction. In this way, the different senses of words can be well captured by our model.

Different from the Duluth system (Pedersen, 2017) which identifies the last word which changed senses between different runs of the WordNet::SenseRelate::AllWords disambiguation algorithm, we do not use the WordNet-based WSD results. Furthermore, we do not heuristically identify the pun word but propose a neural model to achieve this goal.

4.1 Word Sense Disambiguation and Sense Embedding

In order to obtain sense inventory and the sense embeddings for each word, we choose SenseGram (Pelevina et al., 2016). The SenseGram toolkit is available online[2], and it can take as an input the word embeddings and split different senses of the input words. For instance, the vector for the word "table" will be split into "table (data)" and "table (furniture)". SenseGram induces sense inventory from existing word embeddings via clustering of ego-networks of related words. In our work, the Wikipedia corpus is used to train word embeddings (together with contextual embeddings of words) by using word2vec and then the word embeddings are used by SenseGram for inducing sense inventory and sense embeddings. The word similarity graph used by SenseGram is built based on the similarity between word embeddings. Note

---

[2]https://github.com/tudarmstadt-lt/sensegram

that we do not use WordNet as sense inventory because the sense inventory is too fine-grained and many words are not included in WordNet.

Given each target word ω and its context words $C = \{c_1, ..., c_k\}$ in the sentence, we want to assign a sense vector to ω from the set of its sense vectors $S = \{s_1, ..., s_m\}$. We use two simple WSD methods for achieving this. The first WSD strategy is based on the sigmoid function. $\bar{c}_c$ is the mean of the contextual embeddings of words in C and the sense embedding of ω is chosen as

$$s^* = \arg\max_{s_i \in S} \frac{1}{1 + e^{-\bar{c}_c \cdot s_i}} \tag{1}$$

Let $\bar{c}_w$ be the mean of the word embeddings of words in C, which is different from $\bar{c}_c$. The second disambiguation strategy is based on the cosine similarity function.

$$s^* = \arg\max_{s_i \in S} \frac{\bar{c}_w \cdot s_i}{\|\bar{c}_w\| \cdot \|s_i\|} \tag{2}$$

For each WSD strategy, we can set different window sizes of 3 and 50 (the maximum sentence length in the corpus) as different configurations. By obtaining different WSD results, we expect to well capture the characteristics of homographic puns.

4.2 Neural Model Details

The proposed sense-aware neural model differs from the baseline neural model in that it models multiple sequences of word senses corresponding to different WSD results. In other words, the sense-aware model works on the sense level, but the baseline model works on the word level.

The architecture of the sense-aware model is illustrated in Figure 2, which contains several bi-directional LSTM networks. For each WSD result, the sequence of sense embeddings is taken as input for a bi-directional LSTM network. Assuming we have K WSD results, the outputs $h_i^j (j = 1, ..., K)$ by K different bi-directional LSTM networks for the same i-th word (i.e., the i-th time step) are then concatenated into one vector, and the vector is sent to a two-layer feed-forward neural network and a sigmoid function for prediction. The loss function is the same as that of the baseline model. Our sense-aware model can be considered as applying the baseline model on different WSD results and then combining the outputs for prediction.

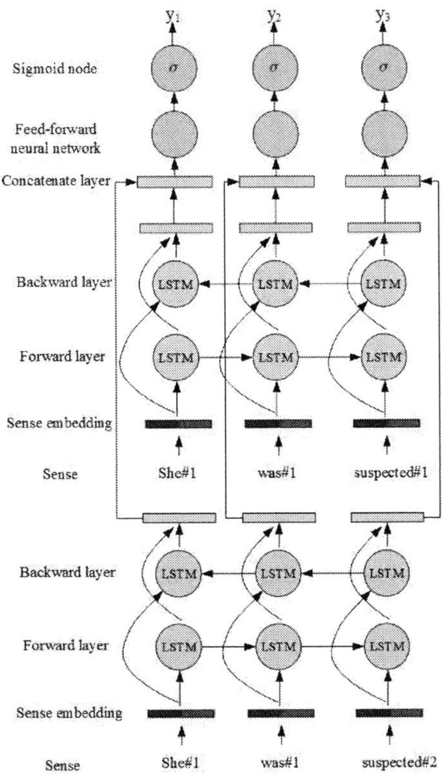

Figure 2: Sense-aware neural model with bidirectional LSTMs

4.3 Model Training

We use stochastic gradient descent to train the neural models with a batch size of 225 and 512 hidden units, and the learning rate is 0.0001 and the size of embeddings and hidden vectors is 300.

5 Experiments

5.1 Dataset

We use the benchmark dataset from SemEval 2017 Task 7. There are a total of 2250 sentences in the dataset, 1607 of which contain a pun. For Pun Location, we only use sentences with pun words for evaluation, the same as the task setting. Since no training data is provided, so we test our models with 10-fold cross validation. We combine the output results on each test set of all 10 folds and then calculate precision, recall and F-score on the combined set. Thus the scores are comparable to the official results based on the whole test set.

5.2 Word Sense Disambiguation

As is mentioned in section 4.1, we can obtain four WSD results with two different strategies and two different window sizes. We make three groups based on four WSD results: Group 1 (G1) contains two WSD results with the first WSD strategy with two window sizes of 3 and 50; Group 2 (G2) contains two WSD results with the second WSD strategy with two window sizes; Group 3 (G3) contains all results in Group 1 and Group 2.

5.3 Evaluation Results

We compared our proposed SAM model (w/ three groups of WSD results) with the baseline model BM. We also apply the bi-directional LSTM model on the sequence of senses for each single WSD result and thus get BiLSTM-WSD1 through BiLSTM-WSD4. Moreover, we apply SVM and CRF models with various features (e.g., ngram, POS tagging, word location, word similarity, etc.) on this task.

Table 1 shows the results. In the table, we also present the results of the best participating system Idiom Savant, and two official baselines (last word and max. polysemy). We can see that the baseline BM model does not perform well, while the CRF model performs very well. The results of BiLSTM-WSD1 through BiLSTM-WSD4 are much better than the BM model, which indicates that the sense-level prediction is more suitable than the word-level prediction. Our proposed SAM model with different groups of WSD results can further improve the performance, because different WSD results may provide complementary information for pun location. The SAM model with G1 performs the best, even outperforming the SAM model with more WSD results (G3), which indicates the necessity for choosing proper WSD results.

6 Conclusion

In this work, we apply the neural network models to the pun location task. We proposed a novel sense-aware neural model to leveraging multiple WSD results. Evaluation results on the benchmark SemEval 2017 dataset demonstrate the efficacy of our proposed model. In future work, we will test with more advanced WSD algorithms and try to address the pun interpretation task.

Method	Precision	Recall	F-Score
SVM	0.717	0.717	0.717
CRF	0.759	**0.759**	0.759
BM	0.751	0.617	0.677
BiLSTM-WSD1	0.751	0.742	0.746
BiLSTM-WSD2	0.754	0.745	0.750
BiLSTM-WSD3	0.735	0.726	0.730
BiLSTM-WSD4	0.742	0.732	0.737
SAM-G1	0.815	0.747	**0.780**
SAM-G2	**0.828**	0.731	0.776
SAM-G3	0.804	0.745	0.773
Idiom Savant	0.664	0.663	0.663
last word	0.470	0.470	0.470
max. polysemy	0.180	0.180	0.180

Table 1: Comparison results.

Acknowledgment

This work was supported by National Natural Science Foundation of China (61772036, 61331011) and Key Laboratory of Science, Technology and Standard in Press Industry (Key Laboratory of Intelligent Press Media Technology). We thank the anonymous reviewers for their helpful comments. Xiaojun Wan is the corresponding author.

References

Samuel Doogan, Aniruddha Ghosh, Hanyang Chen, and Tony Veale. 2017. Idiom savant at semeval-2017 task 7: Detection and interpretation of english puns. In *Proceedings of the 11th International Workshop on Semantic Evaluation (SemEval-2017)*, pages 103–108.

Christiane Fellbaum. 1998. *WordNet: An Electronic Lexical Database.* Cambridge, MA: MIT Press, Cambridge, UK.

Vijayasaradhi Indurthi and Subba Reddy Oota. 2017. Fermi at semeval-2017 task 7: Detection and interpretation of homographic puns in english language. In *Proceedings of the 11th International Workshop on Semantic Evaluation (SemEval-2017)*, pages 457–460.

Michael Lesk. 1986. Automatic sense disambiguation using machine readable dictionaries:how to tell a pine cone from an ice cream cone. In *Acm Special Interest Group for Design of Communication*, pages 24–26.

Elena Mikhalkova and Yuri Karyakin. 2017. Punfields at semeval-2017 task 7: Employing roget's thesaurus in automatic pun recognition and interpretation. *arXiv preprint arXiv:1707.05479*.

Tomas Mikolov, Kai Chen, Greg Corrado, and Jeffrey Dean. 2013. Efficient estimation of word representations in vector space. *Computer Science*.

Tristan Miller and Iryna Gurevych. 2015. Automatic disambiguation of english puns. In *Proceedings of the 53rd Annual Meeting of the Association for Computational Linguistics and the 7th International Joint Conference on Natural Language Processing (Volume 1: Long Papers)*, volume 1, pages 719–729.

Tristan Miller, Christian Hempelmann, and Iryna Gurevych. 2017. Semeval-2017 task 7: Detection and interpretation of english puns. In *Proceedings of the 11th International Workshop on Semantic Evaluation (SemEval-2017)*, pages 58–68.

Tristan Miller and Mladen Turković. 2016. Towards the automatic detection and identification of english puns. *The European Journal of Humour Research*, 4(1):59–75.

Roberto Navigli and Simone Paolo Ponzetto. 2012. Babelnet: The automatic construction, evaluation and application of a wide-coverage multilingual semantic network. *Artificial Intelligence*, 193(6):217–250.

Dieke Oele and Kilian Evang. 2017. Buzzsaw at semeval-2017 task 7: Global vs. local context for interpreting and locating homographic english puns with sense embeddings. In *Proceedings of the 11th International Workshop on Semantic Evaluation (SemEval-2017)*, pages 444–448.

Ted Pedersen. 2017. Duluth at semeval-2017 task 7 : Puns upon a midnight dreary, lexical semantics for the weak and weary. *CoRR*, abs/1704.08388.

Maria Pelevina, Nikolay Arefiev, Chris Biemann, and Alexander Panchenko. 2016. Making sense of word embeddings. In *The Workshop on Representation Learning for Nlp*, pages 174–183.

Aniket Pramanick and Dipankar Das. 2017. Ju-cse-nlp at semeval 2017 task 7: Employing rules to detect and interpret english puns. In *Proceedings of the 11th International Workshop on Semantic Evaluation (SemEval-2017)*, pages 432–435.

Alessandro Raganato, Claudio Delli Bovi, and Roberto Navigli. 2017. Neural sequence learning models for word sense disambiguation. In *Proceedings of the 2017 Conference on Empirical Methods in Natural Language Processing*, pages 1156–1167.

Özge Sevgili, Nima Ghotbi, and Selma Tekir. 2017. N-hance at semeval-2017 task 7: A computational approach using word association for puns. In *Proceedings of the 11th International Workshop on Semantic Evaluation (SemEval-2017)*, pages 436–439.

Ankit Vadehra. 2017. Uwav at semeval-2017 task 7: Automated feature-based system for locating puns. In *Proceedings of the 11th International Workshop on Semantic Evaluation (SemEval-2017)*, pages 449–452.

Olga Vechtomova. 2017. Uwaterloo at semeval-2017 task 7: Locating the pun using syntactic characteristics and corpus-based metrics. In *Proceedings of the 11th International Workshop on Semantic Evaluation (SemEval-2017)*, pages 421–425.

Yuhuan Xiu, Man Lan, and Yuanbin Wu. 2017. Ecnu at semeval-2017 task 7: Using supervised and unsupervised methods to detect and locate english puns. In *Proceedings of the 11th International Workshop on Semantic Evaluation (SemEval-2017)*, pages 453–456.

Dayu Yuan, Julian Richardson, Ryan Doherty, Colin Evans, and Eric Altendorf. 2016. Semi-supervised word sense disambiguation with neural models. *arXiv preprint arXiv:1603.07012.*

A Rank-Based Similarity Metric for Word Embeddings

Enrico Santus[1], Hongmin Wang[2], Emmanuele Chersoni[3] and **Yue Zhang[4]**

`esantus@mit.edu`
`hongmin_wang@cs.ucsb.edu`
`emmanuelechersoni@gmail.com`
`yue_zhang@sutd.edu.sg`

[1] Computer Science and Artificial Intelligence Lab, MIT
[2] Department of Computer Science, University of California Santa Barbara
[3] Aix-Marseille University
[4] ISTD, Singapore University of Technology and Design

Abstract

Word Embeddings (WE) have recently imposed themselves as a standard for representing word meaning in NLP. Semantic similarity between word pairs has become the most common evaluation benchmark for these representations, with vector cosine being typically used as the only similarity metric. In this paper, we report experiments with a *rank-based* metric for WE, which performs comparably to vector cosine in *similarity estimation* and outperforms it in the recently-introduced and challenging task of *outlier detection*, thus suggesting that rank-based measures can improve clustering quality.[1]

1 Introduction

> "All happy families resemble one another, but
> each unhappy family is unhappy in its own way."
> *Anna Karenina*, Leo Tolstoy

Distributional Semantic Models (DSMs) have received an increasing attention in the NLP community, as they constitute an efficient data-driven method for creating word representations and measuring their semantic similarity by computing their distance in the vector space (Turney and Pantel, 2010).

The most popular similarity metric in DSMs is the vector cosine. Compared to Euclidean distances, vector cosine scores are normalized on each dimension and hence are robust to the scaling effect. On the other hand, one limitation of this metric is that it regards each dimension equally, without taking into account the fact that some dimensions might be more relevant for characterizing the semantic content of a word. Such a limitation led to the introduction of alternative metrics based on feature ranking, which have been reported to outperform vector cosine in several similarity tasks (Santus et al., 2016a,b).

Recently, the focus of the research on word representations has been shifting onto the so-called *word embeddings* (WE), which are dense vectors obtained by means of neural network training that achieved significant improvements in several similarity-related tasks (Mikolov et al., 2013a; Baroni et al., 2014). Although the representation type of the embeddings was helpful for reducing the sparsity of traditional count vectors, their nature does not sensibly differ (Levy et al., 2015). Most research works involving WE still adopt vector cosine for similarity estimation, yet little experimentation has been done on alternative metrics for comparing dense representations (exceptions include Camacho-Collados et al. (2015)).

Some attempts to directly transfer rank-based measures from traditional DSMs to WE have faced difficulties (see, for example, Jebbara et al. (2018)). In this paper, we suggest a possible solution to this problem by adapting $APSyn$, a rank-based similarity metric originally proposed for sparse vectors (Santus et al., 2016b,a), to low-dimensional word embeddings. This goal is achieved by removing the parameter N (the extent of the feature overlap to be taken into account) and adding a smoothing parameter that is proven to be constant under multiple settings, therefore making the measure unsupervised.

Our experiments show performance improvements both in *similarity estimation* and in the more challenging *outlier detection* task (Camacho-Collados and Navigli, 2016), which consists in cluster and outlier identification.[2]

---

[1] Enrico Santus and Hongmin Wang equally contributed to this work, which was started while they were both affiliated to the Singapore University of Technology and Design.

[2] Code and vectors used for the experiments are available at https://github.com/esantus/Outlier_Detection.

Proceedings of the 56th Annual Meeting of the Association for Computational Linguistics (Short Papers), pages 552–557
Melbourne, Australia, July 15 - 20, 2018. ©2018 Association for Computational Linguistics

2 Similarity, Relatedness and Dissimilarity: Current Issues in the Evaluation of DSMs

A classical benchmark for DSMs is represented by the estimation of word similarity: evaluation datasets are built by asking human subjects to rate the degree of semantic similarity of word pairs, and the performance is assessed in terms of the correlation between the average scores assigned to the pairs by the subjects and the cosines of the corresponding vectors (*similarity estimation* task).

Similarity as modeled by DSMs has been under debate, as its definition is underspecified. It in fact includes an ambiguity with the more generic notion of *semantic relatedness*, which is present also in many popular datasets (i.e. the concepts of *coffee* and *cup* are certainly related, but there is very little similarity about them), as opposed to 'genuine' *semantic similarity* (i.e. the relation holding between concepts such as *coffee* and *tea*) (Agirre et al., 2009; Hill et al., 2015; Gladkova and Drozd, 2016). Therefore, when testing a DSM, it is important to pay attention to what type of semantic relation is actually modeled by the evaluation dataset. Moreover, researchers pointed out that similarity estimation alone does not constitute a strong benchmark, as the inter-annotator agreement is relatively low in all datasets and the performance of several automated systems is already above the upper bound (Batchkarov et al., 2016). As a consequence, workshops such as RepEval have been organized with the explicit purpose of finding alternative evaluation tasks for DSMs.

A recent proposal is the challenging *outlier detection* task (Camacho-Collados and Navigli, 2016; Blair et al., 2016), which consists in the recognition of *cluster membership*, as well as of a relative degree of *semantic dissimilarity*. The task is described as follows: given a group of words, identify the outlier, namely the word that does not belong to the group (i.e. the one that is less similar to the others). On top of its potential applications (e.g. ontology learning), detecting outliers in clusters is a goal that poses a more strict quality requirement on the distributional representations compared to tests based simply on pairwise comparisons, as it is required that similar words group into semantically meaningful clusters. Clearly, the task involves the identification of discriminative semantic dimensions, which could set the cluster members apart from non-members. Outliers are not necessarily unrelated to the other words: rather, they have a lower degree of similarity with respect to some prominent property of the cluster (e.g. the case of *Los Angeles Lakers* as an outlier in a cluster of *football teams*). In our view, a similarity metric has to exploit such discriminative dimensions to form cohesive clusters.

3 A Rank-Based Metric for Embeddings

We use cosine as a baseline and we test an adaptation of a rank-based measure to the dense features of the word embeddings.

Vector cosine computes the correlation between all the vector dimensions, independently of their relevance for a given word pair or for a semantic cluster, and this could be a limitation for discerning different degrees of dissimilarity. The alternative rank-based measure is based on the hypothesis that similarity consists of sharing many relevant features, whereas dissimilarity can be described as either the non-sharing of relevant features or the sharing of non-relevant features (Santus et al., 2014, 2016b).

This hypothesis could turn out to be very helpful for a task like the outlier detection, where prominent features might be the key to improve clustering quality: semantic dimensions that are shared by many of the cluster elements should be weighted more, as they are likely to be useful for setting the outliers apart. In fact, a cohesive cluster should be mostly characterized by the same 'salient' dimensions, and thus, basing word comparisons on such dimensions should lead to more reliable estimates of cluster membership.

In our contribution, we propose to adapt $APSyn$, a metric originally proposed by Santus et al. (2016a,b), to dense word embeddings representations.[3] $APSyn$ was shown to perform well on both synonymy detection and similarity estimation tasks, and it was recently adapted to achieve state-of-the-art results in thematic fit estimation (Santus et al., 2017). The original $APSyn$ formula is shown in equation 1.

$$APSyn(w_x, w_y) = \sum_{i=0}^{i=N} \frac{1}{AVG(r_{s_x}(f_i), r_{s_{s_y}}(f_i))} \quad (1)$$

For every feature f_i in the intersection between the top N features of two vectors w_x and w_y, we

---

[3]The number of dimensions in word embeddings is in the scale of hundreds, and thus the dimensionality is way lower than in the original DSMs used by Santus and colleagues.

add the inverse of the average rank of such feature, $r_{s_x}(f_x)$ and $r_{s_y}(f_y)$, in the two decreasingly value-sorted vectors s_x and s_y (in traditional vectors, often the parameter $N \geq 1000$, but in WE $N = |f|$). $APSyn$ scores low if the features of the two vectors are inversely ranked and high if they are similarly ranked.

$APSyn$ maps the average feature ranks to a non-linear function, emphasizing the contribution of top-ranked features. Its direct application to dense embeddings would shrink too much the contribution of lower ranks (see Figure 1), with the score mostly affected by the top ~ 25 features. While this is reasonable for the traditional vectors derived from co-occurrence counts, where thousands of smaller contributions can still affect the final score, dense vectors need a smoother curve. While preserving the idea of the non-linear weight allocation across the average feature ranks during the summation, we modify the original $APSyn$ formula by taking the exponential of the feature ranks to a power of a constant value ranging between 0 and 1 (excluded), as shown in equation 2, such that now the number of ranks contributing to the final score is widen to all features (see the smoother curve of $APSynPower$ in Figure 1). We name this variant $APSynPower$ or, shortly, $APSynP$.

$$APSynP(w_x, w_y) = \sum_{i=0}^{i=|f|} \frac{1}{AVG(r_{s_x}(f_i)^p, r_{s_y}(f_i)^p)} \tag{2}$$

The power p added to $APSynP$ formula is a trainable parameter. We trained it on the similarity subset of WordSim dataset, obtaining the optimal value of $p = 0.1$, which has been successfully used in all evaluations, under all settings (i.e. embedding types and training corpora). Such regularity allows us to consider $p = 0.1$ as a constant, therefore dropping p. Since in WE we can drop also the parameter N by defining $N = |f|$, $APSynP$ can be not parametrized at all.

4 Evaluation Settings

4.1 Embeddings

For our experiments, we used two popular word embeddings architectures: the Skip-Gram with negative sampling (Mikolov et al., 2013a,b) and the GloVe vectors (Pennington et al., 2014) (standard hyperparameter settings: 300 dimensions,

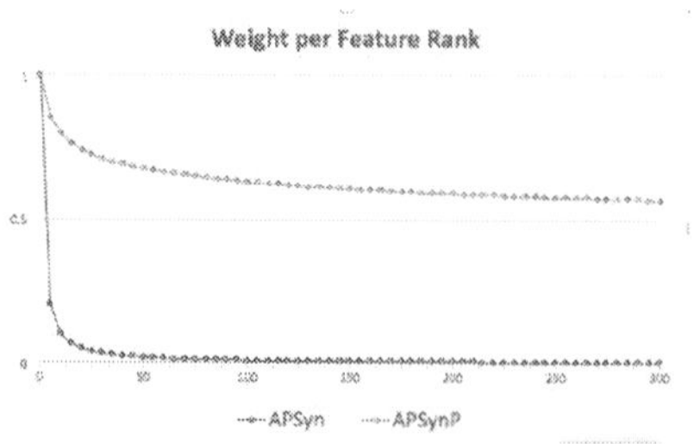

Figure 1: Comparison of weight per feature rank in $APSyn$ and $APSynP$ ($p = 0.1$) across feature ranks ranging from 1 to 300.

context size of 10 and negative sampling).[4]

For comparison with Camacho-Collados and Navigli (2016) on outlier detection, we used the same training corpora: the UMBC (Han et al., 2013) and the English Wikipedia.[5]

4.2 Datasets

As for the similarity estimation task, we evaluate the Spearman correlation between system-generated scores and human judgments. We used three popular benchmark datasets: WordSim-353 (Finkelstein et al., 2001), MEN (Bruni et al., 2014) and SimLex-999 (Hill et al., 2015). It is important to point out that SimLex-999 is the only one specifically built for targeting genuine semantic similarity, while the others tend to mix similarity and relatedness scores.

As for outlier detection, we evaluate our DSMs on the 8-8-8 dataset (Camacho-Collados and Navigli, 2016). The dataset consists of eight clusters, each one with a different topic and consisting in turn of eight lexical items belonging to the cluster and eight outliers (with four degrees of relatedness to the cluster members: C1, C2, C3, C4). In total, the dataset includes 64 sets of 8 words + 1 outlier for the evaluation. For each word w of a cluster W of n words, the authors defined a compactness score $c(w)$ corresponding to the average of all pairwise similarities of the words in $W \setminus \{w\}$. On the basis of the compactness score, they proposed two evaluation metrics: Outlier Position (OP) and Outlier Detection (OD). Given a set W of $n + 1$ words, OP is the rank of the outlier $w_n + 1$ according to the compactness score. Ideally, the rank of the outlier should be n, mean-

---

[4]We also performed experiments with CBOW embeddings (Mikolov et al., 2013b), but results were irregular and inconsistent. We leave therefore their analysis to future work.

[5]Dump of Nov. 2014, approx. 1.7 billion words.

	Skip-Gram			GloVe		
	WordSim-353	MEN	Simlex-999	WordSim-353	MEN	Simlex-999
$Cosine$	**0.736**	**0.758**	0.364	0.511	0.640	0.311
$APSyn$	0.599	0.643	0.343	0.356	0.393	0.174
$APSynP$	0.710	0.737	**0.369**	**0.607**	**0.670**	**0.335**

Table 1: Similarity Estimation, Spearman Correlation by Setting. Embeddings trained on Wikipedia.

	Skip-Gram				GloVe			
	UMBC		Wiki		UMBC		Wiki	
	OPP	Acc.	OPP	Acc.	OPP	Acc.	OPP	Acc.
$CC - Cos$	92.6	64.1	93.8	70.3	81.6	40.6	91.8	56.3
Pairwise								
$APSyn$	93.0	67.2	94.0	68.8	78.7	40.6	89.3	53.1
$APSynP$	**94.0**	**68.8**	**94.5**	**73.4**	**81.8**	**42.2**	**92.8**	**61.0**
Prototype								
$PT - Cos$	93.4	65.6	93.8	68.8	80.3	40.6	90.6	54.7
$APSyn$	92.6	70.3	91.0	62.5	81.6	40.6	88.7	54.7
$APSynP$	**94.0**	**70.3**	**94.9**	**73.4**	**82.2**	**43.8**	**92.0**	**60.9**

Table 2: Outlier Detection, Performance by Setting. *CC-Cos* refers to Camacho-Collados and Navigli (2016)'s pairwise method, while *PT-Cos* refers to the prototype-based one. In bold, best scores per method; in bold and underlined, best scores per corpus-embedding combination.

ing that it has the lowest average similarity with the other cluster elements. The second metric, Outlier Detection (OD), is indeed defined as 1 iff $OP(w_n + 1) = n$, 0 otherwise. Finally, the performance on a dataset composed of $|D|$ sets of words was estimated in terms of *Outlier Position Percentage* (OPP, Eq. 3) and *Accuracy* (Eq. 4):

$$OPP = \frac{\sum_{W \in D} \frac{OP(W)}{|W|-1}}{D} \times 100 \qquad (3)$$

$$Accuracy = \frac{\sum_{W \in D} OD(W)}{D} \times 100 \qquad (4)$$

4.3 Pairwise and Prototype Approaches to Outlier Detection

While for the similarity task scores are always calculated pairwise, for spotting the outlier two different methods were tested: the *pairwise comparisons* and the *cluster prototype*.

In the first case, we reimplemented the method of Camacho-Collados and Navigli (2016): (i) compute the average similarity score of each word with the other words in the cluster; (ii) pick as the outlier the word with the lowest average score. An alternative consists in creating a cluster prototype: (i) for a cluster of N words, we create N prototype vectors by excluding each time one of the words and averaging the vectors of the other ones; (ii) we pick as the outlier the word with the lowest

similarity score with the prototype built out of the vectors of the other words in the cluster.

5 Results and Discussion

Table 1 summarizes the correlations for the similarity task. $APSynP$ outperforms both vector cosine and $APSyn$ in all the datasets described in 4.2 when GloVe embeddings are used. The advantage is statistically significant over the cosine on the MEN dataset ($p < 0.05$) and over $APSyn$ on all datasets ($p < 0.01$).[6] With Skip-Gram embeddings, $APSynP$ performs comparably to vector cosine for relatedness, dominant in WordSim and MEN, while retaining a significant advantage over $APSyn$ on the same datasets ($p < 0.05$). It also performs slightly better than cosine in SimLex-999, and this complies with previous findings of Santus et al. (2016a), who showed that $APSyn$ performs better on genuine similarity datasets. Apparently, the top-ranked vector dimensions (those contributing more to APSyn scores) are more often shared by similar words, than by simply related ones.

Table 2 shows the results for the outlier detection task. The line *CC-Cos* contains the scores by Camacho-Collados and Navigli (2016) as a baseline. The models are divided into *pairwise comparison* and *cluster prototype* (see Section 4.3).

As it can be easily noticed by looking at the bold

---

[6]p-values computed with Fisher's r-to-z transformation.

line, $APSynP$ outperforms the baselines in all settings for both Skip-Gram and GloVe, obtaining higher accuracies and OPPs. Not only $APSynP$ is better at identifying the outlier, but when it is not able to do so, its error is minimum (e.g. the outlier is eventually the second ranked candidate). The best accuracy (73.4 vs. SOA of 70.3) and the best OPP (94.9 vs. SOA of 93.8) are both obtained by $APSynP$ with the prototype approach, using the Skip-Gram trained on Wikipedia. We also tested the significance of the accuracy improvements with the χ^2 test but, also given the small size of the 8-8-8 dataset, the result was negative.

Finally, we observe that the two approaches described in 4.3 do not lead to sensitively different results. The major factors of difference can be found instead in the embeddings (with Skip-Gram outperforming Glove) and in the training corpus (the smaller Wikipedia, 1.7B words, outperforms the bigger UMBC, 3B words).

5.1 Error Analysis

In Table 3, we report the 5 outliers that were most difficult to detect by $APSynP$. Most of them are related to the *German Car Manufacturers* topic, which was ambiguous and populated by rare terms. All outliers in the *Months* and in the *South American countries* clusters (except for the two South-American cities *Rio de Janeiro* and *Bogotá*) are successfully identified under all experimental settings. Finally, the reader can notice that most errors belong to C1 and C2, which are the most challenging classes in the dataset, as these outliers are either very related or very similar to other cluster members.

Cluster	Outlier	Class
GCM	Bridgestone	C1
AJC	Mary	C1
GCM	Michael Schumacher	C3
SSP	Moon	C1
GCM	Samsung	C2
BC	dolphin	C2
ITC	software	C3
BC	dog	C1
GCM	Michelin	C1
ITC	Adidas	C2

Table 3: Outlier Detection: Top 10 common errors across settings and their difficulty class (i.e. C1, C2, C3 and C4). (GCM: German Car Manufacturers; AJC: Apostles of Jesus Christ; SSP: Solar System Planets; BC: Big Cats; ITC: IT Companies).

6 Conclusions

We have introduced $APSynP$, an adaptation of the rank-based similarity measure $APSyn$ (Santus et al., 2016a,b) for word embeddings. This adaptation introduces a power parameter p, which is shown to be constant in multiple tasks (i.e. $p = 0.1$). The stability of this parameter, together with the possibility of dropping the parameter N of $APSyn$ when using WE by setting $N = |f|$, makes the measure unsupervised. We have tested it on the tasks of *similarity estimation* and *outlier detection*, obtaining similar or better performances than vector cosine and the original $APSyn$. $APSynP$ performs more consistently on SimLex-999, showing a preference for genuine similarity, as already noticed by Santus et al. (2016a). We also introduced a new approach to the outlier detection task, based on a cluster prototype. The prototype method is competitive and computationally less expensive than pairwise comparisons.

We leave to future work a systematic comparison of $APSynP$ and other rank-based measures. Pilot tests have shown that other rank-based metrics (e.g. Spearman's Rho) also outperform vector cosine in multiple settings and tasks.

7 Acknowledgments

The authors thank the reviewers for the constructive reviews.

Enrico Santus' research is supported by the Singapore University of Technology and Design (SUTD) and by the Massachusetts Institute of Technology (MIT).

Emmanuele Chersoni's research is supported by an A*MIDEX grant (nANR-11-IDEX-0001-02), funded by the French Government "Investissements d'Avenir" program.

References

Eneko Agirre, Enrique Alfonseca, Keith Hall, Jana Kravalova, Marius Paşca, and Aitor Soroa. 2009. A study on Similarity and Relatedness Using Distributional and Wordnet-based Approaches. In *Proceedings of NAACL-HLT*.

Marco Baroni, Georgiana Dinu, and Germán Kruszewski. 2014. Don't Count, Predict! A Systematic Comparison of Context-counting vs. Context-predicting Semantic Vectors. In *Proceedings of ACL*.

Miroslav Batchkarov, Thomas Kober, Jeremy Reffin, Julie Weeds, and David Weir. 2016. A Critique of Word Similarity as a Method for Evaluating Distributional Semantic Models. In *Proceedings of ACL Workshop on Evaluating Vector Space Representations for NLP*.

Philip Blair, Yuval Merhav, and Joel Barry. 2016. Automated Generation of Multilingual Clusters for the Evaluation of Distributed Representations. *arXiv preprint arXiv:1611.01547*.

Elia Bruni, Nam-Khanh Tran, and Marco Baroni. 2014. Multimodal Distributional Semantics. *Journal of Artificial Intelligence Research*, 49:1–47.

José Camacho-Collados and Roberto Navigli. 2016. Find the Word that Does not Belong: A Framework for an Intrinsic Evaluation of Word Vector Representations. In *Proceedings of ACL Workshop on Evaluating Vector Space Representations for NLP*.

José Camacho-Collados, Mohammad Taher Pilehvar, and Roberto Navigli. 2015. NASARI: a Novel Approach to a Semantically-Aware Representation of Items. In *Proceedings of NAACL-HLT*.

Lev Finkelstein, Evgeniy Gabrilovich, Yossi Matias, Ehud Rivlin, Zach Solan, Gadi Wolfman, and Eytan Ruppin. 2001. Placing Search in Context: The Concept Revisited. In *Proceedings of the 10th international conference on World Wide Web*.

Anna Gladkova and Aleksandr Drozd. 2016. Intrinsic Evaluations of Word Embeddings: What Can We Do Better? In *Proceedings of ACL Workshop on Evaluating Vector Space Representations for NLP*.

Lushan Han, Abhay L Kashyap, Tim Finin, James Mayfield, and Jonathan Weese. 2013. UMBC_EBIQUITY-CORE: Semantic Textual Similarity Systems. In *Proceedings of * SEM*.

Felix Hill, Roi Reichart, and Anna Korhonen. 2015. Simlex-999: Evaluating Semantic Models with (Genuine) Similarity Estimation. *Computational Linguistics*, 41(4):665–695.

Soufian Jebbara, Valerio Basile, Elena Cabrio, and Philipp Cimiano. 2018. Extracting Common Sense Knowledge via Triple Ranking Using Supervised and Unsupervised Distributional Models. *Semantic Web*.

Omer Levy, Yoav Goldberg, and Ido Dagan. 2015. Improving Distributional Similarity with Lessons Learned from Word Embeddings. *Transactions of the Association for Computational Linguistics*, 3:211–225.

Tomas Mikolov, Kai Chen, Greg Corrado, and Jeffrey Dean. 2013a. Efficient Estimation of Word Representations in Vector Space. *arXiv preprint arXiv:1301.3781*.

Tomas Mikolov, Ilya Sutskever, Kai Chen, Greg S Corrado, and Jeff Dean. 2013b. Distributed Representations of Words and Phrases and their Compositionality. *Advances in Neural Information Processing Systems*.

Jeffrey Pennington, Richard Socher, and Christopher D Manning. 2014. Glove: Global Vectors for Word Representation. In *Proceedings of EMNLP*.

Enrico Santus, Emmanuele Chersoni, Alessandro Lenci, and Philippe Blache. 2017. Measuring Thematic Fit with Distributional Feature Overlap. In *Proceedings of EMNLP*.

Enrico Santus, Emmanuele Chersoni, Alessandro Lenci, Chu-Ren Huang, and Philippe Blache. 2016a. Testing Apsyn against Vector Cosine on Similarity Estimation. In *Proceedings of PACLIC*.

Enrico Santus, Tin-Shing Chiu, Qin Lu, Alessandro Lenci, and Chu-Ren Huang. 2016b. What a Nerd! Beating Students and Vector Cosine in the ESL and TOEFL Datasets. In *Proceedings of LREC*.

Enrico Santus, Qin Lu, Alessandro Lenci, and Chu-Ren Huang. 2014. Taking Antonymy Mask Off in Vector Space. In *Proceedings of PACLIC*.

Peter D Turney and Patrick Pantel. 2010. From Frequency to Meaning: Vector Space Models of Semantics. *Journal of Artificial Intelligence Research*, 37:141–188.

Addressing Noise in Multidialectal Word Embeddings

Alexander Erdmann, Nasser Zalmout, Nizar Habash
Computational Approaches to Modeling Language Lab
New York University Abu Dhabi
United Arab Emirates
{ae1541,nasser.zalmout,nizar.habash}@nyu.edu

Abstract

Word embeddings are crucial to many natural language processing tasks. The quality of embeddings relies on large non-noisy corpora. Arabic dialects lack large corpora and are noisy, being linguistically disparate with no standardized spelling. We make three contributions to address this noise. First, we describe simple but effective adaptations to word embedding tools to maximize the informative content leveraged in each training sentence. Second, we analyze methods for representing disparate dialects in one embedding space, either by mapping individual dialects into a shared space or learning a joint model of all dialects. Finally, we evaluate via dictionary induction, showing that two metrics not typically reported in the task enable us to analyze our contributions' effects on low and high frequency words. In addition to boosting performance between 2-53%, we specifically improve on noisy, low frequency forms without compromising accuracy on high frequency forms.

1 Introduction

Many natural language processing tasks require word embeddings as inputs, yet quality embeddings require large, non-noisy corpora. Dialectal Arabic (DA), the low register of highly diglossic Arabic (Ferguson, 1959), is problematically noisy. While the high register, Modern Standard Arabic (MSA), is uniform across educated circles in the Arab World, many varieties of DA are not even mutually intelligible (Chiang et al., 2006). The lexical correspondences across four Arab city dialects in Table 1[1] demonstrate that this variation is not limited to sound change among cognate forms, but involves significant lexical changes due to borrowing, semantic shift, etc.

Rabat	Cairo	Beirut	Doha	MSA	Gloss
مطيشة *mTyšħ*	قوطة *qwTħ*	بندورة *bndwrħ*	طماطم *TmATm*	طماطم *TmATm*	*tomato*
طبلة *Tblħ*	طربيزة *Trbyzħ*	طاولة *TAwlħ*	طاولة *TAwlħ*	مائدة *mAŷdħ*	*table*
لديد *ldyd*	حلو *Hlw*	طيب *Tyb*	لذيذ *lðyð*	لذيذ *lðyð*	*declicious*

Table 1: Lexical correspondences between four urban Arabic dialects and MSA.

Seldom written previously, DA is becoming the dominant form of Arabic on social media, yet annotated data are still scarce (Muhammad Abdul-Mageed and Elaraby, 2018; Israa Alsarsour and Elsayed, 2018; Kareem Darwish and Kallmeyer, 2018). While complex morphology contributes to sparsity in both MSA and DA (Habash, 2010), noise from inter-dialect variation and unstandardized spelling further reduces token-to-type ratios in DA. This limits opportunities to learn accurate vector representations for any given word. Table 2 shows that the MSA token-to-type ratio is over three times larger than DA, controlling for corpus size. This is still not nearly as large as English due to English's morphological simplicity.[2] Furthermore, the percentage of tokens belonging to low frequency types is three times greater in DA.

Many previous works ignore inter-dialect variation, training dialect agnostic embeddings, yet we show that modeling dialects individually yields

---

[1]Examples are drawn from the MADAR lexicon (Bouamor et al., 2018). Arabic script follows CODA guidelines (Habash et al., 2018) and transliteration is presented in the HSB scheme (Habash et al., 2007).

[2]Our DA corpora are described in Section 3 whereas the MSA and English sentences are randomly drawn from the parallel corpus described in Almahairi et al. (2016).

Proceedings of the 56th Annual Meeting of the Association for Computational Linguistics (Short Papers), pages 558–565
Melbourne, Australia, July 15 - 20, 2018. ©2018 Association for Computational Linguistics

	Egyptian	Levantine	MSA	English
Tokens per type	20	19	68	128
Tokens with type frequency < 5	6%	6%	2%	1%

Table 2: Token and type based comparisons between two dialects of Arabic, MSA, and English in corpora of 13 million words each.

strong performances in a dictionary induction task when noise is systematically addressed. To that end, we make three contributions. First, we describe simple but effective adaptations to word embedding tools to maximize the informative content leveraged in each training sentence. Second, we compare methods for representing disparate dialects in one embedding space, by mapping individual dialects into shared space or learning a joint model of all dialects. Finally, we evaluate our techniques via dictionary induction, showing that two metrics not typically reported are quite informative. In addition to improving accuracy 2-53%, our adaptations specifically boost performance on noisy, low frequency forms without compromising accuracy on high frequency forms.

2 Related Work

Common monolingual embedding models are trained to predict either the target word given the context (Continuous Bag of Words) or elements of the context given the target (SkipGram) (Mikolov et al., 2013a). These have been adapted to incorporate word order (Trask et al., 2015) or subword information (Bojanowski et al., 2016) to model syntax, morphology, etc.

Bilingual embeddings are vector representations of two languages mapped into shared space, such that translated word pairs have similar vectors (Gouws et al., 2015; Luong et al., 2015). They facilitate applications from parallel sentence extraction (Grover and Mitra, 2017) to machine translation (Zou et al., 2013; Cholakov and Kordoni, 2016; Artetxe et al., 2017b) and can be used to improve monolingual embeddings (Faruqui and Dyer, 2014). Bilingual embeddings are learned via one of three methods: mapping both spaces into a shared space (Mikolov et al., 2013b), monolingual adaptation of one language's embedding space into another's (Zou et al., 2013), or bilingually training both embeddings simultaneously (AP et al., 2014; Pham et al., 2015). We compare implementations of two state-of-the-art mod-

els for mapping embeddings that use the monolingual adaptation technique, as these best suited our data and resources: VECMAP (Artetxe et al., 2016, 2017a) and MUSE (Conneau et al., 2017). Both are equipped to learn either via supervision or by iteratively mapping with little or no supervision. Recently, another unsupervised approach leveraging local neighborhood structures was evaluated on French, English, and MSA (Aldarmaki et al., 2017). Such approaches address seed data scarcity, but have not previously been applied to sparse corpora lacking standardized spelling. While we address unstandardized spelling indirectly by learning better embeddings for low frequency types, Zalmout et al. (2018), Abidi and Smaïli (2018), and Dasigi and Diab (2011) attempt to map DA spelling variants to each other.

We are the first to use embeddings for multiple specific DA dialects, though DA embeddings are often used for sentiment analysis (Al Sallab et al., 2015; Altowayan and Tao, 2016). One such work, Dahou et al. (2016), uses pre-built dictionaries to deterministically identify phrases in mixed MSA-DA data before training embeddings. In MSA, embeddings have been used in additional tasks like morphological analysis (Zalmout and Habash, 2017) and POS tagging (Darwish et al., 2017).

3 Data

We adopt Zaidan and Callison-Burch (2011)'s 4-way coarse-grained dialect distinction of Gulf (GLF), Maghrebi (MAG), Egyptian (EGY), and Levantine (LEV). We collect corpora for each dialect by concatenating the relevant dialect identified portion of the following corpora: Almeman and Lee (2013)'s web crawl of forums, comments and blogs, Khalifa et al. (2016)'s Gumar corpus of internet novels,[3] the Broad Operational Language Translation corpus of primarily blogs described in Zbib et al. (2012), the dialectal Arabic travel corpus of Bouamor et al. (2018), Zaidan and Callison-Burch (2011)'s online news commentary corpus, and Jarrar et al. (2014)'s corpus of subtitles and tweets. This results in 1.7 million sentences of EGY, 1.5 million GLF, 1.3 million LEV, and 1.1 million MAG. These corpora are each about 200 times smaller than MSA's single-domain Gigaword (Parker et al., 2011), with lack of standard-

---

[3]Gumar's GLF portion is huge, making the GLF corpus less comparable to other dialects. Thus, we removed GLF Gumar as its inclusion did not help performance.

ized spelling and internal domain inconsistency compounding scarcity with noise.

To map dialects' embeddings into shared spaces and evaluate dictionary induction, we generate seed and test dictionaries similar to Artetxe et al. (2016). We use MGIZA (Koehn et al., 2007) to align 8,000 sentences from Bouamor et al. (2018)'s travel corpus. It contains 12,000 five-way parallel sentences between the DA varieties of Beirut (LEV), Cairo (EGY), Doha (GLF), Tunis (MAG), and Rabat (MAG), but we collapse Tunis and Rabat to match Zaidan and Callison-Burch (2011)'s granularity and hold out 4,000 sentences for development on downstream tasks. After alignment, we extract unigram translations from 2,000 sentences to form a bidialectal evaluation dictionary. This yields between 2,500 and 4,000 word pairs, with 1.3 to 1.7 average translations per word depending on the dialect pair. Lastly we realign the remaining 6,000 training sentences and extract a seed dictionary. Three annotators jointly evaluated 400 unigram pairs from the LEV–EGY evaluation dictionary. 89% were acceptable translations.

4 Word Embedding Models

We consider the following models for training word embeddings:

FT refers to a FASTTEXT (Bojanowski et al., 2016) implementation of SkipGram with 200 dimensions and a context window of 5 tokens on either side of the target word. A word's vector is the sum of its SkipGram vector and that of all its component character n-grams between length 2 and 6. Since short vowels are not typically written in Arabic, many affixes only consist of a word start/end token and one character. Thus, these character n-gram parameters outperformed the range of 3 to 6 proposed by Bojanowski et al. (2016) for other languages. In preliminary experiments, FT outperformed WORD2VEC models (Mikolov et al., 2013a; Řehůřek and Sojka, 2010) which lack subword information and hence struggle with Arabic's morphological complexity. We also compared FT to variant implementations with larger and smaller context windows, though FT consistently performed the same or better.

EXT refers to an extended FT model where wide and narrow windowed embeddings, sizes 5 and 1 respectively, are trained separately. Resulting vec-

tors are concatenated to build a 400 dimensional model. Given much work demonstrating that narrow context windows capture more syntactic information and wide windows, semantic information (Pennington et al., 2014; Trask et al., 2015; Goldberg, 2016; Tu et al., 2017), component vectors should complement each other, giving the concatenated vector access to a wider range of linguistic information. To ensure that the improvement came from vector concatenation and not simply from having higher dimensional vectors, we built 400 dimension FT models to compare to EXT, but they did not outperform 200 dimensional FT, likely due to sparsity.

PP+EXT refers to an EXT model trained on a preprocessed corpus where phrases have been probabilistically identified. To identify phrases, we recurse over each sentence R times, each time forming bigram phrases from component unigrams (which could have been longer n-grams in previous iterations) depending on the frequencies of the relevant unigrams and bigrams. We implement this step exactly as described in Mikolov et al. (2013c), but then we copy each output sentence C times and probabilistically decompose the deterministically identified phrases into smaller n-grams.[4] More precisely, for each deterministically identified n-gram phrase, we progress from the first to the $(n-1)^{\text{th}}$ gram, randomly splitting the phrase at that point with probability $\frac{e^n}{\sum_{r=1}^{R} e^r}$. The final result of the probabilistic phrase identification is C potentially unique copies of each sentence containing identified n-gram phrases of length $n \leq 2^R$. We experimented with linear distributions in addition to the exponential one used for phrase splitting, but the exponential performed better. The exponential distribution means that it is less likely to separate at any given potential break point in longer n-grams than in shorter ones.

Like Mikolov et al. (2013c)'s deterministic identification of phrases, PP+EXT avoids training vectors on individual words in non-compositional phrases, yet PP+EXT's probabilistic nature lets the model learn from multiple perspectives of every word/phrase's context, with more informative phrase distributions more likely to appear more frequently. Interestingly, identifying phrases can

---

[4]Using a development set, we found performance to plateau around R=5 and C=15 and thus adopt these parameters, though higher values of C could in theory marginally boost performance at the expense of runtime.

be harmful, as our evaluation is performed on unigrams. We implemented a deterministic version of PP+EXT but it did not outperform the baseline FT as too many unigrams were lost in longer phrases. Thus, identifying phrases probabilistically is crucial to PP+EXT's high performance.

In preliminary experiments, probabilistic phrase identification improved the FT model without extending vectors, yet the performance did not exceed EXT. Hence, we only report PP+EXT scores, as the technique is far more effective when coupled with EXT. The combination of techniques is actually designed to be complementary: FT leverages morphology, EXT combines syntax with semantics, and probabilistic phrase identification increases the number of meaningful contexts used for training. These enable the model to learn better representations for noisy, low frequency forms without requiring additional data.

5 Multidialectal Embedding Space

We consider two options for generating multidialectal embeddings for DA: (a) a dialect agnostic model trained on all DA corpora, and (b) training individual dialect models separately before mapping them into a shared embedding space. While (b) leverages less data per model, (a) is subject to more noise and ambiguity, as many words are unique to certain dialects or have disparate meanings in different dialects. (b) can be seeded with a bidialectal dictionary or parallel sentences. We found the dictionary approach to perform better.

ALLDA is a PP+EXT model trained on a combined corpus of all dialects. To avoid code switching issues, ALLDA assigns words only to those dialects for which its relative frequency in that dialect's corpus is greater than 5% of its maximum relative frequency in any dialect. Thus, a word assigned to multiple dialects will take the same vector in each dialect and be its own nearest neighbor for any dialect pairs where it belongs to both.

VECMAP is Artetxe et al. (2016, 2017a)'s tool that uses a seed dictionary (or shared numerals) to learn a mapping function which minimizes distances between seed dictionary unigram pairs. In data scarce settings, the function can be learned iteratively, inducing a larger seed dictionary each round, yet the noise in our DA corpora prevents this process from getting off the ground, producing scores of zero after a few iterations.

MUSE is Conneau et al. (2017)'s tool, using adversarial learning (and optionally a seed) to identify similarly behaving high frequency anchor words, bootstrapping into fine tuning the mapping of less frequent words. MUSE is specifically designed for data scarce and unsupervised settings. It assumes shared embedding structures to be identifiable, and the authors demonstrate that domain differences can strain this assumption.

6 Experiments and Results

To evaluate the quality of our DA word embeddings, we use the task of dictionary induction. Given source dialect words from the evaluation dictionary, we attempt to recall appropriate translations in the target dialect based on cosine distance in multidialectal embedding space. The standard metric for this task is precision@k=1 (P@1) (Artetxe et al., 2016, 2017a; Conneau et al., 2017), measuring the fraction of source words in the evaluation dictionary for which the nearest target dialect neighbor matches any of the possible translations in the evaluation dictionary.

We, however, are also concerned with how well multiple translations are recalled, as many words become polysemous in DA with short vowels omitted and spelling not standardized. For this reason, many words appearing both in the seed and evaluation dictionaries do not map to the exact same set of possible translations in each. Thus, many precision errors may be forgiveable, so we focus on recall, reporting the metric recall@k=5 (R@5). Lastly, because types appear in a Zipfian distribution and type-based metrics disproportionately reflect accuracy in the tail, we report a frequency weighted recall@k=5 (WR@5) as well.[5] Considering both R@5 and WR@5 avoids the risk of improving performance on high or low frequency types at the expense of the other.

In Table 3, models FT, EXT, and PP+EXT are trained on individual dialects, then mapped using supervised SVECMAP into bidialectal embedding spaces. We experimented with all combinations of mapping algorithms and embedding models, yet SVECMAP consistently outperformed the other mapping algorithms. We also report results for unsupervised UMUSE leveraging PP+EXT embeddings. ID is an identity dictionary mapping

---

[5] R@5 and WR@5 are normalized by the score of an oracle that correctly recalls up to 5 translations of every source word, but no more should more exist. Thus, the maximum score for these metrics is 1, making them comparable to P@1.

	Metric	ID	FT	EXT	SVECMAP PP+EXT	ALLDA PP+EXT	UMUSE PP+EXT
MAG	WR@5	28.9	35.3	42.2	**47.0**	32.6	26.8
⇓	R@5	24.9	36.2	40.4	**51.1**	26.2	14.9
LEV	P@1	33.6	35.3	39.7	**54.0**	33.7	12.2
MAG	WR@5	37.5	46.9	49.7	**50.8**	40.5	42.3
⇓	R@5	30.4	36.9	41.2	**45.2**	29.0	25.4
GLF	P@1	35.0	31.1	37.9	**40.0**	29.6	19.1
MAG	WR@5	42.4	48.2	**48.3**	47.9	45.8	43.1
⇓	R@5	30.7	34.5	39.4	**42.9**	34.0	25.5
EGY	P@1	36.0	29.4	**38.0**	36.6	36.3	20.9
EGY	WR@5	42.9	51.3	51.3	**52.8**	47.8	40.5
⇓	R@5	40.9	48.2	49.9	**52.8**	38.4	33.1
GLF	P@1	47.7	43.3	**48.5**	48.3	41.7	24.0
LEV	WR@5	43.2	50.6	50.4	**51.7**	48.5	40.9
⇓	R@5	33.6	37.8	38.9	**46.4**	31.8	24.7
GLF	P@1	39.0	34.1	37.5	**41.7**	33.1	20.0
LEV	WR@5	44.0	50.3	49.8	**52.4**	50.6	48.1
⇓	R@5	33.0	27.6	39.6	**42.3**	36.5	31.1
EGY	P@1	**39.6**	33.8	38.8	37.7	39.2	25.9

Table 3: Dictionary induction results comparing various multidialectal embedding models mapped via supervised (SVECMAP) and unsupervised (ALLDA, UMUSE) techniques.

all source words to themselves, thus representing dialect similarity. PP+EXT or EXT always outperform the baseline FT, with PP+EXT being the best model in all but one instance according to WR@5 and R@5. PP+EXT successfully addresses noise as its gains are larger on non-frequency weighted R@5 than WR@5; i.e., it improves on low frequency words without compromising high frequency word accuracy. Additionally, the consistency in results for WR@5 and R@5 as compared to P@1 suggests the small k is contributing to noise in the P@1 metric.

While ALLDA generally performs worse than the supervised mapping approaches, it typically performs slightly better on words which were not found in their seed dictionaries according to R@5, likely because it can leverage more data to learn better representations for non-ambiguous, low frequency shared forms. Depending on the intended application, system combination could be ideal, querying ALLDA for low frequency forms appearing in multiple dialects, but not the seed.

	SVECMAP	SMUSE	UMUSE	ALLDA
WR@5	0.70	0.97	0.90	0.99
R@5	0.24	0.48	0.89	0.86
P@1	0.03	0.18	0.68	0.78

Table 4: Correlation between mapping performance and dialect similarity, i.e., the ID baseline, using PP+EXT embeddings.

As for supervised mapping algorithms, Table 4 shows that, depending on the dialect pair in question, SMUSE's adversarial learning approach correlates with ID's metric of dialect similarity 20-30% more strongly than SVECMAP, which takes greater advantage of seed–evaluation domain similarity. Accordingly, SVECMAP beats SMUSE on in-seed forms by 3-23%. That said, SMUSE is more robust to seed coverage, slightly outperforming SVECMAP on out-of-seed forms and UMUSE successfully bootstraps without supervision, unlike UVECMAP. Still, the best performing option in the unsupervised set up is ALLDA. UMUSE's performance does not approach that of supervised alternatives as reported in Conneau et al. (2017). This is likely because they (as do Artetxe et al. (2017a)) impose bilingual data scarcity constraints on high resource languages but do not consider the sparsity effects of noise common in low resource languages. They use large quantities of domain consistent, spelling standardized monolingual data which are not available for DA.

7 Conclusion and Future Work

We presented techniques for generating multidialectal word embeddings from noisy DA corpora. Due to linguistic differences, modeling dialects independently and mapping embeddings into multidialectal space generally outperformed training dialect agnostic embeddings on combined corpora. Our novel techniques include concatenating narrow and wide windowed vectors and probabilistically identifying phrases before training embeddings. These techniques improved performance on bidialectal dictionary induction 2-53% over a state-of-the-art baseline, with most of the improvement realized on noisy, low frequency word forms. Our approach can easily be applied to other, similarly noisy corpora. In future work, we will improve the handling of orthographically ambiguous words, which are very prevalent in DA, and we will evaluate on the downstream applications of machine translation and morphological disambiguation.

Acknowledgments

The second author was supported by the New York University Abu Dhabi Global PhD Student Fellowship program. We are also grateful for the support of the High Performance Computing Center at New York University Abu Dhabi.

References

Karima Abidi and Kamel Smaïli. 2018. An automatic learning of an Algerian dialect lexicon by using multilingual word embeddings. In *11th edition of the Language Resources and Evaluation Conference, LREC 2018*.

Ahmad A Al Sallab, Ramy Baly, Gilbert Badaro, Hazem Hajj, Wassim El Hajj, and Khaled B Shaban. 2015. Deep learning models for sentiment analysis in Arabic. In *ANLP Workshop*. volume 9.

Hanan Aldarmaki, Mahesh Mohan, and Mona Diab. 2017. Unsupervised word mapping using structural similarities in monolingual embeddings. *arXiv preprint arXiv:1712.06961* .

Amjad Almahairi, Kyunghyun Cho, Nizar Habash, and Aaron C. Courville. 2016. First result on Arabic neural machine translation. *CoRR* abs/1606.02680. http://arxiv.org/abs/1606.02680.

Khalid Almeman and Mark Lee. 2013. Automatic building of Arabic multi dialect text corpora by bootstrapping dialect words. In *Communications, signal processing, and their applications (iccspa), 2013 1st international conference on*. IEEE, pages 1–6.

A Aziz Altowayan and Lixin Tao. 2016. Word embeddings for Arabic sentiment analysis. In *Big Data (Big Data), 2016 IEEE International Conference on*. IEEE, pages 3820–3825.

Sarath Chandar AP, Stanislas Lauly, Hugo Larochelle, Mitesh Khapra, Balaraman Ravindran, Vikas C Raykar, and Amrita Saha. 2014. An autoencoder approach to learning bilingual word representations. In *Advances in Neural Information Processing Systems*. pages 1853–1861.

Mikel Artetxe, Gorka Labaka, and Eneko Agirre. 2016. Learning principled bilingual mappings of word embeddings while preserving monolingual invariance. In *EMNLP*. pages 2289–2294.

Mikel Artetxe, Gorka Labaka, and Eneko Agirre. 2017a. Learning bilingual word embeddings with (almost) no bilingual data. In *Proceedings of the 55th Annual Meeting of the Association for Computational Linguistics (Volume 1: Long Papers)*. volume 1, pages 451–462.

Mikel Artetxe, Gorka Labaka, Eneko Agirre, and Kyunghyun Cho. 2017b. Unsupervised neural machine translation. *CoRR* abs/1710.11041. http://arxiv.org/abs/1710.11041.

Piotr Bojanowski, Edouard Grave, Armand Joulin, and Tomas Mikolov. 2016. Enriching word vectors with subword information. *arXiv preprint arXiv:1607.04606* .

Houda Bouamor, Nizar Habash, Mohammad Salameh, Wajdi Zaghouani, Owen Rambow, Dana Abdulrahim, Ossama Obeid, Salam Khalifa, Fadhl Eryani, Alexander Erdmann, and Kemal Oflazer. 2018. The MADAR Arabic dialect corpus and lexicon. In *The International Conference on Language Resources and Evaluation*. Miyazaki, Japan.

David Chiang, Mona Diab, Nizar Habash, Owen Rambow, and Safiullah Shareef. 2006. Parsing Arabic Dialects. In *Proceedings of EACL*. Trento, Italy.

Kostadin Cholakov and Valia Kordoni. 2016. Using word embeddings for improving statistical machine translation of phrasal verbs. *ACL 2016* page 56.

Alexis Conneau, Guillaume Lample, Marc'Aurelio Ranzato, Ludovic Denoyer, and Hervé Jégou. 2017. Word translation without parallel data. *arXiv preprint arXiv:1710.04087* .

Abdelghani Dahou, Shengwu Xiong, Junwei Zhou, Mohamed Houcine Haddoud, and Pengfei Duan. 2016. Word embeddings and convolutional neural network for Arabic sentiment classification. In *COLING*. pages 2418–2427.

Kareem Darwish, Hamdy Mubarak, Ahmed Abdelali, and Mohamed Eldesouki. 2017. Arabic POS tagging: Don't abandon feature engineering just yet. *WANLP 2017 (co-located with EACL 2017)* page 130.

Pradeep Dasigi and Mona Diab. 2011. Codact: Towards identifying orthographic variants in dialectal arabic. In *Proceedings of 5th International Joint Conference on Natural Language Processing*. pages 318–326.

Manaal Faruqui and Chris Dyer. 2014. Improving vector space word representations using multilingual correlation. Association for Computational Linguistics.

Charles F Ferguson. 1959. Diglossia. *Word* 15(2):325–340.

Yoav Goldberg. 2016. A primer on neural network models for natural language processing. *J. Artif. Intell. Res.(JAIR)* 57:345–420.

Stephan Gouws, Yoshua Bengio, and Greg Corrado. 2015. Bilbowa: Fast bilingual distributed representations without word alignments. In *Proceedings of the 32nd International Conference on Machine Learning (ICML-15)*. pages 748–756.

Jeenu Grover and Pabitra Mitra. 2017. Bilingual word embeddings with bucketed cnn for parallel sentence extraction. In *Proceedings of ACL 2017, Student Research Workshop*. pages 11–16.

Nizar Habash, Salam Khalifa, Fadhl Eryani, Owen Rambow, Dana Abdulrahim, Alexander Erdmann, Reem Faraj, Wajdi Zaghouani, Houda Bouamor, Nasser Zalmout, Sara Hassan, Faisal Al Shargi, Sakhar Alkhereyf, Basma Abdulkareem, Ramy Eskander, Mohammad Salameh, and Hind Saddiki. 2018. Unified guidelines and resources for Arabic dialect orthography. In *The International Conference on Language Resources and Evaluation*. Miyazaki, Japan.

Nizar Habash, Abdelhadi Soudi, and Tim Buckwalter. 2007. On Arabic Transliteration. In A. van den Bosch and A. Soudi, editors, *Arabic Computational Morphology: Knowledge-based and Empirical Methods*, Springer.

Nizar Y Habash. 2010. *Introduction to Arabic natural language processing*, volume 3. Morgan & Claypool Publishers.

Esraa Mohamed Reem Suwaileh Israa Alsarsour and Tamer Elsayed. 2018. Dart: A large dataset of dialectal arabic tweets. In Nicoletta Calzolari (Conference chair), Khalid Choukri, Christopher Cieri, Thierry Declerck, Sara Goggi, Koiti Hasida, Hitoshi Isahara, Bente Maegaard, Joseph Mariani, HÃÏ'lÃÍne Mazo, Asuncion Moreno, Jan Odijk, Stelios Piperidis, and Takenobu Tokunaga, editors, *Proceedings of the Eleventh International Conference on Language Resources and Evaluation (LREC 2018)*. European Language Resources Association (ELRA), Paris, France.

Mustafa Jarrar, Nizar Habash, Diyam Akra, and Nasser Zalmout. 2014. Building a corpus for Palestinian Arabic: a preliminary study. In *Proceedings of the EMNLP 2014 Workshop on Arabic Natural Language Processing (ANLP)*. Association for Computational Linguistics, Doha, Qatar, pages 18–27. http://www.aclweb.org/anthology/W14-3603.

Hamdy Mubarak Ahmed Abdelali Mohamed Eldesouki Younes Samih Randah Alharbi Mohammed Attia Walid Magdy Kareem Darwish and Laura Kallmeyer. 2018. Multi-dialect arabic pos tagging: A crf approach. In Nicoletta Calzolari (Conference chair), Khalid Choukri, Christopher Cieri, Thierry Declerck, Sara Goggi, Koiti Hasida, Hitoshi Isahara, Bente Maegaard, Joseph Mariani, HÃÏ'lÃÍne Mazo, Asuncion Moreno, Jan Odijk, Stelios Piperidis, and Takenobu Tokunaga, editors, *Proceedings of the Eleventh International Conference on Language Resources and Evaluation (LREC 2018)*. European Language Resources Association (ELRA), Paris, France.

Salam Khalifa, Nizar Habash, Dana Abdulrahim, and Sara Hassan. 2016. A large scale corpus of Gulf Arabic. *arXiv preprint arXiv:1609.02960* .

Philipp Koehn, Hieu Hoang, Alexandra Birch, Chris Callison-Burch, Marcello Federico, Nicola Bertoldi, Brooke Cowan, Wade Shen, Christine Moran, Richard Zens, et al. 2007. Moses: Open source toolkit for statistical machine translation. In *Proceedings of the 45th annual meeting of the ACL on interactive poster and demonstration sessions*. Association for Computational Linguistics, pages 177–180.

Thang Luong, Hieu Pham, and Christopher D Manning. 2015. Bilingual word representations with monolingual quality in mind. In *Proceedings the North American Chapter of the Association for Computational Linguistics/Human Language Technologies Conference (HLT-NAACL15)*. pages 151–159.

Tomas Mikolov, Kai Chen, Greg Corrado, and Jeffrey Dean. 2013a. Efficient estimation of word representations in vector space. *arXiv preprint arXiv:1301.3781* .

Tomas Mikolov, Quoc V Le, and Ilya Sutskever. 2013b. Exploiting similarities among languages for machine translation. *arXiv preprint arXiv:1309.4168* .

Tomas Mikolov, Ilya Sutskever, Kai Chen, Greg S Corrado, and Jeff Dean. 2013c. Distributed representations of words and phrases and their compositionality. In *Advances in neural information processing systems*. pages 3111–3119.

Hassan Alhuzali Muhammad Abdul-Mageed and Mohamed Elaraby. 2018. You tweet what you speak: A city-level dataset of arabic dialects. In Nicoletta Calzolari (Conference chair), Khalid Choukri, Christopher Cieri, Thierry Declerck, Sara Goggi, Koiti Hasida, Hitoshi Isahara, Bente Maegaard, Joseph Mariani, HÃÏ'lÃÍne Mazo, Asuncion Moreno, Jan Odijk, Stelios Piperidis, and Takenobu Tokunaga, editors, *Proceedings of the Eleventh International Conference on Language Resources and Evaluation (LREC 2018)*. European Language Resources Association (ELRA), Paris, France.

Robert Parker, David Graff, Ke Chen, Junbo Kong, and Kazuaki Maeda. 2011. Arabic Gigaword Fifth Edition. LDC catalog number No. LDC2011T11, ISBN 1-58563-595-2.

Jeffrey Pennington, Richard Socher, and Christopher Manning. 2014. Glove: Global vectors for word representation. In *Proceedings of the 2014 conference on empirical methods in natural language processing (EMNLP)*. pages 1532–1543.

Hieu Pham, Thang Luong, and Christopher D Manning. 2015. Learning distributed representations for multilingual text sequences. In *Proceedings the North American Chapter of the Association for Computational Linguistics/Human Language Technologies Conference (HLT-NAACL15)*. pages 88–94.

Radim Řehůřek and Petr Sojka. 2010. Software Framework for Topic Modelling with Large Corpora. In *Proceedings of the LREC 2010 Workshop on New Challenges for NLP Frameworks*. ELRA, Valletta, Malta, pages 45–50. `http://is.muni.cz/publication/884893/en`.

Andrew Trask, David Gilmore, and Matthew Russell. 2015. Modeling order in neural word embeddings at scale. *arXiv preprint arXiv:1506.02338* .

Lifu Tu, Kevin Gimpel, and Karen Livescu. 2017. Learning to embed words in context for syntactic tasks. *arXiv preprint arXiv:1706.02807* .

Omar F. Zaidan and Chris Callison-Burch. 2011. The Arabic online commentary dataset: an annotated dataset of informal Arabic with high dialectal content. In *Proceedings of the Association for Computational Linguistics*. Portland, Oregon, USA.

Nasser Zalmout, Alexander Erdmann, and Nizar Habash. 2018. Noise-robust morphological disambiguation for dialectal Arabic. In *Proceedings of the 16th Meeting of the North American Chapter of the Association for Computational Linguistics/Human Language Technologies Conference (HLT-NAACL18)*. New Orleans, Louisiana, USA.

Nasser Zalmout and Nizar Habash. 2017. Don't throw those morphological analyzers away just yet: Neural morphological disambiguation for Arabic. In *Proceedings of the 2017 Conference on Empirical Methods in Natural Language Processing*. pages 715–724.

Rabih Zbib, Erika Malchiodi, Jacob Devlin, David Stallard, Spyros Matsoukas, Richard Schwartz, John Makhoul, Omar F Zaidan, and Chris Callison-Burch. 2012. Machine translation of Arabic dialects. In *Proceedings of the 2012 conference of the north american chapter of the association for computational linguistics: Human language technologies*. Association for Computational Linguistics, pages 49–59.

Will Y Zou, Richard Socher, Daniel Cer, and Christopher D Manning. 2013. Bilingual word embeddings for phrase-based machine translation. In *Proceedings of the 2013 Conference on Empirical Methods in Natural Language Processing*. pages 1393–1398.

GNEG: Graph-Based Negative Sampling for word2vec

Zheng Zhang
LIMSI, CNRS, Université Paris-Saclay, Orsay, France
& LRI, Univ. Paris-Sud, CNRS,
Université Paris-Saclay, Orsay, France
`zheng.zhang@limsi.fr`

Pierre Zweigenbaum
LIMSI, CNRS,
Université Paris-Saclay,
Orsay, France
`pz@limsi.fr`

Abstract

Negative sampling is an important component in word2vec for distributed word representation learning. We hypothesize that taking into account global, corpus-level information and generating a different noise distribution for each target word better satisfies the requirements of negative examples for each training word than the original frequency-based distribution. In this purpose we pre-compute word co-occurrence statistics from the corpus and apply to it network algorithms such as random walk. We test this hypothesis through a set of experiments whose results show that our approach boosts the word analogy task by about 5% and improves the performance on word similarity tasks by about 1% compared to the skip-gram negative sampling baseline.

1 Introduction

Negative sampling, as introduced by Mikolov et al. (2013b), is used as a standard component in both the CBOW and skip-gram models of word2vec. For practical reasons, instead of using a softmax function, earlier work explored different alternatives which approximate the softmax in a computationally efficient way. These alternative methods can be roughly divided into two categories: softmax-based approaches (hierarchical softmax (Morin and Bengio, 2005), differentiated softmax (Chen et al., 2015) and CNN-softmax (Kim et al., 2016)) and sampling-based approaches (importance sampling (Bengio et al., 2003), target sampling (Jean et al., 2014), noise contrastive estimation (Mnih and Teh, 2012) and negative sampling Mikolov et al. (2013b)). Generally speaking, among all these methods, negative

sampling is the best choice for distributed word representation learning (Ruder, 2016).

Negative sampling replaces the softmax with binary classifiers. For instance, in the skip-gram model, word representations are learned by predicting a training word's surrounding words given this training word. When training, correct surrounding words provide positive examples in contrast to a set of sampled negative examples (noise). To find these negative examples, a noise distribution is empirically defined as the unigram distribution of the words to the $3/4^{th}$ power:

$$P_n(w) = U(w)^{\frac{3}{4}} / \sum_{i=1}^{|vocab|} U(w_i)^{\frac{3}{4}} \qquad (1)$$

Although this noise distribution is widely used and significantly improves the distributed word representation quality, we believe there is still room for improvement in the two following aspects: First, the unigram distribution only takes into account word frequency, and provides the same noise distribution when selecting negative examples for different target words. Labeau and Allauzen (2017) already showed that a context-dependent noise distribution could be a better solution to learn a language model. But they only use information on adjacent words. Second, unlike the positive target words, the meaning of negative examples remain unclear: For a training word, we do not know what a good noise distribution should be, while we do know what a good target word is (one of its surrounding words).

Our contributions: To address these two problems, we propose a new graph-based method to calculate noise distribution for negative sampling. Based on a word co-occurrence network, our noise distribution is targeted to training words. Besides, through our empirical exploration of the noise distribution, we get a better understanding of the

566

Proceedings of the 56th Annual Meeting of the Association for Computational Linguistics (Short Papers), pages 566–571
Melbourne, Australia, July 15 - 20, 2018. ©2018 Association for Computational Linguistics

meaning of 'negative' and of the characteristics of good noise distributions.

The rest of the paper is organized as follows: Section 2 defines the word co-occurrence network concepts and introduces our graph-based negative sampling approach. Section 3 shows the experimental settings and results, then discusses our understanding of the good noise distributions. Finally, Section 4 draws conclusions and mentions future work directions.

2   Graph-based Negative Sampling

We begin with the word co-occurrence network generation (Section 2.1). By comparing it with the word2vec models, we show the relation between the stochastic matrix of the word co-occurrence network and the distribution of the training word contexts in word2vec. We introduce three methods to generate noise distributions for negative sampling based on the word co-occurrence network:

- Directly using the training word context distribution extracted from the word co-occurrence network (Section 2.2)

- Calculating the difference between the original unigram distribution and the training word context distribution (Section 2.3)

- Performing t-step random walks on the word co-occurrence network (Section 2.4)

We finally insert our noise distribution into the word2vec negative sampling training (Sec. 2.5).

2.1   Word Co-occurrence Network and Stochastic Matrix

A word co-occurrence network is a graph of word interactions representing the co-occurrence of words in a corpus. An undirected edge can be created when two words co-occur within a sentence; these words are possibly non-adjacent, with a maximum distance defined by a parameter d_{max} (Ferrer-i-Cancho and Solé, 2001). Given two words w_u^i and w_v^j that co-occur within a sentence at positions i and j ($i, j \in \{1 \ldots l\}$), we define the distance $d(w_u^i, w_v^j) = |j - i|$ and the co-occurrence of w_u and w_v at a distance δ as $cooc(\delta, w_u, w_v) = |\{ (w_u^i, w_v^j) \mid d(w_u^i, w_v^j) = \delta \}|$. We define the weight $w(d_{max}, w_u, w_v)$ of an edge (w_u, w_v) as the total number of co-occurrences of w_u and w_v

with distances $\delta \leq d_{max}$:

$$w(d_{max}, w_u, w_v) = \sum_{\delta=1}^{d_{max}} cooc(\delta, w_u, w_v).$$

An undirected weighted word co-occurrence network can also be represented as a symmetric adjacency matrix (Mihalcea and Radev, 2011), a square matrix A of dimension $|W| \times |W|$. In our case, W is the set of words used to generate the word co-occurrence network, and the matrix elements A_{uv} and A_{vu} have the same value as the weight of the edge $w(d_{max}, w_u, w_v)$. Then each row of the adjacency matrix A can be normalized (i.e., so that each row sums to 1), turning it into a right stochastic matrix S.

Negative sampling, in the skip-gram model, uniformly draws at random for each training word one of its surrounding words as the (positive) target word. This range is determined by the size of the training context c. In other words, a surrounding word w_s of the training word w_t must satisfy the following condition: $d(w_t^i, w_s^j) \leq c$.

For the same corpus, let us set d_{max} equal to c in word2vec and generate a word co-occurrence network of the whole corpus. Then element S_{uv} in the adjacency matrix extracted from the network represents the probability that word w_v be selected as the target word for training word w_u ($P_{bigram}(w_u, w_v)$ in Eq. 2). Row S_u thus shows the distribution of target words for training word w_u after training the whole corpus. Note that no matter how many training iterations are done over the corpus, this distribution will not change.

$$P_{bigram}(w_u, w_v) = \frac{\sum_{\delta=1}^{d_{max}} cooc(\delta, w_u, w_v)}{\sum_{i=1}^{|vocab|} \sum_{\delta=1}^{d_{max}} cooc(\delta, w_u, w_i)} = S_{uv}$$

$$(2)$$

Networks and matrices are interchangeable. The adjacency matrix of the word co-occurrence network can also be seen as the matrix of word-word co-occurrence counts calculated in a statistical way as in GloVe (Pennington et al., 2014). But unlike Glove, where the matrix is used for factorization, we use word co-occurrence statistics to generate a network, then use network algorithms.

2.2   Training-Word Context Distribution

As discussed in Section 2.1, the stochastic matrix S of the word co-occurrence network represents the context distribution of the training words. Here, we use S directly as one of the three types of bases for noise distribution matrix calculation.

The idea behind this is to perform nonlinear logistic regression to differentiate the observed data from some artificially generated noise. This idea was introduced by Gutmann and Hyvärinen (2010) with the name Noise Contrastive Estimation (NCE). Negative sampling (NEG) can be considered as a simplified version of NCE that follows the same idea and uses the unigram distribution as the basis of the noise distribution. We attempt to improve this by replacing the unigram distribution with a bigram distribution (word co-occurrence, not necessarily contiguous) to make the noise distribution targeted to the training word (see Eq. 2).

Compared to the word-frequency-based unigram distribution, the word co-occurrence based bigram distribution is sparser. With the unigram distribution, for any training word, all the other vocabulary words can be selected as noise words because of their non-zero frequency. In contrast, with the bigram distribution, some vocabulary words may never co-occur with a given training word, which makes them impossible to be selected for this training word. To check the influence of this zero co-occurrence case, we also provide a modified stochastic matrix S' smoothed by replacing all zeros in matrix S with the minimum non-zero value of their corresponding rows.

2.3 Difference Between the Unigram Distribution and the Training Words Contexts Distribution

Contrary to the hypothesis underlying the previous section, here we take into account the positive target words distribution in the training word context distribution. Starting from the 'white noise' unigram distribution, for each training word w_u, we subtract from it the corresponding context distribution of this training word. Elements in this new basis matrix $S_{\text{difference}\,u,v}$ of noise distribution are:

$$P_{\text{difference}}(w_u, w_v) = P_n(w_u) - S_{uv} \quad (3)$$

where w_v is one of the negative examples of w_u, P_n is the unigram distribution defined in Eq. 1 and S is the stochastic matrix we used in Section 2.2. For zeros and negative values in this matrix, we reset them to the minimum non-zero value of the corresponding row $P_{\text{difference}}(w_u)$.

2.4 Random Walks on the Word Co-occurrence Network

After generating the word co-occurrence network, we apply random walks (Aldous and Fill, 2002) to it to obtain yet another noise distribution matrix for negative sampling.

Let us define random walks on the co-occurrence network: Starting from an initial vertex w_u, at each step we can cross an edge attached to w_u that leads to another vertex, say w_v. For a weighted word co-occurrence network, we define the transition probability $P(w_u, w_v)$ from vertex w_u to vertex w_v as the ratio of the weight of the edge (w_u, w_v) over the sum of weights on all adjacency edges of vertex w_u. Using the adjacency matrix A and the right stochastic matrix S presented in Section 2.1, $P_{u,v}$ can be calculated by:

$$P(w_u, w_v) = A_{uv} / \sum_{i=1}^{|A_u|} A_{ui} = S_{uv}.$$

As we want to learn transition probabilities for all training words, we apply random walks on all vertices by making each training word an initial vertex of one t-step random walk at the same time.

The whole set of transition probabilities can be represented as a transition matrix, which is exactly the right stochastic matrix S of the word co-occurrence network in our case. We found that the self-loops (edges that start and end at the same vertex: the main diagonal of an adjacency matrix or a stochastic matrix) in matrix S represent the occurrence of a word in its own context, which may happen in repetitions. We hypothesize they constitute spurious events and therefore test the t-step random walk both on matrix S and its smoothed version R' in which the self-loops are removed. To see the effect of the self-loops, we perform the t-step random walk on both matrices S and R'.

Based on that, the elements of the t-step random walk transition matrix can be calculated by:

$$P_{\text{random-walk}}(w_u, w_v) = S_{uv}^t \; or \; (R')_{uv}^t \quad (4)$$

Ferrer-i-Cancho and Solé (2001) showed that a word co-occurrence network is highly connected. For such networks, random walks converge to a steady state in just a few steps. Steady state means that no matter which vertex one starts with, the distribution of the destination vertex probabilities remains the same. In other words, all S^t columns will have the same value. So we set the maximum step number t_{max} to 4. We will use these t-step random walk transition matrices as the basis for one of our noise distributions matrices for negative sampling.

2.5 Noise Distribution Matrix

Starting from the basic noise distribution matrix, we use the power function to adjust the distribution. Then we normalize all rows of this adjusted matrix to let each row sum to 1. Finally, we get:

$$P_n(w_u, w_v) = (B_{uv})^p / \sum_{i=1}^{|B_u|} (B_{ui})^p \qquad (5)$$

where B is the basic noise distribution calculated according to Eq. 2, 3 or 4 and p is the power.

When performing word2vec training with negative sampling, for each training word, we use the corresponding row in our noise distribution matrix to replace the original unigram noise distribution for the selection of noise candidates.

3 Experiments and Results

3.1 Set-up and Evaluation Methods

We use the skip-gram negative sampling model with window size 5, vocabulary size 10000, vector dimension size 200, number of iterations 5 and negative examples 5 to compute baseline word embeddings. Our three types of graph-based skip-gram negative sampling models share the parameters of the baseline. In addition to these common parameters, they have their own parameters: the maximum distance d_{max} for co-occurrence networks generation, a Boolean *replace_zeros* to control whether or not to replace zeros with the minimum non-zero values, a Boolean *no_self_loops* to control whether or not to remove the self-loops, the number of random walk steps t (Eq. 4) and the power p (Eq. 5).

All four models are trained on an English Wikipedia dump from April 2017 of three sizes: about 19M tokens, about 94M tokens (both are for detailed analyses and non-common parameters grid search in each of the three graph-based models) and around 2.19 billion tokens (for four models comparison). During corpus preprocessing, we use CoreNLP (Manning et al., 2014) for sentence segmentation and word tokenization, then convert tokens to lowercase, replace all expressions with numbers by 0 and replace rare tokens with *UNK*s.

We perform a grid search on the $\sim$19M tokens corpus, with $d_{max} \in \{2, \ldots 10\}$, $t \in \{1, \ldots 4\}$, $p \in \{-2, -1, 0.01, 0.25, 0.75, 1, 2\}$ and $True, False$ for the two Boolean parameters. We retain the best parameters obtained by this grid search and perform a tighter grid search around them on the $\sim$94M tokens corpus. Then based on the two grid search results, we select the final parameters for the entire Wikipedia dump test. We evaluate the resulting word embeddings on word similarity tasks using WordSim-353 (Finkelstein et al., 2001) and SimLex-999 (Hill et al., 2014) (correlation with humans), and on the word analogy task of Mikolov et al. (2013a) (% correct). Therefore, we use the correlation coefficients between model similarity judgments and human similarity judgments for WordSim-353 and SimLex-999 tasks and the accuracy of the model prediction with gold standard for the word analogy task (the metrics in Table 1) as objective functions for these parameter tuning processes.

3.2 Results

The best grid search parameters are shown in Table 2, final evaluation results on the entire English Wikipedia in Table 1. The results show that graph-based negative sampling boosts the word analogy task by about 5% and improves word similarity by about 1%.

As vocabulary size is set to 10000, not all data in evaluation datasets is used. We report here the sizes of the datasets and of the subsets that contained no unknown word, that we used for evaluation: WordSim-353: $353; 261$; SImLex-999: $999; 679$; Word Analogy: $19544; 6032$. We also computed the statistical significance of the differences between our models and the baseline model. Both word similarity tasks use correlation coefficients, so we computed Steiger's Z tests (Steiger, 1980) between the correlation coefficients of each of our models (bigram distribution, difference distribution and random walk distribution) versus the word2vec skip-gram negative sampling baseline. For WordSim-353, differences are significant (*2-tailed p* < 0.05) for difference distribution and random walk distribution for both Pearson and Spearman correlation coefficients; differences are not significant for bigram distribution. For SimLex-999, no difference is significant (all *2-tailed p* > 0.05). The word analogy task uses accuracy, we tested statistical significance of the differences by approximate randomization (Yeh, 2000). Based on 10000 shuffles, we confirmed that all differences between the accuracies of our

	WordSim-353		SimLex-999		Word Analogy		
	Pearson	Spearman	Pearson	Spearman	Semantic	Syntactic	Total
baseline word2vec	66.12%	69.60%	37.36%	36.33%	73.00%	70.67%	71.37%
bigram distr. (Eq. 2)	66.10%	69.77%	**38.05%**	**37.18%**	77.36%[†]	75.55%[†]	76.09%[†]
difference distr. (Eq. 3)	**67.71%**[†]	**71.51%**[†]	37.65%	36.58%	77.14%[†]	**75.98%**[†]	**76.33%**[†]
random walk (Eq. 4)	66.94%[†]	70.70%[†]	37.73%	36.74%	**77.75%**[†]	74.86%[†]	75.73%[†]

Table 1: Evaluation results on WordSim-353, SimLex-999 and the word analogy task for the plain word2vec model and our three graph-based noise distributions on the entire English Wikipedia dump. A dagger[†] marks a statistically significant difference to the baseline word2vec.

distribution	d_{max}	p	others
bigram	3	0.25	*replace_zeros=T*
difference	3	0.01	
random walk	5	0.25	$t = 2$, *no_self_loops=T*

Table 2: Best parameters

models and the accuracy of word2vec skip-gram are statistically significant ($p < 0.0001$).

The time complexity when using our modified negative sampling distribution is similar to that of the original skip-gram negative sampling except that the distribution from which negative examples are sampled is different for each token. We pre-compute this distribution off-line for each token so that the added complexity is proportional to the size of the vocabulary. Specifically, pre-computing the co-occurrences and graphs using corpus2graph (Zhang et al., 2018) takes about 2.5 hours on top of 8 hours for word2vec alone on the entire Wikipedia corpus using 50 logical cores on a server with 4 Intel Xeon E5-4620 processors : the extra cost is not excessive.

Let us take a closer look at each graph-based model. First, the word context distribution based model: we find that all else being equal, replacing zero values gives better performance. We believe a reason may be that for a training word, all the other words should have a probability to be selected as negative examples—the job of noise distributions is to assign these probabilities. We note that for SimLex-999, all combinations of parameters in our grid search outperform the baseline. But unfortunately the differences are not significant. Initially it sounds contradictory that directly using the word context distribution S as the noise distribution: a higher probability denotes that the word w_v is more likely to be the target word of w_u (i.e., positive example). So we tried assigning different negative powers to adjust the distribution

S (Section 2.5) so as to make lower co-occurrence frequencies lead to higher probability of being selected as negative examples. But all these perform poorly for all three tasks.

Second, the difference model: the word analogy task results show a strong dependency on power p: the lower the power p, the higher the performance.

Third, the random-walk model: we observe that all top 5 combinations of parameters in the grid search do random walks after removing self-loops.

4 Conclusion

We presented in this paper three graph-based negative sampling models for word2vec. Experiments show that word embeddings trained by using these models can bring an improvement to the word analogy task and to the word similarity task.

We found that pre-computing graph information extracted from word co-occurrence networks is useful to learn word representations. Possible extensions would be to test whether using this information to select target words (positive examples) could improve training quality, and whether using it to reorder training words could improve training efficiency.

References

David Aldous and James Allen Fill. 2002. Reversible markov chains and random walks on graphs. Unfinished monograph, recompiled 2014, available at http://www.stat.berkeley.edu/~aldous/RWG/book.html.

Yoshua Bengio, Jean-Sébastien Senécal, et al. 2003. Quick training of probabilistic neural nets by importance sampling. In *AISTATS*, pages 1–9.

Welin Chen, David Grangier, and Michael Auli. 2015. Strategies for training large vocabulary neural language models. *arXiv preprint arXiv:1512.04906*.

Ramon Ferrer-i-Cancho and Richard V. Solé. 2001. The small world of human language. *Proceedings of* the *Royal Society of London B: Biological Sciences*, 268(1482):2261–2265.

Lev Finkelstein, Evgeniy Gabrilovich, Yossi Matias, Ehud Rivlin, Zach Solan, Gadi Wolfman, and Eytan Ruppin. 2001. Placing search in context: The concept revisited. In *Proceedings of the 10th international conference on World Wide Web*, pages 406–414. ACM.

Michael Gutmann and Aapo Hyvärinen. 2010. Noise-contrastive estimation: A new estimation principle for unnormalized statistical models. In *Proceedings of the Thirteenth International Conference on Artificial Intelligence and Statistics*, pages 297–304.

Felix Hill, Roi Reichart, and Anna Korhonen. 2014. Simlex-999: Evaluating semantic models with (genuine) similarity estimation. *CoRR*, abs/1408.3456.

Sébastien Jean, Kyunghyun Cho, Roland Memisevic, and Yoshua Bengio. 2014. On using very large target vocabulary for neural machine translation. *arXiv preprint arXiv:1412.2007*.

Yoon Kim, Yacine Jernite, David Sontag, and Alexander M Rush. 2016. Character-aware neural language models. In *AAAI*, pages 2741–2749.

Matthieu Labeau and Alexandre Allauzen. 2017. An experimental analysis of noise-contrastive estimation: the noise distribution matters. In *Proceedings of the 15th Conference of the European Chapter of the Association for Computational Linguistics: Volume 2, Short Papers*, volume 2, pages 15–20.

Christopher D. Manning, Mihai Surdeanu, John Bauer, Jenny Finkel, Steven J. Bethard, and David McClosky. 2014. The Stanford CoreNLP natural language processing toolkit. In *Association for Computational Linguistics (ACL) System Demonstrations*, pages 55–60.

Rada F. Mihalcea and Dragomir R. Radev. 2011. *Graph-based Natural Language Processing and Information Retrieval*, 1st edition. Cambridge University Press, New York, NY, USA.

Tomas Mikolov, Kai Chen, Greg Corrado, and Jeffrey Dean. 2013a. Efficient estimation of word representations in vector space. *CoRR*, abs/1301.3781.

Tomas Mikolov, Ilya Sutskever, Kai Chen, Greg S Corrado, and Jeff Dean. 2013b. Distributed representations of words and phrases and their compositionality. In C. J. C. Burges, L. Bottou, M. Welling, Z. Ghahramani, and K. Q. Weinberger, editors, *Advances in Neural Information Processing Systems 26*, pages 3111–3119. Curran Associates, Inc.

Andriy Mnih and Yee Whye Teh. 2012. A fast and simple algorithm for training neural probabilistic language models. *arXiv preprint arXiv:1206.6426*.

Frederic Morin and Yoshua Bengio. 2005. Hierarchical probabilistic neural network language model. In *Aistats*, volume 5, pages 246–252. Citeseer.

Jeffrey Pennington, Richard Socher, and Christopher D. Manning. 2014. Glove: Global vectors for word representation. In *Empirical Methods in Natural Language Processing (EMNLP)*, pages 1532–1543.

Sebastian Ruder. 2016. On word embeddings - part 2: Approximating the softmax. http://ruder.io/word-embeddings-softmax. Last accessed 11 May 2018.

James H Steiger. 1980. Tests for comparing elements of a correlation matrix. *Psychological bulletin*, 87(2):245.

Alexander Yeh. 2000. More accurate tests for the statistical significance of result differences. In *Proceedings of the 18th Conference on Computational Linguistics - Volume 2*, COLING '00, pages 947–953, Stroudsburg, PA, USA. Association for Computational Linguistics.

Zheng Zhang, Ruiqing Yin, and Pierre Zweigenbaum. 2018. Efficient generation and processing of word co-occurrence networks using corpus2graph. In *Proceedings of TextGraphs-12: the Workshop on Graph-based Methods for Natural Language Processing*. Association for Computational Linguistics.

Unsupervised Learning of Style-sensitive Word Vectors

Reina Akama[*1], **Kento Watanabe**[†2], **Sho Yokoi**[*‡3], **Sosuke Kobayashi**[§4], **Kentaro Inui**[*‡5]
[*]Graduate School of Information Sciences, Tohoku University
[†]National Institute of Advanced Industrial Science and Technology (AIST)
[§]Preferred Networks, Inc.
[‡]RIKEN Center for Advanced Intelligence Project
{[1]reina.a,[3]yokoi,[5]inui}@ecei.tohoku.ac.jp,
[2]kento.watanabe@aist.go.jp,[4]sosk@preferred.jp

Abstract

This paper presents the first study aimed at capturing stylistic similarity between words in an unsupervised manner. We propose extending the continuous bag of words (CBOW) model (Mikolov et al., 2013a) to learn style-sensitive word vectors using a wider context window under the assumption that the style of all the words in an utterance is consistent. In addition, we introduce a novel task to predict lexical stylistic similarity and to create a benchmark dataset for this task. Our experiment with this dataset supports our assumption and demonstrates that the proposed extensions contribute to the acquisition of style-sensitive word embeddings.

1 Introduction

Analyzing and generating natural language texts requires the capturing of two important aspects of language: *what is said* and *how it is said*. In the literature, much more attention has been paid to studies on *what is said*. However, recently, capturing *how it is said*, such as stylistic variations, has also proven to be useful for natural language processing tasks such as classification, analysis, and generation (Pavlick and Tetreault, 2016; Niu and Carpuat, 2017; Wang et al., 2017).

This paper studies the stylistic variations of words in the context of the representation learning of words. The lack of subjective or objective definitions is a major difficulty in studying style (Xu, 2017). Previous attempts have been made to define a selected aspect of the notion of style (e.g., politeness) (Mairesse and Walker, 2007; Pavlick and Nenkova, 2015; Flekova et al., 2016; Preotiuc-Pietro et al., 2016; Sennrich et al., 2016; Niu et al., 2017); however, it is not straightforward to create

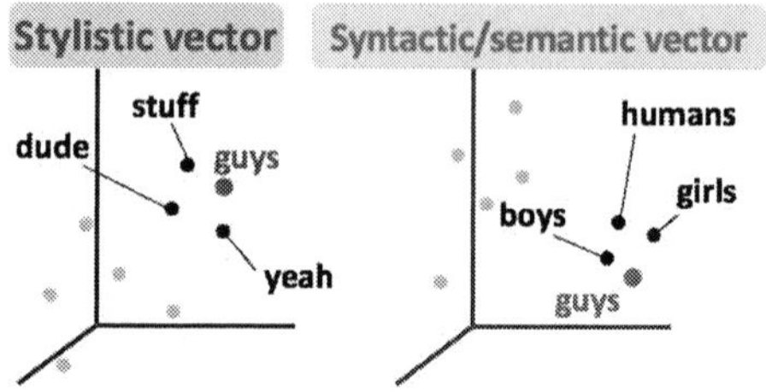

Figure 1: Word vector capturing stylistic and syntactic/semantic similarity.

strict guidelines for identifying the stylistic profile of a given text. The systematic evaluations of style-sensitive word representations and the learning of style-sensitive word representations in a supervised manner are hampered by this. In addition, there is another trend of research forward controlling style-sensitive utterance generation without defining the style dimensions (Li et al., 2016; Akama et al., 2017); however, this line of research considers style to be something associated with a given specific character, i.e., a persona, and does not aim to capture the stylistic variation space.

The contributions of this paper are three-fold. (1) We propose a novel architecture that acquires style-sensitive word vectors (Figure 1) in an unsupervised manner. (2) We construct a novel dataset for style, which consists of pairs of style-sensitive words with each pair scored according to its stylistic similarity. (3) We demonstrate that our word vectors capture the stylistic similarity between two words successfully. In addition, our training script and dataset are available on https://jqk09a.github.io/style-sensitive-word-vectors/.

2 Style-sensitive Word Vector

The key idea is to extend the continuous bag of words (CBOW) (Mikolov et al., 2013a) by distin-

Proceedings of the 56th Annual Meeting of the Association for Computational Linguistics (Short Papers), pages 572–578
Melbourne, Australia, July 15 - 20, 2018. ©2018 Association for Computational Linguistics

guishing nearby contexts and wider contexts under the assumption that a style persists throughout every single utterance in a dialog. We elaborate on it in this section.

2.1 Notation

Let w_t denote the target word (token) in the corpora and $\mathcal{U}_t = \{w_1, \ldots, w_{t-1}, w_t, w_{t+1}, \ldots, w_{|\mathcal{U}_t|}\}$ denote the utterance (word sequence) including w_t. Here, w_{t+d} or $w_{t-d} \in \mathcal{U}_t$ is a context word of w_t (e.g., w_{t+1} is the context word next to w_t), where $d \in \mathbb{N}_{>0}$ is the distance between the context words and the target word w_t.

For each word (token) w, bold face $\boldsymbol{v}_w$ and $\tilde{\boldsymbol{v}}_w$ denote the vector of w and the vector predicting the word w. Let $\mathcal{V}$ denote the vocabulary.

2.2 Baseline Model (CBOW-NEAR-CTX)

First, we give an overview of CBOW, which is our baseline model. CBOW predicts the target word w_t given nearby context words in a window with width δ:

$$\mathcal{C}_{w_t}^{\text{near}} := \{w_{t \pm d} \in \mathcal{U}_t \mid 1 \leq d \leq \delta\} \quad (1)$$

The set $\mathcal{C}_{w_t}^{\text{near}}$ contains in total at most 2δ words, including δ words to the left and δ words to the right of a target word. Specifically, we train the word vectors $\tilde{\boldsymbol{v}}_{w_t}$ and $\boldsymbol{v}_c$ ($c \in \mathcal{C}_{w_t}^{\text{near}}$) by maximizing the following prediction probability:

$$P(w_t | \mathcal{C}_{w_t}^{\text{near}}) \propto \exp\left(\tilde{\boldsymbol{v}}_{w_t} \cdot \frac{1}{|\mathcal{C}_{w_t}^{\text{near}}|} \sum_{c \in \mathcal{C}_{w_t}^{\text{near}}} \boldsymbol{v}_c\right). \quad (2)$$

The CBOW captures both semantic and syntactic word similarity through the training using nearby context words. We refer to this form of CBOW as CBOW-NEAR-CTX. Note that, in the implementation of Mikolov et al. (2013b), the window width δ is sampled from a uniform distribution; however, in this work, we fixed δ for simplicity. Hereafter, throughout our experiments, we turn off the random resizing of δ.

2.3 Learning Style with Utterance-size Context Window (CBOW-ALL-CTX)

CBOW is designed to learn the semantic and syntactic aspects of words from their nearby context (Mikolov et al., 2013b). However, an interesting problem is determining the location where the stylistic aspects of words can be captured. To address this problem, we start with the assumption that a style persists throughout each single utter-

ance in a dialog, that is, the stylistic profile of a word in an utterance must be consistent with other words in the same utterance. Based on this assumption, we propose extending CBOW to use all the words in an utterance as context,

$$\mathcal{C}_{w_t}^{\text{all}} := \{w_{t \pm d} \in \mathcal{U}_t \mid 1 \leq d\}, \quad (3)$$

instead of only the nearby words. Namely, we expand the context window from a fixed width to the entire utterance. This training strategy is expected to lead to learned word vectors that are more sensitive to style rather than to other aspects. We refer to this version as CBOW-ALL-CTX.

2.4 Learning the Style and Syntactic/Semantic Separately

To learn the stylistic aspect more exclusively, we further extended the learning strategy.

Distant-context Model (CBOW-DIST-CTX)

First, remember that using nearby context is effective for learning word vectors that capture semantic and syntactic similarities. However, this means that using the nearby context can lead the word vectors to capture some aspects other than style. Therefore, as the first extension, we propose excluding the *nearby* context $\mathcal{C}_{w_t}^{\text{near}}$ from *all* the context $\mathcal{C}_{w_t}^{\text{all}}$. In other words, we use the *distant* context words only:

$$\mathcal{C}_{w_t}^{\text{dist}} := \mathcal{C}_{w_t}^{\text{all}} \setminus \mathcal{C}_{w_t}^{\text{near}} = \{w_{t \pm d} \in \mathcal{U}_t \mid \delta < d\}. \quad (4)$$

We expect that training with this type of context will lead to word vectors containing the style-sensitive information only. We refer to this method as CBOW-DIST-CTX.

Separate Subspace Model (CBOW-SEP-CTX)

As the second extension to distill off aspects other than style, we use both *nearby* and *all* contexts ($\mathcal{C}_{w_t}^{\text{near}}$ and $\mathcal{C}_{w_t}^{\text{all}}$). As Figure 2 shows, both the vector $\boldsymbol{v}_w$ and $\tilde{\boldsymbol{v}}_w$ of each word $w \in \mathcal{V}$ are divided into two vectors:

$$\boldsymbol{v}_w = \boldsymbol{x}_w \oplus \boldsymbol{y}_w, \quad \tilde{\boldsymbol{v}}_w = \tilde{\boldsymbol{x}}_w \oplus \tilde{\boldsymbol{y}}_w, \quad (5)$$

where $\oplus$ denotes vector concatenation. Vectors $\boldsymbol{x}_w$ and $\tilde{\boldsymbol{x}}_w$ indicate the style-sensitive part of $\boldsymbol{v}_w$ and $\tilde{\boldsymbol{v}}_w$ respectively. Vectors $\boldsymbol{y}_w$ and $\tilde{\boldsymbol{y}}_w$ indicate the syntactic/semantic-sensitive part of $\boldsymbol{v}_w$ and $\tilde{\boldsymbol{v}}_w$ respectively. For training, when the context words are near the target word ($\mathcal{C}_{w_t}^{\text{near}}$), we update both the style-sensitive vectors ($\tilde{\boldsymbol{x}}_{w_t}$, $\boldsymbol{x}_c$) and the syntactic/semantic-sensitive vectors ($\tilde{\boldsymbol{y}}_{w_t}$, $\boldsymbol{y}_c$), i.e., $\tilde{\boldsymbol{v}}_{w_t}$, $\boldsymbol{v}_c$. Conversely, when the context words are

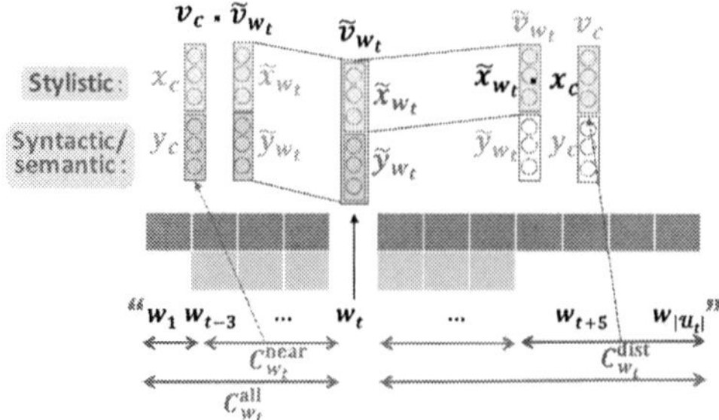

Figure 2: The architecture of CBOW-SEP-CTX.

far from the target word ($\mathcal{C}_{w_t}^{\text{dist}}$), we only update the style-sensitive vectors ($\tilde{x}_{w_t}, x_c$). Formally, the prediction probability is calculated as follows:

$$P_1(w_t | \mathcal{C}_{w_t}^{\text{near}}) \propto \exp\left(\tilde{v}_{w_t} \cdot \frac{1}{|\mathcal{C}_{w_t}^{\text{near}}|} \sum_{c \in \mathcal{C}_{w_t}^{\text{near}}} v_c \right), \quad (6)$$

$$P_2(w_t | \mathcal{C}_{w_t}^{\text{dist}}) \propto \exp\left(\tilde{x}_{w_t} \cdot \frac{1}{|\mathcal{C}_{w_t}^{\text{dist}}|} \sum_{c \in \mathcal{C}_{w_t}^{\text{dist}}} x_c \right). \quad (7)$$

At the time of learning, two prediction probabilities (loss functions) are alternately computed, and the word vectors are updated. We refer to this method using the two-fold contexts separately as the CBOW-SEP-CTX.

3 Experiments

We investigated which word vectors capture the stylistic, syntactic, and semantic similarities.

3.1 Settings

Training and Test Corpus We collected Japanese fictional stories from the Web to construct the dataset. The dataset contains approximately 30M utterances of fictional characters. We separated the data into a 99%–1% split for training and testing. In Japanese, the function words at the end of the sentence often exhibit style (e.g., *desu+wa*, *desu+ze*[1];) therefore, we used an existing lexicon of multi-word functional expressions (Miyazaki et al., 2015). Overall, the vocabulary size $|\mathcal{V}|$ was 100K.

Hyperparameters We chose the dimensions of both the style-sensitive and the syntactic/semantic-sensitive vectors to be 300, and the dimensions of the baseline CBOWs were 300. The learning rate was adjusted individually for each part in $\{x_w, y_w, \tilde{x}_w, \tilde{y}_w\}$ such that "the product of the

---

[1]These words mean the verb *be* in English.

learning rate and the expectation of the number of updates" was a fixed constant. We ran the optimizer with its default settings from the implementation of Mikolov et al. (2013a). The training stopped after 10 epochs. We fixed the nearby window width to $\delta = 5$.

3.2 Stylistic Similarity Evaluation

3.2.1 Data Construction

To verify that our models capture the stylistic similarity, we evaluated our style-sensitive vector x_{w_t} by comparing to other word vectors on a novel artificial task matching human stylistic similarity judgments. For this evaluation, we constructed a novel dataset with human judgments on the stylistic similarity between word pairs by performing the following two steps. First, we collected only style-sensitive words from the test corpus because some words are strongly associated with stylistic aspects (Kinsui, 2003; Teshigawara and Kinsui, 2011) and, therefore, annotating random words for stylistic similarity is inefficient. We asked crowdsourced workers to select style-sensitive words in utterances. Specifically, for the crowdsourced task of picking "style-sensitive" words, we provided workers with a word-segmented utterance and asked them to pick words that they expected to be altered within different situational contexts (e.g., characters, moods, purposes, and the background cultures of the speaker and listener.). Then, we randomly sampled $1,000$ word pairs from the selected words and asked 15 workers to rate each of the pairs on five scales (from -2: *"The style of the pair is different"* to $+2$: *"The style of the pair is similar"*), inspired by the syntactic/semantic similarity dataset (Finkelstein et al., 2002; Gerz et al., 2016). Finally, we picked only word pairs featuring clear worker agreement in which more than 10 annotators rated the pair with the same sign, which consisted of random pairs of highly agreeing style-sensitive words. Consequently, we obtained 399 word pairs with similarity scores. To our knowledge, this is the first study that created an evaluation dataset to measure the lexical stylistic similarity.

In the task of selecting style-sensitive words, the pairwise inter-annotator agreement was moderate (Cohen's kappa κ is 0.51). In the rating task, the pairwise inter-annotator agreement for two classes ($\{-2, -1\}$ or $\{+1, +2\}$) was fair (Cohen's kappa κ is 0.23). These statistics suggest that, at least

Model	ρ_{style}	ρ_{sem}	SYNTAXACC @5	@10
CBOW-NEAR-CTX	12.1	27.8	86.3	85.2
CBOW-ALL-CTX	36.6	24.0	85.3	84.1
CBOW-DIST-CTX	**56.1**	15.9	59.4	58.8
CBOW-SEP-CTX				
x (Stylistic)	**51.3**	**28.9**	68.3	66.2
y (Syntactic/semantic)	9.6	18.1	**88.0**	**87.0**

Table 1: Results of the quantitative evaluations.

in Japanese, native speakers share a sense of style-sensitivity of words and stylistic similarity between style-sensitive words.

3.2.2 Stylistic Sensitivity

We used this evaluation dataset to compute the Spearman rank correlation (ρ_{style}) between the cosine similarity scores between the learned word vectors $\cos(\boldsymbol{v}_w, \boldsymbol{v}_{w'})$ and the human judgements. Table 1 shows the results on its left side. First, our proposed model, CBOW-ALL-CTX outperformed the baseline CBOW-NEAR-CTX. Furthermore, the x of CBOW-DIST-CTX and CBOW-SEP-CTX demonstrated better correlations for stylistic similarity judgments (ρ_{style} = 56.1 and 51.3, respectively). Even though the x of CBOW-SEP-CTX was trained with the same context window as CBOW-ALL-CTX, the style-sensitivity was boosted by introducing joint training with the near context. CBOW-DIST-CTX, which uses only the distant context, slightly outperforms CBOW-SEP-CTX. These results indicate the effectiveness of training using a wider context window.

3.3 Syntactic and Semantic Evaluation

We further investigated the properties of each model using the following criterion: (1) the model's ability to capture the syntactic aspect was assessed through a task predicting part of speech (POS) and (2) the model's ability to capture the semantic aspect was assessed through a task calculating the correlation with human judgments for semantic similarity.

3.3.1 Syntactic Sensitivity

First, we tested the ability to capture syntactic similarity of each model by checking whether the POS of each word was the same as the POS of a neighboring word in the vector space. Specifically, we calculated SYNTAXACC@N defined as follows:

$$\frac{1}{|\mathcal{V}|N} \sum_{w \in \mathcal{V}} \sum_{w' \in \mathcal{N}(w)} \mathbb{I}[\text{POS}(w) = \text{POS}(w')], \quad (8)$$

where $\mathbb{I}[\text{condition}] = 1$ if the condition is true and $\mathbb{I}[\text{conditon}] = 0$ otherwise, the function $\text{POS}(w)$ returns the actual POS tag of the word w, and $\mathcal{N}(w)$ denotes the set of the N top similar words $\{w'\}$ to w w.r.t. $\cos(\boldsymbol{v}_w, \boldsymbol{v}_{w'})$ in each vector space.

Table 1 shows SYNTAXACC@N with $N = 5$ and 10. For both N, the y (the syntactic/semantic part) of CBOW-NEAR-CTX, CBOW-ALL-CTX and CBOW-SEP-CTX achieved similarly good. Interestingly, even though the x of CBOW-SEP-CTX used the same context as that of CBOW-ALL-CTX, the syntactic sensitivity of x was suppressed. We speculate that the syntactic sensitivity was distilled off by the other part of the CBOW-SEP-CTX vector, i.e., y learned using only the *near* context, which captured more syntactic information. In the next section, we analyze CBOW-SEP-CTX for the different characteristics of x and y.

3.3.2 Semantic and Topical Sensitivities

To test the model's ability to capture the semantic similarity, we also measured correlations with the Japanese Word Similarity Dataset (JWSD) (Sakaizawa and Komachi, 2018), which consists of 4,000 Japanese word pairs annotated with semantic similarity scores by human workers. For each model, we calculate and show the Spearman rank correlation score (ρ_{sem}) between the cosine similarity score $\cos(\boldsymbol{v}_w, \boldsymbol{v}_{w'})$ and the human judgements on JWSD in Table 1[2]. CBOW-DIST-CTX has the lowest score ($\rho_{sem} = 15.9$); however, surprisingly, the stylistic vector $\boldsymbol{x}_{w_t}$ has the highest score ($\rho_{sem} = 28.9$), while both vectors have a high ρ_{style}. This result indicates that the proposed stylistic vector $\boldsymbol{x}_{w_t}$ captures not only the stylistic similarity but also the captures semantic similarity, contrary to our expectations (ideally, we want the stylistic vector to capture only the stylistic similarity). We speculate that this is because not only the *style* but also the *topic* is often consistent in single utterances. For example, "サンタ (Santa Clause)" and "トナカイ (reindeer)" are topically relevant words and these words tend to appear in a single utterance. Therefore, stylistic vectors $\{\boldsymbol{x}_w\}$ using all the context words in an utterance also capture the topic relatedness. In addition, JWSD contains topic-related word pairs and synonym pairs; therefore the word vectors that capture the topic similarity have higher ρ_{sem}. We will discuss this point in

---

[2]Note that the low performance of our baseline ($\rho_{sem} = 27.8$ for CBOW-NEAR-CTX) is unsurprising comparing to English baselines (cf., Taguchi et al. (2017)).

| Word w | The top similar words $\{w'\}$ to w w.r.t. cosine similarity | |
	$\cos(\boldsymbol{x}_w, \boldsymbol{x}_{w'})$ (stylistic half)	$\cos(\boldsymbol{y}_w, \boldsymbol{y}_{w'})$ (syntactic/semantic half)
俺 (I; male, colloquial)	おまえ (you; colloquial, rough), あいつ (he/she; colloquial, rough), ねーよ (not; colloquial, rough, male)	僕 (I; male, colloquial, childish), あたし (I; female, childish), 私 (I; formal)
拙者 (I; classical*) *e.g., samurai, ninja	でごさる (be; classical), ござる (be; classical), ござるよ (be; classical)	僕 (I; male, childish), 俺 (I; male, colloquial), 私 (I; formal)
かしら (wonder; female)	わね (QUESTION; female), ないわね (not; female), わ (SENTENCE-FINAL; female)	かな (wonder; childish), でしょうか (wonder; fomal), かしらね (wonder; female)
サンタ (Santa Clause; shortened)	サンタクロース (Santa Clause; -), トナカイ (reindeer; -), クリスマス (Christmas; -)	お客 (customer; little polite), プロデューサー (producer; -), メイド (maid; shortened)
shit	fuckin, fuck, goddamn	shitty, crappy, sucky
hi	hello, bye, hiya, meet	goodbye, goodnight, good-bye
guys	stuff, guy, bunch	boys, humans, girls
ninja	shinobi, genin, konoha	shinobi, pirate, soldier

Table 2: The top similar words for the style-sensitive and syntactic/semantic vectors learned with proposed model, CBOW-SEP-CTX. Japanese words are translated into English by the authors. Legend: (translation; impression).

3.4 Analysis of Trained Word Vectors

Finally, to further understand what types of features our CBOW-SEP-CTX model acquired, we show some words[3] with the four most similar words in Table 2. Here, for English readers, we also report a result for English[4]. The English result also shows an example of the performance of our model on another language. The left side of Table 2 (for stylistic vector x) shows the results. We found that the Japanese word "拙者 (I; classical)" is similar to "ござる (be; classical)" or words containing it (the second row of Table 2). The result looks reasonable, because words such as "拙者 (I; classical)" and "ござる (be; classical)" are typically used by Japanese *Samurai* or *Ninja*. We can see that the vectors captured the similarity of these words, which are stylistically consistent across syntactic and semantic varieties. Conversely, the right side of the table (for the syntactic/semantic vector y) shows that the word "拙者 (I; classical)" is similar to the personal pronoun (e.g., "僕 (I; male, childish)"). We further confirmed that 15 the top similar words are also personal pronouns (even though they are not shown due to space limitations). These results indicate that the proposed CBOW-SEP-CTX model jointly learns two different types of lexical similar-

ities, i.e., the stylistic and syntactic/semantic similarities in the different parts of the vectors. However, our stylistic vector also captured the topic similarity, such as "サンタ (Santa Clause)" and "トナカイ (reindeer)" (the fourth row of Table 2). Therefore, there is still room for improvement in capturing the stylistic similarity.

4 Conclusions and Future Work

This paper presented the unsupervised learning of style-sensitive word vectors, which extends CBOW by distinguishing nearby contexts and wider contexts. We created a novel dataset for style, where the stylistic similarity between word pairs was scored by human. Our experiment demonstrated that our method leads word vectors to distinguish the stylistic aspect and other semantic or syntactic aspects. In addition, we also found that our training cannot help confusing some styles and topics. A future direction will be to addressing the issue by further introducing another context such as a document or dialog-level context windows, where the topics are often consistent but the styles are not.

Acknowledgments

This work was supported by JSPS KAKENHI Grant Number 15H01702. We thank our anonymous reviewers for their helpful comments and suggestions.

---

[3]We arbitrarily selected style-sensitive words from our stylistic similarity evaluation dataset.

[4]We trained another CBOW-SEP-CTX model on an English fan-fiction dataset that was collected from the Web (https://www.fanfiction.net/).

References

Reina Akama, Kazuaki Inada, Naoya Inoue, Sosuke Kobayashi, and Kentaro Inui. 2017. Generating stylistically consistent dialog responses with transfer learning. In *Proceedings of the Eighth International Joint Conference on Natural Language Processing.* pages 408–412.

Lev Finkelstein, Evgeniy Gabrilovich, Yossi Matians, Ehud Rivlin, Zach Solan, Gadi Wolfman, and Eytan Ruppin. 2002. Placing search in context: The concept revisited. *ACM Transactions on Information Systems* 20(1):116–131. https://doi.org/10.1145/503104.503110.

Lucie Flekova, Daniel PreoŢiuc-Pietro, and Lyle Ungar. 2016. Exploring stylistic variation with age and income on twitter. In *Proceedings of the 54th Annual Meeting of the Association for Computational Linguistics.* pages 313–319. https://doi.org/10.18653/v1/P16-2051.

Daniela Gerz, Ivan Vulić, Felix Hill, Roi Reichart, and Anna Korhonen. 2016. Simverb-3500: A large-scale evaluation set of verb similarity. In *Proceedings of the 2016 Conference on Empirical Methods in Natural Language Processing.* pages 2173–2182. https://doi.org/10.18653/v1/D16-1235.

Satoshi Kinsui. 2003. *Vaacharu nihongo: yakuwari-go no nazo (In Japanese).* Tokyo, Japan: Iwanami.

Jiwei Li, Michel Galley, Chris Brockett, Georgios Spithourakis, Jianfeng Gao, and Bill Dolan. 2016. A persona-based neural conversation model. In *Proceedings of the 54th Annual Meeting of the Association for Computational Linguistics.* pages 994–1003. https://doi.org/10.18653/v1/P16-1094.

Francois Mairesse and Marilyn Walker. 2007. Personage: Personality generation for dialogue. In *Proceedings of the 45th Annual Meeting of the Association of Computational Linguistics.* pages 496–503.

Tomas Mikolov, Kai Chen, Greg Corrado, and Jeffrey Dean. 2013a. Efficient estimation of word representations in vector space. In *Proceedings of Workshop at the International Conference on Learning Representations.*

Tomas Mikolov, Ilya Sutskever, Kai Chen, Greg Corrado, and Jeffrey Dean. 2013b. Distributed representations of words and phrases and their compositionality. In *The 26th Annual Conference on Neural Information Processing Systems.* pages 3111–3119.

Chiaki Miyazaki, Toru Hirano, Ryuichiro Higashinaka, Toshiro Makino, and Yoshihiro Matsuo. 2015. Automatic conversion of sentence-end expressions for utterance characterization of dialogue systems. In *Proceedings of the 29th Pacific Asia Conference on Language, Information and Computation.* pages 307–314.

Xing Niu and Marine Carpuat. 2017. Discovering stylistic variations in distributional vector space models via lexical paraphrases. In *Proceedings of the Workshop on Stylistic Variation at the 2017 Conference on Empirical Methods in Natural Language Processing.* pages 20–27. https://doi.org/10.18653/v1/W17-4903.

Xing Niu, Marianna Martindale, and Marine Carpuat. 2017. A study of style in machine translation: Controlling the formality of machine translation output. In *Proceedings of the 2017 Conference on Empirical Methods in Natural Language Processing.* pages 2804–2809. https://doi.org/10.18653/v1/D17-1299.

Ellie Pavlick and Ani Nenkova. 2015. Inducing lexical style properties for paraphrase and genre differentiation. In *Proceedings of the 2015 Conference of the North American Chapter of the Association for Computational Linguistics: Human Language Technologies.* pages 218–224. https://doi.org/10.3115/v1/N15-1023.

Ellie Pavlick and Joel Tetreault. 2016. An empirical analysis of formality in online communication. *Transactions of the Association of Computational Linguistics* 4:61–74.

Daniel Preotiuc-Pietro, Wei Xu, and Lyle H. Ungar. 2016. Discovering user attribute stylistic differences via paraphrasing. In *Proceedings of the 30th AAAI Conference on Artificial Intelligence.* pages 3030–3037.

Yuya Sakaizawa and Mamoru Komachi. 2018. Construction of a japanese word similarity dataset. In *Proceedings of the 11th International Conference on Language Resources and Evaluation.* pages 948–951.

Rico Sennrich, Barry Haddow, and Alexandra Birch. 2016. Controlling politeness in neural machine translation via side constraints. In *Proceedings of the 2016 Conference of the North American Chapter of the Association for Computational Linguistics: Human Language Technologies.* pages 35–40. https://doi.org/10.18653/v1/N16-1005.

Yuya Taguchi, Hideaki Tamori, Yuta Hitomi, Jiro Nishitoba, and Kou Kikuta. 2017. Learning Japanese word distributional representation considering of synonyms (in Japanese). Technical Report 17, The Asahi Shimbun Company, Retrieva Inc.

Mihoko Teshigawara and Satoshi Kinsui. 2011. Modern Japanese 'role language' (yakuwarigo): fictionalised orality in Japanese literature and popular culture. *Sociolinguistic Studies* 5(1):37.

Di Wang, Nebojsa Jojic, Chris Brockett, and Eric Nyberg. 2017. Steering output style and topic in neural response generation. In *Proceedings of the 2017 Conference on Empirical Methods in Natural Language Processing.* pages 2140–2150. https://doi.org/10.18653/v1/D17-1228.

Wei Xu. 2017. From shakespeare to twitter: What are language styles all about? In *Proceedings of the Workshop on Stylistic Variation at the 2017 Conference on Empirical Methods in Natural Language Processing.* pages 1–9. https://doi.org/10.18653/v1/W17-4901.

Exploiting Document Knowledge
for Aspect-level Sentiment Classification

Ruidan He[†‡]**, Wee Sun Lee**[†]**, Hwee Tou Ng**[†]**, and Daniel Dahlmeier**[‡]
[†]Department of Computer Science, National University of Singapore
[‡]SAP Innovation Center Singapore
[†]{ruidanhe,leews,nght}@comp.nus.edu.sg
[‡]d.dahlmeier@sap.com

Abstract

Attention-based long short-term memory (LSTM) networks have proven to be useful in aspect-level sentiment classification. However, due to the difficulties in annotating aspect-level data, existing public datasets for this task are all relatively small, which largely limits the effectiveness of those neural models. In this paper, we explore two approaches that transfer knowledge from document-level data, which is much less expensive to obtain, to improve the performance of aspect-level sentiment classification. We demonstrate the effectiveness of our approaches on 4 public datasets from SemEval 2014, 2015, and 2016, and we show that attention-based LSTM benefits from document-level knowledge in multiple ways.

1 Introduction

Given a sentence and an opinion target (also called an aspect term) occurring in the sentence, aspect-level sentiment classification aims to determine the sentiment polarity in the sentence towards the opinion target. An opinion target or target for short refers to a word or a phrase describing an aspect of an entity. For example, in the sentence *"This little place has a cute interior decor but the prices are quite expensive"*, the targets are *interior decor* and *prices*, and they are associated with positive and negative sentiment respectively.

A sentence may contain multiple sentiment-target pairs, thus one challenge is to separate different opinion contexts for different targets. For this purpose, state-of-the-art neural methods (Wang et al., 2016; Liu and Zhang, 2017; Chen et al., 2017) adopt attention-based LSTM networks, where the LSTM aims to capture sequential patterns and the attention mechanism aims to emphasize target-specific contexts for encoding sentence representations. Typically, LSTMs only show their potential when trained on large datasets. However, aspect-level training data requires the annotation of all opinion targets in a sentence, which is costly to obtain in practice. As such, existing public aspect-level datasets are all relatively small. Insufficient training data limits the effectiveness of neural models.

Despite the lack of aspect-level labeled data, enormous document-level labeled data are easily accessible online such as Amazon reviews. These reviews contain substantial linguistic patterns and come with sentiment labels naturally. In this paper, we hypothesize that aspect-level sentiment classification can be improved by employing knowledge gained from document-level sentiment classification. Specifically, we explore two transfer methods to incorporate this sort of knowledge – pretraining and multi-task learning. In our experiments, we find that both methods are helpful and combining them achieves significant improvements over attention-based LSTM models trained only on aspect-level data. We also illustrate by examples that additional knowledge from document-level data is beneficial in multiple ways. Our source code can be obtained from https://github.com/ruidan/Aspect-level-sentiment.

2 Related Work

Various neural models (Dong et al., 2014; Nguyen and Shirai, 2015; Vo and Zhang, 2015; Tang et al., 2016a,b; Wang et al., 2016; Zhang et al., 2016; Liu and Zhang, 2017; Chen et al., 2017) have been proposed for aspect-level sentiment classification. The main idea behind these works is to develop neural architectures that are able to learn continuous features and capture the intricate relation between a target and context words. However, to sufficiently train these models, substantial aspect-

Proceedings of the 56th Annual Meeting of the Association for Computational Linguistics (Short Papers), pages 579–585
Melbourne, Australia, July 15 - 20, 2018. ©2018 Association for Computational Linguistics

level annotated data is required, which is expensive to obtain in practice.

We explore both pretraining and multi-task learning for transferring knowledge from document level to aspect level. Both methods are widely studied in the literature. Pretraining is a common technique used in computer vision where low-level neural layers can be usefully transferred to different tasks (Krizhevsky and Sutskever, 2012; Zeiler and Fergus, 2014). In natural language processing (NLP), some efforts have been initiated on pretraining LSTMs (Dai and Le, 2015; Zoph et al., 2016; Ramachandran et al., 2017) for sequence-to-sequence models in both supervised and unsupervised settings, where promising results have been obtained. On the other hand, multi-task learning simultaneously trains on samples in multiple tasks with a combined objective (Collobert and Weston, 2008; Luong et al., 2015a; Liu et al., 2016), which has improved model generalization ability in certain cases. In the work of Mou et al. (2016), the authors investigated the transferability of neural models in NLP applications with extensive experiments, showing that transferability largely depends on the semantic relatedness of the source and target tasks. For our problem, we hypothesize that aspect-level sentiment classification can be improved by employing knowledge gained from document-level sentiment classification, as these two tasks are highly related semantically.

3 Models

3.1 Attention-based LSTM

We first describe a conventional implementation of an attention-based LSTM model for this task. We use it as a baseline model and extend it with pretraining and multi-task learning approaches for incorporating document-level knowledge.

The inputs are a sentence $s = (w_1, w_2, ..., w_n)$ consisting of n words, and an opinion target $x = (x_1, x_2, ..., x_m)$ occurring in the sentence consisting of a subsequence of m words from s. Each word is associated with a continuous word embedding $\mathbf{e}_w$ (Mikolov et al., 2013) from an embedding matrix $\mathbf{E} \in \mathbb{R}^{V \times d}$, where V is the vocabulary size and d is the embedding dimension.

LSTM is used to capture sequential information, and outputs a sequence of hidden vectors:

$$[\mathbf{h}_1, ..., \mathbf{h}_n] = \text{LSTM}([\mathbf{e}_{w_1}, ..., \mathbf{e}_{w_n}], \theta_{lstm}) \quad (1)$$

An attention layer assigns a weight α_i to each word in the sentence. The final target-specific representation of the sentence s is then given by:

$$\mathbf{z} = \sum_{i=1}^{n} \alpha_i \mathbf{h}_i \quad (2)$$

And α_i is computed as follows:

$$\alpha_i = \frac{\exp(\beta_i)}{\sum_{j=1}^{n} \exp(\beta_j)} \quad (3)$$

$$\beta_i = f_{score}(\mathbf{h}_i, \mathbf{t}) = tanh(\mathbf{h}_i^T \mathbf{W}_a \mathbf{t}) \quad (4)$$

$$\mathbf{t} = \frac{1}{m} \sum_{i=1}^{m} \mathbf{e}_{x_i} \quad (5)$$

where $\mathbf{t}$ is the target representation computed as the averaged word embedding of the target. f_{score} is a content-based function that captures the semantic association between a word and the target, for which we adopt the formulation used in (Luong et al., 2015b; He et al., 2017) with parameter matrix $\mathbf{W}_a \in \mathbb{R}^{d \times d}$.

The sentence representation $\mathbf{z}$ is fed into an output layer to predict the probability distribution $\mathbf{p}$ over sentiment labels on the target:

$$\mathbf{p} = softmax(\mathbf{W}_o \mathbf{z} + \mathbf{b}_o) \quad (6)$$

We refer to this baseline model as LSTM+ATT. It is trained via cross entropy minimization:

$$J = -\sum_{i \in D} \log \mathbf{p}_i(c_i) \quad (7)$$

where D denotes the overall training corpus, c_i denotes the true label for sample i, and $\mathbf{p}_i(c_i)$ denotes the probability of the true label.

3.2 Transfer Approaches

LSTM+ATT is used as our aspect-level model with parameter set $\theta_{aspect} = \{\mathbf{E}, \theta_{lstm}, \mathbf{W}_a, \mathbf{W}_o, \mathbf{b}_o\}$. We also build a standard LSTM-based classifier based on document-level training examples. This network is the same as the LSTM+ATT apart from the lack of the attention layer. The training objective is also cross entropy minimization as shown in equation (7) and the parameter set is $\theta_{doc} = \{\mathbf{E}', \theta'_{lstm}, \mathbf{W}'_o, \mathbf{b}'_o\}$.

Pretraining (PRET): In this setting, we first train on document-level examples. The last hidden vector from the LSTM outputs is used as the document representation. We initialize the relevant

	Dataset	Pos	Neg	Neu
D1	Restaurant14-Train	2164	807	637
	Restaurant14-Test	728	196	196
D2	Laptop14-Train	994	870	464
	Laptop14-Test	341	128	169
D3	Restaurant15-Train	1178	382	50
	Restaurant15-Test	439	328	35
D4	Restaurant16-Train	1620	709	88
	Restaurant16-Test	597	190	38

Table 1: Dataset description.

parameters $\mathbf{E}, \theta_{lstm}, \mathbf{W}_o, \mathbf{b}_o$ of LSTM+ATT with the pretrained weights, and train it on aspect-level examples to fine tune those weights and learn $\mathbf{W}_a$ which is randomly initialized.

Multi-task Learning (MULT): This approach simultaneously trains two tasks – document-level and aspect-level classification. In this setting, the embedding layer ($\mathbf{E}$) and the LSTM layer (θ_{lstm}) are shared by both tasks, and a document is represented as the mean vector over LSTM outputs. The other parameters are task-specific. The overall loss function is then given by:

$$L = J + \lambda U \qquad (8)$$

where U is the loss function of document-level classification. $\lambda \in (0, 1)$ is a hyperparameter that controls the weight of U.

Combined (PRET+MULT): In this setting, we first perform PRET on document-level examples. We use the pretrained weights for parameter initialization for both aspect-level model and document-level model, and then perform MULT as discussed above.

4 Experiments

4.1 Datasets and Experimental Settings

We run experiments on four benchmark aspect-level datasets, taken from SemEval 2014 (Pontiki et al., 2014), SemEval 2015 (Pontiki et al., 2015), and SemEval 2016 (Pontiki et al., 2016). Following previous work (Tang et al., 2016b; Wang et al., 2016), we remove samples with *conflicting* polarities in all datasets[1]. Statistics of the resulting datasets are presented in Table 1.

We derived two document-level datasets from Yelp2014 (Tang et al., 2015) and the Amazon Electronics dataset (McAuley et al., 2015) respectively. The original reviews were rated on a 5-point scale. We consider 3-class classification and

---

[1] We remove samples in the 2015/6 datasets if an opinion target is associated with different sentiment polarities.

thus label reviews with rating $< 3, > 3$, and $= 3$ as negative, positive, and neutral respectively. Each sampled dataset contains 30k instances with exactly balanced class labels. We pair up an aspect-level dataset and a document-level dataset when they are from a similar domain – the Yelp dataset is used by D1, D3, and D4 for PRET and MULT, and the Electronics dataset is only used by D2.

In all experiments, 300-dimension GloVe vectors (Pennington et al., 2014) are used to initialize $\mathbf{E}$ and $\mathbf{E}'$ when pretraining is not conducted for weight initialization. These vectors are also used for initializing $\mathbf{E}'$ in the pretraining phase. Values for hyperparameters are obtained from experiments on development sets. We randomly sample 20% of the original training data from the aspect-level dataset as the development set and only use the remaining 80% for training. For all experiments, the dimension of LSTM hidden vectors is set to 300, λ is set to 0.1, and we use dropout with probability 0.5 on sentence/document representations before the output layer. We use RMSProp as the optimizer with the decay rate set to 0.9 and the base learning rate set to 0.001. The mini-batch size is set to 32.

4.2 Model Comparison

Table 2 shows the results of LSTM, LSTM+ATT, PRET, MULT, PRET+MULT, and four representative prior works (Tang et al., 2016a,b; Wang et al., 2016; Chen et al., 2017). Significance tests are conducted for testing the robustness of methods under random parameter initialization. Both accuracy and macro-F1 are used for evaluation as label distribution is unbalanced. The reported numbers are obtained as the average value over 5 runs with random initialization for each method.

We observe that PRET is very helpful, and consistently gives a 1–3% increase in accuracy over LSTM+ATT across all datasets. The improvements in macro-F1 scores are even more, especially on D3 and D4 where the labels are extremely unbalanced. MULT gives similar performance as LSTM+ATT on D1 and D2, but improvements can be clearly observed for D3 and D4. The combination (PRET+MULT) overall yields better results.

There are two main reasons why the improvements of macro-F1 scores are more significant on D3 and D4 than on D1: (1) D1 has much more neutral examples in the training set. A classifier

Methods	D1		D2		D3		D4	
	Acc.	Macro-F1	Acc.	Macro-F1	Acc.	Macro-F1	Acc.	Macro-F1
Tang et al. (2016a)	75.37	64.51	68.25	65.96	76.39	58.70	82.16	54.21
Wang et al. (2016)	78.60	67.02	68.88	63.93	78.48	62.84	83.77	61.71
Tang et al. (2016b)	76.87	66.40	68.91	62.79	77.89	59.52	83.04	57.91
Chen et al. (2017)	78.48	68.54	**72.08**	68.43	79.98	60.57	83.88	62.14
LSTM	75.23	64.21	66.79	64.02	75.28	54.10	81.95	58.11
LSTM+ATT	76.83	66.48	68.07	64.82	77.38	60.52	82.73	59.12
Ours: PRET	78.28	68.55	71.32	**68.53**	80.67	68.31	84.87	**70.73**
Ours: MULT	77.41	66.68	68.65	64.57	81.05	65.69	83.27	64.56
Ours: PRET+MULT	**79.11**	**69.73**[*]	71.15	67.46	**81.30**[*]	**68.74**[*]	**85.58**[*]	69.76[*]

Table 2: Average accuracies and Macro-F1 scores over 5 runs with random initialization. The best results are in bold. [*] indicates that PRET+MULT is significantly better than Tang et al. (2016a), Wang et al. (2016), Tang et al. (2016b), Chen et al. (2017), LSTM, and LSTM+ATT with $p < 0.05$ according to one-tailed unpaired t-test.

Settings	D1		D2		D3		D4	
	Acc.	Macro-F1	Acc.	Macro-F1	Acc.	Macro-F1	Acc.	Macro-F1
LSTM only	78.09	67.85	71.04	66.80	78.95	65.30	83.85	67.11
Embeddings only	77.12	67.19	69.12	65.06	80.13	67.04	84.12	70.11
Output layer only	76.88	66.81	69.63	66.07	78.30	64.49	82.55	62.83
Without LSTM	77.45	67.25	69.82	66.63	80.27	68.02	84.80	70.27
Without embeddings	77.97	67.96	70.59	67.16	79.08	65.56	83.94	68.79
Without output layer	78.36	68.06	71.10	67.87	80.82	67.68	84.71	70.48

Table 3: PRET with different transferred layers. Averaged results over 5 runs are reported.

without any external knowledge might still be able to learn some neutral-related features on D1 but it is very hard to learn from D3 and D4. (2) The numbers of neutral examples in the test sets of D3 and D4 are very small. Thus, the precision and recall on neutral class will be largely affected by even a small prediction difference (e.g., with 5 more neutral examples correctly identified, recall is increased by more than 10% on both datasets). As a result, the macro-F1 scores on D3 and D4 are affected more.

4.3 Ablation Tests

Table 2 indicates that a large percentage of the performance gain comes from PRET. To better understand the transfer effects of different layers – embedding layer ($\mathbf{E}$), LSTM layer (θ_{lstm}), and output layer ($\mathbf{W}_o, \mathbf{b}_o$) – we conduct ablation tests on PRET with different layers transfered from the document-level model to the aspect-level model. Results are presented in Table 3. "LSTM only" denotes the setting where only the LSTM layer is transferred, and "Without LSTM" denotes the setting where only the embedding and output layers are transferred (excluding the LSTM layer). The key observations are: (1) Transfer is helpful in all settings. Improvements over LSTM+ATT are observed even when only one layer is transferred. (2) Overall, transfers of the LSTM and embedding

layer are more useful than the output layer. This is what we expect, since the output layer is normally more task-specific. (3) Transfer of the embedding layer is more helpful on D3 and D4. One possible explanation is that the label distribution is extremely unbalanced on these two datasets. Sentiment information is not adequately captured by GloVe word embeddings. Therefore, with a small number of training examples in the negative and neutral classes, the embeddings trained by aspect-level classification still do not effectively capture the true semantics of the relevant opinion words. Transfer of the embedding layer can greatly help in this case.

4.4 Analysis

To show that aspect-level classification indeed benefits from document-level knowledge, we conduct experiments to vary the percentage of document-level training examples from 0.0 to 1.0 for PRET+MULT. The changes of accuracies and macro-F1 scores on the four datasets are shown in Figure 1. The improvements on accuracies with increasing number of document examples are stable across all datasets. For macro-F1 scores, the improvements on D1 and D2 are stable. We observe sharp increases in the macro-F1 scores of D3 and D4 when changing the percentage from 0 to 0.4. This may be related to their extremely

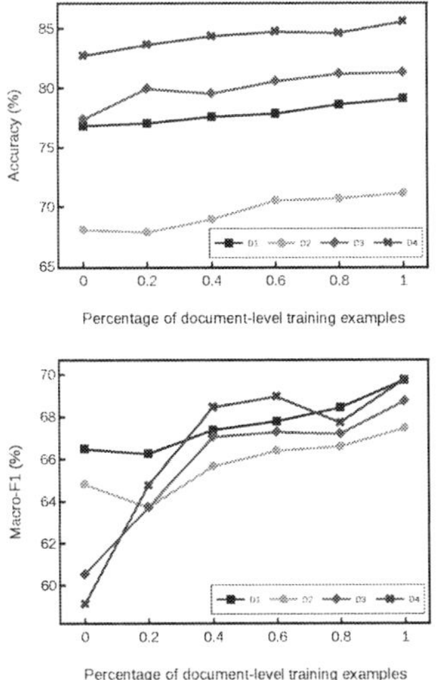

Figure 1: Results of PRET+MULT vs. percentage of document-level training data.

unbalanced label distribution. In such cases, with the knowledge gained from a small number of balanced document-level examples, aspect-level predictions on neutral examples can be significantly improved.

To better understand in which conditions the proposed method is helpful, we analyze a subset of test examples that are correctly classified by PRET+MULT but are misclassified by LSTM+ATT. We find that the benefits brought by document-level knowledge are typically shown in four ways.

First of all, to our surprise, LSTM+ATT made obvious mistakes on some instances with common opinion words. Below are two examples where the target is enclosed in [] with its true sentiment indicated in the subscript:

1. *"I was highly disappointed in the [food]$_{neg}$."*
2. *"This particular location certainly uses substandard [meats]$_{neg}$."*

In the above examples, LSTM+ATT does attend to the right opinion words, but makes the wrong predictions. One possible reason is that the word embeddings from GloVe without PRET do not effectively capture sentiment information, while the aspect-level training samples are not sufficient to capture that for certain words. PRET+MULT eliminates this kind of errors.

Another finding is that our method helps to better capture domain-specific opinion words due to additional knowledge from documents that are

from a similar domain:

1. *"The smaller [size]$_{pos}$ was a bonus because of space restrictions."*
2. *"The [price]$_{pos}$ is 200 dollars down."*

LSTM+ATT attends on *smaller* correctly for the first example but makes the wrong prediction as *smaller* can be negative in many cases. It does not even capture *down* in the second example.

Thirdly, we find that LSTM+ATT made a number of errors on sentences with negation words:

1. *I have experienced no problems, [works]$_{pos}$ as anticipated.*
2. *[Service]$_{neg}$ not the friendliest to our party!*

LSTMs typically only show their potential on large datasets. Without sufficient training examples, it may not be able to effectively capture various sequential patterns. Pretraining the network on larger document-level corpus addresses this problem.

Lastly, PRET+MULT makes fewer errors on recognizing neutral instances. This can also be observed from the macro-F1 scores in Table 2. The lack of training examples makes the prediction of neutral instances very difficult for all previous methods. Knowledge from document-level examples with balanced labels compensates for this disadvantage.

5 Conclusion

The effectiveness of existing aspect-level neural models is limited due to the difficulties in obtaining training data in practice. Our work is the first attempt to incorporate knowledge from document-level corpus for training aspect-level sentiment classifiers. We have demonstrated the effectiveness of our proposed approaches and analyzed the major benefits brought by the knowledge transfer. The proposed approaches can be potentially integrated with other aspect-level neural models to further boost their performance.

References

Peng Chen, Zhongqian Sun, Lidong Bing, and Wei Yang. 2017. Recurrent attention network on memory for aspect sentiment analysis. In *Conference on Empirical Methods in Natural Language Processing (EMNLP 2017)*.

Ronan Collobert and Jason Weston. 2008. A unified architecture for natural language processing: Deep neural networks with multitask learning. In *International Conference on Machine Learning (ICML 2008)*.

Andrew M. Dai and Quoc V. Le. 2015. Semi-supervised sequence learning. In *Neural Information Processing Systems (NIPS 2015)*.

Li Dong, Furu Wei, Chuanqi Tan, Duyu Tang, Ming Zhou, and Ke Xu. 2014. Adaptive recursive neural network for target-dependent Twitter sentiment classification. In *Annual Meeting of the Association for Computational Linguistics (ACL 2014)*.

Ruidan He, Wee Sun Lee, Hwee Tou Ng, and Daniel Dahlmeier. 2017. An unsupervised neural attention model for aspect extraction. In *Annual Meeting of the Association for Computational Linguistics (ACL 2017)*.

Alex Krizhevsky and Ilya Sutskever. 2012. Imagenet classification with deep convolutional neural networks. In *Neural Information Processing Systems (NIPS 2012)*.

Jiangming Liu and Yue Zhang. 2017. Attention modeling for target sentiment. In *Conference of the European Chapter of the Association for Computational Linguistics (EACL 2017)*.

Yang Liu, Sujian Li, Xiaodong Zhang, and Zhifang Sui. 2016. Implicit discourse relation classification via multi-task neural networks. In *AAAI Conference on Artificial Intelligence (AAAI 2016)*.

Minh-Tang Luong, Hieu Pham, and Christopher D. Manning. 2015b. Effective approaches to attention-based neural machine translation. In *Annual Meeting of the Association for Computational Linguistics (ACL 2015)*.

Minh-Thang Luong, Quoc V. Le, Ilya Sutskever, Oriol Vinyals, and Lukasz Kaiser. 2015a. Multi-task sequence to sequence learning. In *International Conference on Learning Representation (ICLR 2015)*.

Julian J. McAuley, Christopher Targett, Qinfeng Shi, and Anton van den Hengel. 2015. Image-based recommendations on styles and substitutes. In *The 38th International ACM SIGIR Conference on Research and Development in Information Retrieval*.

Tomas Mikolov, Ilya Sutskever, Kai Chen, Greg Corrado, and Jeffrey Dean. 2013. Distributed representations of words and phrases and their compositionality. In *Neural Information Processing Systems (NIPS 2013)*.

Lili Mou, Zhao Meng, Rui Yan, Ge Li, Yan Xu, Lu Zhang, and Zhi Jin. 2016. How transferable are neural networks in NLP applications? In *Conference on Empirical Methods in Natural Language Processing (EMNLP 2016)*.

Thien Hai Nguyen and Kiyoaki Shirai. 2015. PhraseRNN: Phrase recursive neural network for aspect-based sentiment analysis. In *Conference on Empirical Methods in Natural Language Processing (EMNLP 2015)*.

Jeffrey Pennington, Richard Socher, and Christopher D Manning. 2014. GloVe: Global vectors for word representation. In *Conference on Empirical Methods in Natural Language Processing (EMNLP 2014)*.

Maria Pontiki, Dimitrios Galanis, Haris Papageorgiou, Suresh Manandhar, and Ion Androutsopoulos. 2015. SemEval-2015 task 12: Aspect based sentiment analysis. In *International Workshop on Semantic Evaluation (SemEval 2015)*.

Maria Pontiki, Dimitrios Galanis, John Pavlopoulos, Haris Papageorgiou, Ion Androutsopoulos, and Suresh Manandhar. 2014. SemEval-2014 task 4: Aspect based sentiment analysis. In *International Workshop on Semantic Evaluation (SemEval 2014)*.

Maria Pontiki, Dimitris Galanis, Haris Papageorgiou, Ion Androutsopoulos, Suresh Manandhar, Mohammed AL-Smadi, Mahmoud Al-Ayyoub, Yanyan Zhao, Bing Qin, Orphée De Clercq, Veronique Hoste, Marianna Apidianaki, Xavier Tannier, Natalia Loukachevitch, Evgeniy Kotelnikov, Núria Bel, Salud Maria Jiménez-Zafra, and Gülşen Eryiğit. 2016. SemEval-2016 task 5: Aspect based sentiment analysis. In *International Workshop on Semantic Evaluation (SemEval 2016)*.

Prajit Ramachandran, Peter J. Liu, and Quoc V. Le. 2017. Unsupervised pretraining for sequence to sequence learning. In *Conference on Empirical Methods in Natural Language Processing (EMNLP 2017)*.

Duyu Tang, Bing Qin, Xiaocheng Feng, and Ting Liu. 2016a. Effective LSTMs for target-dependent sentiment classification. In *International Conference on Computational Linguistics (COLING 2016)*.

Duyu Tang, Bing Qin, and Ting Liu. 2015. Learning semantic representation of users and products for document level sentiment classification. In *Annual Meeting of the Association for Computational Linguistics (ACL 2015)*.

Duyu Tang, Bing Qin, and Ting Liu. 2016b. Aspect level sentiment classification with deep memory network. In *Conference on Empirical Methods in Natural Language Processing (EMNLP 2016)*.

Duy-Tin Vo and Yue Zhang. 2015. Target-dependent Twitter sentiment classification with rich automatic features. In *International Joint Conference on Artificial Intelligence (IJCAI 2015)*.

Yequan Wang, Minlie Huang, Li Zhao, and Xiaoyan Zhu. 2016. Attention-based LSTM for aspect-level sentiment classification. In *Conference on Empirical Methods in Natural Language Processing (EMNLP 2016)*.

Matthew D. Zeiler and Rob Fergus. 2014. Visualizing and understanding convolutional networks. In *European Conference on Computer Vision (ECCV 2014)*.

Meishan Zhang, Yue Zhang, and Duy-Tin Vo. 2016.
Gated neural networks for targeted sentiment anal-
ysis. In *AAAI Conference on Artificial Intelligence
(AAAI 2016)*.

Barret Zoph, Deniz Yuret, Jonathan May, and Kevin
Knight. 2016. Transfer learning for low-resource
neural machine translation. In *Conference on Empirical Methods in Natural Language Processing
(EMNLP 2016)*.

Modeling Sentiment Association in Discourse for Humor Recognition

Lizhen Liu
Information Engineering
Capital Normal University
Beijing, China
liz_liu7480@cnu.edu.cn

Donghai Zhang
Information Engineering
Capital Normal University
Beijing, China
dhzhang@cnu.edu.cn

Wei Song[*]
Information Engineering
Capital Normal University
Beijing, China
wsong@cnu.edu.cn

Abstract

Humor is one of the most attractive parts in human communication. However, automatically recognizing humor in text is challenging due to the complex characteristics of humor. This paper proposes to model sentiment association between discourse units to indicate how the *punchline* breaks the expectation of the *setup*. We found that discourse relation, sentiment conflict and sentiment transition are effective indicators for humor recognition. On the perspective of using sentiment related features, sentiment association in discourse is more useful than counting the number of emotional words.

1 Introduction

Humor can be recognized as a cognitive process, which provokes laughter and provides amusement. It not only promotes the success of human interaction, but also has a positive impact on human mental and physical health (Martineau, 1972; Anderson and Arnoult, 1989; Lefcourt and Martin, 2012). To some extent, humor reflects a kind of intelligence.

However, from both theoretical and computational perspectives, it is hard for computers to build a mechanism for understanding humor like human beings. First, humor is generally loosely defined. Thus it is impossible to construct rules to identify humor. Second, humor is context and background dependent that it expects to break the reader's common sense within a specific situation. Finally, the study of humor involves multiple disciplines like psychology, linguistics and computer science. Recently, humor recognition has drawn more attention (Mihalcea and Strapparava, 2005;

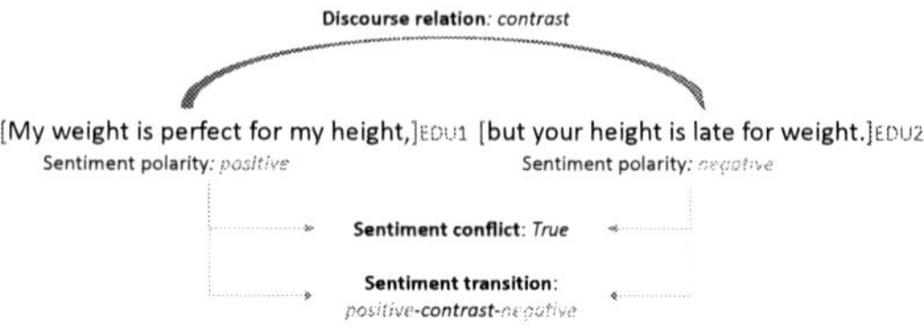

Figure 1: An example of RST style discourse parsing, sentiment polarity analysis and the features we consider in this paper.

Friedland and Allan, 2008; Zhang and Liu, 2014; Yang et al., 2015). The main trend is to design interpretable and computable features that can be well explained by humor theories and easy to be implemented in practice.

In this paper, we propose a novel idea to exploit sentiment analysis for humor recognition. Considering superiority theory (Gruner, 1997) and relief theory (Rutter, 1997), sentiment information should be common in humorous texts to express comparisons between *good* and *bad* or the emotion changes.

Existing work mainly considers statistical sentiment information such as the number of emotional words. We argue that modeling sentiment association at discourse unit level should be a better option for exploiting sentiment information. Such sentiment association in some extent can be used as sentiment patterns to describe the *expectedness* or *unexpectedness*, which is the main idea of incongruity theory (Suls, 1972).

To incorporate discourse information, we exploit RST(Rhetorical Structure Theory) style discourse parsing (Mann and Thompson, 1988) to get discourse units and relations. Combining with sentiment analysis, we derive discourse relation, sentiment conflict and sentiment transition fea-

---

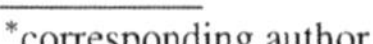

[*]corresponding author

Proceedings of the 56th Annual Meeting of the Association for Computational Linguistics (Short Papers), pages 586–591
Melbourne, Australia, July 15 - 20, 2018. ©2018 Association for Computational Linguistics

tures for humor recognition as shown in Figure 1. The experimental results show that our method can improve the performance of humor recognition on the dataset provided in (Mihalcea and Strapparava, 2005) and exploiting sentiment information at discourse unit level is a better option compared with simply using the number of emotional words as features.

2　Humor Recognition

Humor recognition is typically viewed as a classification problem (Mihalcea and Strapparava, 2005). The main goal is to identify whether a given text contains humorous expressions. Humor is a cognitive process. Thus the interpretability of models is important. Most existing work focuses on designing features motivated by humor theories from different perspectives.

2.1　Humor Theories

The highly recognized theories include superiority theory, relief theory and incongruity theory.

Superiority theory expresses that we laugh because some types of situations make us feel superior to other people (Gruner, 1997). For example, in some jokes, people appear stupid because they have misunderstood an obvious situation or made a stupid mistake.

Relief theory says that humor is the release of nervous energy. The nervous energy relieved through laughter is the energy of emotions that have been found to be inappropriate (Spencer et al., 1860; Rutter, 1997).

Incongruity theory says that humor is the perception of something incongruous, something that violates our common sense and expectations (Suls, 1972) . It is now the dominant theory of humor in philosophy and psychology.

2.2　Baseline Features

Motivated by the humor theories, many researchers design features to describe the characteristics of humor. We mainly follow the recent work of Yang et al. (2015) to build baseline features. The features are summarized as follows.

Incongruity Structure. Inconsistency is considered as an important factor in causing laughter. Following the work of Yang et al. (2015), we describe inconsistency through the following two features:

- The largest semantic distance between word pairs in a sentence

- The smallest semantic distance between word pairs in a sentence

The semantic distance is measured by computing cosine similarity between word embeddings.

Ambiguity. Ambiguity of semantic is a crucial part of humor (Miller and Gurevych, 2015), because ambiguity often causes incongruity, which comes from different understandings of the intention expressed by the author (Bekinschtein et al., 2011). The computation of ambiguity features is based on WordNet (Fellbaum, 2012). We use WordNet to obtain all senses of each word w in an instance s and measure the possibility of ambiguity by computing $\log \prod_{w \in s} num\_of\_sense(w)$, which is used as the value of an ambiguity feature. We also compute the sense farmost and sense closest features as described in (Yang et al., 2015).

Interpersonal Effect. In addition to the commonly used linguistic cues, interpersonal effect may serve an important role in humor (Zhang and Liu, 2014). It is believed that texts containing emotional words and subjective words are more likely to express humor. Therefore, we use the following features based on the resources in (Wilson et al., 2005).

- The number of words with positive polarity

- The number of words with negative polarity

- The number of subjective words

Phonetic Style. Phonetics can also create comic effects. Following (Mihalcea and Strapparava, 2005), we build a feature set which includes alliteration chain and rhyme chain by using CMU speech dictionary[1]. An alliteration chain is a set of words that have the same first phoneme. Similarly, a rhyme chain includes words with the same last syllable. The features are:

- The number of alliteration chains

- The number of rhyme chains

- The length of the longest alliteration chain

- The length of the longest rhyme chain

---

[1] http://www.speech.cs.cmu.edu/cgi-bin/cmudict

KNN. The KNN feature set contains the labels of the top 5 instances in the training data, which are closest to the target instance.

The above five feature sets are denoted as Humor Centric Features(HCF).

Word2Vec Features. Averaged word embeddings are used as sentence representations for classification.

3 Modeling Sentiment Association in Discourse

As described in humor theories and baseline features, emotional words are viewed as important indicators of humorous expressions, which trigger the subjective opinions and sentiment. Previous work only considers the number of words with different sentiment polarity, but ignores the sentiment association in discourse.

Consider the example in Figure 1 again. The first clause expresses a positive sentiment, while the second clause reveals a negative sentiment. The different sentiment polarity forms a kind of contrast or comparison.

Such sentiment association can be explained with main humor theories. For example, superiority theory says humor is the result of suddenly feeling superior when compared with others who are infirm or unfortunate. There are usually two objects, one of the objects is a laugher who feel better than the other, a weak person. The sentiment association between the *perfect weight* and the *late height* highlights such a comparison.

There are also other cases that may have sentiment association between *negatively nervous* and *positively relief* or from *expected sentiment* to *unexpected sentiment*, which can be explained with relief theory (Rutter, 1997) and incongruity theory (Suls, 1972; Ritchie, 1999).

Therefore, sentiment association should be a useful representation to reveal the nature of humor. In this paper, we utilize a discourse parser to get comparable text units and measure sentiment association among them.

3.1 Discourse Parsing

A well-written text is organized by text units which are connected to express the author's intentions through certain discourse relations.

We use the discourse parser implemented by Feng and Hirst (2012) to automatically recognize RST style discourse relations. RST struc-

ture builds a hierarchical structure over the whole text (Mann and Thompson, 1988). A coherent text is represented as a discourse tree, whose leaf nodes are individual text units called elementary discourse unites (EDUs).These independent EDUs can be connected through their relations. The parser can automatically separate a sentence into EDUs and gives discourse relations between EDUs. One of its advantage over others is that it can identify implicit relations, when no discourse marker is given.[2] There are about 77% of sentences in our dataset that don't have explicit connective.

Our goals of using discourse parsing include two aspects: First, we want to investigate whether humorous texts prefer any discourse relations to realize or enhance the effect. Second, EDUs can be used as comparable text units and enable us to measure sentiment association among them. As a result, we derive three types of features.

3.2 Discourse Relation Features

For each instance, we recognize EDUs and the relations connecting them. Then, we design boolean features to indicate the occurrence of discourse relations. The main idea is that some discourse relations such as *contrast* usually indicate a topic transition, which may be used to achieve the effect of unexpectedness.

3.3 Sentiment Conflict Feature

The sentiment conflict we proposed is a specific and descriptive feature to model a kind of incongruity. After dividing an instance into EDUs, we check the sentiment polarity of each EDU using the TextBlob toolkit[3]. The sentiment polarity is either positive, negative or neutral. The sentiment conflict feature is a boolean feature. If there are at least two EDUs and their polarity are opposite (positive vs. negative), the feature is set as *True*.

3.4 Sentiment Transition Features

Besides the heuristically designed sentiment conflict feature, we integrate sentiment polarity and discourse relations. We thought that the expected sentiment might be dependent on the discourse relation. For example, if two clauses have a *sequence* relation, their sentiment polarity may be

---

[2]PDTB-style (Prasad et al., 2008) discourse parsers can be used here as well. But we didn't find proper toolkits that can deal with implicit relations well.

[3]http://textblob.readthedocs.io/en/dev

expected to be the same, while if their relation is *contrast*, their polarity might be different.

For two EDUs with a discourse relation R, we get their sentiment polarity respectively, namely E_1 and E_2, where $E_* \in \{positive, negative, neutral\}$. We design a feature $E_1 \circ R \circ E_2$, where $\circ$ indicates a concatenation operation and E_1 and E_2 are ordered according to the order in which they appear in the instance. For sentence with more than two EDUs, we do this recursively and set a *True* value for every extracted features.

4 Experiments

4.1 Research Questions

We are interested in the following research questions:

- Whether the proposed features are useful for humor recognition?

- Whether the way we manipulate sentiment is more effective compared with previous approaches?

4.2 Settings

We conducted experiments on the dataset used by (Mihalcea and Strapparava, 2005). The dataset contains 10,200 humorous short texts and 10000 non-humorous short texts coming from Reuters titles and Proverbs and British National Corpus(RPBN).

We used the pre-trained word embeddings that are learned using the Word2Vec toolkit (Mikolov et al., 2013) on Google News dataset.[4] We used the implementation of Random Forest in Scikit-learn (Pedregosa et al., 2011) as the classifier. We ran 10-fold cross-validation on the dataset and the average performance would be reported.

4.3 Baselines

- HCF. The method includes the incongruity structure, ambiguity, interpersonal effect, phonetic style features and KNN features.

- HCF w/o KNN. Since KNN features used in HCF are content dependent. We remove KNN features from HCF to have a content free baseline.

---

[4] https://code.google.com/archive/p/word2vec/

	Acc.	P	R	F_1
Base1: HCF	0.787	0.779	0.815	0.797
KNN	0.756	0.733	0.821	0.775
Base2: HCF w/o KNN	0.71	0.706	0.745	0.725
Base3: Word2Vec	0.77	0.775	0.774	0.775
Base4: Base1+Base3	**0.808**	0.81	0.816	**0.813**
Base1+SA	0.799	0.789	0.828	0.808
Base2+SA	0.75	0.747	0.774	0.76
Base3+SA	0.783	0.788	0.787	0.788
Base4+SA	**0.814**	0.812	0.828	**0.82**

Table 1: Humor recognition results. Base1 to Base4 correspond to four baseline settings and SA represents sentiment association features.

- Word2Vec. As described in Section 2.2, this method exploits semantic representations of sentences. It is also content dependent but has better generalization capability.

- HCF+Word2Vec. This method combines HCF and Word2Vec and is the strongest setting as reported in (Yang et al., 2015).

4.4 System Comparisons

Table 1 shows the results, reported with accuracy(Acc.), precision (P), recall (R) and F_1 score. We add sentiment association features (SA) to four baseline settings. In all cases, the performance is improved.

Base2 only uses features that are motivated by humor theories without content features. After adding SA features, Base2 achieves a significant improvement of 4% in accuracy and 3.5% in F_1 score. Since SA features have good interpretability, they complement previous features very well both in theory and practice.

Base1, Base3 and Base4 all consider content features and their performance is significantly better than Base2. However, since the negative instances in the dataset include news titles, it is very likely that the model matches specific topics of the data, rather than capturing the nature of humor. We can see that the KNN method that is based on content similarity only can achieve high scores, which is unreasonable. Even so, SA features still benefit the three baseline settings, although the improvements become small. The results indicate that sentiment association features are useful for humor recognition, especially when domain specific information is not considered.

	Acc.	P	R	F_1
Base2	0.71	0.706	0.745	0.725
Base2-EWC	0.709	0.705	0.742	0.723
Base2-EWC+SA	**0.748**	0.744	0.773	**0.758**
Base4	0.808	0.81	0.816	0.813
Base4-EWC	0.808	0.808	0.818	0.813
Base4-EWC+SA	**0.812**	0.812	0.823	**0.817**

Table 2: Comparing the ways of utilizing sentiment information. Base2 doesn't consider content; Base4 utilizes full information; SA: sentiment association, EWC: emotional word count.

	Acc.	P	R	F_1
Base2	0.71	0.706	0.745	0.725
Base2+DR	0.741	0.737	0.768	0.752
Base2+SC	0.738	0.734	0.764	0.749
Base2+ST	**0.748**	0.743	0.775	**0.759**
Base4	0.808	0.81	0.816	0.813
Base4+DR	**0.813**	0.813	824	**0.818**
Base4+SC	0.811	0.812	0.82	0.816
Base4+ST	**0.813**	0.814	0.823	**0.818**

Table 3: Comparing sentiment association features. Base2 doesn't consider content; Base4 utilizes full information; DR: discourse relation, SC: sentiment conflict, ST: sentiment transition.

4.5 Comparing with Emotional Word Count

Previous work also considers sentiment information but in a different way. Among interpersonal effect features, the numbers of emotional words are used as features, noted as emotional word count, EWC for short. We want to compare the sentiment association features with EWC.

We compare them in two conditions. First, we replace EWC features with SA features in Base2, which doesn't use content information. Second, we replace EWC features with SA features in Base4, which considers all available information. As shown inTable 2, in both conditions, SA features are more effective, indicating the usefulness of analyzing sentiment polarity at EDU level.

4.6 Discussion of Sentiment Association

Table 3 shows the results of adding individual sentiment association features on the basis of Base2 and Base4. All three features are shown to be useful for humor recognition. Sentiment transition is most useful. Again, when removing content features (Base2), the improvements are large. In contrast, if considering content features (Base4), the improvements become small. This is because the content features are already very strong for distinguishing two classes.

Discourse Relation. By analyzing the data, we found that 79% of the humorous instances contain more than one EDU, while 38% of non-humorous messages contain more than one EDU. This means that humorous texts may have more complex sentence structures. The most frequent discourse relations in humorous data include *condition*, *background* and *Contrast*. In contrast, non-humorous texts contain *same-unit* and *attribution* more. The most discriminative relation is *condition*, which accounts for 4.5% in humorous instances and 2% in non-humorous instances. This may be explained with the incongruity theory, where the *setup* of the text prepares an expectation for the readers, while the *punchline* breaks the expectation. *Condition* relation is often used to connect the *setup* and the *punchline*.

Sentiment polarity in Humor. According to the automatic sentiment analysis tool we use, 57% of humorous instances have non-neutral polarity, while 47% of non-humorous instances have non-neutral polarity. This means that humor truly has a positive correlation with sentiment polarities and sentiment analysis should be a useful complement to semantic analysis for measuring incongruity. In addition, as we have shown, measuring sentiment at discourse level should be more important. Combining discourse relations and sentiment polarity performs best.

5 Conclusion

In this paper, we have studied humor recognition from a novel perspective: modeling sentiment association in discourse. We integrate discourse parsing and sentiment analysis to get sentiment association patterns and measure incongruity in a new angle. The proposed idea can be explained with major humor theories. Experimental results also demonstrate the effectiveness of proposed features. This indicates that sentiment association could be a better representation compared with simply analyzing the distribution of sentiment polarity for humor recognition.

Acknowledgements

The research work is funded by the National Natural Science Foundation of China (No.61402304), Beijing Municipal Education Commission (KM201610028015, Connotation Development) and Beijing Advanced Innovation Center for Imaging Technology.

References

Craig A. Anderson and Lynn H. Arnoult. 1989. An examination of perceived control, humor, irrational beliefs, and positive stress as moderators of the relation between negative stress and health. *Basic and Applied Social Psychology* 10(2):101–117.

T. A. Bekinschtein, M. H. Davis, J. M. Rodd, and A. M. Owen. 2011. Why clowns taste funny: the relationship between humor and semantic ambiguity. *Journal of Neuroscience the Official Journal of the Society for Neuroscience* 31(26):9665.

Christiane Fellbaum. 2012. *WordNet*. Blackwell Publishing Ltd.

Vanessa Wei Feng and Graeme Hirst. 2012. Text-level discourse parsing with rich linguistic features. In *Meeting of the Association for Computational Linguistics: Long Papers*. pages 60–68.

Lisa Friedland and James Allan. 2008. Joke retrieval: recognizing the same joke told differently. In *ACM Conference on Information and Knowledge Management*. pages 883–892.

Charles R Gruner. 1997. *The game of humor: A comprehensive theory of why we laugh.*. Transaction PUblishers.

Herbert M. Lefcourt and Rod A. Martin. 2012. Humor and life stress. *Springer Berlin* .

W Mann and Sandra Thompson. 1988. Rhetorical structure theory : Toward a functional theory of text organization. *Text* 8(3):243–281.

William H. Martineau. 1972. *A Model of the Social Functions of Humor*. The Psychology of Humor.

Rada Mihalcea and Carlo Strapparava. 2005. Making computers laugh: investigations in automatic humor recognition. In *Conference on Human Language Technology and Empirical Methods in Natural Language Processing*. pages 531–538.

Tomas Mikolov, Ilya Sutskever, Kai Chen, Greg S Corrado, and Jeff Dean. 2013. Distributed representations of words and phrases and their compositionality. In *Advances in neural information processing systems*. pages 3111–3119.

Tristan Miller and Iryna Gurevych. 2015. Automatic disambiguation of english puns. *Proceedings of the 53rd Annual Meeting of the Association for Computational Linguistics and the 7th International Joint Conference on Natural Language Processing* 1:719–729.

F. Pedregosa, G. Varoquaux, A. Gramfort, V. Michel, B. Thirion, O. Grisel, M. Blondel, P. Prettenhofer, R. Weiss, V. Dubourg, J. Vanderplas, A. Passos, D. Cournapeau, M. Brucher, M. Perrot, and E. Duchesnay. 2011. Scikit-learn: Machine learning in Python. *Journal of Machine Learning Research* 12:2825–2830.

Rashmi Prasad, Nikhil Dinesh, Alan Lee, Eleni Miltsakaki, Livio Robaldo, Aravind K. Joshi, and Bonnie L. Webber. 2008. The penn discourse treebank 2.0. In *International Conference on Language Resources and Evaluation, Lrec 2008, 26 May - 1 June 2008, Marrakech, Morocco*. pages 2961–2968.

Graeme Ritchie. 1999. Developing the incongruity-resolution theory. *Proceedings of the Aisb Symposium on Creative Language* pages 78–85.

Jason. Rutter. 1997. Stand-up as interaction : performance and audience in comedy venues. *University of Salford* 33(4):1 – 2.

Herbert Spencer et al. 1860. The physiology of laughter. *Macmillans Magazine* pages 395–402.

Jerry M. Suls. 1972. A two-stage model for the appreciation of jokes and cartoons: An information-processing analysis. *Psychology of Humor* 331(6019):81–100.

Theresa Wilson, Janyce Wiebe, and Paul Hoffmann. 2005. Recognizing contextual polarity in phrase-level sentiment analysis. In *Proceedings of the conference on human language technology and empirical methods in natural language processing*. Association for Computational Linguistics, pages 347–354.

Diyi Yang, Alon Lavie, Chris Dyer, and Eduard Hovy. 2015. Humor recognition and humor anchor extraction. In *Conference on Empirical Methods in Natural Language Processing*. pages 2367–2376.

Renxian Zhang and Naishi Liu. 2014. Recognizing humor on twitter. In *ACM International Conference on Conference on Information and Knowledge Management*. pages 889–898.

Double Embeddings and CNN-based Sequence Labeling
for Aspect Extraction

Hu Xu[1], Bing Liu[1], Lei Shu[1] and Philip S. Yu[1,2]

[1]Department of Computer Science, University of Illinois at Chicago, Chicago, IL, USA
[2]Institute for Data Science, Tsinghua University, Beijing, China
{hxu48, liub, lshu3, psyu}@uic.edu

Abstract

One key task of fine-grained sentiment analysis of product reviews is to extract product aspects or features that users have expressed opinions on. This paper focuses on supervised aspect extraction using deep learning. Unlike other highly sophisticated supervised deep learning models, this paper proposes a novel and yet simple CNN model [1] employing two types of pre-trained embeddings for aspect extraction: general-purpose embeddings and domain-specific embeddings. Without using any additional supervision, this model achieves surprisingly good results, outperforming state-of-the-art sophisticated existing methods. To our knowledge, this paper is the first to report such double embeddings based CNN model for aspect extraction and achieve very good results.

1 Introduction

Aspect extraction is an important task in sentiment analysis (Hu and Liu, 2004) and has many applications (Liu, 2012). It aims to extract opinion targets (or aspects) from opinion text. In product reviews, aspects are product attributes or features. For example, from "*Its speed is incredible*" in a laptop review, it aims to extract "speed".

Aspect extraction has been performed using supervised (Jakob and Gurevych, 2010; Chernyshevich, 2014; Shu et al., 2017) and unsupervised approaches (Hu and Liu, 2004; Zhuang et al., 2006; Mei et al., 2007; Qiu et al., 2011; Yin et al., 2016; He et al., 2017). Recently, supervised deep learning models achieved state-of-the-art performances (Li and Lam, 2017). Many of these models use

handcrafted features, lexicons, and complicated neural network architectures (Poria et al., 2016; Wang et al., 2016, 2017; Li and Lam, 2017). Although these approaches can achieve better performances than their prior works, there are two other considerations that are also important. (1) Automated feature (representation) learning is always preferred. How to achieve competitive performances without manually crafting features is an important question. (2) According to Occam's razor principle (Blumer et al., 1987), a simple model is always preferred over a complex model. This is especially important when the model is deployed in a real-life application (e.g., chatbot), where a complex model will slow down the speed of inference. Thus, to achieve competitive performance whereas keeping the model as simple as possible is important. This paper proposes such a model.

To address the first consideration, we propose a double embeddings mechanism that is shown crucial for aspect extraction. The embedding layer is the very first layer, where all the information about each word is encoded. The quality of the embeddings determines how easily later layers (e.g., LSTM, CNN or attention) can decode useful information. Existing deep learning models for aspect extraction use either a pre-trained general-purpose embedding, e.g., GloVe (Pennington et al., 2014), or a general review embedding (Poria et al., 2016). However, aspect extraction is a complex task that also requires fine-grained domain embeddings. For example, in the previous example, detecting "speed" may require embeddings of both "Its" and "speed". However, the criteria for good embeddings for "Its" and "speed" can be totally different. "Its" is a general word and the general embedding (trained from a large corpus) is likely to have a better representation for "Its". But, "speed" has a very fine-grained meaning (e.g., how many instructions per second) in the *laptop* domain,

---

[1]The code of this paper can be found at https://www.cs.uic.edu/~hxu/.

Proceedings of the 56th Annual Meeting of the Association for Computational Linguistics (Short Papers), pages 592–598
Melbourne, Australia, July 15 - 20, 2018. ©2018 Association for Computational Linguistics

whereas "speed" in general embeddings or general review embeddings may mean how many miles per second. So using in-domain embeddings is important even when the in-domain embedding corpus is not large. Thus, we leverage both general embeddings and domain embeddings and let the rest of the network to decide which embeddings have more useful information.

To address the second consideration, we use a pure Convolutional Neural Network (CNN) (LeCun et al., 1995) model for sequence labeling. Although most existing models use LSTM (Hochreiter and Schmidhuber, 1997) as the core building block to model sequences (Liu et al., 2015; Li and Lam, 2017), we noticed that CNN is also successful in many NLP tasks (Kim, 2014; Zhang et al., 2015; Gehring et al., 2017). One major drawback of LSTM is that LSTM cells are sequentially dependent. The forward pass and backpropagation must serially go through the whole sequence, which slows down the training/testing process [2]. One challenge of applying CNN on sequence labeling is that convolution and max-pooling operations are usually used for summarizing sequential inputs and the outputs are not well-aligned with the inputs. We discuss the solutions in Section 3.

We call the proposed model <u>D</u>ual <u>E</u>mbeddings <u>CNN</u> (DE-CNN). To the best of our knowledge, this is the first paper that reports a double embedding mechanism and a pure CNN-based sequence labeling model for aspect extraction.

2 Related Work

Sentiment analysis has been studied at document, sentence and aspect levels (Liu, 2012; Pang and Lee, 2008; Cambria and Hussain, 2012). This work focuses on the aspect level (Hu and Liu, 2004). Aspect extraction is one of its key tasks, and has been performed using both unsupervised and supervised approaches. The unsupervised approach includes methods such as frequent pattern mining (Hu and Liu, 2004; Popescu and Etzioni, 2005), syntactic rules-based extraction (Zhuang et al., 2006; Wang and Wang, 2008; Qiu et al., 2011), topic modeling (Mei et al., 2007; Titov and McDonald, 2008; Lin and He, 2009; Moghaddam and Ester, 2011), word alignment (Liu et al.,

2013) and label propagation (Zhou et al., 2013; Shu et al., 2016).

Traditionally, the supervised approach (Jakob and Gurevych, 2010; Mitchell et al., 2013; Shu et al., 2017) uses Conditional Random Fields (CRF) (Lafferty et al., 2001). Recently, deep neural networks are applied to learn better features for supervised aspect extraction, e.g., using LSTM (Williams and Zipser, 1989; Hochreiter and Schmidhuber, 1997; Liu et al., 2015) and attention mechanism (Wang et al., 2017; He et al., 2017) together with manual features (Poria et al., 2016; Wang et al., 2016). Further, (Wang et al., 2016, 2017; Li and Lam, 2017) also proposed aspect and opinion terms co-extraction via a deep network. They took advantage of the gold-standard opinion terms or sentiment lexicon for aspect extraction. The proposed approach is close to (Liu et al., 2015), where only the annotated data for aspect extraction is used. However, we will show that our approach is more effective even compared with baselines using additional supervisions and/or resources.

The proposed embedding mechanism is related to cross domain embeddings (Bollegala et al., 2015, 2017) and domain-specific embeddings (Xu et al., 2018a,b). However, we require the domain of the domain embeddings must exactly match the domain of the aspect extraction task. CNN (LeCun et al., 1995; Kim, 2014) is recently adopted for named entity recognition (Strubell et al., 2017). CNN classifiers are also used in sentiment analysis (Poria et al., 2016; Chen et al., 2017). We adopt CNN for sequence labeling for aspect extraction because CNN is simple and parallelized.

3 Model

The proposed model is depicted in Figure 1. It has 2 embedding layers, 4 CNN layers, a fully-connected layer shared across all positions of words, and a softmax layer over the labeling space $\mathcal{Y} = \{B, I, O\}$ for each position of inputs. Note that an aspect can be a phrase and B, I indicate the beginning word and non-beginning word of an aspect phrase and O indicates non-aspect words.

Assume the input is a sequence of word indexes $\mathbf{x} = (x_1, \ldots, x_n)$. This sequence gets its two corresponding continuous representations $\mathbf{x}^g$ and $\mathbf{x}^d$ via two separate embedding layers (or embedding matrices) W^g and W^d. The first embedding matrix W^g represents general embeddings pre-

---

[2]We notice that a GPU with more cores has no training time gain on a low-dimensional LSTM because extra cores are idle and waiting for the other cores to sequentially compute cells.

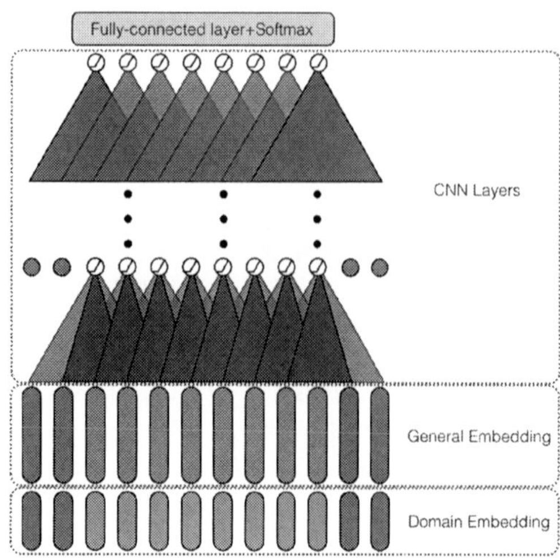

Figure 1: Overview of DE-CNN: red vectors are zero vectors; purple triangles are CNN filters.

trained from a very large general-purpose corpus (usually hundreds of billions of tokens). The second embedding matrix W^d represents domain embeddings pre-trained from a small in-domain corpus, where the scope of the domain is exactly the domain that the training/testing data belongs to. As a counter-example, if the training/testing data is in the *laptop* domain, then embeddings from the *electronics* domain are considered to be out-of-domain embeddings (e.g., the word "adapter" may represent different types of adapters in *electronics* rather than exactly a *laptop* adapter). That is, only laptop reviews are considered to be in-domain.

We do not allow these two embedding layers trainable because small training examples may lead to many unseen words in test data. If embeddings are tunable, the features for seen words' embeddings will be adjusted (e.g., forgetting useless features and infusing new features that are related to the labels of the training examples). And the CNN filters will adjust to the new features accordingly. But the embeddings of unseen words from test data still have the old features that may be mistakenly extracted by CNN.

Then we concatenate two embeddings $\mathbf{x}^{(1)} = \mathbf{x}^g \oplus \mathbf{x}^d$ and feed the result into a stack of 4 CNN layers. A CNN layer has many 1D-convolution filters and each (the r-th) filter has a fixed kernel size $k = 2c+1$ and performs the following convolution

Description	Training #S./#A.	Testing #S./#A.
SemEval-14 Laptop	3045/2358	800/654
SemEval-16 Restaurant	2000/1743	676/622

Table 1: Dataset description with the number of sentences(#S.) and number of aspect terms(#A.)

operation and ReLU activation:

$$x_{i,r}^{(l+1)} = \max\left(0, \left(\sum_{j=-c}^{c} w_{j,r}^{(l)} x_{i+j}^{(l)}\right) + b_r^{(l)}\right), \quad (1)$$

where l indicates the l-th CNN layer. We apply each filter to all positions $i = 1 : n$. So each filter computes the representation for the i-th word along with $2c$ nearby words in its context. Note that we force the kernel size k to be an odd number and set the stride step to be 1 and further pad the left c and right c positions with all zeros. In this way, the output of each layer is well-aligned with the original input $\mathbf{x}$ for sequence labeling purposes. For the first ($l = 1$) CNN layer, we employ two different filter sizes. For the rest 3 CNN ($l \in \{2, 3, 4\}$) layers, we only use one filter size. We will discuss the details of the hyperparameters in the experiment section. Finally, we apply a fully-connected layer with weights shared across all positions and a softmax layer to compute label distribution for each word. The output size of the fully-connected layer is $|\mathcal{Y}| = 3$. We apply dropout after the embedding layer and each ReLU activation. Note that we do not apply any max-pooling layer after convolution layers because a sequence labeling model needs good representations for every position and max-pooling operation mixes the representations of different positions, which is undesirable (we show a max-pooling baseline in the next section).

4 Experiments

4.1 Datasets

Following the experiments of a recent aspect extraction paper (Li and Lam, 2017), we conduct experiments on two benchmark datasets from SemEval challenges (Pontiki et al., 2014, 2016) as shown in Table 4.1. The first dataset is from the *laptop* domain on subtask 1 of SemEval-2014 Task 4. The second dataset is from the *restaurant* domain on subtask 1 (slot 2) of SemEval-2016 Task 5. These two datasets consist of review sentences with aspect terms labeled as spans of characters.

594

We use NLTK[3] to tokenize each sentence into a sequence of words.

For the general-purpose embeddings, we use the glove.840B.300d embeddings (Pennington et al., 2014), which are pre-trained from a corpus of 840 billion tokens that cover almost all web pages. These embeddings have 300 dimensions. For domain-specific embeddings, we collect a laptop review corpus and a restaurant review corpus and use fastText (Bojanowski et al., 2016) to train domain embeddings. The laptop review corpus contains all laptop reviews from the Amazon Review Dataset (He and McAuley, 2016). The restaurant review corpus is from the Yelp Review Dataset Challenge [4]. We only use reviews from restaurant categories that the second dataset is selected from [5]. We set the embedding dimensions to 100 and the number of iterations to 30 (for a small embedding corpus, embeddings tend to be under-fitted), and keep the rest hyper-parameters as the defaults in fastText. We further use fastText to compose out-of-vocabulary word embeddings via subword N-gram embeddings.

4.2 Baseline Methods

We perform a comparison of DE-CNN with three groups of baselines using the standard evaluation of the datasets[6] [7]. The results of the first two groups are copied from (Li and Lam, 2017). The first group uses single-task approaches.

CRF is conditional random fields with basic features[8] and GloVe word embedding(Pennington et al., 2014).

IHS_RD (Chernyshevich, 2014) and **NLANGP** (Toh and Su, 2016) are best systems in the original challenges (Pontiki et al., 2014, 2016).

WDEmb (Yin et al., 2016) enhanced CRF with word embeddings, linear context embeddings and dependency path embeddings as input.

LSTM (Liu et al., 2015; Li and Lam, 2017) is a vanilla BiLSTM.

BiLSTM-CNN-CRF (Reimers and Gurevych, 2017) is the state-of-the-art from the Named Entity Recogntion (NER) community. We use this

baseline[9] to demonstrate that a NER model may need further adaptation for aspect extraction.

The second group uses multi-task learning and also take advantage of gold-standard opinion terms/sentiment lexicon.

RNCRF (Wang et al., 2016) is a joint model with a dependency tree based recursive neural network and CRF for aspect and opinion terms co-extraction. Besides opinion annotations, it also uses handcrafted features.

CMLA (Wang et al., 2017) is a multi-layer coupled-attention network that also performs aspect and opinion terms co-extraction. It uses gold-standard opinion labels in the training data.

MIN (Li and Lam, 2017) is a multi-task learning framework that has (1) two LSTMs for jointly extraction of aspects and opinions, and (2) a third LSTM for discriminating sentimental and non-sentimental sentences. A sentiment lexicon and high precision dependency rules are employed to find opinion terms.

The third group is the variations of DE-CNN.

GloVe-CNN only uses glove.840B.300d to show that domain embeddings are important.

Domain-CNN does not use the general embeddings to show that domain embeddings alone are not good enough as the domain corpus is limited for training good general words embeddings.

MaxPool-DE-CNN adds max-pooling in the last CNN layer. We use this baseline to show that the max-pooling operation used in the traditional CNN architecture is harmful to sequence labeling.

DE-OOD-CNN replaces the domain embeddings with out-of-domain embeddings to show that a large out-of-domain corpus is not a good replacement for a small in-domain corpus for domain embeddings. We use all *electronics* reviews as the out-of-domain corpus for the *laptop* and all the Yelp reviews for *restaurant*.

DE-Google-CNN replaces the glove embeddings with GoogleNews embeddings[10], which are pre-trained from a smaller corpus (100 billion tokens). We use this baseline to demonstrate that general embeddings that are pre-trained from a larger corpus performs better.

DE-CNN-CRF replaces the softmax activation with a CRF layer[11]. We use this baseline to

---

[3] http://www.nltk.org/

[4] https://www.yelp.com/dataset/challenge

[5] http://www.cs.cmu.edu/~mehrbod/RR/Cuisines.wht

[6] http://alt.qcri.org/semeval2014/task4

[7] http://alt.qcri.org/semeval2016/task5

[8] http://sklearn-crfsuite.readthedocs.io/en/latest/tutorial.html

[9] https://github.com/UKPLab/emnlp2017-bilstm-cnn-crf

[10] https://code.google.com/archive/p/word2vec/

[11] https://github.com/allenai/allennlp

Model	Laptop	Restaurant
CRF	74.01	69.56
IHS_RD	74.55	-
NLANGP	-	72.34
WDEmb	75.16	-
LSTM	75.25	71.26
BiLSTM-CNN-CRF	77.8	72.5
RNCRF	78.42	-
CMLA	77.80	-
MIN	77.58	73.44
GloVe-CNN	77.67	72.08
Domain-CNN	78.12	71.75
MaxPool-DE-CNN	77.45	71.12
DE-LSTM	78.73	72.94
DE-OOD-CNN	80.21	74.2
DE-Google-CNN	78.8	72.1
DE-CNN-CRF	80.8	74.1
DE-CNN	**81.59***	**74.37***

Table 2: Comparison results in F_1 score: numbers in the third group are averaged scores of 5 runs as in (Li and Lam, 2017). * indicates the result is statistical significant at the level of 0.05.

demonstrate that CRF may not further improve the challenging performance of aspect extraction.

4.3 Hyper-parameters

We hold out 150 training examples as validation data to decide the hyper-parameters. The first CNN layer has 128 filters with kernel sizes $k = 3$ (where $c = 1$ is the number of words on the left (or right) context) and 128 filters with kernel sizes $k = 5$ ($c = 2$). The rest 3 CNN layers have 256 filters with kernel sizes $k = 5$ ($c = 2$) per layer. The dropout rate is 0.55 and the learning rate of Adam optimizer (Kingma and Ba, 2014) is 0.0001 because CNN training tends to be unstable.

4.4 Results and Analysis

Table 4.3 shows that DE-CNN performs the best. The double embedding mechanism improves the performance and in-domain embeddings are important. We can see that using general embeddings (GloVe-CNN) or domain embeddings (Domain-CNN) alone gives inferior performance. We further notice that the performance on *Laptops* and *Restaurant* domains are quite different. *Laptops* has many domain-specific aspects, such as "adapter". So the domain embeddings for *Laptops* are better than the general embeddings. The *Restaurant* domain has many very general aspects like "staff", "service" that do not deviate much from their general meanings. So general embed-

dings are not bad. Max pooling is a bad operation as indicated by MaxPool-DE-CNN since the max pooling operation loses word positions. DE-OOD-CNN's performance is poor, indicating that making the training corpus of domain embeddings to be exactly in-domain is important. DE-Google-CNN uses a much smaller training corpus for general embeddings, leading to poorer performance than that of DE-CNN. Surprisingly, we notice that the CRF layer (DE-CNN-CRF) does not help. In fact, the CRF layer can improve 1-2% when the laptop's performance is about 75%. But it doesn't contribute much when laptop's performance is above 80%. CRF is good at modeling label dependences (e.g., label I must be after B), but many aspects are just single words and the major types of errors (mentioned later) do not fall in what CRF can solve. Note that we did not tune the hyperparameters of DE-CNN-CRF for practical purpose because training the CRF layer is extremely slow.

One important baseline is BiLSTM-CNN-CRF, which is markedly worse than our method. We believe the reason is that this baseline leverages dependency-based embeddings(Levy and Goldberg, 2014), which could be very important for NER. NER models may require further adaptations (e.g., domain embeddings) for opinion texts.

DE-CNN has two major types of errors. One type comes from inconsistent labeling (e.g., for the restaurant data, the same aspect is sometimes labeled and sometimes not). Another major type of errors comes from unseen aspects in test data that require the semantics of the conjunction word "and" to extract. For example, if A is an aspect and when "A and B" appears, B should also be extracted but not. We leave this to future work.

5 Conclusion

We propose a CNN-based aspect extraction model with a double embeddings mechanism without extra supervision. Experimental results demonstrated that the proposed method outperforms state-of-the-art methods with a large margin.

6 Acknowledgments

This work was supported in part by NSF through grants IIS-1526499, IIS-1763325, and IIS1407927, CNS-1626432, NSFC 61672313, and a gift from Huawei Technologies.

References

Anselm Blumer, Andrzej Ehrenfeucht, David Haussler, and Manfred K Warmuth. 1987. Occam's razor. *Information processing letters*, 24(6):377–380.

Piotr Bojanowski, Edouard Grave, Armand Joulin, and Tomas Mikolov. 2016. Enriching word vectors with subword information. *arXiv preprint arXiv:1607.04606*.

Danushka Bollegala, Kohei Hayashi, and Ken-ichi Kawarabayashi. 2017. Think globally, embed locally—locally linear meta-embedding of words. *arXiv preprint arXiv:1709.06671*.

Danushka Bollegala, Takanori Maehara, and Ken-ichi Kawarabayashi. 2015. Unsupervised cross-domain word representation learning. *arXiv preprint arXiv:1505.07184*.

Erik Cambria and Amir Hussain. 2012. *Sentic Computing Techniques, Tools, and Applications 2nd Edition*.

Tao Chen, Ruifeng Xu, Yulan He, and Xuan Wang. 2017. Improving sentiment analysis via sentence type classification using bilstm-crf and cnn. *Expert Systems with Applications*, 72:221–230.

Maryna Chernyshevich. 2014. Ihs r&d belarus: Cross-domain extraction of product features using crf. In *Proceedings of the 8th International Workshop on Semantic Evaluation (SemEval 2014)*, pages 309–313.

Jonas Gehring, Michael Auli, David Grangier, Denis Yarats, and Yann N Dauphin. 2017. Convolutional sequence to sequence learning. *arXiv preprint arXiv:1705.03122*.

Ruidan He, Wee Sun Lee, Hwee Tou Ng, and Daniel Dahlmeier. 2017. An unsupervised neural attention model for aspect extraction. In *Proceedings of the 55th Annual Meeting of the Association for Computational Linguistics (Volume 1: Long Papers)*, volume 1, pages 388–397.

Ruining He and Julian McAuley. 2016. Ups and downs: Modeling the visual evolution of fashion trends with one-class collaborative filtering. In *proceedings of the 25th international conference on world wide web*, pages 507–517. International World Wide Web Conferences Steering Committee.

Sepp Hochreiter and Jürgen Schmidhuber. 1997. Long short-term memory. *Neural computation*, 9(8):1735–1780.

Minqing Hu and Bing Liu. 2004. Mining and summarizing customer reviews. In *KDD '04*, pages 168–177.

Niklas Jakob and Iryna Gurevych. 2010. Extracting opinion targets in a single- and cross-domain setting with conditional random fields. In *EMNLP '10*, pages 1035–1045.

Yoon Kim. 2014. Convolutional neural networks for sentence classification. *arXiv preprint arXiv:1408.5882*.

Diederik P Kingma and Jimmy Ba. 2014. Adam: A method for stochastic optimization. *arXiv preprint arXiv:1412.6980*.

John Lafferty, Andrew McCallum, and Fernando CN Pereira. 2001. Conditional random fields: Probabilistic models for segmenting and labeling sequence data. In *ICML '01*, pages 282–289.

Yann LeCun, Yoshua Bengio, et al. 1995. Convolutional networks for images, speech, and time series. *The handbook of brain theory and neural networks*, 3361(10):1995.

Omer Levy and Yoav Goldberg. 2014. Dependency-based word embeddings. In *Proceedings of the 52nd Annual Meeting of the Association for Computational Linguistics (Volume 2: Short Papers)*, volume 2, pages 302–308.

Xin Li and Wai Lam. 2017. Deep multi-task learning for aspect term extraction with memory interaction. In *Proceedings of the 2017 Conference on Empirical Methods in Natural Language Processing*, pages 2886–2892.

Chenghua Lin and Yulan He. 2009. Joint sentiment/topic model for sentiment analysis. In *CIKM '09*, pages 375–384.

Bing Liu. 2012. *Sentiment Analysis and Opinion Mining*. Morgan & Claypool Publishers.

Kang Liu, Liheng Xu, Yang Liu, and Jun Zhao. 2013. Opinion target extraction using partially-supervised word alignment model. In *IJCAI '13*, pages 2134–2140.

Pengfei Liu, Shafiq Joty, and Helen Meng. 2015. Fine-grained opinion mining with recurrent neural networks and word embeddings. In *Proceedings of the 2015 Conference on Empirical Methods in Natural Language Processing*, pages 1433–1443.

Qiaozhu Mei, Xu Ling, Matthew Wondra, Hang Su, and ChengXiang Zhai. 2007. Topic sentiment mixture: Modeling facets and opinions in weblogs. In *WWW '07*, pages 171–180.

Margaret Mitchell, Jacqui Aguilar, Theresa Wilson, and Benjamin Van Durme. 2013. Open domain targeted sentiment. In *ACL '13*, pages 1643–1654.

Samaneh Moghaddam and Martin Ester. 2011. ILDA: interdependent lda model for learning latent aspects and their ratings from online product reviews. In *SIGIR '11*, pages 665–674.

Bo Pang and Lillian Lee. 2008. Opinion mining and sentiment analysis. *Found. Trends Inf. Retr.*, 2:1–135.

Jeffrey Pennington, Richard Socher, and Christopher Manning. 2014. Glove: Global vectors for word representation. In *Proceedings of the 2014 conference on empirical methods in natural language processing (EMNLP)*, pages 1532–1543.

Maria Pontiki, Dimitris Galanis, Haris Papageorgiou, Ion Androutsopoulos, Suresh Manandhar, AL-Smadi Mohammad, Mahmoud Al-Ayyoub, Yanyan Zhao, Bing Qin, Orphée De Clercq, et al. 2016. Semeval-2016 task 5: Aspect based sentiment analysis. In *Proceedings of the 10th international workshop on semantic evaluation (SemEval-2016)*, pages 19–30.

Maria Pontiki, Dimitris Galanis, John Pavlopoulos, Harris Papageorgiou, Ion Androutsopoulos, and Suresh Manandhar. 2014. Semeval-2014 task 4: Aspect based sentiment analysis. In *Proceedings of the 8th International Workshop on Semantic Evaluation (SemEval 2014)*, pages 27–35, Dublin, Ireland. Association for Computational Linguistics and Dublin City University.

Ana-Maria Popescu and Oren Etzioni. 2005. Extracting product features and opinions from reviews. In *HLT-EMNLP '05*, pages 339–346.

Soujanya Poria, Erik Cambria, and Alexander Gelbukh. 2016. Aspect extraction for opinion mining with a deep convolutional neural network. *Knowledge-Based Systems*, 108:42–49.

Guang Qiu, Bing Liu, Jiajun Bu, and Chun Chen. 2011. Opinion word expansion and target extraction through double propagation. *Computational Linguistics*, 37(1):9–27.

Nils Reimers and Iryna Gurevych. 2017. Reporting Score Distributions Makes a Difference: Performance Study of LSTM-networks for Sequence Tagging. In *Proceedings of the 2017 Conference on Empirical Methods in Natural Language Processing (EMNLP)*, pages 338–348, Copenhagen, Denmark.

Lei Shu, Bing Liu, Hu Xu, and Annice Kim. 2016. Lifelong-rl: Lifelong relaxation labeling for separating entities and aspects in opinion targets. In *Proceedings of the Conference on Empirical Methods in Natural Language Processing (EMNLP)*.

Lei Shu, Hu Xu, and Bing Liu. 2017. Lifelong learning crf for supervised aspect extraction. In *Proceedings of the 55th Annual Meeting of the Association for Computational Linguistics (Volume 2: Short Papers)*, volume 2, pages 148–154.

Emma Strubell, Patrick Verga, David Belanger, and Andrew McCallum. 2017. Fast and accurate entity recognition with iterated dilated convolutions. In *Proceedings of the 2017 Conference on Empirical Methods in Natural Language Processing*, pages 2670–2680.

Ivan Titov and Ryan McDonald. 2008. A joint model of text and aspect ratings for sentiment summarization. In *ACL '08: HLT*, pages 308–316.

Zhiqiang Toh and Jian Su. 2016. Nlangp at semeval-2016 task 5: Improving aspect based sentiment analysis using neural network features. In *Proceedings of the 10th international workshop on semantic evaluation (SemEval-2016)*, pages 282–288.

Bo Wang and Houfeng Wang. 2008. Bootstrapping both product features and opinion words from chinese customer reviews with cross-inducing. In *IJCNLP '08*, pages 289–295.

Wenya Wang, Sinno Jialin Pan, Daniel Dahlmeier, and Xiaokui Xiao. 2016. Recursive neural conditional random fields for aspect-based sentiment analysis. *arXiv preprint arXiv:1603.06679*.

Wenya Wang, Sinno Jialin Pan, Daniel Dahlmeier, and Xiaokui Xiao. 2017. Coupled multi-layer attentions for co-extraction of aspect and opinion terms. In *AAAI*, pages 3316–3322.

Ronald J Williams and David Zipser. 1989. A learning algorithm for continually running fully recurrent neural networks. *Neural computation*, 1(2):270–280.

Hu Xu, Bing Liu, Lei Shu, and Philip S. Yu. 2018a. Lifelong domain word embedding via meta-learning. In *Proceedings of the 27th International Joint Conference on Artificial Intelligence*. AAAI Press.

Hu Xu, Sihong Xie, Lei Shu, and Philip S. Yu. 2018b. Dual attention network for product compatibility and function satisfiability analysis. In *Proceedings of AAAI Conference on Artificial Intelligence (AAAI)*.

Yichun Yin, Furu Wei, Li Dong, Kaimeng Xu, Ming Zhang, and Ming Zhou. 2016. Unsupervised word and dependency path embeddings for aspect term extraction. *arXiv preprint arXiv:1605.07843*.

Xiang Zhang, Junbo Zhao, and Yann LeCun. 2015. Character-level convolutional networks for text classification. In *Advances in neural information processing systems*, pages 649–657.

Xinjie Zhou, Xiaojun Wan, and Jianguo Xiao. 2013. Collective opinion target extraction in Chinese microblogs. In *EMNLP '13*, pages 1840–1850.

Li Zhuang, Feng Jing, and Xiao-Yan Zhu. 2006. Movie review mining and summarization. In *CIKM '06*, pages 43–50.

Will it Blend? Blending Weak and Strong Labeled Data in a Neural Network for Argumentation Mining

Eyal Shnarch, Carlos Alzate, Lena Dankin, Martin Gleize,
Yufang Hou, Leshem Choshen, Ranit Aharonov, Noam Slonim
IBM Research
{eyals, lenad, leshem.choshen, ranita, noams}@il.ibm.com
{carlos.alzate, martin.gleize, yhou}@ie.ibm.com

Abstract

The process of obtaining high quality labeled data for natural language understanding tasks is often slow, error-prone, complicated and expensive. With the vast usage of neural networks, this issue becomes more notorious since these networks require a large amount of labeled data to produce satisfactory results. We propose a methodology to blend high quality but scarce labeled data with noisy but abundant weak labeled data during the training of neural networks. Experiments in the context of topic-dependent evidence detection with two forms of weak labeled data show the advantages of the blending scheme. In addition, we provide a manually annotated data set for the task of topic-dependent evidence detection.

1   Introduction

In recent years, neural networks have been widely used for natural language understanding tasks. Such networks demand a considerable amount of labeled data for each specific task. However, for many tasks, the process of obtaining high quality labeled data is slow, expensive, and complicated (Habernal et al., 2018). In this work, we propose a method for improving network training when a small amount of labeled data is available.

Several works have suggested methods for generating *weak labeled data* (WLD) whose quality for the task of interest is low, but that can be easily obtained. One approach for gathering WLD is to apply heuristics to a large corpus. For example, Hearst (1992) considered a noun to be the hypernym of another noun if they are connected by the *is a* pattern in a sentence.

Distant supervision is another form of WLD used in various tasks such as relation extraction (Mintz et al., 2009; Surdeanu et al., 2012) and sentiment analysis (Go et al., 2009). Other works use emojis or hashtags as weak labels describing the texts in which they appear (e.g., Davidov et al. (2010) in the context of sarcasm detection).

WLD can be freely obtained, however it comes with a price: it is often very noisy. Therefore, systems trained only on WLD are at a serious disadvantage compared to systems trained on high quality labeled data, which we term henceforth *strong labeled data* (SLD). However, we suggest that the easily accessible WLD is still useful when used alongside SLD, which is naturally limited in size.

In this work we propose a method for blending WLD and SLD in the training of neural networks. Focusing on the argumentation mining field, we create and release a data set for the task of topic-dependent evidence detection. Our evaluation shows that such blending improves the accuracy of the network compared to not using WLD or not blending it. This improvement is even more evident when SLD is not abundantly available.

We believe that blending WLD and SLD is a general notion that may be applicable to many language understanding tasks, and can especially assist researchers who wish to train a network but have a small amount of SLD for their task of interest.

2   Background

2.1   WLD and networks

In the field of neural networks, WLD has mainly been employed for pre-training networks. This was done in related fields such as information retrieval (Dehghani et al., 2017b) and sentiment analysis (Severyn and Moschitti, 2015; Deriu et al., 2017). Contrary to those works, we ex-

Proceedings of the 56th Annual Meeting of the Association for Computational Linguistics (Short Papers), pages 599–605
Melbourne, Australia, July 15 - 20, 2018. ©2018 Association for Computational Linguistics

plore a way to utilize WLD *together* with SLD and *throughout* the training process.

Most similar to our work, Dehghani et al. (2017a) use WLD and SLD together, for sentiment classification. They train two separate networks, one with WLD only, and another with SLD only. They control the magnitude of the gradient updates to the network trained on WLD, using the scores provided by the network trained on SLD. Differently, we blend the two types of labeled data in a single network.

2.2 Argumentation mining

Argumentation mining is attracting a lot of attention (Lippi and Torroni, 2016). One line of research focuses on identifying arguments (claims and evidence/premises) within a text (Stab and Gurevych, 2014; Habernal and Gurevych, 2015; Persing and Ng, 2016; Eger et al., 2017). Another line of work seeks to mine arguments relevant for a given topic or claim, either from a pre-built argument repository where arguments are collected from online debate portals (Wachsmuth et al., 2017), or from unrestricted large scale corpora (Levy et al., 2014; Rinott et al., 2015; Levy et al., 2017). Our work falls into the latter category of *corpus wide topic-dependent* argumentation mining.

Previous work by Rinott et al. (2015) presented the task of detecting evidence texts that are relevant for claims of a given topic. They search in a preselected set of articles, in which the likelihood to find an evidence is considerably higher than in an arbitrary article from the corpus. In this work, we detect evidence directly supporting or contesting the topic (without an intermediate claim), and we search in the entire corpus, with no need for pre-selecting a small set of relevant articles.

2.3 SLD and WLD in argumentation mining

Publicly available strong labeled data (SLD) for argument mining is usually only a couple of thousand instances in size (e.g., Stab and Gurevych (2017) present one of the largest, with around 6,000 annotated positive instances). Recently, Habernal et al. (2018) have commented about the difficulty to collect valuable SLD from crowd sourcing for such tasks.

Several works utilize WLD for argumentation mining; Webis-Debate-16 (Al-Khatib et al., 2016) use the structure of online debates as distant supervision for the task of argument classification.

Sentences from the first paragraph are considered as non-argumentative and the rest of the sentences are considered as argumentative.

For the topic-dependent claim detection task, Levy et al. (2017) showed that retrieving sentences with the word *that* followed by the concept representing the topic, yields candidates that are more likely to contain a claim for that topic than arbitrary sentences which contain the topic concept.

3 BlendNet

We present *BlendNet*, a neural network that is trained on a blend of WLD and SLD.

3.1 Network description

Our network is a bi-directional LSTM (Graves and Schmidhuber, 2005) with an additional attention layer (Yang et al., 2016).

The models are all trained with a dropout of 0.85, using a single dropout mask across all time-steps as proposed by Gal and Ghahramani (2016). The cell size in the LSTM layers is 128, and the attention layer is of size 100. We use the Adam method as an optimizer (Kingma and Ba, 2015) with a learning rate of 0.001, and apply gradient clipping with a maximum global norm of 1.0. Words are represented using the 300 dimensional GloVe embeddings learned on 840B Common Crawl tokens and are left untouched during training (Pennington et al., 2014).

We note that even though we chose this network architecture, there is nothing in the blending method we propose which is restricted to it, and blending can be easily applied to other networks.

3.2 WLD blending

WLD is a pair of disjoint sets, WLD_{pos} and WLD_{neg}. The two sets are constructed such that the probability of finding positive instances in WLD_{pos} is significantly higher than that of finding them in WLD_{neg}. This difference in probabilities is the source of the signal WLD provides. Importantly, the probability in WLD_{pos} can still be rather low.

As mentioned in Section 2.1, using WLD to pre-train neural networks has been proven to be effective. We extend this idea by allowing the use of WLD alongside SLD during the entire training process of the network. Our intuition is that even though WLD signal is noisy, there is potential in its additional massive amount, and integrating it can improve training when SLD is limited in size.

In every epoch (a pass through the entire SLD), the training data is enriched with WLD. However, since WLD is noisy, an exponentially decreasing fraction of it is blended into the network at each epoch.

Formally, we have m *initialization epochs* using the entire WLD with no SLD. After this pre-training phase, we continue with n *blending epochs*, in each using all the available SLD, and a fraction of the WLD which is determined by a *blend factor* $\alpha \in [0..1]$. In the kth blending epoch ($k \in [0..n-1]$) we blend α^k of the WLD with the SLD, and feed the data in a random order to the network. Consequently, the first blending epoch uses full SLD and full WLD, and in every subsequent epoch the amount of WLD decays by a factor of α. The stopping point n will typically be empirically determined. We set it to a number that will guarantee that the last couple of epochs will be composed of mainly SLD, since eventually, this is the better signal for training.

One can come up with different methods for blending WLD and SLD. For instance, start training with all available SLD and gradually blend more and more WLD, or use all available WLD and SLD during the entire training. In Section 5 we refer to some alternatives and show that they do not achieve better results than the one presented above. However, we do not claim that our blending method is the only option or even the best one. The goal of this work is to suggest one method which works.

4 Data sets

We created a data set of 5,785 sentences with manual annotations for the task of topic-dependent evidence detection (this will serve as our SLD). It is available on the IBM Debater Datasets webpage.[1] We use it for training and for evaluation and describe it next. In Section 4.2 we describe two methods for freely obtaining weak labeled data for our task.

4.1 SLD annotation

Our strong labeled data (SLD) consists of pairs of a topic and a sentence. Topics were extracted from several sources, such as Debatepedia, an online

encyclopedia dedicated to debates and argumentation. The data set includes 118 diverse topics, from domains such as politics, science and education. The topics generally deal with one clearly identifiable concept.

The sentences were extracted from Wikipedia and were annotated by crowd-sourcing. We used 10 annotators for each pair of topic and sentence; each annotator either confirms or rejects the sentence as evidence for the topic. We combine the annotators' votes into a binary label by majority. Ties are resolved as non-evidence.

The guidelines for the task present three criteria which all have to be met for a positive label. The sentence must clearly support or contest the topic, and not simply be neutral. It has to be coherent and stand mostly on its own. Finally it has to be convincing, something you could use to sway someone's stance on the topic: a claim is not enough, it has to be backed up.

The annotators agreement is 0.45 by Fleiss' kappa. This is a typical value in such challenging labeling tasks, comparable to previous reports in the literature, e.g., (Aharoni et al., 2014; Rinott et al., 2015). In addition, for 85% of the labeled instances, the majority vote included at least 70% of the annotators, further supporting the quality of the released data.

The 118 topics were randomly split into two sets: 83 topics for training (4,066 sentences), and 35 topics for testing (1,719 sentences). No sentences of the same topic appear in both sets. The prior for positive, i.e., an evidence instance, is about 40% for both sets. In addition, every occurrence of the topic concept in the candidate is replaced with a common token, to keep the training topic-independent. The topic concept is detected by an in-house wikification tool, similar to TagMe (Ferragina and Scaiella, 2010). The README, provided with this paper, includes additional information about the data set and the pre-processing.

4.2 WLD generation

Next we describe two sources of WLD we use in our experiments. For the first source, we use the method described by Levy et al. (2017) for unsupervised topic dependent claim detection. Following them, we construct the set of WLD_{pos} by retrieving sentences from Wikipedia which match the query "that + topic concept", i.e. sentences which contain the word "that" followed by the

---

[1]See `http://www.research.ibm.com/haifa/dept/vst/debating_data.shtml`

concept of the topic (not necessarily adjacent). The WLD_{neg} set is constructed by retrieving sentences that contain the topic concept and are not part of WLD_{pos}. Levy et al. (2017) showed that the likelihood of claims in WLD_{pos} is double the likelihood in WLD_{neg}.

We believe that the query "that + topic concept" is indicative of argumentative content in general, and not just of claims. It is therefore a good fit for constructing WLD for the topic-dependent evidence detection task. Indeed, in the data set, described in Section 4.1, the prior for positive in the entire training set is close to 40%, but among the candidates that match the query, it is much higher – 52%. Applying this WLD method we were able to extract $253,352$ sentences from Wikipedia which contain the topic concept, 25% of them also contain "that" before the topic concept, and they are our WLD_{pos}.

For the second source of WLD, we use the Webis-Debate-16 corpus (Al-Khatib et al., 2016), using their argumentative vs. non-argumentative division. This division was automatically created by mapping the specific structure of idebate.org pages – introduction, points for/against, point/counterpoint – to the two classes. The sentences of the *introduction* are labeled by them as non-argumentative, under the assumption that they neutrally present the topic. We use them as our WLD_{neg}. The other sentences are labeled in Webis-Debate-16 as argumentative, thus we use them as our WLD_{pos}. Out of $16,402$ total instances, 66% are in WLD_{pos}. This data set doubly deserves the status of WLD in our task because the labels do not exactly match the evidence/non-evidence classification, and in addition it is produced automatically based on a coarse-grained mapping that is bound to introduce noise.

5 Experimental setup and results

We use the data set described in Section 4, training the network on the train set and evaluating its accuracy on the test set. We empirically explore several blending configurations and evaluate their impact on the accuracy of the network. To validate our assumption that WLD contribution would be more prominent when SLD is limited, we test each configuration with varying sizes of SLD between 500 and 4,000.

Following some preliminary exploration, on a different data set, we noticed that the parameter m, the number of initialization epochs, does not make a significant difference, and we set it to be 1 (trying $m > 1$ resulted in slightly worse accuracy).

As mentioned in Section 3.2, our stopping criterion was set to ensure that in any configuration, we have four blending epochs in which the input for the network is mostly SLD, i.e. it is at least 95% of the data seen by the network.

For the blending factor we tried $\alpha \in \{0, 0.05, 0.2\}$, and quickly learned that choosing a blending factor value larger than 0.05 is typically ineffective. Since the blending factor determines the numbers of epochs in which the WLD is significant, and since it is reasonable to limit this number due to the noisy nature of the WLD, it is not surprising that a small value of α is preferable. We note that setting $\alpha = 0$ means WLD is only used in the initialization epochs.

Finally, to keep results reliable, as SLD size can get quite small, we repeat each configuration run five times with different SLD slices to reduce variance. For each run we record the best accuracy out of all its epochs and report the micro average of the best accuracies of the five runs.

Figure 1 depicts our results. Blending WLD throughout several epochs of training (the thick green curve with round dots), improves performance over using it only for initialization, as most previous works do (the dashed red curve), and over not using WLD at all (the blue curve with triangles). This effect is significantly more notable as we use less SLD. For example, in the left plot, which presents the usage of Webis-Debate-16 as WLD, we see that using 1,000 instances of SLD with WLD yields results comparable to using 2,500 SLD instances. Similarly, 2,000 SLD instances plus WLD, are comparable to using 3,000 SLD instances. The effect is smaller when the WLD is based on the "that + topic concept" query, but the trend is similar.

One may claim that the signal in WLD is stronger than we hypothesized and therefore the performance improves simply because we are adding labeled data for training. To test this claim we train the network with all available WLD and only it. The single triangles on the Y-axis of each plot show that the accuracy of the network with such training is much lower than using the entire SLD, reflecting the inferior quality of the WLD. In addition, we note that the accuracy on the test set of the "that + topic concept" query, which was

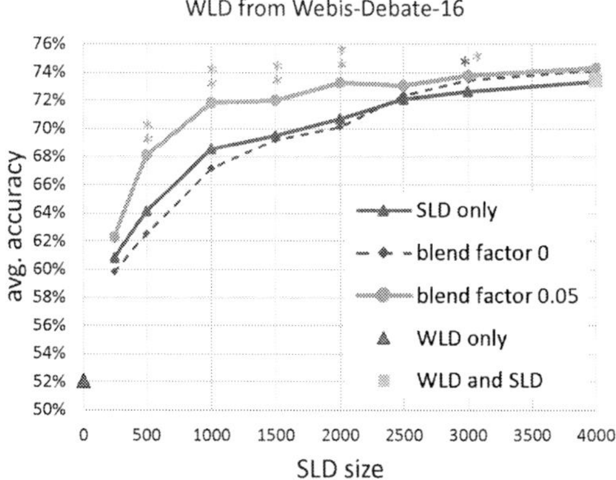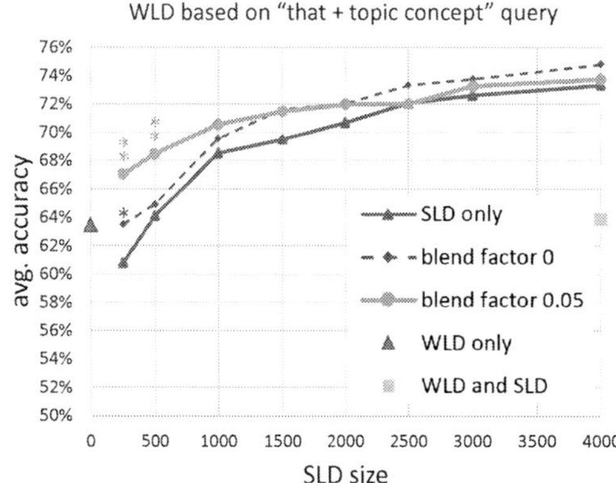

Figure 1: Micro-averaged accuracy on the SLD test set for the different sizes of SLD training data. A single asterisk (*) indicates significant results in comparison to *SLD only* and double asterisks indicate significant results also in comparison to *blend factor 0* (unpaired student t-test with $p < 0.05$).

used to collect one of our WLD types, is only 17%.

Another claim may be that just by utilizing WLD in addition to SLD the accuracy improves, and that there is no need for any blending method. To answer that, we unify the WLD and the SLD, without applying any blending method (single squares on the right border of each plot). For the WLD constructed by the "that + topic concept" query the accuracy is well below the accuracy achieved when using SLD alone, as can be seen in the right plot. On the left plot, we see that unifying the WLD with the SLD does not help nor harm compared to using the SLD alone.

We conclude that even though WLD is not nearly as accurate as SLD, it has the potential to improve performance, if blended correctly.

We also tried gradually *increasing* the amount of WLD in each blending epoch, instead of decreasing it. We tested several increasing factors on both types of WLD. Results were similar to the proposed blending method.

6 Conclusions

Neural networks have become widely useful in natural language understanding tasks. It is often the case that there is not enough high quality labeled data for the target task, leading to significant drops in network performance. On the other hand, for many tasks, weak labeled data can be easily obtained but is usually noisy.

In this work we explore a way to enable a network to take advantage of the large size of WLD without overriding the high quality of SLD.

In the method we present, training starts with initialization epochs in which only the WLD is used. It continues with blending epochs in which the data fed to the network is a dynamic mixture of WLD and SLD. The blending method we presented, assigns higher importance to the vast amount of WLD at the beginning of the training and decreases its impact as training progresses.

We evaluate our blending method on the task of topic-dependent evidence detection, leveraging two WLD sources, and show that it improves performance for each source. The impact of blending increases as the amount of SLD decreases.

Additionally, we release a data set of 5,785 manually labeled sentences to encourage reproducibility and further work on evidence detection.

The impact of the two WLD we tried is evidently different: the Webis corpus seems to help more than the "that + topic concept" query. This calls for future work of understanding what makes a good fit between WLD and SLD. The amount of WLD does not seem to be an important factor, as we see that blending the smaller WLD of the two achieves better performance. It is probably highly related to the quality of the WLD. Sentences retrieved from Wikipedia are of many forms and domains, while the Webis corpus is composed of sentences from debates, which might explain why the network is able to leverage it better.

For future work we intend to examine ways to find better WLD and to make better use of it. For example, instead of choosing one type of WLD, we can combine several WLD types together.

References

Ehud Aharoni, Anatoly Polnarov, Tamar Lavee, Daniel Hershcovich, Ran Levy, Ruty Rinott, Dan Gutfreund, and Noam Slonim. 2014. A benchmark dataset for automatic detection of claims and evidence in the context of controversial topics. In *Proceedings of the first Workshop on Argumentation Mining*, pages 64–68.

Khalid Al-Khatib, Henning Wachsmuth, Matthias Hagen, Jonas Köhler, and Benno Stein. 2016. Cross-domain mining of argumentative text through distant supervision. In *Proceedings of the North American Chapter of the Association for Computational Linguistics: Human Language Technologies*, San Diego, California, 12–17 June 2016, pages 1395–1404.

Dmitry Davidov, Oren Tsur, and Ari Rappoport. 2010. Semi-supervised recognition of sarcastic sentences in twitter and amazon. In *Proceedings of the Fourteenth Conference on Computational Natural Language Learning*, CoNLL, pages 107–116.

Mostafa Dehghani, Aliaksei Severyn, Sascha Rothe, and Jaap Kamps. 2017a. Learning to learn from weak supervision by full supervision. In *Proceedings of the workshop on Meta-Learning at Advances in Neural Information Processing Systems 31(NIPS 2017)*, pages 65–74.

Mostafa Dehghani, Hamed Zamani, Aliaksei Severyn, Jaap Kamps, and W Bruce Croft. 2017b. Neural ranking models with weak supervision. In *Proceedings of the 40th International ACM SIGIR Conference on Research and Development in Information Retrieval*, pages 65–74. ACM.

Jan Deriu, Aurelien Lucchi, Valeria De Luca, Aliaksei Severyn, Simon Müller, Mark Cieliebak, Thomas Hofmann, and Martin Jaggi. 2017. Leveraging large amounts of weakly supervised data for multi-language sentiment classification. In *Proceedings of the 26th International Conference on World Wide Web*, pages 1045–1052. International World Wide Web Conferences Steering Committee.

Steffen Eger, Johannes Daxenberger, and Iryna Gurevych. 2017. Neural end-to-end learning for computational argumentation mining. In *Proceedings of the 55th Annual Meeting of the Association for Computational Linguistics*, Vancouver, Canada, 30 July–4 August 2017, pages 11–22.

Paolo Ferragina and Ugo Scaiella. 2010. Tagme: on-the-fly annotation of short text fragments (by wikipedia entities). In *Proceedings of the 19th ACM international conference on Information and knowledge management*, pages 1625–1628. ACM.

Yarin Gal and Zoubin Ghahramani. 2016. A theoretically grounded application of dropout in recurrent neural networks. In *Advances in neural information processing systems*, pages 1019–1027.

Alec Go, Richa Bhayani, and Lei Huang. 2009. Twitter sentiment classification using distant supervision. Technical report, Stanford.

Alex Graves and Jürgen Schmidhuber. 2005. Framewise phoneme classification with bidirectional lstm and other neural network architectures. *Neural Networks*, 18(5-6):602–610.

Ivan Habernal and Iryna Gurevych. 2015. Exploiting debate portals for semi-supervised argumentation mining in user-generated web discourse. In *Proceedings of the Conference on Empirical Methods in Natural Language Processing*, Lisbon, Portugal, 17–21 September 2015, pages 2127–2137.

Ivan Habernal, Henning Wachsmuth, Iryna Gurevych, and Benno Stein. 2018. The argument reasoning comprehension task: Identification and reconstruction of implicit warrants. In *NAACL*, page to appear. Association for Computational Linguistics.

Marti A. Hearst. 1992. Automatic acquisition of hyponyms from large text corpora. In *Proceedings of the 15th International Conference on Computational Linguistics*, Nantes, France, 23-28 August 1992, pages 539–545.

Diederik P. Kingma and Jimmy Ba. 2015. Adam: A method for stochastic optimization. In *Proceedings of the 3rd International Conference on Learning Representations*, San Diego, 2015.

Ran Levy, Yonatan Bilu, Daniel Hershcovich, Ehud Aharoni, and Noam Slonim. 2014. Context dependent claim detection. In *Proceedings of the 25th International Conference on Computational Linguistics*, Dublin, Ireland, 23–29 August 2014, pages 1489–1500.

Ran Levy, Shai Gretz, Benjamin Sznajder, Shay Hummel, Ranit Aharonov, and Noam Slonim. 2017. Unsupervised corpus–wide claim detection. In *Proceedings of the 4th Workshop on Argument Mining held at EMNLP 2017*, Copenhagen, Denmark, 8 September 2017, pages 79–84.

Marco Lippi and Paolo Torroni. 2016. Argumentation mining: State of the art and emerging trends. *ACM Transactions on Internet Technology (TOIT)*, 16(2):10.

Mike Mintz, Steven Bills, Rion Snow, and Dan Jurafsky. 2009. Distant supervision for relation extraction without labeled data. In *Proceedings of the Joint Conference of the 47th Annual Meeting of the Association for Computational Linguistics and the 4th International Joint Conference on Natural Language Processing*, Singapore, 2–7 August 2009, pages 1003–1011.

Jeffrey Pennington, Richard Socher, and Christopher Manning. 2014. Glove: Global vectors for word representation. In *Proceedings of the 2014 conference on empirical methods in natural language processing (EMNLP)*, pages 1532–1543.

Isaac Persing and Vincent Ng. 2016. End-to-end argumentation mining in student essays. In *Proceedings of the North American Chapter of the Association for Computational Linguistics: Human Language Technologies,* San Diego, California, 12–17 June 2016, pages 1384–1394.

Ruty Rinott, Lena Dankin, Carlos Alzate Perez, Mitesh M. Khapra, Ehud Aharoni, and Noam Slonim. 2015. Show me your evidence - an automatic method for context dependent evidence detection. In *Proceedings of the Conference on Empirical Methods in Natural Language Processing,* Lisbon, Portugal, 17–21 September 2015, pages 440–450.

Aliaksei Severyn and Alessandro Moschitti. 2015. Unitn: Training deep convolutional neural network for twitter sentiment classification. In *Proceedings of the 9th international workshop on semantic evaluation (SemEval 2015),* pages 464–469.

Christian Stab and Iryna Gurevych. 2014. Identifying argumentative discourse structures in persuasive essays. In *Proceedings of the Conference on Empirical Methods in Natural Language Processing,* Doha, Qatar, 25–29 October 2014, pages 46–56.

Christian Stab and Iryna Gurevych. 2017. Parsing argumentation structures in persuasive essays. *Computational Linguistics,* 43:619–660.

Mihai Surdeanu, Julie Tibshirani, Ramesh Nallapati, and Christopher D Manning. 2012. Multi-instance multi-label learning for relation extraction. In *Proceedings of the Conference on Empirical Methods in Natural Language Processing and Natural Language Learning,* Jeju Island, Korea, 12–14 July 2012, pages 455–465.

Henning Wachsmuth, Benno Stein, and Yamen Ajjour. 2017. "pagerank" for argument relevance. In *Proceedings of the 15th Conference of the European Chapter of the Association for Computational Linguistics,* pages 1117–1127.

Zichao Yang, Diyi Yang, Chris Dyer, Xiaodong He, Alex Smola, and Eduard Hovy. 2016. Hierarchical attention networks for document classification. In *Proceedings of the 2016 Conference of the North American Chapter of the Association for Computational Linguistics: Human Language Technologies,* pages 1480–1489.

Investigating Audio, Video, and Text Fusion Methods for End-to-End Automatic Personality Prediction

Onno Kampman, Elham J. Barezi, Dario Bertero, Pascale Fung

Center for AI Research (CAiRE)

Hong Kong University of Science and Technology, Clear Water Bay, Hong Kong

`ejs,dbertero@connect.ust.hk, pascale@ece.ust.hk`

Abstract

We propose a tri-modal architecture to predict Big Five personality trait scores from video clips with different channels for audio, text, and video data. For each channel, stacked Convolutional Neural Networks are employed. The channels are fused both on decision-level and by concatenating their respective fully connected layers. It is shown that a multimodal fusion approach outperforms each single modality channel, with an improvement of 9.4% over the best individual modality (video). Full backpropagation is also shown to be better than a linear combination of modalities, meaning complex interactions between modalities can be leveraged to build better models. Furthermore, we can see the prediction relevance of each modality for each trait. The described model can be used to increase the emotional intelligence of virtual agents.

1 Introduction

Automatic prediction of personality is important for the development of emotional and empathetic virtual agents. Humans are very quick to assign personality traits to each other, as well as to virtual characters (Nass et al., 1995). People infer personality from different cues, both behavioral and verbal, hence a model to predict personality should take into account multiple modalities including language, speech and visual cues.

Personality is typically modeled with the Big Five personality descriptors (Goldberg, 1990). In this model an individual's personality is defined as a collection of five scores in range $[0, 1]$ for personality traits Extraversion, Agreeableness, Conscientiousness, Neuroticism and Openness to Experience. These score are usually calculated by each subject filling in a specific questionnaire. The biggest effort to predict personality, as well as to release a benchmark open-domain personality corpus, was given by the ChaLearn 2016 shared task challenge (Ponce-López et al., 2016). All the best performing teams used neural network techniques. They extracted traditional audio features (zero crossing rate, energy, spectral features, MFCCs) and then fed them into the neural network (Subramaniam et al., 2016; Gürpınar et al., 2016; Zhang et al., 2016). A deep neural network should however be able to extract such features itself. Güçlütürk et al. (2016) took a different approach by feeding the raw audio and video samples to the network. However they mostly designed the network for computer vision, and used the same architecture to audio input without any adaptation or considerations to merge modalities. The challenge was in general aimed at the computer vision community (many only used facial features), thus not many looked into what their deep network was learning regarding other modalities.

In this paper, we are interested in predicting personality from speech, language and video frames (facial features). We first consider the different modalities separately, in order to have more understanding of how personality is expressed and which modalities contribute more to the personality definition. Then we design and analyze fusion methods to effectively combine the three modalities in order to obtain a performance improvement over each individual modality. The readers can refer to the survey by Baltrušaitis et al. (2018) for more information on multi-modal approaches.

2 Methodology

Our multimodal deep neural network architecture consists of three separate channels for audio, text, and video. The channels are fused both in decision-

Proceedings of the 56th Annual Meeting of the Association for Computational Linguistics (Short Papers), pages 606–611
Melbourne, Australia, July 15 - 20, 2018. ©2018 Association for Computational Linguistics

level fusion and inside the neural network. The three channels are trained in a multiclass way, instead of separate models for each trait (Farnadi et al., 2016). The full architecture is trained *end-to-end*, which refers to models that are completely trained from the most raw input representation to the desired output, with all the parameters learned from data (Muller et al., 2006). Automatic feature learning has the capacity to outperform feature engineering, as these learned features are automatically tuned to the task at hand. The full neural network architecture with the three channels is shown in Fig. 1.

2.1 Audio channel

The audio channel looks at acoustic and prosodic (i.e. non-verbal) information of speech. It takes raw waveforms as input instead of commonly used spectrograms or traditional feature sets, as CNNs are able to autonomously extract relevant features directly from audio (Bertero et al., 2016).

Input audio samples are first downscaled to a uniform sampling rate of 8 kHz before fed to the model. During each training iteration (but not during evaluation), for each input audio sample we randomize the amplitude (volume) through an exponential random coefficient $\alpha = 10^{U(-1.5, 1.5)}$, where $U(-1.5, 1.5)$ is a uniform random variable, to avoid any bias related to recording volumes.

We split the input signal into two feature channels as input for the CNN: the raw waveform as-is, and the signal with squared amplitude (aimed at capturing the energy component of the signal). A stack of four convolutional layers is applied to the input to perform feature extraction from short overlapping windows, analyze variations over neighboring regions of different sizes, and combine all contributions throughout the sample.

We used global average pooling operation over the output of each layer to capture globally expressed personality characteristics over the entire audio frame and to combine the contributions of the convolutional layer outputs. After obtaining the overall vector by weighted-average of each convolutional layer output, it is fed to a fully connected layer with final sigmoid layer to perform the final regression operation to map this representation to a score in range $[0, 1]$ for each of the five traits.

2.2 Text channel

The transcriptions for the ChaLearn dataset, provided by the challenge organizers, were obtained by using a professional human transcription service [1] to ensure maximum quality for the ground truth annotations. For this channel we extract `word2vec` *word embeddings* from transcriptions and feed those into a CNN. The embeddings have a dimensionality of $k = 300$ and were pre-trained on Google News data (around 300 billion words). This enables us to take into account much more contextual information than available in just the corpus at hand.

Transcriptions per sample were split up into different sentences. We normalized the text in order to align our corpus with the embedding dictionary. We fed the computed matrix into a CNN, whose architecture is inspired by Kim (2014). Three convolutional windows of size three, four, and five words are slid over the sentence, taking steps of one word each time. These windows are expected to extract compact n-grams from sentences. After this layer, a max-pooling is taken for the outcome of each of the kernels separately to get a final sentence encoding. The representation is then mapped through a fully connected layer with sigmoid activation, to the final Big Five personality traits.

2.3 Video channel

In the video channel, we first take a random frame from each of the videos, which leads to personality recognition from only appearance. We did not use Long Short Term Memory (LSTM) networks because we only need appearance information, not temporal and movement information. Although many works in the ChaLearn competition align faces manually using the famous Viola-Jones algorithm (Viola and Jones, 2004) and crop them from frames (Gürpınar et al., 2016), here we choose not to in order to prevent excessive preprocessing. It has also been found and shown that deep architectures can automatically learn to focus on the face (Gucluturk et al., 2017).

We extract representations from the images using the VGG-face CNN model (Parkhi et al., 2015), with pre-trained VGG-16 weights (Simonyan and Zisserman, 2014). Input images are fed into the model with their three channels (blue, red, and green). Several convolutional layers combined with max-pooling and padding layers follow. We use two final fully connected layers, followed by sigmoid activation to map to the five traits. We only train these two final layers. Fine-tuning pre-

---

[1]http://www.rev.com

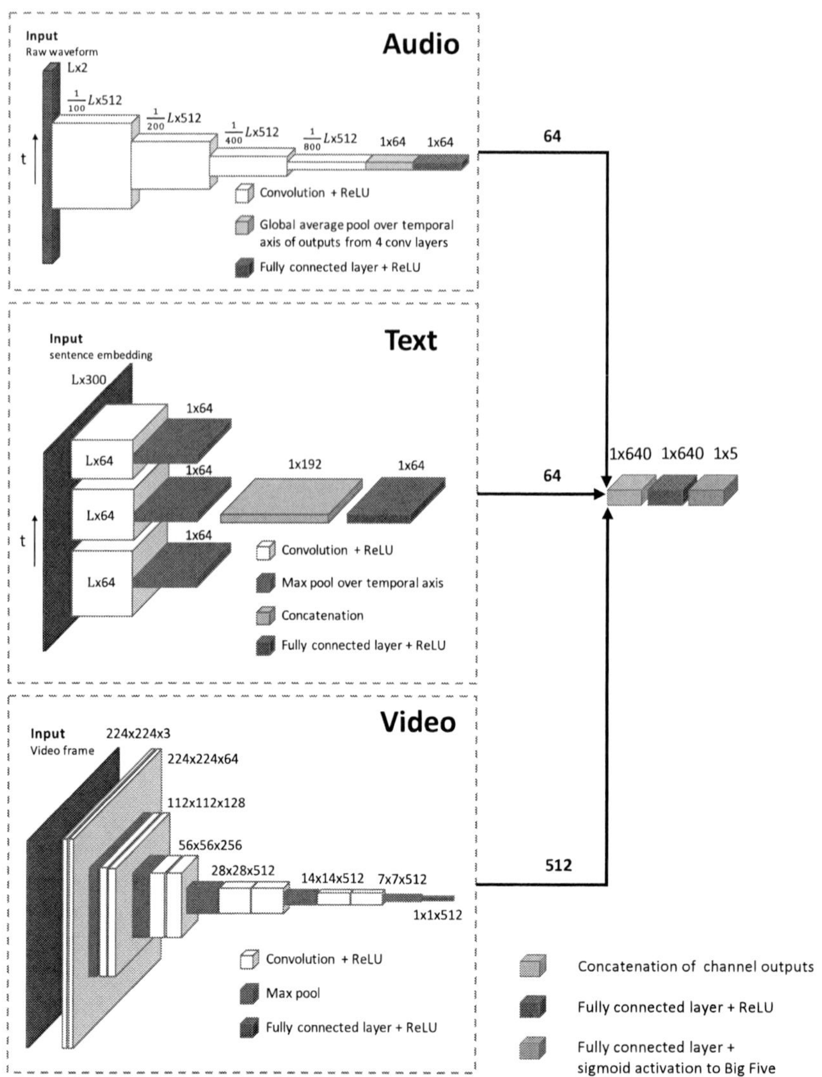

Figure 1: Diagram of the tri-modal architecture for prediction of Big Five traits from audio, text and video input. Concatenating output of the three individual modalities results in an output layer with size of 64+64+512=640.

trained models as such is a common way to leverage on training on large outside datasets and thus the model doesn't need to learn extracting visual features itself (Esteva et al., 2017).

2.4 Multimodal fusion

Humans infer personality from different cues and this motivates us to predict personality by using multiple modalities simultaneously. We look at three different fusing methods to find how to combine modalities best.

The first method is a decision-level fusion ap-proach, done through an ensemble (*voting*) method. The three channels are copies of the fully trained models described above. We want to know the linear combination weights for each modality, for each trait (15 weights in total). The final predictions from our tri-modal model then become $\hat{p}_i = \sum_{j=1}^{N} w_{i,j}\hat{p}_{i,j}$, where p_i represents the ensemble estimator for the score of trait i, j represents the modality (with $N = 3$ the number of modalities), and $w_{i,j}$ and $\hat{p}_{i,j}$ the weights and estimates respectively for trait i for modality j. The weights were found by minimizing the Mean Absolute Error (MAE) on the development set. We choose to have weights per trait because the uni-modal results show that some modalities are better at predicting some traits than others. An important advantage of using this fusion method is that we can read the relevance of the modalities for each of the traits , from the weights.

In the other fusion methods we propose, we first merge the modalities by truncating the final fully connected layers from each of the channels. We then concatenate the previous fully connected layers, to obtain shared representations of the input data. Finally we add two extra fully connected layers on top. For the second method, all layers in the separate channels are frozen, so we basically want the model to learn what combination (could still be a linear one) of channel outputs is optimal. For the third method, we again train this exact architecture, but now we also update the parameters of both the audio and text channels, thus enabling fully end-to-end backpropagation. This enables the model to learn more complex interaction between the different channels. The architecture is illustrated in Fig. 1. The layers in the dashed boxes are frozen (non-trainable) for limited backpropation model, and trainable for full backpropagation model.

3 Experiments

3.1 Corpus

We used the ChaLearn First Impressions Dataset, which consists of YouTube vlogs clips of around 15 seconds (Ponce-López et al., 2016). The speaker in each video is annotated with Big Five personality scores. The ChaLearn dataset was divided into a training set of 6,000 clips and 20% of the training set was taken as validation set during training to tune the hyperparameter, the early stopping conditions and the ensemble method training. We used pre-defined ChaLearn Validation Set of 2,000 clips as the test set.

3.2 Setup

For the audio CNN, we used a window size of 200 (i.e. 25 ms) for the first layer, and a stride of 100 (i.e. 12.5 ms). In the following convolutional layers we set the window size and stride is set to 8 and 2 respectively. The number of filters was kept at 512 for each layer. In the text CNN instead we used a filter size of 128, and apply dropout ($p = 0.5$) to the last layer. In the video CNN we used again 512 filters for each layer.

We trained our model using Adam optimizer (Kingma and Ba, 2014). All models were implemented with Keras (Chollet et al., 2015). We train all models parameters with a regression cost function by iteratively minimizing the average over five traits of the Mean Square Error (MSE) between model predictions and ground truth labels. We also use the MSE with the ground truth to evaluate the performance over the test set.

3.3 Results

Our aim is to investigate the contribution of different modalities for personality detection task. Table 1 includes the optimal weights learned for the decision-level fusion approach. From this table we can read contribution of each of the modalities to the prediction of each trait.

Model	Big Five Personality Traits				
	E	A	C	N	O
Audio	0.44	0.32	0.27	0.45	0.54
Text	-0.03	0.22	0.13	0.03	-0.06
Video	0.59	0.46	0.60	0.52	0.52

Table 1: Optimal weights learned for combining the three modalities for each trait. E, A, C, N, and O stand for Extraversion, Agreeableness, Conscientiousness, Neuroticism and Openness, respectively.

Table 2 displays the tri-modal regression (MAE) performance, individual modalities, multimodal decision-level fusion and the two neural network fusion methods. We also report the average trait scores from the training set labels as a baseline (Mairesse et al., 2007). The neural network fusion with full backpropagation works best with an average MSE score of 0.0938, around 2.9% improvement over the last-layer backpropagation only, and 9.4% over the best separate modality (video). Both in separate and ensemble methods, the results we obtain are lower than just estimating the average from the training set.

The main target in this work is to investigate the effect of audio, visual, and text modalities, and different fusion methods in personality recognition, rather than proposing the method with the best accuracy. However, we still repeat the accuracy of the reported methods in Table 2 and two winners of the ChaLearn 2016 competition DCC (Güçlütürk et al., 2016) and evolgen (Subramaniam et al., 2016) in Table 3. It can be seen that the result for out tri-modal method with fully back-propagation is comparable to the winners.

MAE		Big Five Personality Traits				
Model	Mean	E	A	C	N	O
Audio	.1059	.1080	.0953	.1160	.1077	.1024
Text	.1132	.1177	.0977	.1206	.1167	.1135
Video	.1035	.1040	.0960	.1087	.1064	.1024
DLF	.0967	.0970	.0893	.1049	.0979	.0947
NNLB	.0966	.0970	.0896	.1038	.0973	.0951
NNFB	.0938	.0958	.0907	.0922	.0964	.0938
Train labels avg	.1165	.1194	.1009	.1261	.1209	.1153

Table 2: MAE for each individual modality, fusion approaches and average of training set labels. DLF refers to decision-level fusion, NNLB and NNFB refer to neural network limited backprop and full back respectively.

Mean Acc		Big Five Personality Traits				
Model	Mean	E	A	C	N	O
Audio	.8941	.8920	.9047	.8840	.8923	.8976
Text	.8868	.8823	.9023	.8794	.8833	.8865
Video	.8965	.8960	.9040	.8913	.8936	.8976
DLF	.9033	.9030	.9107	.8951	.9021	.9053
NNLB	.9034	.9030	.9104	.8962	.9027	.9049
NNFB	.9062	.9042	.9093	.9078	.9036	.9062
DCC	.9121	.9104	.9154	.9130	.9097	.9119
evolgen	.9133	.9145	.9157	.9135	.9098	.9130
Train labels avg	.8835	.8806	.8991	.8739	.8791	.8847

Table 3: Mean accuracy for each individual modality, fusion approaches, two winners of the ChaLearn 2016 competition (DCC and evolgen), and average of training set labels.

3.4 Discussion

Looking at the results obtained from various fusion methods in Table 2, we can see that for decision-level and last-layer backpropagation, Neuroticism and Extraversion are the easiest traits to predict, followed by Conscientiousness and Openness. Agreeableness is significantly harder. We also see that the last-layer fusion yields very similar performance as the decision-level approach. It is likely that the limited backpropagation method learns something similar to a linear combination of channels, just like the decision-level method. On the other hand, the full backpropagation method yields significantly higher results for all traits except Agreeableness.

From Table 1 we can also see which modalities carry more information. The text modality is not adding much value to traits other than Agreeableness and Conscientiousness. Extraversion can, on the other hand, be quite easily recognized from tone of voice and appearance. Having said this, we must be careful in deciding which modalities are most suitable for individual traits, since certain traits (e.g. Extraversion) are more evident from a short slice and some (e.g. Openness) need longer temporal information (Aran and Gatica-Perez, 2013). Polzehl et al. (2010) have proposed a method for personality recognition in speech modality on a different corpus. The method is not based on neural network architecture, but they provide a similar analysis that supports our conclusions.

Since the full backpropagation experiments yields much better results than the linear combination model, we can conclude that different modalities interact with each other in a non-trivial manner. Moreover, we can observe that simply adding features from different modalities (represented as concatenating a final representation without full backpropagation) does not yield optimal performance.

Our tri-modal approach is quite extensive and there are more modalities such as nationality, cultural background, age, gender, and personal interests that can be added. All Big Five traits have been found to have a correlation with age (Donnellan and Lucas, 2008). Extraversion and Openness have a negative correlation with age, Agreeableness have a positive correlation, and Conscientiousness scores peak for middle age subjects.

4 Conclusion

We proposed a fusion method, based on deep neural networks, to predict personality traits from audio, language and appearance. We have seen that each of the three modalities contains a signal relevant for personality prediction, that using all three modalities combined greatly outperforms using individual modalities, and that the channels interact with each other in a non-trivial fashion. By combining the last network layers and fine-tuning the parameters we have obtained the best result, average among all traits, of 0.0938 Mean Square Error, which is 9.4% better than the performance of the best individual modality (visual). Out of all modalities, language or speech pattern seems to be the least relevant. Video frames (appearance) are slightly more relevant than audio information (i.e. non-verbal parts of speech).

5 Acknowledgments

This work was partially funded by grants #16214415 and #16248016 of the Hong Kong Research Grants Council, ITS/319/16FP of Innovation Technology Commission, and RDC 1718050-0 of EMOS.AI.

References

Oya Aran and Daniel Gatica-Perez. 2013. One of a kind: Inferring personality impressions in meetings. In *Proceedings of the 15th ACM on International conference on multimodal interaction*. ACM, pages 11–18.

Tadas Baltrušaitis, Chaitanya Ahuja, and Louis-Philippe Morency. 2018. Multimodal machine learning: A survey and taxonomy. *IEEE Transactions on Pattern Analysis and Machine Intelligence* .

Dario Bertero, Farhad Bin Siddique, Chien-Sheng Wu, Yan Wan, Ricky Ho Yin Chan, and Pascale Fung. 2016. Real-time speech emotion and sentiment recognition for interactive dialogue systems. In *Proceedings of the 2016 Conference on Empirical Methods in Natural Language Processing*. Association for Computational Linguistics, Austin, Texas, pages 1042–1047. https://aclweb.org/anthology/D16-1110.

François Chollet et al. 2015. Keras. `https://github.com/fchollet/keras`.

M Brent Donnellan and Richard E Lucas. 2008. Age differences in the big five across the life span: evidence from two national samples. *Psychology and aging* 23(3):558.

Andre Esteva, Brett Kuprel, Roberto A Novoa, Justin Ko, Susan M Swetter, Helen M Blau, and Sebastian Thrun. 2017. Dermatologist-level classification of skin cancer with deep neural networks. *Nature* 542(7639):115–118.

Golnoosh Farnadi, Geetha Sitaraman, Shanu Sushmita, Fabio Celli, Michal Kosinski, David Stillwell, Sergio Davalos, Marie-Francine Moens, and Martine De ***. 2016. Computational personality recognition in social media. *User modeling and user-adapted interaction* 26(2-3):109–142.

Lewis R Goldberg. 1990. An alternative" description of personality": the big-five factor structure. *Journal of personality and social psychology* 59(6):1216.

Yagmur Gucluturk, Umut Guclu, Marc Perez, Hugo Jair Escalante, Xavier Baro, Isabelle Guyon, Carlos Andujar, Julio Jacques Junior, Meysam Madadi, Sergio Escalera, et al. 2017. Visualizing apparent personality analysis with deep residual networks. In *Proceedings of the IEEE Conference on Computer Vision and Pattern Recognition*. pages 3101–3109.

Yağmur Güçlütürk, Umut Güçlü, Marcel AJ van Gerven, and Rob van Lier. 2016. Deep impression: audiovisual deep residual networks for multimodal apparent personality trait recognition. In *Computer Vision–ECCV 2016 Workshops*. Springer, pages 349–358.

Furkan Gürpınar, Heysem Kaya, and Albert Ali Salah. 2016. Combining deep facial and ambient features for first impression estimation. In *Computer Vision–ECCV 2016 Workshops*. Springer, pages 372–385.

Yoon Kim. 2014. Convolutional neural networks for sentence classification. In *Proceedings of the 2014 Conference on Empirical Methods in Natural Language Processing (EMNLP)*. Association for Computational Linguistics, pages 1746–1751.

Diederik Kingma and Jimmy Ba. 2014. Adam: A method for stochastic optimization. *arXiv preprint arXiv:1412.6980* .

François Mairesse, Marilyn A Walker, Matthias R Mehl, and Roger K Moore. 2007. Using linguistic cues for the automatic recognition of personality in conversation and text. *Journal of artificial intelligence research* 30:457–500.

Urs Muller, Jan Ben, Eric Cosatto, Beat Flepp, and Yann L Cun. 2006. Off-road obstacle avoidance through end-to-end learning. In *Advances in neural information processing systems*. pages 739–746.

Clifford Nass, Youngme Moon, BJ Fogg, Byron Reeves, and Chris Dryer. 1995. Can computer personalities be human personalities. In *Conference companion on Human factors in computing systems*. ACM, pages 228–229.

Omkar M Parkhi, Andrea Vedaldi, Andrew Zisserman, et al. 2015. Deep face recognition. In *BMVC*. volume 1, page 6.

Tim Polzehl, Sebastian Moller, and Florian Metze. 2010. Automatically assessing personality from speech. In *Semantic Computing (ICSC), 2010 IEEE Fourth International Conference on*. IEEE, pages 134–140.

Víctor Ponce-López, Baiyu Chen, Marc Oliu, Ciprian Corneanu, Albert Clapés, Isabelle Guyon, Xavier Baró, Hugo Jair Escalante, and Sergio Escalera. 2016. Chalearn lap 2016: First round challenge on first impressions-dataset and results. In *Computer Vision–ECCV 2016 Workshops*. Springer, pages 400–418.

Karen Simonyan and Andrew Zisserman. 2014. Very deep convolutional networks for large-scale image recognition. *arXiv preprint arXiv:1409.1556* .

Arulkumar Subramaniam, Vismay Patel, Ashish Mishra, Prashanth Balasubramanian, and Anurag Mittal. 2016. Bi-modal first impressions recognition using temporally ordered deep audio and stochastic visual features. In *Computer Vision–ECCV 2016 Workshops*. Springer, pages 337–348.

Paul Viola and Michael J Jones. 2004. Robust real-time face detection. *International journal of computer vision* 57(2):137–154.

Chen-Lin Zhang, Hao Zhang, Xiu-Shen Wei, and Jianxin Wu. 2016. Deep bimodal regression for apparent personality analysis. In *Computer Vision–ECCV 2016 Workshops*. Springer, pages 311–324.

An Empirical Study of Building a Strong Baseline
for Constituency Parsing

Jun Suzuki, Sho Takase, Hidetaka Kamigaito, Makoto Morishita, and **Masaaki Nagata**
NTT Communication Science Laboratories, NTT Corporation
2-4 Hikaridai, Seika-cho, Soraku-gun, Kyoto, 619-0237 Japan
{suzuki.jun, takase.sho, kamigaito.hidetaka,
morishita.makoto, nagata.masaaki}@lab.ntt.co.jp

Abstract

This paper investigates the construction of a strong baseline based on general purpose sequence-to-sequence models for constituency parsing. We incorporate several techniques that were mainly developed in natural language generation tasks, e.g., machine translation and summarization, and demonstrate that the sequence-to-sequence model achieves the current top-notch parsers' performance without requiring explicit task-specific knowledge or architecture of constituent parsing.

1 Introduction

Sequence-to-sequence (Seq2seq) models have successfully improved many well-studied NLP tasks, especially for natural language generation (NLG) tasks, such as machine translation (MT) (Sutskever et al., 2014; Cho et al., 2014) and abstractive summarization (Rush et al., 2015). Seq2seq models have also been applied to constituency parsing (Vinyals et al., 2015) and provided a fairly good result. However one obvious, intuitive drawback of Seq2seq models when they are applied to constituency parsing is that they have no explicit architecture to model latent nested relationships among the words and phrases in constituency parse trees, Thus, models that directly model them, such as RNNG (Dyer et al., 2016), are an intuitively more promising approach. In fact, RNNG and its extensions (Kuncoro et al., 2017; Fried et al., 2017) provide the current state-of-the-art performance. Sec2seq models are currently considered a simple baseline of neural-based constituency parsing.

After the first proposal of an Seq2seq constituency parser, many task-independent techniques have been developed, mainly in the NLG

research area. Our aim is to update the Seq2seq approach proposed in Vinyals et al. (2015) as a stronger baseline of constituency parsing. Our motivation is basically identical to that described in Denkowski and Neubig (2017). A strong baseline is crucial for reporting reliable experimental results. It offers a fair evaluation of promising new techniques if they solve new issues or simply resolve issues that have already been addressed by current generic technology. More specifically, it might become possible to analyze what types of implicit linguistic structures are easier or harder to capture for neural models by comparing the outputs of strong Seq2seq models and task-specific models, e.g., RNNG.

The contributions of this paper are summarized as follows: (1) a strong baseline for constituency parsing based on general purpose Seq2seq models[1], (2) an empirical investigation of several generic techniques that can (or cannot) contribute to improve the parser performance, (3) empirical evidence that Seq2seq models implicitly learn parse tree structures well without knowing task-specific and explicit tree structure information.

2 Constituency Parsing by Seq2seq

Our starting point is an RNN-based Seq2seq model with an attention mechanism that was applied to constituency parsing (Vinyals et al., 2015). We omit detailed descriptions due to space limitations, but note that our model architecture is identical to the one introduced in Luong et al. (2015a)[2].

A key trick for applying Seq2seq models to constituency parsing is the *linearization* of parse

---

[1] Our code and experimental configurations for reproducing our experiments are publicly available:
https://github.com/nttcslab-nlp/strong_s2s_baseline_parser

[2] More specifically, our Seq2seq model follows the one implemented in seq2seq-attn (https://github.com/harvardnlp/seq2seq-attn), which is the alpha-version of the OpenNMT tool (http://opennmt.net).

Proceedings of the 56th Annual Meeting of the Association for Computational Linguistics (Short Papers), pages 612–618
Melbourne, Australia, July 15 - 20, 2018. ©2018 Association for Computational Linguistics

Original input	John has a dog .
Output: S-exp.	(S (NP NNP) (VP VBZ (NP DT NN)) .)
Linearized form	$(_\mathrm{S}\ (_\mathrm{NP}$ NNP $)_\mathrm{NP}\ (_\mathrm{VP}$ VBZ $(_\mathrm{NP}$ DT NN $)_\mathrm{NP}\ )_\mathrm{VP}$. $)_\mathrm{S}$
w/ POS normalized	$(_\mathrm{S}\ (_\mathrm{NP}$ XX $)_\mathrm{NP}\ (_\mathrm{VP}$ XX $(_\mathrm{NP}$ XX XX $)_\mathrm{NP}\ )_\mathrm{VP}$. $)_\mathrm{S}$

Table 1: Examples of linearization and POS-tag normalization (Vinyals et al., 2015)

trees (Vinyals et al., 2015). Roughly speaking, a *linearized parse tree* consists of open, close bracketing and POS-tags that correspond to a given input raw sentence. Since a one-to-one mapping exists between a parse tree and its linearized form (if the linearized form is a valid tree), we can recover parse trees from the predicted linearized parse tree. Vinyals et al. (2015) also introduced the *part-of-speech (POS) tag normalization* technique. They substituted each POS tag in a linearized parse tree to a single XX-tag[3], which allows Seq2seq models to achieve a more competitive performance range than the current state-of-the-art parses[4]. Table 1 shows an example of a parse tree to which linearization and POS-tag normalization was applied.

3 Task-independent Extensions

This section describes several generic techniques that improve Seq2seq performance[5]. Table 2 lists the notations used in this paper for a convenient reference.

3.1 Subword as input features

Applying subword decomposition has recently become a leading technique in NMT literature (Sennrich et al., 2016; Wu et al., 2016). Its primary advantage is a significant reduction of the serious out-of-vocabulary (OOV) problem. We incorporated subword information as an additional feature of the original input words. A similar usage of subword features was previously proposed in Bojanowski et al. (2017).

Formally, the encoder embedding vector at encoder position i, namely, $\boldsymbol{e}_i$, is calculated as follows:

$$\boldsymbol{e}_i = \boldsymbol{E}\boldsymbol{x}_k + \sum_{k' \in \psi(w_i)} \boldsymbol{F}\boldsymbol{s}_{k'}, \qquad (1)$$

D	: dimension of the embeddings
H	: dimension of the hidden states
i	: index of the (token) position in input sentence
j	: index of the (token) position in output linearized format of parse tree
$\mathcal{V}^{(e)}$	: vocabulary of word for input (encoder) side
$\mathcal{V}^{(s)}$	: vocabulary of subword for input (encoder) side
$\boldsymbol{E}$	: encoder embedding matrix for $\mathcal{V}^{(e)}$, where $\boldsymbol{E} \in \mathbb{R}^{D \times |\mathcal{V}^{(e)}|}$
$\boldsymbol{F}$	: encoder embedding matrix for $\mathcal{V}^{(s)}$, where $\boldsymbol{F} \in \mathbb{R}^{D \times |\mathcal{V}^{(s)}|}$
w_i	: i-th word (token) in the input sentence, $w_i \in \mathcal{V}^{(e)}$
$\boldsymbol{x}_k$	: one-hot vector representation of the k-th word in $\mathcal{V}^{(e)}$
$\boldsymbol{s}_k$	: one-hot vector representation of the k-th subword in $\mathcal{V}^{(s)}$
$\boldsymbol{u}$	: encoder embedding vector of unknown token
$\phi(\cdot)$	: function that returns the index of given word in the vocabulary $\mathcal{V}^{(e)}$
$\psi(\cdot)$	: function that returns a set of indices in the subword vocabulary $\mathcal{V}^{(s)}$ generated from the given word. e.g., $k \in \psi(w_i)$
$\boldsymbol{e}_i$	: encoder embedding vector at position i in encoder
$\mathcal{V}^{(d)}$	: vocabulary of output with POS-tag normalization
$\mathcal{V}^{(q)}$	: vocabulary of output without POS-tag normalization
$\boldsymbol{W}^{(o)}$	: decoder output matrix for $\mathcal{V}^{(d)}$, where $\boldsymbol{W}^{(o)} \in \mathbb{R}^{|\mathcal{V}^{(o)}| \times H}$
$\boldsymbol{W}^{(q)}$	: decoder output matrix for $\mathcal{V}^{(q)}$, where $\boldsymbol{W}^{(q)} \in \mathbb{R}^{|\mathcal{V}^{(q)}| \times H}$
$\boldsymbol{z}_j$	: final hidden vector calculated at the decoder position j
$\boldsymbol{o}_j$	: final decoder output scores at decoder position j
$\boldsymbol{q}_j$	: output scores of auxiliary task at decoder position j
$\boldsymbol{b}$	: additional bias term in the decoder output layer for mask
$\boldsymbol{p}_j$	: vector format of output probability at decoder position j
A	: number of models for ensembling
C	: number of candidates generating for LM-reranking

Table 2: List of notations used in this paper.

where $k = \phi(w_i)$. Note that the second term of RHS indicates our additional subword features, and the first represents the standard word embedding extraction procedure. Among several choices, we used the byte-pair encoding (BPE) approach proposed in Sennrich et al. (2016) applying 1,000 merge operations[6].

3.2 Unknown token embedding as a bias

We generally replace rare words, e.g., those appearing less than five times in the training data, with *unknown* tokens in the Seq2seq approach. However, we suspect that embedding vectors, which correspond to unknown tokens, cannot be trained well for the following reasons: (1) the occurrence of unknown tokens remains relatively small in the training data since they are obvious replacements for rare words, and (2) Seq2seq is relatively ineffective for training infrequent words (Luong et al., 2015b). Based on these observations, we utilize the unknown embedding as a bias term $\boldsymbol{b}$ of linear layer ($\boldsymbol{W}\boldsymbol{x} + \boldsymbol{b}$) when obtaining every encoder embeddings for overcoming infrequent word problem. Then, we modify Eq. 2 as follows:

$$\boldsymbol{e}_i = (\boldsymbol{E}\boldsymbol{x}_k + \boldsymbol{u}) + \sum_{k' \in \psi(w_i)} (\boldsymbol{F}\boldsymbol{s}_{k'} + \boldsymbol{u}). \qquad (2)$$

Note that if w_i is unknown token, then Eq. 2 becomes $\boldsymbol{e}_i = 2\boldsymbol{u} + \sum_{k' \in \psi(w_i)} (\boldsymbol{F}\boldsymbol{s}_{k'} + \boldsymbol{u})$.

---

[3]We did not substitute POS-tags for punctuation symbols such as ".", and ",".

[4]Several recently developed neural-based constituency parsers ignore POS tags since they are not evaluated in the standard evaluation metric of constituency parsing (Bracketing F-measure).

[5]Figure in the supplementary material shows the brief sketch of the method explained in the following section.

[6]https://github.com/rsennrich/subword-nmt

3.3 Multi-task learning

Several papers on the Seq2seq approach (Luong et al., 2016) have reported that the multi-task learning extension often improves the task performance if we can find effective auxiliary tasks related to the target task. From this general knowledge, we re-consider jointly estimating POS-tags by incorporating the linearized forms without the POS-tag normalization as an auxiliary task. In detail, the linearized forms with and without the POS-tag normalization are independently and simultaneously estimated as o_j and q_j, respectively, in the decoder output layer by following equation:

$$o_j = W^{(o)} z_j, \quad \text{and} \quad q_j = W^{(q)} z_j. \quad (3)$$

3.4 Output length controlling

As described in Vinyals et al. (2015), not all the outputs (predicted linearized parse trees) obtained from the Seq2seq parser are valid (well-formed) as a parse tree. Toward guaranteeing that every output is a valid tree, we introduce a simple extension of the method for controlling the Seq2seq output length (Kikuchi et al., 2016).

First, we introduce an additional bias term b in the decoder output layer to prevent the selection of certain output words:

$$p_j = \mathrm{softmax}(o_j + b). \quad (4)$$

If we set a large negative value at the m-th element in b, namely $b_m \approx -\infty$, then the m-th element in p_j becomes approximately 0, namely $p_{j,m} \approx 0$, regardless of the value of the k-th element in o_j. We refer to this operation to set value $-\infty$ in b as a mask. Since this naive masking approach is harmless to GPU-friendly processing, we can still exploit GPU parallelization.

We set b to always mask the EOS-tag and change b when at least one of the following conditions is satisfied: (1) if the number of open and closed brackets generated so far is the same, then we mask the XX-tags (or the POS-tags) and all the *closed* brackets. (2) if the number of predicted XX-tags (or POS-tags) is equivalent to that of the words in a given input sentence, then we mask the XX-tags (or all the POS-tags) and all the *open* brackets. If both conditions (1) and (2) are satisfied, then the decoding process is finished. The additional cost for controlling the mask is to count the number of XX-tags and the open and closed brackets so far generated in the decoding process.

Dim. of embedding D	300	Dim. of hidden state H	200
Encoder RNN unit	bi-LSTM	Num. of layers L	2
Decoder RNN unit	LSTM with attention	Dropout rate	0.3
Optimizer	SGD	Gradient clipping G	1.0
Learning rate decay	0.9 (after 50 epoch)	Initial learning rate	1.0
Mini-batch size M	16 (shuffled at each epoch)		
Stopping criterion	100 epochs (w/o early stopping)		
Beam size (at Test) B	5		

Table 3: List of model and optimization configurations (hyper-parameters) in our experiments

3.5 Pre-trained word embeddings

The pre-trained word embeddings obtained from a large external corpora often boost the final task performance even if they only initialize the input embedding layer. In constituency parsing, several systems also incorporate pre-trained word embeddings, such as Vinyals et al. (2015); Durrett and Klein (2015). To maintain as much reproducibility of our experiments as possible, we simply applied publicly available pre-trained word embeddings, i.e., `glove.840B.300d`[7], as initial values of the encoder embedding layer.

3.6 Model ensemble

Ensembling several independently trained models together significantly improves many NLP tasks. In the ensembling process, we predict the output tokens using the arithmetic mean of predicted probabilities computed by each model:

$$p_j = \frac{1}{A} \sum_{a=1}^{A} p_j^{(a)}, \quad (5)$$

where $p_j^{(a)}$ represents the probability distribution at position j predicted by the a-th model.

3.7 Language model (LM) reranking

Choe and Charniak (2016) demonstrated that reranking the predicted parser output candidates with an RNN language model (LM) significantly improves performance. We refer to this reranking process as *LM-rerank*. Following their success, we also trained RNN-LMs on the PTB dataset with their published preprocessing code[8] to reproduce the experiments in Choe and Charniak (2016) for our LM-rerank. We selected the current state-of-the-art LM (Yang et al., 2018)[9] as our LM-reranker, which is a much stronger LM than was used in Choe and Charniak (2016).

---

[7]https://nlp.stanford.edu/projects/glove/
[8]https://github.com/cdg720/emnlp2016
[9]We used the identical hyper-parameters introduced in their site: https://github.com/zihangdai/mos.

ID	Method	category	Development Data (PTB Sec.22)				Test Data (PTB Sec.23)			
			Bracketing F_1 (Bra.F)		Complete match (CM)		Bra.F	CM	Bra.F	CM
			ave. ±stdev	min / max	ave. ±stdev	min / max	ave. ±stdev	ave. ±stdev	(dev.max model)	
(a)	Seq2seq w/ attn (+post-proc for valid parse tree)		88.08 ±0.41	87.27 / 88.72	35.80 ±0.78	34.88 / 37.41	88.13 ±0.22	35.05 ±0.79	88.39	35.97
(b)	(a) + Dec.control (§3.4)	dec. mask.	88.35 ±0.37	87.70 / 88.83	35.89 ±0.80	34.94 / 37.47	–	–	–	–
(c)	(b) + Subword (§3.1)	enc. feature	89.76 ±0.23	89.40 / 90.03	39.79 ±0.79	38.47 / 40.88	–	–	–	–
(d)	(c) + Unk bias (§3.2)	enc. featture	90.10 ±0.24	89.77 / 90.54	40.98 ±0.82	39.59 / 42.18	–	–	–	–
(e)	(d) + Pos (§3.3)	dec. multitask	**90.21 ±0.20**	89.85 / 90.48	**41.09 ±0.98**	39.35 / 42.82	90.38 ±0.28	40.76 ±0.74	**90.62**	**41.39**
(f)	(a) + Pre-trained emb. (§3.5)	enc. initialization	89.99 ±0.17	89.75 / 90.34	40.69 ±0.83	39.41 / 41.76	90.14 ±0.12	40.40 ±0.44	90.32	40.89
(g)	(f) + Dec.control (§3.4)	dec. mask.	90.28 ±0.15	90.10 / 90.55	40.78 ±0.84	39.53 / 41.88	–	–	–	–
(h)	(g) + Subword (§3.1)	enc. feature	90.34 ±0.10	90.20 / 90.53	41.19 ±0.64	40.12 / 42.06	–	–	–	–
(i)	(h) + Unk bias (§3.2)	enc. feature	90.92 ±0.17	90.67 / 91.17	**43.38 ±0.57**	42.47 / 44.29	–	–	–	–
(j)	(i) + Pos (§3.3)	dec. multitask	**90.93 ±0.14**	90.68 / 91.07	42.76 ±0.38	42.00 / 43.18	91.18 ±0.12	42.39 ±0.68	**91.36**	**43.50**

Table 4: Results on English PTB data: Results were average (ave), worst (min), and best (max) performance of ten models independently trained with distinct random initial values. Test data was only evaluated on baseline and our best setting ((a), (e), (f) and (j)) to prevent over-tuning to the test data. We confirmed that all our results contained no malformed parse trees.

ID	Method	Dev. Bra.F	Dev. CM	Test Bra.F	Test CM
(k)	(e) + ensemble $A = 8$ (§3.6)	92.32	45.76	**92.18**	**45.90**
(l)	(k) + LM-rerank $C = 80$ (§3.7)	94.31	53.59	**94.14**	**52.69**
(m)	(j) + ensemble $A = 8$ (§3.6)	92.90	47.85	**92.74**	**47.27**
(n)	(m) + LM-rerank $C = 80$ (§3.7)	94.30	54.12	**94.32**	**52.81**

Table 5: Ensembling and reranking results

(a) Mini-batch size M

method	Bra.F	CM
(j) $M = 16$	**90.93**	**42.76**
$M = 64$	89.85	40.94
$M = 256$	89.41	40.41

(b) Gradient clipping G

method	Bra.F	CM
(j) $G = 1$	**90.93**	42.76
$G = 5$	87.36	36.71

(c) Hidden dim H and layer L

method	Bra.F	CM
(j) $H = 200, L = 2$	**90.93**	42.76
$H = 200, L = 3$	90.75	43.00
$H = 200, L = 4$	90.55	42.84
$H = 512, L = 2$	90.59	**43.38**

(d) Beam size B

method	Bra.F	CM
$B = 1$	90.55	42.49
(j) $B = 5$	**90.93**	**42.76**
$B = 20$	90.98	**42.76**
$B = 50$	91.01	**42.76**

(e) usage of subword information (feature or split)

method	Bra.F	CM
(h) word split with $1K$ subword feature	90.93	42.76
$8K$ subword split	87.39	33.62
$16K$ subword split	87.20	31.21

Table 6: Impact of hyper-parameter selections. We only evaluated the development data (PTB Sec. 22) to prevent over-tuning to the test data.

System (Brief description)	Bra.F
[Trained (strictly) from PTB only, no additional resources]	
(Kamigaito et al., 2017) Seq2seq, sup.attention	89.5
(Cross and Huang, 2016a) Shift-reduce	89.95
Ours; Seq2seq	**90.62**
(Watanabe and Sumita, 2015) Shift-reduce	90.68
(Shindo et al., 2012)	91.1
(Cross and Huang, 2016b) Shift-reduce	91.3
(Kamigaito et al., 2017) Seq2seq, sup.attention, ensemble	91.5
(Dyer et al., 2016) Shift-reduce, discriminative	91.7
(Liu and Zhang, 2017) Shift-reduce	91.7
(Stern et al., 2017a) Top-down	91.79
Ours; Seq2seq, ensemble	**92.18**
(Shindo et al., 2012) ensemble	92.4
(Stern et al., 2017b) Top-down, rerank	92.56
(Choe and Charniak, 2016) CKY, LM-rerank	92.6
(Dyer et al., 2016) Shift-reduce, generative	93.3
(Kuncoro et al., 2017) Shift-reduce, rerank	93.6
Ours; Seq2seq, ensemble, LM-rerank(80)	**94.14**
(Fried et al., 2017) Shift-reduce, ensemble, rerank	94.25
[PTB only, but utilizing pre-trained emb. from external corpus for init.]	
(Vinyals et al., 2015) Seq2seq	88.3
(Vinyals et al., 2015) Seq2seq, ensemble	90.5
(Durrett and Klein, 2015) CKY	91.1
Ours; Seq2seq	**91.36**
Ours; Seq2seq, ensemble	**92.74**
Ours best; Seq2seq, ensemble, LM-rerank(80)	**94.32**
[Trained from PTB and other external silver data]	
(Choe and Charniak, 2016) CKY, LM-rerank	93.8
(Fried et al., 2017) Shift-reduce, ensemble, rerank	94.66

Table 7: List of bracketing F-measures on test data (PTB Sec.23) reported in recent top-notch systems: scores with bold font represent our scores.

4 Experiments

Our experiments used the English Penn Treebank data (Marcus et al., 1994), which are the most widely used benchmark data in the literature. We used the standard split of training (Sec.02–21), development (Sec.22), and test data (Sec.23) and strictly followed the instructions for the evaluation settings explained in Vinyals et al. (2015). For data pre-processing, all the parse trees were transformed into linearized forms, which include standard *UNK* replacement for OOV words and *POS-tag normalization* by XX-tags. As explained in Vinyals et al. (2015), we did not apply any parse tree binarization or special unary treatment, which were used as common techniques in the literature.

Table 3 summarizes the model configurations and the optimization settings used in our experiments unless otherwise specified.

4.1 Results

Table 4 shows the main results of our experiments. We reported the Bracketing F-measures (Bra.F) and the complete match scores (CM) evaluated by the EVALB tool[10]. The averages (ave), standard deviations (stdev), lowest (min), and highest (max) scores were calculated from ten independent runs of each setting trained with different random initialization values. This table empirically reveals the effectiveness of individual techniques. Each technique gradually improved the performance, and the best result (j) achieved ap-

---

[10]http://nlp.cs.nyu.edu/evalb/

proximately 3 point gain from the baseline conventional Seq2seq model (a) on test data Bra.F.

One drawback of Seq2seq approach is that it seems sensitive to initialization. Comparing only with a single result for each setting may produce inaccurate conclusions. Therefore, we should evaluate the performances over several trials to improve the evaluation reliability.

The baseline Seq2seq models, (a) and (f), produced the malformed parse trees. We post-processed such malformed parse trees by simple rules introduced in (Vinyals et al., 2015). On the other hand, we confirmed that all the results applying the technique explained in Sec. 3.4 produced no malformed parse trees.

Ensembling and Reranking: Table 5 shows the results of our models with model ensembling and LM-reranking. For ensemble, we randomly selected eight of the ten Seq2seq models reported in Table 4. For LM-reranking, we first generated 80 candidates by the above eight ensemble models and selected the best parse tree for each input in terms of the LM-reranker. The results in Table 5 were taken from a single-shot evaluation, unlike the averages of ten independent runs in Table 4.

Hyper-parameter selection: We empirically investigated the impact of the hyper-parameter selections. Table 6 shows the results. The following observations appear informative for building strong baseline systems: (1) Smaller mini-batch size M and gradient clipping G provided the better performance. Such settings lead to slower and longer training, but higher performance. (2) Larger layer size, hidden state dimension, and beam size have little impact on the performance; our setting, $L = 2$, $H = 200$, and $B = 5$ looks adequate in terms of speed/performance trade-off.

Input unit selection: As often demonstrated in the NMT literature, using subword split as input token unit instead of standard tokenized word unit has potential to improve the performance. Table 6 (e) shows the results of utilizing subword splits. Clearly, $8K$ and $16K$ subword splits as input token units significantly degraded the performance. It seems that the numbers of XX-tags in output and tokens in input should keep consistent for better performance since Seq2seq models look to somehow learn such relationship, and used it during the decoding. Thus, using subword information as features is one promising approach for leveraging subword information into constituency parsing.

4.2 Comparison to current top systems

Table 7 lists the reported constituency parsing scores on PTB that were recently published in the literature. We split the results into three categories. The first category (top row) contains the results of the methods that were trained only from the pre-defined training data (PTB Sec.02–21), *without* any additional resources. The second category (middle row) consists of the results of methods that were trained from the pre-defined PTB training data as well as those listed in the top row, but incorporating word embeddings obtained from a large-scale external corpus to initialize the encoder embedding layer. The third category (bottom row) shows the performance of the methods that were trained using high-confidence, auto-parsed trees in addition to the pre-defined PTB training data.

Our Seq2seq approach successfully achieved the competitive level as the current top-notch methods: RNNG and its variants. Note here that, as described in Dyer et al. (2016), RNNG uses Berkeley parser's mapping rules for effectively handling singleton words in the training corpus. In contrast, we demonstrated that Seq2seq models have enough power to achieve a competitive state-of-the-art performance without leveraging such task-dependent knowledge. Moreover, they need no explicit information of parse tree structures, transition states, stacks, (Stanford or Berkeley) mapping rules, or external silver training data during the model training except general purpose word embeddings as initial values. These observations from our experiments imply that recently developed Seq2seq models have enough ability to implicitly learn parsing structures from linearized parse trees. Our results argue that Seq2seq models can be a strong baseline for constituency parsing.

5 Conclusion

This paper investigated how well general purpose Seq2seq models can achieve the higher performance of constituency parsing as a strong baseline method. We incorporated several generic techniques to enhance Seq2seq models, such as incorporating subword features, and output length controlling. We experimentally demonstrated that by applying ensemble and LM-reranking techniques, a general purpose Seq2seq model achieved almost the same performance level as the state-of-the-art constituency parser without any task-specific or explicit tree structure information.

References

Piotr Bojanowski, Edouard Grave, Armand Joulin, and Tomas Mikolov. 2017. Enriching word vectors with subword information. *Transactions of the Association of Computational Linguistics*, 5:135–146.

Kyunghyun Cho, Bart van Merrienboer, Caglar Gulcehre, Dzmitry Bahdanau, Fethi Bougares, Holger Schwenk, and Yoshua Bengio. 2014. Learning phrase representations using RNN encoder–decoder for statistical machine translation. In *Proceedings of the Conference on Empirical Methods in Natural Language Processing (EMNLP)*, pages 1724–1734.

Do Kook Choe and Eugene Charniak. 2016. Parsing as language modeling. In *Proceedings of the Conference on Empirical Methods in Natural Language Processing (EMNLP)*, pages 2331–2336.

James Cross and Liang Huang. 2016a. Incremental parsing with minimal features using bi-directional lstm. In *Proceedings of the 54th Annual Meeting of the Association for Computational Linguistics (ACL)*, pages 32–37.

James Cross and Liang Huang. 2016b. Span-based constituency parsing with a structure-label system and provably optimal dynamic oracles. In *Proceedings of the Conference on Empirical Methods in Natural Language Processing (EMNLP)*, pages 1–11.

Michael Denkowski and Graham Neubig. 2017. Stronger baselines for trustable results in neural machine translation. In *Proceedings of the 1st Workshop on Neural Machine Translation (WNMT)*.

Greg Durrett and Dan Klein. 2015. Neural CRF parsing. In *Proceedings of the 53rd Annual Meeting of the Association for Computational Linguistics (ACL) and the 7th International Joint Conference on Natural Language Processing*, pages 302–312.

Chris Dyer, Adhiguna Kuncoro, Miguel Ballesteros, and Noah A. Smith. 2016. Recurrent neural network grammars. In *Proceedings of the 2016 North American Chapter of the Association for Computational Linguistics*, pages 199–209.

Daniel Fried, Mitchell Stern, and Dan Klein. 2017. Improving neural parsing by disentangling model combination and reranking effects. In *Proceedings of the 55th Annual Meeting of the Association for Computational Linguistics (ACL)*, pages 161–166.

Hidetaka Kamigaito, Katsuhiko Hayashi, Tsutomu Hirao, Hiroya Takamura, Manabu Okumura, and Masaaki Nagata. 2017. Supervised attention for sequence-to-sequence constituency parsing. In *Proceedings of the Eighth International Joint Conference on Natural Language Processing (Volume 2: Short Papers)*, pages 7–12, Taipei, Taiwan. Asian Federation of Natural Language Processing.

Yuta Kikuchi, Graham Neubig, Ryohei Sasano, Hiroya Takamura, and Manabu Okumura. 2016. Controlling output length in neural encoder-decoders. In *Proceedings of the Conference on Empirical Methods in Natural Language Processing (EMNLP)*, pages 1328–1338.

Adhiguna Kuncoro, Miguel Ballesteros, Lingpeng Kong, Chris Dyer, Graham Neubig, and Noah A. Smith. 2017. What do recurrent neural network grammars learn about syntax? In *Proceedings of the 15th European Chapter of the Association for Computational Linguistics (EACL)*, pages 1249–1258.

Jiangming Liu and Yue Zhang. 2017. Shift-reduce constituent parsing with neural lookahead features. *Transactions of the Association for Computational Linguistics*, 5:45–58.

Minh-Thang Luong, Quoc V. Le, Ilya Sutskever, Oriol Vinyals, and Lukasz Kaiser. 2016. Multi-task sequence to sequence learning. In *Proceedings of the 4th International Conference on Learning Representations (ICLR)*.

Minh-Thang Luong, Hieu Pham, and Christopher D. Manning. 2015a. Effective approaches to attention-based neural machine translation. In *Proceedings of the Conference on Empirical Methods in Natural Language Processing (EMNLP)*.

Minh-Thang Luong, Ilya Sutskever, Quoc Le, Oriol Vinyals, and Wojciech Zaremba. 2015b. Addressing the rare word problem in neural machine translation. In *Proceedings of the 53rd Annual Meeting of the Association for Computational Linguistics (ACL) and the 7th International Joint Conference on Natural Language Processing*.

M. P. Marcus, B. Santorini, and M. A. Marcinkiewicz. 1994. Building a Large Annotated Corpus of English: The Penn Treebank. *Computational Linguistics*, 19(2):313–330.

Alexander M. Rush, Sumit Chopra, and Jason Weston. 2015. A Neural Attention Model for Abstractive Sentence Summarization. In *Proceedings of the Conference on Empirical Methods in Natural Language Processing (EMNLP)*, pages 379–389.

Rico Sennrich, Barry Haddow, and Alexandra Birch. 2016. Neural Machine Translation of Rare Words with Subword Units. In *Proceedings of the 54th Annual Meeting of the Association for Computational Linguistics (ACL)*, pages 1715–1725.

Hiroyuki Shindo, Yusuke Miyao, Akinori Fujino, and Masaaki Nagata. 2012. Bayesian symbol-refined tree substitution grammars for syntactic parsing. In *Proceedings of the 50th Annual Meeting of the Association for Computational Linguistics (Volume 1: Long Papers)*, pages 440–448. Association for Computational Linguistics.

Mitchell Stern, Jacob Andreas, and Dan Klein. 2017a. A minimal span-based neural constituency parser. In *Proceedings of the 55th Annual Meeting of the Association for Computational Linguistics (ACL)*, pages 818–827.

Mitchell Stern, Daniel Fried, and Dan Klein. 2017b. Effective inference for generative neural parsing. In *Proceedings of the Conference on Empirical Methods in Natural Language Processing (EMNLP)*, pages 1695–1700.

Ilya Sutskever, Oriol Vinyals, and Quoc V. Le. 2014. Sequence to sequence learning with neural networks. In *Proceedings of the 28th Annual Conference on Neural Information Processing Systems (NIPS)*.

Oriol Vinyals, Ł ukasz Kaiser, Terry Koo, Slav Petrov, Ilya Sutskever, and Geoffrey Hinton. 2015. Grammar as a Foreign Language. *Advances in Neural Information Processing Systems 28*, pages 2773–2781.

Taro Watanabe and Eiichiro Sumita. 2015. Transition-based neural constituent parsing. In *Proceedings of the 53rd Annual Meeting of the Association for Computational Linguistics (ACL) and the 7th International Joint Conference on Natural Language Processing*, pages 1169–1179.

Yonghui Wu, Mike Schuster, Zhifeng Chen, Quoc V. Le, Mohammad Norouzi, Wolfgang Macherey, Maxim Krikun, Yuan Cao, Qin Gao, Klaus Macherey, Jeff Klingner, Apurva Shah, Melvin Johnson, Xiaobing Liu, Łukasz Kaiser, Stephan Gouws, Yoshikiyo Kato, Taku Kudo, Hideto Kazawa, Keith Stevens, George Kurian, Nishant Patil, Wei Wang, Cliff Young, Jason Smith, Jason Riesa, Alex Rudnick, Oriol Vinyals, Greg Corrado, Macduff Hughes, and Jeffrey Dean. 2016. Google's neural machine translation system: Bridging the gap between human and machine translation. *arXiv preprint arXiv:1609.08144*.

Zhilin Yang, Zihang Dai, Ruslan Salakhutdinov, and William W. Cohen. 2018. Breaking the softmax bottleneck: A high-rank RNN language model. In *Proceedings of the 6th International Conference on Learning Representations (ICLR)*.

Parser Training with Heterogeneous Treebanks

Sara Stymne, Miryam de Lhoneux, Aaron Smith, and Joakim Nivre
Department of Linguistics and Philology
Uppsala University
`firstName.lastName@lingfil.uu.se`

Abstract

How to make the most of multiple heterogeneous treebanks when training a monolingual dependency parser is an open question. We start by investigating previously suggested, but little evaluated, strategies for exploiting multiple treebanks based on concatenating training sets, with or without fine-tuning. We go on to propose a new method based on treebank embeddings. We perform experiments for several languages and show that in many cases fine-tuning and treebank embeddings lead to substantial improvements over single treebanks or concatenation, with average gains of 2.0–3.5 LAS points. We argue that treebank embeddings should be preferred due to their conceptual simplicity, flexibility and extensibility.

1 Introduction

In this paper we investigate how to train monolingual parsers in the situation where several treebanks are available for a single language. This is quite a common occurrence; in release 2.1 of the Universal Dependencies (UD) treebanks (Nivre et al., 2017), 25 languages have more than one treebank. These treebanks can differ in several respects: they can contain material from different language variants, domains, or genres, and written or spoken material. Even though the UD project provides guidelines for consistent annotation, treebanks can still differ with respect to annotation choices, consistency and quality of annotation. Some treebanks are thoroughly checked by human annotators, whereas others are based entirely on automatic conversions. All this means that it is often far from trivial to combine multiple treebanks for the same language.

The 2017 CoNLL Shared Task on Universal Dependency Parsing (Zeman et al., 2017) included 15 languages with multiple treebanks. An additional parallel test set of 1000 sentences, PUD, was also made available for a selection of languages. Most of the participating teams did not take advantage of the multiple treebanks, however, and simply trained one model per treebank instead of one model per language. There were a few exceptions to this rule, but these teams typically did not investigate the effect of their proposed strategies in detail.

In this paper we begin by performing a thorough investigation of previously proposed strategies for training with multiple treebanks for the same language. We then propose a novel method, based on treebank embeddings. Our new technique has the advantage of producing a single flexible model for each language, regardless of the number of treebanks. We show that this method leads to substantial improvements for many languages. Of the competing methods, training on the concatenation of treebanks, followed by fine-tuning for each treebank, also performed well, but this method results in longer training times and necessitates multiple unwieldy models per language.

2 Training with Multiple Treebanks

The most obvious way to combine treebanks for a particular language, provided that they use the same annotation scheme, is simply to concatenate the training sets. This has the advantage that it does not require any modifications to the parser itself, and it produces a single model that can be directly used for any input from the language in question. Björkelund et al. (2017) and Das et al. (2017) used this strategy to parse the PUD test sets in the 2017 CoNLL Shared Task. Little details are given on the results, but while it was successful on

Proceedings of the 56th Annual Meeting of the Association for Computational Linguistics (Short Papers), pages 619–625
Melbourne, Australia, July 15 - 20, 2018. ©2018 Association for Computational Linguistics

dev data for most languages, results were mixed on the actual PUD test sets. For the two Norwegian language variants, concatenation has been proposed (Velldal et al., 2017), but it hurts results unless combined with machine translation.

Training on concatenated treebanks can be improved by a subsequent fine-tuning step. In this set-up, after training the model on concatenated data, it is refined for each treebank by training only on its own training set for a few additional epochs. This enables the models to learn differences between treebanks, but it requires more training, and results in separate models for each treebank. When the parser is applied to new data, there is thus a choice of which fine-tuned version to use. This approach was used by Che et al. (2017) and Shi et al. (2017) for languages with multiple treebanks in the CoNLL 2017 Shared Task. Che et al. (2017) apply fine-tuning to all but the largest treebank for each language, and show average gains of 1.8 LAS for a subset of nine treebanks. Shi et al. (2017) show that the choice of treebank for parsing the PUD test set is important, but do not have any specific evaluation of the effect of fine-tuning.

Another approach, not explored in this paper, is shared gated adversarial networks, proposed by Sato et al. (2017) for the CoNLL 2017 Shared Task. They use treebank prediction as an adversarial task. In this model, treebank-specific BiLSTMs are constructed for all treebanks in addition to a shared BiLSTM which is used both for parsing and for the adversarial task. This method requires knowing at test time which treebank the input belongs to. Sato et al. (2017) show that this strategy can give substantial improvements, especially for small treebanks. For large treebanks, however, there are mostly no or only minor improvements.

Our approach for taking advantage of multiple treebanks is to use a treebank embedding to represent the treebank to which a sentence belongs. In our proposed model, all parameters of the model are shared; the treebank embedding facilitates soft sharing between treebanks at the word level, and allows the parser to learn treebank-specific phenomena. At test time, a treebank identifier has to be given for the input data. A key benefit of using treebank embeddings is that we can train a single model for each language using all available data while remaining sensitive to the differences between treebanks. The addition of treebank embeddings requires only minor modifications to the parser (see section 3.1). To the best of our knowledge this approach is novel when applied to the monolingual case as treebank embeddings. The most similar approach we have found in the literature is Lim and Poibeau (2017), who used one-hot treebank representations to combine data for improving monolingual parsing for three tiny treebanks, with improvements of 0.6–1.9 LAS. It is also related to work on domain embeddings for machine translation (Kobus et al., 2017), and language embeddings for parsing (Ammar et al., 2016).

We previously used a similar architecture for combining languages with very small training sets with additional languages (de Lhoneux et al., 2017a). Language embeddings have also been explored for other cross-lingual tasks such as language modeling (Tsvetkov et al., 2016; Östling and Tiedemann, 2017) and POS-tagging (Bjerva and Augenstein, 2018). Cross-lingual parsing, however, often requires substantially more complex models. They typically include features such as multilingual word embeddings (Ammar et al., 2016), linguistic re-write rules (Aufrant et al., 2016), or machine translation (Tiedemann, 2015). Unlike much work on cross-lingual parsing, we do not focus on a low-resource scenario.

3 Experimental Setup

We perform experiments for 24 treebanks from 9 languages, using UUParser (de Lhoneux et al., 2017a,b). We compare concatenation (CONCAT), concatenation with fine-tuning (C+FT), and treebank embeddings (TB-EMB). In addition we compare these results to using only single treebanks for training (SINGLE). While some of these methods were previously suggested in the literature, no proper evaluation and comparison between them has been performed. For the PUD test data, there is no corresponding training set, so we need to choose a model or set a treebank embedding based on some other treebank. We call this a *proxy* treebank.

For evaluation we use labeled attachment score (LAS). Significance testing is performed using a randomization test, with the script from the CoNLL 2017 Shared Task.[1]

---

[1] https://github.com/udapi/
udapi-python/blob/master/udapi/block/
eval/conll17.py

3.1 The Parser

We use UUParser[2] (de Lhoneux et al., 2017a), which is based on the transition-based parser of Kiperwasser and Goldberg (2016), and adapted to UD. It uses the arc-hybrid transition system from Kuhlmann et al. (2011) extended with a SWAP transition and a static-dynamic oracle, as described in de Lhoneux et al. (2017b). This model allows the construction of non-projective dependency trees (Nivre, 2009).

A configuration c is represented by a feature function $\phi(\cdot)$ over a subset of its elements and, for each configuration, transitions are scored by a classifier. In this case, the classifier is a multi-layer perceptron (MLP) and $\phi(\cdot)$ is a concatenation of the BiLSTM vectors v_i of words on top of the stack and at the beginning of the buffer. The MLP scores transitions together with the arc labels for transitions that involve adding an arc.

For an input sentence of length n with words $w_1, \ldots, w_n$, the parser creates a sequence of vectors $x_{1:n}$, where the vector x_i representing w_i is the concatenation of a word embedding $e(w_i)$ and a character vector, obtained by running a BiLSTM over the m characters $ch_1, \ldots, ch_m$ of w_i:

$$x_i = e(w_i) \circ \text{BiLSTM}(ch_{1:m})$$

Note that no POS-tags or morphological features are used in this parser.

In the TB-EMB setup, we also concatenate a treebank embedding $tb(w_i)$ to the representation of w_i:

$$x_i = e(w_i) \circ \text{BiLSTM}(ch_{1:m}) \circ tb(w_i)$$

Finally, each input element is represented by a BiLSTM vector, v_i:

$$v_i = \text{BiLSTM}(x_{1:n}, i)$$

All embeddings are initialized randomly, and trained together with the BiLSTMs and MLP. For hyperparameter settings we used default values from de Lhoneux et al. (2017a). The dimension of the treebank embedding is set to 12 in our experiments; we saw only small and inconsistent changes when varying the number of dimensions. We train the parser for 30 epochs per setting. For C+FT we apply fine-tuning for an additional 10 epochs for each treebank. We pick the best epoch

based on LAS score on the dev set, using average dev scores when training on more than one treebank, and apply the model from this epoch to the test data.

3.2 Data

We performed all experiments on UD version 2.1 treebanks (Nivre et al., 2017), using gold sentence and word segmentation. We selected 9 languages, based on the criteria that they should have at least two treebanks with fully available training data and a PUD test set. The sizes of the training corpora for the 9 languages are shown in Table 1. The situation is quite different across languages with either treebanks of roughly the same size, as for Spanish, or very skewed data sizes with a mix of large and small treebanks, as for Czech. In all cases we use all available data, except for Czech, where we randomly choose a maximum of 15,000 sentences per treebank per epoch for efficiency reasons.

4 Results

Table 1 shows the results on the test sets of each training treebank and on the PUD test sets. Overall we observe substantial gains when using either C+FT or TB-EMB. On average both C+FT and TB-EMB beat SINGLE by 3.5 LAS points and CONCAT by over 2.0 LAS points when testing on the test sets of the treebanks used for training, and both methods beat both baselines by over 2.0 LAS points for the PUD test set, if we consider the best proxy treebank.

We see positive gains across many scenarios when using C+FT and TB-EMB. First, there are gains for both balanced and unbalanced data sizes, as in the cases of Spanish and French, respectively. Secondly, there are cases with different language variants, as for Portuguese, and different domains, as for Finnish where FTB only contains grammar examples and TDT contains a mix of domains. There are also cases of known differences in annotation choices, as for the Swedish treebanks.

When the data is very skewed, as for Russian, the effect of adding a small treebank to a large one is minor, as expected. While our results are not directly comparable to the adversarial learning in Sato et al. (2017) who used a different parser and test set, the improvements of C+FT and TB-EMB are typically at least on par with and often larger than their improvements. While our im-

			Same treebank test set				PUD test set			
Language	**Treebank**	**Size**	SINGLE	CONCAT	C+FT	TB-EMB	SINGLE	CONCAT	C+FT	TB-EMB
Czech	PDT	68495	86.7	87.5$^+$	**88.3***	87.2$^+$	**81.7**		81.6	81.2
	CAC	23478	86.0	87.8$^+$	88.1$^+$	**88.5**$^+$	75.0	**81.7**	81.3	81.1
	FicTree	10160	84.3	89.3$^+$	**89.5**$^+$	89.2$^+$	66.1		79.8	80.3
	CLTT	860	72.5	86.2$^+$	**86.9**$^+$	86.0$^+$	42.1		80.8	80.9
English	EWT	12543	82.2	82.1	82.5	**83.0**	80.7		81.7*	**81.9***
	LinES	2738	72.1	76.7$^+$	**77.3**$^+$	**77.3**$^+$	62.6	80.0	75.9	74.5
	ParTUT	1781	80.5	83.5$^+$	85.4$^+$	**85.7**$^+$	68.0		78.1	76.9
Finnish	FTB	14981	76.4$^\times$	74.4	80.1*	**80.6***	46.7	73.0	54.6	53.1
	TDT	12217	78.1$^\times$	70.6	**80.6***	80.3*	78.6$^\times$		**81.3***	80.9*
French	FTB	14759	83.2	83.2	83.9*	**84.1***	72.0		76.7	74.1
	GSD	14554	84.5	84.1	85.3	**85.6**$^\times$	79.1	79.4	80.2*	**80.3***
	Sequoia	2231	84.0	86.0$^+$	**89.8***	89.1*	69.5		78.1	77.6
	ParTUT	803	79.8	80.5	89.1*	**90.3***	63.4		78.8	77.5
Italian	ISDT	12838	87.7	**87.9**	87.7	87.6	85.4		85.7	86.0
	PoSTWITA	2808	71.4	76.7$^+$	76.8$^+$	**77.0**$^+$	68.5	86.0	85.7	85.3
	ParTUT	1781	83.4	89.2$^+$	**89.3**$^+$	88.8$^+$	77.4		85.8$^+$	**86.1**$^+$
Portuguese	GSD	9664	88.3	87.3	89.0*	**89.1***	74.0	76.8$^+$	75.2	74.9
	Bosque	8331	84.7	84.2	86.2$^\times$	**86.3***	75.2		77.5$^+$	**77.6**$^+$
Russian	SynTagRus	48814	90.2$^\times$	89.4	**90.4**$^\times$	**90.4**$^\times$	66.0	68.7	66.3	66.4
	GSD	3850	74.7$^\times$	73.4	79.8*	**80.8***	70.1$^\times$		77.6*	**78.0***
Spanish	AnCora	14305	87.2$^\times$	86.2	87.5$^\times$	**87.6**$^\times$	75.2	79.9	77.7	76.4
	GSD	14187	84.7	83.0	85.8$^\times$	**86.2***	79.8		80.8$^+$	**80.9***
Swedish	Talbanken	4303	79.6	79.1	80.2	**80.6**$^\times$	70.3	72.0$^+$	73.2*	**73.6***
	LinES	2738	74.3	76.8	**77.3**$^+$	77.1$^+$	64.0		70.0	69.0
Average			81.4	82.7$^+$	**84.9***	**84.9***	77.9	77.5	80.0*	**80.1***

Table 1: LAS scores when testing on the training treebank and on the PUD test set with training treebank as proxy. For each test set, the best result is marked with bold. Treebank size is given as number of sentences in the training data. Statistically significant differences, at the 0.05-level, from SINGLE are marked with +, from CONCAT with $\times$ and from both these systems with *. For clarity, significance for PUD is only shown for the proxy treebank with the highest score.

provements are, unsurprisingly, largest for smaller treebanks, we do also see some improvements for large treebanks, in contrast to Sato et al. (2017).

Some variation can be observed between languages. In two cases, Italian ISDT and Czech PUD, CONCAT performs marginally better than the more advanced methods, but these differences are not statistically significant. In several cases, especially for small treebanks, CONCAT helps noticeably over SINGLE, whereas it actually hurts for Finnish and Russian. It is, however, nearly always better to combine treebanks in some way than to use only a single treebank. The differences between the two best methods, C+FT and TB-EMB are typically small and not statistically significant, with the exception of Czech PDT, and for some of the small proxy treebanks for PUD.

The PUD test set can be seen as an example of applying the proposed models to unseen data, without matching training data. For all languages, except Czech, the results for C+FT and TB-EMB with the best proxy treebank are significantly better than the equivalent result for SINGLE, and for

six of the nine languages, TB-EMB performs significantly better than CONCAT. It is clear that some treebanks are bad fits to PUD, most notably Finnish FTB and Russian SynTagRus. However, even when a treebank is a bad fit, TB-EMB and C+FT can still improve substantially over using only the single model for the treebank with the best fit, as for Russian where there is a gain of nearly 8 LAS points for TB-EMB over SINGLE, when using GSD as a proxy. For some languages, however, most notably Italian, the choice of proxy treebank makes little difference for TB-EMB and C+FT. It is also interesting to see that in many cases it is not the largest treebank that is the best proxy for PUD. The large difference in results for PUD, depending on which treebank was used as proxy, also seems to point at potential inconsistencies in the UD annotation for several languages.

5 Error Analysis

To complement the LAS scores, we performed a small manual error analysis for Swedish, looking at the results for the PUD data, when translated

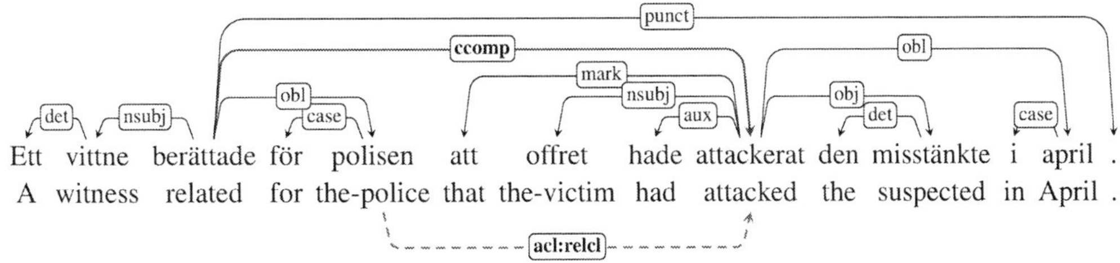

Figure 1: Example sentence from the Swedish PUD treebank with parsing error represented by dashed arc. Translation: "A witness told the police that the victim had attacked the suspect in April."

using different methods and proxy treebanks. The two Swedish treebanks, Talbanken and LinES, are known to differ in the annotation of a few constructions, notably relative clauses and prepositions that take subordinate clauses as complements. The error analysis reveals that the treebank embedding approach allows the model to learn the distinctive "style" of each treebank, while concatenation, even with fine-tuning, results in more inconsistencies in the output. A typical example is shown in Figure 1. When trained with treebank embeddings (and Talbanken as the proxy treebank), the parser produces the correct tree depicted above the sentence. When trained with fine-tuning instead, the parser incorrectly analyzes the subordinate clause as a relative clause (as shown by the dashed arc below the sentence), because the *mark* relation is also used for relative pronouns in the LinES treebank, despite the fact that such structures never occur in Talbanken.

6 Conclusion and Future Work

We have conducted the first large-scale study on how best to combine multiple treebanks for a single language, when all treebanks use the same annotation scheme but may be heterogeneous with respect to domain, genre, size, language variant, annotation style, and quality, as is the case for many languages in the UD project. We propose using treebank embeddings, which represent the treebank a sentence comes from. This method is simple, effective, and flexible, and performs on par with a previously suggested method of using concatenation in combination with fine-tuning, which, however, requires longer training, and produces more models.

We show that both these methods give substantial gains for a variety of languages, including different scenarios with respect to the mix of available treebanks. Our results are also at least on par with a previously proposed, but more complex model, based on adversarial learning (Sato et al., 2017). To improve parsing accuracy, it is certainly worth combining multiple treebanks, when available, for a language, using more sophisticated methods than simple concatenation. We recommend the treebank embedding model due to its simplicity.

The proposed methods work well with a transition-based parser with BiLSTM feature extractors without POS-tags or pre-trained embeddings. In future work, we want to investigate how these methods interact with other parsers, and if the combination methods are useful also for tasks like POS-tagging and morphology prediction.

We did not yet investigate methods for choosing a proxy treebank when parsing new data. The results on the PUD test set could indicate which treebank is likely to be the best proxy for the languages explored here. Other factors that could be taken into account when making this choice include degree of domain match and treebank quality. The user may also simply choose the desired annotation style by selecting the corresponding proxy treebank. For the TB-EMB approach, interpolation of the various treebank embeddings is another possibility.

In the current paper, we explore only the monolingual case, using several treebanks for a single language. Preliminary experiments show that we can combine treebank and language embeddings and add other languages to the mix. Including closely related languages typically gives additional gains, which we will explore in future work.

Acknowledgments

We gratefully acknowledge funding from the Swedish Research Council (P2016-01817) and computational resources on the Taito-CSC cluster in Helsinki from NeIC-NLPL (www.nlpl.eu).

References

Waleed Ammar, George Mulcaire, Miguel Ballesteros, Chris Dyer, and Noah Smith. 2016. Many languages, one parser. *Transactions of the Association of Computational Linguistics*, 4:431–444.

Lauriane Aufrant, Guillaume Wisniewski, and François Yvon. 2016. Zero-resource dependency parsing: Boosting delexicalized cross-lingual transfer with linguistic knowledge. In *Proceedings of the 26th International Conference on Computational Linguistics (COLING)*, pages 119–130, Osaka, Japan.

Johannes Bjerva and Isabelle Augenstein. 2018. Tracking typological traits of Uralic languages in distributed language representations. In *Proceedings of the Fourth International Workshop on Computational Linguistics of Uralic Languages*, pages 78–88, Helsinki, Finland.

Anders Björkelund, Agnieszka Falenska, Xiang Yu, and Jonas Kuhn. 2017. IMS at the CoNLL 2017 UD shared task: CRFs and perceptrons meet neural networks. In *Proceedings of the CoNLL 2017 Shared Task: Multilingual Parsing from Raw Text to Universal Dependencies*, pages 40–51, Vancouver, Canada.

Wanxiang Che, Jiang Guo, Yuxuan Wang, Bo Zheng, Huaipeng Zhao, Yang Liu, Dechuan Teng, and Ting Liu. 2017. The hit-scir system for end-to-end parsing of universal dependencies. In *Proceedings of the CoNLL 2017 Shared Task: Multilingual Parsing from Raw Text to Universal Dependencies*, pages 52–62, Vancouver, Canada.

Ayan Das, Affan Zaffar, and Sudeshna Sarkar. 2017. Delexicalized transfer parsing for low-resource languages using transformed and combined treebanks. In *Proceedings of the CoNLL 2017 Shared Task: Multilingual Parsing from Raw Text to Universal Dependencies*, pages 182–190, Vancouver, Canada.

Eliyahu Kiperwasser and Yoav Goldberg. 2016. Simple and accurate dependency parsing using bidirectional LSTM feature representations. *Transactions of the Association of Computational Linguistics*, 4:313–327.

Catherine Kobus, Josep Crego, and Jean Senellart. 2017. Domain control for neural machine translation. In *Proceedings of the International Conference Recent Advances in Natural Language Processing, RANLP'17*, pages 372–378, Varna, Bulgaria.

Marco Kuhlmann, Carlos Gómez-Rodríguez, and Giorgio Satta. 2011. Dynamic programming algorithms for transition-based dependency parsers. In *Proceedings of the 49th Annual Meeting of the ACL: Human Language Technologies*, pages 673–682, Portland, Oregon, USA.

Miryam de Lhoneux, Yan Shao, Ali Basirat, Eliyahu Kiperwasser, Sara Stymne, Yoav Goldberg, and Joakim Nivre. 2017a. From raw text to universal dependencies - look, no tags! In *Proceedings of the CoNLL 2017 Shared Task: Multilingual Parsing from Raw Text to Universal Dependencies*, pages 207–217, Vancouver, Canada.

Miryam de Lhoneux, Sara Stymne, and Joakim Nivre. 2017b. Arc-hybrid non-projective dependency parsing with a static-dynamic oracle. In *Proceedings of the 15th International Conference on Parsing Technologies*, pages 99–104, Pisa, Italy.

KyungTae Lim and Thierry Poibeau. 2017. A system for multilingual dependency parsing based on bidirectional lstm feature representations. In *Proceedings of the CoNLL 2017 Shared Task: Multilingual Parsing from Raw Text to Universal Dependencies*, pages 63–70, Vancouver, Canada.

Joakim Nivre. 2009. Non-projective dependency parsing in expected linear time. In *Proceedings of the Joint Conference of the 47th Annual Meeting of the ACL and the 4th International Joint Conference on Natural Language Processing of the AFNLP*, pages 351–359, Suntec, Singapore.

Joakim Nivre, Željko Agić, Lars Ahrenberg, Lene Antonsen, Maria Jesus Aranzabe, Masayuki Asahara, Luma Ateyah, Mohammed Attia, Aitziber Atutxa, Liesbeth Augustinus, Elena Badmaeva, Miguel Ballesteros, Esha Banerjee, Sebastian Bank, Verginica Barbu Mititelu, John Bauer, Kepa Bengoetxea, Riyaz Ahmad Bhat, Eckhard Bick, Victoria Bobicev, Carl Börstell, Cristina Bosco, Gosse Bouma, Sam Bowman, Aljoscha Burchardt, Marie Candito, Gauthier Caron, Gülşen Cebiroğlu Eryiğit, Giuseppe G. A. Celano, Savas Cetin, Fabricio Chalub, Jinho Choi, Silvie Cinková, Çağrı Çöltekin, Miriam Connor, Elizabeth Davidson, Marie-Catherine de Marneffe, Valeria de Paiva, Arantza Diaz de Ilarraza, Peter Dirix, Kaja Dobrovoljc, Timothy Dozat, Kira Droganova, Puneet Dwivedi, Marhaba Eli, Ali Elkahky, Tomaž Erjavec, Richárd Farkas, Hector Fernandez Alcalde, Jennifer Foster, Cláudia Freitas, Katarína Gajdošová, Daniel Galbraith, Marcos Garcia, Moa Gärdenfors, Kim Gerdes, Filip Ginter, Iakes Goenaga, Koldo Gojenola, Memduh Gökırmak, Yoav Goldberg, Xavier Gómez Guinovart, Berta Gonzáles Saavedra, Matias Grioni, Normunds Grūzītis, Bruno Guillaume, Nizar Habash, Jan Hajič, Jan Hajič jr., Linh Hà Mỹ, Kim Harris, Dag Haug, Barbora Hladká, Jaroslava Hlaváčová, Florinel Hociung, Petter Hohle, Radu Ion, Elena Irimia, Tomáš Jelínek, Anders Johannsen, Fredrik Jørgensen, Hüner Kaşıkara, Hiroshi Kanayama, Jenna Kanerva, Tolga Kayadelen, Václava Kettnerová, Jesse Kirchner, Natalia Kotsyba, Simon Krek, Veronika Laippala, Lorenzo Lambertino, Tatiana Lando, John Lee, Phng Lê H`ông, Alessandro Lenci, Saran Lertpradit, Herman Leung, Cheuk Ying Li, Josie Li, Keying Li, Nikola Ljubešić, Olga Loginova, Olga Lyashevskaya, Teresa Lynn, Vivien Macketanz, Aibek Makazhanov, Michael Mandl, Christopher Manning, Cătălina Mărănduc, David Mareček, Katrin

Marheinecke, Héctor Martínez Alonso, André Martins, Jan Mašek, Yuji Matsumoto, Ryan McDonald, Gustavo Mendonça, Niko Miekka, Anna Missilä, Cătălin Mititelu, Yusuke Miyao, Simonetta Montemagni, Amir More, Laura Moreno Romero, Shinsuke Mori, Bohdan Moskalevskyi, Kadri Muischnek, Kaili Müürisep, Pinkey Nainwani, Anna Nedoluzhko, Gunta Nešpore-Bērzkalne, Luong Nguyen Thị, Huyen Nguyen Thị Minh, Vitaly Nikolaev, Hanna Nurmi, Stina Ojala, Petya Osenova, Robert Östling, Lilja Øvrelid, Elena Pascual, Marco Passarotti, Cenel-Augusto Perez, Guy Perrier, Slav Petrov, Jussi Piitulainen, Emily Pitler, Barbara Plank, Martin Popel, Lauma Pretkalniņa, Prokopis Prokopidis, Tiina Puolakainen, Sampo Pyysalo, Alexandre Rademaker, Loganathan Ramasamy, Taraka Rama, Vinit Ravishankar, Livy Real, Siva Reddy, Georg Rehm, Larissa Rinaldi, Laura Rituma, Mykhailo Romanenko, Rudolf Rosa, Davide Rovati, Benoît Sagot, Shadi Saleh, Tanja Samardžić, Manuela Sanguinetti, Baiba Saulīte, Sebastian Schuster, Djamé Seddah, Wolfgang Seeker, Mojgan Seraji, Mo Shen, Atsuko Shimada, Dmitry Sichinava, Natalia Silveira, Maria Simi, Radu Simionescu, Katalin Simkó, Mária Šimková, Kiril Simov, Aaron Smith, Antonio Stella, Milan Straka, Jana Strnadová, Alane Suhr, Umut Sulubacak, Zsolt Szántó, Dima Taji, Takaaki Tanaka, Trond Trosterud, Anna Trukhina, Reut Tsarfaty, Francis Tyers, Sumire Uematsu, Zdeňka Urešová, Larraitz Uria, Hans Uszkoreit, Sowmya Vajjala, Daniel van Niekerk, Gertjan van Noord, Viktor Varga, Eric Villemonte de la Clergerie, Veronika Vincze, Lars Wallin, Jonathan North Washington, Mats Wirén, Tak-sum Wong, Zhuoran Yu, Zdeněk Žabokrtský, Amir Zeldes, Daniel Zeman, and Hanzhi Zhu. 2017. Universal dependencies 2.1. LINDAT/CLARIN digital library at the Institute of Formal and Applied Linguistics (ÚFAL), Faculty of Mathematics and Physics, Charles University.

Robert Östling and Jörg Tiedemann. 2017. Continuous multilinguality with language vectors. In *Proceedings of the 15th Conference of the European Chapter of the Association for Computational Linguistics: Volume 2, Short Papers*, pages 644–649, Valencia, Spain.

Motoki Sato, Hitoshi Manabe, Hiroshi Noji, and Yuji Matsumoto. 2017. Adversarial training for cross-domain universal dependency parsing. In *Proceedings of the CoNLL 2017 Shared Task: Multilingual Parsing from Raw Text to Universal Dependencies*, pages 71–79, Vancouver, Canada.

Tianze Shi, Felix G. Wu, Xilun Chen, and Yao Cheng. 2017. Combining global models for parsing universal dependencies. In *Proceedings of the CoNLL 2017 Shared Task: Multilingual Parsing from Raw Text to Universal Dependencies*, pages 31–39, Vancouver, Canada.

Jörg Tiedemann. 2015. Cross-lingual dependency parsing with universal dependencies and predicted PoS labels. In *Proceedings of the Third International Conference on Dependency Linguistics (Depling 2015)*, pages 340–349, Uppsala, Sweden. Uppsala University, Uppsala, Sweden.

Yulia Tsvetkov, Sunayana Sitaram, Manaal Faruqui, Guillaume Lample, Patrick Littell, David Mortensen, Alan W Black, Lori Levin, and Chris Dyer. 2016. Polyglot neural language models: A case study in cross-lingual phonetic representation learning. In *Proceedings of the 2016 Conference of the NAACL: Human Language Technologies*, pages 1357–1366, San Diego, California, USA.

Erik Velldal, Lilja Øvrelid, and Petter Hohle. 2017. Joint UD parsing of Norwegian Bokmål and Nynorsk. In *Proceedings of the 21st Nordic Conference on Computational Linguistics (NODALIDA'17)*, pages 1–10, Gothenburg, Sweden.

Daniel Zeman, Martin Popel, Milan Straka, Hajič Jan, Joakim Nivre, Filip Ginter, Juhani Luotolahti, Sampo Pyysalo, Slav Petrov, Martin Potthast, Francis Tyers, Elena Badmaeva, Memduh Gokirmak, Anna Nedoluzhko, Silvie Cinkova, Jan Hajič jr., Jaroslava Hlavacova, Václava Kettnerová, Zdenka Uresova, Jenna Kanerva, Stina Ojala, Anna Missilä, Christopher D. Manning, Sebastian Schuster, Siva Reddy, Dima Taji, Nizar Habash, Herman Leung, Marie-Catherine de Marneffe, Manuela Sanguinetti, Maria Simi, Hiroshi Kanayama, Valeria dePaiva, Kira Droganova, Héctor Martínez Alonso, Çağrı Çöltekin, Umut Sulubacak, Hans Uszkoreit, Vivien Macketanz, Aljoscha Burchardt, Kim Harris, Katrin Marheinecke, Georg Rehm, Tolga Kayadelen, Mohammed Attia, Ali Elkahky, Zhuoran Yu, Emily Pitler, Saran Lertpradit, Michael Mandl, Jesse Kirchner, Hector Fernandez Alcalde, Jana Strnadová, Esha Banerjee, Ruli Manurung, Antonio Stella, Atsuko Shimada, Sookyoung Kwak, Gustavo Mendonca, Tatiana Lando, Rattima Nitisaroj, and Josie Li. 2017. CoNLL 2017 shared task: Multilingual parsing from raw text to universal dependencies. In *Proceedings of the CoNLL 2017 Shared Task: Multilingual Parsing from Raw Text to Universal Dependencies*, pages 1–19, Vancouver, Canada.

Generalized chart constraints for efficient PCFG and TAG parsing

Stefan Grünewald and **Sophie Henning** and **Alexander Koller**
Department of Language Science and Technology
Saarland University, Saarbrücken, Germany
`{stefang|shenning|koller}@coli.uni-saarland.de`

Abstract

Chart constraints, which specify at which string positions a constituent may begin or end, have been shown to speed up chart parsers for PCFGs. We generalize chart constraints to more expressive grammar formalisms and describe a neural tagger which predicts chart constraints at very high precision. Our constraints accelerate both PCFG and TAG parsing, and combine effectively with other pruning techniques (coarse-to-fine and supertagging) for an overall speedup of two orders of magnitude, while improving accuracy.

1 Introduction

Effective and high-precision pruning is essential for making statistical parsers fast and accurate. Existing pruning techniques differ in the source of parsing complexity they tackle. Beam search (Collins, 2003) bounds the number of entries in each cell of the parse chart; supertagging (Bangalore and Joshi, 1999; Clark and Curran, 2007; Lewis et al., 2016) bounds the number of lexicon entries for each input token; and coarse-to-fine parsing (Charniak et al., 2006) blocks chart cells that were not useful when parsing with a coarser-grained grammar.

One very direct method for limiting the chart cells the parser considers is through *chart constraints* (Roark et al., 2012): a tagger first identifies string positions at which constituents may begin or end, and the chart parser may then only fill cells which respect these constraints. Roark et al. found that begin and end chart constraints accelerated PCFG parsing by up to 8x. However, in their original form, chart constraints are limited to PCFGs and cannot be directly applied to more expressive formalisms, such as tree-adjoining grammar (TAG, Joshi and Schabes (1997)).

Chart constraints prune the ways in which smaller structures can be combined into bigger ones. Intuitively, they are complementary to supertagging, which constrains lexical ambiguity in lexicalized grammar formalisms such as TAG and CCG, and has been shown to drastically improve efficiency and accuracy for these (Bangalore et al., 2009; Lewis et al., 2016; Kasai et al., 2017). For CCG specifically, Zhang et al. (2010) showed that supertagging combines favorably with chart constraints. To our knowledge, similar results for other grammar formalisms are not available.

In this paper, we make two contributions. First, we generalize chart constraints to more expressive grammar formalisms by casting them in terms of *allowable parse items* that should be considered by the parser. The Roark chart constraints are the special case for PCFGs and CKY; our view applies to any grammar formalism for which a parser can be specified in terms of parsing schemata. Second, we present a neural tagger which predicts begin and end constraints with an accuracy around 98%. We show that these chart constraints speed up a PCFG parser by 18x and a TAG chart parser by 4x. Furthermore, chart constraints can be combined effectively with coarse-to-fine parsing for PCFGs (for an overall speedup of 70x) and supertagging for TAG (overall speedup of 124x), all while improving the accuracy over those of the baseline parsers. Our code is part of the Alto parser (Gontrum et al., 2017), available at `http://bitbucket.org/tclup/alto`.

2 Generalized chart constraints

Roark et al. define *begin* and *end* chart constraints. A begin constraint $\overline{B}$ for the string **w** is a set of positions in **w** at which no constituent of width two or more may start. Conversely, an end constraint $\overline{E}$ describes where constituents may not end.

Roark et al. focus on speeding up the standard

Proceedings of the 56th Annual Meeting of the Association for Computational Linguistics (Short Papers), pages 626–631
Melbourne, Australia, July 15 - 20, 2018. ©2018 Association for Computational Linguistics

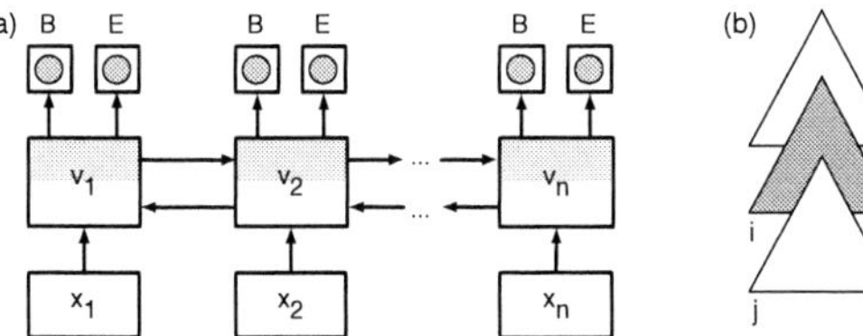

Figure 1: (a) Chart-constraint tagger; (b) TAG adjunction.

CKY parser for PCFGs with chart constraints. They do this by declaring a cell $[i, k]$ of the CKY parse chart as *closed* if $i \in \overline{B}$ or $k \in \overline{E}$, and modifying the CKY algorithm such that no nonterminals may be entered into closed cells. They show this to be very effective for PCFG parsing; but in its reliance on CKY chart cells, their algorithm is not directly applicable to other parsing algorithms or grammar formalisms.

2.1 Allowable items

In this paper, we take a more general perspective on chart constraints, which we express in terms of *parsing schemata* (Shieber et al., 1995). A parsing schema consists of a set $\mathcal{I}$ of *items*, which are derived from initial items by applying inference rules. Once all derivable items have been calculated, we can calculate the best parse tree by following the derivations of the *goal items* backwards.

Many parsing algorithms can be expressed in terms of parsing schemata. For instance, the CKY algorithm for CFGs uses items of the form $[A, i, k]$ to express that the substring from i to k can be derived from the nonterminal A, and derives new items out of old ones using the inference rule

$$\frac{[B, i, j] \quad [C, j, k] \quad A \to B\ C}{[A, i, k]}$$

The purpose of a chart constraint is to describe a set of *allowable items* $\mathcal{A} \subseteq \mathcal{I}$. We restrict the parsing algorithm so that the consequent item of an inference rule may only be derived if it is allowable. If all items that are required for the best derivation are allowable, the parser remains complete, but may become faster because fewer items are derived.

For the specific case of the CKY algorithm for PCFGs, we can simulate the behavior of Roark et al.'s algorithm by defining an item $[A, i, k]$ as allowable if $i \notin \overline{B}$ and $k \notin \overline{E}$.

2.2 Chart constraints and binarization

One technical challenge regarding chart constraints arises in the context of binarization. Chart con-

straints are trained to identify constituent boundaries in the original treebank, where nodes may have more than two children. However, an efficient chart parser for PCFG can combine only two adjacent constituents in each step. Thus, if the original tree used the rule $A \to B\ C\ D$, the parser needs to first combine B with C, say into the substring $[i, k]$, and then the result with D (or vice versa). This intermediate parsing item for $[i, k]$ must be allowable, even if $k \in \overline{E}$, because it does not represent a real constituent; it is only a computation step on the way towards one.

We solve this problem by keeping track in the parse items whether they were an intermediate result caused by binarization, or a complete constituent. This generalizes Roark et al.'s cells that are "closed to complete constituents". For instance, when converting a PCFG grammar to Chomsky normal form, one can distinguish the "new" nonterminals generated by the CNF conversion from those that were already present in the original grammar. We can then let an item $[A, i, k]$ be allowable if $i \notin \overline{B}$ and either $k \notin \overline{E}$ or A is new.

2.3 Allowable items for TAG parsing

By interpreting chart constraints in terms of allowable parse items, we can apply them to a wide range of grammar formalisms beyond PCFGs. We illustrate this by defining allowable parse items for TAG. Parse items for TAG (Shieber et al., 1995; Kallmeyer, 2010) are of the form $[\mathcal{X}, i, j, k, l]$, where i, l are string positions, and j, k are either both string positions or both are NULL. $\mathcal{X}$ is a complex representation of a position in an elementary tree, which we do not go into here; see the literature for details. The item describes a derivation of the string from position i to l. If j and k are NULL, then the derivation starts with an initial tree and covers the entire substring. Otherwise, it starts with an auxiliary tree, and there is a gap in its string yield from j to k. Such an item will later be adjoined at a node which covers the substring from j to k using the following inference rule (see Fig. 1b):

$$\frac{[\mathcal{X}, i, j, k, l] \quad [\mathcal{Y}, j, r, s, k]}{[\mathcal{Y}', i, r, s, l]}$$

Assuming begin and end constraints as above, we define allowable TAG items as follows. First, an item $[\mathcal{X}, i, j, k, l]$ is not allowable if $i \in \overline{B}$ or $l \in \overline{E}$. Second, if j and k are not NULL, then the item is not allowable if $j \in \overline{B}$ or $k \in \overline{E}$ (else there will be no constituent from j to k at which the item could be adjoined). Otherwise, the item is allowable.

2.4 Allowable states for IRTG parsing

Allowable items have a particularly direct interpretation when parsing with Interpreted Regular Tree Grammars (IRTGs, Koller and Kuhlmann (2011)), a grammar formalism which generalizes PCFG, TAG, and many others. Chart parsers for IRTG describe substructures of the input object as *states* of a finite tree automaton D. When we encode a PCFG as an IRTG, these states are of the form $[i, k]$; when we encode a TAG grammar, they are of the form $[i, j, k, l]$. Thus chart constraints describe *allowable states* of this automaton, and we can prune the chart simply by restricting D to rules that use only allowable states.

In the experiments below, we use the Alto IRTG parser (Gontrum et al., 2017), modified to implement chart constraints as allowable states. We convert the PCFG and TAG grammars into IRTG grammars and use the parsing algorithms of Groschwitz et al. (2016): "condensed intersection" for PCFG parsing and the "sibling-finder" algorithm for TAG. Both of these implement the CKY algorithm and compute charts which correspond to the parsing schemata sketched above.

3 Neural chart-constraint tagging

Roark et al. predict the begin and end constraints for a string $\mathbf{w}$ using a log-linear model with manually designed features. We replace this with a neural tagger (Fig. 1a), which reads the input sentence token by token and jointly predicts for each string position whether it is in $\overline{B}$ and/or $\overline{E}$.

Technically, our tagger is a two-layer bidirectional LSTM (Kiperwasser and Goldberg, 2016; Lewis et al., 2016; Kummerfeld and Klein, 2017). In each time step, it reads as input a pair $x_i = (w_i, p_i)$ of one-hot encodings of a word w_i and a POS tag p_i, and embeds them into dense vectors (using pretrained GloVe word embeddings (Pennington et al., 2014) for w_i and learned POS tag embeddings for p_i). It then computes the probability that a constituent begins (ends) at position i from the concatenation $v_i = v_i^{F2} \circ v_i^{B2}$ of the hidden states v^{F2} and v^{B2} of the second forward and backward LSTM at position i:

$$
\begin{aligned}
P(B \mid \mathbf{w}, i) &= \mathrm{softmax}(W_B \cdot v_i + b_B) \\
P(E \mid \mathbf{w}, i) &= \mathrm{softmax}(W_E \cdot v_i + b_E)
\end{aligned}
$$

θ	$\overline{B}$			$\overline{E}$		
	acc	prec	recall	acc	prec	recall
0.5	97.6	97.4	97.8	98.1	98.7	98.7
0.9	96.7	98.8	95.2	97.2	99.4	96.7
0.99	93.7	99.6	87.9	93.0	99.7	90.5

Figure 2: Chart-constraint tagging accuracy.

We let $\overline{B} = \{i \mid P(B|\mathbf{w}, i) < 1 - \theta\}$; that is, the network predicts a begin constraint if the probability of $\overline{B}$ exceeds a threshold θ (analogously for $\overline{E}$). The threshold allows us to trade off precision against recall; this is important because false positives can prevent the parser from discovering the best tree.

4 Evaluation

We evaluated the efficacy of chart-constraint pruning for PCFG and TAG parsing. All runtimes are on an AMD Opteron 6380 CPU at 2.5 GHz, using Oracle Java version 8. See the Supplementary Materials for details on the setup.

4.1 PCFG parsing

We trained the chart-constraint tagger on WSJ Sections 02–21. The tagging accuracy on WSJ Section 23 is shown in Fig. 2. As expected, an increasing threshold θ increases precision and decreases recall. Precision and recall are comparable to Roark et al.'s log-linear model for $\overline{E}$. Our tagger achieves 94% recall for $\overline{B}$ at a precision of 99%, compared to Roark et al.'s recall of just over 80% – without the feature engineering effort required by their system.[1]

We extracted a PCFG grammar from a right-binarized version of WSJ Sections 02–21 using maximum likelihood estimation, applying a horizontal markovization of 2 and using POS tags as terminal symbols to avoid sparse data issues. We parsed Section 23 using a baseline parser which does not prune the chart, obtaining a low f-score of 71, which is typical for such a simple PCFG. We also parsed Section 23 with parsers which utilize the chart constraints predicted by the tagger (on the original sentences and gold POS tags) and the gold chart constraints from Section 23. The results are shown in Fig. 3; "time" is the mean time to compute the chart for each sentence, in milliseconds.

Chart constraints by themselves speed the parser up by factor of 18x at $\theta = 0.5$; higher values of θ did not increase the parsing accuracy further, but

---

[1]Note that the numbers are not directly comparable because Roark et al. evaluate their tagger on Section 24.

Parser	f-score	time	speedup	% gold
Unpruned	71.0	2599	1.0x	4.4
CC ($\theta = 0.5$)	75.0	143	18.2x	91.8
CC (gold)	77.6	143	18.2x	100.0
CTF	67.6	194	13.4x	20.1
CTF + CC ($\theta=0.5$)	72.4	37	**70.1x**	94.3
CTF + CC (gold)	75.3	38	68.4x	100.0

Figure 3: Results for PCFG parsing.

yielded smaller speedups. This compares to an 8x speedup in Roark et al.; the difference may be due to the higher $\overline{B}$ recall of our neural tagger. Furthermore, when we combine chart constraints with the coarse-to-fine parser of Teichmann et al. (2017), using their threshold of 10^{-5} for CTF pruning, the two pruning methods amplify each other, yielding an overall speedup of up to 70x.[2]

4.2 TAG parsing

For the TAG experiments, we converted WSJ Sections 02–21 into a TAG corpus using the method of Chen and Vijay-Shanker (2004). This method sometimes adjoins multiple auxiliary trees to the same node. We removed all but the last adjunction at each node to make the derivations compatible with standard TAG, shortening the sentences by about 40% on average. To combat sparse data, we replaced all numbers by NUMBER and all words that do not have a GloVe embedding by UNK.

The neural chart-constraint tagger, trained on the shortened corpus, achieves a recall of 93% for $\overline{B}$ and 98% for $\overline{E}$ at 99% precision on the (shortened) Section 00. We chose a value of $\theta = 0.95$ for the experiments, since in the case of TAG parsing, false positive chart constraints frequently prevent the parser from finding any parse at all, and thus lower values of θ strongly degrade the f-scores.

We read a PTAG grammar (Resnik, 1992) with 4731 unlexicalized elementary trees off of the training corpus, binarized it, and used it to parse Section 00. This grammar struggles with unseen words, and thus achieves a rather low f-score (see Fig. 4). Chart constraints by themselves speed the TAG parser up by 3.8x, almost matching the performance of gold chart constraints. This improvement is remarkable in that Teichmann et al. (2017) found that coarse-to-fine parsing, which also prunes the substrings a finer-grained parser considers, did not improve TAG parsing performance.

---

[2]Our CTF numbers differ slightly from Teichmann et al.'s because they only parse sentences with up to 40 words and use a different binarization method.

	Parser	f-score	time	speedup	% gold
binarized	Unpruned	51.4	9483	1.0x	5.3
	CC ($\theta = 0.95$)	53.6	2489	3.8x	76.7
	CC (gold)	53.9	2281	4.2x	100.0
	supertag ($k = 3$)	77.5	137	69.4x	29.7
unbinarized	supertag ($k = 3$)	78.5	132	72.0x	30.2
	… + CC (0.95)	78.4	76	**124.3x**	91.6
	… + CC (0.99)	79.2	80	119.2x	86.1
	… + CC (gold)	78.3	74	127.9x	100.0
	… + B/E (0.95)	79.2	87	108.9x	74.5
	… + B/E (0.8)	78.4	84	113.3x	76.9
	supertag ($k = 10$)	79.4	1768	5.4x	1.5
	… + CC (0.95)	80.6	265	35.8x	71.3
	… + CC (0.99)	81.0	288	33.0x	60.3
	… + CC (gold)	81.9	252	37.6x	100.0
	… + B/E (0.95)	81.1	397	23.9x	35.6
	… + B/E (0.8)	80.7	386	24.6x	38.6

Figure 4: Results for TAG parsing.

Supertagging. We then investigated the combination of chart constraints with a neural supertagger along the lines of Lewis et al. (2016). We modified the output layer of Fig. 1a such that it predicts the supertag (= unlexicalized elementary tree) for each token. Each input token is represented by a 200D GloVe embedding.

To parse a sentence $\mathbf{w}$ of length n, we ran the trained supertagger on $\mathbf{w}$ and extracted the top k supertags for each token w_i of $\mathbf{w}$. We then ran the Alto PTAG parser on an artificial string "*1 2 … n*" and a sentence-specific TAG grammar which contains, for each i, the top k elementary trees for w_i, lexicalized with the "word" i and weighted with the probability of its supertag. This allowed us to use the unmodified Alto parser, while avoiding the possible mixing of supertags for multiple occurrences of the same word. We then obtained the best parse trees for the original sentence $\mathbf{w}$ by replacing each artificial token i in the parse tree by the original token w_i.

The sentence-specific grammars are so small that we can parse the test corpus without binarizing them. As Fig. 4 indicates, supertagging speeds up the parser by 5x ($k = 10$) to 70x ($k = 3$); the use of word embeddings boosts the coverage to almost 100% and the f-score to around 80. Adding chart constraints on top of supertagging further improves the parser, yielding the best speed (at $k = 3$) and accuracy (at $k = 10$). We achieve an overall speedup of two orders of magnitude with a drastic increase in accuracy.

Allowable items for TAG. Instead of requiring that a TAG chart item is only allowable if neither the string $[i, l]$ nor its gap $[j, k]$ violate a chart constraint (as in Section 2.3), one could instead adopt a simpler definition by which a TAG chart item is allowable if i and l satisfy the chart constraints, regardless of the gap.[3]

We evaluated the original definition from Section 2.3 ("CC") against this baseline definition ("B/E"). As the results in Fig. 4 indicate, the B/E strategy achieves higher accuracy and lower parsing speeds than the CC strategy at equal values of θ. This is to be expected, because CC has more opportunities to prune chart items early, but false positive chart constraints can cause it to overprune. When θ is scaled so both strategies achieve the same accuracy – i.e., B/E $\theta = 0.8$ for CC $\theta = 0.95$, or CC $\theta = 0.99$ for B/E $\theta = 0.95$ –, CC is faster than B/E. This suggests that imposing chart constraints on the gap is beneficial and illustrates the flexibility and power of the "admissible items" approach we introduce here.

4.3 Discussion

The effect of using chart constraints is that the parser considers fewer substructures of the input object – potentially to the point that the asymptotic parsing complexity is reduced below that of the underlying grammar formalism (Roark et al., 2012). In practice, we observe that the percentage of chart items whose begin positions and end positions are consistent with the gold standard tree ("% gold" in the figures) is increased by CTF and supertagging, indicating that these suppress the computation of many spans that are not needed for the best tree. However, chart constraints prune useless spans out much more directly and completely, leading to a further boost in parsing speed.

Because we remove multiple adjunctions in the TAG experiment, most sentences in the corpus are shorter than in the original. This might skew the parsing results in favor of pruning techniques that work best on short sentences. We checked this by plotting sentence lengths against mean parsing times for a number of pruning methods in Fig. 5 (supertagging with $k = 10$, chart constraints with $\theta = 0.95$). As the sentence length increases, parsing times of supertagging together with chart constraints grows much more slowly than the other methods. Thus we can expect the relative speedup to increase for corpora of longer sentences.

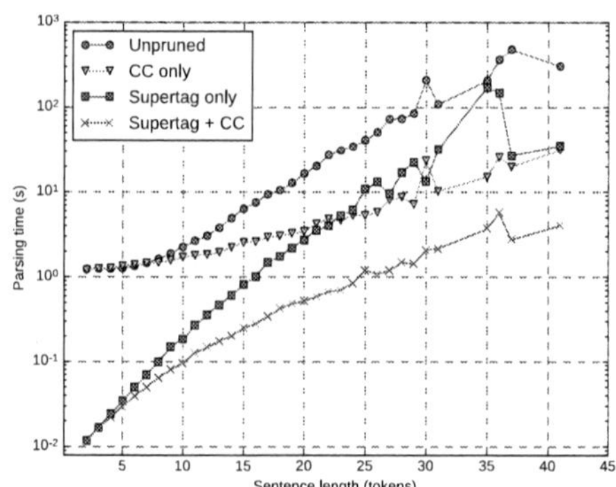

Figure 5: TAG parsing speed as a function of sentence length.

5   Conclusion

Chart constraints, computed by a neural tagger, robustly accelerate parsers both for PCFGs and for more expressive formalisms such as TAG. Even highly effective pruning techniques such as CTF and supertagging can be further improved through chart constraints, indicating that they target different sources of complexity.

By interpreting chart constraints in terms of allowable chart items, we can apply them to arbitrary chart parsers, including ones for grammar formalisms that describe objects other than strings, e.g. graphs (Chiang et al., 2013; Groschwitz et al., 2015). The primary challenge here is to develop a high-precision tagger that identifies allowable subgraphs, which requires moving beyond LSTMs.

An intriguing question is to what extent chart constraints can speed up parsing algorithms that do not use charts. It is known that chart constraints can speed up context-free shift-reduce parsers (Chen et al., 2017). It would be interesting to see how a neural parser, such as (Dyer et al., 2016), would benefit from chart constraints calculated by a neural tagger.

Acknowledgments. We are grateful to Jonas Groschwitz, Christoph Teichmann, Stefan Thater, and the anonymous reviewers for discussions and comments. This work was supported through the DFG grant KO 2916/2-1.

References

Srinivas Bangalore, Pierre Boulllier, Alexis Nasr, Owen Rambow, and Benoît Sagot. 2009. MICA: A

---

[3]We thank an anonymous reviewer for suggesting this comparison.

probabilistic dependency parser based on tree insertion grammars application note. In *Proceedings of NAACL-HLT (Short Papers)*.

Srinivas Bangalore and Aravind K. Joshi. 1999. Supertagging: An approach to almost parsing. *Computataional Linguistics* 25(2):237–265.

Eugene Charniak, Mark Johnson, Micha Elsner, Joseph Austerweil, David Ellis, Isaac Haxton, Catherine Hill, R. Shrivaths, Jeremy Moore, Michael Pozar, and Theresa Vu. 2006. Multilevel coarse-to-fine PCFG parsing. In *Proceedings of NAACL-HLT*.

John Chen and K. Vijay-Shanker. 2004. Automatic extraction of TAGs from the Penn Treebank. In *New developments in parsing technology*, Springer, pages 73–89.

Wenliang Chen, Muhua Zhu, Min Zhang, Yue Zhang, and Jingbo Zhu. 2017. Improving shift-reduce phrase-structure parsing with constituent boundary information. *Computational Intelligence* 33(3):428–447.

David Chiang, Jacob Andreas, Daniel Bauer, Karl Moritz Hermann, Bevan Jones, and Kevin Knight. 2013. Parsing graphs with hyperedge replacement grammars. In *Proceedings of the 51st Annual Meeting of the Association for Computational Linguistics*.

Stephen Clark and James R. Curran. 2007. Wide-coverage efficient statistical parsing with CCG and log-linear models. *Computational Linguistics* 33(4):493–552.

Michael Collins. 2003. Head-driven statistical models for natural language parsing. *Computational Linguistics* 29(4):589–637.

Chris Dyer, Adhiguna Kuncoro, Miguel Ballesteros, and Noah A. Smith. 2016. Recurrent neural network grammars. In *Proceedings of the 2016 Conference of the North American Chapter of the Association for Computational Linguistics: Human Language Technologies*. pages 199–209.

Johannes Gontrum, Jonas Groschwitz, Alexander Koller, and Christoph Teichmann. 2017. Alto: Rapid prototyping for parsing and translation. In *Proceedings of the EACL Demo Session*. Valencia.

Jonas Groschwitz, Alexander Koller, and Mark Johnson. 2016. Efficient techniques for parsing with tree automata. In *Proceedings of the 54th Annual Meeting of the Association for Computational Linguistics*.

Jonas Groschwitz, Alexander Koller, and Christoph Teichmann. 2015. Graph parsing with s-graph grammars. In *Proceedings of the 53rd Annual Meeting of the Association for Computational Linguistics and the 7th International Joint Conference on Natural Language Processing*.

Aravind K. Joshi and Yves Schabes. 1997. Tree-Adjoining Grammars. In G. Rozenberg and A. Salomaa, editors, *Handbook of Formal Languages*, Springer-Verlag, volume 3.

Laura Kallmeyer. 2010. *Parsing Beyond Context-Free Grammars*. Springer.

Jungo Kasai, Bob Frank, Tom McCoy, Owen Rambow, and Alexis Nasr. 2017. TAG parsing with neural networks and vector representations of supertags. In *Proceedings of EMNLP*.

Eliyahu Kiperwasser and Yoav Goldberg. 2016. Simple and accurate dependency parsing using bidirectional LSTM feature representations. *Transactions of the Association for Computational Linguistics* 4:313–327.

Alexander Koller and Marco Kuhlmann. 2011. A generalized view on parsing and translation. In *Proceedings of the 12th International Conference on Parsing Technologies*.

Jonathan K. Kummerfeld and Dan Klein. 2017. Parsing with traces: An $O(n^4)$ algorithm and a structural representation. *Transactions of the ACL* 5:441–454.

Mike Lewis, Kenton Lee, and Luke Zettlemoyer. 2016. LSTM CCG parsing. In *Proceedings of NAACL-HLT 2016*.

Jeffrey Pennington, Richard Socher, and Christopher D. Manning. 2014. GloVe: Global vectors for word representation. In *Proceedings of EMNLP*.

Phil Resnik. 1992. Probabilistic tree-adjoining grammar as a framework for statistical natural language processing. In *Proceedings of the 14th COLING*.

Brian Roark, Kristy Hollingshead, and Nathan Bodenstab. 2012. Finite-state chart constraints for reduced complexity context-free parsing pipelines. *Computational Linguistics* 38(4):719–753.

Stuart Shieber, Yves Schabes, and Fernando Pereira. 1995. Principles and implementation of deductive parsing. *Journal of Logic Programming* 24(1–2):3–36.

Christoph Teichmann, Alexander Koller, and Jonas Groschwitz. 2017. Coarse-to-fine parsing for expressive grammar formalisms. In *Proceedings of the 15th International Conference on Parsing Technologies (IWPT)*. Pisa.

Yue Zhang, Byung-Gyu Ahn, Stephen Clark, Curt Van Wyk, James R. Curran, and Laura Rimell. 2010. Chart pruning for fast lexicalised-grammar parsing. In *Proceedings of COLING*.

Exploring Semantic Properties of Sentence Embeddings

Xunjie Zhu
Rutgers University
Piscataway, NJ, USA
xunjie.zhu@
rutgers.edu

Tingfeng Li
Northwestern Polytechnical
University, Xi'an, China
ltf@mail.nwpu.edu.cn

Gerard de Melo
Rutgers University
Piscataway, NJ, USA
gdm@demelo.org

Abstract

Neural vector representations are ubiquitous throughout all subfields of NLP. While word vectors have been studied in much detail, thus far only little light has been shed on the properties of sentence embeddings. In this paper, we assess to what extent prominent sentence embedding methods exhibit select semantic properties. We propose a framework that generate triplets of sentences to explore how changes in the syntactic structure or semantics of a given sentence affect the similarities obtained between their sentence embeddings.

1   Introduction

Neural vector representations have become ubiquitous in all subfields of natural language processing. For the case of word vectors, important properties of the representations have been studied, including their linear substructures (Mikolov et al., 2013; Levy and Goldberg, 2014), the linear superposition of word senses (Arora et al., 2016b), and the nexus to pointwise mutual information scores between co-occurring words (Arora et al., 2016a).

However, thus far, only little is known about the properties of sentence embeddings. Sentence embedding methods attempt to encode a variable-length input sentence into a fixed length vector. A number of such sentence embedding methods have been proposed in recent years (Le and Mikolov, 2014; Kiros et al., 2015; Wieting et al., 2015; Conneau et al., 2017; Arora et al., 2017).

Sentence embeddings have mainly been evaluated in terms of how well their cosine similarities mirror human judgments of semantic relatedness, typically with respect to the SemEval Semantic Textual Similarity competitions. The SICK dataset (Marelli et al., 2014) was created to better benchmark the effectiveness of different models across a broad range of challenging lexical, syntactic, and semantic phenomena, in terms of both similarities and the ability to be predictive of entailment. However, even on SICK, oftentimes very shallow methods prove effective at obtaining fairly competitive results (Wieting et al., 2015). Adi et al. investigated to what extent different embedding methods are predictive of i) the occurrence of words in the original sentence, ii) the order of words in the original sentence, and iii) the length of the original sentence (Adi et al., 2016, 2017). Belinkov et al. (2017) inspected neural machine translation systems with regard to their ability to acquire morphology, while Shi et al. (2016) investigated to what extent they learn source side syntax. Wang et al. (2016) argue that the latent representations of advanced neural reading comprehension architectures encode information about predication. Finally, sentence embeddings have also often been investigated in classification tasks such as sentiment polarity or question type classification (Kiros et al., 2015). Concurrently with our research, Conneau et al. (2018) investigated to what extent one can learn to classify specific syntactic and semantic properties of sentences using large amounts of training data (100,000 instances) for each property.

Overall, still, remarkably little is known about what specific semantic properties are directly reflected by such embeddings. In this paper, we specifically focus on a few select aspects of sentence semantics and inspect to what extent prominent sentence embedding methods are able to capture them. Our framework generates triplets of sentences to explore how changes in the syntactic structure or semantics of a given sentence affect the similarities obtained between their sentence embeddings.

Proceedings of the 56th Annual Meeting of the Association for Computational Linguistics (Short Papers), pages 632–637
Melbourne, Australia, July 15 - 20, 2018. ©2018 Association for Computational Linguistics

2 Analysis

To conduct our analysis, we proceed by generating new phenomena-specific evaluation datasets.

Our starting point is that even minor alterations of a sentence may lead to notable shifts in meaning. For instance, a sentence S such as *A rabbit is jumping over the fence* and a sentence S^* such as *A rabbit is not jumping over the fence* diverge with respect to many of the inferences that they warrant. Even if sentence S^* is somewhat less idiomatic than alternative wordings such as *There are no rabbits jumping over the fence*, we nevertheless expect sentence embedding methods to interpret both correctly, just as humans do.

Despite the semantic differences between the two sentences due to the negation, we still expect the cosine similarity between their respective embeddings to be fairly high, in light of their semantic relatedness in touching on similar themes.

Hence, only comparing the similarity between sentence pairs of this sort does not easily lend itself to insightful automated analyses. Instead, we draw on another key idea. It is common for two sentences to be semantically close despite differences in their specific linguistic realizations. Building on the previous example, we can construct a further contrasting sentence S^+ such as *A rabbit is hopping over the fence*. This sentence is very close in meaning to sentence S, despite minor differences in the choice of words. In this case, we would want for the semantic relatedness between sentences S and S^+ to be assessed as higher than between sentence S and sentence S^*.

We refer to this sort of scheme as sentence triplets. We rely on simple transformations to generate several different sets of sentence triplets.

2.1 Sentence Modification Schemes

In the following, we first describe the kinds of transformations we apply to generate altered sentences. Subsequently, in Section 2.2, we shall consider how to assemble such sentences into sentence triplets of various kinds so as to assess different semantic properties of sentence embeddings.

Not-Negation. We negate the original sentence by inserting the negation marker *not* before the first verb of the original sentence A to generate a new sentence B, including contractions as appropriate, or removing negations when they are already present, as in:

A: The young boy is climbing the wall made of rock.

B: The young boy isn't climbing the wall made of rock.

Quantifier-Negation. We prepend the quantifier expression *there is no* to original sentences beginning with A to generate new sentences.

A: A girl is cutting butter into two pieces.

B: There is no girl cutting butter into two pieces.

Synonym Substitution. We substitute the verb in the original sentence with an appropriate synonym to generate a new sentence B.

A: The man is talking on the telephone.

B: The man is chatting on the telephone.

Embedded Clause Extraction. For those sentences containing verbs such as *say, think* with embedded clauses, we extract the clauses as the new sentence.

A: Octel said the purchase was expected.

B: The purchase was expected.

Passivization. Sentences that are expressed in active voice are changed to passive voice.

A: Harley asked Abigail to bake some muffins.

B: Abigail is asked to bake some muffins.

Argument Reordering. For sentences matching the structure "⟨somebody⟩ ⟨verb⟩ ⟨somebody⟩ *to* ⟨do something⟩", we swap the subject and object of the original sentence A to generate a new sentence B.

A: Matilda encouraged Sophia to compete in a match.

B: Sophia encouraged Matilda to compete in a match.

Fixed Point Inversion. We select a word in the sentence as the pivot and invert the order of words before and after the pivot. The intuition here is that this simple corruption is likely to result in a new sentence that does not properly convey the original meaning, despite sharing the original words in common with it. Hence, these sorts of corruptions can serve as a useful diagnostic.

A: *A dog is running on concrete and is holding a blue ball*

B: *concrete and is holding a blue ball a dog is running on.*

2.2 Sentence Triplet Generation

Given the above forms of modified sentences, we induce five evaluation datasets, consisting of triplets of sentences as follows.

1. **Negation Detection:** Original sentence, Synonym Substitution, Not-Negation

   With this dataset, we seek to explore how well sentence embeddings can distinguish sentences with similar structure and opposite meaning, while using Synonym Substitution as the contrast set. We would want the similarity between the original sentence and the negated sentence to be lower than that between the original sentence and its synonym version.

2. **Negation Variants:** Quantifier-Negation, Not-Negation, Original sentence

   In the second dataset, we aim to investigate how well the sentence embeddings reflect negation quantifiers. We posit that the similarity between the Quantifier-Negation and Not-Negation versions should be a bit higher than between either the Not-Negation or the Quantifier-Negation and original sentences.

3. **Clause Relatedness:** Original sentence, Embedded Clause Extraction, Not-Negation

   In this third set, we want to explore whether the similarity between a sentence and its embedded clause is higher than between a sentence and its negation.

4. **Argument Sensitivity:** Original sentence, Passivization, Argument Reordering

   With this last test, we wish to ascertain whether the sentence embeddings succeed in distinguishing semantic information from structural information. Consider, for instance, the following triplet.

   > S: Lilly loves Imogen.
   > S^+: Imogen is loved by Lilly.
   > S^*: Imogen loves Lilly.

   Here, S and S^+ mostly share the same meaning, whereas S^+ and S^* have a similar word order, but do not possess the same specific meaning. If the sentence embeddings focus more on semantic cues, then the similarity

between S and S^+ ought to be larger than that between S^+ and S^*. If the sentence embedding however is easily misled by matching sentence structures, the opposite will be the case.

5. **Fixed Point Reorder:** *Original sentence, Semantically equivalent sentence, Fixed Point Inversion*

   With this dataset, our objective is to explore how well the sentence embeddings account for shifts in meaning due to the word order in a sentence. We select sentence pairs from the SICK dataset according to their semantic relatedness score and entailment labeling. Sentence pairs with a high relatedness score and the *Entailment* tag are considered semantically similar sentences. We rely on the Levenshtein Distance as a filter to ensure a structural similarity between the two sentences, i.e., sentence pairs whose Levenshtein Distance is sufficiently high are regarded as eligible.

   Additionally, we use the Fixed Point Inversion technique to generate a contrastive sentence. The resulting sentence likely no longer adequately reflects the original meaning. Hence, we expect that, on average, the similarity between the original sentence and the semantically similar sentence should be higher than that between the original sentence and the contrastive version.

3 Experiments

We now proceed to describe our experimental evaluation based on this paradigm.

3.1 Datasets

Using the aforementioned triplet generation methods, we create the evaluation datasets listed in Table 1, drawing on source sentences from SICK, Penn Treebank WSJ and MSR Paraphase corpus. Although the process to modify the sentences is automatic, we rely on human annotators to double-check the results for grammaticality and semantics. This is particularly important for synonym substitution, for which we relied on Word-Net (Fellbaum, 1998). Unfortunately, not all synonyms are suitable as replacements in a given context.

Table 1: Generated Evaluation Datasets

Dataset	# of Sentences
Negation Detection	674
Negation Variants	516
Clause Relatedness	567
Argument Sensitivity	445
Fixed Point Reorder	623

3.2 Embedding Methods

In our experiments, we compare three particularly prominent sentence embedding methods:

1. GloVe Averaging (GloVe Avg.): The simple approach of taking the average of the word vectors for all words in a sentence. Although this method neglects the order of words entirely, it can fare reasonably well on some of the most commonly invoked forms of evaluation (Wieting et al., 2015; Arora et al., 2017). Note that we here rely on regular unweighted GloVe vectors (Pennington et al., 2014) instead of fine-tuned or weighted word vectors.

2. Concatenated P-Mean Embeddings (P-Means): Rücklé et al. (2018) proposed concatenating different p-means of multiple kinds of word vectors.

3. Sent2Vec: Pagliardini et al. (2018) proposed a method to learn word and n-gram embeddings such that the average of all words and n-grams in a sentence can serve as a high-quality sentence vector.

4. The Skip-Thought Vector approach (SkipThought) by Kiros et al. (2015) applies the neighbour prediction intuitions of the word2vec Skip-Gram model at the level of entire sentences, as encoded and decoded via recurrent neural networks. The method trains an encoder to process an input sentence such that the resulting latent representation is optimized for predicting neighbouring sentences via the decoder.

5. InferSent (Conneau et al., 2017) is based on supervision from an auxiliary task, namely the Stanford NLI dataset.

3.3 Results and Discussion

Negation Detection. Table 2 lists the results for the Negation Detection dataset, where S, S^+, S^* refer to the original, Synonym Substitution, and Not-Negation versions of the sentences, respectively. For each of the considered embedding methods, we first report the average cosine similarity scores between all relevant sorts of pairings of two sentences, i.e. between the original and the Synonym-Substitution sentences (S and S^+), between original and Not-Negated (S and S^*), and between Not-Negated and Synonym-Substitution (S^+ and S^*). Finally, in the last column, we report the Accuracy, computed as the percentage of sentence triplets for which the proximity relationships were as desired, i.e., the cosine similarity between the original and synonym-substituted versions was higher than the similarity between that same original and its Not-Negation version.

On this dataset, we observe that GloVe Avg. is more often than not misled by the introduction of synonyms, although the corresponding word vector typically has a high cosine similarity with the original word's embedding. In contrast, both InferSent and SkipThought succeed in distinguishing unnegated sentences from negated ones.

Table 2: Evaluation of Negation Detection

	$S \wedge S^+$	$S \wedge S^*$	$S^+ \wedge S^*$	Accuracy
Glove Avg	97.42%	98.80%	96.53%	13.06%
P Means	98.49%	99.47%	98.13%	6.82%
Sent2Vec	91.28%	93.50%	85.30%	41.99%
SkipThought	88.34%	81.95%	73.74%	78.19%
Infersent	94.74%	88.64%	85.15%	91.10%

Negation Variants. In Table 3, S, S^+, S^* refer to the original, Not-Negation, and Quantifier-Negation versions of a sentence, respectively. Accuracy in this problem is defined as percentage of sentence triples whose similarity between $S+$ and S^* is the higher than similarity between S and $S+$ and S^+ and S^* The results of both averaging of word embeddings. and SkipThought are dismal in terms of the accuracy. InferSent, in contrast, appears to have acquired a better understanding of negation quantifiers, as these are commonplace in many NLI datasets.

Clause Relatedness. In Table 4, S, S^+, S^* refer to original, Embedded Clause Extraction, and Not-Negation, respectively. Although not particularly more accurate than random guessing, among the considered approaches, Sent2vec fares best in distinguishing the embedded clause of a sentence

Table 3: Evaluation of Negation Variants

	$S \wedge S^+$	$S \wedge S^*$	$S^+ \wedge S^*$	Accuracy
Glove Avg	96.91%	97.99%	97.05%	1.56%
P Means	98.66%	99.07%	98.49%	0.19%
Sent2Vec	90.53%	90.59%	86.87%	1.56%
SkipThought	71.94%	75.40%	73.11%	22.96%
InferSent	84.51%	88.45%	91.63%	85.78%

Table 5: Evaluation of Argument Sensitivity

	$S \wedge S^+$	$S \wedge S^*$	$S^+ \wedge S^*$	Accuracy
Glove Avg	96.17%	99.96%	96.17%	0.00%
P Means	97.94%	99.98%	97.94%	0.00%
Sent2Vec	89.11%	99.80%	89.13%	0.00%
SkipThought	83.44%	95.57%	82.32%	4.71%
Infersent	93.70%	97.98%	94.11%	2.24%

from a negation of said sentence.

For a detailed analysis, we can divide the sentence triplets in this dataset into two categories as exemplified by the following examples:

a) Copperweld said it doesn't expect a protracted strike. — Copperweld said it expected a protracted strike. — It doesn't expect a protracted strike.

b) "We made our own decision," he said. — "We didn't make our own decision," he said. — We made our own decision.

For cases resembling a), the average SkipThought similarity between the sentence and its Not-Negation version is 79.90%, while for cases resembling b), it is 26.71%. The accuracy of SkipThought on cases resembling a is 36.90%, and the accuracy of SkipThought on cases like b is only 0.75% It seems plausible that SkipThought is more sensitive to the word order due to the recurrent architecture. Infersent also achieved better performance on sentences resembling a) compared with sentences resembling b), its accuracy on these two structures is 28.37% and 15.73% respectively.

Table 4: Evaluation of Clause Relatedness

	$S \wedge S^+$	$S \wedge S^*$	$S^+ \wedge S^*$	Accuracy
Glove Avg	94.76%	99.14%	94.03%	4.58%
P Means	97.40%	99.61%	97.08%	2.46%
Sent2Vec	86.62%	92.40%	79.23%	32.92%
SkipThought	54.94%	84.27%	45.48%	19.51%
Infersent	89.47%	95.12%	85.22%	18.45%

Argument Sensitivity. In Table 5, S, S^+, S^* to refer to the original sentence, it Passivization form, and the Argument Reordering version, respectively. Although recurrent architectures are able to consider the order of words, unfortunately, none of the analysed approaches prove adept at distinguishing the semantic information from structural information in this case.

Fixed Point Reorder. In Table 6, S, S^+, S^* to refer to the original sentence, its semantically equivalent one and Fixed Point Inversion Version. As Table 6 indicates, sentence embeddings based on means (GloVe averages), weighted means (Sent2Vec), or concatenation of p-mean embeddings (P-Means) are unable to distinguish the fixed point inverted sentence from the semantically equivalent one, as they do not encode sufficient word order information into the sentence embeddings. Sent2Vec does consider n-grams but these do not affect the results sufficiently.SkipThought and InferSent did well when the original sentence and its semantically equivalence share similar structure.

Table 6: Evaluation of Fixed Point Reorder

	$S \wedge S^+$	$S \wedge S^*$	$S^+ \wedge S^*$	Accuracy
Glove avg	97.74%	100.00%	97.74%	0.00%
P-Means	98.68%	100.00%	98.68%	0.00%
Sent2Vec	92.88%	100.00%	92.88%	0.00%
SkipThought	89.83%	39.75%	37.28%	99.84%
InferSent	95.53%	94.26%	90.64%	72.92%

4 Conclusion

This paper proposes a simple method to inspect sentence embeddings with respect to their semantic properties, analysing three popular embedding methods. We find that both SkipThought and InferSent distinguish negation of a sentence from synonymy. InferSent fares better at identifying semantic equivalence regardless of the order of words and copes better with quantifiers. SkipThoughts is more suitable for tasks in which the semantics of the sentence corresponds to its structure, but it often fails to identify sentences with different word order yet similar meaning. In almost all cases, dedicated sentence embeddings from hidden states a neural network outperform a simple averaging of word embeddings.

Acknowledgments

This research is funded in part by ARO grant no. W911NF-17-C-0098 as part of the DARPA So-cialSim program.

References

Yossi Adi, Einat Kermany, Yonatan Belinkov, Ofer Lavi, and Yoav Goldberg. 2016. Fine-grained Analysis of Sentence Embeddings Using Auxiliary Prediction Tasks. *arXiv.org*.

Yossi Adi, Einat Kermany, Yonatan Belinkov, Ofer Lavi, and Yoav Goldberg. 2017. Analysis of sentence embedding models using prediction tasks in natural language processing. *IBM Journal of Research and Development*, 61(4):3:1–3:9.

Sanjeev Arora, Yuanzhi Li, Yingyu Liang, Tengyu Ma, and Andrej Risteski. 2016a. A latent variable model approach to pmi-based word embeddings. *Transactions of the Association for Computational Linguistics*, 4:385–399.

Sanjeev Arora, Yuanzhi Li, Yingyu Liang, Tengyu Ma, and Andrej Risteski. 2016b. Linear algebraic structure of word senses, with applications to polysemy. *arXiv preprint arXiv:1601.03764*.

Sanjeev Arora, Yingyu Liang, and Tengyu Ma. 2017. A simple but tough-to-beat baseline for sentence embeddings. In *Proceedings of ICLR 2017*.

Yonatan Belinkov, Nadir Durrani, Fahim Dalvi, Hassan Sajjad, and James R. Glass. 2017. What do neural machine translation models learn about morphology? *CoRR*, abs/1704.03471.

A. Conneau, G. Kruszewski, G. Lample, L. Barrault, and M. Baroni. 2018. What you can cram into a single vector: Probing sentence embeddings for linguistic properties. *ArXiv e-prints*.

Alexis Conneau, Douwe Kiela, Holger Schwenk, Loïc Barrault, and Antoine Bordes. 2017. Supervised learning of universal sentence representations from natural language inference data. *CoRR*, abs/1705.02364.

Christiane Fellbaum, editor. 1998. *WordNet: An Electronic Lexical Database*. The MIT Press.

Ryan Kiros, Yukun Zhu, Ruslan Salakhutdinov, Richard S. Zemel, Antonio Torralba, Raquel Urtasun, and Sanja Fidler. 2015. Skip-thought vectors. In *Proceedings of NIPS 2015*. MIT Press.

Quoc Le and Tomas Mikolov. 2014. Distributed representations of sentences and documents. In *Proceedings of ICML 2014*. PMLR.

Omer Levy and Yoav Goldberg. 2014. Linguistic regularities in sparse and explicit word representations. In *Proceedings of the Eighteenth Conference on Computational Natural Language Learning*, pages 171–180, Ann Arbor, Michigan. Association for Computational Linguistics.

Marco Marelli, Stefano Menini, Marco Baroni, Luisa Bentivogli, Raffaella bernardi, and Roberto Zamparelli. 2014. A sick cure for the evaluation of compositional distributional semantic models. In *Proceedings of the Ninth International Conference on Language Resources and Evaluation (LREC-2014)*. European Language Resources Association (ELRA).

Tomas Mikolov, Wen-tau Yih, and Geoffrey Zweig. 2013. Linguistic regularities in continuous space word representations. In *HLT-NAACL*, pages 746–751.

Matteo Pagliardini, Prakhar Gupta, and Martin Jaggi. 2018. Unsupervised learning of sentence embeddings using compositional n-Gram features. In *NAACL 2018 - Conference of the North American Chapter of the Association for Computational Linguistics*.

Jeffrey Pennington, Richard Socher, and Christopher Manning. 2014. GloVe: Global vectors for word representation. In *Proceedings of the 2014 Conference on Empirical Methods in Natural Language Processing (EMNLP 2014)*, pages 1532–1543.

Andreas Rücklé, Steffen Eger, Maxime Peyrard, and Iryna Gurevych. 2018. Concatenated p-mean embeddings as universal cross-lingual sentence representations. *arXiv*.

Xing Shi, Inkit Padhi, and Kevin Knight. 2016. Does string-based neural mt learn source syntax? In *Proceedings of the 2016 Conference on Empirical Methods in Natural Language Processing*, pages 1526–1534, Austin, Texas. Association for Computational Linguistics.

Hai Wang, Takeshi Onishi, Kevin Gimpel, and David A. McAllester. 2016. Emergent logical structure in vector representations of neural readers. *CoRR*, abs/1611.07954.

John Wieting, Mohit Bansal, Kevin Gimpel, and Karen Livescu. 2015. Towards universal paraphrastic sentence embeddings. *CoRR*, abs/1511.08198.

Scoring Lexical Entailment
with a Supervised Directional Similarity Network

Marek Rei[♠◇]   **Daniela Gerz**[♣]   **Ivan Vulić**[♣]
[♠]Computer Laboratory, University of Cambridge, United Kingdom
[◇]The ALTA Institute, University of Cambridge, United Kingdom
[♣]Language Technology Lab, University of Cambridge, United Kingdom
`marek.rei@cl.cam.ac.uk, dsg40@cam.ac.uk, iv250@cam.ac.uk`

Abstract

We present the Supervised Directional Similarity Network (SDSN), a novel neural architecture for learning task-specific transformation functions on top of general-purpose word embeddings. Relying on only a limited amount of supervision from task-specific scores on a subset of the vocabulary, our architecture is able to generalise and transform a general-purpose distributional vector space to model the relation of lexical entailment. Experiments show excellent performance on scoring graded lexical entailment, raising the state-of-the-art on the HyperLex dataset by approximately 25%.

1   Introduction

Standard word embedding models (Mikolov et al., 2013; Pennington et al., 2014; Bojanowski et al., 2017) are based on the distributional hypothesis by Harris (1954). However, purely distributional models coalesce various lexico-semantic relations (e.g., synonymy, antonymy, hypernymy) into a joint distributed representation. To address this, previous work has focused on introducing supervision into *individual* word embeddings, allowing them to better capture the desired lexical properties. For example, Faruqui et al. (2015) and Wieting et al. (2015) proposed methods for using annotated lexical relations to condition the vector space and bring synonymous words closer together. Mrkšić et al. (2016) and Mrkšić et al. (2017) improved the optimisation function and introduced an additional constraint for pushing antonym pairs further apart. While these methods integrate hand-crafted features from external lexical resources with distributional information, they improve only the embeddings of words that have annotated lexical relations

in the training resource.

In this work, we propose a novel approach to leveraging external knowledge with general-purpose unsupervised embeddings, focusing on the directional graded lexical entailment task (Vulić et al., 2017), whereas previous work has mostly investigated simpler non-directional semantic similarity tasks. Instead of optimising individual word embeddings, our model uses general-purpose embeddings and optimises a separate neural component to adapt these to the specific task. In particular, our neural Supervised Directional Similarity Network (SDSN) dynamically produces task-specific embeddings optimised for scoring the asymmetric lexical entailment relation between any two words, regardless of their presence in the training resource. Our results with task-specific embeddings indicate large improvements on the HyperLex dataset, a standard graded lexical entailment benchmark. The model also yields improvements on a simpler non-graded entailment detection task.

2   The Task of Grading Lexical Entailment

In graded lexical entailment, the goal is to make fine-grained assertions regarding the directional hierarchical semantic relationships between concepts (Vulić et al., 2017). The task is grounded in theories of concept (proto)typicality and category vagueness from cognitive science (Rosch, 1975; Kamp and Partee, 1995), and aims at answering the following question: *"To what degree is X a type of Y?"*. It quantifies the degree of lexical entailment instead of providing only a binary *yes/no* decision on the relationship between the concepts X and Y, as done in hypernymy detection tasks (Kotlerman et al., 2010; Weeds et al., 2014; Santus et al., 2014; Kiela et al., 2015; Shwartz et al., 2017).

Graded lexical entailment provides finer-grained

Proceedings of the 56th Annual Meeting of the Association for Computational Linguistics (Short Papers), pages 638–643
Melbourne, Australia, July 15 - 20, 2018. ©2018 Association for Computational Linguistics

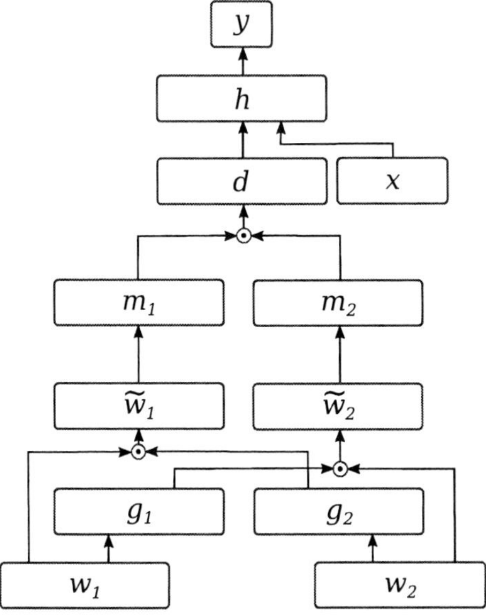

Figure 1: Supervised directional similarity network (SDSN) for grading lexical relations.

judgements on a continuous scale. For instance, the word pair (*girl* → *person*) has been rated highly with 9.85/10 by the HyperLex annotators. The pair (*guest* → *person*) has received a slightly lower score of 7.22, as a prototypical guest is often a person but there can be exceptions. In contrast, the score for the reversed pair (*person* → *guest*) is only judged at 2.88.

As demonstrated by Vulić et al. (2017) and Nickel and Kiela (2017), standard general-purpose representation models trained in an unsupervised way purely on distributional information are unfit for this task and unable to surpass the performance of simple frequency baselines (see also Table 1). Therefore, in what follows, we describe a novel supervised framework for constructing task-specific word embeddings, optimised for the graded entailment task at hand.

3   System Architecture

The network architecture can be seen in Figure 1. The system receives a pair of words as input and predicts a score that represents the strength of the given lexical relation. In the graded entailment task, we would like the model to return a high score for (*biology* → *science*), as biology is a type of science, but a low score for (*point* → *pencil*).

We start by mapping both input words to corresponding word embeddings w_1 and w_2. The

embeddings come from a standard distributional vector space, pre-trained on a large unannotated corpus, and are not fine-tuned during training. An element-wise gating operation is then applied to each word, conditioned on the other word:

$$g_1 = \sigma(W_{g_1} w_1 + b_{g_1}) \tag{1}$$
$$g_2 = \sigma(W_{g_2} w_2 + b_{g_2}) \tag{2}$$
$$\widetilde{w}_1 = w_1 \odot g_2 \tag{3}$$
$$\widetilde{w}_2 = w_2 \odot g_1 \tag{4}$$

where W_{g_1} and W_{g_2} are weight matrices, b_{g_1} and b_{g_2} are bias vectors, $\sigma()$ is the logistic function and $\odot$ indicates element-wise multiplication. This operation allows the network to first observe the candidate hypernym w_2 and then decide which features are important when analysing the hyponym w_1. For example, when deciding whether *seal* is a type of *animal*, the model is able to first see the word *animal* and then apply a mask that blocks out features of the word *seal* that are not related to nature. During development we found it best to apply this gating in both directions, therefore we condition each word based on the other.

Each of the word representations is then passed through a non-linear layer with $tanh$ activation, mapping the words to a new space that is more suitable for the given task:

$$m_1 = tanh(W_{m_1} \widetilde{w}_1 + b_{m_1}) \tag{5}$$
$$m_2 = tanh(W_{m_2} \widetilde{w}_2 + b_{m_2}) \tag{6}$$

where W_{m_1}, W_{m_2}, b_{m_1} and b_{m_2} are trainable parameters. The input embeddings are trained to predict surrounding words on a large unannotated corpus using the skip-gram objective (Mikolov et al., 2013), making the resulting vector space reflect (a broad relation of) semantic relatedness but unsuitable for lexical entailment (Vulić et al., 2017). The mapping stage allows the network to learn a transformation function from the general skip-gram embeddings to a task-specific space for lexical entailment. In addition, the two weight matrices enable asymmetric reasoning, allowing the network to learn separate mappings for hyponyms and hypernyms.

We then use a supervised composition function for combining the two representations and returning a confidence score as output. Rei et al. (2017) described a generalised version of cosine similarity for metaphor detection, constructing a supervised operation and learning individual weights for each feature. We apply a similar approach here and modify it to predict a relation score:

$$d = m_1 \odot m_2 \tag{7}$$

$$h = tanh(W_h d + b_h) \tag{8}$$

$$y = S \cdot \sigma(a(W_y h + b_y)) \tag{9}$$

where W_h, b_h, a, W_y and b_y are trainable parameters. The annotated labels of lexical relations are generally in a fixed range, therefore we base the output function on logistic regression, which also restricts the range of the predicted scores. b_y allows for the function to be shifted as necessary and a controls the slope of the sigmoid. S is the value of the maximum score in the dataset, scaling the resulting value to the correct range. The output y represents the confidence that the two input words are in a lexical entailment relation.

We optimise the model by minimising the mean squared distance between the predicted score y and the gold-standard score $\hat{y}$:

$$L = \sum_i (y_i - \hat{y}_i)^2 \tag{10}$$

Sparse Distributional Features (SDF). Word embeddings are well-suited for capturing distributional similarity, but they have trouble encoding features such as word frequency, or the number of unique contexts the word has appeared in. This information becomes important when deciding whether one word entails another, as the system needs to determine when a concept is more general and subsumes the other.

We construct classical sparse distributional word vectors and use them to extract 5 unique features for every word pair, to complement the features extracted from neural embeddings:

- Regular cosine similarity between the sparse distributional vectors of both words.

- The sparse weighted cosine measure, described by Rei and Briscoe (2014), comparing the weighted ranks of different distributional contexts. The measure is directional and assigns more importance to the features of the broader term. We include this weighted cosine in both directions.

- The proportion of shared unique contexts, compared to the number of contexts for one word. This measure is able to capture whether one of the words appears in a subset of the contexts, compared to the other word. This feature is also directional and is therefore included in both directions.

We build the sparse distributional word vectors from two versions of the British National Corpus (Leech, 1992). The first counts contexts simply based on a window of size 3. The second uses a parsed version of the BNC (Andersen et al., 2008) and extracts contexts based on dependency relations. In both cases, the features are weighted using pointwise mutual information. Each of the five features is calculated separately for the two vector spaces, resulting in 10 corpus-based features. We integrate them into the network by conditioning the hidden layer h on this vector:

$$h = tanh(W_h d + W_x x + b_h) \tag{11}$$

where x is the feature vector of length 10 and W_x is the corresponding weight matrix.

Additional Supervision (AS). Methods such as retrofitting (Faruqui et al., 2015), ATTRACT-REPEL (Mrkšić et al., 2017) and Poincaré embeddings (Nickel and Kiela, 2017) make use of hand-annotated lexical relations for optimising word representations such that they capture the desired properties (so-called *embedding specialisation*). We also experiment with incorporating these resources, but instead of adjusting the individual word embeddings, we use them to optimise the shared network weights. This teaches the model to find useful regularities in general-purpose word embeddings, which can then be equally applied to all words in the embedding vocabulary.

For hyponym detection, we extract examples from WordNet (Miller, 1995) and the Paraphrase Database (PPDB 2.0) (Pavlick et al., 2015). We use WordNet synonyms and hyponyms as positive examples, along with antonyms and hypernyms as negative examples. In order to prevent the network from biasing towards specific words that have numerous annotated relations, we limit them to a maximum of 10 examples per word. From the PPDB we extract the Equivalence relations as positive examples and the Exclusion relations as negative word pairs.

The final dataset contains 102,586 positive pairs and 42,958 negative pairs. However, only binary labels are attached to all word pairs, whereas the task requires predicting a graded score. Initial experiments with optimising the network to predict the minimal and maximal possible score for these cases did not lead to improved performance. Therefore, we instead make use of a hinge loss function that optimises the network to only push these examples to the correct side of the decision boundary:

$$L = \sum_i max((y - \hat{y})^2 - (\frac{S}{2} - R)^2, 0) \quad (12)$$

where S is the maximum score in the range and and R is a margin parameter. By minimising Equation 12, the model is only updated based on examples that are not yet on the correct side of the boundary, including a margin. This prevents us from penalising the model for predicting a score with slight variations, as the extracted examples are not annotated with sufficient granularity. When optimising the model, we first perform one pre-training pass over these additional word pairs before proceeding with the regular training process.

4 Evaluation

SDSN Training Setup. As input to the SDSN network we use 300-dimensional dependency-based word embeddings by Levy and Goldberg (2014). Layers m_1 and m_2 also have size 300 and layer h has size 100. For regularisation, we apply dropout to the embeddings with $p = 0.5$. The margin R is set to 1 for the supervised pre-training stage. The model is optimised using AdaDelta (Zeiler, 2012) with learning rate 1.0. In order to control for random noise, we run each experiment with 10 different random seeds and average the results. Our code and detailed configuration files will be made available online.[1]

Evaluation Data. We evaluate graded lexical entailment on the HyperLex dataset (Vulić et al., 2017) which contains 2,616 word pairs in total scored for the asymmetric graded lexical entailment relation. Following a standard practice, we report Spearman's ρ correlation of the model output to the given human-annotated scores. We conduct experiments on two standard data splits for supervised learning: *random split* and *lexical* split. In the random split the data is randomly divided into training, validation, and test subsets containing 1831, 130, and 655 word pairs, respectively. In the *lexical*

| | Random | | Lexical | |
	DEV	TEST	DEV	TEST
FR	-	0.299	-	0.199
SGNS-DEPS	-	0.250	-	0.253
WN-WuP	-	0.212	-	0.261
SGNS-DEPS (concat+r)	-	0.539	-	0.399
Paragram+CF (cos)	-	0.346	-	0.453
Paragram+CF (mul+r)	-	0.386	-	0.439
SDSN	0.708	0.658	0.547	0.475
SDSN+SDF	0.722	0.671	0.562	0.495
SDSN+SDF+AS	**0.757**	**0.692**	**0.577**	**0.544**

Table 1: Graded lexical entailment detection results on the random and lexical splits of the HyperLex dataset. We report Spearman's ρ on both validation and test sets.

split, proposed by Levy et al. (2015), there is no lexical overlap between training and test subsets. This prevents the effect of *lexical memorisation*, as supervised models tend to learn an independent property of a single concept in the pair instead of learning a relation between the two concepts. In this setup training, validation, and test sets contain 1133, 85, and 269 word pairs, respectively.[2]

Since plenty of related research on lexical entailment is still focused on the simpler binary detection of asymmetric relations, we also run experiments on the large binary detection HypeNet dataset (Shwartz et al., 2016), where the SDSN output is converted to binary decisions. We again report scores for both random and lexical split.

Results and Analysis. The results on two HyperLex splits are presented in Table 1, along with the best configurations reported by Vulić et al. (2017). We refer the interested reader to the original HyperLex paper (Vulić et al., 2017) for a detailed description of the best performing baseline models.

The Supervised Directional Similarity Network (**SDSN**) achieves substantially better scores than all other tested systems, despite relying on a much simpler supervision signal. The previous top approaches, including the Paragram+CF embeddings, make use of numerous annotations provided by WordNet or similarly rich lexical resources, while for SDSN and **SDSN+SDF** only use the designated relation-specific training set and corpus statistics. By also including these extra training instances (**SDSN+SDF+AS**), we can gain additional perfor-

641

	Lexical split			Random split		
	P	R	F	P	R	F
Dual-T	70.5	78.5	74.3	93.3	82.6	87.6
HypeNet-hybrid	80.9	61.7	70.0	91.3	**89.0**	90.1
H-feature	70.0	**96.4**	81.1	92.6	85.0	88.6
SDSN	**82.8**	84.6	83.7	**94.0**	86.7	90.2
SDSN+SDF	82.6	86.0	**84.2**	92.8	88.7	**90.7**

Table 2: Results on the HypeNet binary hypernymy detection dataset.

mance and push the correlation to 0.692 on the random split and 0.544 on the lexical split of HyperLex, an improvement of approximately 25% to the standard supervised training regime.

In Table 3 we provide some example output from the final SDSN+SDF+AS model. It is able to successfully assign a high score to (*captain*, *officer*) and also identify with high confidence that *wing* is not a type of *airplane*, even though they are semantically related. As an example of incorrect output, the model fails to assign a high score to (*prince*, *royalty*), possibly due to the usage patterns of these words being different in context. In contrast, it assigns an unexpectedly high score to (*kid*, *parent*), likely due to the high distributional similarity of these words.

Glavaš and Ponzetto (2017) proposed a related dual tensor model for the binary detection of asymmetric relations (*Dual-T*). In order to compare our system to theirs, we train our model on HypeNet and convert the output to binary decisions. We also compare SDSN to the best reported models of Shwartz et al. (2016) and Roller and Erk (2016), which combine distributional and pattern-based information for hypernymy detection (*HypeNet-hybrid* and *H-feature*, respectively).[3] We do not include additional WordNet and PPDB examples in these experiments, as the HypeNet data already subsumes most of them. As can be seen in Table 2, our SDSN+SDF model achieves the best results also on the HypeNet dataset, outperforming previous models on both data splits.

5 Conclusion

We introduce a novel neural architecture for mapping and specialising a vector space based on limited supervision. While prior work has focused only on optimising individual word embeddings available in external resources, our model uses

---

[3]For more detail on the baseline models, we refer the reader to the original papers.

		S	P
captain	officer	8.22	8.17
celery	food	9.3	9.43
horn	bull	1.12	0.94
wing	airplane	1.03	0.84
prince	royalty	9.85	4.71
autumn	season	9.77	3.69
kid	parent	0.52	8.00
discipline	punishment	7.7	3.32

Table 3: Example word pairs from the HyperLex development set. S is the human-annotated score in the HyperLex dataset. P is the predicted score using the SDSN+SDF+AS model.

general-purpose embeddings and optimises a separate neural component to adapt these to the specific task, generalising to unseen data. The system achieves new state-of-the-art results on the task of scoring graded lexical entailment. Future work could apply the model to other lexical relations or extend it to cover multiple relations simultaneously.

Acknowledgments

Daniela Gerz and Ivan Vulić are supported by the ERC Consolidator Grant LEXICAL: Lexical Acquisition Across Languages (no 648909). We would like to thank the NVIDIA Corporation for the donation of the Titan GPU that was used for this research.

References

Øistein Andersen, Julien Nioche, Edward J. Briscoe, and John Carroll. 2008. The BNC parsed with RASP4UIMA. In *LREC*.

Piotr Bojanowski, Edouard Grave, Armand Joulin, and Tomas Mikolov. 2017. Enriching word vectors with subword information. *Transactions of the ACL*, 5:135–146.

Manaal Faruqui, Jesse Dodge, Sujay Kumar Jauhar, Chris Dyer, Eduard Hovy, and Noah a. Smith. 2015. Retrofitting word vectors to semantic lexicons. In *NAACL-HLT*, pages 1606–1615.

Goran Glavaš and Simone Paolo Ponzetto. 2017. Dual tensor model for detecting asymmetric lexico-semantic relations. In *EMNLP*, pages 1757–1767.

Zellig S. Harris. 1954. Distributional structure. *Word*, 10(23):146–162.

Hans Kamp and Barbara Partee. 1995. Prototype theory and compositionality. *Cognition*, 57(2):129–191.

Douwe Kiela, Laura Rimell, Ivan Vulić, and Stephen Clark. 2015. Exploiting image generality for lexical entailment detection. In *ACL*, pages 119–124.

Lili Kotlerman, Ido Dagan, Idan Szpektor, and Maayan Zhitomirsky-Geffet. 2010. Directional distributional similarity for lexical inference. *Natural Language Engineering*, 16(4):359–389.

Geoffrey Neil Leech. 1992. 100 million words of English: the British National Corpus (BNC).

Omer Levy and Yoav Goldberg. 2014. Dependency-based word embeddings. In *ACL*, pages 302–308.

Omer Levy, Steffen Remus, Chris Biemann, and Ido Dagan. 2015. Do supervised distributional methods really learn lexical inference relations? In *NAACL-HLT*, pages 970–976.

Tomáš Mikolov, Kai Chen, Greg Corrado, and Jeffrey Dean. 2013. Distributed representations of words and phrases and their compositionality. In *NIPS*, pages 3111–3119.

George A. Miller. 1995. WordNet: a lexical database for English. *Communications of the ACM*, 38(11):39–41.

Nikola Mrkšić, Diarmuid Ó Séaghdha, Blaise Thomson, Milica Gašić, Lina Rojas-Barahona, Pei-Hao Su, David Vandyke, Tsung-Hsien Wen, and Steve Young. 2016. Counter-fitting word vectors to linguistic constraints. pages 142–148.

Nikola Mrkšić, Ivan Vulić, Diarmuid Ó Séaghdha, Ira Leviant, Roi Reichart, Milica Gašić, Anna Korhonen, and Steve Young. 2017. Semantic specialisation of distributional word vector spaces using monolingual and cross-lingual constraints. *Transactions of the ACL*, 5:309–324.

Maximilian Nickel and Douwe Kiela. 2017. Poincaré embeddings for learning hierarchical representations. In *NIPS*, pages 6341–6350.

Ellie Pavlick, Pushpendre Rastogi, Juri Ganitkevitch, Benjamin Van Durme, and Chris Callison-Burch. 2015. PPDB 2.0: Better paraphrase ranking, fine-grained entailment relations, word embeddings, and style classification. In *ACL*, pages 425–430.

Jeffrey Pennington, Richard Socher, and Christopher Manning. 2014. Glove: Global vectors for word representation. In *EMNLP*, pages 1532–1543.

Marek Rei and Ted Briscoe. 2014. Looking for hyponyms in vector space. In *CoNLL*, pages 68–77.

Marek Rei, Luana Bulat, Douwe Kiela, and Ekaterina Shutova. 2017. Grasping the finer point: A supervised similarity network for metaphor detection. In *EMNLP*, pages 1537–1546.

Stephen Roller and Katrin Erk. 2016. Relations such as hypernymy: Identifying and exploiting hearst patterns in distributional vectors for lexical entailment. In *EMNLP*, pages 2163–2172.

Eleanor H. Rosch. 1975. Cognitive representations of semantic categories. *Journal of Experimental Psychology*, 104(3):192–233.

Enrico Santus, Alessandro Lenci, Qin Lu, and Sabine Schulte im Walde. 2014. Chasing hypernyms in vector spaces with entropy. In *EACL*, pages 38–42.

Vered Shwartz, Yoav Goldberg, and Ido Dagan. 2016. Improving hypernymy detection with an integrated path-based and distributional method. In *ACL*, pages 2389–2398.

Vered Shwartz, Enrico Santus, and Dominik Schlechtweg. 2017. Hypernyms under siege: Linguistically-motivated artillery for hypernymy detection. In *EACL*, pages 65–75.

Ivan Vulić, Daniela Gerz, Douwe Kiela, Felix Hill, and Anna Korhonen. 2017. Hyperlex: A large-scale evaluation of graded lexical entailment. *Computational Linguistics*, 43(4).

Julie Weeds, Daoud Clarke, Jeremy Reffin, David Weir, and Bill Keller. 2014. Learning to distinguish hypernyms and co-hyponyms. In *COLING*, pages 2249–2259.

John Wieting, Mohit Bansal, Kevin Gimpel, and Karen Livescu. 2015. From paraphrase database to compositional paraphrase model and back. *Transactions of the ACL*, 3:345–358.

Matthew D. Zeiler. 2012. ADADELTA: An adaptive learning rate method. *arXiv preprint arXiv:1212.5701*.

Extracting Commonsense Properties from Embeddings with Limited Human Guidance

Yiben Yang [1], **Larry Birnbaum**[2], **Ji-Ping Wang**[1], **Doug Downey**[2]

[1]Department of Statistics, Northwestern University, Evanston, IL, 60208, USA
[2]Department of Electrical Engineering & Computer Science, Northwestern University, Evanston, IL, 60208, USA
[1]{yiben.yang, jzwang}@northwestern.edu
[2]{l-birnbaum, d-downey}@northwestern.edu

Abstract

Intelligent systems require common sense, but automatically extracting this knowledge from text can be difficult. We propose and assess methods for extracting one type of commonsense knowledge, object-property comparisons, from pre-trained embeddings. In experiments, we show that our approach exceeds the accuracy of previous work but requires substantially less hand-annotated knowledge. Further, we show that an active learning approach that synthesizes common-sense queries can boost accuracy.

1 Introduction

Automatically extracting common sense from text is a long-standing challenge in natural language processing (Schubert, 2002; Van Durme and Schubert, 2008; Vanderwende, 2005). As argued by Forbes and Yejin (2017), typical language use may reflect common sense, but the commonsense knowledge itself is not often explicitly stated, due to reporting bias (Gordon and Van Durme, 2013). Thus, additional human knowledge or annotated training data are often used to help systems learn common sense.

In this paper, we study methods for reducing the amount of human input needed to learn common sense. Specifically, we focus on learning relative comparisons of (one-dimensional) object properties, such as the fact that a cantaloupe is *more round* than a hammer. Methods for learning this kind of common sense have been developed previously (e.g. Forbes and Choi, 2017), but the best-performing methods in that previous work requires dozens of manually-annotated frames for each comparison property, to connect the property to how it is indirectly reflected in text—e.g., if

text asserts that "x carries y," this implies that x is probably *larger* than y.

Our architecture for relative comparisons follows the zero-shot learning paradigm (Palatucci et al., 2009). It takes the form of a neural network that compares a projection of embeddings for each of two objects (e.g. "elephant" and "tiger") to the embeddings for the two poles of the target dimension of comparison (e.g., "big" and "small" for the size property). The projected object embeddings are trained to be closer to the appropriate pole, using a small training set of hand-labeled comparisons. Our experiments reveal that our architecture outperforms previous work, despite using less annotated data. Further, because our architecture takes the property (pole) labels as arguments, it can extend to the zero-shot setting in which we evaluate on properties not seen in training. We find that in zero-shot, our approach outperforms baselines and comes close to supervised results, but providing labels for both poles of the relation rather than just one is important. Finally, because the number of properties we wish to learn is large, we experiment with active learning (AL) over a larger property space. We show that synthesizing AL queries can be effective using an approach that explicitly models which comparison questions are nonsensical (e.g., is Batman taller than Democracy?). We release our code base and a new commonsense data set to the research community.[1]

2 Problem Definition and Methods

We define the task of comparing object properties in two different ways: a three-way classification task, and a four-way classification task. In the three-way classification task, we want to estimate the following conditional probability:

$$P(\mathbf{L}|\mathbf{O_1}, \mathbf{O_2}, \mathbf{Property}), \mathbf{L} \in \{\boxed{<}, \boxed{>}, \boxed{\approx}\}.$$

---

[1]https://github.com/yangyiben/PCE

Proceedings of the 56th Annual Meeting of the Association for Computational Linguistics (Short Papers), pages 644–649
Melbourne, Australia, July 15 - 20, 2018. ©2018 Association for Computational Linguistics

For example, $Prob$(An elephant is larger than a dog) can be expressed as $P(\mathbf{L} = \boxed{>} | \mathbf{O_1} = $ $"elephant", \mathbf{O_2} = "dog", \mathbf{Property} = "size")$. The three-way classification task has been explored in previous work (Forbes and Choi, 2017) and is only performed on triples where both objects have the property, so that the comparison is meaningful. In applications, however, we may not know in advance which comparisons are meaningful. Thus, we also define a four-way classification task to include "not applicable" as the fourth label, so that inference can be performed on any object-property triples. In the four-way task, the system is tasked with identifying the nonsensical comparisons. Formally, we want to estimate the following conditional probability:

$$P(\mathbf{L}|\mathbf{O_1}, \mathbf{O_2}, \mathbf{Property}), \mathbf{L} \in \{\boxed{<}, \boxed{>}, \boxed{\approx}, \boxed{\text{N/A}}\}.$$

2.1 Three-way Model

For each comparison property, we pick an adjective and its antonym to represent the $\{\boxed{<}, \boxed{>}\}$ labels. For example, for the property *size*, we pick "big" and "small". The adjective "similar" serves as the label for $\boxed{\approx}$ for all properties. Under this framework, a relative comparison question, for instance, "Is a dog bigger than an elephant?", can be formulated as a quintuple query to the model, namely {dog, elephant, small, similar, big}. Denoting the word embeddings for tokens in a quintuple query as $X, Y, R_<, R_\approx, R_>$, our three-way model is defined as follows:

$$P(\mathbf{L} = s|Q) = softmax(R_s \cdot \sigma((X \oplus Y)W)),$$

for $s \in \{<, >, \approx\}$, where Q is an quintuple query, $\sigma(\cdot)$ is an activation function and W is a learnable weight matrix. The symbol $\oplus$ represents concatenation. We refer to this method as **PCE** (**P**roperty **C**omparison from **E**mbeddings) for the 3-way task. We also experiment with generating label representations from just a single adjective (property) embedding $R_<$, namely $R_\approx = \sigma(R_< W_2)$, $R_> = \sigma(R_< W_3)$. We refer to this simpler method as **PCE(one-pole)**.

We note that in both the three- and four-way settings, the question "A>B?" is equivalent to "B<A?". We leverage this fact at test time by feeding our network a reversed object pair, and taking the average of the aligned network outputs before the softmax layer to reduce prediction variance. We refer to our model without this technique as **PCE(no reverse)**.

The key distinction of our method is that it learns a projection from the object word embedding space to the label embedding space. This allows the model to leverage the property label embeddings to perform zero-shot prediction on properties not observed in training. For example, from a training example "dogs are smaller than elephants", the model will learn a projection that puts "dogs" relatively closer to "small," and far from "big" and "similar." Doing so may also result in projecting "dog" to be closer to "light" than to "heavy," such that the model is able to predict "dogs are lighter than elephants" despite never being trained on any weight comparison examples.

2.2 Four-way Model

Our four-way model is the same as our three-way model, with an additional module to learn whether the comparison is applicable. Keeping the other output nodes unchanged, we add an additional component into the softmax layer to output the probability of "N/A":

$$h_x = \sigma(XW_a), \ h_y = \sigma(YW_a),$$
$$A_i = h_i \cdot R_> + h_i \cdot R_<,$$
$$P(\mathbf{L} = \boxed{\text{N/A}} | Q) \propto exp(A_x + A_y).$$

2.3 Synthesis for Active Learning

We propose a method to synthesize informative queries to pose to annotators, a form of active learning (Settles, 2009). We use the common heuristic that an informative training example will have a high uncertainty in the model's predictive distribution. We adopt the confidence measure (Culotta and McCallum, 2005) to access the uncertainty of a given example:

$$Uncertainty(x) = 1 - \max_y P(y|x, D_{train}).$$

Good candidates for acquisition should have high uncertainty measure, but we also want to avoid querying outliers. As the vocabulary is finite, it is possible to evaluate the uncertainty measures for all possible inputs to synthesize the most uncertain query. However, such a greedy policy is expensive and prone to selecting outliers. Hence, we adopt a sampling based synthesis strategy: at each round, we generate one random object pair per property, and query the one that achieves the highest uncertainty measure.

A classical difficulty faced by synthesis approaches to active learning is that they may produce unnatural queries that are difficult for a human to label (Baum and Lang, 1992). However, our task formulation includes "similar" and "N/A" classes that encompass many of the more difficult or confusing comparisons, which we believe aids the effectiveness of the synthesis approach.

3 Experiments

We now present our experimental results on both the three-way and four-way tasks.

3.1 Data Sets

We test our three-way model on the VERB PHYSICS data set from (Forbes and Choi, 2017). As there are only 5 properties in VERB PHYSICS, we also develop a new data set we call PROPERTY COMMON SENSE. We select 32 commonsense properties to form our property set (e.g., value, roundness, deliciousness, intelligence, etc.). We extract object nouns from the McRae Feature Norms dataset (McRae et al., 2005) and add selected named entities to form a object vocabulary of 689 distinct objects. We randomly generate 3148 object-property triples, label them and reserve 45% of the data for the test set. We further add 5 manually-selected applicable comparison examples per property to our test set, in order to make sure each property has some applicable testing examples. To verify the labeling, we have a second annotator redundantly label 200 examples and find a Cohen's Kappa of 0.64, which indicates good annotator agreement (we analyze the source of the disagreements in Section 4.1). The training set is used for the passive learning and pool-based active learning, and a human oracle provides labels in the synthesis active learning setting.

3.2 Experimental Setup

We experiment with three types of embeddings: **GloVe**, normalized 300-dimensional embeddings trained on a corpus of 6B tokens (Pennington et al., 2014) (the F&C method (Forbes and Choi, 2017) uses the 100-dimensional version, as it achieves the highest validation accuracy for their methods); **Word2vec**, normalized 300-dimensional embeddings trained on 100B tokens (Mikolov et al., 2013); and **LSTM**, the normalized 1024-dimensional weight matrix from the softmax layer of the Google 1B LSTM language model (Jozefowicz et al., 2016).

For training PCE, we use an identity activation function and apply 50% dropout. We use the Adam optimizer with default settings to train the models for 800 epochs, minimizing cross entropy loss. For zero-shot learning, we adopt a hold-one-property-out scheme to test our models' zero-shot performance.

Finally, for active learning, we use Word2vec embeddings. All the models are trained on 200 random training examples to warm up. We train for 20 epochs after each label acquisition. To smooth noise, we report the average of 20 different runs of **random** (passive learning) and *least confident* (**LC**) pool-based active learning (Culotta and McCallum, 2005) baselines. We report the average of only 6 runs for an *expected model change* (**EMC**) pool-based active learning (Cai et al., 2013) baseline due to its high computational cost, and of only 2 runs for our synthesis active learning approach due to its high labeling cost. The pool size is 1540 examples.

3.3 Results

In Table 1, we compare the performance of the three-way PCE model against the existing state of the art on the VERB PHYSICS data set. The use of LSTM embeddings in PCE yields the best accuracy for all properties. Across all embedding choices, PCE performs as well or better than F&C, despite the fact that PCE does not use the annotated frames that F&C requires (approximately 188 labels per property). Thus, our approach matches or exceeds the performance of previous work using significantly less annotated knowledge. The lower performance of "no reverse" shows that the simple method of averaging over the reversed object pair is effective.

Table 2 evaluates our models on properties not seen in training (zero-shot learning). We compare against a random baseline, and an Emb-Similarity baseline that classifies based on the cosine similarity of the object embeddings to the pole label embeddings (i.e., *without* the projection layer in PCE). PCE outperforms the baselines. Although the one-pole method was shown to perform similarly to the two-pole method for properties seen in training (Table 1), we see that for zero-shot learning, using two poles is important.

In Table 3, we show that our four-way models with different embeddings beat both the majority and random baselines on the PROPERTY

Model	Development						Test					
	size	weight	stren	rigid	speed	overall	size	weight	stren	rigid	speed	overall
Majority	0.50	0.54	0.51	0.50	0.53	0.51	0.51	0.55	0.52	0.49	0.50	0.51
F&C	0.75	0.74	0.71	0.68	0.66	0.71	0.75	0.76	0.72	0.65	0.61	0.70
PCE(LSTM)	0.79	**0.81**	0.75	**0.71**	**0.72**	**0.76**	**0.80**	0.79	0.76	**0.71**	0.71	**0.76**
PCE(GloVe)	0.75	0.75	0.71	0.67	0.69	0.71	0.76	0.75	0.71	0.68	0.68	0.72
PCE(Word2vec)	0.76	0.76	0.73	0.70	0.68	0.73	0.76	0.76	0.73	0.68	0.66	0.72
PCE(one-pole)	**0.80**	**0.81**	**0.77**	0.65	**0.72**	0.75	0.79	**0.79**	**0.77**	0.65	**0.72**	0.75
PCE(no reverse)	0.72	0.74	0.71	0.67	0.67	0.70	0.73	0.75	0.72	0.65	0.68	0.71

Table 1: Accuracy on the VERB PHYSICS data set. PCE outperforms the F&C model from previous work. PCE(one-pole) and PCE(no reverse) use LSTM embeddings.

Model	Development					Test				
	size	weight	stren	rigid	speed	size	weight	stren	rigid	speed
Random	0.33	0.33	0.33	0.33	0.33	0.33	0.33	0.33	0.33	0.33
Emb-Similarity	0.43	0.55	0.51	0.43	0.35	0.37	0.53	0.48	0.43	0.35
PCE(one-pole)	0.73	0.71	0.67	0.53	0.34	**0.74**	0.72	0.68	0.53	0.32
PCE	**0.76**	**0.72**	**0.71**	**0.62**	**0.60**	**0.74**	**0.73**	**0.70**	**0.62**	**0.58**

Table 2: Accuracy of zero-shot learning on the VERB PHYSICS data set(using LSTM embeddings). PCE outperforms the baselines, and using both poles is important for accuracy.

Model	Test
Random	0.25
Majority Class	0.51
PCE(GloVe)	0.63
PCE(Word2vec)	**0.67**
PCE(LSTM)	**0.67**

Table 3: Accuracy on the four-way task on the PROPERTY COMMON SENSE data.

COMMON SENSE data. Here, the LSTM embeddings perform similarly to the Word2vec embeddings, perhaps because the PROPERTY COMMON SENSE vocabulary consists of less frequent nouns than in VERB PHYSICS. Thus, the Word2vec embeddings are able to catch up due to their larger vocabulary and much larger training corpus.

Finally, in Figure 1, we evaluate in the active learning setting. The synthesis approach performs best, especially later in training when the training pool for the pool-based methods has only uninformative examples remaining. Figure 2 helps explain the relative advantage of the synthesis approach: it is able to continue synthesizing informative (uncertain) queries throughout the entire training run.

4 Discussion

4.1 Sources of annotator disagreement

As noted above, we found a "good" level of agreement (Cohen's Kappa of 0.64) for our PROPERTY COMMON SENSE data, which is lower than one might expect for task aimed at common sense. We

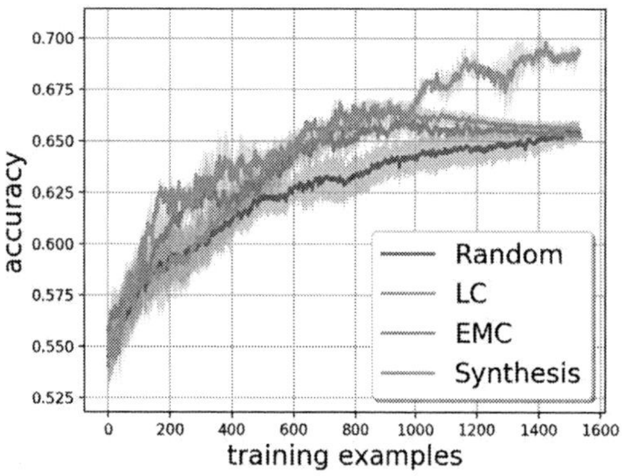

Figure 1: Test accuracy as a function of the number of queried training examples. The synthesis approach performs best.

analyzed the disagreements and found that they stem from two sources of subjectivity in the task. The first is that different labelers may have different thresholds for what counts as similar—a spider and an ant might be marked similar in size for one labeler, but not for another labeler. In our data, 58% of the disagreements are cases in which one annotator marks similar while the other says not similar. The second is that different labelers have different standards for whether a comparison is N/A. For example, in our data set, one labeler labels that a toaster is physically stronger than alcohol, and the other labeler says the comparison is N/A. 37% of our disagreements are due to this type of subjectivity. The above two types of subjectivity account for almost all disagreements

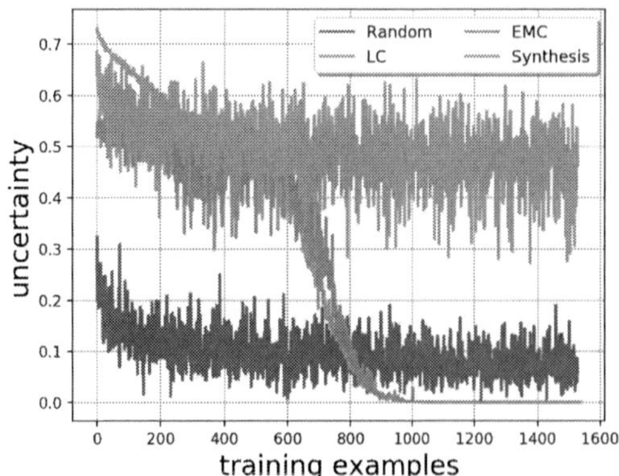

Figure 2: The uncertainty measure of each queried training example. As training proceeds, the synthesis approach continues to select more uncertain examples.

Object	Smallness
restaurant	0.077
gully	0.416
lung	1.182
bow	4.036
scissors	14.492

Table 4: Scores of smallness for 5 randomly picked objects in VERB PHYSICS data set

Word choice	Trained	Zero
fast vs. slow	0.71	0.58
speedy vs. slow	0.71	0.56
fast vs. plodding	0.72	0.48
speedy vs. plodding	0.72	0.51
big vs. small	0.80	0.74
large vs. small	0.80	0.76
big vs. little	0.80	0.71
large vs. little	0.80	0.69

Table 5: Trained and zero-shot accuracies for different word choices

(95%), and the remaining 5% are due to annotation errors (one of the annotators makes mistake).

4.2 Model Interpretation

Since we adopt an identity activation function and a single layer design, it is possible to simplify the mathematical expression of our model to make it more interpretable. After accounting for model averaging, we have the following equality:

$$P(\mathbf{L} =< |Q) \propto$$
$$exp(R_< \cdot ((X \oplus Y)W) + R_> \cdot ((Y \oplus X)W))$$
$$= exp(R_<^T(XW_1 + YW_2) + R_>^T(YW_1 + XW_2))$$
$$\propto exp((R_< - R_>)^T(XW_1 + XW_2)),$$

where $W = W_1 \oplus W_2$. So we can define a *score* of "$R_<$" for a object with embedding X as the following:

$$score(X, R_<) = (R_< - R_>)^T(XW_1 + XW_2).$$

An object with a higher score for $R_<$ is more associated with the $R_<$ pole than the $R_>$ one. For example, score("elephant","small") represents how small an elephant is—a larger score indicates a smaller object. Table 4 shows smallness scores for 5 randomly picked objects from the VERB PHYSICS data set. PCE tends to assign higher scores to the smaller objects in the set.

4.3 Sensitivity to pole labels

PCE requires labels for the poles of the target object property. Table 5 presents a limited sensitivity analysis to pole labels, evaluating the test accuracy of PCE as the pole label varies among different combinations of synonyms for the size and speed relations. We evaluate in both the trained setting (comparable to the results in Table 1) and the zero-shot setting (comparable to Table 2). We see that the trained accuracy remains essentially unchanged for different pole labels. In the zero-shot setting, all combinations achieve accuracy that beats the baselines in Table 2, but the accuracy value is somewhat sensitive to the choice of pole label. Exploring how to select pole labels and experimenting with richer pole representations such as textual definitions are items of future work.

5 Conclusion

In this paper, we presented a method for extracting commonsense knowledge from embeddings. Our experiments demonstrate that the approach is effective at performing relative comparisons of object properties using less hand-annotated knowledge than in previous work. A synthesis active learner was found to boost accuracy, and further experiments with this approach are an item of future work.

Acknowledgments

This work was supported in part by NSF Grant IIS-1351029. We thank the anonymous reviewers for helpful comments.

References

Eric B Baum and Kenneth Lang. 1992. Query learning can work poorly when a human oracle is used. In *International joint conference on neural networks*, volume 8, page 8.

W. Cai, Y. Zhang, and J. Zhou. 2013. Maximizing expected model change for active learning in regression. In *2013 IEEE 13th International Conference on Data Mining*, pages 51–60.

Aron Culotta and Andrew McCallum. 2005. Reducing labeling effort for structured prediction tasks. In *AAAI*, pages 746–751. AAAI Press / The MIT Press.

Maxwell Forbes and Yejin Choi. 2017. Verb physics: Relative physical knowledge of actions and objects. *arXiv preprint arXiv:1706.03799*.

Jonathan Gordon and Benjamin Van Durme. 2013. Reporting bias and knowledge acquisition. In *Proceedings of the 2013 workshop on Automated knowledge base construction*, pages 25–30. ACM.

Rafal Jozefowicz, Oriol Vinyals, Mike Schuster, Noam Shazeer, and Yonghui Wu. 2016. Exploring the limits of language modeling. *arXiv preprint arXiv:1602.02410*.

Ken McRae, George S. Cree, Mark S. Seidenberg, and Chris Mcnorgan. 2005. Semantic feature production norms for a large set of living and nonliving things. *Behavior Research Methods*, 37(4):547–559.

Tomas Mikolov, Ilya Sutskever, Kai Chen, Greg S Corrado, and Jeff Dean. 2013. Distributed representations of words and phrases and their compositionality. In C. J. C. Burges, L. Bottou, M. Welling, Z. Ghahramani, and K. Q. Weinberger, editors, *Advances in Neural Information Processing Systems 26*, pages 3111–3119. Curran Associates, Inc.

Mark Palatucci, Dean Pomerleau, Geoffrey E Hinton, and Tom M Mitchell. 2009. Zero-shot learning with semantic output codes. In Y. Bengio, D. Schuurmans, J. D. Lafferty, C. K. I. Williams, and A. Culotta, editors, *Advances in Neural Information Processing Systems 22*, pages 1410–1418. Curran Associates, Inc.

Jeffrey Pennington, Richard Socher, and Christopher D. Manning. 2014. Glove: Global vectors for word representation. In *Empirical Methods in Natural Language Processing (EMNLP)*, pages 1532–1543.

Lenhart Schubert. 2002. Can we derive general world knowledge from texts? In *Proceedings of the second international conference on Human Language Technology Research*, pages 94–97. Morgan Kaufmann Publishers Inc.

B. Settles. 2009. Active learning literature survey. Computer Sciences Technical Report 1648, University of Wisconsin–Madison.

Benjamin Van Durme and Lenhart Schubert. 2008. Open knowledge extraction through compositional language processing. In *Proceedings of the 2008 Conference on Semantics in Text Processing*, pages 239–254. Association for Computational Linguistics.

Lucy Vanderwende. 2005. Volunteers created the web. In *AAAI Spring Symposium: Knowledge Collection from Volunteer Contributors*, pages 84–90.

Breaking NLI Systems
with Sentences that Require Simple Lexical Inferences

Max Glockner[1], Vered Shwartz[2] and Yoav Goldberg[2]

[1]Computer Science Department, TU Darmstadt, Germany
[2]Computer Science Department, Bar-Ilan University, Ramat-Gan, Israel
{maxg216,vered1986,yoav.goldberg}@gmail.com

Abstract

We create a new NLI test set that shows
the deficiency of state-of-the-art models in
inferences that require lexical and world
knowledge. The new examples are simpler than the SNLI test set, containing sentences that differ by at most one word
from sentences in the training set. Yet,
the performance on the new test set is substantially worse across systems trained on
SNLI, demonstrating that these systems
are limited in their generalization ability,
failing to capture many simple inferences.

1 Introduction

Recognizing textual entailment (RTE) (Dagan
et al., 2013), recently framed as natural language
inference (NLI) (Bowman et al., 2015) is a task
concerned with identifying whether a *premise* sentence entails, contradicts or is neutral with the *hypothesis* sentence. Following the release of the
large-scale SNLI dataset (Bowman et al., 2015),
many end-to-end neural models have been developed for the task, achieving high accuracy on the
test set. As opposed to previous-generation methods, which relied heavily on lexical resources,
neural models only make use of pre-trained word
embeddings. The few efforts to incorporate external lexical knowledge resulted in negligible performance gain (Chen et al., 2018). This raises
the question whether (1) neural methods are inherently stronger, obviating the need of external lexical knowledge; (2) large-scale training data allows
for implicit learning of previously explicit lexical
knowledge; or (3) the NLI datasets are simpler
than early RTE datasets, requiring less knowledge.

Premise/Hypothesis	Label
The man is holding a saxophone The man is holding an electric guitar	contradiction[1]
A little girl is very sad. A little girl is very unhappy.	entailment
A couple drinking wine A couple drinking champagne	neutral

Table 1: Examples from the new test set.

In this paper we show that state-of-the-art NLI
systems are limited in their generalization ability,
and fail to capture many simple inferences that require lexical and world knowledge. Inspired by
the work of Jia and Liang (2017) on reading comprehension, we create a new NLI test set with examples that capture various kinds of lexical knowledge (Table 1). For example, that *champagne* is
a type of *wine* (hypernymy), and that *saxophone*
and *electric guitar* are different musical instruments (co-hyponyms). To isolate lexical knowledge aspects, our constructed examples contain
only words that appear both in the training set and
in pre-trained embeddings, and differ by a single
word from sentences in the training set.

The performance on the new test set is substantially worse across systems, demonstrating that the
SNLI test set alone is not a sufficient measure of
language understanding capabilities. Our results
are in line with Gururangan et al. (2018) and Poliak et al. (2018), who showed that the label can
be identified by looking only at the hypothesis and
exploiting annotation artifacts such as word choice
and sentence length.

Further investigation shows that what mostly
affects the systems' ability to correctly predict
a test example is the amount of similar examples found in the training set. Given that training data will always be limited, this is a rather
inefficient way to learn lexical inferences, stressing the need to develop methods that do this more

---

[1]The contradiction example follows the assumption in
Bowman et al. (2015) that the premise contains the most
prominent information in the event, hence the premise can't
describe the event of a man holding both instruments.

Proceedings of the 56th Annual Meeting of the Association for Computational Linguistics (Short Papers), pages 650–655
Melbourne, Australia, July 15 - 20, 2018. ©2018 Association for Computational Linguistics

effectively. Our test set can be used to evaluate such models' ability to recognize lexical inferences, and it is available at `https://github.com/BIU-NLP/Breaking_NLI`.

2 Background

NLI Datasets. The SNLI dataset (Stanford Natural Language Inference, Bowman et al., 2015) consists of 570k sentence-pairs manually labeled as entailment, contradiction, and neutral. Premises are image captions from Young et al. (2014), while hypotheses were generated by crowd-sourced workers who were shown a premise and asked to generate entailing, contradicting, and neutral sentences. Workers were instructed to judge the relation between sentences *given that they describe the same event*. Hence, sentences that differ by a single mutually-exclusive term should be considered contradicting, as in "The president visited Alabama" and "The president visited Mississippi". This differs from traditional RTE datasets, which do not assume event coreference, and in which such sentence-pairs would be considered neutral.

Following criticism on the simplicity of the dataset, stemming mostly from its narrow domain, two additional datasets have been collected. The MultiNLI dataset (Multi-Genre Natural Language Inference, Williams et al., 2018) was collected similarly to SNLI, though covering a wider range of genres, and supporting a cross-genre evaluation. The SciTail dataset (Khot et al., 2018), created from science exams, is somewhat different from the two datasets, being smaller (27,026 examples), and labeled only as entailment or neutral. The domain makes this dataset different in nature from the other two datasets, and it consists of more factual sentences rather than scene descriptions.

Neural Approaches for NLI. Following the release of SNLI, there has been tremendous interest in the task, and many end-to-end neural models were developed, achieving promising results.[2] Methods are divided into two main approaches. Sentence-encoding models (e.g. Bowman et al., 2015, 2016; Nie and Bansal, 2017; Shen et al., 2018) encode the premise and hypothesis individually, while attention-based models align words in the premise with similar words in the hypothesis, encoding the two sentences together (e.g. Rocktäschel et al., 2016; Chen et al., 2017).

External Lexical Knowledge. Traditional RTE methods typically relied on resources such as WordNet (Fellbaum, 1998) to identify lexical inferences. Conversely, neural methods rely solely on pre-trained word embeddings, yet, they achieve high accuracy on SNLI.

The only neural model to date that incorporates external lexical knowledge (from WordNet) is KIM (Chen et al., 2018), however, gaining only a small addition of 0.6 points in accuracy on the SNLI test set. This raises the question whether the small performance gap is a result of the model not capturing lexical knowledge well, or the SNLI test set not requiring this knowledge in the first place.

3 Data Collection

We construct a test set with the goal of evaluating the ability of state-of-the-art NLI models to make inferences that require simple lexical knowledge. We automatically generate sentence pairs (§3.1) which are then manually verified (§3.2).

3.1 Generating Adversarial Examples

In order to isolate the lexical knowledge aspects, the premises are taken from the SNLI training set. For each premise we generate several hypotheses by replacing a single word within the premise by a different word. We also allow some multi-word noun phrases ("electric guitar") and adapt determiners and prepositions when needed.

We focus on generating only *entailment* and *contradiction* examples, while *neutral* examples may be generated as a by-product. *Entailment* examples are generated by replacing a word with its synonym or hypernym, while *contradiction* examples are created by replacing words with mutually exclusive co-hyponyms and antonyms (see Table 1). The generation steps are detailed below.

Replacement Words. We collected the replacement words using online resources for English learning.[3] The newly introduced words are all present in the SNLI training set: from occurrence in a single training example ("Portugal") up to 248,051 examples ("man"), with a mean of 3,663.1 and a median of 149.5. The words are also available in the pre-trained embeddings vocabulary. The goal of this constraint is to isolate lexical knowledge aspects, and evaluate the models' ability to generalize and make new inferences for known words.

---

[2]See the SNLI leaderboard for a comprehensive list: `https://nlp.stanford.edu/projects/snli/`.

[3]`www.enchantedlearning.com`, `www.smart-words.org`

	SNLI Test	New Test
Instances:		
contradiction	3,236	7,164
entailment	3,364	982
neutral	3,215	47
Overall	9,815	8,193
Fleiss κ:		
contradiction	0.77	0.61
entailment	0.69	0.90
Overall	0.67	0.61
Estimated human performance:		
	87.7%	94.1%

Table 2: Statistics of the test sets. 9,815 is the number of samples with majority agreement in the SNLI test set, whose full size is 9,824.

Replacement words are divided into topical categories detailed in Table 4. In several categories we applied additional processing to ensure that examples are indeed mutually-exclusive, topically-similar, and interchangeable in context. We included WordNet antonyms with the same part-of-speech and with a cosine similarity score above a threshold, using GloVe (Pennington et al., 2014). In *nationalities* and *countries* we focused on countries which are related geographically *(Japan, China)* or culturally *(Argentina, Spain)*.

Sentence-Pairs. To avoid introducing new information not present in the training data, we sampled premises from the SNLI training set that contain words from our lists, and generated hypotheses by replacing the selected word with its replacement. Some of the generated sentences may be ungrammatical or nonsensical, for instance, when replacing *Jordan* with *Syria* in sentences discussing *Michael Jordan*. We used Wikipedia bigrams[4] to discard sentences in which the replaced word created a bigram with less than 10 occurrences.

3.2 Manual Verification

We manually verify the correctness of the automatically constructed examples using crowd-sourced workers in Amazon Mechanical Turk. To ensure the quality of workers, we applied a qualification test and required a 99% approval rate for at least 1,000 prior tasks. We assigned each annotation to 3 workers.

Following the SNLI guidelines, we instructed the workers to consider the sentences as describing the same event, but we simplified the annotation process into answering 3 simple yes/no questions:

1. Do the sentences describe the same event?

2. Does the new sentence (hypothesis) add new information to the original sentence (premise)?

3. Is the new sentence incorrect/ungrammatical?

We then discarded any sentence-pair in which at least one worker answered the third question positively. If the answer to the first question was negative, we considered the label as *contradiction*. Otherwise, we considered the label as *entailment* if the answer to the second question was negative and *neutral* if it was positive. We used the majority vote to determine the gold label.

The annotations yielded substantial agreement, with Fleiss' Kappa $\kappa = 0.61$ (Landis and Koch, 1977). We estimate human performance to 94.1%, using the method described in Gong et al. (2018), showing that the new test set is substantially easier to humans than SNLI. Table 2 provides additional statistics on the test set.[5]

4 Evaluation

4.1 Models

Without External Knowledge. We chose 3 representative models in different approaches (sentence encoding and/or attention): RESIDUAL-STACKED-ENCODER (Nie and Bansal, 2017) is a biLSTM-based single sentence-encoding model without attention. As opposed to traditional multi-layer biLSTMs, the input to each next layer is the concatenation of the word embedding and the summation of outputs from previous layers. ESIM (Enhanced Sequential Inference Model, Chen et al., 2017) is a hybrid TreeLSTM-based and biLSTM-based model. We use the biLSTM model, which uses an inter-sentence attention mechanism to align words across sentences. Finally, DECOMPOSABLE ATTENTION (Parikh et al., 2016) performs soft alignment of words from the premise to words in the hypothesis using attention mechanism, and decomposes the task into comparison of aligned words. Lexical-level decisions are merged to produce the final classification. We use the AllenNLP re-implementation,[6] which does not implement the optional intra-sentence attention, and achieves an accuracy of 84.7% on the SNLI test set, comparable to 86.3% by the original system.

---

[4] github.com/rmaestre/Wikipedia-Bigram-Open-Datasets

[5] We note that due to its bias towards *contradiction*, the new test set can neither be used for training, nor serve as a main evaluation set for NLI. Instead, we suggest to use it in addition to the original test set in order to test a model's ability to handle lexical inferences.

[6] http://allennlp.org/models

Model	Train set	SNLI test set	New test set	Δ
Decomposable Attention (Parikh et al., 2016)	SNLI	84.7%	51.9%	-32.8
	MultiNLI + SNLI	84.9%	65.8%	-19.1
	SciTail + SNLI	85.0%	49.0%	-36.0
ESIM (Chen et al., 2017)	SNLI	87.9%	65.6%	-22.3
	MultiNLI + SNLI	86.3%	74.9%	-11.4
	SciTail + SNLI	88.3%	67.7%	-20.6
Residual-Stacked-Encoder (Nie and Bansal, 2017)	SNLI	86.0%	62.2%	-23.8
	MultiNLI + SNLI	84.6%	68.2%	-16.8
	SciTail + SNLI	85.0%	60.1%	-24.9
WordNet Baseline	-	-	85.8%	-
KIM (Chen et al., 2018)	SNLI	88.6%	83.5%	-5.1

Table 3: Accuracy of various models trained on SNLI or a union of SNLI with another dataset (MultiNLI, SciTail), and tested on the original SNLI test set and the new test set.

We chose models which are amongst the best performing within their approaches (excluding ensembles) and have available code. All models are based on pre-trained GloVe embeddings (Pennington et al., 2014), which are either fine-tuned during training (RESIDUAL-STACKED-ENCODER and ESIM) or stay fixed (DECOMPOSABLE ATTENTION). All models predict the label using a concatenation of features derived from the sentence representations (e.g. maximum, mean), for example as in Mou et al. (2016). We use the recommended hyper-parameters for each model, as they appear in the provided code.

With External Knowledge. We provide a simple WORDNET BASELINE, in which we classify a sentence-pair according to the WordNet relation that holds between the original word w_p and the replaced word w_h. We predict *entailment* if w_p is a hyponym of w_h or if they are synonyms, *neutral* if w_p is a hypernym of w_h, and *contradiction* if w_p and w_h are antonyms or if they share a common hypernym ancestor (up to 2 edges). Word pairs with no WordNet relations are classified as *other*.

We also report the performance of KIM (Knowledge-based Inference Model, Chen et al., 2018), an extension of ESIM with external knowledge from WordNet, which was kindly provided to us by Qian Chen. KIM improves the attention mechanism by taking into account the existence of WordNet relations between the words. The lexical inference component, operating over pairs of aligned words, is enriched with a vector encoding the specific WordNet relations between the words.

4.2 Experimental Settings

We trained each model on 3 different datasets: (1) SNLI train set, (2) a union of the SNLI train set and the MultiNLI train set, and (3) a union of the SNLI train set and the SciTail train set. The motivation is that while SNLI might lack the training data needed to learn the required lexical knowledge, it may be available in the other datasets, which are presumably richer.

4.3 Results

Table 3 displays the results for all the models on the original SNLI test set and the new test set. Despite the task being considerably simpler, the drop in performance is substantial, ranging from 11 to 33 points in accuracy. Adding MultiNLI to the training data somewhat mitigates this drop in accuracy, thanks to almost doubling the amount of training data. We note that adding SciTail to the training data did not similarly improve the performance; we conjecture that this stems from the differences between the datasets.

KIM substantially outperforms the other neural models, demonstrating that lexical knowledge is the only requirement for good performance on the new test set, and stressing the inability of the other models to learn it. Both WordNet-informed models leave room for improvement: possibly due to limited WordNet coverage and the implications of applying lexical inferences within context.

5 Analysis

We take a deeper look into the predictions of the models that don't employ external knowledge, focusing on the models trained on SNLI.

5.1 Accuracy by Category

Table 4 displays the accuracy of each model per replacement-word category. The neural models tend to perform well on categories which are frequent in the training set, such as *colors*, and badly

Dominant Label	Category	Instances	Example Words	Decomposable Attention	ESIM	Residual Encoders	WordNet Baseline	KIM
Cont.	antonyms	1,147	*loves - dislikes*	41.6%	70.4%	58.2%	95.5%	86.5%
	cardinals	759	*five - seven*	53.5%	75.5%	53.1%	98.6%	93.4%
	nationalities	755	*Greek - Italian*	37.5%	35.9%	70.9%	78.5%	73.5%
	drinks	731	*lemonade - beer*	52.9%	63.7%	52.0%	94.8%	96.6%
	antonyms (WN)	706	*sitting - standing*	55.1%	74.6%	67.9%	94.5%	78.8%
	colors	699	*red - blue*	85.0%	96.1%	87.0%	98.7%	98.3%
	ordinals	663	*fifth - 16th*	2.1%	21.0%	5.4%	40.7%	56.6%
	countries	613	*Mexico - Peru*	15.2%	25.4%	66.2%	100.0%	70.8%
	rooms	595	*kitchen - bathroom*	59.2%	69.4%	63.4%	89.9%	77.6%
	materials	397	*stone - glass*	65.2%	89.7%	79.9%	75.3%	98.7%
	vegetables	109	*tomato -potato*	43.1%	31.2%	37.6%	86.2%	79.8%
	instruments	65	*harmonica - harp*	96.9%	90.8%	96.9%	67.7%	96.9%
	planets	60	*Mars - Venus*	31.7%	3.3%	21.7%	100.0%	5.0%
Ent.	synonyms	894	*happy - joyful*	97.5%	99.7%	86.1%	70.5%	92.1%
	total	8,193		51.9%	65.6%	62.2%	85.8%	83.5%

Table 4: The number of instances and accuracy per category achieved by each model.

on categories such as *planets*, which rarely occur in SNLI. These models perform better than the WordNet baseline on entailment examples (*synonyms*), suggesting that they do so due to high lexical overlap between the premise and the hypothesis rather than recognizing synonymy. We therefore focus the rest of the discussion on contradiction examples.

5.2 Accuracy by Word Similarity

The accuracies for *ordinals*, *nationalities* and *countries* are especially low. We conjecture that this stems from the proximity of the contradicting words in the embedding space. Indeed, the Decomposable Attention model—which does not update its embeddings during training—seems to suffer the most.

Grouping its prediction accuracy by the cosine similarity between the contradicting words reveals a clear trend that the model errs more on contradicting pairs with similar pre-trained vectors:[7]

Similarity	0.5-0.6	0.6-0.7	0.7-0.8	0.8-0.9	0.9-1.0
Accuracy	46.2%	42.3%	37.5%	29.7%	20.2%

5.3 Accuracy by Frequency in Training

Models that fine-tune the word embeddings may benefit from training examples consisting of test replacement pairs. Namely, for a given replacement pair (w_p, w_h), if many training examples labeled as contradiction contain w_p in the premise and w_h in the hypothesis, the model may update their embeddings to optimize predicting contradiction. Indeed, we show that the ESIM accuracy on test pairs increases with the frequency in which

their replacement words appear in contradiction examples in the training data:

Frequency	0	1-4	5-9	10-49	50-99	100+
Accuracy	40.2%	70.6%	91.4%	92.1%	97.5%	98.5%

This demonstrates that the model is capable of learning lexical knowledge when sufficient training data is given, but relying on explicit training examples is a very inefficient way of obtaining simple lexical knowledge.

6 Conclusion

We created a new NLI test set with the goal of evaluating systems' ability to make inferences that require simple lexical knowledge. Although the test set is constructed to be much simpler than SNLI, and does not introduce new vocabulary, the state-of-the-art systems perform poorly on it, suggesting that they are limited in their generalization ability. The test set can be used in the future to assess the lexical inference abilities of NLI systems and to tease apart the performance of otherwise very similarly-performing systems.

Acknowledgments

We would like to thank Qian Chen for evaluating KIM on our test set. This work was supported in part by the German Research Foundation through the German-Israeli Project Cooperation (DIP, grant DA 1600/1-1), an Intel ICRI-CI grant, Theo Hoffenberg, and the Israel Science Foundation grants 1951/17 and 1555/15. Vered is also supported by the Clore Scholars Programme (2017), and the AI2 Key Scientific Challenges Program (2017).

---

[7]We ignore multi-word replacements in §5.2 and §5.3.

References

Samuel R. Bowman, Gabor Angeli, Christopher Potts, and D. Christopher Manning. 2015. A large annotated corpus for learning natural language inference. In *Proceedings of the 2015 Conference on Empirical Methods in Natural Language Processing*. Association for Computational Linguistics, pages 632–642. https://doi.org/10.18653/v1/D15-1075.

Samuel R Bowman, Jon Gauthier, Abhinav Rastogi, Raghav Gupta, Christopher D Manning, and Christopher Potts. 2016. A fast unified model for parsing and sentence understanding. In *Proceedings of the 54th Annual Meeting of the Association for Computational Linguistics (Volume 1: Long Papers)*. volume 1, pages 1466–1477.

Qian Chen, Xiaodan Zhu, Zhen-Hua Ling, Diana Inkpen, and Si Wei. 2018. Neural natural language inference models enhanced with external knowledge. In *The 56th Annual Meeting of the Association for Computational Linguistics (ACL)*. Melbourne, Australia.

Qian Chen, Xiaodan Zhu, Zhen-Hua Ling, Si Wei, Hui Jiang, and Diana Inkpen. 2017. Enhanced lstm for natural language inference. In *Proceedings of the 55th Annual Meeting of the Association for Computational Linguistics (Volume 1: Long Papers)*. Association for Computational Linguistics, Vancouver, Canada, pages 1657–1668.

Ido Dagan, Dan Roth, Mark Sammons, and Fabio Massimo Zanzotto. 2013. Recognizing textual entailment: Models and applications. *Synthesis Lectures on Human Language Technologies* 6(4):1–220.

Christiane Fellbaum. 1998. *WordNet*. Wiley Online Library.

Yichen Gong, Heng Luo, and Jian Zhang. 2018. Natural language inference over interaction space. In *International Conference on Learning Representations (ICLR)*.

Suchin Gururangan, Swabha Swayamdipta, Omer Levy, Roy Schwartz, Samuel R Bowman, and Noah A Smith. 2018. Annotation artifacts in natural language inference data. In *The 16th Annual Conference of the North American Chapter of the Association for Computational Linguistics: Human Language Technologies (NAACL-HLT)*. New Orleans, Louisiana.

Robin Jia and Percy Liang. 2017. Adversarial examples for evaluating reading comprehension systems. In *Proceedings of the 2017 Conference on Empirical Methods in Natural Language Processing*. Association for Computational Linguistics, Copenhagen, Denmark, pages 2021–2031. https://www.aclweb.org/anthology/D17-1215.

Tushar Khot, Ashish Sabharwal, and Peter Clark. 2018. SciTail: A textual entailment dataset from science question answering. In *The Thirty-Second AAAI Conference on Artificial Intelligence (AAAI)*. New Orleans, Louisiana.

J Richard Landis and Gary G Koch. 1977. The measurement of observer agreement for categorical data. *biometrics* pages 159–174.

Lili Mou, Rui Men, Ge Li, Yan Xu, Lu Zhang, Rui Yan, and Zhi Jin. 2016. Natural language inference by tree-based convolution and heuristic matching. In *Proceedings of the 54th Annual Meeting of the Association for Computational Linguistics (Volume 2: Short Papers)*. volume 2, pages 130–136.

Yixin Nie and Mohit Bansal. 2017. Shortcut-stacked sentence encoders for multi-domain inference. *arXiv preprint arXiv:1708.02312* .

Ankur Parikh, Oscar Täckström, Dipanjan Das, and Jakob Uszkoreit. 2016. A decomposable attention model for natural language inference. In *Proceedings of the 2016 Conference on Empirical Methods in Natural Language Processing*. Association for Computational Linguistics, Austin, Texas, pages 2249–2255. https://aclweb.org/anthology/D16-1244.

Jeffrey Pennington, Richard Socher, and Christopher Manning. 2014. Glove: Global vectors for word representation. In *Proceedings of the 2014 Conference on Empirical Methods in Natural Language Processing (EMNLP)*. Association for Computational Linguistics, Doha, Qatar, pages 1532–1543. http://www.aclweb.org/anthology/D14-1162.

Adam Poliak, Jason Naradowsky, Aparajita Haldar, Rachel Rudinger, and Benjamin Van Durme. 2018. Hypothesis Only Baselines in Natural Language Inference. In *Joint Conference on Lexical and Computational Semantics (StarSem)*.

Tim Rocktäschel, Edward Grefenstette, Karl Moritz Hermann, Tomas Kocisky, and Phil Blunsom. 2016. Reasoning about entailment with neural attention. In *International Conference on Learning Representations (ICLR)*.

Tao Shen, Tianyi Zhou, Guodong Long, Jing Jiang, Sen Wang, and Chengqi Zhang. 2018. Reinforced self-attention network: a hybrid of hard and soft attention for sequence modeling. *arXiv preprint arXiv:1801.10296* .

Adina Williams, Nikita Nangia, and Samuel R Bowman. 2018. A broad-coverage challenge corpus for sentence understanding through inference. In *The 16th Annual Conference of the North American Chapter of the Association for Computational Linguistics: Human Language Technologies (NAACL-HLT)*. New Orleans, Louisiana.

Peter Young, Alice Lai, Micah Hodosh, and Julia Hockenmaier. 2014. From image descriptions to visual denotations: New similarity metrics for semantic inference over event descriptions. *Transactions of the Association for Computational Linguistics* 2:67–78.

Adaptive Knowledge Sharing in Multi-Task Learning: Improving Low-Resource Neural Machine Translation

Poorya Zaremoodi   **Wray Buntine**   **Gholamreza Haffari**
Faculty of Information Technology, Monash University, Australia
`first.last@monash.edu`

Abstract

Neural Machine Translation (NMT) is notorious for its need for large amounts of bilingual data. An effective approach to compensate for this requirement is Multi-Task Learning (MTL) to leverage different linguistic resources as a source of inductive bias. Current MTL architectures are based on the SEQ2SEQ transduction, and (partially) share different components of the models among the tasks. However, this MTL approach often suffers from task interference, and is not able to fully capture commonalities among subsets of tasks. We address this issue by extending the recurrent units with multiple *blocks* along with a trainable *routing network*. The routing network enables adaptive collaboration by dynamic sharing of blocks conditioned on the task at hand, input, and model state. Empirical evaluation of two low-resource translation tasks, English to Vietnamese and Farsi, show +1 BLEU score improvements compared to strong baselines.

1 Introduction

Neural Machine Translation (NMT) has shown remarkable progress in recent years. However, it requires large amounts of bilingual data to learn a translation model with reasonable quality (Koehn and Knowles, 2017). This requirement can be compensated by leveraging curated monolingual linguistic resources in a multi-task learning framework. Essentially, learned knowledge from auxiliary linguistic tasks serves as inductive bias for the translation task to lead to better generalizations.

Multi-Task Learning (MTL) is an effective approach for leveraging commonalities of related tasks to improve performance. Various recent works have attempted to improve NMT by scaffolding translation task on a single auxiliary task (Domhan and Hieber, 2017; Zhang and Zong, 2016; Dalvi et al., 2017). Recently, (Niehues and Cho, 2017) have made use of several linguistic tasks to improve NMT. Their method shares components of the SEQ2SEQ model among the tasks, e.g. encoder, decoder or the attention mechanism. However, this approach has two limitations: (i) it *fully* shares the components, and (ii) the shared component(s) are shared among *all* of the tasks. The first limitation can be addressed using deep stacked layers in encoder/decoder, and sharing the layers partially (Zaremoodi and Haffari, 2018). The second limitation causes this MTL approach to suffer from task interference or inability to leverages commonalities among a *subset* of tasks. Recently, (Ruder et al., 2017) tried to address this issue; however, their method is restrictive for SEQ2SEQ scenarios and does not consider the input at each time step to modulate parameter sharing.

In this paper, we address the task interference problem by learning how to dynamically control the amount of sharing among all tasks. We extended the recurrent units with multiple *blocks* along with a routing network to dynamically control sharing of blocks conditioning on the task at hand, the input, and model state. Empirical results on two low-resource translation scenarios, English to Farsi and Vietnamese, show the effectiveness of the proposed model by achieving +1 BLEU score improvement compared to strong baselines.

2 SEQ2SEQ MTL Using Recurrent Unit with Adaptive Routed Blocks

Our MTL is based on the sequential encoder-decoder architecture with the attention mecha-

656

Proceedings of the 56th Annual Meeting of the Association for Computational Linguistics (Short Papers), pages 656–661
Melbourne, Australia, July 15 - 20, 2018. ©2018 Association for Computational Linguistics

nism (Luong et al., 2015b; Bahdanau et al., 2014). The encoder/decoder consist of recurrent units to read/generate a sentence sequentially. Sharing the parameters of the recurrent units among different tasks is indeed sharing the *knowledge* for controlling the information flow in the hidden states. Sharing these parameters among *all* tasks may, however, lead to task interference or inability to leverages commonalities among *subsets* of tasks. We address this issue by extending the recurrent units with multiple *blocks*, each of which processing its own information flow through the time. The state of the recurrent unit at each time step is composed of the states of these blocks. The recurrent unit is equipped with a *routing* mechanism to softly direct the input at each time step to these blocks (see Fig 1). Each block mimics an expert in handling different kinds of information, coordinated by the router. In MTL, the tasks can use different subsets of these shared experts.

(Rosenbaum et al., 2018) uses a routing network for adaptive selection of non-linear functions for MTL. However, it is for fixed-size inputs based on a feed-forward architecture, and is not applicable to SEQ2SEQ scenarios such as MT. (Shazeer et al., 2017) uses Mixture-of-Experts (feed-forward sub-networks) between stacked layers of recurrent units, to adaptively gate state information *vertically*. This is in contrast to our approach where the *horizontal* information flow is adaptively modulated, as we would like to minimise the task interference in MTL.

Assuming there are n blocks in a recurrent unit, we share $n-1$ blocks among the tasks, and let the last one to be task-specific[1]. Task-specific block receives the input of the unit directly while shared blocks are fed with modulated input by the routing network. The state of the unit at each time-step would be the aggregation of blocks' states.

2.1 Routing Mechanism

At each time step, the routing network is responsible to softly forward the input to the shared blocks conditioning on the input x_t, and the previous hidden state of the unit h_{t-1} as follows:

$$
\begin{aligned}
s_t &= \tanh(W_x \cdot x_t + W_h \cdot h_{t-1} + b_s), \\
\tau_t &= \mathrm{softmax}(W_\tau \cdot s_t + b_\tau),
\end{aligned}
$$

where W's and b's are the parameters. Then, the i-th shared block is fed with the input of the

---

[1]multiple recurrent units can be stacked on top of each other to consist a multi-layer component

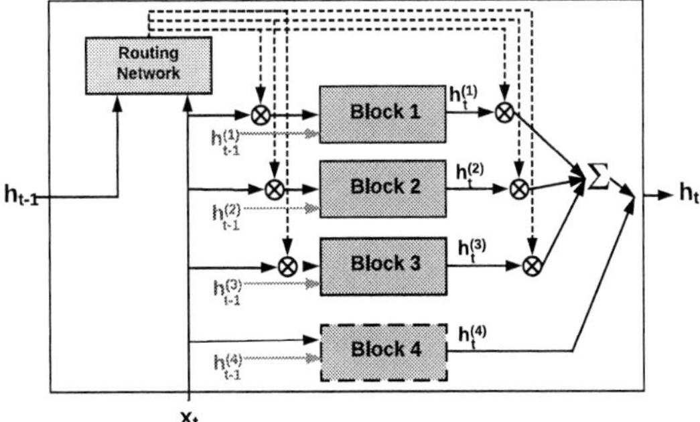

Figure 1: High-level architecture of the proposed recurrent unit with 3 shared blocks and 1 task-specific.

unit modulated by the corresponding output of the routing network $\tilde{x}_t^{(i)} = \tau_t[i]x_t$ where $\tau_t[i]$ is the scalar output of the routing network for the i-th block.

The hidden state of the unit is the concatenation of the hidden state of the shared and task-specific parts $h_t = [h_t^{(shared)}; h_t^{(task)}]$. The state of task-specific part is the state of the corresponding block $h_t^{(task)} = h_t^{(n+1)}$, and the state of the shared part is the sum of states of shared blocks weighted by the outputs of the routing network $h_t^{(shared)} = \sum_{i=1}^{n} \tau_t[i]h_t^{(i)}$.

2.2 Block Architecture

Each block is responsible to control its own flow of information via a standard gating mechanism. Our recurrent units are agnostic to the internal architecture of the blocks; we use the gated-recurrent unit (Cho et al., 2014) in this paper. For the i-th block the corresponding equations are as follows:

$$
\begin{aligned}
z_t^{(i)} &= \sigma(W_z^{(i)}\tilde{x}_t^{(i)} + U_z^{(i)}h_{t-1}^{(i)} + b_z^{(i)}), \\
r_t^{(i)} &= \sigma(W_r^{(i)}\tilde{x}_t^{(i)} + U_r^{(i)}h_{t-1}^{(i)} + b_r^{(i)}), \\
\tilde{h}_t^{(i)} &= \tanh(W_h^{(i)}\tilde{x}_t^{(i)} + U_h^{(i)}h_{t-1}^{(i)} + b_h^{(i)}), \\
h_t^{(i)} &= z_t^{(i)} \odot h_{t-1}^{(i)} + (1 - z_t^{(i)}) \odot \tilde{h}_t^{(i)}.
\end{aligned}
$$

2.3 Training Objective and Schedule.

The rest of the model is similar to attentional SEQ2SEQ model (Luong et al., 2015b) which computes the conditional probability of the target sequence given the source $P_\theta(y|x) = \prod_j P_\theta(y_j|y_{<j}x)$. For the case of training $M + 1$ SEQ2SEQ transduction tasks, each of which is associated with a training set $\mathcal{D}_m := \{(x_i, y_i)\}_{i=1}^{N_m}$, the parameters of MTL architecture $\Theta_{mtl} =$

$\{\boldsymbol{\Theta}_m\}_{m=0}^M$ are learned by maximizing the following objective:

$$\mathcal{L}_{mtl}(\boldsymbol{\Theta}_{mtl}) := \sum_{m=0}^M \frac{\gamma_m}{|\mathcal{D}_m|} \sum_{(\boldsymbol{x},\boldsymbol{y})\in\mathcal{D}_m} \log P_{\boldsymbol{\Theta}_m}(\boldsymbol{y}|\boldsymbol{x})$$

where $|\mathcal{D}_m|$ is the size of the training set for the m-th task, and γ_m is responsible to balance the influence of tasks in the training objective. We explored different values in preliminary experiments, and found that for our training schedule $\gamma = 1$ for all tasks results in the best performance. Generally, γ is useful when the dataset sizes for auxiliary tasks are imbalanced (our training schedule handles the main task).

Variants of stochastic gradient descent (SGD) can be used to optimize the objective function. In our training schedule, we randomly select a mini-batch from the main task (translation) and another mini-batch from a randomly selected auxiliary task to make the next SGD update. Selecting a mini-batch from the main task in each SGD update ensures that its training signals are not washed out by auxiliary tasks.

3 Experiments

3.1 Bilingual Corpora

We use two language-pairs, translating from English to Farsi and Vietnamese. We have chosen them to analyze the effect of multi-task learning on languages with different underlying linguistic structures[2]. We apply BPE (Sennrich et al., 2016) on the union of source and target vocabularies for English-Vietnamese, and separate vocabularies for English-Farsi as the alphabets are disjoined (30K BPE operations). Further details about the corpora and their pre-processing is as follows:

- The English-Farsi corpus has $\sim$105K sentence pairs. It is assembled from English-Farsi parallel subtitles from the TED corpus (Tiedemann, 2012), accompanied by all the parallel news text in LDC2016E93 *Farsi Representative Language Pack* from the Linguistic Data Consortium. The corpus has been normalized using the Hazm toolkit[3]. We have removed sentences with more than 80 tokens in either side (before applying BPE). 3k and 4k sentence pairs were held out for the purpose of validation and test.

- The English-Vietnamese has $\sim$133K training pairs. It is the preprocessed version of the IWSLT 2015 translation task provided by (Luong and Manning, 2015). It consists of subtitles and their corresponding translations of a collection of public speeches from TED and TEDX talks. The "tst2012" and "tst2013" parts are used as validation and test sets, respectively. We have removed sentence pairs which had more than 300 tokens after applying BPE on either sides.

3.2 Auxiliary Tasks

We have chosen the following auxiliary tasks to leverage the syntactic and semantic knowledge to improve NMT:

Named-Entity Recognition (NER). It is expected that learning to recognize named-entities help the model to learn translation pattern by masking out named-entites. We have used the NER data comes from the CONLL shared task.[4] Sentences in this dataset come from a collection of newswire articles from the Reuters Corpus. These sentences are annotated with four types of named entities: persons, locations, organizations and names of miscellaneous entities.

Syntactic Parsing. By learning the phrase structure of the input sentence, the model would be able to learn better re-ordering. Specially, in the case of language pairs with high level of syntactic divergence (e.g. English-Farsi). We have used Penn Tree Bank parsing data with the standard split for training, development, and test (Marcus et al., 1993). We cast syntactic parsing to a SEQ2SEQ transduction task by linearizing constituency trees (Vinyals et al., 2015).

Semantic Parsing. Learning semantic parsing helps the model to abstract away the meaning from the surface in order to convey it in the target translation. For this task, we have used the Abstract Meaning Representation (AMR) corpus Release 2.0 (LDC2017T10)[5]. This corpus contains natural language sentences from newswire, weblogs, web discussion forums and broadcast conversations. We cast this task to a SEQ2SEQ transduction task by linearizing the AMR graphs (Konstas et al., 2017).

---

[2] English and Vietnamese are SVO, and Farsi is SOV.
[3] `www.sobhe.ir/hazm`

[4] https://www.clips.uantwerpen.be/conll2003/ner
[5] https://catalog.ldc.upenn.edu/LDC2017T10

Method	English → Farsi						English → Vietnamese					
	Dev			Test			Dev			Test		
	PPL	TER	BLEU	PPL	TER	BLEU	PPL	TER	BLEU	PPL	TER	BLEU
NMT (Luong et al., 2015b)	55.36	87.9	8.57	56.21	88.2	8.35	18.21	64.92	18.39	16.3	61.37	20.18
MTL (Full) (Niehues and Cho, 2017)	47.43	85.92	8.97	48.23	87.3	8.73	14.56	61.52	20.55	12.5	57.6	22.6
MTL (Partial) (Zaremoodi and Haffari, 2018)	42.6	80.16	10.58	43.09	81.94	10.54	13.32	59.55	22.2	11.34	55.84	24.65
Our MTL (Routing)	**37.95**	**76.30**	**12.06**	**38.57**	**78.18**	**11.95**	**12.38**	**58.52**	**23.06**	**10.52**	**54.33**	**25.65**

Table 1: The performance measures of the baselines vs our MTL architecture on the bilingual datasets.

3.3 Models and Baselines

We have implemented the proposed MTL architecture along with the baselines in C++ using DyNet (Neubig et al., 2017) on top of Mantis (Cohn et al., 2016) which is an implementation of the attentional SEQ2SEQ NMT model. For our MTL architecture, we used the proposed recurrent unit with 3 blocks in encoder and decoder. For the fair comparison in terms the of number of parameters, we used 3 stacked layers in both encoder and decoder components for the baselines. We compare against the following baselines:

- Baseline 1: The vanilla SEQ2SEQ model (Luong et al., 2015a) without any auxiliary task.

- Baseline 2: The MTL architecture proposed in (Niehues and Cho, 2017) which fully shares parameters in components. We have used their best performing architecture with our training schedule. We have extended their work with *deep* stacked layers for the sake of comparison.

- Baseline 3: The MTL architecture proposed in (Zaremoodi and Haffari, 2018) which uses deep stacked layers in the components and shares the parameters of the top two/one stacked layers among encoders/decoders of all tasks[6].

For the proposed MTL, we use recurrent units with 400 hidden dimensions for each block. The encoders and decoders of the baselines use GRU units with 400 hidden dimensions. The attention component has 400 dimensions. We use Adam optimizer (Kingma and Ba, 2014) with the initial learning rate of 0.003 for all the tasks. Learning

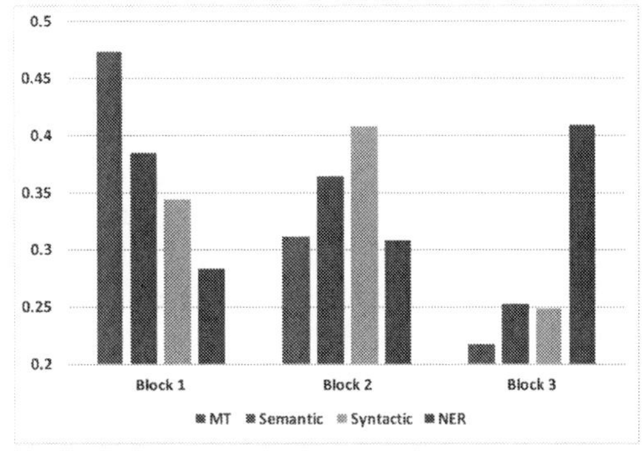

Figure 2: Average percentage of block usage for each task.

rates are halved on the decrease in the performance on the dev set of corresponding task. Mini-batch size is set to 32, and dropout rate is 0.5. All models are trained for 50 epochs and the best models are saved based on the perplexity on the dev set of the translation task.

For each task, we add special tokens to the beginning of source sequence (similar to (Johnson et al., 2017)) to indicate which task the sequence pair comes from.

We used greedy decoding to generate translation. In order to measure translation quality, we use BLEU[7] (Papineni et al., 2002) and TER (Snover et al., 2006) scores.

3.4 Results and analysis

Table 1 reports the results for the baselines and our proposed method on the two aforementioned translation tasks. As expected, the performance of MTL models are better than the baseline 1 (only MT task). As seen, partial parameter sharing is more effective than fully parameter sharing. Furthermore, our proposed architecture with adaptive

---

[6]In preliminary experiments, we have tried different sharing scenarios and this one led to the best results.

[7]Using "multi-bleu.perl" script from Moses (Koehn et al., 2007).

sharing performs better than the other MTL methods on all tasks, and achieve +1 BLEU score improvements on the test sets. The improvements in the translation quality of NMT models trained by our MTL method may be attributed to less interference with multiple auxiliary tasks.

Figure 2 shows the average percentage of block usage for each task in an MTL model with 3 shared blocks, on the English-Farsi test set. We have aggregated the output of the routing network for the blocks in the encoder recurrent units over all the input tokens. Then, it is normalized by dividing on the total number of input tokens. Based on Figure 2, the first and third blocks are more specialized (based on their usage) for the translation and NER tasks, respectively. The second block is mostly used by the semantic and syntactic parsing tasks, so specialized for them. This confirms our model leverages commonalities among subsets of tasks by dedicating common blocks to them to reduce task interference.

4 Conclusions

We have presented an effective MTL approach to improve NMT for low-resource languages, by leveraging curated linguistic resources on the source side. We address the task interference issue in previous MTL models by extending the recurrent units with multiple *blocks* along with a trainable *routing network*. Our experimental results on low-resource English to Farsi and Vietnamese datasets, show +1 BLEU score improvements compared to strong baselines.

Acknowledgments

The research reported here was initiated at the 2017 Frederick Jelinek Memorial Summer Workshop on Speech and Language Technologies, hosted at Carnegie Mellon University and sponsored by Johns Hopkins University with unrestricted gifts from Amazon, Apple, Facebook, Google, and Microsoft. We are very grateful to the workshop members for the insightful discussions and data pre-processing. This work was supported by the Multi-modal Australian ScienceS Imaging and Visualisation Environment (MASSIVE) (www.massive.org.au), and by the Australian Research Council through DP160102686. The first author was partly supported by CSIRO's Data61. We would like to thank the anonymous reviewers for their constructive feedback.

References

Dzmitry Bahdanau, Kyunghyun Cho, and Yoshua Bengio. 2014. Neural machine translation by jointly learning to align and translate. *arXiv preprint arXiv:1409.0473*.

Kyunghyun Cho, Bart van Merrienboer, Caglar Gulcehre, Dzmitry Bahdanau, Fethi Bougares, Holger Schwenk, and Yoshua Bengio. 2014. Learning phrase representations using rnn encoder–decoder for statistical machine translation. In *Proceedings of the 2014 Conference on Empirical Methods in Natural Language Processing (EMNLP)*, pages 1724–1734.

Trevor Cohn, Cong Duy Vu Hoang, Ekaterina Vymolova, Kaisheng Yao, Chris Dyer, and Gholamreza Haffari. 2016. Incorporating structural alignment biases into an attentional neural translation model. In *Proceedings of the 2016 Conference of the North American Chapter of the Association for Computational Linguistics: Human Language Technologies*, pages 876–885.

Fahim Dalvi, Nadir Durrani, Hassan Sajjad, Yonatan Belinkov, and Stephan Vogel. 2017. Understanding and improving morphological learning in the neural machine translation decoder. In *Proceedings of the Eighth International Joint Conference on Natural Language Processing*, pages 142–151.

Tobias Domhan and Felix Hieber. 2017. Using target-side monolingual data for neural machine translation through multi-task learning. In *Proceedings of the 2017 Conference on Empirical Methods in Natural Language Processing*, pages 1501–1506.

Melvin Johnson, Mike Schuster, Quoc V Le, Maxim Krikun, Yonghui Wu, Zhifeng Chen, Nikhil Thorat, Fernanda Viégas, Martin Wattenberg, Greg Corrado, et al. 2017. Google's multilingual neural machine translation system: Enabling zero-shot translation. *Transactions of the Association of Computational Linguistics*, 5(1):339–351.

Diederik Kingma and Jimmy Ba. 2014. Adam: A method for stochastic optimization. *arXiv preprint arXiv:1412.6980*.

Philipp Koehn, Hieu Hoang, Alexandra Birch, Chris Callison-Burch, Marcello Federico, Nicola Bertoldi, Brooke Cowan, Wade Shen, Christine Moran, Richard Zens, Chris Dyer, Ondřej Bojar, Alexandra Constantin, and Evan Herbst. 2007. Moses: Open Source Toolkit for Statistical Machine Translation. In *Proceedings of the 45th Annual Meeting of the ACL on Interactive Poster and Demonstration Sessions*, pages 177–180.

Philipp Koehn and Rebecca Knowles. 2017. Six challenges for neural machine translation. In *Proceedings of the First Workshop on Neural Machine Translation*, pages 28–39.

Ioannis Konstas, Srinivasan Iyer, Mark Yatskar, Yejin Choi, and Luke Zettlemoyer. 2017. Neural amr: Sequence-to-sequence models for parsing and generation. In *Proceedings of the 55th Annual Meeting of the Association for Computational Linguistics*, pages 146–157.

Minh-Thang Luong and Christopher D. Manning. 2015. Stanford neural machine translation systems for spoken language domain. In *International Workshop on Spoken Language Translation*.

Minh-Thang Luong, Hieu Pham, and Christopher D Manning. 2015a. Effective approaches to attention-based neural machine translation. In *Proceedings of the 2015 Conference on Empirical Methods in Natural Language Processing (EMNLP)*. Association for Computational Linguistics.

Thang Luong, Hieu Pham, and Christopher D. Manning. 2015b. Effective Approaches to Attention-based Neural Machine Translation. In *Proceedings of the 2015 Conference on Empirical Methods in Natural Language Processing*, pages 1412–1421.

Mitchell P. Marcus, Mary Ann Marcinkiewicz, and Beatrice Santorini. 1993. Building a large annotated corpus of english: The penn treebank. *Comput. Linguist.*, 19(2):313–330.

Graham Neubig, Chris Dyer, Yoav Goldberg, Austin Matthews, Waleed Ammar, Antonios Anastasopoulos, Miguel Ballesteros, David Chiang, Daniel Clothiaux, Trevor Cohn, et al. 2017. Dynet: The dynamic neural network toolkit. *arXiv preprint arXiv:1701.03980*.

Jan Niehues and Eunah Cho. 2017. Exploiting linguistic resources for neural machine translation using multi-task learning. In *Proceedings of the Second Conference on Machine Translation*, pages 80–89.

Kishore Papineni, Salim Roukos, Todd Ward, and Wei-Jing Zhu. 2002. Bleu: a method for automatic evaluation of machine translation. In *Proceedings of the 40th annual meeting on association for computational linguistics*, pages 311–318.

Clemens Rosenbaum, Tim Klinger, and Matthew Riemer. 2018. Routing networks: Adaptive selection of non-linear functions for multi-task learning. In *International Conference on Learning Representations*.

Sebastian Ruder, Joachim Bingel, Isabelle Augenstein, and Anders Søgaard. 2017. Sluice networks: Learning what to share between loosely related tasks. *CoRR*, abs/1705.08142.

Rico Sennrich, Barry Haddow, and Alexandra Birch. 2016. Neural Machine Translation of Rare Words with Subword Units. In *Proceedings of the 54th Annual Meeting of the Association for Computational Linguistics*, pages 1715–1725.

Noam Shazeer, Azalia Mirhoseini, Krzysztof Maziarz, Andy Davis, Quoc Le, Geoffrey Hinton, and Jeff Dean. 2017. Outrageously large neural networks: The sparsely-gated mixture-of-experts layer. *arXiv preprint arXiv:1701.06538*.

Matthew Snover, Bonnie Dorr, Richard Schwartz, Linnea Micciulla, and John Makhoul. 2006. A study of translation edit rate with targeted human annotation. In *Proceedings of association for machine translation in the Americas*.

Jörg Tiedemann. 2012. Parallel data, tools and interfaces in opus. In *Proceedings of the Eighth International Conference on Language Resources and Evaluation*, pages 2214–2218.

Oriol Vinyals, Ł ukasz Kaiser, Terry Koo, Slav Petrov, Ilya Sutskever, and Geoffrey Hinton. 2015. Grammar as a foreign language. In *Advances in Neural Information Processing Systems 28*, pages 2773–2781.

Poorya Zaremoodi and Gholamreza Haffari. 2018. Neural machine translation for bilingually scarce scenarios: A deep multi-task learning approach. In *Proceedings of the 2018 Conference of the North American Chapter of the Association for Computational Linguistics: Human Language Technologies*.

Jiajun Zhang and Chengqing Zong. 2016. Exploiting source-side monolingual data in neural machine translation. In *Proceedings of the 2016 Conference on Empirical Methods in Natural Language Processing*, pages 1535–1545.

Automatic Estimation of Simultaneous Interpreter Performance

Craig Stewart[1], Nikolai Vogler[1], Junjie Hu[1], Jordan Boyd-Graber[2], Graham Neubig[1]
[1]Language Technologies Institute, Carnegie Mellon University
[2]CS, iSchool, UMIACS, LSC, University of Maryland

Abstract

Simultaneous interpretation, translation of the spoken word in real-time, is both highly challenging and physically demanding. Methods to predict interpreter confidence and the adequacy of the interpreted message have a number of potential applications, such as in computer-assisted interpretation interfaces or pedagogical tools. We propose the task of predicting simultaneous interpreter performance by building on existing methodology for quality estimation (QE) of machine translation output. In experiments over five settings in three language pairs, we extend a QE pipeline to estimate interpreter performance (as approximated by the METEOR evaluation metric) and propose novel features reflecting interpretation strategy and evaluation measures that further improve prediction accuracy.[1]

1 Introduction

Simultaneous Interpretation (SI) is an inherently difficult task that carries significant cognitive and attentional burdens. The role of the simultaneous interpreter is to accurately render the source speech in a given target language in a timely and precise manner. Interpreters employ a range of strategies, including generalization and summarization, to convey the source message as efficiently and reliably as possible (He et al., 2016). Unfortunately, the interpreter is pitched against the limits of human memory and stamina, and after only minutes of interpreting, the number of errors made by an interpreter begins to increase exponentially (Moser-Mercer et al., 1998).

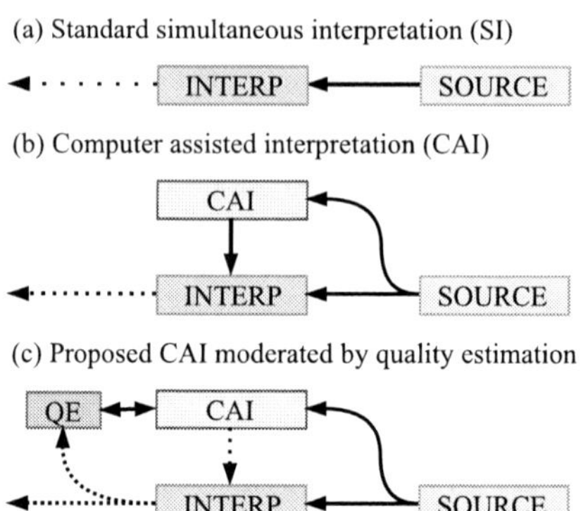

Figure 1: Simultaneous interpretation scenarios

We examine the task of *estimating simultaneous interpreter performance*: automatically predicting when interpreters are interpreting smoothly and when they are struggling. This has several immediate potential applications, one of which being in Computer-Assisted Interpretation (CAI). CAI is quickly gaining traction in the interpreting community, with software products such as Interpret-Bank (Fantinouli, 2016) deployed in interpreting booths to provide live and interactive terminology support. Figure 1(b) shows how this might work; both the interpreter and the CAI system receive the source message and the system displays assistive information in the form of terminology and informational support.

While this might improve the quality of interpreter output, there is a danger that these systems will provide *too much* information and increase the cognitive load imposed upon the interpreter (Fantinouli, 2018). Intuitively, the ideal level of support depends on current interpreter performance. The system can minimize distraction by providing assistance only when an interpreter is struggling. This level of support could be moderated appropriately if interpreter performance can be accurately predicted. Figure 1(c) demonstrates

---

[1]https://github.com/craigastewart/qe_sim_interp

Proceedings of the 56th Annual Meeting of the Association for Computational Linguistics (Short Papers), pages 662–666
Melbourne, Australia, July 15 - 20, 2018. ©2018 Association for Computational Linguistics

how our proposed quality estimation (QE) system receives and evaluates interpreter output, allowing the CAI system to appropriately lower the amount of information passed to the interpreter, maximizing the quality of interpreter output.

As a concrete method for estimating interpreter performance, we turn to existing work on QE for machine translation (MT) systems (Specia et al., 2010, 2015), which takes in the source sentence and MT-generated outputs and estimates a measure of quality. In doing so, we arrive at two natural research questions:

1. Do existing methods for performing QE on MT output also allow for accurate estimation of interpreter performance, despite the inherent differences between MT and SI?

2. What unique aspects of the problem of interpreter performance estimation, such as the availability of prosody and other linguistic cues, can be exploited to further improve the accuracy of our predictions?

The remainder of the paper describes methods and experiments on English-Japanese (EN-JA), English-French (EN-FR), and English-Italian (EN-IT) interpretation data attempting to answer these questions.

2 Quality Estimation

Blatz et al. (2004) first proposed the problem of measuring the quality of MT output as a prediction task, given that existing metrics such as BLEU (Papineni et al., 2002) rely on the availability of reference translations to evaluate MT output quality, which aren't always available. As such, QE has since received widespread attention in the MT community and since 2012 has been included as a task in the Workshop on Statistical Machine Translation (Callison-Burch et al., 2012), using approaches ranging from linear classifiers (Ueffing and Ney, 2007; Luong et al., 2014) to neural models (Martins et al., 2016, 2017).

QuEst++ (Specia et al., 2015) is a well-known QE pipeline that supports word-level, sentence-level, and document-level QE. Its effectiveness and flexibility make it an attractive candidate for our proposed task. There are two main modules to QuEst++: a feature extractor and a learning module. The feature extractor produces an intermediate representation of the source and translation in a continuous feature vector. The goal of the learning module, given a source and translation pair, is to predict the quality of the translation, either as a label or as a continuous value. This module is trained on example translations that have an assigned score (such as BLEU) and then predicts the score of a new example. QuEst++ offers a range of learning algorithms but defaults to Support Vector Regression for sentence-level QE.

3 Quality Estimation for Interpretation

The default, out-of-the-box, sentence-level feature set for QuEst++ includes seventeen features such as number of tokens in source/target utterances, average token length, n-gram frequency, etc. (Specia et al., 2015). While this feature set is effective for evaluation of MT output, SI output is inherently different—full of pauses, hesitations, paraphrases, re-orderings and repetitions. In the following sections, we describe our methods to adapt QE to handle these phenomena.

3.1 Interpretation-specific Features

To adapt QE to interpreter output, we augment the baseline feature set with four additional types of features that may indicate a struggling interpreter.

Ratio of pauses/hesitations/incomplete words: Sridhar et al. (2013) propose that interpreters regularly use pauses to gain more time to think and as a cognitive strategy to manage memory constraints. An increased number of hesitations or incomplete words in interpreter output might indicate that an interpreter is struggling to produce accurate output. In our particular case, both corpora we use in experiments are annotated for pauses and partial renditions of words.

Ratio of non-specific words: Interpreters often compress output by replacing or omitting common nouns to avoid specific terminology (Sridhar et al., 2013), either to prevent redundancy or to ease cognitive load. For example: "The chairman explained the proposal to the delegates" might be rendered in a target language as "he explained it to them." To capture this, we include a feature that checks for words from a pre-determined seed list of pronouns and demonstrative adjectives.

Ratio of 'quasi-'cognates: In related language pairs, often words of a similar root are orthographically similar, for example "artificial"(EN), "artificiel"(FR) and "artificiale"(IT). Likewise in

Japanese, words adapted from English are transcribed in katakana script to indicate their foreign origin. Transliterated words in interpreted speech could represent facilitated translation by language proximity, or an attempt to produce an approximation of a word that the interpreter did not know. We include a feature that counts the number of words that share at least 50% identical orthography (for EN, FR, IT) or are rendered in the interpreter transcript in katakana (JA).

Ratio of number of words: We further include three features from the bank of features provided with QuEst++ that compare source and target length and the amount of transcribed punctuation. Information about utterance length makes sense in an interpreting scenario, given the aforementioned strategies of omission and compression of information. A list, for example, may be compressed to avoid redundancy or may be an erroneous omission (Barik, 1994).

3.2 Evaluation Metric

Novice interpreters are assessed for accuracy on the number of omissions, additions and the inaccurate renditions of lexical items and longer phrases (Altman, 1994), but recovery of content and correct terminology are highly valued. While no large corpus exists that has been manually annotated with these measures, they align with the phenomena that MT evaluation tries to solve. One important design decision is which evaluation metric to target in our QE system. There is an abundance of evaluation metrics available for MT including WER (Su et al.), BLEU (Papineni et al., 2002), NIST (Doddington, 2002) and METEOR (Denkowski and Lavie, 2014), all of which compare the similarity between reference translations and translations. Interpreter output is fundamentally different from any reference that we may use in evaluation because interpreters employ a range of economizing strategies such as segmentation, omission, generalization, and reformulation (Riccardi, 2005). As such, measuring interpretation quality by some metrics employed in MT such as BLEU can result in artificially low scores (Shimizu et al., 2013). To mitigate this, we use METEOR, a more sophisticated MT evaluation metric that considers paraphrases and content-function word distinctions, and thus should be better equipped to deal with the disparity between MT and SI. Better handling of these divergences

for evaluation of interpreter output, or fine-grained evaluation based on measures from interpretation studies is an interesting direction for future work.

4   Data: Interpretation Corpora

For our EN-JA language data we train the pipeline on combined data from seven TED Talks taken from the NAIST TED SI corpus (Shimizu et al., 2013). This corpus provides human transcribed SI output from three interpreters of low, intermediate and high levels of proficiency denoted B-rank, A-rank and S-rank respectively, with 559 utterances from each interpreter. The corpus also provides written translations of the source speech, which we use as reference translations when evaluating interpreter output using METEOR.

Our EN-FR and EN-IT data are drawn from the EPTIC corpus (Bernardini et al., 2016), which provides source and interpreter transcripts for speeches from the European Parliament (manually transcribed to include vocal expressions), as well as translations of transcripts of the source speech. The EN-FR and EN-IT datasets contain 739 and 731 utterances respectively. While the EPTIC translations are accurate, they were created from an official transcript that differs significantly in register from the source speech. As a proxy for our experiments, we generated translations of the original speech using Google Translate, which resulted in much more qualitatively reliable METEOR scores than the EPTIC translations.

5   Interpreter Quality Experiments

To evaluate the quality of our QE system, we use the Pearson's r correlation between the predicted and true METEOR for each language pair (Graham, 2015). As a baseline, we train QuEst++ on the out-of-the-box feature set (Section 2).

We use k-fold cross-validation individually on EN-JA, EN-FR, and EN-IT source-interpreter language pairs with a held-out development set and test set for each fold. For each experiment setting, we run the experiment for each fold (ten iterations for each set) and evaluate average Pearson's r correlation on the development set.

In our baseline setting, we extract features based on the default QuEst++ sentence-level feature set (*baseline*). We ablate baseline features through cross-validation and remove features relating to bigram and trigram frequency and punctuation frequency in the source utterance, creating

	baseline	trimmed	proposed
EN-JA(B-rank)	0.514	0.542	**0.593**
EN-JA(A-rank)	0.487	0.554	**0.591**
EN-JA(S-rank)	0.325	0.334	**0.411**
EN-FR	0.631	0.610	**0.691**
EN-IT	0.569	0.543	**0.576**

Table 1: Pearson's r scores for predicted ME-TEOR for baseline, trimmed and proposed feature sets on the test set (highest accuracy for each dataset indicated in bold).

a more effective trimmed model (*trimmed*).

Subsequently, we add our interpreter features (Section 3.1) and arrive at our *proposed* model. We then repeat each experiment using the test set data from each fold and compare the resulting average Pearson's r scores.

5.1 Results

Table 1 shows our primary results comparing the baseline, trimmed, and proposed feature sets. Our first observation is that, even with the baseline feature set, QE obtains respectable correlation scores, proving feasible as a method to predict interpreter performance. Our trimmed feature set performs moderately better than the baseline for Japanese, and slightly under-performs for French and Italian. However, our proposed, interpreter-focused model out-performs in all language settings with notable gains in particular for EN-JA(A-Rank) (+0.104), achieving its highest accuracy on the EN-FR dataset. Over all datasets, the gain of the proposed model is statistically significant at $p < 0.05$ by the pairwise bootstrap (Koehn, 2004).

5.2 Analysis

We further present two analyses: ablation on the full feature set and a qualitative comparison. Table 2 iteratively reduces the feature set by first removing the 'quasi-'cognate feature (w/o cog); specific words (w/o spec); pauses, hesitations, and incomplete words (w/o fill); and finally sentence length and punctuation differences (w/o length).

Relative difference in utterance length appears to aid Japanese and French above other languages. Cognates are particularly useful in EN-FR and EN-IT; this may be indicative of the corpus domain (European Parliament proceedings being rich in Latinate legalese) or of cognate frequency in those languages. In Japanese, cognates were

	w/o cog	w/o spec	w/o fill	w/o len
EN-JA(B)	+0.007	+0.012	+0.016	-0.053
EN-JA(A)	-0.006	-0.011	-0.012	-0.031
EN-JA(S)	-0.014	+0.001	+0.004	-0.061
EN-FR	-0.013	-0.006	+0.007	-0.054
EN-IT	-0.020	+0.002	+0.020	+0.005
Average	-0.009	-0.001	+0.007	-0.039

Table 2: Relative difference in Pearson's r scores for ablated features after removing cognates, specifics, fillers and length difference (cumulative ablation, left to right). Omission and addition are key features distinguishing SI from translation.

more indicative of quality for the more skilled interpreter (S-rank). While pauses and hesitations seem to aid the model in EN-FR and EN-IT, they appear to hinder EN-JA.

Below is a qualitative EN-IT example with a METEOR score of 0.079 (being substantially lower than the average METEOR score across all datasets; 0.262). The baseline model prediction of its score was 0.127, and our proposed model, 0.066:

SOURCE: *"Will the Parliament grant President Dilma Rousseff, on the very first occasion after her groundbaking groundbreaking election and for no sound formal reason, the kind of debate that we usually reserve for people like Mugabe? So, I ask you to remove Brazil from the agenda of the urgencies."*

INTERP: *"Ehm il Parlamento... dopo le elezioni... daremdar spazio a un dibattito sul ehm sul caso per esempio del presidente Mugabe invece di mettere il Brasile all'ordine del giorno?"*

GLOSS: *"Ehm the Parliament... after the elections... we'll gi- will give way to a debate on the ehm on the case for example of President Mugabe instead of putting Brazil on the agenda?"*

Our model can better capture the issues in this example because it has many interpretation specific qualities (pauses, compression, and omission). This is an example in which a CAI system might offer assistance to an interpreter struggling to produce an accurate rendition.

6 Conclusion

We introduce a novel and effective application of QE to evaluate interpreter output, which could be immediately applied to allow CAI systems to selectively offer assistance to struggling interpreters. This work uses METEOR to evaluate interpreter output, but creation of fine-grained measures to evaluate various aspects of interpreter performance is an interesting avenue for future work.

Acknowledgements

This material is based upon work supported by the National Science Foundation under Grant No. 1748663 and Graduate Research Fellowship No. DGE1745016.

References

Janet Altman. 1994. *Error Analysis in the Teaching of Simultaneous Interpreting: A Pilot Study*. John Benjamins Publishing Company, Edinburgh, Scotland.

Henry Barik. 1994. *A Description of Various Types of Omissions, Additions and Errors of Translation Encountered in Simultaneous Interpretation*. John Benjamins Publishing Company, North Carolina, USA.

Silvia Bernardini, Adriano Ferraresi, and Maja Milievi. 2016. From EPIC to EPTIC exploring simplification in interpreting and translation from an intermodal perspective. *Target. International Journal of Translation Studies*, 28(1):61–86.

John Blatz, Erin Fitzgerald, George Foster, Simona Gandrabur, Cyril Goutte, Alex Kulesza, Alberto Sanchis, and Nicola Ueffing. 2004. Confidence estimation for machine translation. In *Proceedings of the 20th International Conference on Computational Linguistics*, COLING '04, Stroudsburg, PA, USA. Association for Computational Linguistics.

Chris Callison-Burch, Philipp Koehn, Christof Monz, Matt Post, Radu Soricut, and Lucia Specia. 2012. Findings of the 2012 workshop on statistical machine translation. In *Proc. WMT*.

Michael Denkowski and Alon Lavie. 2014. Meteor universal: Language specific translation evaluation for any target language. In *Proc. WMT*.

George Doddington. 2002. Automatic evaluation of machine translation quality using n-gram co-occurrence statistics. In *Proc. HLT*, pages 138–145.

Claudio Fantinouli. 2016. Interpretbank. redefining computer-assisted interpreting tools. In *Proceedings of the 38th Conference Translating and the Computer*, pages 42–55.

Claudio Fantinouli. 2018. Trends in e-tools and resources for translators and interpreters. In *Isabel Durn and Gloria Corpas (eds.)*, pages 153–174.

Yvette Graham. 2015. Improving evaluation of machine translation quality estimation. In *Proc. ACL*, pages 1804–1813.

He He, Jordan Boyd-Graber, and Hal Daumé III. 2016. Interpretese vs. translationese: The uniqueness of human strategies in simultaneous interpretation. In *Proc. NAACL*, pages 971–976.

Philipp Koehn. 2004. Statistical significance tests for machine translation evaluation. In *Proc. EMNLP*, pages 388–395.

Ngoc-Quang Luong, Laurent Besacier, and Benjamin Lecouteux. 2014. LIG system for word level QE task at WMT14. pages 335–341.

André Martins, Ramon Astudillo, Chris Hokamp, and Fabio Kepler. 2016. Unbabel's participation in the WMT16 word-level translation quality estimation shared task. pages 806–811.

André F.T. Martins, Marcin Junczys-Dowmunt, Fabio N. Kepler, Ramn Astudillo, Chris Hokamp, and Roman Grundkiewicz. 2017. Pushing the limits of translation quality estimation. *Transactions of the Association for Computational Linguistics*, 5:205–218.

B Moser-Mercer, A Knzli, and M Korac. 1998. Prolonged turns in interpreting: Effects on quality, physiological and psychological stress. In *INTERPRETING*, pages 47–65.

Kishore Papineni, Salim Roukos, Todd Ward, and Wei-Jing Zhu. 2002. BLEU: a method for automatic evaluation of machine translation. In *Proc. ACL*, pages 311–318.

Alessandra Riccardi. 2005. On the evolution of interpreting strategies in simultaneous interpreting. *Meta*, 50(2):753–767.

Hiroaki Shimizu, Graham Neubig, Sakriani Sakti, Tomoki Toda, and Satoshi Nakamura. 2013. Constructing a speech translation system using simultaneous interpretation data. In *Proc. IWSLT*, pages 212–218.

Lucia Specia, Gustavo Paetzold, and Carolina Scarton. 2015. Multi-level translation quality prediction with quest++. In *Proc. ACL*, pages 115–120.

Lucia Specia, Dhwaj Raj, and Marco Turchi. 2010. Machine translation evaluation versus quality estimation. *Machine Translation*, 24(1):39–50.

Vivek Kumar Rangarajan Sridhar, John Chen, Srinivas Bangalore, Andrej Ljolje, and Rathinavelu Chengalvarayan. 2013. Segmentation strategies for streaming speech translation. In *Proc. NAACL*, pages 230–238.

Keh-Yih Su, Ming-Wen Wu, and Jing-Shin Chang. A new quantitative quality measure for machine translation systems. In *Proceedings of the 14th Conference on Computational Linguistics*.

Nicola Ueffing and Hermann Ney. 2007. Word-level confidence estimation for machine translation. *Computational Linguistics*, 33(1):9–40.

Polyglot Semantic Role Labeling

Phoebe Mulcaire♡   **Swabha Swayamdipta**◇   **Noah A. Smith**♡
♡Paul G. Allen School of Computer Science & Engineering, University of Washington
◇School of Computer Science, Carnegie Mellon University
{pmulc,nasmith}@cs.washington.edu, swabha@cs.cmu.edu

Abstract

Previous approaches to multilingual semantic dependency parsing treat languages independently, without exploiting the similarities between semantic structures across languages. We experiment with a new approach where we combine resources from a pair of languages in the CoNLL 2009 shared task (Hajič et al., 2009) to build a *polyglot* semantic role labeler. Notwithstanding the absence of parallel data, and the dissimilarity in annotations between languages, our approach results in an improvement in SRL performance on multiple languages over a monolingual baseline. Analysis of the polyglot model shows it to be advantageous in lower-resource settings.

1 Introduction

The standard approach to multilingual NLP is to design a single architecture, but tune and train a separate model for each language. While this method allows for customizing the model to the particulars of each language and the available data, it also presents a problem when little data is available: extensive language-specific annotation is required. The reality is that most languages have very little annotated data for most NLP tasks.

Ammar et al. (2016a) found that using training data from multiple languages annotated with Universal Dependencies (Nivre et al., 2016), and represented using multilingual word vectors, outperformed monolingual training. Inspired by this, we apply the idea of training one model on multiple languages—which we call polyglot training— to PropBank-style semantic role labeling (SRL). We train several parsers for each language in the CoNLL 2009 dataset (Hajič et al., 2009): a tra-

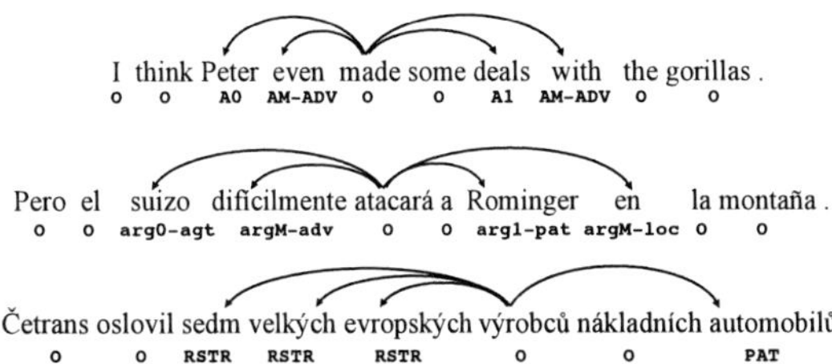

Figure 1: Example predicate-argument structures from English, Spanish, and Czech. Note that the argument labels are different in each language.

ditional monolingual version, and variants which additionally incorporate supervision from English portion of the dataset. To our knowledge, this is the first multilingual SRL approach to combine supervision from several languages.

The CoNLL 2009 dataset includes seven different languages, allowing study of trends across the same. Unlike the Universal Dependencies dataset, however, the semantic label spaces are entirely language-specific, making our task more challenging. Nonetheless, the success of polyglot training in this setting demonstrates that sharing of statistical strength across languages does not depend on explicit alignment in annotation conventions, and can be done simply through parameter sharing. We show that polyglot training can result in better labeling accuracy than a monolingual parser, *especially* for low-resource languages. We find that even a simple combination of data is as effective as more complex kinds of polyglot training. We include a breakdown into label categories of the differences between the monolingual and polyglot models. Our findings indicate that polyglot training consistently improves label accuracy for common labels.

Proceedings of the 56th Annual Meeting of the Association for Computational Linguistics (Short Papers), pages 667–672
Melbourne, Australia, July 15 - 20, 2018. ©2018 Association for Computational Linguistics

	# sentences	# sentences w/ 1+ predicates	# predicates
CAT	13200	12876	37444
CES	38727	38579	414133
DEU	36020	14282	17400
ENG	39279	37847	179014
JPN	4393	4344	25712
SPA	14329	13836	43828
ZHO	22277	21073	102827

Table 1: Train data statistics. Languages are indicated with ISO 639-3 codes.

2 Data

We evaluate our system on the semantic role labeling portion of the CoNLL-2009 shared task (Hajič et al., 2009), on all seven languages, namely Catalan, Chinese, Czech, English, German, Japanese and Spanish. For each language, certain tokens in each sentence in the dataset are marked as predicates. Each predicate takes as arguments other words in the same sentence, their relationship marked by labeled dependency arcs. Sentences may contain no predicates.

Despite the consistency of this format, there are significant differences between the training sets across languages.[1] English uses PropBank role labels (Palmer et al., 2005). Catalan, Chinese, English, German, and Spanish include (but are not limited to) labels such as "arg_0-agt" (for "agent") or "A_0" that may correspond to some degree to each other and to the English roles. Catalan and Spanish share most labels (being drawn from the same source corpus, AnCora; Taulé et al., 2008), and English and German share some labels. Czech and Japanese each have their own distinct sets of argument labels, most of which do not have clear correspondences to English or to each other.

We also note that, due to semi-automatic projection of annotations to construct the German dataset, more than half of German sentences do *not* include labeled predicate and arguments. Thus while German has almost as many sentences as Czech, it has by far the fewest training examples (predicate-argument structures); see Table 1.

---

[1]This is expected, as the datasets were annotated independently under diverse formalisms and only later converted into CoNLL format (Hajič et al., 2009).

3 Model

Given a sentence with a marked predicate, the CoNLL 2009 shared task requires disambiguation of the sense of the predicate, and labeling all its dependent arguments. The shared task assumed predicates have already been identified, hence we do not handle the predicate identification task.

Our basic model adapts the span-based dependency SRL model of He et al. (2017). This adaptation treats the dependent arguments as argument spans of length 1. Additionally, BIO consistency constraints are removed from the original model—each token is tagged simply with the argument label or an empty tag. A similar approach has also been proposed by Marcheggiani et al. (2017).

The input to the model consists of a sequence of pretrained embeddings for the surface forms of the sentence tokens. Each token embedding is also concatenated with a vector indicating whether the word is a predicate or not. Since the part-of-speech tags in the CoNLL 2009 dataset are based on a different tagset for each language, we do not use these. Each training instance consists of the annotations for a single predicate. These representations are then passed through a deep, multi-layer bidirectional LSTM (Graves, 2013; Hochreiter and Schmidhuber, 1997) with highway connections (Srivastava et al., 2015).

We use the hidden representations produced by the deep biLSTM for both argument labeling and predicate sense disambiguation in a multitask setup; this is a modification to the models of He et al. (2017), who did not handle predicate senses, and of Marcheggiani et al. (2017), who used a separate model. These two predictions are made independently, with separate softmaxes over different last-layer parameters; we then combine the losses for each task when training. For predicate sense disambiguation, since the predicate has been identified, we choose from a small set of valid predicate senses as the tag for that token. This set of possible senses is selected based on the training data: we map from lemmatized tokens to predicates and from predicates to the set of all senses of that predicate. Most predicates are only observed to have one or two corresponding senses, making the set of available senses at test time quite small (less than five senses/predicate on average across all languages). If a particular lemma was not observed in training, we heuristically predict it as the first sense of that predicate. For Czech and

Japanese, the predicate sense annotation is simply the lemmatized token of the predicate, giving a one-to-one predicate-"sense" mapping.

For argument labeling, every token in the sentence is assigned one of the argument labels, or NULL if the model predicts it is not an argument to the indicated predicate.

3.1 Monolingual Baseline

We use pretrained word embeddings as input to the model. For each of the shared task languages, we produced GloVe vectors (Pennington et al., 2014) from the news, web, and Wikipedia text of the Leipzig Corpora Collection (Goldhahn et al., 2012).[2] We trained 300-dimensional vectors, then reduced them to 100 dimensions with principal component analysis for efficiency.

3.2 Simple Polyglot Sharing

In the first polyglot variant, we consider multilingual sharing between each language and English by using pretrained *multilingual* embeddings. This polyglot model is trained on the union of annotations in the two languages. We use stratified sampling to give the two datasets equal effective weight in training, and we ensure that every training instance is seen at least once per epoch.

Pretrained multilingual embeddings. The basis of our polyglot training is the use of pretrained multilingual word vectors, which allow representing entirely distinct vocabularies (such as the tokens of different languages) in a shared representation space, allowing crosslingual learning (Klementiev et al., 2012). We produced multilingual embeddings from the monolingual embeddings using the method of Ammar et al. (2016b): for each non-English language, a small crosslingual dictionary and canonical correlation analysis was used to find a transformation of the non-English vectors into the English vector space (Faruqui and Dyer, 2014).

Unlike multilingual word representations, argument label sets are disjoint between language pairs, and correspondences are not clearly defined. Hence, we use separate label representations for each language's labels. Similarly, while (for example) ENG:look and SPA:mira may be semantically connected, the senses `look.01` and `mira.01` may not correspond. Hence, predicate sense representations are also language-specific.

3.3 Language Identification

In the second variant, we concatenate a language ID vector to each multilingual word embedding and predicate indicator feature in the input representation. This vector is randomly initialized and updated in training. These additional parameters provide a small degree of language-specificity in the model, while still sharing most parameters.

3.4 Language-Specific LSTMs

This third variant takes inspiration from the "frustratingly easy" architecture of Daume III (2007) for domain adaptation. In addition to processing every example with a shared biLSTM as in previous models, we add language-specific biLSTMs that are trained only on the examples belonging to one language. Each of these language-specific biLSTMs is two layers deep, and is combined with the shared biSLTM in the input to the third layer. This adds a greater degree of language-specific processing while still sharing representations across languages. It also uses the language identification vector and multilingual word vectors in the input.

4 Experiments

We present our results in Table 2. We observe that simple polyglot training improves over monolingual training, with the exception of Czech, where we observe no change in performance. The languages with the fewest training examples (German, Japanese, Catalan) show the most improvement, while large-dataset languages such as Czech or Chinese see little or no improvement (Figure 2).

The language ID model performs inconsistently; it is better than the simple polyglot model in some cases, including Czech, but not in all. The language-specific LSTMs model performs best on a few languages, such as Catalan and Chinese, but worst on others. While these results may reflect differences between languages in the optimal amount of crosslingual sharing, we focus on the simple polyglot results in our analysis, which sufficiently demonstrate that polyglot training can improve performance over monolingual training.

We also report performance of state-of-the-art systems in each of these languages, all of which make explicit use of syntactic features, Marcheg-

---

²For English we used the vectors provided on the GloVe website `nlp.stanford.edu/projects/glove/`.

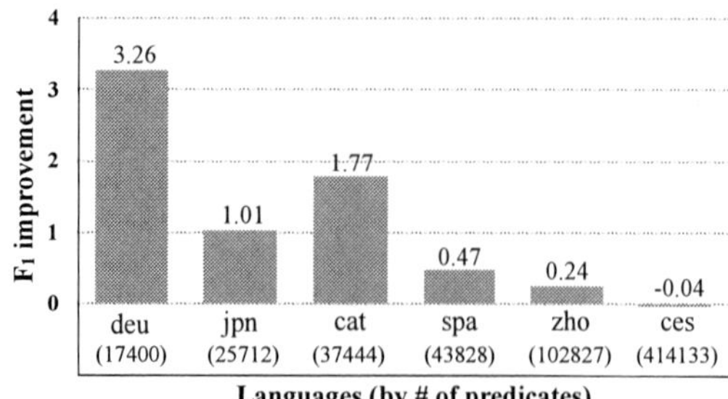

Figure 2: Improvement in absolute F_1 with polyglot training with addition of English. Languages are sorted in order of increasing number of predicates in the training set.

giani et al. (2017) excepted. While this results in better performance on many languages, our model has the advantage of not relying on a syntactic parser, and is hence more applicable to languages with lower resources. However, the results suggest that syntactic information is critical for strong performance on German, which has the fewest predicates and thus the least semantic annotation for a semantics-only model to learn from. Nevertheless, our baseline is on par with the best published scores for Chinese, and it shows strong performance on most languages.

Label-wise results. Table 3 gives the F_1 scores for individual label categories in the Catalan and Spanish datasets, as an illustration of the larger trend. In both languages, we find a small but consistent improvement in the most common label categories (e.g., arg_1 and arg_M). Less common label categories are sensitive to small changes in performance; they have the largest changes in F_1 in absolute value, but without a consistent direction. This could be attributed to the addition of English data, which improves learning of representations that are useful for the most common labels, but is essentially a random perturbation for the rarer ones. This pattern is seen across languages, and consistently results in overall gains from polyglot training.

One exception is in Czech, where polyglot training reduces accuracy on several common argument labels, e.g., PAT and LOC. While the effect sizes are small (consistent with other languages), the overall F_1 score on Czech decreases slightly in the polyglot condition. It may be that the Czech dataset is too large to make use of the comparatively small amount of English data, or that differences in the annotation schemes prevent

effective crosslingual transfer.

Future work on language pairs that do not include English could provide further insights. Catalan and Spanish, for example, are closely related and use the same argument label set (both being drawn from the AnCora corpus) which would allow for sharing output representations as well as input tokens and parameters.

Polyglot English results. For each language pair, we also evaluated the simple polyglot model on the English test set from the CoNLL 2009 shared task (Table 4). English SRL consistently benefits from polyglot training, with an increase of 0.25–0.7 absolute F_1 points, depending on the language. Surprisingly, Czech provides the smallest improvement, despite the large amount of data added; the absence of crosslingual transfer in both directions for the English-Czech case, breaking the pattern seen in other languages, could therefore be due to differences in annotation rather than questions of dataset size.

Labeled vs. unlabeled F_1. Table 5 provides unlabeled F_1 scores for each language pair. As can be seen here, the unlabeled F_1 improvements are generally positive but small, indicating that polyglot training can help both in structure prediction and labeling of arguments. The pattern of seeing the largest improvements on the languages with the smallest datasets generally holds here: the largest F_1 gains are in German and Catalan, followed by Japanese, with minimal or no improvement elsewhere.

5 Related Work

Recent improvements in multilingual SRL can be attributed to neural architectures. Swayamdipta et al. (2016) present a transition-based stack LSTM model that predicts syntax and semantics jointly, as a remedy to the reliance on pipelined models. Guo et al. (2016) and Roth and Lapata (2016) use deep biLSTM architectures which use syntactic information to guide the composition. Marcheggiani et al. (2017) use a simple LSTM model over word tokens to tag semantic dependencies, like our model. Their model predicts a token's label based on the combination of the token vector and the predicate vector, and saw benefits from using POS tags, both improvements that could be added to our model. Marcheggiani and Titov (2017) apply the recently-developed graph

Model	CAT	CES	DEU	ENG	JPN	SPA	ZHO
Marcheggiani et al. (2017)	-	86.00	-	87.60	-	80.30	81.20
Best previously reported	*80.32*	86.00	*80.10*	*89.10*	*78.15*	*80.50*	*81.20*
Monolingual	77.31	84.87	66.71	86.54	74.99	75.98	81.26
+ ENG(simple polyglot)	79.08	84.82	69.97	–	76.00	76.45	81.50
+ ENG(language ID)	79.05	85.14	69.49	–	75.77	77.32	81.42
+ ENG(language-specific LSTMs)	79.45	84.78	68.30	–	75.88	76.86	81.89

Table 2: Semantic F_1 scores (including predicate sense disambiguation) on the CoNLL 2009 dataset. State of the art for Catalan and Japanese is from Zhao et al. (2009), for German and Spanish from Roth and Lapata (2016), for English and Chinese from Marcheggiani and Titov (2017). Italics indicate use of syntax.

	arg_0	arg_1	arg_2	arg_3	arg_4	arg_L	arg_M
Gold label count (CAT)	2117	4296	1713	61	71	49	2968
Monolingual CAT F_1	82.06	79.06	68.95	28.89	42.42	39.51	60.85
+ ENG improvement	+2.75	+2.58	+4.53	+18.17	+9.81	+1.35	+1.10
Gold label count (SPA)	2438	4295	1677	49	82	46	3237
Monolingual SPA F_1	82.44	77.93	70.24	28.89	41.15	22.50	58.89
+ ENG improvement	+0.37	+0.43	+1.35	-3.40	-3.48	+4.01	+1.26

Table 3: Per-label breakdown of F_1 scores for Catalan and Spanish. These numbers reflect labels for each argument; the combination is different from the overall semantic F_1, which includes predicate sense disambiguation.

ENG-only	+CAT	+CES	+DEU	+JPN	+SPA	+ZHO
86.54	86.79	87.07	87.07	87.11	87.24	87.10

Table 4: Semantic F_1 scores on the English test set for each language pair.

Model	CAT	CES	DEU	ENG	JPN	SPA	ZHO
Monolingual	93.92	91.92	87.95	92.87	85.55	93.61	87.93
+ ENG	94.09	91.97	89.01	–	86.17	93.65	87.90

Table 5: Unlabeled semantic F_1 scores on the CoNLL 2009 dataset.

convolutional networks to SRL, obtaining state of the art results on English and Chinese. All of these approaches are orthogonal to ours, and might benefit from polyglot training.

Other polyglot models have been proposed for semantics. Richardson et al. (2018) train on multiple (natural language)-(programming language) pairs to improve a model that translates API text into code signature representations. Duong et al. (2017) treat English and German semantic parsing as a multi-task learning problem and saw improvement over monolingual baselines, especially for small datasets. Most relevant to our work is Johannsen et al. (2015), which trains a polyglot model for *frame*-semantic parsing. In addition to sharing features with multilingual word vectors, they use them to find word translations of target language words for additional lexical features.

6 Conclusion

In this work, we have explored a straightforward method for polyglot training in SRL: use multilingual word vectors and combine training data across languages. This allows sharing without crosslingual alignments, shared annotation, or parallel data. We demonstrate that a polyglot model can outperform a monolingual one for semantic analysis, particularly for languages with less data.

Acknowledgments

We thank Luke Zettlemoyer, Luheng He, and the anonymous reviewers for helpful comments and feedback. This research was supported in part by the Defense Advanced Research Projects Agency (DARPA) Information Innovation Office (I2O) under the Low Resource Languages for Emergent Incidents (LORELEI) program issued by DARPA/I2O under contract HR001115C0113 to BBN. Views expressed are those of the authors alone.

References

Waleed Ammar, George Mulcaire, Miguel Ballesteros, Chris Dyer, and Noah Smith. 2016a. Many languages, one parser. *Transactions of the Association for Computational Linguistics*, 4:431–444.

Waleed Ammar, George Mulcaire, Yulia Tsvetkov, Guillaume Lample, Chris Dyer, and Noah A Smith. 2016b. Massively multilingual word embeddings. arXiv:1602.01925.

Hal Daume III. 2007. Frustratingly easy domain adaptation. In *Proceedings of ACL*.

Long Duong, Hadi Afshar, Dominique Estival, Glen Pink, Philip Cohen, and Mark Johnson. 2017. Multilingual semantic parsing and code-switching. In *Proceedings of CoNLL*.

Manaal Faruqui and Chris Dyer. 2014. Improving vector space word representations using multilingual correlation. In *Proceedings of EACL*.

Dirk Goldhahn, Thomas Eckart, and Uwe Quasthoff. 2012. Building large monolingual dictionaries at the Leipzig corpora collection: From 100 to 200 languages. In *Proceedings of LREC*.

Alex Graves. 2013. Generating sequences with recurrent neural networks. arXiv:1308.0850.

Jiang Guo, Wanxiang Che, Haifeng Wang, Ting Liu, and Jun Xu. 2016. A unified architecture for semantic role labeling and relation classification. In *Proceedings of COLING*.

Jan Hajič, Massimiliano Ciaramita, Richard Johansson, Daisuke Kawahara, Maria Antònia Martí, Lluís Màrquez, Adam Meyers, Joakim Nivre, Sebastian Padó, Jan Štěpánek, et al. 2009. The conll-2009 shared task: Syntactic and semantic dependencies in multiple languages. In *Proceedings of CoNLL*.

Luheng He, Kenton Lee, Mike Lewis, and Luke Zettlemoyer. 2017. Deep semantic role labeling: What works and whats next. In *Proceedings of ACL*.

Sepp Hochreiter and Jürgen Schmidhuber. 1997. Long short-term memory. *Neural Computation*, 9(8):1735–1780.

Anders Johannsen, Héctor Martínez Alonso, and Anders Søgaard. 2015. Any-language frame-semantic parsing. In *Proceedings of EMNLP*.

Alexandre Klementiev, Ivan Titov, and Binod Bhattarai. 2012. Inducing crosslingual distributed representations of words. *Proceedings of COLING*.

Diego Marcheggiani, Anton Frolov, and Ivan Titov. 2017. A simple and accurate syntax-agnostic neural model for dependency-based semantic role labeling. arXiv:1701.02593.

Diego Marcheggiani and Ivan Titov. 2017. Encoding sentences with graph convolutional networks for semantic role labeling. In *Proceedings of EMNLP*, Copenhagen, Denmark.

Joakim Nivre, Marie-Catherine de Marneffe, Filip Ginter, Yoav Goldberg, Jan Hajic, Christopher D. Manning, Ryan T. McDonald, Slav Petrov, Sampo Pyysalo, Natalia Silveira, Reut Tsarfaty, and Daniel Zeman. 2016. Universal dependencies v1: A multilingual treebank collection. In *Proceedings of LREC*.

Martha Palmer, Daniel Gildea, and Paul Kingsbury. 2005. The Proposition Bank: An annotated corpus of semantic roles. *Computational Linguistics*, 31(1):71–106.

Jeffrey Pennington, Richard Socher, and Christopher D. Manning. 2014. GloVe: Global vectors for word representation. In *Proceedings of EMNLP*.

Kyle Richardson, Jonathan Berant, and Jonas Kuhn. 2018. Polyglot semantic parsing in APIs. In *Proceedings of NAACL*.

Michael Roth and Mirella Lapata. 2016. Neural semantic role labeling with dependency path embeddings. arXiv:1605.07515.

Rupesh Kumar Srivastava, Klaus Greff, and Jürgen Schmidhuber. 2015. Training very deep networks. In *NIPS*.

Swabha Swayamdipta, Miguel Ballesteros, Chris Dyer, and Noah A. Smith. 2016. Greedy, joint syntactic-semantic parsing with stack LSTMs. In *Proceedings of CoNLL*.

Mariona Taulé, M. Antònia Martí, and Marta Recasens. 2008. AnCora: Multilevel annotated corpora for Catalan and Spanish. In *Proceedings of LREC*.

Hai Zhao, Wenliang Chen, Jun'ichi Kazama, Kiyotaka Uchimoto, and Kentaro Torisawa. 2009. Multilingual dependency learning: Exploiting rich features for tagging syntactic and semantic dependencies. In *Proceedings of CoNLL*.

Learning Cross-lingual Distributed Logical Representations
for Semantic Parsing

Yanyan Zou and **Wei Lu**
Singapore University of Technology and Design
8 Somapah Road, Singapore, 487372
yanyan_zou@mymail.sutd.edu.sg, luwei@sutd.edu.sg

Abstract

With the development of several multilingual datasets used for semantic parsing, recent research efforts have looked into the problem of learning semantic parsers in a multilingual setup (Duong et al., 2017; Susanto and Lu, 2017a). However, how to improve the performance of a monolingual semantic parser for a specific language by leveraging data annotated in different languages remains a research question that is under-explored. In this work, we present a study to show how learning distributed representations of the logical forms from data annotated in different languages can be used for improving the performance of a monolingual semantic parser. We extend two existing monolingual semantic parsers to incorporate such cross-lingual distributed logical representations as features. Experiments show that our proposed approach is able to yield improved semantic parsing results on the standard multilingual GeoQuery dataset.

1 Introduction

Semantic parsing, one of the classic tasks in natural language processing (NLP), has been extensively studied in the past few years (Zettlemoyer and Collins, 2005; Wong and Mooney, 2006, 2007; Liang et al., 2011; Kwiatkowski et al., 2011; Artzi et al., 2015). With the development of datasets annotated in different languages, learning semantic parsers from such multilingual datasets also attracted attention of researchers (Susanto and Lu, 2017a). However, how to make use of such cross-lingual data to perform cross-lingual semantic parsing – using data annotated for one language to help improve the performance of another lan-

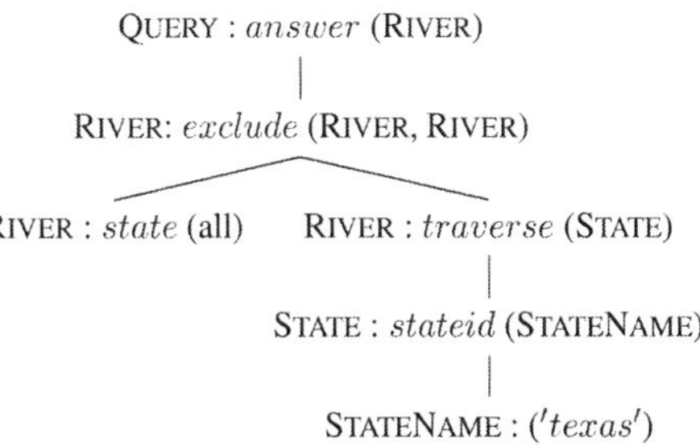

English: which rivers do not run through texas ?
German: welche flüsse fliessen nicht durch texas ?

Figure 1: An example of two semantically equivalent sentences (below) and their tree-shaped semantic representation (above).

guage remains a research question that is largely under-explored.

Prior work (Chan et al., 2007) shows that semantically equivalent words coming from different languages may contain shared semantic level information, which will be helpful for certain semantic processing tasks. In this work, we propose a simple method to learn the distributed representations for output structured semantic representations which allow us to capture cross-lingual features. Specifically, following previous work (Wong and Mooney, 2006; Jones et al., 2012; Susanto and Lu, 2017b), we adopt a commonly used tree-shaped form as the underlying meaning representation where each tree node is a semantic unit. Our objective is to learn for each semantic unit a distributed representation useful for semantic parsing, based on multilingual datasets. Figure 1 depicts an instance of such tree-shaped semantic representations, which correspond to the two semantically equivalent sentences in English and German below it.

For such structured semantics, we consider each semantic unit separately. We learn distributed rep-

673

Proceedings of the 56th Annual Meeting of the Association for Computational Linguistics (Short Papers), pages 673–679
Melbourne, Australia, July 15 - 20, 2018. ©2018 Association for Computational Linguistics

resentations for individual semantic unit based on multilingual datasets where semantic representations are annotated with different languages. Such distributed representations capture shared information cross different languages. We extend two existing monolingual semantic parsers (Lu, 2015; Susanto and Lu, 2017b) to incorporate such cross-lingual features. To the best of our knowledge, this is the first work that exploits cross-lingual embeddings for logical representations for semantic parsing. Our system is publicly available at `http://statnlp.org/research/sp/`.

2 Related Work

Many research efforts on semantic parsing have been made, such as mapping sentences into lambda calculus forms based on CCG (Artzi and Zettlemoyer, 2011; Artzi et al., 2014; Kwiatkowski et al., 2011), modeling dependency-based compositional semantics (Liang et al., 2011; Zhang et al., 2017), or transforming sentences into tree structured semantic representations (Lu, 2015; Susanto and Lu, 2017b). With the development of multilingual datasets, systems for multilingual semantic parsing are also developed. Jie and Lu (2014) employed majority voting to combine outputs from different parsers for certain languages to perform multilingual semantic parsing. Susanto and Lu (2017a) presented an extension of one existing neural parser, SEQ2TREE (Dong and Lapata, 2016), by developing a shared attention mechanism for different languages to conduct multilingual semantic parsing. Such a model allows two types of input signals: single source SL-SINGLE and multi-source SL-MULTI. However, semantic parsing with cross-lingual features has not been explored, while many recent works in various NLP tasks show the effectiveness of shared information cross different languages. Examples include semantic role labeling (Kozhevnikov and Titov, 2013), information extraction (Wang et al., 2013; Pan et al., 2017; Ni et al., 2017), and question answering (Joty et al., 2017), which motivate this work.

Our work involves exploiting distributed output representations for improved structured predictions, which is in line with works of (Srikumar and Manning, 2014; Rocktäschel et al., 2014; Xiao and Guo, 2015). The work of (Rocktäschel et al., 2014) is perhaps the most related to this research. The authors first map first-order logical statements produced by a semantic parser or an information extraction system into expressions in tensor calculus. They then learn low-dimensional embeddings of such statements with the help of a given logical knowledge base consisting of first-order rules so that the learned representations are consistent with these rules. They adopt stochastic gradient descent (SGD) to conduct optimizations. This work learns distributed representations of logical forms from cross-lingual data based on co-occurrence information without relying on external knowledge bases.

3 Approach

3.1 Semantic Parser

In this work, we build our model and conduct experiments on top of the discriminative hybrid tree semantic parser (Lu, 2014, 2015). The parser was designed based on the hybrid tree representation (HT-G) originally introduced in (Lu et al., 2008). The hybrid tree is a joint representation encoding both sentence and semantics that aims to capture the interactions between words and semantic units. A discriminative hybrid tree (HT-D) (Lu, 2014, 2015) learns the optimal latent word-semantics correspondence where every word in the input sentence is associated with a semantic unit. Such a model allows us to incorporate rich features and long-range dependencies. Recently, Susanto and Lu (2017b) extended HT-D by attaching neural architectures, resulting in their neural hybrid tree (HT-D (NN)).

Since the correct correspondence between words and semantics is not explicitly given in the training data, we regard the hybrid tree representation as a latent variable. Formally, for each sentence $\mathbf{n}$ with its semantic representation $\mathbf{m}$ from the training set, we assume the joint representation (a hybrid tree) is $\mathbf{h}$. Now we can define a discriminative log-linear model as follows:

$$P_\Lambda(\mathbf{m}|\mathbf{n}) = \sum_{\mathbf{h} \in \mathcal{H}(\mathbf{n},\mathbf{m})} P_\Lambda(\mathbf{m}, \mathbf{h}|\mathbf{n})$$

$$= \frac{\sum_{\mathbf{h} \in \mathcal{H}(\mathbf{n},\mathbf{m})} e^{F_\Lambda(\mathbf{n},\mathbf{m},\mathbf{h})}}{\sum_{\mathbf{m}',\mathbf{h}' \in \mathcal{H}(\mathbf{n},\mathbf{m}')} e^{F_\Lambda(\mathbf{n},\mathbf{m}',\mathbf{h}'))}} \quad (1)$$

$$F_\Lambda(\mathbf{n}, \mathbf{m}, \mathbf{h})) = \Lambda \cdot \Phi(\mathbf{n}, \mathbf{m}, \mathbf{h})) \quad (2)$$

where $\mathcal{H}(\mathbf{n}, \mathbf{m})$ returns the set of all possible joint representations that contain both $\mathbf{n}$ and $\mathbf{m}$ exactly, and F is a scoring function that is calculated as a dot product between a feature function Φ defined over tuple $(\mathbf{m}, \mathbf{n}, \mathbf{h})$ and a weight vector Λ.

To incorporate neural features, HT-D (NN) defines the following scoring function:

$$F_{\Lambda,\Theta}(\mathbf{n}, \mathbf{m}, \mathbf{h})) = \Lambda \cdot \Phi(\mathbf{n}, \mathbf{m}, \mathbf{h}) + G_{\Theta}(\mathbf{n}, \mathbf{m}, \mathbf{h}) \tag{3}$$

where Θ is the set of parameters of the neural networks and G is the neural scoring function over the $(\mathbf{n},\mathbf{m},\mathbf{h})$ tuple (Susanto and Lu, 2017b). Specifically, the neural features are defined over a fixed-size window surrounding a word in $\mathbf{n}$ paired with its immediately associated semantic unit. Following the work (Susanto and Lu, 2017b), we denote the window size as $J \in \{0, 1, 2\}$.

3.2 Cross-lingual Distributed Semantic Representations

A multilingual dataset used in semantic parsing comes with instances consisting of logical forms annotated with sentences from multiple different languages. In this work, we aim to learn one monolingual semantic parser for each language, while leveraging useful information that can be extracted from other languages. Our setup is as follows. Each time, we train the parser for a target language and regard the other languages as *auxiliary languages*. To learn cross-lingual distributed semantic representations from such data, we first combine all data involving all auxiliary languages to form a large dataset. Next, for each target language, we construct a semantics-word co-occurrence matrix $\mathbf{M} \in R^{m \times n}$ (where m is the number of unique semantic units, n is the number of unique words in the combined dataset). Each entry is the number of co-occurrences for a particular (semantic unit-word) pair. We will use this matrix to learn a low-dimensional cross-lingual representation for each semantic unit. To do so, we first apply singular value decomposition (SVD) to this matrix, leading to:

$$\mathbf{M} = \mathbf{U\Sigma V}^* \tag{4}$$

where $\mathbf{U} \in R^{m \times m}$ and $\mathbf{V} \in R^{n \times m}$ are unitary matrices, $\mathbf{V}^*$ is the conjugate transpose of $\mathbf{V}$, and $\mathbf{\Sigma} \in R^{m \times m}$ is a diagonal matrix. We truncate the diagonal matrix $\mathbf{\Sigma}$ and left multiply it with $\mathbf{U}$:

$$\mathbf{U\tilde{\Sigma}} \tag{5}$$

where $\tilde{\mathbf{\Sigma}} \in R^{m \times d}$ is a matrix that consists of only the left d columns of $\mathbf{\Sigma}$, containing the d largest

	Rank (d)	F		Rank (d)	F
English	30	88.3	Chinese	10	80.0
Thai	20	85.8	Indonesian	30	88.3
German	30	78.3	Swedish	20	83.3
Greek	10	81.7	Farsi	10	76.7

Table 1: Performance on development set. F: F1-measure (%).

singular values. We leave the rank d as a hyperparameter. Each row in the above matrix is a d-dimensional vector, giving a low-dimensional representation for one semantic unit. Such distributed output representations can be readily used as continuous features in $\Phi(\mathbf{n}, \mathbf{m}, \mathbf{h})$.

3.3 Training and Decoding

During the training process, we optimize the objective function defined over the training set as:

$$\mathcal{L}(\Lambda, \Theta) = \sum_i \log \sum_{\mathbf{h} \in \mathcal{H}(\mathbf{n}_i, \mathbf{m}_i)} e^{F_{\Lambda,\Theta}(\mathbf{n}_i, \mathbf{m}_i, \mathbf{h})}$$
$$- \sum_i \log \sum_{\mathbf{m}', \mathbf{h}' \in \mathcal{H}(\mathbf{n}_i, \mathbf{m}')} e^{F_{\Lambda,\Theta}(\mathbf{n}_i, \mathbf{m}', \mathbf{h}')} \tag{6}$$

We follow the dynamic programming approach used in (Susanto and Lu, 2017b) to perform efficient inference, and follow the same optimization strategy as described there.

In the decoding phase, we are given a new input sentence $\mathbf{n}$, and find the optimal semantic tree $\mathbf{m}^*$:

$$\mathbf{m}^* = \underset{\mathbf{m}, \mathbf{h} \in \mathcal{H}(\mathbf{n}, \mathbf{m})}{\arg\max} F_{\Lambda,\Theta}(\mathbf{n}, \mathbf{m}, \mathbf{h}) \tag{7}$$

Again, the above equation can be efficiently computed by dynamic programming (Susanto and Lu, 2017b).

4 Experiments and Results

4.1 Datasets and Settings

We evaluate our approach on the standard Geo-Query dataset annotated in eight languages (Wong and Mooney, 2006; Jones et al., 2012; Susanto and Lu, 2017b). We follow a standard practice for evaluations which has been adopted in the literature (Lu, 2014, 2015; Susanto and Lu, 2017b). Specifically, to evaluate the proposed model, predicted outputs are transformed into Prolog queries. An output is considered as correct if answers that queries retrieve from GeoQuery database are the same as the gold ones . The dataset consists of 880 instances. In all experiments, we follow the experimental settings and procedures in (Lu, 2014,

		English		Thai		German		Greek		Chinese		Indonesian		Swedish		Farsi	
		Acc.	*F*	*Acc.*	*F*	*Acc.*	*F*	*Acc.*	*F*	*Acc.*	*F*	*Acc.*	*F*	*Acc.*	*F*	*Acc.*	*F*
WASP		71.1	77.7	71.4	75.0	65.7	74.9	70.7	78.6	48.2	51.6	74.6	**79.8**	63.9	71.5	46.8	54.1
HT-G		76.8	81.0	73.6	76.7	62.1	68.5	69.3	74.6	56.1	58.4	66.4	72.8	61.4	70.5	51.8	58.6
UBL-S		82.1	82.1	66.4	66.4	75.0	75.0	73.6	73.7	63.8	63.8	73.8	73.8	78.1	78.1	64.4	64.4
TREETRANS		79.3	79.3	78.2	78.2	74.6	74.6	75.4	75.4	-	-	-	-	-	-	-	-
SEQ2TREE†		84.5	-	71.9	-	70.3	-	73.1	-	73.3	-	**80.7**	-	**80.8**	-	70.5	-
SL-SINGLE †		83.5	-	72.1	-	69.3	-	74.2	-	74.9	-	79.8	-	77.5	-	72.2	-
HT-D		**86.8**	**86.8**	80.7	80.7	**75.7**	**75.7**	79.3	79.3	76.1	76.1	75.0	75.0	79.3	**79.3**	73.9	73.9
HT-D (+O)		86.1	86.1	**81.1**	**81.1**	73.6	73.6	**81.4**	**81.4**	**77.9**	**77.9**	79.6	79.6	79.3	**79.3**	**75.7**	**75.7**
HT-D (NN)	J=0	87.9	87.9	82.1	82.1	75.7	75.7	81.1	81.1	76.8	76.8	76.1	76.1	81.1	81.1	75.0	75.0
HT-D (NN)	J=1	88.6	88.6	84.6	84.6	**76.8**	**76.8**	79.6	79.6	75.4	75.4	78.6	78.6	82.9	82.9	76.1	76.1
HT-D (NN)	J=2	**90.0**	**90.0**	82.1	82.1	73.9	73.9	80.7	80.7	81.1	81.1	81.8	81.8	**83.9**	**83.9**	74.6	74.6
HT-D (NN+O)	J=0	86.1	86.1	83.6	83.6	73.9	73.9	82.1	82.1	77.9	77.9	81.1	81.1	82.1	82.1	74.6	74.6
HT-D (NN+O)	J=1	86.1	86.1	**86.1**	**86.1**	72.5	72.5	80.4	80.4	81.4	81.4	82.5	82.5	82.5	82.5	75.7	75.7
HT-D (NN+O)	J=2	89.6	89.6	84.6	84.6	72.1	72.1	**83.2**	**83.2**	**82.1**	**82.1**	**83.9**	**83.9**	83.6	83.6	**76.8**	**76.8**

Table 2: Performance on multilingual datasets. *Acc.*: accuracy (%), *F*: F1-measure (%). +O: including distributed representations for semantic units as features. († indicates systems that make use of lambda calculus expressions as meaning representations.)

2015; Susanto and Lu, 2017b). In particular, we use 600 instances for training and 280 for test and set the maximum optimization iteration to 150. In order to tune the rank d, we randomly select 80% of the training instances for learning and use the rest 20% for development. We report the value of d for each language in Table 1 and the F1 scores on the development set.

4.2 Results

We compare our models against different existing systems, especially the two baselines HT-D (Lu, 2015) and HT-D (NN) (Susanto and Lu, 2017b) with different word window sizes $J \in \{0, 1, 2\}$.

WASP (Wong and Mooney, 2006) is a semantic parser based on statistical phrase-based machine translation. UBL-S (Kwiatkowski et al., 2010) induced probabilistic CCG grammars with higher-order unification that allowed to construct general logical forms for input sentences. TREETRANS (Jones et al., 2012) is built based on a Bayesian inference framework. We run WASP, UBL-S, HT-G, UBL-S, SEQ2TREE and SL-SINGLE [1] for comparisons. Note that there exist multiple versions of logical representations used in the GEO-QUERY dataset. Specifically, one version is based on lambda calculus expression, and the other is based on the variable free tree-shaped represen-

tation. We use the latter representation in this work, while the SEQ2TREE and SL-SINGLE employ the lambda calculus expression. It was noted in Kwiatkowski et al. (2010); Lu (2014) that evaluations based on these two versions are not directly comparable – the version that uses tree-shaped representations appears to be more challenging. We do not compare against (Jie and Lu, 2014) due to their different setup from ours.[2]

Table 2 shows results that we have conducted on eight different languages. The highest scores are highlighted. We can observe that when distributed logical representations are included, both HT-D and HT-D (NN) can lead to competitive results. Specifically, when such features are included, evaluation results for 5 out of 8 languages get improved.

We found that the shared information cross different languages could guide the model so that it can make more accurate predictions, eliminating certain semantic level ambiguities associated with the semantic units. This is exemplified by a real instance from the English portion of the dataset:

Input:	Which states have a river?
Gold:	$answer(state(loc(river(all))))$
Output:	$answer(state(traverse(river(all))))$
Output (+O):	$answer(state(loc(river(all))))$

---

[1] Note that in Dong and Lapata (2016), they adopted a different split – using 680 instances as training examples and the rest 200 for evaluation. We ran the released source code for SEQ2TREE (Dong and Lapata, 2016) over eight different languages. For each language, we repeated the experiments 3 times with different random seed values, and reported the average results as shown in Table 2 to make comparisons. Likewise, we ran SL-SINGLE following the same procedure.

[2] They trained monolingual semantic parsers. In the evaluation phase, they fed parallel text from different languages to each individual semantic parser, then employed a majority voting based ensemble method to combine predictions. Differently, we train monolingual semantic parsers augmented with cross-lingual distributed semantic information. In the evaluation phase, we only have one monolingual semantic parser. Hence, these two efforts are not directly comparable.

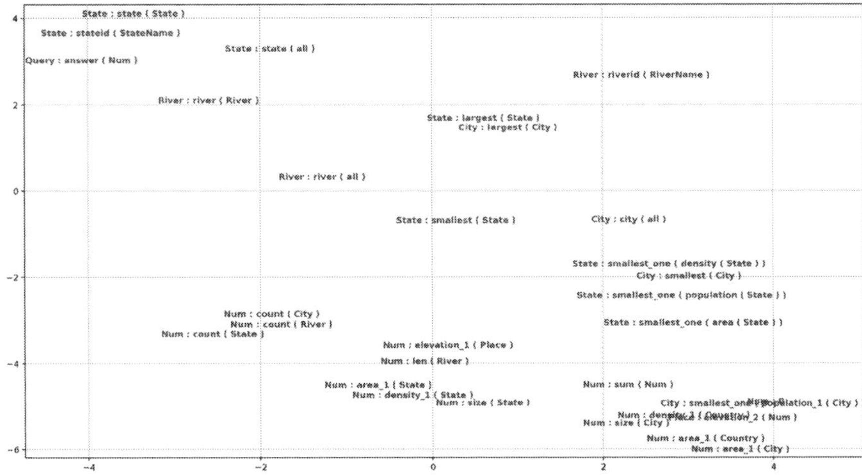

Figure 2: 2-D projection of learned distributed representations for semantics.

Here the input sentence in English is "Which states have a river?", and the correct output is shown below the sentence. Output is the prediction from HT-D (NN) and Output (+O) is the parsing result given by HT-D (NN+O) where the learned cross-lingual representations of semantics are included. We observe that, by introducing our learned cross-lingual semantic information, the system is able to distinguish the two semantically related concepts, *loc* (located in) and *traverse* (traverse), and further make more promising predictions.

Interestingly, for German, the results become much lower when such features are included, indicating such features are not helpful in the learning process when such a language is considered. Reasons for this need further investigations. We note, however, previously it was also reported in the literature that the behavior of the performance associated with this language is different than other languages in the presence of additional features (Lu, 2014).

4.3 Visualizing Output Representations

To qualitatively understand how good the learned distributed representations are, we also visualize the learned distributed representations for semantic units. In the Figure 2, we plot the embeddings of a small set of semantic units which are learned from all languages other than English. Each representation is a 30-dimensional vector and is projected into a 2-dimensional space using Barnes-Hut-SNE (Maaten, 2013) for visualization. In general, we found that semantic units expressing similar meanings tend to appear to-

gether. For example, the two semantic units STATE : *smallest_one* (*density* (STATE)) and STATE : *smallest_one* (*population* (STATE)) share similar representations. However, we also found that occasionally semantic units conveying opposite meanings are also grouped together. This reveals the limitations associated with such a simple co-occurrence based approach for learning distributed representations for logical expressions.

5 Conclusions

In this paper, we empirically show that the distributed representations of logical expressions learned from multilingual datasets for semantic parsing can be exploited to improve the performance of a monolingual semantic parser. Our approach is simple, relying on an SVD over semantics-word co-occurrence matrix for finding such distributed representations for semantic units. Future directions include investigating better ways of learning such distributed representations as well as learning such distributed representations and semantic parsers in a joint manner.

Acknowledgments

We would like to thank the three anonymous ACL reviewers for their thoughtful and constructive comments. We would also like to thank Raymond H. Susanto for his help on this work. This work is supported by Singapore Ministry of Education Academic Research Fund (AcRF) Tier 2 Project MOE2017-T2-1-156, and is partially supported by Singapore Ministry of Education Academic Research Fund (AcRF) Tier 1 SUTDT12015008.

References

Yoav Artzi, Dipanjan Das, and Slav Petrov. 2014. Learning compact lexicons for ccg semantic parsing. In *Proc. of EMNLP.* https://doi.org/10.3115/v1/D14-1134.

Yoav Artzi, Kenton Lee, and Luke S. Zettlemoyer. 2015. Broad-coverage ccg semantic parsing with amr. In *Proc. of EMNLP.* https://doi.org/10.18653/v1/D15-1198.

Yoav Artzi and Luke S. Zettlemoyer. 2011. Bootstrapping semantic parsers from conversations. In *Proc. of EMNLP.* http://www.aclweb.org/anthology/D11-1039.

Yee Seng Chan, Hwee Tou Ng, and David Chiang. 2007. Word sense disambiguation improves statistical machine translation. In *Proc. of ACL.* http://www.aclweb.org/anthology/P07-1005.

Li Dong and Mirella Lapata. 2016. Language to logical form with neural attention. In *Proc. of ACL.* https://doi.org/10.18653/v1/P16-1004.

Long Duong, Hadi Afshar, Dominique Estival, Glen Pink, Philip Cohen, and Mark Johnson. 2017. Multilingual semantic parsing and code-switching. In *Proc. of CoNLL.* https://doi.org/10.18653/v1/K17-1038.

Zhanming Jie and Wei Lu. 2014. Multilingual semantic parsing : Parsing multiple languages into semantic representations. In *Proc. of COLING.* http://www.aclweb.org/anthology/C14-1122.

Bevan Jones, Mark Johnson, and Sharon Goldwater. 2012. Semantic parsing with bayesian tree transducers. In *Proc. of ACL.* http://www.aclweb.org/anthology/P12-1051.

Shafiq Joty, Preslav Nakov, Lluís Màrquez, and Israa Jaradat. 2017. Cross-language learning with adversarial neural networks. In *Proc. of CoNLL.* https://doi.org/10.18653/v1/K17-1024.

Mikhail Kozhevnikov and Ivan Titov. 2013. Cross-lingual transfer of semantic role labeling models. In *Proc. of ACL.* http://www.aclweb.org/anthology/P13-1117.

Tom Kwiatkowski, Luke Zettlemoyer, Sharon Goldwater, and Mark Steedman. 2011. Lexical generalization in ccg grammar induction for semantic parsing. In *Proc. of EMNLP.* http://www.aclweb.org/anthology/D11-1140.

Tom Kwiatkowski, Luke S. Zettlemoyer, Sharon Goldwater, and Mark Steedman. 2010. Inducing probabilistic ccg grammars from logical form with higher-order unification. In *Proc. of EMNLP.* http://www.aclweb.org/anthology/D10-1119.

Percy Liang, Michael Jordan, and Dan Klein. 2011. Learning dependency-based compositional semantics. In *Proc. of ACL.* http://www.aclweb.org/anthology/P11-1060.

Wei Lu. 2014. Semantic parsing with relaxed hybrid trees. In *Proc. of EMNLP.* https://doi.org/10.3115/v1/D14-1137.

Wei Lu. 2015. Constrained semantic forests for improved discriminative semantic parsing. In *Proc. of ACL.* https://doi.org/10.3115/v1/P15-2121.

Wei Lu, Hwee Tou Ng, Wee Sun Lee, and Luke S. Zettlemoyer. 2008. A generative model for parsing natural language to meaning representations. In *Proc. of EMNLP.* https://doi.org/10.3115/1613715.1613815.

Laurens van der Maaten. 2013. Barnes-hut-sne. In *Proc. of ICLR.* https://arxiv.org/pdf/1301.3342.pdf.

Jian Ni, Georgiana Dinu, and Radu Florian. 2017. Weakly supervised cross-lingual named entity recognition via effective annotation and representation projection. In *Proc. of ACL.* https://doi.org/10.18653/v1/P17-1135.

Xiaoman Pan, Boliang Zhang, Jonathan May, Joel Nothman, Kevin Knight, and Heng Ji. 2017. Cross-lingual name tagging and linking for 282 languages. In *Proc. of ACL.* https://doi.org/10.18653/v1/P17-1178.

Tim Rocktäschel, Matko Bošnjak, Sameer Singh, and Sebastian Riedel. 2014. Low-dimensional embeddings of logic. In *Proc. of the ACL 2014 Workshop on Semantic Parsing.* https://doi.org/10.3115/v1/W14-2409.

Vivek Srikumar and Christopher D Manning. 2014. Learning distributed representations for structured output prediction. In *Proc. of NIPS.* http://papers.nips.cc/paper/5323-learning-distributed-representations-for-structured-output-prediction.pdf.

Raymond Hendy Susanto and Wei Lu. 2017a. Neural architectures for multilingual semantic parsing. In *Proc. of ACL.* https://doi.org/10.18653/v1/P17-2007.

Raymond Hendy Susanto and Wei Lu. 2017b. Semantic parsing with neural hybrid trees. In *Proc. of AAAI.* https://www.aaai.org/ocs/index.php/AAAI/AAAI17/paper/view/14843.

Zhigang Wang, Zhixing Li, Juanzi Li, Jie Tang, and Jeff Z. Pan. 2013. Transfer learning based cross-lingual knowledge extraction for wikipedia. In *Proc. of ACL.* http://www.aclweb.org/anthology/P13-1063.

Yuk Wah Wong and Raymond Mooney. 2006. Learning for semantic parsing with statistical machine translation. In *Proc. of NAACL.* https://doi.org/10.3115/1220835.1220891.

Yuk Wah Wong and Raymond Mooney. 2007. Learning synchronous grammars for semantic parsing with lambda calculus. In *Proc. of ACL.* http://www.aclweb.org/anthology/P07-1121.

Min Xiao and Yuhong Guo. 2015. Learning hidden markov models with distributed state representations for domain adaptation. In *Proc. of ACL-IJCNLP*. https://doi.org/10.3115/v1/P15-2086.

Luke S Zettlemoyer and Michael Collins. 2005. Learning to map sentences to logical form: Structured classification with probabilistic categorial grammars. In *Proc. of UAI*. http://dl.acm.org/citation.cfm?id=3020336.3020416.

Yuchen Zhang, Panupong Pasupat, and Percy Liang. 2017. Macro grammars and holistic triggering for efficient semantic parsing. In *Proc. of EMNLP*. https://doi.org/10.18653/v1/d17-1125.

Enhancing Drug-Drug Interaction Extraction from Texts by Molecular Structure Information

Masaki Asada, **Makoto Miwa** and **Yutaka Sasaki**
Computational Intelligence Laboratory
Toyota Technological Institute
2-12-1 Hisakata, Tempaku-ku, Nagoya, Aichi, 468-8511, Japan
{sd17402, makoto-miwa, yutaka.sasaki}@toyota-ti.ac.jp

Abstract

We propose a novel neural method to extract drug-drug interactions (DDIs) from texts using external drug molecular structure information. We encode textual drug pairs with convolutional neural networks and their molecular pairs with graph convolutional networks (GCNs), and then we concatenate the outputs of these two networks. In the experiments, we show that GCNs can predict DDIs from the molecular structures of drugs in high accuracy and the molecular information can enhance text-based DDI extraction by 2.39 percent points in the F-score on the DDIExtraction 2013 shared task data set.

1 Introduction

When drugs are concomitantly administered to a patient, the effects of the drugs may be enhanced or weakened, which may also cause side effects. These kinds of interactions are called Drug-Drug Interactions (DDIs). Several drug databases have been maintained to summarize drug and DDI information such as DrugBank (Law et al., 2014), Therapeutic Target database (Yang et al., 2016), and PharmGKB (Thorn et al., 2013). Automatic DDI extraction from texts is expected to support the maintenance of databases with high coverage and quick update to help medical experts. Deep neural network-based methods have recently drawn a considerable attention (Liu et al., 2016; Sahu and Anand, 2017; Zheng et al., 2017; Lim et al., 2018) since they show state-of-the-art performance without manual feature engineering.

In parallel to the progress in DDI extraction from texts, Graph Convolutional Networks (GCNs) have been proposed and applied to estimate physical and chemical properties of molecular graphs such as solubility and toxicity (Duvenaud et al., 2015; Li et al., 2016; Gilmer et al., 2017).

In this study, we propose a novel method to utilize both textual and molecular information for DDI extraction from texts. We illustrate the overview of the proposed model in Figure 1. We obtain the representations of drug pairs in molecular graph structures using GCNs and concatenate the representations with the representations of the textual mention pairs obtained by convolutional neural networks (CNNs). We trained the molecule-based model using interacting pairs mentioned in the DrugBank database and then trained the entire model using the labeled pairs in the text data set of the DDIExtraction 2013 shared task (SemEval-2013 Task 9) (Segura Bedmar et al., 2013). In the experiment, we show GCNs can predict DDIs from molecular graphs in a high accuracy. We also show molecular information can enhance the performance of DDI extraction from texts in 2.39 percent points in F-score.

The contribution of this paper is three-fold:

- We propose a novel neural method to extract DDIs from texts with the related molecular structure information.
- We apply GCNs to pairwise drug molecules for the first time and show GCNs can predict DDIs between drug molecular structures in a high accuracy.
- We show the molecular information is useful in extracting DDIs from texts.

2 Methods

2.1 Text-based DDI Extraction

Our model for extracting DDIs from texts is based on the CNN model by Zeng et al. (2014). When an input sentence $S = (w_1, w_2, \cdots, w_N)$ is given, We prepare word embedding $\boldsymbol{w}_i^w$ of w_i and word

680

Proceedings of the 56th Annual Meeting of the Association for Computational Linguistics (Short Papers), pages 680–685
Melbourne, Australia, July 15 - 20, 2018. ©2018 Association for Computational Linguistics

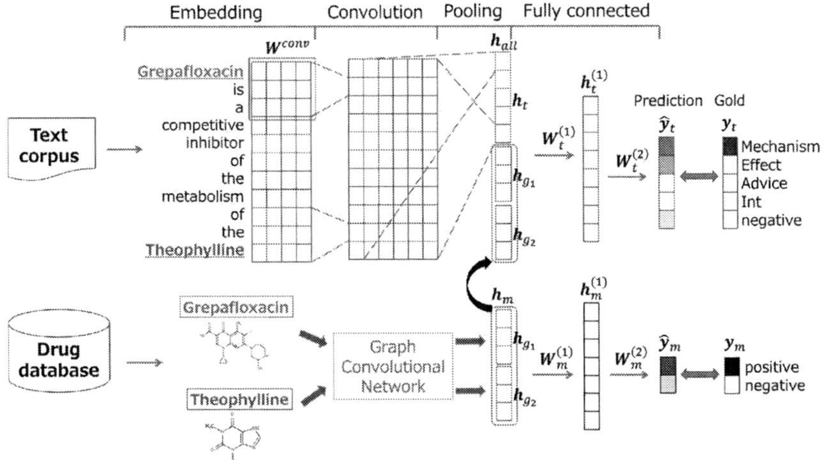

Figure 1: Overview of the proposed model

position embeddings $\boldsymbol{w}_{i,1}^{p}$ and $\boldsymbol{w}_{i,2}^{p}$ that correspond to the relative positions from the first and second target entities, respectively. We concatenate these embeddings as in Equation (1), and we use the resulting vector as the input to the subsequent convolution layer:

$$\boldsymbol{w}_i = [\boldsymbol{w}_i^{w}; \boldsymbol{w}_{i,1}^{p}; \boldsymbol{w}_{i,2}^{p}], \tag{1}$$

where $[;]$ denotes the concatenation. We calculate the expression for each filter j with the window size k_l.

$$
\begin{aligned}
z_{i,l} &= [\boldsymbol{w}_{i-(k_l-1)/2}, \cdots, \boldsymbol{w}_{i-(k_l+1)/2}], &(2)\\
m_{i,j,l} &= \mathrm{relu}(\boldsymbol{W}_j^{conv} \odot \boldsymbol{z}_{i,l} + b^{conv}), &(3)\\
m_{j,l} &= \max_i m_{i,j,l}, &(4)
\end{aligned}
$$

where L is the number of windows, $\boldsymbol{W}_j^{conv}$ and b^{conv} are the weight and bias of CNN, and max indicates max pooling (Boureau et al., 2010).

We convert the output of the convolution layer into a fixed-size vector that represents a textual pair as follows:

$$
\begin{aligned}
m_l &= [m_{1,l}, \cdots, m_{J,l}], &(5)\\
h_t &= [m_1; \ldots; m_L], &(6)
\end{aligned}
$$

where J is the number of filters.

We get a prediction $\hat{y}_t$ by the following fully connected neural networks:

$$
\begin{aligned}
\boldsymbol{h}_t^{(1)} &= \mathrm{relu}(\boldsymbol{W}_t^{(1)}\boldsymbol{h}_t + \boldsymbol{b}_t^{(1)}), &(7)\\
\hat{y}_t &= \mathrm{softmax}(\boldsymbol{W}_t^{(2)}\boldsymbol{h}_t^{(1)} + \boldsymbol{b}_t^{(2)}), &(8)
\end{aligned}
$$

where $\boldsymbol{W}_t^{(1)}$ and $\boldsymbol{W}_t^{(2)}$ are weights and $\boldsymbol{b}_t^{(1)}$ and $\boldsymbol{b}_t^{(2)}$ are bias terms.

2.2 Molecular Structure-based DDI Classification

We represent drug pairs in molecular graph structures using two GCN methods: CNNs for fingerprints (NFP) (Duvenaud et al., 2015) and Gated Graph Neural Networks (GGNN) (Li et al., 2016). They both convert a drug molecule graph G into a fixed size vector $\boldsymbol{h}_g$ by aggregating the representation $\boldsymbol{h}_v^{T}$ of an atom node v in G. We represent atoms as nodes and bonds as edges in the graph.

NFP first obtains the representation $\boldsymbol{h}_v^{t}$ by the following equations (Duvenaud et al., 2015).

$$
\begin{aligned}
\boldsymbol{m}_v^{t+1} &= \boldsymbol{h}_v^{t} + \sum_{w \in N(v)} \boldsymbol{h}_w^{t}, &(9)\\
\boldsymbol{h}_v^{t+1} &= \sigma(\boldsymbol{H}_t^{deg(v)} \boldsymbol{m}_v^{t+1}), &(10)
\end{aligned}
$$

where $\boldsymbol{h}_v^{t}$ is the representation of v in the t-th step, $N(v)$ is the neighbors of v, and $\boldsymbol{H}_t^{deg(v)}$ is a weight parameter. $\boldsymbol{h}_v^{0}$ is initialized by the *atom features* of v. $deg(v)$ is the degree of a node v and σ is a sigmoid function. NFP then acquires the representation of the graph structure

$$\boldsymbol{h}_g = \sum_{v,t} \mathrm{softmax}(\boldsymbol{W}^{t}\boldsymbol{h}_v^{t}), \tag{11}$$

where $\boldsymbol{W}^{t}$ is a weight matrix.

GGNN first obtains the representation $\boldsymbol{h}_v^{t}$ by using Gated Recurrent Unit (GRU)-based recurrent neural networks (Li et al., 2016) as follows:

$$
\begin{aligned}
\boldsymbol{m}_v^{t+1} &= \sum_{w \in N(v)} \boldsymbol{A}_{e_{vw}} \boldsymbol{h}_w^{t} &(12)\\
\boldsymbol{h}_v^{t+1} &= \mathrm{GRU}([\boldsymbol{h}_v^{t}; \boldsymbol{m}_v^{t+1}]), &(13)
\end{aligned}
$$

where $A_{e_{vw}}$ is a weight for the *bond type* of each edge e_{vw}. GGNN then acquires the representation of the graph structure.

$$h_g = \sum_v \sigma(i([h_v^T; h_v^0])) \odot (j(h_v^T)), \qquad (14)$$

where i and j are linear layers and $\odot$ is the element-wise product.

We obtain the representation of a molecular pair by concatenating the molecular graph representations of drugs g_1 and g_2, i.e., $h_m = [h_{g_1}; h_{g_2}]$.

We get a prediction $\hat{y}_m$ as follows:

$$h_m^{(1)} = \mathrm{relu}(W_m^{(1)} h_m + b_m^{(1)}), \qquad (15)$$

$$\hat{y}_m = \mathrm{softmax}(W_m^{(2)} h_m^{(1)} + b_m^{(2)}), \quad (16)$$

where $W_m^{(1)}$ and $W_m^{(2)}$ are weights and $b_m^{(1)}$ and $b_m^{(2)}$ are bias terms.

2.3 DDI Extraction from Texts Using Molecular Structures

We realize the simultaneous use of textual and molecular information by concatenating a text-based and molecule-based vectors: $h_{all} = [h_t; h_m]$. We normalize molecule-based vectors. We then use h_{all} instead of h_t in Equation 7.

In training, we first train the molecular-based DDI classification model. The molecular-based classification is performed by minimizing the loss function $L_m = -\sum y_m \log \hat{y}_m$. We then fix the parameters for GCNs and train text-based DDI extraction model by minimizing the loss function $L_t = -\sum y_t \log \hat{y}_t$.

3 Experimental Settings

In this section, we explain the textual and molecular data and task settings and training settings.

3.1 Text Corpus and Task Setting

We followed the task setting of Task 9.2 in the DDIExtraction 2013 shared task (Segura Bedmar et al., 2013; Herrero-Zazo et al., 2013) for the evaluation. This data set is composed of documents annotated with drug mentions and their four types of interactions: *Mechanism*, *Effect*, *Advice* and *Int*. For the data statistics, please refer to the supplementary materials.

The task is a multi-class classification task, i.e., to classify a given pair of drugs into the four interaction types or no interaction. We evaluated the performance with micro-averaged precision (P),

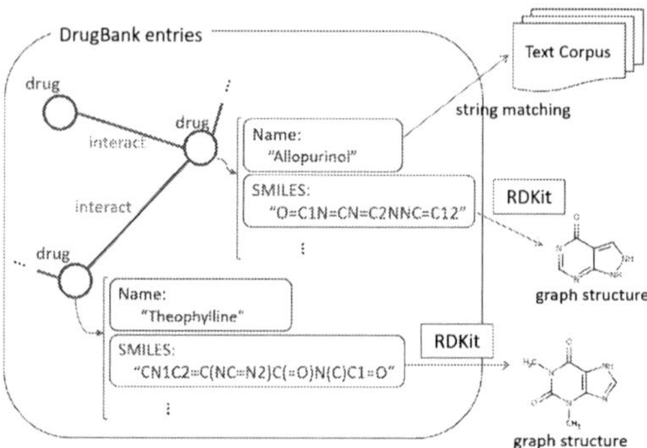

Figure 2: Associating DrugBank entries with texts and molecular graph structures

recall (R), and F-score (F) on all the interaction types. We used the official evaluation script provided by the task organizers.

As preprocessing, we split sentences into words using the GENIA tagger (Tsuruoka et al., 2005). We replaced the drug mentions of the target pair with *DRUG1* and *DRUG2* according to their order of appearance. We also replaced other drug mentions with *DRUGOTHER*. We did not employ negative instance filtering unlike other existing methods, e.g., Liu et al. (2016), since our focus is to evaluate the effect of the molecular information on texts.

We linked mentions in texts to DrugBank entries by string matching. We lowercased the mentions and the names in the entries and chose the entries with the most overlaps. As a result, 92.15% and 93.09% of drug mentions in train and test data set matched the DrugBank entries.

3.2 Data and Task for Molecular Structures

We extracted 255,229 interacting (positive) pairs from DrugBank. We note that, unlike text-based interactions, DrugBank only contains the information of interacting pairs; there are no detailed labels and no information for non-interacting (negative) pairs. We thus generated the same number of pseudo negative pairs by randomly pairing drugs and removing those in positive pairs. To avoid overestimation of the performance, we also deleted drug pairs mentioned in the test set of the text corpus. We split positive and negative pairs into 4:1 for training and test data, and we evaluated the classification accuracy using only the molecular information.

To obtain the graph of a drug molecule, we took

Methods	P	R	F (%)
Liu et al. (2016)	75.29	60.37	67.01
Zheng et al. (2017)	75.9	68.7	71.5
Lim et al. (2018)	74.4	69.3	71.7
Text-only	71.97	68.44	70.16
+ NFP	72.62	71.81	72.21
+ GGNN	73.31	71.81	72.55

Table 1: Evaluation on DDI extraction from texts

DDI Type	Mech.	Effect	Adv.	Int (%)
Text-only	69.52	69.27	79.81	48.18
+ NFP	72.70	72.44	79.56	46.98
+ GGNN	73.83	71.03	81.62	45.83

Table 2: Performance on individual DDI types in F-scores

Methods	Accuracy (%)
NFP	94.19
GGNN	98.00

Table 3: Accuracy of binary classification on DrugBank pairs

Methods	P	R	F	Acc. (%)
NFP	15.56	48.93	23.61	45.78
GGNN	15.11	57.10	23.90	37.72

Table 4: Classification of DDIs in texts by molecular structure-based DDI classification model

as input the SMILES (Weininger, 1988) string encoding of the molecule from DrugBank and then converted it into the graph using RDKit (Landrum, 2016) as illustrated in Figure 2. For the *atom features*, we used randomly embedded vectors for each atoms (i.e., C, O, N, ...). We also used 4 *bond types*: single, double, triple, or aromatic.

3.3 Training Settings

We employed mini-batch training using the Adam optimizer (Kingma and Ba, 2015). We used L2 regularization to avoid over-fitting. We tuned the bias term $b_t^{(2)}$ for negative examples in the final softmax layer. For the hyper-parameters, please refer to the supplementary materials.

We employed pre-trained word embeddings trained by using the word2vec tool (Mikolov et al., 2013) on the 2014 MEDLINE/PubMed baseline distribution. The vocabulary size was 215,840. The embedding of the drugs, i.e., *DRUG1* and *DRUG2* were initialized with the pre-trained embedding of the word *drug*. The embeddings of training words that did not appear in the pre-trained embeddings were initialized with the average of all pre-trained word embeddings. Words that appeared only once in the training data were replaced with an *UNK* word during training, and the embedding of words in the test data set that did not appear in both training and pre-trained embeddings were set to the embedding of the *UNK* word. Word position embeddings are initialized with random values drawn from a uniform distribution.

We set the molecule-based vectors of unmatched entities to zero vectors.

4 Results

Table 1 shows the performance of DDI extraction models. We show the performance without negative instance filtering or ensemble for the fair comparison. We observe the increase of recall and F-score by using molecular information, which results in the state-of-the-art performance with GGNN.

Both GCNs improvements were statistically significant ($p < 0.05$ for NFP and $p < 0.005$ for GGNN) with randomized shuffled test.

Table 2 shows F-scores on individual DDI types. The molecular information improves F-scores especially on type *Mechanism* and *Effect*.

We also evaluated the accuracy of binary classification on DrugBank pairs by using only the molecular information in Table 3. The performance is high, although the accuracy is evaluated on automatically generated negative instances.

Finally, we applied the molecular-based DDI classification model trained on DrugBank to the DDIExtraction 2013 task data set. Since the DrugBank has no detailed labels, we mapped all four types of interactions to positive interactions and evaluated the classification performance. The results in Table 4 show that GCNs produce higher recall than precision and the overall performance is low considering the high performance on DrugBank pairs. This might be because the interactions of drugs are not always mentioned in texts even if the drugs can interact with each other and because hedged DDI mentions are annotated as DDIs in the text data set. We also trained the DDI extraction model only with molecular information by replacing h_{all} with h_m, but the F-scores were quite low ($< 5\%$). These results show that we cannot predict textual relations only with molecular information.

5 Related Work

Various feature-based methods have been proposed during and after the DDIExtraction-2013 shared task (Segura Bedmar et al., 2013). Kim et al. (2015) proposed a two-phase SVM-based approach that employed a linear SVM with rich features that consist of word, word pair, dependency graph, parse tree, and noun phrase-based constrained coordination features. Zheng et al. (2016) proposed a context vector graph kernel to exploit various types of contexts. Raihani and Laachfoubi (2017) also employed a two-phase SVM-based approach using non-linear kernels and they proposed five groups of features: word, drug, pair of drug, main verb and negative sentence features. Our model does not use any features or kernels.

Various neural DDI extraction models have been recently proposed using CNNs and Recurrent Neural Networks (RNNs). Liu et al. (2016) built a CNN-based model based on word and position embeddings. Zheng et al. (2017) proposed a Bidirectional Long Short-Term Memory RNN (Bi-LSTM)-based model with an input attention mechanism, which obtained target drug-specific word representations before the Bi-LSTM. Lim et al. (2018) proposed Recursive neural network-based model with a subtree containment feature and an ensemble method. This model showed the state-of-the-art performance on the DDIExtraction 2013 shared task data set if systems do not use negative instance filtering. These approaches did not consider molecular information, and they can also be enhanced by the molecular information.

Vilar et al. (2017) focused on detecting DDIs from different sources such as pharmacovigilance sources, scientific biomedical literature and social media. They did not use deep neural networks and they did not consider molecular information.

Learning representations of graphs are widely studied in several tasks such as knowledge base completion, drug discovery, and material science (Wang et al., 2017; Gilmer et al., 2017). Several graph convolutional neural networks have been proposed such as NFP (Duvenaud et al., 2015), GGNN (Li et al., 2016), and Molecular Graph Convolutions (Kearnes et al., 2016), but they have not been applied to DDI extraction.

6 Conclusions

We proposed a novel neural method for DDI extraction using both textual and molecular information. The results show that DDIs can be predicted with high accuracy from molecular structure information and that the molecular information can improve DDI extraction from texts by 2.39 percept points in F-score on the data set of the DDIExtraction 2013 shared task.

As future work, we would like to seek the way to model the textual and molecular representations jointly with alleviating the differences in labels. We will also investigate the use of other information in DrugBank.

Acknowledgments

This work was supported by JSPS KAKENHI Grant Number 17K12741.

References

Y-Lan Boureau, Jean Ponce, and Yann LeCun. 2010. A theoretical analysis of feature pooling in visual recognition. In *Proceedings of ICML*. pages 111–118.

David K Duvenaud, Dougal Maclaurin, Jorge Iparraguirre, Rafael Bombarell, Timothy Hirzel, Alan Aspuru-Guzik, and Ryan P Adams. 2015. Convolutional networks on graphs for learning molecular fingerprints. In *Proceedings of NIPS*, pages 2224–2232.

Justin Gilmer, Samuel S. Schoenholz, Patrick F. Riley, Oriol Vinyals, and George E. Dahl. 2017. Neural message passing for quantum chemistry. In *Proceedings of ICML*. pages 1263–1272.

María Herrero-Zazo, Isabel Segura-Bedmar, Paloma Martínez, and Thierry Declerck. 2013. The DDI corpus: An annotated corpus with pharmacological substances and drug–drug interactions. *Journal of biomedical informatics* 46(5):914–920.

Steven Kearnes, Kevin McCloskey, Marc Berndl, Vijay Pande, and Patrick Riley. 2016. Molecular graph convolutions: moving beyond fingerprints. *Journal of computer-aided molecular design* 30(8):595–608.

Sun Kim, Haibin Liu, Lana Yeganova, and W John Wilbur. 2015. Extracting drug–drug interactions from literature using a rich feature-based linear kernel approach. *Journal of biomedical informatics* 55:23–30.

Diederik Kingma and Jimmy Ba. 2015. Adam: A method for stochastic optimization. In *Proceedings of ICLR*.

Greg Landrum. 2016. Rdkit: Open-source cheminformatics.

Vivian Law, Craig Knox, Yannick Djoumbou, Tim Jewison, An Chi Guo, Yifeng Liu, Adam Maciejewski, David Arndt, Michael Wilson, Vanessa Neveu, et al. 2014. DrugBank 4.0: shedding new light on drug metabolism. *Nucleic acids research* 42(D1):D1091–D1097.

Yujia Li, Daniel Tarlow, Marc Brockschmidt, and Richard Zemel. 2016. Gated graph sequence neural networks. In *Proceedings of ICLR*.

Sangrak Lim, Kyubum Lee, and Jaewoo Kang. 2018. Drug drug interaction extraction from the literature using a recursive neural network. *PloS one* 13(1):e0190926.

Shengyu Liu, Buzhou Tang, Qingcai Chen, and Xiaolong Wang. 2016. Drug-drug interaction extraction via convolutional neural networks. *Computational and mathematical methods in medicine* .

Tomas Mikolov, Ilya Sutskever, Kai Chen, Greg S Corrado, and Jeff Dean. 2013. Distributed representations of words and phrases and their compositionality. In *Proceedings of NIPS*. pages 3111–3119.

Anass Raihani and Nabil Laachfoubi. 2017. A rich feature-based kernel approach for drug-drug interaction extraction. *International Journal of Advanced Computer Science and Applications* 8(4):324–330.

Sunil Kumar Sahu and Ashish Anand. 2017. Drug-drug interaction extraction from biomedical text using long short term memory network. *arXiv preprint arXiv:1701.08303* .

Isabel Segura Bedmar, Paloma Martínez, and María Herrero Zazo. 2013. SemEval-2013 Task 9: Extraction of drug-drug interactions from biomedical texts (DDIExtraction 2013). In *Proceedings of the 7th International Workshop on Semantic Evaluations*. pages 341–350.

Caroline F Thorn, Teri E Klein, and Russ B Altman. 2013. PharmGKB: the pharmacogenomics knowledge base. *Pharmacogenomics: Methods and Protocols* pages 311–320.

Yoshimasa Tsuruoka, Yuka Tateishi, Jin-Dong Kim, Tomoko Ohta, John McNaught, Sophia Ananiadou, and Junichi Tsujii. 2005. Developing a robust part-of-speech tagger for biomedical text. In *Panhellenic Conference on Informatics*. pages 382–392.

Santiago Vilar, Carol Friedman, and George Hripcsak. 2017. Detection of drug–drug interactions through data mining studies using clinical sources, scientific literature and social media. *Briefings in bioinformatics* .

Quan Wang, Zhendong Mao, Bin Wang, and Li Guo. 2017. Knowledge graph embedding: A survey of approaches and applications. *IEEE Transactions on Knowledge and Data Engineering* 29(12):2724–2743.

David Weininger. 1988. Smiles, a chemical language and information system. 1. introduction to methodology and encoding rules. *Journal of chemical information and computer sciences* 28(1):31–36.

Hong Yang, Chu Qin, Ying Hong Li, Lin Tao, Jin Zhou, Chun Yan Yu, Feng Xu, Zhe Chen, Feng Zhu, and Yu Zong Chen. 2016. Therapeutic target database update 2016: enriched resource for bench to clinical drug target and targeted pathway information. *Nucleic acids research* 44(D1):D1069–D1074.

Daojian Zeng, Kang Liu, Siwei Lai, Guangyou Zhou, Jun Zhao, et al. 2014. Relation classification via convolutional deep neural network. In *COLING*. pages 2335–2344.

Wei Zheng, Hongfei Lin, Ling Luo, Zhehuan Zhao, Zhengguang Li, Yijia Zhang, Zhihao Yang, and Jian Wang. 2017. An attention-based effective neural model for drug-drug interactions extraction. *BMC Bioinformatics* 18(1):445.

Wei Zheng, Hongfei Lin, Zhehuan Zhao, Bo Xu, Yijia Zhang, Zhihao Yang, and Jian Wang. 2016. A graph kernel based on context vectors for extracting drug–drug interactions. *Journal of biomedical informatics* 61:34–43.

diaNED: Time-Aware Named Entity Disambiguation for Diachronic Corpora

Prabal Agarwal[1], Jannik Strötgen[1,2], Luciano del Corro[3], Johannes Hoffart[3], Gerhard Weikum[1]

[1]Max Planck Institute for Informatics, Saarland Informatics Campus, Saarbrücken, Germany
[2]Bosch Center for Artificial Intelligence, Renningen, Germany
[3]Ambiverse GmbH, Saarbrücken, Germany

```
{pagarwal,weikum}@mpi-inf.mpg.de
jannik.stroetgen@de.bosch.com
{luciano,johannes}@ambiverse.com
```


Abstract

Named Entity Disambiguation (NED) systems perform well on news articles and other texts covering a specific time interval. However, NED quality drops when inputs span long time periods like in archives or historic corpora. This paper presents the first time-aware method for NED that resolves ambiguities even when mention contexts give only few cues. The method is based on computing temporal signatures for entities and comparing these to the temporal contexts of input mentions. Our experiments show superior quality on a newly created diachronic corpus.[1]

1 Introduction

Problem. *Schumacher convinced to win on Sunday.* When this news headline is fed into modern tools for Named Entity Disambiguation (NED), virtually all of them would map the mention *Schumacher* onto the former Formula One champion *Michael Schumacher*, as the best-fitting entity from a Wikipedia-centric knowledge base (KB). However, knowing that *Sunday* refers to August 14, 1949, i.e., ignoring the surface form but exploiting normalized information, it becomes clear that the text actually refers to the German politician *Kurt Schumacher*. State-of-the-art NED methods (see surveys by Hachey et al. (2013), Ling et al. (2015), Shen et al. (2015)) tend to miss this because they are designed and trained for temporally focused input corpora such as current news, and do not cope well with longitudinal archives and other diachronic corpora that span decades. Standard NED benchmarks from CoNLL and TAC do not reflect this difficulty either.

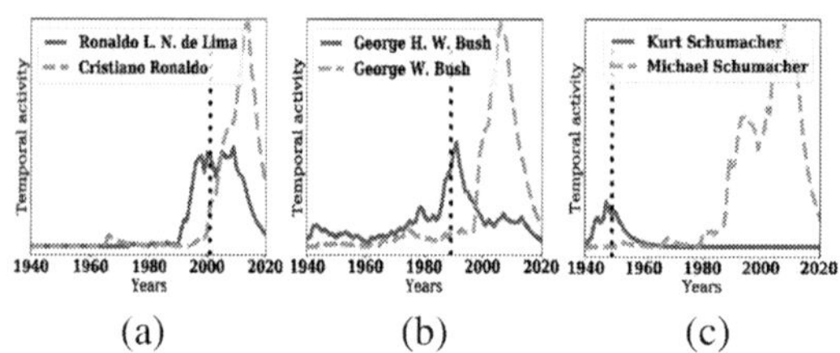

Figure 1: Temporal signatures of candidate entities for the following three sample sentences (vertical lines represent temporal contexts):
a) *Ronaldo comeback cut to 14 minutes.* (2001)
b) *Bush to stress domestic issues in speech.* (1989)
c) *Schumacher convinced to win on Sunday.* (1949)

What is needed here is a better way of capturing *temporal context*, for both the mention *Schumacher* and each of the candidate entities. Figure 1 illustrates "time profiles" for sample entities with highly ambiguous names. Normalized temporal information from the input context, such as *Sunday* (1949-08-14), can provide additional cues for proper disambiguation. The problem addressed in this paper is how to model and capture temporal contexts and how to enhance NED with this novel asset.

Contribution. Our approach to this problem is to compute *temporal signatures* for entities in the KB, and to use these as expressive features when comparing candidate entities against the context of an input mention. Temporal signatures are embeddings that reflect the importance of different years for entities. They are automatically constructed by extracting and normalizing temporal expressions in entity descriptions such as Wikipedia articles. Analogously, temporal signals are captured in the contexts of textual mentions and represented by embeddings.

The time-aware NED method that we devise with these features can robustly cope with inputs

---

[1]The diaNED corpus and the temporal signatures of entities are publicly available: https://www.mpi-inf.mpg.de/yago-naga/dianed/.

Proceedings of the 56th Annual Meeting of the Association for Computational Linguistics (Short Papers), pages 686–693
Melbourne, Australia, July 15 - 20, 2018. ©2018 Association for Computational Linguistics

from diachronic corpora. We propose a new evaluation benchmark, based on the New York Times Archive, spanning more than 20 years, and the history collection *historynet.com*, spanning several centuries. Our experiments demonstrate that time-aware NED substantially outperforms some of the best standard NED tools.

2 Temporal Signatures and Contexts

Better context representation improves disambiguation quality (see, e.g., Shen et al. (2015)). As the underlying entity descriptions (e.g., Wikipedia articles) are not only textually but also temporally related to their mentions, we enrich the context representation with a temporal dimension, which no prior work handles explicitly.

We model the temporal dimension by embedding vectors. The embeddings represent the *temporal signatures* of entities in a KB and the *temporal contexts* of entity mentions in text in a joint vector space. Then, the similarity between them quantifies their temporal relatedness.

Temporal vector space. We use 2,050 dimensions (years 1 AD to 2050) to define the vector space. Coarser and finer granularities than years could be used, but finer ones (e.g., days) are rarely needed for NED and coarser granularities (e.g., centuries) are too vague.[2]

Temporal signatures of entities. We use the temporal tagger HeidelTime (Strötgen and Gertz, 2010; Strötgen and Gertz, 2015) to extract and normalize date expressions from an entity's Wikipedia page[3] and aggregate them by years. This results in a count-based temporal vector $\mathbf{t}_e^{cb} = (t_{0001}, ..., t_i, ..., t_{2050})$ where t_i is the total number of temporal expressions extracted from e's Wikipedia page referring to year i. Temporal expressions of finer granularities are mapped to respective years and expressions of coarser granularities than year are currently ignored.

As the count-based vectors may overfit to the entity descriptions and to avoid discontinuity in the temporal signatures, we apply exponential smoothing and get smoothed temporal vectors

$\mathbf{t}_e^s = (t_{0001}^s, ..., t_i^s, ..., t_{2050}^s)$ such that $t_i^s = \alpha \cdot t_i^{cb} + (1 - \alpha) \cdot t_{i-1}^s$, for $i > 0001$ where α is the smoothing factor with $0 \leq \alpha \leq 1$. For further smoothing, this procedure can be recursively applied n times. In experiments, we set $\alpha = 0.2$ and $n = 2$ based on cross-validation.

Temporal contexts of entity mentions. We exploit temporal expressions in the surrounding text of entity mentions and the texts' publication dates. In news-style articles, entities are likely to be related to the document creation time (dct), while dates in the content are important for other types of documents (Strötgen and Gertz, 2016).

Temporal vectors for mentions $\mathbf{t}_m$ are thus a combination of a one-hot temporal vector $\mathbf{t}_m^{dct} = (0, ..., t_i, ..., 0)$ where $t_i = 1$ if i is the dct's year, and $\mathbf{t}_m^{content}$ containing dates extracted by a temporal tagger in the immediate context of the mention (e.g., in the same sentence or paragraph), aggregated by year. $\mathbf{t}_m^{dct}$ and $\mathbf{t}_m^{content}$ are linearly combined as $\mathbf{t}_m = \lambda \cdot \mathbf{t}_m^{dct} + (1 - \lambda) \cdot \mathbf{t}_m^{content}$ where λ (with $0 \leq \lambda \leq 1$) weights the components.

Relatedness. We calculate the temporal relatedness between a mention and all candidate entities as the cosine similarity between $\mathbf{t}_m$ and $\mathbf{t}_e$.

3 Time-aware NED

To test the importance of time-awareness for NED, we use two settings. We enhance a basic NED system and a state-of-the-art system by enriching both with temporal signatures and contexts.

diaNED-1, as basic NED system, uses a mention-entity prior reflecting entity prominence and a keyphrase-based language model for the similarity of mention and entity contexts (as suggested by Hoffart et al. (2011)). These components are cast into edge weights for a graph over which the final disambiguation is computed. Hyper-parameters for the relative influence of the two components are tuned using an SVM.

We added the temporal dimension to the feature set and retrained the model accordingly to get new feature weights.

diaNED-2 based on Yamada et al. (2016): This is a learning-to-rank-based model. Besides mention-entity priors and string-similarity features, it uses word and entity embeddings trained in a joint vector space to model context and coherence. The intuition is that a good candidate entity vector must be close to the word and entity vectors appearing in the same context.

---

[2]In an analysis of temporal expressions extracted with HeidelTime from the Wikipedia corpus (August 2016 dump), we find that there are on average 18.500 expressions per year value (with year values ranging from `0001 AD` to `2050 AD`) in contrast to only 9.64 expressions per day value (with day values ranging from `0001-01-01` to `2050-12-31`). Therefore, using year level identifiers to define our temporal vector space results in short and non-sparse temporal vectors.

[3]August 2016 Wikipedia dump

Yamada et al. (2016) measures entity context by averaging the word vectors of the proper noun neighbors and calculating the cosine similarity with each candidate entity. Similarly, the coherence between entities is measured by computing the cosine similarity between candidates and the average of the other entities in the neighborhood.

diaNED-2 enhances this model as follows. We compute the cosine similarity between the mention's and the candidate entities' temporal vectors, and normalize the time relatedness scores across candidate entities. Finally, all similarity features are used to train a binary classifier with gradient-boosted decision trees. The top-ranked candidate entity in each pool of candidates is assigned to the mention being evaluated.

4   A Diachronic NED Data Set

Datasets for NED evaluation contain articles published within a short period. Consequently, all mentions share a temporal context making it difficult to evaluate temporal variability. CoNLL-AIDA (Hoffart et al., 2011) are newswire articles from 1996, TAC 2010 (Ji et al., 2010) news and forum articles from 2004–2007, and Microposts-2014 (Cano et al., 2014) tweets from 2011.

To account for this limitation, we create a new diachronic benchmark containing documents with heterogeneous temporal context. As in Microposts-2014, we limit documents to single sentences and headlines from *HistoryNet.com* (*HN*) and *The New York Times corpus* (*NYT*). For the annotation process, we followed the entity annotation guidelines, which have been used for annotating CoNLL-AIDA (Hoffart et al., 2011).

HN is an online resource of world history with information on popular historical topics. Its section *Today in History* contains short texts on what happened on a specific day with a total of 7,061 facts/events (excluding *born today*). Using Stanford NER (Finkel et al., 2005), we extracted 13,773 entity mentions and randomly selected 350 of them. We annotated all entity mentions in respective sentences with their Wikipedia ids. After removing NER errors and out-of-KB entities, the dataset contains 865 gold entity mentions in 334 sentences. Examples are: "*Conrad II* claims the throne in *France*" from 1032 or "The *Old Pretender*, son of *James III* dies" from 1766.

NYT contains more than 1.5 million documents published between 1987 and 2007. After applying the same procedure, the dataset contains 368 manually annotated mentions in 290 news headlines. Examples are "*Arafat*'s Faction is Said to Avoid Guerrilla Actions" from 1989 or "*U.N.* Aide to Meet *Milosevic*, Angering Some" from 1999.

As *HN* texts come without further context, entity mentions are rather explicit. Entity mentions in *NYT*'s headlines are more ambiguous as more information is available in the articles and the entities are mostly, at the time of publication, prominent and obvious to the reader.

Finally, we created a third subset from the 7,061 documents of *HistoryNet.com* with 13,773 entity mentions. It contains the sentences with all the entity mentions which are linked to different entities by diaNED-2 depending on whether it uses its time-awareness or not, i.e., whether diaNED-2 is trained with or without the temporal feature. This set (*HN-timediff*) contains 567 manually annotated entities from 547 documents. It is the most challenging subset as all entity mentions are difficult to disambiguate.

5   Evaluation

To evaluate the importance of temporal information in NED, we focus in our analysis on the newly created *diaNED* corpus. As standard NED datasets CoNLL-AIDA and TAC 2010 contain only articles published within a short period of time, they are not suited for evaluating time-aware NED (cf. Section 4), and experiments on these datasets showed no significant differences between using diaNED-1 and diaNED-2 with or without their time-awareness features.

Note that the temporal contexts in the *HN* sentences and the *NYT* headlines of the diaNED corpus are part of the metadata. Thus, to ensure a fair comparison among all systems, we added the temporal contexts in the form of year information to all documents to allow the non-time-aware systems to exploit the temporal context in case the respective year number occurs as part of the entities' textual context.[4]

5.1   Intra-system Comparison

As described above, we (re-)implemented two NED systems as diaNED-1 and diaNED-2. To al-

---

[4]Disambiguation quality of non-time-aware systems was generally lower without this additional information. The diaNED corpus contains all sentences with and without year information so that evaluation results can be reproduced for both settings.

Feature set	HN subset		NYT subset	
	w/o time	w time	w/o time	w time
Prior	72.26	80.48*	38.14	54.24*
Context	63.63	66.10*	48.31	62.71*

* significant over w/o time (Welch's t-test at level of 0.01)

Table 1: Micro-accuracy of diaNED-1 with and without time-awareness feature.

Feature set	HN subset		NYT subset	
	w/o time	w time	w/o time	w time
Base	89.44	90.23*	85.81	87.36*
String	89.40	90.00*	86.28	87.07*
Context	91.10	91.81*	87.07	88.34*
Coherence	91.16	91.98*	86.83	88.69*

* significant over w/o time (Welch's t-test at level of 0.01)

Table 2: Micro-accuracy of diaNED-2 with and without time-awareness feature.

low the systems to adapt to the diachronic corpus without considering temporal information explicitly, we retrained the systems so that appropriate weights are learnt for each standard feature. Due to the rather small size of the diaNED corpus, we use bootstrapping (i.e., train and evaluate on 50 randomly shuffled versions of the corpus) with and without using the time-awareness feature.

diaNED-1. Table 1 shows micro-accuracy for our basic NED system on the *HN* and *NYT* sets of diaNED. Significant gains are achieved when combining the prior and context features with the time-awareness feature. This demonstrates that NED systems with standard features can be improved by making them time-aware.

diaNED-2. Table 2 shows micro-accuracy for our re-implementation of Yamada et al. (2016)'s initial features with and without the time-awareness feature. As can be seen in the table, adding the temporal feature improves the results significantly in each setting on both sets, which demonstrates that even state-of-the-art systems can be improved by making them time-aware.

5.2 Inter-system Comparison

In Table 3, we compare the time-aware NED approach diaNED-2 to various NED tools available via GERBIL (v. 1.2.5) (Usbeck et al., 2015) and to the recent work by Gupta et al. (2017). As all systems are used with standard settings, we also trained diaNED-2 on standard NED training data (CoNLL-AIDA) with the temporal context of entity mentions being the respective article's year

system	HN	NYT
xLisa-NGRAM (Zhang and Rettinger, 2014)	87.07	66.30
WAT (Ferragina and Scaiella, 2012)	82.26	70.95
PBOH (Ganea et al., 2016)	90.26	71.75
FREME NER (Dojchinovski and Kliegr, 2013)	48.50	45.27
FRED (Consoli and Recupero, 2015)	23.18	15.44
FOX (Speck and Ngomo, 2014)	77.85	54.25
Dexter (Ceccarelli et al., 2013)	69.66	49.12
DBpedia Spotlight(Mendes et al., 2011)	56.92	61.91
AIDA (Hoffart et al., 2011)	82.35	70.14
AGDISTIS (Usbeck et al., 2014)	70.77	50.14
Gupta et al. (2017)	62.82	43.33
reimpl. of (Yamada et al., 2016)	90.87	72.55
diaNED-2 w time	**91.68**	**76.09**

Table 3: F1-scores of various systems on the *HN* and *NYT* subsets of the diaNED benchmark.

	overall	person	location	organization
time-agnostic	27.51	9.63	40.07	33.77
time-aware	42.50	39.91	45.22	40.26

Table 4: Micro-accuracy of diaNED-2 on *HN-timediff* with and without time-awareness feature.

of publication. However, due to the differences in what kind of entities the systems consider and what kind of candidate entity lookup dictionaries they use, the systems are not directly comparable and the performance differences should be interpreted with a grain of salt. Nevertheless, time-awareness further increases the distance between (Yamada et al., 2016) and the second best system significantly, which demonstrates its usefulness for NED.

5.3 Type-based Analysis

To gain further insights about the importance of time-awareness, we analyzed the results of diaNED-2 with and without temporal feature on the *HN-timediff* set of our benchmark (Table 4). On these particularly challenging documents, the time-awareness feature helps to improve NED quality for all entity types. While location and organization entities moderately benefit, there is a huge performance increase for person entities. The explanation that person entities benefit most could be that person entities have comparably short life spans and are thus most time-sensitive.

6 Related Work

Starting with the early work of Bunescu and Paşca (2006), Cucerzan (2007), Mihalcea and Csomai (2007), and Milne and Witten (2008),

NED methods and tools have been greatly advanced and become mature. Many systems use a combination of (i) local features like string similarities, lexico-syntactic characteristics and context between mentions and candidate entities and (ii) global features like the coherence among a set of selected entities. The inference over this feature space is typically performed by probabilistic graphical models, learning-to-rank techniques or algorithms related to such models (see, e.g., Ratinov et al. (2011), Hoffart et al. (2011), Ferragina and Scaiella (2012), Cheng and Roth (2013), Guo and Barbosa (2014), Durrett and Klein (2014), Chisholm and Hachey (2015), Pershina et al. (2015), Lazic et al. (2015), Nguyen et al. (2016), Globerson et al. (2016), Eshel et al. (2017), and Ganea and Hofmann (2017)). The GERBIL framework (Usbeck et al., 2015) provides a unified way of evaluating a wide variety of NED tools and services.

A recent line of work uses representational learning to characterize contexts through embeddings (e.g., He et al. (2013), Sun et al. (2015), Francis-Landau et al. (2016), Yamada et al. (2016), Gupta et al. (2017), Yamada et al. (2017)). These approaches naturally lend themselves towards inference by neural networks such as LSTMs. In our experiments, the Neural Text-Entity Encoder by Yamada et al. (2016) serves as state-of-the-art baseline.

While temporal information was used as a global feature to compute coherence between entity lifespans (Hoffart et al., 2013), no prior work on named entity disambiguation made explicit use of temporal information as a local feature. However, the value of time has been shown in a variety of other information extraction tasks, such as relation extraction (UzZaman et al., 2013; Mirza and Tonelli, 2016), event extraction (Kuzey et al., 2016; Spitz and Gertz, 2016), and slot filling (Ji et al., 2011; Surdeanu et al., 2011; Surdeanu, 2013), as well as in the context of information retrieval (Berberich et al., 2010; Agarwal and Strötgen, 2017) and fact checking (Popat et al., 2017). In this paper, inspired by the importance of temporal information for many NLP tasks, we analyzed its value for NED.

7   Conclusions and Ongoing Work

We proposed the first NED method with explicit consideration of temporal background. As demonstrated in our experiments, this time-awareness improves NED quality over diachronic texts that span long time periods. The diaNED dataset and the temporal signatures of entities are publicly available.[5]

Currently, we integrate a strategy for handling out-of-KB entities to determine how temporal affinity may help in the *nil* detection problem. Furthermore, we plan large-scale experiments with distant supervision data which will also allow to evaluate the effectiveness of considering temporal expressions in the context of the entity mentions as further temporal context information. Finally, using a multilingual temporal tagger (Strötgen and Gertz, 2015), the value of time for NED could be studied for further languages.

Acknowledgments

The authors thank the anonymous reviewers for their valuable comments and suggestions and Ikuya Yamada for providing the word-entity embeddings and his help in the implementation of one of the baseline systems.

References

Prabal Agarwal and Jannik Strötgen. 2017. Tiwiki: Searching Wikipedia with Temporal Constraints. In *Proceedings of the 7th Temporal Web Analytics Workshop*, TempWeb'17, pages 1595–1600.

Klaus Berberich, Srikanta Bedathur, Omar Alonso, and Gerhard Weikum. 2010. A Language Modeling Approach for Temporal Information Needs. In *Proceedings of the 32nd European Conference on Advances in Information Retrieval*, ECIR'10, pages 13–25.

Razvan Bunescu and Marius Paşca. 2006. Using Encyclopedic Knowledge for Named Entity Disambiguation. In *Proceedings of the 11th Conference of the European Chapter of the Association for Computational Linguistics*, EACL'06, pages 9–16.

Amparo E. Cano, Giuseppe Rizzo, Andrea Varga, Matthew Rowe, Milan Stankovic, and Aba-Sah Dadzie. 2014. Making Sense of Microposts (#Microposts2014): Named Entity Extraction & Linking Challenge. In *Proceedings of the 4th Workshop on Making Sense out of Microposts*, Microposts'14, pages 54–60.

Diego Ceccarelli, Claudio Lucchese, Salvatore Orlando, Raffaele Perego, and Salvatore Trani. 2013. Dexter: An Open Source Framework for Entity

---

[5]https://www.mpi-inf.mpg.de/yago-naga/dianed/

Linking. In *Proceedings of the 6th International Workshop on Exploiting Semantic Annotations in Information Retrieval*, ESAIR'13, pages 17–20.

Xiao Cheng and Dan Roth. 2013. Relational Inference for Wikification. In *Proceedings of the 2013 Conference on Empirical Methods in Natural Language Processing*, EMNLP'13, pages 1787–1796.

Andrew Chisholm and Ben Hachey. 2015. Entity Disambiguation with Web Links. *Transactions of the Association for Computational Linguistics*, 3:145–156.

Sergio Consoli and Diego Reforgiato Recupero. 2015. Using FRED for Named Entity Resolution, Linking and Typing for Knowledge Base Population. In *Proceedings of the Semantic Web Evaluation Challenge*, SemWebEval'15, pages 40–50.

Silviu Cucerzan. 2007. Large-Scale Named Entity Disambiguation Based on Wikipedia Data. In *Proceedings of the 2007 Joint Conference on Empirical Methods in Natural Language Processing and Computational Natural Language Learning*, EMNLP-CoNLL'07, pages 708–716.

Milan Dojchinovski and Tomáš Kliegr. 2013. Entityclassifier.eu: Real-Time Classification of Entities in Text with Wikipedia. In *Proceedings of the Joint European Conference on Machine Learning and Knowledge Discovery in Databases*, ECML-PKDD'13, pages 654–658.

Greg Durrett and Dan Klein. 2014. A Joint Model for Entity Analysis: Coreference, Typing, and Linking. *Transactions of the Association for Computational Linguistics*, 2:477–490.

Yotam Eshel, Noam Cohen, Kira Radinsky, Shaul Markovitch, Ikuya Yamada, and Omer Levy. 2017. Named Entity Disambiguation for Noisy Text. In *Proceedings of the 21st Conference on Computational Natural Language Learning*, CoNLL'17, pages 58–68.

Paolo Ferragina and Ugo Scaiella. 2012. Fast and Accurate Annotation of Short Texts with Wikipedia Pages. *IEEE Software*, 29(1):70–75.

Jenny Rose Finkel, Trond Grenager, and Christopher Manning. 2005. Incorporating Non-local Information into Information Extraction Systems by Gibbs Sampling. In *Proceedings of the 43rd Annual Meeting on Association for Computational Linguistics*, ACL'05, pages 363–370.

Matthew Francis-Landau, Greg Durrett, and Dan Klein. 2016. Capturing Semantic Similarity for Entity Linking with Convolutional Neural Networks. In *Proceedings of the 2016 Conference of the North American Chapter of the Association for Computational Linguistics: Human Language Technologies*, NAACL-HLT'16, pages 1256–1261.

Octavian-Eugen Ganea, Marina Ganea, Aurelien Lucchi, Carsten Eickhoff, and Thomas Hofmann. 2016. Probabilistic Bag-Of-Hyperlinks Model for Entity Linking. In *Proceedings of the 25th International Conference on World Wide Web*, WWW'16, pages 927–938.

Octavian-Eugen Ganea and Thomas Hofmann. 2017. Deep Joint Entity Disambiguation with Local Neural Attention. In *Proceedings of the 2017 Conference on Empirical Methods in Natural Language Processing*, EMNLP'17, pages 2609–2619.

Amir Globerson, Nevena Lazic, Soumen Chakrabarti, Amarnag Subramanya, Michael Ringaard, and Fernando Pereira. 2016. Collective Entity Resolution with Multi-Focal Attention. In *Proceedings of the 54th Annual Meeting of the Association for Computational Linguistics*, ACL'16, pages 621–631.

Zhaochen Guo and Denilson Barbosa. 2014. Robust Entity Linking via Random Walks. In *Proceedings of the 23rd ACM International Conference on Information and Knowledge Management*, CIKM'14, pages 499–508.

Nitish Gupta, Sameer Singh, and Dan Roth. 2017. Entity Linking via Joint Encoding of Types, Descriptions, and Context. In *Proceedings of the 2017 Conference on Empirical Methods in Natural Language Processing*, EMNLP'17, pages 2681–2690.

Ben Hachey, Will Radford, Joel Nothman, Matthew Honnibal, and James R. Curran. 2013. Evaluating Entity Linking with Wikipedia. *Artificial Intelligence*, 194:130–150.

Zhengyan He, Shujie Liu, Mu Li, Ming Zhou, Longkai Zhang, and Houfeng Wang. 2013. Learning Entity Representation for Entity Disambiguation. In *Proceedings of the 51st Annual Meeting of the Association for Computational Linguistics*, ACL'13, pages 30–34.

Johannes Hoffart, Fabian M. Suchanek, Klaus Berberich, and Gerhard Weikum. 2013. YAGO2: A Spatially and Temporally Enhanced Knowledge Base from Wikipedia. *Artificial Intelligence*, 194:28–61.

Johannes Hoffart, Mohamed Amir Yosef, Ilaria Bordino, Hagen Fürstenau, Manfred Pinkal, Marc Spaniol, Bilyana Taneva, Stefan Thater, and Gerhard Weikum. 2011. Robust Disambiguation of Named Entities in Text. In *Proceedings of the 2011 Conference on Empirical Methods in Natural Language Processing*, EMNLP'11, pages 782–792.

Heng Ji, Ralph Grishman, and Hoa Dang. 2011. Overview of the TAC2011 Knowledge Base Population Track. In *Proceedings of the 4th Text Analysis Conference*, TAC'11.

Heng Ji, Ralph Grishman, Hoa Trang Dang, Kira Griffitt, and Joe Ellis. 2010. Overview of the TAC 2010 Knowledge Base Population Track. In *Proceedings of the 3rd Text Analysis Conference*, TAC'10.

Erdal Kuzey, Vinay Setty, Jannik Strötgen, and Gerhard Weikum. 2016. As Time Goes By: Comprehensive Tagging of Textual Phrases with Temporal Scopes. In *Proceedings of the 25th International Conference on World Wide Web*, WWW'16, pages 915–925.

Nevena Lazic, Amarnag Subramanya, Michael Ringgaard, and Fernando Pereira. 2015. Plato: A Selective Context Model for Entity Resolution. *Transactions of the Association for Computational Linguistics*, 3:503–515.

Xiao Ling, Sameer Singh, and Daniel Weld. 2015. Design Challenges for Entity Linking. *Transactions of the Association for Computational Linguistics*, 3:315–328.

Pablo N. Mendes, Max Jakob, Andrés García-Silva, and Christian Bizer. 2011. DBpedia Spotlight: Shedding Light on the Web of Documents. In *Proceedings of the 7th International Conference on Semantic Systems*, I-Semantics'11, pages 1–8.

Rada Mihalcea and Andras Csomai. 2007. Wikify!: Linking Documents to Encyclopedic Knowledge. In *Proceedings of the 16th ACM Conference on Information and Knowledge Management*, CIKM'07, pages 233–242.

David Milne and Ian H. Witten. 2008. Learning to Link with Wikipedia. In *Proceedings of the 17th ACM Conference on Information and Knowledge Management*, CIKM'08, pages 509–518.

Paramita Mirza and Sara Tonelli. 2016. CATENA: Causal and Temporal Relation Extraction from Natural Language Texts. In *Proceedings the 26th International Conference on Computational Linguistics*, COLING'16, pages 64–75.

Dat Nguyen, Martin Theobald, and Gerhard Weikum. 2016. J-NERD: Joint Named Entity Recognition and Disambiguation with Rich Linguistic Features. *Transactions of the Association for Computational Linguistics*, 4:215–229.

Maria Pershina, Yifan He, and Ralph Grishman. 2015. Personalized Page Rank for Named Entity Disambiguation. In *Proceedings of the 2015 Conference of the North American Chapter of the Association for Computational Linguistics: Human Language Technologies*, NAACL-HLT'15, pages 238–243.

Kashyap Popat, Subhabrata Mukherjee, Jannik Strötgen, and Gerhard Weikum. 2017. Where the truth lies: Explaining the credibility of emerging claims on the web and social media. In *Proceedings of the 26th International Conference on World Wide Web Companion*, WWW'17, pages 1003–1012.

Lev Ratinov, Dan Roth, Doug Downey, and Mike Anderson. 2011. Local and Global Algorithms for Disambiguation to Wikipedia. In *Proceedings of the 49th Annual Meeting of the Association for Computational Linguistics: Human Language Technologies*, ACL-HLT'11, pages 1375–1384.

Wei Shen, Jianyong Wang, and Jiawei Han. 2015. Entity Linking with a Knowledge Base: Issues, Techniques, and Solutions. *IEEE Transactions on Knowledge and Data Engineering*, 27(2):443–460.

René Speck and Axel-Cyrille Ngonga Ngomo. 2014. Named Entity Recognition Using FOX. In *Proceedings of the International Semantic Web Conference*, ISWC-PD'14, pages 85–88.

Andreas Spitz and Michael Gertz. 2016. Terms over LOAD: Leveraging Named Entities for Cross-Document Extraction and Summarization of Events. In *Proceedings of the 39th International ACM SIGIR Conference on Research and Development in Information Retrieval*, SIGIR'16, pages 503–512.

Jannik Strötgen and Michael Gertz. 2010. HeidelTime: High Quality Rule-based Extraction and Normalization of Temporal Expressions. In *Proceedings of the 5th International Workshop on Semantic Evaluation*, SemEval'10, pages 321–324.

Jannik Strötgen and Michael Gertz. 2015. A Baseline Temporal Tagger for all Languages. In *Proceedings of the 2015 Conference on Empirical Methods in Natural Language Processing*, EMNLP'15, pages 541–547.

Jannik Strötgen and Michael Gertz. 2016. *Domain-sensitive Temporal Tagging*. Synthesis Lectures on Human Language Technologies, Morgan & Claypool Publishers.

Yaming Sun, Lei Lin, Duyu Tang, Nan Yang, Zhenzhou Ji, and Xiaolong Wang. 2015. Modeling Mention, Context and Entity with Neural Networks for Entity Disambiguation. In *Proceedings of the 24th International Conference on Artificial Intelligence*, IJCAI'15, pages 1333–1339.

Mihai Surdeanu. 2013. Overview of the TAC2013 Knowledge Base Population Evaluation: English Slot Filling and Temporal Slot Filling. In *Proceedings of the 6th Text Analysis Conference*, TAC'13.

Mihai Surdeanu, Sonal Gupta, John Bauer, David McClosky, Angel X. Chang, Valentin I. Spitkovsky, and Christopher D. Manning. 2011. Stanford's Distantly-Supervised Slot-Filling System. In *Proceedings of the 4th Text Analysis Conference*, TAC'11.

Ricardo Usbeck, Axel-Cyrille Ngonga Ngomo, Michael Röder, Daniel Gerber, Sandro Athaide Coelho, Sören Auer, and Andreas Both. 2014. AGDISTIS - Graph-Based Disambiguation of Named Entities Using Linked Data. In *Proceedings of the 13th International Semantic Web Conference*, ISWC'14, pages 457–471.

Ricardo Usbeck, Michael Röder, Axel-Cyrille Ngonga Ngomo, Ciro Baron, Andreas Both, Martin Brümmer, Diego Ceccarelli, Marco Cornolti, Didier Cherix, Bernd Eickmann, Paolo Ferragina, Christiane Lemke, Andrea Moro, Roberto Navigli,

Francesco Piccinno, Giuseppe Rizzo, Harald Sack, René Speck, Raphaël Troncy, Jörg Waitelonis, and Lars Wesemann. 2015. GERBIL: General Entity Annotator Benchmarking Framework. In *Proceedings of the 24th International Conference on World Wide Web*, WWW'15, pages 1133–1143.

Naushad UzZaman, Hector Llorens, Leon Derczynski, James Allen, Marc Verhagen, and James Pustejovsky. 2013. SemEval-2013 Task 1: TempEval-3: Evaluating Time Expressions, Events, and Temporal Relations. In *Proceedings of the 7th International Workshop on Semantic Evaluation*, SemEval'13, pages 1–9.

Ikuya Yamada, Hiroyuki Shindo, Hideaki Takeda, and Yoshiyasu Takefuji. 2016. Joint Learning of the Embedding of Words and Entities for Named Entity Disambiguation. In *Proceedings of the 20th SIGNLL Conference on Computational Natural Language Learning*, CoNLL'15, pages 250–259.

Ikuya Yamada, Hiroyuki Shindo, Hideaki Takeda, and Yoshiyasu Takefuji. 2017. Learning Distributed Representations of Texts and Entities from Knowledge Base. *Transactions of the Association for Computational Linguistics*, 5:397–411.

Lei Zhang and Achim Rettinger. 2014. X-LiSA: Cross-lingual Semantic Annotation. *Proc. VLDB Endow.*, 7(13):1693–1696.

Examining Temporality in Document Classification

Xiaolei Huang and **Michael J. Paul**
Information Science
University of Colorado
Boulder, CO 80309, USA
{xiaolei.huang,mpaul}@colorado.edu

Abstract

Many corpora span broad periods of time. Language processing models trained during one time period may not work well in future time periods, and the best model may depend on specific times of year (e.g., people might describe hotels differently in reviews during the winter versus the summer). This study investigates how document classifiers trained on documents from certain time intervals perform on documents from other time intervals, considering both seasonal intervals (intervals that repeat across years, e.g., winter) and non-seasonal intervals (e.g., specific years). We show experimentally that classification performance varies over time, and that performance can be improved by using a standard domain adaptation approach to adjust for changes in time.

1 Introduction

Language, and therefore data derived from language, changes over time (Ullmann, 1962). Word senses can shift over long periods of time (Wilkins, 1993; Wijaya and Yeniterzi, 2011; Hamilton et al., 2016), and written language can change rapidly in online platforms (Eisenstein et al., 2014; Goel et al., 2016). However, little is known about how shifts in text over time affect the performance of language processing systems.

This paper focuses on a standard text processing task, document classification, to provide insight into how classification performance varies with time. We consider both long-term variations in text over time and seasonal variations which change throughout a year but repeat across years. Our empirical study considers corpora containing formal text spanning decades as well as user-generated content spanning only a few years.

After describing the datasets and experiment design, this paper has two main sections, respectively addressing the following research questions:

1. In what ways does document classification depend on the timestamps of the documents?

2. Can document classifiers be adapted to perform better in time-varying corpora?

To address question 1, we train and test on data from different time periods, to understand how performance varies with time. To address question 2, we apply a domain adaptation approach, treating time intervals as domains. We show that in most cases this approach can lead to improvements in classification performance, even on future time intervals.

1.1 Related Work

Time is implicitly embedded in the classification process: classifiers are often built to be applied to future data that doesn't yet exist, and performance on held-out data is measured to estimate performance on future data whose distribution may have changed. Methods exist to adjust for changes in the data distribution (*covariate shift*) (Shimodaira, 2000; Bickel et al., 2009), but time is not typically incorporated into such methods explicitly.

One line of work that explicitly studies the relationship between time and the distribution of data is work on classifying the time period in which a document was written (*document dating*) (Kanhabua and Nørvåg, 2008; Chambers, 2012; Kotsakos et al., 2014). However, this task is directed differently from our work: predicting timestamps given documents, rather than predicting information about documents given timestamps.

Proceedings of the 56th Annual Meeting of the Association for Computational Linguistics (Short Papers), pages 694–699
Melbourne, Australia, July 15 - 20, 2018. ©2018 Association for Computational Linguistics

Dataset	Time intervals (non-seasonal)	Time intervals (seasonal)	Size
Reviews (music)	1997-99, 2000-02, 2003-05, 2006-08, 2009-11, 2012-14	Jan-Mar, Apr-Jun, Jul-Sep, Oct-Dec	653K
Reviews (hotels)	2005-08, 2009-11, 2012-14, 2015-17	Jan-Mar, Apr-Jun, Jul-Sep, Oct-Dec	78.6K
Reviews (restaurants)	2005-08, 2009-11, 2012-14, 2015-17	Jan-Mar, Apr-Jun, Jul-Sep, Oct-Dec	1.16M
News (economy)	1950-70, 1971-85, 1986-2000, 2001-14	Jan-Mar, Apr-Jun, Jul-Sep, Oct-Dec	6.29K
Politics (platforms)	1948-56, 1960-68, 1972-80, 1984-92, 1996-2004, 2008-16	n/a	35.8K
Twitter (vaccines)	2013, 2014, 2015, 2016	Jan-Mar, Apr-Jun, Jul-Sep, Oct-Dec	9.83K

Table 1: Descriptions of corpora spanning multiple time intervals. Size is the number of documents.

2   Datasets and Experimental Setup

Our study experiments with six corpora:

- **Reviews:** Three corpora containing reviews labeled with sentiment: music reviews from Amazon (He and McAuley, 2016), and hotel reviews and restaurant reviews from Yelp.[1] We discarded reviews that had fewer than 10 tokens or a helpfulness/usefulness score of zero. The reviews with neutral scores were removed.

- **Politics:** Sentences from the American party platforms of Republicans and Democrats from 1948 to 2016, available every four years.[2]

- **News:** Newspaper articles from 1950-2014, labeled with whether the article is relevant to the US economy.[3]

- **Twitter:** Tweets labeled with whether they indicate that the user received an influenza vaccination (i.e., a flu shot) (Huang et al., 2017).

Our experiments require documents to be grouped into time intervals. Table 1 shows the intervals for each corpus. Documents that fall outside of these time intervals were removed. We grouped documents into two types of intervals:

- **Seasonal:** Time intervals within a year (e.g., January through March) that may be repeated across years.

- **Non-seasonal:** Time intervals that do not repeat (e.g., 1997-1999).

For each dataset, we performed binary classification, implemented in `sklearn` (Pedregosa et al., 2011). We built logistic regression classifiers with TF-IDF weighted n-gram features ($n \in \{1, 2, 3\}$), removing features that appeared in less than 2 documents. Except when otherwise specified, we held out a random 10% of documents as validation data for each dataset. We used Elastic Net (combined ℓ_1 and ℓ_2) regularization (Zou and Hastie, 2005), and tuned the regularization parameters to maximize performance on the validation data. We evaluated the performance using weighted F1 scores.

3   How Does Classification Performance Vary with Time?

We first conduct an analysis of how classifier performance depends on the time intervals in which it is trained and applied. For each corpus, we train the classifier on each time interval and test on each time interval. We downsampled the training data within each time interval to match the number of documents in the smallest interval, so that differences in performance are not due to the size of the training data.

In all experiments, we train a classifier on a partition of 80% of the documents in the time interval, and repeat this five times on different partitions, averaging the five F1 scores to produce the final estimate. When training and testing on the same interval, we test on the held-out 20% of documents in that interval (standard cross-validation). When testing on different time intervals, we test on all documents, since they are all held-out from the training interval; however, we still train on five subsets of 80% of documents, so that the training data is identical across all experiments.

Finally, to understand why performance varies, we also qualitatively examined how the distribution of content changes across time intervals. To measure the distribution of content, we trained a topic model with 20 topics using `gensim` (Řehůřek and Sojka, 2010) with default parameters. We associated each document with one topic (the most probable topic in the document), and then calculated the proportion of each topic within a time period as the proportion of documents in that time period assigned to that topic. We can then visualize the extent to which the distribution of 20 topics varies by time.

---

[1] `https://www.yelp.com/dataset`
[2] `https://www.comparativeagendas.net/datasets_codebooks`
[3] `https://www.crowdflower.com/data-for-everyone/`

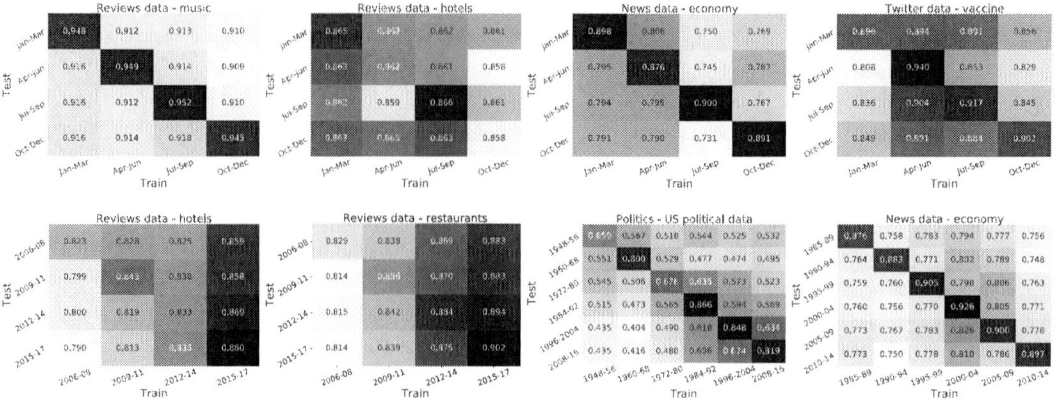

Figure 1: Document classification performance when training and testing on different times of year (top) and different years (bottom). Some corpora are omitted for space.

3.1 Seasonal Variability

The top row of Figure 1 shows the test scores from training and testing on each pair of seasonal time intervals for four of the datasets. We observe very strong seasonal variations in the economic news corpus, with a drop in F1 score on the order of 10 when there is a mismatch in the season between training and testing. There is a similar, but weaker, effect on performance in the music reviews from Amazon and the vaccine tweets. There was virtually no difference in performance in any of the pairs in both review corpora from Yelp (restaurants, not pictured, and hotels).

To help understand why the performance varies, Figure 2 (left) shows the distribution of topics in each seasonal interval for two corpora: Amazon music reviews and Twitter. We observe very little variation in the topic distribution across seasons in the Amazon corpus, but some variation in the Twitter corpus, which may explain the large performance differences when testing on held-out seasons in the Twitter data as compared to the Amazon corpus.

For space, we do not show the descriptions of the topics, but instead only the shape of the distributions to show the degree of variability. We did qualitatively examine the differences in word features across the time periods, but had difficulty interpreting the observations and were unable to draw clear conclusions. Thus, characterizing the ways in which content distributions vary over time, and why this affects performance, is still an open question.

3.2 Non-seasonal Variability

The bottom row of Figure 1 shows the test scores from training and testing on each pair of non-seasonal time intervals. A strong pattern emerges in the political parties corpus: F1 scores can drop by as much as 40 points when testing on different time intervals. This is perhaps unsurprising, as this collection spans decades, and US party positions have substantially changed over time. The performance declines more when testing on time intervals that are further away in time from the training interval, suggesting that changes in party platforms shift gradually over time. In contrast, while there was a performance drop when testing outside the training interval in the economic news corpus, the drop was not gradual. In the Twitter dataset (not pictured), F1 dropped by an average of 4.9 points outside the training interval.

We observe an intriguing non-seasonal pattern that is consistent in both of the review corpora from Yelp, but not in the music review corpus from Amazon (not pictured), which is that the classification performance fairly consistently increases over time. Since we sampled the dataset so that the time intervals have the same number of reviews, this suggests something else changed over time about the way reviews are written that makes the sentiment easier to detect.

The right side of Figure 2 shows the topic distribution in the Amazon and Twitter datasets across non-seasonal intervals. We observe higher levels of variability across time in the non-seasonal intervals as compared to the seasonal intervals.

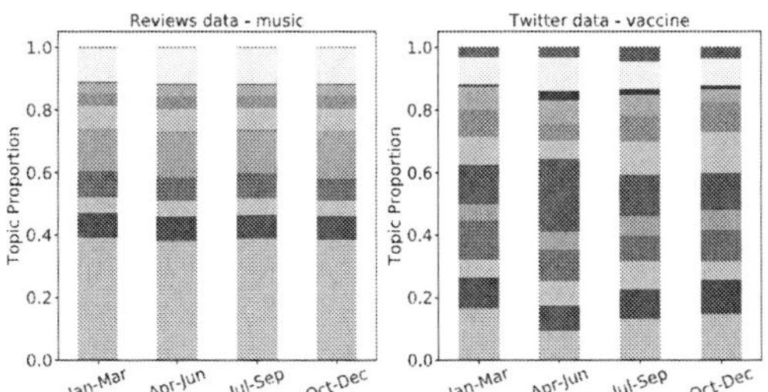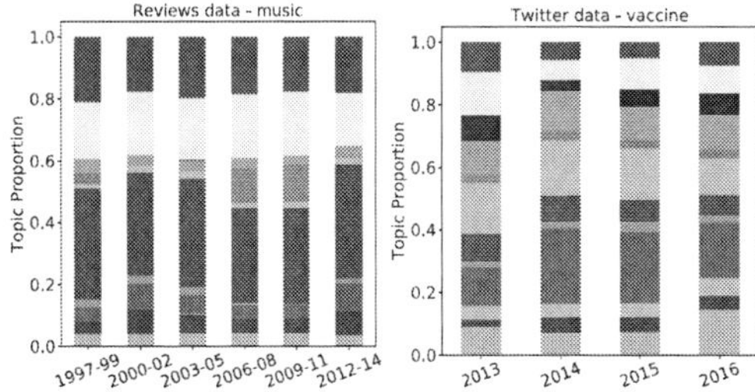

Figure 2: Topic distributions in each time of year (left) and each span of years (right). Topic models are trained independently in the seasonal vs. non-seasonal settings and are not aligned.

3.3 Discussion

Overall, it is clear that classifiers generally perform best when applied to the same time interval they were trained. Performance diminishes when applied to different time intervals, although different corpora exhibit differ patterns in the way in which the performance diminishes. This kind of analysis can be applied to any corpus and could provide insights into characteristics of the corpus that may be helpful when designing a classifier.

4 Making Classification Robust to Temporality

We now consider how to improve classifiers when working with datasets that span different time intervals. We propose to treat this as a *domain adaptation* problem. In domain adaptation, any partition of data that is expected to have a different distribution of features can be treated as a domain (Joshi et al., 2013). Traditionally, domain adaptation is used to adapt models to a common task across rather different sets of data, e.g., a sentiment classifier for different types of products (Blitzer et al., 2007). Recent work has also applied domain adaptation to adjust for potentially more subtle differences in data, such as adapting for differences in the demographics of authors (Volkova et al., 2013; Lynn et al., 2017). We follow the same approach, treating time intervals as domains.

In our experiments, we use the feature augmentation approach of Daumé III (2007) to perform domain adaptation. Each feature is duplicated to have a specific version of the feature for every domain, as well as a domain-independent version of the feature. In each instance, the domain-independent feature and the domain-specific feature for that instance's domain have the same feature value, while the value is zeroed out for the domain-specific features for the other domains.

Data (Seasonal)	Baseline	Adaptation
Reviews (music)	.901	**.919**
Reviews (hotels)	.867	**.881**
Reviews (restaurants)	.874	**.898**
News (economy)	.782	.782
Twitter (vaccines)	**.881**	.880

Table 2: F1 scores when treating each seasonal time interval as a domain and applying domain adaptation compared to using no adaptation.

This is equivalent to a model where the feature weights are domain specific but share a Gaussian prior across domains (Finkel and Manning, 2009). This approach is widely used due to its simplicity, and derivatives of this approach have been used in similar work (e.g., (Lynn et al., 2017)). Following Finkel and Manning (2009), we separately adjust the regularization strength for the domain-independent feature weights and the domain-specific feature weights.

4.1 Seasonal Adaptation

We first examine classification performance on the datasets when grouping the seasonal time intervals (January-March, April-June, July-August, September-December) as domains and applying the feature augmentation approach for domain adaptation. As a baseline comparison, we apply the same classifier, but without domain adaptation.

Results are shown in Table 2. We see that applying domain adaptation provides a small boost in three of the datasets, and has no effect on two of the datasets. If this pattern holds in other corpora, then this suggests that it does not hurt performance to apply domain adaptation across different times of year, and in some cases can lead to a small performance boost.

Data (Non-seasonal)	Baseline	Adaptation	Adapt.+seasons
Reviews (music)	.895	**.924**	.910
Reviews (hotels)	.886	.892	**.920**
Reviews (restaurants)	.831	.879	**.889**
News (economy)	.763	.780	**.859**
Politics (platforms)	.661	**.665**	n/a
Twitter (vaccines)	.910	.903	**.920**

Table 3: F1 scores when testing on the final time interval after training on all previous intervals.

4.2 Non-seasonal Adaptation

We now consider the non-seasonal time intervals (spans of years). In particular, we consider the scenario when one wants to apply a classifier trained on older data to *future* data. This requires a modification to the domain adaptation approach, because future data includes domains that did not exist in the training data, and thus we cannot learn domain-specific feature weights. To solve this, we train in the usual way, but when testing on future data, we only include the domain-independent features. The intuition is that the domain-independent parameters should be applicable to all domains, and so using only these features should lead to better generalizability to new domains. We test this hypothesis by training the classifiers on all but the last time interval, and testing on the final interval. For hyperparameter tuning, we used the final time interval of the training data (i.e., the penultimate interval) as the validation set. The intuition is that the penultimate interval is the closest to the test data and thus is expected to be most similar to it.

Results are shown in the first three columns of Table 3. We see that this approach leads to a small performance boost in all cases except the Twitter dataset. This means that this simple feature augmentation approach has the potential to make classifiers more robust to future changes in data.

How to apply the feature augmentation technique to unseen domains is not well understood. By removing the domain-specific features, as we did here, the prediction model has changed, and so its behavior may be hard to predict. Nonetheless, this appears to be a successful approach.

4.2.1 Adding Seasonal Features

We also experimented with including the seasonal features when performing non-seasonal adaptation. In this setting, we train the models with two domain-specific features in addition to the domain-independent features: one for the season,

and one for the non-seasonal interval. As above, we remove the non-seasonal features at test time; however, we retain the season-specific features in addition to the domain-independent features, as they can be reused in future years.

The results of this approach are shown in the last column of Table 3. We find that combining seasonal and non-seasonal features together leads to an additional performance gain in most cases.

5 Conclusion

Our experiments suggest that time can substantially affect the performance of document classification, and practitioners should be cognizant of this variable when developing classifiers. A simple analysis comparing pairs of time intervals can provide insights into how performance varies with time, which could be a good practice to do when initially working with a corpus. Our experiments also suggest that simple domain adaptation techniques can help account for this variation.[4]

We make two practical recommendations following the insights from this work. First, evaluation will be most accurate if the test data is as similar as possible to whatever future data the classifier will be applied to, and one way to achieve this is to select test data from the chronological end of the corpus, rather than randomly sampling data without regard to time. Second, we observed that performance on future data tends to increase when hyperparameter tuning is conducted on later data; thus, we also recommend sampling validation data from the chronological end of the corpus.

Acknowledgements

The authors thank the anonymous reviews for their insightful comments and suggestions. This work was supported in part by the National Science Foundation under award number IIS-1657338.

---

[4]Our code is available at: `https://github.com/xiaoleihuang/Domain_Adaptation_ACL2018`

References

Steffen Bickel, Michael Brckner, and Tobias Scheffer. 2009. Discriminative learning under covariate shift. *Journal of Machine Learning Research*, 10:2137–2155.

John Blitzer, Mark Dredze, and Fernando Pereira. 2007. Biographies, bollywood, boom-boxes and blenders: Domain adaptation for sentiment classification. In *Association for Computational Linguistics (ACL)*, pages 440–447.

Nathanael Chambers. 2012. Labeling documents with timestamps: Learning from their time expressions. In *Proceedings of the 50th Annual Meeting of the Association for Computational Linguistics (ACL)*, pages 98–106.

Hal Daumé III. 2007. Frustratingly easy domain adaptation. In *Association for Computational Linguistics (ACL)*.

Jacob Eisenstein, Brendan O'Connor, Noah A. Smith, and Eric P. Xing. 2014. Diffusion of lexical change in social media. *PLoS ONE*, 9.

Jenny R. Finkel and Christopher D. Manning. 2009. Hierarchical Bayesian domain adaptation. In *North American Chapter of the Association for Computational Linguistics (ACL)*.

Rahul Goel, Sandeep Soni, Naman Goyal, John Paparrizos, Hanna Wallach, Fernando Diaz, and Jacob Eisenstein. 2016. The social dynamics of language change in online networks. In *The International Conference on Social Informatics (SocInfo)*.

William L. Hamilton, Jure Leskovec, and Dan Jurafsky. 2016. Diachronic word embeddings reveal statistical laws of semantic change. In *Association for Computational Linguistics (ACL)*.

Ruining He and Julian McAuley. 2016. Ups and downs: Modeling the visual evolution of fashion trends with one-class collaborative filtering. In *Proceedings of the 25th International Conference on World Wide Web (WWW)*, pages 507–517. International World Wide Web Conferences Steering Committee.

Xiaolei Huang, Michael C Smith, Michael J Paul, Dmytro Ryzhkov, Sandra C Quinn, David A Broniatowski, and Mark Dredze. 2017. Examining patterns of influenza vaccination in social media. In *Proceedings of the AAAI Joint Workshop on Health Intelligence (W3PHIAI), San Francisco, CA, USA*, pages 4–5.

Mahesh Joshi, Mark Dredze, William W. Cohen, and Carolyn P. Rose. 2013. What's in a domain? multi-domain learning for multi-attribute data. In *North American Chapter of the Association for Computational Linguistics (NAACL) (short paper)*, pages 685–690.

N. Kanhabua and K. Nørvåg. 2008. Improving temporal language models for determining time of non-timestamped documents. In *European Conference on Digital Libraries (ECDL)*.

Dimitrios Kotsakos, Theodoros Lappas, Dimitrios Kotzias, Dimitrios Gunopulos, Nattiya Kanhabua, and Kjetil Nørvåg. 2014. A burstiness-aware approach for document dating. In *Proceedings of the 37th International ACM SIGIR Conference on Research & Development in Information Retrieval (SIGIR)*, pages 1003–1006.

Veronica E. Lynn, Youngseo Son, Vivek Kulkarni, Niranjan Balasubramanian, and H. Andrew Schwartz. 2017. Human centered NLP with user-factor adaptation. In *Empirical Methods in Natural Language Processing (EMNLP)*, pages 1146–1155.

Fabian Pedregosa, Gaël Varoquaux, Alexandre Gramfort, Vincent Michel, Bertrand Thirion, Olivier Grisel, Mathieu Blondel, Peter Prettenhofer, Ron Weiss, Vincent Dubourg, et al. 2011. Scikit-learn: Machine learning in Python. *The Journal of Machine Learning Research*, 12:2825–2830.

Radim Řehůřek and Petr Sojka. 2010. Software Framework for Topic Modelling with Large Corpora. In *Proceedings of the LREC 2010 Workshop on New Challenges for NLP Frameworks*, pages 45–50, Valletta, Malta. ELRA. http://is.muni.cz/publication/884893/en.

Hidetoshi Shimodaira. 2000. Improving predictive inference under covariate shift by weighting the log-likelihood function. *Journal of Statistical Planning and Inference*, 90(2):227 – 244.

Stephen Ullmann. 1962. *Semantics: an introduction to the science of meaning*. Basil Blackwell, Oxford.

Svitlana Volkova, Theresa Wilson, and David Yarowsky. 2013. Exploring demographic language variations to improve multilingual sentiment analysis in social media. In *Empirical Methods in Natural Language Processing (EMNLP)*, pages 1815–1827.

Derry Tanti Wijaya and Reyyan Yeniterzi. 2011. Understanding semantic change of words over centuries. In *Proceedings of the 2011 International Workshop on DETecting and Exploiting Cultural diversiTy on the Social Web*.

D.P. Wilkins. 1993. *From Part to Person: Natural Tendencies of Semantic Change and the Search for Cognates*. Cognitive Anthropology Research Group at the Max Planck Institute for Psycholinguistics.

Hui Zou and Trevor Hastie. 2005. Regularization and variable selection via the elastic net. *Journal of the Royal Statistical Society, Series B*, 67:301–320.

Personalized Language Model for Query Auto-Completion

Aaron Jaech and Mari Ostendorf
University of Washington
{ajaech, ostendor}@uw.edu

Abstract

Query auto-completion is a search engine feature whereby the system suggests completed queries as the user types. Recently, the use of a recurrent neural network language model was suggested as a method of generating query completions. We show how an adaptable language model can be used to generate personalized completions and how the model can use online updating to make predictions for users not seen during training. The personalized predictions are significantly better than a baseline that uses no user information.

1 Introduction

Query auto-completion (QAC) is a feature used by search engines that provides a list of suggested queries for the user as they are typing. For instance, if the user types the prefix "mete" then the system might suggest "meters" or "meteorite" as completions. This feature can save the user time and reduce cognitive load (Cai et al., 2016).

Most approaches to QAC are extensions of the Most Popular Completion (MPC) algorithm (Bar-Yossef and Kraus, 2011). MPC suggests completions based on the most popular queries in the training data that match the specified prefix. One way to improve MPC is to consider additional signals such as temporal information (Shokouhi and Radinsky, 2012; Whiting and Jose, 2014) or information gleaned from a users' past queries (Shokouhi, 2013). This paper deals with the latter of those two signals, i.e. personalization. Personalization relies on the fact that query likelihoods are drastically different among different people depending on their needs and interests.

Recently, Park and Chiba (2017) suggested a significantly different approach to QAC. In their

	Cold Start	Warm Start
1	bank of america	bank of america
2	barnes and noble	basketball
3	babiesrus	baseball
4	baby names	barnes and noble
5	bank one	baltimore

Table 1: Top five completions for the prefix "ba" for a cold start model with no user knowledge and a warm model that has seen the queries espn, sports news, nascar, yankees, and nba.

work, completions are generated from a character LSTM language model instead of by ranking completions retrieved from a database, as in the MPC algorithm. This approach is able to complete queries whose prefixes were not seen during training and has significant memory savings over having to store a large query database.

Building on this work, we consider the task of personalized QAC, advancing current methods by combining the obvious advantages of personalization with the effectiveness of a language model in handling rare and previously unseen prefixes. The model must learn how to extract information from a user's past queries and use it to adapt the generative model for that person's future queries. To do this, we leverage recent advances in context-adaptive neural language modeling. In particular, we make use of the recently introduced FactorCell model that uses an embedding vector to additively transform the weights of the language model's recurrent layer with a low-rank matrix (Jaech and Ostendorf, 2017). By allowing a greater fraction of the weights to change during personalization, the FactorCell model has advantages over the traditional approach to adaptation of concatenating a context vector to the input of the LSTM (Mikolov and Zweig, 2012).

Table 1 provides an anecdotal example from

Proceedings of the 56th Annual Meeting of the Association for Computational Linguistics (Short Papers), pages 700–705
Melbourne, Australia, July 15 - 20, 2018. ©2018 Association for Computational Linguistics

the trained FactorCell model to demonstrate the intended behavior. The table shows the top five completions for the prefix "ba" in a cold start scenario and again after the user has completed five sports related queries. In the warm start scenario, the "baby names" and "babiesrus" completions no longer appear in the top five and have been replaced with "basketball" and "baseball".

The novel aspects of this work are the application of an adaptive language model to the task of QAC personalization and the demonstration of how RNN language models can be adapted to contexts (users) not seen during training. An additional contribution is showing that a richer adaptation framework gives added gains with added data.

2   Model

Adaptation depends on learning an embedding for each user, which we discuss in Section 2.1, and then using that embedding to adjust the weights of the recurrent layer, discussed in Section 2.2.

2.1   Learning User Embeddings

During training, we learn an embedding for each of the users. We think of these embeddings as holding latent demographic factors for each user. Users who have less than 15 queries in the training data (around half the users but less than 13% of the queries) are grouped together as a single entity, $user_1$, leaving k users. The user embeddings matrix $\mathbf{U}_{k \times m}$, where m is the user embedding size, is learned via back-propagation as part of the end-to-end model. The embedding for an individual user is the ith row of $\mathbf{U}$ and is denoted by u_i.

It is important to be able to apply the model to users that are not seen during training. This is done by online updating of the user embeddings during evaluation. When a new person, $user_{k+1}$ is seen, a new row is added to $\mathbf{U}$ and initialized to u_1. Each person's user embedding is updated via back-propagation every time they select a query. When doing online updating of the user embeddings, the rest of the model parameters (everything except $\mathbf{U}$) are frozen.

2.2   Recurrent Layer Adaptation

We consider three model architectures which differ only in the method for adapting the recurrent layer. First is the unadapted LM, analogous to the model from Park and Chiba (2017), which does no personalization. The second architecture was

introduced by Mikolov and Zweig (2012) and has been used multiple times for LM personalization (Wen et al., 2013; Huang et al., 2014; Li et al., 2016). It works by concatenating a user embedding to the character embedding at every step of the input to the recurrent layer. Jaech and Ostendorf (2017) refer to this model as the ConcatCell and show that it is equivalent to adding a term $\mathbf{V}u$ to adjust the bias of the recurrent layer. The hidden state of a ConcatCell with embedding size e and hidden state size h is given in Equation 1 where σ is the activation function, w_t is the character embedding, h_{t-1} is the previous hidden state, and $\mathbf{W} \in \mathbb{R}^{e+h \times h}$ and $b \in \mathbb{R}^h$ are the recurrent layer weight matrix and bias vector.

$$h_t = \sigma([w_t, h_{t-1}]\mathbf{W} + b + \mathbf{V}u) \qquad (1)$$

Adapting just the bias vector is a significant limitation. The FactorCell model, (Jaech and Ostendorf, 2017), remedies this by letting the user embedding transform the weights of the recurrent layer via the use of a low-rank adaptation matrix. The FactorCell uses a weight matrix $\mathbf{W}' = \mathbf{W} + \mathbf{A}$ that has been additively transformed by a personalized low-rank matrix $\mathbf{A}$. Because the FactorCell weight matrix $\mathbf{W}'$ is different for each user (See Equation 2), it allows for a much stronger adaptation than what is possible using the more standard ConcatCell model.[1]

$$h_t = \sigma([w_t, h_{t-1}]\mathbf{W}' + b) \qquad (2)$$

The low-rank adaptation matrix $\mathbf{A}$ is generated by taking the product between a user's m dimensional embedding and left and right bases tensors, $\mathbf{Z}_L \in \mathbb{R}^{m \times e+h \times r}$ and $\mathbf{Z}_R \in \mathbb{R}^{r \times h \times m}$ as so,

$$\mathbf{A} = (u_i \times_1 \mathbf{Z}_L)(\mathbf{Z}_R \times_3 u_i) \qquad (3)$$

where $\times_i$ denotes the mode-i tensor product. The above product selects a user specific adaptation matrix by taking a weighted combination of the m rank r matrices held between $\mathbf{Z}_L$ and $\mathbf{Z}_R$. The rank, r, is a hyperparameter which controls the degree of personalization.

3   Data

Our experiments make use of the AOL Query data collected over three months in 2006 (Pass et al., 2006). The first six of the ten files were used for

---

[1]In the case of an LSTM, $\mathbf{W}'$ is extended to incorporate all of the gates.

training. This contains approximately 12 million queries from 173,000 users for an average of 70 queries per user (median 15). A set of 240,000 queries from those same users (2% of the data) was reserved for tuning and validation. From the remaining files, one million queries from 30,000 users are used to test the models on a disjoint set of users.

4 Experiments

4.1 Implementation Details

The vocabulary consists of 79 characters including special start and stop tokens. Models were trained for six epochs. The Adam optimizer is used during training with a learning rate of 10^{-3} (Kingma and Ba, 2014). When updating the user embeddings during evaluation, we found that it is easier to use an optimizer without momentum. We use Adadelta (Zeiler, 2012) and tune the online learning rate to give the best perplexity on a held-out set of 12,000 queries, having previously verified that perplexity is a good indicator of performance on the QAC task.[2]

The language model is a single-layer character-level LSTM with coupled input and forget gates and layer normalization (Melis et al., 2018; Ba et al., 2016). We do experiments on two model configurations: small and large. The small models use an LSTM hidden state size of 300 and 20 dimensional user embeddings. The large models use a hidden state size of 600 and 40 dimensional user embeddings. Both sizes use 24 dimensional character embeddings. For the small sized models, we experimented with different values of the FactorCell rank hyperparameter between 30 and 50 dimensions finding that bigger rank is better. The large sized models used a fixed value of 60 for the rank hyperparemeter. During training only and due to limited computational resources, queries are truncated to a length of 40 characters.

Prefixes are selected uniformly at random with the constraint that they contain at least two characters in the prefix and that there is at least one character in the completion. To generate completions using beam search, we use a beam width of 100 and a branching factor of 4. Results are reported using mean reciprocal rank (MRR), the standard method of evaluating QAC systems. It is the mean of the reciprocal rank of the true completion in the

---

[2]Code at http://github.com/ajaech/query_completion

Size	Model	Seen	Unseen	All
	MPC	.292	.000	.203
(S)	Unadapted	.292	.256	.267
	ConcatCell	.296	.263	.273
	FactorCell	.300	.264	.275
(B)	Unadapted	.324	.286	.297
	ConcatCell	.330	.298	.308
	FactorCell	.335	.298	.309

Table 2: MRR reported for seen and unseen prefixes for small (S) and big (B) models.

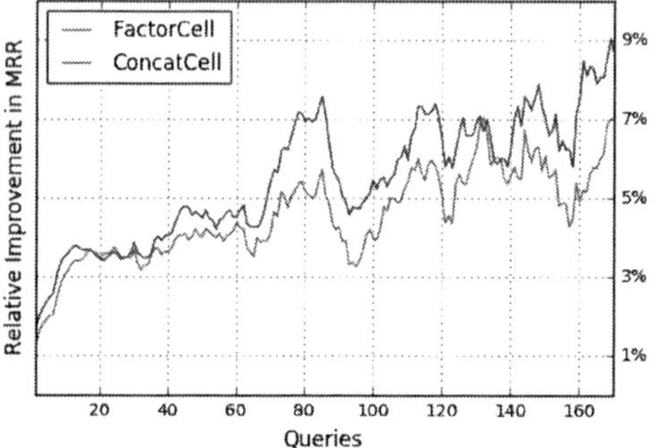

Figure 1: Relative improvement in MRR over the unpersonalized model versus queries seen using the large size models. Plot uses a moving average of width 9 to reduce noise.

top ten proposed completions. The reciprocal rank is zero if the true completion is not in the top ten.

Neural models are compared against an MPC baseline. Following Park and Chiba (2017), we remove queries seen less than three times from the MPC training data.

4.2 Results

Table 2 compares the performance of the different models against the MPC baseline on a test set of one million queries from a user population that is disjoint with the training set. Results are presented separately for prefixes that are seen or unseen in the training data. Consistent with prior work, the neural models do better than the MPC baseline. The personalized models are both better than the unadapted one. The FactorCell model is the best overall in both the big and small sized experiments, but the gain is mainly for the seen prefixes.

Figure 1 shows the relative improvement in MRR over an unpersonalized model versus the number of queries seen per user. Both the Factor-

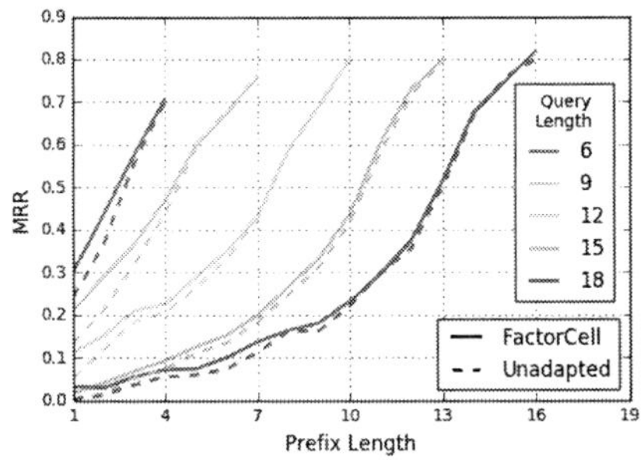

Figure 2: MRR by prefix and query lengths for the large FactorCell and unadapted models with the first 50 queries per user excluded.

Cell and the ConcatCell show continued improvement as more queries from each user are seen, and the FactorCell outperforms the ConcatCell by an increasing margin over time. In the long run, we expect that the system will have seen many queries from most users. Therefore, the right side of Figure 1, where the relative gain of FactorCell is up to 2% better than that of the ConcatCell, is more indicative of the potential of these models for active users. Since the data was collected over a limited time frame and half of all users have fifteen or fewer queries, the results in Table 2 do not reflect the full benefit of personalization.

Figure 2 shows the MRR for different prefix and query lengths. We find that longer prefixes help the model make longer completions and (more obviously) shorter completions have higher MRR. Comparing the personalized model against the unpersonalized baseline, we see that the biggest gains are for short queries and prefixes of length one or two.

We found that one reason why the FactorCell outperforms the ConcatCell is that it is able to pick up sooner on the repetitive search behaviors that some users have. This commonly happens for navigational queries where someone searches for the name of their favorite website once or more per day. At the extreme tail there are users who search for nothing but free online poker. Both models do well on these highly predictable users but the FactorCell is generally a bit quicker to adapt.

We conducted case studies to better understand what information is represented in the user embeddings and what makes the FactorCell different from the ConcatCell. From a cold start user embedding we ran two queries and allowed the model to update the user embedding. Then, we ranked

	FactorCell	ConcatCell
1	high school musical	horoscope
2	chris brown	high school musical
3	funnyjunk.com	homes for sale
4	funbrain.com	modular homes
5	chat room	hair styles

Table 3: The five queries that have the greatest adapted vs. unadapted likelihood ratio after searching for "high school softball" and "math homework help".

the most frequent 1,500 queries based on the ratio of their likelihood from before and after updating the user embeddings.

Tables 3 and 4 show the queries with the highest relative likelihood of the adapted vs. unadapted models after two related search queries: "high school softball" and "math homework help" for Table 3, and "Prada handbags" and "Versace eyewear" for Table 4. In both cases, the FactorCell model examples are more semantically coherent than the ConcatCell examples. In the first case, the FactorCell model identifies queries that a high school student might make, including entertainment sources and a celebrity entertainer popular with that demographic. In the second case, the FactorCell model chooses retailers that carry woman's apparel and those that sell home goods. While these companies' brands are not as luxurious as Prada or Versace, most of the top luxury brand names do not appear in the top 1,500 queries and our model may not be capable of being that specific. There is no obvious semantic connection between the highest likelihood ratio phrases for the ConcatCell; it seems to be focusing more on orthography than semantics (e.g. "home" in the first example).. Not shown are the queries which experienced the greatest decrease in likelihood. For the "high school" case, these included searches for travel agencies and airline tickets—websites not targeted towards the high school age demographic.

5   Related Work

While the standard implementation of MPC can not handle unseen prefixes, there are variants which do have that ability. Park and Chiba (2017) find that the neural LM outperforms MPC even when MPC has been augmented with the approach from Mitra and Craswell (2015) for handling rare

	FactorCell	ConcatCell
1	neiman marcus	craigslist nyc
2	pottery barn	myspace layouts
3	jc penney	verizon wireless
4	verizon wireless	jensen ackles
5	bed bath and beyond	webster dictionary

Table 4: The five queries that have the greatest adapted vs. unadapted likelihood ratio after searching for "prada handbags" and "versace eyewear".

prefixes. There has also been work on personalizing MPC (Shokouhi, 2013; Cai et al., 2014). We did not compare against these specific models because our goal was to show how personalization can improve the already-proven generative neural model approach. RNN's have also previously been used for the related task of next query suggestion (Sordoni et al., 2015).

Our results are not directly comparable to Park and Chiba (2017) or Mitra and Craswell (2015) due to differences in the partitioning of the data and the method for selecting random prefixes. Prior work partitions the data by time instead of by user. Splitting by users is necessary in order to properly test personalization over longer time ranges.

Wang et al. (2018) show how spelling correction can be integrated into an RNN language model query auto-completion system and how the completions can be generated in real time using a GPU. Our method of updating the model during evaluation resembles work on dynamic evaluation for language modeling (Krause et al., 2017), but differs in that only the user embeddings (latent demographic factors) are updated.

6 Conclusion and Future Work

Our experiments show that the LSTM model can be improved using personalization. The method of adapting the recurrent layer clearly matters and we obtained an advantage by using the FactorCell model. The reason the FactorCell does better is in part attributable to having two to three times as many parameters in the recurrent layer as either the ConcatCell or the unadapted models. By design, the adapted weight matrix $\mathbf{W}'$ only needs to be computed at most once per query and is reused many thousands of times during beam search. As a result, for a given latency budget, the FactorCell

model outperforms the Mikolov and Zweig (2012) model for LSTM adaptation.

The cost for updating the user embeddings is similar to the cost of the forward pass and depends on the size of the user embedding, hidden state size, FactorCell rank, and query length. In most cases there will be time between queries for updates, but updates can be less frequent to reduce computational costs.

We also showed that language model personalization can be effective even on users who are not seen during training. The benefits of personalization are immediate and increase over time as the system continues to leverage the incoming data to build better user representations. The approach can easily be extended to include time as an additional conditioning factor. We leave the question of whether the results can be improved by combining the language model with MPC for future work.

References

Jimmy Lei Ba, Jamie Ryan Kiros, and Geoffrey E Hinton. 2016. Layer normalization. *arXiv preprint arXiv:1607.06450*.

Ziv Bar-Yossef and Naama Kraus. 2011. Context-sensitive query auto-completion. In *WWW*, pages 107–116. ACM.

Fei Cai, Maarten De Rijke, et al. 2016. A survey of query auto completion in information retrieval. *Foundations and Trends in Information Retrieval*, 10(4):273–363.

Fei Cai, Shangsong Liang, and Maarten De Rijke. 2014. Time-sensitive personalized query auto-completion. In *CIKM*, pages 1599–1608. ACM.

Yu-Yang Huang, Rui Yan, Tsung-Ting Kuo, and Shou-De Lin. 2014. Enriching cold start personalized language model using social network information. In *ACL*, pages 611–617.

Aaron Jaech and Mari Ostendorf. 2017. Low-rank RNN adaptation for context-aware language modeling. *arXiv preprint arXiv:1710.02603*.

Diederik P Kingma and Jimmy Ba. 2014. Adam: A method for stochastic optimization. *arXiv preprint arXiv:1412.6980*.

Ben Krause, Emmanuel Kahembwe, Iain Murray, and Steve Renals. 2017. Dynamic evaluation of neural sequence models. *arXiv preprint arXiv:1709.07432*.

Jiwei Li, Michel Galley, Chris Brockett, Jianfeng Gao, and Bill Dolan. 2016. A persona-based neural conversation model. *ACL*.

Gábor Melis, Chris Dyer, and Phil Blunsom. 2018. On the state of the art of evaluation in neural language models. *ICLR*.

Tomas Mikolov and Geoffrey Zweig. 2012. Context dependent recurrent neural network language model. In *SLT*, pages 234–239.

Bhaskar Mitra and Nick Craswell. 2015. Query auto-completion for rare prefixes. In *CIKM*, pages 1755–1758. ACM.

Dae Hoon Park and Rikio Chiba. 2017. A neural language model for query auto-completion. In *SIGIR*, pages 1189–1192. ACM.

Greg Pass, Abdur Chowdhury, and Cayley Torgeson. 2006. A picture of search. In *InfoScale*, volume 152, page 1.

Milad Shokouhi. 2013. Learning to personalize query auto-completion. In *SIGIR*, pages 103–112. ACM.

Milad Shokouhi and Kira Radinsky. 2012. Time-sensitive query auto-completion. In *SIGIR*, pages 601–610. ACM.

Alessandro Sordoni, Yoshua Bengio, Hossein Vahabi, Christina Lioma, Jakob Grue Simonsen, and Jian-Yun Nie. 2015. A hierarchical recurrent encoder-decoder for generative context-aware query suggestion. In *CIKM*, pages 553–562. ACM.

Po-Wei Wang, J. Zico Kolter, Vijai Mohan, and Inderjit S. Dhillon. 2018. Realtime query completion via deep language models. *ICLR*.

Tsung-Hsien Wen, Aaron Heidel, Hung-yi Lee, Yu Tsao, and Lin-Shan Lee. 2013. Recurrent neural network based language model personalization by social network crowdsourcing. In *INTERSPEECH*, pages 2703–2707.

Stewart Whiting and Joemon M Jose. 2014. Recent and robust query auto-completion. In *WWW*, pages 971–982. ACM.

Matthew D. Zeiler. 2012. ADADELTA: an adaptive learning rate method. *CoRR*, abs/1212.5701.

Personalized Review Generation by Expanding Phrases and Attending on Aspect-Aware Representations

Jianmo Ni
University of California San Diego
`jin018@ucsd.edu`

Julian McAuley
University of California San Diego
`jmcauley@ucsd.edu`

Abstract

In this paper, we focus on the problem of building assistive systems that can help users to write reviews. We cast this problem using an encoder-decoder framework that generates personalized reviews by expanding short phrases (e.g. review summaries, product titles) provided as input to the system. We incorporate aspect-level information via an aspect encoder that learns 'aspect-aware' user and item representations. An attention fusion layer is applied to control generation by attending on the outputs of multiple encoders. Experimental results show that our model is capable of generating coherent and diverse reviews that expand the contents of input phrases. In addition, the learned aspect-aware representations discover those aspects that users are more inclined to discuss and bias the generated text toward their personalized aspect preferences.

1 Introduction

Contextual, or 'data-to-text' natural language generation is one of the core tasks in natural language processing and has a considerable impact on various fields (Gatt and Krahmer, 2017). Within the field of recommender systems, a promising application is to estimate (or generate) personalized reviews that a user would write about a product, i.e., to discover their nuanced opinions about each of its individual aspects. A successful model could work (for instance) as (a) a highly-nuanced recommender system that tells users their likely reaction to a product in the form of text fragments; (b) a writing tool that helps users 'brainstorm' the review-writing process; or (c) a querying system that facilitates personalized natural language queries (i.e., to find items about which a user would be most likely to write a particular phrase). Some recent works have explored the review generation task and shown success in generating cohesive reviews (Dong et al., 2017; Ni et al., 2017; Zang and Wan, 2017). Most of these works treat the user and item identity as input; we seek a system with more nuance and more precision by allowing users to 'guide' the model via short phrases, or auxiliary data such as item specifications. For example, a review writing assistant might allow users to write short phrases and expand these key points into a plausible review.

Review text has been widely studied in traditional tasks such as aspect extraction (Mukherjee and Liu, 2012; He et al., 2017), extraction of sentiment lexicons (Zhang et al., 2014), and aspect-aware sentiment analysis (Wang et al., 2016; McAuley et al., 2012). These works are related to review generation since they can provide prior knowledge to supervise the generative process. We are interested in exploring how such knowledge (e.g. extracted aspects) can be used in the review generation task.

In this paper, we focus on designing a review generation model that is able to leverage both user and item information as well as auxiliary, textual input and aspect-aware knowledge. Specifically, we study the task of expanding short phrases into complete, coherent reviews that accurately reflect the opinions and knowledge learned from those phrases.

These short phrases could include snippets provided by the user, or manifest aspects about the items themselves (e.g. brand words, technical specifications, etc.). We propose an encoder-decoder framework that takes into consideration three encoders (a sequence encoder, an attribute encoder, and an aspect encoder), and one decoder. The sequence encoder uses a gated recurrent unit

Proceedings of the 56th Annual Meeting of the Association for Computational Linguistics (Short Papers), pages 706–711
Melbourne, Australia, July 15 - 20, 2018. ©2018 Association for Computational Linguistics

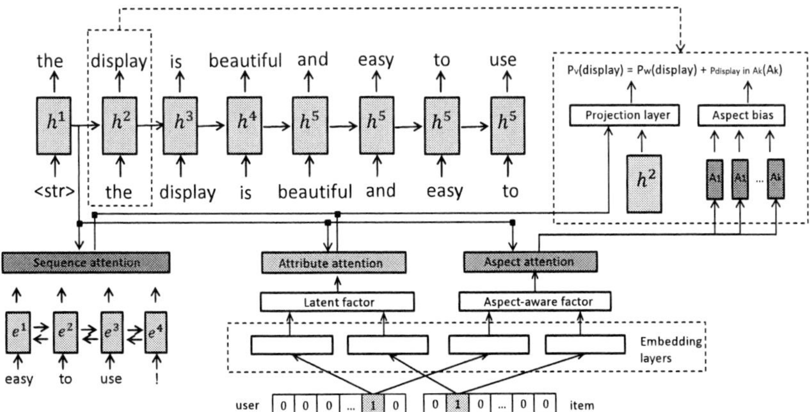

Figure 1: General structure of ExpansionNet.

(GRU) network to encode text information; the attribute encoder learns a latent representation of user and item identity; finally, the aspect encoder finds an aspect-aware representation of users and items, which reflects user-aspect preferences and item-aspect relationships. The aspect-aware representation is helpful to discover what each user is likely to discuss about each item. Finally, the output of these encoders is passed to the sequence decoder with an attention fusion layer. The decoder attends on the encoded information and biases the model to generate words that are consistent with the input phrases and words belonging to the most relevant aspects.

2 Related Work

Review generation belongs to a large body of work on data-to-text natural language generation (Gatt and Krahmer, 2017), which has applications including summarization (See et al., 2017), image captioning (Vinyals et al., 2015), and dialogue response generation (Xing et al., 2017; Li et al., 2016; Ghosh et al., 2017), among others. Among these, review generation is characterized by the need to generate long sequences and estimate high-order interactions between users and items.

Several approaches have been recently proposed to tackle these problems. Dong et al. (2017) proposed an attribute-to-sequence (Attr2Seq) method to encode user and item identities as well as rating information with a multi-layer perceptron and a decoder then generates reviews conditioned on this information. They also used an attention mechanism to strengthen the alignment between output and input attributes. Ni et al. (2017) trained a collaborative-filtering generative concatenative network to jointly learn the tasks of review generation and item recommendation. Zang and Wan (2017) proposed a hierarchical structure to generate long reviews; they assume each sentence is associated with an aspect score, and learn the attention between aspect scores and sentences during training. Our approach differs from these mainly in our goal of incorporating auxiliary textual information (short phrases, product specifications, etc.) into the generative process, which facilitates the generation of higher-fidelity reviews.

Another line of work related to review generation is aspect extraction and opinion mining (Park et al., 2015; Qiu et al., 2017; He et al., 2017; Chen et al., 2014). In this paper, we argue that the extra aspect (opinion) information extracted using these previous works can effectively improve the quality of generated reviews. We propose a simple but effective way to combine aspect information into the generative model.

3 Approach

We describe the review generation task as follows. Given a user u, item i, several short phrases $\{d_1, d_2, ..., d_M\}$, and a group of extracted aspects $\{A_1, A_2, ..., A_k\}$, our goal is to generate a review $(w_1, w_2, ..., w_T)$ that maximizes the probability $P(w_{1:T}|u, i, d_{1:M})$. To solve this task, we propose a method called *ExpansionNet* which contains two parts: 1) three encoders to leverage the input phrases and aspect information; and 2) a decoder with an attention fusion layer to generate sequences and align the generation with the input sources. The model structure is shown in Figure 1.

3.1 Sequence encoder, attribute encoder and aspect encoder

Our sequence encoder is a two-layer bi-directional GRU, as is commonly used in sequence-to-sequence (Seq2Seq) models (Cho et al., 2014). Input phrases first pass a word embedding layer, then go through the GRU one-by-one and finally yield a sequence of hidden states $\{\mathbf{e}_1, \mathbf{e}_2..., \mathbf{e}_L\}$. In the case of multiple phrases, these share the same sequence encoder and have different lengths, L. To simplify notation, we only consider one input phrase in this section.

The attribute encoder and aspect encoder both consist of two embedding layers and a projection layer. For the attribute encoder, we define two general embedding layers $E_u \in \mathbb{R}^{|\mathcal{U}| \times m}$ and $E_i \in \mathbb{R}^{|\mathcal{I}| \times m}$ to obtain the attribute latent factors γ_u and γ_i; for the aspect encoder, we use two aspect-aware embedding layers $E_u' \in \mathbb{R}^{|\mathcal{U}| \times k}$ and $E_i' \in \mathbb{R}^{|\mathcal{I}| \times k}$ to obtain aspect-aware latent factors β_u and β_i. Here $|\mathcal{U}|$, $|\mathcal{I}|$, m and k are the number of users, number of items, the dimension of attributes, and the number of aspects, respectively. After the embedding layers, the attribute and aspect-aware latent factors are concatenated and fed into a projection layer with $\tanh$ activation. The outputs are calculated as:

$$\gamma_u = E_u(u), \gamma_i = E_i(i) \tag{1}$$

$$\beta_u = E_u'(u), \beta_i = E_i'(i) \tag{2}$$

$$\mathbf{u} = \tanh(W_{\mathbf{u}}[\gamma_u; \gamma_i] + \mathbf{b_u}) \tag{3}$$

$$\mathbf{v} = \tanh(W_{\mathbf{v}}[\beta_u; \beta_i] + \mathbf{b_v}) \tag{4}$$

where $W_{\mathbf{u}} \in \mathbb{R}^{n \times 2m}$, $\mathbf{b_u} \in \mathbb{R}^n$, $W_{\mathbf{v}} \in \mathbb{R}^{n \times 2k}$, $\mathbf{b_v} \in \mathbb{R}^n$ are learnable parameters and n is the dimensionality of the hidden units in the decoder.

3.2 Decoder with attention fusion layer

The decoder is a two-layer GRU that predicts the target words given the start token. The hidden state of the decoder is initialized using the sum of the three encoders' outputs. The hidden state at time-step t is updated via the GRU unit based on the previous hidden state and the input word. Specifically:

$$\mathbf{h}_0 = \mathbf{e}_L + \mathbf{u} + \mathbf{v} \tag{5}$$

$$\mathbf{h}_t = \text{GRU}(w_t, \mathbf{h}_{t-1}), \tag{6}$$

where $\mathbf{h}_0 \in \mathbb{R}^n$ is the decoder's initial hidden state and $\mathbf{h}_t \in \mathbb{R}^n$ is the hidden state at time-step t.

To fully exploit the encoder-side information, we apply an attention fusion layer to summarize the output of each encoder and jointly determine the final word distribution. For the sequence encoder, the attention vector is defined as in many other applications (Bahdanau et al., 2014; Luong et al., 2015):

$$\mathbf{a}_t^1 = \sum_{j=1}^{L} \alpha_{tj}^1 \mathbf{e}_j \tag{7}$$

$$\alpha_{tj}^1 = \exp(\tanh(\mathbf{v}_\alpha^{1\top}(W_\alpha^1[\mathbf{e}_j; \mathbf{h}_t] + \mathbf{b}_\alpha^1)))/Z, \tag{8}$$

where $\mathbf{a}_t^1 \in \mathbb{R}^n$ is the attention vector on the sequence encoder at time-step t, α_{tj}^1 is the attention score over the encoder hidden state $\mathbf{e}_j$ and decoder hidden state $\mathbf{h}_t$, and Z is a normalization term.

For the attribute encoder, the attention vector is calculated as:

$$\mathbf{a}_t^2 = \sum_{j \in u,i} \alpha_{tj}^2 \gamma_j \tag{9}$$

$$\alpha_{tj}^2 = \exp(\tanh(\mathbf{v}_\alpha^{2\top}(W_\alpha^2[\gamma_j; \mathbf{h}_t] + \mathbf{b}_\alpha^2)))/Z, \tag{10}$$

where $\mathbf{a}_t^2 \in \mathbb{R}^n$ is the attention vector on the attribute encoder, and α_{tj}^2 is the attention score between the attribute latent factor γ_j and decoder hidden state $\mathbf{h}_t$.

Inspired by the copy mechanism (Gu et al., 2016; See et al., 2017), we design an attention vector that estimates the probability that each aspect will be discussed in the next time-step:

$$s_{ui} = W_s[\beta_u; \beta_i] + \mathbf{b}_s \tag{11}$$

$$\mathbf{a}_t^3 = \tanh(W_\alpha^3[s_{ui}; e_t; \mathbf{h}_t] + \mathbf{b}_\alpha^3), \tag{12}$$

where $s_{ui} \in \mathbb{R}^k$ is the aspect importance considering the interaction between u and i, e_t is the decoder input after embedding layer at time-step t, and $\mathbf{a}_t^3 \in \mathbb{R}^k$ is a probability vector to bias each aspect at time-step t. Finally, the first two attention vectors are concatenated with the decoder hidden state at time-step t and projected to obtain the output word distribution P_v. The attention scores from the aspect encoder are then directly added to the aspect words in the final word distribution. The output probability for word w at time-step t is given by:

$$P_v(w_t) = \tanh(W[\mathbf{h}_t; \mathbf{a}_t^1; \mathbf{a}_t^2] + \mathbf{b}) \tag{13}$$

$$P(w_t) = P_v(w_t) + \mathbf{a}_t^3[k] \cdot \mathbb{1}_{w_t \in A_k}, \tag{14}$$

Table 1: Parameter settings used in our experiments.

Word dimension	Attribute dimension	Aspect dimension	GRU hidden size	Batch Size	Learning Rate	Optimizer
512	64	15	512	16	0.0002	Adam

where w_t is the target word at time-step t, $\mathbf{a}_t^3[k]$ is the probability that aspect k will be discussed at time-step t, A_k represents all words belonging to aspect k and $\mathbb{1}_{w_t \in A_k}$ is a binary variable indicating whether w_t belongs to aspect k.

During inference, we use greedy decoding by choosing the word with maximum probability, denoted as $y_t = \mathrm{argmax}_{w_t}\mathrm{softmax}(P(w_t))$. Decoding finishes when an end token is encountered.

4 Experiments

We consider a real world dataset from *Amazon Electronics* (McAuley et al., 2015) to evaluate our model. We convert all text into lowercase, add start and end tokens to each review, and perform tokenization using NLTK.[1] We discard reviews with length greater than 100 tokens and consider a vocabulary of 30,000 tokens. After preprocessing, the dataset contains 182,850 users, 59,043 items, and 992,172 reviews (sparsity 99.993%), which is much sparser than the datasets used in previous works (Dong et al., 2017; Ni et al., 2017). On average, each review contains 49.32 tokens as well as a short-text summary of 4.52 tokens. In our experiments, the basic ExpansionNet uses these summaries as input phrases. We split the dataset into training (80%), validation (10%) and test sets (10%). All results are reported on the test set.

4.1 Aspect Extraction

We use the method[2] in (He et al., 2017) to extract 15 aspects and consider the top 100 words from each aspect. Table 2 shows 10 inferred aspects and representative words (inferred aspects are manually labeled). ExpansionNet calculates an attention score based on the user and item aspect-aware representation, then determines how much these representative words are biased in the output word distribution.

Table 2: List of representative words for inferred aspects on Amazon Electronics dataset.

Aspects	Representative Words
Service	vendor seller supplier reply refund delivery shipping exchange contacting promptly
Price	price value overall dependable reliable affordable practical budget inexpensive bargain
Screen	screen touchscreen browse display scrolling surfing navigate icon menu surfing text blur reflection
Case	case cover briefcase portfolio padded protective rubberized padding leather skin
Drive	drive disk copying copied fat32 terabyte ntfs data hdd cache
Sound	sound vocal loudness booming bass treble tinny speaker isolation sennheisers
Vision	glossy shiny transparent polish reflective faded lcd shield glass painted
Laptop	lenovo inspiron ibm gateway pentium alienware xps pavilion thinkpad elite
Time	cycle time week day month hour suddenly repeated overnight continuously
Stableness	unscrew securing mounting drill centered tightening screwed attach tighten loosen

4.2 Experiment Details

We use PyTorch[3] to implement our model.[4] Parameter settings are shown in Table 1. For the attribute encoder and aspect encoder, we set the dimensionality to 64 and 15 respectively. For both the sequence encoder and decoder, we use a 2-layer GRU with hidden size 512. We also add dropout layers before and after the GRUs. The dropout rate is set to 0.1. During training, the input sequences of the same source (e.g. review, summary) inside each batch are padded to the same length.

4.3 Performance Evaluation

We evaluate the model on six automatic metrics (Table 3): Perplexity, BLEU-1/BLEU-4, ROUGE-L and Distinct-1/2 (percentage of distinct unigrams and bi-grams) (Li et al., 2016). We compare

---

[1] https://www.nltk.org/

[2] https://github.com/ruidan/Unsupervised-Aspect-Extraction

[3] http://pytorch.org/docs/master/index.html

[4] https://github.com/nijianmo/textExpansion

Table 3: Results on automatic metrics

Model	PPL	BLEU-1(%)	BLEU-4(%)	ROUGE-L	Distinct-1(%)	Distinct-2(%)
Rand	/	20.24	0.45	0.390	1.311	13.681
GRU-LM	35.35	30.79	1.20	/	/	/
Att2Seq	34.21	26.16	1.23	0.403	0.014	0.051
+aspect	34.26	26.87	1.51	0.397	0.018	0.069
ExpansionNet	34.18	26.05	2.21	0.404	0.096	0.789
+title	**30.7**	27.90	2.50	**0.415**	0.099	0.911
+attribute & aspect	31.7	**30.33**	**2.63**	0.408	**0.133**	**1.134**

User/Item	user *A3G831BTCLWGVQ* and item *B007M50PTM*
Review summary	"easy to use and nice standard apps"
Item title	"samsung galaxy tab 2 (10.1-Inch, wi-fi) 2012 model"
Real review	"the display is beautiful and the tablet is very easy to use. it comes with some really nice standard apps."
AttrsSeq	"i bought this for my wife 's new ipad air . it fits perfectly and looks great . the only thing i do n't like is that the cover is a little too small for the ipad air . "
ExpansionNet	"i love this tablet . it is fast and easy to use . i have no complaints . i would recommend this tablet to anyone ."
+title	"i love this tablet . it is fast and easy to use . i have a galaxy tab 2 and i love it ."
+attribute & aspect	"i love this tablet . it is easy to use and the screen is very responsive . i love the fact that it has a micro sd slot . i have not tried the tablet app yet but i do n't have any problems with it . i am very happy with this tablet ."

Figure 2: Examples of a real review and reviews generated by different models given a user, item, review summary, and item title. Highlights added for emphasis.

against three baselines: Rand (randomly choose a review from the training set), GRU-LM (the GRU decoder works alone as a language model) and a state-of-the-art model Attr2Seq that only considers user and item attribute (Dong et al., 2017). ExpansionNet (with summary, item title, attribute and aspect as input) achieves significant improvements over Attr2Seq on all metrics. As we add more input information, the model continues to obtain better results, except for the ROUGE-L metric. This proves that our model can effectively learn from short input phrases and aspect information and improve the correctness and diversity of generated results.

Figure 2 presents a sample generation result. ExpansionNet captures fine-grained item information (e.g. that the item is a tablet), which Attr2Seq fails to recognize. Moreover, given a phrase like "easy to use" in the summary, ExpansionNet generates reviews containing the same text. This demonstrates the possibility of using our model in an assistive review generation scenario. Finally, given extra aspect information, the model successfully estimates that the screen would be an important aspect (i.e., for the current user and item); it generates phrases such as "screen is very respon-

Table 4: Aspect coverage analysis

	# aspects (real)	# aspects (generated)	# covered aspects
Attr2Seq	2.875	**2.744**	0.686
ExpansionNet	2.875	1.804	0.807
+title	2.875	1.721	0.894
+attribute&aspect	2.875	1.834	**0.931**

sive" about the aspect "screen" which is also covered in the real (ground-truth) review ("display is beautiful").

We are also interested in seeing how the aspect-aware representation can find related aspects and bias the generation to discuss more about those aspects. We analyze the average number of aspects in real and generated reviews and show on average how many aspects in real reviews are covered in generated reviews. We consider a review as covering an aspect if any of the aspect's representative words exists in the review. As shown in Table 4, Attr2Seq tends to cover more aspects in generation, many of which are not discussed in real reviews. On the other hand, ExpansionNet better captures the distribution of aspects that are discussed in real reviews.

References

Dzmitry Bahdanau, Kyunghyun Cho, and Yoshua Bengio. 2014. Neural machine translation by jointly learning to align and translate. In *ICLR*.

Zhiyuan Chen, Arjun Mukherjee, and Bing Liu. 2014. Aspect extraction with automated prior knowledge learning. In *ACL*.

Kyunghyun Cho, Bart van Merrienboer, aglar Gülehre, Dzmitry Bahdanau, Fethi Bougares, Holger Schwenk, and Yoshua Bengio. 2014. Learning phrase representations using rnn encoder-decoder for statistical machine translation. In *EMNLP*.

Li Dong, Shaohan Huang, Furu Wei, , Mirella Lapata, Ming Zhou, and Ke Xu. 2017. Learning to generate product reviews from attributes. In *EACL*.

Albert Gatt and Emiel Krahmer. 2017. Survey of the state of the art in natural language generation: Core tasks, applications and evaluation. *JAIR*.

Sayan Ghosh, Mathieu Chollet, Eugene Laksana, Louis-Philippe Morency, and Stefan Scherer. 2017. Affect-lm: A neural language model for customizable affective text generation. In *ACL*.

Jiatao Gu, Zhengdong Lu, Hang Li, and Victor O. K. Li. 2016. Incorporating copying mechanism in sequence-to-sequence learning. In *ACL*.

Ruidan He, Wee Sun Lee, Hwee Tou Ng, and Daniel Dahlmeier. 2017. An unsupervised neural attention model for aspect extraction. In *ACL*.

Jiwei Li, Michel Galley, Chris Brockett, Georgios P. Spithourakis, Jianfeng Gao, and William B. Dolan. 2016. A persona-based neural conversation model. In *ACL*.

Thang Luong, Hieu Pham, and Christopher D. Manning. 2015. Effective approaches to attention-based neural machine translation. In *EMNLP*.

Julian J. McAuley, Jure Leskovec, and Dan Jurafsky. 2012. Learning attitudes and attributes from multi-aspect reviews. In *ICDM*.

Julian J. McAuley, Christopher Targett, Qinfeng Shi, and Anton van den Hengel. 2015. Image-based recommendations on styles and substitutes. In *SIGIR*.

Arjun Mukherjee and Bing Liu. 2012. Aspect extraction through semi-supervised modeling. In *ACL*.

Jianmo Ni, Zachary C. Lipton, Sharad Vikram, and Julian J. McAuley. 2017. Estimating reactions and recommending products with generative models of reviews. In *International Joint Conference on Natural Language Processing*.

Dae Hoon Park, Hyun Duk Kim, ChengXiang Zhai, and Lifan Guo. 2015. Retrieval of relevant opinion sentences for new products. In *SIGIR*.

Minghui Qiu, Yinfei Yang, Cen Chen, and Forrest Sheng Bao. 2017. Aspect extraction from product reviews using category hierarchy information. In *EACL*.

Abigail See, Peter J. Liu, and Christopher D. Manning. 2017. Get to the point: Summarization with pointer-generator networks. In *ACL*.

Oriol Vinyals, Alexander Toshev, Samy Bengio, and Dumitru Erhan. 2015. Show and tell: A neural image caption generator. In *CVPR*.

Yequan Wang, Minlie Huang, Xiaoyan Zhu, and Li Zhao. 2016. Attention-based LSTM for aspect-level sentiment classification. In *EMNLP*.

Chen Xing, Wei Wu, Yu Wu, Jie Liu, Yalou Huang, Ming Zhou, and Wei-Ying Ma. 2017. Topic aware neural response generation. In *AAAI*.

Hongyu Zang and Xiaojun Wan. 2017. Towards automatic generation of product reviews from aspect-sentiment scores. In *International Conference on Natural Language Generation*.

Yongfeng Zhang, Guokun Lai, Min Zhang, Yi Zhang, Yiqun Liu, and Shaoping Ma. 2014. Explicit factor models for explainable recommendation based on phrase-level sentiment analysis. In *SIGIR*.

Learning Simplifications for Specific Target Audiences

Carolina Scarton and **Lucia Specia**
Department of Computer Science, University of Sheffield
Regent Court, 211 Portobello Street, Sheffield, S1 4DP, UK
{c.scarton,l.specia}@sheffield.ac.uk

Abstract

Text simplification (TS) is a monolingual text-to-text transformation task where an original (complex) text is transformed into a target (simpler) text. Most recent work is based on sequence-to-sequence neural models similar to those used for machine translation (MT). Different from MT, TS data comprises more elaborate transformations, such as sentence splitting. It can also contain multiple simplifications of the same original text targeting different audiences, such as school grade levels. We explore these two features of TS to build models tailored for specific grade levels. Our approach uses a standard sequence-to-sequence architecture where the original sequence is annotated with information about the target audience and/or the (predicted) type of simplification operation. We show that it outperforms state-of-the-art TS approaches (up to 3 and 12 BLEU and SARI points, respectively), including when training data for the specific complex-simple combination of grade levels is not available, i.e. zero-shot learning.

1 Introduction

Text simplification (TS) is the task of modifying an original text into a simpler version of it. One of the main parameters for defining a suitable simplification is the target audience. Examples include elderly, children, cognitively impaired users, non-native speakers and low-literacy readers.

Traditionally, work on TS has been divided in lexical simplification (LS) and syntactic simplification (SS). LS (Paetzold, 2016) deals with the identification and replacement of complex words or phrases. SS (Siddharthan, 2011) performs structural transformations such as changing a sentence from passive to active voice. However, most recent approaches learn transformations from corpora, addressing simplification at lexical and syntactic levels altogether. These include either learning tree-based transformations (Woodsend and Lapata, 2011; Paetzold and Specia, 2013) or using machine translation (MT)-based techniques (Zhu et al., 2010; Coster and Kauchak, 2011a; Wubben et al., 2012; Narayan and Gardent, 2014; Nisioi et al., 2017; Zhang and Lapata, 2017). This paper uses the latter type of technique, which treats TS as a monolingual MT task, where an original text is "translated" into its simplified version.

In order to build MT-based models, a parallel corpus of original texts with their simplified counterparts is needed. For English, two main such corpora are available: Wikipedia-Simple Wikipedia (W-SW) (Zhu et al., 2010) and the Newsela Article Corpus.[1] The former is a collection of original Wikipedia articles and their simplified versions created by volunteers. The latter consists of news articles professionally simplified for various specific audiences following the US school grade system. To build simplification models, the pairs of articles in these corpora have been aligned at the level of smaller units using standard algorithms (Coster and Kauchak, 2011b; Paetzold and Specia, 2016; Štajner et al., 2017). Based on the number of sentences involved in these alignments, one can categorise alignments into four types of coarse-grained simplification operations:

- Identical: an original sentence is aligned to itself, i.e. no simplification is performed.
- Elaboration: an original sentence is aligned to a single, rewritten simplified sentence.
- One-to-many: splitting – an original sentence is aligned to 2+ simplified sentences.

---

[1]https://newsela.com/data, v.2016-01-29.

Proceedings of the 56th Annual Meeting of the Association for Computational Linguistics (Short Papers), pages 712–718
Melbourne, Australia, July 15 - 20, 2018. ©2018 Association for Computational Linguistics

- Many-to-one: joining – 2+ original sentences are aligned to a single simplified sentence.

We hereafter refer to the unit of simplification, i.e. one or more original or simplified sentences, as *instances.*

The Newsela corpus is seen as having higher quality than W-SW because its simplifications are created by professionals, following well defined guidelines (Xu et al., 2015). It is also larger which is preferable for training corpus-based models. More interestingly, the Newsela corpus has a feature that has been ignored thus far: Each instance in the corpus was created for readers with a certain school grade level. Each original article has a label indicating its corresponding grade level (from 12 to 2), and may have various simplified versions, each for a different grade level. For example, a level 12 article may have simplified counterparts for levels 8 and 4. In other words, the corpus contains instances where the same input leads to different outputs. Disregarding this factor may lead to suboptimal models. To avoid this problem, previous work (Alva-Manchego et al., 2017; Zhang and Lapata, 2017; Scarton et al., 2018b) has used subsets of the corpus with only certain combinations of complex-simplified article pairs, e.g. adjacent or non-adjacent pairs. This however reduces the amount of data available for training.

We propose a way of making use of this information to build more informed TS models that are aware of different types of target audiences, while still making use of the full dataset for learning. Inspired by the work of Johnson et al. (2017) for MT, we add to each original instance an artificial token that represents the target grade level of that instance in order to guide a sequence-to-sequence attentional encoder-decoder neural approach (Bahdanau et al., 2015) (§2). In a similar vein, we also annotate the coarse-grained type of operation that should be performed to simplify the original instance, under the hypothesis that certain operations are more often used to simplify into certain grade levels. Deciding on the operation is an easier problem than performing the actual operation. We rely on both gold and predicted operation types.

Experiments with models built with these artificial tokens outperform state-of-the-art neural models for TS, with the best approach combining grade level and type of operation (§3). Interestingly, such an approach also enables zero-shot TS, where a simplification for a grade level pair unseen at training time can still be generated during testing. We show that our zero-shot learning models perform virtually as well as our grade/operation-informed models (§4). To the best of our knowledge, this is the first work to build TS models for specific target audiences and to explore zero-shot learning for this application.

2 System architecture

Our approach follows that of Johnson et al. (2017), a multilingual MT approach that adds an artificial token to encode the target language to the beginning of each source sentence in the parallel corpus. With this modified version of the corpus, a single encoder-decoder architecture is used to deal with different language pairs. Based on the tokens, the source sentences are encoded differently according to the target language they have been paired with in the corpus. Such an approach enables zero-shot MT, where a model is able to provide translations for language pairs it has not seem at training time.

We apply three types of data manipulation, where artificial tokens are added to the beginning of original side of both training and test instances:

- **to-grade**: the token corresponds to the grade level of the target instance,
- **operation**: the token is one of the four possible coarse-grained operations that transforms the original into the simplified instance,
- **to-grade-operation**: concatenation of the two above tokens.

Different from the grade level, which can be available at test time simply by knowing the intended reader of the text, information about the operations to be performed, which we extracted from the parallel corpus, will not be available at test time. We use gold labels extracted from the parallel corpus for an oracle experiment but also use a classifier that predicts the operations for the test set based on those in the training data. We built a simple Naive Bayes classifier using the `scikit-learn` toolkit (Pedregosa et al., 2011) and nine features (Scarton et al., 2017):

- number of tokens / punctuation / content words / clauses,
- ratio of the number of verbs / nouns / adjectives / adverbs / connectives to the number of content words.

Table 1 shows examples of the tokens used when an original instance is marked to be simpli-

	to grade level 4	to grade level 2
to-grade	<4> dusty handprints stood out against the rust of the fence near Sasabe.	<2> dusty handprints stood out against the rust of the fence near Sasabe.
operation	<**identical**> dusty handprints stood out against the rust of the fence near Sasabe.	<**elaboration**> dusty handprints stood out against the rust of the fence near Sasabe.
to-grade-operation	<**4-identical**> dusty handprints stood out against the rust of the fence near Sasabe.	<**2-elaboration**> dusty handprints stood out against the rust of the fence near Sasabe.
reference	dusty handprints stood out against the rust of the fence near Sasabe.	dusty handprints could be seen on the fence near Sasabe.

Table 1: Examples of artificial tokens used.

fied to grade level 4 or grade level 2. Since the reference for grade level 4 is a copy of the original, the operation token for this case is <identical>. For level 2 the reference is a rewrite and, therefore, the operation token is <elaboration>.

We use OpenNMT[2] as our encoder-decoder architecture. Both encoder and decoder have two LSTM layers, hidden states of size 500 and dropout = 0.3. Global attention combined with input-feeding is used, as describe in (Luong et al., 2015). A model is trained for each dataset constructed with different artificial tokens for 13 epochs. The best model is selected according to perplexity on the development set. Figure 1 shows the architecture of the neural network, including attention and input-feeding. In this example, <token> represents the artificial token added to the pre-processed data.

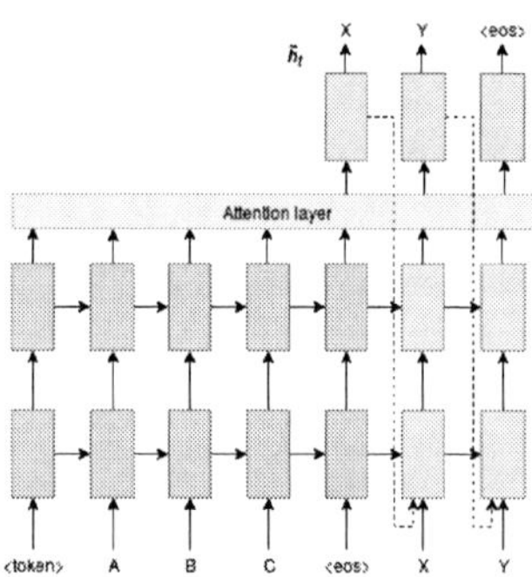

Figure 1: Neural model architecture.

We evaluate our models with BLEU[3] (Papineni et al., 2002) (a proxy for grammaticality assessment), SARI (Xu et al., 2016)[4] (a proxy for simplicity assessment) and Flesch Reading Ease[5] (a

proxy for readability assessment). According to Xu et al. (2016), BLEU shows high correlation with human scores for grammaticality and meaning preservation, whilst SARI shows high correlation with human scores for simplicity. Although previous work have also relied on human judgements of grammaticality, meaning preservation and simplicity, in our case such a type of evaluation is infeasible: we would need to involve judges with specific grade levels or rely on professionals who are experts in grade level-specific simplification to make such assessments.

3   Reader-specific TS models

Our version of the Newsela corpus has $550,644$ instance pairs (11M original tokens and 10M target tokens), which we randomly divided into training ($440,516$ instances: 80%), development ($55,064$ instances: 10%) and test ($55,064$ instances: 10%) sets. Instances were aligned using the method by Paetzold and Specia (2016). Xu et al. (2015) report over 56K original sentences and approximately 305K sentences including the original ones and all simplification types. Our number of instance pairs is higher because we allowed alignments from original to all simplified versions and among simplified versions. An original article 0 may be aligned to up to four simplified versions: 1, 2, 3 and 4. For each article, the alignments were extracted between 0-{1,2,3,4}, 1-{2,3,4}, 2-{3,4} and 3-4, where available. Our corpus is also larger than the ones used in (Alva-Manchego et al., 2017; Scarton et al., 2018b) and (Zhang and Lapata, 2017). While the former use only adjacent levels (e.g. 0-1, 1-2) and the latter only non-adjacent levels (e.g. 0-2, 1-4), we make use of the full dataset.

As baseline we trained a model using OpenNMT and the same hyperparameters as described in §2 on the entire Newsela corpus but without artificial tokens (s2s model). The state-of-the-

---

[2]Torch version: http://opennmt.net/OpenNMT/

[3]The multi-blue.perl script from https://github.com/moses-smt/mosesdecoder

[4]https://github.com/cocoxu/simplification

[5]https://github.com/mmautner/readability

art model is represented by NTS, which was also trained on the entire corpus using a similar Open-NMT architecture with the same hyperparameters but additional pre-trained word embeddings as described in Nisioi et al. (2017).[6]

As shown in Table 2 the NTS system performs slightly worse than the baseline system according to BLEU and SARI. Although concatenating global and local embeddings has led to improvements for the W-SW corpus in (Nisioi et al., 2017), this does not seem to be the case for the Newsela corpus. Our models outperform both the baseline and NTS systems by a large margin. Examples of outputs from all systems can be found in the Supplementary Material.

	BLEU ↑	SARI ↑	Flesch ↑
NTS	61.60	33.40	79.95
s2s	61.78	33.72	79.86
s2s+to-grade	**62.91**	**41.04**	82.91
s2s+operation (pred)	59.83	37.36	**84.96**
s2s+to-grade+operation (pred)	61.48	40.56	83.11
s2s+operation (gold)	63.24	41.81	84.47
s2s+to-grade+operation (gold)	**64.78**	**45.41**	**85.44**

Table 2: Results on the Newsela test set.

The best model is the one built with the $<$to-grade+operation$>$ token with gold operations annotations (last row). The second best system uses the gold $<$operation$>$ token only. Therefore, knowing the operation type to be performed for a given instance provides valuable information. Even though the models with predicted operations ('pred' in Table 2) still outperform the baseline, they lag behind their counterparts built using gold operations. The main reason for that is the very simplistic classifier we used (average accuracy = 0.51, calculated using 10-fold cross-validation). In summary, s2s+to-grade is the best performing model in a real world scenario, given the low performance of 'pred' systems. A more informed classifier should lead to better results, but this left for future work; our goal was to show the potential of this information.

The improvements in SARI are substantial: 7 points over the baseline even with the predicted operations. However, SARI aims to measure simplicity in general (not for specific grade levels). Since human evaluation of the targeted simplification performed by our models is not feasible, we can only approximate the usefulness of our models by using readability metrics such

as the Flesch-Kincaid Grade Level. This metric maps a text into a US grade level, which is the same grading provided in the Newsela corpus and, therefore, relevant for our study. Table 3 shows the Flesch-Kincaid results for the test set divided into the appropriate grade levels considering the outputs of s2s, s2s+to-grade and s2s+to-grade+operation (gold) models. Simplifications generated by s2s+to-grade and s2s+to-grade+operation are scored consistently closer to the appropriate grade, which does not happen with s2s.

	s2s	+to-grade	+to-grade+operation (gold)
$<$10$>$	9.23	11.90	9.93
$<$9$>$	8.85	9.82	8.57
$<$8$>$	7.47	8.46	7.58
$<$7$>$	7.81	7.79	6.89
$<$6$>$	6.99	6.48	5.57
$<$5$>$	5.58	5.05	4.49
$<$4$>$	5.90	3.85	3.28
$<$3$>$	5.15	2.44	1.88
$<$2$>$	3.94	1.57	1.00
MAE	1.09	**0.63**	**0.63**

Table 3: Flesch-Kincaid scores for instances of each grade level simplified using s2s, s2s+to-grade and s2s+to-grade+operation (gold) models.

The last row of Table 3 shows the Mean Absolute Error (MAE) considering the Flesch-Kincaid Grade Level scores for the system outputs as the hypothesis and the expected grade level as the gold scores. Our s2s+to-grade and s2s+to-grade+operation (gold) models show lower error scores than the baseline system, which supports our hypothesis that such models produce more adequate outputs for targeted grade levels.

3.1 Usefulness of the s2s+to-grade model

The main advantage of s2s+to-grade is that a user can inform their grade level and retrieve a personalised simplification. Table 4 shows an example with different simplifications for an out-of-domain instance from the SimPA corpus (Scarton et al., 2018a). The same instance was given as input to the s2s+to-grade model with different artificial tokens according to the grade level that we want to achieve. The s2s system (second row) repeats the original instance (first row). Conversely, our s2s+to-grade model is capable of distinguishing among different levels and produces personalised simplifications for each grade level.

---

[6]Equivalent to their best performing "NTS-w2v" version.

original	We want to reassure you that we take fire safety very seriously and we are doing everything we can to make sure our residents are safe.
s2s	We want to reassure you that we take fire safety very seriously and we are doing everything we can to make sure our residents are safe.
<10>	We want to reassure you that we take fire safety very seriously and we are doing everything we can to make sure our residents are safe.
<9>	We want to reassure you that we take fire safety very seriously and we are doing everything we can to make sure our residents are safe.
<8>	We want to reassure you that we take fire safety very seriously and we are doing everything we can to make sure our residents are safe.
<7>	We want to reassure you that we take fire safety very seriously and we are doing everything we can to make sure our residents are safe.
<6>	We want to reassure you that we take fire safety very seriously. We are doing everything we can to make sure our residents are safe.
<5>	We want to reassure you that we take fire safety very seriously. We are doing everything we can to make sure our residents are safe.
<4>	We want to make sure we take fire safety very seriously. We are doing everything we can to make sure our people are safe.
<3>	We want to make sure people take fire safety very seriously. We are doing everything we can to make sure our people are safe.
<2>	We want to make sure people take fire safety very seriously. We are doing everything we can to make sure people are safe.

Table 4: Examples of s2s+to-grade outputs when an original instance is simplified into different levels.

4   Zero-shot TS models

To show that zero-shot TS is possible, we build models on training data without instances of a certain grade level pair and test them on instances of that grade level pair. Consider the grade level pair $< g_o, g_t >$, where g_o is the grade level of an original instance o, g_t of a target instance t, and t is aligned to o. We test if our "s2s+to-grade" model can generalise for instances of $< \hat{g}_o, \hat{g}_t >$ that have not been seen at training time.

Due to space restrictions, we only show results for three representative grade level pairs. These pairs have a large enough number of training and test instances and cover levels that are closer or further apart from each other. In addition, after removing them the training corpus still has enough instances of the $\hat{g}_t$ as target grade level. Instances of the target but not the original level (or of the target language in MT) must exist for zero-shot to be possible. The distributions of the selected grade level pairs is shown in Table 5.

	# training	# test	# of remaining $\hat{g}_t$
$< 12, 7 >$	30,246	3,825	34,545
$< 12, 4 >$	22,709	2,867	104,833
$< 6, 5 >$	18,122	2,239	79,546

Table 5: Zero-shot data distribution.

In Table 6, the s2s and s2s+to-grade models are the same as in Section 3, i.e. trained with the entire dataset without artificial tokens (s2s) or with artificial tokens (s2s+to-grade). The zero-shot models (s2s+to-grade+zs) are trained with <to-grade> data, but after removing instances of the grade level pair $< \hat{g}_o, \hat{g}_t >$ under investigation, i.e. on a smaller dataset. For $< 12, 7 >$ and $< 12, 4 >$, the zero-shot models outperform the baseline according to all metrics. In terms of SARI, for $< 12, 7 >$ the zero-shot model is only marginally worse than the s2s+to-grade model. Conversely, s2s+to-grade+zs outperforms s2s+to-grade for $<$

$12, 4 >$, which is an impressive result. Finally, for $< 6, 5 >$ all three models perform similarly. This may be explained by the proximity of $\hat{g}_o$ and $\hat{g}_t$, which means that instances must be considerably close to each other and therefore simplifications will be minor and have little impact in the scores.

	BLEU ↑	SARI ↑	Flesch ↑
$< 12, 7 >$			
s2s	63.02	38.43	73.83
s2s+to-grade	64.16	**40.61**	**74.43**
s2s+to-grade+zs	**64.50**	39.83	74.09
$< 12, 4 >$			
s2s	44.56	37.56	79.50
s2s+to-grade	49.43	50.76	91.04
s2s+to-grade+zs	**50.18**	**50.85**	**91.08**
$< 6, 5 >$			
s2s	**69.71**	**26.47**	84.74
s2s+to-grade	69.39	26.32	**87.07**
s2s+to-grade+zs	68.78	26.23	86.80

Table 6: Results of zero-shot experiments for TS.

5   Conclusions

We have presented an approach for TS that benefits from corpora built for various target audiences and allows building better models than general-purpose ones. We have also shown that zero-shot learning is possible for TS, where instances of the original-target audience do not exist. As future work we intend to investigate (i) better classifiers to predict operation types and (ii) multi-task learning as an alternative way of building a single TS model for various specific target audiences. We also plan to run experiments with the W-SW corpus and using an improved classifier to train models with information on operations.

Acknowledgements

This work was supported by the EC project SIMPATICO (H2020-EURO-6-2015, grant number 692819).

References

Fernando Alva-Manchego, Joachim Bingel, Gustavo Paetzold, Carolina Scarton, and Lucia Specia. 2017. Learning how to simplify from explicit labeling of complex-simplified text pairs. In *Proceedings of the Eighth International Joint Conference on Natural Language Processing (Volume 1: Long Papers)*. Asian Federation of Natural Language Processing, Taipei, Taiwan, pages 295–305. http://www.aclweb.org/anthology/I17-1030.

Dzmitry Bahdanau, Kyunghyun Cho, and Yoshua Bengio. 2015. Neural machine translation by jointly learning to align and translate. In *Proceedings of the 3rd International Conference on Learning Representations*. San Diego, CA, ICLR '15. https://arxiv.org/pdf/1409.0473.pdf.

William Coster and David Kauchak. 2011a. Learning to simplify sentences using wikipedia. In *Proceedings of the Workshop on Monolingual Text-To-Text Generation*. ACL, Portland, Oregon, MTTG '11, pages 1–9. http://dl.acm.org/citation.cfm?id=2107679.2107680.

William Coster and David Kauchak. 2011b. Simple english wikipedia: A new text simplification task. In *Proceedings of the 49th Annual Meeting of the Association for Computational Linguistics: Human Language Technologies: Short Papers - Volume 2*. Association for Computational Linguistics, Stroudsburg, PA, USA, HLT '11, pages 665–669. http://dl.acm.org/citation.cfm?id=2002736.2002865.

Melvin Johnson, Mike Schuster, Quoc V. Le, Maxim Krikun, Yonghui Wu, Zhifeng Chen, Nikhil Thorat, Fernanda Viégas, Martin Wattenberg, Greg Corrado, Macduff Hughes, and Jeffrey Dean. 2017. Google's Multilingual Neural Machine Translation System: Enabling Zero-Shot Translation. *Transactions of the Association for Computational Linguistics* 5:339–351. http://aclweb.org/anthology/Q17-1024.

Thang Luong, Hieu Pham, and Christopher D. Manning. 2015. Effective approaches to attention-based neural machine translation. In *Proceedings of the 2015 Conference on Empirical Methods in Natural Language Processing*. Association for Computational Linguistics, Lisbon, Portugal, pages 1412–1421. http://aclweb.org/anthology/D15-1166.

Shashi Narayan and Claire Gardent. 2014. Hybrid simplification using deep semantics and machine translation. In *Proceedings of the 52nd Annual Meeting of the Association for Computational Linguistics (Volume 1: Long Papers)*. Association for Computational Linguistics, Baltimore, Maryland, pages 435–445. http://www.aclweb.org/anthology/P14-1041.

Sergiu Nisioi, Sanja Štajner, Simone Paolo Ponzetto, and Liviu P. Dinu. 2017. Exploring neural text simplification models. In *Proceedings of the 55th Annual Meeting of the Association for Computational Linguistics (Volume 2: Short Papers)*. Association for Computational Linguistics, Vancouver, Canada, pages 85–91. http://aclweb.org/anthology/P17-2014.

Gustavo Paetzold and Lucia Specia. 2013. Text simplification as tree transduction. In *Proceedings of the 9th Brazilian Symposium in Information and Human Language Technology*. Fortaleza, Brazil, STIL, pages 116–125. http://aclweb.org/anthology/W13-4813.

Gustavo Henrique Paetzold. 2016. *Lexical Simplification for Non-Native English Speakers*. Ph.D. thesis, University of Sheffield, Sheffield, UK. http://etheses.whiterose.ac.uk/15332/.

Gustavo Henrique Paetzold and Lucia Specia. 2016. Vicinity-driven paragraph and sentence alignment for comparable corpora. *CoRR* abs/1612.04113. http://arxiv.org/abs/1612.04113.

Kishore Papineni, Salim Roukos, Todd Ward, and Wei-Jing Zhu. 2002. Bleu: A method for automatic evaluation of machine translation. In *Proceedings of the 40th Annual Meeting on Association for Computational Linguistics*. ACL, Philadelphia, Pennsylvania, ACL '02, pages 311–318. https://doi.org/10.3115/1073083.1073135.

F. Pedregosa, G. Varoquaux, A. Gramfort, V. Michel, B. Thirion, O. Grisel, M. Blondel, P. Prettenhofer, R. Weiss, V. Dubourg, J. Vanderplas, A. Passos, D. Cournapeau, M. Brucher, M. Perrot, and E. Duchesnay. 2011. Scikit-learn: Machine learning in Python. *Journal of Machine Learning Research* .

Carolina Scarton, Gustavo Henrique Paetzold, and Lucia Specia. 2018a. SimPA: A Sentence-Level Simplification Corpus for the Public Administration Domain. In *Proceedings of the Eleventh International Conference on Language Resources and Evaluation*. European Language Resources Association (ELRA), Miyazaki, Japan, pages 4333–4338. http://www.lrec-conf.org/proceedings/lrec2018/pdf/542.pdf.

Carolina Scarton, Gustavo Henrique Paetzold, and Lucia Specia. 2018b. Text Simplification from Professionally Produced Corpora. In *Proceedings of the Eleventh International Conference on Language Resources and Evaluation*. European Language Resources Association (ELRA), Miyazaki, Japan, pages 3504–3510. http://www.lrec-conf.org/proceedings/lrec2018/pdf/1063.pdf.

Carolina Scarton, Alessio Palmero Aprosio, Sara Tonelli, Tamara Martín Wanton, and Lucia Specia. 2017. MUSST: A Multilingual Syntactic Simplification Tool. In *Proceedings of the Eighth International Joint Conference on Natural Language Processing (System Demonstrations)*. Asian Federation of Natural Language Processing, Taipei, Taiwan, pages 25–28. http://aclweb.org/anthology/I17-3007.

Advaith Siddharthan. 2011. Text simplification using typed dependencies: A comparison of the robustness of different generation strategies. In *Proceedings of the 13th European Workshop on Natural Language Generation*. Association for Computational Linguistics, Stroudsburg, PA, USA, ENLG '11, pages 2–11. http://dl.acm.org/citation.cfm?id=2187681.2187684.

Sanja Štajner, Marc Franco-Salvador, Simone Paolo Ponzetto, Paolo Rosso, and Heiner Stuckenschmidt. 2017. Sentence alignment methods for improving text simplification systems. In *Proceedings of the 55th Annual Meeting of the Association for Computational Linguistics (Volume 2: Short Papers)*. Association for Computational Linguistics, Vancouver, Canada, pages 97–102. http://aclweb.org/anthology/P17-2016.

Kristian Woodsend and Mirella Lapata. 2011. Learning to Simplify Sentences with Quasi-Synchronous Grammar and Integer Programming. In *Proceedings of the 2011 Conference on Empirical Methods in Natural Language Processing*. Association for Computational Linguistics, Edinburgh, Scotland, UK., pages 409–420. http://www.aclweb.org/anthology/D11-1038.

Sander Wubben, Antal van den Bosch, and Emiel Krahmer. 2012. Sentence simplification by monolingual machine translation. In *Proceedings of the 50th Annual Meeting of the Association for Computational Linguistics: Long Papers - Volume 1*. Association for Computational Linguistics, Stroudsburg, PA, USA, ACL '12, pages 1015–1024. http://www.aclweb.org/anthology/P12-1107.

Wei Xu, Chris Callison-Burch, and Courtney Napoles. 2015. Problems in current text simplification research: New data can help. *Transactions of the Association for Computational Linguistics* 3:283–297. http://www.aclweb.org/anthology/Q15-1021.

Wei Xu, Courtney Napoles, Ellie Pavlick, Quanze Chen, and Chris Callison-Burch. 2016. Optimizing statistical machine translation for text simplification. *Transactions of the Association for Computational Linguistics* 4:401–415. http://www.aclweb.org/anthology/Q16-1029.

Xingxing Zhang and Mirella Lapata. 2017. Sentence simplification with deep reinforcement learning. In *Proceedings of the 2017 Conference on Empirical Methods in Natural Language Processing*. Association for Computational Linguistics, Copenhagen, Denmark, pages 595–605. https://www.aclweb.org/anthology/D17-1063.

Zhemin Zhu, Delphine Bernhard, and Iryna Gurevych. 2010. A monolingual tree-based translation model for sentence simplification. In *Proceedings of the 23rd International Conference on Computational Linguistics*. Association for Computational Linguistics, Stroudsburg, PA, USA, COLING '10, pages 1353–1361. http://dl.acm.org/citation.cfm?id=1873781.1873933.

Split and Rephrase: Better Evaluation and a Stronger Baseline

Roee Aharoni & Yoav Goldberg
Computer Science Department
Bar-Ilan University
Ramat-Gan, Israel
{roee.aharoni,yoav.goldberg}@gmail.com

Abstract

Splitting and rephrasing a complex sentence into several shorter sentences that convey the same meaning is a challenging problem in NLP. We show that while vanilla seq2seq models can reach high scores on the proposed benchmark (Narayan et al., 2017), they suffer from memorization of the training set which contains more than 89% of the unique simple sentences from the validation and test sets. To aid this, we present a new train-development-test data split and neural models augmented with a copy-mechanism, outperforming the best reported baseline by 8.68 BLEU and fostering further progress on the task.

1 Introduction

Processing long, complex sentences is challenging. This is true either for humans in various circumstances (Inui et al., 2003; Watanabe et al., 2009; De Belder and Moens, 2010) or in NLP tasks like parsing (Tomita, 1986; McDonald and Nivre, 2011; Jelínek, 2014) and machine translation (Chandrasekar et al., 1996; Pouget-Abadie et al., 2014; Koehn and Knowles, 2017). An automatic system capable of breaking a complex sentence into several simple sentences that convey the same meaning is very appealing.

A recent work by Narayan et al. (2017) introduced a dataset, evaluation method and baseline systems for the task, naming it "Split-and-Rephrase". The dataset includes 1,066,115 instances mapping a single complex sentence to a sequence of sentences that express the same meaning, together with RDF triples that describe their semantics. They considered two system setups: a text-to-text setup that does not use the accompany-

ing RDF information, and a semantics-augmented setup that does. They report a BLEU score of 48.9 for their best text-to-text system, and of 78.7 for the best RDF-aware one. We focus on the text-to-text setup, which we find to be more challenging and more natural.

We begin with vanilla SEQ2SEQ models with attention (Bahdanau et al., 2015) and reach an accuracy of 77.5 BLEU, substantially outperforming the text-to-text baseline of Narayan et al. (2017) and approaching their best RDF-aware method. However, manual inspection reveal many cases of unwanted behaviors in the resulting outputs: (1) many resulting sentences are *unsupported* by the input: they contain correct facts about relevant entities, but these facts were not mentioned in the input sentence; (2) some facts are *repeated*—the same fact is mentioned in multiple output sentences; and (3) some facts are *missing*—mentioned in the input but omitted in the output.

The model learned to *memorize entity-fact pairs* instead of learning to split and rephrase. Indeed, feeding the model with examples containing entities alone without any facts about them causes it to output perfectly phrased but unsupported facts (Table 3). Digging further, we find that 99% of the simple sentences (more than 89% of the unique ones) in the validation and test sets also appear in the training set, which—coupled with the good memorization capabilities of SEQ2SEQ models and the relatively small number of distinct simple sentences—helps to explain the high BLEU score.

To aid further research on the task, we propose a more challenging split of the data. We also establish a stronger baseline by extending the SEQ2SEQ approach with a copy mechanism, which was shown to be helpful in similar tasks (Gu et al., 2016; Merity et al., 2017; See et al., 2017). On the original split, our models outperform the

Proceedings of the 56th Annual Meeting of the Association for Computational Linguistics (Short Papers), pages 719–724
Melbourne, Australia, July 15 - 20, 2018. ©2018 Association for Computational Linguistics

	count	unique
RDF entities	32,186	925
RDF relations	16,093	172
complex sentences	1,066,115	5,544
simple sentences	5,320,716	9,552
train complex sentences	886,857	4,438
train simple sentences	4,451,959	8,840
dev complex sentences	97,950	554
dev simple sentences	475,337	3,765
test complex sentences	81,308	554
test simple sentences	393,420	4,015
% dev simple in train	99.69%	90.9%
% test simple in train	99.09%	89.8%
% dev vocab in train	97.24%	
% test vocab in train	96.35%	

Table 1: Statistics for the WEBSPLIT dataset.

best baseline of Narayan et al. (2017) by up to 8.68 BLEU, without using the RDF triples. On the new split, the vanilla SEQ2SEQ models break completely, while the copy-augmented models perform better. In parallel to our work, an updated version of the dataset was released (v1.0), which is larger and features a train/test split protocol which is similar to our proposal. We report results on this dataset as well. The code and data to reproduce our results are available on Github.[1] We encourage future work on the split-and-rephrase task to use our new data split or the v1.0 split instead of the original one.

2 Preliminary Experiments

Task Definition In the split-and-rephrase task we are given a complex sentence C, and need to produce a sequence of simple sentences $T_1, ..., T_n$, $n \geq 2$, such that the output sentences convey all and only the information in C. As additional supervision, the split-and-rephrase dataset associates each sentence with a set of RDF triples that describe the information in the sentence. Note that the number of simple sentences to generate is not given as part of the input.

Experimental Details We focus on the task of splitting a complex sentence into several simple ones *without* access to the corresponding RDF triples in either train or test time. For evaluation we follow Narayan et al. (2017) and compute the averaged individual multi-reference BLEU score for each prediction.[2] We split each prediction to

Model	BLEU	#S/C	#T/S
SOURCE	55.67	1.0	21.11
REFERENCE	–	2.52	10.93
Narayan et al. (2017)			
HYBRIDSIMPL	39.97	1.26	17.55
SEQ2SEQ	48.92	2.51	10.32
MULTISEQ2SEQ*	42.18	2.53	10.69
SPLIT-MULTISEQ2SEQ*	77.27	2.84	11.63
SPLIT-SEQ2SEQ*	78.77	2.84	9.28
This work			
SEQ2SEQ128	76.56	2.53	10.53
SEQ2SEQ256	77.48	2.57	10.56
SEQ2SEQ512	75.92	2.59	10.59

Table 2: BLEU scores, simple sentences per complex sentence (#S/C) and tokens per simple sentence (#T/S), as computed over the test set. SOURCE are the complex sentences and REFERENCE are the reference rephrasings from the test set. Models marked with * use the semantic RDF triples.

sentences[3] and report the average number of simple sentences in each prediction, and the average number of tokens for each simple sentence. We train vanilla sequence-to-sequence models with attention (Bahdanau et al., 2015) as implemented in the OPENNMT-PY toolkit (Klein et al., 2017).[4] Our models only differ in the LSTM cell size (128, 256 and 512, respectively). See the supplementary material for training details and hyperparameters. We compare our models to the baselines proposed in Narayan et al. (2017). HYBRIDSIMPL and SEQ2SEQ are text-to-text models, while the other reported baselines additionally use the RDF information.

Results As shown in Table 2, our 3 models obtain higher BLEU scores then the SEQ2SEQ baseline, with up to 28.35 BLEU improvement, despite being single-layer models vs. the 3-layer models used in Narayan et al. (2017). A possible explanation for this discrepancy is the SEQ2SEQ baseline using a dropout rate of 0.8, while we use 0.3 and only apply it on the LSTM outputs. Our results are also better than the MULTISEQ2SEQ and SPLIT-MULTISEQ2SEQ models, which use explicit RDF information. We also present the macro-average[5] number of sim-

---

[1] https://github.com/biu-nlp/sprp-acl2018

[2] Note that this differs from "normal" multi-reference BLEU (as implemented in multi-bleu.pl) since the number of references differs among the instances in the test-

set.

[3] Using NLTK v3.2.5 https://www.nltk.org/

[4] https://github.com/OpenNMT/OpenNMT-py commit d4ab35a

[5] Since the number of references varies greatly from one complex sentence to another, (min: 1, max: 76,283, median: 16) we avoid bias towards the complex sentences with many references by performing macro average, i.e. we first average the number of simple sentences in each reference among the

Input	Prediction
A Fortress of Grey Ice with ISBM 0-7653-0633-6 has 672 pages .	J.V. Jones authored A Fortress of Grey Ice . A Fortress of Grey Ice has 672 pages .
The address , 11 Diagonal Street is located in South Africa where the leader is Cyril Ramaphosa and some Asian South Africans live .	The address , 11 Diagonal Street is located in South Africa . The leader of South Africa is called Cyril Ramaphosa . The leader of South Africa is called Cyril Ramaphosa . The leader of South Africa is called Cyril Ramaphosa .
Alan Shepard Alan Shepard Alan Shepard	Alan Shepard is dead . Alan Shepard was a test pilot .
AFC Ajax AFC Ajax AFC Ajax	AFC Ajax 's manager is Jong Ajax . AFC Ajax N.V. own Sportpark De Toekomst .

Table 3: Predictions from a vanilla SEQ2SEQ model, illustrating unsupported facts, missing facts and repeated facts. The last two rows show inputs we composed to demonstrate that the models memorize entity-fact pairs.

ple sentences per complex sentence in the reference rephrasings (REFERENCE) showing that the SPLIT-MULTISEQ2SEQ and SPLIT-SEQ2SEQ baselines may suffer from over-splitting since the reference splits include 2.52 simple sentences on average, while the mentioned models produced 2.84 sentences.

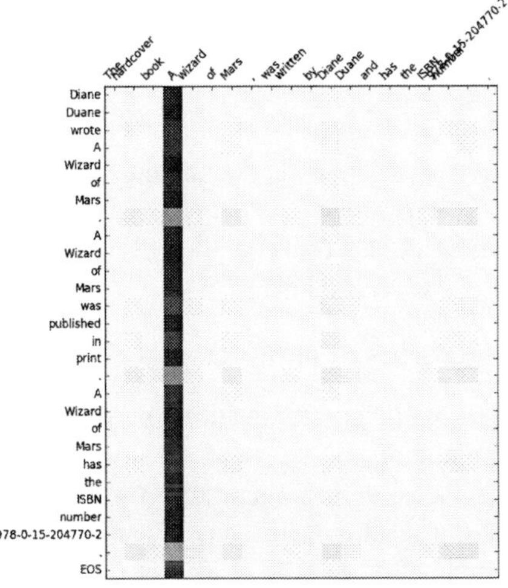

Figure 1: SEQ2SEQ512's attention weights. Horizontal: input. Vertical: predictions.

Analysis We begin analyzing the results by manually inspecting the model's predictions on the validation set. This reveals three common kinds of mistakes as demonstrated in Table 3: unsupported facts, repetitions, and missing facts. All the unsupported facts seem to be related to entities mentioned in the source sentence. Inspecting the attention weights (Figure 1) reveals a worrying trend: throughout the prediction, the model focuses heavily on the first word in of the first entity ("A wizard of Mars") while paying little attention to other cues like "hardcover", "Diane" and

"the ISBN number". This explains the abundance of "hallucinated" unsupported facts: rather than learning to split and rephrase, the model learned to identify entities, and spit out a list of facts it had memorized about them. To validate this assumption, we count the number of predicted sentences which appeared as-is in the training data. We find that 1645 out of the 1693 (97.16%) predicted sentences appear verbatim in the training set. Table 1 gives more detailed statistics on the WEBSPLIT dataset.

To further illustrate the model's recognize-and-spit strategy, we compose inputs containing an entity string which is duplicated three times, as shown in the bottom two rows of Table 3. As expected, the model predicted perfectly phrased and correct facts about the given entities, although these facts are clearly not supported by the input.

3 New Data-split

The original data-split is not suitable for measuring generalization, as it is susceptible to "cheating" by fact memorization. We construct a new train-development-test split to better reflect our expected behavior from a split-and-rephrase model. We split the data into train, development and test sets by randomly dividing the 5,554 distinct complex sentences across the sets, while using the provided RDF information to ensure that:

1. Every possible RDF relation (e.g., BORNIN, LOCATEDIN) is represented in the training set (and may appear also in the other sets).

2. Every RDF triplet (a complete fact) is represented only in one of the splits.

While the set of complex sentences is still divided roughly to 80%/10%/10% as in the original split, now there are nearly no simple sentences in

---

references of a specific complex sentence, and then average these numbers.

	count	unique
train complex sentences	1,039,392	4,506
train simple sentences	5,239,279	7,865
dev complex sentences	13,294	535
dev simple sentences	39,703	812
test complex sentences	13,429	503
test simple sentences	41,734	879
# dev simple in train	35 (0.09%)	
# test simple in train	1 (0%)	
% dev vocab in train	62.99%	
% test vocab in train	61.67%	
dev entities in train	26/111 (23.42%)	
test entities in train	25/120 (20.83%)	
dev relations in train	34/34 (100%)	
test relations in train	37/37 (100%)	

Table 4: Statistics for the RDF-based data split

the development and test sets that appear verbatim in the train-set. Yet, every relation appearing in the development and test sets is supported by examples in the train set. We believe this split strikes a good balance between challenge and feasibility: to succeed, a model needs to learn to identify relations in the complex sentence, link them to their arguments, and produce a rephrasing of them. However, it is not required to generalize to unseen relations. [6]

The data split and scripts for creating it are available on Github.[7] Statistics describing the data split are detailed in Table 4.

4 Copy-augmented Model

To better suit the split-and-rephrase task, we augment the SEQ2SEQ models with a copy mechanism. Such mechanisms have proven to be beneficial in similar tasks like abstractive summarization (Gu et al., 2016; See et al., 2017) and language modeling (Merity et al., 2017). We hypothesize that biasing the model towards copying will improve performance, as many of the words in the simple sentences (mostly corresponding to entities) appear in the complex sentence, as evident by the relatively high BLEU scores for the SOURCE baseline in Table 2.

Copying is modeled using a "copy switch" probability $p(z)$ computed by a sigmoid over a learned composition of the decoder state, the context vector and the last output embedding. It interpolates the $p_{softmax}$ distribution over the target vocabulary and a copy distribution p_{copy} over the source sentence tokens. p_{copy} is simply the computed attention weights. Once the above distribu-

---

[6]The updated dataset (v1.0, published by Narayan et al. after this work was accepted) follows (2) above, but not (1).

[7]`https://github.com/biu-nlp/`
`sprp-acl2018`

		BLEU	#S/C	#T/S
original data split	SOURCE	55.67	1.0	21.11
	REFERENCE	–	2.52	10.93
	SPLIT-SEQ2SEQ	78.77	2.84	9.28
	SEQ2SEQ128	76.56	2.53	10.53
	SEQ2SEQ256	77.48	2.57	10.56
	SEQ2SEQ512	75.92	2.59	10.59
	COPY128	78.55	2.51	10.29
	COPY256	83.73	2.49	10.66
	COPY512	87.45	2.56	10.50
new data split	SOURCE	55.66	1.0	20.37
	REFERENCE	–	2.40	10.83
	SEQ2SEQ128	5.55	2.27	11.68
	SEQ2SEQ256	5.28	2.27	10.54
	SEQ2SEQ512	6.68	2.44	10.23
	COPY128	16.71	2.0	10.53
	COPY256	23.78	2.38	10.55
	COPY512	24.97	2.87	10.04
v1.0	SOURCE	56.1	1.0	20.4
	REFERENCE	–	2.48	10.69
	COPY512	25.47	2.29	11.74

Table 5: Results over the test sets of the original, our proposed split and the v1.0 split

tions are computed, the final probability for an output word w is:

$$p(w) = p(z = 1)p_{copy}(w) + p(z = 0)p_{softmax}(w)$$

In case w is not present in the output vocabulary, we set $p_{softmax}(w) = 0$. We refer the reader to See et al. (2017) for a detailed discussion regarding the copy mechanism.

5 Experiments and Results

Models with larger capacities may have greater representation power, but also a stronger tendency to memorize the training data. We therefore perform experiments with copy-enhanced models of varying LSTM widths (128, 256 and 512). We train the models using the negative log likelihood of $p(w)$ as the objective. Other than the copy mechanism, we keep the settings identical to those in Section 2. We train models on the original split, our proposed data split and the v1.0 split.

Results Table 5 presents the results. On the original data-split, the COPY512 model outperforms all baselines, improving over the previous best by 8.68 BLEU points. On the new data-split, as expected, the performance degrades for all models, as they are required to generalize to sentences not seen during training. The copy-augmented models perform better than the baselines in this case as well, with a larger relative gap which can be explained by the lower lexical overlap between the train and the test sets in the new split. On the v1.0 split the results are similar to those on our split,

Input	Prediction
Madeleine L'Engle who is influenced by George Macdonald wrote " A Severed Wasp " .	A Severed Wasp was written by George Macdonald . A Severed Wasp is from the United States .
The A.C. Lumezzane has 4150 members and play in the Lega Pro League .	A.C. Lumezzane 's ground is in the Lega Pro League . A.C. Lumezzane has 4150 members .
Irish English is the official language of Ireland , which is lead by Enda Kenny and home to Adare Manor .	Adare Manor is located in Ireland . English is the language of Ireland . English is the language of Ireland . (repeated x3)

Table 6: Predictions from the COPY512 model, trained on the new data split.

in spite of it being larger (1,331,515 vs. 886,857 examples), indicating that merely adding data will not solve the task.

Analysis We inspect the models' predictions for the first 20 complex sentences of the original and new validation sets in Table 7. We mark each simple sentence as being "correct" if it contains all and only relevant information, "unsupported" if it contains facts not present in the source, and "repeated" if it repeats information from a previous sentence. We also count missing facts. Figure 2 shows the attention weights of the COPY512 model for the same sentence in Figure 1. Reassuringly, the attention is now distributed more evenly over the input symbols. On the new splits, all models perform catastrophically. Table 6 shows outputs from the COPY512 model when trained on the new split. On the original split, while SEQ2SEQ128 mainly suffers from missing information, perhaps due to insufficient memorization capacity, SEQ2SEQ512 generated the most unsupported sentences, due to overfitting or memorization. The overall number of issues is clearly reduced in the copy-augmented models.

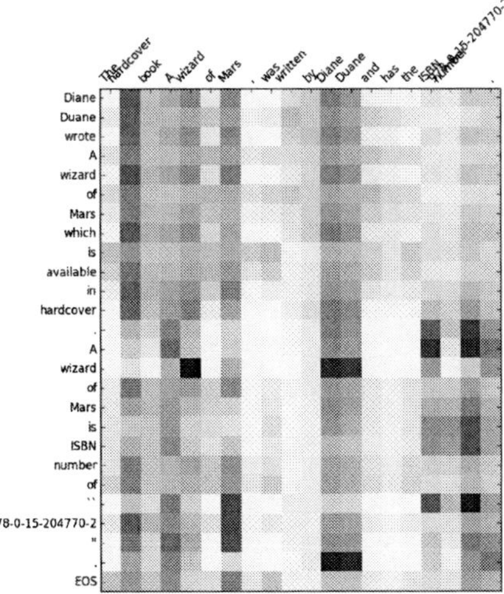

Figure 2: Attention weights from the COPY512 model for the same input as in Figure 1.

Model	unsup.	repeated	correct	missing
original split				
SEQ2SEQ128	5	4	40/49 (82%)	9
SEQ2SEQ256	2	2	42/46 (91%)	5
SEQ2SEQ512	12	2	36/49 (73%)	5
COPY128	3	4	42/49 (86%)	4
COPY256	3	2	45/50 (90%)	6
COPY512	5	0	46/51 (90%)	3
new split				
SEQ2SEQ128	37	8	0	54
SEQ2SEQ256	41	7	0	54
SEQ2SEQ512	43	5	0	54
COPY128	23	3	2/27 (7%)	52
COPY256	35	2	3/40 (7%)	49
COPY512	36	13	11/54 (20%)	43
v1.0 split				
COPY512	41	3	3/44 (7%)	51

Table 7: Results of the manual analysis, showing the number of simple sentences with unsupported facts (unsup.), repeated facts, missing facts and correct facts, for 20 complex sentences from the original and new validation sets.

6 Conclusions

We demonstrated that a SEQ2SEQ model can obtain high scores on the original split-and-rephrase task while not actually learning to split-and-rephrase. We propose a new and more challenging data-split to remedy this, and demonstrate that the cheating SEQ2SEQ models fail miserably on the new split. Augmenting the SEQ2SEQ models with a copy-mechanism improves performance on both data splits, establishing a new competitive baseline for the task. Yet, the split-and-rephrase task (on the new split) is still far from being solved. We strongly encourage future research to evaluate on our proposed split or on the recently released version 1.0 of the dataset, which is larger and also addresses the overlap issues mentioned here.

Acknowledgments

We thank Shashi Narayan and Jan Botha for their useful comments. The work was supported by the Intel Collaborative Research Institute for Computational Intelligence (ICRI-CI), the Israeli Science Foundation (grant number 1555/15), and the German Research Foundation via the German-Israeli Project Cooperation (DIP, grant DA 1600/1-1).

References

Dzmitry Bahdanau, Kyunghyun Cho, and Yoshua Bengio. 2015. Neural machine translation by jointly learning to align and translate. In *Proceedings of the International Conference on Learning Representations (ICLR)*.

Raman Chandrasekar, Christine Doran, and Bangalore Srinivas. 1996. Motivations and methods for text simplification. In *Proceedings of the 16th conference on Computational linguistics*. Association for Computational Linguistics.

Jan De Belder and Marie-Francine Moens. 2010. Text simplification for children. In *Proceedings of the SIGIR workshop on accessible search systems*. ACM.

Jiatao Gu, Zhengdong Lu, Hang Li, and Victor O.K. Li. 2016. Incorporating copying mechanism in sequence-to-sequence learning. In *Proceedings of the 54th Annual Meeting of the Association for Computational Linguistics (Volume 1: Long Papers)*. Association for Computational Linguistics, Berlin, Germany. http://www.aclweb.org/anthology/P16-1154.

Kentaro Inui, Atsushi Fujita, Tetsuro Takahashi, Ryu Iida, and Tomoya Iwakura. 2003. Text simplification for reading assistance: a project note. In *Proceedings of the second international workshop on Paraphrasing-Volume 16*. Association for Computational Linguistics.

Tomáš Jelínek. 2014. Improvements to dependency parsing using automatic simplification of data. In *Proceedings of the Ninth International Conference on Language Resources and Evaluation (LREC'14)*. European Language Resources Association (ELRA), Reykjavik, Iceland.

Guillaume Klein, Yoon Kim, Yuntian Deng, Jean Senellart, and Alexander Rush. 2017. Opennmt: Open-source toolkit for neural machine translation. In *Proceedings of ACL 2017, System Demonstrations*. Association for Computational Linguistics, Vancouver, Canada. http://aclweb.org/anthology/P17-4012.

Philipp Koehn and Rebecca Knowles. 2017. Six challenges for neural machine translation. In *Proceedings of the First Workshop on Neural Machine Translation*. Association for Computational Linguistics, Vancouver. http://www.aclweb.org/anthology/W17-3204.

Ryan McDonald and Joakim Nivre. 2011. Analyzing and integrating dependency parsers. *Computational Linguistics* 37.

Stephen Merity, Caiming Xiong, James Bradbury, and Richard Socher. 2017. Pointer sentinel mixture models. In *Proceedings of the International Conference on Learning Representations (ICLR)*.

Shashi Narayan, Claire Gardent, Shay B. Cohen, and Anastasia Shimorina. 2017. Split and rephrase. In *Proceedings of the 2017 Conference on Empirical Methods in Natural Language Processing*. Association for Computational Linguistics. http://aclweb.org/anthology/D17-1064.

Jean Pouget-Abadie, Dzmitry Bahdanau, Bart van Merrienboer, Kyunghyun Cho, and Yoshua Bengio. 2014. Overcoming the curse of sentence length for neural machine translation using automatic segmentation. In *Proceedings of SSST-8, Eighth Workshop on Syntax, Semantics and Structure in Statistical Translation*. Association for Computational Linguistics, Doha, Qatar. http://www.aclweb.org/anthology/W14-4009.

Abigail See, Peter J. Liu, and Christopher D. Manning. 2017. Get to the point: Summarization with pointer-generator networks. In *Proceedings of the 55th Annual Meeting of the Association for Computational Linguistics (Volume 1: Long Papers)*. Association for Computational Linguistics. http://www.aclweb.org/anthology/P17-1099.

Masaru Tomita. 1986. Efficient parsing for natural languagea fast algorithm for practical systems. int. series in engineering and computer science.

Willian Massami Watanabe, Arnaldo Candido Junior, Vinícius Rodriguez Uzêda, Renata Pontin de Mattos Fortes, Thiago Alexandre Salgueiro Pardo, and Sandra Maria Aluísio. 2009. Facilita: reading assistance for low-literacy readers. In *Proceedings of the 27th ACM international conference on Design of communication*. ACM.

Autoencoder as Assistant Supervisor: Improving Text Representation for Chinese Social Media Text Summarization

Shuming Ma[1], Xu Sun[1,2], Junyang Lin[3], Houfeng Wang[1]
[1]MOE Key Lab of Computational Linguistics, School of EECS, Peking University
[2]Deep Learning Lab, Beijing Institute of Big Data Research, Peking University
[3]School of Foreign Languages, Peking University
{shumingma, xusun, linjunyang, wanghf}@pku.edu.cn

Abstract

Most of the current abstractive text summarization models are based on the sequence-to-sequence model (Seq2Seq). The source content of social media is long and noisy, so it is difficult for Seq2Seq to learn an accurate semantic representation. Compared with the source content, the annotated summary is short and well written. Moreover, it shares the same meaning as the source content. In this work, we supervise the learning of the representation of the source content with that of the summary. In implementation, we regard a summary autoencoder as an assistant supervisor of Seq2Seq. Following previous work, we evaluate our model on a popular Chinese social media dataset. Experimental results show that our model achieves the state-of-the-art performances on the benchmark dataset.[1]

1 Introduction

Text summarization is to produce a brief summary of the main ideas of the text. Unlike extractive text summarization (Radev et al., 2004; Woodsend and Lapata, 2010; Cheng and Lapata, 2016), which selects words or word phrases from the source texts as the summary, abstractive text summarization learns a semantic representation to generate more human-like summaries. Recently, most models for abstractive text summarization are based on the sequence-to-sequence model, which encodes the source texts into the semantic representation with an encoder, and generates the summaries from the representation with a decoder.

The contents on the social media are long, and contain many errors, which come from spelling mistakes, informal expressions, and grammatical mistakes (Baldwin et al., 2013). Large amount of errors in the contents cause great difficulties for text summarization. As for RNN-based Seq2Seq, it is difficult to compress a long sequence into an accurate representation (Li et al., 2015), because of the gradient vanishing and exploding problem.

Compared with the source content, it is easier to encode the representations of the summaries, which are short and manually selected. Since the source content and the summary share the same points, it is possible to supervise the learning of the semantic representation of the source content with that of the summary.

In this paper, we regard a summary autoencoder as an assistant supervisor of Seq2Seq. First, we train an autoencoder, which inputs and reconstructs the summaries, to obtain a better representation to generate the summaries. Then, we supervise the internal representation of Seq2Seq with that of autoencoder by minimizing the distance between two representations. Finally, we use adversarial learning to enhance the supervision. Following the previous work (Ma et al., 2017), We evaluate our proposed model on a Chinese social media dataset. Experimental results show that our model outperforms the state-of-the-art baseline models. More specifically, our model outperforms the Seq2Seq baseline by the score of 7.1 ROUGE-1, 6.1 ROUGE-2, and 7.0 ROUGE-L.

2 Proposed Model

We introduce our proposed model in detail in this section.

2.1 Notation

Given a summarization dataset that consists of N data samples, the ith data sample (x_i, y_i) con-

---

[1]The code is available at https://github.com/lancopku/superAE

Proceedings of the 56th Annual Meeting of the Association for Computational Linguistics (Short Papers), pages 725–731
Melbourne, Australia, July 15 - 20, 2018. ©2018 Association for Computational Linguistics

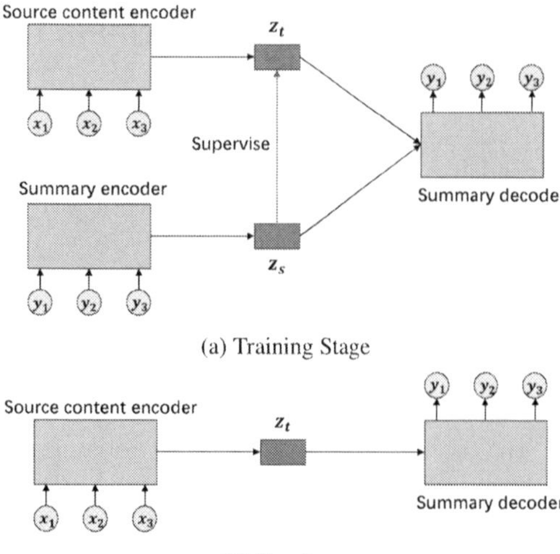

(a) Training Stage

(b) Test Stage

Figure 1: The overview of our model. The model consists of a sequence-to-sequence model and an autoencoder model. At the training stage, we use the autoencoder to supervise the sequence-to-sequence model. At the test stage, we use the sequence-to-sequence model to generate the summaries.

tains a source content $x_i = \{x_1, x_2, ..., x_M\}$, and a summary $y_i = \{y_1, y_2, ..., y_L\}$, while M is the number of the source words, and L is the number of the summary words. At the training stage, we train the model to generate the summary y given the source content x. At the test stage, the model decodes the predicted summary y' given the source content x.

2.2 Supervision with Autoencoder

Figure 1 shows the architecture of our model. At the training stage, the source content encoder compresses the input contents x into the internal representation z_t with a Bi-LSTM encoder. At the same time, the summary encoder compresses the reference summary y into the representation z_s. Then both z_t and z_s are fed into a LSTM decoder to generate the summary. Finally, the semantic representation of the source content is supervised by the summary.

We implement the supervision by minimizing the distance between the semantic representations z_t and z_s, and this term in the loss function can be written as:

$$L_S = \frac{\lambda}{N_h} d(z_t, z_s) \qquad (1)$$

where $d(z_t, z_s)$ is a function which measures the distance between z_s and z_t. λ is a tunable hyperparameter to balance the loss of the supervision and the other parts of the loss, and N_h is the number of the hidden unit to limit the magnitude of the distance function. We set $\lambda = 0.3$ based on the performance on the validation set. The distance between two representations can be written as:

$$d(z_t, z_s) = \|z_t - z_s\|_2 \qquad (2)$$

2.3 Adversarial Learning

We further enhance the supervision with the adversarial learning approach. As shown in Eq. 1, we use a fixed hyper-parameter as a weight to measure the strength of the supervision of the autoencoder. However, in the case when the source content and summary have high relevance, the strength of the supervision should be higher, and when the source content and summary has low relevance, the strength should be lower. In order to determine the strength of supervision more dynamically, we introduce the adversarial learning. More specifically, we regard the representation of the autoencoder as the "gold" representation, and that of the sequence-to-sequence as the "fake" representation. A model is trained to discriminate between the gold and fake representations, which is called a discriminator. The discriminator tries to identify the two representations. On the contrary, the supervision, which minimizes the distance of the representations and makes them similar, tries to prevent the discriminator from making correct predictions. In this way, when the discriminator can distinguish the two representations (which means the source content and the summary has low relevance), the strength of supervision will be decreased, and when the discriminator fails to distinguish, the strength of supervision will be improved.

In implementation of the adversarial learning, the discriminator objective function can be written as:

$$L_D(\theta_D) = - \log P_{\theta_D}(y = 1|z_t) \\ - \log P_{\theta_D}(y = 0|z_s) \qquad (3)$$

where $P_{\theta_D}(y = 1|z)$ is the probability that the discriminator identifies the vector z as the "gold" representation, while $P_{\theta_D}(y = 0|z)$ is the probability that the vector z is identified as the "fake" representation, and θ_D is the parameters of the discriminator. When minimizing the discriminator objective, we only train the parameters of the discriminator, while the rest of the parameters remains unchanged.

The supervision objective to be against the discriminator can be written as:

$$L_G(\theta_E) = -\log P_{\theta_D}(y = 0|z_t) \\ - \log P_{\theta_D}(y = 1|z_s) \quad (4)$$

When minimizing the supervision objective, we only update the parameters of the encoders.

2.4 Loss Function and Training

There are several parts of the objective functions to optimize in our models. The first part is the cross entropy losses of the sequence-to-sequence and the autoencoder:

$$L_{Seq2seq} = -\sum_{i=1}^{N} p_{Seq2seq}(y_i|z_s) \quad (5)$$

$$L_{AE} = -\sum_{i=1}^{N} p_{AE}(y_i|z_t) \quad (6)$$

The second part is the L2 loss of the supervision, as written in Equation 1. The last part is the adversarial learning, which are Equation 3 and Equation 4. The sum of all these parts is the final loss function to optimize.

We use the Adam (Kingma and Ba, 2014) optimization method to train the model. For the hyper-parameters of Adam optimizer, we set the learning rate $\alpha = 0.001$, two momentum parameters $\beta_1 = 0.9$ and $\beta_2 = 0.999$ respectively, and $\epsilon = 1 \times 10^{-8}$. We clip the gradients (Pascanu et al., 2013) to the maximum norm of 10.0.

3 Experiments

Following the previous work (Ma et al., 2017), we evaluate our model on a popular Chinese social media dataset. We first introduce the datasets, evaluation metrics, and experimental details. Then, we compare our model with several state-of-the-art systems.

3.1 Dataset

Large Scale Chinese Social Media Text Summarization Dataset (LCSTS) is constructed by Hu et al. (2015). The dataset consists of more than 2,400,000 text-summary pairs, constructed from a famous Chinese social media website called Sina Weibo.[2] It is split into three parts, with 2,400,591

pairs in PART I, 10,666 pairs in PART II and 1,106 pairs in PART III. All the text-summary pairs in PART II and PART III are manually annotated with relevant scores ranged from 1 to 5. We only reserve pairs with scores no less than 3, leaving 8,685 pairs in PART II and 725 pairs in PART III. Following the previous work (Hu et al., 2015), we use PART I as training set, PART II as validation set, and PART III as test set.

3.2 Evaluation Metric

Our evaluation metric is ROUGE score (Lin and Hovy, 2003), which is popular for summarization evaluation. The metrics compare an automatically produced summary with the reference summaries, by computing overlapping lexical units, including unigram, bigram, trigram, and longest common subsequence (LCS). Following previous work (Rush et al., 2015; Hu et al., 2015), we use ROUGE-1 (unigram), ROUGE-2 (bi-gram) and ROUGE-L (LCS) as the evaluation metrics in the reported experimental results.

3.3 Experimental Details

The vocabularies are extracted from the training sets, and the source contents and the summaries share the same vocabularies. In order to alleviate the risk of word segmentation mistakes, we split the Chinese sentences into characters. We prune the vocabulary size to 4,000, which covers most of the common characters.

We tune the hyper-parameters based on the ROUGE scores on the validation sets. We set the word embedding size and the hidden size to 512, and the number of LSTM layers is 2. The batch size is 64, and we do not use dropout (Srivastava et al., 2014) on this dataset. Following the previous work (Li et al., 2017), we implement the beam search, and set the beam size to 10.

3.4 Baselines

We compare our model with the following state-of-the-art baselines.

- **RNN** and **RNN-cont** are two sequence-to-sequence baseline with GRU encoder and decoder, provided by Hu et al. (2015). The difference between them is that RNN-context has attention mechanism while RNN does not.

- **RNN-dist** (Chen et al., 2016) is a distraction-based neural model, which the attention

Models	R-1	R-2	R-L
RNN-W(Hu et al., 2015)	17.7	8.5	15.8
RNN(Hu et al., 2015)	21.5	8.9	18.6
RNN-cont-W(Hu et al., 2015)	26.8	16.1	24.1
RNN-cont(Hu et al., 2015)	29.9	17.4	27.2
SRB(Ma et al., 2017)	33.3	20.0	30.1
CopyNet-W(Gu et al., 2016)	35.0	22.3	32.0
CopyNet(Gu et al., 2016)	34.4	21.6	31.3
RNN-dist(Chen et al., 2016)	35.2	22.6	32.5
DRGD(Li et al., 2017)	37.0	24.2	34.2
Seq2Seq (our impl.)	32.1	19.9	29.2
+superAE (this paper)	**39.2**	**26.0**	**36.2**
w/o adversarial learning	37.7	25.3	35.2

Table 1: Comparison with state-of-the-art models on the LCSTS test set. R-1, R-2, and R-L denote ROUGE-1, ROUGE-2, and ROUGE-L, respectively. The models with a suffix of 'W' in the table are word-based, while the rest of models are character-based.

Models	2-class (%)	5-class (%)
Seq2seq	80.7	65.1
+superAE	**88.8 (+8.1)**	**71.7 (+6.6)**

Table 2: Accuracy of the sentiment classification on the Amazon dataset. We train a classifier which inputs internal representation provided by the sequence-to-sequence model, and outputs a predicted label. We compute the 2-class and 5-class accuracy of the predicted labels to evaluate the quality of the text representation.

mechanism focuses on the different parts of the source content.

- **CopyNet** (Gu et al., 2016) incorporates a copy mechanism to allow parts of the generated summary are copied from the source content.

- **SRB** (Ma et al., 2017) is a sequence-to-sequence based neural model with improving the semantic relevance between the input text and the output summary.

- **DRGD** (Li et al., 2017) is a deep recurrent generative decoder model, combining the decoder with a variational autoencoder.

- **Seq2seq** is our implementation of the sequence-to-sequence model with the attention mechanism, which has the same experimental setting as our model for fair comparison.

3.5 Results

For the purpose of simplicity, we denote our supervision with autoencoder model as **superAE**. We report the ROUGE F1 score of our model and the baseline models on the test sets.

Table 1 summarizes the results of our superAE model and several baselines. We first compare our model with Seq2Seq baseline. It shows that our

superAE model has a large improvement over the Seq2Seq baseline by 7.1 ROUGE-1, 6.1 ROUGE-2, and 7.0 ROUGE-L, which demonstrates the efficiency of our model. Moreover, we compare our model with the recent summarization systems, which have been evaluated on the same training set and the test sets as ours. Their results are directly reported in the referred articles. It shows that our superAE outperforms all of these models, with a relative gain of 2.2 ROUGE-1, 1.8 ROUGE-2, and 2.0 ROUGE-L. We also perform ablation study by removing the adversarial learning component, in order to show its contribution. It shows that the adversarial learning improves the performance of 1.5 ROUGE-1, 0.7 ROUGE-2, and 1.0 ROUGE-L.

We also give a summarization examples of our model. As shown in Table 3, the SeqSeq model captures the wrong meaning of the source content, and produces the summary that *"China United Airlines exploded in the airport"*. Our superAE model captures the correct points, so that the generated summary is close in meaning to the reference summary.

3.6 Analysis of text representation

We want to analyze whether the internal text representation is improved by our superAE model. Since the text representation is abstractive and hard to evaluate, we translate the representation into a sentiment score with a sentiment classifier, and evaluate the quality of the representation by means of the sentiment accuracy.

We perform experiments on the Amazon Fine Foods Reviews Corpus (McAuley and Leskovec, 2013). The Amazon dataset contains users' rating labels as well as the summary for the reviews, making it possible to train a classifier to predict the sentiment labels and a seq2seq model to generate summaries. First, we train the superAE model and

Source: 昨晚，中联航空成都飞北京一架航班被发现有多人吸烟。后因天气原因，飞机备降太原机场。有乘客要求重新安检，机长决定继续飞行，引起机组人员与未吸烟乘客冲突。

Last night, several people were caught to smoke on a flight of China United Airlines from Chendu to Beijing. Later the flight temporarily landed on Taiyuan Airport. Some passengers asked for a security check but were denied by the captain, which led to a collision between crew and passengers.

Reference: 航班多人吸烟机组人员与乘客冲突。

Several people smoked on a flight which led to a collision between crew and passengers.

Seq2Seq: 中联航空机场发生爆炸致多人死亡。

China United Airlines exploded in the airport, leaving several people dead.

+superAE: 成都飞北京航班多人吸烟机组人员与乘客冲突。

Several people smoked on a flight from Chendu to Beijing, which led to a collision between crew and passengers.

Table 3: A summarization example of our model, compared with Seq2Seq and the reference.

the seq2seq model with the text-summary pairs until convergence. Then, we transfer the encoders to a sentiment classifier, and train the classifier with fixing the parameters of the encoders. The classifier is a simple feedforward neural network which maps the representation into the label distribution. Finally, we compute the accuracy of the predicted 2-class labels and 5-class labels.

As shown in Table 2, the seq2seq model achieves 80.7% and 65.1% accuracy of 2-class and 5-class, respectively. Our superAE model outperforms the baselines with a large margin of 8.1% and 6.6%.

4   Related Work

Rush et al. (2015) first propose an abstractive based summarization model, which uses an attentive CNN encoder to compress texts and a neural network language model to generate summaries. Chopra et al. (2016) explore a recurrent structure for abstractive summarization. To deal with out-of-vocabulary problem, Nallapati et al. (2016)

propose a generator-pointer model so that the decoder is able to generate words in source texts. Gu et al. (2016) also solved this issue by incorporating copying mechanism, allowing parts of the summaries are copied from the source contents. See et al. (2017) further discuss this problem, and incorporate the pointer-generator model with the coverage mechanism. Hu et al. (2015) build a large corpus of Chinese social media short text summarization, which is one of our benchmark datasets. Chen et al. (2016) introduce a distraction based neural model, which forces the attention mechanism to focus on the difference parts of the source inputs. Ma et al. (2017) propose a neural model to improve the semantic relevance between the source contents and the summaries.

Our work is also related to the sequence-to-sequence model (Cho et al., 2014), and the autoencoder model (Bengio, 2009; Liou et al., 2008, 2014). Sequence-to-sequence model is one of the most successful generative neural model, and is widely applied in machine translation (Sutskever et al., 2014; Jean et al., 2015; Luong et al., 2015), text summarization (Rush et al., 2015; Chopra et al., 2016; Nallapati et al., 2016), and other natural language processing tasks. Autoencoder (Bengio, 2009) is an artificial neural network used for unsupervised learning of efficient representation. Neural attention model is first proposed by Bahdanau et al. (2014).

5   Conclusion

We propose a novel model, in which the autoencoder is a supervisor of the sequence-to-sequence model, to learn a better internal representation for abstractive summarization. An adversarial learning approach is introduced to further improve the supervision of the autoencoder. Experimental results show that our model outperforms the sequence-to-sequence baseline by a large margin, and achieves the state-of-the-art performances on a Chinese social media dataset.

Acknowledgements

Our work is supported by National Natural Science Foundation of China (No. 61433015, No. 61673028), National High Technology Research and Development Program of China (863 Program, No. 2015AA015404), and the National Thousand Young Talents Program. Xu Sun is the corresponding author of this paper.

References

Dzmitry Bahdanau, Kyunghyun Cho, and Yoshua Bengio. 2014. Neural machine translation by jointly learning to align and translate. *CoRR*, abs/1409.0473.

Timothy Baldwin, Paul Cook, Marco Lui, Andrew MacKinlay, and Li Wang. 2013. How noisy social media text, how diffrnt social media sources? In *Sixth International Joint Conference on Natural Language Processing, IJCNLP 2013, Nagoya, Japan, October 14-18, 2013*, pages 356–364.

Yoshua Bengio. 2009. Learning deep architectures for AI. *Foundations and Trends in Machine Learning*, 2(1):1–127.

Qian Chen, Xiaodan Zhu, Zhenhua Ling, Si Wei, and Hui Jiang. 2016. Distraction-based neural networks for modeling documents. In *Proceedings of the 25th International Joint Conference on Artificial Intelligence (IJCAI 2015)*, New York, NY. AAAI.

Jianpeng Cheng and Mirella Lapata. 2016. Neural summarization by extracting sentences and words. In *Proceedings of the 54th Annual Meeting of the Association for Computational Linguistics, ACL 2016, August 7-12, 2016, Berlin, Germany, Volume 1: Long Papers*.

Kyunghyun Cho, Bart van Merrienboer, Çaglar Gülçehre, Dzmitry Bahdanau, Fethi Bougares, Holger Schwenk, and Yoshua Bengio. 2014. Learning phrase representations using RNN encoder-decoder for statistical machine translation. In *Proceedings of the 2014 Conference on Empirical Methods in Natural Language Processing, EMNLP 2014*, pages 1724–1734.

Sumit Chopra, Michael Auli, and Alexander M. Rush. 2016. Abstractive sentence summarization with attentive recurrent neural networks. In *NAACL HLT 2016, The 2016 Conference of the North American Chapter of the Association for Computational Linguistics: Human Language Technologies*, pages 93–98.

Jiatao Gu, Zhengdong Lu, Hang Li, and Victor O. K. Li. 2016. Incorporating copying mechanism in sequence-to-sequence learning. In *Proceedings of the 54th Annual Meeting of the Association for Computational Linguistics, ACL 2016*.

Baotian Hu, Qingcai Chen, and Fangze Zhu. 2015. LCSTS: A large scale chinese short text summarization dataset. In *Proceedings of the 2015 Conference on Empirical Methods in Natural Language Processing, EMNLP 2015, Lisbon, Portugal, September 17-21, 2015*, pages 1967–1972.

Sébastien Jean, KyungHyun Cho, Roland Memisevic, and Yoshua Bengio. 2015. On using very large target vocabulary for neural machine translation. In *Proceedings of the 53rd Annual Meeting of the Association for Computational Linguistics, ACL 2015*, pages 1–10.

Diederik P. Kingma and Jimmy Ba. 2014. Adam: A method for stochastic optimization. *CoRR*, abs/1412.6980.

Jiwei Li, Minh-Thang Luong, and Dan Jurafsky. 2015. A hierarchical neural autoencoder for paragraphs and documents. In *Proceedings of the 53rd Annual Meeting of the Association for Computational Linguistics and the 7th International Joint Conference on Natural Language Processing of the Asian Federation of Natural Language Processing, ACL 2015, July 26-31, 2015, Beijing, China, Volume 1: Long Papers*, pages 1106–1115.

Piji Li, Wai Lam, Lidong Bing, and Zihao Wang. 2017. Deep recurrent generative decoder for abstractive text summarization. In *Proceedings of the 2017 Conference on Empirical Methods in Natural Language Processing, EMNLP 2017, Copenhagen, Denmark, September 9-11, 2017*, pages 2091–2100.

Chin-Yew Lin and Eduard H. Hovy. 2003. Automatic evaluation of summaries using n-gram co-occurrence statistics. In *Human Language Technology Conference of the North American Chapter of the Association for Computational Linguistics, HLT-NAACL 2003*.

Cheng-Yuan Liou, Wei-Chen Cheng, Jiun-Wei Liou, and Daw-Ran Liou. 2014. Autoencoder for words. *Neurocomputing*, 139:84–96.

Cheng-Yuan Liou, Jau-Chi Huang, and Wen-Chie Yang. 2008. Modeling word perception using the elman network. *Neurocomputing*, 71(16-18):3150–3157.

Thang Luong, Hieu Pham, and Christopher D. Manning. 2015. Effective approaches to attention-based neural machine translation. In *Proceedings of the 2015 Conference on Empirical Methods in Natural Language Processing, EMNLP 2015*, pages 1412–1421.

Shuming Ma, Xu Sun, Wei Li, Sujian Li, Wenjie Li, and Xuancheng Ren. 2018. Query and output: Generating words by querying distributed word representations for paraphrase generation. In *NAACL 2018*.

Shuming Ma, Xu Sun, Jingjing Xu, Houfeng Wang, Wenjie Li, and Qi Su. 2017. Improving semantic relevance for sequence-to-sequence learning of chinese social media text summarization. In *Proceedings of the 55th Annual Meeting of the Association for Computational Linguistics, ACL 2017, Vancouver, Canada, July 30 - August 4, Volume 2: Short Papers*, pages 635–640.

Julian John McAuley and Jure Leskovec. 2013. From amateurs to connoisseurs: modeling the evolution of user expertise through online reviews. In *22nd International World Wide Web Conference, WWW '13, Rio de Janeiro, Brazil, May 13-17, 2013*, pages 897–908.

Ramesh Nallapati, Bowen Zhou, Cícero Nogueira dos Santos, Çaglar Gülçehre, and Bing Xiang. 2016. Abstractive text summarization using sequence-to-sequence rnns and beyond. In *Proceedings of the 20th SIGNLL Conference on Computational Natural Language Learning, CoNLL 2016, Berlin, Germany, August 11-12, 2016*, pages 280–290.

Razvan Pascanu, Tomas Mikolov, and Yoshua Bengio. 2013. On the difficulty of training recurrent neural networks. In *Proceedings of the 30th International Conference on Machine Learning, ICML 2013, Atlanta, GA, USA, 16-21 June 2013*, pages 1310–1318.

Dragomir R. Radev, Timothy Allison, Sasha Blair-Goldensohn, John Blitzer, Arda Çelebi, Stanko Dimitrov, Elliott Drábek, Ali Hakim, Wai Lam, Danyu Liu, Jahna Otterbacher, Hong Qi, Horacio Saggion, Simone Teufel, Michael Topper, Adam Winkel, and Zhu Zhang. 2004. MEAD - A platform for multidocument multilingual text summarization. In *Proceedings of the Fourth International Conference on Language Resources and Evaluation, LREC 2004*.

Alexander M. Rush, Sumit Chopra, and Jason Weston. 2015. A neural attention model for abstractive sentence summarization. In *Proceedings of the 2015 Conference on Empirical Methods in Natural Language Processing, EMNLP 2015, Lisbon, Portugal, September 17-21, 2015*, pages 379–389.

Abigail See, Peter J. Liu, and Christopher D. Manning. 2017. Get to the point: Summarization with pointer-generator networks. In *Proceedings of the 55th Annual Meeting of the Association for Computational Linguistics, ACL 2017*, pages 1073–1083.

Nitish Srivastava, Geoffrey E. Hinton, Alex Krizhevsky, Ilya Sutskever, and Ruslan Salakhutdinov. 2014. Dropout: a simple way to prevent neural networks from overfitting. *Journal of Machine Learning Research*, 15(1):1929–1958.

Xu Sun, Xuancheng Ren, Shuming Ma, and Houfeng Wang. 2017a. meprop: Sparsified back propagation for accelerated deep learning with reduced overfitting. In *ICML 2017*, pages 3299–3308.

Xu Sun, Bingzhen Wei, Xuancheng Ren, and Shuming Ma. 2017b. Label embedding network: Learning label representation for soft training of deep networks. *CoRR*, abs/1710.10393.

Ilya Sutskever, Oriol Vinyals, and Quoc V. Le. 2014. Sequence to sequence learning with neural networks. In *Advances in Neural Information Processing Systems 27: Annual Conference on Neural Information Processing Systems 2014*, pages 3104–3112.

Sho Takase, Jun Suzuki, Naoaki Okazaki, Tsutomu Hirao, and Masaaki Nagata. 2016. Neural headline generation on abstract meaning representation. In *Proceedings of the 2016 Conference on Empirical Methods in Natural Language Processing, EMNLP 2016, Austin, Texas, USA, November 1-4, 2016*, pages 1054–1059.

Kristian Woodsend and Mirella Lapata. 2010. Automatic generation of story highlights. In *ACL 2010, Proceedings of the 48th Annual Meeting of the Association for Computational Linguistics*, pages 565–574.

Jingjing Xu, Xu Sun, Xuancheng Ren, Junyang Lin, Binzhen Wei, and Wei Li. 2018a. Dp-gan: Diversity-promoting generative adversarial network for generating informative and diversified text. *CoRR*, abs/1802.01345.

Jingjing Xu, Xu Sun, Qi Zeng, Xiaodong Zhang, Xuancheng Ren, Houfeng Wang, and Wenjie Li. 2018b. Unpaired sentiment-to-sentiment translation: A cycled reinforcement learning approach. In *ACL 2018*.

Long Short-Term Memory
as a Dynamically Computed Element-wise Weighted Sum

Omer Levy[*]   **Kenton Lee**[*]   **Nicholas FitzGerald**   **Luke Zettlemoyer**
Paul G. Allen School, University of Washington, Seattle, WA
{omerlevy,kentonl,nfitz,lsz}@cs.washington.edu

Abstract

LSTMs were introduced to combat vanishing gradients in simple RNNs by augmenting them with gated additive recurrent connections. We present an alternative view to explain the success of LSTMs: the gates themselves are versatile recurrent models that provide more representational power than previously appreciated. We do this by decoupling the LSTM's gates from the embedded simple RNN, producing a new class of RNNs where the recurrence computes an element-wise weighted sum of context-independent functions of the input. Ablations on a range of problems demonstrate that the gating mechanism alone performs as well as an LSTM in most settings, strongly suggesting that the gates are doing much more in practice than just alleviating vanishing gradients.

1 Introduction

Long short-term memory (LSTM) (Hochreiter and Schmidhuber, 1997) has become the de-facto recurrent neural network (RNN) for learning representations of sequences in NLP. Like simple recurrent neural networks (S-RNNs) (Elman, 1990), LSTMs are able to learn non-linear functions of arbitrary-length input sequences. However, they also introduce an additional memory cell to mitigate the vanishing gradient problem (Hochreiter, 1991; Bengio et al., 1994). This memory is controlled by a mechanism of gates, whose additive connections allow long-distance dependencies to be learned more easily during backpropagation. While this view is mathematically accurate, in this paper we argue that it does not provide a complete picture of why LSTMs work in practice.

We present an alternate view to explain the success of LSTMs: the gates themselves are powerful recurrent models that provide more representational power than previously realized. To demonstrate this, we first show that LSTMs can be seen as a combination of two recurrent models: (1) an S-RNN, and (2) an element-wise weighted sum of the S-RNN's outputs over time, which is implicitly computed by the gates. We hypothesize that, for many practical NLP problems, the weighted sum serves as the main modeling component. The S-RNN, while theoretically expressive, is in practice only a minor contributor that clouds the mathematical clarity of the model. By replacing the S-RNN with a context-*independent* function of the input, we arrive at a much more restricted class of RNNs, where the main recurrence is via the element-wise weighted sums that the gates are computing.

We test our hypothesis on NLP problems, where LSTMs are wildly popular at least in part due to their ability to model crucial phenomena such as word order (Adi et al., 2017), syntactic structure (Linzen et al., 2016), and even long-range semantic dependencies (He et al., 2017). We consider four challenging tasks: language modeling, question answering, dependency parsing, and machine translation. Experiments show that while removing the gates from an LSTM can severely hurt performance, replacing the S-RNN with a simple linear transformation of the input results in minimal or no loss in model performance. We also show that, in many cases, LSTMs can be further simplified by removing the output gate, arriving at an even more transparent architecture, where the output is a context-*independent* function of the weighted sum. Together, these results suggest that the gates' ability to compute an element-wise weighted sum, rather than the non-linear transition dynamics of S-RNNs, are the driving force behind LSTM's success.

The first two authors contributed equally to this paper.

Proceedings of the 56th Annual Meeting of the Association for Computational Linguistics (Short Papers), pages 732–739
Melbourne, Australia, July 15 - 20, 2018. ©2018 Association for Computational Linguistics

2 What Do Memory Cells Compute?

LSTMs are typically motivated as an augmentation of simple RNNs (S-RNNs), defined as:

$$h_t = \tanh(W_{hh}h_{t-1} + W_{hx}x_t + b_h) \qquad (1)$$

S-RNNs suffer from the vanishing gradient problem (Hochreiter, 1991; Bengio et al., 1994) due to compounding multiplicative updates of the hidden state. By introducing a memory cell and an output layer controlled by gates, LSTMs enable shortcuts through which gradients can flow when learning with backpropagation. This mechanism enables learning of long-distance dependencies while preserving the expressive power of recurrent nonlinear transformations provided by S-RNNs.

Rather than viewing the gates as simply an auxiliary mechanism to address a *learning* problem, we present an alternate view that emphasizes their *modeling* strengths. We argue that the LSTM should be interpreted as a hybrid of two distinct recurrent architectures: (1) the S-RNN which provides multiplicative connections across timesteps, and (2) the memory cell which provides additive connections across timesteps. On top of these recurrences, an output layer is included that simply squashes and filters the memory cell at each step.

Throughout this paper, let $\{x_1, \ldots, x_n\}$ be the sequence of input vectors, $\{h_1, \ldots, h_n\}$ be the sequence of output vectors, and $\{c_1, \ldots, c_n\}$ be the memory cell's states. Then, given the basic LSTM definition below, we can formally identify three sub-components.

$$\widetilde{c}_t = \tanh(W_{ch}h_{t-1} + W_{cx}x_t + b_c) \qquad (2)$$
$$i_t = \sigma(W_{ih}h_{t-1} + W_{ix}x_t + b_i) \qquad (3)$$
$$f_t = \sigma(W_{fh}h_{t-1} + W_{fx}x_t + b_f) \qquad (4)$$
$$c_t = i_t \circ \widetilde{c}_t + f_t \circ c_{t-1} \qquad (5)$$
$$o_t = \sigma(W_{oh}h_{t-1} + W_{ox}x_t + b_o) \qquad (6)$$
$$h_t = o_t \circ \tanh(c_t) \qquad (7)$$

Content Layer (Equation 2) We refer to $\widetilde{c}_t$ as the content layer, which is the output of an S-RNN. Evaluating the need for multiplicative recurrent connections in the content layer is the focus of this work. The content layer is passed to the memory cell, which decides which parts of it to store.

Memory Cell (Equations 3-5) The memory cell c_t is controlled by two gates. The input gate i_t controls what part of the content ($\widetilde{c}_t$) is written to the memory, while the forget gate f_t controls what part of the memory is deleted by filtering the previous state of the memory (c_{t-1}). Writing to the memory is done by adding the filtered content ($i_t \circ \widetilde{c}_t$) to the retained memory ($f_t \circ c_{t-1}$).

Output Layer (Equations 6-7) The output layer h_t passes the memory cell through a tanh activation function and uses an output gate o_t to read selectively from the squashed memory cell.

Our goal is to study how much each of these components contribute to the empirical performance of LSTMs. In particular, it is worth considering the memory cell in more detail to reveal why it could serve as a standalone powerful model of long-distance context. It is possible to show that it implicitly computes an *element-wise weighted sum* of all the previous content layers by expanding the recurrence relation in Equation 5:

$$\begin{aligned}
c_t &= i_t \circ \widetilde{c}_t + f_t \circ c_{t-1} \\
&= \sum_{j=0}^{t} \left(i_j \circ \prod_{k=j+1}^{t} f_k\right) \circ \widetilde{c}_j \qquad (8) \\
&= \sum_{j=0}^{t} w_j^t \circ \widetilde{c}_j
\end{aligned}$$

Each weight w_j^t is a product of the input gate i_j (when its respective input $\widetilde{c}_j$ was read) and every subsequent forget gate f_k. An interesting property of these weights is that, like the gates, they are also soft element-wise binary filters.

3 Standalone Memory Cells are Powerful

The restricted space of element-wise weighted sums allows for easier mathematical analysis, visualization, and perhaps even learnability. However, constrained function spaces are also less expressive, and a natural question is whether these models will work well for NLP problems that involve understanding context. We hypothesize that the memory cell (which computes weighted sums) can function as a standalone contextualizer. To test this hypothesis, we present several simplifications of the LSTM's architecture (Section 3.1), and show on a variety of NLP benchmarks that there is a qualitative performance difference between models that contain a memory cell and those that do not (Section 3.2). We conclude that the content and output layers are relatively minor contributors, and that the space of element-wise weighted sums is sufficiently powerful to compete with fully parameterized LSTMs (Section 3.3).

3.1 Simplified Models

The modeling power of LSTMs is commonly assumed to derive from the S-RNN in the content layer, with the rest of the model acting as a learning aid to bypass the vanishing gradient problem. We first isolate the S-RNN by ablating the gates (denoted as *LSTM – GATES* for consistency).

To test whether the memory cell has enough modeling power of its own, we take an LSTM and replace the S-RNN in the content layer from Equation 2 with a simple linear transformation ($\tilde{c}_t = W_{cx}x_t$) creating the *LSTM – S-RNN* model.

We further simplify the LSTM by removing the output gate from Equation 7 ($h_t = \tanh(c_t)$), leaving only the activation function in the output layer (*LSTM – S-RNN – OUT*). After removing the S-RNN and the output gate from the LSTM, the entire ablated model can be written in a modular, compact form:

$$h_t = \text{OUTPUT}\left(\sum_{j=0}^{t} w_j^t \circ \text{CONTENT}(x_j)\right) \quad (9)$$

where the content layer $\text{CONTENT}(\cdot)$ and the output layer $\text{OUTPUT}(\cdot)$ are both context-*independent* functions, making the entire model highly constrained and mathematically simpler. The complexity of modeling contextual information is needed only for computing the weights w_j^t. As we will see in Section 3.2, both of these ablations perform on par with LSTMs on several tasks.

Finally, we ablate the hidden state from the gates as well, by computing each gate g_t via $\sigma(W_{gx}x_t + b_g)$. In this model, the only recurrence is the additive connection in the memory cell; it has no multiplicative recurrent connections at all. It can be seen as a type of QRNN (Bradbury et al., 2016) or SRU (Lei et al., 2017b), but for consistency we label it as *LSTM – S-RNN – HIDDEN*.

3.2 Experiments

We compare model performance on four NLP tasks, with an experimental setup that is lenient towards LSTMs and harsh towards its simplifications. In each case, we use existing implementations and previously reported hyperparameter settings. Since these settings were tuned for LSTMs, any simplification that performs equally to (or better than) LSTMs under these LSTM-friendly settings provides strong evidence that the ablated component is not a contributing factor. For each task we also report the mean and standard deviation of 5 runs of the LSTM settings to demonstrate the typical variance observed due to training with different random initializations.

Language Modeling We evaluate the models on the Penn Treebank (PTB) (Marcus et al., 1993) language modeling benchmark. We use the implementation of Zaremba et al. (2014) from TensorFlow's tutorial while replacing any invocation of LSTMs with simpler models. We test two of their configurations: *medium* and *large* (Table 1).

Question Answering For question answering, we use two different QA systems on the Stanford question answering dataset (SQuAD) (Rajpurkar et al., 2016): the Bidirectional Attention Flow model (BiDAF) (Seo et al., 2016) and DrQA (Chen et al., 2017). BiDAF contains 3 LSTMs, which are referred to as the phrase layer, the modeling layer, and the span end encoder. Our experiments replace each of these LSTMs with their simplified counterparts. We directly use the implementation of BiDAF from AllenNLP (Gardner et al., 2017), and all experiments reuse the existing hyperparameters that were tuned for LSTMs. Likewise, we use an open-source implementation of DrQA[1] and replace only the LSTMs, while leaving everything else intact. Table 2 shows the results.

Dependency Parsing For dependency parsing, we use the Deep Biaffine Dependency Parser (Dozat and Manning, 2016), which relies on stacked bidirectional LSTMs to learn context-sensitive word embeddings for determining arcs between a pair of words. We directly use their released implementation, which is evaluated on the Universal Dependencies English Web Treebank v1.3 (Silveira et al., 2014). In our experiments, we use the existing hyperparameters and only replace the LSTMs with the simplified architectures. Table 3 shows the results.

Machine Translation For machine translation, we used OpenNMT (Klein et al., 2017) to train English to German translation models on the multimodal benchmarks from WMT 2016 (used in OpenNMT's readme file). We use OpenNMT's default model and hyperparameters, replacing the stacked bidirectional LSTM encoder with the sim-

---

[1] https://github.com/hitvoice/DrQA

Configuration	Model	Perplexity
PTB (Medium)	LSTM	83.9 ± 0.3
	– S-RNN	80.5
	– S-RNN – OUT	81.6
	– S-RNN – HIDDEN	83.3
	– GATES	140.9
PTB (Large)	LSTM	78.8 ± 0.2
	– S-RNN	76.0
	– S-RNN – OUT	78.5
	– S-RNN – HIDDEN	82.9
	– GATES	126.1

Table 1: Performance on language modeling benchmarks, measured by perplexity.

System	Model	EM	F1
BiDAF	LSTM	67.9 ± 0.3	77.5 ± 0.2
	– S-RNN	68.4	78.2
	– S-RNN – OUT	67.4	77.2
	– S-RNN – HIDDEN	66.5	76.6
	– GATES	62.9	73.3
DrQA	LSTM	68.8 ± 0.2	78.2 ± 0.2
	– S-RNN	68.0	77.2
	– S-RNN – OUT	68.7	77.9
	– S-RNN – HIDDEN	67.9	77.2
	– GATES	56.4	66.5

Table 2: Performance on SQuAD, measured by exact match (EM) and span overlap (F1).

plified architectures.[2] Table 4 shows the results.

3.3 Discussion

We showed four major ablations of the LSTM. In the S-RNN experiments (*LSTM – GATES*), we ablate the memory cell and the output layer. In the *LSTM – S-RNN* and *LSTM – S-RNN – OUT* experiments, we ablate the S-RNN. In the *LSTM – S-RNN – HIDDEN*, we remove not only the S-RNN in the content layer, but also the S-RNNs in the gates, resulting in a model whose sole recurrence is in the memory cell's additive connection.

As consistent with previous literature, removing the memory cell degrades performance drastically. In contrast, removing the S-RNN makes little to no difference in the final performance, suggesting that the memory cell alone is largely responsible for the success of LSTMs in NLP.

Even after removing every multiplicative recurrence from the memory cell itself, the model's performance remains well above the vanilla S-

---

Model	UAS	LAS
LSTM	90.60 ± 0.21	88.05 ± 0.33
– S-RNN	90.77	88.49
– S-RNN – OUT	90.70	88.31
– S-RNN – HIDDEN	90.53	87.96
– GATES	87.75	84.61

Table 3: Performance on the universal dependencies parsing benchmark, measured by unlabeled (UAS) and labeled attachment score (LAS).

Model	BLEU
LSTM	38.19 ± 0.1
– S-RNN	37.84
– S-RNN – OUT	38.36
– S-RNN – HIDDEN	36.98
– GATES	26.52

Table 4: Performance on the WMT 2016 multimodal English to German benchmark.

RNN's, and falls within the standard deviation of an LSTM's on some tasks (see Table 3). This latter result indicates that the additive recurrent connection in the memory cell – and not the multiplicative recurrent connections in the content layer or in the gates – is the most important computational element in an LSTM. As a corollary, this result also suggests that a weighted sum of context words, while mathematically simple, is a powerful model of contextual information.

4 LSTM as Self-Attention

Attention mechanisms are widely used in the NLP literature to aggregate over a sequence (Cho et al., 2014; Bahdanau et al., 2015) or contextualize tokens within a sequence (Cheng et al., 2016; Parikh et al., 2016) by *explicitly* computing weighted sums. In the previous sections, we demonstrated that LSTMs implicitly compute weighted sums as well, and that this computation is central to their success. How, then, are these two computations related, and in what ways do they differ?

After simplifying the content layer and removing the output gate (*LSTM – S-RNN – OUT*), the model's computation can be expressed as a weighted sum of context-independent functions of the inputs (Equation 9 in Section 3.1). This formula abstracts over both the simplified LSTM and the family of attention mechanisms, and through this lens, the memory cell's computation can be seen as a "cousin" of self-attention. In fact, we can also leverage this abstraction to visualize the simplified LSTM's weights as is commonly done with attention (see Appendix A for visualization).

However, there are three major differences in how the *weights* w_j^t are computed.

First, the LSTM's weights are *vectors*, while attention typically computes scalar weights; i.e. a separate weighted sum is computed for every dimension of the LSTM's memory cell. Multi-headed self-attention (Vaswani et al., 2017) can be seen as a middle ground between the two approaches, allocating a scalar weight for different subsets of the dimensions.

Second, the weighted sum is accumulated with a dynamic program. This enables a linear rather than quadratic complexity in comparison to self-attention, but reduces the amount of parallel computation. This accumulation also creates an inductive bias of attending to nearby words, since the weights can only decrease over time.

Finally, attention has a probabilistic interpretation due to the softmax normalization, while the sum of weights in LSTMs can grow up to the sequence length. In variants of the LSTM that tie the input and forget gate, such as coupled-gate LSTMs (Greff et al., 2016) and GRUs (Cho et al., 2014), the memory cell instead computes a weighted *average* with a probabilistic interpretation. These variants compute locally normalized distributions via a product of sigmoids rather than globally normalized distributions via a single softmax.

5   Related Work

Many variants of LSTMs (Hochreiter and Schmidhuber, 1997) have been previously explored. These typically consist of a different parameterization of the gates, such as LSTMs with peephole connections (Gers and Schmidhuber, 2000), or a rewiring of the connections, such as GRUs (Cho et al., 2014). However, these modifications invariably maintain the recurrent content layer. Even more systematic explorations (Józefowicz et al., 2015; Greff et al., 2016; Zoph and Le, 2017) do not question the importance of the embedded S-RNN. This is the first study to provide apples-to-apples comparisons between LSTMs with and without the recurrent content layer.

Several other recent works have also reported promising results with recurrent models that are vastly simpler than LSTMs, such as quasi-recurrent neural networks (Bradbury et al., 2016), strongly-typed recurrent neural networks (Bal-

duzzi and Ghifary, 2016), recurrent additive networks (Lee et al., 2017), kernel neural networks (Lei et al., 2017a), and simple recurrent units (Lei et al., 2017b), making it increasingly apparent that LSTMs are over-parameterized. While these works indicate an obvious trend, they do not focus on explaining what LSTMs are learning. In our carefully controlled ablation studies, we propose and evaluate the minimal changes required to test our hypothesis that LSTMs are powerful because they dynamically compute element-wise weighted sums of content layers.

6   Conclusion

We presented an alternate view of LSTMs: they are a hybrid of S-RNNs and a gated model that dynamically computes weighted sums of the S-RNN outputs. Our experiments investigated whether the S-RNN is a necessary component of LSTMs. In other words, are the gates alone as powerful of a model as an LSTM? Results across four major NLP tasks (language modeling, question answering, dependency parsing, and machine translation) indicate that LSTMs suffer little to no performance loss when removing the S-RNN. This provides evidence that the gating mechanism is doing the heavy lifting in modeling context. We further ablate the recurrence in each gate and find that this incurs only a modest drop in performance, indicating that the real modeling power of LSTMs stems from their ability to compute element-wise weighted sums of context-independent functions of their inputs.

This realization allows us to mathematically relate LSTMs and other gated RNNs to attention-based models. Casting an LSTM as a dynamically-computed attention mechanism enables the visualization of how context is used at every timestep, shedding light on the inner workings of the relatively opaque LSTM.

Acknowledgements

The research was supported in part by DARPA under the DEFT program (FA8750-13-2-0019), the ARO (W911NF-16-1-0121), the NSF (IIS-1252835, IIS-1562364), gifts from Google, Tencent, and Nvidia, and an Allen Distinguished Investigator Award. We also thank Yoav Goldberg, Benjamin Heinzerling, Tao Lei, and the UW NLP group for helpful conversations and comments on the work.

References

Yossi Adi, Einat Kermany, Yonatan Belinkov, Ofer Lavi, and Yoav Goldberg. 2017. Fine-grained analysis of sentence embeddings using auxiliary prediction tasks. In *ICLR*.

Dzmitry Bahdanau, Kyunghyun Cho, and Yoshua Bengio. 2015. Neural machine translation by jointly learning to align and translate. In *ICLR*.

David Balduzzi and Muhammad Ghifary. 2016. Strongly-typed recurrent neural networks. In *Proceedings of the 33nd International Conference on Machine Learning, ICML 2016, New York City, NY, USA, June 19-24, 2016*. pages 1292–1300. http://jmlr.org/proceedings/papers/v48/balduzzi16.html.

Yoshua Bengio, Patrice Y. Simard, and Paolo Frasconi. 1994. Learning long-term dependencies with gradient descent is difficult. *IEEE Transactions on Neural Networks* 5(2):157–166.

James Bradbury, Stephen Merity, Caiming Xiong, and Richard Socher. 2016. Quasi-recurrent neural networks. *CoRR* abs/1611.01576.

Danqi Chen, Adam Fisch, Jason Weston, and Antoine Bordes. 2017. Reading wikipedia to answer open-domain questions. In *Proceedings of the 55th Annual Meeting of the Association for Computational Linguistics (Volume 1: Long Papers)*. Association for Computational Linguistics, Vancouver, Canada, pages 1870–1879. http://aclweb.org/anthology/P17-1171.

Jianpeng Cheng, Li Dong, and Mirella Lapata. 2016. Long short-term memory-networks for machine reading. In *Proceedings of the 2016 Conference on Empirical Methods in Natural Language Processing*. Association for Computational Linguistics, Austin, Texas, pages 551–561. https://aclweb.org/anthology/D16-1053.

Kyunghyun Cho, Bart van Merrienboer, Caglar Gulcehre, Dzmitry Bahdanau, Fethi Bougares, Holger Schwenk, and Yoshua Bengio. 2014. Learning phrase representations using rnn encoder–decoder for statistical machine translation. In *Proceedings of the 2014 Conference on Empirical Methods in Natural Language Processing (EMNLP)*. Association for Computational Linguistics, Doha, Qatar, pages 1724–1734. http://www.aclweb.org/anthology/D14-1179.

Timothy Dozat and Christopher D. Manning. 2016. Deep biaffine attention for neural dependency parsing. *CoRR* abs/1611.01734.

Jeffrey L. Elman. 1990. Finding structure in time. *Cognitive Science* 14:179–211.

Matt Gardner, Joel Grus, Mark Neumann, Oyvind Tafjord, Pradeep Dasigi, Nelson Liu, Matthew Peters, Michael Schmitz, and Luke Zettlemoyer. 2017. Allennlp: A deep semantic natural language processing platform. http://allennlp.org/papers/AllenNLP_white_paper.pdf.

Felix A. Gers and Jürgen Schmidhuber. 2000. Recurrent nets that time and count. In *IJCNN*.

Klaus Greff, Rupesh K Srivastava, Jan Koutník, Bas R Steunebrink, and Jürgen Schmidhuber. 2016. Lstm: A search space odyssey. *IEEE Transactions on Neural Networks and Learning Systems* .

Luheng He, Kenton Lee, Mike Lewis, and Luke Zettlemoyer. 2017. Deep semantic role labeling: What works and whats next. In *Proceedings of the Annual Meeting of the Association for Computational Linguistics*.

Sepp Hochreiter. 1991. Untersuchungen zu dynamischen neuronalen netzen. *Diploma, Technische Universität München* 91.

Sepp Hochreiter and Jürgen Schmidhuber. 1997. Long Short-term Memory. *Neural computation* 9(8):1735–1780.

Rafal Józefowicz, Wojciech Zaremba, and Ilya Sutskever. 2015. An empirical exploration of recurrent network architectures. In *ICML*.

Guillaume Klein, Yoon Kim, Yuntian Deng, Jean Senellart, and Alexander M. Rush. 2017. Opennmt: Open-source toolkit for neural machine translation. In *Proc. ACL*. https://doi.org/10.18653/v1/P17-4012.

Kenton Lee, Omer Levy, and Luke Zettlemoyer. 2017. Recurrent additive networks. *arXiv preprint arXiv:1705.07393* .

Tao Lei, Wengong Jin, Regina Barzilay, and Tommi Jaakkola. 2017a. Deriving neural architectures from sequence and graph kernels. In *ICML*.

Tao Lei, Yu Zhang, and Yoav Artzi. 2017b. Training rnns as fast as cnns. *arXiv preprint arXiv:1709.02755* .

Tal Linzen, Emmanuel Dupoux, and Yoav Goldberg. 2016. Assessing the ability of lstms to learn syntax-sensitive dependencies. *TACL* 4:521–535.

Mitchell P. Marcus, Beatrice Santorini, and Mary Ann Marcinkiewicz. 1993. Building a large annotated corpus of english: The penn treebank. *Computational Linguistics* 19:313–330.

Ankur Parikh, Oscar Täckström, Dipanjan Das, and Jakob Uszkoreit. 2016. A decomposable attention model for natural language inference. In *Proceedings of the 2016 Conference on Empirical Methods in Natural Language Processing*. Association for Computational Linguistics, Austin, Texas, pages 2249–2255. https://aclweb.org/anthology/D16-1244.

Pranav Rajpurkar, Jian Zhang, Konstantin Lopyrev, and Percy Liang. 2016. Squad: 100, 000+ questions for machine comprehension of text. In *EMNLP*.

Min Joon Seo, Aniruddha Kembhavi, Ali Farhadi, and Hannaneh Hajishirzi. 2016. Bidirectional attention flow for machine comprehension. *CoRR* abs/1611.01603.

Natalia Silveira, Timothy Dozat, Marie-Catherine de Marneffe, Samuel Bowman, Miriam Connor, John Bauer, and Christopher D. Manning. 2014. A gold standard dependency corpus for English. In *Proceedings of the Ninth International Conference on Language Resources and Evaluation (LREC-2014)*.

Ashish Vaswani, Noam Shazeer, Niki Parmar, Jakob Uszkoreit, Llion Jones, Aidan N. Gomez, Lukasz Kaiser, and Illia Polosukhin. 2017. Attention is all you need. *arXiv preprint arXiv:1706.03762* .

Wojciech Zaremba, Ilya Sutskever, and Oriol Vinyals. 2014. Recurrent neural network regularization. *arXiv preprint arXiv:1409.2329* .

Barret Zoph and Quoc V Le. 2017. Neural architecture search with reinforcement learning. In *ICLR*.

A   Weight Visualization

Given the empirical evidence that LSTMs are effectively learning weighted sums of the content layers, it is natural to investigate what weights the model learns in practice. Using the more mathematically transparent simplification of LSTMs, we can visualize the weights w_j^t that are placed on every input j at every timestep t (see Equation 9).

Unlike attention mechanisms, these weights are vectors rather than scalar values. Therefore, we can only provide a coarse-grained visualization of the weights by rendering their L^2-norm, as shown in Table 5. In the visualization, each column indicates the word represented by the weighted sum, and each row indicates the word over which the weighted sum is computed. Dark horizontal streaks indicate the duration for which a word was remembered. Unsurprisingly, the weights on the diagonal are always the largest since it indicates the weight of the current word. More interesting task-specific patterns emerge when inspecting the off-diagonals that represent the weight on the context words.

The first visualization uses the language model. Due to the language modeling setup, there are only non-zero weights on the current or previous words. We find that the common function words are quickly forgotten, while infrequent words that signal the topic are remembered over very long distances.

The second visualization uses the dependency parser. In this setting, since the recurrent architectures are bidirectional, there are non-zero weights on all words in the sentence. The top-right triangle indicates weights from the forward direction, and the bottom-left triangle indicates from the backward direction. For syntax, we see a significantly different pattern. Function words that are useful for determining syntax are more likely to be remembered. Weights on head words are also likely to persist until the end of a constituent.

This illustration provides only a glimpse into what the model is capturing, and perhaps future, more detailed visualizations that take the individual dimensions into account can provide further insight into what LSTMs are learning in practice.

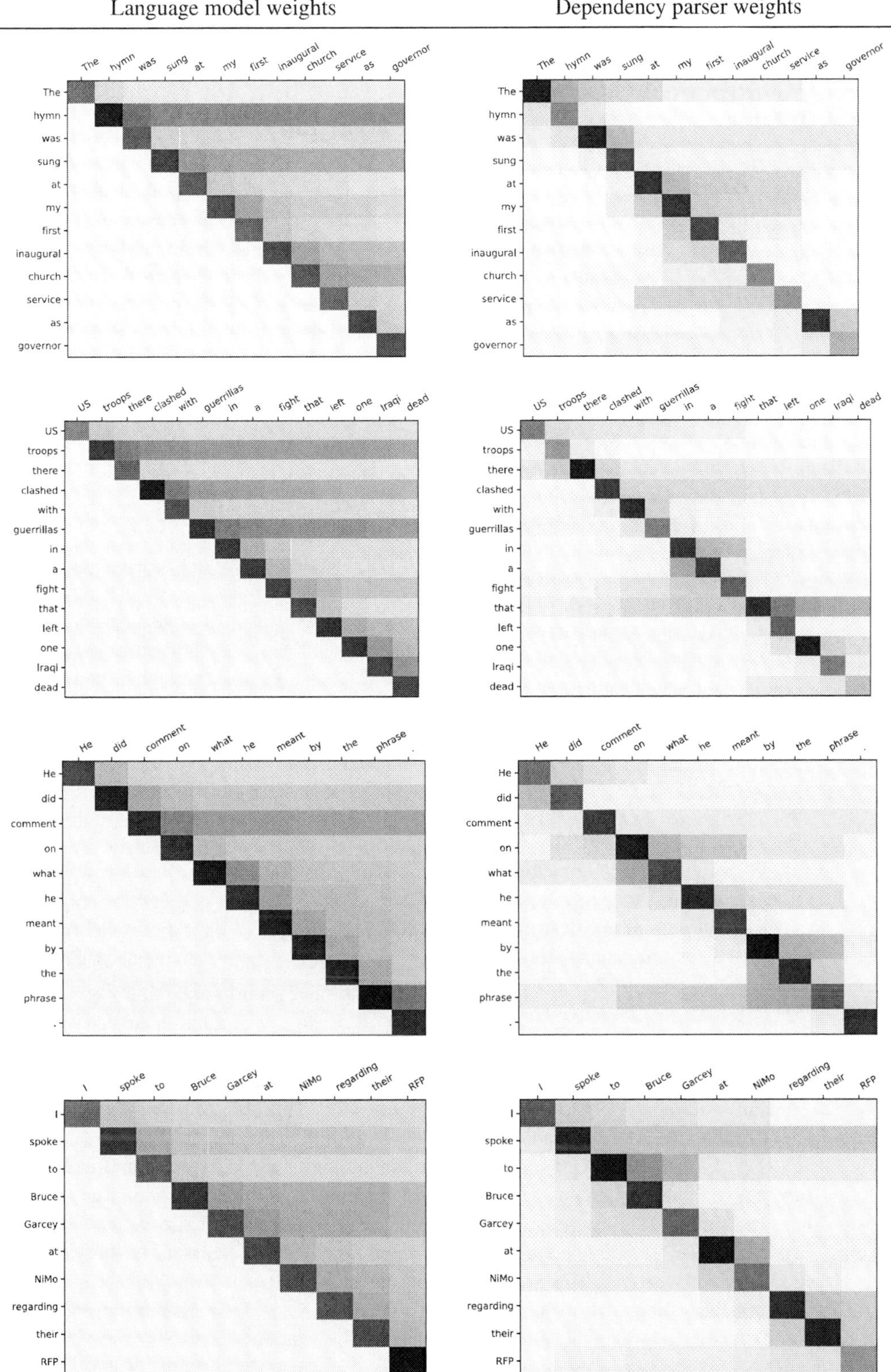

Table 5: Visualization of the weights on context words learned by the memory cell. Each column represents the current word t, and each row represents a context word j. The gating mechanism implicitly computes element-wise weighted sums over each column. The darkness of each square indicates the L^2-norm of the vector weights w_j^t from Equation 9. Figures on the left show weights learned by a language model. Figures on the right show weights learned by a dependency parser.

On the Practical Computational Power of Finite Precision RNNs for Language Recognition

Gail Weiss
Technion, Israel

Yoav Goldberg
Bar-Ilan University, Israel

Eran Yahav
Technion, Israel

{sgailw,yahave}@cs.technion.ac.il
yogo@cs.biu.ac.il

Abstract

While Recurrent Neural Networks (RNNs) are famously known to be Turing complete, this relies on infinite precision in the states and unbounded computation time. We consider the case of RNNs with finite precision whose computation time is linear in the input length. Under these limitations, we show that different RNN variants have different computational power. In particular, we show that the LSTM and the Elman-RNN with ReLU activation are strictly stronger than the RNN with a squashing activation and the GRU. This is achieved because LSTMs and ReLU-RNNs can easily implement counting behavior. We show empirically that the LSTM does indeed learn to effectively use the counting mechanism.

1 Introduction

Recurrent Neural Network (RNNs) emerge as very strong learners of sequential data. A famous result by Siegelmann and Sontag (1992; 1994), and its extension in (Siegelmann, 1999), demonstrates that an Elman-RNN (Elman, 1990) with a sigmoid activation function, rational weights and infinite precision states can simulate a Turing-machine in real-time, making RNNs Turing-complete. Recently, Chen et al (2017) extended the result to the ReLU activation function. However, these constructions (a) assume reading the entire input into the RNN state and only then performing the computation, using *unbounded time*; and (b) rely on having *infinite precision* in the network states. As argued by Chen et al (2017), this is not the model of RNN computation used in NLP applications. Instead, RNNs are often used by feeding an input sequence into the RNN one item at a time, each immediately returning a state-vector that corresponds to a prefix of the sequence and which can be passed as input for a subsequent feed-forward prediction network operating in constant time. The amount of tape used by a Turing machine under this restriction is linear in the input length, reducing its power to recognition of context-sensitive language. More importantly, computation is often performed on GPUs with 32bit floating point computation, and there is increasing evidence that competitive performance can be achieved also for quantized networks with 4-bit weights or fixed-point arithmetics (Hubara et al., 2016). The construction of (Siegelmann, 1999) implements pushing 0 into a binary stack by the operation $g \leftarrow g/4 + 1/4$. This allows pushing roughly 15 zeros before reaching the limit of the 32bit floating point precision. Finally, RNN solutions that rely on carefully orchestrated mathematical constructions are unlikely to be found using backpropagation-based training.

In this work we restrict ourselves to *input-bound recurrent neural networks with finite-precision states (IBFP-RNN)*, trained using backpropagation. This class of networks is likely to coincide with the networks one can expect to obtain when training RNNs for NLP applications. An IBFP Elman-RNN is finite state. But what about other RNN variants? In particular, we consider the Elman RNN (SRNN) (Elman, 1990) with squashing and with ReLU activations, the Long Short-Term Memory (LSTM) (Hochreiter and Schmidhuber, 1997) and the Gated Recurrent Unit (GRU) (Cho et al., 2014; Chung et al., 2014).

The common wisdom is that the LSTM and GRU introduce additional *gating components* that handle the vanishing gradients problem of training SRNNs, thus stabilizing training and making it more robust. The LSTM and GRU are often considered as almost equivalent variants of each other.

Proceedings of the 56th Annual Meeting of the Association for Computational Linguistics (Short Papers), pages 740–745
Melbourne, Australia, July 15 - 20, 2018. ©2018 Association for Computational Linguistics

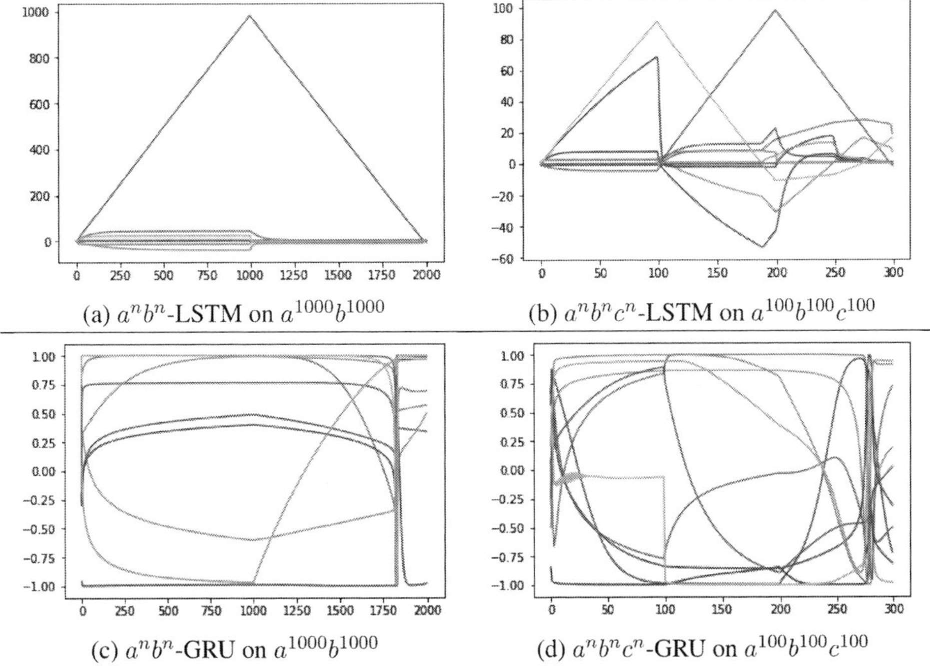

(a) $a^n b^n$-LSTM on $a^{1000} b^{1000}$ (b) $a^n b^n c^n$-LSTM on $a^{100} b^{100} c^{100}$

(c) $a^n b^n$-GRU on $a^{1000} b^{1000}$ (d) $a^n b^n c^n$-GRU on $a^{100} b^{100} c^{100}$

Figure 1: Activations — c for LSTM and h for GRU — for networks trained on $a^n b^n$ and $a^n b^n c^n$. The LSTM has clearly learned to use an explicit counting mechanism, in contrast with the GRU.

We show that in the input-bound, finite-precision case, there is a real difference between the computational capacities of the LSTM and the GRU: the LSTM can easily perform unbounded counting, while the GRU (and the SRNN) cannot. This makes the LSTM a variant of a k-counter machine (Fischer et al., 1968), while the GRU remains finite-state. Interestingly, the SRNN with ReLU activation followed by an MLP classifier also has power similar to a k-counter machine.

These results suggest there is a class of formal languages that can be recognized by LSTMs but not by GRUs. In section 5, we demonstrate that for at least two such languages, the LSTM manages to learn the desired concept classes using back-propagation, while using the hypothesized control structure. Figure 1 shows the activations of 10-d LSTM and GRU trained to recognize the languages $a^n b^n$ and $a^n b^n c^n$. It is clear that the LSTM learned to dedicate specific dimensions for counting, in contrast to the GRU.[1]

2 The RNN Models

An RNN is a parameterized function R that takes as input an input vector x_t and a state vector h_{t-1} and returns a state vector h_t:

$$h_t = R(x_t, h_{t-1}) \qquad (1)$$

The RNN is applied to a sequence $x_1, ..., x_n$ by starting with an initial vector h_0 (often the 0 vector) and applying R repeatedly according to equation (1). Let Σ be an input vocabulary (alphabet), and assume a mapping E from every vocabulary item to a vector x (achieved through a 1-hot encoding, an embedding layer, or some other means). Let $RNN(x_1, ..., x_n)$ denote the state vector h resulting from the application of R to the sequence $E(x_1), ..., E(x_n)$. An *RNN recognizer* (or *RNN acceptor*) has an additional function f mapping states h to $0, 1$. Typically, f is a log-linear classifier or multi-layer perceptron. We say that *an RNN recognizes a language* $L \subseteq \Sigma^*$ if $f(RNN(w))$ returns 1 for all and only words $w = x_1, ..., x_n \in L$.

Elman-RNN (SRNN) In the Elman-RNN (Elman, 1990), also called the Simple RNN (SRNN),

---

[1] Is the ability to perform unbounded counting relevant to "real world" NLP tasks? In some cases it might be. For example, processing linearized parse trees (Vinyals et al., 2015; Choe and Charniak, 2016; Aharoni and Goldberg, 2017) requires counting brackets and nesting levels. Indeed, previous works that process linearized parse trees report using LSTMs and not GRUs for this purpose. Our work here suggests that this may not be a coincidence.

741

the function R takes the form of an affine transform followed by a tanh nonlinearity:

$$h_t = \tanh(Wx_t + Uh_{t-1} + b) \qquad (2)$$

Elman-RNNs are known to be at-least finite-state. Siegelmann (1996) proved that the tanh can be replaced by any other squashing function without sacrificing computational power.

IRNN The IRNN model, explored by (Le et al., 2015), replaces the tanh activation with a non-squashing ReLU:

$$h_t = max(0, (Wx_t + Uh_{t-1} + b)) \qquad (3)$$

The computational power of such RNNs (given infinite precision) is explored in (Chen et al., 2017).

Gated Recurrent Unit (GRU) In the GRU (Cho et al., 2014), the function R incorporates a *gating mechanism*, taking the form:

$$
\begin{aligned}
z_t &= \sigma(W^z x_t + U^z h_{t-1} + b^z) & (4)\\
r_t &= \sigma(W^r x_t + U^r h_{t-1} + b^r) & (5)\\
\tilde{h}_t &= \tanh(W^h x_t + U^h(r_t \circ h_{t-1}) + b^h) & (6)\\
h_t &= z_t \circ h_{t-1} + (1 - z_t) \circ \tilde{h}_t & (7)
\end{aligned}
$$

Where σ is the sigmoid function and $\circ$ is the Hadamard product (element-wise product).

Long Short Term Memory (LSTM) In the LSTM (Hochreiter and Schmidhuber, 1997), R uses a different gating component configuration:

$$
\begin{aligned}
f_t &= \sigma(W^f x_t + U^f h_{t-1} + b^f) & (8)\\
i_t &= \sigma(W^i x_t + U^i h_{t-1} + b^i) & (9)\\
o_t &= \sigma(W^o x_t + U^o h_{t-1} + b^o) & (10)\\
\tilde{c}_t &= \tanh(W^c x_t + U^c h_{t-1} + b^c) & (11)\\
c_t &= f_t \circ c_{t-1} + i_t \circ \tilde{c}_t & (12)\\
h_t &= o_t \circ g(c_t) & (13)
\end{aligned}
$$

where g can be either tanh or the identity.

Equivalences The GRU and LSTM are at least as strong as the SRNN: by setting the gates of the GRU to $z_t = 0$ and $r_t = 1$ we obtain the SRNN computation. Similarly by setting the LSTM gates to $i_t = 1, o_t = 1$, and $f_t = 0$. This is easily achieved by setting the matrices W and U to 0, and the biases b to the (constant) desired gate values.

Thus, all the above RNNs can recognize finite-state languages.

3 Power of Counting

Power beyond finite state can be obtained by introducing counters. Counting languages and k-counter machines are discussed in depth in (Fischer et al., 1968). When unbounded computation is allowed, a 2-counter machine has Turing power. However, for computation bound by input length (real-time) there is a more interesting hierarchy. In particular, real-time counting languages cut across the traditional Chomsky hierarchy: real-time k-counter machines can recognize at least one context-free language ($a^n b^n$), and at least one context-sensitive one ($a^n b^n c^n$). However, they *cannot* recognize the context free language given by the grammar $S \rightarrow x|aSa|bSb$ (palindromes).

SKCM For our purposes, we consider a simplified variant of k-counter machines (SKCM). A counter is a device which can be incremented by a fixed amount (INC), decremented by a fixed amount (DEC) or compared to 0 (COMP0). Informally,[2] an SKCM is a finite-state automaton extended with k counters, where at each step of the computation each counter can be incremented, decremented or ignored in an input-dependent way, and state-transitions and accept/reject decisions can inspect the counters' states using COMP0. The results for the three languages discussed above hold for the SKCM variant as well, with proofs provided in the supplementary material.

4 RNNs as SKCMs

In what follows, we consider the effect on the state-update equations on a single dimension, $h_t[j]$. We omit the index $[j]$ for readability.

LSTM The LSTM acts as an SKCM by designating k dimensions of the memory cell c_t as counters. In non-counting steps, set $i_t = 0, f_t = 1$ through equations (8-9). In counting steps, the counter direction (+1 or -1) is set in $\tilde{c}_t$ (equation 11) based on the input x_t and state h_{t-1}. The counting itself is performed in equation (12), after setting $i_t = f_t = 1$. The counter can be reset to 0 by setting $i_t = f_t = 0$.

Finally, the counter values are exposed through $h_t = o_t g(c_t)$, making it trivial to compare the

---

[2]Formal definition is given in the supplementary material.

counter's value to 0.[3]

We note that this implementation of the SKCM operations is achieved by saturating the activations to their boundaries, making it relatively easy to reach and maintain in practice.

SRNN The finite-precision SRNN cannot designate unbounded counting dimensions.

The SRNN update equation is:

$$h_t = \tanh(Wx + Uh_{t-1} + b)$$

$$h_t[i] = \tanh(\sum_{j=1}^{d_x} W_{ij}x[j] + \sum_{j=1}^{d_h} U_{ij}h_{t-1}[j] + b[i])$$

By properly setting U and W, one can get certain dimensions of h to update according to the value of x, by $h_t[i] = \tanh(h_{t-1}[i] + w_i x + b[i])$. However, this counting behavior is within a $\tanh$ activation. Theoretically, this means unbounded counting cannot be achieved without infinite precision. Practically, this makes the counting behavior inherently unstable, and bounded to a relatively narrow region. While the network could adapt to set w to be small enough such that counting works for the needed range seen in training without overflowing the $\tanh$, attempting to count to larger n will quickly leave this safe region and diverge.

IRNN Finite-precision IRNNs can perform unbounded counting conditioned on input symbols. This requires representing each counter as two dimensions, and implementing INC as incrementing one dimension, DEC as incrementing the other, and COMP0 as comparing their difference to 0. Indeed, Appendix A in (Chen et al., 2017) provides concrete IRNNs for recognizing the languages $a^n b^n$ and $a^n b^n c^n$. This makes IBFP-RNN with ReLU activation more powerful than IBFP-RNN with a squashing activation. Practically, ReLU-activated RNNs are known to be notoriously hard to train because of the exploding gradient problem.

GRU Finite-precision GRUs cannot implement unbounded counting on a given dimension. The $\tanh$ in equation (6) combined with the interpolation (tying z_t and $1 - z_t$) in equation (7) restricts the range of values in h to between -1 and 1, precluding unbounded counting with finite precision. Practically, the GRU can learn to count up to some bound m seen in training, but will not generalize well beyond that.[4] Moreover, simulating forms of counting behavior in equation (7) require consistently setting the gates z_t, r_t and the proposal $\tilde{h}_t$ to precise, non-saturated values, making it much harder to find and maintain stable solutions.

Summary We show that LSTM and IRNN can implement unbounded counting in dedicated counting dimensions, while the GRU and SRNN cannot. This makes the LSTM and IRNN at least as strong as SKCMs, and strictly stronger than the SRNN and the GRU.[5]

5 Experimental Results

Can the LSTM indeed learn to behave as a k-counter machine when trained using backpropagation? We show empirically that:

1. LSTMs can be trained to recognize $a^n b^n$ and $a^n b^n c^n$.

2. These LSTMs generalize to much higher n than seen in the training set (though not infinitely so).

3. The trained LSTM learn to use the per-dimension counting mechanism.

4. The GRU can also be trained to recognize $a^n b^n$ and $a^n b^n c^n$, but they do not have clear

---

[3]Some further remarks on the LSTM: LSTM supports both increment and decrement in a single dimension. The counting dimensions in c_t are exposed through a function g. For both $g(x) = x$ and $g(x) = \tanh(x)$, it is trivial to do compare 0. Another operation of interest is comparing two counters (for example, checking the difference between them). This cannot be reliably achieved with $g(x) = \tanh(x)$, due to the non-linearity and saturation properties of the $\tanh$ function, but is possible in the $g(x) = x$ case. LSTM can also easily set the value of a counter to 0 in one step. The ability to set the counter to 0 gives slightly more power for real-time recognition, as discussed by Fischer et al. (1968).
Relation to known architectural variants: Adding peephole connections (Gers and Schmidhuber, 2000) essentially sets $g(x) = x$ and allows comparing counters in a stable way. Coupling the input and the forget gates ($i_t = 1 - f_t$) (Greff et al., 2017) removes the single-dimension unbounded counting ability, as discussed for the GRU.

[4]One such mechanism could be to divide a given dimension by $k > 1$ at each symbol encounter, by setting $z_t = 1/k$ and $\tilde{h}_t = 0$. Note that the inverse operation would not be implementable, and counting down would have to be realized with a second counter.

[5]One can argue that other counting mechanisms—involving several dimensions—are also possible. Intuitively, such mechanisms cannot be trained to perform unbounded counting based on a finite sample as the model has no means of generalizing the counting behavior to dimensions beyond those seen in training. We discuss this more in depth in the supplementary material, where we also prove that an SRNN cannot represent a binary counter.

counting dimensions, and they generalize to much smaller n than the LSTMs, often failing to generalize correctly even for n within their training domain.

5. Trained LSTM networks outperform trained GRU networks on random test sets for the languages $a^n b^n$ and $a^n b^n c^n$.

Similar empirical observations regarding the ability of the LSTM to learn to recognize $a^n b^n$ and $a^n b^n c^n$ are described also in (Gers and Schmidhuber, 2001).

We train 10-dimension, 1-layer LSTM and GRU networks to recognize $a^n b^n$ and $a^n b^n c^n$. For $a^n b^n$ the training samples went up to $n = 100$ and for $a^n b^n c^n$ up to $n = 50$.[6]

Results On $a^n b^n$, the LSTM generalizes well up to $n = 256$, after which it accumulates a deviation making it reject $a^n b^n$ but recognize $a^n b^{n+1}$ for a while, until the deviation grows.[7] The GRU does not capture the desired concept even within its training domain: accepting $a^n b^{n+1}$ for $n > 38$, and also accepting $a^n b^{n+2}$ for $n > 97$. It stops accepting $a^n b^n$ for $n > 198$.

On $a^n b^n c^n$ the LSTM recognizes well until $n = 100$. It then starts accepting also $a^n b^{n+1} c^n$. At $n > 120$ it stops accepting $a^n b^n c^n$ and switches to accepting $a^n b^{n+1} c^n$, until at some point the deviation grows. The GRU accepts already $a^9 b^{10} c^{12}$, and stops accepting $a^n b^n c^n$ for $n > 63$.

Figure 1a plots the activations of the 10 dimensions of the $a^n b^n$-LSTM for the input $a^{1000} b^{1000}$. While the LSTM misclassifies this example, the use of the counting mechanism is clear. Figure 1b plots the activation for the $a^n b^n c^n$ LSTM on $a^{100} b^{100} c^{100}$. Here, again, the two counting dimensions are clearly identified—indicating the LSTM learned the canonical 2-counter solution—although the slightly-imprecise counting also starts to show. In contrast, Figures 1c and 1d

---

[6]Implementation in DyNet, using the SGD Optimizer. Positive examples are generated by sampling n in the desired range. For negative examples we sample 2 or 3 n values independently, and ensuring at least one of them differs from the others. We dedicate a portion of the examples as the dev set, and train up to 100% dev set accuracy.

[7]These fluctuations occur as the networks do not fully saturate their gates, meaning the LSTM implements an imperfect counter that accumulates small deviations during computation, e.g.: increasing the counting dimension by 0.99 but decreasing only by 0.98. Despite this, we see that the its solution remains much more robust than that found by the GRU — the LSTM has learned the essence of the counting based solution, but its implementation is imprecise.

show the state values of the GRU-networks. The GRU behavior is much less interpretable than the LSTM. In the $a^n b^n$ case, some dimensions may be performing counting within a bounded range, but move to erratic behavior at around $t = 1750$ (the network starts to misclassify on sequences much shorter than that). The $a^n b^n c^n$ state dynamics are even less interpretable.

Finally, we created 1000-sample test sets for each of the languages. For $a^n b^n$ we used words with the form $a^{n+i} b^{n+j}$ where $n \in \mathrm{rand}(0, 200)$ and $i, j \in \mathrm{rand}(-2, 2)$, and for $a^n b^n c^n$ we use words of the form $a^{n+i} b^{n+j} c^{n+k}$ where $n \in \mathrm{rand}(0, 150)$ and $i, j, k \in \mathrm{rand}(-2, 2)$. The LSTM's accuracy was 100% and 98.6% on $a^n b^n$ and $a^n b^n c^n$ respectively, as opposed to the GRU's 87.0% and 86.9%, also respectively.

All of this empirically supports our result, showing that IBFP-LSTMs can not only theoretically implement "unbounded" counters, but also learn to do so in practice (although not perfectly), while IBFP-GRUs do not manage to learn proper counting behavior, even when allowing floating point computations.

6 Conclusions

We show that the IBFP-LSTM can model a real-time SKCM, both in theory and in practice. This makes it more powerful than the IBFP-SRNN and the IBFP-GRU, which cannot implement unbounded counting and are hence restricted to recognizing regular languages. The IBFP-IRNN can also perform input-dependent counting, and is thus more powerful than the IBFP-SRNN.

We note that in addition to theoretical distinctions between architectures, it is important to consider also the practicality of different solutions: how easy it is for a given architecture to discover and maintain a stable behavior in practice. We leave further exploration of this question for future work.

Acknowledgments

The research leading to the results presented in this paper is supported by the European Union's Seventh Framework Programme (FP7) under grant agreement no. 615688 (PRIME), The Israeli Science Foundation (grant number 1555/15), and The Allen Institute for Artificial Intelligence.

References

Roee Aharoni and Yoav Goldberg. 2017. Towards string-to-tree neural machine translation. In *Proceedings of the 55th Annual Meeting of the Association for Computational Linguistics (Volume 2: Short Papers)*, pages 132–140, Vancouver, Canada. Association for Computational Linguistics.

Yining Chen, Sorcha Gilroy, Kevin Knight, and Jonathan May. 2017. Recurrent neural networks as weighted language recognizers. *CoRR*, abs/1711.05408.

Kyunghyun Cho, Bart van Merrienboer, Caglar Gulcehre, Dzmitry Bahdanau, Fethi Bougares, Holger Schwenk, and Yoshua Bengio. 2014. Learning Phrase Representations using RNN Encoder–Decoder for Statistical Machine Translation. In *Proceedings of the 2014 Conference on Empirical Methods in Natural Language Processing (EMNLP)*, pages 1724–1734, Doha, Qatar. Association for Computational Linguistics.

Do Kook Choe and Eugene Charniak. 2016. Parsing as language modeling. In *Proceedings of the 2016 Conference on Empirical Methods in Natural Language Processing*, pages 2331–2336, Austin, Texas. Association for Computational Linguistics.

Junyoung Chung, Caglar Gulcehre, KyungHyun Cho, and Yoshua Bengio. 2014. Empirical Evaluation of Gated Recurrent Neural Networks on Sequence Modeling. *arXiv:1412.3555 [cs]*.

Jeffrey L. Elman. 1990. Finding Structure in Time. *Cognitive Science*, 14(2):179–211.

Patrick C. Fischer, Albert R. Meyer, and Arnold L. Rosenberg. 1968. Counter machines and counter languages. *Mathematical systems theory*, 2(3):265–283.

F. A. Gers and E. Schmidhuber. 2001. Lstm recurrent networks learn simple context-free and context-sensitive languages. *Transactions on Neural Networks*, 12(6):1333–1340.

F. A. Gers and J. Schmidhuber. 2000. Recurrent nets that time and count. In *Proceedings of the IEEE-INNS-ENNS International Joint Conference on Neural Networks. IJCNN 2000. Neural Computing: New Challenges and Perspectives for the New Millennium*, volume 3, pages 189–194 vol.3.

K. Greff, R. K. Srivastava, J. Koutnk, B. R. Steunebrink, and J. Schmidhuber. 2017. Lstm: A search space odyssey. *IEEE Transactions on Neural Networks and Learning Systems*, 28(10):2222–2232.

Sepp Hochreiter and Jürgen Schmidhuber. 1997. Long short-term memory. *Neural computation*, 9(8):1735–1780.

Itay Hubara, Matthieu Courbariaux, Daniel Soudry, Ran El-Yaniv, and Yoshua Bengio. 2016. Binarized neural networks. In D. D. Lee, M. Sugiyama, U. V. Luxburg, I. Guyon, and R. Garnett, editors, *Advances in Neural Information Processing Systems 29*, pages 4107–4115. Curran Associates, Inc.

Quoc V. Le, Navdeep Jaitly, and Geoffrey E. Hinton. 2015. A Simple Way to Initialize Recurrent Networks of Rectified Linear Units. *arXiv:1504.00941 [cs]*.

Hava Siegelmann. 1999. *Neural Networks and Analog Computation: Beyond the Turing Limit*, 1 edition. Birkhäuser Basel.

Hava T. Siegelmann. 1996. Recurrent neural networks and finite automata. *Computational Intelligence*, 12:567–574.

Hava T. Siegelmann and Eduardo D. Sontag. 1992. On the computational power of neural nets. In *Proceedings of the Fifth Annual ACM Conference on Computational Learning Theory, COLT 1992, Pittsburgh, PA, USA, July 27-29, 1992.*, pages 440–449.

Hava T. Siegelmann and Eduardo D. Sontag. 1994. Analog computation via neural networks. *Theor. Comput. Sci.*, 131(2):331–360.

Oriol Vinyals, Lukasz Kaiser, Terry Koo, Slav Petrov, Ilya Sutskever, and Geoffrey Hinton. 2015. Grammar as a foreign language. In *Proceedings of the 28th International Conference on Neural Information Processing Systems - Volume 2*, NIPS'15, pages 2773–2781, Cambridge, MA, USA. MIT Press.

A Co-Matching Model for Multi-choice Reading Comprehension

Shuohang Wang[1], Mo Yu[2], Shiyu Chang[2], Jing Jiang[1]
[1]School of Information System, Singapore Management University   [2]IBM Research
{shwang.2014,jingjiang}@smu.edu.sg
yum@us.ibm.com, shiyu.chang@ibm.com

Abstract

Multi-choice reading comprehension is a challenging task, which involves the matching between a passage and a question-answer pair. This paper proposes a new *co-matching* approach to this problem, which jointly models whether a passage can match both a question and a candidate answer. Experimental results on the RACE dataset demonstrate that our approach achieves state-of-the-art performance.

1 Introduction

Enabling machines to understand natural language text is arguably the ultimate goal of natural language processing, and the task of machine reading comprehension is an intermediate step towards this ultimate goal (Richardson et al., 2013; Hermann et al., 2015; Hill et al., 2015; Rajpurkar et al., 2016; Nguyen et al., 2016). Recently, Lai et al. (2017) released a new multi-choice machine comprehension dataset called RACE that was extracted from middle and high school English examinations in China. Figure 1 shows an example passage and two related questions from RACE. The key difference between RACE and previously released machine comprehension datasets (*e.g.*, the CNN/Daily Mail dataset (Hermann et al., 2015) and SQuAD (Rajpurkar et al., 2016)) is that the answers in RACE often cannot be directly extracted from the given passages, as illustrated by the two example questions (Q1 & Q2) in Figure 1. Thus, answering these questions is more challenging and requires more inferences.

Previous approaches to machine comprehension are usually based on pairwise sequence matching, where either the passage is matched against the sequence that concatenates both the question and a candidate answer (Yin et al., 2016), or the passage is matched against the question alone followed by a second step of selecting an answer using the matching result of the first step (Lai et al., 2017; Zhou et al., 2018). However, these approaches may not be suitable for multi-choice reading comprehension since questions and answers are often equally important. Matching the passage only against the question may not be meaningful and may lead to loss of information from the original passage, as we can see from the first example question in Figure 1. On the other hand, concatenating the question and the answer into a single sequence for matching may not work, either, due to the loss of interaction information between a question and an answer. As illustrated by Q2 in Figure 1, the model may need to recognize what "he" and "it" in candidate answer (c) refer to in the question, in order to select (c) as the correct answer. This observation of the RACE dataset shows that we face a new challenge of matching sequence triplets (*i.e.*, passage, question and answer) instead of pairwise matching.

In this paper, we propose a new model to match a question-answer pair to a given passage. Our *co-matching* approach explicitly treats the question and the candidate answer as two sequences and jointly matches them to the given passage. Specifically, for each position in the passage, we compute two attention-weighted vectors, where one is from the question and the other from the candidate answer. Then, two matching representations are constructed: the first one matches the passage with the question while the second one matches the passage with the candidate answer. These two newly constructed matching representations together form a *co-matching state*. Intuitively, it encodes the locational information of the question and the candidate answer matched to a specific context of the passage. Finally, we apply a hierar-

Proceedings of the 56th Annual Meeting of the Association for Computational Linguistics (Short Papers), pages 746–751
Melbourne, Australia, July 15 - 20, 2018. ©2018 Association for Computational Linguistics

Passage: *My father wasn't a king, he was a taxi driver, but I am a prince-Prince Renato II, of the country Pontinha , an island fort on Funchal harbour. In 1903, the king of Portugal sold the land to a wealthy British family, the Blandys, who make Madeira wine. Fourteen years ago the family decided to sell it for just EUR25,000, but nobody wanted to buy it either. I met Blandy at a party and he asked if I'd like to buy the island. Of course I said yes, but I had no money-I was just an art teacher. I tried to find some business partners, who all thought I was crazy. So I sold some of my possessions, put my savings together and bought it. Of course, my family and my friends-all thought I was mad ... If I want to have a national flag, it could be blue today, red tomorrow. ... My family sometimes drops by, and other people come every day because the country is free for tourists to visit ...*

Q1: *Which statement of the following is true?*	Q2: *How did the author get the island?*
a. *The author made his living by driving.*	a. *It was a present from Blandy.*
b. *The author's wife supported to buy the island.*	b. *The king sold it to him.*
c. *Blue and red are the main colors of his national flag.*	**c. *He bought it from Blandy.***
d. *People can travel around the island free of charge.*	d. *He inherited from his father.*

Table 1: An example passage and two related multi-choice questions. The ground-truth answers are in **bold**.

chical LSTM (Tang et al., 2015) over the sequence of co-matching states at different positions of the passage. Information is aggregated from word-level to sentence-level and then from sentence-level to document-level. In this way, our model can better deal with the questions that require evidence scattered in different sentences in the passage. Our model improves the state-of-the-art model by 3 percentage on the RACE dataset. Our code will be released under `https://github.com/shuohangwang/comatch`.

2 Model

For the task of multi-choice reading comprehension, the machine is given a passage, a question and a set of candidate answers. The goal is to select the correct answer from the candidates. Let us use $\mathbf{P} \in \mathbb{R}^{d \times P}$, $\mathbf{Q} \in \mathbb{R}^{d \times Q}$ and $\mathbf{A} \in \mathbb{R}^{d \times A}$ to represent the passage, the question and a candidate answer, respectively, where each word in each sequence is represented by an embedding vector. d is the dimensionality of the embeddings, and P, Q, and A are the lengths of these sequences.

Overall our model works as follows. For each candidate answer, our model constructs a vector that represents the matching of $\mathbf{P}$ with both $\mathbf{Q}$ and $\mathbf{A}$. The vectors of all candidate answers are then used for answer selection. Because we simultaneously match $\mathbf{P}$ with $\mathbf{Q}$ and $\mathbf{A}$, we call this a *co-matching* model. In Section 2.1 we introduce the word-level co-matching mechanism. Then in Section 2.2 we introduce a hierarchical aggregation

process. Finally in Section 2.3 we present the objective function. An overview of our co-matching model is shown in Figure 2.

2.1 Co-matching

The co-matching part of our model aims to match the passage with the question and the candidate answer at the word-level. Inspired by some previous work (Wang and Jiang, 2016; Trischler et al., 2016), we first use bi-directional LSTMs (Hochreiter and Schmidhuber, 1997) to pre-process the sequences as follows:

$$\mathbf{H}^p = \text{Bi-LSTM}(\mathbf{P}), \mathbf{H}^q = \text{Bi-LSTM}(\mathbf{Q}),$$
$$\mathbf{H}^a = \text{Bi-LSTM}(\mathbf{A}), \quad (1)$$

where $\mathbf{H}^p \in \mathbb{R}^{l \times P}$, $\mathbf{H}^q \in \mathbb{R}^{l \times Q}$ and $\mathbf{H}^a \in \mathbb{R}^{l \times A}$ are the sequences of hidden states generated by the bi-directional LSTMs. We then make use of the attention mechanism to match each state in the passage to an aggregated representation of the question and the candidate answer. The attention vectors are computed as follows:

$$
\begin{aligned}
\mathbf{G}^q &= \text{SoftMax}\left(\left(\mathbf{W}^g \mathbf{H}^q + \mathbf{b}^g \otimes e_Q\right)^{\mathrm{T}} \mathbf{H}^p\right), \\
\mathbf{G}^a &= \text{SoftMax}\left(\left(\mathbf{W}^g \mathbf{H}^a + \mathbf{b}^g \otimes e_Q\right)^{\mathrm{T}} \mathbf{H}^p\right), \\
\overline{\mathbf{H}}^q &= \mathbf{H}^q \mathbf{G}^q, \\
\overline{\mathbf{H}}^a &= \mathbf{H}^a \mathbf{G}^a, \quad (2)
\end{aligned}
$$

where $\mathbf{W}^g \in \mathbb{R}^{l \times l}$ and $\mathbf{b}^g \in \mathbb{R}^l$ are the parameters to learn. $e_Q \in \mathbb{R}^Q$ is a vector of all 1s and it is used to repeat the bias vector into the matrix. $\mathbf{G}^q \in \mathbb{R}^{Q \times P}$ and $\mathbf{G}^a \in \mathbb{R}^{A \times P}$ are the attention

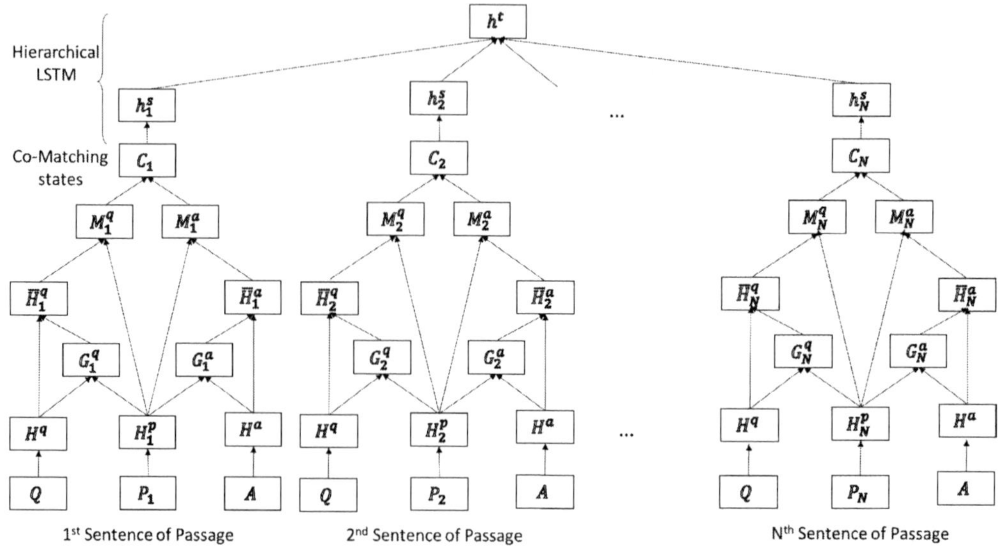

Figure 1: An overview of the model that builds a matching representation for a triplet $\{\mathbf{P}, \mathbf{Q}, \mathbf{A}\}$ (*i.e.*, passage, question and candidate answer).

weights assigned to the different hidden states in the question and the candidate answer sequences, respectively. $\overline{\mathbf{H}}^{q} \in \mathbb{R}^{l \times P}$ is the weighted sum of all the question hidden states and it represents how the question can be aligned to each hidden state in the passage. So is $\overline{\mathbf{H}}^{a} \in \mathbb{R}^{l \times P}$. Finally we can co-match the passage states with the question and the candidate answer as follows:

$$\mathbf{M}^{q} = \mathrm{ReLU}\left(\mathbf{W}^{m}\begin{bmatrix}\overline{\mathbf{H}}^{q} \ominus \mathbf{H}^{p} \\ \overline{\mathbf{H}}^{q} \otimes \mathbf{H}^{p}\end{bmatrix} + \mathbf{b}^{m}\right),$$

$$\mathbf{M}^{a} = \mathrm{ReLU}\left(\mathbf{W}^{m}\begin{bmatrix}\overline{\mathbf{H}}^{a} \ominus \mathbf{H}^{p} \\ \overline{\mathbf{H}}^{a} \otimes \mathbf{H}^{p}\end{bmatrix} + \mathbf{b}^{m}\right),$$

$$\mathbf{C} = \begin{bmatrix}\mathbf{M}^{q} \\ \mathbf{M}^{a}\end{bmatrix}, \tag{3}$$

where $\mathbf{W}^{g} \in \mathbb{R}^{l \times 2l}$ and $\mathbf{b}^{g} \in \mathbb{R}^{l}$ are the parameters to learn. $\begin{bmatrix}\cdot \\ \cdot\end{bmatrix}$ is the column-wise concatenation of two matrices, and $\cdot \ominus \cdot$ and $\cdot \otimes \cdot$ are the element-wise subtraction and multiplication between two matrices, which are used to build better matching representations (Tai et al., 2015; Wang and Jiang, 2017). $\mathbf{M}^{q} \in \mathbb{R}^{l \times P}$ represents the matching between the hidden states of the passage and the corresponding attention-weighted representations of the question. Similarly, we match the passage with the candidate answer and represent the matching results using $\mathbf{M}^{a} \in \mathbb{R}^{l \times P}$. Finally $C \in \mathbb{R}^{2l \times P}$ is the concatenation of $\mathbf{M}^{q} \in \mathbb{R}^{l \times P}$

and $\mathbf{M}^{a} \in \mathbb{R}^{l \times P}$ and represents how each passage state can be matched with the question and the candidate answer. We refer to $\mathbf{c} \in \mathbb{R}^{2l}$, which is a single column of $\mathbf{C}$, as a *co-matching state* that concurrently matches a passage state with both the question and the candidate answer.

2.2 Hierarchical Aggregation

In order to capture the sentence structure of the passage, we further modify the model presented earlier and build a hierarchical LSTM (Tang et al., 2015) on top of the co-matching states. Specifically, we first split the passage into sentences and we use $\mathbf{P}_1, \mathbf{P}_2, \ldots, \mathbf{P}_N$ to represent these sentences, where N is the number of sentences in the passage. For each triplet $\{\mathbf{P}_n, \mathbf{Q}, \mathbf{A}\}, n \in [1, N]$, we can get the co-matching states $\mathbf{C}_n$ through Eqn. (1-3). Then we build a bi-directional LSTM followed by max pooling on top of the co-matching states of each sentence as follows:

$$\mathbf{h}_n^s = \mathrm{MaxPooling}\left(\text{Bi-LSTM}\left(\mathbf{C}_n\right)\right), \tag{4}$$

where the function $\mathrm{MaxPooling}(\cdot)$ is the row-wise max pooling operation. $\mathbf{h}_n^s \in \mathbb{R}^{l}, n \in [1, N]$ is the sentence-level aggregation of the co-matching states. All these representations will be further integrated by another Bi-LSTM to get the final triplet matching representation.

$$\mathbf{H}^s = [\mathbf{h}_1^s; \mathbf{h}_2^s; \ldots; \mathbf{h}_N^s],$$

$$\mathbf{h}^t = \mathrm{MaxPooling}\left(\text{Bi-LSTM}\left(\mathbf{H}^s\right)\right), \tag{5}$$

	RACE-M	RACE-H	RACE
Random	24.6	25.0	24.9
Sliding Window	37.3	30.4	32.2
Stanford AR	44.2	43.0	43.3
GA	43.7	44.2	44.1
ElimiNet	-	-	44.7
HAF	45.3	47.9	47.2
MUSIC	51.5	45.7	47.4
Hier-Co-Matching	**55.8***	**48.2***	**50.4***
- Hier-Aggregation	54.2	46.2	48.5
- Co-Matching	50.7	45.6	46.4
Turkers	85.1	69.4	73.3
Ceiling	95.4	94.2	94.5

Table 2: Experiment Results. * means it's significant to the models ablating either the hierarchical aggregation or co-matching state.

where $\mathbf{H}^s \in \mathbb{R}^{l \times N}$ is the concatenation of all the sentence-level representations and it is the input of a higher level LSTM. $\mathbf{h}^t \in \mathbb{R}^l$ is the final output of the matching between the sequences of the passage, the question and the candidate answer.

2.3 Objective function

For each candidate answer $\mathbf{A}_i$, we can build its matching representation $\mathbf{h}_i^t \in \mathbb{R}^l$ with the question and the passage through Eqn. (5). Our loss function is computed as follows:

$$L(\mathbf{A}_i|\mathbf{P}, \mathbf{Q}) = -\log \frac{\exp(\mathbf{w}^T \mathbf{h}_i^t)}{\sum_{j=1}^{4} \exp(\mathbf{w}^T \mathbf{h}_j^t)}, \quad (6)$$

where $\mathbf{w} \in \mathbb{R}^l$ is a parameter to learn.

3 Experiment

To evaluate the effectiveness of our hierarchical co-matching model, we use the RACE dataset (Lai et al., 2017), which consists of two subsets: RACE-M comes from middle school examinations while RACE-H comes from high school examinations. RACE is the combination of the two.

We compare our model with a number of baseline models. We also compare with two variants of our model for an ablation study.

Comparison with Baselines We compare our model with the following baselines:

• **Sliding Window** based method (Richardson et al., 2013) computes the matching score based on the sum of the tf-idf values of the matched words between the question-answer pair and each sub-passage with a fixed a window size.

• **Stanford Attentive Reader (AR)** (Chen et al., 2016) first builds a question-related passage representation through attention mechanism and then compares it with each candidate answer representation to get the answer probabilities.

• **GA** (Dhingra et al., 2017) uses gated attention mechanism with multiple hops to extract the question-related information of the passage and compares it with candidate answers.

• **ElimiNet** (Soham et al., 2017) tries to first eliminate the most irrelevant choices and then select the best answer.

• **HAF** (Zhou et al., 2018) considers not only the matching between the three sequences, namely, passage, question and candidate answer, but also the matching between the candidate answers.

• **MUSIC** (Xu et al., 2017) integrates different sequence matching strategies into the model and also adds a unit of multi-step reasoning for selecting the answer.

Besides, we also report the following two results as reference points: **Turkers** is the performance of Amazon Turkers on a randomly sampled subset of the RACE test set. **Ceiling** is the percentage of the unambiguous questions with a correct answer in a subset of the test set.

The performance of our model together with the baselines are shown in Table 2. We can see that our proposed complete model, **Hier-Co-Matching**, achieved the best performance among all the public results. Still, there is a huge gap between the best machine reading performance and the human performance, showing the great potential for further research.

Ablation Study Moreover, we conduct an ablation study of our model architecture. In this study, we are mainly interested in the contribution of each component introduced in this work to our final results. We studied two key factors: (1) the co-matching module and (2) the hierarchical aggregation approach. We observed a 4 percentage performance decrease by replacing the co-matching module with a single matching state (*i.e.*, only $\mathbf{M}^a$ in Eqn (3)) by directly concatenating the question with each candidate answer (Yin et al., 2016). We also observe about 2 percentage decrease when we treat the passage as a plain sequence, and run a two-layer LSTM (to ensure the numbers of parameters are comparable) over the whole passage instead of the hierarchical LSTM.

Question Type Analysis We also conducted an analysis on what types of questions our model can handle better. We find that our model obtains similar performance on the "wh" questions such as "why," "what," "when" and "where" questions, on which the performance is usually around 50%. We also check statement-justification questions with the keyword "true" (*e.g.*, "Which of the following statements is true"), negation questions with the keyword "not" (*e.g.*, "which of the following is not true"), and summarization questions with the keyword "title" (*e.g.*, "what is the best title for the passage?"), and their performance is 51%, 52% and 48%, respectively. We can see that the performance of our model on different types of questions in the RACE dataset is quite similar. However, our model is only based on word-level matching and may not have the ability of reasoning. In order to answer questions that require summarization, inference or reasoning, we still need to further explore the dataset and improve the model. Finally, we further compared our model to the baseline, which concatenates the question with each candidate answer, and our model can achieve better performance on different types of questions. For example, on the subset of the questions with pronouns, our model can achieve better accuracy of 49.8% than 47.9%. Similarly, on statement-justification questions with the keyword "true", our model could achieve better accuracy of 51% than 47%.

4   Conclusions

In this paper, we proposed a co-matching model for multi-choice reading comprehension. The model consists of a co-matching component and a hierarchical aggregation component. We showed that our model could achieve state-of-the-art performance on the RACE dataset. In the future, we will adapt the idea of co-matching and hierarchical aggregation to the standard open-domain QA setting for answer candidate reranking (Wang et al., 2017). We will also further study how to explicitly model inference and reasoning on the RACE dataset.

5   Acknowledgement

This work was partially supported by DSO grant DSOCL15223.

References

Danqi Chen, Jason Bolton, and Christopher D. Manning. 2016. A thorough examination of the CNN/Daily Mail reading comprehension task. In *Proceedings of the Conference on Association for Computational Linguistics*.

Bhuwan Dhingra, Hanxiao Liu, Zhilin Yang, William W Cohen, and Ruslan Salakhutdinov. 2017. Gated-attention readers for text comprehension. In *Proceedings of the Conference on Association for Computational Linguistics*.

Karl Moritz Hermann, Tomas Kocisky, Edward Grefenstette, Lasse Espeholt, Will Kay, Mustafa Suleyman, and Phil Blunsom. 2015. Teaching machines to read and comprehend. In *Proceedings of the Conference on Advances in Neural Information Processing Systems*.

Felix Hill, Antoine Bordes, Sumit Chopra, and Jason Weston. 2015. The goldilocks principle: Reading children's books with explicit memory representations. *arXiv preprint arXiv:1511.02301* .

Sepp Hochreiter and Jürgen Schmidhuber. 1997. Long short-term memory. *Neural Computation* 9(8):1735–1780.

Guokun Lai, Qizhe Xie, Hanxiao Liu, Yiming Yang, and Eduard Hovy. 2017. RACE: Large-scale reading comprehension dataset from examinations. *Proceedings of the Conference on Empirical Methods in Natural Language Processing* .

Tri Nguyen, Mir Rosenberg, Xia Song, Jianfeng Gao, Saurabh Tiwary, Rangan Majumder, and Li Deng. 2016. MS MARCO: A human generated machine reading comprehension dataset. *arXiv preprint arXiv:1611.09268* .

Pranav Rajpurkar, Jian Zhang, Konstantin Lopyrev, and Percy Liang. 2016. SQuAD: 100,000+ questions for machine comprehension of text. In *Proceedings of the Conference on Empirical Methods in Natural Language Processing*.

Matthew Richardson, Christopher JC Burges, and Erin Renshaw. 2013. MCTest: A challenge dataset for the open-domain machine comprehension of text. In *Proceedings of the Conference on Empirical Methods in Natural Language Processing*.

Parikh Soham, Sai Ananya, Nema Preksha, and M Khapra Mitesh. 2017. Eliminet: A model for eliminating options for reading comprehension with multiple choice questions. *Openreview* .

Kai Sheng Tai, Richard Socher, and Christopher D Manning. 2015. Improved semantic representations from tree-structured long short-term memory networks. In *Proceedings of the Conference on Association for Computational Linguistics*.

Duyu Tang, Bing Qin, and Ting Liu. 2015. Document modeling with gated recurrent neural network for sentiment classification. In *Proceedings of the Conference on Empirical Methods in Natural Language Processing*.

Adam Trischler, Zheng Ye, Xingdi Yuan, Jing He, Phillip Bachman, and Kaheer Suleman. 2016. A parallel-hierarchical model for machine comprehension on sparse data. In *Proceedings of the Conference on Association for Computational Linguistics*.

Shuohang Wang and Jing Jiang. 2016. Learning natural language inference with LSTM. In *Proceedings of the Conference on the North American Chapter of the Association for Computational Linguistics*.

Shuohang Wang and Jing Jiang. 2017. A compare-aggregate model for matching text sequences. In *Proceedings of the International Conference on Learning Representations*.

Shuohang Wang, Mo Yu, Jing Jiang, Wei Zhang, Xiaoxiao Guo, Shiyu Chang, Zhiguo Wang, Tim Klinger, Gerald Tesauro, and Murray Campbell. 2017. Evidence aggregation for answer re-ranking in open-domain question answering. *arXiv preprint arXiv:1711.05116* .

Yichong Xu, Jingjing Liu, Jianfeng Gao, Yelong Shen, and Xiaodong Liu. 2017. Towards human-level machine reading comprehension: Reasoning and inference with multiple strategies. *arXiv preprint arXiv:1711.04964* .

Wenpeng Yin, Sebastian Ebert, and Hinrich Schütze. 2016. Attention-based convolutional neural network for machine comprehension. *arXiv preprint arXiv:1602.04341* .

Haichao Zhou, Wei Furu, Qin Bing, and Liu Ting. 2018. Hierarchical attention flow for multiple-choice reading comprehension. In *Proceedings of AAAI Conference on Artificial Intelligence*.

Tackling the Story Ending Biases in The Story Cloze Test

Rishi Sharma[1], James F. Allen[1,2],Omid Bakhshandeh[3], Nasrin Mostafazadeh[4*]

1 University of Rochester, 2 Institute for Human and Machine Cognition, 3 Verneek.ai 4 Elemental Cognition

rishi.sharma@rochester.edu, nasrinm@cs.rochester.edu

Abstract

The Story Cloze Test (SCT) is a recent framework for evaluating story comprehension and script learning. There have been a variety of models tackling the SCT so far. Although the original goal behind the SCT was to require systems to perform deep language understanding and commonsense reasoning for successful narrative understanding, some recent models could perform significantly better than the initial baselines by leveraging human-authorship biases discovered in the SCT dataset. In order to shed some light on this issue, we have performed various data analysis and analyzed a variety of top performing models presented for this task. Given the statistics we have aggregated, we have designed a new crowd-sourcing scheme that creates a new SCT dataset, which overcomes some of the biases. We benchmark a few models on the new dataset and show that the top-performing model on the original SCT dataset fails to keep up its performance. Our findings further signify the importance of benchmarking NLP systems on various evolving test sets.

1 Introduction

Story comprehension has been one of the longest-running ambitions in artificial intelligence (Dijk, 1980; Charniak, 1972). One of the challenges in expanding the field had been the lack of a solid evaluation framework and datasets on which comprehension models can be trained and tested. Mostafazadeh et al. (2016) introduced the Story Cloze Test (SCT) evaluation framework to address

this issue. This test evaluates a story comprehension system where the system is given a four-sentence short story as the 'context' and two alternative endings and to the story, labeled 'right ending' and 'wrong ending.' Then, the system's task is to choose the right ending. In order to support this task, Mostafazadeh et al. also provide the ROC Stories dataset, which is a collection of crowd-sourced complete five sentence stories through Amazon Mechanical Turk (MTurk). Each story follows a character through a fairly simple series of events to a conclusion.

Several shallow and neural models, including the state-of-the-art script learning approaches, were presented as baselines (Mostafazadeh et al., 2016) for tackling the task, where they show that all their models perform only slightly better than a random baseline suggesting that richer models are required for tackling this task. A variety of new systems were proposed (Mihaylov and Frank, 2017; Schenk and Chiarcos, 2017; Schwartz et al., 2017b; Roemmele et al., 2017) as a part of the first shared task on SCT at LSDSem'17 workshop (Mostafazadeh et al., 2017). Surprisingly, one of the models made a staggering improvement of 15% to the accuracy, partially due to using stylistic features isolated in the ending choices (Schwartz et al., 2017b), discarding the narrative context. Clearly, this success does not seem to reflect the intent of the original task, where the systems should leverage narrative understanding as opposed to the statistical biases in the data. In this paper, we study the effect of such biases between the ending choices and present a new scheme to reduce such stylistic artifacts.

The contribution of this paper is threefold: (1) we provide an extensive analysis of the SCT dataset to shed some light on the ending data characteristics (Section 3) (2) we develop a new strong classifier for tackling the SCT that uses a variety

* This work was performed at University of Rochester.

Proceedings of the 56th Annual Meeting of the Association for Computational Linguistics (Short Papers), pages 752–757
Melbourne, Australia, July 15 - 20, 2018. ©2018 Association for Computational Linguistics

Context	Right Ending	Wrong Ending
Ramona was very unhappy in her job. She asked for a raise, but was denied. The refusal prompted her to aggressively comb the want ads. She found an interesting new possibility and set up an interview.	She was offered the new job at a higher salary.	Ramona had no reason to want to change jobs anymore.
The teacher was walking with a stack of papers. Outside started to rain. When the teacher tried to walk down a few steps, she ended up falling. The papers flew out of her hands and landed on the ground.	A passer-by helped her up and helped her collect the papers.	The teacher got up and walked home leaving the papers behind.

Table 1: Example Story Cloze Test examples from the SCT-v1.0 corpus.

of features inspired by all the top-performing systems on the task (Section 4) (3) we design a new crowd-sourcing scheme that yields a new SCT dataset; we benchmark various models on the new dataset (Section 5). The results show that the top-performing SCT system on the the leaderboard[1] (Chaturvedi et al., 2017) fails to keep up the performance on our new dataset. We discuss the implications of this experiment to the greater research community in terms of data collection and benchmarking practices in Section 6. All the code and datasets for this paper will be released to the public. We hope that the availability of the new evaluation set can further support the continued research on story understanding.

2 Related Work

This paper mainly extends the work on creating the Story Cloze Test set (Mostafazadeh et al., 2016), hereinafter SCT-v1.0. The SCT-v1.0 dataset was created as follows: full five-sentence stories from the ROC Stories corpus were sampled, then, the initial four sentences were shown to a set of MTurk[2] crowd workers who were prompted to author 'right' and 'wrong' endings. Mostafazadeh et al. (Mostafazadeh et al., 2016) give special care to make sure there were no boundary cases for 'right' and 'wrong' endings by implementing extra rounds of data filtering. The resulting SCT-v1.0 dataset had a validation (hereinafter, SCT-v1.0 Val) and a test set (SCT-v1.0 test), each with 1,871 cases. Table 1 shows two example story cloze test cases from SCT-v1.0 corpus. As for positive training data, they had provided a collection of 100K five sentence stories. Human performance is reported to be 100% on SCT-v1.0.

Mostafazadeh et al. (2016) provide a variety of baseline models for SCT-v1.0, with the best model performing with an accuracy of 59%. The first

shared task on SCT-v1.0 was conducted at the LSDSem'17 workshop (Mostafazadeh et al., 2017), where most of the models performed with 60-70% accuracy. One of the top-performing models, *msap* (Schwartz et al., 2017b,a), built a classifier using linguistic features that have been previously useful in authorship style detection, using only the ending sentences. They used stylistic features such as sentence length, word, and character level n-grams for each ending (fully discarding the context), achieving an accuracy of 72%. In conjunction with their work, Cai et al., (Cai et al., 2017) reported similar observations separately, exposing that features such as sentiment, negation, and length are different between the right and wrong endings. The best model on SCT-v1.0 to this date is *cogcomp*, which is a linear model that uses event sequences, sentiment trajectory, and topical consistency as features, and performs with an accuracy of 77.6%.

This paper takes all their analysis further and introduces a model aggregating all the pinpointed features to shed more light into the stylistic biases isolated in SCT-v1.0 endings.

3 Stylistic Feature Analysis

Despite all the efforts made in the original SCT paper, there was never an extensive analysis of the features isolated in the endings of the stories. We explored the differences among stylistic features such as word-token count, sentiment, and the sentence complexity between the endings, to determine a composite score for identifying sources of bias. For determining the sentiment, we used Stanford CoreNLP (Manning et al., 2014) and the VADER sentiment analyzer (Hutto and Gilbert, 2014). For measuring the syntactic complexity, we used Yngve and Frazier metrics (Yngve, 1960; Frazier, 1985). Table 2 compares these statistics between the right and wrong endings in the SCT-v1.0 dataset. The feature distribution plots can be found in the supplementary material.

---

[1] As of 15th February 2018.

[2] http://mturk.com

	# of Tokens	Stanford Sentiment	VADER Sentiment	Frazier	Yngve
Right ending	8.705	2.04	0.146	1.09	1.15
Wrong ending	8.466	2.02	0.011	1.08	1.17
p-value	6.63×10^{-5}	0.526	3.48×10^{-54}	0.135	0.089

Table 2: The mean value for the 'right endings' and the 'wrong endings' for the two sample T-tests conducted for each feature.

Furthermore, we conducted an extensive n-gram analysis, using word tokens, characters, part-of-speech, and token-POS (similar to Schwartz et al. (Schwartz et al., 2017b)) as features. We see char-grams such as "sn't" and "not" appear more commonly in the 'wrong endings', suggesting heavy negation. In 'right endings', pronouns are used more frequently versus proper nouns used in 'wrong endings'. Artifacts such as 'pizza' are common in 'wrong endings,' which could suggest that for a given topic, the authors may replace an object in a right ending with a wrong one and quickly think up a common item such as pizza to create a 'wrong' one. An extensive analysis of these features, including the n-gram analysis, can be found in the supplementary material.

4 Model

Following the analysis above, we developed a Story Cloze model, hereinafter EndingReg, that only uses the ending features while disregarding the story context for choosing the right ending. We expanded each Story Cloze Test case's ending options into a set of two single sentences. Then, for each sentence, we created the following features:

1. Number of tokens
2. VADER composite sentiment score
3. Yngve complexity score
4. Token-POS n-grams
5. POS n-grams
6. Four length character-grams

All n-gram features needed to appear at least five times throughout the dataset. The features were collected for each five-sentence story and then fed into a logistic regression classifier. As an initial experiment, we trained this model using the SCT-v1.0 validation set and tested on the SCT-v1.0 test set. An L2 regularization penalty was used to enforce a Gaussian prior on the feature-space, where a grid search was conducted for hyper-parameter tuning. This model achieves an accuracy of 71.5% on the SCT-v1.0 dataset which is on par with the highest score achieved by any model using only the endings. Table 3 shows the accuracies ob-

tained by models using only those particular features. We achieve minimal but sometimes important classification using token count, VADER, and Yngve in combination alone, better classification using POS or char-grams alone, and best classification using n-grams alone. By combining all of them we achieve the overall best results.

token-count+VADER+yngve	ngram	pos	char-grams	All
50.3%	69.7%	68.7%	63.4%	71.5%

Table 3: Classification results on SCT-v1.0 using each of the feature sets designated in the columns.

5 Data Collection

Based on the findings above, a new test set for the SCT was deemed necessary. The premise of predicting an ending to a short story, as opposed to predicting say a middle sentence, enables a more systematic evaluation where human can agree on the cases 100%. Hence, our goal was to come up with a data collection scheme that overcomes the data collection biases, while keeping the original evaluation format. As the data analysis revealed, the token count, sentiment, and the complexity are not as important features for classification as the ending n-grams are. We set the following goals for sourcing the new 'right' and 'wrong' endings. They both should:

1. Contain a similar number of tokens
2. Have similar distributions of token n-grams and char-grams
3. Occur as standalone events with the same likelihood to occur, with topical, sentimental, or emotion consistencies when applicable.

First, we crowdsourced 5,000 new five-sentence stories through Amazon Mechanical Turk. We prompted the users in the same manner described in Mostafazadeh et al. (2016). In order to source new 'wrong' endings, we tried two different methods. In Method #1, we kept the original ending sourcing format of Mostafazadeh et al., but imposed some further restrictions. This was done by taking the first four sentences of the newly collected stories and asking an MTurker to write a 'right' and 'wrong' ending for each. The new restrictions were: 'Each sentence should stay within the same subject area of the story,' and 'The number of words in the Right and Wrong sentences should not differ by more than 2 words,' and 'When possible, the Right and Wrong sentences should try to keep a similar tone/sentiment as one another.' The motivation behind this technique was to reduce the statistical differences by asking the user to be mindful of considerations.

In Method #2, we took the five sentences stories and prompted a second set of MTurk workers to modify the fifth sentence in order to make a resulting five-sentence story non-sensible. Here, the prompt instructs the workers to make sure the new 'wrong ending' sentence makes sense standalone, that it does not differ in the number of words from the original sentence by more than three words, and that the changes cannot be as simple as e.g., putting the word 'not' in front of a description or a verb. As a result, the workers had much less flexibility for changing the underlying linguistic structures which can help tackle the authorship style differences between the 'right' and 'wrong' endings.

The results in Table 4, which show classification accuracy when using EndingReg on the two new data sources, show that Method #2 is a slightly better data sourcing scheme in reducing the bias, since the EndingReg model's performance is slightly worse. The set was further filtered through human verification similar to Mostafazadeh et al. (2016). The filtering was done by splitting each SCT-v1.0's two alternative endings into two independent five-sentence stories and asking three different MTurk users to categorize the story as either: one where the story made complete sense, one where the story made sense until the last sentence and one where the story does not make sense for another reason. Stories were only selected if all the three MTurk users verified that the story with the 'right ending' and the corresponding story with the 'wrong ending' were verified to be indeed right and wrong respectively. This ensured a higher quality of data and eliminating boundary cases. This entire process resulted in creating the Story Cloze Test v1.5 (SCT-v1.5) dataset, consisting of 1,571 stories for each validation and test sets.

	Method #1	Method #2
EndingReg	0.709	0.695
cogcomp	0.649	0.641

Table 4: Comparison of initial data sourcing methods

	$n-gram$	$char-gram$	POS
SCT-v1.0	13.9	12.4	16.4
SCT-v1.5	7.0	6.3	7.5

Table 5: Standard deviation of the word and character n-gram counts, as well as the part of speech (POS) counts, between the right and wrong endings.

6 Results

In order to test the decrease in n-gram bias, which was the most salient feature for the classification task using only the endings, we compare the variance between the n-gram counts from SCT-v1.0 to SCT-v1.5. The results are presented in Table 5, which indicates the drop in the standard deviations in our new dataset. Table 6 shows the classification results of various models on SCT-v1.5. The drop in accuracy of the EndingReg model between the SCT-v1.0 and SCT-v1.5 shows a significant improvement on the statistical weight of the stylistic features generated by the model.

Since the main features used are the token length and the various n-grams, this suggests that the new 'right endings' and 'wrong endings' have much more similar token n-gram, pos n-gram, pos-token n-gram and char-gram overlap. Furthermore, the CogComp model's performance has significantly dropped on SCT-v1.5. Although this model seems to be using story comprehension features such as event sequencing, since the endings are included in the sequences, the biases within the endings have influenced the predictions and the weak performance of the model in SCT-v1.5 suggest that this model had picked up on the biases of SCT-v1.0 as opposed to really understanding the context. In particular, the posterior probabilities for each ending choice using their features are quite similar on the SCT-v1.5. These results place the classification accuracy of this top performing model on par with or worse than the models that did not use the ending features of the old SCT-v1.0 dataset (Mostafazadeh et al., 2017), which suggest that the gap that once was held by models using the ending biases seems to be corrected for. Al-

	SCT-v1.0 Val	SCT-v1.0 Test	SCT-v1.5 Test
cogcomp	0.751	0.776	0.608
EndingReg	N/A	0.715	**0.644**
average sentiment	0.489	0.492	0.496
last senti- ment	0.514	0.522	0.525
word2vec	0.545	0.539	0.594
human	1.0	1.0	1.0

Table 6: Classification accuracy for various models on the SCT-v1.0 and SCT-v1.5 datasets.

though we did not get to test all the other models published on SCT-v1.0 directly, we predict similar trends.

It is important to point out that the 64.4% performance attained by our EndingReg model is still high for a model which completely discards the context. This indicates that although we could correct for some of the stylistic biases, there are some other hidden patterns in the new endings that would not have been accounted for without having the EndingReg baseline. This showcases the importance of maintaining benchmarks that evolve and improve over time, where systems should not be optimized for particular narrow test sets. We propose the community to report accuracies on both SCT-v1.0 and SCT-v1.5, both of which still have a huge gap between the best system and the human performance.

7 Conclusion

In this paper, we presented a comprehensive analysis of the stylistic features isolated in the endings of the original Story Cloze Test (SCT-v1.0). Using that analysis, along with a classifier we developed for testing new data collection schemes, we created a new SCT dataset, SCT-v1.5, which overcomes some of the biases. Based on the results presented in this paper, we believe that our SCT-v1.5 is a better benchmark for story comprehension. However, as shown in multiple AI tasks (Ettinger et al., 2017; Antol et al., 2015; Jabri et al., 2016; Poliak et al., 2018), no collected dataset is entirely without its inherent biases and often the biases in datasets go undiscovered. We believe that evaluation benchmarks should evolve and improve over time and we are planning to incrementally update the Story Cloze Test benchmark. All the new versions, along with a leader-board showcasing the state-of-the-art results, will be tracked via CodaLab

```
https://competitions.codalab.org/
competitions/15333.
```

The success of our modified data collection method shows how extreme care must be given for sourcing new datasets. We suggest the next SCT challenges to be completely blind, where the participants cannot deliberately leverage any particular data biases. Along with this paper, we are releasing the datasets and the developed models to the community. All the announcements, new supplementary material, and datasets can be accessed through `http://cs. rochester.edu/nlp/rocstories/`. We hope that this work ignites further interest in the community for making progress on story understanding.

Acknowledgement

We would like to thank Roy Schwartz for his valuable feedback regarding some of the experiments. We also thank the amazing crowd workers, without the work of whom this work would have been impossible. This work was supported in part by grant W911NF15-1-0542 with the US Defense Advanced Research Projects Agency (DARPA) as a part of the Communicating with Computers (CwC) program.

References

Stanislaw Antol, Aishwarya Agrawal, Jiasen Lu, Margaret Mitchell, Dhruv Batra, C. Lawrence Zitnick, and Devi Parikh. 2015. VQA: Visual Question Answering. In *International Conference on Computer Vision (ICCV)*.

Zheng Cai, Lifu Tu, and Kevin Gimpel. 2017. Pay attention to the ending: Strong neural baselines for the ROC story cloze task. In *Proceedings of the 55th Annual Meeting of the Association for Computational Linguistics (Volume 2: Short Papers)*. Association for Computational Linguistics.

Eugene Charniak. 1972. Toward a model of children's story comprehension.

Snigdha Chaturvedi, Haoruo Peng, and Dan Roth. 2017. Story comprehension for predicting what happens next.

Teun A. Van Dijk. 1980. Story comprehension: An introduction. *Poetics*, 9(1):1 – 21. Special Issue Story Comprehension.

Allyson Ettinger, Sudha Rao, Hal Daum III, and Emily M Bender. 2017. Towards linguistically generalizable nlp systems: A workshop and shared task.

In *Proceedings of the First Workshop on Building Linguistically Generalizable NLP Systems*, pages 1–10.

Lyn Frazier. 1985. Natural language parsing. *Cambridge University Press*.

C.J. Hutto and E.E. Gilbert. 2014. Vader: A parsimonious rule-based model for sentiment analysis of social media text. In *Eighth International Conference on Weblogs and Social Media*.

Allan Jabri, Armand Joulin, and Laurens van der Maaten. 2016. Revisiting visual question answering baselines. In *ECCV*.

Christopher D. Manning, Mihai Surdeanu, John Bauer, Jenny Finkel, Steven J. Bethard, and David McClosky. 2014. Stanford corenlp natural language processing toolkit. In *Association for Computational Linguistics (ACL) System Demonstrations*, pages 55–60.

Todor Mihaylov and Anette Frank. 2017. Simple story ending selection baselines. In *Proceedings of the 2nd Workshop on Linking Models of Lexical, Sentential and Discourse-level Semantics (LSDSem)*, Valencia, Spain. Association for Computational Linguistics.

Nasrin Mostafazadeh, Nathanael Chambers, Xiaodong He, Devi Parikh, Dhruv Batra, Lucy Vanderwende, Pushmeet Kohli, and James Allen. 2016. A corpus and cloze evaluation for deeper understanding of commonsense stories. In *Proceedings of the 2016 Conference of the North American Chapter of the Association for Computational Linguistics: Human Language Technologies NAACL HLT 2016*, page 839849.

Nasrin Mostafazadeh, Michael Roth, Annie Louis, Nathanael Chambers, and James F. Allen. 2017. Lsdsem 2017 shared task: The story cloze test. In *Proceedings of the 2nd Workshop on Linking Models of Lexical, Sentential and Discourse-level Semantics*.

Adam Poliak, Jason Naradowsky, Aparajita Haldar, Rachel Rudinger, and Benjamin Van Durme. 2018. Hypothesis Only Baselines in Natural Language Inference. In *Joint Conference on Lexical and Computational Semantics (StarSem)*.

Melissa Roemmele, Sosuke Kobayashi, Naoya Inoue, and Andrew Gordon. 2017. An RNN-based binary classifier for the story cloze test. In *Proceedings of the 2nd Workshop on Linking Models of Lexical, Sentential and Discourse-level Semantics (LSDSem)*, Valencia, Spain. Association for Computational Linguistics.

Niko Schenk and Christian Chiarcos. 2017. Resource-lean modeling of coherence in commonsense stories. In *Proceedings of the 2nd Workshop on Linking Models of Lexical, Sentential and Discourse-level Semantics (LSDSem)*, Valencia, Spain. Association for Computational Linguistics.

Roy Schwartz, Maarten Sap, Ioannis Konstas, Li Zilles, Yejin Choi, and Noah A. Smith. 2017a. The effect of different writing tasks on linguistic style: A case study of the ROC story cloze task. In *Proc. of CoNLL*.

Roy Schwartz, Maarten Sap, Ioannis Konstas, Li Zilles, Yejin Choi, and Noah A. Smith. 2017b. Story cloze task: Uw nlp system. In *Proceedings of the 2nd Workshop on Linking Models of Lexical, Sentential and Discourse-level Semantics*.

Victor Yngve. 1960. A model and an hypothesis for language structure.

A Multi-sentiment-resource Enhanced Attention Network for Sentiment Classification

Zeyang Lei[1,2], Yujiu Yang[1], Min Yang[3], and Yi Liu[2]

Graduate School at Shenzhen, Tsinghua University[1]

Peking University Shenzhen Institute[2]

Shenzhen Institutes of Advanced Technology, Chinese Academy of Sciences[3]

`leizy16@mails.tsinghua.edu.cn, yang.yujiu@sz.tsinghua.edu.cn,`
`min.yang1129@gmail.com, eeyliu@gmail.com`

Abstract

Deep learning approaches for sentiment classification do not fully exploit sentiment linguistic knowledge. In this paper, we propose a Multi-sentiment-resource Enhanced Attention Network (MEAN) to alleviate the problem by integrating three kinds of sentiment linguistic knowledge (e.g., sentiment lexicon, negation words, intensity words) into the deep neural network via attention mechanisms. By using various types of sentiment resources, MEAN utilizes sentiment-relevant information from different representation subspaces, which makes it more effective to capture the overall semantics of the sentiment, negation and intensity words for sentiment prediction. The experimental results demonstrate that MEAN has robust superiority over strong competitors.

1 Introduction

Sentiment classification is an important task of natural language processing (NLP), aiming to classify the sentiment polarity of a given text as positive, negative, or more fine-grained classes. It has obtained considerable attention due to its broad applications in natural language processing (Hao et al., 2012; Gui et al., 2017). Most existing studies set up sentiment classifiers using supervised machine learning approaches, such as support vector machine (SVM) (Pang et al., 2002), convolutional neural network (CNN) (Kim, 2014; Bonggun et al., 2017), long short-term memory (LSTM) (Hochreiter and Schmidhuber, 1997; Qian et al., 2017), Tree-LSTM (Tai et al., 2015), and attention-based methods (Zhou et al., 2016; Yang et al., 2016; Lin et al., 2017; Du et al., 2017).

Despite the remarkable progress made by the previous work, we argue that sentiment analysis still remains a challenge. Sentiment resources including sentiment lexicon, negation words, intensity words play a crucial role in traditional sentiment classification approaches (Maks and Vossen, 2012; Duyu et al., 2014). Despite its usefulness, to date, the sentiment linguistic knowledge has been underutilized in most recent deep neural network models (e.g., CNNs and LSTMs).

In this work, we propose a Multi-sentiment-resource Enhanced Attention Network (MEAN) for sentence-level sentiment classification to integrate many kinds of sentiment linguistic knowledge into deep neural networks via multi-path attention mechanism. Specifically, we first design a coupled word embedding module to model the word representation from character-level and word-level semantics. This can help to capture the morphological information such as prefixes and suffixes of words. Then, we propose a multi-sentiment-resource attention module to learn more comprehensive and meaningful sentiment-specific sentence representation by using the three types of sentiment resource words as attention sources attending to the context words respectively. In this way, we can attend to different sentiment-relevant information from different representation subspaces implied by different types of sentiment sources and capture the overall semantics of the sentiment, negation and intensity words for sentiment prediction.

The main contributions of this paper are summarized as follows. First, we design a coupled word embedding obtained from character-level embedding and word-level embedding to capture both the character-level morphological information and word-level semantics. Second, we propose a multi-sentiment-resource attention module to learn more comprehensive sentiment-specific sentence representation from multiply subspaces

Proceedings of the 56th Annual Meeting of the Association for Computational Linguistics (Short Papers), pages 758–763
Melbourne, Australia, July 15 - 20, 2018. ©2018 Association for Computational Linguistics

implied by three kinds of sentiment resources including sentiment lexicon, intensity words, negation words. Finally, the experimental results show that MEAN consistently outperforms competitive methods.

2 Model

Our proposed MEAN model consists of three key components: coupled word embedding module, multi-sentiment-resource attention module, sentence classifier module. In the rest of this section, we will elaborate these three parts in details.

2.1 Coupled Word Embedding

To exploit the sentiment-related morphological information implied by some prefixes and suffixes of words (such as "Non-", "In-", "Im-"), we design a coupled word embedding learned from character-level embedding and word-level embedding. We first design a character-level convolution neural network (Char-CNN) to obtain character-level embedding (Zhang et al., 2015). Different from (Zhang et al., 2015), the designed Char-CNN is a fully convolutional network without max-pooling layer to capture better semantic information in character chunk. Specifically, we first input one-hot-encoding character sequences to a 1×1 convolution layer to enhance the semantic nonlinear representation ability of our model (Long et al., 2015), and the output is then fed into a multi-gram (i.e. different window sizes) convolution layer to capture different local character chunk information. For word-level embedding, we use pre-trained word vectors, GloVe (Pennington et al., 2014), to map each word to a low-dimensional vector space. Finally, each word is represented as a concatenation of the character-level embedding and word-level embedding. This is performed on the context words and the three types of sentiment resource words [1], resulting in four final coupled word embedding matrices: the $W^c = [w_1^c, ..., w_t^c] \in \mathbb{R}^{d \times t}$ for context words, the $W^s = [w_1^s, ..., w_m^s] \in \mathbb{R}^{d \times m}$ for sentiment words, the $W^i = [w_1^i, ..., w_k^i] \in \mathbb{R}^{d \times k}$ for intensity words, the $W^n = [w_1^n, ..., w_p^n] \in \mathbb{R}^{d \times p}$ for negation words. Here, t, m, k, p are the length of the corresponding items respectively, and d is the embedding dimension. Each W is normalized to better calculate the following word correlation.

[1] To be precise, sentiment resource words include sentiment words, negation words and intensity words.

2.2 Multi-sentiment-resource Attention Module

After obtaining the coupled word embedding, we propose a multi-sentiment-resource attention mechanism to help select the crucial sentiment-resource-relevant context words to build the sentiment-specific sentence representation. Concretely, we use the three kinds of sentiment resource words as attention sources to attend to the context words respectively, which is beneficial to capture different sentiment-relevant context words corresponding to different types of sentiment sources. For example, using sentiment words as attention source attending to the context words helps form the sentiment-word-enhanced sentence representation. Then, we combine the three kinds of sentiment-resource-enhanced sentence representations to learn the final sentiment-specific sentence representation. We design three types of attention mechanisms: sentiment attention, intensity attention, negation attention to model the three kinds of sentiment resources, respectively. In the following, we will elaborate the three types of attention mechanisms in details.

First, inspired by (Xiong et al.), we expect to establish the word-level relationship between the context words and different kinds of sentiment resource words. To be specific, we define the dot products among the context words and the three kinds of sentiment resource words as correlation matrices. Mathematically, the detailed formulation is described as follows.

$$M^s = (W^c)^T \cdot W^s \in \mathbb{R}^{t \times m} \tag{1}$$

$$M^i = (W^c)^T \cdot W^i \in \mathbb{R}^{t \times k} \tag{2}$$

$$M^n = (W^c)^T \cdot W^n \in \mathbb{R}^{t \times p} \tag{3}$$

where M^s, M^i, M^n are the correlation matrices to measure the relationship among the context words and the three kinds of sentiment resource words, representing the relevance between the context words and the sentiment resource word.

After obtaining the correlation matrices, we can compute the sentiment-resource-relevant context word representations X_s^c, X_i^c, X_n^c by the dot products among the context words and different types of corresponding correlation matrices. Meanwhile, we can also obtain the context-word-relevant sentiment word representation matrix X^s by the dot product between the correlation matrix M^s and the sentiment words W^s, the context-word-relevant intensity word representation matrix X^i by the dot product between the intensity words W^i and the correlation matrix M^i, the context-word-relevant negation word representation matrix X^n by the dot product between the negation words W^n and the correlation matrix M^n. The detailed formulas are presented as follows:

$$X_s^c = W^c M^s, X^s = W^s (M^s)^T \qquad (4)$$

$$X_i^c = W^c M^i, X^i = W^i (M^i)^T \qquad (5)$$

$$X_n^c = W^c M^n, X^n = W^n (M^n)^T \qquad (6)$$

The final enhanced context word representation matrix is computed as:

$$X^c = X_s^c + X_i^c + X_n^c. \qquad (7)$$

Next, we employ four independent GRU networks (Chung et al., 2015) to encode hidden states of the context words and the three types of sentiment resource words, respectively. Formally, given the word embedding X^c, X^s, X^i, X^n, the hidden state matrices H^c, H^s, H^i, H^n can be obtained as follows:

$$H^c = GRU(X^c) \qquad (8)$$

$$H^s = GRU(X^s) \qquad (9)$$

$$H^i = GRU(X^i) \qquad (10)$$

$$H^n = GRU(X^n) \qquad (11)$$

After obtaining the hidden state matrices, the sentiment-word-enhanced sentence representation o_1 can be computed as:

$$o_1 = \sum_{i=1}^{t} \alpha_i h_i^c, q^s = \sum_{i=1}^{m} h_i^s / m \qquad (12)$$

$$\beta([h_i^c; q_s]) = u_s^T tanh(W_s[h_i^c; q_s]) \qquad (13)$$

$$\alpha_i = \frac{exp(\beta([h_i^c; q_s]))}{\sum_{i=1}^{t} exp(\beta([h_i^c; q_s]))} \qquad (14)$$

where q^s denotes the mean-pooling operation towards H^s, β is the attention function that calculates the importance of the i-th word h_i^c in the context and α_i indicates the importance of the i-th word in the context, u_s and W_s are learnable parameters.

Similarly, with the hidden states H^i and H^n for the intensity words and the negation words as attention sources, we can obtain the intensity-word-enhanced sentence representation o_2 and the

negation-word-enhanced sentence representation o_3. The final comprehensive sentiment-specific sentence representation $\tilde{o}$ is the composition of the above three sentiment-resource-specific sentence representations o_1, o_2, o_3:

$$\tilde{o} = [o_1, o_2, o_3] \qquad (15)$$

2.3 Sentence Classifier

After obtaining the final sentence representation $\tilde{o}$, we feed it to a softmax layer to predict the sentiment label distribution of a sentence:

$$\hat{y} = \frac{exp(\tilde{W}_o^T \tilde{o} + \tilde{b}_o)}{\sum_{i=1}^{C} exp(\tilde{W}_o^T \tilde{o} + \tilde{b}_o)} \qquad (16)$$

where $\hat{y}$ is the predicted sentiment distribution of the sentence, C is the number of sentiment labels, $\tilde{W}_o$ and $\tilde{b}_o$ are parameters to be learned.

For model training, our goal is to minimize the cross entropy between the ground truth and predicted results for all sentences. Meanwhile, in order to avoid overfitting, we use dropout strategy to randomly omit parts of the parameters on each training case. Inspired by (Lin et al., 2017), we also design a penalization term to ensure the diversity of semantics from different sentiment-resource-specific sentence representations, which reduces information redundancy from different sentiment resources attention. Specifically, the final loss function is presented as follows:

$$L(\hat{y}, y) = -\sum_{i=1}^{N} \sum_{j=1}^{C} y_i^j log(\hat{y}_i^j) + \lambda(\sum_{\theta \in \Theta} \theta^2) \qquad (17)$$

$$+ \mu ||\tilde{O}\tilde{O}^T - \psi I||_F^2$$
$$\tilde{O} = [o_1; o_2; o_3] \qquad (18)$$

where y_i^j is the target sentiment distribution of the sentence, $\hat{y}_i^j$ is the prediction probabilities, θ denotes each parameter to be regularized, Θ is parameter set, λ is the coefficient for L_2 regularization, μ is a hyper-parameter to balance the three terms, ψ is the weight parameter, I denotes the the identity matrix and $||.||_F$ denotes the Frobenius norm of a matrix. Here, the first two terms of the loss function are cross-entropy function of the predicted and true distributions and L_2 regularization respectively, and the final term is a penalization term to encourage the diversity of sentiment sources.

3 Experiments

3.1 Datasets and Sentiment Resources

Movie Review (MR)[2] and Stanford Sentiment Treebank (SST)[3] are used to evaluate our model. MR dataset has 5,331 positive samples and 5,331 negative samples. We adopt the same data split as in (Qian et al., 2017). SST consists of 8,545 training samples, 1,101 validation samples, 2210 test samples. Each sample is marked as very negative, negative, neutral, positive, or very positive. Sentiment lexicon combines the sentiment words from both (Qian et al., 2017) and (Hu and Liu, 2004), resulting in 10,899 sentiment words in total. We collect negation and intensity words manually as the number of these words is limited.

3.2 Baselines

In order to comprehensively evaluate the performance of our model, we list several baselines for sentence-level sentiment classification.

RNTN: Recursive Tensor Neural Network (Socher et al., 2013) is used to model correlations between different dimensions of child nodes vectors.

LSTM/Bi-LSTM: Cho et al. (2014) employs Long Short-Term Memory and the bidirectional variant to capture sequential information.

Tree-LSTM: Memory cells was introduced by Tree-Structured Long Short-Term Memory (Tai et al., 2015) and gates into tree-structured neural network, which is beneficial to capture semantic relatedness by parsing syntax trees.

CNN: Convolutional Neural Networks (Kim, 2014) is applied to generate task-specific sentence representation.

NCSL: Teng et al. (2016) designs a Neural Context-Sensitive Lexicon (NSCL) to obtain prior sentiment scores of words in the sentence.

LR-Bi-LSTM: Qian et al. (2017) imposes linguistic roles into neural networks by applying linguistic regularization on intermediate outputs with KL divergence.

Self-attention: Lin et al. (2017) proposes a self-attention mechanism to learn structured sentence embedding.

ID-LSTM: (Tianyang et al., 2018) uses reinforcement learning to learn structured sentence representation for sentiment classification.

3.3 Implementation Details

In our experiments, the dimensions of character-level embedding and word embedding (GloVe) are both set to 300. Kernel sizes of multi-gram convolution for Char-CNN are set to 2, 3, respectively. All the weight matrices are initialized as random orthogonal matrices, and we set all the bias vectors as zero vectors. We optimize the proposed model with RMSprop algorithm, using mini-batch training. The size of mini-batch is 60. The dropout rate is 0.5, and the coefficient λ of L_2 normalization is set to 10^{-5}. μ is set to 10^{-4}. ψ is set to 0.9. When there are not sentiment resource words in the sentences, all the context words are treated as sentiment resource words to implement the multi-path self-attention strategy.

3.4 Experiment Results

In our experiments, to be consistent with the recent baseline methods, we adopt classification accuracy as evaluation metric. We summarize the experimental results in Table 1. Our model has robust superiority over competitors and sets state-of-the-art on MR and SST datasets. First, our model brings a substantial improvement over the methods that do not leverage sentiment linguistic knowledge (e.g., RNTN, LSTM, BiLSTM, C-NN and ID-LSTM) on both datasets. This verifies the effectiveness of leveraging sentiment linguistic resource with the deep learning algorithms. Second, our model also consistently outperforms LR-Bi-LSTM which integrates linguistic roles of sentiment, negation and intensity words into neural networks via the linguistic regularization. For example, our model achieves 2.4% improvements over the MR dataset and 0.8% improvements over the SST dataset compared to LR-Bi-LSTM. This is because that MEAN designs attention mechanisms to leverage sentiment resources efficiently, which utilizes the interactive information between context words and sentiment resource words.

In order to analyze the effectiveness of each component of MEAN, we also report the ablation test in terms of discarding character-level embedding (denoted as MEAN w/o CharCNN) and sentiment words/negation words/intensity words (denoted as MEAN w/o sentiment words/negation words/intensity words). All the tested factors con-

---

[2] http://www.cs.cornell.edu/people/pabo/movie-review-data/

[3] https://nlp.stanford.edu/sentiment/we train the model on both phrases and sentences but only test on sentences

tribute greatly to the improvement of the MEAN. In particular, the accuracy decreases sharply when discarding the sentiment words. This is within our expectation since sentiment words are vital when classifying the polarity of the sentences.

Methods	MR	SST
RNTN	75.9%#	45.7%
LSTM	77.4%#	46.4%
BiLSTM	79.3%#	49.1%
Tree-LSTM	80.7%#	51.0%
CNN	81.5%	48.0%
NSCL	82.9%	51.1%
LR-Bi-LSTM	82.1%	50.6%
Self-attention	81.7%*	48.9%*
ID-LSTM	81.6%	50.0%
MEAN(our model)	**84.5%**	**51.4%**
MEAN-CharCNN	83.2%	50.0%
MEAN-sentiment words	82.1%	48.4%
MEAN-negation words	82.9%	49.5%
MEAN-intensity words	83.5%	49.3%

Table 1: Evaluation results. The best result for each dataset is in bold. The result marked with # are retrieved from (Qian et al., 2017), and the results marked with * denote the results are obtained by our implementation.

4 Conclusion

In this paper, we propose a novel Multi-sentiment-resource Enhanced Attention Network (MEAN) to enhance the performance of sentence-level sentiment analysis, which integrates the sentiment linguistic knowledge into the deep neural network.

Acknowledgements

This work was supported in part by the Research Fund for the development of strategic emerging industries by ShenZhen city (No.JCYJ20160301151844537 and No. JCYJ20160331104524983).

References

Shin Bonggun, Lee Timothy, and D. Choi Jinho. 2017. Lexicon integrated cnn models with attention for sentiment analysis. In *Proceedings of the 8th Workshop on Computational Approaches to Subjectivity, Sentiment and Social Media Analysis, ACL 2017.*

Kyunghyun Cho, Bart van Merrienboer, Çaglar Gülçehre, Fethi Bougares, Holger Schwenk, and Yoshua Bengio. 2014. Learning phrase representations using RNN encoder-decoder for statistical machine translation. *CoRR*, abs/1406.1078.

Junyoung Chung, Caglar Gulcehre, Kyunghyun Cho, and Yoshua Bengio. 2015. Gated feedback recurrent neural networks. In *Proceedings of ICML 2015.*

Jiachen Du, Ruifeng Xu, Yulan He, and Lin Gui. 2017. Stance classification with target-specific neural attention networks. In *Proceedings of IJCAI 2017.*

Tang Duyu, Wei Furu, Qin Bing, Liu Ting, and Zhou Ming. 2014. Coooolll: A deep learning system for twitter sentiment classification. In *Proceedings of the 8th International Workshop on Semantic Evaluation, SemEval@COLING 2014.*

Lin Gui, Yu Zhou, Ruifeng Xu, Yulan He, and Qin Lu. 2017. Learning representations from heterogeneous network for sentiment classification of product reviews. *Knowledge-Based Systems*, 124:34–45.

Li Hao, Chen Yu, Ji Heng, Muresan Smaranda, and Zheng Dequan. 2012. Combining social cognitive theories with linguistic features for multi-genre sentiment analysis. In *Proceedings of the 26th Pacific Asia Conference on Language, Information and Computation.*

Sepp Hochreiter and Jürgen Schmidhuber. 1997. Long short-term memory. *Neural computation*, pages 1735–1780.

Minqing Hu and Bing Liu. 2004. Mining and summarizing customer reviews. In *Proceedings of SIGKDD 2004.*

Yoon Kim. 2014. Convolutional neural networks for sentence classification. In *Proceedings of EMNLP 2014.*

Zhouhan Lin, Minwei Feng, Cicero Nogueira dos Santos, Mo Yu, Bing Xiang, Bowen Zhou, and Yoshua Bengio. 2017. A structured self-attentive sentence embedding. In *Proceedings of ICLR 2017.*

Jonathan Long, Evan Shelhamer, and Trevor Darrell. 2015. Fully convolutional networks for semantic segmentation. In *Proceedings of CVPR 2015.*

Isa Maks and Piek Vossen. 2012. A lexicon model for deep sentiment analysis and opinion mining applications. *Decision Support Systems*, pages 680–688.

Bo Pang, Lillian Lee, and Shivakumar Vaithyanathan. 2002. Thumbs up?: sentiment classification using machine learning techniques. In *Proceedings of ACL 2002.*

Jeffrey Pennington, Richard Socher, and Christopher Manning. 2014. Glove: Global vectors for word representation. In *Proceedings of EMNLP 2014.*

Qiao Qian, Minlie Huang, Jinhao Lei, and Xiaoyan Zhu. 2017. Linguistically regularized LSTM for sentiment classification. In *Proceedings of ACL 2017*, pages 1679–1689.

Richard Socher, Alex Perelygin, Jean Wu, Jason Chuang, Christopher D Manning, Andrew Ng, and Christopher Potts. 2013. Recursive deep models for semantic compositionality over a sentiment treebank. In *Proceedings of EMNLP 2013*.

Kai Sheng Tai, Richard Socher, and Christopher D. Manning. 2015. Improved semantic representations from tree-structured long short-term memory networks. In *Proceedings of ACL 2015*.

Zhiyang Teng, Duy-Tin Vo, and Yue Zhang. 2016. Context-sensitive lexicon features for neural sentiment analysis. In *Proceedings of EMNLP 2016*.

Zhang Tianyang, Huang Minlie, and Li Zhao. 2018. Learning structured representation for text classification via reinforcement learning. In *Proceedings of AAAI 2018*.

Caiming Xiong, Victor Zhong, and Richard Socher. Dynamic coattention networks for question answering. In *ICLR*.

Zichao Yang, Diyi Yang, Chris Dyer, Xiaodong He, Alex Smola, and Eduard Hovy. 2016. Hierarchical attention networks for document classification. In *Proceedings of NAACL 2016*.

Xiang Zhang, Junbo Zhao, and Yann LeCun. 2015. Character-level convolutional networks for text classification. In *Proceedings of NIPS 2015*.

Xinjie Zhou, Xiaojun Wan, and Jianguo Xiao. 2016. Attention-based lstm network for cross-lingual sentiment classification. In *Proceedings of EMNLP 2016*.

Pretraining Sentiment Classifiers with Unlabeled Dialog Data

Toru Shimizu[1], Hayato Kobayashi[1,2], and Nobuyuki Shimizu[1]

[1]Yahoo Japan Corporation
[2]Riken AIP
{toshimiz,hakobaya,nobushim}@yahoo-corp.jp

Abstract

The huge cost of creating labeled training data is a common problem for supervised learning tasks such as sentiment classification. Recent studies showed that pretraining with unlabeled data via a language model can improve the performance of classification models. In this paper, we take the concept a step further by using a conditional language model, instead of a language model. Specifically, we address a sentiment classification task for a tweet analysis service as a case study and propose a pretraining strategy with unlabeled dialog data (tweet-reply pairs) via an encoder-decoder model. Experimental results show that our strategy can improve the performance of sentiment classifiers and outperform several state-of-the-art strategies including language model pretraining.

1 Introduction

Sentiment classification is a task to predict a sentiment label, such as positive/negative, for a given text and has been applied to many domains such as movie/product reviews, customer surveys, news comments, and social media. A common problem of this task is the lack of labeled training data due to costly annotation work, especially for social media without explicit sentiment feedback such as review scores.

To overcome this problem, Dai and Le (2015) recently proposed a semi-supervised sequence learning framework, where a sentiment classifier based on recurrent neural networks (RNNs) is trained with labeled data after initializing it with the parameters of an RNN-based language model pretrained with a large amount of unlabeled data.

The concept of their framework is simple but effective, and their work yielded many related studies of semi-supervised training based on sequence modeling, as described in Section 4.

In this paper, we take their concept a step further by using a conditional language model with unlabeled dialog data (i.e., tweet-reply pairs) instead of a language model with unpaired data[1]. An important observation of the dialog data that underpins our strategy is that the sentiment or mood in a message often affects messages in reply to it. People tend to write angry responses to angry messages, empathetic replies to sad remarks, or congratulatory phrases to good news.

Our contributions are listed as follows.

- We propose a pretraining strategy with unlabeled dialog data (tweet-reply pairs) via an encoder-decoder model for sentiment classifiers (Section 2). To the best of our knowledge, our proposal is the first such proposal, as clarified in Section 4.

- We report on a case study based on a costly labeled sentiment dataset of 99.5K items and a large-scale unlabeled dialog dataset of 22.3M, which were provided from a tweet analysis service (Section 3.1).

- Experimental results of sentiment classification show that our method outperforms the current semi-supervised methods based on a language model, autoencoder, and distant supervision, as well as linear classifiers (Section 3.4).

2 Proposed Method

Our pretraining strategy simply consists of the following two steps:

---

[1]We use the term "conditional language model" in a narrow sense only for a model trained with explicit source-target pairs, although both RNN-based language and autoencoder models can generate a text from a real-valued context vector.

Proceedings of the 56th Annual Meeting of the Association for Computational Linguistics (Short Papers), pages 764–770
Melbourne, Australia, July 15 - 20, 2018. ©2018 Association for Computational Linguistics

1. Training a dialog (encoder-decoder) model using unlabeled dialog data (tweet-reply pairs) as pretraining.

2. Training a sentiment classifier (encoder-labeler) model using labeled sentiment data (tweet-label pairs) after initializing its encoder part with the encoder parameters of the encoder-decoder model.

The encoder-decoder model is a conditional language model that predicts a correct output sequence from an input sequence (Sutskever et al., 2014). This model consists of two RNNs: an encoder and decoder. The encoder extracts a context of the input sequence as a real-valued vector, and the decoder predicts the output sequences from the context individually.

Our classifier forms an encoder-labeler structure, which consists of the above encoder and a labeler that predicts a sentiment label from the context. Note that the encoder of the classifier is fine-tuned with labeled data, as in (Dai and Le, 2015). The main difference between their approach and ours is that we examine paired (dialog) data for pretraining, while they only showed the usefulness of pretraining with unpaired data.

3 Experiments

3.1 Datasets

We used two datasets, a dialog dataset for pretraining the encoder-decoder model and a sentiment dataset for training (fine-tuning) the sentiment classifier, as shown in Table 1. Those datasets were provided by Yahoo! JAPAN, which is the largest portal site in Japan.

The dialog dataset contains about 22.3 million tweet-reply pairs extracted from Twitter Firehose data. In its preprocessing, we filtered out spam and bot posts by using user-level signals such as the follower count, the friend count, the favorite count, and whether a profile image is set or not. Also, we replaced all the URLs in the text with "[u]" and all the user mentions with "[m]", considering them as noise. The rest of the text was used

	Train	Valid	Test
Dialog	22,300,000	10,000	50,000
Sentiment	80,591	4,000	15,000

Table 1: Details of dialog and sentiment datasets

as it was. On average, source and target (or reply) tweets after preprocessing were 31.5 and 27.8 characters long, respectively. While redistribution of tweets is prohibited, we are planning to publicize tweet IDs of this dataset for reproducibility.[2]

The sentiment dataset includes about 100K tweets with manually annotated three-class sentiment labels: `positive`, `negative`, and `neutral`. The breakdown of `positive`, `negative`, and `neutral` in the training set was 15.0, 18.6, and 66.4%, respectively. Note that the tweets were sampled separately from those of the dialog dataset. The procedure for text preprocessing was the same with that of the dialog dataset. The average length of the tweets after preprocessing was 17 characters. Each tweet was judged by a majority vote of three experienced editors in the company providing the sentiment-analysis service. The inter-annotator agreement ratio assessed with Fleiss' κ was 0.495. The overall annotation work took roughly 300 person-days. This means that the cost is at least 24K dollars, 8 hours $\times$ 300 days $\times$ legal minimum wage in Japan 10 dollars/hour. Considering that the in-house annotators are well-educated, skilled proper employees, the actual cost would be much higher than this rough estimate and much more costly than collecting unlabeled dialog data. In addition, the annotators had gone through a few days of training to become able to appropriately judge the sentiment before they got down to actual annotation work, but the number, 300 person-days, does not include the time for this training.

3.2 Model and Training

The settings of the dialog (encoder-decoder) model are as follows. In both the encoder and decoder, the size of the word-embedding layer is 256 and that of the LSTM-RNN hidden layer is 1024. The size of the output layer is 4000, which is the same as the (character-based) vocabulary size.[3] The encoder and decoder share these hyperparameters as well as the parameters themselves (that is, with regard to the embedding layer and

---

[2]The tweet IDs will be provided from https://research-lab.yahoo.co.jp/en/software/ .

[3]We used a character-based model since it performed better than word-based models in our preliminary experiments. Existing morphological analyzers needed for word-based models have usually been trained by formal text such as that of newspapers and seem not suitable to highly colloquial text seen in tweets, which often includes emoticons and emoji.

recurrent layer). The total number of parameters is 8.9 million.

The settings of the sentiment classifier (encoder-labeler) model are as follows. The encoder part has the same structure and hyper-parameters as that of the dialog model, making them compatible for transferring learned parameters. We reused the dialog model's dictionaries in the classifier model so that the two models could process tweet texts consistently. The labeler consists of a fully connected layer and soft max nonlinearity.

The models were trained with ADADELTA (Zeiler, 2012) with a mini-batch size of 64. The dialog model was trained in five epochs, and the classifier model was tuned with the early-stopping strategy, which stops training when the validation accuracy drops. For ADADELTA's parameters, we fixed the learning rate to 1.0, decay rate ρ to 0.95, and smoothing constant ϵ to 10^{-6} for all training sessions. We evaluated validation costs ten times per epoch and selected the model with the lowest validation cost. The training took 15.9 days on 1 GPU with 7 TFLOPS computational power.

3.3 Compared Models

We compared the following eight models: non-pretrained (Default), proposed dialog pretraining (Dial), current pretraining with unpaired data (Lang, SeqAE) and pseudo labeled data (Emo2M, Emo6M), and classical linear learners (LogReg, LinSVM). The details of these models are given below.

- Default: Trained without pretraining by executing only Step 2 in Section 2.

- Dial: Pretrained with the dialog model described in Section 2.

- Lang, SeqAE: Pretrained with the language model and autoencoder model proposed in (Dai and Le, 2015). The language model is the decoder part of the encoder-decoder model using a zero vector as the initial hidden layer value, and the autoencoder model is the same structure of the encoder-decoder model, where input and output are the same. To make the comparison as fair as possible, we used the reply-side of the dialog dataset for pretraining Lang and SeqAE so that the same supervision information on the

basis of the same tweet-reply pairs would be applied to Lang, SeqAE, and Dial. The number of their pretraining epochs was also equal to that of Dial.

- Emo2M, Emo6M: Pretrained with pseudo labeled data (2M, 6M) based on manually collected emoticons, which consist of 120 positive emoticons and 116 negative ones. This technique is also known as distant-supervision. These pseudo labels were annotated by extracting tweets including one of those emoticons from our dialog data and another 92M tweets. Pretraining was conducted via a two-class sentiment classifier, which is a similar model to Default, since uncertain tweets without emoticons are not always neutral. We confirmed that this two-class classifier can reach more than 90% test accuracy on the emoticon-based test dataset. After pretraining, the parameters of the encoder part were transfered to the final classifier model.

- LogReg, LinSVM: Logistic regression and linear support vector machine (SVM) models of LIBLINEAR (Fan et al., 2008) with bag-of-words features, which consist of 50K unigrams (w/o stopwords), 50K bigrams, and 233 emoticons. These features are based on a state-of-the-art system (Mohammad et al., 2013) that performed best in the SEMEVAL competition (Nakov et al., 2013) and was actually used in the tweet analysis service of the data-providing company. The best parameters were found through a grid-search on the validation set.

3.4 Results

Table 2 shows the macro-average F-measure results of the compared models in Section 3.3 on the sentiment classification task when varying data size (5K to 80K). Each value is the average of five trials with different random seeds for each setting, and a value of a trial is the macro-average of F-measure values of three sentiment classes. The first row (Default) shows the default sentiment classifier model without pretraining. The second row block (Dial to Emo6M) shows the results of the same training as Default after pretraining via different models, while the third block shows those of linear classifiers (non-RNN models). The supplemental materials also include the results measured by accuracy.

	5K	10K	20K	40K	80K
Default	0.517	0.590	0.623	0.653	0.673
Dial	**0.665**[†]	**0.685**[†]	**0.702**[†]	**0.717**[†]	**0.738**[†]
Lang	0.653	0.674	0.692	0.707	0.726
SeqAE	0.568	0.598	0.626	0.649	0.677
Emo2M	0.482	0.532	0.579	0.626	0.664
Emo6M	0.484	0.517	0.565	0.613	0.650
LogReg	0.577	0.609	0.631	0.648	0.675
LinSVM	0.582	0.610	0.627	0.637	0.648

Table 2: Macro-average F-measure of sentiment classification of each model versus labeled data size. `Dial` is our proposed method, and † in its row indicates statistically significant difference from the corresponding value of `Lang` ($p < 0.05$).

Comparing `Dial` with the other models, we can see that our pretraining strategy with dialog data consistently outperformed all the other models: state-of-the-art pretraining strategies with unpaired unlabeled data (`Lang`, `SeqAE`) and pseudo labeled data (`Emo2M`, `Emo6M`), as well as linear learners (`LogReg`, `LinSVM`). This indicates that unlabeled dialog data (tweet-reply pairs) have useful information for sentiment classifiers, as expected in Section 1. In fact, we observed that the pretrained encoder-decoder model seems to generate an appropriate reply, on which the sentiment on the input tweet is well reflected. For example, the reply ":(" was generated for the input tweet "I'm sorry to hear that" (see supplementary material for more examples).

`Lang` also outperformed well but did not overtake `Dial`. The differences between `Dial` and `Lang` are statistically significant[4] for all five training dataset sizes. Interestingly, `SeqAE` was not so effective like `Dial`, despite their model structures are basically the same. This implies that it is practically important to find appropriate data for pretraining, such as dialog data for sentiment classification.

As for the results of distant supervision with emoticons, both `Emo2M` and `Emo6M` performed worse than `Default`, and increasing the dataset size did not change the situation. The reason why these models did not perform as well as other pretraining-based models is considered to be noisy labels, especially in negative ones. We illustrate two instances in the `Emo2M` training data that include an emoticon that is usually negative emoti-

---

[4]Under the significance level of 0.05 with two-tailed t-test assuming unequal variances.

con but can be considered positive:

- 美人すぎるよ可愛い (; ;) , "She is so beautiful, cute (crying emoticon)"

- うらやましいです。おめでとうございます orz, "I envy you. Congratulations (bow-the-knee emoticon)"

Comparing `Default` with `LogReg` and `LinSVM`, we can see that the linear models performed better than the default RNN model without pretraining, when the labeled data size is less than or equal to 20K. However, looking at the results of `Dial`, our method improved `Default` even for these cases (5K to 20K), and `Dial` clearly outperformed the linear models. This means that pretraining is useful especially on the situation where the labeled data size is limited.

4   Related Work

After Dai and Le (2015) proposed the framework of semi-supervised sequence learning, there have been several attempts to extend sequence learning models for different tasks to semi-supervised settings. Cheng et al. (2016) and Ramachandran et al. (2017) studied semi-supervised training of machine translation models via an autoencoder model and language model, respectively. They also used paired data (parallel corpora), but unsupervised training was conducted with reasonable monolingual corpora to compensate for costly parallel corpora, which is opposite to our setting. Zhou et al. (2016a,b) proposed to use parallel corpora for adapting the sentiment resources in a resource-rich language to a resource-poor language. Their purpose was completely different from ours, since making parallel corpora is also costly. The other studies include semi-supervised extensions for predicting the property values of Wikipedia (Hewlett et al., 2017), detecting medical conditions from heart rate data (Ballinger et al., 2018), and morphological reinflection of inflected words (e.g., "playing" to "played"). They did not use paired-text data to leverage their tasks.

Our method can be regarded as a general version of distant supervision since we assume that a reply includes the label information of the corresponding tweet. There have been many studies about distant supervision for sentiment analysis (Read, 2005; Go et al., 2009; Davidov et al., 2010; Purver and Battersby, 2012; Mohammad et al., 2013; Tang et al., 2014; dos Santos and Gatti,

2014; Severyn and Moschitti, 2015; Deriu et al., 2016; Müller et al., 2017), but they basically focused on how to use emoticons and hashtags to leverage performance. One exception is the study by (Pool and Nissim, 2016), in which Facebook reactions were used for distant supervision. Their approach is similar to ours using tweet-reply pairs, but our method is more general since they only used six reply categories (i.e., like, love, haha, wow, sad, and angry), not text replies.

There have been a few studies on sentiment classification in dialogue data (Bertero and Fung, 2016; Bertero et al., 2016). These studies involved sentiment classification based on dialog contexts, which means that they used labeled dialog data, while we used unlabeled dialog data. For tweet data, several studies used reply-features for sentiment classification of tweets (Barbosa and Feng, 2010; Jiang et al., 2011; Vanzo et al., 2014; Bamman and Smith, 2015; Ren et al., 2016; Castellucci et al., 2016). However, they used replies as labeled data for sentiment classification, not unlabeled data for pretraining.

5   Conclusion

We proposed a pretraining strategy with dialog data for sentiment classifiers. The experimental results showed that our strategy clearly outperformed the existing pretraining with unpaired unlabeled data via language modeling and pseudo labeled data via distant supervision, as well as linear classifiers. In the future, we will investigate whether or not we can use other paired data for pretraining of classification tasks. For example, we expect that news article-comment pairs are useful for predicting fake news detection and that question-answer pairs of Q&A sites are useful for recommending questions for answering.

References

Brandon Ballinger, Johnson Hsieh, Avesh Singh, Nimit Sohoni, Jack Wang, Geoffrey H. Tison, Gregory M. Marcus, Jose M. Sanchez, Carol Maguire, Jeffrey E. Olgin, and Mark J. Pletcher. 2018. DeepHeart: Semi-Supervised Sequence Learning for Cardiovascular Risk Prediction. In *Proceedings of the Thirty-Second AAAI Conference on Artificial Intelligence (AAAI 2018)*. To appear. https://arxiv.org/abs/1802.02511.

David Bamman and Noah A. Smith. 2015. Contextualized Sarcasm Detection on Twitter. In *Proceedings of the Ninth International Conference on Web and Social Media (ICWSM 2015)*. pages 574–577. http://www.aaai.org/ocs/index.php/ICWSM/ICWSM15/paper/view/10538.

Luciano Barbosa and Junlan Feng. 2010. Robust Sentiment Detection on Twitter from Biased and Noisy Data. In *Proceedings of the 21st International Conference on Computational Linguistics (COLING 2010)*. Coling 2010 Organizing Committee, pages 36–44. http://www.aclweb.org/anthology/C10-2005.

Dario Bertero and Pascale Fung. 2016. A Long Short-Term Memory Framework for Predicting Humor in Dialogues. In *Proceedings of the 2016 Conference of the North American Chapter of the Association for Computational Linguistics: Human Language Technologies (NAACL-HLT 2016)*. Association for Computational Linguistics, pages 130–135. http://www.aclweb.org/anthology/N16-1016.

Dario Bertero, Farhad Bin Siddique, Chien-Sheng Wu, Yan Wan, Ricky Ho Yin Chan, and Pascale Fung. 2016. Real-Time Speech Emotion and Sentiment Recognition for Interactive Dialogue Systems. In *Proceedings of the 2016 Conference on Empirical Methods in Natural Language Processing (EMNLP 2016)*. Association for Computational Linguistics, pages 1042–1047. https://aclweb.org/anthology/D16-1110.

Giuseppe Castellucci, Danilo Croce, and Roberto Basili. 2016. Context-aware Convolutional Neural Networks for Twitter Sentiment Analysis in Italian. In *Proceedings of Third Italian Conference on Computational Linguistics (CLiC-it 2016) & Fifth Evaluation Campaign of Natural Language Processing and Speech Tools for Italian. Final Workshop (EVALITA 2016)*. http://ceur-ws.org/Vol-1749/paper_029.pdf.

Yong Cheng, Wei Xu, Zhongjun He, Wei He, Hua Wu, Maosong Sun, and Yang Liu. 2016. Semi-Supervised Learning for Neural Machine Translation. In *Proceedings of the 54th Annual Meeting of the Association for Computational Linguistics (ACL 2016)*. Association for Computational Linguistics, pages 1965–1974. http://www.aclweb.org/anthology/P16-1185.

Andrew M Dai and Quoc V Le. 2015. Semi-supervised Sequence Learning. In *Advances in Neural Information Processing Systems 28 (NIPS 2015)*, Curran Associates, Inc., pages 3079–3087. http://papers.nips.cc/paper/5949-semi-supervised-sequence-learning.pdf.

Dmitry Davidov, Oren Tsur, and Ari Rappoport. 2010. Enhanced Sentiment Learning Using Twitter Hashtags and Smileys. In *Proceedings of the 21st International Conference on Computational Linguistics (COLING 2010)*. Coling 2010 Organizing Committee, pages 241–249. http://www.aclweb.org/anthology/C10-2028.

Jan Deriu, Maurice Gonzenbach, Fatih Uzdilli, Aurelien Lucchi, Valeria De Luca, and Martin Jaggi. 2016. SwissCheese at SemEval-2016 Task 4: Sentiment Classification Using an Ensemble of Convolutional Neural Networks with Distant Supervision. In *Proceedings of the 10th International Workshop on Semantic Evaluation (SemEval 2016)*. Association for Computational Linguistics, pages 1124–1128. http://www.aclweb.org/anthology/S16-1173.

Cicero dos Santos and Maira Gatti. 2014. Deep Convolutional Neural Networks for Sentiment Analysis of Short Texts. In *Proceedings of the 25th International Conference on Computational Linguistics (COLING 2014)*. Dublin City University and Association for Computational Linguistics, pages 69–78. http://www.aclweb.org/anthology/C14-1008.

Rong-En Fan, Kai-Wei Chang, Cho-Jui Hsieh, Xiang-Rui Wang, and Chih-Jen Lin. 2008. LIBLINEAR: A Library for Large Linear Classification. *Journal of Machine Learning Research* 9:1871–1874.

Alec Go, Richa Bhayani, and Lei Huang. 2009. Twitter Sentiment Classification using Distant Supervision. Technical report, Stanford Digital Library Technologies Project. https://cs.stanford.edu/people/alecmgo/papers/ TwitterDistantSupervision09.pdf.

Daniel Hewlett, Llion Jones, Alexandre Lacoste, and izzeddin gur. 2017. Accurate Supervised and Semi-Supervised Machine Reading for Long Documents. In *Proceedings of the 2017 Conference on Empirical Methods in Natural Language Processing (EMNLP 2017)*. Association for Computational Linguistics, pages 2011–2020. https://www.aclweb.org/anthology/D17-1214.

Long Jiang, Mo Yu, Ming Zhou, Xiaohua Liu, and Tiejun Zhao. 2011. Target-dependent Twitter Sentiment Classification. In *Proceedings of the 49th Annual Meeting of the Association for Computational Linguistics: Human Language Technologies (ACL-HLT 2011)*. Association for Computational Linguistics, pages 151–160. http://www.aclweb.org/anthology/P11-1016.

Saif Mohammad, Svetlana Kiritchenko, and Xiaodan Zhu. 2013. NRC-Canada: Building the State-of-the-Art in Sentiment Analysis of Tweets. In *Proceedings of the Seventh International Workshop on Semantic Evaluation (SemEval 2013)*. Association for Computational Linguistics, pages 321–327. http://www.aclweb.org/anthology/S13-2053.

Simon Müller, Tobias Huonder, Jan Deriu, and Mark Cieliebak. 2017. TopicThunder at SemEval-2017 Task 4: Sentiment Classification Using a Convolutional Neural Network with Distant Supervision. In *Proceedings of the 11th International Workshop on Semantic Evaluation (SemEval 2017)*. Association for Computational Linguistics, pages 766–770. http://www.aclweb.org/anthology/S17-2129.

Preslav Nakov, Sara Rosenthal, Zornitsa Kozareva, Veselin Stoyanov, Alan Ritter, and Theresa Wilson. 2013. SemEval-2013 Task 2: Sentiment Analysis in Twitter. In *Proceedings of the Seventh International Workshop on Semantic Evaluation (SemEval 2013)*. Association for Computational Linguistics, pages 312–320. http://www.aclweb.org/anthology/S13-2052.

Chris Pool and Malvina Nissim. 2016. Distant supervision for emotion detection using facebook reactions. In *Proceedings of the Workshop on Computational Modeling of People's Opinions, Personality, and Emotions in Social Media (PEOPLES)*. The COLING 2016 Organizing Committee, pages 30–39. http://aclweb.org/anthology/W16-4304.

Matthew Purver and Stuart Battersby. 2012. Experimenting with Distant Supervision for Emotion Classification. In *Proceedings of the 13th Conference of the European Chapter of the Association for Computational Linguistics (ACL 2012)*. Association for Computational Linguistics, pages 482–491. http://www.aclweb.org/anthology/E12-1049.

Prajit Ramachandran, Peter Liu, and Quoc Le. 2017. Unsupervised Pretraining for Sequence to Sequence Learning. In *Proceedings of the 2017 Conference on Empirical Methods in Natural Language Processing (EMNLP 2017)*. Association for Computational Linguistics, pages 383–391. https://www.aclweb.org/anthology/D17-1039.

Jonathon Read. 2005. Using Emoticons to Reduce Dependency in Machine Learning Techniques for Sentiment Classification. In *Proceedings of the ACL Student Research Workshop*. Association for Computational Linguistics, pages 43–48. http://www.aclweb.org/anthology/P/P05/P05-2008.

Yafeng Ren, Yue Zhang, Meishan Zhang, and Donghong Ji. 2016. Context-sensitive Twitter Sentiment Classification Using Neural Network. In *Proceedings of the Thirtieth AAAI Conference on Artificial Intelligence (AAAI 2016)*. AAAI Press, pages 215–221. http://dl.acm.org/citation.cfm?id=3015812.3015844.

Aliaksei Severyn and Alessandro Moschitti. 2015. UNITN: Training Deep Convolutional Neural Network for Twitter Sentiment Classification. In *Proceedings of the 9th International Workshop on Semantic Evaluation (SemEval 2015)*. Association for Computational Linguistics, pages 464–469. http://www.aclweb.org/anthology/S15-2079.

Ilya Sutskever, Oriol Vinyals, and Quoc V Le. 2014. Sequence to sequence learning with neural networks. In *Advances in Neural Information Processing Systems 27 (NIPS 2014)*, Curran Associates, Inc., pages 3104–3112. http://papers.nips.cc/paper/5346-sequence-to-sequence-learning-with-neural-networks.pdf.

Duyu Tang, Furu Wei, Nan Yang, Ming Zhou, Ting Liu, and Bing Qin. 2014. Learning

Sentiment-Specific Word Embedding for Twitter Sentiment Classification. In *Proceedings of the 52nd Annual Meeting of the Association for Computational Linguistics (ACL 2014)*. Association for Computational Linguistics, pages 1555–1565. http://www.aclweb.org/anthology/P14-1146.

Andrea Vanzo, Danilo Croce, and Roberto Basili. 2014. A context-based model for Sentiment Analysis in Twitter. In *Proceedings of the 25th International Conference on Computational Linguistics (COLING 2014)*. Dublin City University and Association for Computational Linguistics, pages 2345–2354. http://www.aclweb.org/anthology/C14-1221.

Matthew D. Zeiler. 2012. ADADELTA: An Adaptive Learning Rate Method. *CoRR* abs/1212.5701.

Xinjie Zhou, Xiaojun Wan, and Jianguo Xiao. 2016a. Attention-based LSTM Network for Cross-Lingual Sentiment Classification. In *Proceedings of the 2016 Conference on Empirical Methods in Natural Language Processing (EMNLP 2016)*. Association for Computational Linguistics, Austin, Texas, pages 247–256. https://aclweb.org/anthology/D16-1024.

Xinjie Zhou, Xiaojun Wan, and Jianguo Xiao. 2016b. Cross-Lingual Sentiment Classification with Bilingual Document Representation Learning. In *Proceedings of the 54th Annual Meeting of the Association for Computational Linguistics (ACL 2016)*. Association for Computational Linguistics, pages 1403–1412. http://www.aclweb.org/anthology/P16-1133.

Disambiguating False-Alarm Hashtag Usages in Tweets for Irony Detection

Hen-Hsen Huang,[1] **Chiao-Chen Chen,**[1] and **Hsin-Hsi Chen**[12]
[1] Department of Computer Science and Information Engineering,
National Taiwan University, Taipei, Taiwan
[2] MOST Joint Research Center for AI Technology and All Vista Healthcare, Taipei, Taiwan
`hhhuang@nlg.csie.ntu.edu.tw, {b04902055,hhchen}@ntu.edu.tw`

Abstract

The reliability of self-labeled data is an important issue when the data are regarded as ground-truth for training and testing learning-based models. This paper addresses the issue of false-alarm hashtags in the self-labeled data for irony detection. We analyze the ambiguity of hashtag usages and propose a novel neural network-based model, which incorporates linguistic information from different aspects, to disambiguate the usage of three hashtags that are widely used to collect the training data for irony detection. Furthermore, we apply our model to prune the self-labeled training data. Experimental results show that the irony detection model trained on the less but cleaner training instances outperforms the models trained on all data.

1 Introduction

Self-labeled data available on the Internet are popular research materials in many NLP areas. Metadata such as tags and emoticons given by users are considered as labels for training and testing learning-based models, which usually benefit from large amount of data.

One of the sources of self-labeled data widely used in the research community is Twitter, where the short-text messages tweets written by the crowd are publicly shared. In a tweet, the author can tag the short text with some hashtags such as #excited, #happy, #UnbornLivesMatter, and #Hillary4President to express their emotion or opinion. The tweets with a certain types of hashtags are collected as self-label data in a variety of research works including sentiment analysis (Qadir and Riloff, 2014), stance detection (Mohammad et al., 2016; Sobhani et al., 2017), fi-

nancial opinion mining (Cortis et al., 2017), and irony detection (Ghosh et al., 2015; Peled and Reichart, 2017; Hee et al., 2018). In the case of irony detection, it is impractical to manually annotate the ironic sentences from randomly sampled data due to the relatively low occurrences of irony (Davidov et al., 2010). Collecting the tweets with the hashtags like #sarcasm, #irony, and #not becomes the mainstream approach to dataset construction (Sulis et al., 2016). As shown in (S1), the tweet with the hashtag #not is treated as a positive (ironic) instance by removing #not from the text.

(S1) *@Anonymous doing a great job...
#not What do I pay my extortionate
council taxes for? #Disgrace #OngoingProblem http://t.co/FQZUUwKSoN*

However, the reliability of the self-labeled data is an important issue. As pointed out in the pioneering work, not all tweet writers know the definition of irony (Van Hee et al., 2016b). For instance, (S2) is tagged with #irony by the writer, but it is just witty and amusing.

(S2) *BestProAdvice @Anonymous More
clean OR cleaner, never more cleaner.
#irony*

When the false-alarm instances like (S2) are collected and mixed in the training and test data, the models that learn from the unreliable data may be misled, and the evaluation is also suspicious.

The other kind of unreliable data comes from the hashtags not only functioning as metadata. That is, a hashtag in a tweet may also function as a content word in its word form. For example, the hashtag #irony in (S3) is a part of the sentence "the irony of taking a break...", in contrast to the hashtag #not in (S1), which can be removed without a change of meaning.

Proceedings of the 56th Annual Meeting of the Association for Computational Linguistics (Short Papers), pages 771–777
Melbourne, Australia, July 15 - 20, 2018. ©2018 Association for Computational Linguistics

(S3) *The #irony of taking a break from reading about #socialmedia to check my social media.*

When the hashtag plays as a content word in a tweet, the tweet is not a good candidate of self-labeled ironic instances because the sentence will be incomplete once the hashtag is removed.

In this work, both kinds of unreliable data, the tweets with a misused hashtag and the tweets in which the hashtag serves as a content word, are our targets to remove from the training data. Manual data cleaning is labor-intensive and inefficient (Van Hee et al., 2016a). Compared to general training data cleaning approaches (Malik and Bhardwaj, 2011; Esuli and Sebastiani, 2013; Fukumoto and Suzuki, 2004) such as boosting-based learning, this work leverages the characteristics of hashtag usages in tweets. With small amount of golden labeled data, we propose a neural network classifier for pruning the self-labeled tweets, and train an ironic detector on the less but cleaner instances. This approach is easily to apply to other NLP tasks that rely on self-labeled data.

The contributions of this work are three-fold: (1) We make an empirically study on an issue that is potentially inherited in a number of research topics based on self-labeled data. (2) We propose a model for hashtag disambiguation. For this task, the human-verified ground-truth is quite limited. To address the issue of sparsity, a novel neural network model for hashtag disambiguation is proposed. (3) The data pruning method, in which our model is applied to select reliable self-labeled data, is capable of improving the performance of irony detection.

The rest of this paper is organized as follows. Section 2 describes how we construct a dataset for disambiguating false-alarm hashtag usages based on Tweets. In Section 3, our model for hashtag disambiguation is proposed. Experimental results of hashtag disambiguation are shown in Section 4. In addition, we apply our method to prune training data for irony detection. The results are shown in Section 5. Section 6 concludes this paper.

2 Dataset

The tweets with indication hashtags such as #irony are usually collected as a dataset in previous works on irony detection. As pointed out in Section 1, the hashtags are treated as ground-truth for training and testing. To investigate the issue of false-alarm

Hashtag	False-Alarm	Irony	Total
#not	196	346	542
#sarcasm	46	449	495
#irony	34	288	322
Total	276	1,083	1,359

Table 1: Statistics of the Ground-Truth Data.

self-labeled tweets, the tweets with human verification are indispensable. In this study, we build the ground-truth based on the dataset released for SemEval 2018 Task 3,[1] which is targeted for fine-grained irony detection (Hee et al., 2018).

In the SemEval dataset, the tweets with one of the three indication hashtags #not, #sarcasm, and #irony, are collected and human-annotated as one of four types: verbal irony by means of a polarity contrast, other verbal irony, situational irony, and non-ironic. In other words, the false-alarm tweets, i.e., the non-ironic tweets with indication hashtags, are distinguished from the real ironic tweets in this dataset. However, the hashtag itself has been removed in the SemEval dataset. For example, the original tweet (S1) has been modified to (S4), where the hashtag #not disappears. As a result, the hashtag information, the position and the word form of the hashtag (i.e., not, irony, or sarcasm), is missing from the SemEval dataset.

(S4) *@Anonymous doing a great job... What do I pay my extortionate council taxes for? #Disgrace #OngoingProblem http://t.co/FQZUUwKSoN*

For hashtag disambiguation, the information of the hashtag in each tweet is mandatory. Thus, we recover the original tweets by using Twitter search. As shown in Table 1, a total of 1,359 tweets with hashtags information are adopted as the ground-truth. Note that more than 20% of self-labeled data are false-alarm, and this can be an issue when they are adopted as training or test data. For performing the experiment of irony detection in Section 5, we reserve the other 1,072 tweets in the SemEval dataset that are annotated as real ironic as the test data.

In addition to the issue of hashtag disambiguation, the irony tweets without an indication hashtag, which are regarded as non-irony instances in previous work, are another kind of misleading data for irony detection. Fortunately, the occurrence of such "false-negative" instances is insignificant due

---

[1] https://competitions.codalab.org/competitions/17468

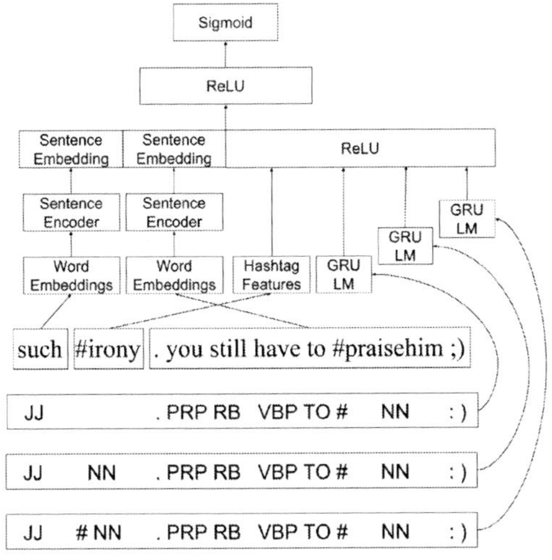

Figure 1: Overview of Our Model for Hashtag Disambiguation.

to the relatively low occurrence of irony (Davidov et al., 2010).

3 Disambiguation of Hashtags

Figure 1 shows our model for distinguishing the real ironic tweets from the false-alarm ones. Given an instance with the hashtag #irony is given, the preceding and the following word sequences of the hashtag are encoded by separate sub-networks, and both embeddings are concatenated with the handcrafted features and the probabilities of three kinds of part-of-speech (POS) tag sequences. Finally, the sigmoid activation function decides whether the instance is real ironic or false-alarm. The details of each component will be presented in the rest of this section.

Word Sequences: The word sequences of the context preceding and following the targeting hashtag are separately encoded by neural network sentence encoders. The Penn Treebank Tokenizer provided by NLTK (Bird et al., 2009) is used for tokenization. As a result, each of the left and the right word sequences is encoded as a embedding with a length of 50.

We experiments with convolution neural network (CNN) (Kim, 2014), gated recurrent unit (GRU) (Cho et al., 2014), and attentive-GRU for sentence encoding. CNN for sentence classification has been shown effective in NLP applications such as sentiment analysis (Kim, 2014). Classifiers based on recurrent neural network (RNN)

have also been applied to NLP, especially for sequential modeling. For irony detection, one of the state-of-the-art models is based on the attentive RNN (Huang et al., 2017). The first layer of the CNN, the GRU, and the attenive-GRU model is the 300-dimensional word embedding that is initialized by using the vectors pre-trained on Google News dataset.[2]

Handcrafted Features: We add the handcrafted features of the tweet in the one-hot representation. The features taken into account are listed as follows. (1) Lengths of the tweet in words and in characters. (2) Type of the target hashtag (i.e. #not, #sarcasm, or #irony). (3) Number of all hashtags in the tweet. (4) Whether the targeting hashtag is the first token in the tweet. (5) Whether the targeting hashtag is the last token in the tweet. (6) Whether the targeting hashtag is the first hashtag in the tweet since a tweet may contain more than one hashtag. (7) Whether the targeting hashtag is the last hashtag in the tweet. (8) Position of the targeting hashtag in terms of tokens. If the targeting hashtag is the ith token of the tweet with $|w|$ tokens, and this feature is $\frac{i}{|w|}$. (9) Position of the targeting hashtag in all hashtags in the tweet. It is computed as $\frac{j}{|h|}$ where the targeting hashtag is the jth hashtag in the tweet that contains $|h|$ hashtags.

Language Modeling of POS Sequences: As mentioned in Section 1, a kind of false-alarm hashtag usages is the case that the hashtag also functions as a content word. In this paper, we attempt to measure the grammatical completeness of the tweet with and without the hashtag. Therefore, language model on the level of POS tagging is used. As shown in Figure 1, POS tagging is performed on three versions of the tweet, and based on that three probabilities are measured and taken into account: 1) $p_{\bar{h}}$: the tweet with the whole hashtag removed. 2) $p_{\bar{s}}$: the tweet with the hash symbol # removed only. 3) p_t: the original tweet. Our idea is that a tweet will be more grammatical complete with only the hash symbol removed if the hashtag is also a content word. On the other hand, the tweet will be more grammatical complete with the whole hashtag removed since the hashtag is a metadata.

To measure the probability of the POS tag sequence, we integrate a neural network-based language model of POS sequence into our model. RNN-based language models are reportedly capa-

---

[2] https://code.google.com/archive/p/word2vec/

ble of modeling the longer dependencies among the sequential tokens (Mikolov et al., 2011). Two millions of English tweets that are entirely different from those in the training and test data described in Section 2 are collected and tagged with POS tags. We train a GRU language model on the level of POS tags. In this work, all the POS tagging is performed with the Stanford CoreNLP toolkit (Manning et al., 2014).

4   Experiments

We compare our model with popular neural network-based sentence classifiers including CNN, GRU, and attentive GRU. We also train a logistic regression (LR) classifier with the hand-crafted features introduced in Section 3. For the imbalance data, we assign class-weights inversely proportional to class frequencies. Five-fold cross-validation is performed. Early-stop is employed with a patience of 5 epoches. In each fold, we further keep 10% of training data for tuning the model. The hidden dimension is 50, the batch size is 32, and the Adam optimizer is employed (Kingma and Ba, 2014).

Table 2 shows the experimental results reported in Precision (P), Recall (R), and F-score (F). Our goal is to select the real ironic tweets for training the irony detection model. Thus, the real ironic tweets are regarded as positive, and the false-alarm ones are negative. We apply t-test for significance testing. The vanilla GRU and attentive GRU are slightly superior to the logistic regression model. The CNN model performs the worst in this task because it suffers from over-fitting problem. We explored a number of layouts and hyper-parameters for the CNN model, and consistent results are observed.

Our method is evaluated with either CNN, GRU, or attentive GRU for encoding the context preceding and following the targeting hashtag. By integrating various kinds of information, our method outperforms all baseline models no matter which encoder is used. The best model is the one integrating the attentive GRU encoder, which is significantly superior to all baseline models ($p < 0.05$), achieves an F-score of 88.49%,

To confirm the effectiveness of the language modeling of POS sequence, we also try to exclude the GRU language model from our best model. Experimental results show that the addition of language model significantly improves the perfor-

Model	Encoder	P	R	F
LR	N/A	91.43%	75.81%	82.89%
CNN	N/A	89.16%	56.97%	69.52%
GRU	N/A	90.75%	77.01%	83.32%
Att.GRU	N/A	87.97%	79.69%	83.62%
Our Method	CNN	90.35%	83.84%	86.97%
Our Method	GRU	90.90%	78.39%	84.18%
Our Method	Att.GRU	90.86%	86.24%	88.49%
w/o LM	Att.GRU	88.17%	80.52%	84.17%

Table 2: Results of Hashtag Disambiguation.

mance ($p < 0.05$). As shown in the last row of Table 2, the F-score is dropped to 84.17%.

From the data, we observe that the instances whose $p_{\bar{s}} \gg p_{\bar{h}}$ usually contain a indication hashtag function as a content word, and vice versa. For instances, (S5) and (S6) show the instances with the highest and the lowest $\frac{p_{\bar{s}}}{p_{\bar{h}}}$, respectively.

(S5) *when your #sarcasm is so advanced people actually think you are #stupid ..*

(S6) *#mtvstars justin bieber #net #not #fast*

5   Irony Detection

We employ our model to prune self-labeled data for irony detection. As prior work did, we collect a set of tweets that contain indication hashtags as (pseudo) positive instances and also collect a set of tweets that do not contain indication hashtags as negative instances. For each positive instance, our model is performed to predict whether it is a real ironic tweet or false-alarm ones, and the false-alarm ones are discarded.

After pruning, a set of 14,055 tweets containing indication hashtags have been reduced to 4,617 reliable positive instances according to our model. We add an equal amount of negative instances randomly selected from the collection of the tweets that do not contain indication hashtags. As a result, the prior- and the post-pruning training data, in the sizes of 28,110 and 9,234, respectively, are prepared for experiments. The dataflow of the training data pruning is shown in Figure 2.

For evaluating the effectiveness of our pruning method, we implement a state-of-the-art irony detector (Huang et al., 2017), which is based on attentive-RNN classifier, and train it on the prior- and the post-pruned training data.

The test data is made by the procedure as follows. The positive instances in the test data are taken from the 1,072 human-verified ironic tweets

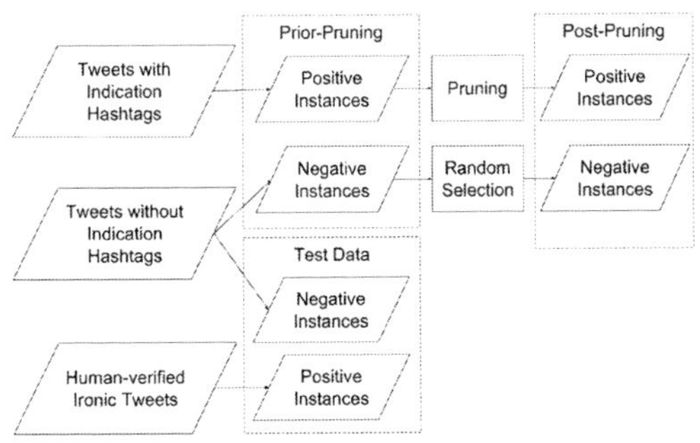

Figure 2: Dataflow of the Training Data Pruning for Irony Detection.

Training Data	Size	P	R	F
Prior-Pruning	28,110	79.04%	84.05%	81.46%
Post-Pruning	9,234	80.83%	85.35%	83.03%
Human Verified	2,166	86.35%	66.70%	75.26%

Table 3: Performance of Irony Detection.

that are reserved for irony detection as mentioned in Section 2. The negative instances in the test data are obtained from the tweets that do not contain indication hashtags. Note that the negative instances in the test data are isolated from those in the training data. Experimental results confirm the benefit of pruning. As shown in Table 3, the irony detection model trained on the less, but cleaner data significantly outperforms the model that is trained on all data ($p < 0.05$).

We compare our pruning method with an alternative approach that trains the irony detector on the human-verified data directly. Under this circumstances, the 1,083 ironic instances for training our hashtag disambiguation model are currently mixed with an equal amount of randomly sampled negative instances, and employed to train the irony detector. As shown in the last row of Table 3, the irony detector trained on the small data does not compete with the models that are trained on larger amount of self-labeled data. In other words, our data pruning strategy forms a semi-supervised learning that benefits from both self-labeled data and human annotation. Note that this task and the dataset are different from those of the official evaluation of SemEval 2018 Task 3, so the experimental results cannot be directly compared.

The calibrated confidence output by the sigmoid layer of our hashtag disambiguation model can be regarded as a measurement of the reliability of an instance (Niculescu-Mizil and Caruana, 2005; Guo et al., 2017). Thus, we can sort

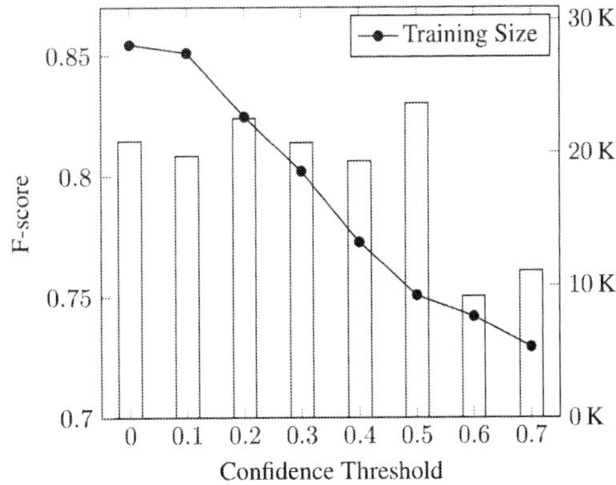

Figure 3: Performance of Irony Detection with Different Threshold Values for Data Pruning.

all self-labeled data by their calibrated confidence and control the size of training set by adjusting the threshold. The higher the threshold value is set, the less the training instances remain. Figure 3 shows the performances of the irony detector trained on the data filtered with different threshold values. For each threshold value, the bullet symbol (•) indicates the size of training data, and the bar indicates the F-score achieved by the irony detector trained on those data. The best result achieved by the irony detector trained on the 9,234 data filtered by our model with the default threshold value (0.5). This confirms that our model is able to select useful training instances in a strict manner.

6 Conclusion

Self-labeled data is an accessible and economical resource for a variety of learning-based applications. However, directly using the labels made by the crowd as ground-truth for training and testing may lead to inaccurate performance due to the reliability issue. This paper addresses this issue in the case of irony detection by proposing a model to remove two kinds of false-alarm tweets from the training data. Experimental results confirm that the irony detection model benefits from the less, but cleaner training data. Our approach can be applied to other topics that rely on self-labeled data.

Acknowledgements

This research was partially supported by Ministry of Science and Technology, Taiwan, under grants MOST-105-2221-E-002-154-MY3, MOST-106-2923-E-002-012-MY3 and MOST-107-2634-F-002-011-.

References

Steven Bird, Edward Loper, and Ewan Klein. 2009. *Natural Language Processing with Python*. O'Reilly Media Inc.

Kyunghyun Cho, Bart van Merrienboer, Çaglar Gülçehre, Fethi Bougares, Holger Schwenk, and Yoshua Bengio. 2014. Learning phrase representations using RNN encoder-decoder for statistical machine translation. *CoRR*, abs/1406.1078.

Keith Cortis, André Freitas, Tobias Daudert, Manuela Huerlimann, Manel Zarrouk, Siegfried Handschuh, and Brian Davis. 2017. Semeval-2017 task 5: Fine-grained sentiment analysis on financial microblogs and news. In *Proceedings of the 11th International Workshop on Semantic Evaluation (SemEval-2017)*, pages 519–535, Vancouver, Canada. Association for Computational Linguistics.

Dmitry Davidov, Oren Tsur, and Ari Rappoport. 2010. Semi-supervised recognition of sarcasm in twitter and amazon. In *Proceedings of the Fourteenth Conference on Computational Natural Language Learning*, pages 107–116, Uppsala, Sweden. Association for Computational Linguistics.

Andrea Esuli and Fabrizio Sebastiani. 2013. Improving text classification accuracy by training label cleaning. *ACM Trans. Inf. Syst.*, 31(4):19:1–19:28.

Fumiyo Fukumoto and Yoshimi Suzuki. 2004. Correcting category errors in text classification. In *Proceedings of Coling 2004*, pages 868–874, Geneva, Switzerland. COLING.

Debanjan Ghosh, Weiwei Guo, and Smaranda Muresan. 2015. Sarcastic or not: Word embeddings to predict the literal or sarcastic meaning of words. In *Proceedings of the 2015 Conference on Empirical Methods in Natural Language Processing*, pages 1003–1012, Lisbon, Portugal. Association for Computational Linguistics.

Chuan Guo, Geoff Pleiss, Yu Sun, and Kilian Q. Weinberger. 2017. On calibration of modern neural networks. In *Proceedings of the 34th International Conference on Machine Learning*, volume 70 of *Proceedings of Machine Learning Research*, pages 1321–1330, International Convention Centre, Sydney, Australia. PMLR.

Cynthia Van Hee, Els Lefever, and Vronique Hoste. 2018. Semeval-2018 task 3: Irony detection in english tweets. In *Proceedings of the 12th International Workshop on Semantic Evaluation (SemEval-2018)*, New Orleans, LA, USA.

Yu-Hsiang Huang, Hen-Hsen Huang, and Hsin-Hsi Chen. 2017. Irony detection with attentive recurrent neural networks. In *European Conference on Information Retrieval*, pages 534–540. Springer.

Yoon Kim. 2014. Convolutional neural networks for sentence classification. In *Proceedings of the 2014 Conference on Empirical Methods in Natural Language Processing (EMNLP)*, pages 1746–1751, Doha, Qatar. Association for Computational Linguistics.

Diederik P. Kingma and Jimmy Ba. 2014. Adam: A method for stochastic optimization. *CoRR*, abs/1412.6980.

Hassan H. Malik and Vikas S. Bhardwaj. 2011. Automatic training data cleaning for text classification. In *Proceedings of the 2011 IEEE 11th International Conference on Data Mining Workshops*, ICDMW '11, pages 442–449, Washington, DC, USA. IEEE Computer Society.

Christopher D. Manning, Mihai Surdeanu, John Bauer, Jenny Finkel, Steven J. Bethard, and David Mc-Closky. 2014. The Stanford CoreNLP natural language processing toolkit. In *Association for Computational Linguistics (ACL) System Demonstrations*, pages 55–60.

Tomas Mikolov, Stefan Kombrink, Anoop Deoras, Lukar Burget, and Jan Cernocky. 2011. Rnnlm-recurrent neural network language modeling toolkit. In *Proc. of the 2011 ASRU Workshop*, pages 196–201.

Saif Mohammad, Svetlana Kiritchenko, Parinaz Sobhani, Xiaodan Zhu, and Colin Cherry. 2016. Semeval-2016 task 6: Detecting stance in tweets. In *Proceedings of the 10th International Workshop on Semantic Evaluation (SemEval-2016)*, pages 31–41, San Diego, California. Association for Computational Linguistics.

Alexandru Niculescu-Mizil and Rich Caruana. 2005. Predicting good probabilities with supervised learning. In *Proceedings of the 22Nd International Conference on Machine Learning*, ICML '05, pages 625–632, New York, NY, USA. ACM.

Lotem Peled and Roi Reichart. 2017. Sarcasm sign: Interpreting sarcasm with sentiment based monolingual machine translation. In *Proceedings of the 55th Annual Meeting of the Association for Computational Linguistics (Volume 1: Long Papers)*, pages 1690–1700, Vancouver, Canada. Association for Computational Linguistics.

Ashequl Qadir and Ellen Riloff. 2014. Learning emotion indicators from tweets: Hashtags, hashtag patterns, and phrases. In *Proceedings of the 2014 Conference on Empirical Methods in Natural Language Processing (EMNLP)*, pages 1203–1209, Doha, Qatar. Association for Computational Linguistics.

Parinaz Sobhani, Diana Inkpen, and Xiaodan Zhu. 2017. A dataset for multi-target stance detection. In *Proceedings of the 15th Conference of the European Chapter of the Association for Computational Linguistics: Volume 2, Short Papers*, pages 551–557, Valencia, Spain. Association for Computational Linguistics.

Emilio Sulis, Delia Irazú Hernández Farías, Paolo
Rosso, Viviana Patti, and Giancarlo Ruffo. 2016.
Figurative messages and affect in twitter. *Know.-
Based Syst.*, 108(C):132–143.

Cynthia Van Hee, Els Lefever, and Veronique Hoste.
2016a. Exploring the realization of irony in twit-
ter data. In *Proceedings of the Tenth International
Conference on Language Resources and Evaluation
(LREC '16)*, pages 1795–1799. European Language
Resources Association (ELRA).

Cynthia Van Hee, Els Lefever, and Veronique Hoste.
2016b. Monday mornings are my fave :) #not exploring the automatic recognition of irony in english tweets. In *Proceedings of COLING 2016,
the 26th International Conference on Computational
Linguistics: Technical Papers*, pages 2730–2739,
Osaka, Japan. The COLING 2016 Organizing Committee.

Cross-Target Stance Classification with Self-Attention Networks

Chang Xu, Cécile Paris, Surya Nepal, and **Ross Sparks**
CSIRO Data61, Marsfield, NSW, Australia
{Chang.Xu, Cecile.Paris, Surya.Nepal, Ross.Sparks}@data61.csiro.au

Abstract

In stance classification, the target on which the stance is made defines the boundary of the task, and a classifier is usually trained for prediction on the same target. In this work, we explore the potential for generalizing classifiers between *different* targets, and propose a neural model that can apply what has been learned from a source target to a destination target. We show that our model can find useful information shared between relevant targets which improves generalization in certain scenarios.

1 Introduction

Stance classification is the task of automatically identifying users' positions about a specific target from text (Mohammad et al., 2017). Table 1 shows an example of this task, where the stance of the sentence is recognized as favorable on the target *climate change is concern*. Traditionally, this task is approached by learning a target-specific classifier that is trained for prediction on the same target of interest (Hasan and Ng, 2013; Mohammad et al., 2016; Ebrahimi et al., 2016). This implies that a new classifier has to be built from scratch on a well-prepared set of ground-truth data whenever predictions are needed for an unseen target.

An alternative to this approach is to conduct a *cross-target* classification, where the classifier is adapted from different but *related* targets (Augenstein et al., 2016), which allows benefiting from the knowledge of existing targets. For example, in our project we are interested in online users' stances on the approvals of particular mining projects in the country. It might be useful to start with a classifier that is adapted from a related target such as *climate change is concern* (presumably available and annotated), as in both cases

Sentence: We need to protect our islands and stop the destruction of coral reef.	
Target: Climate Change is Concern	Stance: Favor

Table 1: An example of stance classification task.

users could discuss the impacts from the targets to some common issues, such as the environment or communities.

Cross-target stance classification is a more challenging task simply because the language models may not be compatible between different targets. However, for some targets that can be recognized as being related to the same and more general domains, it could be possible to generalize through certain aspects of the domains that reflect users' major concerns. For example, from the following sentence, whose stance is against the approval of a mining project, *"Environmentalists warn the $16 billion coal facility will damage the Great Barrier Reef"*, it can be seen that both this sentence and the one in Table 1 mention the same aspect "reef destruction/damage", which is closely related to the "environment" domain.

In this paper, we focus on cross-target stance classification and explore the limits of generalizing models between different but *domain-related* targets[1]. The basic idea is to learn a set of domain-specific aspects from a source target, and then apply them to prediction on a destination target. To this end, we propose CrossNet, a novel neural model that implements the above idea based on the self-attention mechanism. Our preliminary analysis shows that the proposed model can find useful domain-specific information from a stance-bearing sentence and that the classification performance is improved in certain domains.

---

[1] In this work, the source target is chosen based on common sense. Exploring more sophisticated source target selection methods will be our future work.

Proceedings of the 56th Annual Meeting of the Association for Computational Linguistics (Short Papers), pages 778–783
Melbourne, Australia, July 15 - 20, 2018. ©2018 Association for Computational Linguistics

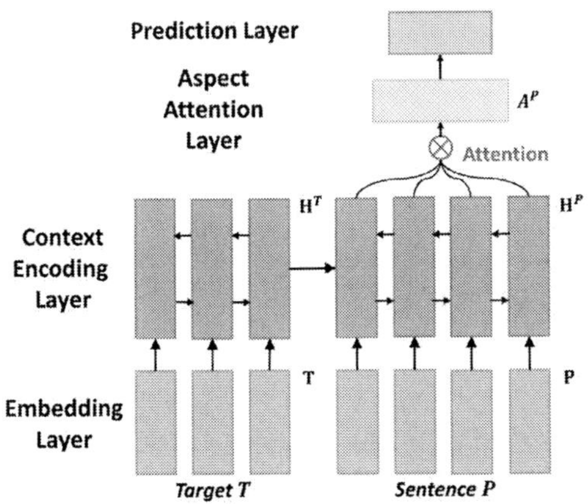

Figure 1: The Architecture of CrossNet.

2 Model

In this section, we introduce the proposed model, CrossNet, for cross-target stance classification. Figure 1 shows the architecture of CrossNet. It consists of four layers from the Embedding Layer (bottom) to the Prediction Layer (top). It works by taking a stance-bearing sentence and a target as input and yielding the predicted stance label as output. In the following, we present the implementation of each layer in CrossNet.

2.1 Embedding Layer

There are two inputs in CrossNet: a stance-bearing sentence P and a descriptive target T (e.g., *climate change is concern* in Table 1). We use word embeddings (Mikolov et al., 2013) to represent each word in the input as a dense vector. The output of this layer are two sequences of vectors $P = \{p_1, ..., p_{|P|}\}$ and $T = \{t_1, ..., t_{|T|}\}$, where p, t are word vectors.

2.2 Context Encoding Layer

In this layer, we encode the contextual information in the input sentence and target. We use a bi-directional Long Short-Term Memory Network (BiLSTM) (Hochreiter and Schmidhuber, 1997) to capture the left and right contexts of each word in the input. Moreover, to account for the impact of the target on stance inference, we borrow the idea of conditional encoding (Augenstein et al., 2016) to model the dependency of the sentence on the target. Formally, we first use a BiLSTM$_T$ to encode the target:

$$[\overrightarrow{h}_i^T \; \overrightarrow{c}_i^T] = \overrightarrow{\text{LSTM}}_T(t_i, \overrightarrow{h}_{i-1}^T, \overrightarrow{c}_{i-1}^T)$$
$$[\overleftarrow{h}_i^T \; \overleftarrow{c}_i^T] = \overleftarrow{\text{LSTM}}_T(t_i, \overleftarrow{h}_{i+1}^T, \overleftarrow{c}_{i+1}^T) \quad (1)$$

where $h \in \mathbb{R}^h$ and $c \in \mathbb{R}^h$ are the hidden state and cell state of LSTM. The symbol $\rightarrow(\leftarrow)$ indicates the forward (backward) pass. t_i is the input word vector at time step i.

Then, we learn a conditional encoding of the sentence P, by initializing BiLSTM$_P$ (a different BiLSTM) with the final states of BiLSTM$_T$:

$$[\overrightarrow{h}_1^P \; \overrightarrow{c}_1^P] = \overrightarrow{\text{LSTM}}_P(p_1, \overrightarrow{h}_{|T|}^T, \overrightarrow{c}_{|T|}^T)$$
$$[\overleftarrow{h}_{|P|}^P \; \overleftarrow{c}_{|P|}^P] = \overleftarrow{\text{LSTM}}_P(p_{|P|}, \overleftarrow{h}_1^T, \overleftarrow{c}_1^T) \quad (2)$$

It can be seen that the initialization is done by aligning the forward (backward) pass of the two BiLSTMs. The output is a contextually-encoded sequence, $H^P = \{h_1^P, ..., h_{|P|}^P\}$, where $h = [\overrightarrow{h}; \overleftarrow{h}] \in \mathbb{R}^{2h}$ with $[;]$ as the vector concatenation operation.

2.3 Aspect Attention Layer

In this layer, we implement the idea of discovering domain-specific aspects for cross-target stance inference. In particular, the key observation we make is that the domain aspects that reflect users' major concerns are usually the core of understanding their stances, and could be mentioned by multiple users in a discussion. For example, we find that many users in our corpus mention the aspect "reef" to express their concerns about the impact of a mining project on the Great Barrier Reef. Based on this observation, the perception of the domain aspects can be boiled down to finding the sentence parts that not only carry the core idea of a stance-bearing sentence but also tend to be recurring in the corpus.

First, to capture the recurrences of the domain aspects, a simple way is to make every input sentence be consumed by this layer (see Figure 1), so that the layer parameters are shared across the corpus for being stimulated by all appearances of the domain aspects.

Then, we utilize self-attention to signal the core parts of a stance-bearing sentence. Self-attention is an attention mechanism for selecting specific parts of a sequence by relating its elements at different positions (Vaswani et al., 2017; Cheng et al., 2016). In our case, the self-attention process is based on the assumption that the core parts of a sentence are those that are compatible with the semantics of the entire sentence. To this end, we introduce a compatibility function to score the semantic compatibility between the encoded sequence $\boldsymbol{H}^P$ and each of its hidden states $\boldsymbol{h}^P$:

$$c_i = \boldsymbol{w}_2^\top \sigma(\boldsymbol{W}_1 \boldsymbol{h}_i^P + \boldsymbol{b}_1) + b_2 \quad (3)$$

where $\boldsymbol{W}_1 \in \mathbb{R}^{d \times 2h}$, $\boldsymbol{w}_2 \in \mathbb{R}^d$, $\boldsymbol{b}_1 \in \mathbb{R}^d$, and $b_2 \in \mathbb{R}$ are trainable parameters, and σ is the activation function. Note that all the above parameters are shared by every hidden state in $\boldsymbol{H}^P$. Next, we compute the attention weight a_i for each $\boldsymbol{h}_i^P$ based on its compatibility score via softmax operation:

$$a_i = \frac{\exp(c_i)}{\sum_{j=1}^{|P|} \exp(c_j)} \quad (4)$$

Finally, we can obtain the domain aspect encoded representation based on the attention weights:

$$\boldsymbol{A}^P = \sum_{i=1}^{|P|} a_i \boldsymbol{h}_i^P \quad (5)$$

where $\boldsymbol{A}^P \in \mathbb{R}^{2h}$ is the domain aspect encoding for sentence P and also the output of this layer.

2.4 Prediction Layer

We predict the stance label of the sentence based on its domain aspect encoding:

$$\hat{\boldsymbol{y}} = \mathrm{softmax}(\mathrm{MLP}(\boldsymbol{A}^P)) \quad (6)$$

where we use a multilayer perceptron (MLP) to consume the domain aspect encoding $\boldsymbol{A}^P$ and apply the softmax to get the predicted probability for each of the C classes, $\hat{\boldsymbol{y}} = \{y_1, ..., y_C\}$.

2.5 Model Training

For model training, we use multi-class cross-entropy loss,

$$\mathcal{J}(\theta) = - \sum_i^N \sum_j^C y_j^{(i)} \log \hat{y}_j^{(i)} + \lambda \|\Theta\| \quad (7)$$

where N is the size of training set. y is the ground-truth label indicator for each class, and $\hat{y}$ is the predicted probability. λ is the coefficient for L_2-regularization. Θ denotes the set of all trainable parameters in our model.

3 Experiments

This section reports the results of quantitative and qualitative evaluations of the proposed model.

Target	%Favor	%Against	%Neither	#Total
CC	59.4	4.6	36.0	564
FM	28.2	53.8	18.0	949
HC	16.6	57.4	26.0	984
LA	17.9	58.3	23.8	933
DT	20.9	42.3	36.8	707

Table 2: SemEval-2016 Task 6 Tweet Stance Detection dataset used in our evaluation.

3.1 Datasets

SemEval-2016: the first dataset is from SemEval-2016 Task 6 on Twitter stance detection, which contains stance-bearing tweets on different targets. We use the following five targets for our experiments: *Climate Change is Concern* (CC), *Feminist Movement* (FM), *Hillary Clinton* (HC), *Legalization of Abortion* (LA), and *Donald Trump* (DT). The class labels are *favor*, *against*, and *neither*, and their distributions are shown in Table 2.

Tweets on an Australian mining project (AM): the second is our collection of tweets on a mining project in Australia obtained using Twitter API. It includes 220,067 tweets posted from January 2016 to June 2017 that contain the project name in the text. We remove all URL-only tweets and duplicate tweets, and obtain a set of 40,852 (unlabeled) tweets. Due to the lack of annotation, this dataset is only used for our qualitative evaluation.

To align with our scenario, the above targets can be categorized into three different domains: Women's Rights (FM, LA), American Politics (HC, DT), and Environments (CC, AM).

3.2 Metric

We use *F1-score* to measure the classification performance. Due to the imbalanced class distributions of the SemEval dataset, we compute both micro-averaged (large classes dominate) and macro-averaged (small classes dominate) F1-scores (Manning et al., 2008), and use their average as the metric, i.e., $F = \frac{1}{2}(F_{\mathrm{micro}} + F_{\mathrm{macro}})$.

To evaluate the effectiveness of target adaptation, we use the metric *transfer ratio* (Glorot et al., 2011) to compare the cross-target and in-target performance of a model: $\mathcal{Q} = \frac{F(S,D)}{F_b(D,D)}$, where $F(S, D)$ is the cross-target F1-score of a model trained on the source target S and tested on the destination target D, and $F_b(D, D)$ is the in-target F1-score of a *baseline* model trained and tested on the same target D, which serves as the performance calibration for target adaptation.

3.3 Training setup

The word embeddings are initialized with the pre-trained 200d GloVe word vectors on the 27B Twitter corpus (Pennington et al., 2014), and fixed during training. The model is trained (90%) and validated (10%) on a source target, and tested on a destination target. The following model settings are selected based on a small grid search on the validation set: the LSTM hidden size of 60, the MLP layer size of 60, and dropout 0.1. The $L2$-regularization coefficient λ in the loss is 0.01. ADAM (Kingma and Ba, 2014) is used as the optimizer, with a learning rate of 10^{-3}. Stratified 10-fold cross-validation is conducted to produce averaged results.

3.4 Classification Performance

This section reports the results of our model and two baseline approaches on cross-target stance classification.

BiLSTM: this is a base model for our task. It has two BiLSTMs for encoding the sentence and target separately. Then, the concatenation of the resulting encodings is fed into the final Prediction Layer to generate predicted stance labels. In our evaluation, this model is treated as the baseline model for deriving the in-target performance calibration $F_b(D, D)$.

MITRE (Augenstein et al., 2016): this is the best system in SemEval-2016 Task 6. It utilizes the conditional encoding to learn a target-dependent representation for the input sentence. The conditional encoding is realized in the same way as the Context Encoding Layer does in our model, namely by using the hidden states of the target-encoding BiLSTM to initialize the sentence-encoding BiLSTM.

Table 3 shows the results (in-target and cross-target) on the two domains: Women's Rights and American Politics. First, it is observed that MITRE outperforms BiLSTM over all target configurations, suggesting that, compared to simple concatenation, the conditional encoding of the target information could be more helpful to capture the dependency of the sentence on the target.

Second, our model is shown to achieve better results than the two baselines in almost all cases (only slightly worse than MITRE on LA under the in-target setting, and the difference is not statistically significant), which implies that the aspect attention mechanism adopted in our model could benefit target-level generalization while it does not hurt the in-target performance. Moreover, by comparing the performance of our model under different target configurations, we see that the improvements brought by our model are more significant on the cross-target task than they are on the in-target task, with an average improvement of 6.6% (cross-target) vs. 3.0% (in-target) over MITRE in F1-score, which demonstrates a greater advantage of our model in the cross-target task.

Finally, according to the transfer ratio results, the general drop from the in-target to cross-target performance (26% averaged over all cases) could imply that while the target-independent information (i.e., the domain-specific aspects) is shown to benefit generalization, it could be important to also consider the information that is specific to the destination target for model building (which has not yet been explored in this work).

3.5 Visualization of Attention

To show that our model can select sentence parts that are related to domain aspects, we visualize the self-attention results on some tweet examples that are correctly classified by our model in Table 4.

We can see that the most highlighted parts in each example are relevant to the respective domain. For example, "feminist", "rights", and "equality" are commonly used when talking about women's rights, and "president" and "dreams" of-

Domain	Target	BiLSTM	MITRE	CrossNet
In-target performance (F1-score)				
Women's	FM	51.4(2.6)*	53.7(3.9)	55.9(4.6)
Rights	LA	59.4(6.4)	61.9(6.3)	61.8(4.7)
American	HC	55.5(4.7)*	56.0(3.1)*	60.0(3.3)
Politics	DT	57.9(6.0)*	59.6(5.8)*	60.2(5.1)
Cross-target performance (F1-score)				
Women's	FM→LA	40.1(2.3)*	40.3(2.2)*	44.2(1.3)
Rights	LA→FM	37.9(2.9)*	39.2(1.5)*	43.1(1.3)
American	HC→DT	43.3(2.4)*	44.2(3.2)	46.1(3.7)
Politics	DT→HC	40.1(2.6)	40.8(2.2)	41.8(3.2)
Transfer ratio				
Women's	FM→LA	0.67	0.67	0.74
Rights	LA→FM	0.74	0.76	0.83
American	HC→DT	0.75	0.76	0.79
Politics	DT→HC	0.72	0.73	0.75

(Standard deviation in parentheses)

* Improvements over baselines at $p < .05$ with paired t-test

Table 3: Classification performance of our model and other baselines on 4 targets: *Feminist Movement* (FM), *Hillary Clinton* (HC), *Legalization of Abortion* (LA), and *Donald Trump* (DT).

ID	Target	Tweet
1	FM→LA	Abortion has nothing to do with feminism. Its about the BABYS body, not yours. (A)
2	LA→FM	All humans, male and female, should have equal political, economic and social rights. Equality. (F)
3	HC→DT	Trumps presidential dreams r about as real as KimJonguns unicorns. (A)
4	DT→HC	Maybe a woman should be President. (F)
5	CC→AM	[N] still will destroy the reef. It is criminal that QLD federal govts are promoting it. (A)
6	CC→AM	[N], who are trying to change our laws, 'forgot' to tell us about their CEO's environmental disaster! (A)

Table 4: The heatmap of the attention weights assigned by the Aspect Attention Layer to the tweets with stance labels *favor* (F) and *against* (A). "[N]" denotes the mining project's name of interest.

Domain	Sample
Women's Rights (FM↔LA)	feminist, victim, fight, equality, children, women, mom, great, love, fight, beautiful, girl, housewife, wrong, fear, safe, good, life, crime
American Politics (HC↔DT)	american, winning, welfare, obama, society, wall, crazy, money, republican, nation, great, vote, amazing, stupid, justice, government, future
Environments (CC→AM)	environment, reverse, needs, bad, weather, solution, important, rain, earth, generation, humans, power, heat, future, strategy, together, idea

Table 5: Samples of the learned domain aspects.

ten appear in text about politics. It is also interesting to note that words that are specific to the destination target may not be captured by the model learned from the source target, such as "abortion" in sentence 1 and "trumps" in sentence 3. This makes sense because those words are rare in the source target corpus and thus not well noticed by the model.

Finally, for our project, we can see from the last two sentences that the model learned from *climate change is concern* is able to concentrate on words that are central to understanding the authors' stances on the approval of the mining project, such as "reef", "destroy", "environmental", and "disaster". Overall, the above visualization demonstrates that our model could benefit stance inference across related targets through capturing domain-specific information.

3.6 Learned Domain-Specific Aspects

Finally, it is also possible to show the learned domain aspects by extracting all sentence parts in a corpus that are highly attended by our model. Table 5 presents a number of samples from the intersections between the sets of highly-attended words on the respective targets in the three domains. Again, we see that these highly-attended words are specific to the respective domains. We

also notice that besides the domain-aspect words, our model can find words that carry sentiments as well, such as "great", "crazy", and "beautiful", which contribute to stance prediction.

4 Conclusion and Future Work

In this work, we study cross-target stance classification and propose a novel self-attention neural model that can extract target-independent information for model generalization. Experimental results show that the proposed model can perceive high-level domain-specific information in a sentence and achieves superior results over a number of baselines in certain domains. In the future, there are several ways of extending our model.

First, selecting the effective source targets to generalize from is crucial for achieving satisfying results on the destination targets. One possibility could be to learn certain correlations between target closeness and generalization performance, which could further be used for guiding the target selection process. Second, our current model for identifying users' stances on mining projects only generalizes from one source target (i.e., *Climate Change is Concern*). However, a mining project in general could affect other aspects of our society such as community and economics. It could be useful to also consider other related sources for knowledge transfer. Finally, it would be interesting to evaluate our model in a multilingual scenario (Taulé et al., 2017), in order to examine its generalization ability (whether it can attend to useful domain-specific information in a new language) and multilingual scope.

Acknowledgments

We thank all anonymous reviewers for their valuable comments. We would also like to thank Keith Vander Linden for his helpful comments on drafts of this paper.

References

Isabelle Augenstein, Tim Rocktäschel, Andreas Vlachos, and Kalina Bontcheva. 2016. Stance detection with bidirectional conditional encoding. In *Proceedings of the Conference on Empirical Methods in Natural Language Processing (EMNLP)*. pages 876–885.

Jianpeng Cheng, Li Dong, and Mirella Lapata. 2016. Long short-term memory-networks for machine reading. In *Proceedings of the Conference on Empirical Methods in Natural Language Processing (EMNLP)*. pages 551–561.

Javid Ebrahimi, Dejing Dou, and Daniel Lowd. 2016. Weakly supervised tweet stance classification by relational bootstrapping. In *Proceedings of the 2016 Conference on Empirical Methods in Natural Language Processing*. pages 1012–1017.

Xavier Glorot, Antoine Bordes, and Yoshua Bengio. 2011. Domain adaptation for large-scale sentiment classification: A deep learning approach. In *Proceedings of the 28th international conference on machine learning (ICML)*. pages 513–520.

Kazi Saidul Hasan and Vincent Ng. 2013. Stance classification of ideological debates: Data, models, features, and constraints. In *Proceedings of the 6th International Joint Conference on Natural Language Processing*. pages 1348–1356.

Sepp Hochreiter and Jürgen Schmidhuber. 1997. Long short-term memory. *Neural Computation* 9(8):1735–1780.

Diederik Kingma and Jimmy Ba. 2014. Adam: A method for stochastic optimization. *arXiv preprint arXiv:1412.6980* .

Christopher D Manning, Prabhakar Raghavan, Hinrich Schütze, et al. 2008. *Introduction to information retrieval*, volume 1. Cambridge university press Cambridge.

Tomas Mikolov, Ilya Sutskever, Kai Chen, Greg S Corrado, and Jeff Dean. 2013. Distributed representations of words and phrases and their compositionality. In *Advances in neural information processing systems (NIPS)*. pages 3111–3119.

Saif Mohammad, Svetlana Kiritchenko, Parinaz Sobhani, Xiao-Dan Zhu, and Colin Cherry. 2016. Semeval-2016 task 6: Detecting stance in tweets. In *SemEval@ NAACL-HLT*. pages 31–41.

Saif M Mohammad, Parinaz Sobhani, and Svetlana Kiritchenko. 2017. Stance and sentiment in tweets. *ACM Transactions on Internet Technology (TOIT)* 17(3):26.

Jeffrey Pennington, Richard Socher, and Christopher D. Manning. 2014. Glove: Global vectors for word representation. In *Proceedings of the Conference on Empirical Methods in Natural Language Processing (EMNLP)*. pages 1532–1543.

Mariona Taulé, M Antonia Martí, Francisco M Rangel, Paolo Rosso, Cristina Bosco, Viviana Patti, et al. 2017. Overview of the task on stance and gender detection in tweets on catalan independence at ibereval 2017. In *2nd Workshop on Evaluation of Human Language Technologies for Iberian Languages, IberEval 2017*. CEUR-WS, volume 1881, pages 157–177.

Ashish Vaswani, Noam Shazeer, Niki Parmar, Jakob Uszkoreit, Llion Jones, Aidan N Gomez, Lukasz Kaiser, and Illia Polosukhin. 2017. Attention is all you need. In *Advances in neural information processing systems (NIPS)*. pages 6000–6010.

Know What You Don't Know: Unanswerable Questions for SQuAD

Pranav Rajpurkar[*] **Robin Jia**[*] **Percy Liang**
Computer Science Department, Stanford University
`{pranavsr,robinjia,pliang}@cs.stanford.edu`

Abstract

Extractive reading comprehension systems can often locate the correct answer to a question in a context document, but they also tend to make unreliable guesses on questions for which the correct answer is not stated in the context. Existing datasets either focus exclusively on answerable questions, or use automatically generated unanswerable questions that are easy to identify. To address these weaknesses, we present SQUADRUN, a new dataset that combines the existing Stanford Question Answering Dataset (SQuAD) with over 50,000 unanswerable questions written adversarially by crowdworkers to look similar to answerable ones. To do well on SQUADRUN, systems must not only answer questions when possible, but also determine when no answer is supported by the paragraph and abstain from answering. SQUADRUN is a challenging natural language understanding task for existing models: a strong neural system that gets 86% F1 on SQuAD achieves only 66% F1 on SQUADRUN. We release SQUADRUN to the community as the successor to SQuAD.

1 Introduction

Machine reading comprehension has become a central task in natural language understanding, fueled by the creation of many large-scale datasets (Hermann et al., 2015; Hewlett et al., 2016; Rajpurkar et al., 2016; Nguyen et al., 2016; Trischler et al., 2017; Joshi et al., 2017). In turn, these datasets have spurred a diverse array of model architecture improvements (Seo et al., 2016; Hu

> **Article:** Endangered Species Act
> **Paragraph:** "... *Other legislation followed, including the Migratory Bird Conservation Act of 1929, a 1937 treaty prohibiting the hunting of right and gray whales, and the* Bald Eagle Protection Act *of 1940. These later laws had a low cost to society—the species were relatively rare—and little opposition was raised.*"
>
> **Question 1:** "*Which laws faced significant opposition?*"
> **Plausible Answer:** later laws
>
> **Question 2:** "*What was the name of the 1937 treaty?*"
> **Plausible Answer:** Bald Eagle Protection Act

Figure 1: Two unanswerable questions written by crowdworkers, along with plausible (but incorrect) answers. Relevant keywords are shown in blue.

et al., 2017; Wang et al., 2017; Clark and Gardner, 2017; Huang et al., 2018). Recent work has even produced systems that surpass human-level exact match accuracy on the Stanford Question Answering Dataset (SQuAD), one of the most widely-used reading comprehension benchmarks (Rajpurkar et al., 2016).

Nonetheless, these systems are still far from true language understanding. Recent analysis shows that models can do well at SQuAD by learning context and type-matching heuristics (Weissenborn et al., 2017), and that success on SQuAD does not ensure robustness to distracting sentences (Jia and Liang, 2017). One root cause of these problems is SQuAD's focus on questions for which a correct answer is guaranteed to exist in the context document. Therefore, models only need to select the span that seems most related to the question, instead of checking that the answer is actually entailed by the text.

In this work, we construct SQUADRUN,[1] a new dataset that combines the existing questions in SQuAD with 53,775 new, unanswerable ques-

---

[*] The first two authors contributed equally to this paper.

[1] SQuAD with adve**R**sarial **U**nanswerable questions

Proceedings of the 56th Annual Meeting of the Association for Computational Linguistics (Short Papers), pages 784–789
Melbourne, Australia, July 15 - 20, 2018. ©2018 Association for Computational Linguistics

tions about the same paragraphs. Crowdworkers crafted these questions so that (1) they are *relevant* to the paragraph, and (2) the paragraph contains a *plausible answer*—something of the same type as what the question asks for. Two such examples are shown in Figure 1.

We confirm that SQUADRUN is both challenging and high-quality. A state-of-the-art model achieves only 66.3% F1 score when trained and tested on SQUADRUN, whereas human accuracy is 89.5% F1, a full 23.2 points higher. The same model architecture trained on SQuAD gets 85.8% F1, only 5.4 points worse than humans. We also show that our unanswerable questions are more challenging than ones created automatically, either via distant supervision (Clark and Gardner, 2017) or a rule-based method (Jia and Liang, 2017). We release SQUADRUN to the public as the successor to SQuAD, and designate it SQuAD 2.0 on the official SQuAD leaderboard.[2] We are optimistc that this new dataset will encourage the development of reading comprehension systems that know what they don't know.

2 Desiderata

We first outline our goals for SQUADRUN. Besides the generic goals of large size, diversity, and low noise, we posit two desiderata specific to unanswerable questions:

Relevance. The unanswerable questions should appear relevant to the topic of the context paragraph. Otherwise, simple heuristics (e.g., based on word overlap) could distinguish answerable and unanswerable questions (Yih et al., 2013).

Existence of plausible answers. There should be some span in the context whose type matches the type of answer the question asks for. For example, if the question asks, *"What company was founded in 1992?"*, then some company should be mentioned in the context. Otherwise, type-matching heuristics could distinguish answerable and unanswerable questions (Weissenborn et al., 2017).

3 Existing datasets

Next, we survey existing reading comprehension datasets with these criteria in mind. We use the

term "negative example" to refer to a context passage paired with an unanswerable question.

3.1 Extractive datasets

In extractive reading comprehension datasets, a system must extract the correct answer to a question from a context document or paragraph. The Zero-shot Relation Extraction dataset (Levy et al., 2017) contains negative examples generated with distant supervision. Levy et al. (2017) found that 65% of these negative examples do not have a plausible answer, making them easy to identify.

Other distant supervision strategies can also create negative examples. TriviaQA (Joshi et al., 2017) retrieves context documents from the web or Wikipedia for each question. Some documents do not contain the correct answer, yielding negative examples; however, these are excluded from the final dataset. Clark and Gardner (2017) generate negative examples for SQuAD by pairing existing questions with other paragraphs from the same article based on TF-IDF overlap; we refer to these as TFIDF examples. In general, distant supervision does not ensure the existence of a plausible answer in the retrieved context, and might also add noise, as the context might contain a paraphrase of the correct answer. Moreover, when retrieving from a small set of possible contexts, as in Clark and Gardner (2017), we find that the retrieved paragraphs are often not very relevant to the question, making these negative examples easy to identify.

The NewsQA data collection process also yields unanswerable questions, because crowdworkers write questions given only a summary of an article, not the full text (Trischler et al., 2017). Only 9.5% of their questions are unanswerable, making this strategy hard to scale. Of this fraction, we found that some are misannotated as unanswerable, and others are out-of-scope (e.g., summarization questions). Trischler et al. (2017) also exclude negative examples from their final dataset.

Jia and Liang (2017) propose a rule-based procedure for editing SQuAD questions to make them unanswerable. Their questions are not very diverse: they only replace entities and numbers with similar words, and replace nouns and adjectives with WordNet antonyms. We refer to these unanswerable questions as RULEBASED questions.

3.2 Answer sentence selection datasets

Sentence selection datasets test whether a system can rank sentences that answer a question higher

Reasoning	Description	Example	Percentage
Negation	Negation word inserted or removed.	Sentence: *"Several hospital pharmacies have decided to outsource high risk preparations …"* Question: *"What types of pharmacy functions have* **never** *been outsourced?"*	9%
Antonym	Antonym used.	S: *"the extinction of the dinosaurs… allowed the tropical rainforest to spread out across the continent."* Q: *"The extinction of what led to the* **decline** *of rainforests?"*	20%
Entity Swap	Entity, number, or date replaced with other entity, number, or date.	S: *"These values are much greater than the 9–88 cm as projected … in its Third Assessment Report."* Q: *"What was the projection of sea level increases in the* **fourth assessment report**?"*	21%
Mutual Exclusion	Word or phrase is mutually exclusive with something for which an answer is present.	S: *"BSkyB… waiv[ed] the charge for subscribers whose package included two or more premium channels."* Q: *"What service did BSkyB* **give away for free unconditionally**?"*	15%
Impossible Condition	Asks for condition that is not satisfied by anything in the paragraph.	S: *"Union forces left Jacksonville and confronted a Confederate Army at the Battle of Olustee… Union forces then retreated to Jacksonville and held the city for the remainder of the war."* Q: *"After what battle did Union forces leave Jacksonville* **for good**?"*	4%
Other Neutral	Other cases where the paragraph does not imply any answer.	S: *"Schuenemann et al. concluded in 2011 that the Black Death… was caused by a variant of Y. pestis…"* Q: *"Who* **discovered** *Y. pestis?"*	24%
Answerable	Question is answerable (i.e. dataset noise).		7%

Table 1: Types of negative examples in SQUADRUN exhibiting a wide range of phenomena.

than sentences that do not. Wang et al. (2007) constructed the QASENT dataset from questions in the TREC 8-13 QA tracks. Yih et al. (2013) showed that lexical baselines are highly competitive on this dataset. WikiQA (Yang et al., 2015) pairs questions from Bing query logs with sentences from Wikipedia. Like TFIDF examples, these sentences are not guaranteed to have plausible answers or high relevance to the question. The dataset is also limited in scale (3,047 questions, 1,473 answers).

3.3 Multiple choice datasets

Finally, some datasets, like MCTest (Richardson et al., 2013) and RACE (Lai et al., 2017), pose multiple choice questions, which can have a "none of the above" option. In practice, multiple choice options are often unavailable, making these datasets less suited for training user-facing systems. Multiple choice questions also tend to be quite different from extractive ones, with more emphasis on fill-in-the-blank, interpretation, and summarization (Lai et al., 2017).

4 The SQUADRUN dataset

We now describe our new dataset, which we constructed to satisfy both the relevance and plausible answer desiderata from Section 2.

4.1 Dataset creation

We employed crowdworkers on the Daemo crowdsourcing platform (Gaikwad et al., 2015) to write unanswerable questions. Each task consisted of an entire article from the original SQuAD dataset. For each paragraph in the article, workers were asked to pose up to five questions that were impossible to answer based on the paragraph alone, while referencing entities in the paragraph and ensuring that a plausible answer is present. As inspiration, we also showed questions from SQuAD for each paragraph; this further encouraged unanswerable questions to look similar to answerable ones. Workers were asked to spend 7 minutes per paragraph, and were paid $10.50 per hour. Screenshots of our interface are shown in Appendix A.1.

We removed questions from workers who wrote 25 or fewer questions on that article; this filter helped remove noise from workers who had trouble understanding the task, and therefore quit before completing the whole article. We applied this filter to both our new data and the existing answerable questions in SQuAD. To generate train, development, and test splits, we used the same partition of articles as SQuAD, and combined the existing SQuAD data with our new data for each split. For the SQUADRUN development and test sets, we removed articles for which we did not col-

	SQuAD	SQUADRUN
Train		
Total examples	87,599	130,319
Negative examples	0	43,498
Total articles	442	442
Articles with negatives	0	285
Development		
Total examples	10,570	11,873
Negative examples	0	5,945
Total articles	48	35
Articles with negatives	0	35
Test		
Total examples	9,533	8,862
Negative examples	0	4,332
Total articles	46	28
Articles with negatives	0	28

Table 2: Dataset statistics of SQUADRUN, compared to the original SQuAD dataset.

lect unanswerable questions. This resulted in a roughly one-to-one ratio of answerable to unanswerable questions in these splits, whereas the train data has roughly twice as many answerable questions as unanswerable ones. Table 2 summarizes overall statistics of SQUADRUN.

4.2 Human accuracy

To confirm that our dataset is clean, we hired additional crowdworkers to answer all questions in the SQUADRUN development and test sets. In each task, we showed workers an entire article from the dataset. For each paragraph, we showed all associated questions; unanswerable and answerable questions were shuffled together. For each question, workers were told to either highlight the answer in the paragraph, or mark it as unanswerable. Workers were told to expect every paragraph to have some answerable and some unanswerable questions. They were asked to spend one minute per question, and were paid $10.50 per hour.

To reduce crowdworker noise, we collected multiple human answers for each question and selected the final answer by majority vote, breaking ties in favor of answering questions and preferring shorter answers to longer ones. On average, we collected 4.8 answers per question. We note that for the original SQuAD, Rajpurkar et al. (2016) evaluated a single human's performance; therefore, they likely underestimate human accuracy.

4.3 Analysis

We manually inspected 100 randomly chosen negative examples from our development set to understand the challenges these examples present. In Table 1, we define different categories of nega-

tive examples, and give examples and their frequency in SQUADRUN. We observe a wide range of phenomena, extending beyond expected phenomena like negation, antonymy, and entity changes. In particular, SQUADRUN is much more diverse than RULEBASED, which creates unanswerable questions by applying entity, number, and antonym swaps to existing SQuAD questions. We also found that 93% of the sampled negative examples are indeed unanswerable.

5 Experiments

5.1 Models

We evaluated three existing model architectures: the BiDAF-No-Answer (BNA) model proposed by Levy et al. (2017), and two versions of the DocumentQA No-Answer (DocQA) model from Clark and Gardner (2017), namely versions with and without ELMo (Peters et al., 2018). These models all learn to predict the probability that a question is unanswerable, in addition to a distribution over answer choices. At test time, models abstain whenever their predicted probability that a question is unanswerable exceeds some threshold. We tune this threshold separately for each model on the development set. When evaluating on the test set, we use the threshold that maximizes F1 score on the development set. We find this strategy does slightly better than simply taking the argmax prediction, possibly due to the different proportions of negative examples at training and test time.

5.2 Main results

First, we trained and tested all three models on SQUADRUN, as shown in Table 3. Following Rajpurkar et al. (2016), we report average exact match and F1 scores.[3] The best model, DocQA + ELMo, achieves only 66.3 F1 on the test set, 23.2 points lower than the human accuracy of 89.5 F1. Note that a baseline that always abstains gets 48.9 test F1; existing models are closer to this baseline than they are to human performance. Therefore, we see significant room for model improvement on this task. We also compare with reported test numbers for analogous model architectures on SQuAD. There is a much larger gap between humans and machines on SQUADRUN compared to SQuAD, which confirms that SQUADRUN is a much harder dataset for existing models.

---

[3] For negative examples, abstaining receives a score of 1, and any other response gets 0, for both exact match and F1.

System	SQuAD test		SQUADRUN dev		SQUADRUN test	
	EM	F1	EM	F1	EM	F1
BNA	68.0	77.3	59.8	62.6	59.2	62.1
DocQA	72.1	81.0	61.9	64.8	59.3	62.3
DocQA + ELMo	**78.6**	**85.8**	**65.1**	**67.6**	**63.4**	**66.3**
Human	82.3	91.2	86.3	89.0	86.9	89.5
Human–Machine Gap	3.7	5.4	**21.2**	**21.4**	**23.5**	**23.2**

Table 3: Exact Match (EM) and F1 scores on SQUADRUN and SQuAD. The gap between humans and the best tested model is much larger on SQUADRUN, suggesting there is a great deal of room for model improvement.

System	SQuAD + TFIDF		SQuAD + RULEBASED		SQUADRUN dev	
	EM	F1	EM	F1	EM	F1
BNA	72.7	76.6	80.1	84.8	59.8	62.6
DocQA	75.6	79.2	80.8	84.8	61.9	64.8
DocQA + ELMo	**79.4**	**83.0**	**85.7**	**89.6**	**65.1**	**67.6**

Table 4: Exact Match (EM) and F1 scores on the SQUADRUN development set, compared with SQuAD with two types of automatically generated negative examples. SQUADRUN is more challenging for current models.

5.3 Automatically generated negatives

Next, we investigated whether automatic ways of generating negative examples can also yield a challenging dataset. We trained and tested all three model architectures on SQuAD augmented with either TFIDF or RULEBASED examples. To ensure a fair comparison with SQUADRUN, we generated training data by applying TFIDF or RULEBASED only to the 285 articles for which SQUADRUN has unanswerable questions. We tested on the articles and answerable questions in the SQUADRUN development set, adding unanswerable questions in a roughly one-to-one ratio with answerable ones. These results are shown in Table 4. The highest score on SQUADRUN is 15.4 F1 points lower than the highest score on either of the other two datasets, suggesting that automatically generated negative examples are much easier for existing models to detect.

5.4 Plausible answers as distractors

Finally, we measured how often systems were fooled into answering the plausible but incorrect answers provided by crowdworkers for our unanswerable questions. For both computer systems and humans, roughly half of all wrong answers on unanswerable questions exactly matched the plausible answers. This suggests that the plausible answers do indeed serve as effective distractors. Full results are shown in Appendix A.2.

6 Discussion

SQUADRUN forces models to understand whether a paragraph entails that a certain span is the answer to a question. Similarly, recognizing textual entailment (RTE) requires systems to decide whether a hypothesis is entailed by, contradicted by, or neutral with respect to a premise (Marelli et al., 2014; Bowman et al., 2015). Relation extraction systems must understand when a possible relationship between two entities is not entailed by the text (Zhang et al., 2017).

Jia and Liang (2017) created adversarial examples that fool pre-trained SQuAD models at test time. However, models that train on similar examples are not easily fooled by their method. In contrast, the adversarial examples in SQUADRUN are difficult even for models trained on examples from the same distribution.

In conclusion, we have presented SQUADRUN, a challenging, diverse, and large-scale dataset that forces models to understand when a question cannot be answered given the context. We are optimistic that SQUADRUN will encourage the development of new reading comprehension models that know what they don't know, and therefore understand language at a deeper level.

Reproducibility. All code, data, experiments are available on the Codalab platform at `https://bit.ly/2rDHBgY`.

Acknowledgments. We would like to thank the anonymous reviewers, Arun Chaganty, Peng Qi, and Sharon Zhou for their constructive feedback. We are grateful to Durim Morina and Michael Bernstein for their help with the Daemo platform. This work was supported by funding from Facebook. R.J. is supported by an NSF Graduate Research Fellowship under Grant No. DGE-114747.

References

S. Bowman, G. Angeli, C. Potts, and C. D. Manning. 2015. A large annotated corpus for learning natural language inference. In *Empirical Methods in Natural Language Processing (EMNLP)*.

C. Clark and M. Gardner. 2017. Simple and effective multi-paragraph reading comprehension. *arXiv preprint arXiv:1710.10723*.

S. N. Gaikwad, D. Morina, R. Nistala, M. Agarwal, A. Cossette, R. Bhanu, S. Savage, V. Narwal, K. Rajpal, J. Regino, et al. 2015. Daemo: A self-governed crowdsourcing marketplace. In *Proceedings of the 28th Annual ACM Symposium on User Interface Software & Technology*. pages 101–102.

K. M. Hermann, T. Koisk, E. Grefenstette, L. Espeholt, W. Kay, M. Suleyman, and P. Blunsom. 2015. Teaching machines to read and comprehend. In *Advances in Neural Information Processing Systems (NIPS)*.

D. Hewlett, A. Lacoste, L. Jones, I. Polosukhin, A. Fandrianto, J. Han, M. Kelcey, and D. Berthelot. 2016. Wikireading: A novel large-scale language understanding task over Wikipedia. In *Association for Computational Linguistics (ACL)*.

M. Hu, Y. Peng, and X. Qiu. 2017. Reinforced mnemonic reader for machine comprehension. *arXiv*.

H. Huang, C. Zhu, Y. Shen, and W. Chen. 2018. Fusionnet: Fusing via fully-aware attention with application to machine comprehension. In *International Conference on Learning Representations (ICLR)*.

R. Jia and P. Liang. 2017. Adversarial examples for evaluating reading comprehension systems. In *Empirical Methods in Natural Language Processing (EMNLP)*.

M. Joshi, E. Choi, D. Weld, and L. Zettlemoyer. 2017. TriviaQA: A large scale distantly supervised challenge dataset for reading comprehension. In *Association for Computational Linguistics (ACL)*.

G. Lai, Q. Xie, H. Liu, Y. Yang, and E. Hovy. 2017. Race: Large-scale reading comprehension dataset from examinations. *arXiv preprint arXiv:1704.04683*.

O. Levy, M. Seo, E. Choi, and L. Zettlemoyer. 2017. Zero-shot relation extraction via reading comprehension. In *Computational Natural Language Learning (CoNLL)*.

M. Marelli, S. Menini, M. Baroni, L. Bentivogli, R. bernardi, and R. Zamparelli. 2014. A SICK cure for the evaluation of compositional distributional semantic models. In *Language Resources and Evaluation Conference (LREC)*.

T. Nguyen, M. Rosenberg, X. Song, J. Gao, S. Tiwary, R. Majumder, and L. Deng. 2016. MS MARCO: A human generated machine reading comprehension dataset. In *Workshop on Cognitive Computing at NIPS*.

M. E. Peters, M. Neumann, M. Iyyer, M. Gardner, C. Clark, K. Lee, and L. Zettlemoyer. 2018. Deep contextualized word representations. In *North American Association for Computational Linguistics (NAACL)*.

P. Rajpurkar, J. Zhang, K. Lopyrev, and P. Liang. 2016. SQuAD: 100,000+ questions for machine comprehension of text. In *Empirical Methods in Natural Language Processing (EMNLP)*.

M. Richardson, C. J. Burges, and E. Renshaw. 2013. Mctest: A challenge dataset for the open-domain machine comprehension of text. In *Empirical Methods in Natural Language Processing (EMNLP)*. pages 193–203.

M. Seo, A. Kembhavi, A. Farhadi, and H. Hajishirzi. 2016. Bidirectional attention flow for machine comprehension. *arXiv*.

A. Trischler, T. Wang, X. Yuan, J. Harris, A. Sordoni, P. Bachman, and K. Suleman. 2017. NewsQA: A machine comprehension dataset. In *Workshop on Representation Learning for NLP*.

M. Wang, N. A. Smith, and T. Mitamura. 2007. What is the jeopardy model? a quasi-synchronous grammar for QA. In *Empirical Methods in Natural Language Processing (EMNLP)*.

W. Wang, N. Yang, F. Wei, B. Chang, and M. Zhou. 2017. Gated self-matching networks for reading comprehension and question answering. In *Association for Computational Linguistics (ACL)*.

D. Weissenborn, G. Wiese, and L. Seiffe. 2017. Making neural QA as simple as possible but not simpler. In *Computational Natural Language Learning (CoNLL)*.

Y. Yang, W. Yih, and C. Meek. 2015. WikiQA: A challenge dataset for open-domain question answering. In *Empirical Methods in Natural Language Processing (EMNLP)*. pages 2013–2018.

W. Yih, M. Chang, C. Meek, and A. Pastusiak. 2013. Question answering using enhanced lexical semantic models. In *Association for Computational Linguistics (ACL)*.

Y. Zhang, V. Zhong, D. Chen, G. Angeli, and C. D. Manning. 2017. Position-aware attention and supervised data improve slot filling. In *Empirical Methods in Natural Language Processing (EMNLP)*.

'Lighter' Can Still Be Dark:
Modeling Comparative Color Descriptions

Olivia Winn
Computer Science Department
Columbia University
`olivia@cs.columbia.edu`

Smaranda Muresan
Data Science Institute
Columbia University
`smara@columbia.edu`

Abstract

We propose a novel paradigm of grounding comparative adjectives within the realm of color descriptions. Given a reference RGB color and a comparative term (e.g., `lighter`, `darker`), our model learns to ground the comparative as a direction in the RGB space such that the colors along the vector, rooted at the reference color, satisfy the comparison. Our model generates grounded representations of comparative adjectives with an average accuracy of 0.65 cosine similarity to the desired direction of change. These vectors approach colors with Delta-E scores of under 7 compared to the target colors, indicating the differences are very small with respect to human perception. Our approach makes use of a newly created dataset for this task derived from existing labeled color data.

1 Introduction

Multimodal approaches to object recognition have achieved a degree of success by grounding adjectives and nouns from descriptive text in image features (Farhadi et al., 2009; Lampert et al., 2009; Russakovsky and Fei-Fei, 2010; Lazaridou et al., 2015). One limitation of this approach, particularly for fine-grained object recognition, is when objects are differentiated not by having unique sets of attributes but by a difference in the strengths of their shared attributes (Wang et al., 2009; Duan et al., 2012; Maji et al., 2013; Vedaldi et al., 2014). In text, this difference is described using comparative adjectives. For example, the sexual dimorphism of the American black duck is described with the phrase "females tend to be *slightly paler*

(a) The grounding of '`darker`' trained on teal data, applied to a teal sample

(b) The grounding of '`darker`' trained on *pink* data, applied to a teal sample

Figure 1: Grounding 'darker'

than males, with ***duller olive*** bills".[1]

In a recent study of pragmatic referring expression interpretation in the context of color selection, Monroe et al. (2017) found that speakers almost always used comparative adjectives when the target color was very similar to a distractor, rather than using multiple positive form adjectives to create a highly specific description of the color independent of its surroundings. Though color has been studied in terms of its contextual dependence and vagueness in grounding (Egré et al., 2013; McMahan and Stone, 2015; Monroe et al., 2016, 2017), no approaches have focused explicitly on learning to ground comparative adjective; in this work we focus on comparative color descriptions.

The presence of distractors in the Monroe et al. (2017) study is important - comparatives describe a change in a feature *with respect to a reference point*. While the description ***light blue*** can be understood to represent a particular subset of colors in RGB, for example, neither '`lighter`' nor '`lighter blue`' have explicit representations; it is only with a reference that we can image what color either might refer to. If the reference color is a deep navy blue, then we imagine the target to be much closer to navy than, for example, a sky blue.

We propose a new paradigm of learning to ground comparative adjectives within the realm of color descriptions: given a reference RGB color and a comparative term (e.g. '`lighter`', '`paler`'),

---

[1] `https://www.allaboutbirds.org/guide/`
`American_Black_Duck/id`

Proceedings of the 56th Annual Meeting of the Association for Computational Linguistics (Short Papers), pages 790–795
Melbourne, Australia, July 15 - 20, 2018. ©2018 Association for Computational Linguistics

our deep learning model learns to ground the comparative as a direction in RB space such that the colors along the vector, rooted at the reference color, satisfy the comparison (Section 3). The reference color does more than quantify the specific RGB values to apply the comparative to: it also affects the grounding of the comparative. For example, 'darker' might seem like a simple change - simply reduce the values of all color channels equally towards 0. But as Fig 1 shows, 'darker' refers to a different direction in RGB space depending on the reference color, and thus we need a reference-dependent approach.

Our approach makes use of a newly created dataset for this task derived from an existing labeled color dataset (McMahan and Stone, 2015) (Section 2). Our results in Section 5 show that our model generates grounded representations of comparative adjectives with an average accuracy of 0.65 cosine similarity to the desired direction of change. These learned vectors approach colors with Delta-E scores of under 7 compared to the target colors, indicating the differences are very small with respect to human perception.

2 Data

We utilize the labeled RGB color data originally collected by Munroe (2010), through an online survey asking participants to provide free-form labels to various RGB samples. This data was then cleaned by McMahan and Stone (2015)[2]. The cleaned data contains 821 color labels, averaging 600 RGB datapoints per label. These labels do not contain comparative adjectives, but many start with adjectives in the positive form (e.g., *dusty*, *bright*). As Lassiter and Goodman (2017) write, "Vague terms ... are generally thought in linguistic semantics to rely on a free threshold variable: 'heavy' is interpreted as 'heaver than θ'." Coming back to the example of *light blue*, implicit in the term is the assumption that there is a reference *blue*, such that *light blue* is understood as 'lighter' than this reference. By representing this referential *blue* with the *blue* RGB samples from the data, we can assume the *light blue* RGB samples are 'lighter' than these references, giving us a quantitative θ in which to ground 'lighter'. Applying this process to the

rest of the labels, we convert the original dataset into 415 tuples (reference color label, comparative adjective, and target color label), such as (*blue*, 'lighter', *light blue*), where each color label is a set of RGB datapoints as in McMahan and Stone (2015). Note that not all labels containing quantifiers could be utilized in this manner; one does not consider *cobalt blue* to be 'more cobalt' than the average *blue*. The new dataset of 415 tuples contains 79 unique reference color labels and 81 unique comparatives and is made available online.[3]

While it is reasonable to believe that the comparative adjective describes the relationship between the colors in general, individual pairs of colors from the data may not display the appropriate θ. Thus, we make the assumption that the comparison holds true for the *average* of the target *light blue* samples, and use the average as our ground truth given the *blue* reference colors and the comparative adjective 'lighter'.

3 Method

We have chosen to represent comparative adjectives in RGB space as directions, such that given ain input RGB reference color r_c and a comparative adjective w our model outputs a vector $\vec{w}_g$ pointing from r_c in the direction of change in RGB, which in training is measured against the direction towars a target color t_c. Fig 1 is a good indication for why this representation is appropriate; our output $\vec{w}_g$ corresponds to the rate of change across the color bar, indicating the direction along with the degree of the compared property increases. All points along this line are representations of w in respect to r_c.

The network architecture consists of two fully connected layers, shown in Fig 2. The comparative is represented as a bi-gram to account for comparatives which necessitate using 'more' (e.g. "more electric"); single-word comparatives are preceded by the zero vector. We used the Google pre-trained word embeddings[4] with d=300 (Mikolov et al., 2013a,b). As these vectors are two orders of magnitude larger than the reference RGB color, we input the reference directly into both layers of the network, helping to mitigate the loss of

---

[2]A few of the labels (such as 'horrible') were manually discarded, as the corresponding set of colors were too widely spread across RGB space for the label to be considered as describing a distinct color.

[3]https://bitbucket.org/o_winn/comparative_colors

[4]https://code.google.com/archive/p/word2vec/

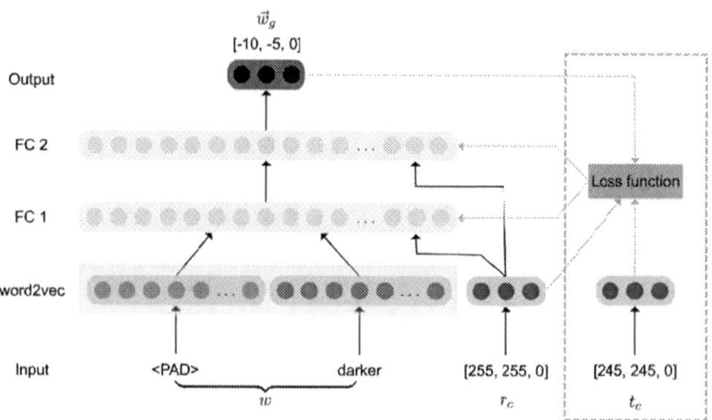

Figure 2: Network Architecture

Data	# Tuples	# Dtpts
Training	271	15.3M
Test (Seen Pairings)	271	2.4M
Test (Unseen Pairings)	29	0.29M
Test (Unseen Ref. Color)	63	2.4M
Test(Unseen Comparative)	41	0.38M
Test (Fully Unseen)	11	58k

Table 1: Data Split

information this dichotomy in size would otherwise produce (an empirical study of various input configurations determined inputting the color into only one of the layers to be insufficient). The output of the first hidden layer has d=30; each layer reduces the dimension of the output by an order of magnitude.

The loss function of the model has two metrics. The first is the cosine similarity between $\vec{w}_g$ and the vector from r_c to t_c. To restrain the length of $\vec{w}_g$, the second metric is the distance between t_c and the result of $\vec{w}_g + r_c$. Training the length of $\vec{w}_g$ to roughly match the distance between r_c and t_c helps it to capture that the difference should be small enough to warrant a comparison rather than separate descriptors, while still representing enough of a difference to be comparable.

4 Experimental Setup

Table 1 shows the data split between training and testing both in terms of tuples (#Tuples column) and in terms of the actual datapoint instances (#Dtpts column) for our experiments. To properly measure the accuracy of our model, our test set covers five input conditions:

- *Seen Pairings.* The reference color label, the comparative adjective and their pairing have been seen in the training data.

- *Unseen Pairings.* The reference color label and the comparative adjective have been seen in the training data, but not their pairing.

- *Unseen Ref. Color.* The reference color label, and thus all the corresponding RGB color datapoints, have not be seen in training, while the comparative has been seen in the training data.

- *Unseen Comparative.* The comparative adjective has not been seen in training, but the reference color label has been seen.

- *Fully Unseen.* Neither the comparative adjective nor the reference color have been seen in the training.

For the conditions where the reference color label has been seen in training, the actual RGB reference color datapoints associated with the labels were different from the ones used in training: 15% of the datapoints from each training reference color label were set aside for testing, providing RGB values close but not equivalent to those seen in training. 10% of the reference color labels were set aside for testing, as were 10% of the comparative words; this amounted to 8 reference colors and 8 comparatives. The number of tuples and actual datapoints instances for each test condition is given in Table 1.

The network was trained at a 0.001 learning rate for 800 epochs, with the output of the first layer of dimension d=30.

792

TEST TYPE	r'_c	w	$\vec{w}_g$	t_c	COS SIM	DELTA-E
Seen Pairings		darker			0.97	0.9
		more greenish			-0.76	20.0
Unseen Pairings		lighter			0.94	4.2
		darker			0.77	12.3
Unseen Ref. Color		lighter			0.93	2.7
		bluer			-0.93	17.4
Unseen Comparative		more neon			0.96	1.3
		more neon			-0.14	26.1
Fully Unseen		paler			0.99	3.5
		rustier			-0.73	18

Figure 3: Examples of learned comparatives for each test condition

5 Results

Figure 3 shows examples of learned groundings of comparatives for each of the five test conditions (Test Type column). It shows the reference RGB color datapoint r'_c (always unseen), the comparative word w, the learned grounding vector $\vec{w}_g$, the target color t_c, and two scores: cosine similarity and Delta-E. The upper sample for each test type is an example of a highly accurate result, while the lower sample exemplifies failure.

Delta-E is a metric for understanding how the human eye perceives color differences (Table 2). This is a useful metric as distances in RGB space are not perceived linearly. Figure 4 shows two example pairs of colors which are spaced equally in terms of distance in RGB, but in terms of the Delta-E metric the green colors are closer together.

As seen in Figure 3, grounding comparatives in directional vectors over RGB allows them to capture a full range of modification of the reference color. Even for some of the error cases the resulting outputs tend to capture directions which are reasonable illustrations of the color the comparative described. Though the '`darker`' grounding example from unseen pairings is incorrectly de-saturating the reference color, it is also in fact making the color darker. Most impressive is the '`paler`' example at the bottom, which is able to capture the direction of the comparative almost perfectly. Regarding failures, we see that they tend

Delta-E	Perception
≤ 1.0	Imperceptible
1 - 2	Requires close observation
2 - 10	Perceivable
11 - 49	More similar than opposite
100	Exact opposites

Table 2: Delta-E Ranges

to be of comparatives words that relate to a different color, such as '`more greenish`' and '`bluer`', rather than comparatives such as '`lighter`'.

Table 3 provides quantitative results in terms of average cosine similarity and average Delta-E. Overall, the average cosine similarity is 0.65, with an average Delta-E of 6.8. Separating the performance by test condition, we see that the conditions where the reference and comparatives were both seen perform the best (independent of whether the pairing was seen in training); again 'seen reference' refers only to the label being seen and not the reference color datapoint itself. The fully unseen case performs the worst by far with respect to cosine similarity, though it is not as deviant in Delta-E. It is again apparent that the performance of the model drops when given comparatives which refer to another color.

Figure 5 shows the comparative '`electric`' applied to colors outside of our dataset. With no known t_cs we cannot quantitatively measure the accuracy, but we can qualitatively assess the re-

Figure 4: Same RGB distance, different Delta-E

Test Condition	Avg Cos	Avg Delta-E
Seen Pairings	0.68	6.1
Unseen Pairings	0.68	7.9
Unseen Ref. Color	0.40	11.4
Unseen Comparative	0.41	10.5
Fully Unseen	-0.21	15.9
Overall	**0.65**	**6.8**

Table 3: Results

sults as plausible.

We also examined whether the model could generate plausible comparative terms given a r_c and t_c. All of the comparatives in the model's vocabulary were applied to r_c, and the corresponding $\vec{w}_g$ were sorted by cosine similarity to given reference-target direction. When given a green reference and a dark green target (both sampled from the test data), the model outputs 'truer', 'deeper', and 'darker' as the closest comparatives.

In Figure 6, given a reference sampled from 'purple' and a target sampled from 'soft purple', the model outputs the 5 most plausible comparatives - 'softer' was the 9th closest. They are presented in descending order by distance between the target color and its projection on the modifying vector. We see that the comparatives the model returns are semantically very similar, as are their corresponding $\vec{w}_g$ vectors.

6 Related Work

Though color has been studied in terms of its contextual dependence and vagueness in grounding

Figure 5: Groundings for 'more electric'

Figure 6: Top comparatives generated by the model

(Egré et al., 2013; McMahan and Stone, 2015; Monroe et al., 2016, 2017), no approaches have focused explicitly on learning to ground comparatives. Related to this work is that of image ranking, which is inherently a form of comparison (Parikh and Grauman, 2011; Yu and Grauman, 2014). However, ranking methods do not ground the comparatives themselves in image features. Besides the fact that no ranked color data exists, ranking methods are not flexible enough to handle the high dependence of color comparatives on the individual reference color.

7 Conclusion

We propose a new paradigm of grounding comparative adjectives describing colors as directions in RGB space such that the colors along the vector, rooted at the reference color, satisfy the comparison. We introduce a new methodology for transforming labeled color data into comparative color data, and propose a simple but effective learning model that is able to accurately modify unseen colors and comparatives. With respect to the desired output, the representations have an average accuracy of 0.65 cosine similarity, and average Delta-E scores of under 7. Our model can also provide plausible descriptions of the difference between a given reference and target pair, as well as the grounded representations of the comparatives generated, providing an explanation for the model decision. This model is the first step towards fine-grained object recognition through comparative descriptions, providing a way to utilize relational descriptive text. This approach could be extended to other properties such as size, texture, or curvature. It could also be used to aid in zero-shot learning from text sources, generating human-understandable explanations for categorization of similar objects, or providing descriptions of new, unknown objects with respect to known ones.

References

Kun Duan, Devi Parikh, David Crandall, and Kristen Grauman. 2012. Discovering localized attributes for fine-grained recognition. In *Computer Vision and Pattern Recognition (CVPR), 2012 IEEE Conference on*, pages 3474–3481. IEEE.

Paul Egré, Vincent De Gardelle, and David Ripley. 2013. Vagueness and order effects in color categorization. *Journal of Logic, Language and Information*, 22(4):391–420.

Ali Farhadi, Ian Endres, Derek Hoiem, and David Forsyth. 2009. Describing objects by their attributes. In *Computer Vision and Pattern Recognition, 2009. CVPR 2009. IEEE Conference on*, pages 1778–1785. IEEE.

Christoph H Lampert, Hannes Nickisch, and Stefan Harmeling. 2009. Learning to detect unseen object classes by between-class attribute transfer. In *Computer Vision and Pattern Recognition, 2009. CVPR 2009. IEEE Conference on*, pages 951–958. IEEE.

Daniel Lassiter and Noah D Goodman. 2017. Adjectival vagueness in a Bayesian model of interpretation. *Synthese*, 194(10):3801–3836.

Angeliki Lazaridou, Georgiana Dinu, Adam Liska, and Marco Baroni. 2015. From Visual Attributes to Adjectives through Decompositional Distributional Semantics. *Transactions of the Association for Computational Linguistics*, 3(0):183–196.

Subhransu Maji, Esa Rahtu, Juho Kannala, Matthew Blaschko, and Andrea Vedaldi. 2013. Fine-grained visual classification of aircraft. *arXiv preprint arXiv:1306.5151*.

Brian McMahan and Matthew Stone. 2015. A bayesian model of grounded color semantics. *Transactions of the Association of Computational Linguistics*, 3(1):103–115.

Tomas Mikolov, Kai Chen, Greg Corrado, and Jeffrey Dean. 2013a. Efficient estimation of word representations in vector space. In *Proceedings of Workshop at ICLR*.

Tomas Mikolov, Wen-tau Yih, and Geoffrey Zweig. 2013b. Linguistic regularities in continuous space word representations. In *Proceedings of the 2013 Conference of the North American Chapter of the Association for Computational Linguistics: Human Language Technologies*, pages 746–751.

Will Monroe, Noah D Goodman, and Christopher Potts. 2016. Learning to generate compositional color descriptions. In *Proceedings of the 2016 Conference on Empirical Methods in Natural Language Processing*.

Will Monroe, Robert XD Hawkins, Noah D Goodman, and Christopher Potts. 2017. Colors in context: A pragmatic neural model for grounded language understanding. *Transactions of the Association for Computational Linguistics*, 5:325–338.

Randall Munroe. 2010. Color survey.

Devi Parikh and Kristen Grauman. 2011. Relative Attributes. *ICCV*, pages 503–510.

Olga Russakovsky and Li Fei-Fei. 2010. Attribute learning in large-scale datasets. In *European Conference on Computer Vision*, pages 1–14. Springer.

Andrea Vedaldi, Siddharth Mahendran, Stavros Tsogkas, Subhransu Maji, Ross Girshick, Juho Kannala, Esa Rahtu, Iasonas Kokkinos, Matthew B Blaschko, David Weiss, et al. 2014. Understanding objects in detail with fine-grained attributes. In *Proceedings of the IEEE conference on computer vision and pattern recognition*, pages 3622–3629.

Josiah Wang, Katja Markert, and Mark Everingham. 2009. Learning models for object recognition from natural language descriptions. In *Proceedings of the 20th British Machine Vision Conference (BMVC2009)*.

Aron Yu and Kristen Grauman. 2014. Fine-Grained Visual Comparisons with Local Learning. In *Proceedings of the IEEE Conference on Computer Vision and Pattern Recognition (CVPR)*.

Author Index